DATE DUE

			PRINTED IN U.S.A.

Literature Criticism from 1400 to 1800

Guide to Gale Literary Criticism Series

For criticism on	Consult these Gale series
Authors now living or who died after December 31, 1999	*CONTEMPORARY LITERARY CRITICISM (CLC)*
Authors who died between 1900 and 1999	*TWENTIETH-CENTURY LITERARY CRITICISM (TCLC)*
Authors who died between 1800 and 1899	*NINETEENTH-CENTURY LITERATURE CRITICISM (NCLC)*
Authors who died between 1400 and 1799	*LITERATURE CRITICISM FROM 1400 TO 1800 (LC)* *SHAKESPEAREAN CRITICISM (SC)*
Authors who died before 1400	*CLASSICAL AND MEDIEVAL LITERATURE CRITICISM (CMLC)*
Authors of books for children and young adults	*CHILDREN'S LITERATURE REVIEW (CLR)*
Dramatists	*DRAMA CRITICISM (DC)*
Poets	*POETRY CRITICISM (PC)*
Short story writers	*SHORT STORY CRITICISM (SSC)*
Black writers of the past two hundred years	*BLACK LITERATURE CRITICISM (BLC)*
Hispanic writers of the late nineteenth and twentieth centuries	*HISPANIC LITERATURE CRITICISM (HLC)*
Native North American writers and orators of the eighteenth, nineteenth, and twentieth centuries	*NATIVE NORTH AMERICAN LITERATURE (NNAL)*
Major authors from the Renaissance to the present	*WORLD LITERATURE CRITICISM, 1500 TO THE PRESENT (WLC)*

ISSN 0740-2880

Volume 54

Literature Criticism from 1400 to 1800

Critical Discussion of the Works of Fifteenth-, Sixteenth-, Seventeenth-, and Eighteenth-Century Novelists, Poets, Playwrights, Philosophers, and Other Creative Writers

Marie Lazzari, Lawrence J. Trudeau
Editors

GALE GROUP

Detroit
New York
San Francisco
London
Boston
Woodbridge, CT

STAFF

Janet Witalec, *Managing Editor, Literature Product*
Marie Lazzari, Lawrence J. Trudeau, *Editors*
Mark W. Scott, *Publisher, Literature Product*

Michelle Lee, *Editor*
Gianna Barberi, Lisa Gellert, *Associate Editors*
Tom Schoenberg, *Assistant Editor*
Patti A. Tippet, Timothy J. White, *Technical Training Specialists*
Kathleen Lopez Nolan, Lynn M. Spampinato, *Managing Editors*
Susan M. Trosky, *Content Director*

Maria L. Franklin, *Permissions Manager*
Edna Hedblad, Kimberly F. Smilay, *Permissions Specialists*
Erin Bealmear, Sandy Gore, Keryl Stanley, *Permissions Assistants*

Victoria B. Cariappa, *Research Manager*
Andrew Guy Malonis, Barbara McNeil, Gary J. Oudersluys, Maureen Richards, Cheryl L. Warnock, *Research Specialists*
Tamara C. Nott, Tracie A. Richardson, *Research Associates*
Scott Floyd, Timothy Lehnerer, Ron Morelli, *Research Assistants*

Dorothy Maki, *Manufacturing Manager*
Stacy Melson, *Buyer*

Mary Beth Trimper, *Composition Manager*
Evi Seoud, *Assistant Production Manager*
Carolyn Fischer, Gary Leach, *Composition Specialists*

Randy Bassett, *Image Database Supervisor*
Robert Duncan, *Imaging Specialists*
Mike Logusz, *Graphic Artist*
Pamela A. Reed, *Imaging Coordinator*

Library of Congress Catalog Card Number 94-29718
ISBN 0-7876-3269-4
ISSN 0740-2880
Printed in the United States of America

10 9 8 7 6 5 4 3 2 1

Contents

Preface vii

Acknowledgments xi

Preface

*L*iterature Criticism from 1400 to 1800 (*LC*) presents critical discussion of world literature from the fifteenth through the eighteenth centuries. The literature of this period is especially vital: the years 1400 to 1800 saw the rise of modern European drama, the birth of the novel and personal essay forms, the emergence of newspapers and periodicals, and major achievements in poetry and philosophy. *LC* provides valuable insight into the art, life, thought, and cultural transformations that took place during these centuries.

Scope of the Series

LC provides an introduction to the great poets, dramatists, novelists, essayists, and philosophers of the fifteenth through eighteenth centuries, and to the most significant interpretations of these authors' works. Because criticism of this literature spans nearly six hundred years, an overwhelming amount of scholarship confronts the student. *LC* organizes this material concisely and logically. Every attempt is made to reprint the most noteworthy, relevant, and educationally available essays available.

A separate Gale reference series, *Shakespearean Criticism,* is devoted exclusively to Shakespearean studies. Although properly belonging to the period covered in *LC*, William Shakespeare has inspired such a tremendous and ever-growing body of secondary material that a separate series was deemed essential.

Each entry in *LC* presents a representative selection of critical response to an author, a literary topic, or to a single important work of literature. Early commentary is offered to indicate initial responses, later selections document changes in literary reputations, and retrospective analyses provide the reader with modern views. The size of each author entry is a relative reflection of the scope of the criticism available in English. Every attempt has been made to identify and include the seminal essays on each author's work and to include recent commentary providing modern perspectives.

Volumes 1 through 12 of the series feature author entries arranged alphabetically by author. Volumes 13-47 of the series feature a thematic arrangement. Each volume includes an entry devoted to the general study of a specific literary or philosophical movement, writings surrounding important political and historical events, the philosophy and art associated with eras of cultural transformation, or the literature of specific social or ethnic groups. Each of these volumes also includes several author entries devoted to major representatives of the featured period, genre, or national literature. With volume 48, the series returns to a standard author approach, with occasional entries devoted to a single important work of world literature. One volume annually is devoted wholly to literary topics.

Organization of the Book

An *LC* entry consists of the following elements:

■ The **Author Heading** cites the name under which the author most commonly wrote, followed by birth and death dates. Also located here are any name variations under which an author wrote, including transliterated forms for authors whose native languages use nonroman alphabets. If the author wrote consistently under a pseudonym, the pseudonym will be listed in the author heading and the author's actual name given in parenthesis on the first line of the biographical and critical information. Uncertain birth or death dates are indicated by question marks. Topic entries are preceded by a **Thematic Heading,** which simply states the subject of the entry. Single-work entries are preceded by the title of the work and its date of publication.

■ The **Introduction** contains background information that introduces the reader to the author, work, or topic that is the subject of the entry.

- A **Portrait of the Author** is included when available.

- The list of **Principal Works** is ordered chronologically by date of first publication and lists the most important works by the author. The genre and publication date of each work is given. In the case of foreign authors whose works have been translated into English, the title and date (if available) of the first English-language edition is given in brackets following the original title. Unless otherwise indicated, dramas are dated by first performance, not first publication. Lists of **Representative Works** by different authors appear with topic entries.

- Reprinted **Criticism** is arranged chronologically in each entry to provide a useful perspective on changes in critical evaluation over time. The critic's name and the date of composition or publication of the critical work are given at the beginning of each piece of criticism. Unsigned criticism is preceded by the title of the source in which it appeared. All titles by the author featured in the text are printed in boldface type. Footnotes are reprinted at the end of each essay or excerpt. In the case of excerpted criticism, only those footnotes that pertain to the excerpted texts are included. Criticism in topic entries is arranged chronologically under a variety of subheadings to facilitate the study of different aspects of the topic.

- Critical essays are prefaced by brief **Annotations** explicating each piece.

- A complete **Bibliographical Citation** of the original essay or book precedes each piece of criticism.

- An annotated bibliography of **Further Reading** appears at the end of each entry and suggests resources for additional study. In some cases, significant essays for which the editors could not obtain reprint rights are included here. Boxed material following the further reading list provides references to other biographical and critical sources on the author in series published by Gale.

Cumulative Indexes

A **Cumulative Author Index** lists all of the authors that appear in a wide variety of reference sources published by the Gale Group, including *LC*. A complete list of these sources is found facing the first page of the Author Index. The index also includes birth and death dates and cross references between pseudonyms and actual names.

A **Cumulative Topic Index** lists the literary themes and topics treated in the series as well as in *Nineteenth-Century Literature Criticism, Twentieth-Century Literary Criticism,* and the *Contemporary Literature Criticism* Yearbook, which was discontinued in 1998.

A **Cumulative Nationality Index** lists all authors featured in *LC* by nationality, followed by the number of the *LC* volume in which their entry appears.

A **Cumulative Title Index** lists in alphabetical order all of the works discussed in the series. Each title listing includes the corresponding volume and page numbers where criticism may be located. Foreign-language titles that have been translated into English are followed by the titles of the translation—for example, *El ingenioso hidalgo Don Quixote de la Mancha* (*Don Quixote*). Page numbers following these translated titles refer to all pages on which any form of the titles, either foreign-language or translated, appear. Titles of novels, dramas, nonfiction books, and poetry, short story, or essay collections are printed in italics, while individual poems, short stories, and essays are printed in roman type within quotation marks.

Citing *Literature Criticism from 1400 to 1800*

When writing papers, students who quote directly from any volume in the Literary Criticism Series may use the following general format to footnote reprinted criticism. The first example pertains to material drawn from periodicals, the second to material reprinted from books.

Eileen Reeves, "Daniel 5 and the *Assayer*:" Galileo Reads the Handwriting on the Wall, " *The Journal of Medieval and Renaissance Studies,* 21, no. 1 (Spring 1991): 1-27; reprinted in *Literature Criticism from 1400 to 1800,* vol. 45, eds. Jelena Krstović and Marie Lazzari (Farmington Hills, Mich.: The Gale Group, 1999), 297-310.

Margaret Anne Doody, *A Natural Passion: A Study of the Novels of Samuel Richardson* (Oxford University Press, 1974), 17-22, 132-35; excerpted and reprinted in *Literature Criticism from 1400 to 1800,* vol. 46, eds. Jelena Krstović and Marie Lazzari (Farmington Hills, Mich.: The Gale Group, 1999), 20-2.

Suggestions are Welcome

Readers who wish to suggest new features, topics, or authors to appear in future volumes, or who have other suggestions or comments are cordially invited to call, write, or fax the Managing Editor:

Managing Editor, Literary Criticism Series
The Gale Group
27500 Drake Road
Farmington Hills, MI 48331-3535
1-800-347-4253 (GALE)
Fax: 248-699-8054

Acknowledgments

The editors wish to thank the copyright holders of the excerpted criticism included in this volume and the permissions managers of many book and magazine publishing companies for assisting us in securing reproduction rights. We are also grateful to the staffs of the Detroit Public Library, the Library of Congress, the University of Detroit Mercy Library, Wayne State University Purdy/Kresge Library Complex, and the University of Michigan Libraries for making their resources available to us. Following is a list of the copyright holders who have granted us permission to reproduce material in this volume of *LC*. Every effort has been made to trace copyright, but if omissions have been made, please let us know.

PHOTOGRAPHS APPEARING IN *LC*, VOLUME 54, WERE RECEIVED FROM THE FOLLOWING SOURCES:

Chatterton, Thomas, photograph of a pen and ink drawing. Corbis-Bettmann. Reproduced by permission. Ronsard, Pierre de, photograph. Archive Photos, Inc. Reproduced by permission.

Thomas Chatterton
1752-1770

(Also wrote under the pseudonym of Probus) English poet, satirist, dramatist, and journalist.

INTRODUCTION

Thomas Chatterton is best known today for the controversy surrounding his fabrication or "forgery" of both the life and poetry of a medieval priest called Thomas Rowley, and for his short, intense life and lonely death as a suicide. Considering the brevity of his life, Chatterton's literary output was remarkable. But perhaps more significant than his own work was his effect on the creative minds that succeeded him. Writers of the Romantic period as well as writers and painters of the Pre-Raphaelite era were inspired by Chatterton, whom they revered as a tragic prodigy or, in the words of the poet William Wordsworth, a "marvellous boy."

BIOGRAPHICAL INFORMATION

Chatterton was born in the commercial port of Bristol, England. His father, a schoolmaster and church clerk, died two months before Chatterton's birth, leaving his young wife almost penniless with two children to raise on a seamstress's small income. Solitary and moody as a child, Chatterton received most of his early education from his sister, who taught him to read. He subsequently developed an avid curiosity for subjects ranging from English heraldry to music, metaphysics, and astronomy. At the age of twelve Chatterton attended a local charity school. Although the unimaginative curriculum there soon extinguished his eagerness for formal education, it is likely that the archaic atmosphere and medieval regimen of the school, once a Carmelite priory, fed a fascination for the past that underlies much of Chatterton's work.

At fourteen Chatterton left school and was apprenticed to a Bristol attorney named John Lambert. Chatterton disliked his apprenticeship and—much to Lambert's annoyance—frequently neglected his legal copying to write poetry. During this period Chatterton had several satirical commentaries published pseudonymously in Bristol and London newspapers. His most enjoyable hours, however, were spent in Bristol's Church of Saint Mary Redcliffe. For several generations members of Chatterton's family had served as sextons in the church, and like his father Chatterton was drawn to the church's old records and parchments. The "Rowley poems" were a direct result of this interest. In 1768 Chatterton claimed to have discov-

ered these apparently medieval literary poems—complete with archaic language, heraldic drawings and antiqued parchments—supposedly written by a fifteenth-century Bristol priest named Thomas Rowley. In fact, Rowley, his poems, and the accompanying documents proved to be inventions of Chatterton's; the only genuinely historical personage mentioned in the documents was William Canynge—a merchant and mayor of Bristol who helped build the Church of Saint Mary Redcliffe. According to Chatterton's fabrication, Canynge was also Rowley's patron and frequent correspondent. At first, the Rowley poems were acclaimed as a historic find. Chatterton even submitted some of the documents to the antiquarian and writer Horace Walpole who was himself initially fooled by their apparent authenticity. Walpole and others began to become suspicious, however, once they learned how young and poorly educated the "discoverer" of the documents was; Chatterton's Rowley poems were subsequently returned to him without further reply.

Embittered but determined, Chatterton left Bristol in 1770 to try to make a living as a writer in London. Although he published some satires and articles—and even one Rowley poem entitled "Elinoure and Juga" (1769)—Chatterton became increasingly impoverished. In what seems to have been a fit of despair, Chatterton poisoned himself with arsenic in his rented room in London just a few months before his eighteenth birthday.

MAJOR WORKS

Although Chatterton's Rowley series, set during the reign of Edward IV, is not in fact the account of an actual priest, as Chatterton claimed, it does have a historical personage—William Canynge—as part of its focus. In the Rowley poems Chatterton magnifies Canynge's importance, presenting him not only as benefactor to the Church of Saint Mary Redcliffe and to the fictional priest Rowley, but also as a patron of the arts surrounded by a circle of poets and painters whose names Chatterton invented or culled from Saint Mary's tombstones. Within his chronicles the fictitious Rowley praises Canynge's munificence and sketches the colorful activities of Church feast days, the vigor of peasant life, and the pageantry of the nobility—all against a background of Saxon history. Through Rowley's chronicles Chatterton also explores the actions of traditional heroes—warriors, rulers, and saints—and defines the merchant of character, such as Canynge, as one who uses his wealth for good, much as traditional heroes had employed social rank, physical prowess, or saintly vocation. Significantly, the merchant of character was a hero for whom there was no strong literary precedent. In "A Brief Account of William Cannings from the Life of Thomas Rowlie Preeste," Chatterton develops the role of Canynge by establishing a relationship between the merchant and Rowley. Their friendship begins with Canynge's patronage of Rowley and grows as Canynge recognizes Rowley's taste and artistry, which are crucial to the designing and building of Saint Mary's. A defining element in the relationship between Rowley and Canynge is money, which measures mutual esteem rather than greed. The style of "A Brief Account" is the same as that of many of the Rowley works: a gossipy, relaxed narrative summary with subtle comic touches.

Chatterton's satiric verses, by contrast, are traditional in format and address society's iniquities—a subject foreign to the Rowley poems. In works such as "The Whore of Babylon" and "Kew Gardens" Chatterton targets influential members of ruling political and religious institutions, indicting the preferments and corruption which he believed had contributed to his own hardship. In poems ranging from playful satire to bitter invective, Chatterton assumes the conventional but far from dispassionate stance of outspoken freethinker—a pose which, while allowing him to vent his grievances, required less innovation than did the Rowley series.

CRITICAL RECEPTION

After Chatterton's death the Rowley poems generated heated debate between those who did and those who did not believe in their authenticity. Ultimately the argument was decided in favor of scholars who judged the poems to be Chatterton's own creation, or "forgery"; as a result, most critics during the period immediately after the young writer's death saw Chatterton as morally reprehensible and untalented. This view changed in the nineteenth century, when Chatterton was mythologized first by the Romantics and later by the Pre-Raphaelites, who saw the young poet as a sensitive, tortured genius destroyed by poverty and critical opinion before he could prove himself as a writer. Indeed, Chatterton's non-Rowley poetry directly influenced the work of the Romantics, using as it does the imagery and rhythms which were to typify Romantic verse, and presenting a portrait of the poet as an intuitive, unfettered spirit in conflict with what was crass, conventional, and insensitive in society.

Today, critical assessments of Chatterton tend to moderate between the two extremes. Most modern scholars take the view that it is a fine line that separates works that have been condemned as forgeries, such as Chatterton's Rowley poems, and others that are labeled simply as fiction; Nick Groom, for one, sees the Rowley poems as calling into question the very notions of authenticiy, forgery, and the construction of history. Concerning Chatterton's poetic abilities, most scholars agree that the young writer's untimely death makes it difficult to evaluate his potential. Ivan Philips, for instance, characterizes Chatterton's verse as "uneven," but goes on to declare: "A writer of paradox and playful irony, Chatterton—for all his immaturity—is a more sophisticated artist than his meagre and melodramatic reputation allows." Regardless of the merits or shortcomings of Chatterton's poems, or of their "truth" or "falsity," they remain significant for many critics because of their impact on subsequent writers. In her analysis of Chatterton's influence on John Keats, Lucy Morrison observes that "Chatterton clearly merits further examination, particularly since his texts have influenced later poets and since they actively participate within ongoing traditions."

PRINCIPAL WORKS

"Elinoure and Juga" (poetry) 1769

The Execution of Sir Charles Bawdin (poetry) 1772

Poems, Supposed to Have Been Written at Bristol, by Thomas Rowley, and Others, in the Fifteenth Century (poetry) 1777

Miscellanies in Prose and Verse (essays and poetry) 1778

The Revenge, A Burletta (drama) 1795

The Works of Thomas Chatterton. 3 vols. (poetry, prose, and letters) 1803

The Poetical Works of Thomas Chatterton. 2 vols. (poetry) 1871

The Complete Works of Thomas Chatterton (poetry, prose, letters, and drama) 1971

CRITICISM

Donald S. Taylor (essay date 1978)

SOURCE: "The Imaginative Matrix: The Rowley World and Its Documents, 1768-1769," in *Thomas Chatterton's Art: Experiments in Imagined History,* Princeton University Press, 1978, pp. 44-78.

[In the following excerpt, Taylor draws a distinction between the documents Chatterton created to establish the medieval world in which the fictional Rowley supposedly lived and the pieces that the ancient poet was purported to have written; further, Taylor argues that Chatterton should not be regarded as a forger because he himself believed in validity of the world that he created.]

In autumn 1768, after the four-and-one-half-year gap in the evidence, we are faced with documents indicating that the Rowley experiment is in full career. The literary works will be the subject of the next chapter, but those works presuppose a larger idea—Chatterton's imagined world of ancient Bristol—an idea not in itself literature and never fully recorded. That imagined world and the documents written to authenticate it will be the concerns of this chapter. The reality of that world for Chatterton is poignantly shown in a reminiscence of his friend William Smith:

> He was always very fond of walking in the fields, and particularly in Redcliffe meadows; and of talking about these manuscripts and reading them there. *Come,* he would say, *you and I will take a walk in the meadow. I have got the cleverest thing for you, that ever was. It is worth half a crown merely to have a sight of it; and to hear me read it to you.* When we were arrived at the place proposed, he would produce his parchment; shew it, and read it to me. There was one spot in particular, full in view of the church, in which he always seemed to take a peculiar delight. He would frequently lay himself down, fix his eyes upon the church; and seem as if he were in a kind of extasy [sic] or trance. Then on a sudden and abruptly, he would tell me, *that steeple was burnt down by lightning: that was the place where they formerly acted plays. . . .* [1]

Our detailed knowledge of the existence, nature, and gradual development of this imagined world must be largely inferential. Other authors have imagined subsuming, engendering ideas of this geographical-historical sort. Even if we take their literary works to be something like interim reports or partial representations, we find the larger ideas difficult to deal with, for they seem to grow and change with each work. Hardy's Wessex, Joyce's Dublin, Faulkner's Mississippi, Sinclair Lewis's Middle West, Blake's England, Georges Simenon's Paris are other countries of the mind. In them, the imagining of physical detail is intense and rich. When such ideas are pronouncedly historical, they seem to stand in many relations to the author's imaginative present—producing it, making it comprehensible, judging it, giving it significance and moment.

The obviously inferential nature of our knowledge of such imagined worlds tends to make us prefer the study of particular works, which seem to lie quite fully before us, available in their entirety. Yet our knowledge of particular works is also largely inferential. Without the active work of our imaginations and the knowledge we so lightly carry, no work can be more than marks on paper, teasing hints of a meaning we know must exist. Our techniques of literary history and criticism, the tools of our imaginations, are inferring tools. To study the larger ideas we must add to these traditional tools of the literary student something akin to that constructive imagination that enables the historian to build lucid pictures of events not now present and not, when they happened, recorded—of such events, say, as the English settlements of Britain—from a diverse body of written, linguistic, and archaeological evidence. In the case of Chatterton the pressure to study the subsuming Rowley idea is particularly strong, since the idea involved, first, inventing a language, second, imagining in detail a physical city through over a millennium of history, and, third, composing authenticating documents. These documents considerably outnumber the Rowleyan literary works.

Here I must pause to explain my own distinction between Rowleyan works and Rowleyan documents. A Rowleyan document is a composition whose major intended effect is the authentication of the Rowley world—either for Chatterton or for some presumed audience—rather than the achieving of literary expression. The literary works have, to be sure, something of this authentication in them, but it is never central. Insofar as the documents contribute to the imaginative structure of the Rowley world and so express Chatterton's feelings about that world, they are also to that extent artistic; but this is not their major intent. They too have their forms, which can be elucidated, but their forms aim at authentication rather than at literary effect. It is the difference between a child's exactly describing an imaginary playmate's clothing and his telling a story about that playmate. Put another way, the works grow from the larger idea, whereas the documents buttress its authenticity.

Since they are not centrally literary, it will not be relevant to this literary history to consider each of the sixty-odd documents. (Since there are documents within documents and groupings of related documents, this number is somewhat arbitrary.) I shall try to suggest their various functions, and I shall treat some of them in detail because of their demonstrable importance to the *literary* history. They are frequently our best evidence for the idea out of which the works grew, and some of them exist in a kind of shadow ground between literature and imaginary history. In a psychological study they would probably be as important as the literary works, and for those who wish to consider them more fully than the purposes of this study would justify, they are all available. [2]

The difference between Chatterton's Rowley world and such subsuming geographical-historical ideas in other authors is that Chatterton will have no truck with the convention of the willing suspension of disbelief. Not only the documents, but also the Rowleyan language and the imagined physical Bristol from pre-Roman times through the fifteenth century keep insisting to us, contrary to everything we know, that this city, these men and women actually existed. The traditional explanation—that Chatterton was a forger, a hoaxer given over to an elaborate lie—allows us to dismiss his insistence on actuality but explains nothing. This evasion has the double disadvantage of not advancing our understanding of Chatterton and not corresponding to the evidence. It is about as helpful as saying that cave paintings show a belief in magic. More fruitful ways of thinking about Chatterton's insistence on the authenticity of his imagined world are available to us.

R. G. Collingwood has compared novelists and historians in a way that can illuminate these special problems.

> Each aims at making his picture a coherent whole. . . . Both the novel and the history are self-explanatory, self-justifying, the product of an autonomous or self-authorizing activity; and in both cases this activity is the *a priori* imagination.
>
> As works of imagination, the historian's work and the novelist's do not differ. Where they do differ is that the historian's picture is meant to be true. The novelist has a single task only: to construct a coherent picture, one that makes sense. The historian has a double task: he has both to do this, and to construct a picture of things as they really were and of events as they really happened. This further necessity imposes upon him obedience to three rules of method, from which the novelist or artist in general is free.
>
> First, his picture must be localized in space and time. The artist's need not; essentially, things that he imagines are imagined as happening at no place and at no date. . . . it was a sure instinct that led [Hardy] to replace Oxford by Christminster, Wantage by Alfredston, and Fawley by Marychurch, recoiling against the discord of topographical fact in what should be a purely imaginary world.
>
> Secondly, all history must be consistent with itself. . . .
>
> Thirdly, and most important, the historian's picture stands in a peculiar relation to something called evidence.[3]

This instructive comparison begs a question that is relevant to our inquiry. Why did Hardy make it almost incumbent upon us to see Oxford in Christchurch, Wantage in Alfredston, and so on? He would appear to have felt the topographical and historical ties as strengthening in some way the impact of his novels. Still, however, the difference between Hardy's Wessex and Chatterton's Bristol is crucial, for Chatterton took his fictional Rowley world as historically and topographically true, and he meant it to be so taken by others. By creating the evidence and working to make it consistent, he is following in some special way of his own Collingwood's three rules of method. Chatterton must, therefore, be studied both as artist and as *some* kind

of historian. His knowledge of Bristol history and of fifteenth-century English, quite inadequate by modern standards, was very rich by the standards of other Englishmen of his day, even educated Bristolians. It can have taken little more than a dangerous prevalence of imagination to convince him that both that world and its language had historic validity. His letter to Walpole of 14 April 1769 argues quite sincerely, I believe, that what he had imagined was the *sort* of thing at least that the existing evidence obliged one to believe.

Again, although we know the Rowley world to be unhistoric, it is, for another reason, quite unproductive to study it as in essence a hoax. Though Chatterton deceived many, deception was not his ultimate goal, and the sort of knowledge we wish to gain about him argues for our studying him as artist rather than as forger. Take, for example, the central figure in his imagined world—Thomas Rowley, his author. Would it not be as delicate a task to draw a precise line of demarcation between Chatterton's Rowley and Sterne's Tristram as between Sterne's Tristram and the narrator of *The History of Tom Jones*? We would not willingly limit ourselves to studying either Tristram or the narrating "Fielding" as exercises in deception. With Chatterton, as with Fielding and Sterne, we must address ourselves to the function of the imagined narrator, to the quality of the imagined world, and to the special language with which he brings that world to life in our minds. Yet we must also remember that, presumably unlike Fielding and Sterne, Chatterton was quite unwilling to view his imagined author as a fiction.

He went about authenticating his Rowley world in three major ways—inventing its special language, imagining the ancient physical city, and writing the Rowleyan documents. All three ways share a common factor—density of imagining, something akin to what literary criticism calls verisimilitude. When we wish to persuade ourselves of the reality of imagined worlds, of fantasies, or dreams, we thicken the imagining, persuading ourselves, as it were, by sheer weight of detail. The Rowleyan language is perhaps the most striking instance of this authenticating density. It is also, in a strange way, the most authentic aspect of the world. Chatterton invented a special language of approximately 1800 words. Contrary to what has been hitherto assumed, this vocabulary is never, apparently, free fantasy. It is thoroughly true to what Chatterton knew of pre-eighteenth-century English, being collected entirely from what were to him authentic sources. The glossary in **Works** cites probable or possible sources for all but fifteen of these 1800 words, which suggests that sources will eventually be found for all. The language, then, was as authentic as Chatterton's detailed, though unsophisticated researches could make it.

Chatterton took the essence of fifteenth-century spelling, syntax, and word forms to be lawlessness. All of his language sources taken together as being equally "old" English—the dictionaries, the glossaries, Gibson's Camden, Leland, Percy, and the others (see *Works,* II, 1178-1179)—

would certainly convey such an impression to any imaginative person not expert in language study. Consequently he can expand his basic 1800-word vocabulary simply by embodying this lawlessness in the spelling and inflections of words from standard eighteenth-century English. His proficiency with this invented language grew steadily and rapidly throughout the Rowley year; to see this one need only compare **"Bristowe Tragedie"** with any of the later Rowley poems—say the **Eclogues.** The invented language grows, then, with the imagined world.

A second sort of authentication by density will be found in the Rowleyan drawings. All are boyish in their lack of skill and, frequently, in their ferocious intensity of detail. There are nearly three hundred of them extant (depending again on what one counts as a distinct drawing); eighty of them are printed in **Works.** The subjects suggest important aspects of the Rowley world. Nearly half are heraldic; the rest are drawings of objects from that world—coins, inscriptions, ruins, churches, gates, windows, statues—historian's objects we might call them. Five are maps of Bristol, Redcliff, and Bristol Castle and environs. It would be my guess that in these drawings and maps something analogous to the development of the Rowleyan language took place. Architectural and monumental Bristol—Redcliff Church and Canynge's tomb therein, to begin with— were as much catalysts and sources for the Rowley world as were old books and dictionaries. I would assume that something in a building, an exposed wall or foundation, the lay of a particular piece of land suggested to Chatterton most of his architectural fantasies. We know that he copied coins, statues, inscriptions from the engraved plates in his antiquarian sourcebooks. His drawings of Bristol Castle are particularly rich and detailed, and there were enigmatic and tantalizing fragments of that fabric still to be seen in his day. The map on page 62 is particularly eloquent: hardly a street of Redcliff fails to receive its heavy quota of buildings and monuments, each eloquent physical testimony to a glorious, actual past.

The more important Rowley documents will be taken up in the next section in their order of composition so as to give some notion of the gradual development of the Rowley world. Here, however, I should like to survey briefly the *kinds* of documents Chatterton composed—another instance of authenticating by density of imagining. A smaller group of documents can be called for convenience of classification "primary," since they purport to be remains rather than discussion and interpretation by Rowley and others (the "secondary" documents). There are four letters from Rowley, fifteen (nearly all of them dated) from his patron Canynge, as well as brief extracts from others. These letters show the shared interests of Canynge and Rowley at different stages of their lives—first youthful high jinks and women; then politics, architecture, art, literature, and history; and finally religion and snug retreat from the world. They also surround some of Rowley's major literary works with documentation of the occasions for writing and of the reception given them.[4] The other "primary" documents are an inscription on the cover of a mass book, a fragment of

a sermon by Rowley on the Holy Spirit in which he quotes from Latin and Greek fathers, nine legal documents (wills clearing Canynge from the Bristol legend that he was tight-fisted with his sons, deeds of endowment of ancient chapels, proclamations by Canynge and Rowley in their roles as judicious, patient preservers of orthodoxy and public order), and an itemized bill to Canynge for various paintings and heraldic decorations he had ordered.[5]

The "secondary" documents are an even more varied assortment. There are two very lengthy genealogies; two long lists of artists, one with heraldic notes; historical sketches of English coining, painting, and Christmas games; and two *catalogues raisonnés* of Canynge's collections of antiquities.[6] There are lengthy historical-topographical-architectural treatises on Bristol, Redcliff, and St. Bartholomew's Priory.[7] There are forty-odd (depending again on how such things are counted) historical notes of various length, mostly by Rowley, on coins, inscriptions, buildings, ancient Bristolians, monuments, churches, and heraldry.[8] There are lists of Bristol and Redcliff officials starting in Norman times, two chronicles, and two biographical sketches.[9] Nearly all seem to borrow their forms from historical and antiquarian writers closely familiar to Chatterton. Each piece has its distinct purpose, but taken together the Rowleyan documents work richly toward the authentication of the imaginary world, the idea that engendered the poetry. Once again we are turned, I feel, toward Collingwood's comparison of the novelist and the historian.

Notes

1. Jacob Bryant, *Observations upon the Poems of Thomas Rowley* (London, 1781), p. 350, as quoted in E. W. H. Meyerstein, *Life of Thomas Chatterton* (New York and London, 1930), p. 164.

2. In E. W. H. Meyerstein, *The Complete Works of Thomas Chatterton: A Bicentenary Edition* (Oxford, 1971), usually with suggestions about literary, biographical or psychological significance.

3. R. G. Collingwood, *The Idea of History* (New York, 1956), pp. 245-246.

4. "Four Letters on Warwyke," "Abstracts from Letters," "Three Rowley Letters," "Lyfe of W: Canynge."

5. "Mass Book Inscription," "Fragment of a Sermon," "Nine Deeds and Proclamations," "Painter's Bill to Canynge."

6. "Extracts from Craishes Herauldry," "Account of the Family of the De Berghams"; "Rowley's Heraldic Account," "Historie of Peyncters yn Englande"; "Of the Auntiaunt Forme of Monies," "The Ryse of Peyncteynge," "The Antiquity of Christmas Games"; "Englandes Glorye Revyved," "Explayneals of the Yellowe Rolle."

7. "A Discourse on Brystowe," the third of "Three Rowley Letters," "The Rolle of Seyncte Bartlemeweis Priorie."

8. "Rowley's Printing Press," "Towre Gate," "Hardinge," "Rowley's Collections for Canynge," "Bristol Castle," "Seyncte Maries Chyrche of the Porte," "Knightes Templaries Chyrche," "The Chyrche Oratorie of the Calendaryes," "Three Tombs," "Note to Map of Bristol," "Saxon Tinctures," "Elle's Coffin," "Churches of Bristol," "Fragments of Anticquitie," "The Court-Mantle," "Saxon Achievements," "Anecdote of Chaucer."

9. Appendix to third of "Three Rowley Letters"; chronicle in third of "Three Rowley Letters," "Chronical 1340-1374"; "Byrtonne," "Lyfe of W: Canynge."

Brian E. Mayne (essay date 1983)

SOURCE: "Thomas Chatterton—The Magnificent Prodigy," in *Mark Twain Journal,* Vol. 21, No. 3, Spring 1983, pp. 46-7.

[In the following essay, Mayne remarks on the variety of Chatterton's works, which include satires, hymns, essays, elegies, and a comic burletta. In addition, the critic observes that even as Chatterton forged the Rowley poems, he internalized the persona of Rowley as his own.]

Thomas Chatterton was seventeen years and nine months old when, on the 25th of August, 1770, discouraged and hopeless, he put an end to his own life. His acknowledged works, written in that short and hectic span, include long satires, elegies, verse epistles, squibs, lampoons, a comic burletta, essays and sketches. These and his life as a schoolboy, apprentice, and pretended antiquarian formed the outer shell of his fascinating character. The core was the serious and deeply emotional 15th century poet Rowley, whose connection with himself he never publicly acknowledged. It was the brilliant and sincere Rowley poems that catapulted Chatterton to literary fame and it is primarily for these creations that he is remembered. However, Chatterton's unique genius cannot be truly recognized unless his various styles are contrasted. It does not seem possible that the same person could have written the sprawling denunciation of **"Kew Gardens,"** the troubled lyrics of **"The Resignation,"** and the beautiful and touching **"An Excellente Balade of Charitie as wroten bie the gode Priest Thomas Rowley, 1464."** Yet all these pieces and more were written by a boy! Chatterton mixed his creative imagination with an astonishing drive and the results have amazed and puzzled intellects for more than two centuries.

He was a posthumous child, brought up by a mother he deeply loved. When he was eleven he wrote a hymn for Christmas Day. Here is one stanza from it:

How shall we celebrate the day
When God appeared in mortal clay,
The mark of worldly scorn?
When the archangel's heavenly lays
Attempted the Redeemer's praise,
And hailed salvation's morn?

Both in metre and religious sentiment these are good lines for a boy who had been esteemed a dunce. Chatterton had been removed from his first school for stupidity; at his next one he was considered very dull, but allowed to stay.

When he was twelve he finished a long poem entitled **"Elinoure and Juga"** and, by the time he was fourteen, he had so thoroughly acquired a knowledge of antiquated English that he was able to fool grave scholars with his fabricated Rowley poems. He forged a series of antique parchments that gave rise to excited discussions in learned circles. When he was sixteen a new bridge was finished at Bristol and he sent a Bristol newspaper the account of the opening of the old bridge 300 years before. Soon he was inventing ancient sermons for theologians; poems for wealthy people, which he claimed had been written by their ancestors hundreds of years before; and to antiquarians he would send accounts of ancient buildings as they looked when first completed. All were accepted as gospel truth by his many dupes. One of his most daring forgeries was an account of the eminent "Caravellers and Peyncters" of Bristol, which he sent to Walpole, who was then writing a history of British painters. Walpole, although at first deceived, submitted the manuscripts to two judges of ancient literature who pronounced them forgeries.

Chatterton's **"Battle of Hastings,"** written when he was sixteen, has a strain of noble dignity that has been hard to match. Here are a few lines:

Fitz Salnarville, Duke William's favourite knyght,
To noble Edelwarde his life did yeilde;
With hys tylte launce hee stroke with thilk a might
The Norman's bowels steemde upon the feeld.
Old Salnarville beheld his son lie ded
Against Erle Edelwarde his bowe-strynge drewe;
But Harold at one blow made tweine his head;
He dy'd before the poignant arrowe flew.
So was the hope of all the issue gone,
And in one battle fell the sire and son.

After his seventeenth birthday, Chatterton went to London to engage in a literary life. He entered with high hopes and began at once to write for magazines and newspapers, and at first met with enough success to encourage him in splendid dreams of fame and fortune. He wrote glowing accounts to his mother and sister of what he intended to achieve and spent his earnings on presents for them. But his bright hopes faded and he could scarcely earn enough to keep body and soul together. His lofty mood changed to one of despair. Too proud to make known his wants or to ask for assistance, he was soon on the verge of starvation.

Just two months before he died he returned to whatever comfort Rowley could give him and wrote his most poignant poem, **"An Excellente Balade of Charitie"**:

> Look in his gloomed face, his spryghte there scanne;
> Howe woe-be-gone, how withered, forwynd, deade!
> Haste to thie church-glebe-house, ashrewed manne!
> Haste to thie kiste, thie onlie dortoure bedde.
> Cale as the claie which will gre on thie hedde
> Is Charitie and Love aminge highe elves;
> Knightis and Barons live for pleasure and themselves.

One evening in the fall of 1770, when he had not eaten for three days, his landlady invited him to dine with her. With characteristic pride he assured her that he was neither hungry nor in want and shut himself up in his room. Thus poor Chatterton, haughty, conceited, and yet stung to the quick by his lack of immediate success, could find no way out of his troubles—except by a dose of arsenic. The brief life of the greatest prodigy in the history of English Literature had ended. He was buried in a pauper's grave near London.

The last bitter verses reflect his final contempt for Bristol:

> Farewell Bristolia's dingy piles of brick,
> Lovers of Mammon, worshippers of Trick!
> Ye spurned the boy who gave you antique lays,
> And paid for learning with your empty praise.
> Farewell ye guzzling aldermanic fools,
> By nature fitted for Corruption's tools!
> I go to where celestial anthems swell;
> But you, when you depart will sink to Hell.
> Farewell my Mother!—cease my anguished soul,
> Nor let distraction's billows o'er me roll!—
> Have mercy, Heaven! When I here cease to live,
> And this last act of wretchedness forgive!

It was after his death that the discussion about the poetry which he claimed was written by Thomas Rowley began. The best authorities agreed that the old poems must have been written by Chatterton only, and Rowley was the *nom de plume* under which he had sought to hide his own work believing, no doubt, that more fame would attach to them with Rowley's name than the works themselves would bring.

The most remarkable among the poems ascribed to Rowley are **"The Tragedy of Aella,"** **"The Battle of Hastings,"** **"Execution of Sir Charles Bawdin,"** **"The Tournament,"** and **"A Description of Cannynge's Feast."**

Almost a century after Chatterton's death the eminent semanticist and lexicographer Skeat put in what was then considered the final word as to how the Rowley poems had been written. He claimed Chatterton had found his old words in Speght's edition of Chaucer and in an early dictionary, that the Rowley poems were first written in modern English, and then rewritten with the substitution of archaic words for modern equivalents—with Chatterton using exaggerated spelling in line with what he had found in Speght's Chaucer. One wonders what conclusions Skeat

might have drawn had he been familiar with present-day research into multiple personalities—or what speculations he might have made had he been a believer in reincarnation.

Whatever the real solution is to the Chatterton mystery, there is little doubt that, as a Boy Wonder, he stands at the very top of history's list of such prodigies. We may condemn him for his forging activities and we may damn him for his haughty conceit, but we can only respect and wonder at his astonishing achievements.

Bibliography

Beers, H. A. *A History of English Romanticism in the Eighteenth Century.* London: Holt [c. 1898].

"Chatterton, Thomas," *Dictionary of National Biography.* ed. Leslie Stephen and Sidney Lee. 63 vols. London: Smith, Elder and Co., 1885-1900.

Ellinger, Esther P. *Thomas Chatterton, The Marvelous Boy.* London: Humphrey Milford Oxford University Press. 1930.

Galton, F. *Hereditary Genius.* New York: Appleton. 1871.

McCurdy, Harold G. "The Childhood Pattern of Genius," *Readings for an Introduction to Psychology,* ed. Richard A. King. Second ed. New York: McGraw-Hill Book Co. 1966.

Sampson, George. *The Concise Cambridge History of English Literature.* Cambridge: The Cambridge University Press. 1941.

Wilcox, Charles. *Poetical Works of Chatterton.* Abridged ed. Boston: Little, Brown & Company. 1857.

Maryhelen C. Harmon (essay date 1987)

SOURCE: "Melville's 'Borrowed Personage': Bartleby and Thomas Chatterton," in *ESQ,* Vol. 33, No. 1, 1st Quarter, 1987, pp. 35-44.

[In the following essay, Harmon argues that Chatterton's life served as the inspiration for Herman Melville's story "Bartleby, the Scrivener," which chronicles the short, dreary life of a solitary copyist—a job that Chatterton held before leaving Bristol.]

> Chatterton! methinks I hear thy name.
>
> —Samuel Taylor Coleridge[1]

In his Preface to the 1966 edition of *Melville's Reading,* Merton M. Sealts, Jr., observed that Melville's "literary use of important surviving books remains to be studied; the implications of many known purchases and borrowings have yet to be assessed."[2] In the interim since this comment, a number of source studies have appeared,[3] but none assessing Melville's possible utilization of his two annotated volumes of the poetical works of the eighteenth-century "Bristol Boy" Thomas Chatterton, which he listed in his *Journal of a Visit to London and the Continent*[4] as "obtained in London 1849" and valued enough to have rebound near the dirty bookstall in Chancery Lane where he bought them.[5] Volume One, in addition to Chatterton's poetry, includes the lengthy "Notices of His Life," and it is here, as well as in the poetry, that a surprising number of previously unnoticed "singular coincidences" are found that link not only the biographic facts and careers of the two writers, but also, and of greatest consequence, two exceedingly disparate narratives: the life of the poet and law-office scrivener Chatterton and Melville's tale of Bartleby.

Melville unquestionably examined the contents of both Chatterton volumes, for he not only inscribed each by pen with his name and the date purchased ("Dec. 19, 1849"), but also marked numerous passages throughout in pencil, using his characteristic check mark or vertical line in the margin. Volume Two was later presented to his brother-in-law, John C. Hoadley, and its dedication, dated January 6, 1854, supports the argument that Melville read both Chatterton volumes between their purchase in 1849 and 1854; Jay Leyda, in *The Melville Log,* states his belief that Melville in all likelihood read his Chatterton volumes at sea on his return voyage from Europe sometime before February in 1850.[6] At any rate, Melville certainly became familiar with the details of Chatterton's life and with "the strange ambiguity of his character" (C, p. cxi), during a critical period of his literary germination that produced not only "Bartleby, the Scrivener" and others of the collected *Piazza Tales,* but also *Moby-Dick* and *Pierre.*

It is not surprising that Melville was drawn to Chatterton, whose "forte . . . was pathos" (C, p. 319). Here was a ready-made personal emblem—a literary genius, author of sweeping epics, and quintessential romantic whose fate at the hands of Philistines had inspired panegyrics for almost a century after his death. Perhaps Melville experienced a "shock of recognition" when he read about Chatterton, seeing himself as a reincarnation of the earlier self-impelled isolato. Certainly he incorporated many details from Chatterton's life and character in his creation of Bartleby, a figure many see as an autobiographical "parable of the artist."[7] Both Melville and Bartleby "at first prefer to copy, . . . prefer solitude, both are suspected of being mentally unbalanced, and both are inclined to suicide,"[8] traits the two share with Chatterton. Furthermore, scriveners, like authors, are paid only for the number of pages they produce, a piece-work means of employment galling to Melville.

As to his acquaintance with Chatterton's poetry, Melville utilized, in slightly altered form, a stanza of the minstrel's song from *Aella* as an epigraph to Sketch Eighth, "Norfolk Isle and the Chola Widow," in "The Encantadas or Enchanted Isles," a collection written in the same period as "Bartleby." That stanza, along with all the other minstrel songs, Melville marked with a marginal pencil line in his edition. Also, "Cock-a-Doodle-Doo!" published in *Harp-*

er's in December 1853 (when the second half of "Bartleby" appeared in *Putnam's*), includes a parody of a stanza of Wordsworth's "Resolution and Independence" reflecting on the desolate fate of poets and citing thoughts of Chatterton, "the marvelous Boy, the sleepless Soul that perished in his pride," as a stimulus for his cheerless meditations. Earlier lines of this poem, which Melville could not have failed to note, allude to "all the ways of men, so vain and melancholy," and to anxiety concerning "Solitude, pain of heart, distress, and poverty,"[9] circumstances certainly descriptive of both Chatterton and Bartleby.

What did Melville find worthy of marking in his two volumes of the life and works of Chatterton that might appear later in "Bartleby, the Scrivener"? The Preface begins with the editor and biographer C. B. Willcox's compelling declaration that "Perhaps there was never an age in which the literary world were more devoted to studies which involve metaphysical disquisition or analytical reasoning" (C, p. i) than that of which he wrote. Chatterton's chronicler aims "to gratify that class of readers who recognize in the study of man the proper and most ennobling study of their race, and who find delight in examining into the darkest mysteries of the human heart, and exploring the most hidden springs of the human will" (C, pp. i-ii).

Thus the tone is set for "the most curious investigation" (C, p. i) of the life of Chatterton. The verbose and often sentimental biographer emphasizes his subject's "dark destiny" and "perpetual struggles," the brevity of life, and "the solemn agony and terrific grandeur of his death" (C, p. ii). Seeing Chatterton's life as "a kind of psychological romance" (C, p. xxix), Willcox unequivocally declares that such personal qualities and events render Chatterton "at once a sublime study for the poet, and a character of the most absorbing interest to the psychologist" (C, p. ii).

These introductory statements, which Melville marked with a long, vertical pencil mark in the margin, are akin in tone, verbosity, and sentimentality with those of his lawyer, who sees scriveners as an "interesting and somewhat singular set of men," the willful Bartleby obviously obsessing him. Although confident of his powers as a raconteur ("if I pleased, [I] could relate divers histories"[10] of other scriveners), he chooses the brief and fragmentary encounter with Bartleby as his sublime study. The elusive figure proves to be, like Chatterton, "a character of the most absorbing interest to the psychologist," a role the lawyer assumes in his narrative as he seeks to analyze in retrospect his enigmatic employee. Melville describes Bartleby as "inscrutable" (M, p. 35), "unaccountable" (M, p. 27), one "of whom nothing is ascertainable" (M, p. 13), whose actions prove increasingly to be a "sore perplexity" (M, p. 22) both to the lawyer and to the reader who shares his bafflement. Chatterton also troubled his chronicler, for Willcox begged his readers to be patient "till we have rightly unravelled the mysteries of his character" (C, p. lxxii).

Working with what he gleaned from previous versions of Chatterton's biography, Willcox, after his lengthy and melodramatic prefatory apologia, then feels impelled—like Melville's lawyer—to proceed with details of the brief life of his fated subject. He begins with the circumstances of the poet's birth and environment, likewise convinced that "some such description is indispensable to an adequate understanding of the chief character about to be presented" (M, p. 13). Melville's lawyer too sensed the need to know where Bartleby was born, for him to tell him *any thing* about himself, to which inquiries the scrivener replied, of course, "I would prefer not to" (M, p. 20). Therefore there can be no "complete life," as "few passages in the life of Bartleby" are discovered, and Melville's lawyer laments that "no materials exist for a full and satisfactory biography of this man" (M, p. 13); Chatterton's chronicler, in a similar vein, complained, "there are no documents to which we can refer for facts; there are no biographical notices which we can consult. . . . All that is to be told must be . . . woven, as best it can, into the form of a narrative" (C, p. cxx). Thus both Willcox and the fictional lawyer resolutely intend to fill in themselves in compensation for what they see as "an irreparable loss to literature" (M, p. 13).

Melville read that Chatterton's early years were spent as a "charity-boy" at Colston's school in Bristol, a seven-year period that a twentieth-century biographer, E. H. W. Meyerstein, describes in almost Bartleby-like terms: Chatterton "was now immured in . . . a training prison . . . near the heart of the noisy city . . ."[11] In 1767, at age fourteen, the youth was apprenticed as a scrivener to Mr. John Lambert, whose offices, like those of Melville's lawyer in New York, were in two different locations during Chatterton's employment, first in Small Street (the suggestion of Wall Street is uncanny), then in two rooms opposite the Bristol Exchange, that city's equivalent of Wall Street. Under the terms of Chatterton's employment, he was provided "food, clothing, and lodging by his master" (C, p. xlix). Melville depicts Bartleby as also dependent on his employer, by one stratagem or another, for his subsistence, keeping "bachelor's hall" in the law chambers, "his constant abiding place and home" (M, p. 29) where he "ate, dressed, and slept" (M, p. 27). Further, in their final confrontation in the office, the lawyer invites Bartleby to go home with him; and when Bartleby is imprisoned in the Tombs, the lawyer pays the grub-man "to provide [Bartleby] with something good to eat" (M, p. 43).

The financially comfortable and "unambitious" Lambert was described by Meyerstein "as a kindhearted man, who read a great deal" (p. 67) but, like Bartleby's employer, had "distinctly limited perception."[12] At first he had little difficulty with his scrivener, "who was always accessible" (C, p. lxxvii) in the same way that Bartleby *was always there* (M, p. 26). Chatterton was "of a melancholy and contemplative disposition" (C, p. li) and "not disposed to be over-communicative" (C, p. lv), like Melville's "silent man" (M, p. 44). The young scrivener at first produced, like Bartleby, "an extraordinary quantity of writing" for

this conservative attorney: "Chatterton was a good apprentice. There are still extant in his hand-writing a folio book of law forms and precedents, containing three hundred and thirty-four closely written pages" (C, p. li). In a strikingly similar phrase, Melville describes a certain work of Bartleby as "five hundred pages, closely written . . ." (M, p. 20).

In order to accomplish such a volume of work along with his literary endeavors, which by now occupied much of his time, Chatterton "seldom slept, and would even write by moonlight" (C, p. lx); Bartleby also "ran a day and night line, copying by sun-light and by candlelight" (M, p. 19). He "never went to dinner," "never eat[ing] a dinner, properly speaking" (M, p. 23). Nor did Chatterton eat regularly; ("Of his meals he was ever oblivious;" C, p. xxviii), "living upon a tart only" (C, p. lxi). Twice in the Chatterton "Life" the young man's taste for gingerbread tarts is mentioned; these flat cakes or tarts were indeed one of his few foods,[13] a close parallel to the diet of Bartleby. Chatterton "never tasted strong or spiritous liquors" (C, p. lxi), while Bartleby "never drank beer like Turkey, or tea or coffee even, like other men" (M, p. 28). As Chatterton's biographer observed, such a life "is rather singular" (C, p. lxvi), a descriptive term Melville uses four times in "Bartleby" (M, pp. 13, 15, 19, 26).

Needless to say, at first Lambert was well-pleased with his diligent new scrivener and gave "the highest testimony to the worth of Chatterton . . . to his regularity in his profession, his punctual attendance on all the duties required of him"; he "never knew him in bad company, or suspected him of any inclination thereto" (C, p. li-lii). In similar phrasing, Melville's lawyer remarked about Bartleby's "freedom from dissipation," for "it was not to be thought of for a moment that Bartleby was an immoral person" (M, p. 27).

A crisis occurred, however, when Chatterton submitted anonymously to local officials, who were planning a celebration of the anniversary of the construction of the Bristol Bridge, a parchment purporting to be an original fifteenth-century document describing the dedication. The scrivener was suspected of being the author, and several citizens confronted him, beseeching him, like Bartleby, "to verify the accuracy of his copy," as it were. When he adamantly refused, Chatterton, who had indeed created the spurious document, "was assailed with threats, to which he retaliated with haughtiness, and flatly refused to give any account. Finding him invincible, they assumed another tone, spoke to him in a gentle manner, talked of patronage and assistance . . ." (C, p. lxv). In a similar scene, Melville's lawyer confronts Bartleby, and Nippers intrudes indignantly, calling Bartleby "a stubborn mule" (M, p. 31). Yet "Bartleby moved not a limb," preferring "not to be a little reasonable" (M, p. 30). Then the lawyer gently called him into his office, but receiving no reply, "in a still gentler tone" (M, p. 30), he repeated his summons. Bartleby, however, was obdurate: "his countenance remained immovable" (M, p. 30). About Chatterton, Willcox cited the opinion that "there is a degree of heroism in his obstinacy" as he "inflexibly persisted to the last," increasingly "more determined in asserting what he had once asserted" (C, p. 308).

A telling marginal notation by Melville in the "Life" of Chatterton appears beside the context of the controversy that ensued when the young scrivener unsuccessfully sought the patronage of Horace Walpole, the renowned connoisseur and man of letters. Like Bartleby, Chatterton "had considerable time to himself." He spent it not only copying legal documents but also creating the pseudo-medieval chronicles of Thomas Rowley, a fictitious fifteenth-century Bristol cleric, samples of which Chatterton sent Walpole. Intrigued at first, Walpole became suspicious about their authenticity and sought to know more about the discoverer of such curious manuscripts. Imprudently Chatterton informed him of his age and station in life, after which Walpole, fearing exploitation, abruptly withdrew interest in Chatterton's chronicles. The young man, however, was resolute, for throughout his brief life, when challenged "to verify the accuracy of his writings," he steadfastly claimed that certain of his poems and essays were originally the work of Rowley, and that he merely copied them, scrivenerlike, from antique manuscripts he discovered in a local church. Walpole was convinced, nevertheless, that the "singularly impertinent" (C, p. ciii) Chatterton "was deliberately practicing a deception on him" (C, p. cvi). Yet the image of Chatterton continued to haunt Walpole like an "intolerable incubus," even after the youth's death. Just as the New York lawyer admitted that "In vain I persisted that Bartleby was nothing to me" (M, p. 40), Walpole also was never to free himself of the specter of a pale scrivener.

In Willcox's biography, the word "forger" appears repeatedly to describe Chatterton as creator of the putative author Rowley's works. Perhaps the word is the seed of Melville's grub-man's impression that Bartleby was "a gentleman forger" (M, p. 44). Willcox remarked about the irony of Walpole, himself a literary "forger" in his original ascription of *The Castle of Otranto*,[14] assailing Chatterton for misrepresenting himself both as petitioner and as perpetrator of the Rowley attribution. Melville noted the biographer's rhetorical question about the Walpole controversy: "So might Chatterton have appealed—Was not *my* Rowley a 'borrowed personage,' and am not I therefore excusable?" (C, p. xcvii-xcviii). Sir Walter Scott is quoted in the 1842 edition of Chatterton's life and works that Melville purchased as having the opinion that Chatterton "probably deprecated the doubtful fame of an ingenious but detected imposter, and *preferred* the internal consciousness, that, by persisting in the deception he had commenced, future ages might venerate the power of Chatterton, under patronage of the fictitious Rowley."[15] The facts, then, are that Thomas Chatterton was a scrivener/forger, that Bartleby, also a scrivener, was thought to be imprisoned for forgery, and that Melville penciled a passage describing Chatterton's complex "house of forgery" (C, p. cxviii).

The lawyer Lambert's satisfaction with Chatterton's work as an apprentice was short-lived. He began to observe certain "strange peculiarities," especially that his enigmatic young man was becoming increasingly "gloomy and sullen, exhibiting frequent fits of ill temper" (C, p. li). "For days together he would scarcely utter a word. He would enter . . . without deigning to address a single inmate; would occupy his stool at the office in rigid silence, noticing the observations of his fellow-clerks only with a supercilious, sarcastic smile of contempt" (C, p. lxxvii). Elsewhere Willcox describes Chatterton as "silent and gloomy for long intervals together, speaking to no one, and appearing angry when noticed or disturbed" (C, p. lxiv). Chatterton's "intervals of silence, when with difficulty he could be got to speak or make answer to an inquiry" (C, p. liii), are uncannily like Bartleby's "great stillness," "austere reserve," and "morbid moodiness" (M, pp. 26, 28, 29).

"What had *he* in common with his vulgar associates?" (C, p. lx), Chatterton felt, loathing "the mechanical and always detested duties of his clerkship" (C, p. xlvii*n*). The robotlike nature of scrivener's work also struck Melville, whose Bartleby "wrote on silently, palely . . . mechanically." It was clear that for Chatterton "the disgust which he had conceived for his profession continued to increase" (C, p. lv), much like Nippers, who had "a certain impatience of the duties of a mere copyist" and "wanted . . . to be rid of a scrivener's table altogether." Just as Bartleby was spied upon, so was Chatterton. Lambert would "watch his actions, and if possible, detect him off his post" (C, p. liii). But Chatterton relentlessly "maintained a gloomy reserve, speaking to no one—retreating into his own invisible world" (C, p. lxxvii), silently asserting his "pride, the reserve, the native and unconquerable haughtiness" (C, p. xxvii) of his being.

Such erratic behavior increasingly infuriated the Bristol lawyer, as it does his New York counterpart, and Lambert came to recognize that his employee's neurotic conduct, "already the source of much uneasiness" (C, p. xxiii)—"the silence, the solitude . . . his eccentric habits, his singularities of behavior" (C, p. 308)—"were not attributed to a true cause" (C, p. lxxvii*n*.); Chatterton was, as Melville would describe Bartleby, "the victim of innate and incurable disorder" (M, p. 29). Similarly, Bartleby becomes "a phenomenon totally alien to [the lawyer's] experience and sensibilities,"[16] causing, as the elderly man complains, "a whisper of wonder" to run "all through the circle of my professional acquaintance," "perplexing my visitors, and scandalizing my professional reputation" (M, p. 38).

Chatterton's "fits of absence were remarkable" (C, p. lxxvii); these "moody intervals in which he would be long invincibly silent" (C, p. xxii) increased alarmingly, his life becoming a "total abstraction from all the external world" (C, p. liii). Chatterton too spent time in "dead-wall revery," "would often look stedfastly . . . without speaking, or seeming to see . . . for a quarter of an hour or more" (C, p. lxxvii), with gray eyes (C, p. cxlii), like those of

Bartleby. Melville echoes the same terminology: twice in "Bartleby" the lawyer looks "steadfastly" at his scrivener (M, pp. 20, 32). The tense situation soon became unendurable for both Chatterton and his employer; the youth "was continually insulting him and making his life miserable" (C, p. liii). No doubt to Lambert, as to Melville's lawyer, "his perverseness seemed ungrateful, considering the undeniable good usage and indulgence he had received" (M, p. 30), but nothing could be resolved. As Chatterton himself later wrote of his "confinement" in the sterile office routine, "Bristol's mercenary walls were never destined to hold me" (C, p. 712). "The irksomeness of his profession, and the disgust which he had conceived for its restraint, continued to increase, and he soon came to the determination . . . to abandon it altogether" (C, p. cviii). Like Bartleby, "he had permanently given up copying," "had decided upon doing no more writing," and "his decision was irreversible" (M, pp. 31, 32).

One day, while Lambert was rummaging in Chatterton's desk (he too probably thought, like Bartleby's employer, that "the desk is mine, and its contents too"; M, p. 28), he discovered an alarming document, Chatterton's "Last Will and Testament," in which the young man announced his decision to commit suicide in the office the following day. He wrote, "I must either live a slave—a servant, have no will of my own . . . —or DIE" (C, p. cxvii). Lambert, with relief, immediately dismissed him, for like Bartleby's lawyer, he wanted no scandal, sharing the "conviction that the easiest way of life is the best" (M, p. 14). Thus he resolved his predicament of employing the difficult young man with such a "proud and unconquerable will" (C, p. cxliii).

Here the signal correspondence between the life of Chatterton and Melville's Bartleby is most evident: in each narrative, a tolerant yet exasperated lawyer is sorely tested by a remarkably similar exercise of will by an eccentric and threatening young employee. Bartleby's lawyer is so distressed by his scrivener's "strange willfulness" (M, p. 23) that he seeks a resolution of his dilemma by consulting Jonathan Edwards' *Freedom of the Will* and is thereby inspired to accept his situation with grace as "predestined from eternity," and would have done so, he rationalized, were it not "for the unsolicited and uncharitable remarks" (M, p. 37) of his professional colleagues. In Bristol there was "the general impression that [Chatterton] was going mad" (C, p. lxxvii). Bartleby provoked similar fears, Ginger Nut finding him "a little luny," the lawyer asking "Are you moon-struck?" and later concluding that "he is a little deranged."[17] Perhaps the instability of both scriveners stemmed from the incompatibility of their jobs to their natures; certainly Chatterton was torn between mechanical copying and the obsession with "his own peculiar business"—"copying" the Rowley chronicles that he claimed to have found—just as Bartleby, as Newton Arvin observes, was reduced to the uninspired and intolerable drudgery of a scrivener (p. 242).

After he quit copying for Lambert, Chatterton left Bristol almost immediately for London, in April 1770. Prefiguring Melville's descriptions of Bartleby's prison of "grimy . . . bricks" (M, p. 19) and his view of a "lofty brick wall, black by age" (M, p. 14), in verses said to have been found after his death, Chatterton wrote, "Farewell, Bristolia's dingy piles of brick."[18] His final gesture to those few who wished him well was to purchase and distribute ginger tarts. "Little now remained to be said of Chatterton," Willcox concluded, "and that little consists of no stirring adventures, and of no incidents that can satisfy curiosity or afford amusement to any but those who love a simple story" (C, p. cxx), much as Bartleby's chronicler expresses a similar sense of finality in similar terms: "there would seem little need for proceeding further in this history" (M, p. 45).

The final brief phase in London of Chatterton's life again resembles Bartleby's. He began "miserably to starve," existing on a "morsel of bread, the penny tart and draught of spring water" (C, p. cxxxiv). He settled in a tiny garret room in Brooke Street, like Bartleby's move "from the four walls of the law office to four walls of the city prison."[19] Again his plight resembles Bartleby's, whose "miserable friendlessness and loneliness are here revealed! His poverty is great, but his solitude, how horrible!" (M, p. 27). Offered food by a solicitous neighbor, Chatterton "scorned subsistence" (C, p. lx-viii*n*), "angrily refused to be fed—*to be kept alive*—by the bread of charity" (C, p. cxxxvii); though starving, "nothing could induce him again to satisfy his hunger at another's expense" (C, p. cxxxviii). When a kindly benefactor "begged him to take some dinner with her, knowing that he had eaten nothing throughout that period, he was offended at her expressions—refused the invitation, and assured her that he was not hungry" (C, p. cxxxvii). In Bartleby's words, he "prefer[red] not to dine today" (M, p. 44). In his squalid room he had two viewless dormer windows, and "friendless, lone, and unassisted" (C, p. cxxxvii), the young man "in that window . . . loitered for some hours before he retired to his last rest,"[20] literally his ultimate "dead-wall revery" (M, p. 31). That same night, August 24, 1770,[21] Chatterton drank arsenic, lay down just as Bartleby did in the prison yard, and died a suicide.[22]

After an inquest, "a coroner's verdict of insanity was returned" (C, p. clx). He was seventeen years old, his life, like Bartleby's, a short story. Willcox describes the "solemn agony and terrific grandeur" of Chatterton's death (C, p. i), when "the sleeper awoke" for the final time "to find his only pillow was a stone" (C, p. cxxxvi); the dead Bartleby is found "lying on his side, his head touching the cold stones," seeming "profoundly sleeping" (M, pp. 44-45). "It is not our intention," Chatterton's biographer gravely concludes, "to profane the chamber of death, or to portray with unavailing and heartless minuteness, the dark imaginings and mental convulsions of 'the sleepless boy that perished in his pride'"; the details, "are not to be coldly delineated in words, but are to be realized by the thinking and sympathetic heart alone" (C, p. cxxxix). In like manner Melville's lawyer demurred, choosing not to describe the analogous scene verbally, confident that "Imagination will readily supply the meager recital" of the denouement (M, p. 45). Each victim would be buried without dignity, Chatterton "among paupers" (C, p. clx) and Bartleby "among uncaring strangers" (M, p. 28).

Turning philosophic, Willcox admitted that he found it "difficult to form a just appreciation of the character" (C, p. cxlii) of the strange young man whose life he documented to "its most melancholy termination" (C, p. cx), especially poignant being the details of "his departure from the world, in which we are all pilgrims and strangers" (C, p. cxxxix). Equally philosophic is Bartleby's baffled narrator, assigning the pathetic scrivener to eternal sleep with "kings and counsellors" (M, p. 45). Melville read in his Chatterton volumes the biographer's conclusion about the brief life of his subject, what he felt was "a tale half-told" (C, p. 319n), "only a melodrama, and no complete tragedy" (C, pp. lxxxi-lxxxii).

In the conclusion of "Bartleby," the lawyer recounts a "vague report," "one little item of rumor" (M, pp. 13, 45), in his frustrated efforts to analyze his subject, to enhance his melodramatic narrative so "sentimental souls might weep" (M, p. 13): that Bartleby had previously worked in the Dead Letter Office in Washington. Willcox's "Life" records curious parallels, first that in Chatterton's deathroom "the floor was covered with a multitude of small fragments of paper" (C, p. cxxxix), the poems he destroyed, communications destined never to reach anyone's eyes. Further, "it is related that Dr. Fry, the head of St. Johns College, Oxford, very shortly after the unhappy end of the young poet, proceeded to Bristol . . . to befriend and assist [Chatterton]" (C, p. clxi). On discovering that his venture was futile, that he was too late "on errands of life," Fry realized that an interval of only a few days thwarted his offer of help to one who "died despairing." Similarly, Melville described Bartleby as one "who died unhoping," one who died stifled by unrelieved calamities" (M, p. 45). Another biographer reports an additional incident regarding Chatterton's request on the day before his suicide "to a very respectable friend for some money. . . . The money was sent, with an assurance that he might have more, if he wanted it";[23] in this "dead letter" there was "a bank-note sent in swiftest charity:—he whom it would relieve, nor eats nor hungers any more" (M, p. 45). The young Bristol poet had directed this inscription to be inscribed in "a Mourning Ring" in his "Last Will and Testament": "Alas! poor Chatterton—"; "Ah Bartleby! Ah humanity!" concludes Melville's lawyer (M, p. 45).

Melville was an omnivorous reader, "ever dependent upon his sources,"[24] gorging himself on whatever he could lay his hands on, but unlike Bartleby, for whom "there was no pause for digestion," what Melville read stayed with him: "the books that really spoke to Melville became an immediate part of him to a degree hardly matched by any other of our great writers in their maturity."[25] As an extreme depiction of dejection, denial of self, and retreat from any

kind of creative involvement in life, Melville's realization of Bartleby is a powerful study in the ultimate effect of Chatterton's story. Each scrivener would convey a legacy of depression to haunt his employer, whether the lawyer in Bristol or the lawyer in New York, as well as those who read of their similar plights, Chatterton's story providing both a model and imagery for what Melville felt compelled to dramatize as a telling and cautionary statement about the perils of a totally unrealized life. Surely, as so many critics have observed, in "Bartleby" Melville was expressing his doubts and frustrations about reversals in his own literary career; yet he was also writing more universally a parable about human endeavor that all men might heed.

I argue that Melville recognized a kindred spirit in Chatterton, an "appeal . . . hardly to be resisted" (M, p. 16), and that familiarity with the two volumes of his life and works so impressed him with its "fraternal melancholy" that he incorporated in Bartleby's genealogical substance something of the scrivener/artist Chatterton. Melville read and marked the lament that the life of Thomas Chatterton had "never been drawn by the hand of a master" (C, p. cxin); the biography of Bartleby related by Melville's Master in Chancery is evidence that there was not to be another such "irreparable loss to literature" (M, p. 13).

Notes

1. The epigraph is from "Monody on the Death of Chatterton," first version.

2. Sealts, *Melville's Reading* (Madison: Univ. of Wisconsin Press, 1966), p. v.

3. See, for example, the compilation by Gordon E. Bigelow in "The Problem of Symbolist Form in Melville's 'Bartleby the Scrivener,'" *Modern Language Quarterly*, 31 (1970), 345-346; and Lewis Leary's "B is for Bartleby" in *Bartleby the Inscrutable* (Hamden, Conn.: Archon Books, 1979), pp. 13-27.

4. Eleanor Melville Metcalf, ed., *Journal of a Visit to London and the Continent by Herman Melville, 1849-1850* (Cambridge, Mass.: Harvard Univ. Press, 1948), p. 75. An ironic coincidence is the site of Melville's purchase of the Chatterton volumes—Chancery Lane; Melville's elderly lawyer is a Master in Chancery. Another is that Chancery Lane is only a few blocks from Brooke Street, where Chatterton died.

5. *The Poetical Works of Thomas Chatterton with Notices of His Life, History of the Rowley Controversy, a Selection of his Letters, and Notes Critical and Explanatory,* 2 vols. (Cambridge: Printed for W. P. Grant, 1842). Sealts includes the volumes as entry 137 in his compendium of Melville's reading. Although the edition was published anonymously, the editor and biographer was C. B. Willcox. Citations from this text of

Melville's will be shown parenthetically with the abbreviation C and page number.

I wish to express my gratitude to the curators of the Berg Collection in the New York Public Library for granting me permission to inspect these two books of Melville's, from which a record of his notations was made. Metcalf (Melville's granddaughter) remarks that "these volumes of Chatterton contain numerous interesting markings in Melville's usual manner . . ." (p. 152).

6. Leyda, *The Melville Log* (New York: Harcourt, Brace, 1951), I, 363.

7. See Richard Chase's *Herman Melville: A Critical Study* (New York: Macmillan, 1949), p. 146. Chatterton's influence might also be seen in *Pierre* (1852), which concerns the agonies of a writer who like Chatterton finds no audience, is obsessed with his own genealogy, and kills himself in a prison in a big city.

8. Henry A. Murray, "Bartleby and I" in *Melville Annual 1965, A Symposium: Bartleby the Scrivener,* ed. Howard P. Vincent (Kent, Ohio: Kent State Univ. Press, 1966), pp. 13-14.

9. For a detailed discussion of Melville's adaptation of Wordsworth's poem, see Marvin Fisher's *Going Under* (Baton Rouge: Louisiana State Univ. Press, 1977), pp. 171-173.

10. Melville, *The Piazza Tales and Other Prose Pieces: 1839-1860* (Evanston and Chicago: Northwestern Univ. Press and Newberry Library, 1987) p. 13; hereafter cited as M with page number.

11. Meyerstein, *A Life of Thomas Chatterton* (New York: Russell and Russell, 1930), p. 27.

12. Leo Marx, "Melville's Parable of the Walls," *Sewanee Review,* 61 (1953), 605.

13. Meyerstein records that Chatterton "was in the habit of buying tarts at Mr. Freeling's, a gingerbread baker" in Bristol (347*n.*).

14. Walpole claimed on the title page that the manuscript was "translated by Wm. Marshal, Gent., from the original Italian of ONUPHRIO MURALTO, supposedly first printed at Naples in the black letter, in the year, 1529." Compare this ascription with a typical one of Chatterton's: "As wroten bie the gode Prieste Thomas Rowley, 1464."

15. This passage is quoted in II, 624*n;* italics mine.

16. R. Bruce Bickley, Jr., *The Method of Melville's Short Fiction* (Durham, N. C.: Duke Univ. Press, 1975), p. 36. A biographer of Chatterton, John H. Ingram, reported that "the well-to-do solicitor was too interested in his own well-being . . . to consider any such dereliction in any member" of his staff; *The True Chatterton* (London: T. Fisher Unwin, 1910), p. 54.

17. Melville read Lord Byron's opinion: "Chatterton, *I* think, was mad" (C, p. clx). Byron is mentioned on two other occasions in this text and is the only literary figure alluded to in "Bartleby": the lawyer avers "that the mettlesome poet Byron" (M, p. 20) certainly would not have verified copy either. As to Chatterton's mental state, in 1871 J. Addington Symonds analyzed his condition, "the deeply seated duality of his nature," and concluded that he suffered from what later psychoanalysts would term schizophrenia; *The Academy,* 39, December 15, 1871, 549-550. Although Symonds' purpose was to review the 1871 edition of Chatterton's poetry, his keen insight inspired future critics to pursue this direction in their studies. Arvin analyzed "Bartleby" as "a wonderfully intuitive study in what would now be called schizophrenia, and in Melville himself there were certainly the germs of schizophrenic detachment"; *Herman Melville* (New York: Viking Press, 1950), p. 243. Elizabeth Hardwick also notes Bartleby's "schizophrenic deterioration"; *Bartleby in Manhattan and Other Essays* (New York: Random House, 1962) p. 218.

18. The 1842 edition of Chatterton's life and works was reprinted in 1857 and included "The Last Verses Written by Chatterton," which begins with this line; Meyerstein, pp. 446-447.

19. Bickley, p. 43, n. 15.

20. Herbert Croft, *Love and Madness* (London: G. Kearsley, 1886), p. 223.

21. Joel Conarroe argues in "Melville, Bartleby and Charles Lamb," *Studies in Short Fiction* 5 (Winter 1968), 113-118, that Melville's reading in 1849 included an essay of Lamb's suggesting the contemplative martyr St. Bartholemew (also known as "Bartlemy") as a prototype for the scrivener. By an incredible coincidence, the Feast Day of St. Bartlemy is August 24, the day of Chatterton's death. As to the possible similarity he cites between the name Bartleby and that of St. Bartlemy, there is also a suggestion in the "Life" of Chatterton that Melville read about the Dean of Bristol, who is remembered in Chatterton's "Will," Dr. Cutts Barton (C, p. 628); the youth leaves him his Religion, a sentiment that may have struck Melville's interest. The grub-man, Mr. Cutlets, who is named in the *Putnam's* version of "Bartleby, the Scrivener," also echoes the name of the "lazy dean" Chatterton satirically maligned.

22. The famous painting of Chatterton's death scene by Henry Wallis (1856), now exhibited in the Tate Gallery in London, is highly idealized. The young poet's body is not distorted as it would have been after the convulsions caused by the poison. Windows open out to a pleasant view, and there is a plant on the sill. More realistic is the floor, littered with scraps of his destroyed poems.

23. Croft, p. 196; also quoted in Meyerstein, p. 439.

24. Bickley, p. 27. Leon Howard agrees, asserting that the "essence of [Bartleby] was distilled from Melville's reading"; *Herman Melville* (Berkeley: Univ. of California Press, 1951), p. 108.

25. F. O. Matthiessen, *American Renaissance* (New York: Oxford Univ. Press, 1941), p. 122.

Louise J. Kaplan (essay date 1987)

SOURCE: "Introduction," in *The Family Romance of Imposter-Poet Thomas Chatterton*, Macmillan-Atheneum, 1987, pp. 1-11.

[In the following essay, Kaplan provides a psychoanalytic portrait of Chatterton, describing him as a "typical, if extreme," adolescent who was also haunted by the absence of a father who died before he was born. Chatterton, the critic notes, spent his short life searching for his father in the form of the medieval personages that he fabricated.]

Thomas Chatterton was in many ways a typical adolescent. During the seventeen years of his life, he was an exuberant player in the artistic, intellectual, religious, political, and sexual adventures we have come to expect of not-quite-adults. Even his suicide marked him as a typical, if extreme, example of the *Sturm und Drang* image of adolescence. But he was not merely an ordinary adolescent. He was an impostor, and indeed he grew up in the precise family environment that is believed to promote imposturousness. He was a fatherless boy raised by an adoring, idealizing mother and sister, both of whom encouraged his tendencies toward grandiosity and exceptionality. Chatterton was an artistically gifted boy whose poetic talents flourished during adolescence.

In fact I came to Chatterton through my work on adolescence. While sorting out my research and notes for the concluding sections of my last book, *Adolescence,* I thought that Thomas Chatterton, the now nearly forgotten eighteenth-century poet who became an emblem for the English romantic movement, would be the ideal figure to represent the prototypically male disorder, the impostor. However, as I looked further into the circumstances of his life history, I found that his imposturous deeds and indeed his character were far more out of the ordinary than I had expected. I had imagined impostor types to be more straightfoward—obvious con men and manipulators. But Chatterton was different. In the first place, he was not even a genuine plagiarizer. A plagiarizer imitates or appropriates the writings of another person and represents them as his own original work. He is a pure and simple faker, whose motives of financial reward and personal aggrandizement are relatively uncomplicated. But Chatterton actually wrote the poems that he pretended were written by a fifteenth-century priest. He never took on the identity of another person the way a true impostor would. Further-

more, it was nearly impossible to discern where his genuine artistic passions left off and his criminal impulses began.

Felix Krull, Thomas Mann's brilliantly realized fictional confidence man, an out-and-out liar, cheat, and plagiarizer, was decidedly better suited to my immediate purposes. Some of the ambiguities in Chatterton's character are also present in Krull. As Mann commented on his novel, "It is in essence the story of an artist; in it the element of the unreal and illusional passes frankly over into the criminal." But despite this general ambiguity, Mann's fictional confidence man exemplifies with greater clarity the language and mentality of the criminal than could Thomas Chatterton, who never quite grasped the criminal nature of his poetic enterprise and who never had a Thomas Mann to give artistic shape to his confused mental life.

Krull was the example I selected to use in *Adolescence,* but I could not abandon Chatterton. I had grown attached to him and wanted to give him a book of his own, a biography that would do justice to the richness and complexity of his life, particularly to the peculiar relationship between artistic creation and falsehood that is expressed in his literary endeavors. I was intrigued by the dilemmas of his moral character, his motives for writing imposturous poetry, and the external circumstances and internal motives surrounding his suicide.

Another facet of Chatterton's imposturousness commanded my attention. Obviously, a man who pretends to be another man has an uncertain sense of personal identity. What is not so obvious is that underlying that manifest uncertainty of selfhood is a fragility of *masculine* gender identity. As psychoanalysts have come to appreciate, an impostor's sexual orientation is as ambiguous as his moral orientation. The sexual dilemmas are not whether the impostor's sexual orientation is homosexual or heterosexual; the dilemmas concern the perverse quality of his relationships with his sexual partners, whether they are male or female. Impostors are predisposed to acquiring sexual perversions such as sadomasochism, transvestism, fetishism, exhibitionism, voyeurism. And when they become involved in less-complicated sexual relations with women they nevertheless are pseudogenital in the psychological sense; that is, while they are able to employ their penises without ritualized or manifestly perverse scenarios, they emphasize scoring, performance, orgasm in the partner not as the giving of pleasure but as vanquishment and defeat. They view erection as risk, enmity, deception, survival.

Unlike Felix Krull, who we are told courts and seduces married and unmarried women, Thomas Chatterton's actual sexual behavior remains a mystery. He was rumored to be a profligate, a libertine, far too enamored of too many of the young ladies in his Bristol neighborhood, far too well acquainted with the mantua-makers and dulcineas of London. One widespread theory had it that he committed suicide because he was afflicted with syphilis or perhaps an untreatable gonorrhea.

What is certain is that under his own identity he wrote a few scandalous works, among them an obscene poem celebrating the size and marvelous abilities of an exhibitionist's penis and a doggerel verse deriding a capacious vagina and that in the last year of his life he wrote as a freethinker on all matters—religious, political, social, and sexual. Though some critics would cite these writings as evidence of Chatterton's sexual perversions, such "wild" hypotheses are unfounded. The significant issues concern the unique and puzzling relationships between Chatterton's acknowledged freethinking writings and the conflicts expressed in his imposturous works, which were noble, pure, and saintly.

My special interest in the relationships among artistic creation, falsehood, and perversion, which Chatterton's life illustrates, began in my clinical work where many years ago I encountered several overtly perverse patients who were simultaneously caught up in various fabrications of reality—pathological lying, hoaxing, plagiarism, swindling. About fifteen years ago, I took into treatment a nine-year-old boy who, quite unknown to anyone in his family, was consumed by a secret voyeuristic involvement with the live-in housekeeper, an attractive forty-year-old woman who was unconsciously seductive toward my patient. It was not until the second year of analysis that my patient alerted me to his voyeurism.

From the beginning I worked with the boy to modulate the severe anxieties that had brought him into treatment. He was terrified that his parents would abandon him. His day-fantasies and dream life were haunted by outer-space creatures that were poised to hack off, burn off, or otherwise mutilate his arms, legs, ears, eyes, and penis. The year after my patient and I began to address the connection between his voyeurism and these terrifying abandonment and mutilation anxieties, puberty arrived, and the surface clinical picture altered. His overt perversion diminished considerably. His anxieties became more manageable. For some time thereafter, however, his considerable intellectual and creative energies were put in the service of convincing me, his teachers, and his family that events that were untrue were true. He had become a pathological liar. At that juncture, I remembered something crucial about the relationship between perversion and pathological lying. Otto Fenichel, a disciple of Freud's, put it: "If it is possible to make someone believe that untrue things are true, then it is also possible for true things, the memory of which threatens me, are untrue."

Sexual perversions in men center on a fear of the female genitals. The true things that are to be falsified are the penisless female genitals—the vagina, the labia, the tiny erect clitoris. Pathological lying and imposturousness can make these undeniably true facts of life at least momentarily deniable, Petty lies, hoaxes, practical jokes, plagiarisms, and imposturous acts—known as character perversions—originate in the same anxieties and serve similar purposes as manifestly sexual perversions such as fetishism, voyeurism, exhibitionism, transvestism. The analyst

Jacob Arlow, who first identified the perverse nature of these denials of reality, illustrated the connections between character perversions and sexual perversions:

> The petty lie is the equivalent of the fetish—it is something which is interposed between the individual and reality in order to ward off the perception of true reality and to substitute instead perceptions which facilitate ambiguity and illusion, both of which can temper for the patient the harsh reality of female anatomy.

Coincidentally, during the same period I was engaged in a prolonged diagnostic evaluation of a five-year-old boy who was in analysis with a colleague of mine. The boy demonstrated a conscious wish to be a girl and an impulse to dress up in his mother's clothing—an impulse that he resisted valiantly but his mother subtly encouraged.

I was struck by the similarities in family background and psychological dynamics of these two boys. The prominent features of each developmental history were an absent or absentee father and a mother who had unsettled the child's narcissistic balance by inviting the fantasy that he had the power to gratify her every wish and desire and eventually fulfill her own exalted version of masculinity. When the exalted maternal ideal of masculinity replaces or overshadows the masculine ideal as represented by the father, this produces the emotional hothouse in which manifest perversions and character perversions, including certain failures of identification such as imposturousness, seem to flourish.

Literary imposture occupies its own niche within imposturousness. It flourished in England during the eighteenth century. The century started off with George Psalmanazar, a French impostor who, in his mid-twenties, came to London posing as a native of Formosa and after translating the Anglican catechism into Formosan, a language he invented, produced (in Latin) the totally fictitious *Historical and Geographical Description of Formosa*. At the century's end, William Henry Ireland fabricated two "lost" Shakespearean plays, *Vortigern and Rowena,* and *Henry II*. And in between were literally scores of others.

The masks of the literary impostors of the eighteenth century were diverse; some were manufacturers of fake legal documents, some printers of spurious books, some tellers of false tales, some creators of some form of false literature. But as I have pointed out, the literary impostor is not, strictly speaking, a plagiarizer. He is more complex in that he represents his own hard-won labors as having originated in someone else's mind. He claims to bring lost documents to light, and in so doing dupes the world into believing that something which is not true is true.

Thomas Chatterton, one of the more famous eighteenth-century impostor-poets, can be distinguished from his fellow literary impostors by the poetic verisimilitude he brought to the long-ago past that he invented. An interpretative reading of Psalmanazar's exotic Formosa or James Macpherson's glorified Irish heroes might also reveal a psychological longing for an ideal father figure. But Chatterton's fabrication of the fifteenth-century Sir William Canynge, the noble merchant prince through whom he tried to fill in the gaps in his own identity, represents a longing for a father that is startlingly transparent. As I embark on this full narrative of that young man's literary exploits and brief, tragic life, I hope that my explorations will enrich the psychoanalytic perspective on the dynamic relationships among creativity, falsehood, and perversion. I hope also that I can communicate to readers outside the psychoanalytic profession something of the richness of the psychoanalytic version of the relationship between sexuality and morality.

While I have not yet made explicit the two main themes of this narrative on the life of Thomas Chatterton, it must already be apparent that I am speaking of imposturousness as a male rather than a female disorder. In the course of relating the tale of this young man's life, I shall be exploring the psychological ramifications of the absence (and by extension of the presence) of a father in a boy's life.

One of my motives in writing about a father-son relationship was to redress the balance at a time when at last so many women writers have been appreciating the depth and meaning of the mother-daughter bond. Since female relationships play so large a part in the upbringing of impostors and impostor-poets, I will be inquiring into mother-son, sister-brother bonds and what these might mean in the father's absence. But my major emphasis will be on the longing for a father, a universal human longing that is all the more significant because we have begun to live in a father-absent culture, where large numbers of boys and girls are being raised in households made fatherless by illegitimacy, abandonment, divorce, and most recently the decision of women to bear and bring up children as single parents. Lest I give the impression that this turn of events might hasten us toward a matriarchal paradise, I want to underline that I am exploring not a positive or potentially beneficial phenomenon but the detrimental effects of an absence.

The week I was preparing this introduction, Stanley Kunitz published an article for the *New York Times Book Review* entitled "The Poet's Quest for the Father," in which he concludes:

> Out of 20th century American poetry emerges, as a collective creation, the mythic image of the absent father. His absence explains why he haunts the modern imagination. He has died of natural causes, or by suicide, or in the wars of the century. It is astonishing how many American poets have lost their fathers at an early age. . . . Often the father is more than absent; he is lost, as he has been lost to himself for most of his adult life, crushed by his burdens, rendered impotent by fatigue and anxieties, reduced to a number, a statistical integer, in the army or the factory or the marketplace. The son goes in search of the father, to be reconciled in a healing embrace. In that act of love he restores his father's lost pride and manhood. Perhaps he also finds himself.

I agree with Kunitz that the absent father can serve as an inspiration for poetry and that poetry can act as a healing embrace between father and son. And I appreciate how earlier in the essay he offers an impressive list of women poets who have written about their fathers. Even so, as he points out, "The song of daughters is different from that of sons, and the scope of my essay does not permit me to add to its complications." With this crucial distinction I also concur, because I regard *The Family Romance of the Impostor-Poet Thomas Chatterton* as a biography about masculine psychology as distinct from, though not, as I shall be explaining, dichotomous with, feminine psychology.

A few words concerning the reasoning that led to my original choice of the impostor as a representative of masculine conflicts are in order here. In the concluding section of my book on adolescence I contrast two rare emotional disorders that come to fruition during puberty, one of them prototypically feminine, the other prototypically masculine. The prototype for the feminine disorder, anorexia nervosa, is a typically adolescent, typically feminine solution to the dilemmas of becoming an adult. It entails the pursuit of a caricature of femininity—a pure and saintly attitude toward all forms of desire (not merely the avoidance of food); a nymphlike physical appearance devoid of body fat, hips, breasts, or any other grown-up feminine attribute. The moral and sexual life of the anorectic have been arrested at a childlike ideal of what it means to be female.

When it came to conceptualizing the male counterpart to anorexia, I was confronted with all the paradoxes inherent in contemporary research and thinking on issues of femininity and masculinity. Therefore I adopted a few strategies that I hoped would minimize the ideologies and intellectual shortcomings that usually result from these paradoxes.

The first of these was to avoid the statistical and normative solutions that have been promulgated by quite a number of feminist writers. Phyllis Chesler's influential notion, for example, that women internalize aggressive feelings while men externalize them was derived from a more or less numerical base: men are victimizers—killers, robbers, burglars, muggers—while women are victimized—they destroy themselves, succumbing to depression and hysteria. Women tend to become mental patients rather than criminals. Among psychotics, the men are the violent paranoids, the women the self-mutilating, silly hebephrenics. Men are sadists while women are masochists. This sort of head-counting approach to mental illness is often supplemented by the assumption that masculinity is synonymous with being strong and active while femininity is associated with being weak and passive.

I was wary of such dichotomizing of feminine and masculine traits. Such approaches to the gender dilemma also claim that one set of traits—feminine or masculine—is better than the other. While it is tempting to succumb to the appeal of the superiority of "the feminine approach to science," "the feminine universe," "feminine dialogue," "feminine morality," I am generally suspicious of the motives underlying any "better or worse" interpretation of the differences between the sexes. Often, I believe, when people dichotomize differences they regress to the very stereotypes they are so conscientiously striving to avoid.

I started with some basic numbers. Anorexia, a rare disorder in its full-fledged primary form to begin with, is rare in males, who comprise at most ten percent of all anorectics. The impostor, also a rare disorder in its primary form, is with few exceptions nonexistent among females. When I intentionally selected these apparently dichotomized disorders, I did not intend to demonstrate that females are more likely to solve gender dilemmas by manipulating their bodies while men are more likely to solve these dilemmas by manipulating others. I wanted to demonstrate how a seeming dichotomy, when explored from a psychoanalytic developmental perspective, reveals other more subtle dynamic issues. The anorectic and the impostor are distinctly different disorders but both are aftermaths of a developmental arrest in which an "absence of the father" usually exerts a significant influence.

When no one comes along to intrude on the intimacies of the mother-infant dialogue, the child's moral sense continues to be dominated by the concrete prohibitions and permissions of the nursery. The "voice of the father" (or any powerful third force that makes it clear to the child that his mother is not his possession) awakens the child to the complex moral authority of the larger social order. The father's presence in the mother's life and the mother's presence in the father's convey to the child the painful but necessary knowledge of the differences between the sexes and the generations. This bitter reminder that he is small, vulnerable, deficient in grown-up desires and capacities motivates a young child to become like his powerful parents and acquire some of their moral authority. Thus, in exchange for banishment by his parents, the child is permitted to participate in the principles of law and order that govern the social world in which he will grow up. The primitive nursery morality that gathers its dreadful power from the possibility of abandonment, absence, weaning, mutilation, and defilement is tamed and to a large extent replaced by inner conscience and the less awesome anxieties that arise from guilt. The primitive gender ideals of femininity and masculinity are also modified. As development proceeds, they become less stereotyped and rigid, more humane and rich with complexity.

The anorectic and the impostor represent alternative sex-gender scripts that never evolved beyond the simplified ideals of femininity and masculinity conveyed to a child during infancy. These infantile ideals, if unmodified and enriched by later development, will eventuate in pathological solutions to the dilemmas of arriving at genital maturity during adolescence. Neither the anorectic nor the impostor dares to risk the challenges of adult gender identity offered by the adolescent process. Though these pathological solutions are typically feminine and typically mas-

culine, they cannot be construed as paired opposites with assigned valuations such as weak/strong, clean/dirty, good/bad, subjective/objective, passive/active. They are examples of what happens to a sex-gender script when the infantile gender ideal as conveyed by the mother during the earliest months and years of life does not confront the challenges posed later on by the three-person socialized version in which the father also plays a part. A weak articulation of the oedipal triangle—an "absence of the father"—leaves both boys and girls extremely vulnerable to unfocused, generalized anxieties about abandonment and mutilation. The anorectic and the impostor are prototypes of all who remain in the never-never land of moral and genital ambiguity because they are too frightened to assume the complex demands of adult moral responsibility and adult gender identity.

Thomas Chatterton, though he did suffer from a character perversion, was *not* a full-fledged impostor. He was a youth who struggled to find a way toward adult moral life and gender identity despite the absence of an actual father in his life. Because he was artistically gifted—a poet who could portray his quest for an adult ideal of manhood—he left a record of these struggles for all of us.

In conclusion I will relate an incident that occurred a few months before I completed this life of Chatterton, during a discussion period after I had presented a paper based on the life of Chatterton at a psychoanalytic conference. Since my paper dealt primarily with the borders between art and crime described earlier in this introduction, I requested that Judith Rossner be the official discussant rather than a psychoanalyst. Rossner recognized immediately that I was writing about the meaning of literary impostures and pathological lying, and in keeping with the spirit of the occasion, she decided to play a literary prank on the audience—the invention of a female literary impostor. Her invention was so convincing that many listeners thought they remembered reading Nell Shapiro's "A Servant's Diary," a "lost" manuscript purportedly written by one Estella Martinez and then "discovered" by Nell.

Judith Rossner told the audience she wanted to stimulate discussion on an issue that concerned her:

> The question that recurred as I read Louise's paper had to do not with its accuracy but with the limitations of her observations on Chatterton and on literary impostors in general. That is to say, all of her references, as well as those of Dr. Chasseguet-Smirgel, were to men, but they set me to thinking about women and imposture.

Rossner went on to point out that after all girls did have a head start on castration anxiety and that in any event

> As a bored world becomes increasingly determined to erase those sexual distinctions that seem to have been crucial in arresting mankind's boredom, we shall doubtless see an increasing number of women supplying their missing pieces by faking advanced degrees . . . performing surgery they know almost as well as if

they'd really gone to medical school . . . selling millions of gallons of corn oil stored in nonexistent storage tanks in New Jersey . . . and publishing manuscripts they've found in their grandmother's attics that are later revealed to have been written and placed there by themselves.

This was in fact the issue that dominated the discussion period, which dealt not only with the general problem of creativity and imposture but more specifically with the premise that women did have and were entitled to have the same perversions and character perversions as men. At first my male colleagues on the panel took a professional view and supported my thesis that the perversions and character perversions I had described were primarily male territories. Before too long, however, a few of them lost their analytic objectivity and began to react like ordinary besieged men. They began to blur the distinctions between technical language and everyday usage. One analyst, for example, found himself defending the commonplace notion that women were just as guilty of exhibitionism as men. Didn't they sit in front of the mirror all day, trying on clothes, putting on makeup, and so on? Strange alliances were made. Some feminist members of the audience supported this male analyst's argument by proposing that prostitutes and specialty call girls were as perverse as their male clients. Quite a few agreed that when it came to petty lies women were more accomplished than men. Equal rights had won the day.

Before presenting my paper I had discussed my premises with a few writers and psychoanalysts. One of them, William Grossman, predicted what might happen: "You'll see. The minute you begin to illustrate a few of the ways in which men and women are different you will get dozens of examples of how they are alike. Just listen. You will gather more fascinating and useful data than if you had set up months of interviews directly addressing the questions, 'Do you know of women who engage in perverse sexual acts like exhibitionism, fetishism, voyeurism?'; 'Do you have female patients who are practical jokers, impostors, or pathological liars?'" He was right.

That afternoon's discussion encouraged me to begin the research for my next book, which will examine female perversions and character perversions and their resemblances to or differences from male perversions and character perversions.

For now, I return to *The Family Romance of the Impostor-Poet Thomas Chatterton,* which is much less a sinister tale of sexual perversion than it is a study of the slender border between art and crime. I expect that some readers may question whether Thomas Chatterton's fate was in fact prototypically masculine. But I imagine even they will consent to my general thesis that, for Chatterton at least, an "absence of the father" stimulated his imposturous acts and also set him on his quest for poetic nobility. The first part of the *Romance* is about the healing embrace between Thomas Chatterton and Sir William Canynge, the fifteenth-century father through whom Chatterton hoped to find his own manhood. In the second part, we see what happened to Chatterton when he lost that father.

References

"The Impostor," *Adolescence,* pp. 283-317.

Phyllis Greenacre, "The Impostor," in *Emotional Growth I*; "The Family Romance of the Artist," and "The Relation of the Impostor to the Artist," in *Emotional Growth II* (New York: International Universities Press, 1971).

Thomas Mann. "it is in essence," preface to *Stories of Three Decades,* trans. H. T. Lowe-Porter (New York: Modern Library, 1936), p. vii; hereafter referred to as Mann.

The formula for the relationship between perversion and pathological lying appears in Otto Fenichel, "The Economics of Pseudologia Phantastica," in *Collected Papers of Otto Fenichel,* 2nd ser. (New York: W. W. Norton, 1954), p. 133; hereafter referred to as Fenichel.

Jacob Arlow, "Character Perversion," in *Currents in Psychoanalysis,* ed. Irwin M. Marcus (New York: International Universities Press, Inc., 1971), pp. 317-336; hereafter referred to as Arlow. "The petty lie is," p. 326.

Literary Impostors in Eighteenth-Century England

Murray Warren, *A Descriptive and Annotated Bibliography of Thomas Chatterton* (New York and London: Garland Publishing, Inc., 1977), pp. 13-15. Warren presents a heavily abbreviated list of English literary impostors, among them Thomas Birch (1705-1766), who fabricated England's first newspaper, *Englishe Mercurie, imprinted at London by Her Highness's Printer, 1588;* Charles Betram (1723-1765), who produced an alleged ancient manuscript by Richard of Cirencester; John Jordon (1746-1809), the composer of some fraudulent tales on the life of Shakespeare; John Pinkerton (1758-1826), author of the spurious *Select Scottish Ballads;* and Allan Cunningham (1748-1842), who contributed many spurious entries to a collection of the *Remains of Nithedale and Galloway Song.*

Then, of course, there was Horace Walpole, the first person to detect the imposturous nature of Chatterton's poetry. He set an example for legitimate scholars by announcing on the title page that his own *The Castle of Otranto* was translated by a fictitious William Marshall, Gent. from the original Italian of Onuphrio Muralto, Canon of the Church of St. Nicholas, at Otranto, and claiming that the work, originally printed at Naples in 1529, was "found in the library of an ancient Catholic family in the north of England."

Horace Walpole's literary imposture: Wilmarth Sheldon Lewis, *Horace Walpole,* Bollingen Series xxxv, 9 (New York: Pantheon Books, 1960), 157.

Stanley Kunitz, "The Poet's Quest for the Father," *New York Times Book Review,* 22 February 1987, p. 37.

Judith Rossner, discussion on "Perversion, Falsehood, Creativity," by Louise J. Kaplan, at conference on *Character Perversions,* Council of Psychoanalytic Psychotherapists, October 19, 1986.

Woodstock Books (essay date 1990)

SOURCE: "Introduction," in *The Rowley Poems* by Thomas Chatterton, Woodstock Books, 1990, n.p.

[In the following essay, the anonymous critic contends that Chatterton's popularity with later writers such as John Keats and William Wordsworth had more to do with the romance surrounding Chatterton's youth, his suicide, and his forged poetry than with the specific quality of his literary output.]

In September 1819, two days after composing *To autumn*—'Season of mists and mellow fruitfulness'—Keats remarks in a letter, 'I always somehow associate Chatterton with autumn'. To which he adds, apparently without connection:

> He is the purest writer in the English Language. He has no French idiom, or particles like Chaucer—'tis English Idiom in English Words. I have given up *Hyperion*—there were too many Miltonic inversions in it . . . English ought to be kept up.

The previous autumn Keats had spent nursing his dying younger brother, Tom. That he should 'somehow associate' the season with early death is not surprising, and Chatterton had taken arsenic at the age of seventeen. Chatterton, for Keats's generation, had the aura of myth that Keats himself was later to achieve, standing for promise, talent, genius, cut off before its time. One thing that he did not commonly stand for was purity of language. His poetry was after all a fake, allegedly 'wroten bie the gode Prieste Thomas Rowley, 1464'.

It may be that Wordsworth would have understood Keats's train of thought. Worried by Coleridge's dejection and addiction, he had written in *The leech gatherer* of 'fear that kills . . . And mighty poets in their misery dead':

> I thought of Chatterton, the marvellous boy,
> The sleepless soul who perished in his pride,
> Of him who walked in glory and in joy
> Behind his plough upon the mountain-side . . .

That Wordsworth was indeed thinking about Chatterton is confirmed by his use of the archaic spenserian stanza of *An excellent balade of charitie.* Behind *The leech gatherer* lies Coleridge's *Monody on the death of Chatterton* (printed in this edition for the first time), where he too had brooded on the fates of earlier poets. As modern representatives, Chatterton and Burns are linked in Wordsworth's mind, partly because they both died young (Burns, not very), partly by primitivist assumptions about language, such as Keats is tacitly making. Though one wrote in

Scots, the other in a bogus medieval English, they are united as working-class writers whose language expressed the feelings of the heart, and seemed a guarantee of Wordsworth's own position.

Apart from Wallace's dramatic painting of his suicide, *The leech gatherer* has proved the most lasting contribution to Chatterton's myth. The myth had been building, however, since 1770, the year of Wordsworth's birth. As with Macpherson's spurious 'translations' of Ossian, controversy had played a big part. Readers were intrigued to know whether the *Balade* and other poems did indeed belong to the fifteenth century. Could a Bristol charity-school boy, with no scholarly training, really have forged them? The fraud had been exposed by Tyrwhitt as early as 1777, in *Poems supposed to have been written by Thomas Rowley*; but Sharpe, in his Preface to the 1794 volume, has no wish to close off the discussion. As editor, his 'sole design'

> is to furnish the public with a neat Edition of these Poems, which, whether the Author of them may have been ROWLEY, or CHATTERTON, or some third person, (as has been ridiculously supposed) fully entitle him to be ranked in the fourth place among our British Poets.

Chaucer, Spenser, Milton, Chatterton—there were some (as Hazlitt complains in his lecture of 1818) who went still further and talked as if Chatterton was the greatest genius since Shakespeare. Hazlitt is at his most incisive:

> He did not show extraordinary powers of genius, but extraordinary precocity. Nor do I believe he would have written better had he lived. He knew this himself, or he would have lived. Great geniuses, like great kings, have too much to think of to kill themselves.

It was scarcely charitable, but brings the discussion down to earth:

> As to those who are really capable of admiring Chatterton's genius, or of feeling an interest in his fate, I would only say, that I never heard any one speak of any one of his works as if it were an old well-known favourite, and had become a faith and a religion in his mind. It is his name, his youth, and what he might have lived to have done, that excite our wonder and admiration.

'I was very disappointed by his treatment of Chatterton', was the comment of Keats, after the lecture; but to a large extent Hazlitt must be right. Even Wordsworth, whose admiration is genuine, is forced to emphasize Chatterton's precocity, and sounds a little general in his praise. 'I asked Wordsworth this evening', Crabb Robinson writes in 1842,

> wherein Chatterton's excellence lay. He said his genius was universal; he excelled in every species of composition, so remarkable an instance of precocious talent being quite unexampled. His prose is excellent, and his powers of picturesque description and satire great.

Interestingly, Coleridge's view was that Chatterton's poems had never been popular. 'The very circumstance', he writes in 1797 (only three years after publishing the

Monody), 'which made them so much talked of—their *ancientness*—prevented them from being generally read'.

Chatterton's spelling is certainly a problem. Many are daunted by the Scottish poetry of Burns, and almost no one can now hear the Dorset cadences of Barnes and Hardy, the Lincolnshire of Tennyson. What looks difficult, or different, isn't read. But Chatterton is not dialect. He knows some middle English, and enjoys inventing more ('slughorne', for instance, famously picked up by Browning in *Childe Roland*), but, as Hazlitt astutely points out, the secret of his 'imposture' lies 'in the repetition of a few obsolete words, and the mis-spelling of common ones':

> the whole controversy might have been settled . . . from this single circumstance, that the poems read as smooth as any modern poems, if you read them as modern compositions; and that you cannot read them, or make verse of them at all, if you pronounce or accent the words as they were spoken at the time when the poems were pretended to have been written.

We no more have to be frightened by Chatterton's *ancientness* than we are by that of *The ancyent marinere* (1798). His rhythms are strong and fluent, and as he carries us along we can enjoy the game that he is playing. **The dethe of Syr Charles Bawdin** (recollected by Blake in *The Marriage of Heaven and Hell*) is an excellent example:

> Howe oft ynne battaile have I stoode,
> Whan thousands dy'd arounde;
> Whan smokynge streemes of crimson bloode
> Imbrew'd the fatten'd grounde:
> Howe dydd I knowe thatt ev'ry darte,
> That cutte the airie waie,
> Myghte nott fynde passage toe my harte,
> And close myne eyes for aie?

Equally accomplished, and equally accessible, is the Shakespearean **Mynstrelles Songe** from *Aella*:

> See! the whyte moone sheenes onne hie;
> Whyterre ys mie true loves shroude;
> Whyterre yanne the mornynge skie,
> Whyterre yanne the evenynge cloude;
> Mie love ys dedde,
> Gon to hys deathe-bedde,
> Al under the wyllowe tree.

As Keats so memorably said, 'Tis English Idiom in English Words.'

Chatterton seems to have had a collection of medieval documents, filched by his sexton father from a coffer in St Mary Redcliffe. His spellings (like Dickens's spellings of working-class speech) are there to create an atmosphere, without causing actual difficulty to the reader. Many are in fact perfectly possible in a fifteenth-century scribe. As well as being a distinguished poet and forger, Chatterton was obviously a fascinated linguist. Glossing his improbable coinage, 'glommed', he writes in a footnote to the *Balade*:

Clouded, dejected. A person of some note in the literary world is of opinion, that *glum* and *glom* are modern cant words; and from this circumstance doubts the authenticity of Rowley's Manuscripts. Glum-mong in the Saxon signifies twilight, a dark or dubious light; and the modern *gloomy* is derived from the Saxon *glum*.

It may not prove the authenticity of Rowley's manuscripts, but Chatterton's etymology is largely correct. Like Keats, he believed that 'English ought to be kept up'.

Lucy Morrison (essay date 1996)

SOURCE: "Chatterton and Keats: The Need for Close Examination," in *Keats-Shelley Review*, No. 10, Spring 1996, pp. 35-50.

[In the following essay, Morrison argues that John Keats's poem "To Autumn" was strongly influenced by several poetic works produced by Chatterton. The critic observes that Keats preserves but softens the death imagery present in Chatterton's evocations of autumn, and remarks that Keats tried hard to overcome Chatterton's influence in order to present his own original voice.]

John Keats's philosophical writings shed some light upon his awareness of the influence of other writers upon him, whether consciously or subconsciously. As with any writer who is also a reader, Keats does not deny that material he reads exerts an influence upon his own writings:

> It is a wretched thing to confess; but it is a very fact that not one word I ever utter can be taken for granted as an opinion growing out of my identical nature—how can it when I have no nature?[1]

'To Autumn' clearly demonstrates a heavy reliance upon Thomas Chatterton's Thyrde Mynstrelle's song in the play **'Aella'** as well as upon other Chatterton texts, including **'Elegy to the Memory of Mr. Thomas Phillips, of Fairford,'** and **'An Excelente Balade of Charitie.'** This connection has not been fully investigated hitherto, although critics have discussed Keats's fondness for Chatterton's work and have drawn comparisons between an assortment of lines by the two authors.[2]

Through critical examination of the writing process, it can be shown that the alterations made to the texts under consideration may be attributed to an awareness of similarities to other texts, and the process also demonstrates that the text of a poem as published today nevertheless manifests a heavy debt to other texts. Although the author's intention can never be conclusively established, the writing process can suggest the workings of the author's mind and perhaps indicate the difficulties of an author striving for originality, and the alterations perceived can be interpreted as being due to this natural determination for originality.

Keats wrote 'To Autumn'[3] at the beginning of the season, on Sunday, September 19th, 1819, following his return to

Winchester from five days spent in London trying to raise money to relieve his brother George's financial difficulties in America, and Keats indicated the walk as his inspiration in a letter to John Hamilton Reynolds two days later:

> How beautiful the season is now—How fine the air. A temperate sharpness about it. Really, without joking, chaste weather—Dian skies—I never lik'd stubble-fields as much as now—Aye better than the chilly green of the Spring. Somehow a stubble-plain looks warm—in the same way that some pictures look warm—This struck me so much in my Sunday's walk that I composed upon it.[4]

This section of Keats's letter has frequently been quoted as the obvious source of inspiration for the poem, and the walk was clearly a contributing factor, but there has been no thorough acknowledgement of the poem's debt to Chatterton or of the similarities between Keats's poem and Chatterton's work.

There are five versions of 'To Autumn' available, and the published version invariably used in the modern classroom differs quite substantially from Keats's own draft.[5] Facsimiles of the drafts are available in Jack Stillinger's edition of *John Keats: Poetry Manuscripts at Harvard, a Facsimile Edition*. But while investigating the surface material alterations which the poem undergoes, it is simultaneously necessary to acknowledge the alterations in terms of a search for originality and thus in terms of Keats's assumed awareness of the similarities between his own text and those of Chatterton.

Although **'Aella'** is Chatterton's principal text associated with Keats's 'To Autumn,' other Chatterton poems also need to be considered, as connections to several of Chatterton's works are evident and should not be overlooked: 'Besides the third minstrel's song from **"Aella,"** other relaxed, spontaneous melodies of Chatterton's perhaps also flooded Keats's mind.'[6] Although Nai-Tung Ting does not elucidate to which 'melodies' she is referring, other texts by Chatterton are clearly echoed by Keats. Claude Lee Finney suggests that the alterations in the drafting process be viewed as relatively insignificant and concerned mainly with spelling and word choice: 'Comparing these manuscripts, we find some revision of phraseology but no essential change in imagery, emotion, and thought.'[7] It is the 'revision of phraseology' which presents clear evidence of the echoes of Chatterton's work, and these would thus seem to be of prime significance in establishing the connections between texts.

Robert Gittings recognises that 'To Autumn' 'echoes so much his [Keats's] own description of his walk that it might seem unnecessary to seek any literary source as well,'[8] but Keats's walk must not be relied upon as unique inspiration. Importantly, Gittings acknowledges this supposition by concluding that 'such there was, recognized quite consciously by Keats in the words "I somehow always associate Chatterton with autumn."'[9] Keats's *Letters* at the time of writing this poem clearly identify Chatterton as a source for his writing and this contemporary comment should not be ignored.

The first available draft of Keats's poem would seem to differ from the published version primarily in its spelling and word order, perhaps due to Keats's hurry in writing the poem down following his walk. But even the misspelled words throw some light upon Keats's thoughts behind the words. In the first stanza, the sun is 'natturing' rather than 'maturing,'[10] and although the difference could be attributed to a hasty spelling error, it could be that Keats was trying to convey the ideas of the sun's essential role within nature, and, furthermore, the necessity of the sun in order to achieve the ripeness of autumn.

Keats's opening lines are unaltered throughout the drafting process, as the season is introduced as one of peaceful and unthreatening lethargy, although there is an underlying implication that the season and the sun are in a conspiracy which is not wholly well-intentioned: 'Season of mists and mellow fruitfulness, / Close bosom-friend of the maturing sun.'[11] The opening line suggests a completion whilst simultaneously indicating a decline, a relaxation as one of death. Although the season clings to the 'maturing sun,'[12] trying to elicit its beneficial warmth, autumn cannot prevent the sun's withdrawal of its bounty. Keats wrote that 'The setting sun will always set me to rights.'[13] The days are certain to grow shorter as the year progresses irrevocably towards the darkness of winter. 'The autumn fogs over a rich land is like the steam from cabbage water'[14] presents an image of the season suggesting distaste two weeks before writing 'To Autumn,' but the aforesaid 'fogs' are altered to become more ambiguous and less disagreeable 'mists' within the text of the poem. Although Keats's inspiration might have come from his walk in Winchester, his previous dislike for the season is combined with the pleasantness of his walk to create a unique autumn: Keats cannot deny autumn's function as the simultaneous fulfilment of life and harbinger of the succeeding winter's death.

Chatterton also introduces autumn in **'Aella'** in connection with the sun, but his season is 'blake and sonne-brente.'[15] Chatterton's own notes on the same page[16] suggest that 'blake' stands for nakcd; but, read aloud, the word is more similar to the colour black, which symbolically suggests darkness and death. The sun is presented as excessive, since it harms by burning, and the implication behind Chatterton's first line is similar to that of Keats in that both lines suggest an air of evil lurking within or beyond the season. Just as an excess of sun causes painful burning, so the season of autumn described thus is harmful in that it presents an absoluteness which can be succeeded only by death. In both texts, the autumn introduced at the start of the poem is one which is harmful in its course, and even though Keats suggests that the maturing process is 'mellow,'[17] the implication would seem to be that autumn is deceptive in its slow ripening, as winter's death draws undeniably closer all the while.

Although the next two lines of Keats's text are essentially unaltered, the order of the fruit and the vines in line four is reversed, so that the first draft and transcripts read 'Conspiring with him how to load and bless / The Vines with fruit that round the thatch eves run.'[18] The revised version is easier to read and the capitalisation of the vines which lends them emphasis disappears, so that the revised version directs attention to the fruit which is the blessing of life's fulfilment. The alteration has the effect of weighing the rhythm of the line, as the positioning of the line-break compels the reader to pause before identifying the object of the verb 'bless,' and the reversal of the order delays its fulfilment still further. Wolf Z. Hirst suggests further that the word structure imitates the desired effect of the poem: 'The convoluted phrase "bless / With fruit and vines that round the thatch-eves run" with its inversion and difficulty in articulation makes the tongue imitate the entwining creepers as they hug wall and roof.'[19] Yet Hirst does not support his assertion with any analysis of the linguistic features involved and even misquotes the poem by replacing 'the' with 'and' and thus altering the line entirely.

Keats's line 'To bend with apples the moss'd Cottage trees'[20] remains unaltered throughout the drafting process, and clearly demonstrates a similarity to Chatterton's 'Whann the fayre apple, rudde as even skie, / Do bende the tree unto the fructyle ground.'[21] In both texts, the apples are the impetus behind the bowing of the fruit trees, and Chatterton's image would seem to have been the suggestion behind Keats's line, especially since Chatterton employs a similar image in another poem: 'The apple rodded from its palie greene / And the mole peare did bende the leafy spraie.'[22] Keats's apples remain colourless, but Chatterton's apple and soft pear both bend the tree just as Keats's apples do. The fruit at its prime can usefully develop no further, and these visual images primarily suggest an air of admiration for the achievements of nature in its ripeness and growth amidst the stillness. Yet this ripeness is on the verge of becoming cloying; and although the fruit blesses the vines, it also loads them, as the trees are bent with their burden of apples.

The remaining six lines of the first stanza do not vary significantly throughout the drafting process. The hurried 'sweeness' of the sixth line of the first draft becomes 'ripeness' in Woodhouse's transcript, and the hurried 'furuits' of the first draft becomes singular 'fruit' in Woodhouse's copy. Again, this error could be attributed to hurried spelling, or could perhaps be linked to Keats's recent readings of Chatterton with its supposed medieval spellings. Keats's attention to detail is clear, as the fruit varies not only in spelling, but also between the singular and plural. Today's 'sweet kernel' was formerly 'white,'[23] and Woodhouse mistakenly writes 'yet' for 'still' in his transcript.[24] Yet it is remarkable to note how essentially little this first stanza alters during the drafting process, perhaps indicating that the first available draft is in fact Keats's transcript of a previous composition.

Gittings suggests that 'The "white kernel" of line eight gains its adjective from the autumnal song in Chatterton's *Aella,*'[25] assumably referring to Chatterton's line 'Whan al the hyls wythe woddie sede ys whyte.'[26] Perhaps Chatterton's white seed did inspire Keats to adopt the same colour in application to the kernel or seed of his hazel shells, but as Gittings goes on to point out, 'The "white" kernel inevitably went when the earlier change to "ripeness" left the adjective "sweet" available.'[27] Finney notes that 'The first draft of the ode reproduces some of Chatterton's words, especially words depicting the colors of autumn,'[28] and I would agree that the colour change is not due solely to Gittings's suggestion that an alternative adjective became available, but rather that the alteration is in part due to Keats's awareness of the similarity. As Ting asserts: 'It appears quite obvious, besides, that Keats sometimes took pains to disguise or suppress his more apparent borrowings from Chatterton.'[29] This seemingly minor adjustment is perhaps indicative of the alterations throughout the drafting process due to Keats's awareness of his own echoes of Chatterton's work.

The combination of infinite autumns is personified in the second stanza, and the movement is again into autumn as the first line clearly refers to previous autumns and to the expected successors: 'Who hath not seen thee oft amid thy store?'[30] Yet Keats altered this line in his own first draft, since it originally read 'Who hath not seen thee? for thy haunts are many,'[31] and this original line seems to pose problems in connecting to the following lines within the stanza, perhaps explaining the adjustment. But this alteration could alternatively have been inspired by Chatterton's **'Aella,'** and Keats's revision demonstrates a clear similarity to a line of Chatterton's: 'Ofte have I seene thee atte the none-daie feaste.'[32] The repetition of exact word choice is obvious and Keats's line could be almost a development upon Chatterton's, as Keats uses the same words and merely broadens the address and adapts it to fit his own personifications of autumn. Gittings dismisses similar turns of phrase: 'Yet these, though strong, are only immediate and verbal influences,'[33] but it seems clear that the verbal influences indicate Keats's debt to Chatterton and cannot be summarily dismissed. The singular 'store' of the final version is also perhaps more attuned to Chatterton's singular occasion and further limits the realm of autumn. The store could refer to the fruits of the seasons or to the stored death of the personified autumn.

The following personification of autumn is primarily specific, suggesting a search 'for thee,'[34] but is altered by Keats to become more sweeping in its compass, since the suggestion comes that this personified autumn can be found 'abroad.'[35] The personification is depicted in attitudes of stillness and recline, of repose and idleness. She is 'careless on a granary floor, / Thy hair soft-lifted by the winnowing wind,'[36] and her stasis bears an element of uselessness, as she is without care and can remain motionless only while the light wind of nature tries without success to arouse her. Following this image, there are five lines in the original draft which are deleted:

While bright the sun slants through the (husky)
barn;—
orr on a half reap'd furrow sound asleep
Or sound asleep in a half reaped field
Dos'd with read poppies; while thy reeping hook
Spares form some slumbrous minutes while wam
slumpers creep.[37]

The second line above was a revision of the third, but
Keats seems here to be struggling with words and ideas
which do not co-ordinate with the rest of the poem. John
Bayley goes so far as to suggest that 'he [Keats] is using,
I think, a conscious Chattertonism; and so also, perhaps, is
the phrase "husky barn,"'[38] but fails to clarify the parallel
further than his own individual interpretation and association. Critics see Keats's deletions as due to a desire to
avoid similarities with other writers while simultaneously
failing to give specific references, but this cancelled section is interesting primarily in terms of the final two lines.

As Finney points out, 'The personification of autumn as a
reaper, the most essential element in Keats's ode, was derived from Chatterton's song;'[39] and, although Finney does
not go into detail regarding this assertion, Chatterton's
work can be seen clearly as a starting point for Keats's
personifications. In Chatterton's autumnal minstrel's song,
the personification is not a gentle and ineffective woman,
but rather a man and a perpetrator of violence. Autumn is
depicted as a man who will 'guylteynge the fallenge lefe'
and carry the 'riped shefe,'[40] and is therefore imagined as
the enactor and bearer of death. Keats's eradicated 'reeping hook' would seem to fit Chatterton's manly personification rather than his own gentler image. Chatterton's personification similarly cannot halt nature's murderous
process of 'bryngeynge oppe Wynterr to folfylle the yere,'[41]
and Keats's original also did not allow the natural growth
any lasting respite: 'Spares for some slumbrous minutes
the next swath.'[42] Just as Chatterton's personification
causes death and simultaneously and inevitably heralds the
death of the year, so Keats's image suggests that any respite from the approaching onslaught is only momentary.

The murderous hook is not completely lost, since Keats's
personification is depicted 'sound asleep'[43] with only half
the furrow reaped 'while thy hook / Spares the next swath
and all its twined flowers.'[44] It is only in sleep that any
part of the personified autumn's nature can escape its fate:
her murderous and sacrificial sickle is allayed only by her
momentary respite. The swath also becomes invested with
flowers in the revision, and this addition not only softens
the harshness of the image, but also incorporates a feminine aspect and suggests that the death is a gentle one,
perhaps indicating Keats's acceptance of the inevitability
of death.

The final four lines of this stanza also soften Chatterton's
harsh personification of the murderous season, as the images are of stasis and almost of peacefulness:

And sometimes like a gleaner thou dost keep
Steady thy laden head across a brook;

Or by a cyder-press, with patient look
Thou watchest the last oozings hours by hours.[45]

The final image was suggested perhaps by Chatterton's
line in presenting autumn performing its duties: 'From
purple clusters prest the foamy wine.'[46] Chatterton's image
is more active, but Keats's personification of autumn is
one of relaxation and a lack of assertion. Although the personifications are different in temperament, the suggestion
of autumn fulfiling life and creating out of the ripeness is
shared, and Keats's image would therefore seem not to be
wholly original.

Keats's personification rests by the life-giving water, her
posture symbolically intimating her acceptance of the transition of the seasons, or she lies in the torpid passing of
time, motionless, as she watches the last ounce of life being squeezed out of the complete apples. The closing mood
of this stanza is one of resignation, as the movement and
fulfilment of life is passed over in passing through autumn
and only death remains. The drafting changes in these four
lines are minor and are concerned primarily with the emphasis placed upon the words. The description of the head
changes from 'leaden' to 'laden'[47] and 'the brook'[48] becomes 'a Brook.'[49] The first alteration implies an unspe-
cific weight upon the head of the reaper rather than em-
phasising the weight itself of her head, and perhaps
suggesting a consciousness of the destruction reaped by
autumn. The second change serves to release the image
from any specific conjuring of the author, and broadens
the sweep of the reference to include any images conjured
in the minds of the readers.

Addressing autumn in a direct appeal at the start of the
third stanza, spring is presented as almost inferior. Despite
the promise of life and development of spring, autumn has
the ultimate music in her ability for completion. Keats's
'Where are the songs of spring? Ay, where are they? /
Think not of them, thou hast thy music too,—'[50] remains
unaltered throughout the revision process, and is sharply
reminiscent of Chatterton's 'rough October has his pleasures too.'[51] Chatterton's poem presents all the seasons
with their various redeeming attributes, such as 'golden
autumn, wreath'd in rip'ned corn,'[52] and despite singing
the praises of each of the seasons, Chatterton finds special
features within autumn. Similarly, Keats compels the image of spring to arise within the readers' minds by mentioning it, and dismisses the privileges of life and beauty
traditionally associated with spring and suggests that autumn is comparably wonderful in its own way. The similarity between lines is again clear, since the same words
are employed and the two lines have similar turns of
phrase, and the lack of revision of Keats's lines again reinforces his recent reading of Chatterton's texts and
Keats's conscious or unconscious alignment between their
work.

Although the clouds of Keats's poem are blooming over
the day, which is dying without protest,[53] they are nevertheless 'barred'[54] and do not possess the power to break

free and wander over the sky. The 'barred clouds bloom' of the first draft is in fact altered from Keats's originally differently coloured image: 'a gold cloud gilds.'[55] The original is reminiscent of Chatterton's reaper, with his 'goulde honde guylteynge,'[56] and it would seem that Keats was aware of the similarity, one which perhaps inspired him to make the alteration, as Ting has noted: 'The line in "To Autumn" ("While a gold cloud gilds the soft dying day,") . . . clearly reminiscent of Chatterton, . . . were both [sic] omitted in publication.'[57]

Keats alters the succeeding lines also in order to further build the images upon one another, since the 'rosy hue' of the 'stibble plains,' originally due to the day's 'touching,'[58] is altered to rely upon the 'while': 'And touch the stubble-plains with rosy hue.'[59] Thus the colours of the two separate images are combined to produce the setting sun colour of dusk, symbolising the end of the day and the end of life before winter's bleak onset. The gnats are left mourning for the passing of the seasons, at the mercy of nature's will: 'borne aloft / Or sinking as the light wind lives or dies.'[60] The wind originally 'lives and dies,'[61] and the alteration serves to emphasize the combination of life and death within the season. Just as the wind's actions are fluctuating and unpredictable, so autumn promises the absolute fulfilment of life while simultaneously heralding the inevitable death to follow.

The lambs are now 'full-grown'[62] and have lost the carefree time of youth and development. Only the 'red-breast'[63] or robin is left in this changed season, surely indicative of the onset of winter as the swallows gather for migration. The 'gathering swallows'[64] of the final version were originally 'gather'd swallows,'[65] and the alteration again serves to imply the motion of the seasons and to perpetuate the omnipotent movement of autumn. The swallows cannot be in stasis, as all nature is always fluctuating and moving in the progressive cycle. The animals seem aware of the approaching darkness and accept the perpetual process of ripening, decay, and death.

The poem closes with death at the end of autumn, but also in a mood of acceptance of nature's cycle. The final glance is towards the sky, towards the heavenly region of human death and accompanying peace. The progression is one into and through autumn, entering on the boundary and completion of the cycle and departing as the approaching winter encroaches upon the scene and only death lies ahead. Just as the fullness of the fruit attracted Adam to sin, so the fulfilment of autumn and its promise of life can result only in death.

Chatterton's final lines are perhaps the most important to a reading of Keats's 'To Autumn': 'Thann, bee the even foule, or even fayre, / Meethynckes mie hartys joie ys steynced wyth somme care.'[66] Keats acknowledged Chatterton's emotion and reproduces it within his own poem: although beauty is to be found in autumn, there is always an accompanying feeling of death with the natural completion. Paradoxically, however much autumn ripens life and

develops it to its ultimate capacity, it inevitably simultaneously augurs death. The 'care' of autumn is the ambiguity of the season, as the promised fulfilment of life can be succeeded only by death. It would seem that Chatterton's lines were prominent in Keats's thoughts as he wrote his own poem, since the tone of Keats's poem duplicates the sentiment of Chatterton.

It is not only the tone and sentiment of Chatterton's text which are reproduced by Keats, as there are also similarities in melody. The stanzas of 'To Autumn' are altered from the quatrain-sestet with the rhyming scheme ababcdecde that can be found in the Petrarchan sonnet form of 'Ode to a Nightingale,'[67] to the quatrain-septet with a rhyming scheme of abab-cdecdde. Walter Jackson Bate adroitly acknowledges that the unexpected delay of the tenth line denies the stanza a sense of completion and thus complements the theme: 'The ode stanza is given a more prolonged effect; and the prolonging of fulfillment is itself an intrinsic part of the theme of the ode.'[68] The rhyming couplets in the ninth and tenth lines of the stanzas of 'To Autumn' echo the rhyming couplets to be found at the end of each stanza in Chatterton's **'Aella,'** but Keats's extra line at the end of each stanza denies any conventional adoption of closure.

Keats wrote of his admiration for Chatterton's language as the 'purest' and dismisses his own 'Hyperion' for having 'too many Miltonic inversions in it,'[69] stressing his preference for Chatterton's language as being 'entirely northern.'[70] In considering 'To Autumn,' Geoffrey Hartman asks the reader to

> consider the northernisms. . . . There is hardly a romance language phrase: sound-shapes like sallows, swallows, borne, bourn, crickets, croft, predominate. And, finally, the poise of the stanza's ending, on the verge of flight like joy always bidding adieu.[71]

The northernisms which Hartman identifies but does not define are perhaps a further indication of Keats's attachment to Chatterton's language, but the melodic fondness which Bailey recalls[72] is far more convincingly demonstrated in Keats's text.

Supplementary to the clear word and phrase reproduction seen in 'To Autumn,' the text seems also to replicate Chatterton's melody or rhythm. Bailey recalls Keats's fondness for Chatterton's line 'Come with acorn cup and thorn,'[73] and E. C. Pettet points out that 'in his own practice Keats certainly made a very considerable use of the melodic principle embodied in this admired line from Chatterton.'[74] Pettet uses line twenty-nine of 'To Autumn' as an example: 'Or sinking as the light wind lives or dies.'[75] The interwoven vowel sounds of Chatterton's 'come' and 'cup,' 'acorn' and 'thorn' are repeated by Keats's 'sinking' and 'lives,' 'light' and 'dies.' Pettet points out also that the line 'While barred clouds bloom the soft-dying day'[76] 'forms the antithesis of Chatterton's "Come with acorn cup and thorn" . . .' since 'though there are of course two strong alliterations, all eight of the principal vowel sounds are different.'[77] Thus Keats's poem can be seen both to reproduce Chatterton's melody and to juxtapose and contrast this with Keats's own melodic style.

Douglas Bush points out that 'it is generally agreed that this poem is flawless in structure, texture, tone, and rhythm,'[78] but he states that 'Keats's notion of Chatterton's English was unsophisticated,'[79] whereas Gittings finds virtue in Keats's identification with Chatterton's English:

> Direct borrowings from the minstrel's song of Autumn in Chatterton's *Aella* are apparent in the first draft, but alter under Keats's hand to more rich and positive form, though he retained the essential simplicity of Chatterton.[80]

Keats's poem remains objective and consciousness is almost absorbed into the poem; and, although the shared sentiment of Chatterton and Keats is clear, the images are adequate in themselves and in their symbolic suggestiveness as the real and the ideal are concretely presented.

Autumn is the paradoxical area between life and death, between warmth and chill. Keats takes his reader into autumn nearly at its closure and almost imperceptibly moves through autumn towards the unavoidable death. He has accepted the undeniable fact of man's mortality as the immediate successor to the fullness of life, seemingly suggested to him by Chatterton's lines. As Shakespeare's Edgar stated prior to his triumph over his wicked brother:

> Men must endure
> Their going hence even as coming hither,
> Ripeness is all.[81]

Keats has accepted life's cycle, serenely acknowledging the loss of life prior to the creation of new life. Three months after writing 'To Autumn,' Keats was to suffer a haemorrhage which led to his own death.

It is only by considering all available versions of Keats's text that their clear connections to Chatterton's work can be established, and only through this consideration can influence be duly acknowledged. The alterations and awareness of the context in which the text was produced indicate to some extent that Keats was aware of Chatterton's influence, whether consciously or unconsciously. There is a sense of continuation between texts within the poetic tradition, demonstrated by the perpetuating concern with the theme of autumn evident in the texts of the authors under consideration. But extensive textual examination of all extant versions is also essential in contemplating the texts, and Chatterton clearly merits further examination, particularly since his texts have influenced later poets and since they actively participate within ongoing traditions.

Notes

1. *Letters* 157-58.
2. See Robert Gitting's 'Keats and Chatterton' *KSJ* 4, and Nai-Tung Ting's 'The Influence of Chatterton on Keats' *KSJ* 5, and 'Chatterton and Keats: A Reexamination' *KSJ* 30.
3. *Poetical Works* 218-19.
4. *Letters* 152.
5. In order to refer to each of the drafts in analysing the changes therein, Jack Stillinger's extremely useful coded system to be found in his editing of *The Poems of John Keats* (476-77) has been adapted, and the transcript by George Keats and the modern Published Oxford edition of the poem are also considered:

   D refers to Keats's own draft

   L refers to the copy sent by Keats to Richard Woodhouse in a letter

   CB refers to the transcript by Charles Brown, revised by Keats and corrected by Woodhouse

   GK refers to the transcript by George Keats

   RW refers to the transcript by Woodhouse

   M refers to the published version in the Oxford edition of Keats's poetical works.
6. 'Chatterton and Keats' 116.
7. 706.
8. *The Living Year* 187.
9. *The Living Year* 187.
10. *D*, line 2.
11. *M*, 1-2.
12. *M*, 2.
13. *Letters* 38.
14. *Letters* 286.
15. 'Aella,' line 296.
16. 1986 Carcanet Edition, 50.
17. *M*, 1.
18. *D, L, CB, GK, RW*, 3-4.
19. 151.
20. *M*, 5.
21. 'Aella,' 302-03.
22. 'An Excelente Balade of Charitie,' 3-4.
23. *D, L, RW*, 8.
24. *RW*, 9.
25. *The Odes of Keats* 75.
26. 300.
27. 75.
28. 709.
29. 'The Influence of Chatterton on Keats' 108.
30. *M*, 12.
31. *D*, 12.
32. 'Aella' 163.
33. *The Living Year* 188.

34. *D*, 13.

35. *D*, 13.

36. *M*, 14-15.

37. *D*, 15-16.

38. 10.

39. 708.

40. 297, 299.

41. 298.

42. *D*, 18.

43. *M*, 16.

44. *M*, 17-18.

45. *M*, 19-22.

46. from 'Elegy to the Memory of Mr. Thomas Phillips, of Fairford,' hereafter 'Elegy' line 22.

47. *CB*, 20.

48. *D, CB, GK*, 20.

49. *RW*, 20.

50. *M*, 23.

51. 'Elegy' 53.

52. 21.

53. 'soft-dying' *M*, 25.

54. *M*, 25.

55. *D*, 25.

56. 'Aella' 297.

57. 'The Influence of Chatterton on Keats' 108.

58. *D*, 26.

59. *M*, 26.

60. *M*, 28-29.

61. *D, L, RW*, 29.

62. *M*, 30.

63. *M*, 32.

64. *M*, 33.

65. *D, L, RW*, 33.

66. 'Aella' 304-05.

67. *Poetical Works* 207-09.

68. 581.

69. *Letters* 292.

70. *Letters* 325.

71. 94.

72. 276.

73. 276.

74. 92.

75. *M*, 29.

76. *M*, 25.

77. 93.

78. 176.

79. 173.

80. *John Keats* 349.

81. *King Lear* 5.2-11.

Works Cited

Bailey, Benjamin. 'To R. M. Milnes.' 7 May 1849. Letter 253 in *The Keats Circle: Letters and Papers and More Letters and Poems of the Keats Circle*. Ed. Hyder Edward Rollins. 2nd ed. Vol. 1. Cambridge, MA: Harvard UP, 1965, p. 276.

Bate, Walter Jackson. *John Keats*. Cambridge, MA: Belknap P, 1964, p. 581.

Bayley, John. *Keats and Reality*. [Folcroft, PA]: Folcroft, 1969, p. 10.

Bush, Douglas. *John Keats: His Life and Writings*. New York: Macmillan, 1967, pp. 173, 176.

Chatterton, Thomas. *Thomas Chatterton: Selected Poems*. Ed. Grevel Lindop. Manchester: Carcanet, 1986, pp. 30-33, 42-72, 73-76.

Finney, Claude Lee. *The Evolution of Keats's Poetry*. Vol. 2. New York: Russell, 1963, pp. 706, 708, 709.

Gittings, Robert. *John Keats*. London: Penguin, 1979, p. 349.

———. *John Keats: The Living Year, 21 September 1818 to 21 September 1819*. Cambridge, MA: Harvard UP, 1954, pp. 187, 188.

———. 'Keats and Chatterton.' *Keats-Shelley Journal* 4 (1955): 47-54.

———. ed. *The Odes of Keats and Their Earliest Known Manuscripts*. Ohio: Kent State UP, 1970, p. 75.

Hartman, Geoffrey. 'Poem and Ideology: A Study of "To Autumn."' *John Keats: Modern Critical Views*. Ed. Harold Bloom. New York: Chelsea, 1985, p. 94.

Hirst, Wolf Z. *John Keats*. Boston: Twayne, 1981, p. 151.

Keats, John. *John Keats: Poetry Manuscripts at Harvard, a Facsimile Edition*. Ed. Jack Stillinger. 8 vols. Cambridge, MA: Belknap P, 1990, pp. 36-37, 173-74, 259-61.

———. *Keats: Poetical Works*. Ed. H. W. Garrod. Oxford: Oxford UP, 1987, pp. 207-09, 218-19.

———. *Letters of John Keats*. Ed. Robert Gittings. Oxford: Oxford UP, 1990, pp. 38, 152, 157-58, 286, 292, 325, 413.

———. *The Poems of John Keats*. Ed. Jack Stillinger. Cambridge, MA: Belknap P, 1978, pp. 476-77.

Pettet, E. C. *On the Poetry of Keats.* Cambridge: Cambridge UP, 1957, pp. 92, 93.

Shakespeare, William. *King Lear. The Riverside Shakespeare.* Boston: Houghton, 1974, p. 1291.

Ting, Nai-Tung. 'Chatterton and Keats: A Reexamination.' *Keats-Shelley Journal* 30 (1981): pp. 100-17.

————. 'The Influence of Chatterton on Keats.' *Keats-Shelley Journal* 5 (1956): pp. 103-8.

Nick Groom (essay date 1998)

SOURCE: "Thomas Chatterton Was a Forger," in *The Yearbook of English Studies: Eighteenth-Century Lexis and Lexicography,* edited by Andrew Gurr, Vol. 28, 1998, pp. 276-91.

[In the following excerpt, Groom tries to define forgery in light of the Rowley manuscript controversy that occurred after Chatterton's death; in his discussion, Groom focuses on the complex debate concerning the difference between history and fiction and the importance of authorial intention in deciding whether a document is indeed a forgery.]

> At that point Don Giuseppe would explain to him at length how the work of the historian is all deception, all fraud; how there was more merit in inventing history than transcribing it from old maps and tablets and ancient tombs; how, therefore, in all honesty, their efforts deserved an immensely larger compensation than the work of a real historian, a historiographer who enjoyed the benefits of merit and status.
>
> 'It's all fraud. History does not exist. Perhaps you think the generations of leaves that have dropped from that tree autumn after autumn still exist? The tree exists; its new leaves exist; but these leaves will also fall; in time, the tree itself will disappear—in smoke, in ashes. . . . What we are making, you and I, is a little fire, a little smoke with these limbs, in order to beguile people, whole nations—every living human being . . . History!'[1]
>
> (Leonardo Sciasca, *The Council of Egypt*).

Thomas Chatterton was a forger. What does this statement, this knowledge, mean? Chatterton forged literature: he forged language, he forged scholarly credentials, he forged sources. Yet he was not a mere forger: only the works attributed to Thomas Rowley and his set are called forgeries. Chatterton's other pieces in his two-volume *Works* are literature, as opposed to literary forgeries (in a sense, they are aberrant works in the canon of a forger). This essay will focus on Rowley: is it enough to say that Thomas Chatterton forged the works attributed to Thomas Rowley?

The definition of forgery begs a thousand questions: questions of intention and reception, counterfeit and plagiarism, imitation and pastiche, mimesis and representation. In a word, it always refers to a set of conditions outside the text. It is criminal evidence of authorial intention, or (in the case of the death of the forger) it is an enigma ravelled about the discourses of scholarly opinion. The word anticipates both the problem to be solved, and the solution. But Chatterton, I will argue, produced forgeries-within-forgeries which magnify the clumsiness of attempts to explain away his work, and which radically challenged notions of history and writing in the eighteenth century.

In Chatterton's work, meaning is always escaping into the remnants of things, language bristles like a hedgehog rolled up beneath spikes, or blurs into the scorch marks of decaying manuscripts. The reader is left to puzzle over quills or cinders. Indeed in **'Clifton'** (unforged), Chatterton suggests that history may appear to evade its own process by side-stepping into language and then shrouding itself in mildew upon the worm-eaten page.

Yet the page itself is rotting away, enacting the very process of time:

> O'er the historick page my fancy runs,
> Of Britain's fortunes, of her valiant sons,
> You castle, erst of Saxon standards proud,
> Its neighbouring meadows dy'd with Danish bloody
> . . .
> But for its ancient use no more employ'd,
> Its walls all moulder'd and its gates destroy'd;
> In Hist'ry's roll it still a shade retains,
> Tho' of the fortress scarce a stone remains.[2]

Thus in the shade of 'Hist'ry's roll', we see only the sign of writing having passed, not the language itself. In fact, meaning decays as inevitably as the fragile medium of the medieval manuscript. This essay will argue that the manuscript defied eighteenth-century literary antiquarianism. It was in opposition to the print ideology of scholarship, and so was judged to be fundamentally inauthentic. But the manuscript (especially in the Rowley corpus) inevitably remained a vehicle, a mode of transference, or a metaphor, for history—a version of history that would embarrass literary antiquarianism. The argument draws on my own earlier work, and has been indirectly inspired by a minor constellation of theoretical essays.[3]

On 8 February 1777, Thomas Tyrwhitt published the first volume of Rowley poetry: ***Poems, supposed to have been written at Bristol, by Thomas Rowley and Others, in the Fifteenth Century.*** The collection contained a selection of ancient poems and dramatic verse, mainly by one Thomas Rowley. These literary remains had been discovered in St Mary Redcliffe Church in Bristol in the late 1760s by a teenager called Thomas Chatterton, a Colston charity boy and an attorney's clerk. Chatterton's father had begun rifling through the old chests in the muniment room in the 1750s, and his posthumous son followed him in these wormy habits. Chatterton, a voracious reader and a prolific writer, claimed in about 1768 to have discovered the works of Thomas Rowley, a fifteenth-century priest, in an old chest in the muniment room over the north porch of the church. The Rowley corpus was enormous, including poems, prose, drawings, and maps, and appeared to be a major literary find. Chatterton had produced more and more examples while living and working in Bristol before moving to London a few months before his death in 1770, either adolescent suicide or dreadful accident. He was only seventeen. Soon after, these 'Rowley Poems' found themselves at the centre of an argument concerning their authenticity, first in Bristol and Bath, then in London. With the 1777 edition, these sparks of doubt were blown into an inferno of controversy which raged for the next two or three decades. It was eventually concluded that the works were all forged by the boy. History was written rather than rewritten.

The proofs were (and in a sense still are) conclusive, and so the story of Chatterton is already anticipated in its telling—anticipated as a story explaining and explaining away the phenomenon of 'literary forgery'. But a doubt remains in the plausible accounts of the eighteenth-century literati, not in the Romantic mythography of Wordsworth and Coleridge and Keats, nor in the postmodern intertextuality of Peter Ackroyd. A single page from the 1777 edition of the **Rowley Poems** presents a riddle. The title-page of Tyrwhitt's **Rowley Poems** highlighted the manuscript status of Rowley: 'THE GREATEST PART NOW FIRST PUBLISHED FROM THE MOST AUTHENTIC COPIES, WITH AN ENGRAVED SPECIMEN OF ONE OF THE MSS.'[4] This engraving, 'The Accounte of W. Canynges Feast', was a startling image, displaying extravagantly archaic calligraphy, exotic Gothic lettering, and featuring illustrations of two heraldic shields. The visual impact of the document was further enhanced by its position in the volume: facing the printed transcript of **'The Accounte of W. Canynges Feast'**, which looked desolate in comparison. . . . The relationship between the typographic text and the unique engraving of a Rowley manuscript is both fascinating and bewildering.

Despite the sparse image of print compared with the magnificence of the parchments, the form of Rowley on the printed page was still grotesquely strange: Chatterton forged a pseudo-medieval language. He scavenged archaic words from the glossaries of Chaucer and Thomas Percy's *Reliques of Ancient English Poetry,* and had a Shakespearean talent for comparable neologism and coinage. And he garbed this odd pastiche in an idiosyncratic, supposedly archaic orthography. Chatterton invented a poetic Rowleyan language by doubling consonants, substitutions ('y' for 'i' and 'c' for 'k'), and (indeed like Percy in his *Reliques*) adding redundant e's to most words.[5] Antiquity was guaranteed by redundancy and copiousness, like Gothic architecture (indeed, very like the Gothic of St Mary Redcliffe). All these orthographic oddities were faithfully reproduced in the **Rowley Poems** and **Miscellanies in Verse and Prose** (a follow-up volume printed in 1778), and the very lines drew attention to their rough physicality:

> Geofroie makes vearse, as handycraftes theyr ware;
> Wordes wythoute sense fulle groffyngelye* he twynes,

Cotteynge hys storie off as wythe a sheere;
*foolishly. [Chatterton's note.][6]

For the majority of readers, readers of the posthumous, printed editions, this bizarre language was the most immediately compelling aspect of Rowley. It barked and rasped with a guttural new poetic voice, echoing from the iron depths of fantastic medieval armour, even if it was easily strangled by deft wit.[7]

In his *History of English Poetry* in 1781, the pioneering literary historian and poet, Thomas Warton, modernized the **'Notbrowne Mayde'** to challenge Edward Capell's dating of the poem.[8] This technique of textual analysis was based on the assumption that history was integral rather than superficial to a poem, but was ultimately simply a force acting on language, a factor of linguistic change, a structuring principle: that language is writ on the roll of history and offered the sign of times passed.

The technique was full of all the confidence of burgeoning literary history: indeed it could be seen as its whole rationale, the demonstration of historical change and literary improvement. There was none of the abysmal semantic melancholy that Chatterton suggests in **'Clifton'** and elsewhere. In consequence, translation and pastiche were enthusiastically propounded by 'anti-Rowleyans' as demystifiers in the debates about the poems. William Mason deployed the device most tellingly in *An Archeological Epistle to the Reverend and Worshipful Jeremiah Milles* (1782): the 'Epistlle to Doctoure Mylles' was a piece of verse describing the controversy and its participants in Rowleyan language, and the effect was both absurd and hallucinatory. George Hardinge added a little Rowley pastiche, 'To the Dygne Reader' to his play *Rowley and Chatterton in the Shades: or, Nugae Antiquitae et Novae* (1782). The Shakespearean editor Edmond Malone, too, in his pamphlet *Cursory Observations on the Poems attributed to Thomas Rowley* (1782), took delight in rewriting Chatterton's poems: 'Chatterton in Masquerade' was a translation of **'Narva and Mored'** into Rowleyan, while 'Chatterton Unmasked' modernized the Rowleyan **'First Eclogue'**.

Of most interest is an unsigned letter to the *Public Advertiser,* dated 19 March 1782, in homage to Mason's 'Epistlle to Doctoure Mylles' (the pastiche of a forgery). The correspondent suggests that other authors be garbed in 'Archaeological Language' to affect a sort of textual alchemy: 'This, however, I would not call *Translation,* but *Transmutation,* for a very obvious Reason.' The opening of *Paradise Lost* and the famous soliloquy from *Hamlet* are offered as tongue-in-cheek examples:

> Offe mannes fyrste bykrous volunde wolle I singe,
> And offe the fruicte offe yatte caltyfnyd tre
> Whose lethall taste ynto thys Worlde dydde brynge
> Both mothe and tene to all posteritie.
> To blynne or not to blynne the denwere is;
> Gif ytte bee bette wythinne the spryte to beare

The bawsyn floes and tackels of dystresse,
Or by forloynyng amenuse them clere.

Ironically, this transmutation does dazzle us like newly-minted gold as we recognize the familiar in a new radiance. It is reminiscent of R. L. C. Lorimer's recent Scottish *Macbeth*

Whuff, cannle-dwop!
Life's nocht but a scug gangin, a bauch actor
as strunts an fykes his ae hour on the stage.[9]

The perspective of the text is strictly from the present looking to the past (sidelong, in the case of Lorimer); history is focused like a spectacle before the gaze of the present. There could be no more powerful demonstration that eighteenth-century literary antiquarianism heralded the genealogy of the perfection of the art of writing.[10] History came of age in the genius of the present.

Having proved to their satisfaction that Chatterton's Rowley language actually supported their theories of linguistic integrity, the antiquarians pursued this theme by considering each word as an object, with its own linear history. Reviewing the **Rowley Poems** in 1777, Ralph Griffiths called them *'Mock Ruins'*, (although the volume contained no fragments), and in 1782, Warton observed, 'A builder of ruins is seldom exact throughout in his imitation of the old-fashioned architecture.'[11] He presented Chatterton's work as a visual pastiche: 'In dictionaries of old English, he saw words detached and separated from their context: these he seized and combined with others, without considering their relative or other accidental signification.'[12] Malone too described the poems in architectural terms: 'Many of the stones which this ingenious boy employed in his building . . . are as old as those at Stone-henge; but the beautiful fabrick that he has raised is tied together by modern cement, and is covered by a stucco of no older date than that of Wyat and Adams.'[13] He gave several examples of Chatterton's plagiarisms from the cultural monument of the canon. Indeed, spotting Rowley's sources was a game started in the *St. James's Chronicle* in 1778 and enthusiastically prosecuted by another Shakespearean, George Steevens. This device effectively foiled a discussion of the poetical merits of Rowley by implying that any verse could be composed in this allusive way, that it was entirely dependent on earlier writers, that it was parasitic and derivative and plagiarized.

Jacob Bryant, a fearsomely and erratically learned defender of Rowley, was scornful of Chatterton's supposed use of dictionaries and glossaries: 'We may as well suppose, that a pedlar built York cathedral by stealing a tile, or a stone, in every parish he passed through.'[14] But Vicesimus Knox was nonplussed:

Thyself thou has emblazoned; thine own monument thou hast erected. . . . Thou hast built an artificial ruin. The stones are mossy and old, the whole fabric appears really antique to the distant and the careless spectator; even the connoisseur, who pores with spectacles on the

single stones, and inspects the mossy concretions with an antiquarian eye, boldly authenticates its antiquity; but they who examine without prejudice, and by the criterion of common sense, clearly discover the cement and the workmanship of a modern mason.[15]

Why the architectural imagery? Horace Walpole, in his *Anecdotes of Painting in England,* had famously made antiquarianism visionary, a way of feeling the 'magic hardiness' of the Gothic: 'One must have taste to be sensible of the beauties of Grecian architecture; one only wants passions to feel Gothic.'[16] He described the English Gothic past as an enormous painting or piece of architecture, both visual and tactile—'vaults, tombs, painted windows, gloom, and perspectives'—analogous to his own medieval simulation, Strawberry Hill. Walpole's Gothic metonyms derived from the persistent use in earlier works of architectural images to describe old language. For example, Elizabeth Cooper's *The Muses Library* compared the 'Gothique Rudeness' of Chaucer and Spencer [*sic*] to the 'Monumental Statues of the Dead', and John Weever's *Ancient Funeral Monuments* (quoted by Chatterton) had an ecclesiastical Gothic atmosphere of black-letter inscriptions and crypts which is redolent of Walpole, and Rowley too.[17] Gothic was a sentimental reading of the past in which archaic language was objectified and fetishized. Moreover, as with architectural uses of porticoes or arched windows, each medieval word, even each unexpected use of a 'k' or doubled consonant or redundant 'e', was a gesture that alluded to the whole culture and recalled history. They functioned as relics, or rather meaning was securely encased in these encrusted reliquaries. Like bits and pieces of saints (or in antiquarian cabinets of curiosities, like the remains of secular heroes and heroines) the presentation of words in this ritual way seemed to suggest that they shared in the physical reality of some event—history—but also transcended it. They were fragments of true meaning, with the authority of their own existence.

Why was this metaphor so insistent? It is not enough to state that Chatterton's art rose with the archive, was an odd contortion of a print culture which favoured ready retrieval devices such as glossaries and dictionaries. Rowley's works were discovered in a church muniment room, and Rowley was in one sense a sepulchre. But the sepulchre was empty, there was no poetry among the vellum scraps Chatterton and his father collected. Chatterton is suggesting that meaning has an origin outside of history.

This is apparent in his weaving of text and commentary: the double narratives of medieval poetry and editorial annotations. Chatterton's editorial persona provided a constant commentary and at times drowned out the poetry. Sometimes nearly every word in a line would be footnoted. The reader was prevented from reading the pieces: the poetry represented its own disappearance under the tide of the present. When the pieces were published, the reader was bullied into seeing in them merely the sign of ancient poetry: the polyvalency of archaisms and footnotes. Annotation was ostentatious: to conspicuously display erudition served to authenticate the poems within the discourses of scholarship.

Rowley was split into many voices. For the antiquarians, the question was to discover where these voices began, either in the 1760s or the 1460s, but the question of origins also carried the big cultural question, where did our history, our national past, begin? Rowley does not offer the convenient linearity of Warton's scheme, precisely because he is not part of the great tradition: he is an outsider, whether real (interred in the muniment room) or not. Rowley's history is fragmentary, a decaying palimpsest too fragile to scrape clean. In the shady muniment room, where the vellum scraps were gathered like so many sibylline leaves, the broken texts could only be a metaphor for the past. There was nothing really there.

So English literary history was no longer confined to the past in the 1760s when Rowley was emerging. The works appeared in a highly charged literary context, at the moment of the construction of the canon of English poetry in Percy's *Reliques,* and were published at the moment of literary history's being written in Warton's *History of English Poetry* (1774-81). In fact, Rowley actually featured in the second volume of Warton's *History* (1778) in a twenty-five page section, which was in press some time before Tyrwhitt's edition.

Warton had published the first volume of his authoritative *History* in 1774, in which a preliminary dissertation had stressed the importance of literacy: indeed, the essay 'On the Introduction of Learning into England' reads like a bibliolator's Grand Tour. Literacy flourished all over Gothic Europe. King Alfred promoted no illiterate priests and translated Latin authors into his native Saxon, while 'the conqueror himself patronised and loved letters' and demonstrated his power and control over his new land by outlawing the Saxon tongue.[18] In this case, literate language had created problems for the native Saxons: the Normans would not accept Saxon documents of property rights because they implied a rejection of the new ruler, and this necessitated the 'pious fraud' of forging monastic charters (reminiscent of the Donation of Constantine) (I, 3 n.). Moreover, forgery was an inevitable part of medieval manuscript culture: copying and plagiarizing from manuscripts were the only way of disseminating and circulating texts. But precisely because of this, it became a characteristic against which eighteenth-century print culture and scholarship defined itself.

Warton's *History* did raise concern about the status of sources. Although his first volume was derived from manuscripts, Warton made no mention of the uniqueness of his texts, nor the nature of chirographic culture: he was wary of mentioning the word 'manuscript' at all. One of the aims of the *History* seems to have been to create an anthology or 'general repository of our antient poetry', although Warton explicitly denied this (I, 208). Because so much of Warton's material had not previously been pub-

lished he quoted his illustrations at length, reprinting the earliest extant manuscript of a poem under the assumption that it provided the most reliable text (I, 101).

In the second volume of his *History of English Poetry,* Warton encountered Caxton, and very briefly described the impact of moveable type: it played a vital part in disseminating literature, 'contributed to sow the seeds of a national erudition, and to form a popular taste'; and 'multiplied English readers, and these again produced new vernacular writers' (II, 122, 124 n.). But because Warton had treated the chirographic texts of pre-Caxton verse as if they had the authority of typographic texts, he did not suggest that Caxton's innovation in any way revolutionized the word on the page. The transition between manuscript and print culture was elided. Eighteenth-century scholarship was grounded in print and printed books, which itself implied a linear history. Literature, the object of antiquarian study, necessarily predated it, but scholarship had the capaciousness enabled by print to comprehend it. English verse did not arrive with Caxton's press; its origins had to be presented as lost in the mists and myths of time (and as competitors with the Celts and other northern pretenders), but also recoverable through historical theory and research. Warton was writing a teleological history of English poetry; he only stressed that print provided the instruments of modern scholarship.

Warton devoted a whole section of his second volume to Rowley. For this chapter, he quoted long passages of Rowley as part of his larger argument of literary progress. The technique enabled him to juxtapose Rowley with the fifteenth-century verse that supported his argument, and so to deny the incongruous Rowley a place in the system he was perfecting. Although the Rowley remains were constantly invoked and scrutinized by Warton, no referent such as **'The Accounte of W. Canynges Feast'** was provided. And although Warton described his analyses of calligraphy, ink, and parchment, this forensic account had to be taken on trust because these very features were not reproducible in a printed book.

Rowley appeared then at the moment the canon became an issue: who was to be included or excluded from Warton's epoch-making work? The work of Percy and Warton, not to mention Samuel Johnson in the *Dictionary* and the *Lives,* was about uncovering the printable manuscript: recognizing the manuscripts in which inherent typography was most lucidly articulated. Print was the yardstick of antiquarian evidence. The cause and consequence of the canon, formulated in the eighteenth century, was that typographic structures were perceived to be inherent in manuscripts. And it was this print-determined selectivity that literary forgery exposed.

Rowley attempted to find or construct a place outside the all-pervasive culture of typography, and therefore insisted on all the untypographic elements of the medium: calligraphy, ink, paper or parchment, as well as provenance, damage, and supplementarity. They forced print to insist and re-insist upon its totalitarianism, because these untranslatable aspects of the manuscript exposed the absolutist assumptions of typography. To establish that Rowley was spurious, Warton did not in fact visit Bristol, or even handle a Rowleian manuscript: they were described to him in correspondence which, being ideally suited to printing, he of course published. The manuscript was treated as an entirely inauthentic document, because it was unsuited to being printed—though it was never declared to be inauthentic, except in cases such as the Rowley controversy.

So the actual conceptual problem that Rowley's manuscript posed the eighteenth-century literary antiquarians—is there anything more to letters than typography?—was never actually answered. The works of Chatterton were declared 'forgeries' by Warton, and others, and dismissed to an incoherent twilight, because if this work, called forgery, did find a place outside typography, it could, like Archimedes and his place to stand on, move the world. All literature might be forged.

This is the challenge posed by the manuscript, the crux of Chatterton-Rowley so dramatically played out in the two (printed) pages of **'The Accounte of W. Canynges Feast'**. The whole dreadful significance of the Rowley hoard lay in Chatterton's use of the found manuscript. Manuscripts subverted print: the *manuscrit trouvé,* complete with lacunae and illegible letters, could not be adequately reproduced on the printed page of eighteenth-century literary histories. While exposing the profound limitations of print, the page exercised an extraordinary fascination upon contemporaries. It was reproduced in all the editions of Rowley and in commentaries as late as 1809, and was discussed, almost without exception, in Rowley Controversy books, pamphlets, and magazine articles.[19] This was a tantalizing glimpse of the real thing, the supposed manuscript, although it was, of course, just a particularly well-disguised printed page.

The page collapses definitions of forgery and originality. This manuscript is supposedly original (and yet in an important sense it is still a copy). It is a forgery of a work which is original, yet which (it is claimed by detractors) has no original. It exposes a contradiction, or paradox, in the very definition of forgery: while an economic forger, a counterfeiter, is able to forge a bank note (that is, make an exact copy of something which already exists), such as a £5 note, the same forger is not able to pass off an original forgery, such as a £3 note. But art and literary forgers do forge works that might never have previously existed. So, strangely, the text is sign and proof of both authenticity and fraudulence. It is both true and untrue (and was employed as evidence on both sides of the authenticity debate). So it seems that the whole idea of forgery becomes impossibly refracted. The word loses its authority to present and solve a problem, because Chatterton has produced, (posthumously) on this page, and more radically in his vellum Rowley manuscripts, forgeries-within-forgeries. They secrete the odour of an intricate textual problem, but the secret they reveal is that there is no se-

cret, and no basis for literary antiquarian criticism. We see a printed skeleton, clothed (on the right) with the flesh of chirography. But it is, at its core, for Tyrwhitt and Warton and Walpole, a printed artefact. The manuscript, within the metaphysics of typography, is simply a corruption of print, a deviation from it. All manuscripts are already typographic on these terms, but still the manuscript is more: it has an excess, a capacity uncontained by the typeface and engraving.

For this reason, the manuscript *per se* was not part of published literary antiquarianism: it was an image rather than an object, a shadow cast upon the screen of print. Of course Percy, Warton, Capell, and Walpole all used manuscripts, but they did not publish engravings of manuscripts as textual artefacts, nor did they clearly acknowledge their indebtedness to manuscript sources. The jockeying for ancient sources between Percy and James Macpherson in *Five Pieces of Runic Poetry* (1763) and the *Reliques,* and the collected *Ossian* (1765) respectively, demonstrated that not just the emergent canon but cultural identity was at stake. But evidently there was a great deal of confusion about the status afforded to literary-antiquarian evidence. The over-scrupulous editing of Edward Capell and 'Don' Bowle was contrasted with the sentimental panache of Richard Hurd and Walpole; and both Macpherson and Percy ran into difficulties when they tried to present manuscripts.

Because Chatterton produced manuscripts that could be circulated, rather than transcriptions or proofsheets, there are enormous differences between his work and that of Macpherson and Percy and other antiquarians. Editors with ambitions to publish experienced great difficulties expressing themselves on the printed page, but Chatterton side-stepped these problems by concentrating on the manuscripts, leaving others to plan the publication.[20] Although Chatterton verified his source as Macpherson and Percy had verified theirs, by local testimonial, internal proofs, and supporting argument, he alone introduced forensic evidence. It was the latter that precipitated the Rowley controversy: the existence of palpable objects was missing from *Ossian* and *Reliques.* No matter how hard the antiquarians tried in claiming that old Gothic words had the 'magic hardiness' of old Gothic buildings, it was clear that they did not have the ephemeral precision of a manuscript. Chatterton slotted Rowley between Macpherson's late recognition of the necessity of manuscripts and Percy's mirage of the source (his jealously guarded folio manuscript). Critics and scholars alike were able to exercise their wit and erudition on their impression of one of these actual documents. Indeed, because only two Rowley pieces were published in Chatterton's lifetime (the **'Bridge Narrative'** in *Felix Farley's Bristol Journal,* 1 October 1768, and **'Elinoure and Juga'** in the *Town and Country Magazine,* May 1769), we are left with a body of material which created a controversy motivated in part by the problems in printing it.

Chatterton cheerfully embraced the protean nature of manuscript culture. A lengthy closing footnote to the **'Bris-**

towe Tragedy' stressed the importance of this context. After verifying the beheading of Bawdin with reference to the historian John Stow, Chatterton wrote asking for more evidence:

> But a more Authentick Evidence of this Fact I met with in an old Parchment Roll, in which among other Curiosities preserv'd in the Cabinet of Mr Canynge, is mentioned . . . .
>
> I shall conclude this with remarking, that if Gentlemen of Fortune wou'd take the trouble of looking over the Manuscripts in their Possession, which are only valued for their Antiquity, it might possibly throw Light upon many obscure Passages in and help to establish a more Concise History of our Native Country, than even *Cambden's Britania.*

> (*Works*, 1, 20 n.)

Chatterton's reinvention of manuscript sources received its fullest exposition in **'A Brief Account of William Cannings from the Life of Thomas Rowlie Preeste'.** This short prose piece explained how Canynge ordered Rowley to 'goe to all the Abbies and Pryoryes, and gather together auncient drawynges, if of any Account; at any Price' (1, 51). The Wapolean Canynge was interested in old English painters, but the Chattertonian Rowley was more concerned with manuscripts, and discovered a Saxon parchment at the 'Minster of oure Ladie and Saincte Godwyne', which he bought and set 'diligentlie to translate and worde it in Englishe Metre' (1, 52, 54). A year later he had the **'Battle of Hastynges'.** Over eight hundred years, the poem had been transmitted from Turgotus to Rowley to Chatterton. The nature of the source affected the poem and its presentation, and the uniqueness of the source was stressed because it determined the text. In this case, Chatterton complained in his editorial introduction that the poem was incomplete:

> AN Ancient poem called the Battle of Hastynges written by Turgot a Saxon Monk in the *Tenth* Century and translated by Thomas Ronlie [*sic*: a deliberate error by Chatterton's editorial persona] the remaynyng Part of this Poem I have not been happy enough to meet with—

> (1, 26-27)

which was hardly surprising after eight centuries. But the transmission of the poem did more than reinscribe, did more than record the impact of history upon the text. The silence of the absent part is not Chatterton's suppressed rejoicing at having found an excuse not to finish the piece, but the resounding silence of history. Language has passed without a trace, only the rump of the poem remains.

The manuscript as a metaphor for history, a vehicle for the liquidation of language, was reflected in Rowley's other activities. Canynge employed Rowley to compile lists of inscriptions, recording relics of antique text on a parchment which Chatterton reduced to a hopeless fragment itself (1, 117-18, facing p. 116). Fragmentation verified the manuscript source in the act of destroying it, and the inevitable attempts of readers to fill in the gaps with conjec-

tural emendations was cruelly satirized by Chatterton. In the effervescent prose skit **'Memoirs of a Sad Dog',** he had Baron Otranto misread a broken and eroded gravestone, 'James Hicks lieth here, with Hester his wife', as '*Hic jacet corpus Kenelmae Sancto Legero. Requiescat*' (1, 659). The fragmentary stone was a memorial to lost languages rather than a testament to antiquarian genius.

The shift of focus, from writing to history, from print to manuscript, from language to silence, that Rowley precipitated created a contagious game of Chinese whispers, or rather, a wild paper chase. If ancient manuscripts spoke most eloquently of their silence and meaninglessness, modern manuscripts (in the guise of transcripts) larded this profound silence with the clamour of voices, all saying the same thing but every one speaking in a different tongue. Tyrwhitt had provided the **Rowley Poems** with an 'Introductory Account of the Several Pieces contained in this Volume', which detailed provenance, textual variants, historical background, references, and sources (pp. xv-xxv). George Catcott and William Barrett, original Bristol supporters of Rowley, had gradually disseminated transcripts to trusted allies, who in turn had copied the texts to enlist supporters, and so on. This had been going on for seven years, so the Rowley texts existed in countless variants. They had spawned a subculture of migratory and self-duplicating manuscripts that further upset the authority of print and actually mirrored the clamorous manuscript culture of Rowley. If a manuscript copy of a genuine ancient manuscript could be made by Chatterton or Catcott, a facsimile (or counterfeit) manuscript copy could also be made: a forgery of a forgery. This copy would not necessarily invalidate the original document, but as the 'original forgery' needed not exist anyway, it made the concept of the original superfluous. Transcripts were marauders: wonderfully ambiguous signs which harried the unanimous uniformity of print with ever-mutating texts, so they too became engaged in another ceaseless Chattertonian attack upon the assumption that typography was the fundamental medium of literature and the empirical unit of literary history.

This sort of argument was elaborated by pro-Rowleians such as Henry Dampier, who responded to Warton with *Remarks upon the Eighth Section of the Second Volume of Mr. Warton's History of English Poetry.*[21] Dampier answered some of Warton's points—the staining of the paper, the colour of ink—while at the same time denying that the extant manuscripts represented any definite grounds for refutation anyway: 'The proofs that even this manuscript is a forgery, are by no means incontestable; nor if they were, would it follow the course, that all or any of the other manuscripts must necessarily be so too' (p. 30). If the parchments were fakes, it meant that they could be Chatterton's counterfeits of genuine documents, and another link in the chain of transmission from the fifteenth century to the eighteenth. (Dampier also criticized Warton's instinctive citation of Percy's glossary to the *Reliques* as a Rowley source. It simply showed the literati closing ranks.)

Rayner Hickford argued with most awareness on the issue of sources, in *Observations on the Poems attributed to Rowley*. Hickford was not afraid to argue that sources, and therefore meaning, were endlessly deferred: for example, he brilliantly demonstrated that the provenance of **'Verses to Johne Ladgate, with Johne Ladgate's Answer'** was a maze of chirographic transmission.[22] Hickford also pointed out that Rowley himself was not unlike certain eighteenth-century editors, and was prepared to rewrite ancient history, to *'clean it from it's rust'* (p. 13).

But the most obsessive defence came from the grinding pen of Jacob Bryant. Bryant's doorstop of a book, *Observations upon the Poems of Thomas Rowley* (1781), was an unstable juggernaut pulled along by sheer erudition. Writing as if through gritted teeth, he insisted that the lexical peculiarities of Rowley were caused by the influence of oral dialects on chirographic culture:

> Before the art of printing became of general use, it is scarcely possible to conceive, but that people must have written in dialects: for they had no standard, by which they could be regulated; and if there had existed any thing of this nature in any particular place, it could not have been universally kept up, for want of that intercourse and correspondence, which are so essential to its influence and authority.
>
> (p. 8)

Bryant's whole method was based on what he perceived to be the shortcomings of scribal culture, and it was the scholar's unflinching duty to scrape away these transcriptural mistakes. Bryant attempted to reconstitute the archetypal manuscripts from which Chatterton had worked. His scholarship was visionary: an absolute recovery and reconstitution of what was incoherently expressed:

> Whether the Mss. was at all impaired, and the words in some degree effaced: or whether it were owing to his ignorance, and carelessness, I know not: but thus much is certain, that the terms are sadly transposed, and changed, to the ruin of the context.
>
> (p. 95)

Bryant brought his etymological researches to Rowley: as John Cleland had suggested a few years earlier (1768), 'The antientest way of spelling a word is ever the best guide to the decomposition of it'.[23] No letter or word was secure from interrogation and revision, no phrase or meaning was contained, but seeped hermetic inference, enabling Bryant to rewrite Rowley. He queried whether it was possible for the Bristol youth to be familiar with as much arcane lore as he was himself:

> There are many dark hints and intimations, with which he [Chatterton] was totally unacquainted. From these secret allusions I have been induced to think, that some of these poems were not even of the age of Rowley, but far antecedent: being composed by some person, or persons, who were not far removed from the times and events, which they celebrate [e.g. **'Hastings'**].
>
> (p. 206)

Bryant therefore interpreted literature as a semiotic medium: cultural significance was only conducted to those familiar with a structure underlying everyday language. In this way Bryant extended his notion of language to the whole system of signs—Chatterton's biography, manuscript provenance, etymology, aesthetics, intertextuality—which constituted the reception of Rowley. The distinction between text and context was entirely dissolved. Ultimately, texts for Bryant were only part of a large cultural code; they did not constitute it: in fact they constituted a celebration of his own abstruse learning.

Bryant's work reads like a crusade down the road of history, a road littered with manuscripts, with ashes, indeed with cinders. Derrida has proposed the metaphor of the cinder to describe the trace, and we may perceive in the manuscript, read 'In Hist'ry's roll' (itself subject to reduction by tearing, mildew, and cinders), what is left after language has been exhausted.[24] Crumbling manuscripts are both fragile and tenacious, they are on the border between things and words, and they may carry us down the path that leads to origins. But they testify to the passing of language, not to language itself; the manuscript is always already too late, it is record of something done and gone. Chatterton aged a manuscript by holding it over a flame and thereby fading the words to leave 'the mellow vestiges of evanscent ink'.[25] If the manuscript carries us down the path that leads to origins, there are only cinders there.

'The Accounte of W. Canynges Feast' is now in the British Library.[26] It is a tiny document (the 1777 facsimile is full size). The text runs to all edges of the parchment; there is a complete absence of margins, whitespace, titles, and in these versions, notes. And it is black as soot.

On 9 March 1784, William Jessop wrote to Thomas Percy on the subject of the *Reliques of Ancient English Poetry*:

> Oh for a ray of Chatterton's genius. Had I this, I should soon send you a roll ten yards long of worm-eaten vellum, which should, here and there, amidst undecypherable hieroglyphics, exhibit to you a legible distambour upon the miserable substratum with silk and gold of your own property.[27]

The manuscript source was acknowledged 'undecypherable'; it stretched like a canvas for the editor to embroider. Antiquarian literary history spun its loquacious myths out of the indecipherable, incomprehensible silence of history. The most poignant Rowley manuscripts that remain are those that Taylor lists as 'illegible antiqued parchments': unreadable manuscripts that gave up their secrets when no one was reading. Writing has passed 'O'er the historick page', and passed away.

Notes

1. *The Council of Egypt* (1963), trans. by Adrienne Foulkes (London: Harvill, 1993), pp. 63-64.

2. *The Complete Works of Thomas Chatterton,* ed. by Donald S. Taylor, 2 vols (Oxford: Clarendon Press, 1971). 1, 343.

3. See *Narratives of Forgery,* ed. by Nick Groom, *Angelaki,* 1.2 (1993); Nick Groom, 'Celts, Goths, and the Nature of the Literary Source', in *Tradition in Transition: Women Writers, Marginal Texts, and the Eighteenth-Century Canon,* ed, by Alvaro Ribeiro, SJ, and James G. Basker (Oxford: Clarendon Press, 1996), pp. 275-96; Jean Baudrillard, 'Gesture and Signature: Semiurgy in Contemporary Art', in *For a Critique of the Political Economy of the Sign,* trans. by Charles Levin (n.p.: Telos Press, 1981), pp. 102-11; Jacques Derrida, 'Signature Event Context', in *Margins of Philosophy,* ed. and trans. by Alan Bass (Chicago: University of Chicago Press, 1982), pp. 307-30; Michel Foucault, 'Nietzsche Genealogy History', in *The Foucault Reader,* ed. by Paul Rabinow (Harmondsworth: Penguin, 1984).

4. *Poems, supposed to have been written at Bristol, by Thomas Rowley and Others, in the Fifteenth century,* ed. by Thomas Tyrwhitt (London, 1777), sig. al^r.

5. *The Poetical Works of Thomas Chatterton,* ed. by Walter W. Skeat, 2 vols (London: Bell & Daldy, 1872), 11, xxxv-xl, 1176-80.

6. *Rowley Poems,* p. 69: *Works,* I, 176.

7. See Richard Holmes, 'Thomas Chatterton: The Case Re-Opened', *Cornhill Magazine,* 178 (1970), 230.

8. *The History of English Poetry,* 3 vols (London, 1774-81), III, 136.

9. *Times Literary Supplement,* 18 September 1992. p. 14.

10. See David Fairer, 'Organizing Verse: Burke's *Reflections* and Eighteenth-Century English Poetry' (forthcoming, *Romanticism*).

11. *Monthly Review,* 28 (1777), 256. After printing the 'Testimony of George Catcott' in the May issue (originally his 'Introduction' and 'Remarks'), the June *Review* concluded 'We do not hesitate to pronounce that these Poems are the original production of Rowley, with many alterations and interpolation by Chatterton' (pp. 312, 449). The sceptical *Gentleman's Magazine* printed the song of Robin and Alice from 'Aella', 'With some trivial Alterations': it was completely modernized (*Gentleman's Magazine,* 47 (1777), 275).

12. Thomas Warton, *An Enquiry into the Authenticity of the Poems attributed to Rowley* (London, 1782), p. 43.

13. Edmond Malone, *Cursory Observations on the Poems attributed to Thomas Rowley, A Priest of the Fifteenth Century* (London, 1782), pp. 11-12.

14. Jacob Bryant, *Observations upon the Poems of Thomas Rowley: in which the Authenticity of those Poems is Ascertained* (London, 1781), p. 423.

15. 'On the Poems attributed to Rowley', in *Essays Moral and Literary,* 2 vols (London, 1782), II, 251.

16. *Anecdotes of Painting in England,* 3 vols (Twickenham, 1762), II, 107-08.

17. Elizabeth Cooper [and William Oldys], *The Muses Library; or, A Series of English Poetry, from the Saxons to the Reign of King Charles II,* 2 vols (London, 1737), I, xii[i]; John Weever, *Antient Funeral Monuments, of Great-Britain, Ireland, and the Islands Adjacent* (1631), 2nd edn (London, 1767), 'A Discourse on Funeral Monuments, &c.', p. vi. This prefatory Discourse defined monument not simply as physical testaments to human lives or achievements, but 'to speak properly of a monument . . . it is a receptacle or sepulchre, purposely made, erected, or built, to receive a dead corps, and to preserve the same from violation'. Chatterton claimed to have discovered the Rowley works in William Canynge's chest in the muniment room over the north porch of St Mary Redcliffe, Bristol. Chatterton referred to Weever in 'Antiquity of Christmas Games' (*Works,* I, 411) and 'Memoirs of a Sad Dog' (*Works,* I, 659).

18. Warton, I, sig, f. I^v.

19. In 1809 John Sherwen tried to resume the defence of Rowley, but despite the passage of a quarter of a century, could offer no new angle on the question. He resorted to 'The Accounte of W. Canynges Feast' in order to solve two textual cruces and thereby authenticate the poems. He suggested 'hath' for 'han' and 'Yche corse' for 'Syke keene' (*Introduction to an Examination of Some Part of the Internal Evidence, respecting the Antiquity and Authenticity of Certain Publications, said to have been found in Manuscripts at Bristol, Written by a Learned Priest and Others, in the Fifteenth Century; but generally considered as the Suppositious Productions of an Ingenious Youth of the Present Age* (Bath, 1809), p. 130).

20. Ian Haywood, 'Chatterton's Plans for the Publication of the Forgery', *RES,* 36 (1985), 58-68 (reprinted in *The Making of History: A Study of the Literary Forgeries of James Macpherson and Thomas Chatterton in relation to Eighteenth-Century Ideas of History and Fiction* (London: Associated University Press, 1986), pp. 175-84). See also Michael F. Suarez, 'What Thomas Knew: Chatterton and the Business of getting into Print', in *Angelaki,* 1.2 (1993), 83-94; Jonathan Barry, 'The History and Antiquities of the City of Bristol: Chatterton in Bristol', in *Angelaki,* 1.2 (1993), 55-58; Jonathan Barry, 'Provincial Town Culture, 1640-1789: Urbane or Civic?', in *Interpretation and Cultural History,* ed. by Joan H. Pittock and Andrew Wear (London: Macmillan, 1991), 198-223, p. 219); Jonathan Barry,

'Representations of the Past in Bristol: 1625-1789' (unpublished typescript, pp. 26-27). I am grateful to Dr Barry for making this research available to me.

21. (London, [1780(?)]). This has also been attributed to Francis Woodward. See E. H. W. Meyerstein, *A Life of Thomas Chatterton* (London: Ingpen & Grant, 1930), p. 470 n.

22. *Observations on the Poems attributed to Rowley* (London, 1782), pp. 11-12.

23. John Cleland, *The Way to Things by Words, and to Words by Things, being a Sketch of an Attempt at the Retrieval of the Antient Celtic, or, Primitive Language of Europe* (London, 1768), p. 83.

24. Jaques Derrida, *Cinders,* trans. by Ned Lukacher (Lincoln and London: University of Nebraska Press, 1991).

25. Warton, *An Enquiry,* p. 3.

26. London, British Library, Add. MS 5766A, fol. 6.

27. Oxford, Bodleian Library, MS Percy b. 1, fol. 3ʳ.

FURTHER READING

Bibliography

Warren, Murray. *A Descriptive and Annotated Bibliography of Thomas Chatterton.* New York: Garland Publishing, Inc., 1977, 130 p.
 Includes an introduction which looks at Chatterton's roles as forger versus poet, and lists Chatterton's own works as well as literary criticism on Chatterton and literature based on his life.

Biography

Ackroyd, Peter. *Chatterton.* New York: Grove Press, 1987, 234 p.
 Presents an anecdotal and conjectural story of Thomas Chatterton's life.

Kelly, Linda. *The Marvellous Boy: The Life and Myth of Thomas Chatterton.* London: Weidenfeld and Nicolson, 1971, 141 p.

Examines the details of Chatterton's life as well as the events surrounding the "Rowley Controversy"; also discusses the ways in which the later Romantic writers and Pre-Raphaelite writers and painters mythologized Chatterton.

Criticism

Goldberg, Brian. "Romantic Professionalism in 1800: Robert Southey, Herbert Croft, and the Letters and Legacy of Thomas Chatterton." *ELH* 63, No. 3 (Fall 1996): 681-706.
 Discusses the manner in which Chatterton's fate influenced the Romantic poet Robert Southey as he set about defining writing as a profession.

Kuist, James M. "Introduction." In *Cursory Observations on the Poems Attributed to Thomas Rowley* by Edmond Malone, 1782. Reprint. Los Angeles: William Clark Memorial Library, University of California, 1966, pp. i-xiv.
 Examines Malone's contribution to the "anti-Rowley" side of the debate regarding the authenticity of Chatterton's Rowley poems.

Lewis, Roger C. "A Misattribution: Oscar Wilde's 'Unpublished Sonnet on Chatterton.'" *Victorian Poetry* 28, No. 2 (Summer 1990): 164-69.
 Asserts that a poem on Chatterton that was thought to have been written by Oscar Wilde was in fact written by the Pre-Raphaelite poet and painter Dante Gabriel Rossetti; the poem is included in the article.

Taylor, Donald S. "Introduction." In *The Complete Works of Thomas Chatterton: A Bicentenary Edition,* edited by Donald S. Taylor with Benjamin B. Hoover, pp. xxv-xlv. Oxford: The Clarendon Press, 1971.
 Provides a chronology of the publication of Chatterton's works and discusses the difficulties inherent in locating accurate versions of the youthful writer's works.

Ting, Nai-Tung. "Chatterton and Keats: A Reexamination." *Keats-Shelley Journal* XXX (1981): 100-17.
 Argues that John Keats's poetry was influenced by the rhythms and descriptive language of Chatterton's work, but that the profundity of Keats's poetical insight remains uniquely his own.

Additional coverage of Chatterton's life and career is contained in the following sources published by the Gale Group: *Dictionary of Literary Biography,* **Vol. 109;** *DISCovering Authors: Modules*—**Poets Module.**

Jonathan Edwards
1703-1758

American theologian, essayist, homilist, and journal writer.

INTRODUCTION

A preeminent theologian of the eighteenth century, Edwards is one of the most controversial figures in American religious history. As the author of the fiery sermon, "Sinners in the Hands of an Angry God," which graphically describes the torment of souls damned to hell, Edwards is remembered as the archetypal "fire and brimstone" preacher. As the author of theological treatises on such subjects as freedom of the will and the nature of virtue, he is considered a highly disciplined and original thinker. Edwards has thus acquired a dual reputation, alternately dismissed as a Puritan religious fanatic and lauded as one of America's most brilliant philosopher-theologians.

BIOGRAPHICAL INFORMATION

Edwards was born in East Windsor, Connecticut, the son and grandson of pastors. During his childhood, Edwards demonstrated a precocious intellectual curiosity and an abiding interest in scientific and theological issues. In 1716, just before his thirteenth birthday, Edwards entered the Collegiate School (later Yale University) in New Haven. After graduating in 1720 Edwards stayed on for two years to study theology. During this time he experienced an intensely emotional religious conversion, which determined the course of his life and career. In 1727, he was married, ordained, and called to the pastoral ministry at the venerable Northampton church led by his grandfather, Solomon Stoddard, in the Massachusetts Bay Colony. When Stoddard died in 1729, Edwards became the sole pastor of the church, where he began to achieve fame and notoriety for his stern and unyielding sermons, and for presiding over the series of religious revivals that swept through New England in the 1730s and 1740s. Later known as the Great Awakening, these revivals and the resultant conversions stimulated considerable evangelical, missionary, and philanthropic activity. Although Edwards applauded the spiritual fervor and atonement produced by the revival movement, and himself delivered many of the sermons that precipitated the dramatic responses for which the revivals were noted, he nonetheless deplored the excessive emotionalism and mass hysteria of the movement, and over time he lamented what he perceived as a lack of true conversions.

After more than two decades as pastor of the Northampton church, Edwards became increasingly embroiled in conflict with the members of his congregation, particularly over his insistence on stringent eligibility requirements for membership and participation in the sacrament of communion. In 1750 a council representing ten churches in the region ended the pastoral relationship between Edwards and the Northampton congregation. Rather than continue in active parish ministry, Edwards elected to become a missionary to the Housatonic Indians in the pioneer town of Stockbridge, Massachusetts. During the seven years he remained there, Edwards wrote many of his important theological theses, including *The Freedom of the Will, The Great Christian Doctrine of Original Sin Defended, Concerning the End for Which God Created the World,* and *The Nature of True Virtue.* In 1757 Edwards, whose essays had attracted considerable attention, was asked to accept the presidency of Princeton University, then known as the College of New Jersey. He did so, somewhat reluctantly, early in 1758. Five weeks later, after contracting small pox from an unperfected inoculation, he died.

MAJOR WORKS

To understand Edwards's life and thought, and therefore his works, requires a knowledge of his theological credo, that of Puritanical Calvinism. Edwards was an adamant opponent of what he considered the dangerous heresy of New England Arminianism, which proposed that any individual could earn God's grace through good works and adherence to Christian doctrine. He believed in the existence of a God of absolute sovereignty, through whose will and grace alone could humanity achieve salvation. He further believed that only a certain group of the elect would be chosen to receive God's grace while the vast majority would be doomed. To Edwards, God was a constant, all-pervasive presence in the world, and it was God alone who lent to all existence its validity. All of Edwards's work focused on articulating this viewpoint and eliciting a sincere and appropriate response from his audience. His sermons reflect the vigor of their author and the unyielding nature of his doctrine, while the treatises reflect his commanding intellect and orderly rationalism. The beliefs incorporated in the sermons and the treatises are in no way inconsistent; only the mode of expression in the two genres is notably different: in his sermons, Edwards appealed to his audience's emotions; in the essays, he spoke to their reason. In such works Edwards crossed traditional boundaries of separate disciplines by embracing scientific inquiry and integrating scientific thought, particularly Isaac Newton's theories in the field of physics, in the development of some of his theological arguments. In *The Freedom of the Will*, Newton's theory of cause and effect provides the backbone of Edwards's case for determinism. Emerging scientific knowledge about the structure and biology of the natural world was also incorporated into Edwards's observations about the relationships between Creation and the Creator

During the decades anticipating the tricentenary of Edwards's birth, increased attention has been paid to his unpublished writings. In 1953 an effort was begun by historian Perry Miller to publish a modern, critical edition of Edwards's entire oeuvre, including previously unpublished sermons and manuscripts. Forty-six years later, seventeen of a projected twenty-seven volumes of writings have been released by the Yale University Press in the series, *The Works of Jonathan Edwards*, along with *A Jonathan Edwards Reader* (1995) and *The Sermons of Jonathan Edwards: A Reader* (1999).

CRITICAL RECEPTION

Critical assessment of Edwards has remained fairly constant throughout the centuries. Reinhold Niebuhr eulogized Edwards as "America's first and foremost theologian," and others agree that his theological treatises are carefully reasoned. Some commentators, however, contend that Edwards's theses, logical and precise as they are, nevertheless reach false conclusions because their premises, rooted in Calvinist doctrine, are assumed, not proven. Those who

dismiss Edwards's rigid theology and unyielding sermons rightly point out that many of his views were extreme even by the strictest Puritan standards of his time. But even critics who do not accept the fundamentals of his theology acknowledge that the treatises show evidence of Edwards's keen intelligence and remarkable range of knowledge. Scholars also note that Edwards's work demonstrates the influence of intellectual and philosophical thought outside the confines of Calvinist theology. In matters of philosophy outside the range of traditional Calvinist thought, critics have long commented that Edwards's reading of John Locke and René Descartes had a significant influence on his thinking about empiricism and salvation. Perhaps it is the contradictory juxtaposition of Edwards's strict, Puritanical rhetoric with the clarity and perception of his natural and moral philosophy—and the still-emerging portrait of the man behind the sermons—that captures the attention of late twentieth-century critics and scholars who continue to study Edwards, his work, and his centuries-long impact on the theology and politics of a nation that was barely in its infancy during his lifetime.

PRINCIPAL WORKS

God Glorified in the Work of Redemption, By the Greatness of Man's Dependence upon Him in the Whole of It (sermon) 1731

A Divine and Supernatural Light, Immediately Imparted to the Soul by the Spirit of God, Shown to Be Both a Scriptural, and Rational Doctrine (sermon) 1734

*A Faithful Narrative Of The Surprizing Work of God In The Conversion of Many Hundred Souls in Northampton, and the Neighbouring Towns and Villages (essay) 1737

The Distinguishing Marks Of a Work of the Spirit of God (sermon) 1741

Sinners in the Hands of an Angry God (sermon) 1741

Some Thoughts Concerning the Present Revival of Religion In New-England (sermon) 1742

A Treatise Concerning Religious Affections (essay) 1746

An Account of the Life of the Late Reverend Mr. David Brainerd, Minister of the Gospel (essay) 1749

An Humble Inquiry Into The Rules of the Word of God Concerning The Qualifications Requisite to a Compleat Standing and full Communion In the Visible Christian Church (essay) 1749

A Farewel-Sermon Preached at the first Precinct in Northampton, After the People's Publick Rejection of their Minister, and Renouncing their Relation to Him (sermon) 1751

Misrepresentations Corrected, And Truth Vindicated, In A Reply to the Rev. Mr. Solomon Williams's Book, intitled, The True State of the Question concerning the Qualifications (essay) 1752

†A Careful and Strict Enquiry Into The Modern Prevailing Notions Of That Freedom of Will, Which is Supposed to

be Essential To Moral Agency, Vertue and Vice, Reward and Punishment, Praise and Blame (essay) 1754

The Great Christian Doctrine of Original Sin Defended (essay) 1758

‡*Personal Narrative* (journal) 1765; published in *The Life and Character Of The Late Reverend, Learned, and Pious Mr. Jonathan Edwards,* 1799

§*Two Dissertations, I. Concerning the End for which God Created the World. II. The Nature of True Virtue* (essays) 1765

A History Of the Work of Redemption (essay) 1774

Puritan Sage: Collected Writings of Jonathan Edwards (sermons, essays, and journal) 1953

The Works of Jonathan Edwards. 17 vols. (sermons, essays, and journal) 1957-99

A Jonathan Edwards Reader (essays, sermons) 1995

The Sermons of Jonathan Edwards: A Reader (sermons) 1999

*This work is a revision of an unpublished letter.

†This work is commonly referred to as *The Freedom of the Will.*

‡This work was written in 1739.

§This work was written between 1755 and 1758.

CRITICISM

Clyde A. Holbrook (essay date 1987)

SOURCE: "Nature, Morality, and Holiness," in *Jonathan Edwards, The Valley and Nature: An Interpretive Essay,* Associated University Presses, Inc., 1987, pp. 98-122.

[In the following excerpt, Holbrook discusses Edwards's appropriation of the principles of proportion and harmony in nature to describe the relationship between humankind and God, and he analyzes the relationship between nature, morality, and holiness in Edwardsean thought.]

Among the learned of the eighteenth century, few words carried more authority and prestige than *nature*. In no small part the enthusiasm with which the word was embraced was due to its ambiguous meaning. In its most obvious sense the word signified the entire range of sensed physical objects that encircled human life. But science was pushing beyond so naive a meaning and in doing so increasingly laid bare the laws that gave order to the apparent diversity of the physical world. Nature was no longer what one saw and felt around oneself, but was the order itself. Nature not only "obeyed" laws, but essentially was order as dictated by laws. Once this identification of nature with laws and principles was made, it was not uncommon to suppose that these laws and principles described nature not only as it was but also as it ought to be. In this way nature as description was surreptitiously turned into a norm that proved adaptable to human affairs. In some fashion or other nature was seen as a standard by which to judge what was acceptable by rational people. To speak of

an act, thought, or belief as being in accord with nature was to stake a claim for its undeniable truth, for it represented the essential correctness believed to exist in physical and law-abiding nature. By this indefinite standard social and political arrangements and morality generally could be estimated as to their relative validity. Nature had become a norm to which "right-thinking," rational people could repair, undisturbed by whatever opinions otherwise divided them. Here was a solid basis by which to guide human life. If one believed in God, then nature was His creation, which showed in all phases how human life was to be lived. If one did not believe in God, there still stood nature accomplishing the same end. Nature provided common ground for both believer and doubter. However, in fact, as the social and political events of the century showed, the word *nature* settled few important disputes. *Nature* could be bent to the interests of its proponents. When used conservatively it sanctioned any already settled social and political order on the assumption that this order reflected the steady, unchanging, and universal condition of physical nature. In the service of a more radical outlook, *nature* stood for human rights that were suppressed by the status quo defended by the conservatives. Both parties appealed to nature as a norm of what was right, but each party read nature according to its own interests. In religious matters the same clash of interests existed. Freethinkers latched on to *nature,* with its correlate of right reason, to deny the legitimacy of religion—that is, Christianity, with its appeal to the supernatural and miracles. Less radical thinkers salvaged what they could by championing belief in a God of nature shorn of most of the attributes of the biblical deity. Edwards, like many others who held to more traditional religious beliefs, was called upon to interpret nature and reason in such a way that their importance would not be endangered by the supernaturalism of the Christian faith. He had to do justice to nature and yet give an account of spiritual realities that did not reduce them to a nature conceived in merely physical terms. However, nature as a system of laws and principles from the mind of God was acceptable to him. In that respect Edwards was quite in tune with a major segment of learned opinion of his period. The difference from that opinion was to show itself in how he employed these laws and principles in respect to the religious and moral life.

Edwards accepted nature as meaning the actuality of the sensible corporeal and external world. This usage is especially evident in his youthful **"Diary,"** where no doubt was expressed as to the physical reality of his body in conflict with his appetites and religious ponderings. His correspondence with friends abroad and with the Princeton trustees shows the same unsophisticated acceptance of physical nature. Even his typology that referred to the actuality of historical events and natural objects in the Bible was based upon what he believed were concrete realities. The symbolism in the **"Personal Narrative"** followed the same pattern. In some periods of his life nature was physically real to him. However, his interest in science, the metaphysics of idealism, and his sense of the spiritual world pointed him in a different direction. Beyond this external and physically sensed world was another one. He repeatedly stated that this sensible world was but a shadow of the spiritual, and this was a large step in the direction of recognizing nature as consisting in a system of laws and principles akin to spiritual reality. In his most extreme statements he totally denied the existence of physical matter, bodies, as he said, having "no proper being of their own." That he had problems with consistently working out this view of nature as idea I have already demonstrated, but it was the most compelling of his conceptions of nature. In nature as sensibly experienced he found the principles of its orderliness, and upon them much of the order of the spiritual and ideal world depended. Nature was the ideas themselves, the "naked ideas" he once had sought, manifested in external nature but not confined to that domain. The word *nature* stood for a harmonious system of ideas existing by virtue of human perception and God's knowledge. Therefore to speak of nature was to all intents and purposes to speak of a metaphysic of nature rather than of a visible, tangible and existing world independent of human consciousness. This metaphysic of nature I suggest was the "nature" that exercised a profound and determinative influence on Edwards's view of the religious and ethical life.

This contention does not at a stroke eliminate for Edwards the importance of sensibly perceived nature. Analogy drawn from the ordinary world of human affairs or nature was still appealed to for understanding spiritual matters. Edwards, for example, used what transpired in daily experience to clarify what went on in the higher world when he wrote, "We never could have any notion what understanding or volition, love or hatred are, either in created spirits or in God, if we never experienced what understanding and volition, love and hatred are in our own minds."[1] The superior or real world might itself be ideal, but there still remained that inferior world from which truth could be drawn. This opinion was widely shared by other thinkers of the period. George Turnbull contended that natural philosophy, when carried through to the end, reduced phenomena to "good general laws" that became moral philosophy. Bishop Thomas Burnet went farther, to claim that since moral and natural phenomena were both part of God's world, "they run the same course and are so proportional to each other that man's moral and spiritual states may be gauged by examining the condition of nature." It is not clear what meaning of nature he had in mind, but the connection between two different kinds of experience is evident. Berkeley himself is credited with having compared gravity to benevolence and social attraction on the grounds that throughout "the moral and intellectual as well as the natural and corporeal" worlds there was "a certain correspondence of parts, similitude of operation and unity of design."[2] Edwards might have agreed in varying degrees with each of these comments as analogies, but Turnbull seems to have come the closest to Edwards's intent in respect to moral thought. When nature is reduced to its principles and laws, it did for Edwards convert into moral philosophy, as Turnbull suggested. And to

describe nature metaphysically was to describe ideal reality itself, and at the same time to lay a foundation for analogy.

For Edwards God's world was not only an analogical or typological one, but a coherent reality where laws and principles discernible in external nature also operated in the realm of spirit. From the beginning he had been aware of the order, harmony, and beauty of the nature about him. But for his questing mind it was not sufficient to behold and revel in this beauty. He sought the root ideas by which this beauty was made possible. And he found them in the forms of attraction, cohesion, consent, proportionality, and symmetry.[3] But these principles, when expressed in the metaphysics of nature, were not to be understood simply as analogies, but as the very structure of a reality that encompassed both sensible and ideal reality. The entire world, being one under God, could be expected to exhibit in both areas the same overriding principles by which beauty or excellence was created. Accordingly, the reason why the "sweet harmony between the various parts of the universe" was "an image of mutual love" was that the same structures were operative at both levels, the world being one.[4] Edwards spelled out this insight in Miscellany 651, in which he argued that inanimate, animate, and human beings were all governed by "exactly the same laws." This he took to be a strong argument that the world had but one Creator and governor. The analogy "between the corporeal and spiritual parts of the creation" further established his thesis that the whole is the creation of but one wisdom and design.[5] In short, the analogies Edwards found throughout nature that pointed to and expressed spiritual reality hinged upon the prior assumption of the unity of the whole world whose laws and principles operated at every level. Analogy without this grounding in the unity and relationship of all things would have been left without a metaphysical reason. It is not difficult, therefore, to see his treatment of true virtue as exhibiting the manner in which morality also was in conformity with the ideal structures underlying the analogies found in nature. The metaphysics of nature enabled him to give an account of virtue that partook of the beauty of the corporeal world, since both manifested the same principles of order.

In the first instance true virtue for Edwards was "that consent, propensity and union of heart to being in general, which is immediately exercised in a general good will." The beauty of this disposition rested not on discord or discontent, but as any intelligent being is in some way always related to being in general, it consisted in "union and consent with the great whole."[6] Clearly then, consent or agreement was at the heart of true virtue. However, an interesting question may be raised as to the status of consent in the wider context of Edwards's thought. Was consent an actual feature of nature sensibly experienced or otherwise interpreted? Or was it a unique relation between spiritual beings, quite independent of sensible nature? In favor of the latter option stands Edwards's explicit admission that his use of the word *consent* in reference to the excellence of bodies was one borrowed from spiritual beings. Consent, so considered, made of the consents of corporeal nature an analogy to the higher world. Furthermore it underlined the unique status of what Edwards called "proper consent." "There is no proper consent but that of minds," he wrote, "which when it is of minds towards minds, it is love and when of minds towards other things it is choice."[7] Yet the word *consent* was peculiarly appropriate in respect to nature in the light of other aspects of Edwards's philosophy and science. When we bear in mind his conviction that the whole world was one under God, we can understand that, however the realm of nature be characterized, it possessed features that had their counterparts in the superior world of spirit, as did the superior world in the lower one. His essay on the **"Reality of the World"** was replete with references to the "many sorts of consent" in the corporeal world, wherein lay "the sweetest and most charming beauty."[8] He intended those consents to be images of the beauty of the spiritual world, but it is significant that the best way he had of delineating this beauty was to turn first to the consents in the corporeal world. There he found the evidence of a consent that not only reflected but also gave form to spiritual consent.

The notion of consent or agreement may be seen in a larger perspective when nature is considered metaphysically. Excellence in respect to bodies, Edwards had made clear, depended on similarity between them, or agreement. If there was disagreement, the result produced pain or lack of pleasure in perceiving beings. This state he labeled "the greatest and only evil," whereas agreement was "the greatest and only good." Excellence or beauty then depended on consents or agreements, the lack of which gave rise to deformity or "false beauty."[9] This insight allowed Edwards to conclude that "the beauty of figures and motion, when one part has such consonant proportion with the rest as representing a general agreeing and consenting together" is "very much the image of love in all parts of a society united by a sweet consent and charity of heart." In a slightly different sense he suggested "sensible things, by virtue of the harmony and proportion that is seen in them, carry the appearance of perceiving and willing being."[10] In these passages analogy was used, but they also cast consent or agreement in terms of metaphysical reality. It is not purely sensibly experienced nature that is at stake, but certain metaphysical principles such as harmony and proportion that govern consent. Nature is here being interpreted in conformity with metaphysical principles that are detectable in nature as sensibly experienced, but are extracted to be in conformity with Edwards's contention that nature was essentially idea, and for him reality was mentalistic. Consent then, as idea, was embedded in the very nature of reality, and had a wider meaning than that attributed to consent as a spiritual relation between human beings. Consent could then be construed not only as an analogy between nature as sensibly experienced and the spiritual dimension, but as part and parcel of reality. I take it that in part this was Fiering's meaning in denying that the relation between the physical world and God's continuous activity was simply a matter of analogy. "There is an actual metaphysical connection," he wrote, "between

the perceived world and divine activity, explicable in terms of Edwards's philosophical idealism."[11]

Edwards's scientific speculation on the universe also gave support to the more inclusive meaning of consent. He had paid especial attention to the power of attraction, cohesion, and gravity in nature. Without gravity the whole corporeal world would vanish, and atoms cleave to each other by this same power of attraction, which insures cohesion. "There must," Edwards concluded, "be an universal attraction in the whole system of things from the beginning to the end." Indeed, so powerful and pervasive was the power of attraction that if there was the least change in one atom, all other atoms would also be changed, thus making the universe other than what it now is.[12] Similarly changes in the least particles of the human body, Edwards surmised, would cause a thought to arise, "which in length of time (yea, and that not very great) might occasion a vast alteration through the whole world of mankind."[13] Thus the mutual attraction operative in nature can be seen as testimony to the idea of consent, for as things are drawn to each other and affect each other, they do so by means of what is similar in each part to the other. In seizing upon the power of attraction in nature, Edwards had grasped a fundamental metaphysical principle, whose influence was not confined to natural phenomena. Attraction was but a form of consent which, understood as metaphysical truth, was writ large over all of God's creation. The consent of minds was the supreme instance of an all-embracing metaphysic whose agreements unified the whole universe. Therefore it was not an exception to the way the universe acted, but its chief exemplification at the conscious level. To this fact Edwards paid tribute by defining excellency as consent of being to being and supremely in "being's consent to entity," that is, God. On the basis of this consent he could go on to add that "the more consent is, and the more extensive, the greater is the excellency."[14]

At the human level consent is an affection. When experienced consciously, attraction or consent as an aspect of the metaphysics of nature becomes vastly more than an abstract unitive relation of inert particles. It is a deeply felt union of selves with selves or selves with God. It is love. But love or affection was to be no unbridled passion. At the height of the Great Awakening Edwards had come to understand that intense surges of emotion taken as evidence of grace needed to be in subservience to principle, and for that principle has metaphysic of nature came into play in another way.

This principle was proportionality. He had developed the importance of this concept in his account of beauty in the corporeal world where delicate ratios and proportion reigned. When he spoke of excellency, he turned to descriptions of equalities, ratios, and proportions exhibited by globes, circles, and parallel and perpendicular lines. Everywhere he looked, Edwards found excellency to inhere in "harmony, symmetry and proportion." "There is no other way that sensible things can consent one to another but by equality, or by likeness, or by proportion." Harmony was observable about him in notes of music, the beauty of figures and motion, the pen drawings of flowers, the human body, the features of a face or the structure of buildings, all of which were examples of proportional consent. "I can conceive of no other reason why equality and proportion should be pleasing to him that perceives, but only that it has an appearance of consent."[15] Proportionality and consent were fellow principles in the idea of excellency and beauty.

Nowhere was this connection between consent and proportionality more evident to Edwards than in his conception of God, who by any definition of perfection manifested true virtue at its highest point. Proportion was then not simply to be confined to things in the corporeal world. Like consent, it was to be understood as ingrained in the ideal reality of the world. Although Edwards plainly stated that there was no proportion between universal being, that is, God, and finite being, no matter how great the degree of the latter, this did not signify that God's love of Himself failed in respect to proportionality.[16] God's "infinite beauty" lay in "his mutual love of himself" and this was to be seen in the doctrine of the Trinity.[17] Since God was supremely excellent and since any single entity by itself would lack duality and therefore the basis for consent between itself and other entities, there must be a plurality in God by which He exercises a "mutual love of himself."[18] This is a rendering of true virtue in God that employs another metaphysical principle, that of duality or polarity, without which consent would be impossible. Duality also plays its part when God's knowledge of Himself as the proper object of love or consent is considered. To know Himself, something "distinct from his meer direct existence" must be known, just as in human beings there must be something that occasions reflection that is differentiated from the reflection itself. Since God is supremely excellent, He must as it were have Himself as the object of reflection, and this is made possible by the presence of Himself in the Trinity.[19] And what He knows is that He is the greatest being and therefore, by the principle of proportionality, rightly loves or consents to Himself. Above all else, since "that object who has the most of being, or has the greatest share of existence, 'other things being equal' . . . will have the greatest share of the propensity and benevolent affections of the heart."[20] This being so in respect to persons, so also it is true for God, whose being far exceeds that of all else.

In ***The End For Which God Created the World*** Edwards rehearsed the theme of proportionality and quantity of being by setting up a hypothetical situation to make his point. He postulated that some imaginary eternal being of disinterested perfect wisdom and rectitude could judge the proper balance of regard due to God on the one hand, and the created order on the other. This being, having weighed the degrees of existence and moral excellence in both, would of course find that God outweighed the remainder of the world "in such proportion" that He should have the "greatest share of regard." However, in fact, there was no need for this hypothetical third party, since God Himself possessed the perfect discernment and rectitude by which He impartially judged in His own favor.[21] Thus, by the principle of proportionality God was established as the sole object of true virtue, for both Himself and human beings.

Edwards proposed that even in heaven proportionality reigned in respect to true virtue. There the "symmetry and proportion in God's workmanship" found in the world functioned in the celestial love enjoyed by the saints. In heaven the saints would practice affections in perfect degree and proportion. "Love is in proportion to the perfection and amiableness of the objects beloved, and therefore it must necessarily cause delight in them when they see that the happiness and glory of others are in proportion to their amiableness, and so in proportion to their love to them." Or more simply stated, "Just in proportion as any person is beloved, in the same proportion is his love desired and prized."[22] If anywhere true virtue would be realized to its fullest, heaven would indeed be the place.

As proportion ruled the display of true virtue in heaven, so it also did on earth. As it played its part in the production of harmonious sound and color vibrations, so it also applied to spiritual harmonies, where "the proportions are vastly oftener redoubled and respect more beings." In fact, to get to the root of the matter Edwards claimed that being was itself "nothing else but proportion."[23] No wonder then that true virtue, which had to do with consent to being, should itself reflect proportionality. Its validity was to be in proportion to the greatness of the object to which it was addressed, the infinite Being or Being in general. And its expression among fellow human beings was to follow the same pattern. When writing in justification of revivalism Edwards had let it be known that Christian love should be extended "to one and another only in that proportion in which the image of God is seen in them."[24] And by the time he penned ***The Nature of True Virtue*** he had not deviated from the conviction that true virtue as love should be meted out to others in agreement with proportionality. In this would also be a beauty. The amiableness of true virtue lay in consent and benevolence and "in a proportion compounded of the greatness of the benevolent being, in the degree of being and the degree of benevolence." It followed then that one who loves Being in general will value the same good will wherever he sees it and will value it even more if he sees it in two beings rather than in one. Then there would be more being favoring being on a strictly quantitative basis. What this means is that when true virtue does its work, it fastens on other human beings who have the same temper of benevolence and consent to being in general. One loves others in proportion to the degree of being and benevolence they have. "And that is to love beings in proportion to their dignity."[25]

But Edwards's enchantment with the idea of proportionality in this case comes to a strange end, for it stands at complete odds with the Christian message of salvation. That message one might have thought extended true virtue or love to those who most needed it, not only to those who already possessed it. If love to others was to be meted out on the basis of their amount of being and benevolence, Christian virtue could not only lack spontaneity but be limited to a very small segment of the human population. Edwards might well have settled for a "small segment" with his idea of election of the saints. But would this not be a far remove from Jesus' words criticizing those who love only those who love them? (cf. Matt. 5:47) It is precisely those who lack consent to being and lack moral excellence that most need the ministrations of true Christian love. Or, as Paul Tillich read the Christian Gospel, it had to do with "the acceptance of the unacceptable." Edwards, on the other hand, was so far under the spell of proportionality that he accepted the commonplace truth that like attracted like in due proportion on earth as in heaven.[26]

In his earlier writings Edwards had addressed this flaw in his later metaphysical calculations. There he pictured true virtue, although slightly tainted by ulterior motives, as being directed to both the good and the bad. "We should do good to all men as we have opportunity" that they may be benefited and won to Christ. The truly virtuous person is obliged to do good to enemies, for that is "the only retaliation that becomes us as Christians. . . ." True love is universal benevolence and good will, and properly embraces friends and enemies, the thankful and unthankful.[27] The *True Virtue* glancingly struck the same theme when, in distinguishing secondary virtue from true virtue, he stressed that the general beauty of true virtue was comprehensive "as related to everything with which it stands connected."[28] From that assertion it would follow that since all people are related to Being in general in one way or another, benevolence should be exercised to all persons regardless of their spiritual estate.

When all is told of true virtue, it remains a correct relation to Being in general, consisting of cordial consent or love to Being in general, exercised in proportion both as to the greatness of the deity and as to one's fellow men in proportion to their dignity or degree of being and excellence. The priority of being, however, seems to have been the foundation of the beauty and excellence found in true virtue. Had he not stated that "existence or entity is that into which all excellency is to be resolved"? The greatness of being, that is, God, "considered alone is the more excellent because he partakes more of being. . . ."[29] Accordingly, nothing could be of the nature of true virtue unless it had for its direct and immediate object "being in general or the great system of universal existence."[30] What was not clear was why people should be incited to love and practice benevolence to others by a vivid awareness of Being in general. Why should greatness of being in infinite degree evoke cordial consent to itself or in turn prompt love to created beings? At most sheer "is-ness" in infinite degree that exceeded all finitude might produce wonder, awe, or fear, but certainly not cordial consent. That may be the reason Edwards could say "No proportion is the cause or ground of the existence of such a thing as benevolence to being," although elsewhere he had already affirmed that being was nothing else but proportion. A

shift in his thought seems to have occurred at this juncture when he asserted that proportion of being "is the consequence of the existence of benevolence and not the ground of it."[31]

This pronouncement looks like a reversal of his emphasis upon the priority of being in true virtue, but it was an insight quite in keeping with his claim that God's goodness "moved him to give both being and beauty" to objects in the world.[32] Edwards supported this priority of benevolence in God by an example drawn from nature. Bodies that attract each other do so in proportion to their degree of matter, but—and this was his point—this proportion is due to the mutual attraction itself, not simply to proportionality. Thus, in respect to being's consent to being, he could write, "If being, in itself considered, were not pleasing, being's consent to being would not be pleasing, nor would disagreeing with being be displeasing." Consent then, as one central feature of true virtue or excellency, was inherent in being itself. God as "the infinite, universal and all-comprehending existence" had within Himself not simply a preponderance of sheer existence, but His being by its very nature was excellent and beautiful, and this was what attracted human beings to loving consent. One could love Being in general because God as Being in general exhibited loving consent in his very nature. Existence, of which God was the supreme exemplar, was "that into which all excellency is to be resolved."[33] There could be no distinction between being and excellence. The two were inextricably bound together.

This alliance of being with excellence escaped the notice of some of his early critics, who seized upon his frequent references to being as such to show the inadequacy of his conception of true virtue. *Being* is one of those essential metaphysical terms that either gathers to itself all the sensed differentiation of actual existence or is one so vague as to be devoid of any specific meaning. In the first sense the term *being* adds nothing to the fact that things, people, laws, and so on, exist. In the second sense the term can be bent to the design of the one who uses it. Although Edwards did not in the final analysis intend either of these meanings, his manner of writing gave ample opportunity for critics to blast him for playing fast and loose with an idea void of identifying attributes. The Reverend William Hart so read Edwards on true virtue, and concluded that Edwards's notion of Being in general was offered to religious folk as a being without perception, will, or ethical qualities. Being, abstractly considered, Hart argued, "is neither wise nor foolish, neither morally good nor evil, neither self-existent nor created and dependent upon neither God nor creature." Most cuttingly in the face of Edwards's talk of benevolence, he added, "It has no relation to the benevolent mind." In short, being dressed up as Being in general in infinite degree was a featureless metaphysical abstraction and not at all the God of Christian faith.[34] Whatever the shortcomings of Hart's little book, and there were many, he succeeded in fastening on Edwards the charge that abstract metaphysical reasoning produced something that did not in the least resemble the God of the Bible and vital piety. One could not identify the conclusions of abstract speculation with a deity that loved, decided, hated, judged, and redeemed humanity. Being in general was a shapeless something or other that just was and did nothing. Edwards's love of metaphysics had run him aground on the hard rock of the difference between his Calvinist biblical faith and metaphysics.

Hart seems to have taken the alternative that being was an empty notion. Robert Hall, an English clergyman, took the opposite view, namely that being in general referred to every single item in the universe. The inadequacy of Edwards's notion of morality lay in what Hall took to be the necessity of a truly virtuous person cordially to consent to every single item or person in the world. And that was an impossible goal. Instead of beginning with an affection for something called Being in general, Hall argued, men should first be made benevolent and unselfish in their private affections. "As in the operations of intellect we proceed from the contemplation of individuals to the formation of general abstractions, so in the development of the passions, in like manner we advance from private to public affections." Otherwise men are taught "to love the whole species more by loving every particular part less." Furthermore, in agreement with Hart, the notion of pursuing the good of the whole in its abstractness "is a motive so loose and indeterminate, and embraces such an infinity of relations, that before we could be certain what action it prescribed, the season of action would be past."[35] For Hall it was not sin that prevented men from cordially consenting to Being in general. It was sheer entanglement in metaphysical relations that frustrated any efforts in that direction. Even divine grace or "a new sense" would seem to have been incapable of untangling the formidable network of relations into which Edwards had snared people.

There is a specious validity in Hall's analysis, for which Edwards himself was partly to blame. Edwards had written that "among created beings one single person must be looked upon as inconsiderable in comparison of the generality; and so his interest is of little importance compared with the interest of the whole system." In fact when the interest of a single person or part of the whole is held to be of more importance than the whole of being, it is vicious and sinful.[36] Furthermore Edwards's insistence upon proportionality and the quantification of being as essential to true virtue opened him to the criticism of Hall. His famous, if not notorious note on love "in proportion to the degree of existence" led to his claim that "an archangel must be supposed to have more existence and to be every way farther removed from nonentity, than a worm."[37] This observation undoubtedly owed much to Edwards's hierarchical view of nature in a Neoplatonic mode of thought. In his *End for Which God Created the World* he had described God's beauty, power, and wisdom as poured forth as from a fountain, or the sun, thus making created beings the lower in the order the less they participated in God's nature. Saints, however, received the outpouring of God's nature and thus resonated back to God his original emanation, and stood higher.[38] If Hall had read this work, he

would have found further evidence that the theory of the quantity of being and excellence gave shape to an ethical and metaphysical outlook that moved in the opposite direction from his insistence upon the importance of individuals and the danger of their loving Being in general more and "loving each other less."

But had these critics read Edwards correctly as to the meaning of Being in general? Did Edwards mean to equate Being in general with every single feature of the created world? Or did he mean that Being in general was a term without specifiable meaning, as Hart supposed? The first alternative was a truism that yielded no religious or metaphysical rewards. And the second was in danger of becoming identified with nothing in particular. And as Edwards had announced that "there should absolutely be nothing at all is utterly impossible . . ." a state of absolute nothing is a state of absolute contradiction.[39] Even to talk about nothing except in relation to something that exists is to suppose being in some sense. Thus ontology asserts itself in the very texture of rational discourse. Being therefore could not be a void of which everything and nothing could be said with equal validity. It had structure, and at a minimum it was proportion, which was one sign of its excellency or beauty. Excellence would be impossible if being were not presupposed as its ontological ground, and being without proportion would not be excellent or beautiful. And to Edwards's mind Being in general was that supreme excellence. The dividing point between Edwards and his critics was his firm, but often untidily expressed conviction that Being in general was not any kind of being or sum of beings that existed in the finite world, with God regarded merely as a superior form thereof, but essentially of the same kind.[40]

At this point it is important to recall again that for Edwards being itself was nothing else but proportion. This enigmatic statement presupposed a plurality of relations within being, in respect to which proportionality had definite meaning. "One alone, without reference to any more, cannot be excellent," since without relations there would be no place for consent, the archetype of which was the Trinity itself.[41] God as Being in general was the unique model of true excellence, whose internal relations were adumbrated in relations with nature and perceiving beings. Being in general was not then to be regarded as a structureless "something" without attributes, subject to deformation by human desires or ignorance. God was not a simple unity, but a complex one constituted of an infinite number of relations, the principal one of which was consent. In this lay His goodness, beauty, and excellence, which acted as a lure for saintly souls. Being in general was obviously related to being in the world, but as the power and excellence that permeated and upheld them. Yet it was not totally identified with them. The world was *one* under God, but it *was* not God or Being in general. The difference Edwards had made clear when he stated that there was no proportion between the greatness of the natural, finite world and God.[42] So God was in and with the world, but never to be assimilated to it. This was not pantheism in any literal sense, as I have previously argued, but a metaphysical position that is best described as pa- nentheism, which retains the transcendence of God to His world and saves divine engagement with it at all points. In that lay His sovereignty.

One who lived or consented to Being in general was not, as Hall supposed, driven first to establish benevolent rela- tions with every single human before ascending to a love of Being in general. Nor, for Edwards, was this a state in which motivation would be loose and indeterminate. In loving Being in general in proportion to its being and ex- cellence, one is also disposed to dispense love to other hu- man beings in proportion to their degrees of existence and benevolence. Contrary to Hall's opinion, Edwards saw that private affections left to themselves or energized by the most strenuous human effort never overcome their self- interested position. They do not of themselves expand to encompass all beings or Being in general. And even if ever larger numbers of finite beings are encompassed with affection, one does not finally bridge the gap between natural affections and love of God for His own sake and not for what one hopes to get from such a relation. To consent to Being in general is first to chasten, purify, and convert private affections at their root and open them to the widest possible comprehension of reality. Then they reflect the beauty, goodness, wisdom, and power resident in Being in general and radiate the same to other beings. And this state of affairs transcends mere morality. It is ho- liness, the supreme goal of the spiritual life.

Most people do not live on the breathless heights of true virtue or holiness. The moral habitat of natural man is a secondary kind of morality that has its own kind of beauty, but one that does not reach to the level of spiritual enjoy- ment. To this kind of morality Edwards paid a great deal of attention in order to set off its inadequacy from the standpoint of true virtue.

Edwards's treatment of natural morality begins with his announcement that the consent found in spiritual beauty has its counterpart in the beauty of natural things, even in inanimate things. It consists, as we might expect, in regu- larity, order, uniformity, symmetry, proportion, and har- mony.[43] As such, it is some image of true spiritual beauty. The correspondence also includes consent, but at this point the first difference between it and true virtue appears. Both types of morality involve consent, but true virtue is set off from natural morality by its cordial consent. Natural agree- ment, although it is an image of genuine union, is entirely different, "the will, disposition or affection of the heart having no concern in it, but consisting only in uniformity and consent of nature, form, quantity etc." Cordial con- sent, on the other hand, "consists in concord and union of mind and heart." The first kind of consent is due to natural causes or principles; the second is an insight into the union itself. It is the immediate view of that wherein the beauty fundamentally lies and is therefore pleasing to the virtuous mind.[44] Secondary beauty is a term that applies not only to material and external things, but also to immaterial reali-

ties. "If uniformity and proportion be the things that affect and appear agreeable to the sense of beauty, then," asked Edwards, "why should not uniformity and proportion af- fect the same sense in immaterial things as well . . . if there be equal capacity of discerning it in both?[45] His em- phasis on the principle of proportionality first seen in na- ture has led one author to argue that proportionality is the essential factor in secondary virtue and has no application to true virtue.[46] Yet, as demonstrated, proportionality had its part to play in several ways in respect to true virtue and the nature of God, the perfect being. Consequently, pro- portionality cannot be used as the identifying mark of sec- ondary virtue, important as it was.

This fact becomes equally apparent in opposition to this same author's criticism that beauty was for Edwards the clue to his thought, for beauty, even of the purely spiritual kind, was marked by proportionality. To speak meaning- fully of Edwards's notion of beauty demanded that it in- clude not only affection or consent, but right knowledge and structure. The beauty of true virtue depended upon cordial consent, but equally important was the cognitive factor. Consent, no matter how cordial, would be left with- out direction as to its proper object and range without knowledge of God. Edwards was keenly aware in the re- vivals of the danger that people of heated emotions would seize upon any uprush of feelings as indicative of divine grace. To guard against this antinomian threat he main- tained that correct knowledge was necessary. Although he admitted "it is not easy, precisely to fix the limits of man's capacity as to love of God; yet in general we may deter- mine that his capacity of love is coextended with his ca- pacity of knowledge. The exercise of the understanding opens the way for the other faculty," that is, affection.[47] He had previously made his point clear by stating that the first objective ground of gracious affections was "the transcen- dently excellent and amiable nature of divine things as they are in themselves; and not any conceived relation they bear to self, or self-interest."[48] And in the *True Virtue* he reemphasized the point by claiming that "the first ob- ject of a virtuous benevolence," simply considered, was Being in general.[49] Unfortunately for man, sin had entered to mar and disfigure this beautiful relationship, and love of God had been misdirected to self and accordingly reduced its range to finite entities. "Sin, like some powerful astrin- gent, contracted his soul to the very small dimensions of selfishness."[50] Breadth and comprehensiveness of knowl- edge had been surrendered, and as a result affections, with- out that necessary knowledge, had been devoted to a "pri- vate circle or system of beings" that were but a fraction of the whole of existence, inclusive of God. In the case of true virtue, knowledge was enlarged and invigorated by divine grace, and centered then on God alone.[51] And in that was beauty.

Equally important to beauty of true and secondary virtue was the need of structure, which proportionality provided. The beauty Edwards attributed to true virtue could not be realized without harmony among beings, which presup- posed not only consent but proportionality. As nature was a harmonious system, so also, thought Edwards, was true virtue. In his analysis of excellence he had concluded that proportion was more pleasing than deformity or disproportion because "disproportion or inconsistency is contrary to being," which is nothing else but proportion.[52] So being, Being in general, and the affections directed to Being in general must in high degree be beautiful because of the proportionality that insured structure.[53]

Without these three factors of cordial consent, knowledge, and proportionality, beauty could not exist as a feature of true virtue. But no one of them by itself could distinguish secondary or inferior beauty from true beauty. However, if one chooses to concentrate on the end product of these three factors, it may be said that beauty was the central idea of his system, but it must not be forgotten that that beauty depended on the integral relations between cordial consent, knowledge, and proportionality that made beauty possible. When these relations are placed to the forefront, then one can agree with Fiering that beauty "is not itself an ultimate category." It is a derivative of relations.[54]

What then sets off secondary beauty or common morality from true virtue? Proportionality by itself cannot do it. Cordial consent fails the test, since intensity of the emotions can be found among even the greatest of sinners, whose affections rest upon finite entities including themselves. Knowledge does not of itself draw the line between secondary and true virtue. Yet there must be a line to be drawn between the two.

The primary place where the distinction occurs is in a consideration of what is meant by cordial consent. In one important sense it is a warm-hearted agreement between the soul and Being in general. It is a matter of the affections in their most dynamic operations. It is an immediate sensation or intuition, not one built upon arguments, "any more than tasting the sweetness of honey, or perceiving the harmony of a tune, is by argumentation or connections and consequences."[55] There is something more than argument in cordial consent. That factor is intuitive insight or knowledge. What makes true virtue appealing is not simply the intensity of one's affections, but the perception of the union itself, and that quality secondary virtue or beauty lacks.[56] This higher kind of knowledge was for Edwards quite different from the natural appreciation of agreement and proportion that men find in both nature and moral matters.

Secondary virtue is due to a law of nature that God has implanted in all rational persons, but they "do not reflect in that particular agreement and proportion which . . . is the ground and rule of beauty in the case." They remain ignorant of what in fact constitutes the beauty of the world, but are pleased with it nevertheless. They are unable to penetrate to the essence of beauty, as does true virtue when it stirs the heart to cordial consent. As such, secondary virtue is an entirely different thing from a truly virtuous taste and "has no connection with virtue."[57]

Cordial consent as a form of cognition sees what indeed makes beauty to be itself, and that is to see the proper relation between the affections and their true object. Natural, unconverted people could, with an intensity equal to that assumed to exist in true virtue, relish and enjoy relations among things in the natural world and even justice in ethical matters. Their affections, however, were thereby fixed upon finite objects, including themselves. True virtue or valid gracious affections fixed upon that which possessed the highest degree of excellence and being. As he had written in the **"Miscellanies,"** "'Tis from the nature of the object loved rather than from the degree of the principle [love] in the lover."[58] Therefore secondary virtue is set off from true virtue not by the degree of affection or agreement exercised, but by the object to which that agreement yields itself, and that is God, the perfect being. This insight led Edwards to diverge from other benevolence and moral-sense philosophers who to his mind had confused secondary with primary moral beauty. Of them, with Hutcheson and Wollaston particularly in mind, he commented, "They do not wholly exclude a regard to the Deity but yet mention it so slightly, that they leave one room and reason to suspect they esteem it as less important and a subordinate part of true morality." But if God plays some part in morality, he added, then it must be that respect to God is the chief ingredient in true virtue.[59] Philosophies that teach benevolence or generosity toward mankind and other virtues without "apprehension of God's supreme glory and worthiness and an answerable supreme esteem of and love to Him" are "not true schemes of philosophy" and are "fundamentally wrong."[60] There may indeed be a moral sense in human beings that enables them to be gratified by displays of virtue, and prompts them to love others who love them, but this moral sense is at a secondary level of the ethical manifold and "is entirely different from a sense or relish of the original essential beauty of true virtue."[61] The fault remains in the moral-sense theory when its proponents wrongly suppose that this natural virtue is identical with true virtue. Yet the natural moral sense "so far as it is disinterested" is the same as conscience, which of course was part of man's natural moral equipment.[62] Nevertheless, the omission of the divine object by definition condemns this philosophy as totally inadequate.

This inadequacy bears as its consequence the lack of comprehensive insight and affection. Whereas true virtue directs benevolence to Being in general, the natural moral sense is always limited to "private systems" and that term refers not only to self-interested individuals but to the most far-reaching, inclusive systems of finite beings. Humanity for Edwards would still be a "private system," because all existence is not exhausted by any collection of human, living, or inanimate entities for that matter. As long as natural affection embraces only a part of universal existence, it "bears no proportion to the great all-comprehending system."[63] Thus to rest one's affections on that which is disproportionate to Being in general is to settle for an inferior type of virtue, which when regarded as selfishness is in outright opposition to true virtue.

Self-interest then suffers from a myopic view of existence. "The reason why men are so ready to take their private affections for true virtue, is the narrowness of their views," and of course that means they leave "the divine Being out of view" or regard him as "a kind of shadowy, imaginary being."[64] Yet self-interest has its uses. It is necessary to society and by means of it men do disapprove of vices and immorality and approve such virtues as meekness, peaceableness, benevolence, charity, generosity, justice, and the social virtues in general, which tend to the welfare of mankind.[65] Surely sinners seek and love their own happiness, which is to be found in the esteem and love others have for them, although again this yearning for happiness is centered in self rather than graced by the disinterestedness that accompanies true benevolence. In an absolute sense Edwards was willing to affirm that the degree of men's happiness may be the same in saint and sinner when directed toward others, but he was quick to add, "the proportion that their love of self bears to their love for others, may not be the same."[66] Yet he was unwilling to deny that this kind of affection should be entirely abolished. It was needful for the good of man and society, and totally to root it out would be "to reproach and oppose the wisdom of the Creator."[67]

On the other hand he was loath to accept at face value the notion that self-love, following "the laws of nature," created mutual love. There was no metaphysical necessity for this to be the case, since to suppose that it could be otherwise implied no contradiction. To illustrate his point he plunged into a tangled argument that depended upon the operations of nature. Because bodies have solidity, cohesion, and gravitation toward the center of the earth, he argued, it did not follow by metaphysical necessity that "a weight suspended on the beam of a balance should have greater power to counterbalance a weight on the other side, when that body was at a distance from the fulcrum, than when it was near." There is no logical contradiction involved that it should be otherwise. Similarly there is no absolute metaphysical necessity, because there is an internal mutual attraction of the parts of the earth whereby the whole becomes one solid coherent body, that other bodies around it should also be attracted by it. The only contradiction that could occur would be due to the fact that these arrangements contradicted "that beautiful proportion and harmony, which the Author of Nature observes in the laws of nature." Edwards concluded by analogy, "By a like order of nature a man's love to those who love him, is no more than a certain expression or effect of self-love." Consequently, there is no more true virtue in a man's loving his friends from self-love than there is in the motive of self-love itself.[68]

This excursion into the natural realm may show that Edwards's thoughts on morality were never far distant from his metaphysics of nature, but it is doubtful that the arguments he proposed very much clarified the status of self-love. He certainly, for example, had not shown why "metaphysical necessity" and natural law were not both products of God's arbitrary will and therefore were indistinguishable from each other. He had instead virtually disavowed that there was any connection between "metaphysical necessity" and natural law, thus introducing confusion into his argument that presumably made self-love a natural law of human life.

Edwards seems to have been of two minds concerning the difference between this secondary virtue inclusive of self-love, moral sense, and conscience, and true virtue. He had made it clear that the two had nothing to do with each other, inferior virtue being in outright opposition to primary virtue. Yet there were strong connections between the two. Both were forms of beauty that inevitably conformed to the general definition of beauty as proportionality, agreement, and harmony. In fact, without recourse to ideas derived from secondary virtue Edwards would have been hard pressed to describe the higher beauty of true virtue. Instead he might well have been reduced to inarticulate ejaculations of delight over true virtue, as also he would have been over the taste of honey. Instead he wrote, "Some image of the true, spiritual, original beauty . . . consisting in being's consent to being, or the union of spiritual beings in a mutual propensity and affection of heart" was detectable in the beauty of sensed objects.[69] Although this opinion followed Edwards's tendency to believe that spiritual realities were models for inferior things, the converse was true, since in fact he had patterned his ethics upon what he had learned from his metaphysics of nature. The distinction between the two orders of morality also was endangered at another point, in spite of Edwards's claim that natural men had no access to true virtue. These same persons, he admitted, by natural conscience could approve true virtue "from that uniformity, equality, and justice which there is in it."[70] Apparently there was some limited access to true virtue by those who did not participate in it. They could at least recognize in it the principles derived from the metaphysics of nature.

Nevertheless, the gap between the two moralities was repeatedly emphasized. Edwards insisted that delight in natural beauty was in no way dependent on the possession of true virtue. Those elevated to the realm of true virtue did not therefore have a livelier appreciation of the beauty of "squares and cubes" or other indications of order in the world about them. Appreciation of the natural world was not increased in proportion to the height of one's virtue, as seen in the fact that "very vicious and lewd" persons possess a sense of natural beauty. So it must be obvious that as awareness of natural beauty is not dependent on appreciation of spiritual beauty, neither is appreciation of spiritual beauty dependent on that of natural beauty. Each is independent of the other.[71] Edwards had apparently changed his mind slightly on this point. In his *Religious Affections* he admitted that natural man might have a sense of the natural perfection of God, but he insisted that this sense more frequently occurred in the saints. By means of grace the saints' perception of the natural attributes of God was enhanced, and so also presumably would be the perception of those divine principles which constituted the beauty of the natural world. If this was the case, their delight in the natural world and the natural attributes of God that were seen in that world would be in proportion to the degree of one's true virtue represented in aesthetic sensitivity.[72] However, it did not follow that delight in natural beauty led automatically to delight in the spiritual beauty of true virtue. The relation between the two kinds of beauty was asymmetrical. Spiritual beauty would enhance sensitivity to natural beauty, but appreciation of natural beauty would never mount to the heights of spiritual beauty. There remained the dictum that there was no proportion between the whole of finite existence and the infinite Being, God. And on that ground Edwards was convinced, in spite of some evidence to the contrary, that no path led from natural morality to the beauty of true virtue. The intervening step of a "new sense" due to divine grace, which would span the gap, had to be taken.

There was another way of construing the nature of true virtue that was also largely influenced by Edwards's conception of nature. The world after all was one whole. It remained therefore to show how this idea of a unitary, harmonious world played its part in the structure of true virtue or holiness. This was accomplished by an insistence not only upon harmony of all parts of the sensed world, but preeminently by the notion of the hierarchy of all creation. This idea was what has come to be known as "The Great Chain of Being." Edwards, in keeping with this popular eighteenth-century notion, described the world of nature as one of a descending series of types of beings ranging from God downward through angels, men, animals, vegetation, and inanimate nature. The world as an object both of the senses and of spiritual perception was an organic harmony created or emanated from and presided over by the perfect being, God. If, as we have seen, Edwards's metaphysics of nature tended to analytically skeletonize both nature and virtue, the chain of being remedied that fault by spelling out an interdependent creation built on a vertical scale of being. Edwards was captivated by this essentially Neoplatonic scheme, which at one and the same time did justice to proportionality of beings and protected differences within the created world without breaching the difference between it and God. The chain-of-being concept extended into heaven as well as into the lower world. In heaven there would be some souls of a higher degree of being and excellence than those of lesser status. Above both stood the angels, with similar degrees of dignity, to whom the saints were subordinate. And below both those ranks were others filled by natural men, on down through animals with varying degrees of being until one reached inanimate nature, beyond which there would be nothing.

The social and political world found the same hierarchical principle at work. In his thoughts in **"God's Moral Government"** Edwards expressed his belief that God had so constituted all things with an eye to "beauty, good order and regulation, proportion and harmony" that the very system of the natural world in its seasons, in the formation of plants and the various parts of the human body, all reflected this divine order. Since mankind was the highest type of being within this world, possessed of intelligence,

perception, mind, and action, it too shared in the pattern of subordination and superordination, lest by failing to obey the laws of social coherence humanity fall into discord, confusion, and ruin. As all natural bodies in the created world were united as individual entities [atoms?] in one body by mutual dependence and subserviency, so human society should also reflect the same order and harmony. Specifically, God has intended "moral subordination amongst men," so there should be princes and governors "to whom honor, subjection and obedience should be paid." Children were to be governed by parents, as "is most evidently founded in nature." God has appointed that there be moral rulers "that are the wiser and stronger" over the "less knowing and weaker." It logically followed for Edwards that the same pattern applied to the relation between mankind and God. "In maintaining communication or converse" between the two, "one must yield to the other, must comply with the other; there must be a union of wills; one must be clothed with authority, the other with submission."[73] Thus the chain of being put the stamp of approval upon the *status quo,* supporting a conservative moral and political outlook. There was to be no place for human pride or any tendency to move oneself from one's appointed station, and certainly there were no grounds for revolutionary action in the face of what obviously was the way God had created his world from top to bottom. Social relations were as much a part of the laws of nature as was nature itself.[74]

However, there was another aspect of this system that Arthur O. Lovejoy properly called the temporalizing of the chain. Movement by human beings was possible, as to their intelligence, will, and spiritual endowments. The conception of the destiny of man as an unending progress also entered the picture. Joseph Addison could claim "There is not . . . a more pleasing and triumphant consideration in religion than this of the perpetual progress which the soul makes towards the perfection of its nature, without ever arriving at a period in it . . . it must be a prospect pleasing to God himself, to see his creation ever beautifying in his eyes, and drawing nearer to him, by greater degrees of resemblance." And Leibniz concluded his *Principles of Nature and Grace* with the words that human happiness should consist "in a perpetual progress to new pleasures and perfections."[75]

These words could have been penned by Edwards, with one major exception. This lay in the fact that sin stood in the way, and by no amount of purely individual effort could one pass from sin to spiritual perfection. Furthermore, in Edwards's reading of it, the chain of being was less like a ladder to be climbed than a series of spiritual attainments to which one was lured by the beauty, power, and wisdom of God. The "climb," if that was what it was, was an ascent only for those who were saints, not an open invitation to natural human beings to strive to achieve their potentiality, as the Enlightenment moralists of the period supposed. But all else that the rationalistic purveyors of the chain-of-being philosophy claimed was acceptable to Edwards. There was to be for the saints, those endowed with true virtue, a never-ending progress of union with God in eternity, but they never would become God. The goal of unity with God and its blessedness could be approached or realized only asymptotically. "The time," Edwards wrote, "will never come when it can be said it is attained to, in the most absolutely perfect manner." Distance was still presupposed, in keeping with the principles of proportionality and hierarchy. Yet, "it is no solid objection against God's aiming at an infinitely perfect union of the creature with himself, that the particular time will never come when it can be said, the union is now infinitely perfect . . . there never will come the moment that now this infinitely valuable good has been actually bestowed."[76]

The metaphysical scene in which this portrayal of true virtue was set is one that takes the natural phenomena of the sun and a fountain to express the vital interchange between the saints and God. God, like a fountain or sun, overflows in His goodness and power, both creating the world and establishing the manner in which the saints will forever approach to a total union with Him. But for the word *creating* Edwards substituted the Neoplatonic term *emanation.* The relation of God to His world is not that of ruler exercising his sovereign rights over subjects so much as that of an infinitely fertile source of being and excellence that overflows into the world, filling the saints with His own nature, which is reflected back to Him. To the saints He communicates knowledge of Himself, which is "the image of God's own knowledge of himself." It is a participation in God as particular beams of the sun are communicated by the light and glory of that body. God emanates in an equally free-flowing manner His holiness, by which the creature partakes of God's own moral excellency. So the creature's holiness consists in love, which is the comprehension of all true virtue as it centers preeminently in God. "If holiness in God consist chiefly in love to himself, holiness in the creature must chiefly consist in love to him."[77] Then happiness comes, the happiness that God has in Himself and His glory. This also is "something of God" in which the human subject is confirmed and united to God "in proportion as the communication is greater or less."[78]

All in all, the end for which the world was created is God's own glory. And that glory is "often represented by an effulgence, or emanation, or communication of light, from a luminary of fountain of light."[79] The saints' holiness or true virtue consists in their knowing, esteeming, loving, rejoicing in, and praising God, all of which is an exhibition of God's glory in them. So there is an interplay between the two. God's fullness is received by the saint and reflected back to the luminary, and this is emanation and remanation, as Edwards put it. True virtue is at last holiness, which is loving participation in the deity, whose glory is thereby manifested. God, it may be said, is the final lure that attracts the believer, whose will is determined by that which one loves. As he stated it in the **"Freedom of the Will,"** "the will always *is* as the greatest apparent good, or as what appears most agreeable . . ." and that is not to say that the will is under compulsion to love God,

but rather is determined to love Him by the vision of the great Being.[80] One is irresistibly drawn to rest one's destiny in that which one loves above all else. Beyond that state of affairs, whereby God is glorified, no one can go.

Insofar as Edwards formulated his later conception of the saints' advance to true virtue and holiness on the model of the chain of being, he was using one that supposedly had been fashioned on the order of nature, although in fact its origin lay more in a metaphysical theory of nature than in an empirical view of it. Into that model the figures of the sun and fountain fitted as apt representations of the Neoplatonic tradition, although it was in significant ways different from the Newtonian world picture Edwards had developed earlier. Nevertheless, the pattern of nature found within the chain of being governed Edwards's way of describing how by degrees and proportionality true virtue came about. His aesthetic sensitivity to beauty in nature and his metaphysical ponderings on the ways of nature were translated to the higher plane of spiritual truth. It is no wonder that Edwards's more pedestrian critics found little by which to guide daily moral decisions in this transformation of ethics into holiness. True, in a certain way to guide one's steps by the principle of proportionality would curb the more extravagant exercises of self-interest, and conscience, implanted in all mankind "to be as it were in God's stead," could distinguish right from wrong, and might even put men "upon seeking true virtue."[81] But in the final analysis such secondary virtue could not of itself be lifted up to the breathless heights of holiness. Since true virtue was not simply a higher kind of morality on a scale of ethical achievement, it was an experience with which natural humanity was by and large unacquainted. It was a state of transformed consciousness and being that transcended the ethics of right and wrong and the demands of duty. It was an ecstasy, unachievable by human effort, that was intrinsically valuable and therefore useless as a means to anything beyond itself.

Nicolai Hartmann, although an atheist, has described such an experience as "radiant virtue," which flowed outward from the inherent richness of being in the human subject.[82] And Edwards's true virtue was precisely such a radiant virtue, given by God, of which morality as commonly understood was the most important by-product, but not the central point. Like Augustine's famous dictum, it was a matter of loving God and, from that source, doing what one wills.

Notes

1. TV 64.

2. Earl R. Wasserman, "Nature Moralized: The Divine Analogy in the Eighteenth Century," *ELH, A Journal of English Literary History,* no. 20 (March 1953), 1, 51, 57, 61.

3. Cf., e.g., SPW 231, no. 16; 236, nos. 31, 36; 248, no. 55.

4. Cf. To 27.

5. Cf. ibid., 261-62, Misc. 651.

6. TV 3-4.

7. SPW 362, no. 45.

8. Cf. ibid., 305-6.

9. Ibid., 335; cf. also 344.

10. Cf. ibid., 380, no. 62.

11. Fi 84-85.

12. Cf. SPW 235, no. 23b; 357, no. 40.

13. Cf. ibid., 343.

14. Ibid., 336.

15. Ibid., 380, no. 62; cf. 382, no. 62.

16. Cf. ibid., 381, no. 62.

17. Cf. ibid., 363-64, nos. 4, 9.

18. Cf. To 258, Misc. 117; TV 23; SPW 337.

19. Cf. He 99.

20. TV 9.

21. Cf. CW 201, 203.

22. CF 479-85. Cf. Misc. 369, 403, 431, 681, 817, 822 on degrees and proportions of saints' glory and happiness. (Schafter transcript)

23. SPW 336.

24. GA 470.

25. Cf. TV 12.

26. Cf. CF 479, 482, 485.

27. Cf. ibid., 145, 150-51.

28. TV 3.

29. Cf. SPW 381.

30. Cf. TV 5.

31. TV 38.

32. Ibid., 6.

33. SPW 381.

34. Cf. The Reverend William Hart, *Remarks on President Edwards's Dissertation Concerning the Nature of True Virtue* (New Haven, Conn.: T. and S. Green, 1771), 4.

35. Cf. Robert Hall, *Works in Four Volumes* (New York: Harper and Brothers, 1849), 1:43. Hall was a prominent Baptist preacher in England, 1764-1831. Cf. Ho 123-25.

36. Cf. CW 215.

37. TV 9.

38. CW 255.

39. Cf. SPW 202, 206.

40. Cf. Douglas J. Elwood, *The Philosophical Theology of Jonathan Edwards* (New York: Columbia University Press, 1961), 29; Joseph Haroutunian, *Piety Versus Moralism* (New York: Henry Holt and Co., 1932), 78.

41. Cf. SPW 337.

42. Cf. ibid., 381, no. 62.

43. Cf. TV 28.

44. Ibid., 31.

45. Ibid., 35.

46. Cf. Roland Delattre, *Beauty and Sensibility in the Thought of Jonathan Edwards* (New Haven: Yale University Press, 1968), 9, 18, 20, 23, 24, 26.

47. OS 141.

48. RA 240.

49. TV 8, 14.

50. CF 227.

51. Cf. TV 4, 5.

52. Cf. To 21-25. On the question of whether in the eighteenth century harmony in music immediately pleases, see John Neubauer, *The Emancipation of Music from Language* (New Haven and London: Yale University Press, 1986), esp. 160, 175-76, 178, 179.

53. Ho 206, n. 12; 207, n. 17; 209, n. 35.

54. Cf. Fi 81.

55. TV 98-99.

56. Cf. ibid., 33.

57. Cf. ibid., 32, 40, 41.

58. To 205, no. 7 39.

59. Cf. ibid., 16-17, 26; Ho 102.

60. Cf. To 147-48, cor. 1.

61. TV 51; for other criticisms by Edwards of the moral-sense philosophers, see ibid., 48-60.

62. Cf. ibid., 70.

63. Ibid., 22.

64. Ibid., 87.

65. Cf. ibid., 57, 89.

66. Cf. CF 284.

67. Cf. GA 470.

68. Cf. TV 47-48.

69. Ibid., 30.

70. Ibid., 68.

71. Ibid., 40-41.

72. Cf. RA 266.

73. Cf. MG 566-72.

74. Cf. Gerald R. Cragg, *Puritanism in the Period of the Great Persecution, 1660-1688* (Cambridge: Cambridge University Press, 1957), 230.

75. In Arthur O. Lovejoy, *The Great Chain of Being* (Cambridge, Mass.: Harvard University Press, 1942), 247, 248.

76. CW 257.

77. Ibid., 217.

78. Ibid., 210-11.

79. Ibid., 250.

80. FW 144, 12.

81. TV 90, 853.

82. Nicolai Hartmann, *Ethics,* (London: George Allen and Unwin; New York, The Macmillan Co., 1932), 2:332-38.

Works Cited

PRIMARY SOURCES

AW *Apocalyptic Writings. Works of Jonathan Edwards,* vol. 5. Edited by Stephen J. Stein. New Haven and London: Yale Univeristy Press, 1977.

CF: *Charity and Its Fruits.* Edited by Tryon Edwards. New York: Robert Carter and Brothers, 1852.

CW: *Dissertation Concerning the End for which God Created the World. The Works of President Edwards in Four Volumes,* A Reprint of the Worcester Edition, vol. 2. New York: Leavitt and Allen, 1843.

DB: *The Life of David Brainerd. Works of Jonathan Edwards,* vol. 7. Edited by Norman Pettit. New Haven and London: Yale Univeristy Press, 1985.

Dw: *Memoir of his Life. The Works of President Edwards with a Memoir of His Life in Ten Volumes*; vol. 1. New York: Published by S. Converse, 1829; *Types of the Messiah and Notes on the Bible.The Works of President Edwards with a Memoir of His Life in Ten Volumes,* vol. 9. New York: G. and C. and H. Carville, 1830. Known as the Dwight edition. (Sereno Dwight, ed.)

FS: *Forty Sermons on Various Subjects. The Works of President Edwards in Four Volumes,* A Reprint of the Worcester Edition, vol. 4. New York: Leavitt and Allen, 1843.

FW: *Freedom of the Will. Works of Jonathan Edwards,* vol. 1. Edited by Paul Ramsey. New Haven: Yale University Press; London: Oxford University Press, 1957.

GA: *The Great Awakening. Works of Jonathan Edwards,* vol. 4. Edited by C. C. Goen. New Haven and London: Yale University Press, 1972.

He: *Treatise on Grace and other posthumously published writings.* Edited by Paul Helm. Cambridge and London: James Clarke and Co., Ltd., 1971.

HR: *A History of the Work of Redemption. The Works of President Edwards in Four Volumes,* A Reprint of the Worcester Edition, vol. 1. New York: Leavitt and Allen, 1843.

IS: *Images or Shadows of Divine Things.* Edited by Perry Miller. New Haven: Yale University Press; London: Geoffrey Cumberledge, Oxford University Press, 1948.

MG: *God's Moral Government. The Works of President Edwards in Four Volumes,* A Reprint of the Worcester Edition, vol. 1. New York: Leavitt and Allen, 1843.

OS: *Original Sin. Works of Jonathan Edwards,* vol. 3. Edited by Clyde A. Holbrook. New Haven and London: Yale University Press, 1970.

RA: *Religious Affections. Works of Jonathan Edwards,* vol. 2. Edited by John E.Smith. New Haven and London: Yale University Press, 1959.

SPW: *Scientific and Philosophical Writings. Works of Jonathan Edwards,* vol. 6. New Haven and London: Yale University Press, 1980.

To: *The Philosophy of Jonathan Edwards* Edited by Harvey G. Townsend. Eugene: University of Oregon Press, 1958.

TV: *The Nature of True Virtue.* Foreword by William K. Frankena. Ann Arbor Paperbacks. Ann Arbor: University of Michigan Press, 1960.

SECONDARY SOURCES

Fi: Norman Fiering, *Jonathan Edwards's Moral Thought and Its British Context.* Chapel Hill: The University of North Carolina Press, 1981.

Ho: Clyde A. Holbrook, *The Ethics of Jonathan Edwards.* Ann Arbor: University of Michigan Press, 1973.

Lo: Mason I. Lowance Jr., *The Language of Canaan.* Cambridge, Mass. and London: Harvard University Press, 1980.

Th: Keith Thomas, *Man and the Natural World.* New York: Pantheon Press, 1983.

Helen Petter Westra (essay date 1988)

SOURCE: "Jonathan Edwards on 'Faithful and Successful Ministers,'" *Early American Literature,* Vol. 23, No. 3, 1988, pp. 281-90.

[In the following essay, Westra examines two sermons preached by Edwards for the ordination of fellow clergy—one from 1736, the other from 1754. She contrasts the "jubilant" tone of the former with the gravity of the latter, and concludes that the sermons reflect the evolution of Edwards's assessment of the relative joys and hardships of the pastoral ministry, based on his personal experiences at the Northampton church from 1727 to 1750.]

Jonathan Edwards' revivalist leadership and rhetoric of sensation in New England's Great Awakening have become commonplace parts of the American religious tradition. Urged by ministerial friends in Boston and London,

Edwards himself wrote *A Faithful Narrative of the Surprising Conversions* to provide elaborate documentation of the religious fervor that began in his Northampton, Massachusetts, church and spread, by his count, to at least thirty-two Connecticut River Valley communities (*Works* IV: 22-23). In describing these waves of revival, he paid special attention to the signs of religious ardor in his own congregation, "alive in God's service, everyone earnestly intent on the public worship, every hearer eager to drink in the words of the minister as they came from his mouth" (*Works* IV: 151).

As history reveals, however, the extraordinary intensity of these "renewals" or "quickenings" could not be sustained in Northampton or elsewhere, and by 1750 the power of Edwards' evangelical pulpit had been drastically diminished by a series of ecclesiastical debates and battles that toppled him from his Northampton pastorate. Today, some 250 years after the 1734-35 awakenings spurred by Edwards' leadership, we can discover in his manuscript sermons vivid evidence of the powerful effects these revivals and his subsequent pastoral failures in Northampton had on his firmly held views of gospel ministry. These views are articulated pointedly in the sermons Edwards preached for the ordinations of fellow clergymen, sermons which over the course of his ministry clearly reflected the shifts and developments in his pastoral consciousness at critical moments in his own ecclesiastical career.

Among the many sermons in the extensive Edwards manuscript collection at Yale's Beinecke Library are the first and the last of these ordination sermons that Edwards delivered; each comments fervently on the office of gospel minister and each is informed significantly by contemporaneous events in Edwards' life. In a sense, these two ordination sermons—one on Luke 10:17-18 and one on Acts 20:28—could be said to bracket his most active and renowned years of public ministry.[1]

His first ordination sermon, delivered in 1736, is shaped strongly by the 1734-35 revivals; his final ordination sermon, written in 1754 and delivered on two separate occasions, is marked painfully by Edwards' dismissal from Northampton. Like most of the approximately 1,200 manuscript sermons covering his thirty-six years of preaching (1722–58), his 1736 and 1754 ordination messages have never been published and are therefore little known. Today it seems timely to transcribe key passages from these two unpublished sermons so they can again speak after centuries of silence.

I

In 1736, after the first wave of extraordinary spiritual awakenings had reverberated through the colonies and Northampton's exemplary piety had gained wide repute, Edwards was invited to deliver a sermon for the ordination of a fellow pastor. This November 17, 1736, unpublished sermon that Edwards preached at Lambstown (a Worcester County settlement that later became the town of Hard-

wick, Massachusetts, on a branch of the Ware River) is a lively, lyrical celebration of the minister as God's trusted, faithful, and above all, joyful servant. The doctrine of the sermon, based on Luke 10:17-18, maintains: "When those ministers of the gospel that have been faithful and successful come to give an account of their success to their Lord that hath sent them, Christ and they will rejoice together" (5).

Of great interest is the fact that the date of this sermon follows very closely that of Edwards' letter to the Rev. Benjamin Coleman of Boston (*Works* IV: 151), the letter (later published and made famous as *A Faithful Narrative of the Surprising Work of God*) being a detailed account of "the late wonderful work of God in this [town of Northampton] and some other towns of this county [of Hampshire]" (*Works* IV: 113).

Edwards' letter to Coleman repeatedly described the revivals as an "extraordinary pouring out of the Spirit of God," but the missive also carefully recounted his own ministerial role in the late great "work of God upon souls" (*Works* IV: 120). The narrative particularly refers to sermons he had preached preliminary to and during the awakenings,[2] sermons he believed to have been "remarkably blessed" in producing "immediate saving fruit" (*Works* IV: 168). The November 6 letter also rejoiced much in the signs of religious ardor in his own congregation. "It was no longer the tavern," wrote Edwards, "but the minister's house, that was thronged far more than ever the tavern had been wont to be" (*Works* IV: 161). Religion had become the central interest in Northampton, and in all of this the minister was a pivotal figure.

The ordination sermon that Edwards preached that November Sunday at Lambstown is of particular historic interest in its consistently optimistic, even exuberant spirit. The key words—"joy," "rejoice," "joyful," "rejoicing," "successful ministers," "faithful ministers"—mark its highly celebrative tone. Edwards repeatedly asserts that the minister's labor is awesomely "great"; the divine Master is infinitely "great"; the minister's success is gloriously "great"; and the minister's vocation greatly surpasses all other earthly vocations:

> There is no employment that the children of men are employed in wherein they have such opportunity [as they do in gospel ministry] to lay a foundation for their own blessedness. Faithfulness in serving God in any calling will be crowned with glorious rewards, but there seems to be promises of distinguished and peculiar honor and joy in a faithfulness in this work [of gospel ministry]. . . .
>
> This employment may well be looked on as a yet more excellent and honorable employment on the account of the joy that the success of it occasions to Christ. The very business of those that are called to this employment is to do that in which Christ exceedingly rejoices.
>
> Surely that must be great and excellent indeed that the Lord of angels and men takes such notice of and so rejoices in. 'Tis not that honorable . . . to be employed

to do that which when done rejoices the heart of the son of God? The work of ministers is to recover lost souls and bring them to eternal happiness, which is that work that Christ himself came into the world and shed his blood for. (23-25)

Infused with the joys of his own remarkable pastoral and evangelistic successes, Edwards' 1736 ordination sermon bypasses any careful exploration of the rigors, complexities, or difficulties inherent in gospel ministry. Rather, it offers a richly impressive, eschatological view of the spiritual rejoicing and eternal rewards awaiting faithful ministers:

> Let us who are employed in or about to be employed in this work [of gospel ministry] consider how blessed a day that day will [be] to us whereon we return to our Lord to give an account, if we have been faithful and successful. Let us consider how it will be when we die, which we surely must. And let us consider how it will be at the day of judgment when we see those persons standing with us at Christ's right hand shining in glory that we have been the instruments of the conversion and salvation of and of the building up in holiness. . . .
>
> And when we shall be admitted unto fellowship and intimate conversation with our Lord and relate to him our labours and self-denial through his grace and the blessed success we had worked on one person and another . . . we have reason to conclude from the word of God that they shall be admitted as friends to converse freely with him, no less freely than the disciples on earth did. (28-29)

The sermon also resonates with lively spousal, parental, and natal imagery, images reflecting Edwards' keen interest in typology and correspondences. The images warmly picture the minister as a solicitous spiritual father and midwife to souls and as Christ's intimate friend, the trusted steward who happily prepares Christ's bride for union with the divine bridegroom:

> And what honor is this that is conferred on the children of men that they [ministers] should be employed in setting the crown of joy upon Christ's head in that they are the instruments of bringing to pass the work of conversion which is the marriage between Christ and his spouse. The day of [a soul's] conversion is the day of Christ's espousal and the day of that exceeding gladness of his heart. It is thought to have been a custom among the Israelites that on the wedding day the mother of the bridegroom put a crown upon his head to be a crown and joy and rejoicing which is mystically applied to Christ in Cant. 3:11. "Go forth, O ye daughters of Zion and behold King Solomon with his crown wherewith his mother crowned him. . . ." By King Solomon is evidently meant Christ. And by his mother and his bride, [by] both is meant the church, but by his mother seems especially to be meant the church as holding forth the word of Christ and administering his ordinances whereby souls are converted and as it were brought forth and brought to a spiritual marriage with Christ and therefore the ministers of the gospel seem especially to be intended by his mother for the travaill

[*sic*] of pain with souls 'til Christ be formed in them. Gal. 4:19. Christ said of his disciples, they are my brethren and sister and mother. These therefore when they are the instruments of converting souls and their espousal to Christ, they do as it were put a crown of gladness on Christ's head.

> And what an honor is that . . . that a faithful minister is an instrument of the conversion of . . . such persons, that brings a soul to espousal with Christ and occasions gladness in his heart and adds a jewel to his crown of rejoicing.
>
> And hereafter when they [ministers] come to give an [account] to their Lord of their success, they shall then behold the crown of joy which they have set on Christ's head, and Christ will at the same time give the same souls to them to be their own crown of rejoicing and thus they shall have communion in the same crown of joy which shows the exceeding blessedness of this work. (25-27)

With the exception of a brief warning of the divine judgment awaiting ministers who neglect the souls in their charge, the sermon maintains a spirit of delight and rejoicing throughout. It is informed by the same kind of elation that Edwards expressed in *A Faithful Narrative* when he described Northampton as a town that "seemed to be full of the presence of God: it never was so full of love, nor so full of joy. . . . There were remarkable tokens of God's presence in almost every house. It was a time of joy in families on the account of salvation's being brought unto them. . . . the congregation was alive in God's service" (*Works* IV: 151). In this context, Edwards' first ordination sermon stands as a vigorous, animated affirmation of ministry delivered by a preacher whom many had come to view as a grand and blessed success and whom the world was fast recognizing as the leader of a remarkable American revival, a preacher who could say of his church, "we are evidently a people blessed . . . and in this corner of the world God dwells and manifests his glory" (*Works* IV: 127).

II

In 1754, nearly twenty years after his first invitation to preach an ordination sermon, Edwards selected Acts 20:28 as the basis of the message that would constitute his last ordination sermon. Edwards' personal note on the top left-hand side of the first page identifies the sermon as one "prepared for the [May 28, 1754] installment of Mr. Billing" and then "preached also at No. 3 July, 1756 at Mr. Jones' Ordination." By this time, Edwards was serving the tiny frontier settlement of Stockbridge, Massachusetts; he had been dismissed as Northampton's pastor because the community leaders no longer respected his zealous orthodoxy, his spiritual direction, or his insistence that persons seeking communicant membership in the church be required to make a public profession of their faith in God.

In sharp contrast to the warm-hearted, jubilant tone of 1736, the 1754 sermon is pensive, dark, and defensive. This sermon on Acts 20:28 possesses none of the buoyant, cheerful optimism present in the 1736 picture of ministers cheerfully and successfully working among Christ's people.

This last, grave ordination sermon is profoundly shaped by Edwards' personal experiences of rejection, anguish, and defamation as a gospel minister deposed from his pulpit. The sermon does not meditate on the joy and success of ministers but rather looks directly at the ineffably perfect example of Christ's suffering, selflessness, obedience, and humility as the pattern to be emulated, particularly by gospel ministers. Edwards' sermon doctrine and intent are explicit: "My design . . . is to consider Christ's expending his own blood for the salvation and happiness of the souls of men, in the view both of an inducement and a direction to ministers to exert themselves for the same end" (4).

One of the few Stockbridge sermons entirely written rather than simply outlined, this text plays upon extremities; the infinite lowliness and utter vileness of men and women as enemies of Christ stand in dramatic contrast to Christ's infinite dignity, benevolence, perfection, and sacrificial love. Edwards' rhetorical method is to push the listener step by step to an awareness that the magnitude of Christ's redemptive gift is beyond human comprehension. At times the language becomes incantatory:

> It was the blood of one of infinite dignity and glory, and it was blood that was infinitely precious, and what was done in shedding of it for sinners was a thing infinitely great and infinitely greater than if the greatest earthly potentate had shed his blood, yea, or that of all the princes on earth, yea, an infinitely greater than the highest created angel, yea, and not only so, but an infinitely greater thing than if the whole glorious host of those pure and glorious spirits [had given up their lives], . . . in that it was the blood of God. (9-10)

Edwards continues thus to repeat "infinite" upon "infinite" to magnify and intensify Christ's exaltation as well as his humiliation. And it is this Christ, Edwards claims repeatedly in the sermon, that ministers must not only *represent* but also *imitate* and *resemble*:

> 'Tis undoubtedly the duty of ministers to . . . be willing to bring themselves even to the utmost as to all temporal things and even to their own death, if they should be called to it in divine providence, yea, to undergo the most tormenting and ignominious death as many of Christ's ministers have been called to it and have actually done it. (37-38)

> [Christ] shed his blood . . . at a time when he received the worst treatment from those that he shed his blood for. Their ingratitude was at the height. This teaches ministers [that] Christ did this in opposition to the greatest temptation of Satan. This should be encouraging to ministers. (42-43)

> Ministers in the whole course of their labor in the ministry should have a constant regard to the example of Jesus Christ. . . . Shedding his blood for the salvation and happiness of the souls of men should be regarded

by ministers thus to induce and direct them in exerting themselves for the same. (46-47)

> The work of the ministry is in many respects as Christ's own work, the work of being savior. . . . Christ was a minister of the gospel. He was sent forth as the Father's minister. . . . Ministers are not only appointed to carry on Christ's work of saving souls but also shedding of Christ's blood in every respect. 2 Cor. 5:20. (49-50)

> Let it be considered that if ministers do exert themselves for the happiness of the souls of men in imitation of him who has purchased them with his own blood, how excellently and honorably they will be employed. (52)

Pointing directly to the martyrdom of the apostles and remembering, no doubt, his own ministerial anguish, Edwards teaches that it is especially the duty of ministers "to submit willingly and cheerfully to self-denial and suffering." Christ's self-sacrifice and benevolence, says Edwards in the sermon's application, are "an example for all the followers of Christ, but more especially an example for ministers to teach them in what manner they ought to behave themselves in their work" (46).

Once again, Edwards' language is heavy with superlatives as he attempts to excite his listeners to consider the exemplary Christ in "the greatest test" of his love, "the highest manifestation" of his obedience, his "exercise of the fullest humility," his "most admirable kindness toward his most injurious, spiteful, and contemptuous enemies when they were in the highest exercise of their cruelty," and his suffering "the most terrible effects of [his enemies'] vile malignancy [when] they showed the most ingratitude" (44-47).

Having presented a view of the quintessentially awesome and perfect Christ, the sermon subsequently moves to collapse this great gap between the divinely sovereign Christ and his ministers: "Christ is the church's head and ruler and ministers under Christ are rulers of the church" (51). Edwards joins Christ and his ministers together by underscoring the ways in which self-abnegating, faithful ministers not only serve but also reflect Christ: "The relation of ministers to the church of God is in many respects an image of that which Christ stands in" (50). Edwards has thus masterfully managed his message at first to magnify the great abyss separating perfect Savior and sinful creature; but ultimately, in the sermon's conclusion, the emphasis on the infinite span between God and fallen sinners paradoxically gives way to an emphasis on the benevolent union between Christ and the redeemed. And most particularly in the gospel minister is Christ's love, compassion, and concern for souls concretely embodied: "The work of the ministry is the same in many respects as Christ's own work, the work of being savior" (49). Through the graciously instrumental words, lives, and persons of his ministers, says Edwards, Christ performs his great work of redemption.

After Edwards was dismissed from his Northampton parish in 1750, his preaching was directed primarily to a small group of white settlers at Stockbridge and to a group of illiterate Mohawk and Housatonic Indians for whom he preached very simple sermons from outlines or revisions of his old Northampton sermons. Yet the March 1754 ordination sermon demonstrates that Edwards was still able to achieve the strategic use of incremental and impressive language as he had done so forcefully in his earlier revival and imprecatory sermons. His practiced sense of incantation and rhythm, amassed details, and climactic rhetoric operates inexorably in this sermon to celebrate Christ's self-denial, humility, and obedience.

The dark tones and imagery of this last ordination sermon, however, also demonstrate Edwards' deep awareness that the task of gospel ministry had cost him great personal pain, heartache, and haunting humiliation. Throughout his ministry he had asserted that the preaching of Christ's faithful ministers demonstrates God's counsels, reveals God's mind, and shows forth God's glory. Yet, exactly when Edwards had believed himself faithful and diligent in protecting the sanctity of the Lord's Supper and in defending orthodoxy, his parishioners had overruled and rejected his leadership and had forced him to leave the church he had served for twenty-three years.

Thus, this last ordination sermon reveals Edwards continuing to grapple with this central paradox in his ministerial vision: the life-saving message he is "sent forth" to deliver sometimes falls on deaf or antagonistic ears. The minister's pressing desire is that the souls under his care be touched, awakened, nourished, and saved by the gospel he preaches. He believes his irrefragable mandate is to be one of Christ's "faithful and successful ministers." To this end, the gospel minister strives always to resemble and exemplify Christ. But this Christ is infinitely perfect, infinitely beautiful, infinitely meek, patient, and majestic; this Christ is wholly beyond the capability of even the most faithful, righteous, long-suffering minister to imitate and represent.

It has been noted that many of the most cogent and telling expressions of Edwards' theological thought and pastoral concerns are yet to be uncovered in the unpublished sermon manuscripts. Wilson Kimnach, editor of the forthcoming Yale sermon edition of Edwards' *Works,* considers the sermon manuscripts "unrivaled as a chronicle of the man and his art in the midst of life" (197). Indeed, the unpublished ordination sermons on Luke 10:17-18 and on Acts 20:28 demonstrate that though Edwards' pastoral experiences definitely colored his vision of ministry, he never wavered in his belief that the gospel ministry was a sacred task to "care for souls," a commission that required a lifetime of faithfulness in guiding and guarding those in his charge. To view Edwards' long career as gospel minister particularly through the medium of his sermons is to observe him not only as he reacted joyously to what he considered "the blessed successes" of that office but also as he gave expression to the heaviness and deep disappoint-

ments he felt when it appeared that his prophetic messages from his Master had gone unheard.

Notes

1. The sermon manuscripts in the Edwards Manuscript Collection at the Beinecke Library are filed according to the biblical text upon which the sermon doctrine is based. The sermon passages included in this essay are my transcriptions from Edwards' holograph sermons; where words are undecipherable or require interpolation, I have placed my insertions in brackets. I have added minimal punctuation to Edwards' notoriously punctuationless prose. For the sermon on Luke 10:17-18, I have followed pagination penciled lightly (by some former reader) on the manuscript; however, for the sermon on Acts 20:28, I have disregarded earlier penciled pagination (clearly not Edwards') because numbers here fail to count left-hand pages. The quotations here from unpublished manuscripts appear with the permission of the Beinecke Rare Book and Manuscript Library, Yale University.

2. This letter was Edwards' enormously expanded version of an earlier May 30, 1735, letter to Coleman. Coleman abridged this November 6 letter and appended it to a volume of sermons, *The Duty and Interest of a People* by William Williams, published later in 1736. As C. C. Goen indicates (*The Great Awakening* 112), this was the first American publication of any of Edwards' accounts of the Great Awakening.

Works Cited

Edwards, Jonathan. *The Great Awakening.* Ed. C. C. Goen. Vol. IV of *The Works of Jonathan Edwards.* 7 vols. New Haven: Yale Univ. Press, 1972.

———. "Sermon on Acts 20:28." Beinecke Library, Yale Univ.

———. "Sermon on Luke 10:17-18." Beinecke Library, Yale Univ.

Kimnach, Wilson. "Literary Techniques of Jonathan Edwards." Dissertation. Univ. of Pennsylvania, 1971.

Allen C. Guelzo (essay date 1989)

SOURCE: "The Waning of Edwardseanism: From Asa Burton to Lyman Beecher," in *Edwards on the Will: A Century of American Theological Debate,* Wesleyan University Press, 1989, pp. 208-39.

[In the following essay, Guelzo traces Edwardseanism's decline as a significant intellectual and theological force

by examining the philosophies of post-Edwardsean figures, including Asa Burton, Timothy Dwight—a grandson of Edwards—and Lyman Beecher.]

Almost every theological party, faction, or movement in New England from 1758 (the death of Edwards) until 1858 (the deaths of Nathaniel William Taylor and Bennet Tyler) defined itself in some way or other according to "Edwards on the will." One measure of the sheer impact of *Freedom of the Will,* was the extent to which it made volition, and especially reconciliationist theories of volition, the principal topic of New England discourse. Of all the efforts to cope with the theory of will spawned by *Freedom of the Will,* the New Divinity was the most ingenious, and had the most intense following, so much so that it is safe to suggest that the New Divinity represents the most vital and fecund intellectual movement in the early republic. Indeed, if intellectual vitality were all that counted, the New Divinity would never have fallen into the oblivion to which it was so long consigned.

There are three basic reasons why the New Divinity passed into intellectual eclipse: one was a problem inherent in its popular strategy, another was a problem in its leadership, and another—the largest—was the successful resurgence of Old Calvinism at Yale in the 1820s, which displaced Edwards's peculiar brand of voluntarism in New England affections with an intellectualist libertarianism. The demise of Edwardseanism dragged down with it the credibility of a reconciliationism built on an Augustinian voluntarism.

In another sense, the demise of Edwardseanism was part of the overall triumph of Scottish "common sense" philosophy within the structure of American religion and American higher education. And in still one further sense, the resurgence of Old Calvinism, particularly in the form of Nathaniel William Taylor, affords a bridge by which the parochialism of Richard Mather and Solomon Stoddard is linked to Horace Bushnell. It must be remembered that Old Calvinism represented the mainstream of New England orthodoxy, while Edwardseanism spoke for one strand of thought, the strand of separatism, standing aloof and critical on the fringe. To give it its due, Edwardseanism proved to be, for almost a century, a position to be reckoned with, and that was because Edwards had endowed it with the philosophical fruits of his genius. Thus, the intellectual progression from Edwards to Hopkins to Emmons is perhaps the single most interesting phenomenon in the history of American thought. But it remained a fringe position all the same, and all that Old Calvinism required to reassert its hegemony was someone to devise a satisfactory alternative to *Freedom of the Will* and its concomitants.

This would not have been possible, however, had not the ingenuity of Edwardseanism reached its zenith in Nathanael Emmons and thereafter declined. The first sign of decay in the New Divinity was its increasing incapacity to sustain the level of anxiety it sought to promote, and which smoothed the way to the embrace of its other teachings. In

short, when it pricked people, they no longer bled. Part of that developed as a simple result of the law of diminishing returns. The New Divinity depended for its *popular* impact on the shock value of its preachings: no "use of means," no unregenerate doings, absolute benevolence, willingness to be damned for the glory of God, willingness (as in Emmons) to preach one's own offspring into hell for the sake of that glory. None of these items, strictly speaking, was ever more than logically peripheral to the theological core of Edwardseanism, but they moved to the fore because of their usefulness in promoting the atmosphere of crisis in which the exercise of the will Edwards had described could be seen to be all-in-all. These ideas became battering rams, to jar complacent parishioners out of their pews and onto their knees, acknowledging their perfect natural ability to repent and wailing over the moral inability that showed how sinful they were.

These ideas were also high-explosive, and they often backfired, but they just as often worked. They would, however, work only for a while, until the noise of them became routine enough that crisis ceased to flow from their application. The Great Awakening was the prime example that an undiluted diet of spiritual shock will last only so long. That the New Divinity kept it going so long in revivals that kept on flaring up until the turn of the century is a tribute to their adeptness and to the depths of thought locked away in *Freedom of the Will.* But even that formula could go only so far, and so the crises ceased to come. And in losing their capacity for crisis, the New Divinity men lost their reason for being. Edwards had originally sought to revive Calvinism as the only true means of staving off mechanism, for in his mind only Calvinism was capable of restoring that sense of supernatural immediacy Malebranche, Berkeley, and even Newton had sought to reinject into the universal machine. Hence, as much as the New Divinity talked of *law,* they meant only God's laws for himself; they denied the other forms of law (like the "use of means," and even causality itself) to make way for God's gracious arbitrariness toward his creation, the sense of a God on whose string we are dangled like a spider over the pit.

Hence, too, the psychology of the Exercise scheme, making all of man's consciousness float timorously on the waves of God's power; hence, the governmental scheme of the atonement, which left God no more obligated to save one soul after Calvary than he had been before Calvary. The difficulty with maintaining this sense of immediacy was that it was so often in the minority.[1] The New Divinity had chosen the route of immediacy when most of the rest of Anglo-American culture went over to theories of natural law, general providence, and commonsense libertarianism, and they came to lack an essential item of any successful intellectual system, simple *respectability.* When the battering rams of New Divinity rhetoric ceased to make breaches in men's hearts, the atmosphere of immediacy and crisis evaporated, and, with it, the New Divinity's principal consolation for the lack of respectability. After that, one by one, the underpinnings of the New Divinity psychology began to collapse.

This process is, by its nature, elusive of description and datability, but one can certainly see some of it in Asa Burton, the king of the Tasters. Burton was what we may call a "second-generation" Hopkinsian: born in 1752, graduate of Dartmouth and student of Levi Hart, Burton found in Edwardseanism "a new field in divinity" and during his fifty-six-year pastorate of Thetford, Vermont, acquired a formidable reputation as a preacher and preceptor. When his theological lessons were finally published in 1824 as *Essays on Some of the First Principles of Metaphysics,* they were hailed not just as the most thorough statement of the Taste Scheme but as "one of the great influential philosophical books of the world." What made Burton remarkable, however, was not that he had managed to state with greater felicity a case which had earlier been made by other Tasters like Smalley.[2] Burton had seen as clearly as anyone the problem posed for divine justice by the likes of Emmons, suspending as Emmons did the sinful exercises of men on the immediate agency of God. In search of a solution, Burton turned not only to Edwards and Smalley but to "every author who had made the mind the subject of his investigation, who was then in print." It was, at length, in the Scottish philosophers that Burton found satisfaction. From them, and from his own "reasoning, writing, and close application of the mind," he formulated a Taste scheme with a strongly Scottish tinge.[3]

To begin with, Burton broke apart the unity of the faculties that Edwards had proposed a generation earlier in **The Religious Affections** and **Freedom of the Will.** "If we . . . say that the mind is nothing more than a composition of thoughts or ideas, feelings and volitions, or as some have said, a bundle or union of exercises, then . . . we must alter" the English language.[4] His authority for prying the faculties back apart was, fundamentally, intuition. "From our thoughts," Burton insisted, "we infer the faculty called the understanding . . . and from our volitions we infer the faculty termed the will, which chooses or rejects," and the two must not be confused.[5] But in addition to these two faculties, whose existence (if not their exact relationship) had been fully acknowledged by Edwards, Burton also proposed to add another faculty of the mind, that of Taste, which he defined as "another faculty of the mind distinct from the understanding and from the will."[6] Burton described Taste as the "*feeling* faculty," or, alternately, "the heart," the "spring of action," and the "moral faculty." None of these faculties was permitted to obtrude upon the other: "The understanding *perceives,* but never *feels;* the heart *feels,* but never perceives anything."[7]

What happened, then, in volition was not a complex act but a fall of dominoes. Motives do not act on the will, nor does the will become as the greatest apparent good is. Instead, motives "affect" the heart; the heart in turn prompts the will; the will then acts to determine external conduct. Burton frankly allowed that the real cause of the will is *in* man. "The real active cause, which determines the will, or

gives rise to volition, is in man, and a property of his nature."[8] The will itself may not have been self-determined, but, in Burton's scheme, the man choosing was.

Burton seems to have been quite aware that he had altered the alignment of heart and will within the framework of Edward's voluntarism. "Scarcely any writer that I now recollect has considered the heart and will to be distinct faculties," Burton conceded; "they have generally been treated as one and the same."[9] What Burton did not recollect, or perhaps never knew, was that his tripartite division of the mind resembled nothing so much as the same three-way division of the mental faculties made by the Scots Presbyterian John Witherspoon and the Unitarian Samuel West. And with them, such a division had been made for the purpose of showing that the feelings were so hopelessly divided over their objects that it was the task of the will to arbitrate.[10]

This collapse of intellectual confidence within the New Divinity was accompanied by what can only be called the overall failure of nerve and imagination on the part of its leadership. By 1787 Ezra Stiles (with perhaps no little satisfaction) noted that the real "Pillars" of Edwardseanism had been removed or were "shaken or falling," and that their places were not likely to be filled.

> President Edwards has been dead 29 years, or a generation; Dr. Bellamy is broken down both body & mind with a Paralytic Shock, & can dictate & domineer no more; Mr. Hopkins still continues, but past his force, having been somewhat affected by a Fit & nervous Debilitation; Mr. West is declining in Health, & besides was never felt so strong Rods as the others. . . . The very New Divinity Gentlemen say they perceive a Disposition among several of their Brethren to struggle for Preheminence—partly Dr. Edwards, Mr. Trumbull, Mr. Judson, Mr. Smalley, Mr. Spring, Mr. Robinson, Mr. Strong of Hartford, Mr. Dwight, Mr. Emmons, &c. They all want to be Luthers. But they will none of them be equal to those strong Reasoners, President Edwards & Mr. Hopkins. . . . Geniuses never imitate. Imitation may rise to something above laudable & very useful Mediocrity but can never reach originality.[11]

Stiles was, of course, premature to predict the intellectual demise of the New Divinity men in so wholesale a fashion: although Bellamy died in 1790, Hopkins lived on until 1803 (publishing in the meanwhile his greatest work, *The System of Doctrines,* in 1793) and West survived to 1818. Stiles was also wrong to shortchange the second generation so severely: Emmons, Spring, Edwards the Younger, Smalley, and Strong all had yet to reach their prime. But all the same, Stiles was right in one respect: the second generation was talented but it lacked the speculative daring that had made Hopkins and Emmons so remarkable. And though they still had yet to flower at the time of Stiles's prediction, their flowring was comparatively brief. Between Bellamy's death in 1790 and Hopkins's in 1803 the younger Edwardseans published a number of lengthy and interesting works, like Spring's *Moral Disquisitions* of 1789 and Nathan Strong's *Doctrine of*

Eternal Misery in 1796; but after that, the fountain dried up. Edwards the Younger, probably the sharpest mind of the second generation, died prematurely in 1801 and never came to fulfillment as a theologian. What appear afterward from Edwardsean pens are mostly sermon anthologies, those traditional *nunc dimittis* volumes of the New England clergy. The only major treatise to appear from a New Divinity author after the turn of the century was Burton's *Essays,* and even these had been circulating in manuscript for twenty years or more before their publication. The second generation were not quite the mediocrities Stiles made them out to be, but they were not up to the level of their preceptors either.

Where Stiles's accusation of mediocrity fits best is on the third generation of the New Divinity men. This is not to say that these students-of-the-students-of-the-students-of-Edwards were not without talent. From 1815 to 1845 Hopkinsian ideas were still being preached with much of the old ruthless consistency by Edward Dorr Griffin, a student of Edwards the Younger, an enormously talented revivalist and president of Williams College; by Bennet Tyler, who early on served as a lieutenant to Azel Backus, Bellamy's successor in Litchfield County and later a president of Dartmouth and founder of the Theological Institute of Connecticut; by Leonard Woods, pupil of Emmons and for thirty-eight years professor of theology at Andover Theological Seminary; and by Asahel Nettleton, probably the most successful revivalist in New England's history of revivals after Whitefield, responsible by Bennet Tyler's breathless estimate for the "AWAKENING" of *"no less than thirty thousand souls."* Still, it is difficult not to read their essays, papers, and memoirs and not conclude that in their hands Edwardsean voluntarism had lost its wonted force, and that the preachers of reconciliationism had fallen back on platitudes.[12]

Outwardly, the old flame of Edwardsean immediacy still seemed to burn in Tyler and Woods, in particular. But, inwardly, it is plain that the fuel for that flame had been exhausted, and that the precedent glimpsed in Asa Burton at the turn of the century had, further on, become routine. Although Tyler insisted that "moral necessity implied something more than simple certainty,"[13] Leonard Woods doubted whether moral necessity could be construed as meaning *more* than certainty. "All that we can say of men's dispositions of characters implies" nothing more than "that we can with more or less certainty predict what will be our feelings and actions on future occasions." To speak, for instance, of the necessity of depraved behavior in fallen men means simply *"that we can predict with certainty that it will in due time act itself out."*[14] In the same way, motives to sinful behavior acted on depraved men not as a cause (efficient *or* occasional) but as an "influence" that "induces" rather than guarantees certain results.

> God himself constantly makes use of motives or rational considerations to induce men to right actions. This constitutes the whole system of influence, employed by the inspired writers and by the ministers and of God

himself. Man is so formed as to be influenced to act by motives, and in no other way.[15]

To be sure, the results of such motives were *certain*—they would happen as though they were really necessary anyway—but without the sense of immediacy that necessity implied. As with Burton, the cause of men's sins could be attributed to the routine likelihood of certain behavioral features in men themselves.

No surprise, then that both Tyler and Woods also adopted the tripartite psychology of Taste that figured so prominently in Burton's *Essays.* Woods bluntly said that "it is a source of no small confusion in Edwards's Treatise on the Will, that he considers all the *affections* and *desires* as acts of the *will,"* and he found it strange that "it has been said by some that volition, or the act of the will, always controls the affections."[16] Woods instead appealed to "consciousness" to prove that "the will, instead of having any direct control of the affections, is itself controlled by them."[17] And the "Affection is excited, and from its very nature must be excited, by a suitable object present in the mind's view, not by an act of will soliciting or requiring."[18] Tyler emphatically agreed. "There are certain laws of mind by which all our mental operations are governed," Tyler explained: "the will is controlled by the affections," and every motion of the affections to control the will is in turn caused "when a material object is presented to one of our senses," producing a sensation "without any act of the will."[19] Thus, the faculties of understanding, affection, and will are acted upon by each other rather than acting together, and, as with Burton, they act in a set sequence that needs no divine intervention beyond the dangling of a motive in the path; and yet, the sequence follows through of its own inherent weight, and not because of a necessary connection between motive and willing.

But that, of course, was precisely the weak link that the Exercisers and the Old Calvinists had pressed on: Did God make Adam sin by his immediate agency? If so, are then men not puppets, suffering from a natural inability to do good? If not, is there really any meaning to the word *necessity* with reference to human action? It is one measure of the flaccidity of these later Edwardseans that, unable or unwilling to work out an answer, they sought refuge from the dilemma by a singularly un-Edwardsean appeal to *fact.* Tyler would only declare that divine agency is a "fact," and human responsibility is a "fact" too—"that we can not see *how* they are consistent, is no evidence against the truth of either."[20]

The appeal to the simple, a posteriori facts of sin and sovereignty was itself a signal of a sharp methodological departure from the confident assertiveness of Edwards's a priori reasoning. This insistence on *facts* as an invocation of philosophical cloture was indicative of the degree to which New England Edwardseans (outside of Emmons) had abandoned immaterialism as their intellectual foundation in favor of the more respectable "Baconian" empiricism of the "moral sense" philosophers. So it is again no surprise to discover the disturbing degree to which not only Burton but Tyler and Woods embraced intuition as the ultimate arbitrator. "Appeal directly," Woods encouraged his students, "to man's moral sense," for every man will find by consulting his moral sense that he is intuitively (if not logically) a free and responsible creature.

> These remarks disclose an important principle, namely: that *the feeling* of obligation is founded in the very constitution of the *human mind;* that it is an ultimate fact in our moral nature. And this is only saying, that God has made us moral and accountable creatures; that he has so formed us, that we are the proper subjects of law, and have an inward consciousness that obedience is our duty, and that disobedience is totally wrong and worthy of punishment.[21]

From there, Woods had nowhere else to go but further into the same amorphous libertarianism conceded by Alexander and Witherspoon. On those terms, Woods was ready to recognize a will, competent not only to mark out its own directions, but even to rearrange the moral disposition of the soul. The power to change our dispositions, said Woods, "is doubtless much greater than is commonly supposed." True, this power "is indirect and limited"—how could it not be when the consciousness could discover little of the existence of such underlying dispositions?—but all the same, Woods considered it "a well known fact, that some men by patient efforts acquire an ability to regulate their views and trains of thought in a manner quite above what others would consider practicable."[22]

The principal dissenter from this movement into "common sense" moralism was Edward Dorr Griffin, who with Enoch Pond (one of Emmons's last pupils) formed the last guard of the Exercisers. Griffin did not share Woods's confidence that "consciousness" can "extend farther than to intellectual and moral exercise" and discover the existence of that which may "*precede* action."[23] Griffin, to be sure, was willing to speak of the existence of a "temper," and even of a "heart" which "must be regarded as the seat of the feelings."[24] But by that, Griffin only meant what Emmons had meant, another species of exercise. The sinner's depravity of *heart* is merely "that *proneness to gratify himself,* growing out of the absence of love to God and the presence of self-love turned to selfishness." That which "constitutes the corrupt nature or temper" is simply "that *combination of inward circumstances* out of which will infallibly arise the exercises of selfishness and enmity against God." Accordingly, "the new nature" is not a new or renewed substance or heart, but new exercises; "not a new *existence,* but a new *relation* between the feelings towards self and towards God."[25]

Naturally this invited the predictable question: If we are nothing essentially but exercises upheld by an immediate divine agency, then how exactly did Adam or anyone else after him fall into sin? "How then can a holy being apostasize?" Griffin's answer, like that of his preceptor Emmons, was unflinching:

> Not until the heart ceases to be inclined to fall in with the motives which moved it before. That cessation cannot be produced by good motives, and before it takes place bad motives cannot operate. It cannot therefore be the effect of motives. It must result from some influence, or some withdrawment of influence, behind the scene. If it results from a positive influence, God must be the efficient cause of sin; if it results from the withdrawment of an influence, the influence withdrawn was that which before inclined the heart to holy action; and that is the very efficiency for which we plead. Without resorting to efficiency and its withdrawment, how can we account for the fall of holy beings?[26]

But if God is responsible for all human exercises, how then can there be freedom? At that, even Griffin hesitated, and, like Tyler and Woods, he shrugged his shoulders.

> It has been asked on our side, How can our faculties be constantly dependent and their operations forever dependent? There is nothing gained by anything delusive or by concealing any part of the truth. I admit therefore that the argument for divine efficiency involved in this question is not logical.[27]

Not to be logical: that for an Edwardsean was a significant concession, since so much of the argument of *Freedom of the Will* hung upon nice logical distinctions and connections between terms. Even for as sturdy an Exerciser as Griffin, the Edwardsean world had grown cold.

This shying away from the immediacy of Edwardsean voluntarism is evident not just on the theoretical level but even in the practical terms of Asahel Nettleton's revival preaching. In 1812 Nettleton, a Yale graduate (1805) and intimate friend of Tyler, commenced a circuit of itinerant revival preaching that produced the most striking series of "harvests" since the 1740s. He was the principal figure of the Second Great Awakening, and until typhoid fever permanently disabled him in 1822, he was the greatest revivalist Edwardseanism had ever produced; indeed, he was the revivalist for which Edwardseanism had always looked as a justification of its New Divinity. It is apparent from Nettleton's own writings that he took that responsibility so self-consciously that descriptions of his revivals are rhetorically patterned after Edwards's *Faithful Narrative,* right down to the case studies offered. But despite his unquestioned success, Nettleton relied for effect not on the shock tactics of the older New Divinity revivalism but on his uncanny skills as a casuist. His methods required quiet, not crisis, and instead of promoting anxiety, he preferred to defuse it.

> When prayer was ended and the people were standing, he made a very close application of the subject to their hearts, in a short address, which was very silently and solemnly heard. He requested them to retire without making a noise. "I love to talk to you, you are so still. It looks as though the Spirit of God were here. Go away as still as possible. Do not talk by the way, lest you forget your own hearts."[28]

This was a far cry from the awesome boisterousness of Bellamy or the arrogance of Stephen West. No wonder Heman Humphrey had to go out of his way to affirm that Nettleton was indeed "an Edwardean," and Gardiner Spring had to be careful, half a century later, to remind his readers that Nettleton was a genuinely Hopkinsian product.[29]

In sum, then, by the 1820s the third generation of Edwardseans had run out of uses and applications for *Freedom of the Will.* The enormous burst of creative development of the premises laid down in *Freedom of the Will* had spent itself by the 1820s, and the generation of Tyler, Woods, Nettleton, and Griffin had, by and large, settled for rearranging and restacking the ideas of their predecessors to fit a less hospitable time. And the fault lay not so much in the New Divinity, which (abstractly considered) still had sufficient energy to carry them along on its back, as in the inability of the New Divinity men to do more with it.

But beyond the diminished capacities of the New Divinity leadership, there was another reason why the New Divinity was beginning to falter, and that was the means by which it translated the Edwardsean legacy from one generation of divines to another. Beginning in the first decade of the nineteenth century, massive changes were taking place in the ways lawyers, physicians, and divines were being taught their functions. The teaching of those specialized kinds of marketable knowledge in law, in medicine, and in divinity which came to be known as the "professions" were slowly being transferred out of the law office, the doctor's parlor, or the pastor's study into the law school, the medical school, and the theological seminary. The number of medical schools in the United States, for instance, jumped from three in 1800 to thirty-five in 1840, while the number of medical school graduates leapt from fifty in 1810 to 2,923 in 1850.[30] Similarly, the Congregationalists, who had no formal "seminaries" at all in 1800, suddenly hurried to found Andover Theological Seminary (1808), Bangor Theological Seminary (1815), the Theological Department at Yale (1822), and the Harvard Divinity School (approximately 1819, since this is when the first full faculty of theology existed at Harvard; Divinity Hall was not dedicated until 1826). The Presbyterians also sponsored their own flurry of seminary building, and within twenty-five years they had founded Princeton Theological Seminary (1812), Auburn Theological Seminary (1818), Union Seminary in Richmond (1824), Western, or Allegheny, Theological Seminary (1827), Columbia Theological Seminary (1828), Lane Theological Seminary (1829) and Union Theological Seminary in New York City (1836).[31]

The advantages of this movement for the theologians were threefold: first, by creating a professional level of training in a specialized theological institution, the ministry preserved at least the semblance of being on the same professional plane as law and medicine. Second, enormous power was concentrated in the hands of a very few practitioners of the profession, allowing them to impose uniformity on theological studies and also to limit, through admission and graduation policies, the number of fellow practitioners—in a word, it limited the pool of available competition. Third, the seminaries helped generate demand for their own services by creating a marketplace. Or, to put it another way, concentrating the production of professional practitioners under one roof made it easier for consumers of professional theological services to do their shopping. A graduate from a certain law school immediately carried an easily identifiable code, so to speak, depending on the reputation of that school; and theological seminaries made it vastly easier for churches to recruit candidates from a supply of ideologically predictable clergy.

To this social reorganization of knowledge the New Divinity men remained strikingly indifferent, just as they had been indifferent to most other schemes of social reconstruction. But this indifference was, this time, to be their undoing, for the parlor seminaries of Emmons and Bellamy became, after 1808 and the founding of the first Congregational Seminary at Andover, their albatross. Unable to rival the new seminaries in output or respectability, the log colleges went the same way as cottage industries in New England, leaving the seminaries in monopolistic control of clerical education. It was the unhappy fate of the New Divinity, who had spurned every aspect of a church-in-society, to be undone by shifts in the socializing of education.

The Old Calvinists, by contrast, profited immensely from this shift. They might have been derivative, unoriginal, and manipulative, but by the 1820s so were the Edwardseans. On the other hand, the Old Calvinists were anything but indifferent to the wants and needs of an audience. Precisely because they preached a church-in-society, they had learned to adapt to the demands of change in society. Dedicated to dominating social situations rather than propagating doctrinal systematics, they had no difficulty in founding and then using institutions that would foster still further domination.

What happened in the founding of Andover Seminary is the best example of how the Old Calvinists regained much of what they had lost to Edwardseanism, and did it not by outthinking them but by outmaneuvering them.[32] The story of Andover Seminary, simply put, begins with the capture of the Hollis Professorship of Divinity at Harvard by the Unitarian Henry Ware in 1805, a capture that, in symbolic terms, meant the seizure by heterodoxy of a system of clergy education that had stood intact for almost two centuries in New England. Previously the Hollis chair had been routinely filled by Old Calvinists, and although that did not enchant the Edwardseans, an Old Calvinist was the best they could expect at Harvard, and at least a man like David Tappan, who occupied the Hollis chair until his death in 1803, was far from an outright heretic. Ware the Unitarian was, and his election to the chair sent a tremor of alarm through New England.

Samuel Spring proposed, as a counter-measure, to organize a theological academy at either Franklin or West Newbury, Massachusetts, with his brother-in-law Emmons as instructor of theology. The proposal met with characteristically small response from Spring's fellow Hopkinsians, and might have gone for nothing had not the Old Calvinist Jedidiah Morse offered a counterproposal. Suggesting that Unitarianism represented a threat sufficiently vast to entice the New Divinity men out of their shells and into an alliance with Old Calvinism, Morse urged Spring to join him in founding a school in which both orthodox factions could jointly repel an infidel threat they could not repulse separately. Spring was at first hesitant to unite with those "who will not give up the half-way covenant, and are forever pleading for the duty which pertains to the BEST actions of sinners," but by degrees he warmed to the plan. Even though Morse insisted that someone less notorious than Emmons would have to be chosen as the professor of theology and a site less notorious than Franklin found, Spring was soothed by assurances that another Hopkinsian would be selected for the post, and that subsequent faculty appointments would always be neatly balanced between Old Calvinists and New Divinity men. Presumably, New Divinity money and Hopkinsian students would never be diverted or decoyed into other channels. Hence, when the new school opened in Andover, Massachusetts, in 1808, the professorship of theology went to Leonard Woods, the pastor of West Newbury and pupil of Emmons, while the professorship of biblical literature went to Moses Stuart, the protégé and successor of James Dana at the Center Church in New Haven.

This relationship, as Emmons had predicted, did not work nearly as well as Spring had envisioned (one Old Calvinist chuckled over the Andover graduate whose "sermon was all confusion—sometimes directing to repent, and sometimes to read and pray, in order to prepare for repentance"). Woods proved to be a bruised reed, and seemed every year to move further away from Emmons into a fuzzy amalgam of Edwardseanism and Scottish philosophy. The one undoubted Exerciser to join the faculty, Edward Dorr Griffin, lasted only two years as professor of pulpit eloquence, from 1809 to 1811, before moving on to the Park Street Church in Boston. And then, as Emmons had also predicted, once Samuel Spring had been removed by death in 1819, the Old Calvinist trustees felt free to stack the faculty with men of their own stripe. Emmons "apprehended that Hopkinsians, thus amalgamated with those whom they looked upon as Moderate Calvinists, would lose their distinctive character, so that the Hopkinsian party would after a time be extinct," and, Cassandralike, he was only too right.

But even Emmons could not disenchant the Hopkinsians from the aura of legitimacy that a seminary, or a seminary education, displayed. By successfully inveigling the New Divinity men to cooperate in the foundation of Andover, and then smothering them once they were inside, the Old Calvinists captured for their own use what became the sole institution for educating and legitimizing future clergymen in Massachusetts. Nor did the process of cooptation end there. In 1808 Morse and Spring also arranged the merger of the only New Divinity magazine, the *Massachusetts Missionary Magazine,* with Morse's *Panoplist*—and with similar results.[33] To Emmons's horror, and over his vehement opposition, Morse also succeeded in engineering the creation of a General Association of Congregationalists in Massachusetts, and although between 1806 and 1811 Morse was able to persuade only half the local Congregational associations to participate, that was bad enough to Emmons, who looked upon his own local Mendon (Massachusetts) Association with suspicion as trampling on the separate autonomy of individual congregations. By 1822, when Old Calvinists in Connecticut imitated the Andover seminary by establishing a divinity school at Yale, the New Divinity influence had been so diminished that no similar offer to cooperate was ever made.[34]

This resurgence of Old Calvinism was built upon more than just the cooptation of theological education. Even more serious was the appropriation by Old Calvinism of the figure of Edwards himself, a process which in some sense had been going for some time, but which became a major strategy at Yale under the aegis of Timothy Dwight between 1795 and 1817. Although Old Calvinism had never exactly disinherited Edwards, it had also issued severe and sustained criticisms of him, and a major rehabilitation of Edwards's reputation would seem a fairly tall order. But, for one thing, Old Calvinism had only ever needed to appropriate Edwards's piety, practical devotion, and preaching, not his doctrines; and, for another, Old Calvinism had in Timothy Dwight precisely the agent best suited to bring such an appropriation to pass. Indeed, the passage of Timothy Dwight out of Edwardseanism and into Old Calvinism is indicative, first, that the problems Congregational orthodoxy had to confront after the Revolution were greater than those posed in Edwards's day by polite Arminianism, and second, that the Edwardsean formula for volition would not only fail to drive men back to God, but would in the new circumstances of republican America actually open Congregationalism to infidelity.

Dwight certainly started off with all the credentials a legitimate Edwardsean could want: the grandson of Edwards and student of his uncle, Edwards the Younger, Dwight had been marked by Ezra Stiles in 1787 as one of the would-be Luthers seeking to seize preeminence among the New Divinity. The young Dwight wore his Edwardsean connections proudly enough. His anti-Old Calvinist satire, *The Triumph of Infidelity,* lauded his grandfather as "That moral Newton/And that second Paul," and in the same year that Stiles figured him for an Edwardsean, Dwight had announced that he "had as lieve communicate with all the devils in Hell as with that corrupt Church" of Northampton, then presided over by the Old Calvinist Solomon Williams.[35] Dwight also had carved out such a brilliant reputation for himself as a tutor at Yale in the 1770s that there had been talk of installing him rather than Stiles as president of Yale—talk Stiles darkly attributed to the Connecticut New Divinity men. In any event, Stiles won the presidency and Dwight resigned his tutorship, and a very promising career seemed to have gone up in smoke.[36]

Over the next two decades, Dwight survived both an external and an internal revolution. Buffeted by personal and family reverses, disappointed that the American Revolution had only opened up "strong temptations, for the sacrifice of integrity at elections, for caballing, bribery, faction, private ambition, bold contentions for place and power, and that civil discord, which is naturally accompanied by the prostration of Morality and Religion," and softened by the twelve tranquil years he spent as pastor of the Connecticut village of Greenfield, Dwight lost his taste for separatism and theological acrimony.[37] The man who had once refused to commune with Old Calvinists, and who was now granting that even a Papist could be a true Christian, had found that there were other, more ominous, dangers to worry about than sinners using the means of grace.

When at last Dwight returned to Yale triumphant in 1795 as Stiles's successor, he was less afraid of unregenerate doings than of the incursions made by French deism, infidelity, and atheism, and Dwight's ideological delousing of Yale in the 1790s has since become a piece of American folklore. He was also less afraid of the utility of a church-in-society, and of the organic unity of a covenantal community. He had seen in Greenfield the very real benefits yielded by parish nurture, and the equally enjoyable rewards of a parish which, if it could not be pure, could at least be decent. In "Farmer Johnson's Political Catechism," Dwight framed a question that his Edwardsean preceptors would not have dreamed of asking:

> Q. How does religion make a man useful to his fellow?
>
> A. By rendering him just, sincere, faithful, kind and public-spirited, from principle. It induces him voluntarily, and always, to perform faithfully in the several duties of social life. . . . All the real good of society springs from the performance of these duties, and cannot exist without them.[38]

Moreover, Dwight had also had a good look at just who was most strenuously advocating the separation of church and community, and it was not always the New Divinity purists. The come-outerism of the New Divinity, however well-intentioned, was playing into the hands of the atheists, the Jacobins, and the Jeffersonians, who sought to divide church from society in the interests of conquering both. Old Calvinism might have sunk its roots into the base earth of social impurity, but at least those roots would hold the society together as a covenantal unit against the erosion of infidelity, and for Dwight that was no small achievement. "From the intimate and inseparable connection between morality and religion," Dwight advised Yale seniors, "arises a most manifest necessity of religion for a nation."[39]

Hence, Dwight threw himself into the struggle to preserve Connecticut's church establishment. He campaigned vigorously to continue public support of the ministry ("Where will you get your ministers if you do not support them by law?") and scorned as unworthy and even suspicious the Baptists' plea of conscientious objection to church taxes ("those who do not wish to avail themselves personally of the direct benefits of religion, might as well plead an exemption from the support of roads, bridges, . . . because they do not use them, as excuse themselves from the support of the public preaching of the Gospel").[40]

Ironically, by the time Dwight took up his cudgels on behalf of the establishment, not all that much remained of it. Connecticut had been forced since 1727 to grant equal support to the Anglicans, and the Act of Toleration had extended public support to all Protestant churches in proportion to their membership. In 1792 Stiles had been forced to allow laymen onto the Yale Corporation in order to get state aid for the college; in 1793 a proposal to divert money from the sale of Connecticut's land claims in Ohio to the support of the ministry went down to humiliating defeat; and in 1795 the control of Connecticut's schools was passed from the ministers to lay societies. But Dwight was arguing for a principle, and against the individualism not only of the Republicans in the state but of the New Divinity in the churches. No lasting union, he warned, had ever been founded on the voluntarism of the naturally able.

> Government, since the days of *Mr. Locke,* has been extensively supposed *to be founded in the Social Compact.* No opinion is more groundless than this. . . . It supposes, that they entered into grave and philosophic deliberations; individually consented to be bound by the will of the majority; and cheerfully gave up the wild life of savage liberty, for restraints, which however necessary and useful, no savage could ever brook for a day.[41]

Having unshackled himself from one of the principal corollaries of the New Divinity, he began to work backward, piece by piece, to the theory of will at the New Divinity's core. As he went, Dwight's new persona as an ex-Edwardsean did not escape attention. In Hartford, one wit sarcastically contrasted the two Dwights, new and old:

> A minister of the Gospel, who ought to be an example to all men, sets at his desk in 1788, hates Yale College, hates Doctors [James] Dana and [Charles] Chauncy—is in contest with most of his brethren—hates sin and Pinckney, and a thousand more conscious men, puts it all into rhyme—issues it without his name—attacks without mercy men, who had been gaining fair characters before he was born. In 1800 is a President of a College, ay the head of a corporation of which his *milky Preacher* [i.e., James Dana] in the above poem is a member—is in high favor with the Clergy, and begins to rebuild the waste of character made by his indignant pen—and first foremost hails his former *hackney coachman of whores* as a pious man and real christian.[42]

And Dwight, for his part, candidly admitted that he was no longer the would-be Luther of Hopkinsianism. James Patriot Wilson, the Philadelphia Hopkinsian, was told by Dwight "that there were no Hopkinsians among them at Yale."[43] To John Ryland, one of Hopkins's English Baptist correspondents, Dwight declared in 1805, "I am not a

Hopkinsian. . . . Their Systems I know, but do not believe; I think some of them [are] in danger of injuring seriously, the faith once delivered to the Saints."[44]

At Yale the principal evidence behind these declarations—and one which Dwight was the first to offer—was his repudiation of the rhetorical tactics of New Divinity voluntarism (Archibald Alexander had it repeatedly drawn to his attention in 1802 that Dwight "drew back from the opinion that God is the author of sin, and also from making a willingness to be damned a sign of grace") and especially his advocacy of the "use of means."[45] "The kingdom of God, as established by his pleasure, is a kingdom of means, regularly connected with their ends," Dwight wrote.[46] In passages reminiscent of Moses Hemmenway and Moses Mather—and it is incidentally of significance that Dwight's four-volume *Travels in New England and New York* makes no mention of New Divinity preachers, but reserves high praise for Moses Mather and other Old Calvinists—Dwight argued that the Old Testament afforded plenteous examples of the covenantal necessity of unregenerate doings.

> God required *Moses* to command all sinners, of that nation, to labour; to cultivate their own ground; to circumcise their children; to celebrate the passover; to offer sacrifices; to be present at the public worship of God; to hear and learn his word from the mouth of their priests; and to teach all these things to their children. It will not, I presume, be questioned that Moses, in enjoining these things upon sinful *Israelites,* as well upon the virtuous ones, acted lawfully; or, in other words, was guilty of no sin. But what was lawful for *Moses,* in this case, is in itself lawful. Accordingly, it was lawfully done by all the Ministers, who followed him in the *Jewish* Church. It cannot therefore fail to be lawful to Christian Ministers, unless it has been plainly forbidden.[47]

And when an objector tried to fasten a logical inference on him—*"Do not sinners grow worse under convictions of Conscience, and in the use of Means?"*—Dwight impatiently dismissed the question as being beyond the experience of mortals to answer. "I am ignorant; and shall remain so, until I can search the heart, and measure the degrees of depravity."[48] The Hopkinsian students at Yale—among whom were Nettleton and Tyler—shook their heads in disbelief to hear Dwight preach so. Nettleton, who had come to Yale with Edwards's writings as his Gospel, and with Exercisers like Spring, West, and Samuel Whitman as his authorities, usually sat and listened to Dwight "without hesitation," but "on this point he differed from him, as did also a large part of the pious in New England."[49]

But Dwight was prepared to shock the pious still further, for, long before Nettleton heard those utterances from the pulpit of the Yale chapel, Dwight had stabbed even deeper at the heart of Edwardseanism. His encounter with David Hume (albeit secondhand, in the pages of Bishop George Horne) had convinced him that Hume's notion of causality was a sure ticket to atheism.

Mr. Hume declares,

> That there is no perceptible connection between cause and effect;

> That the belief of such connection is merely a matter of custom;

> That experience can show us no such connection;

> That we cannot with any reason conclude, that, because an effect has taken place once, it will take place again.[50]

But how different was this from Emmons? or Hopkins? or even Edwards himself on consciousness? Like James Dana thirty years before, Dwight concluded that "the Theology of a part of this country appears to me to be verging, insensibly perhaps, to those who are chiefly concerned, but with no very gradual step, towards a *Pantheism,* differing materially, in one particular only, from that of *Spinosa.*" In reaction, Dwight insisted that, by *cause,* "it will be observed, that I am speaking of what is called *the efficient cause*" and he denied as "totally erroneous" the "assertion" of "Mr. Hume . . . that *the connection between cause and effect exists,* or rather *is perceived, only in the Names.*"[51] In rejecting that, Dwight had shaken not only the New Divinity but the whole premise upon which the argument from moral and natural necessity was built.

His equation of Hume with Emmons eliminated any possibility of further interest in the Exercise scheme. *"That God by an immediate agency of his own, creates the sinful volitions of mankind,* is a doctrine, not warranted, in my view, either by Reason, or Revelation."[52] But he found little solace in the Taste scheme, not only because "the existence of the substratum itself cannot be proved," but principally because of the recurring problem the Tasters always had of explaining how, granting the existence of a *fixed* nature, and granting that Adam's fixed nature had been fixed as a *holy* one, Adam could possibly have committed sin—apart from the direct agency of God so beloved of the Exercisers.[53] This forced a not-entirely-willing Dwight to two conclusions. Unable to embrace either of the Edwardsean alternatives, Dwight first sought refuge from explanation by claiming metaphysical ignorance. "The nature of the cause itself, and the nature and manner of its efficiency, are in most instances, too subtle, or too entirely hidden from our view, either to be perceived at all, or to be so perceived, as to become the materials of real and useful knowledge."[54] When he spoke of nature, he meant only

> a state of mind, generally existing, out of which holy volitions may, in one case, be fairly expected to arise and sinful ones, in another. . . . From these, we learn that it is not so powerful, nor so unchangeable, as to incline the mind, in which it exists so strongly to holiness, as to prevent it absolutely from acting in a holy manner.[55]

Once the Edwardsean causality went, the absolutism went with it, and after that one could speak only of certainties and fair expectations rather than moral necessities.

Secondly, and almost inevitably, Dwight began to alter his grandfather's fundamental doctrine of the will's freedom.

This process can be glimpsed in the organization of Dwight's Yale sermons (published in 1818-1819 in five volumes as a systematic theology), for, as Leon Howard noted in 1943, the published volumes contain more sermons than Dwight actually preached, and probably include sermons from the Greenfield days that did not fit into the Yale school calendar and were not revised.[56] Hence one can find Dwight assuring an audience at one point that God "certainly *will,* and *man* certainly *will not, be the Efficient.*" But in other sermons Dwight adjusts this to read, "Such a change then, as Regeneration or Renovation, exists in man, and is produced by the power of the Holy Ghost; yet is as truly active and voluntary in this change, as in any other conduct."[57] And to fend off criticism, he, too, invoked mystery:

> Many questions may indeed be started concerning the nature and extent of the agency of the Holy Ghost in our renovation, our own agency, and the consistency of these doctrines; which may perplex the authors of them and their readers, and which may never be answered to their satisfaction. Still it will be exactly true, and highly important to us, that we must be born again; and that by the power of the Holy Ghost, exerted in co-incidence with our own agency; whether we do, or do not know any more of the subject than Nicodemus himself knew.[58]

As time went by, Dwight professed even more uncertainty about what went on in volition: "Concerning the Will, we are still more in the dark" and "have not yet determined in what Moral Obligation consists; or how far it extends: nor are we agreed concerning the nature of sin, or its guilt; or concerning the merit of virtue." Indeed, Dwight added, "we understand imperfectly the very *Reason,* by which we make discoveries."[59]

Dwight's disavowals of reason's capacity to explain volition, however much they express his humility, were also his excuse for falling back upon intuition as the primary evidence of freedom. "Men are intuitively conscious of their own free agency, being irresistably sensible, that they act spontaneously, and without any co-ercion or constraint."[60] Motives disappear from discussion, as does connection; and a vocabulary, if not the substance, of self-determination takes their place.

> The certainty, perceived by mere mental inspection, that the changes passing in my own mind are produced by my own active power, is a higher certainty, than that, with which I perceive any other changes to be accomplished by any other active power. . . . Besides, if *we* are not agents, or active causes, possessing active powers, by which we can originate certain changes in the state of things, but are mere chains of ideas and exercises, it will be difficult to assign a reason, why GOD is not, also, a mere chain of ideas and exercises.[61]

Where Dwight talked about motives, it was not in connection with volition, but divine Providence. God's rule of the universe is a moral government, and "a moral government is founded by motives."[62] But what Dwight meant by motives in this sense was not that which the "will was as,"

but an "influence"—and, since he had confined causality to efficiency, influence could only hope to induce certainty indirectly rather than by absolute connection.

> It will not be pretended, that all extraneous influence on the mind destroys its freedom. *We* act upon the minds of each other, and often with complete efficacy; yet it will not be said, that we destroy each other's freedom of acting. God, for aught that appears, may act, also, on our minds, and with an influence, which shall be decisive; and yet not destroy, nor even lessen, our freedom.[63]

But Timothy Dwight's greatest gift to Old Calvinism was his ancestry. Old Calvinism had always, in a general way, wanted to make Edwards out to be one of them, both to embarrass the Hopkinsians and to drape themselves in his reputation. Dwight, the grandson of Edwards and student of Edwardseanism, now made that possible. He never explicitly repudiated his famous grandfather, and indeed was fond of insisting that he was entirely in harmony with the Edwardseans on such issues as the atonement and imputation. He showed, in fact, what James Dana had not been able to show, that one did not have to be an Edwardsean and subscribe to *Freedom of the Will* to claim legitimate descent from Edwards. Dwight further legitimized this conclusion by aggressively promoting that ultimate imprimatur of Edwardseanism—the revival—three times during his tenure at Yale, in 1802, 1808, and 1813.[64]

Relying on the unquestionable authority of his lineage—no small matter, that; Samuel Spring had risked his life under British fire at Quebec to rescue another Edwards grandson, the scapegrace Aaron Burr—and on his position at Yale, Dwight in effect retouched Edwards as a respectable Old Calvinist. Old Calvinists would not hesitate thereafter to publicly denominate themselves as Edwards's heirs, even while they privately muttered criticisms into their notebooks. The New Divinity men, having nothing in their leadership to match "Pope" Dwight, were at the same time often drawn into the bargain, and the wavering and hesitating we hear from pristine Edwardseanism, on the part of Tyler and Woods, owes as much to Dwight's influence (in the cases of Tyler and Nettleton, direct influence) as to their own defects as creative thinkers.

If Dwight was responsible for the cooptation of the New Divinity's theology, it was Lyman Beecher who was most responsible for similarly coopting the New Divinity's revivalism. Beecher has emerged as the most famous of Dwight's students at Yale, and it is in fact to Beecher that we owe the famous account of Dwight's cleansing-of-the-temple at Yale in 1797. Beecher adored Dwight as "second only to St. Paul" (thereby bumping Edwards from the niche Dwight had accorded him) and "loved him as my own soul"—which, considering Beecher's capacity for self-esteem, is saying a great deal.[65] Dwight apparently returned some of the sentiment, for (according to Beecher) Dwight "loved me as a son," and seems to have been the moving force in getting Beecher translated from his first church on Long Island (ironically, this was the old church where David Brainerd had once candidated and where Samuel Buell had spent a half century as incumbent) to the strategic pulpit of Litchfield, Connecticut (which had been vacated by the New Divinity man Abraham Fowler. Thus did Beecher become an apostle of Yale to the fiefdom of Joseph Bellamy).[66] Dwight had picked his man with the precision of moral necessity, for the substance of Beecher's entire colorful career was a dedication to preserving the power and place of the church-in-society. Like Dwight, Beecher was less concerned about picking out the pure within the church than about trying to keep the church from being displaced by infidel forces from without. For Dwight in the 1790s it had been French atheism; for Beecher in the 1810s it was the Unitarians.[67] For Dwight and Beecher alike, the disestablishment of orthodoxy was a cultural and personal disaster. "We shall become slaves," Beecher warned, "and slaves to the worst of masters." And when, a year after Dwight's death, a coalition of dissenting sects and secular politicians (including Edwards's youngest son, the irreligious lawyer Pierpont Edwards) succeeded in terminating Connecticut's public support of the ministry, Beecher sat "on one of the old-fashioned, rush-bottomed kitchen chairs, his head drooping on his breast, and his arms hanging down," moaning, "THE CHURCH OF GOD."[68]

Like Dwight again, Beecher regarded the purism of the New Divinity men as a dangerous luxury in the face of such threatening enemies. As one of Dwight's postcollegiate theology students at Yale, Beecher "read Hopkins's Divinity, but did not take him implicitly," and forty years later Beecher was still assuring audiences that "the doctrine for which I contend is not new divinity, but old Calvinism."[69] Like so many others, Beecher stumbled at the problem of how Adam's sinless nature could have been changed into a sinful one without either God being immediately responsible or Adam being responsible through self-determination. He spurned Emmons, as he wrote to his daughter Catharine (who was then sitting under Emmons's preaching), because he could not accept Emmons's reduction of consciousness to a chain of ideas.[70] Rejecting Emmons and the Exercisers, he had hardly more time for the Tasters, and he judged them guilty of the very natural inability they sought to escape. If God

> could command a change of moral tastes or instincts which are a part of the soul's created constitution, upon which the will cannot act but which do themselves govern the will, as absolutely as the helm governs the ship; then also the things required would be a natural impossibility, and could not be reconciled with free agency and accountability.[71]

More troubling for Beecher than the problem of how Adam could be condemned for a sinful nature he didn't create was how infants who died in infancy could also be thus damned. The problems are really not all that different—in essence, both ask how that which is innocent can be made out to be guilty when it is agreed that the innocent are not actually able to make themselves guilty. And Beecher was hardly the first to put the problem in those terms; Emmons

had done it in one of his most horrific sermons, with the predictable conclusion that God made infants, as he had made Adam, put forth sinful exercises. But by the 1820s it had become routine for the critics of Edwardseanism to replace the abstract person of Adam with the more painfully familiar image of dying infants, probably because a nineteenth-century imagination which might not have balked at consenting to the dispatch of Adam or Aaron Burr to perdition was sentimentally revolted at consigning what was now perceived as an inoffensive infant to the eternal flames.

Beecher's solution was to rewrite the meaning of "depraved nature" as it applied to infants—and, presumably, to Adam. As early as January 1822 Beecher confided, "For some time past, I have noticed a leaning of my mind to *heresy* on this long-disputed and very difficult topic."[72] In March 1825 he spelled out what he meant in a letter to Asahel Hooker (Bennet Tyler's old theological teacher) in which Beecher, with what would once again prove to be something less than originality, proposed that the concept of a *nature* in infants be retained, and even that this *nature* be regarded as the *certain* cause of sin, but without regarding that *nature* as itself sinful or sin as ever more than the *certain* result of it. Like Dwight, he did not try to pretend that the way out of the dilemma of the cause of sin was to redefine causality. Beecher could not but believe that causality was efficiency. But he could redefine what the agent of that efficiency was like, and so he did. As he explained to Hooker,

> That nature in infants which is the ground of the certainty that they will be totally, actually depraved as soon as they are capable of accountable action—which renders actual sin certain, I call a depraved nature; and yet I do not mean by 'depraved nature' the same exactly which I mean by the term as applied to the accountable sinful exercises of the hearts of adult men. Nor does Edwards or Bellamy. Edwards calls it 'a prevailing effectual tendency in their nature' to that sin which brings wrath and eternal undoing; but he does not consider it as being sin in itself considered, in such a sense as to deserve punishment.[73]

Of course it was perfectly possible, as Emmons had done, to set the moment of accountable, and certainly sinful, action so close to birth as to make negligible the difference between becoming a sinner and being born that way. But it was the principle of the idea that Beecher enjoyed: no one was born sinful, nor was their subsequent sinning the exercise of God.

And what role did Beecher now propose to ascribe to the will, since action now took place apart from the control of either God or nature? That would be easier to say if Beecher had been a systematic theologian; as it was, Beecher's intellect revolved around two poles only. "If I understand my own mode of philosophizing, it is the Baconian," he declared. "Facts and the Bible are the extent of my philosophy."[74] But even that is a revelation of Beecher's affection for the Scottish philosophy, and his comments in the 1830s indicate his predilection toward the Scots' intuitive libertarianism.

> Of nothing are men more thoroughly informed, or more competent to judge unerringly, than in respect to their mode of voluntary action, as coerced or free. . . . Our consciousness of the mode of mental action in choice, as uncoerced and free, equals our consciousness of existence itself; and the man who doubts either, gives indication of needing medical treatment instead of argument. . . . There is a deep and universal consciousness in all men as to their freedom of choice; and in denying this, you reverse God's constitution of man.[75]

Of course, Beecher did not propose to grant to the will "complete exemption from any kind or degree of influence from without." But for him, *influence* was as strong a word as he would use to describe the action of motives. When Beecher spoke of "God's government" as "a moral government, by motive and not by force," he had really come to think in terms of human, republican government, not moral necessity, to explain God's divine sovereignty over men.[76] God's will was manifested in terms of incentives, not decrees; of coaxings, not commands.

> What is family government, what is civil government, what is temptation, exhortation, or persuasion; what are the influences of the Holy Spirit, but the means, and the effectual means of influencing the exercises of the human heart, and the conduct of human life? . . . Natural government is direct, irresistable impulse. Moral government is persuasion; and the result of it is voluntary action in the view of motives. . . . The influence of motives cannot destroy free agency; for it is the influence of persuasion only, and results only in choice, which, in the presence of understanding and conscience, is free agency.[77]

At this point, with causality confined to efficiency, and efficiency reduced to producing certainty rather than necessity, Beecher had crossed the boundary separating Edwardsean reconciliationism from the foothills of libertarianism.

But in all this, Beecher was merely partaking of Dwight's new-fashioned Old Calvinism, and his invocation of Edwards and Bellamy in the letter on infant depravity is an indication of the degree to which the image of Edwards was being successfully coopted by Old Calvinism. Like Dwight, Beecher embraced the Edwardsean doctrine of the atonement. Once more one finds the explanation of the atonement as a justification of moral government:

> The gospel is not, as some have imagined, an expedient to set aside a holy, just, and good law, in order to sustain an inferior one, brought down more nearly to the depraved inclinations of men. God did not send his Son, to betray his government, and compromise with rebels, by repealing the law which offended them. He sent his Son, to vindicate and establish this law, to redeem mankind from the curse, and to bring them back to the obedience of the same law from which they had revolted.[78]

Extending that still further, Beecher consistently draped himself in a vocabulary which, on the surface, implied his solidarity with *Freedom of the Will.* "From Augustine to Edwards, and from Edwards to this day, the ability of man, as a free agent, has been taught as consisting in a biased and perverted will," Beecher told the students at Andover, thus neatly blocking himself in with Edwards; and to western Presbyterians, Beecher submitted a bewildering reading list when he wrote, "the authors which contributed to form and settle my faith, were Edwards, Bellamy, Witherspoon, Dwight and [Andrew] Fuller."[79]

But Beecher, more an organizer than a thinker, aimed less at coopting Edwardsean ideas than at coopting New Divinity activism—in this case, revivals. "It has already been made apparent," his son Edward explained, "that the one idea of Dr. Beecher was the promotion of revivals of religion, not merely in his own congregation, but as a prominent instrumentality for the conversion of the world, and the speedy introduction of the millenial reign of our Lord Jesus Christ."[80] As early as 1809 Beecher was stimulating revival on Long Island, and in 1822 in Litchfield, even as he was doubting infant depravity, Horace Mann (who had spent his youth writhing under Emmons's sermons in Franklin) heard Beecher preach a particularly *"hopkinsian"* revival, perhaps made all the more so by Beecher's use of Asahel Nettleton on the spot as his revivalistic coadjutor.[81]

The mention of Nettleton in conjunction with Beecher points to the fact that Beecher coopted not only New Divinity revivalism but also the revivalists themselves. It is significant that the recognition Nettleton enjoyed in New England as a revivalist did not begin until 1813, when Beecher invited Nettleton to come and preach in the Litchfield area, and thereafter much of Nettleton's career was centered in Litchfield County, probably under Beecher's management and perhaps for the purpose of deflecting criticism from Beecher in the old Bellamy territory. When Nettleton came to New Haven and preached his greatest revival at Yale College in 1820, he did so in the company of Lyman Beecher. Nettleton would afterwards deeply resent the implication that he was nothing but Beecher's man, but others believed it, and in 1827 Charles Grandison Finney would interpret Nettleton's actions at the New Lebanon Conference as those of a stalking horse for Beecher.

Charles Grandison Finney affords yet another and more striking example of Beecher's ability to manipulate the later Hopkinsians. Although Finney is unquestionably the best known of all nineteenth-century revivalists, he is more often interpreted as an expression of Jacksonian America than of Edwardsean New England, and yet it is only against the backdrop of the latter that his career has any real meaning. We know little about his early religious training, and not much more about him at all before 1818, except that he was born in Warren, Connecticut, in 1792, moved with his parents to upstate New York in 1794, and undertook a brief stint as a schoolteacher back in Connecticut after 1810. He began to be noticed only after his return to Adams, New York, in 1818, where he studied law and where, in 1821, he experienced a violent conversion that impelled him to leave the law and become an itinerant evangelist.

Finney liked to think of himself as self-taught, but it soon became obvious that, wherever his ideas had come from, they had a strong Hopkinsian tinge:

> Soon after I was converted I called on my pastor, and had a long conversation with him on the atonement. He was a Princeton student, and of course held the limited view of the atonement—that it was made for the elect and available to none else. Our conversation lasted nearly half a day. He held that Jesus suffered for the elect the literal penalty of the Divine law; that he suffered just what was due to each of the elect on the score of retributive justice. I objected that this was absurd . . . on the contrary it seemed to me that Jesus only satisfied public justice, and that that was all that the government of God could require. . . . I asked him if the Bible did not require all who hear the gospel to repent, believe the Gospel, and be saved. He admitted that it did require all to believe and be saved. But how could they believe and accept a salvation which was not provided for them?[82]

And for the next six years he preached what sounded very much like the New Divinity:

> Instead of telling sinners to use the means of grace and pray for a new heart, we called on them to make themselves a new heart and a new spirit, and pressed the duty of instant surrender to God. . . . We taught them that while they were praying for the Holy Spirit, they were constantly resisting him; and that if they would once yield to their own convictions of duty, they would be Christians. We tried to show them that every thing they did or said before they had submitted, believed, given their hearts to God, was all sin, was not that which God required them to do, but was simply deferring repentance and resisting the Holy Ghost.[83]

Indeed, for one who claimed to be sui generis, Finney showed marked resemblances to the Exercisers. "I assumed that moral depravity is, and must be, a voluntary attitude of the mind," Finney remembered, and in his first published sermon he defined the *"spiritual heart"* as a *deepseated but voluntary preference of the mind,"* and regeneration as a change in "that abiding preference of our minds, which prefers sin to holiness."[84] A far from friendly observer, James Waddel Alexander, heard the same things from Finney in New York in 1837, and likewise concluded that Finney's sermon was "an odious caricature of old Hopkinsian divinity."

How did Finney come by these ideas? Perhaps they came from his Connecticut-born parents, perhaps from others in that flood of immigrants from New England into upstate New York in the 1790s that turned the area into a virtual Yankee colony; perhaps it was his own sojourn as a teacher in New England—whatever the source, the New Divinity

element in his preaching struck a sympathetic note among the New England immigrants in New York, and that sympathy accounts for much of his fabulous success as a revivalist there. What must also go into the calculus of his success was the brazen impudence of his manner.

> They used to complain that I let down the dignity of the pulpit; that I was a disgrace to the ministerial profession; that I talked to the people in a colloquial manner; that I said "you," instead of preaching about sin and sinners, and saying "they"; that I said "hell," and with such emphasis as often to shock the people; furthermore, that I urged the people with such vehemence, as if they might not have a moment to live; and sometimes they complained that I blamed the people too much. One doctor of divinity told me that he felt a great deal more like weeping over sinners, than blaming them. I replied that I did not wonder, if he believed that they had a sinful nature, and that sin was entailed upon them, and that they could not help it.[85]

But even these criticisms were nothing new to the Hopkinsian past, and the very things had once been said of Emmons, and with perhaps the same savage retort. Indeed, Finney's most heavily criticized innovation—calling convicted sinners to come forward to an "anxious bench"—was itself merely Finney's way of calling attention to the fact that the sinner had full natural ability to perform any of the duties of repentance.

Those innovations irritated Asahel Nettleton, and when Nettleton met Finney in Albany in 1826, he was appalled not only by Finney's loudmouthed mannerisms but also that Finney had been using Nettleton's name as sanction for them. Incensed, Nettleton called on Beecher to join him in denouncing Finney as an enthusiastic fraud; Beecher, knowing of Finney only from what Nettleton told him, and not wishing to see his condominium with the Hopkinsians wrecked by an upstart New Divinity fireball, joined Nettleton in issuing a booklet containing several letters condemning Finney's "new measures." Finney's lieutenants (and probably Finney himself, though he later denied it) were alarmed at this damaging rebuff. They approached Beecher to achieve a compromise (which says something about perceptions of the relationship of Beecher and Nettleton), and a meeting of New Englanders and New Yorkers was arranged for New Lebanon, New York, in June 1827.[86]

It has to be emphasized that the New Lebanon Conference, much as it has been misdescribed by Perry Miller and others, was not a doctrinal confrontation between young, anti-intellectual, Jacksonian semi-Pelagians and old, crabbed, Tory Calvinists. Calvinism in fact never came up for debate, principally because all in attendance—including Finney—considered themselves in one way or another Calvinists.[87] It was basically an argument about methods in revivals, and it cannot be said even to have accomplished much about that, since the conference broke up with Beecher threatening Finney,

Finney, I know your plan, and you know I do; you mean to come to Connecticut, and carry a streak of fire to Boston. But if you attempt it, as the Lord liveth, I'll meet you at the state line, and call out all the artillery men, and fight every inch of the way to Boston, and then I'll fight you there.[88]

The real significance of the conference lies in what happened to Nettleton. He had been prostrated by typhus in 1822, a disease that terminated his active career and left him a semi-invalid until his death in 1844. He had not wanted to come to the New Lebanon Conference, regarding advice as a mercy wasted on the likes of Finney. At Beecher's urging, he attended anyway, and regretted it, for he must have made a poor comparison to the vigor of Finney. Was that comparison apparent to Beecher? Something close to it must have been, for a year later Beecher hurried to Philadelphia to make his peace with Finney, and in 1831, far from stopping Finney at the state line, Beecher invited him to Boston to preach in his own pulpit.

The conclusion is obvious but unpleasant: Nettleton's enfeebled constitution left Beecher without a reliable revivalist to employ; Finney, although rough around the edges, was no less Hopkinsian than Nettleton, no less successful, and considerably more healthy; ergo, Beecher shelved Nettleton (and it is noticeable how in Nettleton's papers the references to Beecher grow chillier and more bitter from now on) and, after reflecting on his extravagant threatenings, embraced Finney. And it is true not only that Finney afterwards operated under Beecher's management, and even went west to Ohio when Beecher went there, but that Finney's whole manner changed after these events. Finney's great Rochester revival of 1831 was noted for its "phenomenal dignity," and his lectures on revivals in New York City in 1835 were full of Old Calvinistlike utterances about the need for Christian activity in politics and the suspension of Sabbath mails.[89] But all the same, he never completely set aside his Hopkinsianism. His notorious definition of revivals, in those New York City lectures, as "not a miracle, nor dependent on a miracle" but "a purely philosophical result of the right use of the constituted means" was not a profession of Arminianism, but merely Finney's way of reinforcing the old Edwardsean conviction that "sinners are not bound to repent because they have the Spirit's influence, or because they can obtain it, but because they are moral agents, and have the powers which God requires them to exercise."[90]

Much as Beecher strove to take over the revival tactics and the revivalists of the New Divinity, he was noticeably more eager to absorb the second of those two quantities than the first. Beecher was not captured by New Divinity revivalism—he captured it. For one thing, he never stopped preaching that telltale mark of Old Calvinism, the "use of means," something which set him dramatically apart from Finney and Nettleton. After moving to Boston in 1828 to deal face to face with the Unitarians, Beecher preached,

Do you say, "What shall I do?" One thing I will tell you, that if you do not do something more than you

have, you will be lost. . . . Will you go to some solitary place to-night, and there kneel down and pray? You are conscious you can do it. Will you do it? Will you open your Bible and read a chapter? and lest you should not know where to look I will tell you. Read the first chapter of Proverbs, and then kneel, confess your sins, and try to give yourself up to God for the rest of your life. Then seek the instruction of your minister or Christian friends; break off all outward and known sins; put yourself in the way of all religious influences, and I will venture to say you can not pursue this course a fortnight, a week, without finding a new and blessed life dawning within you.[91]

More important, Beecher preached up revivals, not for the purpose of calling the saints out of the world, but rather to thrust them back into it to Christianize it—not to better identify the pure, but to energize the orthodox to combat public infidelity. Although Beecher believed in the establishment as firmly as Dwight, he had seen as early as his arrival in Litchfield that the handwriting of secularism was on the wall. To cope with the termination of the establishment, and, along with it, the reality of a church-in-society, Beecher resorted to the creation of those myriad voluntary societies with which his name has so often been associated, thereby creating a kind of ad hoc establishment that, while it could no longer exercise the direct power of the old church, could nevertheless still exert considerable influence in Connecticut life.

The word *influence* is of enormous significance here, for the truth is that the entire movement of theological vocabulary in both the Old Calvinists and the latter-day New Divinity men—from necessity to certainty—from motives that cause the will to motives that influence it—is a sort of code, measuring the onset of disestablishment by measuring the degree to which the power and place of the church and clergy had slipped from being the monitor of a moral society to being an agency for private religious exercise. In one sense, Edwards himself was acknowledging this by abandoning any notion of justifying Calvinism on the grounds of natural necessity and deploying the concept of moral necessity. What was not clear in his time, however, was whether the recourse to occasional causality glorified the power of God (by denying that the minister is the efficient of salvation in awakenings), or whether it was instead a recognition of the power of the congregations (to sack ministers at will). As Beecher and his compatriots perceived matters (and it was irrelevant whether that perception had ever approximated reality), it had once been a necessity that the citizen stand in awe of the "queues and shoebuckles, and cocked hats, and gold-headed canes" of the ministers; after 1818 in Connecticut, the best one could hope for was the certainty of social respect.[92] The clergy were disabled now from being causes; they could only be influences. Much as Beecher railed against disestablishment, after 1818 he could only accept, with as much grace as possible, that the role of the clergy in Connecticut would henceforth remain passive.[93]

The organization of the voluntary societies was for Beecher and the others a symbol of their helpless acceptance of the demolition of the church-in-society. At the same time, though, Beecher strove to make the most of this acceptance. If the voluntary societies were limited only to the exercise of influence, very well then, it would be an influence of such a degree as would come as close as possible to the necessity once exerted by the old establishment. And yet, precisely because these organizations were voluntary, they were also sterile: one could be born into the church, but not into the American Tract Society. Casting about for a means to populate the societies, Beecher found it expedient to hit upon the revivals, and upon New Divinity men to conduct them. It might have been only bluff that caused Beecher to describe this process as *"the best thing that ever happened to the State of Connecticut,"* or maybe it was his own conviction, after all, that cutting the ministers loose from the establishment would force them to work all the harder. "They say ministers have lost their influence," Beecher said to his daughter, Catharine; "the fact is, they have gained."[94] That may have been true—if everything in the past and present were measured by the yardstick of *influence*. The ministers had actually lost something more than influence; they had lost necessity, and if Old Calvinism demonstrated anywhere its wonted penchant for resourcefulness and adaptability, it is in how they appropriated Edwardsean ideas, practices, and even reputations to shore up their loss and try to make it good. Dwight and Beecher had begun that process of cooptation. Nathaniel William Taylor would finish it.[95]

Notes

1. There was bound to be disagreement about the actual numbers of thoroughgoing Edwardseans, ranging from the estimate of Joel Hawes, who thought that Connecticut was substantially dominated by Old Calvinists, to Heman Humphrey, who claimed that all of Connecticut was Hopkinsian; see Leonard Woods, *History of Andover Theological Seminary* (Boston, 1885), 29-30.

2. James Hoopes, "Calvinism and Consciousness from Edwards to Beecher," in *Jonathan Edwards and the American Experience* (New York: Oxford University Press, 1988), 217-218.

3. Asa Burton, *The Life of Asa Burton Written by Himself* (Thetford, VT, 1973), 62.

4. Asa Burton, *Essays on Some of the First Principles of Metaphysicks, Ethicks, and Theology* (Portland, ME: A. Shirley, 1824), 15.

5. Ibid., 17.

6. Ibid., 53.

7. Ibid., 70.

8. Ibid., 100.

9. Ibid., 84.

10. Bruce Kuklick, *Churchmen and Philosophers: From Jonathan Edwards to John Dewey* (New Haven: Yale University Press, 1985), 57-58.

11. Ezra Stiles, *The Literary Diary of Ezra Stiles, D.D.*, ed. F. B. Dexter (New York: Charles Scribner, 1901), 3:274-275.

12. Bennet Tyler, *The Life and Labours of Asahel Nettleton*, ed. Andrew Bonar (1854; rept. London: Banner of Truth Trust, 1975), 19; "Leonard Woods" and "Edwards Dorr Griffin" in *DAB;* Tyler, *Lectures in Theology*, ed. Nahum Gale (Boston, 1859), 128. For discussions in conventional Edwardsean terms of the standard *loci* of New Divinity theology, see Leonard Woods, *Works* (Boston: John P. Jewett, 1851), 3:555, and Nettleton, *Remains of the Late Rev. Asahel Nettleton, D.D.*, ed. Bennet Tyler (Hartford: Robins and Smith, 1845), 356-357 on natural ability; Woods, *Works*, 3:23, Heman Humphrey, *Revival Sketches and Manual* (New York, 1859), 431, and W. B. Sprague, *Lectures on Revivals of Religion* (1852; rept. London: Banner of Truth Trust, 1978), 47-48, 52, 68-69 on the use of means; and Tyler, *Lectures*, 337-338; Tyler, *Memoir of the Life and Character of the Rev. Asahel Nettleton* (Boston: Doctrinal Tract and Book Society, 1844), 216; Richard Chipman, *A Discourse on the Nature and Means of Ecclesiastical Prosperity* (Hartford, CT: 1839), and Edward Dorr Griffin, *The Life and Sermons of Edward Dorr Griffin*, ed. W. B. Sprague (1839; rept. London: Banner of Truth Trust, 1987), 1:474-478, and also Griffin, *Sermons, Not Before Published* (New York: M. W. Dodd, 1844), 28-29 for moral absolutism.

13. Tyler, *Lectures*, 256, 270, 281.

14. Woods, *Works*, 2:114-115, 131.

15. Leonard Woods, *An Essay on Native Depravity* (Boston, 1835), 64.

16. Woods, "Remarks on Cause and Effect," in *Works*, 5:106.

17. Ibid., 2:97-98.

18. Woods, *Native Depravity*, 155.

19. Tyler, *Lectures*, 298-299.

20. Ibid., 315, 358.

21. Woods, "Letters to Young Ministers," in *Works*, 5:23.

22. Ibid., 2:70, 143.

23. Woods, *Native Depravity*, 190-191.

24. Griffin, *Sermons* (1844), 152-153.

25. Edward Dorr Griffin, *The Doctrine of Divine Efficiency* (New York, 1833), 65.

26. Ibid., 91.

27. Ibid., 168.

28. Tyler, *Memoir of Nettleton*, 124.

29. Ibid., 357; Gardiner Spring, *Personal Reminiscences of the Life and Times of Gardiner Spring* (New York, 1866), 2:16.

30. *Historical Statistics of the United States, Colonial Times to 1970* (Washington, DC: U.S. Government Printing Office, 1975), 1:76.

31. Bruce Kuklick, *Churchmen and Philosophers: From Jonathan Edwards to John Dewey* (New Haven: Yale University Press, 1985), 86.

32. Basic discussion of the founding of Andover can be found in Conrad Wright, *The Beginnings of Unitarianism* (Boston: Starr King Press, 1955), 274-280; Woods, *History of the Andover Theological Seminary,* 72-94; Joseph W. Phillips, *Jedidiah Morse and New England Congregationalism* (New Brunswick, NJ: Rutgers University Press, 1983), 138-140; Spring, *Personal Reminiscences,* 1:303-328.

33. Stephen Berk, *Calvinism versus Democracy: Timothy Dwight and the Origins of American Evangelical Orthodoxy* (Hamden, CT: Archon Books, 1974), 178-183.

34. Phillips, *Morse,* 144-146; see also H. B. Stowe in *The Autobiography of Lyman Beecher* (New York: Harper and Brothers, 1865), 2:280, and Daniel T. Fiske, "New England Theology," in *Bibliotheca Sacra* 22 (July 1865), 476.

35. Leon Howard, *The Connecticut Wits* (Chicago: University of Chicago Press, 1943), 214-215; Stiles, *Literary Diary,* 3:274.

36. Edmund S. Morgan, *The Gentle Puritan: A Life of Ezra Stiles* (New Haven: Yale University Press, 1962), 417.

37. Timothy Dwight, *Theology Explained and Defended In a Series of Sermons* (Middletown, CT, 1818-1819), 2:18; Berk, *Calvinism Versus Democracy,* 45-46; Howard, *Connecticut Wits,* 354.

38. Kenneth Silverman, *Timothy Dwight* (New York: Twayne Publishers, 1969), 105.

39. Timothy Dwight, *Decisions of Questions Discussed by the Senior Class in Yale College in 1813 and 1814* (New York, 1833), 84.

40. Ibid., 88.

41. Dwight, *Theology,* 4:133; Charles Roy Keller, *The Second Great Awakening in Connecticut* (New Haven: Yale University Press, 1942), 62-65.

42. Silverman, *Timothy Dwight,* 102.

43. James Waddel Alexander, *The Life of Archibald Alexander, D.D.* (New York: Charles Scribner, 1854), 241.

44. Berk, *Calvinism versus Democracy,* 72.

45. J. W. Alexander, *Life of Archibald Alexander,* 240.

46. Dwight, *Theology,* 1:255.

47. Ibid., 4:530-531.

48. Ibid., 4:520, 528.

49. Nettleton to Philader Parmele, c. 1809, in Nettleton Manuscript Collection, Hartford Theological Seminary, Hartford; see also Tyler, *Memoir of Nettleton,* 36-37.

50. Timothy Dwight, *Sermons* (New Haven: Hezekiah Howe, 1828), 1:327.

51. Dwight, *Theology,* 1:4, 6, 246.

52. Ibid., 1:245-246.

53. Ibid., 1:387.

54. Ibid., 1:457.

55. Ibid., 3:39.

56. Howard, *Connecticut Wits,* 356.

57. Dwight, *Theology,* 4:463.

58. Dwight, "Secret Things Belong to God," in *Sermons,* 1:20.

59. Dwight, "Man Cannot Find Out a Religion Which Will Render Him Acceptable to God," in ibid., 1:72-73.

60. Dwight, *Theology,* 1:248-249.

61. Ibid., 1:410-411.

62. Ibid., 3:45.

63. Ibid., 3:166.

64. Ralph H. Gabriel, *Religion and Learning at Yale* (New Haven: Yale University Press, 1958), 70-77; Roland Bainton, *Yale and the Ministry* (New York: Harpers, 1957), 115.

65. Stuart C. Henry, *Unvanquished Puritan: A Portrait of Lyman Beecher* (Grand Rapids, MI: William B. Eerdmans, 1973), 42.

66. Beecher, *Autobiography,* 1:44.

67. Ibid., 2:52, 53, 56.

68. Ibid., 1:344.

69. Ibid., 1:69; Lyman Beecher, *Views in Theology* (Cincinnati: Truman and Smith, 1836), 59.

70. Beecher, *Autobiography,* 1:509.

71. Lyman Beecher, *Dependence and Free Agency* (Boston, 1832), 10.

72. Beecher, *Autobiography,* 1:472.

73. Ibid., 2:26.

74. Ibid., 2:175.

75. Beecher, *Views in Theology,* 42-43, 45.

76. Beecher, *Autobiography,* 2:578.

77. Beecher, "The Bible a Code of Laws," in *Sermons Delivered on Various Occasions* (Boston, 1828), 140, 141.

78. Beecher, "The Government of God Desirable," in *Sermons* (1828) 18-19.

79. Beecher, *Dependence and Free Agency,* 32-33.

80. Beecher, *Autobiography,* 2:581-582.

81. Mann, in Ann Douglas, *The Feminization of American Culture* (New York: Alfred Knopf, 1977), 42.

82. Charles Grandison Finney, *Memoirs of Charles G. Finney* (1876; Old Tappan, NJ: Fleming Revell, 1908), 42-43.

83. Ibid., 189.

84. Finney, "Sinners Bound to Change Their Own Hearts," in *Notions of Americans, 1820-1860,* ed. David Grimstead (New York: George Braziller, 1970), 78.

85. Finney, *Memoirs,* 83; see also Whitney R. Cross, *The Burned-Over District: The Social and Intellectual History of Enthusiastic Religion in Western New York, 1800-1850* (1950; rept. New York: Harper & Row, 1965), 151-164.

86. John F. Thornbury, *God Sent Revival: The Story of Asahel Nettleton and the Second Great Awakening* (Grand Rapids, MI: Evangelical Press, 1977), 158-173; George Hugh Birney, "The Life and Letters of Asahel Nettleton, 1783-1844," Ph.D. dissertation, Hartford Theological Seminary, 1943, 114-137.

87. Thornbury, *God Sent Revival,* 174-179; Birney, "Life and Letters of Nettleton," 151; the minutes of the New Lebanon Conference were surreptitiously printed in the Unitarian magazine *Christian Examiner and Theological Review* 4 (1827), 357-370.

88. Beecher, *Autobiography,* 2:101; Finney, *Memoirs,* 220.

89. Cross, *Burned-Over District,* 155, 164-168.

90. Charles Grandison Finney, *Lectures on the Revival of Religion* (Old Tappan, NJ: Fleming Revell, n.d.), 5, 116.

91. Beecher, *Autobiography,* 2:116-117.

92. Beecher, *Autobiography,* 1:344.

93. David L. Weddle, "The Law and the Revival: A 'New Divinity' for the Settlements," in *Church History* 47 (June 1978), 196, 199; Conrad Cherry, *Nature and Religious Imagination from Edwards to Bushnell* (Philadelphia: Fortress Press, 1980), 126-127.

94. Beecher, *Autobiography,* 1:344.

95. One of the great confusions about the motives of those who participated in the Second Great Awakening and those who organized the voluntary societies which sprang to life at virtually the same time concerns the degree to which the revivalists hoped to use the awakening to feed the societies and thus recover whatever measure of social control they thought they had lost. Some, such as Clifford Griffin, Charles Cole, and Timothy L. Smith, argued for a direct linkage, and with various degrees of moral comment on the appropriateness of such a connection. Others, such as Lois Banner, Richard Shiels, and Richard Birdsall, have insisted that the revivalists of the Second Great Awakening had no ulterior manipulative motives, and that the revivals were individualistic in orientation, with little connection to the organization of voluntary societies. I am suggesting that, in fact, both arguments may be true—depending on the area and the people concerned. Shiels, for instance, comes to his conclusion—that the revivals were not intended to recover lost political ground for the clergy—by lumping both old-line Edwardseans like Charles Backus in with Beecher and Dwight, and then taking Backus's disavowals of politics as coverage for the likes of Beecher. In that sense, Shiels does just what Beecher hoped people would do—mistake him for an Edwardsean. I am quite sure that Backus meant every word he said about the clergy needing to disassociate themselves from politics, but he said that because he was a New Divinity man, and therefore in a different league from Beecher. When Beecher, and every other Old Calvinist, talked revival, he meant something entirely different, which perhaps explains Fred J. Hood's point that the voluntary societies were top-heavy with Calvinists of the "old side" persuasion. Edwardsean revivalism, it is true, had little interest in saving the world as it was; but Edwardseans were not the only people who had learned how to play the revival game. Hence, the necessity for careful distinctions between New Divinity Calvinists and Old Calvinists, even up through the nineteenth century. See Richard D. Shiels, "The Second Great Awakening in Connecticut: Critique of the Traditional Interpretation," in *Church History* 49 (December 1980); 411-414, and Richard D. Birdsall, "The Second Great Awakening and the New England Social Order," in *Church History* 39 (1970) 358; also, Douglas, *Feminization of American Culture,* 35-49.

Kenneth P. Minkema (essay date 1990)

SOURCE: "The Authorship of 'The Soul,'" *Yale University Library Gazette,* Vol. 65, Nos. 1-2, October 1990, pp. 26-32.

[In the following essay, Minkema presents evidence that "The Soul," an essay long presumed to have been written by Edwards as a youth, was actually written by his sister, Esther. This article has been slightly modified by Minkema from the form in which it originally appeared.]

In the earliest efforts at recounting the life and collecting the writings of Jonathan Edwards (1703-58), a romantic legend grew about the youth of this foremost colonial American philosopher and theologian. This legend, which expanded throughout the nineteenth century, described a prodigy, a boy genius proficient in Latin at the age of eight, who wandered through the swamps of East Windsor, Connecticut, making precocious scientific observations. In twentieth-century biographies these stories were accorded the stature of historical truth, but they were based on the misdating of a collection of scientific essays supposedly written by Edwards in his childhood; they include **"Of Insects," "Of the Rainbow," "The Mind," "Notes on Natural Science,"** and the famous **"Spider Letter."**

Only recently has Thomas A. Schafer's painstaking analysis of the watermarks, inks, and handwriting in Edwards's manuscripts exploded some longstanding assumptions. For example, Edwards's great-grandson Sereno E. Dwight surmised on the basis of an undated draft of the **"Spider Letter"** that it was composed before Edwards matriculated at Yale College in 1716. Only in 1980 was the fair copy of the letter found, bearing the date 31 October 1723, three years after Edwards had graduated from Yale. **"Of Insects,"** thought to have been written by Edwards in 1714-15, when he was eleven or twelve, actually dates from 1719-21, when he had virtually completed his undergraduate education. Myths are slow to die, yet through labors such as these a more accurate picture of Edwards's early life is slowly emerging.

Now one more blow can be dealt to the myth surrounding Edwards. **"The Soul,"** a composition long thought to be the earliest extant production of Edwards's pen, was first published by Dwight in 1829, in his ten-volume edition of his great-grandfather's works. No doubt Dwight had discovered it among the family papers while researching his biographical account of Edwards. He assumed that Edwards had written it when he was ten or eleven.[1] In 1896 Egbert C. Smyth defended Dwight's dating against questions raised at the end of the nineteenth century.[2]

In his 1980 Edition of Edwards's scientific writings, Wallace E. Anderson relegated **"The Soul"** to an appendix in his volume, stating that every physical aspect of the document itself "gives almost conclusive evidence against [Edwards's] authorship of it."[3] In particular, the watermark of **"The Soul"** matched that of a batch of paper used in 1725 by Jonathan's father, the Rev. Timothy Edwards (1669-1758). On the reverse side of the manuscript of **"The Soul"** appears a memorandum written by Timothy to one of his daughters, who is about to go on a trip to Boston. In it he asks her to pick up two books that had first been published in 1724 and 1725. In addition, comparisons of orthography and spelling reveal marked discrepancies between **"The Soul"** and early manuscripts by Edwards.

Who then was the author of **"The Soul"**? A small, uncatalogued collection of Edwards family letters and diaries in the Beinecke Rare Book and Manuscript Library provides the key: a letter from Jonathan's oldest sister, Esther Edwards (1695-1766), to their sister Hannah Edwards (1713-73). Although undated, this letter can be placed during the first half of 1735.[4] Collation of the letter and essay provides conclusive evidence that both were written by the same person. There are similarities in formation in the lowercase "f," the simple but elegant rendering of the capital "I," and the capital "P" and "L." Virtually all initial instances of "C" and "L" are capitalized. The abbreviation "w^d" appears consistently in both documents (a deviation from the eighteenth-century convention of "wo'd"). There is a tendency to render "u" as "o," as in "suposition" (1735 letter) and "soperior" (**"The Soul"**). In addition, the orthography has the same overall appearance, and the spacing between letters and words is consistent. Perhaps most distinctive is the downward slope of the lines.

An earlier letter from Esther to her father, now at the Connecticut Historical Society, is dated from Nov. 20, 1718.[5] **"The Soul"** differs from it so much that one would hesitate to attribute it to Esther. But in 1718, probably seven to nine years before **"The Soul"** was written, Esther was only twenty-three years old, and her hand would therefore have been steadier and her letter articulation more exact. And she may have taken special care in writing to her father, who was known for his obsessive attention to detail. The other letter, written to her sister seventeen years later, would not have been subject to criticism for poor penmanship and composition.

"The Soul," probably written sometime between 1725, the date of Esther's trip to Boston—for it is to her that the memorandum on the opposite side is addressed—and 1727, when she married the Rev. Samuel Hopkins of Springfield, Massachusetts, is but a draft of a letter. Nonetheless there are similarities between the 1718 letter and **"The Soul,"** such as the formation of the capital "E" and "H" as well as of the lowercase "r" and "f." The lines of this letter also have the characteristic slope, though in this case it is slightly upward. When the three items are placed together, one can observe the evolution of Esther's handwriting.

Esther's authorship of **"The Soul"** demonstrates the level of family culture that was maintained in the East Windsor parsonage, where a strong emphasis was placed on education and self-improvement. Jonathan and his ten sisters were tutored by their father in a rigorous college preparatory curriculum; the older sisters even had the responsibility of teaching Jonathan in their parents' absence. All the sisters learned Latin, some of them learned Greek, and all but one went to finishing schools in Boston.[6] All of Jonathan's sisters were well versed in classical and current learning and exhibited an intellectual acuity that casts doubt on current assumptions about female learning in colonial New England.

The acumen that Esther demonstrates in **"The Soul"** may therefore have been quite typical of the productions of the Edwards sisters. Esther was apparently amused by a Hobbesian speculation that someone in town had made on the nature of the soul—most likely one of the many local boys who boarded at the parsonage during their preparation for college. In response she sat down and drafted a reply that is filled with wit and satire—brands of humor noticeably lacking in her brother Jonathan—and that reveals a grounding in Neoplatonic, antimaterialist philosophy.

[The Soul]

I am informed that you have advanced a notion that the soul is material and keeps with the body till the resurrection. As I am a professed lover of novelty, you must allow me to be much entertained by this discovery which, however old in some parts of the world, is new in this.

I am informed that you have advanced an notion that the soul is material and attends the body till the resurrection. As I am a professed lover of novelty, you must imagine I am very much entertained by this discovery (which, however in some parts of the world, is new to us). But suffer my curiosity a little further—I would know the manner of the kingdom before I swear allegiance. First, I would know whether this material soul keeps within the coffin? And, if so, whether it might not be convenient to build a repository for it? In order to which, I would know what shape it is of, whether round, triangular, or four-square, or whether it is a number of long fine strings reaching from the head to the foot? And, whether it does not live a very discontented life? I am afraid, when the coffin gives way, the earth will fall in and crush it. But, if it should choose to live above ground, and hover about the grave, how big it is—whether it covers all the body, or is assigned to the head or breast? Or how, if it covers all the body, what it does when another body is laid upon that? Whether the first gives way, and if so, where is the place of retreat? But, suppose the souls are not so big but that ten or a dozen of them may be about one body, whether they will not quarrel for the highest place? And as I must insist much upon my honor and property, I would know where I must quit my dear head if a superior soul comes in the way. But above all, I am concerned to know what they do where a burying place has been filled twenty, thirty or one hundred times. If they are atop of one another, the uppermost will be so far off that it can take no care of the body. I strongly suspect they must march off every time there comes a new set. I hope there is some good place provided for them, but doubt the undergoing so much hardship, and being deprived of the body at last, will make them illtempered. I leave it with your physical genius to determine whether some medicinal applications might not be proper in such cases; and subscribe your proselyte when I can have solution of these matters.

* * *

Dear Sister

My mind was fully bent to have Given you A visit this weak if Providence had Permited indeed [I] was so much set I s^d have over Come Considerable defeculties rather than fail'd but yet am Obliged to stay at home my Little Daughter hannah being very ill brok out into sores about her faice & much swell'd in her throat at-

tend[ed] at times wth a feavour Pain in the head sickness at the stomach &c I had Considerable Opportunity wth Unkele Williams of weston & did wth as much Equality & justis as I Could Lay the Case between M^r R[ockwell] & you^7 before him tho' the one half was not told him he is vehemently against your haveing anything more to do wth him he represented his Confidence of your unhapiness by a variety of Exsprssions [he] w^d have me tell you from him y^t you must Cloathe your self wth resolution & must Put an end to it & ye Lik to[o] tedious to relate but one thing I may not omit he says Let your obbligations be w^t they will: ye Liber[ty] y^t he Gave you at our house desolves y^m all. however if you Cannot get Resolution & strength of mind anough to do it, father and Mother must for it must be done. but no more of this. I w^d i[n]form you y^t Mr Woodbridge is still very ill he has still ye relicks of his distemper hanging above him & as he soposes ye janduce set in wth it I am my self much better in helth than w^n you was hear the time appointed for Mr Bricks Ordination is the 8 of October. you must note y^t w^t uncle W^ms said was upon soposition y^t what I said was true I think I kept a Great ways w^tin ye bounds of truth.

we are Like to have a high time at springfei[l]d I have been very urgent wth Mother to Let you be wth me a Little while she [said] you w^d not be willing these are to Let you know y^t you shall be very wellcome yours-E[sther] H[opkins]

* * *

Hartford November ye 20th 1718.
Honored father,

I Went yesterday over to weathersfeild and I understand that the Scholars intend to go to Newhaven next tuesday and if you please to send my Brother to newhaven with them I am of opinion that it will be much heasier than for him to go down alone Because the [other] scholars have hired a man to go with them to bring back all their Horses and ther not being a present opportunity for ye conveying of their chests theither they do intend to Carry their books and Cloaths for their parts [ ] and if you will please to write a letter to my uncle [ ] for and in other respects to take care of my brother It is very probable [that] may save you the [ ] of going down and in case he ben [ ] By me [ ] respect it is verry likely that an oppertunyty will present [ ] of conveying theither what he leaves behind him, and I suppose you will come down to Weathersfeild with him which will prevent any farther truble about my going homeHonoured father, from your dutyful Child
Esther Edwards

Notes

1. Sereno E. Dwight, "Life of President Edwards," *The Works of President Edwards, with a Memoir of His Life* (New York: Converse, 1829-30), 1:20n.

2. Egbert C. Smyth, *Some Early Writings of Jonathan Edwards* (Worcester: Charles Hamilton, 1896), 5-6.

3. *The Works of Jonathan Edwards: Scientific and Philosophical Writings,* ed. Wallace E. Anderson (New Haven and London: Yale University Press, 1980), 402.

4. In the letter, Esther refers to "Mr. Brick's Ordination." Robert Breck, who was controversial for his reputed Arminianism, was to be ordained at Springfield on 8 October 1735. At the instigation of the Rev. William Williams of Hatfield, Massachusetts, and the Rev. Thomas Clap of Windham, Connecticut, the ordination council had Breck arrested when he arrived. Breck was eventually ordained by ministers from Boston in early 1736, a procedure condemned as subverting the authority of the local ministerial association. Jonathan Edwards also opposed the ordination, and assisted in writing a defense of the council's actions. Patricia Tracy, *Jonathan Edwards, Pastor: Religion and Society in Eighteenth-Century Northampton* (New York: Hill and Wang, 1979), 120-21.

5. The letter is badly damaged. In my transcription (by permission of the Connecticut Historical Society, Hartford), empty brackets indicate damage to the manuscript or indecipherable text and words in brackets indicate conjectural readings.

6. Dwight, *"Life of President Edwards,"* 16-17.

7. The "case" that Esther refers to was between Hannah and Matthew Rockwell, who claimed the right by private contract to Hannah's hand in marriage. Hannah resisted his demands until he finally married someone else in 1743. See Kenneth P. Minkema, "The Edwardses: A Ministerial Family in Eighteenth-Century New England" (Ph.D. diss., University of Connecticut, 1988), 117-18.

The edited text of "The Soul" given in this article is reproduced by permission of Yale University Press from *The Works of Jonathan Edwards: Scientific and Philosophical Writings,* ed. Wallace E. Anderson (New Haven and London: Yale University Press, 1980), 405-6.

Larzer Ziff (essay date 1991)

SOURCE: "The World Completed," in *Writing in the New Nation: Prose, Print, and Politics in the Early United States,* Yale University Press, 1991, pp. 1-17.

[In the following essay, Ziff examines An Account of the Life of the Late Reverend Mr. David Brainerd, Minister of the Gospel, *which was Brainerd's personal diary, as edited and published by Edwards. Brainerd was a younger minister who was engaged to one of Edwards's daughters at the time of his death. Ziff suggests that although the work is seldom studied by critics of Edwards's writings, the journal in its edited form is significant among his works, in part because Brainerd's life story was edited by*

Edwards to ensure that it exemplified Edwards's theological and philosophical ideals, and in part because it is historically the most popular work of Jonathan Edwards.]

On April 1, 1743, David Brainerd began his missionary task in the Indian village of Kaunameek, situated between Stockbridge in the Colony of Massachusetts and Albany in the Colony of New York. He was just entering upon his twenty-fifth year and to that date had given no sign that he was particularly suited for the labors he was undertaking. Indeed, it could well be conjectured that Brainerd pursued his relatively thankless duties because, given his background and character, he had little other choice.

Brainerd had been licensed to preach by the Association of Ministers of Danbury in his native Connecticut less than a year before his arrival at Kaunameek under the auspices of the Correspondents of the Society in Scotland for the Propagation of Christian Knowledge. But unlike almost all others so empowered, he held no college degree. The year before he had been expelled from Yale for ungracious conduct after having been there three years. He had entered as a twenty-one-year-old freshman, older by some three or four years than the others in his class, and this awkward circumstance seemed all too much in keeping with the previous events in his life. His father, at one time Speaker of the House in the Connecticut Assembly and, at the time of his death when David was nine, a member of the Governor's Council, had left some farmland to his children. But there were ten of them—David was the sixth of his father's children—and whatever distinction or patrimony fell to him, buried as he was in the pack and lacking the vigor of his siblings, was heavily diluted by the time his mother died, leaving him orphaned at fourteen. When he went to East Haddam to live with his married sister he was still an adolescent, but one who, in his own words, was "something sober, and inclined rather to melancholy than the contrary extreme."[1] At no time in his subsequent brief life did he appear to emerge from this characteristic condition of morose withdrawal. The tuberculosis that killed him at age twenty-nine was accelerated by the smoke and damp of frontier bivouacs, long journeys through the wilds of the western river valleys—the Connecticut, the Delaware, the Susquehanna—and the severity of northeastern winters, and it appears to have intensified his habit of brooding retreat into himself. Brainerd seemed singularly unfit for a career that demanded some capacity to make his personal influence felt, some small power to make himself liked by strangers, some modicum of ability to look outward from his own life into the daily reality of others. It is not surprising that lacking these he was not, in practical terms, a very successful missionary.

After a year Brainerd left Kaunameek, first asking his Indian parishioners to move to Stockbridge to place themselves under the ministry of John Sargent, and in June 1744 he took up missionary work at the Forks of Delaware (near today's Easton, Pennsylvania), moving shortly afterward to an Indian settlement at Crossweeskung (near today's Freehold, New Jersey), where he enjoyed what small success in gaining converts he was to have as a missionary. By early 1747 his rapidly failing health forced him to abandon his labors, and he made his way to Northampton and the home of his fiancée, Jerusha Edwards, where tended by her he died that October.

Yet in spite of the unremarkable facts of his career, few Protestant missionaries have exerted an influence as far-reaching as David Brainerd's. He may have failed to bring significant numbers to Christianity, but his life, as transmitted in one or another published version of his diary, profoundly affected the history of Protestant missionaries. Even during his lifetime, the society that employed him published excerpts from his diary in two separate tracts, and after his death John Wesley and, more fully, Jonathan Edwards, father of his fiancée, published two of a number of other versions. The effect of these publications was momentous. Francis Asbury, who in 1771 commenced Methodism's first mission to Africa, found in the Brainerd of the diary a "Model of meekness, moderation, temptation and labor, and self-denial"; Henry Martyn, the great Anglican missionary to India, read the diary when he was a student at Cambridge in 1802 and wrote, "I long to be like him"; David Livingston, missionary to Africa, similarly responded to the diary; and as recently as 1956, the American missionary Jim Elliott, in the jungles of Ecuador on the mission which would claim his life, wrote, "Confession of pride—suggested by David Brainerd's Diary yesterday—must become an hourly thing with me."[2]

The fullest and best-known version of the diary of David Brainerd, so effective that it has come to stand as the very embodiment of the man, is that first published in Boston in 1749 by Jonathan Edwards: *An Account of the Life of the late Reverend Mr. David Brainerd, Minister of the Gospel.* Edwards's editing, fueled by both his admiration for Brainerd and the pressing political message he found in Brainerd's spiritual career, converted Brainerd's diary into the classical model it has become. Today, however, when Edwards is valued for the logic, power, and scope of his theological, philosophical, and psychological expositions, his *Life of Brainerd* is relatively unread compared with such works as his treatise on the will. But historically the *Life of Brainerd* remains the most popular of his works.

From the mid-1730s through his publication of the Brainerd life, Jonathan Edwards had been a central agent in the series of emotional religious revivals that swept through the colonies with so great an effect that they were labeled "The Great Awakening." He knew that movement was viewed with skepticism if not hostility by many leaders of the older and more polished communities of the seaboard. Indeed, Brainerd's expulsion from Yale was connected with the awakening fervor that led him to incautious behavior at a college whose president, Thomas Clap, distrusted the emotionalism of popular religious meetings as he sought to maintain a standard of intellectual decorum at his institution.[3]

Edwards further realized that since he himself had claims to membership in the colonial elite—claims based on family, education, scholarship, and native genius—his assertion that grossly physical demonstrations did not preclude the presence of grace could be viewed by many of his peers as a betrayal of his class and profession. Northampton was not so distant from London as to blur Edwards's perception of the dominant neoclassical temperament of the leading minds of his day. "Was there ever," he asked rhetorically, "an age wherein strength and penetration of reason, extent of learning, exactness of distinction, correctness of style, and clearness of expression did so abound?"[4]

Yet in the face of this recognition, he maintained that such apparently delusive and disagreeably vulgar manifestations as "trembling, groaning, being sick, crying out, panting, and fainting,"[5] comported with true religion; that, indeed, such physicality was more vitally attached to a sense of the evil of sin and the love of God than were the decorous explications of redemption that prevailed in the churches of the colonies' leaders. "Our people don't so much need to have their heads stored, as to have their hearts touched," he said, "and they stand in the greatest need of that sort of preaching that has the greatest tendency to do this" (*The Revival of Religion in New England,* p. 388).

Accordingly, he took to print in order to state his case, employing the medium traditionally controlled by the intellectual class most opposed to popular and oral, thus irresponsible and anarchic, demonstrations. His masterpiece on the subject, *A Treatise Concerning Religious Affections* (1746), was an acute psychological analysis of the connection between emotional state and physical manifestation and a model of precision in the distinctions it drew between affections generated by the imagination and those inspired by grace. It was, thus, a defense of essentially oral, subjective, emotional phenomena conducted in print according to objective, rational principles.

Edwards realized that objectifying religious experience by describing it in print presented dangers, because however precisely one formulated general psychological principles, the ultimate distinction between true and false religion resided in the particulars of the subjective experience. A failure to appreciate the details of each case led to the formulaic application of rules; led, that is, to the clogging of the vital emotional channels through which God's grace flowed. To comprehend the workings of salvation one must perforce know the particular circumstances of the life of the affected.

Accordingly, Edwards sought to supplement his psychological analyses of religious experience with a presentation of case histories. In *A Faithful Narrative of the Surprising Work of God* (1736), he reported such histories from the viewpoint of a recorder who after the event had received the spiritual details from the mouths of those shaken by grace and had talked also with those closest to them. But in Brainerd's diary he had a treasury: the extended spiritual autobiography of a Christian recorded in detail as it was experienced day by day. It was, so to speak, exactly what Edwards required to cap an argument that in other works had been advanced through a priori reasoning.

Yet read today, Brainerd's diary, personal, intense, and frequently tortured as it is, nevertheless also seems formulaic. This is because Brainerd, in common with others of his time and convictions, expresses himself in a vocabulary and according to paradigms taken principally from the Bible and then distributed in accordance with Calvinist theology. To readers who do not inhabit his sources as familiarly as did he, Brainerd's locutions appear to be very much like those of many others, which is to say that in today's terms his highly personal document does not seem very personal at all. Only those familiar with the models that structure Brainerd's expression can detect the particularity of his agonics and his triumph.

Conversely, however, if what moved Brainerd's readers in the days of his popularity now fails similarly to impress the secular reader, there are moments in his work which formerly passed without remark that now leap from his page as indications of a structure of feeling that we discern more acutely than Brainerd precisely because we do not inhabit that structure. Such moments are often connected with the way in which the saint is separated from the sinner not only theologically but socially. In the seventeenth-century days of American Puritanism, saints were accorded political privileges and with their worldly distinction thus assured had little need to keep apart from sinners in their everyday doings. But the rekindled fervor of the Awakening occurred in the more secular days of royal governors and political preferment of a range of nominal Christians, and, as a consequence, the newly zealous sought to mark their distinction by practicing social exclusion.

So, for example, Brainerd spoke of how he marveled that those who "called themselves Christians . . . could talk of all the world, and spend their time in jesting and the like and never say a word of spiritual concerns or anything of that dreadful wilderness that I had been led along through." He yearned, he said, to escape from them and "get alone in the woods, or any other place of retirement." When he contemplated what was called Christian society, he was sometimes led to think "I was a creature alone and by myself and knew not of any that felt as I did" (*Life of Brainerd*, pp. 141-42). He wrote this particular passage four years before he began missionary work, revealing in it the psychological predisposition that sent him into the literal American wilderness that corresponded to the metaphoric wilderness of his inner struggle. If Brainerd went to the wilds in order to lead the native inhabitants out of their spiritual desolation, it also appears that on a less conscious level he sought to recapture the isolation in which he had first experienced God's grace within him, an experience that could be more keenly relived among manifest pagans than among those he saw as the hypocrites of Christian society.

On a Sunday two weeks after his arrival at Kaunameek Brainerd wrote:

> In the morning was again distressed as soon as I waked, hearing much talk about the world and the things of it: Though I perceived the men were in some measure afraid of me; and I discoursed something about sanctifying the Sabbath, if possible, to solemnize their minds. But when they were at a little distance, they again talked freely about secular affairs. Oh, I thought, what a hell it would be to live with such men to eternity. (*Life of Brainerd,* p. 204)

The anticipated bliss of the social exclusiveness to be enjoyed in eternity feeds Brainerd's distaste for the society this world affords. He also perceives that his clerical garb, his sober demeanor, and his unrelenting attention to spiritual decorum make him an object of fear, and it is this perception that provides the most extraordinary passage in his diary.

On September 21, 1745, a Lord's Day, Brainerd visited the Indians encamped on Juniata Island in the Susquehanna and attempted to gather them together in order to preach to them through an interpreter. But he found them so fully engaged in ceremonies designed to counter a fever then raging among them that they paid him no heed. Watching the ceremonies, Brainerd wrote, "Their monstrous actions tended to excite ideas of horror, and seemed to have something in them (as I thought) peculiarly suited to raise the devil, if he could be raised by anything odd, ridiculous, and frightful" (*Life of Brainerd,* p. 327). Waiting out the powwow for some three hours, he resumed his attempt to talk to them about Christianity, but they soon scattered, leaving him so "greatly sunk" in spirits that he thought the day "the most burdensome and disagreeable Sabbath that ever I saw" (p. 328). In this depressed condition, he recalled and recorded an incident that had occurred some months earlier. Its singularity merits quotation in full:

> When I was in these parts in May last, I had an opportunity of learning many of the notions and customs of the Indians, as well as of observing many of their practices: I then travelling more than an hundred and thirty miles upon the river above the English settlements; and having in that journey a view of some persons of seven or eight distinct tribes, speaking so many different languages. But of all the sights I ever saw among them, or indeed anywhere else, none appeared so frightful or so near akin to what is usually imagined of infernal powers; none ever excited such images of terror in my mind, as the appearance of one who was a devout and zealous reformer, or rather restorer, of what he supposed was the ancient religion of the Indians. He made his appearance in his pontifical garb, which was a coat of bears' skins, dressed with the hair on, and hanging down to his toes, a pair of bearskin stockings, and a great wooden face, painted the one half black, the other tawny, about the color of an Indian's skin, with an extravagant mouth, cut very much awry; the face fastened to a bearskin cap which was drawn over his head. He advanced toward me with the instrument in his hand

that he used for music in his idolatrous worship, which was a dry tortoiseshell, with some corn in it, and the neck of it drawn on to a piece of wood, which made a very convenient handle. As he came forward he beat his tune with the rattle, and danced with all his might, but did not suffer any part of his body, not so much as his fingers, to be seen: And no man would have guessed by his appearance and actions that he could have been a human creature if they had not had some intimation of it otherways. When he came near me I could not but shrink away from him, although it was then noonday, and I knew who it was, his appearance and gestures were so prodigiously frightful! He had a house consecrated to religious uses, with divers images cut out upon the several parts of it. I went in and found the ground beat almost as hard as a rock with their frequent dancing in it. I discoursed with him about Christianity, and some of my discourse he seemed to like; but some of it he disliked entirely. He told me that God had taught him his religion, and that he never would turn from it, but wanted to find some that would join heartily with him in it; for the Indians, he said, were grown very degenerate and corrupt. He had thoughts, he said, of leaving all his friends and travelling abroad, in order to find some that would join him; for he believed God had some good people somewhere that felt as he did. He had not always, he said, felt as he now did, but had formerly been like the rest of the Indians, until about four or five years before that time: Then, he said, his heart was very much distressed, so that he could not live among the Indians, but got away into the woods and lived alone for some months. At length, he says, God comforted his heart and showed him what he should do; and since that time he had known God and tried to serve him; and loved all men, be they who they would, so as he never did before. He treated me with uncommon courtesy, and seemed to be hearty in it. And I was told by the Indians that he opposed their drinking strong liquor with all his power; and if at any time he could not dissuade them from it, by all he could say, he would leave them and go crying into the woods. It was manifest he had a set of religious notions that he had looked into for himself, and not taken for granted upon bare tradition; and he relished or disrelished whatever was spoken of a religious nature, according as it either agreed or disagreed with his standard. And while I was discoursing he would sometimes say, "Now that I like; so God has taught me," etc. And some of his sentiments seemed very just. Yet he utterly denied the being of a devil, and declared there was no such a creature known among the Indians of old times, whose religion he supposed he was attempting to revive. He likewise told me that departed souls all went southward, and that the difference between the good and the bad was this: that the former were admitted into a beautiful town with spiritual walls, or walls agreeable to the nature of souls; and that the latter would forever hover round those walls, and in vain attempt to get in. He seemed to be sincere, honest and conscientious in his own way, and according to his own religious notions, which was more than I ever saw in any other pagan: And I perceived he was looked upon and derided amongst most of the Indians as a precise zealot that made a needless noise about religious matters. But I must say there was something in his temper and disposition that looked more like true reli-

gion than anything I ever observed amongst other heathens. (*Life of Brainerd,* pp. 329-30)

On an island at the junction of the Juniata and Susquehanna rivers, David Brainerd had met his double.[6] Both men had undergone profound religious conversions which had launched them on their missions; both strove to make every outward appearance comport with the spiritual truth revealed to them; both were regarded by their fellows as tiresome precisians at best and objects of fear at worst. In covering himself in bear skins, the Indian prophet emphasized his total difference from the encroaching Europeans who were contributing to the degeneration of his fellows and at the same time he symbolized the regenerative forces available for the redemption of his fellows. Like the bear skins, Brainerd's clerical garb at the same time emphasized his total difference from an opposed culture and symbolized the redemptive force available to those who adhered to his culture. For a magic moment a charge of identity surged between the two missionaries as they recognized that the similar demands made by their gods suggested their kinship.

But Brainerd, as fearful spiritually of the shaman's similarity to him as he had earlier been fearful physically of the shaman's difference, sought to distance himself from the Indian and found the way in their opposing views not on God but on the question of the devil's existence. Within Brainerd's demonology, to deny the reality of the devil was to serve him. In insisting upon their difference, however, Brainerd did not dismiss the shaman into his own culture, granting him a separate if different identity. Rather, he held him fast within the Christian myth, an example of the devil's sway among the heathens, a theological role that blended with the cultural role of the savage. Both were parts of the Christian American's drama of identity wherein the repressed yet luring self was externalized and then attacked.[7]

In seeking to revive what he regarded as the true old Indian religion, the shaman sought also to revive his fellows' national identity, to restore them to a sense of what it meant to be a Delaware and an Indian uncompromised by European habits. In seeking to convert the Indians he visited, Brainerd was annihilating their cultural identity by subordinating it to the roles they had to play in his cosmic Christian drama. As the shaman's mission was national, so Brainerd's was imperial.[8] To convert the heathen was to be an agent of providential history, an instrument in the working out of God's predetermined plan for the world. Although one could not be certain as to the precise place in God's script at which one had arrived at a given historical moment, still the Bible provided a clear scenario for the whole plot from the creation to the apocalypse. America was the designated site for prescribed acts in the drama of the history of the world, a drama which would achieve its climax only after the conversion of the heathen. The Indian prophet, on the other hand, in his attempt to return to (or maintain) the world that prevailed before the European invasion, appears to have held a view of history as essentially complete, although from the slimness of the evidence we can only conjecture this. Such a view accounted for the arrival of the European by reading him back into the period before the invasion in terms of signs that had anticipated his presence.

Discussing the Aztecs' absorption of the Spanish conquest into their history, Tzvetan Todorov writes: "The Aztecs perceive the conquest—i.e., the defeat—and at the same time, mentally overcome it by inscribing it within a history conceived according to their requirements (nor are they the only people to have done such a thing): the present becomes intelligible and at the same time less inadmissible, the moment one can see it already announced in the past. And the remedy is so well adapted to the situation that, hearing the narrative, everyone believes he remembers that the omens had indeed appeared *before* the conquest."[9] To cite this is not to assert an identity between sixteenth-century Aztecs and eighteenth-century Delawares in gross perpetuation of the irresponsible habit of lumping all Indian people from all preinvasion times into a homogeneous mass.[10] It is, rather, to provide a well-observed example of the way in which a view of history as always complete, always, that is, having fulfilled the divine plan, can incorporate into it the evidence of "new" events instead of giving way to a linear view of history as change.

Strikingly, once the contrast between a view of history as linear and a view of it as complete is noted, then a similarity between Puritan and Indian presents itself. The theory of providential history arose from a reading of the New Testament in a way encouraged by the testament itself, one that saw the advent of Jesus as a fulfillment of what had already been written in the Old Testament. In a like manner, the future history of the world is already patterned forth in the New Testament, so that what will occur tomorrow can, once it happens, be related to its reference in the Bible in a procedure not unlike the reading of omens after the fact.

The intellectual habit of seeing the world as complete even as it unfolds, of, that is, finding an already occurred double for what is just now occurring, is manifest in the writings of Jonathan Edwards published in the same period as his edition of the *Life of Brainerd. In Some Thoughts Concerning the Revival of Religion in New England* (1742), for example, he wrote: "God has made as it were two worlds here below, the old and the new (according to the names they are now called by), two great habitable continents. . . . This new world is probably now discovered that the new and most glorious state of God's church on earth might commence there; that God might in it begin a new world in a spiritual respect when he creates the *new heavens* and the *new earth*." He went on to treat America as a geographical correlative of the New Testament: "The other continent hath slain Christ, and has from age to age shed the blood of the saints and martyrs of Jesus, and has often been as it were deluged with the Church's blood: God has therefore probably reserved the honor of building the glorious temple to the daughter, that

has not shed so much blood, when those times of the peace and prosperity and glory of the church shall commence, that were typified by the reign of Solomon." The last world to be "discovered," America will be the first world to experience the coming of the days of glory. "'Tis probable that that will come to pass in spirituals," Edwards said, "that has in temporals, with respect to America; that whereas, till of late, the world was supplied with its silver and gold and earthly treasures from the old continent, now it's supplied chiefly from the new, so the course of things in spiritual respects will be in like manner turned" (*The Revival of Religion in New England,* p. 355).

Seeing America as the realization of what has unalterably been determined imparted a cosmic consequence to the lives of ordinary people. Their spiritual experiences became events in world history; what happened in a church revival in a remote part of the colonies was a step in the progress of the divine plan for the universe. The common man could see himself as a participant in matters of far greater public consequence than those that were managed by his social betters in the commercial and political centers of the land. The text that accompanied Edwards's message about the role of America was one that consistently relocated authority, taking it from its traditional places and lodging it in the lowly believer.

"When God is about to do some great work for his church," he wrote, "his manner is to begin at the lower end; so when he is about to renew the whole habitable earth, 'tis probable that he will begin in this utmost, meanest, youngest and weakest part of it, where the church of God has been planted last of all; and so the first shall be last, and the last first" (*The Revival of Religion in New England,* p. 356). The immediate referent of "this utmost . . . weakest part" is America, where the church was "planted last" after its Near Eastern origin and European development. Beyond that referent, however, lies another to the churches of Edwards's frontier as youngest and weakest when compared to those of the Atlantic seaboard, and beyond this lies a third to the socially lowest members of the church as opposed to the socially dominant who have not experienced an awakening. His text denies the subordination of colonial American to imperial English culture, of frontier to capital society, of lower to upper class. While his explicit terms limit the relocation of power to spiritual matters, at the same time they declare that such are the greatest matters in history. So thorough is Edwards's relocation of power that it extends even to his own authority. "I condemn," he said, "ministers' assuming or taking too much upon them, and appearing as though they supposed that they were the persons to whom it especially belonged to dictate, direct and determine" (p. 291), and he took care to dissociate himself from such behavior.

It can be argued that Edwards's emphasis on the spiritual authority of the believer prepared his followers for the revolution in which they assumed political authority, a revolution Edwards did not live to see. But that revolution and the republic that succeeded it were, as will be seen, preeminently creatures of print culture while Edwards's outlook is shaped by the assumptions of oral culture.

At the root of the American Puritan tradition was the belief that the presence of the Holy Spirit in the believer took precedence over laws, that the divine influence was experienced as a flow rather than through forms. The presence of the Word was a necessary precondition for the efficacy of words; the Holy Spirit had written the Bible and only those who had that Spirit knew how to read the Bible. As John Calvin had said, "Scripture, carrying its own evidence along with it, deigns not to submit to proofs and arguments but owes the full conviction with which we ought to receive it to the testimony of the Spirit."[11] In everyday terms this resulted in a heavy emphasis placed on spontaneity in preaching and prayer, and a deep suspicion of set forms since they were seen as hollow substitutes for, rather than the outgrowth of, the presence of the Spirit. By Edwards's time, however, Puritanism had had some five generations of existence as the way of the establishment rather than the way of dissent, and the emphasis on spontaneity had been modified by codes of decorum. The Great Awakening was a popular reaction against the spiritual authority of the ministerial class and its allies who exerted their control through the maintenance of forms that they were especially qualified by training to administer. It was the rebellion of an oral culture valuing immanence against a literary culture valuing representation.

Jonathan Edwards recognized, to be sure, that no matter how valid the insistence upon immanence—the living presence of the Holy Spirit—and the distrust of representation—the investing of authority in laws of conduct and a class that administered them—the resulting fervor could grow into a wildfire of delusion. Anarchic behavior might be justified by claims that since the Holy Spirit authorized it all rules to the contrary were inapplicable. The chaos that threatened was not, he perceived, to be checked by attacking the anarchic behavior itself; indeed, to do so would be to align himself with the Awakening's opponents who impugned the integrity of spiritual experience by deriding its outer manifestations. Rather, since the Holy Spirit was always consistent with itself so that its presence in an individual could lead neither to conduct that was in conflict with the conduct of another individual equally guided nor to conflict with the words of the Bible that it had written, when such conflict appeared to occur it was not the behavior itself but its sources that required analysis. It is not correct, he agreed, to judge of the truth of the presence of the Spirit by the way a Christian conducts himself; to do so is to put the law in the place of grace. But it is necessary to recognize that certain standards of conduct—he called them "holy practice"—inevitably followed from the profession of grace (*Religious Affections,* pp. 458-59). The created world is determined, not subject to re-creation. When the consciousness is awakened by grace it sees that world in a new light, as if one previously blind to color now saw all its hues. But it does not see, nor is it empow-

ered to create, a different world. The divine plan still dictates that the world is as it is and shall be as it shall be, independently of human will.

Accordingly, Edwards centered his analysis on the ways grace is to be distinguished from the imagination, which seems like but in truth is completely different from it. The imagination is the faculty Satan employs to delude persons into repeating his own revolt by leading them to believe they have the power to affirm a new order. The greater part of Edwards's attention in his *Religious Affections* was devoted to exposing the imagination as the source of experiences that were mistakenly regarded as inspired by grace, and in his editing of the Brainerd diary he omitted visions that Brainerd recorded when he suspected them to be products of the imagination.

Edwards's belief that the created world was complete and his consequent censure of imaginative re-creations are opposed to the values promoted in a print culture. The first novels to be published in America appeared in the same decade as Edwards's writings in defense of the Great Awakening, the very first of them Samuel Richardson's *Pamela* printed by Benjamin Franklin in 1740. The rapid increase in the number of novels published in America signaled the coming of age of print culture. Unlike poetry and drama, the novel is preeminently a product of the printing press. Although connected to oral story telling, the novel is, uniquely, written only to be printed. Its popularity in a society is a mark of the degree to which that society's perceptions are shaped by the assumptions that govern print. The coincidence of Edwards's popular influence reaching its highest point in the decade when the novel commenced its entry into American life suggests that the oral culture that had empowered Edwards's writings had reached flood point and was soon to ebb.

David Brainerd's self was his God-given soul, and his drama was the drama of coming to terms with that given. It was a drama of self-awareness. The new culture of print promoted one's ability to be what one represented oneself as being. It replaced self-awareness with self-knowledge. As Ormond Seavey wrote in studying Benjamin Franklin, "In place of the dramatic possibilities made available by self-awareness, self-knowledge organized life narratively, in the manner of novels or autobiographies."[12]

The transition from a culture of immanence to a culture of representation is a central feature of the writings that are considered in the following pages, writings framed by Crèvecoeur's *Letters from an American Farmer* and the journals of Meriwether Lewis and William Clark. Personal narratives, travel accounts, natural histories, and novels are read with an eye to what they capture of the relation of literary to other forms of representation, the construction of self in writing, and the conquest of the wild through letters, themes that recurred in the literature of a people who were consolidating the first modern republic. So to read these texts is to seek to enter into their historical reality rather than to reconstruct it, although, to be sure, any contention about the way in which those in a past period perceived reality is vulnerable to the objection that if the work being interpreted is bound by the historical situation of its author then the interpretation is bounded by the historical situation of the interpreter.[13] This is undoubtedly so. But the recognition that our perception of reality is inescapably shaped by our times stimulates a desire to enter into the consciousness of the people of an earlier period rather than discourages such an attempt. To arrive at a sense of another day is to interrogate today.

Notes

1. Jonathan Edwards, *The Life of David Brainerd,* ed. Norman Pettit (New Haven, 1985), p. 101. My account of Brainerd relies heavily upon Professor Pettit's excellent introduction.

2. *Life of Brainerd,* pp. 3-4, where a number of others influenced by Brainerd are cited.

3. Some years later Clap supported the Awakening and invited revivalists to preach at Yale.

4. Jonathan Edwards, *Some Thoughts Concerning the Revival of Religion in New England,* in *The Great Awakening,* ed. C. C. Goen (New Haven, 1959), pp. 387-88.

5. Jonathan Edwards, *Religious Affections,* ed. John E. Smith (New Haven, 1959), p. 135.

6. In so saying I echo Elmire Zolla, who writes, "It is as though Brainerd had met his double," *The Writer and the Shaman* (New York, 1973), p. 48, although I disagree with other parts of his book.

7. Speaking more generally of Brainerd's attitude toward Indians, Richard Slotkin notes, "He is not seeking to make them English so much as to discover and exorcise the Indian in himself," *Regeneration through Violence* (Middletown, Conn., 1973), p. 198.

8. I agree when Roy Harvey Pearce says that for missionaries such as Brainerd "conversion was everything and civilizing nothing," and that "savages were to be converted on the frontier, apart from the immediately baneful influence of civilization," *Savagism and Civilization* (Berkeley, 1988), p. 33. But this does not preclude the fact that the missionary effort served the expansionist politics of "civilization."

9. Tzvetan Todorov, *The Conquest of America,* trans. Richard Howard (New York, 1984), p. 74.

10. This and related heresies are identified in Robert F. Berkhofer, Jr., *The White Man's Indian* (New York, 1978), pp. 25-26.

11. John Calvin, *Institutes of the Christian Religion,* trans. Henry Beveridge (London, 1953), 1:72.

12. Ormond Seavey, *Becoming Benjamin Franklin* (University Park, Penn., 1988), p. 41. Seavey's distinction between self-awareness and self-knowledge is based, as he explains, on that of Georges Gusdorf in his *La Découverte de soi* (Paris, 1948).

13. I return to this consideration in the afterword.

Gerald R. McDermott (essay date 1992)

SOURCE: "That Glorious Work of God and the Beautiful Society: The Premillennial Age and the Millennium," in *One Holy and Happy Society: The Public Theology of Jonathan Edwards,* Pennsylvania State University Press, 1992, pp. 37-92.

[In the following excerpt, McDermott asserts that an examination of the social and political implications of millennialism in Edwards's writings and sermons reveals that his societal orientation was universal, rather than provincial, as has been ascribed to him, and that his eschatology was apolitical. Despite the doctrine of national covenant associated with Edwards, writes McDermott, his vision of the "one holy and happy society" that was to come was not one centered in the colonies of New England, but rather a global community of the saved that would transcend national and political boundaries.]

Although Edwards's doctrine of the national covenant, long buried in unpublished sermons, has come to attention only recently, Edwardsean millennialism has been open to public view for more than two centuries. Significant portions of some of his most important published works were devoted to its explication. As a result, it has received considerable critical attention. Some scholars have noted how Edwards's millennial doctrine implicitly challenged contemporary social mores,[1] but others have held that Edwards's vision of future glory constituted an idolatrous civil religion. Sacvan Bercovitch, for example, wonders at Edwards's "astonishing arrogance, both on his own behalf and on behalf of his region and continent." The Northampton pastor, Bercovitch claims, was a case study in religious and nationalistic "provincialism"; his exaggerated sense of New England's role in the eschatological drama of redemption "drew out the proto-nationalistic tendencies of the New England Way."[2]

That Edwards's millennialism characterized America or New England as a redeemer nation with a mission to save other peoples is a familiar theme. C. C. Goen's 1959 article opened the discussion by suggesting that Edwards began to "entertain the idea that God might have purposed to realize the biblical prophecies in America as a land to accomplish the renovation of the world."[3] Subsequent commentaries on Edwards's eschatology have elaborated on the theme. New England for Edwards was the "city on a hill" that would knit together "all of Protestant America"[4] and then, on behalf of the world, inaugurate the final stage of earthly history, the millennium.[5] America was to be the center of future glory, "a locus for the building of the earthly Jerusalem, that 'New heavens and new earth' prophesied by Isaiah."[6] The religious imagination should focus on the New World as the scene of God's future glorious acts, for "the wilderness-to-become-paradise is America."[7] Even before the advent of the eschaton, America had things to teach the world, for America, in Edwards's view, was "a brighter type of heaven."[8] Bercovitch claims for Edwards the thesis that perception of America's importance in the history of redemption is the key to Christian epistemology: one can understand nature in general only if one perceives "Christ's *magnalia Americana*."[9] The most recent illustration of the redeemer-nation interpretation is John Wilson's conclusion that Edwards invested the American experience "with preeminent significance for concluding the drama of Christian redemption."[10]

Some scholars have proposed a link between Edwards's millennialism and various incarnations of "self-interest" in later American culture. Thus, for example, Edwards "and his postmillennial disciples" are said to have provided Calvinists "with a radical justification for early nationalism" that served to baptize the status quo in the waters of divine approbation. In the words of James Maclear, "they tended to accept and sanctify American institutions and social values."[11] Among those values was laissez-faire economics, which Edwards's millennialism is said to have stimulated by using American commerce as a type of the millennium and by equating "conversion, national commerce, and the treasures of a renovated earth."[12]

A second value recently associated with Edwards's eschatology is the idea of American progress. Associated with the millennium, American economic and social progress became part of the deity's plan for world redemption. Thus the American political and social orders, which during the Great Awakening were regarded with suspicion by Edwardsean New Lights, came to be seen through the diffracting lens of Edwardsean eschatology as divinely appointed custodians of the work of redemption.[13]

Although many students of Edwards's eschatology have found it to be self-indulgently nationalistic—at least at certain points in Edwards's career[14]—and some have connected Edwards's millennialism and later American egoism, a minority of critics have argued that Edwards's eschatology was apolitical. James West Davidson maintains that Edwards's millennium is privatistic in the sense that it describes an inner, spiritual world that transcends existing political institutions. Liberty reigns but existing civil governments are not overthrown. So the "liberty" therein described need not be political. Furthermore, the millennial vision requires regeneration, but many—perhaps most—members of society are unregenerate. Therefore, one cannot speak of a wholesale political change.[15] Nathan Hatch reaches the same conclusion but by a different route. He argues that Edwards was too pessimistic in his forecasts of the historical future to hitch his eschatology to the chariots of secular parties. Whereas Calvinists during and after the Revolution linked the advent of the millennium to the new

American republic, Edwards insisted that the millennium would come by spiritual means such as the preaching of the gospel.[16]

What *were* the social and political implications of Edwards's millennialism? Did his eschatology really exalt America to a position of spiritual and political preeminence in cosmic history? Was America to be both the catalyst to inaugurate the millennium and the center of that final, glorious stage of history? If New England and America were central to Edwards's eschatology, both as agents to bring on history's culmination and as most favored nations during that reign of glory, then Edwards's eschatology was inconsistent with his (national) covenantal theology. For in the last chapter we saw that in Edwards's view of the national covenant, New England was not a redeemer nation, but a bad example that the world would be wise to avoid. New England had sinned so grievously that, as Edwards stopped to contemplate its eschatology, he foresaw not future glory but the possibility of imminent destruction.[17] He wondered only why it had not already come. If in Edwards's eschatology New England was to be the locus of the earthly reign of Christ, then his public theology was full of inner contradictions.

It is my thesis in this chapter that on the point at hand Edwards's thought is consistent. There is no conflict between his doctrine of the national covenant and his millennialism. If the former casts a dark cloud of judgment over the colonies, the latter relegates them to obscurity by its overwhelming emphasis on the international dimensions of the millennium. Edwards's eschatology is dominated by an unyielding concentration on the coming global community that implicitly relativizes all merely national concerns and condemns all egoistic nationalism. Before the majestic dimensions of the "one holy and happy society"[18] that is to come, New England and America fade into insignificance.

Scholars have properly concentrated on Edwards's millennialism for clues to his thinking on other issues. The work of redemption within human history was an obsession for Edwards, and the union of nations and peoples in the millennium was the next and last earthly phase of that work of redemption. His vision of the millennium's realities and his anticipation of the "glorious work of God's Spirit"[19] that would bring it to fruition so pervaded his thinking that nearly every one of his central doctrines is illuminated by an unfolding of the millennial vision. It is sometimes remarked, for instance, that Edwards's doctrine of divine sovereignty was as exalted as any in the history of Christian thought.[20] Yet Edwards's doctrine cannot be appreciated fully unless it is understood that every event in history is divinely orchestrated to prepare for the millennium.

Divine typology in history and nature is another characteristic feature of Edwards's theology. For Edwards, typology pointed not only to past redemption and present spiritual realities, but to future events in history as well.[21] Yet the most exciting future events were the millennium and "that glorious work of God's Spirit" leading up to it. Every sunrise, for instance, was for Edwards a type of the bright glory to come in the millennium.[22]

An understanding of Edwards's millennialism will, similarly, shed much light on his public theology. For we shall see that it was in the "one amiable society" (*HWR*, 483) of the millennium, not his own, that Edwards was absorbed. It was the "one holy city, one heavenly family" (*HA*, 339) that looms in the background of nearly every treatise and many of his sermons, and that fills many pages of his private notebooks. In short, in his religious imagination Jonathan Edwards was a world citizen. The parochialism and egoistic nationalism ascribed to him would have struck him as myopic and characteristic only of unregenerate, natural virtue.[23] I shall demonstrate this thesis first by describing the intensity of Edwards's absorption with the millennium and its antecedent events, then by delineating in detail the contours of each of those periods—the millennium and the "glorious work of God's Spirit" preceding it—and drawing out the implications of each for Edwards's public theology.

EDWARDS'S ENTERTAINMENT AND DELIGHT

Jonathan Edwards was not the first New Englander to be interested in the millennium. Religious leaders since the Founding had spoken and written of it. In 1710 Increase Mather wrote that belief in the millennium "has ever been received as a Truth in the Churches of *New-England*." Yet from the first generation eschatology was seldom a central concern for religious leaders. John Winthrop wrote very little about the millennium in his voluminous writings, and "[Thomas] Shepard and [Thomas] Hooker, after John Cotton the two most prolific writers in New England of the 1640s, had far less than he to say upon millennial topics." The focus of Shepard's *Ten Virgins* is Christ's Second Coming, not a final earthly age of glory. John Norton refers to the fullness of the Gentiles in *The Answer,* but this notion plays no significant role in the book.[24]

Religious leaders of New England's later generations "rarely preached specifically on millennial prophecies pointing to the end of time, and when they did it was generally in the most undogmatic and speculative of terms."[25] Michael Wigglesworth's *Day of Doom* (1662), the most popular eschatological statement of the seventeenth century, pointed its readers to hell, not the millennium.[26] The jeremiahs in mid and late century found little or no use for millennial eschatology.[27] Eighteenth-century election sermons show a similar pattern. The millennium is either absent or merely a rhetorical flourish.[28] Even those who celebrated the millennial import of Cape Breton and other events in the French and Indian War were nevertheless unwilling to say that the war was the climactic battle against the Antichrist.[29] In sum, millennialism was a paradigm used more for comprehending the meaning of occasional crises than for understanding everyday life.[30]

For Jonathan Edwards, however, the millennium was a continual obsession. What William Ellery Channing once said of Samuel Hopkins, Edwards's closest disciple, could be said with equal accuracy of Edwards, "The millennium was more than a belief to him. It had the freshness of visible things. He was at home in it. His book on the subject has an air of reality, as if written from observation."[31] Edwards cultivated a lifelong fascination with the millennial prophecies of Scripture. When he wrote his ***Personal Narrative*** at the age of thirty-six, he recalled being dazzled by the millennial future in his twentieth year: "Sometimes Mr. Smith and I walked there [in New York] together, to converse on the things of God; and our conversation used to turn much on the advancement of Christ's kingdom in the world, *and the glorious things that God would accomplish for his church in the latter days.*"[32] We know that Edwards's recollection of concern for eschatology in his twentieth year was not inaccurate because in a diary entry from the same year we find him lamenting the insufficiency of his prayers for the millennium.[33] This engrossment with eschatology continued throughout his life. In a letter in 1741 to a newly converted "dear young friend" in reply to a request for instructions on how to "maintain a religious life," Edwards urged her to pray that God "would carry on his glorious work which he has now begun, till the world shall be full of his glory."[34] Six years later, when David Brainerd was dying in Edwards's home, the two often discussed the coming glorious days of the church, and the young man's "vehement thirstings" for the millennial age only sharpened the pastor's own eschatological hopes (*David Brainerd,* 532). Stephen J. Stein notes that Edwards continued to make millennial entries in his private notebooks to the end of his career (*AW*, 10, 32). It is a telling sign of the fascination eschatology held for Edwards that the Revelation was the only book of the Bible on which he wrote a separate commentary.[35]

For Edwards the millennial age was of more than just speculative or even theological interest. Devotion to it gave him emotional satisfaction and release. In the ***Personal Narrative*** he relates that over the sixteen years since his twentieth year "my mind has been much *entertained and delighted* with the scripture promises and prophecies, which relate to the future glorious advancement of Christ's kingdom upon earth" ("PN," 68; emphasis added). News of the advancement of Christ's kingdom toward its earthly culmination in the millennium would, by his own admission, "much animate and refresh" the sickly and often weary pastor ("PN," 64). Ten years later, he was still finding "entertaining" the news of developments in Scotland that suggested progress in the work of redemption toward the millennium.[36] Stein infers that Edwards's millennial fixation provided comfort "throughout the years of great personal stress and turmoil," particularly in the 1740s when growing tensions between him and his Northampton congregation finally resulted in his ejection.[37]

Theologically, the millennium was crucial because of its place in Edwards's understanding of Providence. All of history was ordered by God in such a way as to lead to a foreordained result—the kingdom of his Son. As Edwards put it, the universe is like a "chariot in which God rides and makes progress towards the last end of all things."[38] So the millennium, as the last earthly stage in that process, is the culmination of all the ages of human history.

> All the changes that are brought to pass in the world, from age to age, are ordered in infinite wisdom in one respect or other to prepare the way for the glorious issue of things, that shall be when truth and righteousness shall finally prevail, and he, whose right it is, shall take the kingdom. . . . The mighty struggles and conflicts of nations, and shakings of kingdoms, and those vast successive changes that are brought to pass, in the kingdoms and empires of the world, from one age to another, are as it were travail pangs of the creation, in order to bring forth this glorious event. (*HA,* 346)

For Edwards, history and the millennium were inseparable. The first was preparation for the second; the second, the *telos* of the first. Therefore, neither could be understood without the other. Edwards demonstrated the inseparability of the two in his mind in two places in his **"Personal Narrative."** In the first instance, when describing his days in New York, he mentioned the two in the same breath: "Our [Edwards and John Smith] conversation used to turn much on the advancement of Christ's kingdom in the world, *and* the glorious things that God would accomplish for his church in the latter days" ("PN," 65). Later in the **"Narrative,"** after saying that "the histories of the past advancement of Christ's kingdom have been sweet to me," Edwards turned immediately to the millennium and its prelude: "And my mind has been much entertained and delighted with the scripture promises and prophecies, which relate to the future glorious advancement of Christ's kingdom upon earth" (68). For Edwards, the process of redemption in human history was "most fundamental to Christianity."[39] And since the millennium was the last earthly stage of that history, no part of the history could be properly evaluated without consideration of its earthly *telos.* Only the future could give proper meaning to both past and present.

Edwards eagerly scanned his contemporary world for signs of progress in that process of which the millennium was the culmination. "If I heard the least hint," he wrote in the **"Narrative,"** "of any thing that happened, in any part of the world, that appeared, in some respect or other, to have a favourable aspect, on the interests of Christ's kingdom, my soul eagerly catched at it. . . . I used to be eager to read public newsletters, mainly for that end; to see if I could not find some news, favourable to the interest of religion in the world" ("PN," 64). Stein tells us that Edwards "retained the habit in later years" (*AW,* 10) and during the French and Indian War "followed developments closely because the outcome had implications for the view of history he had shaped in his reflections on Revelation" (32). In 1749 Edwards begged a Scottish correspondent to give him "information of whatever appears in your parts of the world, favourable to the interests of the kingdom of Christ."[40] His *Notes on the Apocalypse,* written throughout his adult life, reveal copious attention given to world events—political, military, and ecclesiastical—that by his

lights indicated the beginning of the destruction of the Antichrist and the worldwide outpouring of the Spirit of God.[41]

Besides seeing the millennium anticipated in contemporary history, Edwards found it prefigured in biblical history and nature. In his private notebooks Edwards wrote that he found typological anticipations of the coming glorious days of the Church in the fall of Sodom and Gomorrah, the prophecies about Israel's return to the land, Achsah's intercession with her father, the destruction of Sisera, the reign of Solomon, the Jews' victory in the time of Esther, and many other biblical events.[42] When he turned to observe the beauty of the world about him, Edwards found images of the millennium there too. Both spring and the dawn, for example, are types of the "commencement of the glorious times of the church."[43]

Thus Edwards was gripped by the millennium. Yet, as I have mentioned in passing, the millennium was only the penultimate goal of God's work of redemption of the elect. The ultimate goal was the final assemblage of the kingdom in heaven, far removed from earth and *after* the completion of the millennium.[44] This would be a state "manifestly different from the millennium." It would represent the return of all things to God after their beginning in God: "In the beginning of this revolution all things come from God, and are formed out of a chaos; and in the end, all things shall return into a chaos again, and shall return to God, so that he that is *Alpha,* will be the *Omega.*"[45] Thus progress in the work of redemption is ultimately circular. This is why Edwards chose the wheel as the best representation of divine providence.[46]

Although the millennium was not the ultimate goal of the history of redemption, it nevertheless excited more of Edwards's attention than any other phase in that history. This was due to the place Edwards thought he occupied within the history of providence. In his estimation the present generation was standing on the threshold of the age that would precipitate the millennium. As we shall see below, this preparatory age would last far beyond Edwards's lifetime; Edwards never expected to see the dawn of the millennium himself. But to live in the preparatory age was exciting enough. Besides, he thought that he was one of a handful of divines called by God in the latter days to teach and reprove the Church, and thus prepare it for eventual participation in the millennium.[47] So, while he knew that the millennium was only a penultimate stage before ultimate glory, anticipation of its penultimate glory was captivating enough to hold his attention for more than thirty-eight years.

Let us now attempt to imagine the spectacle that so captivated Edwards by sketching the outlines of his millennial vision. We will begin by examining the chronology of the millennial age because (1) it demonstrates where Edwards thought he stood within the history of redemption, and (2) the time of the beginning of the millennial age has been almost universally misunderstood by students of Edwards's thought.

THE SHAPE OF THE MILLENNIUM CHRONOLOGY

For Edwards the millennium would be Christ's *third* coming to set up his kingdom. His *first* coming was in the apostolic era when he set up his kingdom in a spiritual sense and destroyed his enemies by starting the church. The end of this era was marked by the destruction of Jerusalem. The *second* coming effected the "destruction of the heathen Roman empire" in Constantine's time. The *fourth* and last coming will be "his coming to the last judgment, which is the event principally signified in scripture by Christ's coming in his kingdom" (*HWR*, 351).

Contrary to prevailing scholarly opinion, this third coming of Christ in the millennium was not expected by Edwards till the distant future. And, I would argue, Edwards held this view consistently throughout his career. When he was twenty years old (in 1723), he wrote in his private notebook that he did not anticipate the final destruction of "Satan's kingdom till the year 2000" (*AW*, 77, 129). In 1747 he submitted this chronology to public scrutiny in *An Humble Attempt.* Moses Lowman was correct, he maintained, to place the Antichrist's end after 2000. One of the first series of blows against the Antichrist's reign (a worldwide series of revivals) was to come soon, but the final blow (the final destruction of the Antichrist and thus the beginning of the millennium) was not to come until the seventh millennium of human history (A.D. 2000-3000).[48]

Between his first prediction in his private notebook and his public forecast in *An Humble Attempt,* Edwards made another prediction that has caused commentators to stumble ever since. The problem hinges on the interpretation of a phrase in *Some Thoughts Concerning the Revival* (1742). In an oft-cited passage relating the Great Awakening to God's future work of redemption Edwards proclaimed that "this work of God's Spirit, that is so extraordinary and wonderful, is the dawning, or at least a prelude, of that glorious work of God, so often foretold in Scripture, which in the progress and issue of it, shall renew the world of mankind." The phrase in question is "that glorious work of God," which Edwards says later in the passage "must be near" (*ST*, 353). Almost every interpreter of Edwards's eschatology has construed this remark to be a reference to the millennium, and thus a prediction that the millennium was imminent.[49] If they are correct, Edwards had reversed his earlier conviction that the millennium lay in the distant future, and was taking a stand that he would contradict for the remainder of his life. Even Stein, who thinks he refers to the millennium, concedes, "This heady proclamation published in 1743 was neither in character with Edwards's earlier pronouncements on the revivals nor totally consistent with his own private reflections" (*AW*, 26).

In fact, there is good reason to believe that Edwards here referred not to the millennium but to a long period of intermittent revival that would lead up to the millennium. Four to five years earlier Edwards already had made it clear that the millennium would be a state of peace and rest—at least until the great apostasy at its end.[50] In contrast, the revivals leading up to it would be marked by conflict and struggle as the forces of the Antichrist did battle with the newly emerging kingdom of the Son. So the period *before* the millennium would be a time of change and unrest, but the millennium itself would be a changeless epoch of peace.

> The millennium is the sabbatism of the church, or the time of her rest. But surely the days of her sabbatism or rest don't begin, till she ceases to be any longer in travail. . . . And as long as the church still remains struggling and laboring, to bring to pass this effect, her travail ceases not; . . . The church from Christ's time to the millennium, is in a state of warfare, or her militant state; but during that sabbatism, [she] shall be in a triumphant state. The proper time of the church's rest and triumph can't be said to be come, till all her enemies are subdued. (*HA*, 178-79)

The problem with the conventional interpretation is that the passage in question, upon which the interpretation is based, describes a work of God that is still in a process of development and change. It is "that glorious work of God, so often foretold in Scripture, which *in the progress and issue of it,* shall renew the world of mankind!" (*ST*, 353; emphasis added). Edwards here describes a progressive, and therefore gradual, transition in the world, during which the world will be renewed. The emphasis is on a developmental process: "which *in the progress and issue of it,* shall renew the world." The world shall be renewed, but only "in the progress" of that glorious work of God—that is, as the work of God progresses through its duration. Three years earlier, in his sermons on the history of the work of redemption, Edwards had taught quite explicitly that the "great work of God" that would pave the way for the millennium would be wrought "gradually" and amidst "violent and mighty opposition."[51] Yet, as we have seen, Edwards had represented the millennium itself as a state of rest and completion that does not begin until the process of development and conflict has been completed.

It makes much more sense to understand Edwards in the *Some Thoughts* passage as he himself interpreted the passage two years later—that he was referring to the long process preceding the onset of the millennium, not the millennium itself: "It has been slanderously reported and printed concerning me, that I have often said that the millennium was already begun . . . but the report is very diverse from what I have ever said."[52] In words nearly identical to the ones we have just seen from *Some Thoughts* he said that he had always regarded the recent awakenings "as forerunners of those glorious times so often prophesied of in the Scripture, and that this was the first dawning of that light, and beginning of that work which, *in the progress and issue of it,* would *at last* bring on the church's latter-day glory" (*GA*, 560; emphasis added). The "work" that would "progress," in other words, was distinct from "the church's latter-day glory." Lest anyone still think that Edwards had ever considered the millennium imminent or arrived, he added that he had also said on earlier occasions that this work would be accompanied by conflict and struggle:

> There are many that know that I have from time to time added, that there would probably be many sore conflicts and terrible convulsions, and many changes, revivings and intermissions, and returns of dark clouds, and threatening appearances, before this work shall have subdued the world, and Christ's kingdom shall be everywhere established and settled in *peace, which will be the lengthening of the millennium, or day of the church's peace,* rejoicing and triumph on earth, so often spoken of. (*GA,* 560; emphasis added)

In the letter quoted above Edwards denied that he had predicted an imminent millennium, and insisted that he had always assumed a long process of revival and turmoil preceding the millennium. The pattern found here is the same one found in other descriptions of the latter days: the period leading up to the millennium will be a gradual development involving both revival and opposition, whereas the millennium itself will begin only when development has ceased and peace and rest have begun.[53]

There is also the puzzling statement in part 4 of *Some Thoughts* that the New England awakenings might "prove to be the dawning of a general revival" (*ST,* 466). For Edwards, the millennium was never considered, properly speaking, a revival. Edwards understood a revival to be episodic and progressive, but the millennium as uniform and static. In a revival souls change—from unsaved to saved, darkness to light. In the millennial era, on the other hand, souls remain essentially the same: they enter the era in the light (after seeing the light during the glorious days preceding the millennium) and continue in the light until the end and beyond. The millennium will not see the emotional and religious upheavals that occur in a revival.[54] This is why Edwards never used the word "millennium" in any of the *Some Thoughts* passages that allegedly predict an American millennium—a fact which has never been satisfyingly explained.[55] He certainly was not averse to use of the word, for he had previously used it in his private notebooks and would later use it in his published treatises.[56] But he did not use it here because it was not what he meant. "General revival" was a better term for "that great work of God's Spirit," because it consisted of precisely that: a worldwide series of revivals.

The interpretation here suggested—that Edwards foresaw in the immediate future not the millennium but a long age of intermittent revival preceding the millennium—is supported by consideration of Edwards's predecessors in the Reformed eschatological tradition. Examination of that tradition indicates that Edwards was advancing not novel doctrine but a variation of what had become a recurring theme. Thomas Brightman (1562-1607), who was the first Englishman in the mainstream of Reformed thought to break with the Augustinian interpretation of eschatology, forecast a "Middle Advent of Christ," beginning about 1650, the first hundred years of which would see a pro-

gressive reformation in both the Church and the world. By Christ's spiritual help the Church would gradually prosper, the Jewish nation would convert, and the papist and Turkish armies would be destroyed. At the end of that century of progressive reformation, perfection would be secured. The "pleasantness" that "belong[ed] to the first beginning [before the fall]" would be enjoyed by the saints for at least another five centuries until Christ's final coming. In Brightman, then, we see a period of revival and conflict effected by divine effusions before a period of peaceful perfection.[57]

John Cotton (1584-1652) was the foremost millennialist of the New England founders.[58] Like Brightman, he predicted a period of progressively increasing blessing for the Church and gradual destruction of her enemies. (Unlike Brightman, however, Cotton looked for the personal return of Christ to inaugurate the millennium). The Church would approach "full stature and beauty" in a period of "gradual increase," and while it was gradually increasing its size and influence, the Protestant armies would be mobilized to defeat—over a period of time—the Roman and Turkish menaces, as well as the Anglican episcopacy. During this time the world would still be far from millennial perfection. Many individuals and nations would remain unconverted, and Satan would still tempt the saints. The condition of mortality would remain.[59] Cotton was not alone among his contemporaries in projecting an age of gradually increasing glory for the Church before the onset of the millennium. "Few if any theorists of the 1640s and 1650s saw the millennial order as the creation of an instant. It was the way of the Middle Coming both to build upon previous beginnings and to propel events toward completion through a process of gradual development."[60]

Similar projections can be found in the eschatologies of Reformed thinkers at the beginning of the eighteenth century. Both Moses Lowman (1680-1752) and Petrus Van Mastricht (1630-1706), whose eschatology and influence on Edwards are discussed in more detail below, believed that the end of history would be preceded by an era of divine effusions gradually prospering the Church and ruining her enemies. Lowman, whose *Paraphrase and Notes on the Revelation* was the single work most often cited by Edwards in his apocalyptic notebook and treatises, speculated that the destruction of mystical Babylon would proceed gradually until after the year 2000, when the millennium would commence (*AW,* 57). Van Mastricht wrote in the last volume of his greatest work that the near future held either the Last Judgment or a "New Reformation" that would see the internal renewal of the church and a purifying divine judgment on the unregenerate.[61]

James Davidson's study of millennial thought in eighteenth-century New England shows a similar pattern. Most commentators on eschatology held to an "afflictive model of progress" wherein a series of revivals, accompanied by afflictions, would precede the millennium. Things would get worse as the millennium drew near, for as the Church prospers, Satan fights harder against it. The redemption of the world consists of both merciful effusions poured out on the Church and punishing judgments poured out on the world. Even the Church will be chastised in order to purify it. Thus the last age before the millennium will combine mercy and judgment, deliverance and affliction. As Samuel Willard put it, a time was coming when "the privileges of the Church both spiritual and temporal shall be great to admiration, but still it will have a mixture of darkness in it."[62]

This time of tumult stood in stark contrast to a time, of which many also spoke, when human nature would be changed, courts would not be abused, standing armies would be unnecessary, and factions would not exist. Of Edwards's contemporaries, the English dissenting theologian Thomas Ridgley (1667-1734), whose systematic theology was familiar to Edwards, perhaps came closest to distinguishing the two periods. Before the millennium, Ridgley wrote, there would be "a greater fullness of the Gentiles . . . a greater degree of the effusion of the Spirit . . . a more glorious light shining throughout the world, than has ever done." Apparently there would also be afflictions, for the millennium itself would be "perfectly free from all those *afflictive* dispensations of providence, which would tend to hinder the preaching and success of the gospel." The Antichrist will have been subdued, so the saints will be "enjoying as much peace, as they have reason to expect in any condition short of heaven."[63]

Ridgley came close to articulating the distinction, but it was Edwards who most clearly developed the two-stage chronology. Others may have assumed such a distinction without expressing it. Perhaps some, caught up by millennial enthusiasm during and after the French and Indian Wars, saw no distinction at all. Hence their audiences could be forgiven for concluding that Christ was about to come to earth to launch his thousand-year reign. Edwards, on the other hand, took care to point out that the New England revivals were signs of a long period mixed with glory and affliction, and that the millennial age, properly speaking, was still hundreds of years in the future.[64]

In sum, all of these considerations—Edwards's descriptions of the millennium as a static period of peace and rest and the preceding period as a time of change and conflict, his statement that the Great Awakening might be the prelude to a general revival, and the compatibility of this interpretation with those of Edwards's Reformed predecessors—suggest that Edwards was telling the truth when he protested that he had never predicted an imminent millennium. Instead, he had always anticipated "that glorious work of God's Spirit" which would last many generations past his own before the dawning of the millennium itself.

The significance of Edwards's denial of an imminent millennium can be seen when it is contrasted with the views of some of Edwards's predecessors and contemporaries. By postponing the millennium to the twenty-first century, Edwards was rejecting the imminentism of—among others—the Mathers. In the early part of the eighteenth century Increase Mather expected Christ to return within a matter of a few years to inaugurate the millennium. His son Cotton was even more fervent in his expectation of the end-time glory. Unlike his father, he was willing to set a date for Christ's return—1716. After that prophecy failed, he was still writing in 1724 that the millennium could begin at any time.[65]

Edwards was also rejecting the imminentism of many clerical contemporaries. Eighteenth-century revivals, both before and during the Great Awakening, were interpreted as signs that the eschaton was at hand. As early as 1706, for example, Samuel Danforth proclaimed after a revival at Taunton, "The Time of the pouring out of the SPIRIT upon all Flesh may be at the Door." Fifteen years later, Eliphalet Adams understood a rash of conversions at Windham as a sign that the times were "drawing nearer" when the "whole Earth may be filled with the Knowledge of the Glory of the Lord." Great Awakening revivals produced similar expectations. In South Carolina they were hailed as the harbinger of the new age. A Pennsylvania New Side cleric pronounced them proof that "the Kingdom of God is come unto us at this Day." Weekly reports publicizing the progress of the revivals in Thomas Prince's *Christian History,* the Boston periodical published in 1744 and 1745, were punctuated periodically with millennial acclamations. The colonial victory at Cape Breton in 1745 was seen as "an Earnest of our Lords taking to himself the entire Possession of this *New World.*"[66]

The chronology of the Edwardsean millennium has two more salient features: its end and its length. The Edwardsean millennium was to be a period of absolute stability and peace for the vast majority of its duration. Only at its very end would there be a break in its bliss, when the newly freed Satan would lead a great apostasy.[67] After his rebellion is put down, the Last Judgment shall ensue. Then the Church will be lifted to the highest heavens as one glorious society, and the earth will be burned to become a furnace for the wicked.[68]

Concerning the length of the millennium, some of Edwards's contemporaries had supposed the "thousand years" of Revelation to be only a figure of speech to represent a very long time.[69] Edwards, however, insisted that the number was literal. For if it were any longer, he argued, a population explosion would render the planet unlivable. Because of the absence of wars and disease in the millennium, the human race would be "multiplying so fast"—even if it doubles but once in a century—that there would not be room enough for all to coexist comfortably after one thousand years.[70]

If the time and duration of the millennium are important for any investigation of Edwards's civil religion, the *location* of the millennium is no less important. For if the eschaton is to be precipitated by a particular nation, or centrally located in one nation, then that nation will assume preeminence in the history of redemption. Thus we turn to the geography of the millennium.

MILLENNIAL GEOGRAPHY

For too long scholars have attributed to Edwards, on the basis of a misreading of the **Some Thoughts** passage, the belief that the millennium would begin or be centered in America. Edwards, referring to the same "work of God" discussed above, said that "there are many things that make it probable that this work will begin in America."[71] Thus Edwards appears to have contradicted himself, since at the beginning of his career he had written in his private notebooks that the millennium would be centered in Canaan.[72] But, as we have seen, the work of God predicted in the *Some Thoughts* passage is a series of revivals and conflicts preceding the millennium, not the millennium itself. In this passage Edwards claimed only that this work of preparation, which in **An Humble Attempt** he estimated would last two hundred and fifty years (*HA,* 411), would probably begin in America.

Edwards's claim that the millennium itself would begin in Canaan was not unprecedented. In England, both Thomas Brightman (1562-1607) and Daniel Whitby (1638-1726) had claimed the same. Whitby, a liberal theologian whose eschatology Edwards read, portrayed the millennium as primarily a spiritual revival of the Jewish church. Some New England thinkers held similar views. John Cotton believed that the New Jerusalem would rise far from American shores, and Increase Mather wrote that Europe was to be the locus of the millennium.[73]

Edwards placed the center of the millennium in Canaan,[74] and described the millennium itself in international terms. "The kingdom of God . . . shall *not* be like the kingdoms of earthly kings, set up with outward pomp, *in some particular place,* which shall be especially the royal city, and seat of the kingdom" (*DM,* 235; emphasis added). Rather, it "shall universally prevail, and . . . be extended over the whole habitable earth" (*HA,* 333). No people or part of the globe shall be unaffected: "All countries and nations, even those which are now most ignorant, shall be full of light and knowledge" (*HWR,* 480). "All nations from one end of the earth to the other are subdued by the spiritual David, and firmly and quietly established in subjection to his crown."[75]

By positing an international millennium, Edwards was departing from what was more a popular—than clerical—image of the final glorious age. As noted above, John Cotton and Increase Mather rejected the notion of an American millennium. Although Cotton Mather at various points in his career looked for an American millennium, he finally realized that New England should not be confused with the New Jerusalem. Militia captain Edward Johnson, on the other hand, believed that New England was "the place where the Lord will create a new Heaven, and a new Earth in, new Churches, and a new Common-wealth together." Chief Justice Samuel Sewall was convinced that the "Divine Metropolis" would be seated on the American continent (in Mexico, to be precise). Early in the eighteenth century Joseph Morgan's *History of the Kingdom of Bara-*suah, which predicted that Christ's Kingdom would be in the New World, was popular.[76]

Edwards rejected such regionalism. That he propounded an American millennium is a notion without support in either his published works or private notebooks. He would have agreed with those critics who have dismissed the notion as parochial and tribalist—certainly ill-suited to a deity who superintends the entire cosmos. That Edwards at one point suggested that the centuries-long process precipitating the millennium might begin in America does not undermine this thesis, as will be shown below in the discussion of "that glorious work of God."

As others have noted,[77] Edwards did not construct his elaborate millennium vision in a vacuum. He fashioned his eschatology amid the turmoils of the Great Awakening and the struggles with his parishioners that culminated in ejection from his own pulpit. It will come as no surprise, then, to learn that many features of his millennium appear implicitly critical of Northampton religion, society, and economics. In this respect Edwards resembles the "great utopians" whose utopias were not otherworldly, escapist dreams but thoughtful critiques of their societies. Frank and Fritzie Manuel write, "Paradoxically, the great utopians have been great realists. They have an extraordinary comprehension of the time and place in which they are writing and deliver themselves of penetrating reflection on socioeconomic, scientific, or emotional conditions of their moment in history."[78]

Not only was Edwards's millennium a subtle reflection on eighteenth-century Northampton and New England, but it was not so bizarre that it seemed irrelevant. Like every great utopia, it "startles and yet is recognized as conceivable." Rather than fantasizing an unrealistic escape from the present, he sketched a future "that satisfies a hunger or stimulates the mind and the body to the recognition of a new potentiality."[79] It should be no surprise, then, that historians have attributed important social and political movements in colonial and early America to the stimulus of Edwards's millennial vision.[80]

MILLENNIAL RELIGION

In religion, the millennium would be everything Northampton was not. It would embody every virtue and every mark of piety that Edwards longed to see among his parishioners.[81] In the millennial time "religion shall in every respect be uppermost in the world." Political leaders would be "eminent in holiness," possessed by "vital piety." Arminianism and other deviations from Calvinism would be "exploded." Theological problems that long had perplexed the faithful would be solved: "There shall then be a wonderful unraveling the [sic] difficulties in the doctrines of religion, and clearing up of seeming inconsistencies. . . . Difficulties in Scripture shall then be cleared up, and wonderful things shall be discovered in the word of God that were never discovered before. . . . [H]eaven shall be, as it were, opened to the church of God on earth" (*HWR,* 480-81).

Piety would be genuine and sincere, not hypocritical: "Religion shall not be an empty profession as it now mostly is, but holiness of heart and life shall abundantly prevail." Religion would not be privatistic, confined only to the home and church, but would be "inscribed on every thing, on all men's common business and employments, and the common utensils of life."[82] In other words, businessmen, who had come under blistering attack in Edwards's sermons for their indifference to the constraints of Christian charity,[83] would apply a zeal for holiness to their trade. Here then are examples of how Edwards's eschatological vision both was shaped by pastoral concerns and served to rebuke (implicitly) the social standards of his day.

In another implicit reproach to Northampton, whose divisiveness was legendary,[84] Edwards promised that in the millennium the church would be marked by "excellent order" (*HWR,* 484). It would not "be rent with a variety of jarring opinions," but the true government and discipline of the church would then be settled and put into practice (*HA,* 339). Northampton church members probably read between the lines, "Parishioners will respect the minister and accept his teaching and discipline."

Nor would the Church be wracked by the wild claims of "enthusiasts" to have heard voices from God. In a tacit denunciation of Great Awakening enthusiasts,[85] Edwards explained that in the "future and glorious times of [the church's] latter-day prosperity and blessedness" there will not be "prophets, and men endowed with the gifts of tongues and of working miracles, as was the case in the times of the apostles." For the millennium will be the time for only the best, and such charismatic gifts are inferior. The Spirit of God will then be poured out in the "more excellent way" of love, not miracles or impressions of the divine voice.[86]

Millennial religion was not to be limited to the polite society of Western whites. Transcending the social mores of New England's religious liberals, Edwards proclaimed that "the Negroes and Indians will be divines" and theological treatises would be "published in Africa, in Ethiopia, in Turkey" (*HWR,* 480). While many in the eighteenth century acknowledged that in native intellectual and religious capacity blacks were equal to whites, most could not seem to overcome their astonishment at the blacks' "stupidity."[87] It is not clear from either his published tomes or unpublished notebooks if Edwards shared this view of blacks, but it is clear that his sights were trained on their future accomplishments. In the millennium, he claimed, blacks would attain religious virtuosity and publish learned tomes. He prophesied that "the most divine and angelic strains [will come] from among the Hottentots," an African tribe that was used in the eighteenth century as a symbol of intellectual and cultural inferiority. "The press," he went on,

"shall groan in wild Tartary," the central Asian habitat known in Edwards's day for its savagery.[88]

In the seventeenth and eighteenth centuries there was some debate over the manner in which Christ would reign during the millennium—in bodily form or spiritual presence.[89] Like most of his contemporaries, Edwards came down on the side of the spiritualists. Christ's body would not be on earth but remain in heaven. His reign on earth would be "by his Spirit." This would be "more glorious and happy for his church than his human presence would be," Edwards explained, because from heaven Christ would be better able to strengthen the church's faith and "greatly to encourage & comfort them" (*Miscellanies,* no. 827).

Millennial religion, then, was to be free from hypocrisy, strife, charismatic enthusiasm, and racism. All of these qualities concern religious *relations*—no surprise for a thinker who believed, as we shall see in the next chapter, that being consists primarily in relations. Hence it was natural for him to give considerable attention to social relations in the millennial age.

MILLENNIAL SOCIETY

Jonathan Edwards spent his life pursuing the good and the beautiful, both of which he found in the union of intelligent beings devoted to being-in-general.[90] All existence, he proposed, is based on proportion, which is the relation between two things, and beauty on proportions that exhibit agreement—if you will, union—of some sort.[91] All earthly beauties are simply mirrors of the archetype of beauty, the heavenly union of beings in common consent to being-in-general (*TV,* 564-65). Union, therefore, is a signal quality of both the beautiful and the good. Edwards even maintained that all true happiness—even God's—depends upon affectionate union in a society: "The happiness of the deity, as all other true happiness, consists in love and society."[92] Little wonder, then, that when Edwards looked to what he considered to be God's penultimate gift to his Church—the millennium—he found it to be a society of intelligent beings in *union*.[93]

Edwards's invocations of the harmony of millennial society have a lyrical sound to them, as if midway between ordinary consciousness and poetic rapture. "A time wherein the whole earth shall be united as one holy city, one heavenly family, men of all nations shall as it were dwell together, and sweetly correspond one with another as brethren and children of the same father. . . . A time wherein this whole great society shall appear in glorious beauty, in genuine amiable Christianity, and excellent order. . . . And then shall all the world be united in peace and love in one amiable society."[94] Heimert notes that Edwards's preoccupation with oneness was a subtle critique of the divisions the Great Awakening had fostered.[95] These passages are also further evidence that the tribalism of which Edwards has been accused is inconsistent with the eschatological vision he actually held.

Edwards found the cause of this remarkable, unprecedented unity in a new sort of human heart that was then to emerge. What was just beginning to blossom in ordinary history would then be fully in bloom. The human heart would be full of "great peace and love," and therefore would overflow with all the other Christian virtues. "Then shall *flourish* in an *eminent* manner those Christian virtues of meekness, forgiveness, long-suffering, gentleness, goodness and brotherly kindness, those excellent fruits of the Spirit" (*HWR,* 483; emphasis added). Human nature would still have the same sinful nature as in all the eras before the millennium, but because of great effusions of the Spirit the religious virtue of the human heart would be exponentially multiplied. The result would be a universal diffusion of excellence of character. "Men in their temper and disposition shall then be like the lamb of God, the lovely Jesus. The body shall be conformed to the head" (ibid.).

The consequence would be "the most universal peace, love and sweet harmony" in society. People would donate their material resources to help their fellows in need.[96] Millennial man, energized with copious doses of Christian virtue, would revolutionize both political and ecclesiastical relations. "All nations in all parts, on every side of the globe, shall then be knit together in sweet harmony, all parts of God's church assisting and promoting the knowledge and spiritual good one of another" (*HWR,* 483-84).[97]

The millennial society would be the mirror image of the heavenly society of saints, angels, and the Trinity—intelligent beings united in common consent to being-in-general. And since there is "true, spiritual original beauty . . . [in] the union of minds or spiritual beings in a mutual propensity and affection of heart," the millennial society will be "a beautiful society." Beauty shall reside in each of the members as well, for "all the world [shall then be] as one church, one orderly, regular, beautiful society, one body, all the members in beautiful proportion." Compared to all ages past, this "whole great society" in its "glorious beauty" shall be the "perfection of beauty."[98]

A beautiful society is a happy society. In the millennium God's saints will become "unspeakably happy in the view of his glory" (*HA,* 338). For Edwards the happiness of the saints was a common theme. Although he insisted that the Christian life was a pilgrimage through a foreign land with an abundance of suffering, and observed that the Christian's life is usually more troubled than the unbeliever's,[99] he never tired of promising great joy and happiness to the faithful, both in this life and the next. The happiness of the saints, he often remarked, is the intention of the Creator. God created human beings for happiness (*Miscellanies,* no. 87) and delights in their happiness (no. 679). Early in his private notebooks he wrote that their happiness was the highest end of the creation (*Miscellanies,* no. 3). Much later he explained that God's ultimate end in creation "consists in two things, viz., in God's infinite perfection being exerted & so manifested, that is, in God's glorifying Himself; and second, His infinite happiness being communicated & so making the creature happy." Both aspects of God's ultimate end "are sometimes in Scripture included in one world, namely, God's being glorified" (*Miscellanies,* no. 1066). In his notebook on Revelation Edwards wrote that even the damnation of the wicked is for the happiness of the blessed.[100]

MILLENNIAL ECONOMICS

The last era of human history would be showered with "great temporal prosperity." "Wealth" was to be abundant. Agriculture would be promoted "through the remarkable blessing of heaven" so that farms "shall be abundantly fruitful." Life expectancy would increase dramatically as human beings enjoy health and long life. With health abounding and wars having ceased there would be "a great increase of children." The result would be a population boom. "At the end of the thousand years, there would be more than a million inhabitants on the face of the earth, where there is one now." Then would be fulfilled the scriptural prophecies "that his redeemed ones should be as numerous as the drops of dew."[101]

Edwards was keenly aware of the political manipulations that governed the economy of his day.[102] The political and economic concerns of his own Hampshire County were dominated, more than most New England counties, by "a lively interplay of personal power, patronage, and paternalism." Israel Williams (Edwards's cousin) and his cronies exercised a "most imposing" influence over the social and financial affairs of the region. In Perry Miller's words, they were "grafters and land-grabbers."[103]

The Edwardsean millennial economy, in contrast, would prosper without the benefit of underhanded dealings. With his eye no doubt on the brisk river trade that plied the nearby Connecticut River, Edwards told his congregation that "the art of navigation that is now improved so much in fear, with covetousness and pride, and is used so much by wicked, debauched men, shall be consecrated to God, and improved for holy uses." Northampton merchants who profited from Valley navigation—and all who had any inkling of the economy's dependence on Valley trade and its "river gods"—must have seen the millennial ideal "as a severe indictment of a society beginning to take its cues from an amoral marketplace and the hidden hand of self-interest."[104]

In the final two sections of this portrait of the Edwardsean millennium we shall examine two topics of particular relevance to the relationship of the millennium to Edwards's public theology: knowledge and technology is one; politics, the other. Both were used by Edwards to point away from narrow nationalism to a global society, a "spiritual federalism" transcending all parochial concern for one's own land or people. Knowledge and technology in the eschaton would be used primarily to link far-flung corners of the globe in one global society, and the politics of the final earthly age would serve the harmonious relations of an international family of nations.

KNOWLEDGE AND TECHNOLOGY

Millennial commerce would be aided by the explosion of knowledge to come in that age. Then the earth would see a "vast increase of knowledge and understanding" (*HA,* 338). "Great light and knowledge" would fill the world (*HWR,* 480). Inventions and new discoveries would be commonplace: "To what they know now, there will continually be something new and surprising discovered in one part of the world and another" (*Miscellanies,* no. 26). Discoveries were to be both natural and religious. Secular inventions of the eighteenth century, Edwards figured, were divinely ordained clues to the religious discoveries that were to come in the millennium. "The late invention of telescopes . . . is a type and forerunner of the great increase in the knowledge of heavenly things that shall be in the approaching glorious times of the Christian church" (*Images,* 102).

The millennium as a storehouse of knowledge was a stock in trade of both religious and secular utopias. In New England, John Cotton, Increase Mather, and Cotton Mather connected the development of knowledge with the end of the world. In England, Anglican latitudinarians and Nonconformists in the late seventeenth and early eighteenth centuries said Christians would prepare themselves for the millennium by accumulating scientific knowledge and spreading the faith. Daniel 12:4 ("Many shall run to and fro, and knowledge shall be increased") was a favorite of the millennial Puritan heirs to Francis Bacon, who were eager to advance the causes of Christ, knowledge, and empire. For seventeenth-century Pansophists on the continent such as Leibniz and Comenius, calm and orderly science was a way to God in the end-time. Secular utopians of the eighteenth century such as the Marquis de Condorcet (1743-94) fantasized unlimited progress powered by scientific knowledge.[105]

For Edwards, the purpose of this knowledge explosion was to be religious. Labor-saving devices would be developed so "that they shall have more time for more noble exercise," i.e., religious meditation and action. Communications would be improved, Edwards explained, so that there would be "more expedite, easy, and safe communication between distant regions than now." But Edwards was not satisfied with mere improvement. Thought of the millennium's glory encouraged him to expect revolutionary changes. "Who can tell but that God will yet make it more perfect so that there need not be such a tedious voyage in order to hear from the other hemisphere," for the purpose of uniting the new global community of the spirit? "And so the countries about the Poles need no longer be hid to us, but the whole earth may be as one community, one body in Christ."[106] We are therefore presented with the ironic picture of a "provincial" parson envisioning immediate intercontinental communication and the shrinking of far-flung nations to one global village. Edwards's projection of millennial technology as the infrastructure of a new global community is further evidence that in his religious imagination this supposedly insular pastor had long since exploded the bounds of his native land and nation.

POLITICS

Just as the geography of Edwards's millennium was nearly always conceived in international terms, the politics of his eschaton were always interpreted internationally. The millennial disposition—that is, the quantitatively improved human nature discussed above—would affect "all countries and nations." No nation would be excluded. "Now the Kingdom of Christ shall in the most strict and literal sense extend to all nations and the whole earth." "Great knowledge shall prevail *everywhere.*"[107] In one section of *An Humble Attempt* Edwards underscored the universality of the millennium's effects upon every people and nation by consecutively quoting ten biblical passages, all of which contained the word "all," some of them repeating the word over and over again: "all the nations, "all the families of the earth," "all nations" (four times), "all flesh" (three times), etc. By sheer force of repetition Edwards impressed upon his auditors his conviction that no political unit would remain unvanquished before the millennial revolution (*HA,* 329-30).

That revolution[108] would not, however, dissolve all political boundaries into a single world government. The many nations of the world would come into unity, but the unity would be spiritual, resulting in "sweet harmony" among nations still existing individually. In other words, this was not to be a totalitarian world government that demolishes all previous political units, but a federal system respecting the integrity of existing polities. Christ was to be head over all, and his subordinates, the political leaders of each nation, were to rule their domains in accordance with his will. "All nations" would thus remain as nations; they would even manifest "different forms of government, very many."[109] But now they would be "knit together" spiritually by the new millennial character into "one amiable society" (*HWR,* 483).

Edwards's spiritual federalism was analogous to his understanding of the relationship between the regenerate believer and Christ. At conversion, he taught, the believer "becomes one" with Christ, but without losing his separate identity.[110] Just as a hyperbola approaches its asymptote infinitely without ever touching it, throughout eternity the believer approaches closer and closer to perfect union with Christ, but without ever finally merging into undifferentiated unity. So too, in Edwards's spiritual federalism, each nation in the millennium would subsist in such spiritual unity with all other nations that the world of nations would become as "one heavenly family," "as one community[,] one body in Christ."[111] Yet each nation would retain its separate identity and government throughout the duration of the glorious era.

The inevitable result of this international spiritual unity of nations would be world peace. "There shall then be universal peace and good understanding among all the nations of the world, instead of confusion, wars, and bloodshed." International goodwill would be so demonstrable that political leaders would dismantle their military establishments. "So it is represented as if all instruments of war should be destroyed as having become useless."[112] Edwards was not implicitly recommending unilateral disarmament to George II in the interests of Christian love. For armies were to be disbanded in the millennium because international amity would render them "useless." But in 1739 Edwards could give no assurance to his king that all nations were dwelling "quietly and safely, without fear of enemy,"[113] and therefore in no need of armies. In fact, during the French and Indian War Edwards demonstrated that he held to the just war tradition and considered it sometimes obligatory for the Christian to bear arms.[114] Edwards was instead suggesting that arms and war were necessary only in a world where Satan and sin were unchecked, and that the coming kingdom of the Christ would be free from their horrors.

Edwards's description of the *nature* of political power in the millennium confutes the position that the Edwardsean millennium was apolitical.[115] "Liberty" shall reign throughout the earth, he declared. That this liberty is political and not just religious he demonstrated *implicitly* when he said that "the absolute and despotic power of the kings of the earth shall be taken away," and *explicitly* when he stated that "every nation shall be a free people, not only with a freedom from spiritual slavery, but from civil too, from the tyrannical and absolute power of men" (*AW,* 136-37). Edwards understood the Micah 4:4 passage ("wherein every man shall sit under his own vine tree and under his own fig tree") as referring to political liberty and "not understood only in a mystical and spiritual sense" (*AW,* 137).[116] Throughout his life Edwards identified the Antichrist with political powers—both the Catholic nations of Europe and the Muslim Turks. So when he called the saints to action to bring on the millennium, they could be forgiven if they understood the call to have political import.

Relying on a statement in the private notebooks (*AW,* 136), Davidson claims that because Edwards disavowed the overthrow of civil government in the millennium, his idea of the millennium was apolitical. Yet that statement prefaces the assertion that "the absolute and despotic power of the kings of the earth *shall be taken away,* and liberty shall reign throughout the earth" (emphasis added). At the very least, this vision of political revolution—albeit by nonmilitary means—was an implicit denunciation of all eighteenth-century political systems that exercised absolute and despotic power. Hence his millennium had political significance. But the passage most likely says more. It conflates the "glorious work of God" preceding the millennium (when "the civil . . . polities of the nations, shall be overthrown") and the millennium itself (when no "civil government shall in any measure be overthrown")[117] in order to emphasize that in the millennium "the absolute and despotic power of the kings of the earth" shall have been "taken away, and liberty shall reign throughout the earth." The denial of coups d'état *during* the millennium did not

therefore rule out political revolution in the period preceding the millennium. That the millennium would be prepared by political upheaval is further confirmed by Edwards's statement in *Some Thoughts* that Christ would "strike through kings" who opposed the Awakening and "fill the places with dead bodies."[118] Edwards's vision of the millennium thus served to judge all polities falling short of full liberty and warned political leaders of the perils they risked by not supporting the revivals that would lead to the millennium.[119]

Edward's millennium was not a critique, however, of the ruling Hanoverian kings. Unlike his disciples in the Revolutionary era, he considered them to be paragons of political virtue. "Kings shall rather be as the judges were before Saul (whose government was that which was best pleasing to God), and as the kings of England now are in civil matters."[120]

Neither New England nor America figure in the Edwardsean millennium to any significant extent. Although the millennialism of other Great Awakening leaders reflected "an acute sense of American religious mission" and a strong sense of "provincial American patriotism,"[121] Edwards's references to his colony and land were almost uniformly negative. As argued above, the discussion of America in *Some Thoughts* concerns the long period preceding the millennium, not the millennium itself. In *The History of the Work of Redemption* Edwards states, "Then shall this vast continent of America, that now in so great part of it is covered with barbarous ignorance and cruelty, be everywhere covered with glorious gospel light and Christian love." The America to which Edwards here refers is "heathenism," i.e., the native American tribes that were "worshipping the devil" (*HWR,* 471-73). Their gift of glorious gospel light is not a special favor but the local application of a general, worldwide phenomenon. Throughout *The History of the Work of Redemption* the millennium is described in nothing but international terms (479-86). The last mention Edwards made of America and the millennium was in his *Humble Attempt* (1747). There America was portrayed as spiritually bankrupt, and the premillennial revivals as spiritual rescue operations for an otherwise doomed land.

> And how lamentable is the moral and religious state of these American colonies? Of New England in particular? What fierce and violent contentions. . . . How much is the gospel ministry grown into contempt, and the work of the ministry . . . in danger of sinking amongst us? How many of our congregations and churches rending in pieces? . . . What wild and extravagant notions, gross delusions of the devil, and strange practices have prevailed? . . . How apparently are the hearts of the people, everywhere, uncommonly shut up against all means and endeavors to awaken sinners and revive religion? Vice and immorality, of all kinds, withal increasing and unusually prevailing? May not an attentive view and consideration of such a state of things well influence the people that favors the dust of Zion, to earnestness in their cries to God for *a gen-*

eral outpouring of his Spirit, which only can be an effectual remedy for these evils? (Emphasis added)[122]

THAT GLORIOUS WORK OF GOD: THE PREMILLENNIAL REVIVALS

We have now seen the outlines of Edwards's millennium, and its implications for his public theology. This last section of the chapter explores "that glorious work of God," the long introductory period that is to prepare for and eventually bring on the millennium. An examination of this period will shed further light on Edwards's public theology, particularly the critical passage in **Some Thoughts,** which, as I have argued above, refers not to the millennium but to this introductory work of God's Spirit. I will first sketch the significant features of this period, and then discuss its implications for Edwards's public theology.

As we saw above, Edwards considered the millennium to be Christ's third "coming in his kingdom." The fourth coming at the Last Judgment is the coming "principally signified in Scripture by Christ's coming in his kingdom" (*HWR,* 351), but the millennium was to be the third "great event" (ibid.) in providence by which God advances the progress of history toward its culmination. Each of these four great events are preceded by periods of revival and tumult. " 'Tis observable that it has been God's manner in every remarkable new establishment of the state of his visible church, to give a remarkable outpouring of his Spirit" (ibid., 266). The spiritual effusion that will precede Christ's third coming at the millennium is to be "the last and the greatest . . . very extraordinary, and such as never has yet been seen" (*DM,* 230).[123] In its "progress and issue" it "would at last bring on the church's latter-day glory" (*GA,* 560).

The "bringing on" would be slow and gradual. In his 1739 sermon series on the work of redemption, Edwards warned his congregation that this last great work of the Spirit would progress only gradually (*HWR,* 458). Eight years later, in **An Humble Attempt,** he dared to speculate on its actual length. It would take "one half century," he proposed, for religion "in the power and purity of it," to "gain the upper hand through the *Protestant* world." Another "one half century" would be needed to "gain the ascendant in that which is now the *popish* world." A third half-century would be necessary to "prevail and subdue the greater part of the *Mahometan* world, and bring in the *Jewish* nation, in all their dispersions." Finally, "in the next whole century, the whole *heathen* world should be enlightened and converted to the Christian faith, throughout all parts of Africa, Asia, America and Terra Australis." In other words, it would be two hundred fifty years before this great work of God's Spirit would accomplish all that was necessary before the millennium could begin. That great era of peace and rest for the church would not come until about the year 2000.[124]

Edwards's confidence in the progressive nature of history, particularly in this last phase, begs the question of influence on his thinking. Much scholarly attention has been given to the influence of English eschatology, particularly that of Moses Lowman, on Edwards's millennialism.[125] But credit must be given as well to Dutch Reformed scholasticism, which may have influenced Edwards indirectly through Lowman and directly through Petrus van Mastricht.

Lowman studied under disciples of Johannes Cocceius (1603-1669) at Leiden and Utrecht from 1698 to 1710. Cocceius taught a dispensational, progressive view of history that was very influential in seventeenth-century Dutch universities. Influenced by a sixteenth-century Italian Protestant who developed Joachimist speculations, Cocceius believed that Scripture foretells an impending new age in which the Antichrist will fall, the Jews will be converted, and the kingdom of Christ will come to earth by the preaching of the gospel.[126]

As a result of Cocceius' prestige, the Netherlands became a breeding ground for millennial eschatology in the late seventeenth and early eighteenth centuries. Typical of consensus thinking was Willem a Brakel's *Redelyk Godsdienst* ([Reasonable Service], 1700), which proclaimed that history's end was near, though not imminent. The millennium would come after the Antichrist is defeated, and was to be a period of peace, godliness, and knowledge of God. The earth would be fruitful, Christ would be present spiritually, and there would be little want or suffering.[127]

Lowman probably knew of Brakel's work. Brakel may have influenced Lowman's view that the destruction of the Church's enemies was gradually being accomplished and would culminate in their total defeat, to be followed by the millennium. Since we know that Edwards "struggled mightily in his notebook with the interpretation of Lowman" (*AW,* 7), we can infer that Dutch eschatology may have influenced Edwards through Lowman.

But we have better evidence of the possibility of Dutch influence on Edwards's eschatology. In a letter that has survived, Edwards wrote to a disciple that Petrus van Mastricht's *Theoretico-Practica Theologia* was "much better than Turretine or any other book in the world, excepting the Bible, in my opinion." Mastricht (1630-1706) was a precisianist pietist who succeeded Gisbert Voetius as professor of theology at Utrecht in 1677. The 1714 edition of his *Theologia,* to which Edwards referred, contains a 240-page section entitled "Dispensation of the Covenant of Grace." This section teaches a progressive view of history in which the covenant of grace is "renewed and widened" through time, though not without waxing and waning. Like Edwards, Mastricht looked to a future Day of Wrath and the possibility of a "New Reformation," when the faith of the regenerate would quicken and judgments would be poured out on the unregenerate. Mastricht was not the first to introduce the concepts of progressive history or end-time revival to Edwards, for both were common in late seventeenth-and early eighteenth-century New England. But we can say, at least, that Edwards shared Mastricht's opinion that history was progressing toward a telos and that better times lay in store for the church.[128]

Edwards also agreed with Mastricht, however, that before the end the Church would have to endure much tribulation. The two hundred and fifty years before the millennium would be full of "many sore conflicts and terrible convulsions" (*GA*, 560). Satan was not one to surrender without a fight; he would marshal his powerful forces from all around the globe for an all-out battle against God's forces. This "afflictive model of progress"[129] was familiar to Edwards; it seemed to him a familiar pattern in history that as the Church prospered there were "dark clouds and threatening appearances." "The most glorious times of the church are always the most dismal times to the wicked and impenitent. . . . The accomplishment of the terrible destruction of God's enemies, and the glorious prosperity of his church, usually go together."[130]

The "destruction of God's enemies" related to this third coming of Christ was being effected by seven "vials of wrath," which God had been pouring out on the Antichrist since before the Reformation (*AW*, 11). For Edwards, as for most Protestants since the Reformation, the Roman Catholic Church was the worst enemy of the church of Christ, the very embodiment of the spirit of the Antichrist. In his private notebooks he compared the Roman papacy to "a viper or some loathsome, poisonous, crawling monster," whose nefarious influence destroyed true religion in the Middle Ages. In a 1734 sermon he referred to the pope as "the anti[Christ]ian monster." Since the time of John Wyclif, God had been pursuing a twofold strategy to defend his kingdom against the forces of the Antichrist: while pouring out the Spirit in selective revivals to build up his Church, he simultaneously poured out vials of wrath upon the Church's enemies.[131]

God will have poured out seven vials before the Antichrist's final destruction at the end of this last "glorious work of God" (*AW*, 298). After reading Moses Lowman in 1739 Edwards concluded that the fifth vial had been poured out in the Reformation, when Luther and other Reformers dealt serious blows to Rome's influence and prestige. By 1747 he had decided that the sixth vial, which would consist of "the taking away from the Church of Rome the supplies and help she has had from the principal powers that have hitherto supported her" (23), "may well be speedily expected" because Rome's riches were showing signs of significant depletion (*HA*, 421). The kings of Spain and Portugal had recently forbade "going to Rome for investitures, etc., thereby cutting off two great streams of the Pope's wealth [and] popish princes were now taxing the clergy" (*AW*, 300). Another sign was "the late peeling and impoverishing the Pope's temporal dominions in Italy, by the armies of the Austrians, Neapolitans, and Spaniards" (*HA*, 421).[132]

The sixth vial would be poured out for most of the duration of the two hundred fifty years of the glorious work of God. By these executions of God's wrath, and the revivals

his Spirit would produce, Deism, Roman Catholicism, Islam, and Judaism would gradually diminish in power and influence. Then, just before the end of this period, would occur a final great battle. "All the forces of Antichrist, and also Mohammedanism and heathenism, should be united, all the forces of Satan's visible kingdom through the whole world of mankind. . . . This will be, as it were, the dying struggles of the old serpent, a battle wherein he will fight as one that is almost desperate." The fighting will be desperate and "violent," but "Christ and his church shall in this battle obtain a complete and entire victory over their enemies." The hidden weapon that gives Christ the winning edge is the last and seventh vial, whose pouring out was finally to ensure the victory.[133]

AMERICA'S ROLE

Edwards's description of this last great work of God before the millennium, which I have just summarized, makes little mention of New England or America. In fact, with the exception of the oft-quoted *Some Thoughts* passage, America plays no role at all in his public descriptions of this era—the era, by the way, of most immediate relevance for him and his readers. In the passage from *Some Thoughts,* as we have seen, Edwards wrote that the "glorious work of God" might begin in America, and soon. If there was any inconsistency in Edwards's thought, it was here. Only in this work, in 1742, did he highlight America's role in the final ages;[134] neither before nor after this time did Edwards give America or New England a positive role to play in God's shepherding of history.

Yet even here, where America was to be the probable scene of the beginning of that glorious work of God, American leadership was ironic. God would start with America only because she was the "utmost, meanest, youngest, and weakest part" of the world, in order "to make it plain the work was of him."[135] This is a restatement of what he had recorded in his private notebooks at about the same time, where he stated that in the latter days the Church would enter prosperity and spiritual joy by "successive seasons of the pouring out of the Spirit of God . . . and the first outpouring of the Spirit will be the *least glorious*" (emphasis added). As if to underline the ambiguous meaning of America's "leadership" role, Edwards described the return of the church of God in the latter days "by several companies that will come in one after another in successive seasons of the pouring out of the Spirit of God, with a space between [each]: . . . They that are brought in [first] are not only inferior among men, but the least pure, beautiful, and amiable as Christians in their experience and practice."[136]

In the passage from *Some Thoughts,* Edwards further underscored the ambiguity of America's role by arguing that she was chosen out of regard for aesthetic "balance." Since "the old continent has crucified Christ . . . 'tis probable that, in some measure to balance these things, the most glorious renovation of the world shall originate from the new continent." Edwards's God is concerned about continental "equality." His "providence observes a kind of equal distribution of things." Hence, since the Gentiles "first received the true religion from the Jews," God has so ordered it that the Jews should now receive the Gospel from the Gentiles—in order "that there might be a kind of equality in the dispensations of providence."[137]

The tone throughout the discussions of America and the millennium in *Some Thoughts* is consistently tentative. Most projections were conjectural, introduced by the particle "if."[138] This hesitancy increased toward the end of the work, as if Edwards became less optimistic during the course of his writing—a period that coincided with the further development of contention and division in New England.[139] On the last page of the work Edwards's uncertainty was most marked. Suddenly new conditions were added that had to be fulfilled before this glorious work of God could be said to have begun in America. The country must "*fully* and freely . . . acknowledge his glorious power and grace" in the awakening, "and engage with one heart and soul, and by due methods, the endeavor to promote it" (*ST,* 530). In short, the gainsayers and fence sitters of New England had to stop opposing the revival, and jump on the bandwagon to support it enthusiastically—hardly a realistic hope at the end of 1742. From Edwards's pessimistic evaluations of his fellow countrymen we can infer that as the writing of *Some Thoughts* progressed, the author may have begun to lose confidence in his earlier prediction of a probable American beginning for that glorious work of God's Spirit.

When we turn from *Some Thoughts* to his other works in which he discussed the millennium or the great work preceding it, we find that America is never mentioned. In *Faithful Narrative* (1737) Edwards ascribed no eschatological significance to the 1735-36 awakening in the Connecticut Valley—even while two British and four American ministers did, and in the prefaces to the same work.[140] In his 1739 sermons on the history of the work of redemption, Edwards refused to speculate on the timing or the location of the glorious work of God to come: "We know not where this pouring out of the Spirit shall begin, or whether in *many* places at once, or whether what has already taken place ben't some forerunner and beginning of it" (*HWR,* 460). In his letter to Whitefield in 1740 the Northampton divine could only "*hope* this is the dawning of a day of God's mighty power."[141] When writing a Scottish friend about the awakenings, he made no connection between America and either the millennium or revivals introducing it (*GA,* 558-60). In *An Humble Attempt* (1747) particular nations faded into insignificance before the dominating universality of "those great effusions of the Holy Spirit" (333) that would "bring on that advancement of Christ's church and kingdom" (320). When New England and America were mentioned, they were held up as the most egregious examples of nations that were spiritually bankrupt, of nations most in need of awakenings to save them from perdition (357-58).

In all of Edwards's descriptions of the long period of revivals and international tumults that were to precede the millennium, then, America was either absent, vilified, or given leadership by default.[142] When the political dimensions of that glorious work are examined, what stands out is its international scope. "And doubtless one nation shall be enlightened and converted after another. . . . [T]he gospel shall be preached to every tongue and kindred and [nation and people] before [the] fall of Antichrist; so we may suppose that it will soon be gloriously successful to bring in multitudes, and from many nations" (*HWR,* 459, 461). Even the means used to bring on the glorious work would involve international cooperation, with no mention of any one nation as leader: "In the text we have an account *how* this future glorious advancement of the church of God should be brought on, or introduced; viz., by great multitudes in different towns and countries taking up a *joint resolution,* and coming into an express and visible *agreement,* that they will, by united and extraordinary *prayer,* seek to God that he would come and manifest himself, and grant the tokens and fruits of his gracious presence" (*HA,* 314; Edwards's emphases).

Not only is the glorious work international in scope throughout its duration, and effected by prayer societies from many lands, but the forerunners of this work are international as well. Edwards found revivals in England, Scotland, Russia, and India to be portents of the glorious work to come.[143] In a 1748 letter to a Scottish correspondent he opined that recent religious stirrings among British politicians and clerics "appear to be happy presages and forerunners of yet better and greater things that are coming."[144] Thus six years after *Some Thoughts* he found "forerunners" (the same word used of the New England revivals in *Some Thoughts*) of the glorious work thousands of miles away from New England. At roughly the same time he began to see other forerunners close to home, but among a people other than his fellow Yankees. The awakening among native Americans taught by David Brainerd was also "a *forerunner* of something yet much more glorious and extensive of that kind" (*David Brainerd,* 533). And Brainerd's "vehement thirstings of soul" for a glorious work was another sign to Edwards that "God has a design of accomplishing something very glorious for the interest of his Church before long" (534). After *Some Thoughts,* then, Edwards de-Americanized his premillennial schema, and saw God planting seeds of the future revivals all around the earth.

Some scholars have seen in Edwards's repeated calls to the Church to pray for the glorious work to begin, and his faith in the efficacy of such prayer, an identification of eschatological revivals as the fruit of human achievement. James Holstun calls this "catalytic millennialism." The catalytic millennialist shows the way to the reign of Christ on earth, or even how to constitute that reign. He aims to create the virtuous citizen by creating the ideal social order. As James Harrington put it, "'Give us good orders, and they will make us good men' is the maxim of a legislator and the most infallible in the politics." Holstun cites

Czech pedagogue John Amos Comenius (1592-1670) as a catalytic millennialist because Comenius thought he would create a regenerated millennial nation by an educational reformation.[145]

Alan Heimert attempts to cast Edwards as a catalytic millennialist by using texts like the following: "All will not be accomplished at once, as by some great miracle, as the resurrection of the dead at the end of the world will be at once. But this work is a work that will be accomplished by means, by the preaching of the gospel, and the use of the ordinary means of grace."[146] This analysis, however, presupposes that Edwards's referent was the millennium instead of the long series of revivals preceding the millennium. It also ignores the next paragraph, in which Edwards suggested the dependence of ordinary or "natural" means on the Holy Spirit for efficacy: "But I proceed now to show how this glorious work shall be accomplished. 1. [God's] Spirit shall be gloriously poured out for the wonderful revival and propagation of religion" (*HWR*, 460).

Two paragraphs later Edwards suggested what he knew from personal experience, that preaching without the power of the Spirit cannot bring revival: "And there shall be a glorious pouring out of the Spirit with this clear and powerful preaching of the gospel, to make it successful for reviving those holy doctrines of religion which are now chiefly ridiculed in the world" (461). Elsewhere Edwards made this more explicit. After saying that God "is pleased to represent himself as it were at the command of his people" (*HA*, 353), several pages later he qualified that in a discussion of the grace that brings revival: "There is very much to convince us, that God alone can bestow it, and show our entire and absolute dependence on him for it. The insufficiency of human abilities to bring to pass any such happy change in the world . . . does now remarkably appear" (359).

These passages demonstrate that Edwards was what Holstun calls a "hermeneutical millennialist," one who recognizes the "irreducible distance" between future final events and one's attempts to clarify and prophesy them.[147] For Edwards the glorious work of God to precede the millennium could never be at the beck and call of human beings, much less degenerate Americans. God would send it in answer to prayer, but both the prayer and its answers were nevertheless still the fruit of God's sovereign grace. He thus preserved a fundamental discontinuity between human achievement—American or Hottentot—and the eschaton.

Edwards reinforced this discontinuity by noting the disjunction in all revivals between religious states before and after an awakening. "It has usually been so from the beginning of the world, that the state of the church has appeared most dark, just before some remarkable deliverance and advancement" (*HA*, 360). This disjunction underlined for Edwards the absence of any necessary connection between human effort or goodness and the divine effusions, either in the eschaton or at any other time: "[This] has of-

ten been God's opportunity for the magnifying his power, mercy and faithfulness towards her . . . [so] as to magnify God's free grace and sovereign mercy" (361).

Perhaps the most intriguing passage in the Edwards corpus that bears on this subject is an entry in his private notebook written at the end of the 1730s, just before the beginning of the Great Awakening. The entry suggests that Edwards thought of himself as a latter-day prophet whose mission was to correct the Church of her errors, the worst of which was her presumption of virtue and exalted status. "Before the end of the church's suffering state," he wrote, God will raise up "a number of eminent ministers . . . [to] reprove his own [church] & show her her errours." Their ministry will be similar to that of Elihu, who showed Job's three friends their errors, and their "spirit and power" will be that of "Elias." They will "convince his professing people of their meanness emptiness blindness & sinfullness & his sovereignty & greatness."[148]

That Edwards saw himself as one of these eminent ministers is hinted when he explains that "the church *now* exceedingly needs" the reproaches of these men.[149] When Edwards wrote a Scottish correspondent several years later (1743), it was more apparent that he had self-consciously taken upon himself the prophetic mantle: "God is now going and returning to his place, till we acknowledge our offense, and *I* hope to humble his Church in New England, and purify it, and so fit it for yet greater comfort, that he designs in due time to bestow upon it" (*GA*, 540; emphasis added). Perhaps this self-appointed role can help explain why such a substantial part of his spoken ministry consisted of stern reproofs to his parishioners for their failure to integrate their beliefs.

The most interesting part of the *Miscellanies* entry is its identification of pride and self-righteousness as the greatest sin of an eschatological people: "her greatest errour being her being so insensible of these things & her entertaining so many conceits to the contrary of these things" (*Miscellanies*, no. 810). The 1743 letter indicates the same. Edwards told his correspondent that he hoped to "humble" the church in New England (*GA*, 540). As he saw it, pride was the most besetting sin of New England after the awakenings. It was also a sign of greater danger. For a professing people to be ignorant of its corruption was itself symptomatic of moral and religious ruin.

The entry in the *Miscellanies* thus states, approximately three years before *Some Thoughts,* that the most heinous sin for an eschatological people to commit is to think more highly of itself than it ought to think. Presumption of exalted status in the history of redemption is therefore ungodly hubris, and the sort that could prove mortal. If America gloated over her religious favors, forgetting her profligacy, then judgment and destruction threatened. Edwards's most important duty, as an eschatological prophet, was to expose and condemn all self-righteousness and pride. The Northampton theologian may himself have succumbed to pride and self-righteousness by writing such an entry, but he knew that he could not identify his people with God's end-time purposes without risking the betrayal of his prophetic calling.

THE SIGNIFICANCE OF EDWARDS'S MILLENNIALISM

Jonathan Edwards's millennialism represents a "new departure"[150] in two respects. First, as this chapter has shown, for Edwards the millennium was central to his theology. For many thinkers in the Reformed tradition the millennium was often a theological appendage. Although it cannot be claimed that the millennium was the *center* of Edwards's theology, this chapter has argued that eschatology was consistently prominent in, and even essential to, much of his thought. His philosophy of history and his use of biblical typology, for instance, cannot be understood apart from the millennium. Eschatology was such a prominent constituent of Edwards's thought that it spilled over into his private life, providing both "delight" and emotional solace during his many years of professional conflict at Northampton and Stockbridge. That Edwards's theology was future-oriented and even partially determined by consideration of the future, is perhaps better understood in this century when both biblical and systematic theologies have been shaped by eschatological concern.

Second, Edwards's eschatology functioned as social critique. The prominence of eschatology in his thought and the great prestige of the man in his own time[151] combined to give Edwards's millennialism a prophetic voice of considerable power. So when this scrupulous visionary trained his potent imaginative sights on the future global society, his American auditors knew that he would never countenance any nationalism devoid of benevolence to "the universal system of being" (*TV*, 554). And if their consciences were not pricked by his vivid depiction of a millennial society that implicitly judged their own, their indignation was stirred against this preacher whose eschatological vision boldly challenged their motives and mores. Perhaps Northampton never would have expelled its pastor if he had been less severe in his denunciations of their sins. But that was hardly possible, given his own estimate of the eschatological calling he had been given. His conviction that God had called him as an end-time prophet to deflate America's exalted claims for herself only sharpened his criticisms and foreclosed any chance of reconciliation.

Edwards's social critique was stirred by his eschatological vision. But when he turned from derogation to prescription, he looked first through the prisms of philosophical ethics and theology. That is, it was one thing to use the millennium as a template against which to judge New England society. But it was quite another to prescribe how mid-eighteenth-century New England society actually ought to be structured and operated. For this task Edwards drew from his deliberations on being, love, and God.

Notes

1. Miller, *Jonathan Edwards*, 327; Heimert, *Religion and the American Mind*, 99, 102; Robert B. Westbrook, "Social Criticism and the Heavenly City of Jonathan Edwards," *Soundings* 59 (1976): 397-409; Ruth H. Bloch, *Visionary Republic: Millennial Themes in American Thought, 1756-1800* (Cambridge, Mass. 1985), 18-19.

2. Bercovitch, *The American Jeremiad*, 105.

3. Goen, "Jonathan Edwards: A New Departure in Eschatology," 29; see also his introduction to *GA*, 71-72.

4. Bercovitch, *The American Jeremiad*, 106.

5. Heimert, *Religion and the American Mind*, chap. 2; Goen, "Jonathan Edwards: A New Departure in Eschatology," 29, 40; Cushing Strout, *The New Heavens and New Earth: Political Religion in America* (New York, 1974), 29; Conrad Cherry, ed., *God's New Israel: Religious Interpretations of American Destiny* (Englewood Cliffs, N.J., 1971), 55-59; Lowance, *The Language of Canaan*, 179, 187, 190; Bercovitch, *The American Jeremiad*, 106, 124, and *The Puritan Origins*, 154-56; *AW*, 26.

6. Lowance, *The Language of Canaan*, 187. See also Jay Fliegelman, *Prodigals and Pilgrims: The American Revolution against Patriarchal Authority, 1750-1800* (Cambridge, 1982), 191.

7. Bercovitch, *The Puritan Origins*, 154. Both Bercovitch and Lowance wrongly identify the "new heavens and new earth" as the millennium. For Edwards the new heavens and new earth are to come *after* the millennium, when the kingdom of the Son is finally and fully consummated, far from this earth in another part of the universe: "The everlasting residence and reign of Christ & his church will be heaven, & not this lower [earth] purified and refined." *Miscellanies*, Beinecke Rare Book and Manuscript Library, Yale University, New Haven, Connecticut, nos. 743, 946. All citations from the *Miscellanies* will refer only to Edwards's numbering—not page numbers of various modern editions—since there are various editions available. Unless otherwise indicated the Yale edition is being cited.

8. Heimert, *Religion and the American Mind*, 236.

9. Bercovitch, *The Puritan Origins*, 155-56.

10. John Wilson, introduction to *HWR*, 82. See also his "Religion at the Core of American Culture," in *Altered Landscapes: Christianity in America, 1935-1985*, ed. David W. Lotz et al. (Grand Rapids, Mich., 1989), 373.

11. Bercovitch, *The American Jeremiad*, 108; Lowance, *The Language of Canaan*, 179; Maclear, "The Republic and the Millennium," 196.

12. Bercovitch, *The American Jeremiad*, 109, 157, 185.

13. Ibid., 108; Goen, "Jonathan Edwards: A New Departure in Eschatology," 26, 39-40. Other scholars have been more hesitant to connect Edwards with

later nationalism and self-interest. Wilson, for instance, says only that Edwards's *History of the Work of Redemption* "legitimated the social experiment that was the new American culture." Introduction to *HWR,* 82. Alan Heimert was more positive, finding the source for the Revolutionary era's "ideal of continental union" in Edwards's focus on the union of Americans to pray for the millennium. Heimert, *Religion and the American Mind,* 100, 95.

14. Even Ernest Lee Tuveson and Bercovitch, both of whom read Edwards as promoting America as a redeemer nation, concede that Edwards seems to have reversed himself midway through his career. Tuveson, *Redeemer Nation,* 101; Bercovitch, *The American Jeremiad,* 99.

15. James West Davidson, *The Logic of Millennial Thought: Eighteenth-Century New England* (New Haven, 1977), 220-21, 226-32, 258-59.

16. Hatch, *The Sacred Cause of Liberty,* 1-2, 32-36, 167.

17. In the Christian tradition judgment does not necessarily forfeit future participation in the work of redemption. For, as the biblical author put it, "The time has come for judgment to *begin* with the household of God." (1 Peter 4:17 RSV) The judgment that Edwards saw looming for New England, however, would bring New England's usefulness to an end. It would result in New England's "destruction," and the transference of her covenant to a people more worthy of it: "God may give other countreys much of this mercy & us no more of it."

18. Edwards uses this phrase in a letter to a Scottish correspondent to describe the transnational community of the millennial age. It is not clear from the context whether he was referring to the time of worldwide revival preceding the millennium, or to the millennium itself. But in either case, his vision is of the global society to come that will transcend all national boundaries. *AW,* 446.

19. This is Edwards's phrase for the worldwide series of revivals that would precede and bring on the millennium. It will be discussed in the last section of this chapter. *HWR,* 391; see also *ST,* 353.

20. See, for instance, Douglas J. Elwood, *The Philosophical Theology of Jonathan Edwards* (New York, 1960), 155-60; Norman Fiering, "The Rationalist Foundations of Jonathan Edwards's Metaphysics," in *Jonathan Edwards and the American Experience,* ed. Hatch and Stout, 79; and Wallace E. Anderson, ed., *Scientific and Philosophical Writings,* vol. 6 in *The Works of Jonathan Edwards* (New Haven, 1980), 26-27.

21. The best survey of Edwards's typology—despite his misunderstanding of Edwards on America and the millennium—is Lowance, *The Language of Canaan,* 178-207, 249-95.

22. Jonathan Edwards, *Images or Shadows of Divine Things,* ed. Perry Miller (New Haven, 1948), 92. [All references to this work are to page number of this edition, not to item number. Also, this work will be cited as *Images,* both in notes, and parenthetically in the text.]

23. As indeed he argued; see *TV,* 554-56, 609-12.

24. Increase Mather, *A Discourse Concerning Faith and Fervency in Prayer, and the Glorious Kingdom of the Lord Jesus Christ, on Earth, Now Approaching* (Boston, 1710), 1; cited in Bloch, *Visionary Republic,* 11; Robert Middlekauf, *The Mathers: Three Generations of Puritan Intellectuals, 1596-1728* (New York, 1971), 322; Bozeman, *To Live Ancient Lives,* 234; John Norton, *The Answer to the Whole Set of Questions of . . . William Apollonius,* trans. Douglas Horton (1648; Cambridge, Mass., 1958), 7.

25. Stout, *The New England Soul,* 8.

26. Michael Wigglesworth, *Day of Doom,* in *The American Puritans: Their Prose and Poetry,* ed. Perry Miller (Garden City, N.Y., 1956), 282.

27. Mitchell, Stoughton, Oakes, and Torrey turned to it only briefly; it did not play any significant role in their jeremiads. Bozeman, *To Live Ancient Lives,* 338; Davidson, *The Logic of Millennial Thought,* 54, 60-61, 67.

28. In Samuel Danforth's "Repentance" (Boston, 1727), for instance, there is no mention of the millennium. For examples of sermons where mention of the millennium was merely a rhetorical flourish, see Charles Chauncy, "Marvellous Things" (Boston, 1745), and Thomas Prince, "The Natural and Moral Government" (Boston, 1749). Millennialism was even less prominent in eighteenth-century England. Because of the lingering public associations of millennialism with the radicalism of the Puritan Revolution, millennialism "became an almost exclusively academic and theoretical concern." Neither the radical Whigs in the political opposition nor the preachers of the Methodist revival gained a reputation for millennial thought. Bloch, *Visionary Republic,* 10.

29. Stout, *The New England Soul,* 246-47, 253-55.

30. Stout concludes that the importance of millennialism in colonial New England has been "abused through overemphasis." Stout, *The New England Soul,* 8, It must be pointed out, however, that Increase and Cotton Mather anticipated Edwards's absorption with the millennium. In his last years Increase began to insist that belief in the millennium was a test of true faith. Cotton Mather, Robert Middlekauf argues, moved eschatology to the center of New England theology, displacing even the doctrines of Calvin as the key to the meaning of God's sovereignty. Middlekauf, *The Mathers,* 183, 323-24.

31. Edwards was Hopkins's chief inspiration and mentor on millennial topics. William Ellery Channing, *Works,* 6 vols. (Boston, 1841), 4:353; cited in Joseph A. Conforti, *Samuel Hopkins and the New Divinity Movement: Calvinism, the Congregational Ministry, and Reform in New England Between the Great Awakenings* (Grand Rapids, Mich., 1981), 173.

32. Jonathan Edwards, "Personal Narrative," in *Jonathan Edwards: Representative Selections,* ed. Clarence H. Faust and Thomas H. Johnson (New York, 1962), 65 [henceforth cited as "PN" in notes and text]; emphasis added.

33. *The Life of President Edwards,* vol. 1 of *Works,* ed. Dwight, 102.

34. Ibid., 151-52.

35. *AW,* 1. In contrast, it was the only book on which Calvin did *not* write a commentary. For Calvin's views of Revelation and eschatology, see Heinrich Quistorp, *Calvin's Doctrines of the Last Things* (London, 1955), and David E. Holwerda, "Eschatology and History: A Look at Calvin's Eschatological Vision," in *Readings in Calvin's Theology,* ed. Donald K. McKim (Grand Rapids, Mich., 1984), 311-42.

36. Dwight, *The Life of President Edwards,* 278.

37. *AW,* 47. It is interesting that his daughter Esther Burr used the millennial hope similarly, as a source of solace amidst daily frustrations caused by people: "What a charming place this world would be of [*sic*] it was not for the inhabitants—O I long for the blessed and glorious when this World shall become a Mountain of Holiness." Cited in Iain H. Murray, *Jonathan Edwards: A New Biography* (Edinburgh, 1987), 409. In their magisterial survey of Western utopias, Frank and Fritzie Manuel observe that it is characteristic of "utopian personalities," who are typically angry with the world and disgusted with society, to "withdraw from this world into a far simpler form of existence which they fantasy." We shall see below that Edwards's portrayal of the millennium was a subtle critique of eighteenth-century New England. Frank E. Manuel and Fritzie P. Manuel, *Utopian Thought in the Western World* (Cambridge, Mass., 1979), 27.

38. "Miscellaneous Observations on the Holy Scriptures" [the "Blank Bible"] (MS, Yale coll.), 169, cited in *AW,* 49.

39. Wilson, introduction to *HWR,* 10.

40. Dwight, *The Life of President Edwards,* 278.

41. "Notes on the Apocalypse," in *AW,* 95-305. Stein refers to Edwards's "lifelong preoccupation with the fortunes of the church militant through the ages and in the *present,* as well as his concern with the glories of the church triumphant, anticipated on earth and fulfilled ultimately in heaven." Stephen J. Stein, "Providence and the Apocalypse in the Early Writings of Jonathan Edwards," *Early American Literature* 13 (1978): 263. Edwards's careful attention in his private notebooks to contemporary events belies the oft-heard claim that Edwards was uninterested in the social and political realities of his day. For examples of this claim, see Herbert Wallace Schneider, *The Puritan Mind* (New York, 1930), 106-7; Perry Miller, "Jonathan Edwards's Sociology of the Great Awakening," *New England Quarterly* 21 (1948): 51; Anson P. Stokes, *Church and State in the United States* (New York, 1950), 241; Gerhard Alexis, "Jonathan Edwards and the Theocratic Ideal," *Church History* 35 (1966): 329; and Mead, *The Old Religion in the Brave New World,* 4, 52-53.

42. *Notes on the Bible,* vol. 9 of *Works,* ed. Dwight, 224, 232, 296-99, 316, 330-31.

43. *Images,* 92, 124.

44. Thus Stein notes, "Accordingly, in the sermons on Isaiah 51.8 the millennium took second place to heaven, the object of all God's dealings with the church." *AW,* 24.

45. "Notes on the Apocalypse," in *AW,* 142; "Notes on Scripture" (MS, Yale coll.) no. 389, cited in *AW,* 54.

46. *AW,* 53-54. This is the familiar Neoplatonic theme of return to the primordium. Edwards was familiar with the Neoplatonic tradition through his reading of Cambridge Platonists such as John Smith and seventeenth-century Puritan writers such as Richard Sibbes, John Flavel, and John Owen. See John E. Smith's introduction to *RA,* 53, 60-62, 65-66, 68-70; and Simonson, *Jonathan Edwards,* 33.

47. *Miscellanies,* no. 810; *AW,* 303.

48. *HA,* 394, 410. Moses Lowman (1680-1752) was a dissenting clergyman whose *Paraphrase and Notes on the Revelation* (London, 1737) greatly interested Edwards. *AW,* 55.

49. Charles Chauncy, Edwards's contemporary and adversary, was the first. *Seasonable Thoughts on the State of Religion in New-England* (Boston, 1743), 372-75. For more recent such interpretations, see, for example, Miller, *Jonathan Edwards,* 326; Goen, "Jonathan Edwards: A New Departure in Eschatology," 29-30, and introduction to *GA,* 71-72; Mason I. Lowance, Jr., "Typology, Millennial Eschatology, and Jonathan Edwards," in *Critical Essays on Jonathan Edwards,* ed. William J. Scheick (Boston, 1980), 191; Bloch, *Visionary Republic,* 17; and Peter Gay, *A Loss of Mastery: Puritan Historians in Colonial America* (Berkeley and Los Angeles, 1966), 16. Some may have been led astray by Goen's insertion of the heading "The Millennium Probably to Dawn in America" over the passage in question. *GA,* 353.

50. "Notes on the Apocalypse," in *AW,* 177-79. The dating for this is based on the work of Thomas Schafer, as described in *AW,* 78. Schafer estimates that no. 77 of "Notes on the Apocalypse" was written in the 1738-39 period.

51. *HWR,* 392, 394. This is in a long passage describing "that glorious work," 390-404; only on 404 does his description of the millennium begin. In this (the first) section are many allusions to the distinction between the "glorious work of God's Spirit" and the millennium. The prophecy of Daniel 12:11, for instance, of two periods or levels of glory, one at the end of 1290 days, and the other at the end of 1335 days, tell us "that something very glorious should be accomplished at the end of the former period ["that glorious work"], but something much more glorious at the end of the latter [the millennium]." *HA,* 393. In *HA* he said that this first period will see "a *gradual* progress of religion," and that "that great work of God's Spirit" (Language almost identical to that in the *Some Thoughts* passage) "before it is finished, will issue in Antichrist's ruin." Surely that will involve process and conflict. *HA,* 410-11, 425.

52. Letter to William McCulloch, 5 March 1744, in *GA,* 560.

53. These statements were made both before and after the writing of *Some Thoughts,* which suggests that he did not change his mind on this schema. *AW,* 177-79 (written in 1738-39); *HA,* 405, 410 (written in 1747).

54. Compare his descriptions of revivals in *Faithful Narrative* and *Some Thoughts,* particularly his portrayal of the remarkable changes wrought in both individual and corporate consciousness and behavior by conversion, with his description of the millennium, as a period of peace and stability. *FN,* 147-204; *ST,* 331-47.

55. Only Stein seems to have noted its absence, but thinks it merely evidence of Edwards's reluctance to express publicly his private millennialism. *AW,* 28.

56. For examples of usage in his private notebooks, see 177-79, 181 (1738-39); for an example from his public works, see *HA,* 410.

57. Thomas Brightman, *A Revelation of the Apocalyps* (Amsterdam, 1611), 626, 113-14, 634-37, 678, and *A Commentary on the Canticles* (London, 1644), 1077; cited in Bozeman, *To Live Ancient Lives,* 248. For Brightman's eschatology, see Bozeman, *To Live Ancient Lives,* 207-9, 248-49, and Richard Bauckham, *Tudor Apocalypse* (Oxford, 1978), 139-43, 205-31.

58. Stout, *The New England Soul,* 48.

59. John Cotton, *A Brief Exposition with Practical Observations upon the Whole Book of Canticles* (London, 1655), 181, and *A Brief Exposition of the Whole Book of Canticles, or, Song of Solomon* (London, 1642), 221-22; cited in Bozeman, 244-45. For Cotton's eschatology, see Bozeman, *To Live Ancient Lives,* 237-62, and Stout, *The New England Soul,* 19-20, 48-49.

60. Bozeman, *To Live Ancient Lives,* 244.

61. Petrus Van Mastricht, *Beschouwende en Praktikale Godgeleerdheit,* trans. Henricus Pontanus (Rotterdam, 1749), 4:481.

62. See Davidson, *The Logic of Millennial Thought,* 122-75; Samuel Willard, "The Checkered State of the Gospel Church" (Boston, 1701), 22.

63. Davidson, *The Logic of Millennial Thought,* 226-37. Edwards quoted from Ridgley's *Body of Divinity* in his treatise on the Trinity, cited in Thomas H. Johnson, "Jonathan Edwards's Background of Reading," *Publications of the Colonial Society of Massachusetts* 28 (1930-33): 207-8; Thomas Ridgley, *A Body of Divinity,* 4 vols. (London, 1731; first American edition, 1814-15), 2:368, 373, 392.

64. Imminentism was prevalent even after the 1740s. Charles Chauncy and Jonathan Mayhew disagreed on the timing of Christ's bodily return, but both spread hopes for the speedy culmination of history. Mayhew expected a fundamental transformation of the world in the near future. In the 1750s, books by Anglican Richard Clark, Scottish Presbyterian David Imrie, and seventeenth-century English Presbyterian Christopher Love used numerology, extrabilical sources, and personal revelation to predict the beginning of the millennium in the following decade. Reprints of two seventeenth-century premillennialist Puritans, William Torry and Ezekiel Cheever, further encouraged the belief that the millennium could soon begin. Even Joseph Bellamy, Edwards's friend and disciple, was ambiguous on the timing of the millennium in his oft-reprinted sermon on the millennium. Bloch, *Visionary Republic,* 28-32, 22-28. Joseph Bellamy, "The Millennium," in *The Great Awakening: Documents Illustrating the Crisis and Its Consequences,* ed. Perry Miller and Alan Heimert (Indianapolis, 1967), 609-35.

65. Middlekauf, *The Mathers,* 181, 337, 348.

66. Thomas Prince, Jr., *The Christian History,* 2 vols. (Boston, 1744-45), 1:111, cited in Davidson, *The Logic of Millennial Thought,* 149; Eliphalet Adams, *A Sermon Preached at Windham* (New London, Conn., 1721), vi, 40, cited in Davidson, *The Logic of Millennial Thought,* 149; Bloch, *Visionary Republic,* 16; Joseph Sewall, *The Lamb Slain* (Boston, 1745), 6, cited in Stout, *The New England Soul,* 237.

67. This is why Edwards said that during the millennium "the Christian church shall for the most part [be] in a state of peace and prosperity." *HWR,* 479. The notion of a final stand by Satan at the end

of the millennium was routine in England and New England. See, for example, the description of Lowman's version in *AW,* 57.

68. *HWR,* 409, 420.

69. *Miscellanies,* no. 836. See Davidson, *The Logic of Millennial Thought,* 84-97, for the range of topics on which expositors did not interpret Revelation literally.

70. *Miscellanies,* no. 836. In contrast, Ridgley refused to take a position on whether the "thousand years" was literal or figurative. Ridgley, *A Body of Divinity,* 2:391.

71. *ST,* 353. They have also used *Images,* 147, which was written at nearly the same time as *ST* and probably refers as well to the glorious work of God to precede the millennium, not the millennium itself. Dating estimated by Thomas A. Schafer.

72. "Notes on the Apocalypse," in *AW,* 134.

73. Bozeman, *To Live Ancient Lives,* 218; Peter Toon, "The Latter Day Glory," in *Puritans, the Millennium, and the Future of Israel: Puritan Eschatology 1600 to 1660,* ed. Peter Toon (Cambridge, 1870), 30; Davidson, *The Logic of Millennial Thought,* 142, 145; Bozeman, 230; Increase Mather, *A Discourse Concerning the Danger of Apostacy* (Boston, 1685), 56, 61, cited in Bozeman, *To Live Ancient Lives,* 339n. On Increase Mather's eschatology, see Middlekauf, *The Mathers,* 179-87.

74. "The most glorious part of the church will hereafter be there [Canaan], at the center of the kingdom of Christ, communicating influences to all other parts." Edwards noted that Canaan was strategically located, at the center of the Old World in the midst of three continents and therefore positioned with respect to waterways that all other parts of the world could be reached easily. "Notes on the Apocalypse," in *AW,* 134.

75. "Notes on the Apocalypse," in *AW,* 181.

76. Cotton Mather, *Theopolis Americana* (Boston, 1710), 42, cited in Davidson, *The Logic of Millennial Thought,* 150; Johnson, *Wonder-Working Providence,* in *The Puritans,* ed. Perry Miller and Thomas H. Johnson (New York, 1938), 145; Samuel Sewall, *Phenomena Quaedam Apocalyptica* (Boston, 1697), 1-2, 45, cited in Davidson, *The Logic of Millennial Thought,* 67; Joseph Morgan's *History of the Kingdom of Barasuah,* ed. Richard Schlatter (1715; reprint, Cambridge, Mass., 1946), cited in Bloch, *Visionary Republic,* 12. Johnson and Sewall did not use the word "millennium," so it is not clear that that is precisely what they had in mind. But it is clear that they believed their land would have preeminence in God's future dispensation.

77. See, for example, Bercovitch, *The American Jeremiad,* 105.

78. Manuel and Manuel, *Utopian Thought,* 28-29.

79. Ibid.

80. See, for example, Goen, "Jonathan Edwards: A New Departure in Eschatology"; Heimert, *Religion and the American Mind;* and Bloch, *Visionary Republic.*

81. For a lucid study of Edwards's struggles as a pastor, see Patricia J. Tracy, *Jonathan Edwards, Pastor: Religion and Society in Eighteenth-Century Northampton* (New York, 1980).

82. *HWR,* 481; *HA,* 339; *HWR;* 481-82. The prominence of religious piety in Edwards's millennium was not novel in New England eschatology, but illustrates the difference between the religious utopias of England and New England, on the one hand, and continental Europe, on the other. In the latter, science and knowledge, not religion, drive the shafts that turn the wheels. For the Christian Pansophists of the seventeenth century (Bruno, Bacon, Campanella, Andreae, Comenius), the reorganization of knowledge was fundamental to the reformation of society. Though consciously religious, the Pansophists nevertheless placed their faith in the power of scientific knowledge, not piety, to modify human conduct. For Gottfried Leibniz (1646-1714), the moral and religious fate of Christian civilization depended on science, which would be the primary instrument for spreading Christianity. For Robert Turgot (1727-81), who drafted a utopian philosophy of history as a Christian apologetic, the key to progress was nonetheless not religion but intellectual and scientific innovation. Manuel and Manuel, *Utopian Thought,* 205-21, 392-410, 463-83.

83. See, for example, Edwards's condemnation of merchants who profit from the law of supply and demand: they "take advantage" of the "necessity of poor indigent people" and thereby commit the "violent" sin of "oppression." "Dishonesty, or the Sin of Theft and Injustice," in vol. 6 of *Works,* ed. Dwight, 522. Miller claimed that it was this kind of attack that led to Edwards's dismissal. Miller, *Jonathan Edwards,* 324. Calvin, in contrast, "thought well of commerce" and "praised merchants for their service to the community." William J. Bouwsma, *John Calvin: A Sixteenth-Century Portrait* (New York, 1988), 197-98.

84. As Edwards put it, "There had also long prevailed in the town a spirit of contention between two parties, into which they had for many years been divided . . . they prepared to oppose one another in all public affairs." *FN,* 144-46.

85. "Enthusiasm" may be defined as "belief in immediate inspiration by divine or superhuman power; it leads to acting on impulses thought to come directly from the Holy Spirit. In extreme cases it may lead to a sort of frenzied possession." C. C. Goen, *Revivalism and Separatism in New England, 1740-1800* (New Haven, 1962), 20n. Edwards

argued that "immediate revelations" thought to be from God were no evidence of regeneration and could be from Satan or the natural imagination, and reproved George Whitefield on this score when Whitefield visited Northampton. *RA,* 142, 213-18, 286-88; Dwight, *The Life of President Edwards,* 147. For more on New Light "enthusiasm" during the Great Awakening, see Edwin Scott Gaustad, *The Great Awakening in New England* (Gloucester, Mass., 1965), 77-79, and Goen, *Revivalism and Separatism,* 19n, 32, 48n, 174, 182.

86. Jonathan Edwards, *Charity and Its Fruits,* in *Ethical Writings,* ed. Ramsey, 361-62.

87. Cotton Mather, *The Negro Christianized* (Boston, 1706), 25, cited in Winthrop D. Jordan, *White Over Black: American Attitudes Toward the Negro, 1550-1812* (Chapel Hill, N.C., 1968), 187. Like Samuel Sewall and Samuel Davies, Mather believed that black "stupidity" could be eliminated by education. See Jordan, *White Over Black,* 101-265, for early and mid-eighteenth-century attitudes toward blacks.

88. *Miscellanies,* no. 26; *Oxford English Dictionary,* 2d ed. (1989), 7:430, 17:651.

89. Davidson, *The Logic of Millennial Thought,* 75.

90. Roland A. DeLattre has argued similarly in *Beauty and Sensibility in the Thought of Jonathan Edwards* (New Haven, 1968).

91. Jonathan Edwards, "The Mind," in *Scientific and Philosophical Writings,* ed. Anderson, 336; *TV,* 564.

92. Jonathan Edwards, *Treatise on Grace,* ed. Tyron Edwards (1852; reprint, Edinburgh, 1969), 64.

93. *HA,* 339; emphasis added. It is no surprise, either, that God's ultimate gift to his church was also a society in union: the heavenly society in eternity after the end of the millennium. *Miscellanies,* no. 743; ibid., no. 946.

94. *HA,* 339; *HWR,* 483.

95. Heimert, *Religion and the American Mind,* 99. But he mistakenly claims for Edwards the equation of God and the Christian commonwealth. Instead, for Edwards the good Christian commonwealth is an earthly *sign* of the heavenly community of God with the church triumphant. Heimert, *Religion and the American Mind,* 124; *TV,* 564-65.

96. *HA,* 339; *HWR,* 484: men will express their love in "deeds of charity." Edwards never explains, however, why charity will be needed during a time that he also claims will see universal prosperity.

97. As far as I know, Edwards never specifies what form of polity his millennial church will take—whether congregational, for instance, or presbyterian.

98. *TV,* 564; *HWR,* 484; *HA,* 339.

99. Edwards, "The Christian Pilgrim," in *Jonathan Edwards: Representative Selections,* ed. Faust and Johnson, 130-36; *HWR,* 283, 389; sermon on Matthew 25:46, April 1739, cited in John H. Gerstner, *Jonathan Edwards: A Mini-Theology* (Wheaton, Ill., 1987), 109.

100. "Notes on the Apocalypse," in *AW,* 137.

101. *HA,* 339; *HWR,* 484-85; ibid.; *HA,* 340; *HWR,* 484-85; ibid.; *HA,* 342-43; *Miscellanies,* no. 1131. Like most eighteenth-century utopias, Edwards's was based on an agricultural economy. Manuel and Manuel, *Utopian Thought,* 20; Holstun, *A Rational Millennium,* 73.

102. For a sensitive, extended analysis of Edward's economics, see Mark Valeri, "The Economic Thought of Jonathan Edwards," *Church History* 60, no. 1 (March 1991): 37-54.

103. Gregory H. Nobles, *Divisions Throughout the Whole: Politics and Society in Hampshire County, Massachusetts, 1740-1775* (Cambridge, Mass., 1983), 35; Miller, *Jonathan Edwards,* 250.

104. *HWR,* 484; Westbrook, "Social Criticism and the Heavenly City," 409. "Edwards's exposition of the millennial expectation . . . [was] alone . . . powerful enough to check the depredations of the river gods." Miller, *Jonathan Edwards,* 321. Edwards perhaps would have been suspicious of the millennial economy of the Fifth Monarchy Men, which was based on commerce rather than agriculture. This sect was made up primarily of urban mercantilists who were conscious of developing an economic polity for an island kingdom dependent on trade. Manuel and Manuel, *Utopian Thought,* 360.

105. Middlekauf, *The Mathers,* 333; Bloch, *Visionary Republic,* 10; Holstun, *A Rational Millennium,* 50; Manuel and Manuel, *Utopian Thought,* 207, 493-515. Edwards's attitude toward knowledge differed, however, from the sectarian utopists of the English Revolution. That is, unlike the Levellers, Ranters, and Diggers, Edwards was not opposed to the university system or higher degrees. See Manuel and Manuel, *Utopian Thought,* 354.

106. *Miscellanies,* no. 262. There was a "down side" to the communication revolution to come: it would aid the apostasy at the end of the millennium by allowing it to spread around the globe almost immediately. *Miscellanies,* no. 835.

107. *HWR,* 473, 480; Abelove, ed., "Jonathan Edwards's Letter of Invitation to George Whitefield," 488; *HWR,* 405.

108. I use the word "revolution" in the same way that Edwards often used it, to denote radical changes—"overturnings," as he often put it—in every sphere of life, including political. See, for example, *HWR,* 430-31. Revolution in society is an

analogue writ large of the revolution that takes place in a soul during conversion. This is not to suggest, however, that Edwards consciously merged history with the experiences of the private self. See William Scheick, "The Grand Design: Jonathan Edwards's *History of the Work of Redemption*," in *Critical Essays*, ed. Scheick, 177-88, and John Wilson's astute corrective in his introduction to *HWR*, 98-100.

109. *HWR*, 483-84; "Notes on the Apocalypse," in *AW*, 136-37.

110. As Conrad Cherry has put it, "The saint participates in, but is not absorbed in, the Holy Spirit." Cherry, *The Theology of Jonathan Edwards*, 88. See also *RA*, 341.

111. *HA*, 339; *Miscellanies*, no. 262. The political model that I have found closest to this among early modern utopias is Leibniz's world polity, in which individual cultures would preserve their national characters as indestructible monads. Manuel and Manuel, *Utopian Thought*, 405.

112. *HWR*, 482, 483; ibid.

113. Ibid.

114. "A people of G[od] may be called of G[od] to go forth to war against their Enemies." Sermon on 1 Kings 8:44-45, 4 April 1745, Fast for Success in the Expedition against Cape Breton, 3. In the remainder of this sermon Edwards outlined the circumstances in which a professing people may feel justified in going to war: (1) when the rights of a public society are invaded and the preservation of the community requires it; and (2) when a people are obliged by a "Just alliance or Covenant" contracted with another people for their "mutual defense and Preservation." An individual is "called of God" to go to war when he is called by "those that are in authority unless it be notoriously manifest that the war is unjust." Ibid., 10-12.

115. Scholars such as Davidson and Hatch properly emphasize the priority, for Edwards, of spiritual over political forces in history. Yet the political effects of those spiritual forces were not unimportant for Edwards, as an overemphasis on the spiritual forces can imply.

116. Bloch is therefore wrong to say that Edwards did not specify whether this liberty was a quality of civil as well as religious life. Bloch, *Visionary Republic*, 20.

117. Understanding the passage as a conflation—Edwards's combination of the two periods into one general period of transformation—is the only way to make sense of the seemingly contradictory statements contained within it.

118. *ST*, 371. The context refers to the Awakening, which rulers were to support. This is another indication that Edwards in *Some Thoughts* considered the Awakening to be of the tumultuous period preceding the millennium, not the beginning of the millennium itself. For, as we have seen, Edwards had said that the millennium would be peaceful, but the period preceding it full of conflict.

119. Hatch's contrast between Edwards and later "civil millennialists" is too sharp. Their millennialism was heavily charged with political meaning, but his was not without its political implications for both future and present. Hatch, *The Sacred Cause of Liberty*, 167.

120. "Notes on the Apocalypse," in *AW*, 136. In this respect Edwards was like nearly all of his contemporaries. Yet on some occasions, as we shall see in the next two chapters, Edwards attacked the abuse of power by the royal court.

121. Bloch, *Visionary Republic*, 47.

122. *HA*, 357-58. In the text it is clear that the "general outpouring of his Spirit" is one of the revivals to be expected in the period before the millennium. Compare this passage with *HA*, 410-11.

123. Edwards's belief that this glorious work of God's spirit would be the greatest ever seen explains how he could think that if the Great Awakening was indeed the beginning of this, then "the New Jerusalem in this respect has begun to come down from heaven." *ST*, 346.

124. *HA*, 411. The same process is described in more detail, but without specification of its duration, in *HWR*, 467-70.

125. See, for instance, *AW*, 22-23, 55-59; Davidson, *The Logic of Millennial Thought*, 153-57; Goen, "Jonathan Edwards: A New Departure in Eschatology." My understanding of the relationship of Edwards's millennialism to Dutch scholasticism is indebted to James Kennedy. Other treatments of Edwards and the Dutch scholastics include Bogue, *Jonathan Edwards and the Covenant of Grace*, and James P. Martin, *The Last Judgment in Protestant Theology from Orthodoxy to Ritschl* (Edinburgh, 1963).

126. *Dictionary of National Biography* (Oxford, 1917), vid. "Lowman"; Dietrich H. Kromminga, *The Millennium in the Church* (Grand Rapids, Mich., 1963), 205-6; Jürgen Moltmann, "Jacob Brocard als Vorlaeufer der Reich-Gottes-Theologie und der Profetischen Schriftauslegung der Johannes Coccejus," *Zeitschrift für Kirchengeschichte* 71 (1960): 110-29; Grete Moeller, "Föderalismus und Geschichtsbetrachtung im 17. u. 18. Jahrhundert," *Zeitschrift für Kirchengeschichte* 1931, nos. 3 and 4, 404-40; Jürgen Moltmann, "Geschichtstheologie und Pietisches Menschenbild bei Johannes Coccejus und Theodor Untereyck," *Evangelische Theologie* 19 (1959): 346-47.

127. Kromminga, *The Millennium,* 206; Willem a Brakel, *Redelyk Godsdienst,* part 3 (Leiden, 1882), 287-96, 309, 325.

128. Jonathan Edwards, "Letter to Joseph Bellamy, 15 January 1747," *New England Quarterly* 1 (1928): 229; Richard A. Muller, *Post-Reformation Reformed Dogmatics,* vol. 1, *Prolegomena to Theology* (Grand Rapids, Mich., 1987), 48; Mastricht, *Beschouwende en Praktikale Godgeleerdheit,* 3:709-10; 4:481.

129. Davidson, *The Logic of Millennial Thought,* 127-75.

130. *HWR,* 527-28; *Notes on the Bible,* 222; see also *Miscellanies,* no. 356, 810.

131. *Miscellanies,* no. hh, cited in *AW,* 11; Sermon on Matthew 18:7, 18; "Notes on the Apocalypse, in *AW,* 208; *HWR,* 420-21.

132. See also *AW,* 305 (written at about the same time as *HA,* 421).

133. *HWR,* 463-64; see also *HA,* 196-97, 394.

134. It must be noted, however, that at about the same time as *ST* (dating estimated by Thomas A. Schafer), Edwards penned in his private notebooks an allusive reference to America and the latter-day glory. America, he wrote, was "a type and forerunner of what is approaching in spiritual things." *Images,* 102. In this period he also changed his interpretation of the "distant isles" of Isaiah 60:9. Earlier, he had thought them to "principally" refer to Europe; *Miscellanies,* no. g; "Notes on the Apocalypse," in *AW,* 142. But in *ST* he identified them as a reference to America. *ST,* 353.

135. This accusation may seem inconsistent with Edwards's praise for America's spiritual privileges, which we saw in the last chapter. But for Edwards there was no inconsistency. Americans had been given greater spiritual privileges than any other people, but because they had abused those privileges, their guilt was correspondingly greater.

136. *ST,* 356; *Notes on the Bible,* 232; ibid. This latter entry, which is no. 417, has been dated by Schafer at approximately late 1742 or early 1743. It suggests that Edwards has America in mind because Edwards had in the same period written, in *Some Thoughts,* that the Great Awakening was the "first fruits of that glorious day." *ST,* 354. Furthermore, in his private notebook he wrote that the recipients of the "first outpouring of the Spirit" were full of "spiritual pride and self-confidence," the same charge he leveled at New Englanders just a year later in a letter to a Scottish correspondent: "[God] saw our spiritual pride and self-confidence." *Notes on the Bible,* 232; letter to William McCullough, 5 March 1744, in *GA,* 559.

137. *ST,* 354-55.

138. Stein first noticed this. *AW,* 28.

139. In the summer of 1742, for instance, "James Davenport was wrecking the Awakening." Miller, *Jonathan Edwards,* 203. See Gaustad, *The Great Awakening,* 61-79, and Goen, *Revivalism and Separatism,* 48-67.

140. *GA,* 208, 210, 131-32, 137, 141; there are also Edwards's letters to Benjamin Colman, cited by Stein in *AW,* 20.

141. Abelove, "Jonathan Edwards's Letter," 488.

142. The fact that Edwards's closest disciples (Joseph Bellamy, Samuel Hopkins, and Jonathan Edwards, Jr.), who carefully read their mentor's published works and private notebooks, developed eschatologies that were decidedly untribalist supports my contention that Edwards's eschatology transcended provincial, nationalistic concerns. Mark Valeri reports that "like most New Divinity preachers and unlike many Old Light, Arminian and Separatist pastors, Bellamy resisted the kind of civil millennialism or civil religion that flowered during the American Revolution." Bellamy, Hopkins, and Edwards, Jr., interpreted the millennium as the ultimate establishment of benevolence, not primarily as the triumph of an American, nationalistic order. This explains, writes Valeri, why during the 1780s and 1790s New Divinity preachers were critics of populist and democratic nationalism. Mark Valeri, "Joseph Bellamy: Conversion, Social Ethics, and Politics in the Thought of an Eighteenth-Century Calvinist" (Ph.D. diss., Princeton University, 1985), 175, 176-77.

143. See Johan Anthony Dejong, *As the Waters Cover the Sea: Millennial Expectations in the Rise of Anglo-American Missions, 1640-1810* (Kampen, 1970), 127; Miller, *Jonathan Edwards,* 317.

144. Dwight, *The Life of President Edwards,* 262.

145. Holstun, *A Rational Millennium,* 43, 46-47. Other examples of this sort of millennialism cited by Holstun were John Eliot, the early Winstanley, and Harrington; cited in Holstun, 46. The seventeenth-century Pansophists (Giordano Bruno of Nola, Francis Bacon, Tommaso Campanella, and Johann Andreae) demonstrate the same pattern; Manuel and Manuel, *Utopian Thought,* 205-21.

146. *HWR,* 458-59; Heimert, *Religion and the American Mind,* chap. 2. Davidson makes a similar claim: Edwards "was one of the first Americans to argue explicitly that a noncatastrophic interpretation of Christ's coming would provide believers with the confidence necessary to establish the kingdom." Davidson, *The Logic of Millennial Thought,* 270. Edwards argued that believers should have the confidence to pray for the coming of the kingdom, not establish it by their own efforts. *HA,* 395.

147. Holstun, *A Rational Millennium,* 45-46. Holstun cites Richard Baxter, the radical medieval sects described in Norman Cohn's *Pursuit of the*

Millennium, and the Anabaptists at Muenster, as hermeneutical millennialists.

148. *Miscellanies,* no. 810; see a parallel passage in *AW,* 303. This notion of the necessity of a great man to effect world-historical movement in a final age is common to seventeenth- and eighteenth-century utopias, both religious and secular. Leibniz, for example, thought of himself as chosen by God to be the great intermediary between China and Europe as adviser to Peter the Great. Turgot considered the "genius" to be the dynamic agent of progress as history moves toward perfection. Condorcet believed that at crucial moments in history the intervention of genius was necessary to point out the value of a new and better way of doing things. Manuel and Manuel, *Utopian Thought,* 393, 408, 469-70, 495.

149. John Calvin felt he had a similar calling, as a prophet and teacher "to bring the world to order." His calling, however, did not have the eschatological urgency of Edwards's. Bouwsma, *John Calvin,* 191.

150. As this chapter has indicated, Goen misconstrues the nature of Edwards's "new departure." Edwards was by no means the first postmillennialist in New England, and he did not prophesy an imminent American millennium. Goen, "Jonathan Edwards: A New Departure in Eschatology."

151. See the end of Chapter 5 for a discussion of Edwards's influence in the eighteenth century.

List of Abbreviations

AW: Apocalytic Writings, ed. Stephen J. Stein, vol. 5 of *The Works of Jonathan Edwards.*

CF: Charity and Its Fruits, in *Ethical Writings,* ed. Paul Ramsey, vol. 8 of *The Works of Jonathan Edwards.*

DM: The Distinguishing Marks, in *The Great Awakening,* ed. C. C. Goen, vol. 4 of *The Works of Jonathan Edwards.*

FN: A Faithful Narrative, in *The Great Awakening,* ed. C. C. Goen, vol. 4 of *The Works of Jonathan Edwards.*

GA: The Great Awakening, ed. C. C. Goen, vol. 4 of *The Works of Jonathan Edwards.*

HA: An Humble Attempt, ed. Stephen J. Stein, vol. 5 of *The Works of Jonathan Edwards.*

HWR: History of the Work of Redemption, ed. John F. Wilson, vol. 9 of *The Works of Jonathan Edwards.*

OS: Original Sin, ed. Clyde A. Holbrook, vol. 3 of *The Works of Jonathan Edwards.*

"PN": "Personal Narrative," in *Jonathan Edwards: Representative Selections,* ed. Clarence H. Faust and Thomas H. Johnson.

RA: Religious Affections, ed. John E. Smith, vol. 2 of *The Works of Jonathan Edwards.*

ST: Some Thoughts Concerning the Revival, in *The Great Awakening,* ed. C. C. Goen, vol. 4 of *The Works of Jonathan Edwards.*

TV: The Nature of True Virtue, ed. Paul Ramsey, vol. 8 of *The Works of Jonathan Edwards.*

Marc M. Arkin (essay date 1993)

SOURCE: "The Great Awakener," in *The New Criterion,* Vol. II, No. 9, May 1993, pp. 59–62.

[In the following review of John E. Smith's Jonathan Edwards: Puritan, Preacher, Philosopher, *Arkin stresses "the powerful aesthetic strain in Edwards's thought, particularly his moral theology, which expressly equated virtue with the beauty of moral acts."]*

On July 8, 1741, the Congregational Church of Enfield, Connecticut, passed into the history books. On that day, the assembled parishioners were treated to perhaps the single most famous sermon in American history, **"Sinners in the Hands of an Angry God."** Preached on the ominous text "Their foot shall slide in due time" (Deut. 32:35), the sermon featured the unforgettable image of the sinner suspended over the fires of hell, dangling from a slender thread like a spider or "some loathesome insect," whose fate is held by a God who "abhors you and is dreadfully provoked." Tradition has it that the visiting minister—a stranger to the congregation—delivered the sermon in a monotone, staring at the bellrope at the back of the church, while terrified churchgoers fell from their pews in agony at their unredeemed state. Strong men clung to the pillars of the meetinghouse and begged for mercy.

The speaker was not the celebrated George Whitefield, the Billy Graham of his day, who had lately toured New England with such spectacular success; nor was it any of the other itinerant evangelists who were beginning to upset the settled order of the colonial churches in the religious upheaval known as the Great Awakening. It was Jonathan Edwards, the greatest American theologian of the eighteenth century—and possibly of any other. Not simply a religious figure, Edwards was also, as John E. Smith claims in his new monograph [*Jonathan Edwards: Puritan, Preacher, Philosopher*], the most acute American philosophical thinker before Charles Sanders Peirce, the late-nineteenth-century founder of pragmaticism.

Edwards was born in 1703 into the New England clerical elite. His father, Timothy Edwards, was the pastor of the Congregational Church in East Windsor, Connecticut. His maternal grandfather was Solomon Stoddard, whose influential pastorate in Northampton, Massachusetts, had yielded five separate seasons of religious revival and had earned him the unofficial title of "Pope of the Connecticut River Valley." Edwards attended the nascent Yale College, then an evangelical institution whose motto, "Lux et Veritas," was selected to differentiate it from the mere "Veritas" of its graceless rival on the Charles. After a brief pastorate in New York City and a stint as academic tutor at Yale, Edwards was ordained associate pastor of his eighty-four-year-old grandfather's congregation in 1727, becoming pastor when Stoddard died two years later. By this time, Edwards had discovered the new philosophy of John Locke and in his notebooks had marked out the major themes that would occupy the rest of his life: philosophical idealism, empirical observation, and a deep concern for the personal experience of religion.

At first, Edwards found his congregation "very insensible of the things of religion." Then, late in 1734, while in the middle of a closely reasoned sermon series on justification by faith, Edwards noticed a change. Through the spring and summer, the town enjoyed one of those seasons of religious quickening it had experienced under Stoddard, a revival of religion that quickly spread throughout the Connecticut River Valley. By 1737, when Edwards published his *Faithful Narrative of the Surprising Work of God,* the so-called "frontier revival" had waned; it was long cold a year later, when the *Discourses* that occasioned the revival appeared in print.

For the next eight years, Edwards distinguished himself as a participant in the Great Awakening, of which the Northampton revival was a precursor, and as a polemicist for experiential religion within the confines of traditional Calvinist doctrine. His most notable work of this period was *A Treatise Concerning Religious Affections* (1746). In it, Edwards placed the wellspring of true religion in the lively inclinations that determine the heart and "the fountain of all the affections" in Christian love. Then, in 1748, a bitter dispute arose within his congregation. The chief cause was Edwards's insistence on an experiential test for admission to church membership, a practice abjured by his grandfather. The flashpoint occurred when Edwards proposed to discipline the children of some prominent Northampton families for circulating a "bad book," a midwives' manual. Edwards was dismissed from his church in 1750, after twenty-three years of service, with a wife and seven dependent children.

Rescue came in the form of a call to Stockbridge, Massachusetts, a frontier town where the Society for the Propagation of the Gospel in New England and the Bay Colony's Board of Commissioners for Indian Affairs maintained a mission. Despite the strain of a double ministry, the Stockbridge years became the most productive of Edwards's life. During that time, he published the works familiarly known as *Freedom of the Will* (1754) and *The Great Christian Doctrine of Original Sin Defended* (1758). He also prepared the manuscript of *The Nature of True Virtue* (1755, first published in 1765) and began his epic narrative, *A History of the Work of Redemption.* Recognition of this remarkable intellectual outpouring came with a call to become president of Princeton University. Unfortunately, Edwards arrived in Princeton while the town was suffering a smallpox epidemic. Shortly after his installation in 1758, he died of an unsuccessful inoculation, not yet fifty-five years old.

Since the time of Perry Miller, the Harvard scholar who rediscovered the American Puritans, Edwards's reputation has been on the ascendant. Miller himself led the renewed interest in Edwards with his 1949 biography and his still matchless essay "From Edwards to Emerson," which grasped the essential continuity between Edwards's search for the "images and shadows of divine things" in nature and the Transcendentalism of later New England thinkers shed of the baggage of original sin. Nevertheless, like Hegel or Kant, Edwards is one of those thinkers that almost everyone likes to cite and almost no one has the fortitude to read. Laboring under a "ponderous prose" style, Edwards's philosophical works often suffer from being the other half of a polemical debate in which his opponents—and their positions—have long since passed into well-deserved obscurity. Even at their most vital, they partake of a sensibility not easily accessible to the modern reader.

John E. Smith is Clark Professor Emeritus of Philosophy at Yale, and, since 1963, the general editor of the first critical edition of Edwards's writings, now running to some ten volumes. In this short book he has set out either to remedy Edwards's "inaccessibility" or to take advantage of it, depending on your perspective. Drawing largely from his own reading of Edwards and from the excellent critical introductions to the Yale series—particularly those of the philosopher Paul Ramsey and the late religious historian Clyde Holbrook—Smith provides a critical summary of each of Edwards's most important works. Beginning with a very brief biographical sketch, Smith sets the tone with a chapter entitled "Edwards's Thought and the Philosophy of Locke," which considers Edwards's creative appropriation of Lockean categories. Thereafter, Smith moves seriatim through chapters more or less devoted to summarizing *Religious Affections* and Edwards's other defenses of heart religion, *Freedom of the Will, Original Sin, The Nature of True Virtue,* and the unfinished *History of the Work of Redemption.*

While this treatment may be very useful for the perplexed graduate student faced with the original text, it has somewhat more limited value for the general reader. In particular, those looking for an intellectual biography of Edwards will be disappointed. In the first place, Smith's monograph lacks a sense of the development—or the unity—of Edwards's thought. In fact, it is rather weak with regard both to historical context and to chronology; this reader had to consult other reference works to obtain the dates of some of Edwards's works mentioned in this essay.

Instead, Smith seems concerned to place Edwards within the modern intellectual mainstream, stressing the empiricist bent in his thought and, somewhat improbably, attempting to palm off Edwards's sacred history as being uniquely "a century ahead of his time in his understanding of the historical order." As anyone familiar with Cotton Mather's *Magnalia Christi Americana* (1702) would acknowledge, New England divines spilled an inordinate amount of ink searching for the hand of God in history. In fact, Edwards's central aim was to search the historical record so that men might know when exactly God "shall take the kingdom," hardly a modern perspective. The task had a particular urgency since, for Edwards, "what is now seen in America, and especially in New England, may prove the dawn of that glorious day."

By reading Edwards out of his own context, Smith tends to downplay two very remarkable aspects of his thought and the extraordinary tension between them. The first is Edwards's perfect orthodoxy within the New England Calvinist tradition. Beginning with the first premise of the absolute sovereignty of God—a sovereignty so complete that Edwards could not admit of secondary causes such as free will—Edwards adhered to each and every doctrine of traditional Reformed theology: total depravity, unconditional election, limited atonement, irresistible grace, and the perseverance of the saints. These were the touchstone of Edwards's world view.

The second is the powerful aesthetic strain in Edwards's thought, particularly his moral theology, which expressly equated virtue with the beauty of moral acts. Edwards described God as "infinitely the most beautiful and excellent [Being]: and all the beauty to be found throughout the whole creation, is but the reflection of the diffused beams of that Being." True virtue is nothing less than the love of being to that beauty which is Being in general. God's creative urgency is the continuous overflowing of His own love to Being. Original sin is the loss of man's ability to participate in this cycle of divine love; as images of divine beauty, natural beauty and virtue give the truly spiritual a foretaste of the divine. In this light, one might well consider the following passage from Edwards's **Personal Narrative:**

> The first instance that I remember of that sort of inward, sweet delight in God and divine things that I have lived much in since was on reading those words (1 Tim. 1:17), *Now unto the King eternal, immortal, invisible, the only wise God, be honor and glory forever and ever.* . . . Not long after I first began to experience these things . . . I walked abroad alone, in a solitary place in my father's pasture for contemplation. And, as I was walking there and looking upon the sky and clouds, there came into my mind so sweet a sense of the glorious *majesty* and *grace* of God, that I know not how to express. . . . God's excellency, his wisdom, his purity and love, seemed to appear in every thing; in the sun, moon, and stars; in the clouds, and blue sky; in the grass, flowers, trees; in the water, and in all nature.

Is it any wonder that William Ellery Channing placed Edwards among the pantheists, for whom the mystery is why there is anything else in creation but God? And yet, at the same time, Edwards truly felt the radical separation of fallen man from the beauty of both this world and the world unseen. Perhaps the most serious limitation of Smith's essay is that it fails to convey this most immediate element of Edwards's thought and thus does not encourage its audience to seek what is most vital in the original.

Richard E. Brantley (essay date 1993)

SOURCE: "An Anglo-American Nexus," in *Coordinates of Anglo-American Romanticism: Wesley, Edwards, Carlyle and Emerson,* University Press of Florida, 1993, pp. 7-42.

[In the following excerpt, Brantley discusses the relationship between the ideas and work of Methodist founder John Wesley in England and those of preacher and theologian Edwards in the colonies of New England. He traces their respective responses to the philosophy of John Locke and their subsequent legacy to nineteenth-century religious and philosophical thought.]

Commonplaces stand in need of scrutiny. The special relationship between England and the United States is more than merely political, more than merely linguistic, and even more than broadly cultural, for it is at once, and perennially, intellectual and emotional. An especially useful metaphor for this relationship is the special relationship between the Englishman John Wesley and the American Jonathan Edwards. Although they never consciously cooperated with one another, they contributed to a variety of relations between their respective lands. Wesley founded Methodist movements in both England and the United States, and Edwards joined forces with the Briton George Whitefield, who undertook the arduous journey to the colonies in order to participate in the Great Awakening. Wesley and Edwards inspired popular evangelicalism in Britain and America from the 1730s, through the American Revolution, to the end of the nineteenth century. By regarding them as emblematic, I seek to delineate an especially enduring, because still resonating, Anglo-American mode of thought and feeling. The intellectual sway and fervor of Wesley and Edwards contributed to Anglo-American experience.

Whether or not the special relationship between England and the United States rests in large part, even now, on an intellectual as well as emotional frame of reference to nature and to spirit, this frame is not only the considered construct of Wesley and Edwards but also their joint legacy to the nineteenth century. Constituting an Anglo-American *genius loci,* Wesley and Edwards express and disseminate their shared definition of feeling and thought. Through their concerted roles as social forces, through an often indirect but sometimes direct and always propitious process of cultural osmosis, they make up the very model of an Anglo-American sensibility. Their religious methodologies are not, after all, so far removed from even such early twentieth-century methods as the verification principles of the British A. J. Ayer and the pragmatism of the American John Dewey. Many such "representative men"[1] (one would say "representative people") participate in the same binational entity, the same "nature-culture coevolution"[2] of Anglo-American relations.

This chapter, by examining the influence of Wesley and Edwards from the broadest possible perspective, and by addressing their common ground as one single subject, surveys an especially fertile ground of Anglo-American expression. I will consider them philosophically, rather than exclusively theologically, and approach them as methodologically alert, even where they thought themselves simply orthodox. I seek to demonstrate that they shared the same essentially Lockean insights that, as I have previously argued, informed much of British literature and theology from 1740 to 1840. I acknowledge differences between them, yet I discover their common ground, the full character of their two-way special relationship. The twin pioneers of transatlantic revivalism are brothers of both soul and mind in that both men appropriate Lockean empiricism for religious methodology. Indeed, the philosophical as well as religious epistemology of this charismatic diumvirate of the Anglo-American world exemplifies the Anglo-American imagination.

Edwards: An Orientation

Although recent scholarship on Edwards emphasizes his conservatism and his relation to Scottish Commonsense philosophy,[3] Locke was a formative influence on the Commonsense school. Edwards's indebtedness to Locke[4] is consistent with conservative principles in that Locke takes account of both empiricism and "a theocentric framework."[5] Terrence Erdt traces Edwards's language to its conservative source in Calvin and emphasizes the aesthetic dimension of that language; he also acknowledges that an understanding of Edwards's sense-language is central to an understanding of Edwards.[6] Roland Delattre argues that especially according to *The Nature of True Virtue* (1765) divine being is both present to humankind as beauty and known to humankind through emotion.[7] Similarly, though with explicit reference to Locke, I maintain an aesthetic-epistemological emphasis in my approach to Edwards's theology.

Sacvan Bercovitch regards with new respect the pioneering argument of Perry Miller that Edwards is a Lockean.[8] While I share this new respect, it is time to discover new complexities in the Lockean view of Edwards. As I confirm Wallace E. Anderson's conviction that Edwards "accepted Locke's view that it is a wholly contingent matter that each mind receives the sensory information it does,"[9] I consider the consensus that although Lockean ideas of sensation represent real qualities of bodies, real qualities in Edwards's works are often identified only with "the fixed order and relations of ideas."[10] Moreover, although Miller's argument is exclusively sense-oriented, my view of Locke's empiricism is that it is both sense- and reason-based, a view consistent with Edwards's immersion in the categories of sense perception and his desire for the consent of mind to mind.

Whatever the merits, then, of the labels *idealist, Platonist, scholastic, Calvinist,* and *mystic,* the labels *empiricist* and *sensationalist* are particularly apt for Edwards in his eighteenth-century context. The "radical theism" that Robert W. Jenson describes embraces what he sees as Edwards's most characteristic themes: God's relation to nature and history, religious experience, the presence of Christ, and the perfected human community.[11] But "radical theism" also includes the precisely philosophical, because specifically Lockean, theme of the here and now. Although Edwards rejects Newton's cosmology of the universe as a machine, he does not reject Locke's livelier, more down-to-earth world picture. Despite Edwards's life-long struggle with his age's Arminian tendency toward autonomous individuality, his radical theism preserves Locke-derived faith in individual experience.

Wesley and Edwards: An Overview

Charles Rogers, in his attempt to differentiate the pair, disclaims for Edwards any affinity with Wesley's views about providence in general and predestination in particular.[12] Wesley's comments about Edwards's *The Freedom of the Will* (1754) deplore its doctrines of irresistible grace and unconditional election.[13] Wesley's comments, however, approve of Edwards where Edwards posits the experiential context of the soul as a given of religious life: "The soul [quoted Wesley] is now connected with a material vehicle, and placed in the material world. Various objects here continually strike upon one or other of the bodily organs."[14] Albert C. Outler, on the basis of Wesley's published abridgments of five works by Edwards, suggests that Edwards was a formative influence on Wesley.[15] Without losing sight of Rogers's point of view, I concur with Outler's: although Edwards referred to Wesley just once, and disparagingly,[16] Wesley rejoiced in Edwards. Accordingly, I seek to establish the intellectual as well as emotional sense in which they should be linked.

Frederick Dreyer sees them as intellectual polar opposites.

> Edwards's thought was ultimately ontological and proceeded from the premise of necessary being. Wesley's was psychological and proceeded from the premise of self-consciousness. Wesley is satisfied with the apparent truths that ordinary mortals do in fact perceive. Edwards insists upon the necessary truths they ought to perceive.[17]

Except that I would substitute *epistemological* for *psychological,* I am in accord with Dreyer's estimate of Wesley, and Dreyer's estimate of Edwards rings true in that Edwards's ontological moods indeed recur. His early essay **"On Being,"** for example, rests on a rationalistic base, the "platonic traditions of idealism";[18] and toward the end of his career, he clearly retreats from any ostensible harmony of empiricism and faith to a rather intransigent rationalism, a rationalism of the supernatural, if you will. Wesley does not follow this path, for while believing in the supernatural as much as anyone, Wesley holds to the senses and to sense-based reason.

In midcareer, however, Edwards comes close to having it both ways, as Wesley does throughout his life. Against the view of Edwards as exclusively ontological, I contend that his theology, like Wesley's, is often epistemological, and I accordingly emphasize that Lockean empiricism provides a philosophic reason for linking Wesley with Edwards. In "Wesley and Edwards: A Hypothesis," Appendix A of my *Locke, Wesley, and the Method of English Romanticism,* I suggest that Edwards derives his theological method from Locke's theory of knowledge. Wesley uses Locke's language to devise an analogy between the natural senses and the "spiritual sense"; he even conceives of a continuum joining scientific method and rational empiricism to natural and revealed religion. Edwards, too, in midcareer at least, envisions this analogy or continuum.

A DOCUMENT

The shortest way to bring the pair into my field of vision is through Wesley's abridgment (1773) of Edwards's *A Treatise concerning Religious Affections* (1746). This last of Wesley's abridgments of five works by Edwards[19] culminates Wesley's thirty-year response to Edwards's works and hence constitutes Wesley's most mature judgment of those works. *Religious Affections* marks the central juncture of Edwards's development, at the midpoint of his career, and is thus the best representative of his mind and method.

Appearing in volume 23 of Wesley's collected works of 1771-74, *An Extract from a Treatise concerning Religious Affections* omits the entire preface of Edwards's work, the second, third, and fourth of the twelve major sections of part three, many shorter passages, and many words and phrases.[20] Published in 1762, the edition of *Religious Affections* that Wesley used is itself an abridgment by William Gordon.[21]

Although Gregory S. Clapper, in the only other full-length study of Wesley's abridgment, acknowledges that "Gordon's abridgment was about two-thirds of the original" and that "Wesley's was one-sixth," Clapper demonstrates that neither the "excisions and revisions" of Gordon nor those of Wesley "pervert the essential thrust of Edwards's work."[22] To compare Wesley's abridgment with Gordon's, then, is to compare it with *Religious Affections,* too. Wesley's abridgment is not only true to the original, but also "better," that is, less prolix.

Although Wesley often objected to works he carefully read,[23] and although his more than two hundred abridgments sometimes include matter with which he disagreed,[24] his abridgment of *Religious Affections* is so painstaking, polished, and selective that it indicates well his attraction to Edwards's sensibility. By analyzing the abridgment, I characterize Wesley's distillation of Edwards and hence Edwards's influence on Wesley. As occasion rises, I point to parallels between the abridgment and Wesley's works. Nothing Wesley ever wrote materially contradicts either the abridgment or any other version from Edwards's prime;

indeed, what appears in the abridgment finds strikingly similar expression throughout Wesley's works.

The abridgment not only omits, but also alters, and some of the alterations are substantive.[25] As an Arminian who believes that "Christ died for *every Soul* of Man,"[26] Wesley excises Edwards's Calvinism and its doctrine of the elect. Where Edwards inveighs against the view that "mine own hands hath saved me," Wesley balks and quotes nothing,[27] thus suggesting that one bears partial responsibility for one's own salvation. Where Edwards says "the convenant is ordered in all things, and sure," Wesley is silent,[28] thus refusing predestinarian tincture. "Continuance in duty," writes Edwards, is "difficult to [one's very] nature," which is full of "blindness, deceit, self-flattery, self-exaltation, and self-confidence," and he adds, for good measure, that even "the saint . . . has sight of his own corruptions," but Wesley gives no quarter to this extreme belief in human frailty.[29]

Such omissions suggest an anti-Calvinist rationale for Wesley's numerous rejections of Edwards's harsh, uncharitable language. Where Edwards speaks of some religious affections as "false and counterfeit," Wesley calls them merely "mixed or degenerating,"[30] as though to soften the implication of hardened duplicity. Where Edwards argues that "persons may have a kind of religious love, and yet have no saving grace," Wesley, who often says that love and grace are so far from being thus mutually exclusive that they are in fact one and the same, keeps quiet.[31] Where Edwards insists on phrases like "great corruption," "strait and narrow way," "fears of hell," "the duty of self-denial," "deserved eternal burnings," "the infinitely hateful nature of sin," and "the infinitely inferior nature of men," Wesley will have none of it.[32] Indeed, Wesley will have very little Calvinist language of any kind, however innocuous, for though the word *saints,* with its overtones of the perseverance thereof, appears four times,[33] he usually goes to great lengths to avoid even this mild Calvinism. He replaces Edwards's "true saints," "eminent saints," "the character of the saints," and "the minds of the saints" with "Christians," "believers," "good men," "we," "those," or almost anything else he can think of.[34]

"The Eye altering alters all," declared William Blake,[35] which means not only that the organs of perception are creative, that the eye changes what it sees, but also that "the Eye altering" is changed by what it sees, that all is changed within. Similarly, though Wesley's emendatory powers transform some doctrines and improve the style of *Religious Affections,* his editorial eye is itself improved, his "doors of perception" "cleansed,"[36] by his encounter with and his obvious reverence for Edwards's methodology. Although Wesley's thought guides his editorial hand to the point of bias, the abridgment includes, as Wesley's Note to the Reader puts it, those "many remarks and admonitions" of Edwards's "which may be of great use to the children of God."[37]

Clapper, pointing out such parallels between *Religious Affections* and Wesley's works as reliance on Scripture and the theme of humble joy, concludes that

> if one were to give an irenic reading of their differences, one might say that Wesley and Edwards agreed about the sovereignty of God, but that while Edwards expressed this sovereignty through his Calvinist doctrines of predestination and the bondage of the will, Wesley expressed the same thing by emphasizing prevenient grace and the perfecting possibilities of the spirit.[38]

Since the agreement between Wesley and Edwards about the sovereignty of God did not prevent Wesley from rejecting Edwards's *language* of sovereignty at least three times in the abridgment,[39] one might quibble with part of Clapper's statement. But the statement rings true with regard to the abridgment as a whole, which, as Clapper demonstrates, is both careful to epitomize the four basic parts of Edwards's text and consistent with the basic tenets of Wesley's texts.

Finally, though, the abridgment represents more than the merely theological commonality of Wesley and Edwards. Although "edification was Wesley's ultimate criterion when evaluating the written word," Wesley, as even Clapper acknowledges, "shared Edwards's interest in science and philosophy."[40] Although Wesley's Note to the Reader complains that Edwards "heaps together so many curious, subtle, metaphysical distinctions, as are sufficient to puzzle the brain, and confound the intellects of all the plain men and women in the universe," that is, although the abridgment eschews Edwards's ontology, the abridgment is decidedly epistemological wherever Edwards is so.[41] Just as Lockean epistemology avoids regarding mind as superior to, or independent of, sense experience, so Wesley downplays diction that might be construed as rationalist. Where Edwards speaks of "the more vigorous and sensible exercises of the inclination and will of the soul," Wesley, by writing "the more vigorous and sensible exercises of the will,"[42] omits spiritual, mentalist elements, while he retains sense-language. Where Edwards writes, "It may be enquired what are the affections of the mind," Wesley omits "of the mind."[43] Since the fourth of Edwards's twelve distinguishing signs of "Truly Gracious and Holy Affections" asserts the intellectual component in the affections—"Gracious affections do arise from the mind's being enlightened, rightly and spiritually to understand or apprehend divine things"—it may seem strange that the intellectual Wesley omitted it, until one realizes how close it is to rationalism, that is, to a reason insufficiently involved in, or insufficiently tempered by, sense experience.[44]

In line with the fact that Edwards's reasoning is not always sense-based, an entire category of passages appears to have been altered because, although philosophical or methodological enough, they are not sufficiently empirical to suit Wesley. Where Edwards complains of those who "tell you a long story of conversion" or "a fair story of illuminations and discoveries," Wesley, who likes accounts

of experiential efficacy, eliminates the complaint.[45] From Edwards's phrase "doctrinal knowledge," Wesley drops "doctrinal,"[46] as though to include natural knowledge in knowledge conducive to religion. "Ministers," writes Edwards, sometimes insist too much on "distinctness and clearness of method," for the Spirit does not "proceed discernibly in the steps of a particular established scheme, one half so often as is imagined."[47] But Wesley finds no place for this passage:[48] although his "empiricism" is not unacquainted with paradox, he likes method to be clear and distinct.[49]

Thus manipulating as well as preserving the original, Wesley's editorial procedure is motivated in decisive measure by the Lockean presuppositions of his theology. Where Edwards's theology is consistent with those presuppositions, where his theology is "empirical," Wesley tends to make it more so. Witness, for example, his twofold strategy of quoting Edwards's endorsement of experiential priorities—"Without affections, one is wholly destitute of the saving influences of the Holy Spirit"—and omitting an adjacent passage in which Edwards creates some doubt about the very affectional life he advocates: "As there is no true religion, where there is nothing else but affection; so there is no true religion, where there is no affection."[50] Where Edwards speaks of "holy desire exercised in longings, hungerings, and thirstings after God," Wesley omits "longings," as though to lessen subjectivity and so to intensify the sensationalist implications of this biblical and somehow eighteenth-century phraseology.[51]

Wesley is justified in detecting empirical assumptions and empirical language in *Religious Affections,* which is reconcilable with, and even measures up to, Wesley's own Lockean tastes and expectations, his experiential bias and, above all, his doctrine of the "spiritual sense."[52] Notably, he tampers least with passages most clearly resembling his Lockean method. These passages, totaling twenty-two of the abridgment's sixty-five pages,[53] form the focus of this chapter. They constitute both a precise transformation of Lockean method and what Wesley thought was the broadest agreement between Edwards and himself. Here I consider this strain of passages both in itself and in context; I elaborate on a theological equivalent of Locke's philosophy, demonstrating the Lockean ground of both Wesley and Edwards as found in the abridgment. I enunciate a "spiritual sense" as much American as British.

Wesley's and Edwards's evangelical faiths draw in part from both the processes and the forms of late seventeenth-century empiricism, even as they laterally displace them. Wesley's editing is so thoroughly informed by Locke's *Essay concerning Human Understanding* (1690) that the abridgment emerges, without falsifying the original, as a theologizing of Locke's empiricism. To abridge is "to shorten" or even "to curtail," but the abridgment of *Religious Affections* is no mere summary, no mere abstraction, and no mere "selection of essential facts." Wesley's configuring of Edwards's "epistemology" is, in addition, a condensation that epitomizes the original without diluting it and honors the original by enhancing it. Wesley decided that **Religious Affections** is complexly but manifestly empirical, and I agree. This midpoint of Edwards's thought is indeed characterized by the same Locke-derived emphasis on experience, natural as well as spiritual, to be found in Wesley's Methodism. Wesley's abridgment, by heightening that emphasis, epitomizes the "epistemology" common to him and Edwards. Where most alike and nearest the generic level of revival imagination, they are at once methodically intellectual and in resonance with the enabling powers of empirical premises.

By the abridgment, then, I mean a bridge indeed. It is the intersection of the thought of Wesley and the thought of Edwards. The one's Arminianism and the other's Calvinism lie outside the abridgment. Wesley did not stake his theological reputation on the abridgment, nor did Edwards approve it as faithful to his thought. The abridgment contains, however, what they share, not so much the theological as the philosophical thought, the Locke-inspired emphasis on the experiential, which they then each express in their evangelical theologies and practices. So when I use the term "the abridgment" in this work, I mean the areas where the thought of Wesley and the thought of Edwards coincide.

A READING

"Even deliberately to write against something," observes Denis Donoghue, "is to take one's bearings from it."[54] The abridgment takes its bearings from Lockean epistemology without being subsumed by it. In advocating experience as the way to knowledge, the abridgment is historically akin to and even agrees with Locke's preaching of sensation as the key to empirical knowledge. Locke, in homage to Descartes, intuits himself and deduces God:

> For nothing can be more evident to us, than our own Existence. . . . Thus from the Consideration of our Selves, . . . our Reason leads us to the Knowledge . . . That *there is an eternal, most powerful, most knowing Being.*[55]

Locke goes on to insist, however, that "the *Knowledge of the Existence* of any other thing we can have only by *Sensation,*"[56] and his epistemology of sensation is his major contribution to the ways of knowing. The abridgment, especially its twenty-two pages of Lockean method, appropriates this epistemology not only to say how one knows that natural things exist but also to indicate in what manner, and according to what similitude, one knows all spiritual things, including selves and God's own Self. Although spirit and sense would seem opposites (they can be thought of as antipodes and hence complements), the abridgment, without being either loose in applying to theology the language of sensation or glib about spiritual knowledge, attempts to locate the religious in the empirical and vice versa. Thus the abridgment suggests a way of overcoming the split between the natural and the supernatural, and indeed envisions the terms of their unification. Although the abridgment and Locke's *Essay* are not always consistent

with one another, and the relation between them is one of give-and-take, they share a frame of reference and a set of methodological assumptions, a language, and an interest in the same issues.

The abridgment, first of all, falls clearly in line with Locke's stand against enthusiasm, which, *mirabile dictu,* is no more antireligious than Wesley and Edwards are fanatical. "Immediate *Revelation,*" observes Locke,

> being a much easier way for Men to establish their Opinions, and regulate their Conduct, than the tedious and not always successful Labour of strict Reasoning, it is no wonder, that some have been very apt to pretend to Revelation, and to perswade themselves, that they are under the peculiar guidance of Heaven.[57]

The abridgment similarly urges caution in speaking of, and in making claims to, immediate revelation:

> The manner of the Spirit's proceeding in them that are born of the Spirit, is very often exceeding mysterious. It is oftentimes as difficult to know the way of the Spirit in the new birth, as in the first birth: "As thou knowest not what is the way of the Spirit, or how the bones do grow in the womb of her that is with child: Even so thou knowest not the work of God, that worketh all."[58]

Thus both the *Essay* and the abridgment flatly state that the Spirit's workings hardly ever fall under the power of either human understanding or human observation.

Unlike the *Essay,* however, the abridgment proclaims the *fact* of the Spirit's proceeding and even implies, in radical homage to Locke, that the Spirit's workings sometimes significantly fall under the powers of both human understanding and human observation. Locke, on one occasion, acknowledges that God can "excite [men] to Good Actions by the immediate influence and assistance of the Holy Spirit, without any extraordinary Signs accompanying it,"[59] but Locke is primarily concerned to prevent the recurrence of mid-seventeenth-century Puritan excess.[60] His *Essay,* accordingly, though admitting the possibility of visitation, warns that people who claim it are most probably mad. The abridgment concedes that many who claim it are wrong and even that some who claim it are mad. It argues, nonetheless, that visitation is a very possible event for religious people: "How greatly," lament Wesley and Edwards, "has the doctrine of sensibly perceiving the immediate power of the Spirit of God, been ridiculed."[61] "Sensibly perceiving," although making an unLockean point, employs a Lockean criterion.

Almost in spite of itself, the same paragraph that warns that "no man can tell whence [the Spirit] came, or whither it went" (cf. John 3.8) uses empirical language. The paragraph, even though indirectly and by analogy, appeals to the powers of observation and perception in "we, as it were, hear the sound of it, the effect of it is discernible."[62] This language, indeed, is based on more than analogy, for "the effect of it is discernible" connotes sense perceptions as tests or validations of something prior. "We, as it were, hear the sound of it" (even with the "as it were") rings with immediacy and presence, and so stops just short of denoting the senses as preconditions for divine experience.

The abridgment often gives so much credit to Locke's experiential criteria that it entertains a thought at which Locke would be horrified, namely, the direct sensation of God's effects and presence. The following quotation, for example, places all bets on the world of sense experience: "Men will trust their God no further than they know him, and they cannot be in the exercise of faith in him one ace further than they have a sight of his fulness and faithfulness in exercise."[63] "A sight of" need not mean physical sight, but the statement implies that regarding all matters of fact and causation, including the divine, Edwards, and Wesley through him, have the courage of Locke's convictions about experiential vision.

In their evocation of Locke's trust in eyewitness accounts, moreover, Edwards and Wesley wax particularly philosophic:

> Those are very improperly called witnesses of the truth of any thing, who only declare they are of opinion, such a thing is true. Those only are proper witnesses who testify that they have seen the truth of the thing they assert.[64]

Even here, of course, ambiguities arise, for one sees not the thing, but the truth of the thing; but far from meaning only that the senses are outward analogues to inner perception, this strong statement indicates, too, the clear possibility of perceiving God and his effects directly.

Finally, in the question, "What is a tender heart, but one that is easily impressed with what ought to affect it?"[65] the abridgment evinces not only Lockean diction[66] but also, and more importantly, the entire Lockean as well as Wordsworthian premise of "wise passiveness."[67] The self in both the *Essay* and the abridgment is valued, then, insofar as it is receptive, though with a remaining ambiguity about whether "tender heart" is specifically a metaphor for receptivity to the Spirit. It mattered greatly to both the philosopher and the revivalists what is happening to us at a particular time, and what acts upon us from without.

Consider, next, their telling word *impulse. Impulse* for Locke, Wesley, and Edwards, besides meaning "something opposed to deliberate reflection, as in the phrase 'to act on impulse,'" can indicate "a movement stirred in us from without, an influence upon the individual of some force in the outer universe."[68] Here, for example, is Locke's ambiguously subjective and objective use of *impulse.* Attacking those who claim "illumination from the Spirit of God," he observes that "whatsoever odd Action they find in themselves a strong inclination to do, that *impulse* is concluded to be a call or direction from Heaven, and must be obeyed."[69] In their own mood of attacking "self-deceivers" who claim, falsely, the "discoveries and elevations" of immediate revelation, Edwards and Wesley similarly observe

that "the chief grounds of the confidence of many of them are *impulses* and supposed revelations, sometimes with texts of Scripture, and sometimes without. These *impulses* they have called the witness of the Spirit."[70] Locke for his part, and Wesley and Edwards for theirs, refuse to credit the enthusiasts' objective meaning, but the *Essay* elsewhere employs the word in its objective sense:

> How often may a Man observe in himself, that whilst his Mind is intently employ'd in the contemplation of some Objects; and curiously surveyed some ideas that are there, it takes no notice of impressions of sounding Bodies, made upon the organ of Hearing, with the same alteration, that uses to be for the producing the Idea of a Sound? A sufficient *impulse* there may be on the Organ; but it not reaching the Observation of the Mind, there follows no perception.[71]

And Wesley and Edwards, insofar as they agree that even spiritual experience can be an external force that focuses on the individual soul and shapes it in the arena of human history, would concur in an objective usage of *impulse* such as one finds in a theological treatise published during Locke's lifetime: *Discourse of Angels, . . . also Something Touching Devils, Apparitions, and Impulses* (1701).[72]

Here, with a simultaneously objective and religious meaning, albeit without the word *impulse,* is the abridgment's premise that both natural and spiritual experiences write on the mind's blank tablet:

> Indeed the witness or seal of the Spirit, consists in the effect of the Spirit of God in the heart, in the implantation and exercises of grace there, and so consists in experience: And it is beyond doubt, that this seal of the Spirit is the highest kind of evidence of our adoption, that ever we obtain: But in these exercises of grace in practice, God gives witness, and sets to his seal, in the most conspicuous, eminent and evident manner.[73]

Although the senses are in this case implicitly more proof than entry, the imagery of the stamp and the seal is not far from the metaphor of mind as tabula rasa, receiving the impressions of experience. This same combination of Lockean theory and spiritual theology is to be found, say, in Charles Wesley's hymns:

> Where the indubitable seal
> That ascertains the kingdom mine?
> The powerful stamp I long to feel,
> The signature of love divine.[74]

Such emphasis on faith through experience, or rather on faith *as* experience, is everywhere evident in Wesley's abridgment of Edwards's treatise. The abridgment typically declares that "the Scripture represents faith as that by which men are brought into a good estate, and therefore it cannot be the same thing, as believing that they are already in one."[75] Faith is no more innate than ideas and no less dependent than ideas on the nourishment of experience: it is far from either an inherent capacity or a blind leap. The abridgment goes on to attack those "under the notion of . . . living upon Christ and not experiences."[76] Such a notion "directly thwart[s] God's wise constitution of things," for far from being mutually exclusive, Christ and experience are intimately interinvolved.

I have previously defined the epistemology of Locke as "an experiential continuum with understanding at one pole and physical sensation at the other."[77] Thus an ever-increasing though by no means innate strength of reason forms such an important part of Locke's empiricism that his empiricism should be said to include a specific appeal to this a posteriori brand of reasoning. Of all the works of Edwards's that Wesley might have chosen to abridge, *A Treatise concerning Religious Affections* shows perhaps the greatest balance between Edwards's immersion in the categories of sense perception and his desire for the consent of mind to mind. Of all five works of his that Wesley did abridge, **Religious Affections** offers the fullest range of Lockean "empiricism," namely, the same balance between sense and reason that characterizes Wesley's method.[78]

As for the abridgment's categories of sense perception, note, first, that "the influence of some extrinsic force upon [our] minds"[79] connotes the purely natural means whereby we passively receive impressions from without. Boldly, the abridgment often makes no distinction "between the influences of the Spirit of God, and the natural operations of our own minds."[80] This lack of difference is not so much to demythologize the Spirit as to honor experience. While Locke would separate the Spirit from natural operations, Wesley and Edwards do not. And while Locke would elevate natural operations by making them independent of "mere" faith, Wesley and Edwards elevate "mere" natural operations by relating them to, by mentioning them in the same breath as, the Spirit. "For any to expect the influence of the Spirit, without a diligent improvement of the appointed means, is presumption," declares the abridgment in obvious dialogue with Locke.[81] The abridgment adds: "To expect that he will operate upon their minds, without means subservient to the effect, is enthusiastical." So willingly, that is, does the Spirit condescend to work through the natural operations of our minds that spiritual and natural operations can be all but identical, or, to use the words of the abridgment, "It is frequently God's manner to make his hand visible."[82]

The abridgment laments the fact that such "sense perception" of the divine is often mistaken for enthusiasm: recall "how greatly has the doctrine of sensibly perceiving the immediate power of the Spirit of God, been ridiculed." Even where the abridgment speaks exclusively of the spiritual means whereby we receive impressions, it does so in empirical terms, or at least in terms that duplicate theologically the Lockean fascination with extrinsic power over the mind:

> And if persons tell of effects in their own minds, that seem to them not to be from the natural operations of their minds, but from the supernatural power of some

other agent, should it at once be looked upon as a sure evidence of delusion, because things seem to them to be as they are?[83]

Between the abridgment and the *Essay,* in this regard, is a particularly striking connection. Here is the *Essay:*

> Thus we see the holy Men of old, who had *Revelations* from God, had something else besides that internal Light of assurance in their own Minds, to testify to them, that it was from God. They were not left to their own Perswasions alone, that those Perswasions were from God; But had outward Signs to convince them of the Author of those Revelations.[84]

And here is the abridgment:

> And so it was in most of the conversions of particular persons we have an account of in the New Testament: They were not wrought on in a silent, secret, gradual, and insensible manner; but with those manifest evidences of a supernatural power, wonderfully and suddenly causing a great change.[85]

Thus both Locke and Wesley/Edwards require rigorous standards of certification from the religiously inclined, but Wesley and Edwards, more broadly experiential than Locke himself, extend Lockean methods of inquiry to non-Lockean subject matter. By giving credence to "effects in their own minds" as well as to external signs, they include the internal in the catalogue of experience. They imply, thereby, that the senses can be thought of as analogous to, as indispensable for conceiving, the "sense" of inward evidence: while "effects *in* their own minds" draws a boundary around the mind, confining experience to it, "*effects* in their own minds" points to an action or impingement on the mind, such as would only occur through the avenue of the senses.

Wesley and Edwards, accordingly, seem aware that extrinsic power over the mind functions philosophically as well as religiously. The abridgment's expression of receptivity to external influence can be conventionally religious and explicitly biblical:

> I know of no reason why being affected with a view of God's glory, should not cause the body to faint, as well as being affected with a view of Solomon's glory. . . . My soul thirsteth for thee, my flesh longeth for thee, in a dry and thirsty land where no water is. . . . When I heard, my belly trembled, my lips quivered at the voice, and rottenness entered into my bones, and I trembled in myself.[86]

The following quotation, however, evinces not only heart-religion, but also, in equal measures, metaphysics and epistemology: "God has so disposed things as though every thing was contrived to have the greatest possible tendency to reach our hearts in the most tender part, and move our affections most sensibly."[87] This statement, as intellectual as it is emotional, rests on the assumption, the philosophical theology, that sense perception is blessedly constituted to receive every good and perfect gift.[88]

The abridgment, though, hardly depicts the mind as completely passive: Edwards's desire for the consent of mind to mind amounts, at times, to near rationalism, as though the mind were sufficient unto itself; and Wesley, though never himself so nearly mind-intoxicated, allows Edwards to express his desire. Whereas "passions" are the "more sudden" and "more violent" "actings of the will," such "affections" as "hope, love, desire, joy, sorrow, gratitude, compassion, and zeal" are "actings of the will" wherein the mind is more "in its own command."[89] The abridgment, then, though neither Cartesian in particular nor French in general, is, nonetheless and strangely, mentalist as well as Anglo-American.

The abridgment agrees even here, however, with Lockean reason as sense-based, for the affections, and not just the passions, are finally sense-related. Mind in the abridgment is between the extremes of active and passive, and truth in the abridgment is between the extremes of mind and matter.

Take, for example, the close interaction of mind and body. The issue is rampant in the age (it appears in medical treatises, and even in Descartes); Locke gives it his full attention.[90] The abridgment's lengthy argument that mind affects body and vice versa is similarly experiential, similarly other-directed, and almost nontheoretical in tone. "Such are the laws of union of soul and body," declares the abridgment, "that the mind can have no vigorous exercise, without some effect upon the body." The abridgment adds: "Yea, it is questionable, whether an embodied soul ever so much as thinks one thought, or has any exercise at all, but there is some corresponding motion in some part of the body."[91] Here, mind is tacitly superior to senses, for mental experience occurs prior to, and causes, activation of the body. Yet even here, the relation between mental experience and the body is the very evidence of mind's superiority, which, according to the abridgment as well as the *Essay,* consists in a place above, but not aloof from the senses.

The mind, then, far from being independent of the senses, depends on them for its very identity, and its participation in the senses provides the evidence of God's acting in it. For when almost mind-intoxicated, and even when God-intoxicated, the abridgment comes no closer than it does at all other times, and no closer than does Locke, to the pure rationalism that views the mind's identity, and even its experience, as independent of the senses. Wesley and Edwards affirm, finally, a mind/body interaction in which body is often as active as, and sometimes even prior to, mind. After reiterating a certain primacy of mind—to wit, "Such seems to be our nature, that there never is any vigorous exercise of the will, without some effect upon the body, in some alteration of the motions of its fluids, especially of the animal spirits"—the abridgment includes the following significant addendum: "And on the other hand, the constitution of the body, and the motion of its fluids, may promote the exercise of the affections."[92] Here experience affects, and precedes, the mental, and insofar as "body

promotes the exercise of the *affections,*" by which the revivalists mean *religious* affections, the senses are not only receptors for divine truth but also building blocks of spiritual wisdom.

In Wesley's and Edwards's thought, as in Locke's, mind and world form a dialectic, if not a continuum and a harmonic whole. Reality appears to the reader of the *Essay* as a coalescence of subject and object: recall Locke's use of *impulse.* The abridgment, by teaching that mind extends to body and vice versa, implies that mind-body synthesis contacts external reality and vice versa.[93]

"Following the lead of the classical British experience-philosophy," wrote John E. Smith in his modern edition of **Religious Affections,** "Edwards placed primary emphasis upon first-person experience."[94] Smith does not explicitly apply this comment to **Religious Affections,** but the comment can help explain the treatise's emphasis on the practical and on action in matters of religion. The comment applies as well to that same emphasis in both the abridgment and other Wesley writings.

For the obvious reason that *his* experiential emphasis derives from British experience-philosophy, Wesley is careful to represent this aspect of Edwards's sensibility.

> The business of religion is from time to time compared to those exercises, wherein men are wont to have their hearts and strength greatly engaged, such as *running, wrestling,* and *warring.* . . . And as true religion is of a practical nature, and the affections are the springs of men's actions, it must consist very much in them.[95]

Or again:

> The tendency of grace in the heart to holy practice, is direct; and the connexion close and necessary. True grace is not an inactive, barren thing, for it is, in its very nature, a principle of holy action.[96]

These statements exemplify the "epistemology" of Wesley and Edwards. The first celebrates intense experience both as analogue to faith and as precondition for it. The second, besides implying an immediate connection between spiritual influx and practical charity (recall "grace *in* the heart"), contends that the connection between spiritual and natural experience is all but unmediated, that is, that spiritual experience intersects with, superimposes itself on, and, however fleetingly, becomes one with, natural experience.

The statements are broader and more inclusive than any narrowly "scientific" epistemology: "He that has knowledge only, without affection," say Wesley and Edwards, "never is engaged in the business of religion."[97] This statement can be understood in the light of another of Smith's general remarks about Edwards, namely, that he attempted "to bring the individual back to a sense of his own individuality and to the need for a broader conception of human understanding, one that does not eliminate everything but science from its concern."[98] (By "individuality," clearly,

Smith means the significance of self rather than, or in addition to, its sinfulness.) Smith points out, finally, that Edwards's emphasis on first-persons experience "took the form of the new *sense* or *taste* without which faith remains at the purely notional level."[99] Wesley's abridgment includes all of Edwards's statements regarding this "spiritual sense." Here I discuss several, as they accurately appear in the abridgment.

This doctrine, first of all, is Bible-based: "The Scripture is ignorant of any faith in Christ or the operation of God," say Wesley and Edwards, "that is not grounded in a spiritual sight of Christ."[100] They add proof texts. "True faith in Christ," they write, "is never exercised any further than persons 'behold as in a glass, the glory of the Lord,' and have 'the knowledge of the glory of God in the face of Jesus Christ.'"[101] The abridgment's opening passage, concerning the persecuted Christians to whom Paul wrote, constitutes a biblically oriented announcement of the "spiritual sense":

> There was nothing visible that could induce them thus to suffer, and could carry them through such trials. But though there was nothing that the world saw, or that they themselves saw with their bodily eyes, that thus supported them, *yet* they had a supernatural principle of love to something unseen; they loved Jesus Christ, whom they *saw spiritually*.[102]

One thinks, in this connection, of John 20.29 ("Blessed are they that have not seen, and yet have believed"). Note that, even where indicating what lies beyond the grasp of sense and even where mainly quoting the Bible, the abridgment's doctrine of the "spiritual sense" employs sensate language for a distinctively historical reason. Although neither Wesley nor Edwards could avoid the Lockean hegemony, both of them exploit it. They read certain proof texts in the context of the empiricist climate, as though to enhance both the climate and the texts. Both of them reflect a sense bias in their most biblical understanding of spiritual experience, for even in that understanding, they interpret such experience in alignment with an earthly methodology: they appeal to sense experience, if only as analogue.

Their other depictions of the "spiritual sense" are more philosophical than biblical, and as much philosophical as theological. The doctrine, to the extent that it covers immediate revelation, or the Spirit's operations in the present, carries authentically Lockean implications of the senses as tests, and even as manifesters and harbingers. For purposes of consideration in this light, this tough-minded passage is worth requoting: "Men will trust their God no further than they know him, and they cannot be in the exercise of faith in him one ace further than they have a sight of his fulness and faithfulness in exercise."[103] "A sight of" intimates a not so much analogical or metaphorical as literal dimension of the "spiritual sense," for in the absence of such labels as *spiritual,* the connotation is of physical sight, as though the knowledge of God were direct or metaphysical.

In the following statement of the "spiritual sense," moreover, the abridgment shows itself fully epistemological:

> In those gracious affections which are wrought through the saving influences of the Spirit of God, there is a new inward perception or sensation, entirely different in its nature, from any thing that ever their minds were the subjects of, before they were sanctified. If grace be, in the sense above described, an entirely new kind of principle; then the exercises of it are also entirely a new kind of exercise. And if there be in the soul a new sort of exercises which it knew nothing of before, and which no improvement, composition, or management of what it was before conscious of, could produce, or any thing like it; then it follows that there is, as it were, a new spiritual sense in the mind, or an entirely new kind of perception or spiritual sensation, which is in its whole nature different from any former kinds of sensation.[104]

True, this statement tends toward the analogical, and in its insistence that God works a *new* sense into the mind-soul, it does not sound Lockean or empirical. But this "spiritual sense," though wholly unlike the physical senses, is almost consciously Lockean in its explicit adherence to tabula rasa and hence to the pivotal powers of experience in general. In speaking of the minds of newborn people, that is, converts, as the *subjects* of inward perception or sensation, Wesley and Edwards imply the rationalist point that mind is always ultimate, always prior to senselike spiritual experience. Clearly, they seek the consent of mind to mind even as their language of sense perception waxes most Lockean. "Subjects *of,*" however, is ambiguous. The phrase implies that minds are subjected or subordinated to spiritual sensation, which in this case, though inward, is other than, added to or prior to, mind. In spiritual experience, then, and not just in natural experience, the priority lies not in mind alone, nor even exclusively in senselike avenues to something rich and strange, but in the interchange highlighting now one, and now the other.

Although Locke implies that immediate revelation is unlikely or even impossible, because all thought comes from sense perception rather than from the extrasensory, he argues, nonetheless, that biblical revelation is true because it showed itself in action. Wesley and Edwards, in their doctrine of the "spiritual sense," apply this argument to their brief for immediate revelation, which, if confirmed after the fact by the criteria of natural experience, is true. Wesley and Edwards, of course, hold that supernatural intakings and reshapings of the mind constitute ultimate reality, but they use Locke to defend such visitations against charges of enthusiasm. In the passage just quoted, for example, the inward perception does not exist before the natural time, and does not inhere apart from the natural place, of particular spiritual influx. This notion is Lockean insofar as it assumes that grace, like everything else, is dependent on experience. Tough-mindedly experience-oriented rather than exclusively analogistic, the passage iterates the senselike perception of God's things as "a new sort of exercises which [the soul] knew nothing of before."

Thus Wesley and Edwards do not so much follow what Locke thinks as in their own way practice how he thinks and even how he speaks. Although they need not be labeled Lockean (their vision was their own), they do not hesitate to use Locke's distinguished epistemology. The piety of Wesley and Edwards is "natural":[105] not only do they believe in the God of nature, and not only do they think that sense experience can point to, if not include, God, but they also base their supernatural religion on experience. Not only do they assume that what happens in one's inward life is significant in the same way as what happens in one's sense experience but they also link, as their journals indicate, their sanctifications to the passage of time. They assume, in short, that what happens in one's inward life may interact with, and grow out of, what happens in one's sense experience. For them, experience both constitutes matter and mind, considered separately and together, and binds the senses to the soul.

A passage toward the end of the abridgment is perhaps most telling in suggesting this philosophical theology. It duplicates Edwards's attempt to describe faith through the language of both rational empiricism and scientific method. It not only elaborates, but also distills, the doctrine of the "spiritual sense," that is, "that sense of Divine things, which governs [our] heart and hands."[106]

> Not only does the most important part of Christian experience lie in spiritual practice, but nothing is so properly called by the name of experimental religion: For that experience which is in these exercises of grace, that prove effectual at the very point of trial, is the proper experiment of the truth of our godliness, wherein its victorious power is found by experience. This is properly Christian experience, wherein we have opportunity to see, by actual experience and trial, whether we have a heart to do the will of God, and to forsake other things for Christ, or no.[107]

By our experience, that is, we see God's prior reshapings of our hearts; but the passage indicates, too, that the range of spiritual experience can be identical with the range of natural experience. Indeed, the diction is so fully experientialist as to include an insistently scientific tenor: *by actual experience and trial, see, experiment, prove, practice,* and, not least (uncharacteristically for Wesley) the redundant uses of *experience*—all denote the particular empirical method whereby such religious problems as the knowledge of revelation appear to be raised by and solved by one's sense-oriented as well as mental life. Wesley is more empirical than even the Edwards of *Religious Affections.* But the Edwards of *Religious Affections,* as Wesley recognizes, employs the language of actual experience and trial, and both Wesley and Edwards hold that subjectivity corresponds with and, when God-suffused, commands objective truth.

This experiential assumption informs, and may even determine, one of their most characteristic doctrines, namely, assurance. Wesley's version of it derives not just from the Moravians' emphasis on Romans 8.15—"For ye have not received the Spirit of bondage again to fear; but ye have received the Spirit of adoption, whereby we cry, Abba, Father"—but also from Locke's emphasis on "Assurance" as the label for "the highest degree of Probability" in the realm of empirical belief.[108] Wesley, therefore, has his philosophic reason for amply representing Edwards's doctrine of assurance, which, as a thoroughly experiential interpretation of the Bible, is itself a doctrine of the age of Locke. Edwards and Wesley both write:

> God, in the plainest manner, revealed and testified his special favour to Noah; Abraham; Isaac; Jacob, Moses, David, and others. Job often speaks with the greatest *assurance.* David, throughout the book of Psalms, almost every where speaks in the most positive manner of God as his God. Hezekiah appeals to God, as one that knew, "he had walked before him in truth and with a perfect heart;" (2 Kings xx.3;) the Apostle Paul, through all his epistles, speaks in an *assured* strain, ever speaking positively of his special relation to Christ, and his interest in, and expectation of, the future reward.[109]

In sum, then, Wesley and Edwards do not subscribe to the notion of tabula rasa when they believe that we are born with a heavy burden of sin, but their equally characteristic emphasis on conversion admits of Lockean sanction. Conversion ascribes so much importance to what might happen, not only at inner moments but also in one's experience in the world, that whatever precedes such experiential sea-change is by comparison mere tabula rasa. Edwards, a Calvinist, does not assume as much responsibility as Wesley, an Arminian, does for the working out of one's own salvation. But Edwards's doctrine of "testing the spirits" gives even him, in the words of Smith, "some basis for judging the state of his own soul."[110] Although Edwards and Wesley through him warn against making "too much of [our] own doings, to the diminution of the glory of free grace," they finally ask, "Which way is it inconsistent with the freeness of God's grace, that holy practice should be a sign of God's grace?"[111] The nearest analogue to this emphasis on experience as test and not as conduit is the doctrine of good works, but the emphasis makes so much of our "own doings" that it emerges as implicitly Lockean, and the doctrine of the "spiritual sense" is where Edwards's similarity to both Locke and Wesley seems most pertinent.

I submit, now, by way of rounding off my Wesleyan-Lockean perspective on *Religious Affections,* Wesley's most Lockean statement of the "spiritual sense." The statement, from *An Earnest Appeal to Men of Reason and Religion* (1743), includes an explicit subscription to the fundamental, though only potentially theological, tenet of tabula rasa:

> Before it is possible for you to form a true judgment of the things of God, it is absolutely necessary that you have a *clear apprehension* of them, and that your ideas thereof be all *fixed, distinct,* and *determinate.* And seeing our ideas are not all innate, but must originally come from our senses, it is certainly necessary that you

have senses capable of discerning objects of this kind: Not those only which are called natural senses, which in this respect profit nothing, as being altogether incapable of discerning objects of a spiritual kind; but spiritual senses, exercised to discern spiritual good and evil. It is necessary that you have *the hearing ear,* and *the seeing eye,* emphatically so called; that you have a new class of senses opened in your soul, not depending on organs of flesh and blood, to be "the evidence of things not seen" [cf. Heb. 11:1], as your bodily senses are of visible things; to be the avenues to the invisible world, to discern spiritual objects, and to furnish you with ideas of what the outward "eye hath not seen, neither the ear heard" [cf. I Cor 2:9].[112]

This statement, formulated a scant three years before *Religious Affections* first appeared, accords with Edwards's "spiritual sense," which, whether in its analogistic dimension or in its implication that even the natural senses are visionary, proceeds, too, from Lockean assumptions. Like Wesley's *Appeals to Men of Reason and Religion* (1743-45), *Remarks upon Mr. Locke's Essay on Human Understanding* (1781), and *On Living without God* (1790),[113] Edwards's *Treatise concerning Religious Affections* teaches four points: (1) we receive an inrush of spirit and then "see" abstractions manifested in our sensible experience; (2) we walk avenues to the invisible; (3) we receive the divine from the visible; and (4) we discover the divine in the visible. Where Locke coalesces sense experience with mind, Wesley and Edwards coalesce nature with spirit. To state the conclusion another way, the "spiritual sense" of Wesley and Edwards joins rational empiricism to both theistic natural religion and immediate revelation.

A COMPARISON

In *Locke, Wesley, and the Method of English Romanticism,* I argue, among other things, that Wesley's abridgment (1730) of *The Procedure, Extent, and Limits of Human Understanding* (1728) by Peter Browne (d. 1735), Bishop of Cork and Ross, is a key to Wesley's thought: the abridgment demonstrates the Lockean affinity between Browne and Wesley. Wesley's access to Locke—through Browne—parallels, and serves to gloss, Wesley's access to Locke through Edwards. Since both the abridgment of *Religious Affections* and the abridgment of *The Procedure* theologize Locke's *Essay* even more thoroughly than do the originals, a brief comparison of the two abridgments can serve to reinforce my view of the Lockean agreement between Wesley and Edwards.

First, as highlighted by the abridgment of *The Procedure,* here is Browne's doctrine of analogy:

Metaphor is mostly in Words, and is a Figure of Speech; Analogy a Similis Ratio or Proportion of Things, and an excellent and necessary Method or Means of Reason and Knowledge. Metaphor uses Ideas of Sensation to express Immaterial and heavenly Objects, to which they can bear no real Resemblance or Proportion [e.g., "I am the Good Shepherd"]; Analogy substitutes the Operations of our Soul, and notions mostly formed out of them, to represent Divine Things

to which they bear a Real tho' Unknown Correspondency and Proportion [e.g., "God is love"]. In short, Metaphor has no real Foundation in the Nature of the Things compared; Analogy is founded in the Very Nature of the Things on both Sides of the Comparison.[114]

This doctrine, as I have indicated, derives from Locke's emphasis on analogy as "the only help we have in inferring unseen causes." Locke's view that a "wary reasoning from Analogy leads us often into the discovery of Truths . . . which would otherwise lie concealed" (1) emphasizes the transcendent otherness of the Creator, (2) intimates, nonetheless, the accessibility of divine truth, (3) implies that just as there is unity among things above and just as there is unity among things below, so there is correspondence, if not continuity, between the natural and the spiritual worlds, (4) devalues metaphor because of the arbitrary nature of its comparisons (here, Locke is the true son of Puritans who preferred simile to metaphor), (5) proposes analogy as a nonfigurative, philosophically correct means of expression this correspondence of things, and (6) recommends analogy as our "great Rule of Probability" in theological inquiry.[115] Although thinking by an analogy of opposition that emphasizes the distance between this world and another was attacked both by skeptics such as David Hume and by such orthodox thinkers as Samuel Johnson,[116] Locke's analogy was one of proportionality. His analogy, indeed, was so far from being outmoded that it was adapted by such as Browne and Wesley, who made it the prolegomenon to all future epistemologies of faith.

No more than Locke, of course, does either Browne or Wesley wax glib about the relation between God and the world, for like Locke, both Browne and Wesley limited what could be predicated of God. But while Aquinas predicated much through "the assumption of the neo-Platonist scale of Being,"[117] Browne and Wesley predicated much through the Locke-related instrument of sense-language. With the possible exception of the attempt by the later Edwards to conceive of spirit through a congruence of abstractions and logical harmony, it is not feasible to talk about spirit except by analogy to the senses. Christ's method of parables is nothing more nor less than such analogy, as are the medieval fourfold method of exegesis and the analogies of Luther. But the version of analogy in Browne and Wesley is especially empirical in its view of the senses as providing evidence, if not as providing a source, of spiritual knowledge. Just as in Lockean terms sense perception of a human being is the only means of knowing him or her, so in terms of Browne and Wesley the feeling of love is such a good access to the nature of God that it amounts to a "spiritual sense" of him. The feeling of love, with its implication of sexual union, is at once so deep and so relational that it out-senses the senses.

Thus the abridgment of *The Procedure* delineates the analogistic dimension of the spiritual sense, but analogy in the abridgment of *The Procedure* as a whole does not so much indicate the difference between humanity and God as occupy the continuum joining nature to revelation, and such analogy of proportionality is matched by the abridgment of *Religious Affections.* Characteristically, for example, Wesley and Edwards employ that analogy's very form:

> As the affections not only belong to the human nature, but are a great part of it; so holy affections do not only belong to true religion, but are a very great part of it. . . . And as in worldly things, worldly affections are the springs of men's actions; so in religious matters, the spring of their actions is religious affections.[118]

Or again:

> As the taste of honey is diverse from the ideas men get of honey by only looking on and feeling it, so the new sense of spiritual and Divine things is entirely diverse from any thing that is perceived in them, by natural men.[119]

Here, somewhat surprisingly, the abridgment implies that, like the sense of taste, the spiritual sense renders a truth that is deep precisely because it is imageless: compare Demogorgon's "the deep truth is imageless" from Shelley's *Prometheus Unbound.* These samples of the abridgment, moreover, are so analogistic, so detached from the world, that they evince distrust of the senses. But the distrust is directed more to the sense-image world of metaphor, with its distance from the spiritual world, than toward the sense-related instrument of analogy, which describes interiority or spiritual experience according to the model of perception. Taste, after all, is a sense like seeing and hearing, albeit with an image so deep as not to resemble the images of sight and sound.

The abridgment, necessarily or not, retains senselike criteria as the only means available to Lockean temperaments with a need to express the methods of the soul. The term *affections,* significantly, belongs to the language of sense impression and sense perception. Far from abandoning such language, Wesley and Edwards use a strange, vaguely oxymoronic, but nonetheless efficacious version of it, namely, *religious* or *holy affections,* to express a precise analogy between, if not the interpenetrations of, the spirit realm and the world of natural experience.

This doctrine, then, proportional rather than oppositional, helps Wesley and Edwards as Browne's doctrine helps him, namely, to believe that what is both felt and thought approaches, without dispelling the mystery of, what has been and is being revealed. Without quite valuing the familiar for its own sake, the doctrine of Wesley and Edwards honors the familiar as an especially faithful counterpart to what would otherwise lie entirely outside the range of human expression. The senses convince the intellect of what they have to tell. What is felt and thought, in turn, proves spiritually verdicial, that is, theologically equivalent to philosophical seeing and philosophical believing.

Thus, on the relative certainty of natural knowledge, the spiritual sense of Wesley and Edwards establishes the probable truth of a theistic (distinct from Deistic or pantheistic) natural religion, and even of revelation. The twin pioneers of transatlantic revivalism search for an inclusive, intellectually current way of describing how the mind knows God, and how anyone can verify another's faith. They find that way in Lockean doctrine.

An Epitome

Although close reading, especially of Wesley's abridgment of Edwards's *Religious Affections,* recommends itself as "the fascination of what's difficult,"[120] I am concerned, here, to facilitate what is difficult, without losing the fascination of, say, philosophical theology as semiotics. I want to abstract, without diluting, the complex empiricism of Wesley and Edwards.

When teaching that mind is where divine experience takes place, the abridgment puts grace prior to the senses, which become mere physical analogues to inward spiritual experience. Insofar as the experience of Wesley and Edwards is an "experience" of God as otherworldly, a consent of being to being beyond self and senses, the abridgment demonstrates additional non-Lockean ends.

Its validation of those ends, however, its proof that spiritual experience has occurred, appeals to the senses and so amounts to a sufficiently Lockean means. Spiritual inrush, though merely analogous to sense perception, appears in a strong Lockean light, for Locke's view that impressions striking the senses are worthy guides to knowledge informs, and indeed enables, the trust of Wesley and Edwards in influxes "flooding [the] soul with glory divine."[121]

An especially intriguing trait of this philosophical theology is its implication that the senses are indispensable for an experience of the divine. The senses are secondary when they are tests for inwardness and analogies to communicate supernatural reality to a Lockean world. But the senses are primary when they are attendants on, and preconditions for, faith, that is, when natural experience not only sets the terms of, but also either becomes or combines with, spiritual experience. At "a quarter to nine" on the evening of May 24, 1738, in Aldersgate Street, London, Wesley's heart was "strangely warmed" (shades, or foreshadowing, of Blake's talking with Isaiah in the Strand).[122] This famous conversion, this spiritual watershed of English cultural life, has as much to do with time, place, and the specific circumstances of Wesley's sense experience as with his state of mind. Such a nearly empirical recipe for grace is a particular means of the abridgment, which, above all, holds to the senses.

Since Locke's tenet that one's very language depends on the senses was a given of the intellectual climate,[123] all expressions of the divine were necessarily Lockean, that is, sensuous, including the most analogistic and, for that matter, most rationalistic expressions. But the paradox of the God-centered yet sincere self is the crux in the abridgment, the sense-language of which, in accord with the abridgment's understanding of the senses themselves, is now analogue to, and now validation, manifestation, and harbinger of, spiritual experience. Whether a literal or a figurative reading of Locke, whether an uneasy attempt to incorporate senses into near-rationalism or a balance between sense perception and the consent of mind to mind, the abridgment is saturated with Lockean language. Even its consciousness of God not only submits to what Wordsworth, after Locke, calls "the language of the sense,"[124] but also arrives through that language. The very title, virtually the same as the original's, implies the Locke-derived oxymoron "spiritual sense," for **Religious Affections** ambiguously straddles the line between faith and experience.

Natural experience and spiritual experience, then, are not stark oppositions for Wesley and Edwards, whose spiritual experience, like their natural experience, is Lockean, that is, of both the mind and the senses. Just as Lockean epistemology conceives of a link between sense and reason, matter and mind, so the philosophical theologies of Wesley and Edwards, their appropriations of Locke for religious methodology, conceive of a bridge that transports us from nature to grace, returns us from grace to nature, and joins nature and grace, justifying the reality of both. This spiritual sense is even more flexible and even more up-to-date than Lockean epistemology, for it out-Lockes Locke, or carries him to his logical conclusion. It applies to the religious arena that secular trust in experience that helped the early modern mind to position itself in the natural world.

The spiritual sense of Wesley and Edwards rests, specifically, on a view of experience more inclusive, and a respect for experiential criteria greater, than Locke's. While Lockean experience is primarily natural and Lockean theology is almost entirely apart from nature, they both stress the participation of God in creation, and so enlist spirit in the catalogue of experience. The spiritual sense of Wesley and Edwards, indeed, for its part in the eighteenth century's burgeoning discipline of philosophical theology, is imaginative. For by its imaging of heavenly joy on earth, if not by its hope of earthly joy in heaven, it draws on the model of sense perception to detect, and express, a radically immanent Christianity. And by so modernizing Christianity, Wesley and Edwards lay the intellectual as well as emotional groundwork for religious expression not simply in the Anglo-American Enlightenment, but in the Anglo-American world of the nineteenth century as well.

Notes

1. I allude to Emerson's *Representative Men* (1850), a collection of essays on Plato, Emanuel Swedenborg, Montaigne, Shakespeare, Napoleon, and Goethe. Some of Emerson's other works, I suggest, add Wesley and Edwards to the list.

2. I adapt the phrase "gene-culture coevolution" to my purposes. The phrase is used throughout Edward O. Wilson, *Sociobiology.*

3. See, e.g., Norman Fiering, *Jonathan Edwards's Moral Thought and Its British Context;* William J.

Wainwright, "Jonathan Edwards and the Language of God"; and Nathan O. Hatch and Harry S. Stout, eds., *Jonathan Edwards and the American Experience.*

4. For samples of Perry Miller's argument for Edwards as a Lockean, see Miller's *Jonathan Edwards* and his "Jonathan Edwards and the Sense of the Heart."

5. For Locke's "theocentric framework," see Richard Ashcroft, "Faith and Knowledge in Locke's Philosophy"; David Gauthier, "Why Ought One Obey God? Reflections on Hobbes and Locke"; James Farr, "The Way of Hypotheses: Locke on Method"; and W. M. Spellman, *John Locke and the Problem of Depravity.* Spellman's positioning of Locke on the Latitudinarian *via media* between Calvinism and Deism is especially persuasive. For Locke's empiricism, see, e.g., John W. Yolton, *John Locke and the Compass of Human Understanding,* and Roger Woolhouse, *Locke's Philosophy of Science and Knowledge.*

6. Terrence Erdt, *Jonathan Edwards: Art and the Sense of the Heart.*

7. Roland Delattre, *Beauty and Sensibility in the Thought of Jonathan Edwards: An Essay in Aesthetics and Theological Ethics.*

8. Sacvan Bercovitch, *The American Jeremiad,* 107-8. Edwards's model of mind, according to James Hoopes, is Lockean in that it is unitary, for both Edwards and Locke regard "mind" and "thought" as synonymous, and they do not recognize the unconscious mind. Edwards's commitment to the "way of ideas," however, out-Lockes Locke's, for while Locke's model of soul allows for spiritual substance, Edwards's "soul" is made up of ideas only. See James Hoopes, "Calvinism and Consciousness from Edwards to Beecher."

9. Wallace E. Anderson, "The Development of Edwards' Philosophical Thought," 101-2.

10. See the discussion in Anderson, "The Development of Edwards' Philosophical Thought," 101-2. See also Edward H. Davidson, "From Locke to Edwards"; Claude A. Smith, "Jonathan Edwards and the 'Way of Ideas'"; and Paul Helm, "John Locke and Jonathan Edwards: A Reconsideration." Michael J. Colacurcio's emphasis on Edwards's career after 1750, and especially on *The Great Christian Doctrine of Original Sin Defended,* leads to a perhaps too-narrow focus on his capacity for "idealist imagination": "what makes Edwards everywhere Edwards is some absolutely fundamental bias of imagination in favor of idealism." Edwards's career as a whole includes empiricist as well as idealist elements and is aptly summed up (if again with more idealist bias than the entire career warrants) in this observation by Colacurcio: "A capacity to suspect that reality might be very subtle, and a power to suspend belief long enough to

wonder *how* subtle, may tell us more than anything else about the unity and priorities of a mind which saw spiders and thought 'teleology,' which learned of atoms and guessed 'power,' which experienced both nature and grace and leaped to 'idea,' and which ultimately contrived to hand the whole world, including its own consciousness and that of every other man, over to *God Alone.*" See Michael J. Colacurcio, "The Example of Edwards: Idealist Imagination and the Metaphysics of Sovereignty," esp. 96, 98.

11. Robert W. Jenson, *America's Theologian: A Recommendation of Jonathan Edwards,* esp. 3.

12. Charles Rogers, "John Wesley and Jonathan Edwards."

13. See *The Works of the Rev. John Wesley, A.M.,* ed. Thomas Jackson, 10.463, 467, 475.

14. Ibid., 10.460.

15. Albert Outler, *John Wesley,* 16.

16. See Rogers, "John Wesley and Jonathan Edwards," 36.

17. Many thanks to Frederick Dreyer for corresponding with me about his work, which includes his "Faith and Experience in the Thought of John Wesley" and his "Evangelical Thought: John Wesley and Jonathan Edwards."

18. The essay and Harvey G. Townsend's discussion of it are in Townsend, ed., *The Philosophy of Jonathan Edwards from His Private Notebooks,* xi-xiii, 1-20.

19. The other four of Edwards's works abridged by Wesley are *A Faithful Narrative of the Surprising Work of God in the Conversion of many hundred souls in Northampton* (1736); *The Distinguishing Marks of a Work of the Spirit of God* (1741); *Some Thoughts concerning the Present Revival in New England* (1742); and *An Account of the Life of the Late Reverend Mr. David Brainerd* (1749). Wesley's abridgments of these works are *A Narrative of Many Surprising Conversions in Northampton and Vicinity* (1744); *The Distinguishing Marks of a Work of the Spirit of God* (1744); *Thoughts concerning the Present Revival of Religion* (1745); and *An Extract of the Life of the Late Rev. Mr. David Brainerd* (1768).

20. See John Wesley, ed., *An Extract from a Treatise concerning Religious Affections,* in *The Works of the Rev. John Wesley,* and the discussion in *The Works of Jonathan Edwards,* ed. John E. Smith, vol. 2: *A Treatise concerning Religious Affections,* 79. My quotations of the abridgment are from a widely available reprint of it in the following collection of Wesley's abridgments: John Wesley, ed., *A Christian Library: Consisting of Extracts from and Abridgments of the choicest Pieces of Practical Divinity which have been published in the English Tongue;* see 30.308-76.

21. See Jonathan Edwards, *A Treatise concerning Religious Affections: In Three Parts,* ed. William Gordon.

22. Gregory S. Clapper, "'True Religion' and the Affections: A Study of John Wesley's Abridgment of Jonathan Edwards's Treatise on the Religious Affections," 418.

23. See, e.g., Frank Baker, "A Study of John Wesley's Readings."

24. See, e.g., T. Walter Herbert, *John Wesley as Editor and Author,* 75-79.

25. Many of the alterations are more aesthetically motivated than pursuant to Wesley's fears about whether his readers would follow Edwards's thought. Characteristically, Wesley excises verbiage, thus clarifying Edwards's intentions and enhancing his treatise. The following instance is typical (brackets enclose Wesley's omissions): "The kindling [and raising] of gracious affections is like kindling a flame, the higher it is raised, the more ardent it is [and the more it burns, the more vehemently does it tend and seek to burn]" (Gordon's edition of Edwards, *A Treatise concerning Religious Affections,* 211, and Wesley, "An Extract from a Treatise concerning Religious Affections," in *A Christian Library,* 30.363). See also Edwards, *Treatise,* 50, and Wesley, "Extract," 334; Edwards, 54-55, and Wesley, 336; Edwards, 202, and Wesley, 359; and Edwards, 205, and Wesley, 361. Wesley's omissions of many biblical quotations constitute a major means by which he achieves economy of expression: see Edwards, 39-41, and Wesley, 329; Edwards, 42, and Wesley, 330; Edwards, 43, and Wesley, 330; Edwards, 53, and Wesley, 335; Edwards, 54, and Wesley, 336; Edwards, 79-80, and Wesley, 344; Edwards, 81, and Wesley, 344; Edwards, 82, and Wesley, 344; Edwards, 157, and Wesley, 346; Edwards, 188, and Wesley, 353; Edwards, 199, and Wesley, 358; Edwards, 200, and Wesley, 359; Edwards, 204, and Wesley, 360; Edwards, 255-56, and Wesley, 374; and Edwards, 256-57, and Wesley, 374. Gordon, like Edwards, tolerates repetitiousness; Wesley does not: see Edwards, 17-18, and Wesley, 317; Edwards, 65, and Wesley, 342; Edwards, 74-79, and Wesley, 343; Edwards, 87-155, and Wesley, 346; Edwards, 170-71, and Wesley, 349; Edwards, 192-93, and Wesley, 355; Edwards, 202, and Wesley, 359; Edwards, 214-15, and Wesley, 363; Edwards, 217, and Wesley, 364; Edwards, 225-26, and Wesley, 366; Edwards, 237-53, and Wesley, 367; and Edwards, 244-47, and Wesley, 368. Wesley achieves his combination of brevity and fidelity to the original in part by omitting subtopics of a clearly established line of argument: for an especially notable example, see Edwards, 167-70, and Wesley, 349.

26. I take this epitome of Arminianism from Hymn 17 of the Wesley brothers' *Collection of Hymns, for the Use of the People Called Methodists.* For a characterization of the Wesleys' Arminianism see Richard E. Brantley, "Charles Wesley's Experiential Art."

27. See Edwards, *Religious Affections,* 33, and Wesley, "Extract," 326.

28. See Edwards, *Religious Affections,* 53, and Wesley, "Extract," 335.

29. See Edwards, *Religious Affections,* 55-56, and Wesley, "Extract," 336; and Edwards, *Religious Affections,* 217-21, and Wesley, "Extract," 364.

30. See Edwards, *Religious Affections,* 38, and Wesley, "Extract," 329.

31. See Edwards, *Religious Affections,* 38, and Wesley, "Extract," 329. See also Richard E. Brantley, *Locke, Wesley, and the Method of English Romanticism,* 53, 68, 233 n. 44.

32. See Edwards, *Religious Affections,* 21, and Wesley, "Extract," 319; Edwards, 171-72, and Wesley, 349; Edwards, 179-80, and Wesley, 352; Edwards, 200, and Wesley, 358; Edwards, 201, and Wesley, 359; Edwards, 203, and Wesley, 360; and Edwards, 260-63, and Wesley, 376.

33. See Edwards, *Religious Affections,* 50, and Wesley, "Extract," 334; Edwards, 53, and Wesley, 335; Edwards, 66, and Wesley, 342; and Edwards, 86, and Wesley, 345.

34. See Edwards, *Religious Affections,* 9, and Wesley, "Extract," 314; Edwards, 24, and Wesley, 321; Edwards, 42, and Wesley, 330; Edwards, 60, and Wesley, 340; Edwards, 79, and Wesley, 343; Edwards, 85-86, and Wesley, 345; Edwards, 177, and Wesley, 351; Edwards, 204, and Wesley, 360; Edwards, 211, and Wesley, 363; and Edwards, 223-24, and Wesley, 365.

35. I refer to Blake's "The Mental Traveller" (1801-5?).

36. I refer to Blake's *The Marriage of Heaven and Hell* (1793).

37. Wesley, "Extract," 308.

38. See Clapper, "'True Religion' and the Affections," 417. "Against the encroachments of Arminian liberalism, which emphasized human reason, free will, and a benevolent Deity," wrote John Patrick Diggins (in a statement pointing to the difficulty of irenically reading Arminianism and Calvinism), "Edwards waged a rearguard defense of Calvinism's essential principles: man's utter depravity and inability to influence salvation through good works; the election of a few by a transforming grace that cannot be resisted; the uncertainty of the state of one's soul, even for the elect, hence the perseverance of the saints; and within this drama of redemption and damnation, the inscrutability of God's nature." See Diggins, "Puritans and Pragmatists," 39.

39. See Edwards, *Religious Affections,* 60-61, and Wesley, "Extract," 340; Edwards, 61-63, and Wesley, 340; and Edwards, 70-73, and Wesley, 343.

40. Clapper, "'True Religion' and the Affections," 418.

41. For a paradoxical argument that Edwards's ontology is finally epistemological, that according to Edwards's thought "dispositions and habits . . . can mediate between being and becoming, permanence and process," see Sang Hyun Lee, *The Philosophical Theology of Jonathan Edwards,* esp. 3, 115-70.

42. See Edwards, *Religious Affections,* 3, and Wesley, "Extract," 311.

43. Ibid. See also Edwards, 2, and Wesley, 310; and Edwards, 189-91, and Wesley, 354.

44. See the discussion in Clapper, "'True Religion' and the Affections," 418-19.

45. See Edwards, *Religious Affections,* 30-31, and Wesley, "Extract," 324; and Edwards, 198, and Wesley, 358. See also Brantley, *Locke, Wesley, and the Method of English Romanticism,* 15, 17, 125.

46. See Edwards, *Religious Affections,* 8, and Wesley, "Extract," 313.

47. Edwards, *Religious Affections,* 48-49.

48. See Wesley, "Extract," 333, where the passage would have appeared.

49. See Brantley, *Locke, Wesley, and the Method of English Romanticism,* 20-21.

50. See Edwards, *Religious Affections,* 18-19, and Wesley, "Extract," 317.

51. See Edwards, *Religious Affections,* 9, and Wesley, "Extract," 315. See also Edwards, 22, and Wesley, 319; Edwards, 26-27, and Wesley, 321-22; and Edwards, 33-34, and Wesley, 326-27.

52. See Brantley, *Locke, Wesley, and the Method of English Romanticism,* 15, 48-49, 61-62, 89, 100, 250 n. 31.

53. For Edwards's most overt "empiricism," and for Wesley's fidelity to it, see Edwards, *Religious Affections,* 13, and Wesley, "Extract," 312-13; Edwards, 17, and Wesley, 317; Edwards, 18, and Wesley, 317-19; Edwards, 33, and Wesley, 325-26; Edwards, 43, and Wesley, 330; Edwards, 48, and Wesley, 333-35; Edwards, 58-60, and Wesley, 338-39; Edwards, 86-87, and Wesley, 345-46; Edwards, 166, and Wesley, 348; Edwards, 221-22, and Wesley, 364-65; Edwards, 224-25, and Wesley, 365; Edwards, 253-55, and Wesley, 372-73; and Edwards, 256, and Wesley, 374-75. Clapper, in "'True Religion' and the Affections," 419, recognizes "spiritual empiricism" in what the

abridgment includes of the treatise's third part, but "spiritual empiricism" is scattered throughout the abridgment.

54. Denis Donoghue, *The Third Voice: Modern British and American Verse Drama,* 18.

55. John Locke, *Essay,* 4.9.3 and 4.10.6 in *An Essay concerning Human Understanding,* ed. Peter H. Nidditch, 618, 621. Subsequent references to this edition are abbreviated "Nidditch."

56. Locke, *Essay,* 4.11.1; Nidditch, 630.

57. Locke, *Essay,* 4.19.5; Nidditch, 698-99.

58. Wesley, "Extract," 333. Cf. Eccles. 11.5.

59. Locke, *Essay,* 4.19.16; Nidditch, 705.

60. "God when he makes the Prophet," Locke observes, "does not unmake the Man," and Locke adds that God "leaves all Man's Faculties in their natural State, to enable him to judge of his Inspirations, whether they be of divine Original or no. . . . We cannot take it for a *Revelation,* or so much as for true, till we have some other Mark that it is a *Revelation,* besides our believing that it is so. . . . *Gideon* was sent by an Angel to deliver Israel from the *Midianites,* and yet he desired a Sign to convince him, that this Commission was from God" (*Essay,* 4.19.14-15; Nidditch, 704).

61. Wesley, "Extract," 325.

62. Ibid., 333.

63. Ibid., 339.

64. Ibid., 346. Cf. Locke, *Essay,* 4.18.10; Nidditch, 696.

65. Wesley, "Extract," 317.

66. For Locke's discussion of "constant impressions" in the mind, see Locke, *Essay,* 1.2.2-5; Nidditch, 49-51.

67. I refer to Wordsworth's "Expostulation and Reply" (1798).

68. See the discussion in Hugh Sykes Davies, "Wordsworth and the Empirical Philosophers." Davies focuses on Wordsworth's objective usage of *impulse,* as in this stanza from "The Tables Turned" (1798): "One *impulse* from a vernal wood / May teach you more of man, / Of moral evil and of good, / Than all the sages can" (my italics).

69. Locke, *Essay,* 4.19.6; Nidditch, 699 (my italics).

70. Wesley, "Extract," 337 (my italics).

71. Locke, *Essay,* 2.9.4; Nidditch, 144 (my italics).

72. Richard Saunders, *A Discourse of Angels: Their Nature and Office, or Ministry; also Something Touching Devils, Apparitions, and Impulses.*

73. Wesley, "Extract," 374.

74. Hymn 280, Wesley and Wesley, *A Collection of Hymns, for the Use of the People Called Methodists*

(1780); see the discussion in G. H. Vallins, *The Wesleys and the English Language,* 87.

75. Wesley, "Extract," 340.

76. Ibid., 342.

77. See Brantley, *Locke, Wesley, and the Method of English Romanticism,* 12.

78. See, for example, in Brantley, *Locke, Wesley, and the Method of English Romanticism,* 37-44, how Wesley's definition of faith "delineated, for the first time, revelation's inward as well as outward setting and hence its commensurability with empirical philosophy's subject/object emphasis." The other four of Edwards's works abridged by Wesley are "Lockean," too, but unlike Locke's *Essay,* as well as unlike Edwards's *Religious Affections,* they stress experience to the point of subordinating reason.

79. Wesley, "Extract," 325.

80. Ibid.

81. Ibid.; cf. Locke, *Essay,* 4.19; Nidditch, 697-706.

82. Wesley, "Extract," 326.

83. Ibid., 325.

84. Locke, *Essay,* 4.19.15; Nidditch, 705.

85. Wesley, "Extract," 326.

86. Ibid., 322. Cf. Matt. 6.29, Ps. 73.1, and Heb. 3.16.

87. Wesley, "Extract," 319.

88. This strain of the abridgment's experiential theology, incidentally, finds an illuminating counterpart in another "both/and" permutation of Locke by Wordsworth; here, from "Expostulation and Reply," is the full context of "wise passiveness": "The eye—it cannot choose but see; / We cannot bid the ear be still; / Our bodies feel, where'er they be, / Against or with our will. / Nor less I deem that there are Powers / Which of themselves our minds impress; / That we can feed this mind of ours / In a wise passiveness."

89. Wesley, "Extract," 312.

90. Locke, *Essay,* 2.10.5; Nidditch, 151-52.

91. Wesley, "Extract," 321.

92. Ibid., 312.

93. Although Wordsworth, in the following lines from his "Prospectus" to *The Recluse,* does not address the issue of perception as Wesley and Edwards do, that is, although he does not on this occasion apprehend divine reality through the senses as analogues, tests, and receptors, he otherwise gets this "Wesleyan-Edwardsean," indeed this Lockean, point just right: "My voice proclaims / How exquisitely the individual Mind / (And the progressive powers perhaps no less / Of the whole species) to the external World / Is fitted;—and how exquisitely, too— / Theme this but little heard of among men— / The external World is fitted to the

Mind; / And the creation (by no lower name / Can it be called) which they with blended might / Accomplish:—this is our high argument."

94. Edwards, *A Treatise concerning Religious Affections,* ed. Smith, 46.

95. Wesley, "Extract," 312-13.

96. Ibid., 364-65.

97. Ibid., 313.

98. Edwards, *A Treatise concerning Religious Affections,* ed. Smith, 46.

99. Ibid., 46 (my italics).

100. Wesley, "Extract," 338.

101. Cf. 2 Cor. 3.18; 4.6.

102. Wesley, "Extract," 310 (my italics).

103. Ibid., 339.

104. Ibid., 345-46.

105. One thinks, in this connection, of Wordsworth's "natural piety": "My heart leaps up when I behold / A rainbow in the sky: / So was it when my life began; / So is it now I am a man; / So be it when I shall grow old, / Or let me die! / The child is father of the Man; / And I could wish my days to be / Bound each to each by natural piety." These lines are thoroughly Lockean: see the discussion in Samuel F. Pickering, Jr., *John Locke and Children's Books in Eighteenth-Century England,* 160-68. The abridgment, in its Lockean dimension, is consistent with them. "Natural piety" is secularized piety, or so goes the wisdom about Wordsworth, but the phrase connotes a faith in the God of nature, and as Wordsworth responds to the rainbow, so Wesley and Edwards claim "sense perception" of God's promises.

106. Wesley, "Extract," 373.

107. Ibid.

108. Locke, *Essay,* 4.16.6; Nidditch, 661-62.

109. Wesley, "Extract," 335 (my italics).

110. Edwards, *A Treatise concerning Religious Affections,* ed. Smith, 17.

111. Wesley, "Extract," 375.

112. John Wesley, *The Appeals to Men of Reason and Religion,* ed. Gerald R. Cragg, 57.

113. See the discussion in Brantley, *Locke, Wesley, and the Method of English Romanticism,* 48-53, 99-100, 109, 113, 116, 144, 221-23.

114. Peter Browne, *The Procedure, Extent, and Limits of Human Understanding,* 141-42.

115. See Locke's, *Essay,* 4.16.12; Nidditch, 667.

116. See, for example, the discussion in Leopold Damrosch's review of Brantley, *Locke, Wesley, and the Method of English Romanticism in Eighteenth-Century Studies* 19 (1986): 438-41.

117. Anders Jeffner, *Butler and Hume on Religion: A Comparative Analysis,* 185.

118. Wesley, "Extract," 313.

119. Ibid., 346.

120. I refer to W. B. Yeats's "The Fascination of What's Difficult" (1910).

121. I refer to H. J. Zelley's hymn, "Heavenly Sunshine" (1898). See William J. Reynolds, ed., *Baptist Hymnal,* 472.

122. For Wesley's account of his conversion, see *The Journal of the Rev. John Wesley, A. M.,* ed. Nehemiah Curnock, 1.475-76.

123. See Kenneth MacLean, *John Locke and English Literature of the Eighteenth Century,* and Hans Aarsleff, *From Locke to Saussure: Essays on the Study of Language and Intellectual History.*

124. I refer to Wordsworth's "Lines, Written a Few Miles Above Tintern Abbey" (1798).

A. Owen Aldridge (essay date 1993)

SOURCE: "Enlightenment and Awakening in Edwards and Franklin," in *Benjamin Franklin, Jonathan Edwards, and the Representation of American Culture,* edited by Barbara B. Oberg and Harry S. Stout, Oxford University Press, 1993, pp. 27-41.

[In the following essay, Aldridge compares and contrasts Benjamin Franklin, as representative of the Enlightenment, with Edwards, as representative of the Awakening—two men and societal movements that shared approximately the same eighteenth-century time period. Aldridge outlines obvious disparities between the men and their respective affiliations, but he also highlights numerous points on which the two men were in agreement, albeit for separate, and sometimes opposing, reasons.]

The contrary perspectives of the religious movement known in America as the Great Awakening and the intellectual movement embracing most of Europe and America known as the Enlightenment may be seen in the attitudes of a representative of each movement, Jonathan Edwards and Benjamin Franklin, respectively. Illustrating basic attitudes toward life, Edwards reflected that "Christ recommended rising early in the morning, by his rising from the grave very early,"[1] and Franklin in the guise of Poor Richard assured his readers that activity in the prime of the morning makes a man healthy, wealthy, and wise. Here spiritual and secular values and motives are clearly separate but, nevertheless, not completely opposed. Likewise the Awakening and the Enlightenment seem by definition to be antithetical, but they are not necessarily incompatible. In historical terms, the Great Awakening was a religious revival that swept the American colonies from New England to Georgia, according to some scholars between 1739 and 1744, and, according to others, between 1734 and 1749. In theological terms, the Great Awakening was the process by which God was presumably establishing Christ's kingdom in America. Edwards described the movement as "a great and wonderful event, a strange revolution, an unexpected surprising overturning of things, suddenly brought to pass. . . . It is the work of new creation which is infinitely more glorious than the old. . . . The New Jerusalem in this respect has begun to come down from heaven, and perhaps never were more of the prelibations of heaven's glory given upon earth."[2]

Franklin offered no parallel definition of the Enlightenment, but a superb one is to be found in the works of one of his French admirers, the abbé André Morellet:

> It is this ardor for knowledge, this activity of mind which does not wish to leave an effect without seeking the cause, a phenomenon without explanation, an assertion without proof, an objection without a reply, an error without combating it, an evil without seeking the remedy, a possible good without seeking to obtain it; it is this general movement of minds which has marked the eighteenth century and which will constitute its glory forever.[3]

Franklin had almost as much faith that the goals of the Enlightenment would flourish upon the earth as Edwards had concerning those of the Awakening. "God grant," Franklin wrote in 1789, "that not only the Love of Liberty, but a thorough Knowledge of the Rights of Man, may pervade all the Nations of the Earth, so that a Philosopher may set his Foot anywhere on its Surface and say 'This is my Country.'"[4]

In the broadest sense, Edwards may be considered an exponent of a philosophical concept associated with European writers prior to the Great Awakening. The ontology of his essay **"Of Being,"** affirming that everything in the universe has existence only in God's mind, coheres with the notion in Shakespeare and Calderón that life is a dream. Franklin on the Enlightenment side reflects the notion that existence is "a mighty maze! but not without a plan," as Pope had said, and Franklin's personal history embodied his effort to fix "a regular design" in his own life.[5]

Paradoxically, Edwards expressed an Enlightenment goal that seems to belong instead to Franklin, that of thinking big or comprehending in a single system the entire universe of knowledge. Edwards proposed but never brought to completion the writing of an encyclopedic work comprising the history of three worlds, heaven, earth, and hell, "considering the connected successive events and alterations in each." His projected *History of the Work of the Redemption* would be a spiritual parallel to the *Universal History* that was actually published in England. He also at one time proposed to discover and write about a "thousand things" in natural philosophy "by nice observations of the spheroid of the world."[6] Franklin never conceived of a grand synthesis of any kind, but in actual life he became involved in almost every intellectual occupation of the age and wrote about most of them. Franklin represented a related Enlightenment attitude, cosmopolitanism, that was completely alien to Edwards. Even on the Awakening side, Edwards was provincial. He may be contrasted with the evangelist George Whitefield, called the "Grand Itinerant," who proclaimed that "the world is my parish," as Thomas Paine was later to boast, "My country is the world, and my religion is to do good." Franklin made four round trips across the Atlantic, and Whitefield made even more, but Edwards hesitated to cross a single time, even though offered a pastorate in Scotland. Edwards condemned Jews, Pharisees, Papists, and Mohammedans as wicked men who compounded with God in their forms of worship,[7] while Franklin complacently affirmed ecumenical principles. Franklin had favored erecting a meeting house in Philadelphia, which most of the city associated with the Great Awakening, but he had supported the building not "to accommodate any particular Sect, but the Inhabitants in general, so that even if the Mufti of Constantinople were to send a Missionary to preach Mahometanism to us, he would find a pulpit at his Service."[8] Edwards's view of geography divided the world into two spheres, the old and the new, that is, America and Europe.[9] He argued that the people of his own land were "more committed to our care than the people of China, and we ought to pray more for them."[10] China he described as "wild Tartary."[11] Franklin, on the other hand, wanted the *Rights of Man* to be known in all the nations of the earth; he admired the works of Confucius and told his friend Benjamin Vaughan that he was "very fond of reading about China" and "that if he were a young man he should like to go to China."[12]

In essence, the Awakening accepted Biblical authority, and its partisans were swayed by emotion. The Enlightenment rejected all authority, and its exponents followed reason, experiment, and history. Yet adherence to one of these movements did not automatically eliminate influence by the other. Edwards was touched by the Enlightenment without embracing it fully, and Franklin encountered the Awakening in personal relations with his family and close associates. Although each man's principal commitment to life was in a different sphere, both possessed a number of common interests. On the Enlightenment side, Edwards became familiar with the science of Newton in his college years, and as a philosopher he attempted to resolve problems raised by John Locke and the deists Anthony Collins and Mathew Tindal. Franklin absorbed deistical thinking long before becoming familiar with Newtonian science. He and Edwards were introduced to electricity about the same time; Franklin by the public experiments of Archibald Spencer, and Edwards by those of Ebenezer Kinnersley.[13] Franklin preceded Edwards, however, in publishing thoughts on the freedom of the will. On the Awakening side, the movement literally represented for Edwards not only an extraordinary work of the creator, but the great end of all God's other works.[14] For Franklin, the Awakening was merely the intensified expression of a religious system with which he had been familiar since boyhood, but one that he had experienced primarily as a spectator.

Edwards and Franklin would have responded in quite contrary ways to the injunction of Poor Richard in 1755, "Think of three Things, whence you came, where you are going, and to whom you must account." The Awakening and the Enlightenment were most sharply divided over "whence you came"—involving the nature of man's past. Edwards and his fellow theologians found the answer in the doctrine of original sin, defined by Edwards as "the *innate sinful depravity of the heart*," deriving from the first sin of Adam together with "the liableness or exposedness of Adam's posterity, in the divine judgment, to partake of the punishment of that Sin."[15] Franklin, in company with such Enlightenment figures as Rousseau, Voltaire, and Hume, maintained to the contrary that man was by nature good or at least not prepossessed by evil. He found this comfortable doctrine in Lord Shaftesbury, whom he frequently quoted or paraphrased. He specifically opposed Calvinist theology, affirming that the concept of *"our lost and undone State by Nature"* is an absurdity used "to fright and scare an unthinking Populace out of their Senses, and inspire them with Terror, to answer the little selfish Ends of the Inventors and Propagators."[16] Franklin also portrayed the universe itself as reflecting benevolence rather than depravity. "Most happy are we," he wrote, "the sons of men, above all other creatures, who are born to behold the glorious rays of the sun, and to enjoy the pleasant fruits of the earth." He believed that after a life of using reason in doing good, we are rewarded with "the sweet sleep of death, pleasant as a bed to a weary traveller after a long journey."[17] In regard to man's future, the two movements were also far apart. Edwards at the height of the Great Awakening felt that the dawn of the New Age or Christ's kingdom on earth was not only at hand, but that the earliest stages would take place in America.[18] In his best-known sermon, he observed that "God seems now to be hastily gathering in his elect in all parts of the land; and probably the greatest part of adult persons that ever shall be saved, will be brought in now in a little time." Even after the Great Awakening had run its course, Edwards's vision remained fixed upon the kingdom of heaven and a delayed rather than an imminent millennium. Although he believed that loving God required doing good to man, he felt that this earthly service was a subordinate duty. Franklin believed, to the contrary, that doing good to man was the most effective means of serving God. His prospect of the future both for himself and for mankind pertained to the terrestrial, not the heavenly, world. Although he expressed no formal utopian dream, he believed that what he called "true science" was making extraordinary progress. Specifically placing the concept of millennium in a secular framework, he wrote to Joseph Priestley late in life:

> It is impossible to imagine the Height to which may be carried, in a thousand years, the Power of Man over Matter. We may perhaps learn to deprive large Masses of their Gravity, and give them absolute Levity, for the sake of easy Transport. Agriculture may diminish its Labour and double its Produce; all Diseases may by sure means be prevented or cured, not excepting even that of Old Age, and our Lives lengthened at pleasure even beyond the antediluvian Standard.[19]

How Edwards reacted to the question of "to whom you must account" is a rather complex matter. From the standpoint of the Scriptures, he obviously believed that he must answer directly and personally to Christ and that on the day of redemption he would appear among either the saints or the sinners.[20] But awareness of the plan of redemption gave him little help in managing his day-to-day conduct. The Bible offered strong motives to virtue but no universal rule for deciding which actions are virtuous and which not. Edwards affirmed that men must act out of a sense of duty. In his miscellanies he seemed to accept the "dictates of the natural, common and universal moral sense of mankind in all nations and ages."[21] While maintaining that "devotion and not mutual love, charity, justice, beneficence, etc. is the highest end of man,"[22] he also insists on the paramount obligation of works of charity. Although he speaks of those things that are our duty as "being required by moral rules, or absolute positive commands of God,"[23] nowhere does he declare whether rules of conduct are based upon Scriptures, rational decision, or conscience. In his philosophical system, he placed conscience on a lower level than what he called true virtue and attributed moral goodness only to "a sense and relish of the essential beauty of virtue."[24] But this metaphysical virtue provided no practical guidelines for conduct. Edwards was forced, therefore, to fall back upon his own notions of behavior even though his ultimate accounting was to God. In a set of "Resolutions" composed in his twentieth year, he determined to do whatsoever "I think to be most to the glory of God and my own good, profit and pleasure" and "to do whatever I think to be my *duty,* and most for the good and advantage of mankind in general." He was accountable to God but followed his own notions of right and wrong.

For Franklin, the problem of accountability is not in the least complex. Although he believed in a deistical God throughout his life, there is no evidence that he ever acknowledged a personal relationship with Christ. Indeed, in a statement in his private "Articles of Belief and Acts of Religion" at the age of twenty-two, he specifically denied the possibility of personal communication with the supreme being. In his words, "I imagine it great Vanity in me to suppose, that the *Supremely Perfect,* does in the least regard such an inconsiderable Nothing as Man . . . I cannot conceive otherwise, than that He *the Infinite Father,* expects or requires no Worship or Praise from us, but that he is even INFINITELY ABOVE IT."[25]

At that time, Franklin conjectured that each of the planets had its own god, and he granted a measure of communication between this inferior god and his created beings. "Let me then not fail to praise my God continually," Franklin proposed, "for it is his Due, and it is all I can return for his many Favours and great Goodness to me; and let me resolve to be virtuous, that I may be happy, that I may please Him, who is delighted to see me happy." Shortly after setting forth his articles of belief, Franklin conceived of "the bold and arduous project of arriving at moral perfection." As he explains at length in his *Autobiography,* he decided what he considered to be the thirteen principal virtues, defined them, entered them into a notebook with spaces for marking infractions against them, and gave a week's attention to each one successively, hoping eventually to go through a period of thirteen weeks without a single infraction. He even carried the project to his discussion group or Junto as a question to be debated: "Can a man arrive at Perfection in this Life as some Believe?"[26]— and he later envisioned calling the scheme his "Art of Virtue." Although he recognized the "blessing of God" in his quest for moral perfection, he considered himself accountable only to himself. In comments on his thirteen virtues, he tried to show the means and manner of obtaining each one, thereby distinguishing his method "from the mere Exhortation to be good, that does not instruct and indicate the Means, but is like the Apostle's Man of verbal Charity, who only, without showing to the Naked and the Hungry *how* or where they might get Clothes or Victuals, exhorted them to be fed and clothed.—James ii. 15, 16."[27] This is an implied criticism of the type of charity preached by Edwards and other adherents to the Great Awakening—noble and sublime in sentiment, but deficient in practical application. One can only imagine, on the other hand, how Edwards and his fellow divines would have reacted to Franklin's footnote, "Nothing so likely to make a man's fortune as virtue." Franklin elsewhere, however, as a good Shaftesburian, affirmed the beauty of virtue—although not at all in Edwards's sense of love "to being in general" as expounded in his *Nature of True Virtue.* Franklin considered his own Art of Virtue to be of universal utility and an alternative to religious-based ethics for those who do not accept Christianity.[28] His view that it could lead to moral perfection was compatible with the perfectionist doctrine of the Wesleys, completely rejected by Edwards, that man could be completely cleansed of sin.

Edwards also discussed the possibility of several different gods having created the several stars in the sky, but he rejected the notion on the grounds that "the parts of these different systems are not only communicated to and diffused through one another, but act upon one another; and this is a mutual action and reaction between their different blended parts by the same laws of matter and motion." It would, therefore, be unreasonable to suppose anything "other than that this action and reaction are both by the laws and influence of the same God."[29] Edwards did not, however, examine a hypothesis, like Franklin's, that there might be one supremely perfect god, father of the subordinate gods of each individual star. At the time he made his comments on polytheism, Edwards knew considerably more about Newtonian philosophy than Franklin did. As early as 1716, he had access to the Yale copy of the *Principia,* and his youthful essay **"Of Being"** indicates that he made full use of it. Franklin as late as 1746 does not seem to have read, or at least digested, any of Newton, for in a letter to one of his friends in that year, he affirmed that he was not able to comprehend "the concept of *Vis Inertiae essential to Matter.*"[30]

The intricacy and sublimity of the cosmos or the far reaches of the universe represented for Franklin, as for many other minds of the Enlightenment, deists and Christians alike, a proof of the existence of a divine creator. Franklin in his youth derived his belief in a supremely perfect being when, in his words, he stretched his "Imagination thro' and beyond our System of Planets, beyond the visible fix'd Stars themselves, into that Space that is every Way infinite." Later in life Franklin does not seem to have taken seriously this mode of reasoning or imagining that in the eighteenth century was called physico-theology. During his sojourn in France, he parodied the related notion of discerning purpose in the universe through the life cycle of plants and animals and the structure of the human body. In a private letter he complimented the benevolent wisdom of the creator for adjusting the human elbow so that the wine glass could be raised precisely to the mouth.[31] Caustically he reported in his *Memoirs* the explanation offered by an Indian chief that the great Spirit, who made everything in the universe for some use, pronounced that rum should be used for Indians to get drunk with. Franklin added, "indeed if it be the Desire of Providence to extirpate these Savages in order to make room for Cultivators of the Earth, it seems not improbable that Rum may be the appointed Means."[32] Edwards was aware of this kind of natural theology, which he adopted in his early letter on spiders.[33] He traced back to John Locke the related notion that recognition of the wonders of nature leads to knowledge of the existence of god, but rejected it entirely. "If we look over all the accounts we have of the several nations of the earth, and consider everything that has been advanced by any or all of the philosophers," he affirmed, "we can meet with nothing to induce us to think that the first religion of the world was introduced by the use and direction of mere natural reason."[34] To the contrary, man's reason and speculations lead to "false and ill-grounded notions" of the creator. In Edwards's view, divine revelation alone has provided man with the correct notion of the "true nature and the true worship of the deity."[35] He even suggested that the imagination interferes with human perception of the universe and the divine workmanship it reflects. In somewhat rhapsodical terms, he affirmed that "the universe is created out of nothing every moment and if it were not for our imaginations, which hinder us, we might see that wonderful work performed continually which was seen by the morning stars when they sang together."[36] Yet Edwards also used teleological arguments in one of his proofs of God's existence. "The being of God," he affirmed, "may be argued from the desirability and need of it,"[37] a remarkable declaration that comes close to prefiguring Voltaire's famous pronouncement, "If there were no God, it would be necessary to invent him." Edwards argued that we have the moon and stars to keep us from being miserable in the darkness of night, that in Greenland where the sun's rays are oblique, the sun stays longer above the horizon as compensation, and that since camels are forced to go for a long time without water in desert areas, they have a large vessel within them to carry water.[38] Edwards also treated at some length "the wisdom of God" in contriving the mechanism of the human eye, the roundness of the earth, the position of the planets, and the motion of the comets.[39]

Despite Edwards's placing of revelation above reason, he was as a philosopher a confirmed rationalist. It is a paradox, therefore, for Vernon L. Parrington to call him an "anachronism" in the Age of Reason. Rationalism, another scholar has said, "is not the whole of Edwards's philosophy, but it is the basis of it."[40] His *Freedom of the Will* is a masterly exercise in logic that seldom refers to Scripture, and his *Nature of True Virtue* is based entirely on reason. In defining reason, Edwards combines ratiocination with intuition or self-evidence, and he argues that the reasoning process comprises the experience of mankind, including history, tradition, and memory together with the testimony of our senses.[41] In his treatise on the religious affections he affirms that in matters of religion intuition may supersede reason, that "a soul may have a kind of intuitive knowledge of the divinity of the things exhibited in the gospel; not that he judges the doctrines of the gospel to be from God, without any argument or deduction at all; but it is without any long chain of arguments; the argument is but one, and the evidence direct; the mind ascends to the truth of the gospel by but one step."[42] This is as close as he ever came to asserting, as Franklin did more than once, "the great uncertainty . . . in metaphysical reasonings."[43] Edwards did not, however, accept special revelation that is not directly related to the Scriptures. In his remarks on the Awakening, he vigorously repudiated the notion that anything may be made known by inspiration or immediate revelation "that is not taught in the scripture as the words lie in the *Bible*."[44] There is nothing paradoxical in characterizing Franklin as an exponent of the notion of the Age of Reason, even though he was more of an experimenter than a rationalist. He seems not to have clung to an early affirmation "that no Authority is more convincing to Men of Reason than the Authority of Reason itself."[45] In later years, he contrasted reason with "a good sensible Instinct" and suggested that the latter is to be preferred. He also wrote to a friend in France that reason must be fallible "since two people like you and me can draw from the same principles conclusions diametrically opposite. This reason seems to me a guide quite blind. A good and certain instinct would be worth much more to us."[46] In both of these references, instinct applies to all matters, not only to religion, and Franklin says merely that it would be desirable to have, not that it actually exists. Edwards, on the other hand, firmly believed in the existence of his intuition in religious matters. He based his philosophical treatises upon the principles of reason while at the same time asserting that revelation is a superior source of knowledge. Franklin carried out experiments in many scientific areas, rejected supernatural revelation, and used reason primarily in practical affairs. Edwards was America's greatest artisan of metaphysical reasoning or "dialectical pyrotechniques,"

as one scholar has it.[47] Franklin distrusted the process and inveighed extensively against it.

Both Edwards and Franklin, in company with several other writers of the Enlightenment and the Awakening, denied freedom of the will, but they did so from opposing principles and propositions. In a sense, their two discourses are not comparable, as Franklin's was written when he was a mere teenager, and he soon after repudiated its principal doctrine; Edwards's treatise was in some ways the crowning intellectual achievement of his life, and he never wavered from the principles it comprises. Franklin's discussion was limited to a slight pamphlet of twenty-nine pages, although given the title of a *Dissertation,* and Edwards's amounted to a book of more than three hundred pages. The principles in both works are, nevertheless, respectively representative of the two historical currents we are considering, Enlightenment and Awakening. I obviously cannot at this time summarize all of Edwards's arguments against free will, but I can state the major ones. He argues that all of our actions are based upon the strongest motive at each apparent exercise of choice; that every action is determined by our mental volitions even though there may be no physical requirement for that action; and that every action of every individual is part of a chain of cause and effect operating within that individual and at the same time interconnected with every other activity in the universe. Franklin's argument is essentially a variation of the last of those three, with greater emphasis on the role of god as the interconnecting principle. Indeed, in Franklin's pamphlet, god and the universe are absolutely equivalent, and his system is a purely mechanistic one. He affirms as the foundation of his argument that people of "every Sect and Opinion" admit "a first Mover, who is called GOD, Maker of the Universe," and who is "all-wise, all-good, all powerful." God is, therefore, directly and uniquely responsible for every action in the universe, including everything to which we give the name evil. And if man "is thus limited in his Actions, being able to do only such Things as God would have done; then he can have no such Thing as Liberty, Free-will or Power to do or refrain an Action." In Edwards's thought, god, the universe, and man are separate entities, but are interconnected by the spirit of god. His system is spiritual rather than mechanical. Edwards disposes of the problem of evil by means of a distinction between mental volition (required action) and lack of physical restraint (or freedom), a distinction he characterizes as between moral and natural necessity. He thereby makes man responsible for evil since man is physically free to refrain from any immoral action. Franklin, however, does not allow responsibility for actions that are considered evil to be transferred from God to man. He insists that since all actions depend upon God, all are equally good. In other words, he completely removes the distinction between virtue and vice. In Franklin's words, "we must allow that all Things exist now in a Manner agreeable to His Will, and in consequence of that are all equally Good, and therefore equally esteem'd by Him." To buttress this proposition, Franklin adds an argument that all creatures on earth experience an exact balance of pleasure and pain. Men may have different quantities and qualities of sensation, but since each man's total experience of either pleasure or pain is exactly in proportion to the opposite feeling, the result is perfect equality for all mankind.

Soon after publishing his pamphlet, Franklin had second thoughts about his mechanistic universe, bordering as it does on atheism, and he therefore wrote a lecture "On the Providence of God in the Government of the World," which he delivered to his fellow tradesmen in Philadelphia. He later summarized it as based upon the proposition "'That almost all men in all ages and countries have at times made use of prayer.' Thence I reasoned, that if all things are ordained, prayer must among the rest be ordained. But as prayer can produce no change in things that are ordained, praying must then be useless and an absurdity. God would therefore not ordain praying if everything else was ordained. But praying exists, therefore all things are not ordained."[48] Edwards knew nothing about Franklin's dissertation or his lecture, but about the same time that Franklin was delivering the latter, he wrote in his **"Miscellanies"** an explanation of how God could intervene in the system of creation without upsetting his predetermined chain of cause and effect. The explanation depends upon foreknowledge. In Edwards's words, "God decrees all things harmoniously and in excellent order, one decree harmonizes with another, and there is such a relation between all the decrees as makes the most excellent order. Thus, God decrees rain in drought because He decrees the earnest prayers of His people, or thus, He decrees the prayers of His people because He decrees rain . . . God decrees the latter event because of the former no more than he decrees the former because of the latter."[49] Somewhat later (April 1753), Edwards wrote to his son Timothy in terms surprisingly similar to Franklin's: "Whatever your circumstances are, it is your duty not to despair, but to hope in infinite mercy, through a Redeemer. For God makes it your duty to pray to him for mercy; which would not be your duty, if it was allowable for you to despair." Edwards's argument of foreknowledge may take care of the harmony of prayer and predetermined events, but it hardly reconciles God's interfering by special providence in a scheme of predetermined events without changing the course of these events. If God's interference or providence is part of the pre-established pattern, it cannot be considered as an authentic interposition. The law of cause and effect is obviously incompatible with divine intervention. Edwards's sermons are no more satisfactory. In his ***The Most High a Prayer Hearing God*** (1735-36), he affirms that God hears the prayers of men and that he exercises his mercy, but Edwards still does not put the two statements together in an assertion that individual prayers are responded to. He merely cites examples from the Old Testament that affirm a direct relationship.[50] Indeed, Edwards specifically declares that "the mercy of God is not moved or drawn by any thing in the creature; but the spring of God's beneficence is within himself only; he is self moved; and whatsoever mercy he bestows, the reason and ground of it is not to be sought for in the creature, but in God's own good pleasure."[51] Even on the affirmative side,

Edwards says merely that "God can answer prayer, though he bestow not the very thing for which we pray. He can sometimes better answer the lawful desires and good end we have in prayer another way."[52] He also declares unequivocally that "God is pleased sometimes to answer the prayers of unbelievers" by granting their requests, but he immediately reduces the force of this statement by adding that "God may, and sometimes does, hear the cries of wicked men, as he hears the hungry ravens, when they cry."[53] Essentially the relationship in Edwards's system of prayers, God, and subsequent events related to these prayers is the same as that between the individual's moral conduct and his eventual salvation or damnation. These relationships have all been determined by God in a pattern of pre-established harmony. In his **"Miscellanies,"** Edwards explains that decrees of our everlasting state as well as our prayers and strivings have been present with God from all eternity. In his metaphysical system of idealism, all creation is nothing but an idea of God, and therefore no chronological succession or pattern of sequence exists. This theory, however, applies to God and not to ordinary mortals, who do reside in a system of chronological relationships as well as in one of cause and effect.

Edwards believed that God could intervene in the system of nature for other purposes besides the answering of prayer. On one occasion he cited the Old Testament narrative in which "God changed the course of nature, and caused the sun to go from the West to the East."[54] Here Scripture certainly supersedes Newton, the theology of the Awakening outranking the science of the Enlightenment. Franklin in his lecture on divine providence less dramatically reached the same conclusion concerning God's intervention. In his words, "the Deity sometimes . . . sets aside the Events which would otherwise have been produc'd in the Course of Nature, or by the Free Agency of Man."[55] In *Poor Richard,* Franklin appealed to Newton to refute a common Enlightenment notion, "the opinion of all the modern philosophers and mathematicians that the planets are habitable worlds. If so," Franklin asked, "what sort of constitutions must those people have who live in the planet Mercury? where, says Sir Isaac Newton, the heat of the sun is seven times as great as it is with us; and would make our Water boil away."[56]

Franklin did not long retain the confidence expressed in his youthful lecture that a benevolent providence is the foundation of all religion. In a letter in 1769 to the star of the Great Awakening, George Whitefield, he expressed doubt that divine providence attends regularly to human affairs. "I rather suspect, from certain circumstances," he wrote, "that though the general government of the universe is well administered, our particular little affairs are perhaps below notice, and left to take the chance of prudence or imprudence, as either may happen to be uppermost. It is, however, an uncomfortable thought, and I leave it."[57] One wonders whether Franklin really changed his mind back again during the War for Independence when he attributed military successes to the "Interposition of Providence" or when in his *Memoirs,* he acknowledged "that I owe the mention'd Happiness of my past Life to his kind Providence, which led me to the Means I us'd and gave them success."[58] Franklin's indecision concerning the workings of providence obviously has relevance to his opinion concerning the efficacy of prayer. His early articles of belief assume that the creator of the world is a good being who is pleased with the praise and thanksgiving of his subjects, but nothing is said about personal petitions to God or to the possibility of their being answered. Throughout the rest of his life Franklin had a great deal to say about the utility of prayer—the psychological comfort it provides to the individual and the sense of order and common purpose it gives to the community, but he never expressed an opinion that particular prayers are answered. In 1773 he published in collaboration with an English nobleman an abridgment of the Anglican *Book of Common Prayer,* to which he contributed an explanatory preface, and soon after he prepared a revision of the Lord's Prayer for his own use. These experiments or exercises support his conviction, previously expressed to his daughter, that a ritual of prayer and praise is more important in the divine service than a sermon or other discourse.[59] One of the most drastic changes Franklin made in his abridgment of the *Book of Common Prayer* was the elimination of those psalms that "imprecate, in the most bitter terms, the vengeance of God on our adversaries, contrary to the spirit of Christianity, which commands us to love our enemies, and to pray for those that hate us and despitefully use us." He also omitted as objectionable the Commination and "all cursing of mankind." It is conceivable, although never previously suggested in print, that Franklin may have had in mind the sinner psychology of New England theology as well as Anglican formal prayers in his opposition to the attributing of imprecations to God and the portraying of God as vengeful. Although Edwards was skilled, as we all know, in portraying the punishment meted out by an angry god, he nevertheless also took a stand against pulpit prayers that joined "a sort of imprecation with their petition for others" or, as he expressed it, "a sort of cursing men in our prayer, adding a curse with our blessing."[60] At the Constitutional Convention, Franklin made a speech advocating daily prayers during its deliberations. In this speech he affirmed his conviction *"that GOD governs in the Affairs of Men,"* a reversal of his skeptical opinion expressed to Whitefield. But even here he did not hold out the hope that specific prayers or petitions would be answered.

Although prayer is commonly considered by Edwards and others to be an emotional experience or, in Edwards's terms, an outpouring of the religious affections, Franklin did not indicate emotion as an aspect of prayer—and in his writings he paid little attention to emotion in general, except for warning against the harmful passions, especially avarice, the love of money; ambition, the love of power; and pride, the hardest to subdue. Both Edwards and Franklin came under the influence of Lord Shaftesbury's *Inquiry concerning Virtue,* which, among other things, made the passions respectable in British moral philosophy, but while Edwards looked upon virtue as a type

of affection, Franklin considered it in purely rational terms. Edwards throughout his works makes a distinction between head and heart, which does not exist anywhere in Franklin's thought, even though it is paramount in another Enlightenment model, Thomas Jefferson. The workings of heart or the emotions may be traced in the lives of both Edwards and Franklin, however, in the area of social welfare, one of the illustrations of the confluence of Enlightenment and Awakening.

On one occasion, Franklin's sister had admonished him from the perspective of her "New England Doctrines" for slighting the duties of worship and for believing that good works alone are sufficient to gain entry into heaven. After absolving himself of the first charge by reminding her of his private book of devotions and of the second by affirming in somewhat equivocal terms that "there are few, if any, in the World so weake as to imagine that the little Good we can do here, can *merit* so vast a Reward hereafter," he urged her to read Edwards's more tolerant view in his ***Thoughts*** concerning the revival.[61] Here Edwards considers "the Expressions of our Love to GOD, by obeying his moral commands of Self-denial, Righteousness, Meekness, and Christian Love, in our Behavior among Men" of much greater importance than ceremonial acts of worship such as praying, hearing, singing, and attending religious meetings.[62] In a later passage Edwards insists that a religion of deeds is more important than a religion of words, contrary to the usual disparaging of good works among those preaching justification by faith. Edwards further conjectured that "the remarkable Hearing that God has given Mr. Whitefield, and the great success with which he has crowned him, may well be thought to be very much owing to his laying out himself so abundantly in charitable designs."[63] Franklin also respected Whitefield for his charitable designs, particularly for his project of erecting an orphanage at Savannah. In a long passage in his *Memoirs,* he explains how in advance of hearing Whitefield speak he had resolved not to respond at all to fundraising appeals, but that under the spell of Whitefield's admirable oratory he decided successively to donate his coppers, his silver, and finally all the money on his person, including five pistoles in gold. This is a rare instance of Franklin's succumbing to an emotional appeal. It is also a prime example of the overlapping of the Enlightenment and the Awakening, the good works of the first merging with the acts of charity of the second.

Notes

1. A. Owen Aldridge, *Benjamin Franklin and Nature's God* (Durham, N.C., 1967), p. 19.

2. *Works of President Edwards,* 8 vols. (Worcester, Mass., 1808-9), 3: 145-46.

3. Aldridge, *Benjamin Franklin and Nature's God,* p. 5.

4. *Writings of Benjamin Franklin,* 10 vols. ed. Albert Henry Smyth (New York, 1905-7), 10: 172.

5. *PBF, 1:* 100.

6. *WJE, 6:* 230.

7. *Works of President Edwards, 8:* 345.

8. *Benjamin Franklin's Autobiography,* ed. J. A. Leo Lemay and P. M. Zall (New York, 1986), p. 88.

9. *Works of President Edwards, 3:* 154.

10. *Ibid., 3:* 287.

11. *The Philosophy of Jonathan Edwards from His Private Notebooks,* ed. Harvey G. Townsend (Eugene, Ore., 1955), p. 207.

12. *Works of Benjamin Franklin,* 10 vols., ed. Jared Sparks (Boston, 1836-40), *2:* 241.

13. Ola E. Winslow, *Jonathan Edwards, 1703-1758* (1940; rep. New York, 1961), p. 117.

14. *Works of President Edwards, 3:* 144.

15. *WJE, 3:* 107. Emphasis in original.

16. *PBF, 2:* 114. Emphasis in original.

17. *Writings of Benjamin Franklin,* ed. J. A. Leo Lemay (New York, 1987), pp. 232-33.

18. *Works of President Edwards, 3:* 153.

19. *Writings of Benjamin Franklin,* ed. Smyth, 9: 10.

20. *Works of President Edwards, 2:* 362.

21. *Philosophy of Jonathan Edwards,* ed. Townsend, pp. 71, 161, 225.

22. *Ibid.,* p. 237.

23. *Works of President Edwards, 3:* 257.

24. Norman Fiering, *Jonathan Edwards's Moral Thought and Its British Context* (Chapel Hill, N.C., 1981), p. 358.

25. *PBF, 1:* 102. Emphasis in original.

26. *Ibid., 1:* 261. Emphasis in original.

27. *Benjamin Franklin's Autobiography,* ed. Lemay and Zall, p. 74.

28. *PBF, 7:* 105.

29. *Philosophy of Jonathan Edwards,* ed. Townsend, pp. 108-9.

30. *PBF, 3:* 85. Emphasis in original.

31. *Writings of Benjamin Franklin,* ed. Smyth, pp. 7, 436-37.

32. *Benjamin Franklin's Autobiography,* ed. Lemay and Zall, p. 102.

33. *WJE, 6:* 168.

34. *Philosophy of Jonathan Edwards,* ed. Townsend, pp. 212-13.

35. *Ibid.,* p. 213.

36. *Ibid.,* p. 17.

37. *Ibid.,* p. 79.

38. *Ibid.,* p. 179.

39. *WJE, 6:* 307-10.

40. *Philosophy of Jonathan Edwards,* ed. Townsend, p. viii.

41. *Ibid.,* p. 221.

42. *WJE, 2:* 298-99.

43. *Writings of Benjamin Franklin,* ed. Lemay, pp. 435, 1016, 1359.

44. *Works of President Edwards, 3:* 243.

45. *PBF, 1:* 265.

46. Aldridge, *Benjamin Franklin and Nature's God,* p. 74.

47. *WJE, 3:* 96.

48. *Writings of Benjamin Franklin,* ed. Lemay, p. 1016.

49. *Philosophy of Jonathan Edwards,* ed. Townsend, p. 134.

50. *Works of President Edwards, 8:* 57.

51. *Ibid., 8:* 55.

52. *Ibid., 8:* 69.

53. *Ibid., 8:* 64.

54. *Ibid., 3:* 158.

55. *PBF, 1:* 268.

56. *Ibid., 3:* 345.

57. *Writings of Benjamin Franklin,* ed. Lemay, p. 845.

58. *Writings of Benjamin Franklin,* ed. Smyth, *9:* 261.

59. *PBF, 11:* 450.

60. *Works of President Edwards, 3:* 298.

61. *PBF, 2:* 385. Emphasis is in original.

62. *Works of President Edwards, 3:* 343.

63. *Ibid., 3:* 349.

Abbreviations

PBF: *The Papers of Benjamin Franklin* (New Haven, Yale Univ. Press, 1959–)

WJE: *Works of Jonathan Edwards* (New Haven: Yale Univ. Press, 1957–)

Ruth H. Bloch (essay date 1993)

SOURCE: "Women, Love, and Virtue in the Thought of Edwards and Franklin," in *Benjamin Franklin, Jonathan Edwards, and the Representation of American Culture,* edited by Barbara B. Oberg and Harry S. Stout, Oxford University Press, 1993, pp. 134-151.

[In the following essay, Bloch discusses what she terms the ambiguous and inconsistent treatment of women, love, and virtue in the writings of Edwards and Benjamin Franklin, noting that each, in his own way, inadvertently helped set the stage for the romanticists who would follow.]

As major American intellectuals in the midst of the transition from Puritanism to the new Protestant middle-class morality of the late eighteenth and early nineteenth centuries, Jonathan Edwards and Benjamin Franklin stood at an important juncture in the development of ideas about women and marital love. Although neither of them wrote extensively about relationships between men and women, their often implicit ideas reveal difficulties they had reconciling traditional Puritan with newer points of view. Their shared preoccupation with human morality, as well as their personal relationships with women, unavoidably raised basic questions about the role of human attachment in the generation of virtue. Their often internally contradictory answers to these questions at once resisted and encouraged broader changes in the American cultural understanding of women and love.

The Puritans before them, as many historians have shown, accorded marriage fundamental social value as the core of the "little common-wealth" of the family. Regarded as the basic unit of society, familial relationships served as the primary locus of religious education and the enforcement of the moral code. Love between men and women, defined largely in terms of duty, was conceived as a consequence rather than a precondition of marriage. Wives were deemed valuable as both economic and spiritual "helpmates," and traditional criticism of women as dangerously sexual and prone to sinful temptation was gradually giving way to a positive image of female piety and domestic devotion. Love of God, which was always, of course, to supersede conjugal love, was in the late seventeenth century increasingly symbolized in terms of marital bonds.[1]

During the eighteenth century, this earlier positive conception of women and marriage was transformed into a newly sentimental understanding of marital love. No longer stressing the tension between divine and human love, moral commentators increasingly viewed virtue as based in sympathetic connections between human beings. Influential British moral philosophers such as the Earl of Shaftesbury, Francis Hutcheson, and their popularizers rooted virtue in the emotions and posited the existence of an innate moral sense. A growing emphasis on the redemptive qualities of human love, including romantic love between men and women, as something distinct from sexual attraction, pervaded both religious and secular literature. Writings on courtship and marriage commonly attributed especially keen moral sensibilities to women, who as wives and mothers promised to cultivate benevolent emotions in men. According to this increasingly gendered ideal of virtue, feminine intuition and empathy balanced masculine industriousness and self-reliance. Whereas the earlier Puritans had typically characterized good wives as dependable assistants to men, late-eighteenth-century domestic moralists highlighted gender differences and the psychological interdependence of husbands and wives.[2]

On first impression, neither Edwards nor Franklin seems to have contributed to the development of this sentimental conception of women and human love. Neither was particularly concerned with the family as a social institution. Neither regarded virtue as either produced or realized in human relationships. Whatever their differences, the fundamental perspectives of both on the sources of human morality remained essentially individualistic. Virtue was never for either of them the result of emotional involvement with other people. It was instead a quality internal to the individual—for Edwards the product of the gracious awakening of one's spiritual sense, and for Franklin the disciplined quest for worldly happiness. Each in his own way assumed benevolent social relationships to be a necessary outcome of virtue, but neither regarded marriage or the family as distinctive or especially valuable arenas for the expression of virtue.

Both Edwards and Franklin found relations between men and women more problematic, however, than the ostensible clarity of these positions suggests. While biographers have, of course, paid attention to each of their relationships with women, they have made little effort to relate their personal attitudes and experiences to the general framework of their thought.[3] The dominant tendency of both men was to disregard or to trivialize the issues of gender difference and domestic attachments. Yet they each employed gender imagery and periodically sought to define the moral status of marriage. Inasmuch as their thinking did touch on these issues, they both played unwitting but significant parts in constructing the sentimental outlook toward women and marriage that was emerging in the middle of the eighteenth century. Their sporadic and often inconsistent comments about these matters also reveal underlying tensions in their moral theories. These tensions point to the intrusion of their complex personal relationships and deep-seated cultural assumptions about women into the seemingly gender-neutral structure of their thought.

To my knowledge, Edwards left no sustained discussion of his views on women or on love between the sexes. What documentation exists consists of several pieces of indirect evidence: his philosophical speculations about the relationship of the so-called natural affections and instincts to true virtue; his use of examples of women and sexual transgressions in his evangelical writings and ministry; and a few moving expressions of his love for his wife, Sarah. Taken together and set against the backdrop of major events in his life and the general development of his thought, these scattered bits and pieces fall into a discernible pattern.

Edwards was essentially of two minds about the moral status of love between women and men. He held, on the one hand, that love between human beings could be spiritual and, on the other, that such love was fundamentally selfish and instinctual. At times he elevated love above sex and self-interest, at other times he reduced it to them. Similarly torn between an idealization of female spirituality and an abhorrence of female seductiveness, he vacillated in his religious use of feminine symbolism. His overt position was always, of course, to maintain the genderless and transcendent quality of grace. Toward the end of his life, partly in response to pivotal experiences in his own marriage and ministry, this insistence finally drove him to assume a more absolute position equating love between the sexes with sinful self-love. This position was never, however, entirely consistent, and, despite all his efforts to differentiate love of God from human love, an ambiguous and suggestive connection remained between them.

No concept was as fundamental to Edwards's thought as love. The "first and chief" affection propelling the will, love caused desire, hope, joy, and gratitude; the negative affections of hatred, fear, and anger resulted from the absence of love.[4] Love was, he wrote in his **"Notes on the Bible,"** "the sum of all saving virtue."[5] The most holy affection, love of God, was for him the essence of religious experience, the source of beauty, and the basis of virtue. The all-inclusive object of this spiritual love, which Edwards termed "being in general," of course rendered it different in kind from the mundane and unregenerate love of fellow human beings. Indeed, as Norman Fiering has argued, one of Edwards's major intellectual projects was to distinguish himself from the Scottish sentimentalists by denying the moral sufficiency of mere natural affections.

Yet, despite these clear intentions, problems of definition remained. On the one hand, Edwards consistently maintained that love of other human beings—whether of the opposite sex, one's children, neighbors, or humanity generally—arose from self-love rather than from true benevolence. Only love of God, which he variously called spiritual love or Christian love, was essentially selfless. On the other hand, he wavered considerably in his assessment of the morality of self-love, especially when it involved love of other people.[6] Until the early 1740s he often wrote eloquently in defense of the value of love between human beings, even allowing for an intermixture of divine and human love. Around the time of his engagement to Sarah he maintained that love between the sexes was the same "inclination" as Christ felt toward his spouse, the church. Far from hindering one's attraction to the opposite sex, "love of God only refines and purifies it."[7] Although love between human beings remained for him fundamentally an expression of self-love, it was not, he reasoned in 1732, the "simple" self-love that delights only in one's own exclusive good. Instead, the "compounded" self-love that delights in the good of another "is not entirely distinct from love of God, but enters into its nature."[8] In a 1738 sermon entitled *The Spirit of Charity the Opposite of a Selfish Spirit,* he similarly argued that the personal happiness derived from seeking the good of others "is not selfishness, because it is not a confined self-love."[9] "The self which he loves is, as it were, enlarged and multiplied, so that in those same acts wherein he loves himself he loves others. And this is the Christian spirit . . . divine love or Christian charity."[10] Condemning the wickedness of the heathen, who lacked natural affection, he strenuously objected to the "notion that no other love ought to be allowed but spiritual love, and that all other love is to be abolished as carnal, . . . and that therefore love should go out to one

another only in that proportion in which the image of God is seen in them."[11] To the contrary, he advocated love on the natural basis of family ties, even at one point claiming "the nearer the relation, the greater is the obligation to love."[12]

Edwards's dual perspective on human love as distinct from, and yet infused by, the love of God, shifted significantly sometime prior to 1755, when he published *True Virtue.* Earlier he had simply insisted that love of other people be "well-regulated" or kept "under the government of the love of God."[13] In *True Virtue,* however, he emphasized a direct antagonism between natural and religious affections. Love of other people, as he now put it, "is contrary to the tendency of true virtue" and "will set a person against general existence, and make him an enemy to it."[14] The only virtuous love was directly dependent on love of God.[15] For the regenerate, love of other human beings varied in proportion not to the nearness of their familial relationship but to the degree of their holiness. "When anyone under the influence of general benevolence sees another being possessed of the like general benevolence, this attaches his heart to him, and draws forth greater love to him."[16] Mere natural, particular love for one's children or for one's husband or wife Edwards classified as narrow and instinctual self-love, in opposition to "a principle of general benevolence."[17]

This shift in focus within his theory of human love can, as Norman Fiering has suggested, be partly explained by Edwards's increased intellectual efforts to refute the naturalistic premises of sentimental philosophy.[18] Whereas his earlier discussion of human love assumed the presence of grace, he now turned to refute the benevolists' argument for a natural, universal principal of love independent of grace. The difference between his earlier and later perspectives reflects these different intellectual premises. Yet there was a personal dimension to Edwards's intellectual development as well, involving two critical experiences of his middle age: the growing disaffection of his parish and the spiritual crisis of his wife Sarah. Patricia Tracy's study of his pastoral life shows Edwards to have been singularly preoccupied with the danger of youthful sexual transgressions, a concern that may well have reflected a painful history of adultery and divorce in his own family.[19] His sermons during the revival of 1734-35 passionately denounced both parental negligence and the "sensual filthiness" and "abominable lasciviousness" of the town's young.[20] The practices of premarital "bundling" and late-night "frolicking" received his particularly strenuous criticism.[21] Indeed, one of his chief objectives as a minister was to purify souls by divesting religious affections of dangerous sexual tendencies: " . . . certainly the mutual embraces and kisses of persons of different sexes, under the notion of Christian love and holy kisses, are utterly to be disallowed and abominated, as having the most direct tendency quickly to turn Christian love into unclean and brutish lust."[22] For this reason, he made it his policy during the revivals that informal religious meetings be sexually segregated. In his account of the 1735 Northampton revivals he focused on the conversion of a young woman, "one of the greatest company-keepers of the town," whose change of heart "seemed to be almost like a flash of lightning, upon the hearts of young people all over the town and upon many others."[23]

Successful in the short run, Edwards's efforts to arouse the consciences of the wayward young men and women of Northampton almost immediately resulted in a wave of youthful conversions. Later on, however, his tenacious efforts to enforce strict moral discipline apparently cost him the support of much of his original youthful constituency. In the "bad books" incident, he infuriated many parishioners by publicly humiliating a group of young men who had surreptitiously examined anatomical drawings of women in a midwife's manual and then knowingly jeered at a female companion.[24] In another case, Edwards tried hard to force the marriage of parents of an illegitimate child, despite the fact that their sexual affair was over and their families had already agreed on a financial settlement.[25] In these episodes Edwards acted in part to defend the reputation of women victimized by irresponsible young men, as well as to serve, as he put it, "the well being of society."[26] But instead of awakening religious consciences, these disciplinary efforts only contributed to the growing resentment of his ministry. Edwards's later categorization of love between men and women as unregenerate instinct can be understood in part as a response to his failed pastoral exertions.

The second development in his personal life that throws light on Edwards's shifting theories about human love was his wife Sarah's religious experience of 1742. In sharp contrast to his response to the sexual impulses of parish youth, his relationship with Sarah Pierrepont had from the beginning an otherworldly quality. His well-known, lyrical description of her, written shortly after they met, sets her in blissful solitary communion with nature and God: "She loves to be alone, walking in the fields and groves, and seems to have someone invisible always conversing with her."[27] However much sexual passion may have permeated their marriage, Edwards left no written record of his attraction to her. His few recorded words about their relationship stress only their attachment through faith. As he poignantly assured her on his deathbed, "the uncommon union that has so long subsisted between us has been of such a nature as I trust is spiritual and therefore will continue for ever."[28] Unlike earlier Puritans who worried lest marital love become obsessive desire and thereby displace the love of God, Edwards seems to have distinguished sharply between examples of illicit sexuality and the spiritual love of his marriage.

His idealization of Sarah's spirituality took extensive written expression only once, in *Some Thoughts Concerning the Present Revival* of 1743. Borrowing from her account of her recent religious crisis, he described it as a model spiritual experience. To a degree, his use of her as an ideal of religious piety was continuous with the promotion of female examples of faith in his previous evangelical writ-

ing. In *A Faithful Narrative* of 1736, the most salient illustrations of the glorious work of the spirit were women: the notorious loose young woman whose reformation catalyzed a round of conversions, an "aged woman" who suddenly saw scripture in a new light, the invalid Abigail Hutchinson, and the four-year-old Phoebe Bartlett. In this earlier choice of female examplars, Edwards conformed to a growing tendency among New England ministers to associate women with religious faith.[29] But what distinguished Edwards's depiction of Sarah in 1743 was precisely his refusal to identify her as a woman. His description meticulously omitted all mention of gender. The exemplary character modeled after Sarah became in print simply "the person," rupturing Edwards's earlier pattern of associating piety with femininity.

Heavily editing Sarah's own written account of her experience, Edwards expunged all references to the intimate interpersonal context of her crisis. Her version poignantly reveals her dependency on his approval of her, confessing her special sensitivity to "the esteem and love and kind treatment of my husband."[30] As she tells her story, the sources of her spiritual anxieties of 1742 were twofold, both resulting from her deep attachment to Edwards: she became upset because he reprimanded her for being tactless in a conversation with a relative, and she felt acutely jealous of the visiting minister Samuel Buell, who proved to be a more popular preacher than he.[31] After her conversion experience, she described herself as having reached a greater spiritual distance from Edwards. "If the feelings and conduct of my husband were to be changed from tenderness and affection, to extreme hatred and cruelty, and that every day, I could so rest in God that it would not touch my heart, or diminish my happiness."[32] Edwards's published rendition, to the contrary, omits this entire emotional context, only reporting briefly that the joys of grace removed the "person's" former melancholy and censoriousness.[33]

These deletions go far beyond an understandable effort to maintain anonymity. They reveal Edwards's refusal to accord the experience of human love a role in spiritual regeneration, evidence from his own marriage notwithstanding. Whereas he might well have used the occasion to expound upon the way that mortal attachments are superseded by the love of God, he eliminated the marital drama altogether. Sarah's account commendably affirmed the transcendent quality of divine love, but it also more ambiguously pointed to the religious repercussions of mundane human attachments. Edwards left out the entire interpersonal emotional process and chose to endorse only the spiritual conclusion.

Indeed, Sarah's successful disengagement from Edwards may well have pushed him still further towards disparaging the moral value of natural human love, the position he articulated most clearly in his later treatise on *True Virtue*. The scarce evidence permits only the most tentative interpretation of their emotional relationship, but Sarah's experience of religious transcendence seems to be linked to an unusual degree of tension between them. As Patricia Bonomi has suggested, perhaps 1742 marked a period of crisis in their marriage, which led to their assuming a greater emotional distance. Without expressing overt hostility, Sarah's account, written exclusively for Jonathan, dwells repeatedly on his rival's superior preaching, and in it she claims to have finally "rejoiced" over Buell's success. The spacing of the births of their children also suggests the possibility of increased estrangement. Only in 1742 did they not conceive a child within two years of the previous birth—a pattern Bonomi has found otherwise unbroken during more than twenty years of childbearing.[34] On a personal level, Sarah's religious experience and the possibly related change in their marriage can be placed alongside Edwards's disappointment in the revivals and his increased antagonism to the optimistic philosophical arguments of the British sentimentalists.[35] What he most disliked in the moral philosophers—their confidence in the benign quality of human relationships—his wife's inspiring (and perhaps also painful) emotional detachment from him had already powerfully and intimately challenged.

Corresponding to Edwards's growing pessimism about the value of human love was a revealing shift in his use of gender imagery. His earlier description of subjective religious experience had used the passive, often implicitly feminine and sexual metaphors of taste, sight, physical incorporation, and infantile dependency: "an inward sweetness," "the light of the sun," the soul "swallowed up," "intercourse . . . as a child with a father."[36] While this passively sensual language continued to be used in his later accounts, in the 1746 *Religious Affections* he employed far more aggressive and explicitly male symbolism to convey the intensity of religious affections. "The business of religion is . . . compared to those exercises, wherein men are wont to have their hearts, and strength greatly exercised and engaged; such as running, wrestling or agonizing for a great prize or crown, and fighting with strong enemies that seek our lives, and warring as those that by violence take a city or kingdom."[37] And, whereas his earlier evangelical writings had highlighted female conversion experiences, his *Life of David Brainerd* of 1749 exalted a singularly male model of piety. Bravely forsaking the comforts of family and community to venture into heathen lands, pushing himself to the point of death in the service of God, Brainerd's life of continuous "striving and violence in religion," as Edwards put it, could hardly contrast more with the childishness of Phoebe Bartlett or the sickbed confinement of Abigail Hutchinson.[38]

Despite these notable changes in both his perspective on natural affection and his use of gender symbolism, Edwards never fully resolved the thorny moral and spiritual questions posed by human love. Insisting upon the centrality of love in religious life, he equivocated in his judgments about the value of love between people, particularly in relationships between men and women. For a time he assumed an ambiguous compromise position in which human love occupied a kind of middle ground between love of God and base self-love. During the same period he publicly elevated examples of female piety, while consistently expressing abhorrence of female physical seductiveness and sexual desire. In these ways, Edwards can even be seen as indirectly contributing to the more positive evaluation of romantic love and female morality that was gradually developing in the eighteenth century. Yet, in his insistence on the absolute superiority of divine love, he powerfully resisted these sentimental implications. In the 1740s, in response to a combination of intellectual and personal experiences, he began moving toward the more extreme position taken in *True Virtue* of 1755. Uncompromising in his moral castigation of all forms of human attachment, he finally relegated love between men and women simply to the category of instinct. By instinct he first and primarily meant sexual drive. But even in this passage he equivocated, agreeing with Hutcheson and Hume that the "kind affections between the sexes" arose not only from "sensitive pleasure" but from "a disposition both to mutual benevolence and mutual complacence." He acknowledged that God implanted such affections not just to reproduce the race but to provide, more diffusely, for "the comfort of mankind."[39] The notion that human beings instinctively promote the comfort of mankind through their love of the opposite sex is not a view ordinarily associated with Edwards. For all his efforts to deflate the moral and spiritual status of human love, Edwards still left a small opening for the sentimental naturalist arguments about marriage that were gaining currency by the middle of the eighteenth century.

Franklin's relationship to the wider development of middle-class domestic morality is in many respects more straightforward. According to his basic moral philosophy, the pursuit of private, this-worldly happiness promoted rather than undermined the larger moral good. As Poor Richard once expanded on the image of a pebble thrown in a lake, he described self-love as benignly radiating outward to encompass "Friend, Parent, Neighbor, . . . all [the] human Race."[40] For Franklin there was no intrinsic conflict between promoting one's own happiness, benevolently promoting the happiness of others, and pleasing God. As he outlined strategies for achieving success, moreover, he frequently designated marriage as a key to both personal happiness and a beneficial social life. "The good or ill hap of a good or ill life," the almanac put it, "Is the good or ill choice of a good or ill wife."[41] Repeatedly, he characterized single men as "the odd halves of scissors" or as lone volumes "of a set of books."[42] "A Man without a Wife, is but half a Man."[43]

For Franklin, of course, virtue inhered not in one's inner disposition but in one's outwards acts. Just as Edwards drew from a side of Puritanism in his emphasis upon the emotional experience of grace, Franklin enlarged upon the Puritan commitment to vocations. His writing on women and marriage stressed above all the practical affairs of the domestic economy and the larger social benefits of reproducing the race. As wives, frugal and hardworking women served as invaluable assistants to upwardly mobile men.

Franklin frequently drew the equation between good wives and money. "A good Wife and Health," read one of Poor Richard's typical aphorisms, "Is a Man's best Wealth."[44] Commenting in a letter to his sister on his nephew Benny's bride, he wrote, "If she does not *bring* a fortune she will help to *make* one. Industry, frugality, and prudent economy in a wife, are . . . in their effects a fortune."[45]

As mothers, women possessed perhaps even greater value, for in Franklin's view fertility was an index to social happiness. Linked to inexpensive tastes, a high birthrate such as that found in America, he argued, stemmed from the affordability of early marriage made possible by frugal women.[46] Deploring the single life of many English acquaintances, he reported, "The great Complaint is the excessive Expensiveness of English Wives."[47] Franklin's spirited speech in the persona of the unwed mother Polly Baker satirically underscores her "natural and useful Actions" in adding citizens to the commonwealth. Far from attacking marriage, she boasts all her Franklinesque qualifications to marry, "having all the Industry, Frugality, Fertility, and Skill in Oeconomy appertaining to a good Wife's Character."[48]

For all Franklin's appreciation of the economic and reproductive aspects of marriage, he made considerably less room for intimate relationships than Edwards. The ultimate goal of personal happiness inhered, in his view, in material success, sound health, and good reputation.[49] He used the term love in a highly diffuse manner. "*Love* and be *loved*," advised an aphorism he included twice in his almanac.[50] In letters home he sent love to his wife, family, and friends with no effort to discriminate among them, once jokingly acknowledging his wish to have "everybody" love him.[51] Benevolence and efforts to make others happy ranked high for him as human virtues, but he always described the recipients of these acts impersonally. His famous discussion of the "art of virtue" altogether dispenses with such traditional interactive virtues as charity, mercy, kindness, and fidelity. The thirteen virtues included on his list were instead all purely individual and instrumental, chosen for their usefulness in the attainment of happiness for the autonomous self.[52]

Franklin's quality of individual detachment permeated not only his moral theory but his attitude toward his own life. The *Autobiography*'s well-known accounts of his own singularly unromantic courtships perhaps best illustrate this point. He indignantly broke off one engagement when he suspected the family of cheating him out of a dowry. His eventual marriage to the penniless Deborah Read, whom he had several years earlier planned to marry but had forgotten about during his trip to England, as he tells it, came only after his painful discovery that he could command no better price on the marriage market.[53] A similarly utilitarian perspective on marriage led him much later to oppose as "a very rash and precipitate step" the engagement of his daughter Sarah to the debt-ridden Richard Bache.[54]

The repeated effort to secure financial position through marriage was consistent with his apparently affectionate but doggedly practical relationship with his wife. His praise of her centered on her helpfulness in his business, her frugal and efficient housekeeping, and her unwavering loyalty. The song he composed about her for a club of male friends, entitled *I Sing My Plain Country Joan,* expressed appreciation of her down-to-earth qualities in an implicit critique of more exalted ideas of romance.[55] However genuine his regard for her, the emotional content of their marriage clearly dwindled to next to nothing through the fifteen years of separation while he was negotiating for America abroad. Their correspondence was mainly about household matters. He professed homesickness, and doubtless meant it, but was at the same time able to lead a largely satisfying life without her. She claimed that the reason she stayed home was her fear of the sea, but one suspects that both he and she preferred that the "plain country Joan" not risk embarrassment by joining him in the polite social circles of England and France.

In the meantime, beginning already prior to his departure, Franklin developed a series of personal relationships with younger people, particularly young women, to whom he freely gave paternalistic advice. Late in life, during his years in France, he especially cultivated the role of fatherly flirt. Even in his most effusive and charming moments, however, "Cher Papa," as he was known among his female admirers, characteristically used humor to keep his emotional distance.[56] An ironic tone even permeates what we know of his ostensible efforts to proposition Madame Brillon and to propose marriage to Madame Helvetius. Madame Helvetius commented to a friend that Franklin "loved people only as long as he saw them."[57]

Yet beneath Franklin's evasive humor and cool utilitarianism vied deeply conflicting conceptions of women. His scattered comments on sexuality, courtship, and marriage presented dichotomous images of women as irrelevant and invaluable, undermining and uplifting. His focus remained, of course, on men, with himself as the primary model. In the fundamentally male quest of virtue and economic success, women played a profoundly ambiguous role. For Franklin, individual self-reliance was an essential value, the key to the attainment of happiness. Yet within the context of his culture women unavoidably represented the opposite qualities of dependency and attachment. Faced with this basic problem, Franklin wavered between praising women as productive assistants and criticizing them as wasteful spendthrifts. In neither capacity could they comfortably fit into a theory extolling the achievements of autonomous males.

Just as Edwards's ideas about human love played themselves out in his portrayal of Sarah Edwards, Franklin's ambivalence about women are perhaps best revealed in his conflicting assessments of Deborah Franklin. True to his public admonitions about the financial value of a well-chosen wife, the dominant image he conveyed of Deborah was that of "a good & faithful Helpmate," hard-working and economical.[58] Toward the end of his life he fondly re-called in a letter to one of his young female correspondents: "Frugality is an enriching virtue; a Virtue I never could acquire in myself; but I was once lucky enough to find it in a Wife, who thereby became a Fortune to me."[59] The main passage about Deborah in the *Autobiography*, illustrating the proverb, "He that would thrive / Must ask his Wife," similarly counts his good fortune in having a wife "as much dispos'd to Industry & Frugality as myself."[60] Yet immediately following this proud depiction of their mutual parsimony, Franklin relates the famous anecdote about finding his breakfast one day "in a China Bowl with a Spoon of Silver." Presenting this episode as an example of the way "Luxury will enter Families, and make a Progress, in Spite of Principle," he describes his wife as having "no other Excuse or Apology to make but that she thought *her* Husband deserved a Silver Spoon & China Bowl as well as any of his Neighbors."[61] This contrary, critical view of his wife as a frivolous consumer appears most vividly in his private correspondence. His letters from England periodically remind her to be "careful of your Accounts," warning her of his declining income and even raising the specter of poverty.[62] "I know you were not very attentive to Money-matters in your best Days," he chastised her.[63] He gave her a memorandum book and pressed her, unsuccessfully, to keep a close record of her expenses.[64] In the last years of her life, while she suffered from partial paralysis and deteriorating memory, Franklin put her on an inadequate allowance and refused to acknowledge her financial difficulties, even though she was borrowing from friends.

Vacillating between his proud appreciation of Deborah's economic value and his harsh criticism of her excessive expenditures, Franklin seems to have been genuinely unsettled in his basic evaluation of her worth as his wife. This double image of her as both frugal and extravagant expressed Franklin's ambivalence about women generally. Especially in his relatively youthful writings of the 1720s and 1730s, women often appear as vain, lazy, irresponsible, and hopelessly addicted to the latest expensive fashions.[65] His essay on the industrious Anthony Afterwit, driven to despair by his wife's status-seeking and luxurious taste, seems modeled, in part, on his own experience with Deborah's purchase of the china bowl and silver spoon.[66] Repeatedly, in his public and private writings, he juxtaposed the symbols of tea tables and spinning wheels: "Many estates are spent in the getting/Since women for tea forsook spinning and knitting."[67] Often Franklin issued his warning against female acquisitiveness in the context of a comic battle of the sexes. In the opening issues of *Poor Richard's Almanack,* for example, Richard's wife Bridget, whom he regards as "excessive proud," carps at him about their poverty and the necessity of her "spinning in her shift of tow" while he uselessly gazes at stars.[68] In addition to impugning them for their vanity, Franklin frequently caricatured women as malicious gossips, overly talkative, and domineering.[69] He ridiculed the sexual pride of aging, unwanted spinsters who had found too many faults with suitors when young and poked fun at the unfulfilled needs of frustrated widows and old maids.[70]

Taken together, these numerous misogynist pieces depict women as sexually demanding, haughty, and contentious. In keeping with these images, Franklin himself occasionally used the comic mask of a female pseudonym in order brazenly to publicize controversial opinions and attack adversaries.[71] At one point, following Defoe, the young Franklin even had the forceful widow Silence Dogood argue for better female education on the grounds that female failings were mostly due to ignorance, a position that, however, Franklin never espoused elsewhere.[72] Instead he insisted that the proper antidote to overbearing women was male domination. As Poor Richard put it, "Ill thrives that hapless Family that shows / A Cock that's silent and a Hen that crows."[73] Objecting in the *Pennsylvania Gazette* to a recent critique of marriage as a form of slavery for women, Franklin responded, "Every Man that is really a Man is Master of his own Family; and it cannot be Bondage to have another submit to one's Government."[74]

Later on, beginning in the 1740s, Franklin increasingly developed a less hostile (if also less humorous) outlook on women and marriage. Whereas in the early issues of *Poor Richard,* only lawyers receive as much ridicule as wives, after 1738, and especially after 1748, the number of verses and aphorisms that comment on women or marriage dramatically declined.[75] The few that are printed were notably less misogynist as well, giving way to practical recommendations to marry and sensible bits of advice about the prudent choice of a spouse.[76] By 1746 even the acrimonious Richard and Bridget had settled into an idyllic, harmonious, and prosperous married life.[77]

Occasionally in this later period Franklin even espoused a more sentimental attitude. One verse extolled women's benign, civilizing influence; another claimed that men were drawn to women not by their bodies but by their "souls."[78] Deploring the destructive influence of sophisticated taste and high fashion, pieces that dispensed marital advice idealized uncorrupted wives for their "native Innocence," being "form'd in Person and in Mind to please."[79] In other writings as well, Franklin increasingly underscored the benign aspects of innate gender differences. "It is the Man and Wife united that make the compleat human Being," he wrote in his famous 1745 letter on the choice of a mistress; "Separate, she wants his Force of Body and Strength of Reason; he, her Softness, Sensibility, and acute Discernment."[80] Women, he variously observed in the later decades of his life, were less rivalrous and more impressionable than men.[81] In a letter to Madame Brillon of 1780 he went so far as to claim to trust feminine intuition more than male intellect, "for women, I believe, have a certain feel, which is more reliable than our reasonings."[82]

In the end, however, for all these lighthearted concessions to a sentimental ideal of women, Franklin remained as much opposed to idealized expressions of romantic love as Edwards. As he wrote characteristically in a spoof on hot air balloons in the Parisian press, "an element ten times lighter than inflammable air" can be found "in the promises of lovers and of courtiers and in the sighs of our widowers."[83] The dominant tendency of his thought held that virtue was a quality of autonomous males, an attitude well illustrated by the membership restriction in his proposed United Party of Virtue to "young and single Men only."[84] According to his proverbial expression, "it is hard for an empty Sack to stand upright," virtue hinged on the achievement of economic independence.[85] As dependents, women were at best aides, at worst parasites, in this prototypically masculine quest. The fundamental lack of clarity in Franklin's view of women—the vacillation among images of vain and impulsive consumers, industrious helpmates, and intuitive innocents—suggests the underlying difficulty he had determining the relationship of women to his model of the self-reliant, upwardly mobile man. For Edwards, to the contrary, virtue was a quality of genderless saints in communion with God, extended diffusely to all people as part of "being in general." Both men stopped well short of a sentimental conception of women or of love between human beings. In this, though in sharply contrasting ways, both remained faithful to their common Puritan past.

Yet, in other respects, each of them unwittingly helped set the stage for the transformed gender ideology of the late eighteenth century. In his depiction of female exemplars of piety, Edwards took measured steps in the direction of upholding a female standard of virtue. Even the elderly Franklin did so briefly in his extravagant statements about female moral intuition and judgment. Still more importantly, however, Edwards's insistence upon the centrality of love in religious life, coupled with his ambiguous description of the spiritual and moral status of human attachments, point toward more positive interpretations of martial love. Franklin's most decisive contribution lay instead in the formulation of a new male utilitarian standard of virtue. Although he himself only vaguely and inconsistently endorsed an alternative feminine ideal, he defined the male standard against which the sentimental female one was quick to emerge.

Despite the fact that neither of these figures systematically addressed the issue of gender or romantic love, their sketchy and often contradictory depictions of women and marriage point to their troubled ambivalence as much as their intellectual indifference. To a degree, their difficulties with the subject can be understood biographically as the product of each of their very different relations to women. When considered from a wider historical perspective, however, both the omissions and the inconsistencies point to their transitional position as theorists of human psychology and morality. Edwards's towering achievement consisted in integrating modern moral philosophy with Calvinist pietism, an accommodation that problematized the relationship between religious and natural affections despite his own repeated efforts to draw a sharp distinction between them. Franklin, too, was poised between Puritanism and contemporary secular thought, in his case balancing a traditional commitment to hard work and frugality—

norms he applied to men and women both—against a more resolutely masculine and utilitarian endorsement of the value of individual economic success. Romantic love between men and women, I would suggest, symbolized the ambiguous and even threatening element of human interdependence and emotional fusion. While these two intellectuals managed for the most part to avoid this increasingly troublesome issue, it would emerge with full force in the sentimental literature and religious moralizing of the following generation.

Acknowledgments: I should like to thank Joyce Appleby, Patricia Bonomi, Daniel Walker Howe, and Thomas Shafer for their helpful readings of an earlier draft of this paper.

Notes

1. The many works on the Puritan family and women from which this paragraph is drawn include Edmund S. Morgan, *The Puritan Family: Religion and Domestic Relations in Seventeenth-Century New England,* rev. ed. (New York, 1966); Laurel Thatcher Ulrich, *Good Wives: Image and Reality in the Lives of Women in Northern New England, 1650-1750* (New York, 1980); Carol F. Karlsen, *The Devil in the Shape of a Woman: Witchcraft in New England* (New York, 1987); Margaret Masson, "The Typology of the Female as a Model for the Regenerate," *Signs: Journal of Women in Culture and Society,* 2 (1976): 304-15; and Gerald F. Moran, "Sisters' in Christ: Women and the Church in Seventeenth-Century New England," in *Women in American Religion,* ed. Janet Wilson James (Philadelphia, 1980), pp. 47-65.

2. The less extensive literature on this transitional period includes Nancy F. Cott, *The Bonds of Womanhood: Women's 'Sphere' in New England, 1780-1835* (New Haven, 1978); Linda Kerber, *Women of the Republic: Intellect and Ideology in Revolutionary America* (Chapel Hill, N.C., 1980); Mary Beth Norton, *Liberty's Daughters: The Revolutionary Experience of American Women, 1750-1800* (Boston, 1980); and Ruth H. Bloch, "The Gendered Meanings of Virtue in Revolutionary America," *Signs: Journal of Women in Culture and Society,* 11 (Fall 1987): 37-58. On Scottish moral philosophy, see Norman Fiering, *Jonathan Edwards's Moral Thought and Its British Context* (Chapel Hill, N.C., 1981); Daniel Walker Howe, "Why the Scottish Enlightenment Was Useful to the Framers of the American Constitution," *Comparative Studies in Society and History, 31* (July 1989): 572-87; and John Dwyer, *Virtuous Discourse: Sensibility and Community in Late Eighteenth-Century Scotland* (Edinburgh, 1987).

3. See especially Elisabeth D. Dodds, *Marriage to a Difficult Man: The 'Uncommon Union' of Jonathan and Sarah Edwards* (Philadelphia, 1971); Claude-Anne Lopez, *Mon Cher Papa: Franklin and*

the Ladies of Paris (New Haven, 1966); and Claude-Anne Lopez and Eugenia W. Herbert, *The Private Franklin: The Man and His Family* (New York, 1975).

4. *WJE, 2:* 107-8.

5. *The Works of President Edwards,* ed. Sereno Dwight, 10 vols. (New York, 1830), *9:* 511.

6. See also Fiering, *Edwards's Moral Thought,* pp. 150-199.

7. "Miscellanies," no. 189, as quoted in *WJE, 8:* 617-18, n. 3. Thomas Shafer alerted me to this passage and pointed out that JE probably wrote it in the spring or early summer of 1725, about the time of his engagement.

8. "Miscellanies," no. 530, in *The Philosophy of Jonathan Edwards from His Private Notebooks,* ed. Harvey G. Townsend (Eugene, Ore., 1955), pp. 203-4.

9. *WJE, 8:* 258.

10. *Ibid.*

11. *Ibid., 4:* 469-70.

12. "Great Care Necessary, Lest We Live in Some Way of Sin" (1734), *Works of President Edwards,* 4 vols., (New York, 1843), *4:* 522.

13. *WJE, 4:* 470. Fiering notes that JE turned his full attention to exposing the deceptions of self-love only in *True Virtue* (though there are earlier foreshadowings in "Miscellanies" nos. 473 and 534 of the earlier 1730s). See Fiering, *Edwards's Moral Thought,* p. 174.

14. *WJE, 8:* 555.

15. *Ibid.,* pp. 558-59.

16. *Ibid.,* p. 546. See also pp. 545, 571. This argument is presaged in *WJE, 2:* 257.

17. *WJE, 8:* 605.

18. Fiering, *Edwards's Moral Thought,* pp. 174, 197.

19. Patricia J. Tracy, *Jonathan Edwards, Pastor: Religion and Society in Eighteenth-Century Northampton* (New York, 1979), pp. 56, 218-19, n. 38.

20. "The Justice of God in the Damnation of Sinners" (1735), *Works of President Edwards, 4:* 233-34. For a long quotation from this sermon, see Tracy, *Jonathan Edwards,* pp. 81-82. See also *WJE, 4:* 146.

21. "Joseph's Great Temptation and Gracious Deliverance," *Works of President Edwards, 4:* 595-96.

22. *WJE, 4:* 468.

23. *Ibid.,* p. 149.

24. Tracy, *Jonathan Edwards,* pp. 160-64; Thomas H. Johnson, "Jonathan Edwards and the 'Young Folks' Bible," *New England Quarterly,* 5 (1932): 437-514.

25. Tracy, *Jonathan Edwards,* pp. 164-66; Kathryn Kish Sklar, "Culture Versus Economics: A Case of Fornication in Northampton in the 1740s," *University of Michigan Papers in Women's Studies,* Special Issue, May 1978, pp. 35-56.

26. Sklar, "Culture Versus Economics," p. 45, as quoted from Jonathan Edwards Papers, Folder n.d. 2, item 15, Andover Newton Theological School, Newton Centre, Mass.

27. Sereno E. Dwight, *The Life of President Edwards* (New York, 1830), pp. 114-15.

28. *Ibid.,* p. 578.

29. *WJE, 4:* 158. On earlier feminine religious imagery, see Moran, "'Sisters' in Christ," and Masson, "The Typology of the Female."

30. Dwight, *Life of President Edwards,* p. 172.

31. *Ibid.,* pp. 171-72. For a similar interpretation, see Julie Ellison, "The Sociology of 'Holy Indifference': Sarah Edwards' Narrative," *American Literature, 56* (1984): 479-95.

32. Dwight, *Life of President Edwards,* p. 183.

33. *WJE, 4:* 334-35.

34. Patricia Bonomi, "Comment," unpublished paper, National Conference on Jonathan Edwards and Benjamin Franklin, Yale University, February 24, 1990.

35. Fiering, *Edwards's Moral Thought,* p. 174.

36. Dwight, *Life of President Edwards,* pp. 60-61, 65, 132-33; *WJE, 4:* 194-95, 332.

37. *WJE, 2:* 100.

38. *Ibid., 7:* 500.

39. *Ibid., 8:* 603-5.

40. *PBF, 3:* 5.

41. *Ibid.,* p. 8; also *2:* 9.

42. *Ibid., 15:* 184; *The Works of Benjamin Franklin,* 10 vols. (New York, 1904), *10:* 81; *Autobiography and Other Writings,* ed. Kenneth Silverman (New York, 1986), p. 207.

43. *PBF, 5:* 471; see also *2:* 396.

44. *Ibid., 3:* 62; see also *2:* 5, and *Autobiography,* ed. Silverman, p. 88.

45. *PBF, 7:* 216; see also *3:* 479-80.

46. *Ibid., 4:* 227-43.

47. *Ibid., 9:* 175.

48. *Ibid., 3:* 120-25.

49. On how BF's definition of happiness reduces to the instrumental satisfaction of natural, physical wants,

see Herbert Schneider, *The Puritan Mind* (New York, 1930), p. 251; Flower and Murphey, *History of Philosophy, 1:* 110-11.

50. *PBF, 6:* 324; also *5:* 471.

51. Benjamin Franklin, *Dr. Benj. Franklin and the Ladies* (Mt. Vernon, N.Y., 1939), pp. 17-18.

52. *The Autobiography of Benjamin Franklin,* ed. Leonard Labaree *et al.* (New Haven, 1964), pp. 91-92.

53. *Ibid.,* pp. 74-75.

54. *PBF, 15:* 185.

55. *Ibid., 2:* 353-54.

56. These relationships are described vividly in Lopez, *Mon Cher Papa.*

57. *Ibid.,* pp. 261-62.

58. *Autobiography,* ed. Labaree, p. 76.

59. "To Miss Alexander," Passy, June 24, 1782, in *Dr. Benj. Franklin and the Ladies,* p. 32.

60. *Autobiography,* ed. Labaree, p. 88.

61. *Ibid.,* pp. 88-89.

62. *PBF, 6:* 425, and *14:* 193-94.

63. *Ibid., 18:* 91.

64. *PBF, 7:* 167-68, and *10:* 100-01.

65. See, for example, *PBF, 1:* 21-23, 240-43.

66. *Ibid.,* pp. 237-40. Also see Gary E. Baker, "He That Would Thrive Must Ask His Wife: Franklin's Anthony Afterwit Letter," *Pennsylvania Magazine of History and Biography, 109* (January 1985): 27-41.

67. *PBF, 1:* 315. See also pp. 100 and 239; and *The Private Correspondence of Benjamin Franklin,* 2 vols. (London, 1817), *1:* 42.

68. *PBF, 1:* 311. See also *2:* 137, 169, 191, 371.

69. For example, *ibid., 1:* 39-40, 243-48, 316, and *2:* 139, 223, 235, 369, 400.

70. *Ibid., 1:* 37-38; *2:* 166-67, 251, 399; *3:* 65.

71. Examples are the pseudonyms Silence Dogood, *ibid., 1:* 8-46; Cecilia Single, pp. 20-43; and Martha Careful and Caelia Shortface, pp. 112-13.

72. *PBF, 1:* 18-21.

73. *Ibid.,* p. 356.

74. *Ibid., 2:* 22-23.

75. Whereas I counted twenty-two short pieces on women and marriage in the almanac from 1733 through 1738 (3.6 per issue), there were only ten in 1739-44 (1.6 per issue), twelve in 1745-50 (2 per issue), and two in 1751-58 (less than 0.5 per issue).

76. For example, *PBF, 2:* 294; *3:* 62; *5:* 471.

77. *Ibid., 3:* 60.

78. *Ibid.,* pp. 65, 66.

79. *Ibid.,* pp. 103, 342.

80. *Ibid.,* pp. 30-31.

81. *Ibid., 8:* 92.

82. Letter to Mme Brillon, November 29, 1780, as quoted in Lopez, *Mon Cher Papa,* p. 82.

83. Lopez, *Mon Cher Papa,* p. 222.

84. *Autobiography,* ed. Labaree, pp. 103-5.

85. *Ibid.,* p. 106.

Abbreviations

PBF: *Papers of Benjamin Franklin* (New Haven, Yale Univ. Press, 1959–)

WJE: *Works of Jonathan Edwards* (New Haven, Yale Univ. Press, 1957–)

Stephen R. Yarbrough (essay date 1993)

SOURCE: "The Edwardsean Legacy," in *Delightful Conviction: Jonathan Edwards and the Rhetoric of Conversion,* edited by Stephen R. Yarbrough and John C. Adams, Greenwood Press, 1993, pp. 79-93.

[In the following essay, Yarbrough discusses the visible influence of Edwardsean thought on the work of the theologians and philosophers who came after Edwards, as well as the less visible effect of Edwards's theology on American literary writers, as exemplified by Harriet Beecher Stowe.]

Describing Jonathan Edwards' influence is a difficult task, speculative, if not necessarily revisionist, at best. In the first place, influence is itself an extraordinarily problematic critical concept. Its mechanisms, although clarified considerably by Harold Bloom, remain subject to a strenuous debate.[1] Second, Edwards as a minister and theologian was so very self-consciously orthodox that distinguishing his influence from that of other Congregationalists is, in many instances, impossible.

Publication history complicates the problem, for although when he died many of Edwards' sermons and treatises were in print, the notebooks containing his metaphysical speculations were not; and if we, nearly two and a half centuries later, can easily discern the relationship between his metaphysics and his theology, we can also doubt that those coming immediately after Edwards could detect the ramifications of his peculiar formulations. As we have seen, even after some of the more important documents were collected, edited, and published in 1829, Sereno Dwight's misdating of these materials led scholars to misjudge their importance to his mature work.

Finally, we have the problem of historicity: an audience's situation will always condition any judgments of Edwards' significance. Critics have labeled Edwards as a thinker "representative" of his culture, as "the last Medieval American" (*LM* 116), and as a pre-modernist revolutionary misunderstood by his benighted contemporaries. These judgments and others like them say as much or more about the critics' own times and predilections as they do about Edwards. The present study, as well, is no different.

Written in the postmodern era, this study cannot but describe Edwards' work through discursive strategies in many ways completely foreign to him—indeed, foreign to Edwards scholars until very recently. For example, Edwards' theory of language, described by Miller and others as being influenced by Locke, as no doubt it is, seems more structural, if not poststructural, than empirical when we note that Edwards' differentiation between the speculative and sensible relationships to signs—which he believed to be his most important philosophical distinction—rests upon his claim that the ideas to which signs refer derive their ideality from a framework or context of ideas and signs.

As we have seen, for Edwards these frames may be more or less "excellent"; that is, they may in varying degrees approximate the total, infinite frame of God's consciousness. Since reference to this total frame is unattainable except through divine influence, without that influence the truth, even when written plainly in the Bible, is, in postmodern parlance, "undecidable," illusory. Thus Edwards' contention—that "the universe is one vast general frame consisting of an innumerable multitude of lesser frames," and that if it were not for God one random "wandering particle" would be sufficient to "destroy the harmony" of the whole system (*PJE* 101)—sounds remarkably like a tenet of Derridean deconstruction.

A postmodernist such as Barbara Johnson can ask, "If 'comprehension' is the framing of something whose limits are undeterminable, how can we know what we are comprehending?" (J 336). Her final answer seems uncannily familiar: "If we could be sure of the difference between the determinable and the undeterminable, the undeterminable would be comprehended within the determinable. What is undecidable is whether a thing is decidable or not" (J 349). As Edwards would have put it in his time, if we could be sure of the difference between faith and apostasy, then faith would not be faith, but apostasy. Precisely *what* we must believe is *that* we must believe.

Similarly, Edwards' reconfiguration, or abandonment, of faculty psychology may seem to modern eyes "as far from the psychology of our time as from that of the middle ages" ("CCEB" 207), but to the postmodernist, his characterizing the self as a mirror image may seem to foreshadow Jacques Lacan's revision of Freud's substantive ego into a positioned subject. Edwards explicitly rejects Locke's definition of personal identity as the continuity of consciousness, that is, as an explicitly maintained referral to personal memories.

From a post-Lacanian perspective, this rejection is more than a philosophical tour de force designed to avert Arminian attacks upon original sin. More than explaining how the soul may be responsible for an act it did not perform and cannot remember, Edwards' description of "dependent identity" (*OS* 400)—the notion that personal identity is not self-perpetuating but is generated through repeated references to an original pattern—serves to explain not only why "men may be and often are ignorant of their own hearts" (*PJE* 73), that is, why they may be unconscious of their true motivations, but also why they may be incapable of acting upon their conscious, rational judgments. Essentially, Edwards describes the fallen self as a floating signifier that no longer has its "place" within a semiotic system. At least his descriptions of degeneracy can be read that way.

If, historically distant as we are from Edwards' writing, we discover embryonic formulations of present-day concerns, how much more so may Edwards' language have provided rhetorical patterns guiding subsequent writers' arguments, some perhaps subverting Edwards' original. Whether specific ideas, concerns, terminology, or rhetorical strategies, what is passed down may transform in meaning considerably as it assumes a new function in a new situation. Similarly, a later writer employing an entirely different style, diction, and genre may be furthering a purpose a prior writer originally conceived. Thus, a later writer's relation to an earlier may be essentially conservative, one fully intending to pass on the legacy, however it may be (mis)conceived, to the next generation; it may be antagonistic, fully intending to discredit and disempower; or it may be agonistic and revisionary, diverting earlier rhetorical energies into new channels and new purposes.

INFLUENCE VISIBLE

Since the present book is concerned with rhetorical influence, and specifically with the influence of Edwards' conversion rhetoric, we will discuss only briefly Edwards' undeniable, visible influences—on writers after Edwards who specifically defended, extended, modified, or attacked his work. These influences could include his impact not only upon subsequent theological and philosophical developments, what we might call the conceptual legacy, but also upon American religious and social history, or what we might call the ministerial legacy. The latter, however, is confined primarily to the effects of Edwards' revivalist activities, and these, as we have seen, were not unique to Edwards, except for his immediately influential published defenses of the revival.

The conceptual legacy was passed, first and foremost, to a group of disciples who taught and wrote during the decades immediately following Edwards' death. These leaders of the New Divinity movement, as its detractors labeled it, included Joseph Bellamy (1719-90), Samuel Hopkins (b. 1721), Jonathan Edwards, Jr. (1754-1801), and Nathaniel Emmons (1745-1840). Clearly, each of these men intended to conserve, explicate, and expand Edwards' theology. Whether they preserved it or killed it has been a matter of debate. Most recent scholars, taking their cue from Sydney E. Ahlstrom's *A Religious History of the American People* (1972), have concluded along with him that Edwards "did not have a single disciple who was true to his essential genius" (*RHAP* 311) and that the New Divinity, in particular, "degraded Puritan theology by turning it into a lifeless system of apologetics" (*RHAP* 405).

Ahlstrom attributes the continuing degradation of Edwards' subtler thought to the simple fact that "no generation has been able to read and consider Edwards's complete works" (*RHAP* 312). Other scholars blame the decline on historical factors. Conrad Cherry, for instance, follows Joseph Haroutunian in his claim that, with the coming of the humanitarian movement, even for Calvinists moralism began to replace pietism (*PVM*). Cherry, claiming that the New Divinity took "the first step down the path to making theology legal in emphasis and nature didactic in import" (*NRI* 70), believes that "much of the theological preoccupation with law was a consequence of the self-confident democratic feelings spreading in the New Republic" (*NRI* 68).

Other scholars position their explanation of the New Divinity's decline from Edwards nearer to Ahlstrom's point about textual unavailability. James Hoopes, for example, suggests that because key Edwardsean texts remained unpublished, Edwards' disciples were "unaware of his idealist metaphysics" and consequently "unwittingly played into enemy [i.e., Arminian and Antinomian] hands by accepting the Lockean notion of the soul as a substance formed by experience" ("CCEB" 208 215). Ultimately, Hoopes contends, second-generation post-Edwards figures such as Lyman Beecher, who accepted the Lockean definition of substantive identity, would repudiate those fundamental Edwards doctrines—on free will, original sin, and infant damnation—that relied upon Edwards' repudiation of Locke's definition.

Unlike Ahlstrom, Haroutunian, Cherry, and Hoopes, some recent historians, most notably William Breitenbach, have decried the "myth" that Edwards' "most loyal disciples have been [his] betrayers" (B 177). Arguing against the "piety-versus-moralism" model of Puritan studies, Breitenbach discredits the "plot" typically imposed upon New England's religious history: "This interpretation, familiar to all students of American religion, describes a pure theocentric piety descending from the crags of Calvinism by way of covenant theology and worldly prosperity into the meadows of moralism, Arminianism, and Unitarianism, and finally losing itself—some would say, finding itself—in the swamps of Transcendentalism" (B 178).

Breitenbach strenuously objects to those who cast the New Divinity ministers either as fighting against or collaborating with encroaching moralists. No battle between Moralists and Pietists took place. To the contrary, the "*dominant* New England theological tradition," he asserts, "the clerical orthodoxy, was one of piety *and* moralism." Both Ed-

wards and his New Divinity disciples followed in this tradition, occupying "the familiar middle ground, defending it against the extremes of Antinomianism and Arminianism" (B 179).

In many respects, Breitenbach's defense of the New Divinity is quite convincing. Nevertheless, it cannot be denied that even Edwards' most talented followers tended to overemphasize tenets that Edwards himself more carefully conditioned. For example, Bellamy insisted that God permits sin in order to perfect the universe, and Hopkins extended the concept of "disinterested benevolence" toward the "complete willingness to be damned if it be for the greater glory of God" (*RHAP* 408). This extension, as we have seen, is rhetorically implied, in some Edwardsean sermons, but it ignores the Edwardsean caveat that self-love is persistent, so that the self one is willing to damn is only one's "old" self.

After the New Divinity, the most important reform movement began with Timothy Dwight (1758-1817), Jonathan Edwards' grandson, president of Yale, and founder of the New Haven Theology. Dwight is known primarily for continuing his grandfather's tradition of promoting a mutually supportive relationship between Protestantism and empirical science while opposing Deistic claims of the sufficiency of natural religion.

Dwight's followers, including Lyman Beecher (1775-1863) and Nathaniel William Taylor (1786-1858), ushered in the Second Great Awakening, which occurred between 1797 and 1801. Taylor, Dwight's secretary and most promising student at Yale, provided the movement's intellectual foundation. Like Dwight, he was as strongly influenced by the Scottish Common Sense school as he was by Edwards. His greatest contribution was his clarification of Edwards' defence of original sin. As Ahlstrom puts it, "Taylor's fundamental insistence was that no man becomes depraved but by his own act" (*RHAP* 420). Sin, although inevitable, is not causally necessary. As we have seen, Edwards argued precisely this in his ***Original Sin.*** Oddly, Taylor, perhaps overly influenced by Arminian arguments against Edwards, presumed that he was correcting Edwards.

Taylor did go on to differ from Edwards, however, when he claims that man is never completely a determined part of nature but has always a "power to the contrary"—a capacity to negate the inclinations. Edwards, of course, would have replied that that is why men may act civilly out of self-love. Taylor's revision of Edwards provided a pseudo-Calvinistic justification for the humanitarian efforts, social benevolence, and moral reform movements—including temperance and abolition—that would characterize late eighteenth- and nineteenth-century American religion.

In Taylor's writing, the encyclopedic ideal and the notion of God as Moral Governor, both found in Edwards' continuation of the Richardsonian tradition, shifted emphasis. Edwards did indeed identify good actions with obedience, but for him devotion was the ultimate end of Christian practice. For Taylor, also, "the design of God's government" was "the happy harmony of the whole," but for him Christian practice resolved in the production of happiness for others (*NRI* 118-19). Edwards, no doubt, would have leveled the same argument at Taylor that he did at the Deists Taylor would abhor: like the watch found on the beach, the harmony of its parts is to no avail unless it serves the purpose intended by its maker. As Conrad Cherry has explained, in Taylor's view "the happiness which God is disposed to accomplish was not Edwardsean joyful appropriation and reflection of the power of God's presence; it was, instead, 'the love of doing good'" (*NRI* 125).

Taylor, Dwight, and other New Haven theologians were the last important American writers who depended significantly on Jonathan Edwards' work and reputation. Others, certainly, read and responded to his work, including Unitarians such as William Ellery Channing (1780-1842), who abandoned fundamental Calvinistic doctrines such as the trinitarian godhead, predestination, and original sin. Paradoxically, more so than the New Haven group, he saw human striving's end in communion with God and grace's end in disinterested benevolence. However, as his biographer Arthur W. Brown has pointed out, although in his early years Channing's "sense of piety was in kind and degree not very dissimilar from that of Jonathan Edwards," in later years "Edwardean piety would disappear; and he would love mankind for its dynamic potential of human goodness" (*WEC* 28). Like the Scottish philosophers Channing admired, he would come to believe in conscience as an inborn impulse toward benevolent feeling. Other Unitarians, such as Ralph Waldo Emerson, would move into Transcendentalism, in direct opposition to, if not disdain of, trinitarian Congregationalism and institutional religion in general.

Horace Bushnell (1802-76) was perhaps the only nineteenth-century American writer to display any real Edwardsean spirit. A student of Nathaniel Taylor's, Bushnell maintained the essential Calvinist doctrines of original sin and the need for grace. Drawing heavily upon European romantic thought and literature, Bushnell, according to Cherry, "recovered a symbolic view of religious truth very much like that of Jonathan Edwards" (*NRI* 159). Like Edwards, he focused sharply upon the problem of language as being central to the religious problem, although Coleridgean influence led him, of course, in quite different directions. Moreover, unlike most of his contemporaries who saw the proper end of human action in such principles as social harmony or duty to law, for Bushnell it was love, understood in a way not too distant from Edwards' consent to being. Finally, just as Edwards attempted to mediate between the New and Old Lights in his time by applying to the controversy his distinction between the sensible and the speculative, in works such as his *God in Christ* Bushnell expressed hope that his distinction between figurative and literal language would synthesize Calvinism and Unitarianism (*GIC* 85).

As social religion gained popularity in the nineteenth century, Edwards' importance declined, except perhaps as a ritual target for attacks. Mark A. Noll has noted that "during the nineteenth century at least forty-one substantial refutations of Edwards' major books appeared" ("JENT" 269). Of course, later significant influences can be traced, as Bruce Kuklick has shown with respect to John Dewey ("JEAP" 252-55) and as Sydney A. Ahlstrom has suggested of H. Richard Niebuhr (*RHAP* 940-41). For the most part, however, after 1850 Edwards' theology was less an active theological force and more a topic only of historical interest.

INFLUENCE INVISIBLE

Edwards' influence upon American literary rhetoric has been hardly touched upon by scholarship,[2] largely because that influence has been often indirect and sometimes indistinguishable from Puritanism's more general influence. Because of this lack of prior scholarship, we cannot offer an extensive survey of Edwards' unacknowledged influence upon American literary writing. Instead, we offer one example of the direction future scholarship might take.

CONFUSED CONVERSIONS: EDWARDS AND HARRIET BEECHER STOWE

From Stockbridge in the summer of 1751, Edwards wrote to the Reverend Thomas Gillespie of Carnock, Scotland, attempting to explain why he had been dismissed from his Northampton pulpit. The letter carefully, almost artfully, blames himself as much as his congregation for the strife and controversy, and it ends by weighing the success of the revivals he had engendered:

> Many may be ready from things that are lately come to pass to determine that all Northampton religion is come to nothing, and that the famed awakenings and revivals of religion in that place prove to be nothing, but strange tides of a melancholy and whimsical humor. But they would draw no such conclusion if they exactly knew the true state of the case, and would judge it with full calmness and impartiality of mind. (*GA* 565-66)

Edwards' refusal to concede the failure of the awakenings is understandable. Their perceived success justified, in his and the world's eyes, his dogma's rightness and his methods' efficacy.

Yet Edwards did concede, many times, that considerable backsliding occurred after the revivals, that most who appeared full of religion one month were obviously full of the world the next. He was, in addition, clearly distressed by the split between the New and Old Lights. His dismissal was only one of many signs that, although as a social movement the revivals were an obvious success, as instruments of spiritual change his sermons' effects were less than certain. Perhaps his sensing of that possibility made him all the more willing to be exiled from his typical audience and devote himself to writing treatises.

This much is certain: the results of Edwards' sermon rhetoric were largely unwanted. He regretted, and possibly feared, the mass hysteria, the submission to spiritual irrationality, the increased democratization and devaluation of religious authority, and the clerical community's subsequent polarization that accompanied, and can be rightly said to have resulted partially from, the sermon rhetoric he had developed.

Of course, many of these unwanted effects can be explained in terms of historical forces and conditions—economic, political, demographic, and intellectual—which would allow us to describe Edwards' audiences' responses as being well beyond his rhetorical control. At the same time, however, because later generations, including those proponents of social religion who disclaimed his Calvinist dogma, considered Edwards to be the revivalist preacher par excellence, his rhetorical techniques influenced religious conversion practices long after the historical conditions that might explain their effects had disappeared. When Edwards' conversion techniques were applied in a later age, by people of different faith, in a different genre, and yet produced analogous unwanted effects, we can conclude that the rhetorical strategies themselves were as much to blame for the effects as any extraneous factors.

One instance of such a later application ending in a similar rhetorical failure is Harriet Beecher Stowe's *Uncle Tom's Cabin*. Although Stowe's best-seller was "probably the most influential book ever written by an American" (*SD* 122), precisely because it made her into, as President Lincoln supposedly addressed her upon their meeting, "the little lady who made this big war" (*JWW* 480), it was a rhetorical failure in the sense that its effects did not match her intentions.

Today we may doubt that the book alone caused the war. In any case, as John William Ward has noted, "if *Uncle Tom's Cabin* played some small part in the coming of the war, one should remember that this is not the direction in which the book points." Stowe's "only hope" for her book, according to Ward, "was that men with changed hearts" would alter their own compliance with the horrible institution of slavery (*JWW* 492). Similarly, Jane Tompkins has argued that *Uncle Tom's Cabin* dramatized "the notion that historical change takes place only through religious conversion" (*SD* 133), and that although the book "was spectacularly persuasive in conventional political terms: it helped convince a nation to go to war," it was "a political failure" because "Stowe conceived her book as an instrument for bringing about the day when the world would be ruled not by force, but by Christian love" (*SD* 141).

If critics have noted Stowe's rhetorical failure, in the sense of her book's achieving unwanted effects, none have attempted to explain why it failed. Even Tompkins, who unlike her predecessors offers an explanation of why it achieved popularity, says only that "if history did not take the course [Stowe and other female sentimental writers]

recommended, it is not because they were not political, but because they were insufficiently persuasive" (*SD* 141).

Tompkins' explanation of the book's popular success is that it depends upon a "storehouse of assumptions" held by its predominantly female, Protestant audience, to whom it offers an alternative, matriarchal system, one in which "the home is the center of all meaningful activity" and "women perform the most important tasks" (*SD* 127 141). Yet this still does not explain the martial response of the men who went to war or of the women who encouraged them. On this question, Tompkins' answer is no more helpful than that of the male critics she chastises for regarding the book's success "as some sort of mysterious eruption, inexplicable by natural causes" (*SD* 218n).

The Civil War was the last thing Stowe wanted her book to bring about, just as democratization and spiritual irrationality were the last things Edwards wanted his sermons to bring about. For both, changing their audiences' hearts would result in the desired social goal, not the other way around. The social goal did not have to precede the individual change of heart. Edwards did not seek the millennium because then the people would convert; Stowe did not seek just law because then the people would be just. Why, then, did their audiences tend to respond inappropriately?

For both authors the problem was the same; a confusion, on their audiences' part, of conversion with persuasion. Persuasion seeks to discover common ground and then works from that ground toward mutually sharable attitudes and ideas to induce mutually desirable actions. Kenneth Burke has located the central principle of persuasion in what he calls *identification.* "You persuade a man," says Burke, "only insofar as you can talk his language by speech, gesture, tonality, order, image, attitude, idea, *identifying* your ways with his" (*RM* 55). When considered as identification, persuasion must presume that beneath divisiveness and disagreement is an underlying cohesiveness, a sameness of substance, as Burke would put it, that, once assented to, allows transformations to be worked that more coherently unify postures, ideas, goals, concepts, and so forth, that initially seemed incommensurate. For this reason, although "the rhetorician may have to change the audience's opinion in one respect . . . he can succeed only insofar as he yields to that audience's opinions in other respects" (*RM* 56). Persuasion works to resolve superficial, although perhaps divisive, differences among people who are, or who can perceive themselves as being, fundamentally identical.

Conversion, however, works on a contrary principle. It assumes that although a community's members may share the same opinions, attitudes, ideas, language—everything—in common, they may in substance differ fundamentally. Moreover, the superficially shared surface may conceal that crucial difference. Accordingly, conversion systematically dis-covers the grounds upon which individuals historically established their values and purposes, revealing the inadequacy of those grounds and the individuals' incapacity to establish proper grounds, thus preparing them to surrender unconditionally to an exterior, transcendent authority.

As we have seen, Edwards' conversion sermons, both with imagery (as in **"Sinners in the Hands of an Angry God"**) and with logic (as in **"True Grace Distinguished from the Experience of Devils"**), strive persistently to undercut the individual's confidence in his or her opinions, values, and especially attitudes. Such a dis-covering of the abyss over which the forms of personal and social identity hover is especially necessary to Calvinist conversion because the doctrine of God's sovereignty implies that finite beings are ultimately without free will. "Persuasion," as Burke reminds us, "involves choice, will; it is directed to a man only insofar as he is *free*" (*RM* 50). But conversion sermons are directed to their listeners' bound will. The sermons do not attempt to persuade listeners to choose rightly but to convince them that they cannot choose rightly and should submit to God's will.

In an eighteenth-century Puritan community like Northampton, of course, the ministerial and civic authorities represented God's will. Accordingly, the self-loathing accompanying the conversion experience could not be deflected toward the social structure that conditioned the self being loathed. At the same time, however, the self could not surrender to the social system either, even though the system stood for the transcendent authority being sought. Encyclopedic society was a complex of symbolic substitutions for an ideal subordination of self to God.

For this reason, although taken with seriousness, temporal relationships were not taken too seriously, for in the afterlife they would mean nothing. "The things and relations of this life," said Thomas Hooker, "are like prints left in Sand, there is not the least appearance or remembrance of them. The King remembers not his Crown, the Husband the Wife, Father the Child" (quoted in *PF* 20). As Edmund S. Morgan has explained:

> For a child to make too much of its parents, a wife of her husband, a subject of his king was to place the creature before the creator, to reverse the order of creation, to repeat the sin of Adam. All social relations must be maintained with a respect to the order of things, in full recognition of the fact that man "ought to make God his immediate end." (*PF* 21)

When such an attitude toward social relationships, including authoritative ones, has been so long-standing, submission to a cult of personality or to a secular system is unlikely, although, one might argue, in George Whitefield's case it may have come close. Even so, Calvinist dogma militates against the individual's directing either loathing or adulation toward the social structure and its representatives.

Thus, in a Puritan community, conversion, when it goes wrong, can go one of two ways: it can become an extra-institutional revelling in emotion among individuals persuaded to share in presumably the same joyful experience; or, for those unpersuaded whose psychic defenses are nevertheless broken by the conversion process, it can become self-destructive, perhaps suicidal. In both cases, the energy released by the systematic breakdown of the individual's self-mastery is directed inward. Conflict with others can result only when the legitimacy of the individual's experience is denied, as it was by the Old Lights. However, although an us-them mentality did arise from the Old Lights' denial, their denial could not prevent the experience. Since revivalist experience did not depend upon the cooperation of others, Edwardsean converts had no motive to coerce others to submit along with them.

For a number of reasons, the conversion strategy at work in *Uncle Tom's Cabin* produced quite different, more violent responses. Like her brother Henry Ward Beecher, Harriet Beecher Stowe may have rebelled against her grandfather Lyman Beecher's Taylorism, his inflammatory anti-Catholic agitation, and his paranoid fears of a foreign, Roman Catholic conspiracy to control the Mississippi Valley; nevertheless, she inherited from him the keen sense of conversionist strategy that had made him the most successful revivalist of the Second Great Awakening. What Stowe wished to convert her audience to, however, was poles apart from the Calvinist God of Jonathan Edwards.

In the "Concluding Remarks" of *Uncle Tom's Cabin* she addresses her readers directly, telling them exactly what they should do:

> But, what can any individual do? Of that, every individual can judge. There is one thing that every individual can do,—they can see to it that *they feel right.* An atmosphere of sympathetic influence encircles every human being; and the man or woman who *feels* strongly, healthily, and justly on the great interests of humanity, is a constant benefactor to the human race. See, then, to your sympathies in this matter! (*UTC* 472)

Stowe, like many in the humanitarian movement, discounted original sin. Though believing in a permanent principle of self-love, she and others also believed in a natural, God-created principle of "disinterested benevolence," a seat of sympathy and compassion, a divine principle informing the conscience which, because she also believed in free will, enabled the individual to contradict self-interest. A heart kept free of self-interest could feel the difference between virtue and vice.

This and similar views, developed during the eighteenth century by David Hume, Francis Hutcheson, William Wollaston, and others, came to Stowe primarily through her father and other New Divinity ministers, who were greatly influenced by them. Wollaston's description in *The Religion of Nature Delineated* is typical:

> There is something in *human* nature . . . which renders us obnoxious to the pains of others, causing us to sympathize with them. . . . It is grevous to see or hear

(and almost to hear of) any man, or even any animal whatever, in *torment.* . . . It is therefore according to *nature* to be affected with the sufferings of other people and the contrary is *inhuman* and *unnatural.* (quoted in F 249)

In *The Nature of True Virtue,* Edwards attacked the association of conscience and sympathy with virtue.[3] The assumption that sympathy was God-given and therefore God-like led ultimately to the conclusion that a benevolent God would not condemn sinners to everlasting torment, especially for a sin they had inherited and not chosen to commit. Edwards' analysis sought to show that, as Norman Fiering puts it, "The highly touted moral sense is reducible to natural conscience, which is itself reducible to a primitive sense of desert and the natural desire for logical self-consistency, or rather, to the discomfort resulting from self-contradiction" (F 147). As a result, sympathy can be misplaced and self-serving.

Earlier, in *Some Thoughts Concerning the Revival,* Edwards had linked dependence upon conscience to spiritual pride:

> But spiritual pride is the most secret of all sins. There is no sin so much like the Devil as this, for secrecy and subtlety, . . . undiscerned and unsuspected, and appearing as an angel of light. . . . It is a sin that has, as it were, many lives; if you kill it, it will live still; if you mortify it and suppress it in one shape, it rises in another; if you think it is all gone, yet it is there still. There are a great many kinds of it, that lie in different forms and shapes, one under another, and encompass the heart like the coats of an onion; if you pull one off there is another underneath. We had need therefore to have the greatest watch imaginable, over our hearts, with respect to this matter, and to cry most earnestly to the great Searcher of hearts, for his help. "He that trusts his own heart is a fool" [Prov. 28:26]. (*GA* 416-17)

Edwards would not have been surprised to hear that conversions to sympathy would contribute to the start of a bloody civil war.

Stowe's strategy of conversion to sympathy was simple: it sought to undermine the grounds for overriding the primitive, immediate, sympathetic response to others' distress that she assumed all individuals but the most corrupt felt. Thus from the beginning the strategy was more persuasive than convertive, for, being an humanitarian and not a Calvinist, she assumed that her readers, Southerners included, were fundamentally and originally good. She further assumed that two related forces had worked against her readers' natural sympathy. One was the force of habit and tradition that allowed Southerners, who witnessed slavery's horrors daily, simply not to feel in their hearts what they saw with their eyes. The other was the force of distance and abstraction that prevented Northerners from recognizing the slaves' basic humanity and allowed them to ignore their plight.

The latter case and Stowe's strategy against it is best illustrated by Chapter 9, "In Which it Appears that a Senator is But a Man." The chapter opens to a domestic scene involving Ohio state Senator Bird, who had recently returned from the legislature after arguing and winning the case for the Fugitive Slave Act of 1850, "a law," as his wife describes it, "forbidding people to give meat and drink to those poor colored people that come along" (*UTC* 91). On the senate floor, Bird, we learn later, had been

> as bold as a lion about [the Act], and "mightily convinced" not only himself, but everybody that heard him;—but then his idea of a fugitive was only an idea of the letters that spell the word,—or at most, the image of a little newspaper picture of a man with a stick and bundle, with "Ran away from the subscriber" under it. The magic of the real presence of distress,—the imploring human eye, the frail, trembling hand, the despairing appeal of helpless agony,—these he had never tried. (*UTC* 102)

Stowe's employment of Edwards' distinction between speculative and sensible knowledge is obvious here. It implies that all the Senator's legal, rational argument is founded upon an empty concept of the fugitive, a mere sign, and that "the real presence" of one living slave would confound all his logic.

This, in fact, is exactly the tactic Mrs. Bird uses in her argument against her husband's position. Better stated, Mrs. Bird refuses to argue at all. When the Senator tells her, "I can state to you a very clear argument, to show—," she interrupts, "Oh, nonsense, John! you can talk all night, but you would n't do it. I put it to you, John,—would *you,* now, turn away a poor, shivering, hungry creature from your door, because he was a runaway?" (*UTC* 93). "Clear argument" is "nonsense." The Senator's contention that "we must put aside our private feelings" is overturned by Mrs. Bird's reply that "obeying God never brings on public evils" (*UTC* 93).

The issue becomes simply whether her husband is the kind of person who could act on mere law and reason in the face of human distress. Mrs. Bird refuses to believe that he could. She counters his every attempt to defer his personal feeling, whether to duty ("You know it is n't duty,—it can't be a duty!") or to reason ("I hate reasoning, John,—especially on such subjects"). The husband is silenced; his status as a good man is, in his wife's eyes, on the line.

Shortly after this conversation, Eliza and her child appear at the Bird's home seeking asylum. The Senator sheds tears—hiding them, of course—upon witnessing their misery. He has, as the novel has told us, "a particularly humane and accessible nature" (*UTC* 93), so we are not surprised that without being asked he arranges to convey Eliza to safety. "Your heart is better than your head, in this case, John" (*UTC* 100), his wife assures him, yet the reader is well aware that John's heart is in turmoil. As he sinks into "deep meditation" while "anxiously" putting on his boots before leaving with Eliza and her son, he mutters, "It's a confounded awkward, ugly business . . . and that's a fact! It will have to be done, though, for aught I see,—hang it all!" (*UTC* 99). Because he "feels right," he has been thrown into the role of a hypocrite and criminal, and about that he cannot feel right. His conversion cannot be complete and satisfying because the system he serves is evil.

Senator Bird's predicament typifies that of Stowe's entire Northern audience. Since prior to the novel's publication the Fugitive Slave Act had been passed, what was once a Southern problem was now incontrovertibly an American problem: "Nothing of tragedy can be written, can be spoken, can be conceived, that equals the frightful reality of scenes daily and hourly acting on our shores, beneath the shadow of American law, and the shadow of the cross of Christ" (*UTC* 471). The North could no longer deny the slavery on our shores; it could no longer psychologically separate itself from the South. As John William Ward says, "No longer could it be maintained that it was 'they,' the Southerners, who supported slavery; it was 'we,' the people of the United States, who did" (JWW 488).

Stowe's novel, by making present the suffering of a people who for the North had been only abstract, distant figures—"only an idea of the letters that spell the word"—had made it possible for Northerners to feel for the slaves, but it was impossible for Northerners to "feel right" without first rectifying the system. Like Edwards, Stowe had sought to convert her readers, to undermine Southern justifications for slavery and Northern justifications for tolerating it. Like Edwards' call to repent, Stowe's call in the novel was meant for individuals. Nevertheless, she identified her audience as the "men and women of America" (*UTC* 471). Their social identity responded since it was their social identity that was condemned.

The psychology of sympathy explains why, although they came to see Southerners as part of "us" rather than as "them," Northerners were willing to exert violence toward them. In Stowe's book sympathy arises from imaginatively projecting oneself into another's situation, and the capacity for sympathy increases to the extent that the experience calling for compassion is shared. In Chapter 9, Mrs. Bird, who only a few pages before had told her husband that "folks do n't run away when they are happy" (*UTC* 93), asks Eliza why she had run away when by her own admission her master and mistress had been kind. Eliza responds by asking, "Ma'am, . . . have you ever lost a child." Mrs. Bird, bursting into tears, says, "Why do you ask that? I have lost a little one." And to this Eliza replies confidently, "Then you will feel for me" (*UTC* 97).

Consistently throughout the novel the slaves' misery demands sympathy, whereas the slave owners, such as Eliza's owners, the Shelbys, who might have been candidates for sympathy, find their demands for it undercut. Shelby, who sells Eliza's child out of the "cruel necessity" of impending foreclosure, shares his wife's self-condemnation for being "a fool to think I could make anything good out of such a deadly evil" as slavery "under laws like ours" (*UTC* 45). Their kindness is rendered cruel by the system with which they comply.

Far more unsympathetic than the Shelbys, however, is the disgusting slave trader who forced Shelby to sell the child, Haley, "a man of leather,—a man alive to nothing but trade and profit,—cool, and unhesitating, and unrelenting, as death and the grave" (*UTC* 46). Haley, more than any other single character, represents the slavery system, and he is, as Wollaston said of the unsympathetic, "*inhuman* and *unnatural.*"

In *Uncle Tom's Cabin,* those capable of sympathy characteristically respond passionately and violently toward those who act unsympathetically. Mrs. Bird was ordinarily a quiet, restrained woman: "There was only one thing that was capable of arousing her, and that provocation came in on the side of her unusually gentle and sympathetic nature;—anything in the shape of cruelty would throw her into a passion" (*UTC* 92). The book goes on to tell how once, upon finding out her sons had been involved in "stoning a defenseless kitten," Mrs. Bird "whipped them" and "tumbled" them off to bed without any supper. The moral was that the "boys never stoned another kitten" (*UTC* 92).

Beyond implying that cruelty can be stopped only if violent punishment is enforced upon those who cause it, this little tale also suggests that the violence is even more understandable when the cruel party is part of oneself, part of the sympathetic one's family. Just as Edwards' conversions produced self-loathing toward the convert's sinful self, Stowe's, too, produced self-loathing, but toward that part of "us" that necessitated the Northern sympathetic response—the Southern slave owners. In effect, Stowe's novel implicitly demanded that its Northern readers obey the biblical injunction "If thine eye offend thee, pluck it out"—in short, that they wage war against the South.

Both Edwards and Stowe assumed that the horrors they presented as the products of a sinful perspective would induce individuals to change. They did, but not always as individuals. Edwards' and Stowe's rhetoric defined, or really created, their audiences, and simultaneously it asked them to separate themselves from the evil part of the identities the rhetoric had bestowed upon them. But when they heard as an audience, they were persuaded as an audience. Edwards' and Stowe's discourse did create a desire for change, but what their audiences saw fit to do as a group proved antithetical to what the authors would have had them do as individuals. The results, rhetorically speaking, were catastrophic.

For good or ill, Jonathan Edwards' influence on American life and letters extends far deeper and more extensively than we suppose. His legacy, like his life, is quietly persistent, a gift or a curse to those who encounter it. His vision of the abyss cannot with impunity be ignored; his alternative to the abyss cannot with serenity be contemplated. Still, his conviction, although perhaps only a fantasy for postmodernity, is as delightful to imagine as it is wistful to admire.

Notes

1. Harold Bloom's theory of influence, developed in such works as *The Anxiety of Influence* (1973), *A Map of Misreading* (1975), and *Poetry and Repression* (1976), although solely a theory of poetic influence, nevertheless provides the best guide available of the various subtle forms of influence relations among writers. His main point for the present study is that later writers always and necessarily revise earlier ones, inevitably seeking with their language to conceal either their departures from or reliance upon their precursors. In Bloom's work, such revision is revealed to have psychological origins; here, however, although for the most part content simply to identify instances of influence, we are more concerned with socio-historical origins.

2. George S. Lensing's "Robert Lowell and Jonathan Edwards: Poetry in the Hands of an Angry God" (*South Carolina Review* 6 [1974]: 7-17), Robert E. Morsberger's "'The Minister's Black Veil': 'Shrouded in a Blackness, Ten Times Black'" (*New England Quarterly* 46 [September 1973]: 454-63), Mason I. Lowance Jr.'s "From Edwards to Emerson to Thoreau: A Revaluation" (*American Transcendental Quarterly* 18 [Spring 1973]: 3-12), and Melinda Kaye Willard's "Jonathan Edwards and Nathaniel Hawthorne: Themes from the Common Consciousness" (*DAI* 39 [1979]: 6136A) are among the few scholarly works devoted to examining Edwards' influence on American literature.

3. Norman Fiering has extensively analyzed the intellectual context of Edwards' arguments in *The Nature of True Virtue* (see F 139-260). Fiering argues that "Edwards' reflections on the sympathetic emotions and their meaning were largely a reaction to Hutcheson, whom he had been reading extensively in the 1750s" (F 256).

Abbreviations

B: Breitenbach, William. "Piety and Moralism: Edwards and the New Divinity." In *Jonathan Edwards and the American Experience,* ed. Nathan O. Hatch and Harry S. Stout, 177–204. New York and Oxford: Oxford University Press, 1988.

"CCEB": Hoopes, James. "Calvinism and Consciousness from Edwards to Beecher." In *Jonathan Edwards and the American Experience,* ed. Nathan O. Hatch and Harry S. Stout, 205–24. New York and Oxford: Oxford University Press, 1988.

F: Fiering, Norman. *Jonathan Edwards's Moral Thought and Its British Context.* Chapel Hill: University of North Carolina Press, 1981.

GA: Edwards, Jonathan. *The Great Awakening. See* Miller and Smith.

GIC: Bushnell, Horace. *God in Christ.* Hartford, Conn.: Brown and Parsons, 1849.

J: Johnson, Barbara. "The Frame of Reference: Poe, Lacan, Derrida." In *Contemporary Literary Criticism: Literary and Cultural Studies,* ed. Robert Con Davis and Ronald Schleifer, 322–50. 2nd ed. New York and London: Longman, 1989.

"JEAP": Kuklick, Bruce. "Jonathan Edwards and American Philosophy."

"JENT": Noll, Mark A. "Jonathan Edwards and Nineteenth-Century Theology."

JWW: Ward, John William. Afterword. *See* Stowe.

LM: Gay, Peter. *A Loss of Mastery: Puritan Historians in Colonial America.* Berkeley: University of California Press, 1966.

Miller and Smith: Miller, Perry, and John E. Smith, gen. eds. *The Works of Jonathan Edwards.* New Haven and London: Yale University Press. Vol. 1, *Freedom of the Will,* ed. Paul Ramsey, 1957; vol. 2, *Religious Affections,* ed. John E. Smith, 1959; vol. 3, *Original Sin,* ed. Clyde A. Holbrook, 1970; vol. 4, *The Great Awakening,* ed. C. C. Goen, 1972; vol. 5, *Apocalyptic Writings,* ed. Stephen J. Stein, 1977; vol. 6, *Scientific and Philosophical Writings,* ed. Wallace E. Anderson, 1980; vol. 7, *The Life of David Brainard,* ed. Norman Pettit, 1985; vol. 8, *Ethical Writings,* ed. Paul Ramsey, 1989; vol. 9, *A History of the Work of Redemption,* ed. John F. Wilson, 1989.

NRI: Cherry, Conrad. *Nature and Religious Imagination: From Edwards to Bushnell.* Philadelphia: Fortress Press, 1980.

OS: Edwards, Jonathan. *Original Sin. See* Miller and Smith.

PF: Morgan, Edmund S. *The Puritan Family: Religion and Domestic Relations in Seventeenth-Century New England.* 2nd ed. New York: Harper and Row, Harper Torchbooks, 1966.

PJE: Townsend, Harvey G., ed. *The Philosophy of Jonathan Edwards from His Private Notebooks.* Eugene: University of Oregon Press, 1955.

PVM: Haroutunian, Joseph. *Piety versus Moralism: The Passing of the New England Theology.* 1932. Reprinted. New York: Harper and Row, Harper Torchbooks, 1970.

RHAP: Ahlstrom, Sydney E. *A Religious History of the American People.* New Haven and London: Yale University Press, 1972.

RM: Burke, Kenneth. *A Rhetoric of Motives*. 1950. Reprinted. Berkeley, Los Angeles, and London: University of California Press, 1969.

SD: Tompkins, Jane. *Sensational Designs: The Cultural Work of American Fiction, 1790–1860*. New York and Oxford: Oxford University Press, 1985.

Stowe: *See UTC*.

UTC: Stowe, Harriet Beecher. *Uncle Tom's Cabin*. Afterword by John William Ward. New York and Toronto: New American Library, 1966.

WEC: Brown, Arthur W. *William Ellery Channing*. Twayne's United States Authors Series, no. 7, New Haven: College and University Press, 1961.

Joseph A. Conforti (essay date 1995)

SOURCE: "The Second Great Awakening and the Cultural Revival of Edwards," in *Jonathan Edwards, Religious Tradition, and American Culture*, University of North Carolina Press, 1995, pp. 36-61.

[In the following excerpt, Conforti traces an early nineteenth-century rekindling of interest in Edwardsean thought in American Protestantism, from the publication of the first American edition of his works in 1808 to the commemorative naming after Edwards of a new church in Northampton, Massachusetts in 1883.]

The elevation of Jonathan Edwards to a position of major cultural authority was central to the New Divinity-inspired process of creating an American revivalistic tradition. To trace the trajectory of Edwards's reputation and influence as well as the publishing history of his works is to recognize how the eminent theologian did not move toward the center of American evangelical culture until the nineteenth century. New Divinity men initiated the development of an Edwardsian structure of authority as part of the effort to transform the largely New England colonial awakening into a great, general, and formative *American* event that could be invoked to influence the course of the Second Great Awakening.[1]

The spiritual "harvests" in the Connecticut River Valley in the mid-1730s had first thrust Edwards into regional prominence. His reputation then grew with the expansion of revivals in New England in the early 1740s and with his vigorous defenses of their authenticity. But the sudden decline of religious ardor, beginning in 1743, eroded Edwards's recently established authority, a process that continued when his own congregation rebelled against him in 1750. Edwards went into exile on the Massachusetts frontier, a typical obscure settlement for a stigmatized minister. Even Edwards's call to the presidency of Princeton eight years later did little to repair the damage that the demise of revivalistic religion and the antagonism of his own congregation had done to his reputation. Edwards died within weeks of returning from his frontier exile.

To be sure, Princeton's summons demonstrated that Edwards was still highly regarded in some evangelical circles. Yet Edwards's standing in the decades after the colonial awakening must not be overestimated. High esteem, bordering on reverence, for Edwards in post-awakening America was limited to the New England wing of the Presbyterian church and to a then small group of New Divinity Congregationalists. In fact, it was in Scotland, not in America, that Edwards continued to speak to a significant audience in the second half of the eighteenth century. During those decades, Scottish Presbyterian leaders, with whom Edwards had conducted a lengthy correspondence in the 1740s and 1750s, reprinted many of the theologian's works. "It is a humiliating fact," Edwards A. Park, professor of theology at Andover Seminary, remarked a century later, "that several of Edwards's writings were sent to Scotland for publication, because our community would not patronize them." Only a few obituaries announced Edwards's tragic death in 1758, and they suggest that there was no great outpouring of grief. Moreover, Samuel Hopkins, Edwards's most devoted New Divinity disciple, who authored the first biography of the theologian and who prepared some of his works for posthumous publication, abandoned plans for a complete edition of Edwards's writings because he feared there would not be enough buyers.[2]

The first American edition of Edwards's works was not published until 1808; by then an Edwardsian cultural renaissance was underway—a phase of the New Divinity reification of the colonial awakening and creation of an American revivalistic tradition. The cultural revival of Edwards—like the transformation of the historical significance of the colonial awakening—offers persuasive evidence of how the New Divinity movement had grown in size and influence to a position of dominance within New England Congregationalism by the early nineteenth century. Once again, what the New Divinity originated, leaders of the benevolent empire extended. Denominational, interdenominational, and commercial presses inundated the antebellum evangelical community with Edwardsian publications; the American Tract Society alone published over a million copies of Edwards's works.[3] At the same time an ever-expanding religious periodical press created an Edwardsian journalistic industry which examined nearly every aspect of the eminent divine's life and thought.

Edwards's new cultural authority and his exalted place in nineteenth-century evangelical hagiography derived from three sources. First, Edwards came to be admired as a man of remarkable, even saintly, piety; his private writings were exhumed and became sacred public property that furnished a model of genuine evangelical spirituality. Second, as the "father" of the Great Awakening, Edwards was invoked as the major American authority on individual conversion and mass revivalism. Finally, the theological and metaphysical Edwards, admired abroad and vigorously promoted by New Divinity men at home, emerged as a cultural and intellectual icon whose thought was defended, "improved upon," and even occasionally wheeled out simply to "dignify" evangelical theological efforts.[4]

Evangelicals enshrined Edwards as the most distinguished eighteenth-century founding father of America's righteous empire. In the process, they sometimes cut his figure and trimmed his thought to fit the "Methodized" fashions of the day; yet, at the same time, they often summoned Edwards to restrain disquieting expressions of populism and perfectionism in antebellum piety, revivalism, and theology. The revival of Edwards involved far more than a simple rediscovery by antebellum evangelicals of the eminent divine's continuing cultural relevance. Nor was the cultural revival merely the cumulative effect of individual influence, individual interests, and individual texts. Rather, the Edwardsian revival was part of the cultural politics and cultural production of the Second Great Awakening. Edwards's cultural authority was not simply rediscovered; it was created through a process of social and cultural production that involved new religious institutions: presses and periodicals, reform societies and agencies, and theological seminaries. Moreover, the cultural revival of Edwards did not involve the retrieval of an already constituted tradition. Antebellum evangelicals created an American religious tradition around Edwards's figure. They "classicized" Edwards and his writings and in turn used his religious authority to "traditionalize" nineteenth-century piety, revivalism, and theology.

. . . . .

The contrast between the two most important early biographies of Edwards, one written after the colonial revivals and the other at the height of the Second Great Awakening, reflects the evolution of his standing in America. In 1765, Samuel Hopkins published a slim biography of Edwards that served for more than a generation as the authoritative "life" of the theologian. Hopkins's volume originated as an introductory memoir that accompanied Edwards's *Sermons on Various Important Subjects.* Hopkins completed the memoir in anticipation of the publication of other Edwardsian manuscripts and perhaps even a collected edition of the theologian's works. Such New Divinity editorial projects, however, typically failed to win the support of American publishers in the decades after Edwards's death.[5]

Though Hopkins, like other first generation New Divinity ministers, revered his mentor, he was careful not to deify Edwards. Hopkins's memoir introduced the private Edwards to the public, publishing for the first time confessional and devotional works that would become sacred Edwardsian texts—classics of evangelical spirituality—during the Second Great Awakening. Hopkins included in his life of the theologian the *Personal Narrative,* Edwards's lyrical account of his conversion, written some twenty years after the experience. Hopkins also published for the first time Edwards's youthful **"Resolutions"** for moral and spiritual development and extracts from his private diary.

For a disciple and close friend of Edwards, Hopkins exercised considerable restraint in presenting both the public and private lives of his teacher. Impelled more by familiar religious didacticism than by filiopietism, Hopkins disavowed any desire simply to "tell the world how eminently great, wise, holy and useful President Edwards was." Hopkins endeavored to write not "a mere encomium on the dead, but a faithful and plain narration of matters of fact, together with his [Edwards's] own internal exercises, expressed in his own words." Though not hiding his esteem for Edwards, even in the face of publishers' reluctance to reprint the theologian's works or to issue manuscript material that his New Divinity literary executors possessed, Hopkins saw his biography as not "so much an act of friendship to the *dead,* as of kindness to the *living;* it being only an attempt to render a life that has been greatly useful, yet more so."[6]

Hopkins's brief biography spawned other sketches of Edwards in the late eighteenth and early nineteenth centuries. But neither Hopkins's volume nor the vignettes it inspired met the needs of the cultural work of the Second Great Awakening: the invention of an American revival tradition, the reification of the colonial awakening, and the use of the past to arbitrate the religious controversies of the present. Thus, in an act of personal filiopietism that contributed significantly to the cultural production of the Second Great Awakening, Sereno Edwards Dwight published a lengthy memoir of his great-grandfather in 1829. Dwight's memoir served as the introductory volume to a collected edition of Edwards's works.[7] While other collected editions were already available in America, none provided the kind of biographical information that Dwight, the principal custodian of Edwards's papers, presented. More than 600 pages long, Dwight's volume ranked as one of the most detailed American biographies published up to that point and testified to the enormous evangelical interest in Edwards. Where Hopkins had published only about half of Edwards's youthful **"Resolutions"** on moral and spiritual development, Dwight included all seventy. Where Hopkins had only partially opened a window on Edwards's domestic life, Dwight provided his readers with details about the theologian's wife, Sarah, their childrearing practices, and their household economy. Where Hopkins had merely outlined the circumstances surrounding Edwards's dismissal from his Northampton church, Dwight went on, page after densely packed page, examining the dispute and vindicating Edwards. Above all, Dwight's exhaustive volume enlarged upon Edwards's role as the "father" of the "great" colonial awakening.

A reverential, filiopietistic view of Edwards informed Dwight's voluminous memoir. Since the apostolic era, Dwight proclaimed, no individual had done more to unfold scriptural truth and advance evangelical Christianity.

> And when we remember, in addition to all this, that we can probably select no individual, of all who have lived in that long period, who has manifested a more ardent or elevated piety towards God, a warmer or more expended benevolence towards Man, or greater purity, or

disinterestedness of character—one who gave the concentrated strength of all his powers, more absolutely, to the one end of glorifying God in the salvation of Man;—and then reflect, that at the age of *fifty-four,* in the highest vigor of all his faculties, in the fullness of his usefulness, when he was just entering on the most important station of his life, he yielded to the stroke of death, we look toward his grave, in mute astonishment, unable to penetrate those clouds and darkness, which hover around it.[8]

Dwight's extravagant historical assessment both reflected and contributed to what one might call the Second Great Awakening's "reinvention" of Edwards: the elevation of the theologian to the status of major cultural authority, the canonization of his works, and the creation of an Edwardsian religious tradition. Dwight's memoir was frequently reprinted, and almost every evangelical who wrote about Edwards relied on it for the first and last word on the theologian's life and career.[9] In short, Dwight, the family curator of both Edwards's image and of his unpublished papers, superseded Hopkins as the historical authority on New England's most illustrious religious luminary.

Edwards's profound personal piety, rather than his intellectual brilliance, emerged as the central motif of Dwight's memoir and of the numerous depictions of the theologian that it influenced. His personal piety and the works of practical divinity that grew out of his commitment to experimental religion established the basis for Edwards's broad appeal to both Calvinist and non-Calvinist evangelicals during the Second Great Awakening. Despite the distinctly doctrinal cast of Edwards's major theological works, "no denomination has ever yet been able to appropriate his name to themselves," the *Christian Spectator* observed in 1821. "In this respect he has attained higher honor than Calvin, or Luther, or Zwingle [*sic*]. As no sect of christians has ever been able to appropriate the name *Christian* exclusively to themselves, so no sect will ever be denominated Edwardean."[10]

During the course of the Second Great Awakening, Edwards's deep piety, private writings, and works of practical divinity enabled moderate Congregationalists, Old and New Side Presbyterians, and even Methodists to bypass the metaphysical Edwards and to co-opt the New Divinity's exclusive claim to Edwardsian tradition.[11] Ordinary evangelicals came to know Edwards through his private writings and works of practical divinity, which were extensively republished and widely disseminated, rather than through his powerful theological treatises. In particular, Edwards's *Personal Narrative,* his brief spiritual autobiography/conversion narrative, and his private "Resolutions" for spiritual and moral improvement appealed to a diverse evangelical audience and established the literary foundation for Edwards's image as a man of saintly piety.[12] The *Personal Narrative* was reprinted in pamphlet form by, among others, the American Tract Society and the Congregational Board of Publication. The former edition, titled the *Conversion of President Edwards,* was first issued in 1827, and by 1875, 124,000 copies had been dis-

tributed.[13] Edwards's **"Resolutions"** were also printed separately and distributed widely. Joseph Emerson, the Edwardsian minister of the Third Congregational Church in Beverly, Massachusetts, published the first separate edition of the **"Resolutions"** in 1807. He combined Edwards's work with the articles of Faith and Covenant of the Third Church as a devotional manual for members. Emerson's effort proved so successful that he prepared a new edition of his work, which was adopted by churches in Massachusetts, Vermont, and New Hampshire.[14] The publishing history of the *Personal Narrative* and the **"Resolutions"** suggests how local, denominational, and interdenominational religious institutions all made contributions to the cultural revival of Edwards.

Evangelical commentary on Edwards's private writings focused on the saintly spirituality embodied in these works and urged Christians to aspire to an Edwardsian level of piety. Edwards's humility came to be seen as a dominant theme of his life and as the foundation of his piety, enabling moderate evangelicals to fashion a tradition that could be invoked against the perceived spiritual excesses of Finneyites and Methodists. In the *Religious Affections,* a newly canonical text for Second Great Awakeners, moderates found a useful expression of the "evangelical humiliation" that, it was argued, shaped Edwards's spiritual life and private writings. Edwards defined evangelical humility as "a sense a Christian has of his own utter insufficiency, despicableness, and odiousness with an answerable frame of heart."[15] Such an understanding of genuine religious affections derived from the familiar Puritan view that the individual with the most reason for hope and comfort was the one who felt most lost and undeserving. In an age of new-measures revivalism and religious perfectionism, Edwards's figure and his brand of piety were employed as an antidote to spiritual pride and nascent antinomianism. "It has often appeared to me," the eminent divine wrote in the *Personal Narrative,* "that if God should mark iniquity against me, I should appear the very worst of all mankind; of all that have been, since the beginning of the world, to this time." Evangelical humiliation originated in the converted person's new sense of God's majesty. The true convert's humility intensified as an awareness of God increased. Thus Edwards couldn't "bear the thought of being no more humble than other Christians. It seems to me, that though their degrees of humility may be suitable for them, yet it would be a vile self-exaltation in me, not to be the lowest in humility of all mankind."[16]

Evangelical humiliation comprehended a denial not only of self-exaltation, but of worldly pleasure as well. Indeed, worldly self-denial was an important sign that spiritual pride and self-love, which were affections or inclinations of the heart, had been subdued. Edwards's **"Resolutions"** furnished evangelicals with a brief, readable work of practical piety that complemented the high-flown quest for evangelical humility described in the *Personal Narrative.* Composed by Edwards when he was nineteen years old, the seventy resolutions comprised the practical efforts he made to sanctify his heart and root his life in the denial of self-centeredness and worldliness. Some resolutions were directed at the regulation of daily life: "Resolved, to maintain the strictest temperance in eating and drinking." Others expressed the lofty objective behind such self-denial: "*Resolved,* never henceforth, till I die, to act as if I were any way my own, but entirely and altogether God's." Still others established daily, weekly, monthly, and yearly schedules of self-examination to monitor his faithfulness to the resolutions.[17]

Perhaps more than any other of his writings, the **"Resolutions"** shaped the nineteenth-century evangelical image of Edwards's piety. Biographers portrayed his life as a fulfillment of the **"Resolutions"** constructing a towering model of piety for all Christians to emulate. Youthful aspiration became adult, reality, as Edwards was allowed to define his own character. One resolution summed up the personal attributes that, following Dwight's biographical interpretation, became the standard evangelical portrait of Edwards: "Resolved, To endeavor, to my utmost, to deny whatever is not most agreeable to a good and universally sweet and benevolent, quiet, peaceable, contented and easy, compassionate and generous, humble and meek, submissive and obliging, diligent and industrious, charitable and even, patient, moderate, forgiving and sincere temper."[18] Armed with Edwards's authority and saintly image, evangelical leaders set out on their mission of morally domesticating antebellum Americans.

Many evangelicals echoed the judgment of Sereno Dwight, who proclaimed that Edwards's **"Resolutions"** were "the best uninspired summary of christian duty, the best directory to high attainments in evangelical virtue, which the mind of man has hitherto been able to form."[19] The **"Resolutions"** invited favorable comparison with Benjamin Franklin's more famous quest for moral improvement. Franklin's effort, the author of the Sunday School Union's biography of Edwards noted, was admirable but limited to "mere moral precepts." To be a Christian, however, required more than morality; "and never has this applied with such fullness and beautiful symmetry as in the 'Seventy Resolutions,' which Edwards laid down for the guidance of his social and religious actions." Edwards's quest for sanctification was so superior to Franklin's that the **"Resolutions"** ought "to be written by every christian in letters of gold; or rather to be engraved on the tablets of his memory."[20]

Evangelicals often used the **"Resolutions"** to help them establish and Edwardsian moral regimen in their lives, as Basil Manly, Jr., a southern Baptist, demonstrated. Inspired by Edwards, Manly initiated a process of periodic intensive self-examination in 1841, though he felt spiritually inadequate in comparison to America's Augustine. "When I contrast the feeling of my heart with the exercises of that blessed man of God, Jon. Edwards," Manly recorded in his diary, "I am astonished at the coldness of my own heart." Using Edwards's work as a model, Manly drew up a list of one hundred resolutions to aid him in his pursuit of moral and spiritual sanctification.[21]

Such enthusiastic imitators and promoters of the private Edwards repeatedly commented on the "childlike piety" the eminent divine expressed in the **"Resolutions"** and the *Personal Narrative.* Evangelical leaders seized on the contrast between Edwards's humble, childlike piety and his "muscular," unrivaled intellect to support the reigning commonsense philosophy, which held that no matter how much people differed in mental ability and social standing, they were all created morally equal.[22] God bestowed on humankind a universal or common moral sense that helped establish a basic ethical order in the world. Through conversion and the cultivation of this moral sense, conscience, or intuitive affection, all individuals could strive for the kind of evangelical piety that Edwards had attained. Thus, however intimidating and original Edwards's intellect appeared, his equally profound, yet humble, childlike piety remained a realistic model for evangelical spiritual and moral aspirations. Edwards's piety and the commonsense philosophy enabled evangelicals to democratize the distinguished theologian. As one evangelical put it in a biographical sketch of Edwards: "It is peculiarly sweet to observe that in matters of spiritual concern the philosopher and the ploughman, if truly regenerated, have the same feelings, and speak the same language: They all 'eat of the same spiritual meat, and drink of the same spiritual rock, which follows them, and that rock is Christ.'"[23] In short, all converts—the renowned Edwards included—belonged to a spiritual family whose members bore a striking resemblance. Edwards's piety, then, differed only in degree, not in kind, from other family members.

. . . . .

Second Great Awakeners canonized Edwards's *Personal Narrative,* esteeming it as a classic—an American archetype of the conversion narrative, an established and familiar evangelical religious genre. Similarly, the *Faithful Narrative,* Edwards's account of the Northampton and Connecticut Valley revivals of 1734-35, was canonized as the prototype of a more recent evangelical religious genre—the revival narrative. As Michael Crawford has recently argued, Edwards's *Faithful Narrative* "was the first extended account and analysis of a season of religious awakening in a congregation, let alone in a full thirty communities." Edwards's *Faithful Narrative,* which was published in 1737, "established a new religious genre, creating a model of American revival narratives for a century to come."[24]

Yet the publishing history of the *Faithful Narrative* suggests that neither its archetypal importance and influence nor the revival narrative's development in America was fully realized until the Second Great Awakening. First published in England, the *Faithful Narrative* was not extensively reprinted in America during the era of the colonial revivals. The publication of the *Faithful Narrative* in London and Edinburgh in 1737 encouraged American editions in 1738, but not thereafter. Indeed, in the mid-eighteenth century, it was Scottish Presbyterians and English evangelicals who recognized the novelty of

Edwards's account and who published seven editions by 1750. The *Faithful Narrative* was not widely reprinted in America until the Second Great Awakening. Nor, for that matter, was the revival narrative fully established in evangelical culture until publications such as the *Connecticut Evangelical Magazine* institutionalized such accounts as part of their religious and inspirational fare.[25] Second Great Awakeners' appropriation and canonization of the *Faithful Narrative* extended to other Edwardsian revivalistic works, whose republication was an integral part of the invention of the "great" colonial awakening and of Edwards's elevation to the status of founding father of the American revivalistic tradition.

The century preceding the outburst of revivalism in the 1730s, evangelicals argued, witnessed an uninterrupted erosion of American piety, culminating in a religiously deplorable state of affairs. Uncritically accepting the formulaic history of declension that became a convention of the revival narrative beginning with Edwards, nineteenth-century evangelicals often pointed to the Halfway Covenant, uninspired preaching, and creeping moralism as signs of the grievous condition of American church life. "The clergy were, for the most part, grave men," Lyman Beecher claimed in the *Spirit of the Pilgrims* in 1829, "but in some instances, had . . . lost the spirit of religion, and in others, it may be feared, had never felt it."[26] Edwards became "God's chief instrument of all born in this land for . . . restoring prosperity to our American Sion," the *Congregational Quarterly* boasted. "One such man . . . is sufficient alone to redeem the nation, the church, the age to which he belonged."[27] In this dominant evangelical view, Edwards single-handedly ignited the colonial awakening, fanned its flames with the assistance of the likes of George Whitefield and Gilbert Tennent, and labored—though not always successfully—to prevent it from raging out of control. "He was," evangelicals concluded, "the father of the Great Awakening."[28]

But Edwards's authority on revivalism did not derive simply from the evangelical belief that he had sired the Great Awakening. Rather, as the Presbyterian minister Charles Spaulding emphasized in 1832, Edwards also gave birth to the "science of revivals."[29] His deep personal piety and profound intellect, evangelicals noted repeatedly, combined to make Edwards an expert on experimental religion. Edwards's rich devotional life and his quest for holiness established an unrivaled personal understanding of religious affections. Such piety sanctified his powerful intellect and enabled him to become an "eminently discriminating" observer of both individual and mass conversions.[30] Furthermore, the father of the Great Awakening was afforded unequaled opportunities to study the operation of the Holy Spirit in individuals, families, churches, and entire communities over a number of years.

Understandably, then, nineteenth-century evangelicals invested Edwards's revivalistic writings with an authority that far exceeded their eighteenth-century reception and reputation. When, in the midst of the fervor and contro-versy over Finney's new measures, a publisher approached Charles Spaulding to write a work on revivalism, the Presbyterian minister concluded that, since he could not equal, let alone surpass, Edwards, it made more sense to republish the master. In 1832, he published *Edwards on Revivals,* which contained selections from the theologian's work on the colonial awakening.[31] These works—*A Faithful Narrative of the Surprising Works of God* (1737), *The Distinguishing Marks of a Work of the Spirit of God* (1741), *Some Thoughts Concerning the Present Revival of Religion in New England* (1742), and *A Treatise Concerning Religious Affections* (1746)—were among the most popular and frequently reprinted Edwardsian volumes in the nineteenth century. They were also the kind of Edwardsian works that John Wesley, Bishop Francis Asbury, and other Methodist leaders deeply admired, regularly reissued, and enthusiastically recommended to their clergy and laity.[32] Edwards's revivalistic works were equally popular with the American Tract Society. Between 1833 and 1875, to cite just one example, the Society distributed 171,000 copies of Edwards's concluding remarks to *Some Thoughts Concerning the Present Revival of Religion in New England.* Edwards's writings on the colonial awakening, the Reverend William B. Sprague, the influential Presbyterian historian of the American clergy, proclaimed in 1833, "have done more than any other uninspired productions to maintain the purity of revivals, from the period in which they were written to the present." Even if Edwards "had rendered the church no other service," Sprague maintained, "for this alone she would have embalmed his memory."[33]

Edwards's *Religious Affections* came to be appreciated as a contribution to the "science of revivalism," though creative editing, as we have seen, was required to transform it into an accessible religious classic. Recoiling from the emotional excesses of the colonial revivals, Edwards offered a tempered interpretation of genuine spirituality in the *Religious Affections.* By sorting through Edwards's signs of genuine spirituality and by distilling his swollen rhetoric, antebellum evangelicals offered the public a work of practical divinity, which—like Edwards's **"Resolutions"** and *Personal Narrative*—supported evangelical humility and self-denying, sanctified behavior, not self-exalting antinomianism and prideful enthusiasm. The *Religious Affections* helped make the examination of a prospective church member "a rational ordeal," a writer in the *Christian Review* commented in 1841. "This book ought to be labelled the 'Pastor's Manual for the Inquirer's Room' . . . [,] the only work . . . in the English language in any degree entitled to such designation." Another evangelical writing in the *New Englander* agreed that the *Religious Affections* had become "the text-book of christendom on experimental religion." Even religious rationalists acknowledged, at the same time they lamented, the authority that Edwards's treatise carried during the Second Great Awakening. The Unitarian John Brazer, for instance, described the *Religious Affections* in the *Christian Examiner* in 1835 as "a book which is now in unquestioned repute, and which . . . has been referred to and quoted, reprinted and circulated by the predominant class of Christians in this country, with a deference only less than that which is paid to the Bible itself."[34]

Edwards's *History of the Work of Redemption* went through a similar process of canonization during the Second Great Awakening and added to his stature as the preeminent authority on revivalism. Based on sermons he delivered in Northampton during 1739, Edwards's *History of Redemption* drew on scriptural evidence and Christian history to place revivals at the center of the providential plan for human redemption. Edwards offered not a new departure in eschatology, but an original contribution to evangelical historiography. As the most comprehensive recent history of colonial revivalism documents clearly, Edwards "made the phenomenon of the revival the key element in the drama of redemption. He conceived of revivals as the engine that drives redemption history."[35]

Yet, neither Edwards's *History of Redemption,* nor his millennial perspective on revivals, appears to have found a secure place in American evangelical culture until the Second Great Awakening. In fact, Edwards's *History of Redemption* was one of his posthumous works that his New Divinity disciples were unable to place with an American publisher. Jonathan Edwards, Jr., shipped this work to Scotland, where it was first issued in 1774. The publisher included an advertisement with an appeal to the evangelical community for support: "Whether the publisher shall favor the world with any more of these valuable remains, will probably in a good measure depend on the encouragement this work meets with."[36] Scottish evangelicals proved to be more receptive to Edwardsian works than their mid-eighteenth-century American counterparts. The *History of Redemption* was not published in America until 1782 (a reprint of the Scottish edition) and not regularly reissued and extensively distributed until the Second Great Awakening. Perhaps the most influential American edition of this work was first issued in 1838 as part of the Tract Society's "Evangelical Family Library." More than 60,000 copies of this edition were circulated at midcentury.[37] By then revivalism had become an enduring, widespread, and even institutionalized rite within evangelical Protestantism, and not the short-lived, geographically limited outbursts of the colonial period, including the era of the "great" awakening. Edwards's *History of Redemption* contributed the drama of redemption to the powerful revivalistic religious culture that emerged during the Second Great Awakening. The work encouraged antebellum evangelicals to link America's two great awakenings and to invoke Edwards's authority in the service of nineteenth-century millennialism.

One evangelical described the *History of Redemption* in 1827 as "one of the most popular manuals of Calvinistic theology."[38] The work proved to be popular both with lay readers and revivalistic preachers. Edwards's account offered antebellum evangelicals an understanding of history as a grand narrative propelled by a divine "design and a covenant of redemption" that God "carries on from the fall of man to the end of the world."[39] Edwards presented biblical and doctrinal explanations of the historical drama in accessible sermonic form that encouraged human contributions to the work of redemption through individual conversion and revivalism. Indeed, the *History of Redemption* served to "universalize" the revivals of the Second Great Awakening, situating them in a cosmic scheme of redemption and exciting interest in such evangelical causes as missionary work at home and abroad.[40]

Thus, nineteenth-century evangelicals added the *History of Redemption* to the canon of Edwardsian works on revivalism. Edwards emerged as an authority not only on personal piety and individual conversion, but also on the "morphology" of revivals and their millennial significance. As the father of the great colonial revival, Edwards had laid the groundwork for the Second Great Awakening, one nineteenth-century evangelical concluded, by persuading "a generation that feared more than they knew about revivals of their utility and benefit."[41]

. . . . .

Of course the Edwards who was presented to the evangelical public in the 1820s, 1830s, and 1840s by architects of the benevolent empire was different from the Edwards who had been resurrected by the New Divinity men in the early stages of the Second Great Awakening. New Divinity men were theological improvers and not simply advocates of Edwardsian piety and revivalism. They sought to create and extend theological, as well as pietistic and revivalistic, traditions derived from the era of the colonial awakening and to resist the Methodization of orthodoxy on all fronts. As we shall see, "Edwards on the will," as Alan C. Guelzo has recently put it, continued to present moral, philosophical, and doctrinal problems that influenced religious discourse through the middle of the nineteenth century.[42] But Edwards's hyper-Calvinist works were not the texts that were canonized and propagated to a broad lay audience during the Second Great Awakening. The popular piety of the Awakening led evangelical leaders to foreground the "Methodistical" side of Edwards beginning in the 1820s—a process of cultural reinterpretation that enabled moderate Calvinists, such as Lyman Beecher and Charles G. Finney, to challenge the New Divinity's exclusive claim to Edwardsian religious tradition. Edwards's newly established authority on personal piety, conversion, and revivalism also encouraged Old School Presbyterians to downplay the metaphysical Edwards of *Freedom of the Will* and *Original Sin,* to dismiss New Divinity doctrinal improvements, and to claim an orthodox Calvinist Edwards as their own. While Princeton's Archibald Alexander boasted of Edwards in 1844, "few men ever attained, as we think, higher degrees of holiness, or made more accurate observations on the exercises of others," his fellow Old School Presbyterians resisted both the New School Methodization of Edwards and the New Divinity theological appropriation of his legacy.[43]

As the multidenominational authority of a Methodized Edwards became institutionalized in antebellum evangelical culture, the metaphysical, Calvinist Edwards—and theology in general—became increasingly relegated to seminaries, specialized religious journals, and a professionalized ministry. With Congregationalists and Presbyterians in the forefront, fourteen seminaries were opened between 1808, when Andover was established as America's first postgraduate theological school, and 1836.[44] Some of these seminaries published their own journals, representing an academic phase of the antebellum religious print culture that was so central to the invention of the Great Awakening and to the cultural revival of Edwards. In 1828, for example, Lyman Beecher and Professor Chauncey Goodrich purchased the *Christian Spectator* as a quarterly for the theological faculty of Yale, as well as for the promotion of Nathaniel Taylor's New Haven theology.

Taylor and the *Christian Spectator* offered one strategy for acknowledging and employing the authority of Edwardsian tradition without accepting the hyper-Calvinism of the metaphysical Edwards: invoking Edwardsian rhetoric while justifying improvements on the master. Such a strategy made seminary journals the front line in the war of words over Edwards's theological legacy. "It is not the first, nor the thousandth time," Asahel Nettleton complained to Princeton's Samuel Miller in 1835, "that Edwards has been claimed as vindicating the measures and doctrines which everyman who is acquainted with his works knows he did most sadly deplore and publicly condemn."[45] A year earlier, Nettleton and other New Divinity men, claiming to be legitimate religious descendants of Edwards, deputized themselves as his official theological guardians and established their own seminary in Connecticut. The Theological Institute of Connecticut (later Hartford Seminary) was located in East Windsor, a short distance from Edwards's birthplace. In fact, the cornerstone of the new seminary was a step-stone from the Edwards homestead and signified, as the dedication address described it, the founders' determination to preserve the doctrines "of our Pilgrim Fathers—of Edwards, of Bellamy, of Smalley, of Dwight,—and a host of other distinguished divines of our country."[46]

Led by seminary journals, but overflowing into the broader religious periodical press, evangelicals' efforts to reconcile and appropriate the metaphysical and the Methodized Edwards produced a paper was whose volume surpassed the output of the mid-eighteenth-century pamphlet skirmishes that had marked the emergence of an Edwardsian New Divinity school of theology. The seminary paper was sent divinity students, among others, scurrying to consult Edwards's publications. In the 1830s, for example, Edwards's collected **Works** was withdrawn from the Yale library at almost twice the rate of the next most circulated volume.[47] As Samuel Miller accurately noted in 1837, "for the last half century no other American writer in the school of theology has been so frequently quoted, or had any thing like such deference manifested to his opinions as President Edwards."[48] Yet such deference to Edwards and acknowledgment of his cultural authority was discharged and appro-

priated in a variety of ways. Some evangelicals simply downplayed the metaphysical Edwards for the Methodized Edwards; others combined Edwardsian rhetoric and "improvements" to traditionalize their alterations of Edwards's thought; still others sought to neutralize the New Divinity by upholding an orthodox Calvinist Edwards, rather than the highly original metaphysician.

The emergence of Edwards as a kind of American cultural icon undergirded each of these appropriations.[49] Moreover, the theologian as cultural icon helped reduce the distance between the metaphysical Edwards and the Methodized Edwards, between the seminary Edwards and the Tract Society Edwards. In addition, the transformation o the theologian into a cultural icon enabled a spectrum of evangelicals to affirm Edwards's intellectual brilliance without necessarily accepting his specific doctrinal stands.

Foreign respect and admiration for Edwards's mind and writings reinforced his intellectual authority and helped shape his cultural image in America. Nineteenth-century evangelicals rediscovered and publicized European, particularly Scottish, esteem for America's preeminent theologian. Edwards became a kind of religious Hawthorne, his cultural figure and body of work repeatedly invoked to counter European intellectual condescension toward America.[50] Edwards was the one American religious thinker whose works included impressive private spiritual writings, penetrating analyses of revivalistic religion, and powerful theological dissertations. Evangelicals proudly cited the judgment of the *North British Review* that Edwards's works constituted "the only considerable literary monument of American Puritanism." Edwards was not simply the "first American to command by his arguments and opinions the attention of Protestant Christendom," a writer argued in the *Congregational Quarterly,* but he was the first and only American religious thinker to achieve a lofty international reputation. "He gave America that rank in the religious world that Washington gave it in patriotic statesmanship and Franklin in philosophy."[51]

In a monotonous biographical refrain, evangelicals repeated the praises of Edwards sung by Dugald Stewart, the respected commonsense philosopher at the University of Edinburgh. Edwards, Stewart remarked, is the "one metaphysician whom America has to boast, who, in logical acuteness and subtlety, does not yield to any disputant in the universities of Europe."[52] Evangelicals seized on statements that supported Stewart's glowing assessment of Edwards, such as the views of Thomas Chalmers, professor of moral philosophy at St. Andrew's in Scotland. "There is no European Divine to whom I make such frequent appeals in my class rooms as I do to Edwards," Chalmers asserted, "no book of human composition which I more strenuously recommend than his Treatise on the Will." Edwards's famous volume, Chalmers claimed, "helped me more than any uninspired book to find my way through all that might otherwise have proved baffling and transcendental and mysterious in the peculiarities of Calvinism."[53]

Evangelicals fashioned a heroic account of a frontier philosopher who rose from the wild forest of America to reach a sophisticated university audience in Europe. Edwards's intellectual ascent betokened a kind of New World originality and sheer mental muscularity that evangelicals played off against popular nineteenth-century perceptions of European corruption and effeteness. As a reviewer of a new edition of Edwards's works conceded in the *Christian Spectator* in 1821, Europe held significant cultural advantages over America. Unlike England, America's abundant economic opportunity, short history, and modest libraries and colleges presented "obstacles" to cultural achievement. Yet, "in every branch of knowledge which there are motives and means to cultivate," Americans had demonstrated that they measured up to or exceeded the intellectual accomplishments of England. "In proof of this we refer to Edwards as an author. He has commanded the admiration of Europeans, even his enemies; among who [*sic*] have been opposed to his conclusions, have done ample justice to the strength of his reasoning powers."[54]

For other evangelicals, such as the Reverend Increase Tarbox, secretary for the American Education Society, Edwards's intellectual attainments demonstrated that America offered important compensations that offset the cultural advantages of Europe. While it was certainly true, Tarbox argued on the pages of the Andover's *Bibliotheca Sacra,* that America could not match Europe "in refinement, general culture, and all the dainty delicacies of learning," American thinkers like Edwards were not weighed down by history, custom, and established cultural institutions. Edwards possessed a mind "more profoundly new, fresh, original . . . than any which the old world could boast." From the "shadows of a wilderness wellnigh unbroken," Tarbox rhapsodized, Edwards offered "a glimpse at least of the primeval man before the fall" that was imposing "for the beauty of his face and person, lordly in the easy sweep and grasp of his intellect, wonderful in his purity of soul and simple devotion to truth." Edwards's vigorous, original intellect thrived in the American wilderness, where it was free to develop "by an inward force rather than by outward formative power." Had Edwards been born and bred in Europe, his mind would have been "cramped," "confined," and "impeded" by supposed cultural advantages.[55]

In the process of transforming Edwards into a cultural icon, biographers apotheosized the mind that produced such formidable and internationally renowned works as *Freedom of the Will.* Just as Edwards displayed an advanced piety in boyhood, constructing a prayer hut in the woods near his Connecticut home that nineteenth-century travelers pointed out as "a hallowed location,"[56] so too, biographers stressed, the youthful Edwards showed an intellectual precocity that foreshadowed the adult genius. Edwards's juvenile writings revealed an impressive "mature and manly mind" which complemented the more "feminine" affective side of the evangelical boy wonder that the private works of his youth reflected. Edwards's account of the movement of the wood spider through the New England forest, which he wrote at the age of eleven, was consistently cited as evidence of his precocious powers of observation and analysis. "Here was a young philosopher of the Baconian stamp and spirit," one evangelical enthused, "who probably hardly knew as yet that such a man as Bacon ever lived."[57]

Edwards's supposed mastery of Locke at the age of thirteen, "when most boys would scarcely have betaken themselves to any thing more profound than 'Robinson Crusoe,'" followed by the composition of notes on "The Mind," furnished additional evidence for evangelical awe of the youthful Edwards's intellectual ability.[58] While religious liberals and secular commentators regretted that Edwards had squandered his genius by using it to defend Calvinism, evangelicals were grateful that from an early age Edwards's piety served "to enlarge, as well as purify," his mind.[59] "But for his piety," Lyman Beecher wrote to his son George recommending the close study of Edwards's life and writings, "he might have been a skeptic more dangerous than Hume or Voltaire; but for the command of religion over all his powers he might have been one of the more dangerous, as he certainly was one of the most original and fearless of speculators."[60]

Of course, as the founders of both Andover Seminary and the Theological Institute of Connecticut asserted, New England Congregationalists could lay special claim to their "moral Newton," as Timothy Dwight described his grandfather.[61] Even Harriet Beecher Stowe, who once glibly dismissed Edwards's theology as "the refined poetry of torture,"[62] claimed, along with other lapsed Calvinists, that it was neither possible, nor desirable, to uproot an intellectual tradition so firmly attached to New England soil. While Stowe regretted that Edwards had opened the floodgates of Calvinist discussion in New England, she nevertheless conceded that there was something noble in the regional and American intellectual tradition that flowed from his thought. In many respects, she made clear in an essay on Calvinism, she admired Edwards and his New Divinity disciples, "who, leviathan-like have made the theological deep of New England boil like a pot, and the agitation of whose course remains to this day." Only a "shallow mind," Stowe insisted, would fail to recognize something "sublime" in the intricate intellectual maneuvers of Edwardsian thinkers, who "have constituted in New England the strong mental discipline needed by a people who were an absolute democracy."[63]

While rationalist descendants of the Puritans belittled Edwardsianism as a provincial, and therefore embarrassing, intellectual expression, New England's Calvinist evangelicals concurred with Stowe's assessment. Samuel Hopkins, Joseph Bellamy, and other New Divinity theologians possessed a kind of raw Edwardsian mental power, one writer suggested in an essay entitled "Jonathan Edwards and the Old Clergy," which appeared in the *Continental Monthly* at midcentury. "I doubt," the author argued, "if Britain and Germany, with their combined universities could have equaled during the last century the New England pulpit in mental acuteness or philosophical discrimination."[64] As we shall see, the mid-nineteenth-century effort, spearheaded by Edwards A. Park at Andover and the Doctrinal Tract and Book Society in Boston, to publish the collected works and filiopietistic memoirs of Edwards's eighteenth-century New Divinity disciples was part of a successful and influential endeavor to codify, celebrate, and perpetuate one hundred years of Edwardsian theological tradition. To supporters of Park's work of historical reconstruction, there seemed to be little doubt that Edwards and his theological disciples both reflected and contributed to the shaping of the New England and American mind. Perhaps Edwardsian preaching cultivated Yankee ingenuity, one evangelical speculated: "Those who listened to the preaching of such men could not avoid becoming thinkers. . . . A man who could think out the most subtle theories of the pulpit could think out the most elaborate machinery."[65]

Clearly, the mental power that Edwards and his "Farmer-Metaphysician" votaries displayed in their backwoods pulpits and that placed New England and America on the theological map remained, contemporaries were reassured, part of the region's and the nation's lifeblood. Edwardsian ministers in general, and their teacher's "pen" in particular, the Reverend John Todd of Northampton argued in two addresses delivered in 1833 and 1834, shaped "the moral character of New England (and of consequence, that of the rest of this country)." New England's "strong, energetic, untiring" character was merely Edwards's writ large and could be "read" across the American landscape: "in the forests that melt before it, in the sails that whiten the seas,—in the canals and rail-roads, in the factories—on the brow of the whale ship,—in the Temperance Reformation and throughout the world, wherever noble enterprise is to be found."[66]

Edwards's cultural figure was assimilated to what now appears as familiar and contrived rhetoric about Yankee ingenuity, character, and moral energy. But the Yankee cultural identity was still in the process of emerging during the era of the Second Great Awakening, and evangelical writers contributed significantly to its formation. One sees the Yankee identity emergent in the poetry of Timothy Dwight, the moralistic geography of Jedidiah Morse, and the fiction of Harriet Beecher Stowe. More secular sources, such as visual representations of America's "Jonathans," also shaped the creation of the Yankee character.[67] As a cultural icon, Edwards became a "Brother Jonathan" of his own in the nineteenth century.

. . . . .

Esteemed cultural icon, father of the Great Awakening and of American revivalism, and embodiment of a lofty standard of evangelical piety, Edwards was exhibited as the leading luminary in a heroic generation that laid the foundation for the developing nineteenth-century righteous empire. Presbygationalists, in particular, regularly associated Edwards with the revered Founding Fathers of the nation. Such extravagant filiopietism led some evangelicals to

caution against the tendency of their contemporaries to derogate from nineteenth-century religiosity because "they judge of the piety of the past from a few picked specimens as Baxter, Bunyan, Henry, Edwards, Brainard [*sic*], and others whose lives or writings form part of our current literature."[68] Of course, in the process of transforming Edwards into an eighteenth-century founding father of America's righteous empire, nineteenth-century factotums of filiopietism performed a kind of historical face-lift to remove the major blemish on Edwards's image. After all, in what Sereno Dwight described as "one of the most painful and most surprising events recorded in the Ecclesiastical history of New England,"[69] Edwards was dismissed in 1750 from the Northampton church that he had served for twenty-three years and that had been the "birthplace" of the colonial awakening. How could this church, which seemingly had been spiritually regenerated by impressive outbursts of revival religion, turn its back on a man of such piety, intellect, and evangelical skill, branding him at middle age with the stigma of dismissal?

Samuel Hopkins had offered an explanation of the controversy, but his brief account was not an adequate defense of Edwards. It remained for Sereno Dwight to furnish evangelical America with a detailed historical apologia for Edwards. The sizable portion of his biography of Edwards that Dwight devoted to the dismissal testified to the personal and historical importance of his coming to terms with the unfortunate event. One quarter of the *Life of Edwards* (150 pages, not counting Dwight's reprinting of Edwards's entire **Farewell Sermon**) dealt with the dismissal; and this account, like the biography as a whole, became the authoritative evangelical interpretation of the controversy upon which subsequent writers drew.

The intrusion of Unitarians into the cultural debate over Finney's new measures and the legacy of colonial revivalism lent special urgency to Dwight's historical apologetic. From the late 1820s through the 1830s, the *Christian Examiner and Theological Review* and other Unitarian journals sustained a running critical commentary on both specific evangelical excesses and the "revival system" in general. James Walker, minister in Charlestown, editor of the *Christian Examiner* between 1831 and 1839, and subsequently professor of moral philosophy at Harvard as well as president of the university, emerged as the most intelligent and combative Unitarian antagonist of the evangelicals. Indeed, Walker adopted the strategies and the persona of Charles Chauncy, Edwards's major eighteenth-century rationalist foe. As evangelicals quoted chapter and verse from Edwards and republished the great revivalist's writings with commentaries designed either to legitimate or repudiate new measures, so, too, Walker appealed to Chauncyh and strove to undermine evangelical invocation of Edwards's cultural authority.[70]

Of particular importance to Dwight's elaborate defense of Edwards in the church dismissal controversy was a lengthy article, entitled "The Revival under Whitefield," that Walker published in the *Christian Examiner* in 1827. The history of the colonial awakening, Walker claimed, provided a forum for a rational, "less prejudice[d]" examination of the emotionally charged, divisive issues that the revivalism of the 1820s aroused. In his own way, Walker invested the "great" colonial awakening with enormous historical significance, though his reconstruction of that seminal event diverged from the evangelicals' historical scripts. Walker's analysis, for example, suggested that the Second Great Awakening was in the process of unfolding as a historical rerun of the First, with the same contrived origins, the same failed promise, and the same opportunities for proponents of rational religion on the one hand and for "nothingarians" on the other. Far from being "naturally inspired by the circumstances or the subject," Walker argued, revivalism was aroused "by artificial means, and so directed and controlled, by its contrivers and managers, that it might answer their purposes." Yet, once passions became "excited inordinately," it was as difficult to manage them "as to control the storms when they are wildest." Walker recalled the fate of the distinguished Edwards to show the destructive consequences of religious enthusiasm, even to those who had "gotten up" a revival and who had labored to control it.[71]

Walker conceded the evangelical view that Edwards was an impressive historical figure—a man of "great piety" who displayed a "strong natural turn for metaphysical investigation" and who "was as remarkable for his abilities in managing a revival, as in getting it up in the first instance." Perhaps no other minister, Walker concluded, "ever possessed so much influence over his people in time of a revival, and . . . none on the whole, ever exerted it with more judgment and discretion" than Edwards. And yet the revivalistic message, even in the hands of such a saintly, skilled preacher as Edwards, excited enthusiasm and false expressions of piety that the father of the colonial awakening could not control.[72]

Consider, Walker stressed, how the history of Northampton after the colonial awakening established the wisdom of Chauncy's courageous dissent from the popular enthusiasm of revivalistic religion. More than any other community in eighteenth-century America, Northampton had been supposedly purified by the recurring fires of revivalism ignited by the "most reknowned" preacher of the era. One might expect, then, that the town "long continued the abode of peace and virtue, so that in all after time, if any durst lisp a syllable against revivals, men might say 'look at Northampton.'" Instead, within months of the decline of the revival, the town was embarrassed by an obscene book episode involving children of some of the most prominent families in the First Church. Edwards's handling of the incident became the first in a series of divisive issues that pitted the membership against the distinguished revivalist and "that were a scandal to the whole country."[73] The church that had witnessed the birth of the colonial awakening dismissed the "father" of American revivalism in 1750. To Walker, the historical lesson for Second Great Awakeners was clear: if such a distinguished revivalist and student of religious affections as Edwards could not prevent false piety and religious enthusiasm from corrupting his own church, could lesser men a century later contain the destructive consequences of the new generation of James Davenports who had invaded America's churches?

Sereno Dwight prepared what amounted to a bulging legal brief in his *Life of Edwards* that directly responded to Walker's incisive, and often sarcastic, interpretation of Edwards's dismissal and that endeavored to erase this blot from the historical record by transforming it into a morally sublime and providentially inspired episode. Dwight overwhelmed his readers with detailed discussions of the background to the dispute, the political maneuvering that led to the calling of an ecclesiastical council, the politics of that council, and the "uncharitable" treatment of Edwards after the dismissal decision was rendered. He portrayed Edwards as a hero, as a martyr who embodied *"evangelical integrity*—a settled unbending resolution to do what he thought right, whatever self-denial or sacrifices it might cost him." Dwight emphasized that his exhaustive review of the dismissal uncovered no evidence that Edwards was ever accused of neglecting his pastoral duties or of private misconduct. "The only charges brought against him, were, that he had changed his opinion, with regard to the Scriptural Qualification for admission to the Church; that he was very pertinacious in adhering to his new opinions; and that, in this way, he gave his people a great deal of trouble."[74]

Dwight defended Edwards on each score, transforming him into a spiritual brother of the notable martyrs of Anglo-American Protestantism. Certainly Edwards had reversed himself on Solomon Stoddard's practice of opening church membership, and therefore communion, to all individuals who led moral lives, not just to those who had experienced conversion. But, Dwight argued, when Edwards first arrived in Northampton to assist his grandfather, the initial controversy over open communion had subsided and the practice had become well established in the Connecticut River Valley. In light of local popular and clerical opinion, and with the authority of his venerated grandfather behind open communion, "it is not surprising that a young man of *Twenty-three* should conclude, that the practice was probably right, and adopt it of course."[75]

After extensive study, Edwards determined that neither scripture, not New England ecclesiastical history, supported open communion. Though he was in middle age, had eight children, and benefited from "the largest salary paid by any country congregation in New England," he decided to challenge the entrenched practice, recognizing that he would alienate not only his own church, but also local ministers, who would most likely recommend his dismissal. "Rare indeed is the instance," Dwight observed, "in which any individual has entered on the investigation of a difficult point in casuistry, with so many motives to bias his judgment."[76] Edwards's heroic stand against popular opinion was a testimony to his character and a fulfillment of the self-denying piety of the "Resolutions." Moreover, for Dwight and for other evangelicals writing in the age of Andrew Jackson and Charles G. Finney, Edwards's dismissal became a kind of parable on the excesses of democracy, an "example," in the words of one prominent Presbyterian who adopted Dwight's interpretation, "of the blindness and violence of popular feeling, even in a population of the most enlightened, sober, and reflecting character."[77]

In the end, Dwight skillfully exonerated revivalism and arraigned Stoddardeanism for subverting genuine evangelical religion in Northampton and for pitting against Edwards a corrupt church erected through lax admission standards. Because of long-standing Stoddardean practice, Edwards was unable to use ecclesiastical "safeguards" that were critical to protecting the spiritual purity of the church, especially in periods of revivalism. Thus, his church "must have embodied within its pale, an unhappy proportion of hypocrisy, worldly-mindedness and irreligion"; and these elements, "on the first plausible occasion," rose in opposition to "the prevalence of truth, and the welfare of real religion." Even after his dismissal, Edwards displayed humble disinterested benevolence toward church members, who descended to even deeper depths of disgrace. Since the church had no minister, Edwards, still concerned for his former flock's spiritual well-being, offered to supply the vacant pulpit until a minister was settled. In response, the church voted to prohibit Edwards from preaching to anyone from his old pulpit.[78]

From a nineteenth-century historical perspective, it became clear to Dwight that Edwards's dismissal actually served the designs of "an All-wise Providence." The Stockbridge years, despite their poverty and hardship, gave Edwards the time to pursue theological studies and to make major contributions to the advancement of religious truth. If he had continued in Northampton, where his pastoral responsibilities were "so numerous and engrossing," Edwards would not have been able to fulfill his providential role. Instead, "at the best time of life, when his powers had gained their greatest energy," he settled in Stockbridge and produced "four of the ablest and most valuable works, which the church of Christ has in its possession."[79]

By marshaling a carefully selected, but still impressive, array of evidence favorable to Edwards, Dwight transformed defeat into a heroic stand against and providential victory over popular sentiment run amok. Dwight's ex cathedra interpretation, based in part on family documents to which only he—as the curator of a major portion of Edwards's manuscripts—had access, decidedly influenced subsequent biographers and contributors to religious journals, who often described the grandeur of Edwards's stand and the moral lessons that the dismissal episode offered. "With the single exception of the history of Christ," Noah Porter, professor of moral philosophy and metaphysics at Yale, wrote in the *Christian Spectator* in 1831, two years after the publication of Dwight's biography of Edwards, "it would be difficult to find a more wonderful example than is here presented, of wisdom, patience, meekness, conde-

scension, and firmness, on the one hand, or of infatuation, and violent inflexible resistance of truth, kindness and obligation on the other."[80]

In the midst of evangelical America's "rediscovery" of Edwards's heroic stand—which, of course, was only one aspect of the larger Edwards cultural revival—Northamptonites found an opportunity to expiate the historical sins of their community. By the early 1830s, the First Church of Northampton had outgrown its meetinghouse. In a peaceful settlement, a separation was effected in the church and a new society organized. By a unanimous vote, the members of the new church agreed to name it after Edwards. "How little did Edwards think," the Reverend John Todd remarked in the address delivered when the cornerstone of the new meetinghouse was laid on, appropriately, July 4, 1833, "that a church would ever arise here, cherishing as her heart's blood the doctrines which he taught, and calling herself and her Temples by his name because his dear memory lingers on earth."[81] The process of "reinventing" Jonathan Edwards involved not only the canonization of texts, but also the consecration of sacred shrines and relics—the Edwards church, the step-stone from the Edwards family homestead, the site of the youthful Edwards's prayer hut. The creation of such Edwards "antiquities" offers compelling evidence that the eminent divine's religious relevance was not simply rediscovered in the nineteenth century; it was a product of the cultural work of the Second Great Awakening.

Notes

1. The excellent collection of essays edited by Nathan O. Hatch and Harry S. Stout that broadly examines Edwards's influence does not address his importance to and in the Second Great Awakening, though Mark A. Noll offers some suggestive comments. See Noll, "Jonathan Edwards and Nineteenth-Century Theology," in *Jonathan Edwards and the American Experience,* ed. Nathan O. Hatch and Harry S. Stout (New York, 1988), pp. 260-87.

2. Edwards A. Park, *Memoir of the Life and Character of Samuel Hopkins, D.D. . . .* (Boston, 1852), p. 217. On Edwards and Scotland, see Harold P. Simonson, "Jonathan Edwards and His Scottish Connections," *Journal of American Studies* 21 (1987): 353-76. For reactions to Edwards's death and on his eighteenth-century reputation, see Donald Louis Weber, "The Image of Jonathan Edwards in American Culture" (Ph.D. diss., Columbia University, 1978), chap. 1, esp. p. 69f.; see also Daniel B. Shea, "Jonathan Edwards: The First Two Hundred Years," *Journal of American Studies* 14 (August 1980): 181-97.

3. This is the estimate of Thomas Johnson, ed., *The Printed Writings of Jonathan Edwards: A Bibliography* (1940; reprint, New York, 1968), p. xi.

4. Noll, "Edwards and Nineteenth-Century Theology," p. 260. Allen C. Guelzo, *Edwards on the Will: A*

Century of American Theological Debate (Middletown, Conn., 1989), pp. 147, 276. My discussion of Edwards as a cultural icon has been influenced by Guelzo's suggestive comments, but I disagree with his notion that Edwards became little more than a kind of cultural artifact by the late 1820s.

5. One important exception was the publication together in 1765 of Edwards's dissertations on *The Nature of True Virtue* and *Concerning the End for Which God Created the World*.

6. Samuel Hopkins, *The Life and Character of the Late Reverend Mr. Jonathan Edwards*, in *Jonathan Edwards: A Profile*, ed. David Levin (New York, 1969), p. 2.

7. S. E. Dwight, *The Life of President Edwards*, vol. 1 of *The Works of President Edwards, with a Memoir*, ed. Sereno E. Dwight, 10 vols. (New York, 1829).

8. Ibid., p. 624.

9. See, for example, Noah Porter, "Review of the Works of President Edwards," *Quarterly Christian Spectator* 3 (September 1831): 337-51; American Sunday School Union's *The Life of President Edwards* (Philadelphia, 1832); and Samuel Miller, *Life of Jonathan Edwards*, vol. 8 of *The Library of American Biography*, ed. Jared Sparks (New York, 1837).

10. "'Review' of the *Works of President Edwards*, edited by Samuel Austin," *Christian Spectator* 3 (June 1821): 300.

11. Guelzo offers the best discussion of theological efforts to co-opt the New Divinity. See *Edwards on the Will*, esp. pp. 221-22, 228-29, 242-43.

12. See, for example, "Life and Character of Rev. Jonathan Edwards," *Connecticut Evangelical Magazine and Religious Intelligencer* 1 (May 1808): 161-78 and (June 1808): 201-12; Euopius, "On a Resolution of President Edwards," *Christian Spectator* 7 (January 1825): 14ff.; "Interesting Conversions: Jonathan Edwards," *Religious Monitor and Evangelical Repository* 6 (February 1830): 414ff.; American Sunday School Union's *Life of Edwards*, esp. chap. 3; and William B. Sprague, *Annals of the American Pulpit*, 9 vols. (New York, 1857-69), 1:330.

13. *Conversion of President Edwards* (New York, [1827]); Johnson, *Printed Writings of Edwards*, p. 95.

14. Joseph Emerson, *Articles of Faith, and Form of Covenant, Adopted by the Third Congregational Church in Beverly, at Its Formation, November 9, 1801 . . . To Which Are Added Resolutions of President Edwards.* Published by Order of the Church for the use of the Members (Boston, 1807); Johnson, *Printed Writings of Edwards*, p. 101f.

15. Jonathan Edwards, *Religious Affections*, ed. John E. Smith, vol. 2 of *Works of Jonathan Edwards*, 13 vols. (New Haven, Conn., 1959), p. 311.

16. Edwards, quoted in Dwight, *Life of Edwards*, p. 311.

17. Ibid., pp. 69, 71. All seventy resolutions are reprinted on pp. 68-73.

18. Ibid., p. 71.

19. Ibid., p. 73.

20. American Sunday School Union's *Life of Edwards*, p. 26; see also Porter, "Review of the Works of Edwards," p. 342f.; Miller, *Life of Edwards*, esp. p. 190; and Joseph P. Thompson, "Jonathan Edwards, His Character, Teaching, and Influence," *Bibliotheca Sacra* 18 (October 1861): 813ff.

21. Manly is quoted and described in Anne C. Loveland, *Southern Evangelicals and the Social Order, 1800-1860* (Baton Rouge, La., 1980), p. 15.

22. Dwight, *Life of Edwards*, p. 587; Erasmus Middleton, "Jonathan Edwards, D.D.," in *Evangelical Biography*, 4 vols. (Philadelphia, 1798), 1:429; Miller, *Life of Edwards*, pp. 172, 190; "Edwards as a Sermonizer," *Christian Review* 10 (March 1845): 37; and [George MaGoun], "President Edwards as a Reformer," *Congregational Quarterly* 1 (April 1869): 265. On nineteenth-century evangelicals and the commonsense philosophy, see William G. McLoughlin, ed., *The American Evangelicals, 1800-1900* (New York, 1968), pp. 1-10; Mark A. Noll, "Common Sense Traditions and American Evangelical Thought," *American Quarterly* 37 (Summer 1985): 216-38; and Noll, *Princeton in the Republic, 1768-1822: The Search for a Christian Enlightenment in the Era of Samuel Stanhope Smith* (Princeton, N.J., 1989).

23. Middleton, "Jonathan Edwards, D.D.," p. 429.

24. Michael J. Crawford, *Seasons of Grace: Colonial New England's Revival Tradition in Its British Context* (New York, 1991), pp. 124, 189.

25. Johnson, *Printed Writings of Edwards*, pp. 4-15, lists the editions of the *Faithful Narrative*. In 1736, what was to become the *Faithful Narrative* was published in part as an appendix to another American work. But the 1737 English edition was the first complete edition. Bennett Tyler, the influential Edwardsian minister, edited revival narratives from the *Connecticut Evangelical Magazine* and the Massachusetts Sabbath School Society and published them in an important volume. See *New England Revivals, as They existed at the Close of the Eighteenth, and the Beginning of the Nineteenth Centuries. Compiled Principally from Narratives First Published in the Connecticut Evangelical Magazine* (Boston, 1846). Thomas Prince published transatlantic revival narratives during the era of the so-called "great" awakening. But his *Church History*

(Boston, 1743-45) was a short-lived effort that did not establish the revival narrative in evangelical culture.

26. [Lyman Beecher], "Letters on the Introduction and Progress of Unitarianism in New England," *Spirit of the Pilgrims* 2 (March 1829): 122.

27. [MaGoun], "Edwards as a Reformer," p. 265.

28. Ibid.; see also "Edwards as a Sermonizer," esp. p. 53; "Review of Edwards on the Affections," *Christian Review* 6 (December 1841): 492; and Joseph Tracy, *The Great Awakening: A History of the Revival of Religion in the Time of Edwards and Whitefield* (Boston, 1841), esp. pp. 1-18.

29. Charles Spaulding, *Edwards on Revivals* (New York, 1832), p. x.

30. Rev. W. D. Snodgrass, quoted in ibid., p. vii.

31. Ibid., p. xi; see also William B. Sprague, *Lectures on Revivals of Religion* (Albany, 1832), passim.

32. Robert C. Monk, *John Wesley: His Puritan Heritage* (New York and Nashville, 1966), p. 221; Frank Baker, *From Wesley to Asbury: Studies in American Methodism* (Durham, N.C., 1976), esp. p. 71; "Edwards and Wesley," *National Magazine* 3 (October 1853): 308-11.

33. Johnson, *Printed Writings of Edwards*, p. 31; Sprague, *Lectures on Revivals*, p. 218f.

34. "Review of Edwards on the Affections," p. 501f.; "President Edwards on Charity and Its Fruits," *New Englander* 10 (May 1852): 227; John Brazer, "Essays on the Doctrine of Divine Influences," *Christian Examiner* 18 (March 1835): 52; and see also [E. H. Byington], "The Theology of Edwards, as Shown in His Treatise Concerning Religious Affections," *American Theological Review* 1 (May 1859): 199.

35. Crawford, *Seasons of Grace*, p. 132.

36. Jonathan Edwards, *A History of the Work of Redemption. Containing the Outline of a Body of Divinity in a Method Entirely New* (Edinburgh, 1774), p. ii.

37. Johnson, *Printed Writings of Edwards*, pp. 85-94.

38. Edwards W. Grinfield, *The Nature and Extent of the Christian Dispensation with Reference to the Salvability of the Heathen* (London, 1827), p. 427. I am indebted to John F. Wilson for this reference. See "Editor's Introduction," in Jonathan Edwards, *A History of the Work of Redemption,* ed. John F. Wilson, vol. 9 of *Works of Jonathan Edwards* (New Haven, Conn., 1989), pp. 87-88.

39. Edwards, *History of Redemption*, p. 116.

40. Chapter 4 discusses Mary Lyon's combination of Edwardsian millennialism, revivalism, and disinterested benevolence in the service of missionary work. I have found John Wilson's brief discussion (pp. 79-83) of the nineteenth-century reception of the *History of Redemption* useful. But I disagree that Edwards's ideas became so "diffused" that they were hardly Edwardsian. I also disagree with Wilson's similar assessment (pp. 83-84) of Edwards's more strictly theological legacy, namely, that debate "over technical points among ecclesiastics . . . took on a life of its own" largely divorced from Edwards. In one case, the appropriation of Edwards becomes too generalized and in the other too specialized.

41. [MaGoun], "Edwards as a Reformer," p. 269. The term "morphology" of revival is Crawford's; see *Seasons of Grace,* chap. 9.

42. Guelzo, *Edwards on the Will,* chaps. 7, 8. Also see Bruce Kuklick, *Churchmen and Philosophers: From Jonathan Edwards to John Dewey* (New Haven, Conn., 1985), and James Hoopes, *Consciousness in New England: From Puritanism and Ideas to Psychoanalysis and Semiotics* (Baltimore, Md., 1989).

43. Alexander, quoted in Guelzo, *Edwards on the Will,* p. 207. See also George M. Marsden, *The Evangelical Mind and the New School Presbyterian Experience: A Case Study of Thought and Theology in Nineteenth-Century America* (New Haven, Conn., 1970), and Earl Pope, *New England Calvinism and the Disruption of the Presbyterian Church* (New York, 1987).

44. These included Princeton (1812), Harvard (1815), Bangor (1816), Auburn (1818), General (1819), Yale (1822), Union of Virginia (1824), Western (1827), Columbia (1828), Lane (1829), McCormick (1830), East Windsor (1834), and Union of New York (1836). In *The Spiritual Self in Everyday Life: The Transformation of Personal Religious Experience in Nineteenth-Century New England* (Boston, 1989), Richard Rabinowitz offers suggestive discussions of the New Divinity, the relegation of theology to seminaries, and alterations in nineteenth-century evangelical religious sensibilities.

45. Nettleton, quoted in Guelzo, *Edwards on the Will,* p. 271. My discussion of the appropriation of Edwards's theology has been influenced by Guelzo and Noll, "Edwards and Nineteenth-Century Theology," pp. 260-87.

46. Curtis Manning Geer, *The Hartford Theological Seminary, 1834-1934* (Hartford, Conn., 1934), pp. 62-63.

47. John T. Wayland, *The Theological Development of Yale College, 1822-1858* (1933; reprint, New York, 1987), p. 238. For this reference I am indebted to Douglas Sweeney, "Nathaniel William Taylor and the Edwardsian Tradition: A Reassessment," a paper presented at the conference on "The Writings of Jonathan Edwards: Text and Context," Indiana University, June 1994.

48. Miller, *Life of Edwards,* p. 215.

49. Guelzo offers several perceptive comments on Edwards as a cultural icon that suggests how some nineteenth-century polemicists appropriated his figure but not necessarily his theology. See *Edwards on the Will,* pp. 147-48.

50. See Richard Brodhead's discussion of the nineteenth-century canonization of Hawthorne's work and his creative American genius in *The School of Hawthorne* (New York, 1986).

51. [MaGoun], "Edwards as a Reformer," p. 265; Porter, "Review of the Works of Edwards," p. 300; Increase N. Tarbox, "Jonathan Edwards," *Bibliotheca Sacra* 26 (April 1869): 245; William Tyler, "Genius," *Bibliotheca Sacra* 12 (April 1855): 296; Timothy Dwight, *Travels in New England and New York,* 4 vols. (New Haven, Conn., 1823), 4:323-28; and Shea, "Jonathan Edwards," p. 188f.

52. Stewart made this statement in *A General View of the Progress of Metaphysical, Ethical, and Political Philosophy Since the Revival of Letters in Europe: First Dissertation* (Boston, 1822), part 2, p. 256; references to Stewart's assessment are too numerous to cite, but some representative examples may be found in Dwight, *Life of Edwards,* p. 603; American Sunday School Union's *Life of Edwards,* p. 133; and Miller, *Life of Edwards,* p. 183.

53. William B. Sprague, "Jonathan Edwards," in *Annals of the American Pulpit,* ed. William B. Sprague, 9 vols. (New York, 1857-69), 1:334; Miller, *Life of Edwards,* p. 172; Tarbox, "Jonathan Edwards," p. 246; and [MaGoun], "Edwards as a Reformer," p. 265.

54. Porter, "Review of the Works of Edwards," p. 299.

55. Tarbox, "Jonathan Edwards," pp. 255, 261ff.; see also Dwight, *Life of Edwards,* pp. 9, 603.

56. Charles Osgood, "Jonathan Edwards and the New Calvinism," in *Studies in Christian Biography or Hours with Theologians and Reformers* (New York, 1850), p. 352.

57. Dwight, *Life of Edwards,* p. 587; Tarbox, "Jonathan Edwards," p. 259; Miller, *Life of Edwards,* p. 8; and American Sunday School Union's *Life of Edwards,* p. 11. See also Evert A. Duyckinck and George L. Duyckinck, *Cyclopedia of American Literature,* 2 vols. (New York, 1856), 1:92, and Benjamin Silliman, "Juvenile Observations of President Edwards on Spiders," *American Journal of Science and Arts* 21 (January 1832): 109-15.

58. Sprague, "Jonathan Edwards," p. 329; see also "Life of Edwards," *Connecticut Evangelical Magazine,* p. 162; Dwight, *Life of Edwards,* pp. 33-40; and Porter, "Review of the Works of Edwards," pp. 338-42. Wallace Anderson argues that Locke was probably not even available to Edwards when he was thirteen. See Anderson, ed., *Scientific and*

Philosophical Writings, vol. 6 of *Works of Jonathan Edwards* (New Haven, Conn., 1980), pp. 16-18.

59. Miller, *Life of Edwards,* p. 191.

60. *The Autobiography of Lyman Beecher,* ed. Barbara M. Cross, 2 vols. (Cambridge, Mass., 1961), 2:177.

61. Dwight's description of Edwards appeared in *The Triumph of Infidelity: A Poem* (1788) and was quoted by nineteenth-century evangelicals. See, for example, Edwards A. Park, "New England Theology," *Bibliotheca Sacra* 9 (January 1852): 182.

62. Harriet Beecher Stowe, *The Minister's Wooing* (Boston, 1859; reprint, New York, 1967), p. 245.

63. Stowe, quoted in Charles H. Foster, *The Rungless Ladder: Harriet Beecher Stowe and New England Puritanism* (Durham, N.C., 1954), pp. 101-2; see also Lawrence E. Buell, "Calvinism Romanticized: Harriet Beecher Stowe, Samuel Hopkins, and *The Minister's Wooing,*" *Emerson Society Quarterly* 24 (1978): 119-32.

64. W. Frothingham, "Jonathan Edwards and the Old Clergy," *Continental Monthly* 1 (March 1862): 210; see also Park, "New England Theology," pp. 184-85, and Edward Beecher, "The Works of Samuel Hopkins," *Bibliotheca Sacra* 10 (January 1853): 63-82.

65. Frothingham, "Jonathan Edwards and the Old Clergy," p. 265. Memoirs and collected works of New Divinity men included the following: Jonathan Edwards, Jr. (1842), Joseph Bellamy (1850), Samuel Hopkins (1852), and Nathanael Emmons (1861).

66. John Todd, *Address at the Laying of the Corner Stone of the Edwards Church in Northampton, Mass., July 4, 1833* (Northampton, Mass., 1834), pp. 50, 55; see also Todd, *The Pulpit—Its Influence upon Society: A Sermon Delivered at the Dedication of the Edwards Church in Northampton, Mass., December 25, 1833* (Northampton, Mass., 1834). On Edwards's theological followers as Farmer Metaphysicians, see Joseph A. Conforti, *Samuel Hopkins and the New Divinity Movement: Calvinism, the Congregational Ministry, and Reform in New England between the Great Awakenings* (Grand Rapids, Mich., 1981), p. 10.

67. The admirable Yankee emerges in works like Timothy Dwight's *Greenfield Hill* (1794), Jedidiah Morse's *American Geography* (1789), which was widely used in the nineteenth century, and numerous stories and books of Stowe. On the figure of the Yankee in art, see Sarah Burns, "Jonathans," in *Pastoral Inventions: Rural Life in Nineteenth-Century Art and Culture* (Philadelphia, 1989), pp. 149-67; and Elizabeth Johns, "An Image of Pure Yankeeism," in *American Genre Painting: The Politics of Everyday Life* (New Haven, Conn., 1991), pp. 24-59.

68. A. P. Marvin, "Three Eras of Revivals in the U.S.," *Bibliotheca Sacra* 16 (April 1859): 290f.; see also [MaGoun], "Edwards as a Reformer," p. 265, and Spaulding, *Edwards on Revivals,* esp. p. vii.

69. Dwight, *Life of Edwards,* p. 298.

70. See Joseph A. Conforti, "Edwardsians, Unitarians, and the Memory of the Great Awakening," in *American Unitarianism, 1805-1865,* ed. Conrad Edick Wright (Boston, 1989), pp. 31-50.

71. [James Walker], "The Revival under Whitefield," *Christian Examiner* 4 (1827): 465, 480-81.

72. Ibid., pp. 468-69.

73. Ibid., pp. 490-91.

74. Dwight, *Life of Edwards,* pp. 428, 593. Patricia J. Tracy, *Jonathan Edwards, Pastor: Religion and Society in Eighteenth-Century Northampton* (New York, 1989), offers a provocative social history of Edwards's ministry including his dismissal.

75. Dwight, *Life of Edwards,* p. 435.

76. Ibid., p. 436.

77. Miller, *Life of Edwards,* p. 431.

78. Dwight, *Life of Edwards,* p. 431f.

79. Ibid., p. 447.

80. Porter, "Review of the Works of Edwards," p. 349f.

81. Todd, *Address at Edwards Church,* p. 51.

Joseph A. Conforti (essay date 1995)

SOURCE: "Colonial Revival: Edwards and Puritan Tradition in American Culture, 1870-1903," in *Jonathan Edwards, Religious Tradition, and American Culture,* University of North Carolina Press, 1995, pp. 145-85.

[In the following excerpt, Conforti discusses the post-Civil War resurgence of interest in Edwardsean thought and Puritan theology in the United States, as revealed through American literature, renewed academic attention, commemorative events, and the dedication of memorial and historic locations where Edwards and other famous Puritans had lived or died.]

Neither the postbellum dissolution of the New England theology and of Calvinism in general, nor the attendant emergence of social Christianity, which increasingly supplanted revivalistic evangelical religion in mainline Protestant churches, proclaimed the end of American culture's engagement with Jonathan Edwards. Quite the contrary, the passing of the New England theology established new interpretive opportunities for the creation of a post-Calvinist Puritan tradition that met the cultural needs of the present. The formulation of a usable post-Calvinist Puritan past was part cultural consolidation, part cultural reaction. New England-based orbred elites sought narratives of the origins of American culture that consolidated the

political and military victory over the South. Moreover, in the face of the urban, industrial, and ethnic transformation of America these same secular and religious elites spearheaded an interest in and nostalgia for a heroic colonial past—a heavily reactionary perspective that, while acknowledging Puritanism's imperfections, still celebrated its spirit and achievements as the most important moral and cultural presence in the founding and development of America.[1] As the "last" or "greatest" Puritan, Edwards remained central to new narratives of the relationship between religious tradition and the shaping of American culture.

Shortly before and after the Civil War, Harriet Beecher Stowe and Henry Ward Beecher completed novels in which they attempted to come to terms with their Edwardsian and Puritan heritage. In their flight from Calvinism, both Stowe and her brother clung to Puritanism as a moral and cultural force; they displayed an ambivalence toward their religious tradition—an ambivalence that would not be completely erased in later post-Calvinist assessments of Puritanism by individuals who were more culturally distant from that heritage than the children of Lyman Beecher. Between 1852 and 1864, Stowe lived in Andover, Massachusetts, where her husband, Calvin, served on the seminary faculty. The Stowes were friends and neighbors of Edwards A. Park; Stowe read the Abbot Professor's biographies of Hopkins and Emmons, discussed the works with him, and used them in two historical novels in which she began to retrieve Puritanism as a moral and cultural force from its thralldom to Calvinism.

The Minister's Wooing (1859) is set in Newport, Rhode Island, in the 1790s with Samuel Hopkins, "the patron saint of the Negro race" in the town, as "the hero." Stowe does not temper Hopkins's hyper-Calvinist views of divine sovereignty, as Park did; she rejects them, as she does "the refined poetry of torture" in Edwards's sermons. Yet, Stowe embraces disinterested benevolence, especially as it informed the ethos of the Edwardsian ministry: "Their whole lives and deportment bore thrilling witness to their sincerity. Edwards set apart special days of fasting, in view of the dreadful doom of the lost. . . . Hopkins fasted every Saturday. David Brainerd gave up every refinement of civilized life to weep and pray at the feet of hardened savages, if by any means he might save one."[2] Hopkins's disinterested benevolence inspires two heroic acts of self-sacrifice in *The Minister's Wooing.* He challenges slaveowners and slave traders in his own congregation, and he gives up his fiancée, Mary Scudder, when her young beau, who had been presumed drowned, returns to Newport. Even as Stowe uses fiction to negotiate her retreat from the faith once delivered to the saints, she extols the "nobility" and the "grand side" of the "strivings of the soul" encouraged by New England theology, and she eulogizes the "lives of eminent purity and earnestness" of its "noblest" representatives.[3]

In the mid-1860s, Stowe moved to Hartford, Connecticut, and joined the Episcopal Church. The second of her four

New England novels, *Oldtown Folks* (1869), drew on her husband's childhood recollections to evoke life in a small Massachusetts community at the turn of the nineteenth century. *Oldtown Folks* is offered as a memoir by an adult male narrator. Horace Holyoke was orphaned as a boy and taken in by his Grandmother Badger, a severe but loving Puritan matriarch whose favorite reading, her precious "blue book," was Joseph Bellamy's *True Religion Delineated*. Oldtown's Calvinist minister, Dr. Moses Stern, was none other than Nathanael Emmons, Calvin Stowe's teacher. Stern's theological system was comparable to a "skillful engine of torture" powered by "the mental anguish of the most perfect sense of helplessness, with the most torturing sense of responsibility." Still, like Grandmother Badger, Oldtown's throwback to the Puritan patriarchs of ancient times possessed redeeming virtues that gave him a certain nobility. If Stern's "devotion to the King Eternal" exhibited "something terrible and painful," it also displayed qualities which were "grand and in which we can take pride, as fruit of our own nature."[4]

Seemingly inspired by his sister, Henry Ward Beecher turned to local color fiction to separate the theological dross from the precious elements in his New England religious heritage. In 1867, Beecher published *Norwood; or, Village Life in New England,* a novel set in a town that closely resembles Northampton. Norwood is located twenty miles north of Springfield and situated on a hill overlooking the Connecticut River Valley. Moreover, like Northampton, Norwood was established "not far from thirty years after the Pilgrims' landing." Norwood's minister, Jedidiah Buell, is portrayed as an Edwardsian thinker, "a high and noble man, trained to New England theology, but brought to excessive distress by speculations and new views."[5] Buell is presented as an embodiment of a tradition of logical theology that has left New England Calvinist thinkers, "Edwards, perhaps, excepted," deficient in poetic sensibilities and poorly prepared to address the moral and emotional needs of Christians. Yet Beecher shares his sister's pride in New England's religious heritage and social ideals. He sees hope for Buell and his Norwood parishioners in the liberation of Puritan tradition from the constrictions of Calvinism. Beecher's spokesman, medical Dr. Reuben Wentworth, even praises New England theologians for dealing "with the great moral truths in such a manner that the imagination of their people has been powerfully developed."[6]

Stowe and Beecher, of course, differed in several ways from late-nineteenth-century colonial revival interpreters of Puritan and Edwardsian tradition. Lyman Beecher's offspring wrestled with an intensely personal religious past. They also belonged to a generation that had become embroiled in controversies over Calvinist theology and revivalism. In addition, when Stowe and Beecher published their novels, Edwardsianism remained a vital, if receding, presence in American religion. The cultural and religious disengagement from Calvinism during the last three decades of the nineteenth century enabled writers and thinkers to reassess the Puritan heritage with even more sympathy than Stowe and Beecher displayed. There were dissenters, to be sure; and most respectful interpreters of the Puritans were ambivalent enough about the past to accept the wisdom of Hawthorne's historical perspective: "Let us thank God for having given us such ancestors; and let each successive generation thank him not less fervently, for going one step further from them in the march of ages."[7]

But the Puritan past became usable precisely because it was now distant. In a post-Calvinist, postrevival era, Unitarians and Anglicans joined Congregationalists and Presbyterians in a new "politics of Puritan historiography"[8] that addressed the cultural needs of the moment and that led to the first outpouring of Puritan studies. Scholars developed Puritan origins narratives for American history and literature. Pilgrim and Puritan monuments proliferated on the landscape, visual narratives of the tradition and spirit that had triumphed in the Revolution and the Civil War and to which immigrants required acculturation. Commemorations of historic colonial events and of town and church foundings provided occasions for lay and religious elites to perorate on America's glorious Anglo-Puritan past and to invoke religious tradition against such Victorian era symptoms of moral degeneration as political machines, labor strife, saloons, and consumerism. "A foreigner might think," Oliver Wendell Holmes observed in a biographical sketch of Edwards in 1880, "that the patron saint of America was Saint Anniversary."[9]

In the aftermath of the demise of the New England theology, Edwards endured as a dominant cultural figure in newly constructed narratives examining the Puritan origins of American history and American literature. Furthermore, Edwards became the subject of a major and highly successful late-nineteenth-century biography, part of the larger Victorian interest in and appreciation for the virile character, rock-ribbed sense of duty, and spiritual aspirations embodied in the lives of Puritan leaders. Stockbridge and Northampton issued new calls for Edwards's services. Rapidly changing communities, the sites of Edwards's pastorates, commemorated him, erected monuments in his honor, and preserved or invented Edwardsian "antiquities." Saint Anniversary in Stockbridge and Northampton demonstrates not only the vigor of the colonial revival impulse at the local level; it reveals the cultural backlash that Puritan ancestor worship became.

. . . . .

Even before the convening of their Pilgrim Memorial Convention in 1870, American Congregationalists, who held special claim on Puritan tradition and Edwards, sought to stress a common history and ecclesiastical practice, not Calvinist theology, as a denominational bond. Meeting in Boston in 1865, the National Council discussed a statement of faith and debated whether it should include a proposed acknowledgment of "the system of truths which is commonly known among us as Calvinism."[10] Opposition from a minority of the more than five hundred delegates assembled threatened to divide the Council and to jeopardize continuing denominational work in the West and new religious opportunities in the recently defeated South. An excursion to Plymouth, where the representatives reconvened on Burial Hill, appears to have established the historic atmosphere that helped fashion a compromise. The "Burial Hill Declaration" omitted any reference to Calvinism; it also offered a statement so general that, as one denominational historian observed, the document seemed "better suited to an address on an historic occasion than to a creed for local and permanent use."[11]

Five years later, the commemoration of the two hundred and fiftieth anniversary of the founding of Plymouth Colony ushered in what can only be called the golden age of Congregational historiography. From the ruins of the New England theology, denominational energy was diverted to collecting, preserving, and interpreting historical evidence, an early stage of the colonial revival creation of a usable Puritan past. Led by Henry Martyn Dexter (1821-90) and Williston Walker (1860-1922), denominational historians hailed Edwards as "so saintly a man" and as the "father of modern Congregationalism"[12] who overturned Solomon Stoddard's Presbyterian church practices; they also moved far beyond doctrinal history to recover the Puritan as a moral and cultural figure. Dexter graduated from Yale and Andover, served churches in New Hampshire and Boston, and edited the *Congregationalist,* a denominational journal of history and biography. Dexter published his monumental *The Congregationalism of the Last Three Hundred Years as Seen in Its Literature* in 1880. Over 1,000 pages long, Dexter's volume included a 300-page bibliography of published material and manuscript items that stimulated historical research on Congregationalism. Dexter boasted that in his veins "were blended the blood" of a "restless and sometimes testy Puritan" founder of Massachusetts Bay with the blood of Plymouth's Pilgrim leaders. "I began almost to esteem it a filial duty," he confessed, "to study closely our primitive annals." In *As to Roger Williams, and His "Banishment" from Massachusetts Plantations* (1876), Dexter's esteem for his Puritan ancestors even led him to defend them as wisely acting out of self-preservation in expelling the famous religious dissenter.[13]

Dexter also inspired the historical work of Williston Walker, a graduate of Yale (where he served as professor of church history) and Hartford Seminary, who claimed that Congregationalism "contributed far beyond any other polity to the fashioning of the political ideals of the United States."[14] Through such works as *Creeds and Platforms of Congregationalism* (1893), *A History of the Congregational Churches in the United States* (1894), and *Ten New England Leaders* (1901), which included a long, sympathetic essay on Edwards as a latter-day Puritan, Walker succeeded Dexter as the leading authority on the history of Congregationalism.

The development of Congregational House—a denominational headquarters and library—paralleled the historical work of Dexter and Walker. Originating at midcentury un-

der the advocacy of Edwards A. Park, the Congregational Library Association grew into the Congregational House in Boston, which by the 1890s possessed thousands of books and pamphlets and became the major repository of material on denominational history. In 1898, a new, stately eight-story Congregational House was completed on Beacon Hill to accommodate expanding historical interests and denominational needs. Four bas-relief tablets depicting major historical events in the founding of New England were commissioned for the front of the building: the Mayflower Compact, the Pilgrims worshiping on Clark's Pond in Plymouth Harbor, the founding of Harvard College, and John Eliot preaching to the Indians.[15]

Such visual representations of the Pilgrim-Puritan origins of America multiplied—like the saloons that sprouted in ethnic working-class neighborhoods—across New England and outside the region as well. While the Pilgrims and Plymouth became "national" historical icons in the late nineteenth century, Puritan history occasioned far more commemorations, casting of bronze, and molding of granite. Augustus Saint-Gaudens sculpted the most impressive Puritan statue, which was unveiled in Springfield, Massachusetts, in 1887 (Figure 1). Saint-Gaudens's nine-foot bronze statue, "The Puritan," both humanized and aggrandized his subject, creating a visual analogue for colonial revival interpretations of the Puritan character. Pennsylvania's New England Society even commissioned Saint-Gaudens to sculpt a replica of the Springfield statue for Philadelphia.[16] Moreover, Saint-Gaudens's work clearly influenced subsequent Puritan statuary, such as Salem's bronze of Roger Conant.

The erection of statues and monuments to such Puritan stalwarts as John Harvard, John Winthrop and John Eliot accompanied the progress of Saint Anniversary in New England. Edwardsian tradition became part of a seemingly indulgent celebration of a glorious past that was in part a response to Victorian excesses of a different sort. In the late nineteenth century, residents of Enfield, Connecticut, dedicated a rock-monument on the town green consecrating the site where Edwards delivered "Sinners in the Hands of an Angry God" A short while later, Haddam citizens erected a plaque on the homesite of John and David Brainerd. In addition, as we shall see, the historically minded leaders of Stockbridge and Northampton scattered Edwards and colonial memorials throughout their communities. Puritan artifacts, which were placed in public places and not just on church grounds and private property, were far from simply objects of nostalgia that reassured Anglo-Puritan descendants buffeted by change. Rather, they were civic-religious monuments that appropriated public space, linked place to past, and through such historicizing sought to stabilize the present by, among other things, promoting a respect for tradition and interest in Americanization among growing numbers of non-Anglo citizens.

Furthermore, bas-reliefs, bronze statues, granite monuments, memorial boulders, and commemorative plaques composed a visual narrative that buttressed the emergent

Puritan origins lines of interpretation in public addresses, magazine articles, and American history and American literature texts. In the post-Calvinist era, Congregationalists had to share their interest in and appreciation for America's Puritan heritage with former religious opponents, even Unitarians. The Puritans "believed that a free people should govern itself by a higher law than their own desire," George Hoar, Massachusetts's Unitarian senator, declared. "Duty and not self-indulgence, and future good in this world and the other, and not a present and immediate good, were the motives upon which they acted."[17] Descendants of the Puritans, like Hoar, contributed to a colonial revival historical perspective that appealed across denominational lines—fusing as it did nostalgia, ancestor worship, Anglo-Saxon racialism and jeremiadlike criticism of the perceived degradation of Victorian America.

Such an ideologically charged view of the past informed a spate of books—scholarly and popular—that constituted the first flowering of Puritan studies. Even leaden tomes like George Ellis's *The Puritan Age in Massachusetts, 1629—1685* (1888) prospered through several editions. More popular was a run of Puritan biographies which seemed to begin with Alexander V. G. Allen's highly successful 1889 study of Edwards (discussed below) and which continued through the 1890s.[18] Barrett Wendell's *Cotton Mather, The Puritan Priest* (1891) ranks among the most interesting and controversial of these biographical works; it shows how descendants carefully picked the bones of ancestors and thereby fashioned a usable Puritan past. Mather had been the Unitarian whipping boy whose behavior in the Salem witch trials predicted the revivalistic "fanaticism" of the Calvinist-inspired awakenings of the eighteenth and nineteenth centuries. During the bicentennial year of the witchcraft trials, however, Harvard English professor Barrett Wendell published an admiring biography of Mather that did not flinch from his involvement in the episode but at the same time suggested some exculpatory evidence: witchcraft was a popular belief, as was confidence in spectral evidence, which Mather rejected. Mather was never "deliberately dishonest," for throughout his life "he never ceased striving, amid endless stumblings and errors to do his duty." Wendell, who believed New England life was "the source of what is best in our America," showered praise on Mather for "strenuously" and "devoutly" pursuing what he thought was right. Wendell, as one scholar has observed, "identified the Puritan spirit with little more specific than the strenuous life."[19] In the hands of interpreters like Wendell, colonial history—as Puritan iconography suggested—became the fount of restorative moral and cultural values for the maladies of Victorian society.

Boston minister Ezra Hoyt Byington was one successful historian of the Puritans who extended Wendell's line of interpretation. In *The Puritan in England and New England,* which went through four editions between 1896 and 1900, Byington partially excused the Puritans' persecution of witches while conceding that the religious founders of America were not "perfect models" for his contemporaries because they were "not as tolerant as we have learned to be." But despite such limitations, the Puritans were still "in the best sense progressive, and our age owes very much to their fidelity to truth and to freedom." If the Puritans had embodied the "gentleness" and tolerance of the Pilgrims, the New England character, whose traits were now under cultural assault and social abandonment, "would not have given its impress to a great nation like this republic."[20]

The popularity of *The Puritan in England and New England* led Byington to complete a second volume, *The Puritan as a Colonist and Reformer* (1899), which contained a long chapter on "Jonathan Edwards and the Great Awakening." Byington's work was a response to what he saw as the "increasing interest" in and "higher appreciation" of the "Puritan spirit." Byington infused this spirit with Anglo-Saxon racialism, and he lauded the "freedom," "enterprise," and "faith" that cultivated an English "instinct" for successful colonization. Edwards and the Great Awakening, he asserted, represented an extension of the reforming Puritan tradition that had colonized America. The distinguished divine's preaching and writing revitalized spirituality and theology in New England and reversed the "remarkable declension of religious life in the Puritan churches."[21]

Byington did not call for a new Edwards or a new Mather, but at least one participant in a major church symposium, entitled *The New Puritanism,* held in 1897, was unable to summon such restraint. A colonial revival Puritan tradition emerged not only from the books of clerical and academic historians; it was forged in the addresses, publications, and commemorative artifacts of church, town, and historical anniversaries. The semicentennial of the prestigious Plymouth Church in Brooklyn was one such occasion. Lyman Abbott, who succeeded Henry Ward Beecher as the pastor of Plymouth Church, carefully sifted through New England history to distinguish the "Old" from the "New" Puritanism. Abbott applauded Edwardsian tradition for its encouraging among Christians "a profound sense, if a somewhat morbid sense, of their guilt and sinfulness," as well as a "very profound, if not altogether healthful, reverence for God." But the "fatalism" of Edwards's *Freedom of the Will* separated the Old and the New Puritanism; the latter began to evolve in the nineteenth century as the moral energy and "social conscience" of Puritanism and Edwardsianism were rescued from Calvinist theology.[22]

In an address on "Puritan Principles in the Modern World," New Jersey minister Amory Bradford went beyond Abbott and called for a "revival of Puritanism." Bradford seemed uninterested in distinguishing between old and new phases of religious tradition. He praised powerful Puritan figures from Cromwell to Edwards, while berating Victorian America for its "vice," "luxury and effeminacy" and for producing literature that was "in great part becoming mere dirt." Bradford issued a call for the reaffirmation of "traditional" Puritan values: "for character; for clean living as a condition of public service; for recognition of responsibility to God; for the supremacy of the spirit."[23]

Alice Morse Earle was probably among the auditors in the Plymouth Church listening to Abbott, Bradford, and others descanting on the New Puritanism. One of many transplanted New Englanders living in Brooklyn Heights, Earle devised her own historical response to the changes that so disquieted Bradford; she reveals yet another dimension to the colonial revival creation of a usable Puritan past. A prolific author of enormously popular historical works, Earle adapted the techniques of local color fiction to produce richly textured, evocative studies that lauded the virtue and stability of the colonial world. In her skilled hands, a nostalgic glow and descriptive detail often carried—and sometimes masked—the same ideological freight with which Bradford overburdened his audience. *The Sabbath in Puritan New England* was one of Earle's most successful works; first published in 1891, it went through twelve editions in little more than a decade. The book's conclusion resonated with the positive rhetoric and nostalgic historical appraisal that characterized the late-nineteenth-century colonial revival view of the Puritans: "Patient, frugal, God fearing and industrious, cruel and intolerant sometimes, but never cowardly, sternly obeying the word of God in the spirit and the letter, but erring sometimes in the interpretation thereof,—surely they had no traits to shame us, to keep us from thrilling with pride at the drop of their blood which runs in our backsliding veins."[24] It was only a short step from such a seemingly balanced, yet laudatory, assessment to President Theodore Roosevelt's expression of admiration for Edwards because he "always acted in accordance with the strongest sense of duty, and there wasn't a touch of the mollycoddle about him."[25]

Earle's popular works, like commemorations, monuments, and textbooks written for schools, helped disseminate an elite, almost nativist construction of Puritan tradition to a wide audience. This historical perspective encountered resistance not only from southerners, immigrants, and citizens of communities with strong New England Societies who could not trace their origins to the region; the colonial revival view of the past even provoked dissent among New England's Puritan descendants. Brooks Adams's *The Emancipation of Massachusetts* (1886), for example, advanced older notions of an oppressive Puritan theocracy from which his ancestors were gradually, but thankfully, liberated.[26] Three years later, Harvard historian John Fiske admonished his former student for failing "to define the elements of wholesome strength" in the Massachusetts theocracy and for restricting his vision to "its elements of crudity and weakness." The fervent Puritan, Fiske argued in *The Beginnings of New England* (1889), was also "in every fibre a practical Englishman with a full share of plain common sense." Avoiding the pitfalls of medieval "otherworldliness," the New England Puritans sowed the "seeds" of self-government and of American Constitutionalism. Far from emancipating themselves from colonial religious tradition, Fiske suggested, contemporary Americans needed to reaffirm the "Puritan's ethical conception of society."[27]

Edwards's life and cultural figure were woven into new colonial revival assessments of Puritan tradition. It is perhaps fortunate that Edwards A. Park did not complete his long-planned biography of Edwards, which undoubtedly would have remained fixed in the doctrinal polemics surrounding the New England theology rather than meeting the post-Calvinist cultural needs of Puritan descendants. So, too, late-nineteenth-century Puritan ancestors were spared an extended treatment of Oliver Wendell Holmes's interpretation of Edwards, offered in an 1880 essay that revealed how the famous poet continued to ride his own one-hoss shay—an outmoded antebellum Unitarian distaste for the Calvinism and revivalism of New England's Puritan heritage. Edwards's sermonizing, Holmes observed, showed his skill in the "apparatus of torture"; his life amounted to a "short and melancholy" existence; his Calvinism was all "Scotch theological thistle." Edwards's God was "not a Trinity but a Quarternity," Holmes insisted. "The fourth Person is an embodied abstraction, to which he gave the name of *Justice*." Edwards's Calvinist system remained "to the last degree barbaric, mechanical, materialistic, pessimistic." Even members of Holmes's Unitarian literary circle objected to such a limited view of Edwards, the "Protestant saint."[28]

Nine years later, the first full-scale Edwards biography of the post-Calvinist era was presented to the public. Alexander V. G. Allen's *Jonathan Edwards,* like Wendell's biography of Mather and the broader historical assessment of Puritan tradition of which it was a part, offered a highly sympathetic, though not uncritical, interpretation of its subject. Allen's study was part of Houghton Mifflin's prestigious "American Religious Leaders" series, described as "Biographies of Men who have had great influence on Religious Thought and Life in the United States."[29] Allen produced a biography that assimilated Edwards's life and thought into the new post-Calvinist recovery of a usable Puritan past; reprinted in 1890, 1891, 1896, and 1899, Allen's study remained the only major modern biography of Edwards until the 1930s.

A native of Vermont, Allen had spent a year at Andover Seminary, with Park as his teacher, while preparing for the Episcopal priesthood. He went on to serve as professor of church history at the Episcopal Seminary in Cambridge, Massachusetts. Allen combined a knowledge of and a distance from Edwardsian theological and revivalistic traditions that enabled him to transcend the historical perspectives of Park and Holmes and to produce a biography that met the colonial revival cultural needs of Puritan descendants. "I have not found myself devoid of sympathy with one who has filled so large a place in the minds of New England people," Allen announced in his preface. "Edwards is always and everywhere interesting, whatever we may think of his theology." While Allen examined Edwards's theology, he defended studying the great Puritan "on literary and historical grounds alone."[30] Not surprisingly, the Edwards who emerged from Allen's biography was, like the colonial revival Puritans in general, more an artifact in the cultural strife of the late nineteenth century than the embodiment of a continuing doctrinal or religious presence in American life.

Allen piled on Edward's figure "the concentrated vitality and aggressiveness of the occidental people,—of the Anglo-Saxon race in particular, of which he was a consummate flower blossoming in a new world." The product of a "typical Puritan household," Edwards embodied what, from a genteel Victorian religious slant, appeared as an admirable "ascetic tendency" that "entered so largely into the composition of the New England character." Moreover, the "strength and nobility" of that temperament derived from the kind of "conscious self-direction of the will" which Edwards displayed and which "became the characteristic of New England Puritanism."[31] Edwards sprang from the pages of Allen's biography as a flesh and Anglo-Saxon blood typification of Saint-Gaudens's cultural icon.

Allen devoted a lengthy section of his study to the era of the Great Awakening, drawing on Joseph Tracy for details and uncritically accepting his line of interpretation. Writing from a postrevival vantage point, Allen could look back on the awakening as a colonial relic, rather than as an episode directly related to controversies in the present. The awakening represented a response to declension from the "unique and beautiful experiment of the Puritan fathers." Through revivalistic religion Edwards endeavored to reaffirm "the principle of Puritanism." To be sure, sermons like **"Sinners in the Hands of an Angry God"** overflowed with sulfurous rhetoric. Modern readers, however, needed to view such Edwardsian productions in relationship to a colonial "standard of speech, in accordance with which they should be judged, rather than by the gentler, more sentimental standard of later times."[32]

Beyond such "allowances," Allen conceded, there remained a "vehemence" in sermons like **"Sinners in the Hands of an Angry God"** that derived from "the fundamental principles of the preacher's theology." Still, Edwards's preaching included expressions of "marvelous tenderness," not just Dantesque descriptions of a divine inferno.[33] Allen's assessment of Edwards the preacher, like so much else in his interpretation of the divine's life, found favor with Williston Walker. In his lengthy sketch of Edwards in *Ten New England Leaders,* Walker followed Allen and argued that, "though the terrors of the law fill a large place in his pulpit utterances, no man of his age pictured more glowingly than Edwards the joys of the redeemed, the blessedness of the Union with Christ or the felicities of the Knowledge of God."[34] Both Allen and Walker seemed to suggest that neither literary interest in the rhetoric of the Enfield sermon, nor the legacy of antebellum disputes over religious enthusiasm, should distort their era's view of Edwards the preacher.

Indeed, a growing disengagement of mainline Protestantism from revivalism enabled Allen to look back at the colonial awakening with a kind of religious detachment. The "morbid tendencies" and "similar phenomena" associated with the awakening "have always attended those epochs when humanity is seen striving in some unusual way to realize the spiritual as distinct from and above the natural." Allen's sympathetic post-Calvinist, postrevival assessment of the "Great Awakening" did not extend to David Brainerd, who seemed beyond cultural redemption. Brainerd's notoriety, Allen observed, had not "entirely faded"; but he seemed the embodiment of a "morbid psychology," not "genuine religious experience."[35] Walker agreed with the Episcopalian historian; Brainerd's "morbid, introspective self-examinations" and his seesaw emotions amounted to a "sorry illustration . . . of the noble ideal of the full-rounded, healthful Christian life." Samuel Hopkins, not Brainerd, stood as the Edwardsian disciple who seemed to preserve the values—moral courage, self-sacrifice, an iron sense of duty—that colonial revival students of the Puritan spirit like Allen admired and celebrated.[36]

Allen's discussion of Edwards's theology attempted to disentangle "the local and the transitory" elements in his thought—namely, Calvinism—from that which remained "imperishable" and universal—namely, the quest for transcendental spiritual truth and experience that spoke to the nondogmatic religious needs of Victorian America. Since the "spell" of *Freedom of the Will* finally "has been broken," Allen argued, one could see that Edward's enduring works were his study of the ***Religious Affections*** and sermons like **"A Divine and Supernatural Light,"** not **"Sinners in the Hands of an Angry God"** (a revival-era Calvinist remnant). Indeed, images of *"light"* and *"sweetness"* so permeated Edwards's writings, Allen claimed, that the colonial divine was the "forerunner of the later New England transcendentalism quite as truly as the author of a modified Calvinism."[37]

Two generations before Perry Miller, Allen wed Edwards to Emerson, establishing the same religious bonds that the distinguished Harvard scholar delineated. The mystical element in Edwards produced a kind of transcendental hunger for the "beauty" and "sublimity" of God and the creation. Edwards's pursuit of divine illumination made light "a word that controls his thoughts." His "direct vision into divine things" produced written analyses similar to "transcendental modes of speech." For Allen, **"A Divine and Supernatural Light"** in particular seemed to resemble "so closely the later transcendental thought of New England as almost to bridge the distance between Edwards and Emerson."[38]

Thus, Allen's biography added a post-Calvinist Edwardsian spiritual legacy to his positive assessment of Puritanism as a moral-cultural force, a tradition that he saw distilled and powerfully expressed in Edwards's life. Andover's Egbert Smyth praised Allen's study for demonstrating that "Edwards is today a living power; Hopkinsianism, Emmonsism, Edwardseanism even are outlived." While some unreconstructed Calvinists assailed Allen for transforming Edwards into a pantheist, other reviewers commended him for not allowing his rejection of Calvinism to obstruct a fair historical appraisal of the theologian.[39] Reviewers failed to note that Allen's interpretation of Edwards as a link between Puritanism and transcendentalism drew on work in the emerging field of American literature. Colonial revival-era literary scholars developed their own Puritan origins narrative that reserved a prominent place for Edwards.

. . . . .

The development of American literature as a field of study coincided with, and responded to the same cultural needs as, the colonial revival. Not surprisingly, then, the newly established formal study of American literature shaped, and was shaped by, the colonial revival creation of a usable Puritan tradition. As Nina Baym has argued, the post-Civil War New England elites who pioneered the study of American literature "realized that the nation was an artifice and that no single national character undergirded it." Like their fellow historians, from whom they were often indistinguishable, early scholars of American literature offered "the carefully edited New England Puritan as the national type." Historians of American literature hoped to fashion a common heritage—a kind of cultural Puritanism or republicanism—that would inculcate in natives and immigrants alike values deemed "necessary for the future: self-reliance, self-control, and acceptance of hierarchy."[40] Thus, the same needs and opportunities for cultural consolidation and cultural assimilation that informed the historical "recovery" of the Puritan tradition pervaded the study of American literature. An origins narrative emerged that made Puritanism the necessary "prologue" to the great American literature of the nineteenth-century "New England Renaissance," a term coined by Barrett Wendell.[41] Academic descendants of the Puritans dominated the beginnings and early history of American literary study. Some even had clerical backgrounds, a distinct advantage in an era when literature was promoted as a companion and even as a substitute—in the public schools, at least—for religion. Moses Coit Tyler, the "father" of American literary history, was one reborn Congregational minister.

A native of Connecticut, who traced his ancestry back to Plymouth Colony, Tyler graduated from Yale in 1857, studied at Andover Seminary for two years, and served short terms as a Congregational minister in New York State. Tyler resigned his second church in 1862, and five years later joined the University of Michigan, where he taught English and rhetoric. In 1881, he moved on to Cornell and became professor of American history and literature. Tyler joined the Episcopal Church and was ordained to the priesthood in 1883, the same year he confessed that his soul "constantly says, 'Thou ought to be preaching the Gospel, rather than teaching American history, or writing books about it.'"[42] In fact, Tyler did continue to preach through his textbooks on the history of American litera-

ture, joining other descendants of the Puritans in responding to the changing face of the late nineteenth century by celebrating America's colonial foundations.

In 1875, Tyler proposed that his publisher, George Putnam, underwrite the cost of a colonial literature survey that would take advantage of the new interest in the past stimulated by the approach of the centennial of American independence. Such a text would also fill a need created by the emergence of college and high school courses on American literature. Tyler did not meet the centennial deadline; *A History of American Literature* was not published until 1878. The two-volume work—the first extended survey of its kind—provided an account of American literature from its beginnings to 1765.[43] Tyler's work was cited by Alexander V. G. Allen and influenced the biographer's view of Edwards's place in American literature. On a broader level, Tyler's volumes decidedly shaped the major interpretations of American literature down to Wendell's own survey, *A Literary History of America* (1900), and beyond.

After an opening chapter on the English background, Tyler devoted seventeen chapters to American literature, twelve of which focused on New England. "Since the year 1640," Tyler boasted, "the New England race has not received any notable addition to its original stock, and today their Anglican blood is as genuine and as unmixed as that of any county in England." Moreover, unlike other less racially pure parts of America, New England was established as a "thinking community." Though this "thrifty and teeming" intellectual society did not produce belles lettres—that is, "real" literature—its voluminous body of writing, which derived from or was molded by religion, became important from the perspective of the history of ideas.[44] First, Puritan writing revealed venerable New England character traits, which Tyler seemed intent on transmitting to his readers. Tyler, like other colonial revival students of the Puritans, acknowledged the "dark side" of his ancestors. But in preacherly pronouncements, he extolled the mental discipline, moral stamina, and earnestness of the Puritans: "They were not acquainted with indolence: they forgot fatigue; they were stopped by no difficulties; they knew they could do all things that could be done."[45]

An appreciation for such enduring "American" character traits constituted one reason for the study of Puritan writing; understanding the source of subsequent American literary expression comprised another. The "narrowness of Puritanism," Tyler observed, "stunted and stiffened" the development of literature in America. The Puritans' creed and the lack of "symmetry" to their culture "crushed down" the elements essential to belles lettres. Yet, the Puritans retained an aesthetic sense, "and in pure and wholesome natures such as theirs its emergence was only a matter of natural growth."[46] Once delivered from the repression of Calvinism, Puritan mental training, moral energy, and spiritual aesthetics found expression through literature. Not Tyler, whose study ended in 1765, but New England scholars who quickly followed in his train picked up the scent and proceeded to "Puritanize" the writers of the nineteenth-century literary renaissance. "Edwards to Emerson" was enfolded in a narrative of Puritan origins and consummation that explained the development of American literature.

Tyler's own treatment of Edwards is revealing. The fifteen pages he devoted to Edwards were only exceeded by the seventeen he gave to Cotton Mather. Tyler held up Edwards as the product of the "gentlest and most intellectual New England stock." His early life and youthful intellectual accomplishments illustrated how the "thinking community" was sustained by "educational efforts wrought on the people of New England by their rugged theological drill." Edwards's "Resolutions," though marred by "puerile severity," bore witness to "traits of a personal character full of all nobility."[47]

In a succession of vivid images Tyler brought Edwards to life as the "logical drill-master of innumerable minds." Edwards's power as a preacher derived from his attention to the "minuteness of imaginative detail." His words, descending from the pulpit like "drop after drop of the molten metal, of the scalding oil, fell steadily upon the same spot, till the victim cried out in shrieks of agony." Of course, Edwards's imaginative impulse was constrained by "that ganglion of heroic, acute, and appalling dogmas named after John Calvin." Nevertheless, Edwards displayed "the fundamental virtues of a writer" even if he did not produce beautiful literature. The "precision, clearness, and simplicity" of much of his writing and his "bold, original, and poetic imagery" suggested how Puritanism was a sort of cultural quarry whose moral sense, intellectual rigor, and religious imagination supplied the building blocks for American literature.[48]

Tyler's *A History of American Literature*, like the bronze and granite totems being hoisted into place by his contemporaries, was in its own way a monument to the Puritans. Tyler's volume, though far from uncritical of his New England ancestors, resounded with the colonial revival appreciation of the Puritans that was emerging in more strictly historical works. Tyler's study proved to be monumental in another sense; it shaped the study of American literature for more than a generation. Tyler's publisher, for example, issued the first comprehensive survey of American literature from the beginnings to the late nineteenth century in 1887. Authored by the New England born and educated Dartmouth College professor, Charles F. Richardson, *American Literature, 1607-1885* consisted of two volumes: one devoted to American thought and the other to poetry and fiction. American "literature," Richardson claimed, was "only about eighty years old," but colonial religious treatises, sermons, and "records of sight and experience" represented "index figures pointing to future triumphs." In fact, Richardson claimed, the Puritans stood as "the direct precursors and the actual founders of most that is good in American letters."[49]

Other influential professorial descendants of the Puritans put the issue more bluntly. New England's "intellectual activity," Barrett Wendell submitted, "so far exceeded that of any other part of the country that literary history of other regions may be neglected." Wendell's "New England Renaissance" was really an "American Renaissance," as it would be renamed by a later Harvard professor. Wendell also proposed the now canonical pairing of Edwards and Franklin "as representing two distinct aspects of American character." Edwards embodied ideals of religion and morality "inherent in the lasting tradition of the English Bible." Franklin illustrated political and social ideals, "equally inherent in the equally lasting tradition of the English law."[50]

In the two decades after the publication of Tyler's seminal text, American literary histories multiplied. Authors responded to both an expanding educational market for such volumes and to the cultural needs of their era - promoting national pride, a respect for tradition, even a moral code. As Wendell's *A Literary History of America* suggests, Edwards's cultural figure undergirded the Puritan origins narrative that circulated from text to text. Consider Frances Underwood's *The Builders of American Literature* (1893). A Unitarian literary critic, Underwood authored *Quabbin: The Story of a Small Town with Outlooks on Puritan Life* (1893), a richly textured, almost local color, history of his home community that stands as arguably the finest colonial revival-era New England town history. In *The Builders of American Literature,* Underwood did not allow his Unitarianism to interfere with his assessment of the Puritans and of Edwards. It was certainly true, Underwood conceded, that the "unloveliness" of the Puritans' temperament, "the severity of their discipline, and their disdain for sentiment" impeded literary expression in New England. But the Puritans did not journey to America "to indite poems and romances" or "to dance around Maypoles." The Puritans undertook "the great work of founding the colonies on an enduring basis," and for this task their religious spirit and values served them—and posterity—well. For Underwood, Edwards hovered over the colonial era as "the last great Puritan divine." As the "flower of the Puritan race and culture in New England," Edwards demonstrated colonial religion's abiding virtues as well as its antiquated defects. Ensnared in Puritanism's "gloominess, ascetism, narrowness, and provincial spirit," Edwards also exemplified its "logic, its inflexible purpose; its reverence, personal holiness, and steadfast faith."[51]

In the literary histories of the 1880s and 1890s, Edwards became not only an exemplar of the two sides of Puritanism; he emerged as a sort of cultural sepulcher in which Puritan tradition was deposited and held for safe transmission to the nineteenth century. "The dignities of a whole corp of Puritan ancestry are centered in him," one literary historian declared in 1897; "they bridged him over boyhood: he must have strode across the years of fun and pranks on the stilts of his forefathers." Since he was an "intellectual saint rapt into high communion with the Invisible," as another turn-of-the-century literary scholar observed, Edwards's writing was approached as a cultural switchback slowly moving American literature toward its highest expression in the nineteenth-century renaissance. Edwards, the author of *An Introduction to American Literature* (1898) asserted, "is both the spiritual descendant of Cotton Mather and of Michael Wigglesworth, and the spiritual ancestor of Dr. Channing, the great leader of New England Unitarianism, and Emerson, the thinker of later times."[52] Edwards appeared as a towering canonical figure in these early literary texts that valued the history of ideas, that privileged New England writing, that approached colonial works as the prolegomenon to the nineteenth-century renaissance, and that used literature to promote cultural nationalism and Anglo-Puritan moral values.

. . . . .

Monuments, commemorative addresses, historical studies and biographies, and literary histories—these were all cultural productions influenced by the late-nineteenth- and early-twentieth-century interest in and appropriation of the colonial past. Monuments, historical sites, and the homes of famous figures also stimulated the cultural appetite of a growing traveling public—consumers of what is now called heritage tourism. Pilgrimages to colonial shrines and to restored or preserved homes and villages brought temporary relief from the dizzying changes of the late nineteenth century, while arousing nostalgia and respect for a seemingly more simple and virtuous past.

In guidebook accounts that paralleled the narratives in American history and literary texts, the New England past came disproportionately to define the cultural heritage for which tourists went in search. Boston's Edwin Bacon, for instance, published two large and successful guidebooks at the turn of the century: *Historic Pilgrimages in New England* and *Literary Pilgrimages in New England*. Both works employ the visit of a young Western friend of the author who makes summer journeys to the East to acquire cultural knowledge and reaffirm ancestral roots. Advertisements described *Historic Pilgrimages* as follows:

> This is the vivid story of early New England, told while standing upon the very spots where the stirring Colonial drama was enacted. The famous places where the Puritans and Pilgrims planted their first homes, the ancient buildings, and the monuments to the wise and dauntless founders of the great commonwealth are visited, and, while in the atmosphere of the association, the thrilling narrative of the past is recorded.[53]

Literary Pilgrimages takes the author and his culturally starved young companion to the homes and "haunts" of New England writers as well as to the "scenes of their writing."[54]

Stockbridge and Northampton were two of these literary shrines; here the travelers tarried and reflected on "the great eighteenth century metaphysician, who has been called the last and finest product of the Puritans of America." The sojourners recorded their encounter with

Edwardsian monuments, markers, and artifacts, even reproducing some of them in the guidebook.[55] In fact, when Bacon published *Literary Pilgrimages* in 1902, the residents of Stockbridge and Northampton were still in the process of consecrating their townscapes with new Edwards mementos, a process that had begun after the Civil War and that had tracked the progress of the colonial revival. Stockbridge and Northampton afford a view of the colonial revival interest in the Puritan past from the local level. Very different communities in the late nineteenth century, they exemplify varied aspects of the colonial revival, of the renewed interest in Puritan heritage, and of the process of commemoration at the local level that erected less grand monuments to religious tradition than Saint-Gaudens's "Puritan."

Though encircled by mill villages in the river valleys of the Berkshire Hills and by Irish millhands and railroad workers, Stockbridge developed in the post-Civil War era as a fashionable and quaint resort town. The sense of antiquity encouraged by new, cultivated historical associations enhanced the appeal of such "ancient" New England towns. As early as 1868, the First Congregational Church in Stockbridge dedicated four tablets to its first ministers, including Edwards and Stephen West, his New Divinity successor. At the commemoration address, Reverend Nathaniel Eggleston, First Church's pastor, noted that the "Edwards Place abides yet," reference to the theologian's home in Stockbridge which became a late-nineteenth-century landmark. At the time, Eggleston voiced concern over such privately owned "landmarks of our ancestors," fearing that they might cease "to function as aids to memory." Churches, however, offered a location to "erect memorials that will remain when dwellings, subject to the laws of private property, shall be gone."[56] Public space as well, the citizens of Stockbridge would soon discover, presented a more visible and dominant civic location for memorializing a glorious past.

Colonial revival sentiment in Stockbridge received a boost not only from the arrival of major New England historical anniversaries; it drew impetus from the first gathering of the Edwards family, which was held in the town in 1870. Nearly two hundred descendants of Edwards responded to the invitation to attend the meeting. Two days of celebration ensued; between lectures about their distinguished progenitor and ancestral self-congratulations, the descendants visited Edwards shrines, such as the theologian's home on Main Street. Edwards's alma mater furnished a large tent under which his ancestors came together for food and refreshments. Yale also sent President Theodore Dwight Woolsey, himself a descendant of Edwards, who served up appropriate commemorative fare. "He [Edwards] and others among the best Puritans of New England," Woolsey proclaimed, "succeeded in the crowning struggle of the human soul to rise above earthly things, and to lead a spiritual life on the principles of Christ's gospel."[57]

Some speakers, though not direct descendants of Edwards, took pride in a personal connection to the theologian and contributed to the meeting's ancestor worship, as well as to distress about the preservation of the past. Boston minister I. N. Tarbox was, like Edwards, a native of East Windsor, Connecticut, and he reported on disquieting changes in the town—the kind of alterations that provoked colonial revival guardians of the past. The Edwards homesite in Connecticut was "now occupied by one of our adopted fellow-citizens from Ireland, by the name of Christopher McNary." While the Irishman resides on a "spot that is famous," Tarbox complained, "he seems not aware of the privileges in this regard." Such a benighted fellow was "not well read up in Edwardean history," among his other educational deficiencies. "The association of the past disturbs him not," content as McNary was "raising tobacco."[58]

Colonial artifacts, which became part of the antique mania of the late nineteenth century, functioned like historical monuments to secure associations with the past. Edwardsian artifacts were abundantly displayed, and even manufactured, for the participants in the Stockbridge family meeting. Edwards A. Park, for instance, offered manuscripts showing how Edwards compensated for a shortage of paper by writing in newspaper margins, on advertisements, and even on "paper patterns which his daughters had used for making fans and collars, which they sold in order to defray the family expenses." Edwards's "genius" triumphed though he labored "without the fit apparatus."[59] Beneath portraits of Edwards and Sarah and the insignia of the family coat of arms, sacred relics that ranged from the theologian's Yale valedictory address to his wife's wedding dress were exhibited. Edwards's silver porringer was passed around the dinner table like a communion cup from which his descendants sipped coffee as they imbibed his Puritan spirit—a spirit, one speaker averred, that needed to be preserved and combined "with the advancing science and culture of the age."[60] Wood that had been salvaged from the old Indian meeting house where Edwards had preached was carved into "little useful and ornamental articles" for family members. These sacred Edwardsian keepsakes and a group photograph near the site of the Indian church would help sustain the ancestral afterglow of the family meeting.[61]

Commenting on the late-nineteenth-century vogue of family reunions and ancestor worship, Michael Kammen has observed that such filio-pietism served "primarily to enhance the living more than to honor the dead."[62] In Stockbridge, Edwards's descendants basked in rhetoric to their ancestor that included gratefulness to Divine Providence for the blood coursing through their veins. Speakers and auditors celebrated everything from the contributions of family members to the Civil War to the clan's D.D.'s and LL.D.'s that, one versifying descendant remarked, were "like leaves in the autumn breeze," if not "thick as peas." In the flush of family celebration, the descendants determined that it was their "duty to raise . . . some enduring monument" to their ancestor that would "remind the traveler, in a distant age, alike of the virtues of the man and

the piety of his race."[63] Two years later a large granite memorial monument to Edwards was unveiled at an intersection on Main Street.

The Edwards commemoration stimulated the placement of other historical markers on the Stockbridge townscape, a sacred place that descendants had voted to designate as the "traditional home of the Edwards family."[64] These visible associations with the past burnished an aura of antiquity and stability into the townscape that added to the quaint village's appeal as a tourist resort; "Olde Stockbridge," an up-to-date past, began to take shape. But neither the cultural needs of colonial revival tourists, nor the ancestor worship of the Edwards family, prevented the demolition of the "Edwards Place" at the turn of the century. On the sacred site, however, a memorial sundial was erected and from the landmark's boards numerous mementos were fashioned and, apparently, sold to visitors.[65]

When the Edwards family chose Stockbridge as its official "hometown," Northampton had also come under consideration. The rejection of Northampton resulted from more than the fact that the community had turned its back on its illustrious Puritan minister. Post-Civil War Northampton, in its size, economic activity, and ethnic diversity, contrasted sharply with the Berkshire village of Stockbridge. It was precisely this contrast that made colonial revival fascination with the Anglo-Puritan past in general, and with Edwards in particular, so much stronger in Northampton than Stockbridge. Northampton, which shed its town status in 1883, resembled midsized communities like Salem, Massachusetts, whose rich and controversial colonial heritage and rapidly changing socioeconomic order made them focal points of the colonial revival.[66] Certainly, if the native citizens of Salem could retrieve a usable Puritan past from the remains of their colonial history, Northamptonites faced a far less daunting task.

Even before Northampton's interest in the colonial past accelerated in the 1890s, its Yankee citizens confronted many reminders of Edwards and the heritage he represented. Both the First Church, which was held up as the "birthplace" of the colonial awakening, and the Edwards Church, founded in 1833, remained thriving parishes in the center of town. Recently erected obelisks to the Edwards and Dwight families stood in the old cemetery not far from the bustling civic and commercial district. The Edwards elms, trees that the theologian had planted in front of his home on King Street, were a famous local landmark; they would be photographed or illustrated in books discussing Puritan heritage and be reproduced as postcards. On the homesite stood the Whitney Mansion, which became a boardinghouse for business travelers and tourists and which was often mistaken as the Edwards homestead.[67]

By the 1890s, these and other historical artifacts seemed inadequate to anchor the community to its colonial past. Northampton, with a population of nearly 17,000 by 1895, had a long history of manufacturing on the banks of the

Mill River. But the production of cloth, machinery, tools, and items from buttons to toothbrushes grew significantly in the late nineteenth century—until the recession of 1893, from which the city only slowly recovered. Part of this recovery entailed the growth of unions, which increased from seven in 1898 to thirty-five by 1903.[68] Most unsettling of all, perhaps, these changes were accompanied by significant alterations in the ethnic and religious composition of Northampton. Irish Catholics had maintained a strong presence in the city since midcentury, but growing numbers of French Canadians were drawn to Northampton from the 1880s, and they would be followed, from the 1890s onward, by Polish and Italian contract laborers and Russian Jews. By the beginning of the new century, when Polish immigration began to swell, upward of half of the city's residents claimed foreign-born parents. Immigration had already disrupted Northampton's civic institutions, venerable legacies of the community's Puritan past. As early as 1891, for example, Irish and French Catholic schools opened and dramatically affected public school enrollment: one school was closed down and three others lost half of their students.[69]

In the midst of such changes, Yankee natives responded with more than nostalgia for "Olde Northampton." They also launched commemorative activities that, along with other actions, comprised a significant cultural backlash. Edwards's historical figure took on iconic power in the cultural politics of late-nineteenth- and early-twentieth-century Northampton.

In the mid-1890s, Northamptonites began planning and organizing for the two hundred and fiftieth anniversary of the city, which had been established in 1654. One committee was charged with collecting material and artifacts relating to Northampton's early history. As in other communities, the approach of the city's anniversary and a changing social landscape gave birth to the local historical society. The committee members soon realized that the documents and artifacts gathered for the commemoration would need a permanent home. Moreover, a Northampton Historical Society would arrest the erosion of interest in and knowledge of the city's past that resulted from the influx of immigrants, many of whom could barely speak English. And what better place to establish the historical society than on the homesite of Northampton's most distinguished historical father, shaded by the remaining and well-publicized Edwards elm (the other had blown down in 1885).[70]

The committee began to work to acquire and remodel the Whitney Mansion, or "Ye Olde Whitney House," as it was apparently renamed when it started taking in boarders. Plans called for a combination historical society, museum, and headquarters of the Daughters of the American Revolution, a sort of Northampton heritage center on the location consecrated by Edwards. The commemorative committee and its supporters were unable to complete the legal and financial arrangements to purchase and renovate the Whitney Mansion; the historical society was then estab-

lished at another location in Northampton. But a historical tablet was placed on the property identifying it as the Edwards homesite.[71]

Other efforts to preserve Northampton's colonial past and commemorate Edwards coincided with the founding of the Northampton Historical Society. In 1898, James Russell Trumbull published the first volume of his celebratory *History of Northampton, Massachusetts from its Settlement in 1654* (the second volume was published in 1902). A full portrait of Edwards graced the frontispiece of the book. Trumbull's history bulged to 1,200 pages, but he did not venture beyond 1800.[72]

In 1898, also, what was purported to be Edwards's granite doorstep was hauled from the Whitney Mansion and placed on the lawn in front of the town's impressive and recently completed library, the first of several stone memorials to Northampton's religious heritage.[73] That same year, a local real estate developer—offering his own contribution to the preservation of colonial tradition—laid out Edwards Square. A small development of modest middle-class homes, Edwards Square encircled the Edwards elm and homesite. Almost immediately, Edwards Square became the site of a fortress-like armory, a monument to change that was different from, but not unrelated to, the newly placed colonial markers on Northampton's landscape. Built between 1899 and 1900, the armory served as police headquarters and National Guard barracks. Northampton followed the lead of many much larger communities that built armories in the last two decades of the nineteenth century. Usually located in stable middle-class neighborhoods, armories enabled the National Guard to store arms, drill, and respond effectively to social disorder, including violent strikes.[74] In Northampton, at least, the armory did not become a nerve center of state repression; rather, it seemed to function not unlike historical monuments, as a reassuring symbol of the community's ability to cope with and contain change.

While sounds of civic and domestic construction reverberated on both sides of the Edwards homesite, members of the First Congregational Church moved ahead with their plans to pay tribute to the theologian. The church established a committee in 1897 to plan an appropriate memorial to Edwards. Money was raised from church members, other residents of Northampton, descendants of Edwards, and admirers in New England and abroad. The committee could not wait until 1903, the bicentennial of Edward's birth, to honor the distinguished divine. They unabashedly decided to memorialize Edwards on the one hundred and fiftieth anniversary of his dismissal from the First Church! In June 1900, an Edwards descendant unveiled a five-by-eight-foot bronze bas-relief of the colonial pastor completed by the sculptor Herbert Adams. Offering an image of Edwards in the act of preaching what some said was his farewell sermon, the bronze tablet commemorated his now heroic figure with flattering biblical verse.[75]

A daylong series of academic and clerical addresses, which were published by Houghton Mifflin as *Jonathan Edwards: A Retrospect,* accompanied the unveiling ceremonies. In his introduction to the volume, editor H. Norman Gardiner, chairman of the Edwards Memorial Committee and professor of philosophy at Smith College, declared that the bronze tablet "represents neither the contrition nor the pride of the local church." Instead, he offered the memorial as recognition of "a widely spread, and to a certain extent, newly awakened regard for the genius and character of its subject" as well as of a "sympathetic interest in what appeared to many as a simple act of historic justice."[76]

Alexander V. G. Allen's address rehearsed the major points of his popular biography. Edwards was an American Dante, with poetic "imagination," "tenderness," and spiritual "insight"; his enduring writings included **"The Sermon on Spiritual Light"** and his "greatest work," *Religious Affections.* Egbert Smyth offered the Andover view that had not reassured Edwards A. Park years earlier. The memorial tablet stood for "something more than a *return* to Edwards." It meant instead "*a going on* with him," an acknowledgment "that we still have him with us and will continue to have,—*him,* the noblest Roman of us all." Yale's George Park Fisher, dean of the Divinity School, brought Edwards's valedictory address to the commemoration, just as President Woolsey had to the Edwards family meeting thirty years earlier. Fisher praised Edwards as "the Saint of New England," and stressed that three of the theologian's descendants had served in the presidency of Yale for almost half of the nineteenth century. Yale's acquisition of the major Edwards manuscript collections in 1900 strengthened the special institutional claim on the Edwardsian legacy that Fisher made. Speaking for Northampton, Reverend Henry Rose, pastor of the First Church, reminded the audience that Edwards had described the town as "a city set on a hill." Rose was determined to preserve Northampton's distinctive religious heritage as the famed "centre of the mighty religious phenomena known in history under the name of the Great Awakening."[77]

Other speakers from Northampton, Boston, and Princeton recited hymns that contributed to a kind of colonial revival Protestant version of a beatification ceremony. Yankee Northamptonites and other Anglo-Puritan descendants found new opportunities after the turn of the century to continue commemorating Edwards. Indeed, 1903 proved to be the high-water mark of colonial revival celebrations of Edwards as an embodiment of Puritan tradition.

. . . . .

The Northampton commemoration not only gained the notice of the local and denominational press; it was reported in *Harper's* and the *New York Times.* In fact, two weeks before the commemoration the *Times* had editorialized on the need, almost "as a matter of patriotism," for a new edition of Edwards's works and for a biography even "less critical and more human" than Alexander V. G. Allen's.[78]

Edwards's induction into the American Hall of Fame in 1900 lent support to the *Times*'s call, reinforced the filiopietistic activities of Northamptonites, and provides additional evidence of Edwards's eminence in American culture.

The Hall of Fame was yet another late colonial revival attempt to define and institutionalize America's heritage in the face of a shifting social order that seemed to lack centripetal cultural force. Built with a gift from an anonymous donor to New York University, the Hall of Fame was intended as a kind of American pantheon "to stimulate patriotism and high endeavor by commemorating those virtues in persons who have passed away and by collecting busts, portraits, and mementos of these our great." Induction was open to distinguished Americans who had been dead for at least ten years. The benefactor of the Hall of Fame established a careful selection process that was intended to avoid "mistakes of enthusiasm or of prejudice." Nominations were submitted to a panel composed of one hundred distinguished men and women. Nominations and elections were to be held every five years with fifty inductees who had received at least fifty-one of the judges' votes gaining admission to the historical sanctuary after they had also been endorsed by the faculty senate of the university.[79]

With the Hall of Fame building completed, the first election was held in 1900. But only 29 of the 234 nominees received more than fifty-one votes. (They were all men, with Mary Lyon receiving the highest number of votes among nominated women.) Edwards was among the select group. Indeed, he outpolled Nathaniel Hawthorne eighty-one to seventy-three.[80]

Little wonder, then, that the bicentennial of Edwards's birth three years later occasioned extensive commemoration. Widely reported in the religious and secular press, the memorialization of Edwards stretched from Andover, Northampton, Springfield, and Stockbridge in Massachusetts, and Hartford, New Haven, and South Windsor in Connecticut, to New York City, Princeton, and churches from the Midwest to California. Andover hosted the most elaborate commemoration—two days of hymns and addresses accompanied by a full exhibit of Edwards manuscripts and artifacts. At Yale, Williston Walker offered the keynote address on Edwards, while in South Windsor the commemorators visited the theologian's birthplace and his father's grave.[81]

Everywhere Edwards was hailed as a sacred Anglo-Puritan, and thus American, cultural icon. Speaking to audiences both in Stockbridge and Princeton, Professor John DeWitt, for instance, extolled Edwards as the notable representative of a northern European "spiritual race." Reminding his auditors that 1903 was also the centennial of Emerson's birth, DeWitt observed, "The day belongs, not to the great Puritan who gave up the Puritan conception of the universe for its interpretation by poetry and letters, but to the great Puritan who denied himself the high satisfactions of literature, that through his distinctively Christian doctrine of God and men he might be the friend and aider of those who would live in the spirit."[82] In the shadow of Saint-Gaudens's statue, a speaker in Springfield allowed that Edwards's theology was antiquated, but the tradition he represented, "the spirit of Puritanism, is bone of our bone, flesh of our flesh."[83]

In the decades leading up to the Edwards bicentennial, cultural exigencies had sparked colonial revival nostalgia, ancestor worship, and commemoration, which in turn shaped academic studies of America's historical and literary heritage—a "national" heritage of New England origin. The Puritan was refashioned by influential descendants into a kind of post-Calvinist ecumenical figure in whom the moral and cultural spirit of Protestantism, and thus of Americanism, reposed. For many, the Puritan spirit offered the religious leaven for Victorian America. Edwards as "a Puritan of Puritans" was commemorated and enshrined as an American cultural icon.

To a considerable extent, colonial revivalists' uses of Puritan tradition emerged as an effort to construct and impose on a dynamic and seemingly unwieldy nation what can only be described as a civil religion. In celebrating the religious origins of American history and literature, in upholding Anglo-Puritan character traits and moral values, in raising religious or quasi-religious historical monuments, and in using textbooks, public schools, and civic space to accomplish these ends, descendants of the Puritans invoked their heritage to define the American way. Such efforts, however, did encounter significant resistance—and not just from southerners. Northampton Catholics, for example, not only established their own schools; they celebrated their own cultural heritage. In the town's two hundred and fiftieth commemoration, historical floats sponsored by the Knights of Columbus and the St. Jean Baptiste Society joined floats depicting Minutemen and other aspects of Northampton's colonial and Revolutionary past. And when a Polish National Catholic Church was later built on the Edwards homesite, the members rebuffed attempts to preserve the historical tablet that designated the location as hallowed ground.[84] The tablet ended up in the Northampton Historical Society, where it is stored today.

Notes

1. The colonial revival has been studied primarily in relationship to material culture—architecture, domestic interiors, and antiques—and to the centennial celebration of 1876. I am using the term to refer to a broad interest in the colonial past that was fueled by cultural nationalism and cultural reaction in the late nineteenth and early twentieth centuries. The colonial revival perspective on American culture was reflected in and constituted by a variety of artifacts and activities, both popular and elite, that are the subject of this chapter. My understanding of the colonial revival is informed by the suggestive essays in Alan Axelrod, ed., *The Colonial Revival in America* (New York, 1985). Also see Karal Ann Marling, *George Washington Slept Here: Colonial Revivals and American Culture* (Cambridge, Mass., 1988).

2. Harriet Beecher Stowe, *The Minister's Wooing* (Boston, 1859; reprint, New York, 1967), pp. 101, 245, 246.

3. Ibid., p. 18. On Stowe and Puritanism, see Lawrence E. Buell, *New England Literary Culture: From Revolution through Renaissance* (New York, 1986), chap. 11, and Charles H. Foster's still useful *The Rungless Ladder: Harriet Beecher Stowe and New England Puritanism* (Durham, N.C., 1954).

4. Stowe, *Oldtown Folks* (1869; reprint, New Brunswick, N.J., 1987), pp. 317, 318, 322.

5. Beecher, *Norwood; or, Village Life in New England* (New York, 1867), pp. 2-3. The description of Buell is from Beecher's preface to the 1887 edition. It is quoted in William G. McLoughlin, *The Meaning of Henry Ward Beecher: An Essay on the Shifting Values of Mid-Victorian America* (New York, 1970), p. 63.

6. Beecher, *Norwood,* p. 326.

7. Quoted in Buell, *New England Literary Culture,* p. 206.

8. This term is Buell's, who uses it to examine how antebellum views of the Puritan past were shaped by Calvinist-Unitarian disputes over theology and revivalism. See ibid., chap. 9.

9. The sketch of Edwards is reprinted in Oliver Wendell Holmes, *Pages from an Old Volume of Life: A Collection of Essays, 1857-1881* (Boston, 1883); the quotation is on p. 361.

10. Williston Walker, *A History of the Congregational Churches in the United States* (New York, 1894), pp. 397-98.

11. Ibid., p. 399. For the background and the "Burial Hill Declaration" itself, see also Walker, *Creeds and Platforms of Congregationalism* (New York, 1893), pp. 553-69.

12. Henry Martyn Dexter, *The Congregationalism of the Last Three Hundred Years as Seen in Its Literature* (New York, 1880), p. 448; Albert E. Dunning, *Congregationalists in America: A Popular History of Their Origins, Belief, Polity, Growth and Work* (Boston, 1894), p. 263.

13. Dexter, *Congregationalism of the Last Three Hundred Years,* p. v; Dexter, *As to Roger Williams, and His "Banishment" from Massachusetts Plantations* (Boston, 1876).

14. Walker, *History of the Congregational Churches,* p. 438.

15. For background information on the Congregational Library Association, see ibid., pp. 384-85. Dr.

Harold Worthley of the library has also furnished me with information about the association, the building, and the bas-reliefs.

16. For a suggestive discussion of Saint-Gaudens's work and of Puritan iconography, see Michael Kammen, *Mystic Chords of Memory: The Transformation of Tradition in American Culture* (New York, 1991), pp. 206-15. Kammen's brief discussion of the Puritan tradition in the late nineteenth century has informed my own analysis. Less helpful is Jan C. Dawson, *The Unusable Past: America's Puritan Tradition, 1830 to 1930* (Chico, Calif., 1984).

17. Quoted in Kammen, *Mystic Chords of Memory,* p. 212.

18. George Ellis, *The Puritan Age in Massachusetts, 1629-1685* (Boston, 1888). Among the biographies published were the following: Joseph H. Twichell, *John Winthrop, First Governor of the Massachusetts Colony* (New York, 1891); George L. Walker, *Thomas Hooker* (New York, 1891); Abijah Marvin, *The Life and Times of Cotton Mather* (Boston, 1892); Alice M. Earle, *Margaret Winthrop* (New York, 1895); and Nathan H. Chamberlain, *Samuel Sewall and the World He Lived In* (Boston, 1897). Of course antebellum religious controversies had stimulated historical interest in the Puritans. But the colonial revival surge of historical studies of the Puritans was broader and deeper and embraced secular scholarship emerging in colleges and universities.

19. Barrctt Wcndcll, *Cotton Mather, The Puritan Priest* (1891; reprint, Cambridge, Mass., 1926), pp. 1, 78-79, 301, 305. In his introduction to a 1963 paperback edition of Wendell's biography, Alan Heimert comments on Mather and the strenuous life; see *Cotton Mather, The Puritan Priest* (New York, 1963), p. xviii. See also Wendell's views on the Puritans in *Stelligeri and Other Essays* (New York, 1893).

20. Ezra Byington, *The Puritan in England and New England,* 4th ed. (1900; reprint, New York, 1972), pp. x, 113, 335-81.

21. Ezra Byington, *The Puritan as a Colonist and Reformer* (Boston, 1899), pp. vii, 55, 273.

22. Lyman Abbott, "The New Puritanism," in *The New Puritanism,* ed. Lyman Abbott (New York, 1898), pp. 28, 33, 38.

23. Amory Bradford, "Puritan Principles in the Modern World," in ibid., pp. 85, 96, 99.

24. Alice M. Earle, *The Sabbath in Puritan New England* (1891; 8th ed., New York, 1898), p. 327. See "Alice Morse Earle," in *Dictionary of American Biography,* ed. Allen Johnson and Dumas Malone, 10 vols. (New York, 1927-36), 3:593-94. Earle is a crucial figure in the colonial revival construction of an early American past, but she receives only

passing mention in works such as Kammen's *Mystic Chords of Memory* and Axelrod's *Colonial Revival in America.* Earle's publications were more influential than similar works, such as Mary Caroline Crawford's *The Romance of Old New England Churches* (Boston, 1903), which contained a chapter on the Edwards family. Earle's books even reached a wider audience than colonial revival novels, such as Frank Samuel Child's *A Puritan Wooing: A Tale of the Great Awakening* (New York, 1898).

25. Quoted in M. X. Lesser, *Jonathan Edwards: A Reference Guide* (Boston, 1981), p. 136.

26. Adams, *The Emancipation of Massachusetts* (Boston, 1886). See also Dawson, *The Unusable Past,* pp. 94-97.

27. John Fiske, *The Beginnings of New England* (Boston, 1889), pp. viii, 105, 148, 278. Another dissenting Adams responded to Fiske. See Charles Francis Adams, Jr., *Three Episodes of Massachusetts History* (Boston, 1892) and *Massachusetts: Its Historians and Its History* (Boston, 1893).

28. Holmes, "Jonathan Edwards," in *Pages from an Old Volume,* pp. 368, 387, 389, 394, 395; for the reference to Edwards as a Protestant saint and for criticism of Holmes's essay by his literary circle, see Mrs. John T. Sargent, ed., *Sketches and Reminiscences of the Radical Club of Chestnut Street, Boston* (Boston, 1880), pp. 362-75.

29. See the advertisement and list of publications at the end of the first edition of Allen's biography (Boston, 1889).

30. Allen, *Jonathan Edwards,* p. vi.

31. Ibid., pp. 7, 22, 32, 111.

32. Ibid., pp. 52, 55, 116, 299.

33. Ibid., pp. 104, 116.

34. Williston Walker, "Jonathan Edwards," in *Ten New England Leaders* (New York, 1901), p. 236. See also Walker, "Jonathan Edwards," in *Great Men of the Christian Church* (Chicago, 1908), pp. 339-53, and I. N. Tarbox, "Jonathan Edwards as a Man, and the Ministers of the Last Century," *New Englander,* n.s., 7 (September 1884): 615-31.

35. Allen, *Jonathan Edwards,* pp. 160, 246.

36. Walker, *Ten New England Leaders,* p. 243. Hopkins was one of the ten leaders whose lives and careers Walker sympathetically chronicled.

37. Allen, *Jonathan Edwards,* pp. 68, 219, 299, 386, 388.

38. Ibid., p. 68.

39. Egbert Smyth, "Professor Allen's 'Jonathan Edwards,'" *Andover Review* 13 (March 1890): 285-304; George Park Fisher, "Review of Professor Allen's Life of Jonathan Edwards," *New Englander*

and Yale Review 52 (January 1890): 85-88; J. W. Wellman, "A New Biography of Jonathan Edwards," *Our Day* 5 (March and April 1890): 195-219, 288-307.

40. Nina Baym, "Early Histories of American Literature: A Chapter in the Institutionalization of New England," *American Literary History* 1 (Fall 1989): 460. See also Kermit Vanderbilt, *American Literature and the Academy* (Philadelphia, 1986), chaps. 6-8, and Richard Brodhead, *The School of Hawthorne* (New York, 1986), esp. chap. 3.

41. Philip F. Gura uses the word "prologue" to describe the long-standing approach to early American literature that examines colonial writing not on its own terms but primarily in its relationship to nineteenth-century literature. See "The Study of Colonial American Literature, 1966-1987: A Vade Mecum," *William and Mary Quarterly* 45 (April 1988): 308. Wendell coined the term the "Renaissance of New England," in *A Literary History of America* (1900; reprint, New York, 1968), p. 9.

42. Quoted in Michael Kammen, "Moses Coit Tyler: The First Professor of American History in the United States," in *Selvages and Biases* (Ithaca, N.Y., 1987), p. 227. In addition to Kammen's essay, Kermit Vanderbilt's chapter on Tyler is also helpful; see *American Literature and the Academy,* chap. 6.

43. Tyler, *A History of American Literature,* 2 vols. (1878; reprint, New York, 1895). Volume 1 covered 1607-76 and volume 2, 1676-1765.

44. Tyler, *History of American Literature,* 1:94-95, 98.

45. Ibid., pp. 101, 109.

46. Ibid., pp. 113-14.

47. Ibid., 2:178, 180, 186.

48. Ibid., pp. 188, 190, 192.

49. Charles F. Richardson, *American Literature, 1607-1885,* 2 vols. (New York, 1887), 1: ix, xvii. See also Vanderbilt's helpful discussion of Richardson's background and professional life in *American Literature and the Academy,* chap. 7.

50. Wendell, *Literary History of America,* pp. 36, 82; see also Wendell, *Stelligeri and Other Essays,* p. 121.

51. Frances Underwood, *The Builders of American Literature* (Boston, 1893), pp. 3-4, 40. See also Underwood, *Quabbin: The Story of a Small Town with Outlooks on Puritan Life* (1893; reprint, Boston, 1986). Robert Gross's introduction to this reprint offers an excellent analysis of Underwood's life and historical perspective.

52. Donald G. Mitchell, *American Land and Letters* (New York, 1897), pp. 60-61; Walter C. Bronson, *A Short History of American Literature* (1900; reprint, Boston, 1906), p. 33; and Henry S. Pancoast, *An Introduction to American Literature* (New York, 1898), p. 66. See also Henry A. Beers, *Initial Studies in American Letters* (Cleveland, Ohio, 1895), pp. 34-36; F. V. N. Painter, *Introduction to American Literature* (Boston, 1897), pp. 51-58; Lorenzo Sears, *American Literature in the Colonial Period* (Boston, 1902), pp. 3-4, 91-94; and Charles Wells Moulton, ed., *The Library of Literary Criticism of English and American Authors,* 8 vols. (Buffalo, N.Y., 1901-4), 3:380-95.

53. Edwin Bacon, *Historic Pilgrimages in New England* (New York, 1900). The advertisement is in the back of Bacon, *Literary Pilgrimages in New England* (New York, 1902).

54. Bacon, *Literary Pilgrimages,* p. 2. For an excellent analysis of the colonial revival interest in the homes of famous people, which led to the creation of house museums, see Celia Betsky, "Inside the Past: The Interior and the Colonial Revival in American Art and Literature, 1860-1914," in *Colonial Revival in America,* ed. Axelrod, pp. 241-77.

55. Bacon, *Literary Pilgrimages,* pp. 432-38, 460-61.

56. Nathaniel Eggleston, *In Memoriam: A Discourse Preached November 1, 1868, on the Occasion of the Erection of Tablets in the Old Church at Stockbridge, Mass., In Memory of Its Former Pastors, John Sergeant, Jonathan Edwards, Stephen West, David D. Field* (New York, 1869), pp. 9-10, 33. On the history of Stockbridge, see Sarah Cabot Sedgwick and Christina Sedgwick Marquand, *Stockbridge, 1739-1939, A Chronicle* (Great Barrington, Mass., 1939).

57. Theodore Dwight Woolsey, "Commemorative Address," in *Memorial Volume of the Edwards Family Meeting at Stockbridge, Mass., September 6-7 A.D. 1870* (Boston, 1871), p. 72.

58. I. N. Tarbox, "On the Early Life of Jonathan Edwards," in ibid., p. 86.

59. Edwards A. Park, "Characteristics of Edwards," in ibid., pp. 119-20.

60. Henry Gale, "Remarks," in ibid., p. 197.

61. *Memorial Volume,* pp. 22, 163-65, 184.

62. Kammen, *Mystic Chords of Memory,* p. 222.

63. *Memorial Volume,* pp. 13, 177.

64. Ibid., p. 183. Other historical markers included an Indian monument dedicated to "The Friends of Our Fathers," a memorial chime tower at the First Church, and a memorial grove to the Reverend David Dudley Field, minister from 1819 to 1837.

65. "Jonathan Edwards Celebrations," *Congregational and Christian World* 88 (October 17, 1903): 537; see also "Jonathan Edwards Memorial Sundial in Front of the Riggs Foundation," typescript, Stockbridge Library. On Stockbridge as a resort after the Civil War, see Sedgwick and Marquand,

Stockbridge, 1739-1939, chap. 12. On the "colonializing" of another western New England resort town in the late nineteenth century, see William Butler, "Another City upon a Hill: Litchfield, Connecticut, and the Colonial Revival," in *Colonial Revival in America,* ed. Axelrod, pp. 15-51.

66. The colonial revival in Salem led, among other things, to the extensive preservation work of the Essex Institute, the restoration of the House of Seven Gables, and the erection of a Puritan statute to Roger Conant. There is no study of which I am aware of the colonial revival in Salem, but such historicizing activities are mentioned in William B. Rhoads, "The Colonial Revival and the Americanization of Immigrants," in *Colonial Revival in America,* ed. Axelrod, pp. 349-50, and in Jane Holtz Kay, *Preserving New England* (New York, 1986), pp. 38, 45.

67. Z. Eastman, "Jonathan Edwards About His Elms," *Hampshire Gazette* (August 19, 1879), p. 1. In addition to the new monument to Edwards, there was an earlier memorial to him placed next to the gravestones of David Brainerd and Jerusha Edwards; see "In Bridge Cemetery," *Hampshire Gazette* (November 13, 1894), p. 2. On the two churches, see Donald Keyes, *The First Church of Christ in Northampton: A Centennial Celebration of the Fifth Meeting House, 1878-1978* (Northampton, Mass., 1978), esp. p. 28. On the Edwards homesite and Whitney Mansion, see "False Impression Held About House in Northampton," *Springfield Union and Sunday Republican* (August 30, 1931), p. 4A (clipping in Edwards File, Northampton Historical Society); and Charles J. Dean, "Finds the Whitney House and the Jonathan Edwards House Were Not the Same," *Hampshire Gazette* (February 14, 1936), pp. 9, 13.

68. See Archibald V. Galbraith, "Industrial History, 1860-1900," Leo Leopold, "Northampton Labor Unions," and Harold Faulkner, "How Our People Lived," in *The Northampton Book, Chapters from 300 Years in the Life of a New England Town, 1654-1954* (Northampton, Mass., 1954), pp. 233-39, 260-67, 268-76.

69. John Francis Manfredi, "Immigration to Northampton," Virginia Corwin, "Religious Life in Northampton, 1800-1954," and John Smith, "The Origin and Development of the Parochial School System," in *The Northampton Book,* pp. 331-36, 383-93, 194-200. For the larger context of native Yankee response to these changes, see Barbara Miller Solomon's classic study, *Ancestors and Immigrants: A Changing New England Tradition* (Chicago, 1956).

70. "Celebration - Northampton 250th" (File, Historical Society, Northampton, Mass.); see also *Northampton Historical Localities Illustrated, 1654-1904,* compiled by the Committee on Historical Localities for the 250th Anniversary of the Settlement of the Town, June 5, 6, 7 (Northampton, Mass., 1904), and "False Impression Held About House in Northampton," p. 4A.

71. "Edwards Tablets," *Hampshire Gazette* (October 6, 1905), p. 3; "False Impression Held About House in Northampton," p. 4A.

72. James Russell Trumbull, *History of Northampton, Massachusetts from Its Settlement in 1654,* 2 vols. (Northampton, Mass., 1898, 1902). See also *Prospectus of Meadow City Quarter-Millennial Book* (Northampton, Mass., 1904), p. viii.

73. See *Hampshire Gazette* (August 2, 1898), p. 6. Later the original stepping stone of the First Church was hauled to the site of the present church and placed in the front with a plaque. Also, a stone marker was placed at the original site of the First Church. See *Hampshire Gazette* (November 11, 1912), p. 3, (October 18, 1917), p. 4, and (July 30, 1920), p. 3.

74. On the development of Edwards Square and the building of the armory, see "Inventory of Historic Houses," nos. 610, 611 (Historical Society, Northampton, Mass.). On the history of armories, see Robert N. Fogelson, *America's Armories: Architecture, Society, and the Public Order* (Cambridge, Mass., 1989).

75. Background information on the commemoration is contained in the "Report" of the chairman of the memorial committee in *Jonathan Edwards: A Retrospect,* ed. H. Norman Gardiner (Boston, 1901), pp. 165-68. See also *Hampshire Gazette* (June 23, 1900), pp. 1, 8.

76. *Jonathan Edwards: A Retrospect,* p. ix.

77. Alexander V. G. Allen, "The Place of Edwards in History," Egbert Smyth, "The Influence of Edwards on the Spiritual Life of New England," George Park Fisher, "Greetings from Yale University," Henry Rose, "Edwards in Northampton," in ibid., pp. 10, 12, 16, 48, 78, 79, 96.

78. "An American Philosopher of the Eighteenth Century," editorial, *New York Times* (June 11, 1900), p. 6; "Tablet to Jonathan Edwards," ibid. (June 23, 1900), p. 7; "The Jonathan Edwards Memorial," *Harper's Weekly* 44 (June 23, 1900): 574. I am indebted to M. X. Lesser, *Jonathan Edwards: A Reference Guide,* for calling my attention to these notices.

79. The history of the Hall of Fame is detailed in George Cary Eggleston, *The American Immortals* (New York, 1901). The quotations are on p. x, and pp. 337-49 contain a biographical sketch of Edwards. See also Henry Mitchell MacCracken, *The Hall of Fame* (New York, 1901).

80. Eggleston, *The American Immortals,* pp. xi, xv; Lesser, *Jonathan Edwards: A Reference Guide,* p. 103.

81. Reports and material generated by this commemoration are far too numerous to cite. A good summary may be found in "Jonathan Edwards Celebrations," *Congregationalist and Christian World* 88 (October 17, 1903): 537; see also Lesser, *Jonathan Edwards: A Reference Guide,* pp. 111-20. The Andover and Stockbridge commemorations led to the publication of books; see *Exercises Commemorating the Two-Hundredth Anniversary of the Birth of Jonathan Edwards, Held at Andover Theological Seminary, October 4 and 5, 1903* (Andover, Mass., 1904) and *Jonathan Edwards: The Two Hundredth Anniversary of his Birth. Union Meeting of the Berkshire North and South Conferences, Stockbridge, Mass., October Fifth, 1903* (Stockbridge, Mass., 1903). On the commemoration in California, see Henry Kingman, *Jonathan Edwards: A Commemorative Address in Observance of the Bicentenary of His Birth, at the First Congregational Church, Berkeley, California, October 5, 1903* (Berkeley, 1904).

82. John DeWitt, "Jonathan Edwards: A Study," in *Exercises* at the Stockbridge commemoration, pp. 39-40.

83. Rev. Newton Hall, quoted in *Springfield Daily Republican* (October 5, 1903), p. 4. Racial elements in the commemoration of Edwards were part of the larger Anglo-Saxon complex in the assessment of the Puritan heritage. Edwards even became a case study in eugenics at the turn of the century that gained currency and found favor with some bicentennial commemorators. In *Jukes-Edwards: A Study in Education and Heredity* (Harrisburg, Pa., 1900), A. E. Winship compared the hereditary genius and success of Edwards's descendants with the descendants of a clan of "degenerates" who were dubbed the Jukes. "The whole teaching of the culture of animals and plants," Winship concluded, "leaves no room to question the persistency of character, and this is so grandly exemplified in the descendants of Mr. Edwards that it is interesting to see what inheritances were focused in him" (p. 20).

84. See the material on the parade in "Celebrations - Northampton 250th"; on the Polish National Church and the historical marker, see "False Impression Held About House in Northampton," p. 4A, and "King Street," (File, Historical Society, Northampton, Mass.).

Anri Morimoto (essay date 1995)

SOURCE: Introduction to *Jonathan Edwards and the Catholic Vision of Salvation,* Pennsylvania State University Press, 1995, pp. 1-11.

[In the following essay, Morimoto, writing from his point of view as a Japanese Christian scholar, asserts that Edwards's vision of salvation is of significance not only within the context of eighteenth-century colonial America, but also with respect to Roman Catholic theology, past and present.]

"Puritanism is the essence of Protestantism, and Jonathan Edwards is the quintessence of Puritanism,"[1] wrote Perry Miller. To Miller, Edwards was the theologian who defined both Protestantism and Puritanism. Another critic, Robert Jenson, recommended Edwards as "America's Theologian"—not just *an* American theologian who happened to be born and to live in America, but *the* most American of theologians, a man whose theology "meets precisely the problems and opportunities of specifically American Christianity and of the nation molded thereby."[2] If we give credit to these characterizations, we find in Edwards Puritanism, Protestantism, and American Christianity all realized in their purest forms.

In this book, my question is not whether Edwards encompassed *all* of these forms or *less* of them, but whether he possessed *more.* Learning from Edwards would be of little more than historical interest if Edwards were a mere representative—even the best representative—of a particular school of thought within a particular time and context. Naturally, his thought is somewhat defined by the context and the agenda of his own day. Yet, like Augustine, Thomas Aquinas, and John Calvin, Edwards offers us insights that are applicable beyond his own temporal, spatial, and confessional limitations. What is truly representative of a particular type always has a quality that transcends that particularity. With the present study I aim to establish Edwards as a theologian whose vision of salvation is significant not only to eighteenth-century Puritan America but to all people—whether Protestant or Roman Catholic, Puritan or Eastern Orthodox, American or Japanese—who share the basic premise of the Scripture that God's transformative power brings forth a new creation.

As a Calvinist Puritan of eighteenth-century New England, Edwards may not seem very promising for interdenominational dialogue. Yet, contrary to the popular caricature of a narrow-minded, dogmatic "Puritan," Edwards learned much from the theology of the continental Roman Catholic tradition and allowed himself to be profoundly influenced by it. I document examples of unpublicized ecumenical interchanges within Edwards's own theological milieu. His vision of human salvation can therefore offer today's Protestant theology valuable help in reformulating and revitalizing its own understanding of salvation, without forcing it to surrender or compromise its genuine Protestant concerns. Indeed, ecumenical dialogue should not mean watering down the particularities to the lowest common denominator; it should enrich and deepen theological tradition and conviction. It is my hope that the reader will find in Edwards the potential for such mutual enrichment across the presupposed boundaries.

The implication of this dispositional view is not limited to the Christian community. As I argue in Chapter 3, Edwards's soteriology envisions a new and radical paradigm for understanding the salvation of people who are called "non-Christians." Reformed theology has not been very optimistic in this prospect. It teaches that those who die unevangelized or unconverted are destined to eternal damnation. Repugnant to the idea of a God who creates but does nothing to save, theologians of various convictions have recently tried to lay out various paradigms—whether pluralistic, universal, or inclusive—to suggest otherwise. Partly because of my own cultural and religious background, I feel compelled to develop a soteriology that is inclusive yet theologically responsible. Edwards has been regarded as a theologian who peremptorily and almost sadistically condemns unbelievers to eternal damnation. The image of a hell-fire preacher should be carefully relocated in his unexpectedly broad understanding of salvation. By extending the implication of his dispositional view a little further, Edwards's theology could help us reconsider the destiny of those who stand outside the visible circle of Christian faith. Most theologians no longer regard unbelievers as *massa damnata* (damned masses), but would they say that the Christian proclamation is no longer necessary or meaningful? In Edwards's view of faith, the division between Christians and non-Christians is not simply a division between those who have faith and those who do not. Rather the difference lies in whether or not the disposition into faith has been actualized.

Jonathan Edwards lived in an age in which traditional ways of understanding the nature of reality were being radically reconceived in response to the challenges of science and philosophy. In the first two decades of the eighteenth century, books by John Locke (1632-1704) and Isaac Newton (1643-1727) were transported across the Atlantic Ocean to awaken the minds of progressive New England thinkers. Although recent evidence has discounted the legend of a thirteen-year-old Edwards poring over Locke's *Essays* in a dark Yale library room, a young Edwards was no doubt exposed to the thought of both Locke and Newton and became aware of the challenges posed to theology.[3] Edwards was a theologian by profession, but in those days no one could be a theologian without also being a profound metaphysician and, to a varying extent, an amateur scientist; he was no exception. But in Edwards's efforts to restate the traditional doctrines of Calvinist theology in the language of his own time, he accomplished—perhaps without so realizing—what neither Locke nor Newton could accomplish.

While die-hard scholasticism, with its Aristotelian worldview, was on the wane, new theses did not spring automatically from the collapsing castle of medieval scholasticism. Newton had to struggle hard to work out a nonimpact causation theory. Locke too was still probing, although without reaching a definite conclusion, whether it was really possible to abandon the concepts and paradigms of Aristotelian metaphysics altogether. In such a time of transition, Edwards's reflections on the nature of reality made

a qualitative leap from the metaphysics of form and substance to a dispositional ontology that is still relevant today. This dispositional view of reality is carefully described and analyzed in a work by Sang H. Lee, *The Philosophical Theology of Jonathan Edwards,*[4] to which the present study owes its inception. In the following pages, I try to recapitulate Lee's argument, but I refer the reader to this important monograph for deeper understanding. My aim here is to describe more fully the theological implications that this dispositional view of reality has on Edwards's "soteriology," or "theories of salvation"—that is, a theological discipline that deals with ways to understand aspects of human salvation.

At the age of twenty-seven and barely four years into his ministry in a frontier congregation in Northampton, Connecticut, Jonathan Edwards had the honor of being invited to deliver a public lecture in Boston in 1731. This "Thursday Lecture," as it was called, was an occasion for inquiring New England Puritans to listen to their ministers parade the best of their theological talents. Understandably, Edwards prepared his manuscript scrupulously, and within a month after its favorable reception the lecture was published. The title of his first published work is of a typical New England style—long: **"God Glorified in the Work of Redemption, by the Greatness of Man's Dependence upon him, in the Whole of it."** This lecture represents the gist of Edwards's thought in its formative years, and scholars often recognize important concepts of his later days here in embryonic form. I find Edward's vision of salvation articulated in it very clearly.

Edwards takes as his scriptural text 1 Corinthians 1:30 (King James),[5] "Christ Jesus is made unto us wisdom and righteousness and sanctification and redemption," and ascribes both justification and sanctification to the grace of God. He defines these two manifestations of grace somewhat enigmatically as "objective good" and "inherent good." While not neglecting the objective good, Edwards's soteriology uniquely accents the inherent good that redeemed persons have by salvation. Grace transforms human beings so that they may have "spiritual excellency and joy by a kind of participation [in] God." They are not only *counted* as righteous, but are themselves *made* excellent "by a communication of God's excellency" and *made* holy "by being made partakers of God's holiness."[6] For Edwards, salvation means a palpable reality of regeneration. To be saved is to participate in the fullness of God by the communication of God's own nature to humanity. God "communicates" himself to human beings, and human beings "participate" in the nature of God. This vision of salvation is attested to in Scripture (2 Pet. 1:4) and is shared by the Roman Catholic and Eastern Orthodox churches. According to Thomas Aquinas, the end of grace is to make human beings "partakers of the divine nature," while the Eastern Orthodox term for this vision is "divinization" or "deification" (*theosis*).[7] It is this soteriology of ontological transformation that I analyze in Edwards.

Participation, according to Paul Tillich, is an ontological concept that relates an individual subject to an objective and transcendent reality, without destroying the former's self-identity.[8] It is neither complete "absorption" nor complete "separation," and it is possible only when both elements of transcendence and immanence are present. In Edwards's soteriology, the locus where these two elements meet is the "new disposition" created by infused grace. In the Boston lecture, Edwards elaborates on the meaning of "participation" and "communication."

> The saints have both their spiritual excellency and blessedness by the gift of the Holy Ghost, or Spirit of God, and his dwelling in them. They are not only caused by the Holy Ghost, but are in the Holy Ghost as their principle. The Holy Spirit becoming an inhabitant, is a vital principle in the soul: he, acting in, upon, and with the soul, becomes a fountain of true holiness and joy, as a spring is of water, by the exertion and diffusion of itself.[9]

God communicates his own nature to human beings, which results in a new "principle" of the heart. This principle is created by the infusion of the Holy Spirit, Edwards says, who then "dwells" in the regenerate persons as "the vital principle in the soul" by which they spontaneously and voluntarily act out in faith and holy practice.

What is important to note here is Edwards's concept of "a vital principle in the soul" that "exerts" itself. Called more often "disposition" or "habit" in other contexts, this "principle" is a key word in his soteriology and ontology. In Edwards's dispositional view, all being—whether corporeal or spiritual—is a disposition, an active tendency to realize itself in certain ways. Being is no longer described as substance and form, as in the Aristotelian tradition. Being is, for Edwards, essentially a network of laws that prescribe certain actions and events to take place on specified occasions. These laws are active and purposive tendencies, or dispositions, that automatically come into "exertion" when the specified circumstances are met. A chair in a room, for example, is not a chair by itself that has certain qualities. It is rather a result of the exercise of laws governing the nature of that particular chair to exist in such and such a manner. This dispositional conception of being can therefore mediate between various categories traditionally thought to be antithetical—such as substance and accident, being and action, or being and becoming.

The theological upshot of this conception of disposition is that it makes all being radically and constantly dependent on the causal power and activity of God, while at the same time affirming the relative permanence of the created world. On one hand, the existence of the world is totally dependent on God. It is God who has established and who works in and through these laws, bringing entities into being according to the conditions that specify the enactment of these laws. On the other hand, the specific integrity of the created world is secured and upheld by the permanence of the laws that have an objective and ontological reality. The laws that God has established are essentially permanent, and they necessarily and unfailingly come into exercise as specified. This permanence and certainty gives being an integrity of its own.[10]

Translated into soteriological language, this conception of being as the exercise of laws has two aspects. First, it affirms the immediate and continual activity of God in and through the reality of the new creation. By the infusion of grace, God creates in human nature a new disposition. In order for this new disposition to exist and operate, God must be continually at work in and through it. In this sense, the reality of human salvation is totally dependent on the sovereign activity of God. Divine grace never becomes encapsulated in a static human quality. Salvation is not something achieved once and for all and then relegated to human possession. It must be given anew every moment by God's immediate and continual activity from above. I call this the "Protestant concern" in soteriology.

Second, this new disposition is an active and purposive tendency that is exercised necessarily and without fail when conditions are met. Contrary to common understanding, a disposition or habit, according to Edwards, is not a description of likelihood; a disposition as a prescriptive law exerts itself unfailingly and necessarily upon preordained occasions. God works according to the laws he has established, and these laws, once established, are essentially permanent (*potentia ordinata*). This certainty gives the reality of salvation an enduring character. The transformative power of grace effectuates in human nature a real and qualitative change—something tangible and palpable—that is far more than a hypothesis. The regenerate persons enjoy an abiding reality of salvation created within them. I call this the "Catholic concern" in soteriology.

The strength of Edwards's soteriology is that it fuses Protestant and Catholic concerns into one form. To use Tillich's terms, Edwards's soteriology is a well-balanced combination of "Protestant Principle" and "Catholic Substance."[11] The same combination can be expressed by the scholastic terms *gratia increata* (uncreated grace) and *gratia creata* (created grace). Uncreated grace (the Holy Spirit) operates in and through created grace (the new disposition). One can also associate these two aspects of grace with Peter Lombard and Thomas Aquinas: Lombard represents the "Protestant concern," or the tradition of uncreated grace, and Thomas represents the "Catholic concern," or the tradition of created grace. With his dispositional view of reality, Edwards succeeds in mediating the truths of both traditions, arguing for an abiding reality of salvation in humanity, while not undermining God's sovereign grace.

The kind of emphasis Edwards put on the human reality of salvation has often caused suspicion and misgiving in Protestant circles; his genuine theological concerns have been sadly misrepresented. In the middle of the nineteenth century, Tryon Edwards surreptitiously tampered with the text of Edwards's *Charity and Its Fruits* before publication in order to conceal his great forefather's emphatic use of the word "infusion," which to Tryon sounded too "Roman Catholic."[12] George Boardman recognized the precedence of regeneration to justification in Edwards's theology and thought that an explanation was due.[13] In this century, Perry Miller notes that Edwards felt "a necessity of saying something more" than the standard Protestant doctrine of forensic justification.[14] Thomas Schafer also writes that Edwards "went beyond the doctrine of justification."[15]

Comparable efforts to "defend" Edwards's "Protestant-ness" have been made as well. Conrad Cherry argues that Edwards remained Protestant by underscoring the direct indwelling of the Holy Spirit in the regenerate.[16] Paul Ramsey emphatically reassures his readers that, despite the seeming coincidence of Edwards's thought with the Roman Catholic position, Edwards has a "deep family resemblance" to Calvin and other Reformed theologians.[17]

There is truth in each of these assertions. Two preliminary remarks, however, should be made for the sake of clarity. First, Edwards himself seems not to have noticed the obvious similarity his theology has with Roman Catholic theology. His writings hardly show any effort to differentiate or contrast his thought to Roman Catholic understandings of salvation. This may sound surprising in view of Edwards's thorough acquaintance with the anti-Roman polemics of the preceding generation. Even his most explicitly Protestant discourse, "Justification by Faith alone," was directed against those Edwards called "Arminians," not against Roman Catholics.[18] On Edwards's theological horizon, Roman Catholicism did not present itself as something to be confronted or to be reconciled with.[19] The reader should therefore keep in mind that any comparative statement I make in the following pages is instead part of my own effort to better understand Edwards's soteriology on a broad scale.

Second, a distinction should be made between interpretation and value-judgment. It is one thing to say that Edwards's soteriology has a substantial affinity with Roman Catholic soteriology, and quite another to say that it is therefore to be praised or condemned. Though at some points my interpretation concurs with the results of previous studies, my attitude toward the perceived facts is different from those who have seen this affinity as a problem—or even a "scandal" in the biblical sense of the word—that should be concealed or circumvented. As I point out in several contexts, this defensive motivation has often placed undue pressure on the text to make it *look* "Protestant," resulting in misrepresentations of Edwards's true concerns. Furthermore, in light of recent successes of ecumenical dialogues between Protestants and Roman Catholics, it would be indeed unfortunate if the opportunity that Edwards's soteriology offers for a reevaluation of the strengths of both soteriologies is ignored. I want to reconfirm and give positive recognition to the contiguity of Edwards's soteriology with the Roman Catholic tradition, especially as represented by Thomas Aquinas, without depreciating the essential continuity of his theology with that

of Calvin and other Reformed theologians. To achieve this task, I look to recent ecumenical interchanges for support. Edwards's concern for the reality of ontological transformation is consonant, I believe, not only with contemporary Roman Catholic theology but also fundamentally with biblical testimony regarding the transformative power of divine grace.

Notes

1. Perry Miller, *Jonathan Edwards* (1949; reprint, Amherst: University of Massachusetts Press, 1981), 301. Note also "Puritanism is what Edwards is," and "he extracted the essense of Puritanism" (194).

2. Robert Jenson, *America's Theologian: A Recommendation of Jonathan Edwards* (New York: Oxford University Press, 1988), 3.

3. For Edwards's exposure to the writings of Locke and Newton, see Wallace E. Anderson's Introduction to *The Works of Jonathan Edwards* [hereafter *WY*], vol. 6: *Scientific and Philosophical Writings*, ed. Wallace E. Anderson (New Haven: Yale University Press, 1980), 1-143.

4. Sang H. Lee, *The Philosophical Theology of Jonathan Edwards* (Princeton: Princeton University Press, 1988).

5. Biblical quotations are from the New Revised Standard Version unless otherwise stated, as here.

6. Sermon, "God glorified in Man's Dependence," in *The Work of President Edwards in Four Volumes* [hereafter *WW*], (1808-9; reprint, New York: Jonathan Levitt and John F. Trow, 1843), 4:174-75. Perry Miller took advantage of the mysteriousness of these words and interpreted them as "Newton and natural law" and "Locke and perception" so as to suit his own interpretative scheme (Miller, *Jonathan Edwards,* 98). My reading is less constrained, since in another sermon Edwards explicitly uses these words in relation to justification and sanctification. See "The Wisdom of God, displayed in the way of Salvation," *WW,* 4:145.

7. *Summa Theologica,* 1-2.110.3. On *theosis,* see Vladimir Lossky, *The Mystical Theology of the Eastern Church,* trans. The Fellowship of St. Alban and St. Sergius (Cambridge: James Clarke & Co., 1957; reprint, Crestwood, N.Y.: St. Vladimir's Seminary Press, 1976), 196-216 and passim. See also George Maloney, *A Theology of "Uncreated Energies"* (Milwaukee: Marquette University Press, 1978), chap. 3. Jaroslav Pelikan notes its bearing on Edwards's theology in *Christian Doctrine and Modern Culture (since 1700),* vol. 5 of *The Christian Tradition: A History of the Development of Doctrine* (Chicago University of Chicago Press, 1989), 161.

8. Paul Tillich, *Systematic Theology* (Chicago: University of Chicago Press, 1951), 1:177.

9. "God glorified in Man's Dependence," 175.

10. See Lee, *Philosophical Theology*, 34-75. See also Anderson's Introduction to *WY*, 6:68-136. See Chapter 3 of this volume for further discussion.

11. Tillich, *Systematic Theology*, 3:223,245.

12. See Paul Ramsey's Introduction to *Charity and Its Fruits*, in *WY*, vol. 8: *Ethical Writings*, ed. Paul Ramsey (New Haven: Yale University Press, 1989), 59-60 n. 5.

13. George Nye Boardman, *A History of New England Theology* (New York: A. D. F. Randolph, 1899; reprint, New York: Garland, 1987), 155-56.

14. Miller, *Jonathan Edwards*, 76.

15. Thomas A. Schafer, "Jonathan Edwards and Justification by Faith," *Church History* 20 (1951): 64.

16. Conrad Cherry, *The Theology of Jonathan Edwards: A Reappraisal* (Gloucester, Mass.: Peter Smith, 1974), 29-31, 37, 41-43.

17. See Appendix 4 to *WY*, 8:739-50.

18. See, for example, Preface to "Justification by Faith alone," in *The Works of President Edwards in Ten Volumes* [hereafter *WD*] (New York: S. Converse, 1829-30), 5:349.

19. "Papists," as Edwards calls them, are classified in the same category with "heathens or atheists" (Sermons, "Natural men in a dreadful condition," *WD*, 8:12; "Man's Natural Blindness in the things of Religion," *WW*, 4:22). This was not uncommon for a New England Puritan. See, for example, Harry S. Stout, *The New England Soul: Preaching and Religious Culture in Colonial New England* (New York: Oxford University Press, 1986), 48-49. Edwards's firsthand knowledge of Roman Catholic theology did not go beyond conventional literature. See John F. Wilson's Appendix B, "Jonathan Edwards' Notebooks for *A History of the Work of Redemption*," *WY*, vol. 9: *A History of the Work of Redemption*, ed. John F. Wilson, 547.

William J. Wainwright (essay date 1995)

SOURCE: "Jonathan Edwards and the Heart," in *Reason and the Heart: A Prolegomenon to a Critique of Passional Reason*, Cornell University Press, 1995, pp. 7-54.

[In the following essay, Wainwright discusses the treatment of reason and benevolence in Edwards's thought and asserts that Edwards successfully integrated the conflicting influences of rationalism and the Calvinist Reformed tradition in his philosophy.]

Jonathan Edwards was strongly influenced by continental rationalists such as Malebranche, by some of the Cambridge Platonists (Henry More, for example), and by the empiricists (especially Locke). He was also excited by Newton and the new science. Although these traditions were diverse, they had an important feature in common—an almost uncritical confidence in reason's power and scope. Edwards's practice reflects this confidence. Philosophical arguments are deployed to demolish critics, justify the principal Christian doctrines, and erect a speculative metaphysics (a subjective idealism like Berkeley's). But Edwards was also a Calvinist who shared the Reformed tradition's distrust of humanity's natural capacities and its skepticism about natural theology.

The impact of these diverse strands is reflected in the apparent ambiguity of Edwards's remarks on reason. Thus, on the one hand, he can say that, "arguing for the being of a God according to the natural powers from everything we are conversant with is short, easy, and what we naturally fall into" (Misc. 268, T 78)[1] or claim that we can know that a just God governs the world by the "light of nature." Conscience that sees "the relation and agreement there is between that which is wrong or unjust and punishment" and finds unpunished wrongs "shocking" naturally leads us to conclude that God is "a just being" (Misc. 353, T 110-111). Yet he can also insist that, in thinking about God, reason is baffled by "mystery," "paradox," and "seeming inconsistence." (Examples are an omnipresence without extension, an immutability [which Edwards thinks implies duration] without succession, and the idea of a "perfect knowledge of all . . . things of external sense, without any sensation or any reception of ideas from without" [Misc. 1340, T 231].) Even though "the invisible things of God are indeed to be understood by the things that are made," uninstructed reason invariably errs (Misc. 986, T 212). It is "almost impossible [for example] for unassisted reason" to demonstrate "that the world, and all things contained therein, are effects, and had a beginning." A person who was "left to himself" "would be apt to reason" that because causes and effects must be "similar and conformable, matter must have a material cause" and "evil and irregularity . . . must be attributed to an evil and unwise cause." Indeed, without assistance, "the best reasoner in the world . . . might be led into the grossest errors and contradictions" (Misc. Obs., 185-86). If "God never speaks to or converses at all with mankind," we would most likely think "there is no being that made and governs the world" or that, if there is, it is not "properly an intelligent, volitive being" (Misc. 1298, T 218).

Even though Edwards thinks that reason *can* prove God's existence, determine the nature of many of His attributes, discern our obligations to Him, and establish the credibility of scripture, he believes that grace is needed both to help "the natural principles against those things that tend to stupefy it and to hinder its free exercise" (Misc. 626, T 111) and to "sanctify the reasoning faculty and assist it to see the clear evidence there is of the truth of religion in rational arguments" (Misc. 628, T 251).

In many respects, Edwards simply restates Puritan commonplaces. Although they conceded that "some of the things 'plainly proved' by scripture could also be detected by the 'light of natural reason,'" Puritans emphasized reason's powerlessness.[2] Robert Bolton, for instance, thought that if "a man looke upon Gods wayes onely with the eye of reason they are foolishnesse to him." Thomas Adams said, "there is no greater ods in the world than betweene our owne reason and God's wisdome." Peter Sterry maintained that "To seek out spiritual things by the scent and sagacity of reason were to plough with an Oxe and an Asse. . . . You cannot reach the things of reason by the hand of sense. . . . You cannot understand spirituall things Rationally. . . . Some say, that all truths which come by revelation of the Spirit, may also be demonstrated by Reason. But if they be, they are then no more Divine, but humane truths; They lose their certainty, beauty, efficacy; . . . Spirituall truths discovered by demonstrations of Reason, are like the Mistresse in her Cook-maid's clothes." According to the great Puritan divine William Perkins, one "must reject his owne naturall reason, and stoppe up the eyes of his naturall minde, like a blinde man, and suffer himselfe wholly to be guided by God's spirit in the things of God." And the Puritan mystic Francis Rous commended those who "have . . . quenched their owne naturall lamps, that they might get them kindled above by the Father of Lights."[3]

As John Morgan points out, Puritan strictures on reason reflect the Reformed (and ultimately Augustinian and Pauline) insistence on human corruption. Reason is not exempt from the consequences of the Fall. Although natural reason may discover some truths about God (along with many errors), it is incapable of grasping His saving actions on our behalf. Puritan strictures also reflect their emphasis on an "experimental knowledge" of God's favor toward us. According to Arthur Dent, "the knowledge of the reprobate is like the knowledge which a mathematicall geographer hath of the earth and all the places in it, which is but a generall notion and a speculative comprehension of them. But the knowledge of the elect is like the knowledge of a traveller which can speake of experience and feeling, and hath beene there and seene and knowen the particulars."[4] Or, as William Baxter said;

> I do, therefore, neither despise evidence as unnecessary, nor trust to it alone as the sufficient total cause of my belief; for if God's grace do not open mine eyes, and come down in power upon my will, and insinuate into it a sweet acquaintance with the things unseen, and a taste of their goodness to delight my soul, no reasons will serve to stablish and comfort me, however undeniable soever; the way to have the firmest belief of the Christian faith, is to draw near and taste, and try it, and lay bare the heart to receive the impression of it, and then, by the sense of its admirable effects, we shall know that which bare speculation could not discover.[5]

Edwards shares these attitudes. What distinguishes him from other Puritan divines is not his learning or use of philosophical resources[6] but his philosophical acumen and the fact that the intellectual currents that most influenced him (continental rationalism and British empiricism) are those that have both shaped modern philosophy and underlie the dominant view of rationality.

The following sections explore Edwards's position in detail. The first discusses his remarks on mystery and paradox and defends the claim that Edwards believed in the possibility of natural theology. The second examines his discussion of the sense of the heart, and the third shows why Edwards thought that grace is needed to reason properly.

THE POSSIBILITY OF NATURAL THEOLOGY

Edwards's remarks about mystery, paradox, and the impossibility of discovering spiritual truths do not preclude natural theology.

The inconsistencies Edwards alludes to, for instance, are only "*seeming* inconsistencies" and "*seeming* contradictions" (my emphases); they are not real ones. And the only sense in which theology is incomprehensible is that we lack "clear ideas of the things that are the subject of" its truths (Misc. 1100, T 213). We know *that* God necessarily exists, for example, but not *how* this can be true. Or we know "that the Godhead was united to man so as to be properly looked upon [as] the same person" but not "how it was effected" (Misc. 1340, T 234).[7]

But the most important point is this. "Paradox" and "incomprehensibility" also characterize other disciplines whose credentials are beyond dispute. Mathematical truths concerning "surd quantities and fluxions" are incomprehensible in the same sense, and "the reasonings and conclusions of the best metaphysicians and mathematicians concerning infinities are attended with paradoxes and seeming inconsistencies" (Misc. 1100, T 213; Misc. 1340, T 230). Philosophy provides other examples. Reason cannot "comprehend, or explain, or show, or conceive of any way that" minds and bodies can interact although it is obvious that they do (Misc. 1340, T 222). And when we attempt to formulate idealism (which Edwards believes to be both true and demonstrable), "we have got so far beyond those things for which language was chiefly contrived, that *unless we use extreme caution* we cannot speak . . . without literally contradicting ourselves" (Mind 355, my emphasis).

Paradoxes attend these disciplines because they deal with matters remote from "the common business and vulgar affairs of life, things obvious to sense and men's direct view." Their subject matters are not "the objects and affairs which earthly language was made to express," and the truths they discern "are not agreeable to such notions . . . and ways of thinking that grow up with us and are connatural to us" (Misc. 1340, T 227-28). The difficulties that attend theology are no greater in kind (although greater in degree) than those attending other disciplines dealing with "high" and "abstract" matters. It would be as illegitimate to conclude that natural or revealed theology is impossible, then, as to conclude that mathematics or metaphysics are.

Edwards's remarks concerning the impossibility of knowing God apart from revelation should be treated with the same caution. The following is typical. If people are not "led by revelation and direct teaching into a right way of using their reason, in arguing from effects to causes, etc., they would remain forever in the most woeful doubt and uncertainty concerning the nature and the very being of God. This appears not only by the state of the heathen world . . . but also by what appears among those who in these late ages have renounced divine revelation, even the wisest and greatest of 'em," such as Hobbes, Toland, Shaftesbury, and Hume (Misc. 1297, T 214).

I believe that Edwards wishes to make two points. The first is that "uninstructed" reason is powerless; no one is capable of erecting the fabric of *any* discipline on his or her own. The second is that we are powerless to *discover* theological truths although reason can *demonstrate* the truth of (many of) them *after* they have been revealed. Neither implies the impossibility of natural theology.

Miscellany 1297 is instructive. "The state of the heathen world" and "what appears among . . . the wisest and greatest of" the modern "deistical writers" shows that men and women who are not "led by revelation and direct teaching" fall into error. But the deists' errors are greater than those made by people "before the Gospel." For the heathen philosophers did not despise the revelation they had "by tradition from their ancestors, the ancient founders of nations, or from the Jews, which led 'em to embrace many truths contained in the Scripture." Nor did they reject everything beyond their comprehension. The ancients were willing to learn from tradition and to accept truths they did not fully understand, because they did not "proceed in" the deists' "exceeding haughtiness and dependence on their own mere singular understanding, disdaining all dependence on teaching." Nor did they "proceed with" the deists' "enmity against moral and divine truth having not been so irritated by it" (T 214, 217-18).

Sound reasoning is a social product. It presupposes instruction in an intellectual tradition and membership in a community that shares it. Intellectual traditions include beliefs about a subject matter, methods for resolving problems concerning it, and shared values that guide the process of inquiry. Traditions are not static. Beliefs are dropped and added. Sometimes the community is forced to modify its values or revise its methods of investigation.[8] Contributions to this process, however, are normally restricted to those who have been initiated into the community and have thus mastered its intellectual traditions, employ its methods of inquiry, and share its values.[9] As Edwards remarks, "knowledge bears an exact proportion to instruction. Why [else] does the learned and well educated reason better than the mere citizen? . . . There is no fallacy more gross than to imagine reason, utterly untaught

and undisciplined, capable of the same attainments in knowledge as reason well refined and instructed" (Misc. Obs. 186).

Contributions to science or philosophy, for example, are seldom made by outsiders. Isolated reason is impotent. If we stand aloof from the scientific or philosophical community and (relying only on our "own singular understandings") refuse to accept anything we have not worked out on our own or fully understood, we are not likely to contribute to science or philosophy, or even to understand them. If we are also hostile to them, we are still less likely to do so. Why should religion be different? Why suppose that those who cut themselves off from the religious community and its intellectual traditions,[10] rely only on their own reasonings, refuse to accept anything they have not fully understood, and are indifferent to religion or hostile to it are likely to establish truths about God?

Viable religious traditions are unlike other intellectual traditions, however, in one important respect. They can only be inaugurated by God. "In ordinary articles of knowledge, our sense and experience furnish reason with ideas and principles to work on. . . . But in respect to God, it can have no right idea nor axiom to set out with, till he is pleased to reveal it" (Misc. Obs. 186). "That the ancient philosophers and wiser heathen had so good notions of God as they had seems to be much more owing to tradition, which originated from divine revelation, than from their own invention" (Misc. 1340, T 231-32). Revelation is needed because "the first principles of religion, being of a high and spiritual nature, are harder to be found out than those of any other science . . . the minds of men are gross and earthly, used to objects of sense; and all their depraved appetites and corrupt dispositions, which are by nature opposite to true religion, help to increase the natural weakness of their reason" (Misc. Obs. 193).

Nevertheless, "it is one thing" to "strike upon" a point, and quite another "to work out a demonstration of" it "once it is proposed" (Misc. Obs. 185). "It is very needful that God should declare unto mankind what manner of being he is," but reason "is sufficient to confirm such a declaration after it is given, and enable us to see its consistence, harmony, and rationality, in many respects" (Misc. Obs. 217). "After once suggested and delivered," God's declarations are seen to be "agreeable to reason" (Misc. 1340, T 232). That there is only one God, for example, "is what we, now the gospel has so taught us, can see to be truth by our own reason . . . it can easily be shown by reason to be demonstrably true" (*HR* 398-99).

What Edwards denies is that correct ideas of God would have occurred to us if humanity had been left to its own devices. Whether this is true or not[11] is irrelevant to the possibility of natural theology. For the process of discovery is *in general* nonrational. (There are no rational procedures for discovering illuminating new scientific hypotheses, for example, or perspicacious interpretations of literary texts.) Whatever their origins, reason has ideas of God. Having them, it can show that they are not fictions; the truths of natural religion (that God exists, that He is sovereign, righteous, and so on) are demonstrable.

Natural reason can also ascertain that scripture is God's revelation and, knowing this, it can learn truths it could not acquire in other ways.

"Divine testimony" cannot be opposed to reason, evidence, or argument because it is a *rule* of reason, a *kind* of evidence, and a *type* of argument like the "human testimony of credible eye-witnesses," "credible history," "memory," "present experience," "geometrical mensuration," "arithmetical calculation," and "strict metaphysical distinction and comparison" (Misc. Obs. 228).[12] The statement that "Scripture is reliable" resembles such rules as "The testimony of our senses may be depended on," "The agreed testimony of all we see and converse with continually is to be credited," and "The testimony of history and tradition is to be depended on, when attended with such and such credible circumstances" (Misc. 1340, T 221). Principles such as these can be established, or at least certified, by reason[13] and then used to establish other truths that cannot be established without their help ("Fire engines are red," for example, or "Christ atoned for our sins").

That reason can be appropriately used to assess the credentials of a rule of reasoning does not imply that opinions formed by a reason that does not employ the rule can be used to determine the truth or falsity of opinions established *by* its means. The naked eye, for example, "determines the goodness and sufficiency" of the optic glass, yet it would be absurd for a person to "credit no representation made by the glass, wherein the glass differs from his eye" and to refuse to believe, "that the blood consists partly of red particles and partly of limpid liquor because it all appears red to the naked eye" (Misc. Obs. 227). It would be equally absurd to reject truths that can be established by a reason that employs the rule "Memories are generally reliable" because what memory reports cannot be established by a reason that does not. It is just as unreasonable to discount what can be discovered by a reason that employs the rule that scripture is credible on the grounds that truths learned in this way cannot be established by a reason that rejects it.[14]

Although this passage does not explain *how* "Scripture is credible" can be established or certified, what Edwards has in mind is reasonably clear. The strongest evidence for scripture's divine authority is its spiritual beauty—a feature that natural reason cannot detect. Only those with converted hearts can perceive, taste, and relish the stamp of divine splendor on scripture and thus be *certain* of its teachings. (More on this shortly.) The unsanctified are nonetheless capable of acquiring a *probable* conviction of their truth. Scripture's authority is certified by miracles and fulfilled prophecy, the harmony between revealed and natural religion, scripture's beneficial effect on morality, and so on.[15] "None will doubt," says Edwards, "but that

some natural men do yield a kind of assent . . . to the truths of the Christian religion, from the rational proofs or arguments that are offered to evince it" (*RA* 295). Probabilistic arguments for the truth of the gospel can be drawn from history, and "lately . . . these . . . have been set in a clear and convincing light" by the "learned" (*RA* 305). By exercising its natural faculties, reason can know that scripture is God's declaration and can therefore use "Scripture is reliable" as a rule to extend its knowledge.

Natural reason is thus capable of establishing the authority of scripture as well as the truths of natural religion. Why, then, does it so often find it difficult to do so? Not because the *evidence* is not obvious enough. Because these truths nearly concern us, God would not be good if He had not clearly declared them[16] (*OS* 155-57). We have sufficient "means of knowledge," therefore, as well as "a sufficient capacity" (*OS* 148). What is lacking is "a disposition to improve" the "light" God has given us (*OS* 149).

The following two sections examine the ways in which grace repairs our damaged dispositions. The role that moral and spiritual virtues play in sound reasoning about divine matters will become evident as we proceed.

THE SENSE OF THE HEART

Jonathan Edwards is well known for his insistence on a "practical," or "experimental," religion that engages the human heart. At its core is a sense of God's excellence and loveliness, or of the beauty and splendor of divine things.

The savingly converted enjoy "gracious discoveries" of "God, in some of his sweet and glorious attributes manifested in the gospel, and shining forth in the face of Christ"—for example, "the all-sufficiency of the mercy and grace of God" or "the infinite power of God, and his ability to save them. . . . In some, the truth and certainty of the Gospel in general is the first joyful discovery they have. . . . More frequently Christ is distinctly made the object of the mind, in his all-sufficiency and willingness to save sinners" (*FN* 171).[17] Recalling his own conversion, Edwards says:

> The first instance that I remember of that sort of inward, sweet delight in God and divine things that I have lived much in since, was on reading those words, I Tim. i. 17. *Now unto the King eternal, immortal, invisible, the only wise God, be honor and glory for ever and ever, Amen.* As I read the words, there came into my soul, and was as it were diffused through it, a sense of the glory of the Divine Being; a new sense, quite different from any thing I ever experienced before. Never any words of scripture seemed to me as these words did. I thought with myself, how excellent a Being that was, and how happy I should be, if I might enjoy that God, and be rapt up to him in heaven, and be as it were swallowed up in him for ever! (*PN* 59).

Again, Edwards tells us, "I remember the thoughts I used then to have of holiness. . . . It appeared to me, that there was nothing in it but what was ravishingly lovely; the highest beauty and amiableness . . . a *divine* beauty; far purer than anything here upon earth" (PN 63). "God," he says, "has appeared to me a glorious and lovely Being, chiefly on account of his holiness. . . . The doctrines of God's absolute sovereignty, and free grace, in showing mercy to whom he would show mercy; and man's absolute dependence on the operations of God's Holy Spirit, have very often appeared to me as sweet and glorious doctrines. These doctrines have been much my delight" (PN 67).

Some express their new experiences by the terms "sight or discovery," others by "a lively or feeling sense of heart" (*FN* 171-72). Both expressions refer to a new understanding of spiritual notions. Those who have these experiences find that phrases such as "a spiritual sight of Christ," "faith in Christ," "poverty of spirit," and so on, had not previously conveyed "those special and distinct ideas to their minds which they were intended to signify; in some respects no more than the names of colors are to convey the ideas to one that is blind from birth" (*FN* 174). But now "things of religion" seem "new to them . . . preaching is a new thing . . . the bible is a new book" (*FN* 181). Indeed, "the light and comfort which some of them enjoy . . . causes all things about 'em to appear as it were beautiful, sweet and pleasant to them: all things abroad, the sun, moon and stars, the clouds and sky, the heavens and earth, appear as it were with a cast of civine glory and sweetness upon them" (*FN* 183).

This section examines Edwards's attempt to make philosophical and theological sense of these experiences. It is divided into six parts. The first two discuss the nature of the idea of spiritual beauty and Edwards's reasons for thinking that our apprehension of beauty is a kind of sensation or perception. The third explores the implications of Edwards's theory for the epistemic status of religious belief, and the fourth and fifth examine his defense of the objectivity of the new "spiritual sense." The last part explores the bearing of Edwards's remarks on current discussions.

A New Simple Idea

The objects of a sense or feeling of the heart are (1) "actual [i.e., lively, clear, and distinct] ideas," (2) of things pertaining to the will or affections, (3) that involve a "feeling of sweetness or pleasure, or of bitterness or pains." They include (the ideas of)[18] (1) "beauty and deformity," "good or evil," as well as "excellency," "value," "importance" and their opposites, (2) delight and pleasure and pain and misery, (3) affective and conative attitudes, dispositions, and states ("desires and longings, esteem . . . hope, fear, contempt, choosing, refusing . . . loving, hating, anger," (4) "dignity," "terrible greatness, or awful majesty," "meanness or contemptibleness," and so on, and (5) the nonevaluative characteristics on which beauty and deformity, pleasure and pain, and attributes such as dignity or majesty depend.[19] The object of a sense or feeling of the

heart is, in essence, good and evil, and what pertains to it. Natural good or evil is "good or evil which is agreeable or disagreeable to human nature as such." Spiritual good or evil is what is agreeable or disagreeable to people with "spiritual frames," that is, to those who, because the Spirit dwells within them, love being in general (i.e., God and the beings that derive from Him, are absolutely dependent on Him, and reflect Him) (Misc. 782, T 113-26).

The "immediate object of this spiritual sense" is "the beauty of holiness" (*RA* 260), "the spiritual excellency, beauty, or sweetness of divine things" (Misc. 782), "true moral or spiritual beauty" (*TV* 548), "the highest and primary beauty" (*TV* 561)—a "new simple idea" that cannot be produced by the "exalting, varying or compounding of that kind of perceptions or sensations which the mind had before" (*RA* 205).

What kind of idea is this? Or, put another way, what does Edwards mean by "(true) beauty?" His remarks are open to at least three interpretations: that (1) "beauty" refers to the delight or pleasure that holy things evoke in people with spiritual "frames" or "tempers," (2) "beauty" refers to a dispositional property, the tendency of holy things to produce this pleasure or delight in the converted, and (3) "beauty" designates a love of being in general, that is, the consent of being to being that holiness consists in.

There is some evidence that Edwards held the first or second view. He asserts, for example, that "That form or quality is called 'beautiful,' . . . the view or idea of which is immediately pleasant to the mind . . . this agreeableness or gratefulness of the idea is what is called beauty . . . we come by the idea or sensation of beauty . . . by immediate sensation of the gratefulness of the idea [thing] called 'beautiful'" (*TV* 619). In **"The Mind"** 1 (332) Edwards assimilates beauty and excellence and then says, "We would know, why proportion is more excellent than disproportion, that is, why proportion is pleasant to the mind and disproportion unpleasant." Passages such as these imply that beauty is some kind of pleasure or agreeableness,[20] or a tendency to produce it in appropriate circumstances.

We probably should not attribute the second (dispositional) view to Edwards. If "(true) beauty" referred to the tendency to produce a unique sort of delight in those with spiritual frames, the idea of beauty would be a complex idea or "mixed mode."[21] This conflicts with the claim that spiritual beauty is a new simple idea (*RA* 205).[22]

There are also problems in attributing the first view to Edwards. The philosophers who most influenced Edwards (Locke and the Cartesians) explicitly denied that ideas of pleasure and pain tell us anything about the nature of the objects that produce them.[23] The idea of true beauty does. Edwards explicitly rejects the suggestion that "the idea we obtain by this spiritual sense could in no respect be said to be a knowledge or perception of anything besides what was in our own minds," or that it is "no representation of anything without." On the contrary, the idea of spiritual beauty is "the representation and image of the moral perfection and excellency of the Divine Being . . . of which we could have no true idea without it" (*TV* 622-23).[24]

A more compelling reason for doubting that Edwards identified beauty with pleasure (or a tendency to produce it) is that he so often speaks as if it were an *objective* property of the things that have it. One of Edwards's central theses is that God's nature and activity are overwhelmingly beautiful, and that the spiritual and natural beauty of creatures is a reflection of, or participation in, God's own beauty. The tenor of passages expressing these claims seems inconsistent with the suggestion that beauty is no more than a sensation which holy things produce in the suitably disposed (or a power to produce it). Edwards was strongly influenced by Locke and other empiricists. But he also belongs to a Puritan tradition that contains an important Platonic strand.[25] It may therefore be significant that Platonism thinks of beauty as an objective property.

Finally, a number of texts appear to identify beauty with the consent of being to being. This, too, seems inconsistent with the notion that beauty is some sort of pleasure or delight.

In **"The Mind"** 1, for example, Edwards assimilates beauty and excellency and then says, "excellency *consists in* the similarities of one being to another—not merely equality and proportion, but any kind of similarness. . . . This is an universal *definition* of excellency: The consent of being to being, or being's consent to entity" (336, my emphasis). Edwards continues to speak this way in later works. He says, for example, that "the true beauty and loveliness of all intelligent beings does primarily and most essentially *consist in* their moral excellency or holiness," that is, in their benevolence or love of being in general. "Holiness *is* . . . the beauty of the divine nature" (*RA* 257, my emphasis; cf. 258-59). In ***The Nature of True Virtue,*** Edwards asserts that true benevolence "is the thing wherein true moral or spiritual beauty primarily *consists.* Yea, spiritual beauty *consists wholly in* this and in" what proceeds from it (*TV* 648, my emphasis). "There is [also] another, inferior, secondary beauty, which is some image of this . . . which *consists in* a mutual consent and agreement of different things, in form, manner, quantity, and visible end or design; called by the various names of regularity, order, uniformity, symmetry, proportion, harmony, etc." (*TV* 561, my emphasis). Passages of this kind imply that beauty just *is* (i.e., is identical with) some kind of agreement. Primary or spiritual beauty is one and the same thing as benevolence or the "consent or agreement, or union of being to being," and secondary beauty is identical with symmetry, harmony, or proportion, that is, "uniformity in the midst of variety" (*TV* 561-62).

But there are also serious objections to *this* interpretation. Edwards often speaks as if beauty were a property *of* holiness and hence not the *same* thing as holiness. In the ***Religious Affections,*** for example, he speaks of "the loveliness

of the moral excellency of divine things . . . the beauty and sweetness of their moral excellency" (253 f.), "the beauty of their moral excellency," "the beauty of his holiness," "the beauty of his moral attributes" (256), "the loveliness of divine things . . . viz., . . . the beauty of their moral perfection" (271), "the beauty of the moral perfection of Christ" (273), "the beauty of holiness, or true moral good" (274), and so on. Edwards also asserts that the unconverted can see everything that pertains to God's and the saints' moral attributes *except* their "beauty and amiableness" (*RA* 264), thus implying some sort of distinction between these attributes and their beauty. Finally, beauty is a *simple* idea. The consent of (conscious) being to being, however, is complex.[26]

In short, there is textual evidence for the claim that Edwards identified true beauty with a spiritual sensation or a tendency to produce it and also for the claim that he identified it with consent. Both views appear incompatible with some of Edwards's other positions. The first seems inconsistent with his belief that the apprehension of beauty is a "perception" of something existing "without" the mind, and the second is inconsistent with his conviction that beauty is a simple idea. Can a coherent position be constructed from Edwards's remarks? He may have been driving at this: Beauty is identical with benevolence or agreement in somewhat the same way in which water is identical with H_2O or in which (according to materialists) consciousness is identical with certain arrangements of matter. (This accommodates the fact that one can perceive benevolence or agreement without perceiving its beauty even though its beauty "consists in" benevolence or agreement.) But benevolence is also the "objective" or "physical" basis of a dispositional property (the tendency to produce a new simple idea in those with converted hearts). The new idea is a delight or pleasure in being's consent to being which somehow "represents" or is a "perception of" it.

On this interpretation, the idea of true beauty resembles Locke's ideas of primary and secondary qualities. Spiritual delight is, in Locke's words, a simple "sensation or perception in our understanding" like our ideas of color or solidity. (*HU* 2.8.8). The dispositional property is what Locke calls a "quality," a "power to produce those ideas in us" (ibid.). Benevolence is the objective configuration underlying this power and corresponds to the microstructure of bodies that underlie their tendency to excite ideas of primary and secondary qualities in minds like ours. Like simple ideas of primary and secondary qualities, the new spiritual sensation "represents" or is a "perception" of its object. Just as "extension" or "red" can refer to the idea, the power, or the physical configuration that is the base of the power, so "beauty" can refer to the sensation, to the relevant dispositional property, or to benevolence. (My interpretation thus accounts for the ambiguity of Edwards's remarks.)[27]

Edwards's account of spiritual perception is subject to some of the same difficulties as Locke's account of sense perception.[28] Is it, in any way, *less* satisfactory? It may be in one respect. If I am right, the idea of true beauty is a kind of delight or relish and *also* an apparent cognition. *Can* something be both? It is not sufficient to argue that perceptions of objectively real value properties can be inherently affective (and thus pleasurable or painful), for Edwards does not think of pleasure and pain in this way. Pleasures and pains are not qualities or affective dimensions of more complex experiences. They are discrete internal sensations. But if spiritual pleasure *is* a kind of internal delight or thrill, how can it *also* be a true representation of something existing without? Ordinary pleasures and pains differ from visual or auditory impressions in lacking what Berkeley called "outness"; they do not seem to point beyond themselves. Either spiritual pleasure is unlike ordinary pleasure in this respect, or it is not an apparent cognition.

In the next subsection we will see *why* Edwards calls the feeling of spiritual pleasure a "perception." Whether this resolves the difficulty, however, is doubtful.

SPIRITUAL SENSING

Even though the spiritual sense is closely connected with a person's will or inclination,[29] it is a cognitive faculty—"a new foundation laid in the nature of the soul, for a new kind of exercises of the . . . faculty of *understanding*" (*RA* 206, my emphasis).[30] A sense of the heart involves a person's will or inclination because "when the mind is sensible" of spiritual beauty "that implies a sensibleness of sweetness and delight in the presence of the idea of it", "the mind . . . relishes and feels." But "there is [also] the nature of instruction in it"; it is a "kind of understanding" (*RA* 272).

Why does Edwards speak of this new cognition as a kind of perception or sensation? Partly because the idea of a spiritual sense was a Puritan commonplace. For example, John Owen said that God "gives . . . a spirituall sense, a Taste of the things themselves upon the mind, Heart and Conscience." According to Richard Sibbes, "It is knowledge with a taste . . . God giveth knowledge *per modum gustus*." Francis Rous said that "after we have tasted those heavenly things . . . from this taste there ariseth a new, but a true, lively, and experimental knowledge of the things so tasted. . . . For even in natural fruits there are certain relishes . . . which nothing but the taste it self can truly represent and shew unto us. The West-Indian Piney [pineapple] cannot be so expressed in words, even by him that hath tasted it, that he can deliver over the true shape and character of that taste to another that hath not tasted it."[31] Edwards was indebted to his predecessors for the idea of a spiritual sensation. His development of that concept, however, is heavily influenced by empiricists such as Locke and (possibly) Hutcheson.[32]

The object of the spiritual sense is a new simple idea, and Edwards shared Locke's conviction that simple ideas come "from experience" (*HU* 2.1.2). As Francis Hutcheson said, "Reasoning or intellect seems to raise no new species of ideas but [only] to discover or discern the relation of" ideas "received by some immediate powers of perception internal or external which we may call sense" (*Illustrations* 135).

Spiritual understanding also involves a kind of relish or delight, and Edwards follows Locke and Hutcheson in thinking that being pleased or pained, like a feeling of tactual pressure or being appeared to redly, is a kind of sensation or perception. (All three believe that pleasure and pain are simple ideas.)

Then again, the new simple idea occurs involuntarily, and Edwards associates sensation with passivity (cf. Subjects 29). This too was a commonplace. For example, Hutcheson said that a sense is "a determination of the mind to receive any idea from the presence of an object . . . independent on our will" (*Inquiry*, Second Treatise, I, I).

Finally, the mind's apprehension of true or spiritual beauty is immediate (noninferential). As Edwards says, "this manner of being affected with the" beauty of a thing "depends not . . . on any reasonings . . . but on the frame of our minds whereby they are so made that" as soon as we perceive or cognize it, it "appears beautiful" (*TV* 619).[33] A comparison with Hutcheson is again instructive, for Hutcheson argued that the power of receiving the idea of beauty should be called a "sense" because "we are struck at the first with the beauty" (*Inquiry*, Second Treatise, I, XII).

It is thus clear *why* Edwards speaks of the new cognition as a perception or sensation. Whether he should have done so is another matter.

There is little force in the third and fourth considerations. Our sensations (and the beliefs directly based on them) appear involuntary and immediate, but so too does our recognition of the fact that $2 + 2 = 4$. Passivity and immediacy are not peculiar to ideas derived from (internal or external) sensation.

The first two considerations carry more weight. Locke and Hutcheson identify reason with reasoning. Reason is sharply distinguished from the will and its affections and from the senses. Its sole function is to manipulate ideas received from other sources. Edwards shares these views.[34] Reason does not have an affective dimension and is not the source of new simple ideas. The cognition of true beauty, on the other hand, *has* an affective dimension since it involves relish or delight. Furthermore, its object is a new simple idea. Spiritual cognition must therefore be some kind of sensation or perception.

This conclusion seems inconsistent with other aspects of Edwards's position. A number of Hutcheson's critics took exception to his moral sense theory because they believed that (1) at least some moral propositions are necessarily true, and (2) necessary truths are discerned by reason.[35] Hutcheson maintained that the moral sense grasps the goodness of benevolent actions and dispositions, that is, perceives that benevolence is (morally) good. His critics objected that "benevolence is good" is necessarily true and that necessary truths are apprehended by *reason*. It is therefore significant that Edwards, too, apparently believed that moral truths are necessary.[36] Nor is he likely to have thought that the connection between benevolent actions and dispositions and spiritual beauty is only contingent—that holiness or benevolence might not have been truly beautiful. But if "holiness is beautiful" *is* necessarily true, Edwards seems committed to the view that our knowledge of at least some necessary truths is derived from a sense, that is, that some necessary truths are perceived by a kind of sensation. And this is not plausible.

One *may* be able to apprehend the redness of a table without apprehending *that* the table is red. (Perhaps animals and infants do.) But *can* one apprehend the moral goodness of a benevolent action without apprehending *that* the action is morally good or apprehend its spiritual beauty without apprehending *that* it is truly beautiful? This seems doubtful. The idea of beauty derives from experience in the sense that one acquires it by encountering beautiful objects. But the idea of beauty does not seem to be a discrete feeling or sensation (like a feeling of sexual pleasure or a raw sensation of redness) that is *first* received from experience and *then* incorporated in a judgment. On the contrary, receiving the idea of beauty appears to *be* judging that what one is contemplating is beautiful. Edwards seems committed to claiming that this judgment is necessarily true. Does it make any sense, then, to speak of a person's apprehension of a thing's beauty as some kind of internal or external sensing?

If one were to interpret spiritual cognition as an "intellectual intuition" with affective overtones, one could avoid this problem as well as that raised at the end of the last subsection. Spiritual "perception" would then be something like our immediate recognition of the prima facie rightness of an instance of justice or kindness on a view like W. D. Ross's. Edwards was familiar with at least one account of this type, that of the Cambridge Platonist John Smith.

Like Edwards, Smith insisted on the inadequacy of a merely notional or intellectual understanding of spiritual things. He, too, thought that divine truths can only be understood by those who lead holy lives, and he, too, spoke of a "spiritual sensation." "The soul," said Smith, "itself hath its sense, as well as the body: and therefore David . . . calls not for speculation but sensation, Taste and see how good the Lord is." But Smith's spiritual sensation is an act of "that reason that is within us . . . [the] eye of the soul . . . our intellectual faculty." This intellectual intuition or perception of reason *incorporates* love or delight but is not identical with them.[37] (Smith does not find this problematic because he shares the Platonic view that reason itself has an affective dimension. Knowing the good involves loving it and delighting in it).[38]

A view such as Smith's sidesteps the two problems confronting Edwards—how a feeling of delight can also be an apparent cognition, and how a necessary truth can be grasped by a kind of sensation. Edwards's commitment to empiricism precluded this solution. Philosophers such as Locke identified reason with ratiocination and insisted that simple ideas originate in experience (internal or external sensation). Because Edwards accepted these theses, he could not construe spiritual cognitions as rational intuitions. Whether they are essential to his epistemology, however, is debatable.[39]

The Cognition of Spiritual Truths

Although the spiritual sense's direct object is true beauty or excellency, it also has an indirect object—spiritual facts or truths. There are two cases to consider.

In the first, the spiritual sense enables us to recognize the truth of propositions that are logically or epistemically related to the excellency of divine things. For example: Our apprehension of Christ's beauty and excellency produces a conviction of His sufficiency as a Mediator (Misc. 782, T 126; *RA* 273, 302). To grasp the appropriateness of God's end in creation, namely, the communication of His glory *ad extra,* one must perceive its beauty. An appreciation of the splendor of God's glory is also needed to comprehend the fitness of the means He employs to secure it and thus understand His wisdom (*RA* 274, 302). Nor can one discern "the amiableness of the duties . . . that are required of us" unless one perceives the excellency of divine things (*RA* 274). Or again, one must see the beauty of holiness to appreciate the "hatefulness of sin" (*RA* 274, 301) and thus be convinced of the justice of divine punishment and our inability to make satisfaction (*RA* 302). The spiritual sense, then, enables us to grasp the truth of a number of important doctrines.

But it also helps us grasp the truth of the gospel scheme as a whole (*RA* 291-92). A conviction of the gospel's truth is an inference from the beauty or excellency of what it depicts, namely, "God and Jesus Christ . . . the work of redemption, and the ways and works of God" (DSL 8). "There is a divine and superlative glory in these things" that distinguishes "them from all that is earthly and temporal" (DSL 8). A spiritual person "truly sees' this glory (*RA* 298); his perception of it is as immediate and direct as a perception of color or the sweetness of food (DSL 18). (This was not, of course, a new idea. Thus, Richard Sibbes said, "God . . . causeth him to see a divine majesty shining forth in the scriptures, so that there must be an infused establishing by the Spirit to settle the heart in this first principle . . . that the Scriptures are the word of God." Or again, "How do you know the word to be the word? It carrieth proof and evidence in itself. It is an evidence that the fire is hot to him that feeleth it, and that the sun shineth to him that looks on it; how much more doth the word. . . . I am sure I felt it, it warmed my heart, and converted me.")[40]

A conviction of the gospel's truth "is an effect and natural consequence of this perception" (DSL 8). The perception and conviction are nonetheless distinct. The mind *infers* the truth and reality of the things the gospel contains from its *perception* of their spiritual beauty. There is, however, no "long chain of arguments; the argument is but one, and the evidence direct; the mind ascends to the truth of the gospel but by one step, and that is its divine glory" (*RA* 298-99; cf. Misc. 782, T 126).[41] Because only one step is involved, we can truly say that the divinity, or reality, or truth of the gospel is "as it were" known intuitively, that "a soul may have a kind of intuitive knowledge of the divinity [or truth, or reality] of the things exhibited in the gospel" (*RA* 298).[42]

The mind's object differs in the two cases. In the first, it is a comparatively specific doctrinal proposition that is logically or epistemically connected with other propositions that affirm that some person or characteristic or activity or state of affairs is truly amiable or beautiful or excellent. Our spiritual sense enables us to *perceive* the truth of the latter and from this we *infer* the truth of the former. In the second, the mind's object is the content of the gospel as a whole—what Paul Ricoeur has called "the world of the text."[43] The central or controlling features of this world—God, Christ, and the scheme of salvation—are *perceived* to be truly beautiful. On the basis of this perception one immediately concludes that the biblical world is not fictional like those depicted in *The Brothers Karamazov* or *Moby-Dick,* but *real.*

Edwards's view has some interesting implications. If my interpretation is correct, the new spiritual sense does not involve a direct or immediate or quasi-perceptual awareness of God Himself. Instead, God's reality is *inferred* from the excellency and beauty of the things depicted in scripture. As we have seen, however, the inference "is without any long chain of arguments; the argument is but one, and the evidence direct." Because of the inference's spontaneity and immediacy, a person can even be said to have "a kind of intuitive knowledge" of divinity (*RA* 298). Edwards's interpretation of the redeemed's knowledge of God's reality thus resembles Descartes's and Locke's account of our knowledge of other minds and physical objects. These things are not directly perceived, but their reality or presence is spontaneously and immediately inferred from sensations or impressions that *are* directly apprehended. Edwards thinks our knowledge of God is similar. Although God is not *directly* perceived, His reality is no more remote or uncertain than other minds or physical objects are in Locke's view.

If I am right, Edwards's position differs from a basic beliefs approach. One's belief in God is not basic like our memory beliefs, or perceptual beliefs, or beliefs in simple necessary truths but is, instead, inferential. On the other hand, the inference on which one's belief is based does not involve a long or complicated chain of reasoning, and it is as spontaneous and compelling as our (alleged) inference to other minds or the reality of the physical world.

The redeemed's belief in God is thus similar to some of Hume's natural beliefs—the belief in the continued existence of unperceived physical objects, for example, and (on some interpretations) the belief in a designer.[44] It differs in that the *basis* of the inference is a new simple idea that God bestows on the regenerate and because (in Edwards's opinion) the inference is *sound.*

THE OBJECTIVITY OF THE SPIRITUAL SENSE

The final chapter of *The Nature of True Virtue* attempts to show that "the frame of mind, or inward sense . . . whereby the mind is disposed to" relish true virtue for its spiritual beauty, is not "given arbitrarily" but agrees "with the necessary nature of things" (*TV* 620). But the "frame of mind" that disposes a person to delight in true beauty (i.e., to be pleased with benevolence) is benevolence itself. Edwards concludes that it will be sufficient to show that *benevolence* agrees with the nature of things.

Edwards's strategy, in other words, is this. True benevolence is the mechanism underlying the new spiritual sense. If we can show that benevolence has a foundation in the nature of things, we can conclude that the spiritual sense, too, is aligned with reality. Edwards's task, then, is to prove that benevolence agrees with the "necessary nature of things." He has four arguments for this conclusion. The first two are unconvincing. The third and fourth are more persuasive.

Edwards's first argument is this:

> 1. A being with understanding and inclinations necessarily desires its own happiness (i.e., it desires what it wants or desires or finds agreeable).
>
> 2. Benevolence is the disposition to benefit being *in general.*
>
> 3. Therefore, a being with understanding and inclinations must approve of benevolence (for it benefits *him*). (From 1 and 2.)
>
> 4. Hence, if a being with understanding and inclinations approves of vice (i.e., of malevolence or indifference to being in general), then his attitudes are inconsistent. (From 3.)
>
> 5. Virtue (benevolence) can be approved without inconsistency.
>
> 6. If virtue (benevolence) can be approved without inconsistency and vice (malevolence or indifference) cannot, then virtue agrees with the nature of things and vice does not.
>
> 7. Therefore, virtue agrees with the nature of things and vice does not. (From 4, 5, and 6.) (*TV* 621-22).

The argument, if sound, shows that virtue agrees with the nature of things in the sense that loving virtue is a more rational (i.e., coherent) response to reality than loving vice.

But the proof is not persuasive. A person is not inconsistent in approving and disapproving (or not approving) of the same thing if he or she approves and disapproves (or fails to approve) of it in different respects. And this is surely the case here. The wicked approve of benevolence when it benefits them but hate it, or are indifferent toward it, when it benefits others. They approve of (or are indifferent to) malevolence or indifference when directed toward others but not when directed toward themselves. These attitudes may be reprehensible but they are not inconsistent. Let us therefore turn to Edwards's second argument:

> 1. Benevolence is "agreement or consent of being to being."
>
> 2. Being or "general existence" is the nature of things.
>
> 3. Therefore, benevolence agrees with the nature of things (*TV* 620). The argument establishes its conclusion by identifying the nature of things with what is (viz., being in general) and identifying agreement with being's consent to being.

This too seems unconvincing. Edwards's argument only establishes a tautology—that consent to being (i.e., benevolence) is consent to (i.e., agreement with) being (i.e., the nature of things). What *needs* to be shown is that benevolence or consent to being is an *appropriate* response to the nature of things, and his argument does not do this.

But this criticism, although correct, is superficial. For it neglects the argument's theistic context. Edwards believes that being in general is *God* and the "particular beings" that depend on Him and manifest His glory. A consent to, or love of, being in *this* sense is surely an appropriate response to it. The theistic metaphysics becomes explicit in Edwards's third argument.

> 1. God "is in effect being in general." (All being either is God or unconditionally depends on Him.)
>
> 2. It is "necessary, that God should agree with himself, be united with himself, or love himself."
>
> 3. Therefore, God is necessarily benevolent. (From 1 and 2—in loving Himself, God loves "being in general" and is therefore benevolent.)
>
> 4. Consequently, benevolence agrees with the nature of God. (From 3.)
>
> 5. Now, whatever agrees with the nature of what "is in effect being in general" agrees with the nature of things.
>
> 6. Therefore, benevolence agrees with the nature of things. (From 1, 4, and 5.) (*TV* 621).

The third argument uses "agreement" in yet another sense. Edwards's point is roughly that the nature of things is divine benevolence. Human benevolence agrees with it because it is its image.

Edwards is an occasionalist like Malebranche, an idealist like Berkeley, and a mental phenomenalist like Hume.

What are "vulgarly" called causal relations are mere constant conjunctions. *True* causes necessitate their effects. Because God's will alone meets this condition, God is the only true cause. He is also the only true substance. Physical objects are collections of "corporeal ideas" (ideas of color, for example, or solidity, resistance, and so on). Minds are series of "thoughts" or "perceptions." Any substance underlying perceptions, thoughts, and corporeal ideas would be something that "subsisted by itself, and stood underneath and kept up" physical and mental properties. But God alone subsists by Himself, stands underneath, and keeps up thoughts, perceptions, solidity, color, and other corporeal qualities (ideas). Hence, "the substance of bodies [and minds] at last becomes either nothing, or nothing but the Deity acting in that particular manner . . . where he thinks fit."[45] The only real cause and the only real substance are thus God Himself. God's essence, however, is love. The real nature of things, then, is an infinite and omnipotent benevolence.

Our benevolence "agrees with" this in the sense that it resembles it or is an image of it. The thrust of Edwards's argument is therefore this. Benevolence is appropriate because it mirrors reality. Nature's activity is really *God's* activity. (Because God is the only true substance and the only true cause, He is *natura naturans*.) Love is thus "natural" because it imitates the activity of "Nature" itself.

Edwards's theistic metaphysics is also implicit in his fourth argument.

> 1. Harmony among beings is more agreeable to the nature of things than disharmony.
>
> 2. Benevolence (the consent of being to being) promotes (or is) harmony among beings.
>
> 3. Therefore, benevolence agrees with the nature of things. (*TV* 100-101)

Edwards assumes that whatever promotes harmony in a system accords or agrees with its nature. This is plausible when the system is organic or social. In Edwards's opinion, being in general *is* an organic or social system. The only things that exist without qualification are minds, and minds form a social system in which God is sovereign.[46]

Benevolence, then, has a "foundation in the nature of things." Because the spiritual sense is an *expression* of benevolence, Edwards concludes that it, too, is founded "in the nature of things." "The idea we obtain by this spiritual sense" is thus "a knowledge or perception" of something outside our minds, a true "representation" of something "without," namely, God's moral perfection and excellence and its created reflections (*TV* 622f).

Edwards's defense of the objectivity of the new spiritual sense has four steps. (1) Benevolence agrees with the nature of things. The world is an interconnected system of minds and ideas in which the only true substance and cause are an infinite and omnipotent love. Human benevolence, therefore, is an appropriate or fitting response to reality. (2) A delight in benevolence also agrees with reality. Benevolence is pleased by benevolence; it relishes it, or delights in it, for its own sake (*TV* 546-49). If benevolence is an appropriate response to reality, so, too, then, is benevolence's delight in benevolence. (3) Delight in benevolence is identified with a perception of its spiritual beauty. (4) The redeemed's spiritual perceptions are veridical. Spiritual sensations are a "representation" of something "without," that is, they are noetic or perceptionlike. In Berkeley's words, they have "outness." The second step established that our spiritual sense is in order, that its motions are appropriate to reality. If spiritual sensations were merely subjective feelings such as indignation and admiration or physical pleasure and pain, then the second step would only show that these feelings are appropriate affective responses to their objects. But the third step informs us that spiritual sensations *are not* mere feelings; they are apparent cognitions. Because the apparent cognitions are an appropriate response to reality, they are a "knowledge or perception" of something "without"; the representations are "true representations."

How successful is Edwards's defense? The first two steps are plausible. Although Edwards's occasionalism, idealism, and mental phenomenalism undoubtedly strengthened his belief in benevolence's agreement with the nature of things, similar conclusions follow from any theistic (or at least Christian) metaphysics. The second step is also plausible. An essential feature of an appropriate response is itself appropriate. And Edwards's fourth step follows from his second and third.

The problem is the third step. Because Edwards's identification of spiritual perception with a kind of pleasure is suspect (see the first two subsections), his defense is not fully successful. Nevertheless, Edwards's reflections provide a promising start. Benevolence may really *be* spiritual perception's underlying mechanism. The nature of this perception, though, and its relation to benevolence, need further clarification.

The Appeal to Theistic Metaphysics and the Problem of Circularity

The most instructive feature of Edwards's defense is the way it uses theistic metaphysics. I suspect that any persuasive justification of a spiritual sense's reliability will do the same. Is it therefore circular? It is not *if* theistic metaphysics can be established without appealing to spiritual perceptions. Does Edwards think it can? He believes that theistic metaphysics is supported by natural reason and sometimes suggests that the rational evidence is sufficient. On the other hand, he also talks as if it often will not *seem* sufficient to those with unconverted hearts.

If Edwards is right, justifications of spiritual perceptions are not circular in the sense that they employ premises that explicitly or implicitly assert that spiritual perceptions are reliable. Nor are they circular in the sense that they employ premises that *in principle* can only be known to be true by those who rely on their spiritual sense. As we shall see in the following section, however, there is a de facto psychological or causal connection between having spiritual perceptions and appreciating the force of the evidence for a theistic metaphysics and thereby appreciating the force of justifications of the spiritual sense's reliability. It seems, then, both that these justifications are not logically or epistemically circular *and* that those who lack spiritual perceptions, or distrust them, will normally find them unpersuasive.

An example may clarify my point. Suppose that someone sees the force of an inductive argument for the guilt of his brother only after he has been persuaded of his brother's guilt. (Perhaps his brother confessed.) Is the argument circular? Is it circular for him? Not clearly. The nature of his noetic equipment is not such that he cannot know the premises without knowing the conclusion. Indeed, he may have firmly believed that the premises are true. Nor is its nature such that he *cannot* see that the premises establish the conclusion. The fault is not with his noetic equipment but with his attachment to his brother, which blinded him to the force of the evidence and prevented him from using his noetic equipment properly. The relation between believing the conclusion and recognizing the force of the argument for it is thus extrinsic or accidental. His inability to appreciate the weight of the evidence prior to accepting the argument's conclusion is the result of a psychological or moral aberration, not a matter of logic or a consequence of the nature of his cognitive faculties.

Edwards's view is similar. The reliability of our spiritual sense can be justified by a theistic metaphysics that is itself adequately supported by evidence accessible to natural reason. But sin blinds us to the evidence's force. There is thus a causal connection between spiritual perception and rational persuasion. Appeals to spiritual perceptions play no role, however, in the justificatory process itself. If this is correct, it seems misleading to say that the reliability of the spiritual sense cannot be justified without circularity. But this is a difficult issue, and we will return to it in Chapter 4.

The Bearing of Edwards's Theory on Contemporary Discussions

Edwards's account of the sense of the heart goes some way toward filling an important gap in contemporary discussions—the failure adequately to explain *how* theistic belief-producing mechanisms operate. The issue is important for two reasons.

First, the nature of the mechanism has a bearing on its reliability. For example, Freud offers several accounts of the nature of the theistic belief-producing mechanism that, if true, cast doubt on its reliability. Theists can defuse criticisms of this sort by providing alternative and equally plausible accounts of the mechanism's operation that do not impugn its reliability.

The second reason is this. On reading the *Vedas,* an Advaitin may find himself spontaneously believing that they express the Nirguna Brahman. On reading the *Iśa Upanishad* or having a monistic mystical experience, he may find himself spontaneously believing that all differences are unreal or that the impersonal Brahman is ultimate. On surveying the evidence, he may conclude that Advaita Vedānta has fewer difficulties than its rivals and is therefore more likely to be true. If these beliefs are true, theism is false. On the face of it, the theist's beliefs and the Advaitin's beliefs are formed in similar ways. The same sort of belief-producing mechanism seems involved in both cases. If it is, then if one is reliable, so presumably is the other. And yet they cannot *both* be reliable, for they produce conflicting beliefs. Hence, neither seems reliable.

What is needed is an explanation of the difference between theistic and (for example) Advaitin or Mahāyāanan belief-producing mechanisms, together with an indication of why the former are reliable and the latter are not.

Edwards may provide some assistance here for he has the beginnings of an account of how one theistic belief-producing mechanism operates. His account is also the *right* sort. If the mechanism is (a function of?) benevolence rather than wish fulfillment or the working out of an oedipal complex, there may be less reason for thinking it untrustworthy. Again, if (1) the disposition to form true religious beliefs is a function of benevolence or love, (2) benevolence or love agrees with the nature of things, and (3) the love of being in general is either absent or less fully developed in Advaita or Mahāyāan, one has some indication of why the theist's religious belief-producing mechanism is more reliable than the latter's.[47]

My point, of course, is not that Edwards *has* provided a fully adequate account but that some account is needed to defuse certain sorts of criticism and that the kind of account Edwards presents is the *right* kind.

These brief remarks are not sufficient to allay the spectres of subjectivism and relativism; those issues will be addressed in Chapters 4 and 5. Our task now is to look at Edwards's account of religious reasoning more closely.

Sanctified Reason

Edwards uses "reason" in two closely related senses. Sometimes the term refers to "ratiocination, or a power of inferring by arguments" (DSL 18). At others it refers to "the power . . . an intelligent being has to judge of the truth of propositions . . . immediately by only looking on the propositions" as well as to ratiocination (Misc. 1340, T 219).[48] The difference between these characterizations is not important; in either case, "reason's work is to perceive truth and not excellency" (DSL 18). Excellency and what pertains to it are perceived by the heart. Even though Edwards concedes that there is a more extended sense in which "reason" refers to "the faculty of mental perception in general" (DSL 18), he clearly prefers the stricter usage.

His official view is that of other modern philosophers who deny that reason has an affective dimension (a love of the good, for example, or a delight in excellence).[49]

Grace affects reason as well as the heart. "Common grace" helps the faculties "to do that more fully which they do by nature," strengthening "the natural principles [e.g., conscience] against those things that tend to stupify [*sic*] it and to hinder its free exercise." "Special grace," on the other hand, "causes those things to be in the soul that are above nature; and causes them to be in the soul habitually" (Misc. 626, T 111). Special grace sanctifies by infusing benevolence or true virtue (viz., the love of being in general). Infused benevolence is the basis of a new epistemic principle; a sense of the heart that tastes, relishes, and perceives the beauty of holiness (i.e., benevolence). By its means, the sanctified acquire a new simple idea (the idea of "true beauty") that the unredeemed lack.[50] Because this idea is needed to understand divine matters properly, the "saints" are in a superior epistemic position. One cannot rightly understand God's moral attributes, for example, if one does not perceive their beauty. Nor can one adequately grasp truths that logically or epistemically depend on God's holiness and its splendor such as the infinite heinousness of sin or the appropriateness of God's aiming at His own glory. The saints also behold old data with new eyes. They perceive the stamp of divine splendor on the world's order and design, and on the events recorded in sacred history. They thereby acquire a more accurate sense of this evidence's force and impressiveness.

The perception of spiritual beauty was discussed in the preceding section. This section focuses on another epistemic effect of special grace. The new principle that God infuses "sanctifies the reasoning faculty and assists it to see the clear evidence there is of the truth of religion in rational arguments, and that in two ways, viz., as it removes prejudices and so lays the mind more open to the force of arguments, and also secondly, as it positively enlightens and assists it to see the force of rational arguments . . . by adding greater light, clearness and strength to the judgment" (Misc. 628, T 251).[51] There is nothing intrinsically supernatural about many of these benefits. The *cause* of the mind's reasoning soundly is supernatural, but the effect (sound reasoning) need not be;[52] the spirit simply helps us use our natural epistemic faculties rightly.

What sorts of "prejudices" interfere with reason's "free exercise"? "Opinions arising from imagination" are one example. They "take us as soon as we are born, are beat into us by every act of sensation, and so grow up with us from our very births; and by that means grow into us so fast that it is almost impossible to root them out, being as it were so incorporated with our very minds that whatsoever is objected to them, contrary thereunto, is as if it were dissonant to the very constitution of them. Hence, men come to make what they can actually perceive by their senses, or immediate and outside reflection into their own souls, the standard of possibility and impossibility"

(Prejudices 196). Biases arising from temperament, education, custom, and fashion furnish other examples (Mind 68 and Subjects 384 and 387).

Sin's essence is a failure to obey the love commandment. Those who do not love being in general love "private systems." Their loves are partial, extending to only some beings. They are also inordinate; lives are centered on the self or more extensive private systems rather than on God (who is "in effect" being in general) and the creatures who are absolutely dependent on Him and reflect His glory.[53]

Sin has noetic consequences. Edwards refers, for example, to "the great subjection of the soul in its fallen state to the external senses" (Misc. 782, T 122). (This subjection is presumably a consequence of the soul's inordinate love of temporal goods.)[54] Again, self-love blinds us to everything that does not bear on immediate self-interest (OS 145-57). In addition, "the mind of man is naturally full of enmity against the doctrines of the gospel" that cause "arguments that prove their truth . . . to lose their force upon the mind" (RA 307). (God crosses our self-love and love of temporal things, and this arouses hostility.)[55]

Our corrupt inclinations even affect our sense of what is and is not reasonable. "Common inclination or the common dictates of inclination, are often called common sense." A person who says that the doctrine of eternal damnation offends common sense is using the expression in this way. But the inclinations behind this judgment have been shaped by an insensibility to "the great evil of sin." They are therefore corrupt (Misc. Obs. 253).

William James has suggested that our judgments of credibility reflect what we have a use for, what vitally concerns us. "In . . . the sense in which we contrast reality with simple unreality, and in which one thing is said to have more reality than another, and to be more believed, reality means simply relation to our emotional and active life. This is the only sense that the word ever has in the mouths of practical men. In this sense whatever excites and stimulates our interests is real."[56] "The natural propensity of man is to believe that whatever has great value for life is thereby certified as true."[57] Our judgments of truth and reality, in other words, are (partly) functions of our emotional engagement. Edwards would agree. If our interests are badly misdirected, our judgments of what is and is not credible will be correspondingly distorted.

Grace frees the mind from these "prejudices." An unprejudiced reason, however, is not dispassionate. For it is affected by epistemically benign feelings and inclinations. A love of wider systems alone checks self-interest. Nor is it sufficient to replace hostility toward religion with indifference or neutrality; the heart must be receptive to it. An unprejudiced reason is also affected by natural motions of the heart as well as by true benevolence (gratitude for one's being, for example, or a sense that it would be unfitting for the injustice that evades human tribunals to escape punishment).[58] And because our love of temporal goods is not subordinate to a love of eternity, it is inordinate, and the latter is needed to correct it.[59]

Another point is relevant as well. Natural reason reveals many truths about God and our relation to Him. Yet even at the level of nature these truths are not properly understood if the heart lacks a due sense of the natural good and evil in them[60] (a proper sense of the natural unfittingness of disobeying the world's sovereign, for example, a horror of the natural evils consequent on offenses against Him, or a proper sense of the natural benefits He has bestowed on us and of the obligations these gifts create).

I conclude, then, that common grace not only inhibits the action of passional factors corrupting reason; it also causes better natural affections to influence it (at least temporarily). Sanctifying grace replaces the effects of corrupt affections by the influences of true benevolence. A reason that is exercising itself "freely" and without "prejudice," therefore, is affected by passional factors.

But grace does more than remove the impediments ("prejudices") hindering reason's free exercise by restructuring our affections. It adds "greater light, clearness and strength to the judgment." Edwards refers us to **Miscellany 408** for "one way" in which it does so.[61] That entry argues that ideas of spiritual things "appear more lively and with greater strength and impression" after conversion and that, consequently, "their circumstances and various relations and connections between themselves and with other ideas appear more" (Misc. 408, T 249-50).

How does the spirit accomplish this? By focusing the mind's attention on "actual ideas." Thought has a tendency to substitute signs for ideas, to use signs without having the "actual" (i.e., lively, clear, and distinct) ideas they signify. The signs may be words or (confused) ideas of "some sensible part, . . . effect, . . . or concomitant, or a few sensible circumstances" of what we are thinking about (Misc. 782, T 116).[62] Our ability to make this substitution is advantageous because some actual ideas are not easy to elicit and because thought would be too slow without it; it serves us well for "many of the common purposes of thinking." Nevertheless, it is a disadvantage when "we are at a loss concerning a connection or consequence, or have a new inference to draw, or would see the force of some new argument," for the "use of signs . . . causes mankind to run into a multitude of errors" (Misc. 782, T 117-18). The tendency to make this substitution is strongest when the ideas terms signify are ideas of "kinds and sorts," or things "of a spiritual nature, or things that consist in the ideas, acts, and exercises of minds" (Misc. 782, T 115). This tendency infects all (and not merely religious) thinking and can be remedied by attending to ideas instead of the signs that express them.[63]

Actual ideas and attention are closely connected. An idea will not become actual unless one "dwells" on it; "attentive reflection" is necessary. Indeed, "attention of the mind" itself consists "very much" in "exciting the actual idea and making it as lively and clear as we can" (Misc. 782, T 118). But attention is difficult. Even in temporal affairs, taking an "ideal view" (having actual ideas) often depends "not merely on the force of our thoughts but the circumstances we are in, or some special accidental situation and concurrence of things in the course of our thoughts and meditations, or some particular incident in providence that excites a sense of things" (ibid. 121-22). As for *eternal* matters, our attention is distracted by "the great subjection of the soul . . . to the external senses" and by "the direction of the inclinations . . . [away] from . . . things as they are" (ibid. 122). Grace remedies this defect, for one of its effects is to "engage the attention of the mind, with more fixedness and intenseness to that kind of objects; which causes it to have a clearer view of them" (DSL 9-10). Grace "makes even the speculative notions more lively" by assisting and engaging "the attention of the mind" (*RA* 307). Yet why should such extraordinary measures be necessary?

Actual ideas of kinds or sorts are clear and distinct ideas "of those things that are principally essential" in the idea, those things wherein it "most essentially consists" (Misc. 782, T 113, 114). Edwards is undoubtedly thinking of Locke's theory of ideas. Our ideas of God, human nature, and perplexity (Edwards's examples) are complex. The idea of God, for instance, is constructed from the ideas of "supremacy, of supreme power, of supreme government, of supreme knowledge, of will, etc;" (Ibid. 113). Actual ideas of complex ideas such as these involve actual ideas of the ("principally essential"?) simple ideas that compose them.

Actual ideas of things pertaining to good or evil present another difficulty. One cannot have them without being suitably affected, pleased or displeased as the case may be. Actual ideas of these things involve the heart.

Finally, actual ideas of "the ideas, acts, and exercises of minds" are "repetitions of those very things." One cannot have them without experiencing what they are ideas of (Misc. 238, T 247).[64] (Actual ideas of the will or inclination, or the affections, and of things pertaining to them, will thus also involve the heart. An idea of love, for example, is a repetition of it, and love's seat is the heart.)

Our failure to attend to actual ideas has two causes. Sometimes we substitute words and images for ideas we have. Sometimes we lack relevant simple ideas. Both can adversely affect religious reasoning. Those parts of the idea of God that everyone has (ideas of His power, knowledge, and justice, for instance) are not attended to or, when they are, do not affect us with a proper sense of the natural good or evil associated with them. Other parts are simply missing. Without the simple idea of true beauty, people cannot understand God's holiness and the facts that depend on it such as the infinite heinousness of sin or the infinite importance of holiness. Nor can the "carnal" understand genuine benevolence and other properties and qualifications which the elect share with God. Because the

idea of true benevolence is a repetition of it, the truly benevolent alone have an actual idea of it. Those who are not benevolent only discern its circumstances, effects, and so on, "explaining" the idea of benevolence to themselves and others in "general terms" that do not adequately delimit it (Misc. 123, T 245f).[65]

It should by now be clear how sin affects reasoning. Our immersion in temporal concerns distracts us so that we do not attend to our ideas. Our subjection to the senses aggravates the tendency to substitute words and other sensible signs for ideas, and our disordered loves make it difficult for us to appreciate even natural goods and evils associated with religion. (For example, our blunted conscience blinds us to the natural fittingness of obeying God's commands, and our inordinate attachment to the present life leads us to neglect more important natural goods that extend beyond it.) A lack of true benevolence (which is sin's essence) makes it impossible to understand God's holiness (which consists in it) or to appreciate its beauty.

We are now also in a position to understand why rational arguments for religious truths are not always convincing. **Miscellanies 201** (T 246-47) and **408** (T 249-50) imply that a conviction of reality is created by (1) an idea's clarity and liveliness, (2) its internal coherence and coherence with our other ideas, and (3) its agreement with "the nature and constitution of our minds themselves." Why, then, do religious ideas so often fail to carry conviction? Partly because the clarity and intensity of spiritual ideas is a function of "the practice of virtue and holiness' (Misc. 123, T 246) and our own practice falls woefully short, and partly because the "tempers" or "frames" of the ungodly are not suited to them. (See William James's claim that what seems true and real to us is what we have use for.) It is possible that those without spiritual frames cannot even discern their coherence. Sang Hyun Lee argues that because beauty, on Edwards's view, consists in harmony or proportion, a perception of beauty is a perception of harmony.[66] If proportion and pleasing order are included in coherence, unaided reason may have difficulty grasping it; for it may miss the "sweet harmony" among the ideas of religion and between those ideas and other ideas. (Consider those who reject religion because it does not seem to "fit" or "hang together" with science, although they concede there is no formal inconsistency.)

Special or sanctifying grace remedies these defects by enabling us to attend more easily to the actual ideas the words of religion stand for and by disposing the heart to be suitably affected by the natural and supernatural good and evil associated with them. Common grace has similar effects, but (because it does not replace the love of private systems with true benevolence) it does not furnish the mind with actual ideas of true virtue and true beauty and only affects it with a sense of the relevant *natural* goods and evils.

The sense of divine beauty alone is intrinsically supernatural. A reason that has been freed from the bonds of imagination, prejudice, and narrow self-interest, attends to ideas of God's being, power, knowledge, justice, munificence, and other "natural" attributes and is suitably affected by the natural good and evil associated with them is not functioning above its nature.[67] A reason that has been strengthened in these ways is capable, however, of seeing the force of rational arguments for the truths of "natural religion" (i.e., for truths about God that depend neither logically nor epistemically on the ideas of holiness and true beauty). A suitably disposed natural reason is thus capable of establishing God's existence and general nature, and some of our obligations toward Him. Truths that depend on the ideas of holiness and true beauty can also be established by rational arguments, but the force of these can only be appreciated by people with spiritual frames.

EDWARDS AND EVIDENTIALISM

Edwards was the philosophical heir of rationalists and empiricists whose confidence in reason was comparatively unqualified. He was the theological heir of a Reformed tradition that distrusted humanity's natural capacities. Did he succeed in coherently weaving these apparently inconsistent strands together? The answer, I believe, is a qualified "Yes."

The key is a distinction between good rational arguments and the conditions necessary for their acceptance. I may have a good argument against smoking, for example, but my desire to smoke prevents me from appreciating its force. What is needed is not a better argument but a reorientation of my desires.

Edwards's position is roughly this. Although reason is capable of generating good rational arguments for God's existence, His providential government of human affairs, predestination, and many other theological and metaphysical doctrines, self-deception, prejudice, self-interest, and other passional factors make it difficult for us to see their force. These faults cannot be corrected by applying Descartes's rules for correct thinking, Locke's "measures . . . to regulate our assent and moderate our persuasion,"[68] or other methods of this sort. What is needed is a set of excellences that are themselves expressions of morally desirable character traits and rightly ordered affections. The defects distorting human reasoning are deeply rooted in human nature and can only be eliminated by the appropriate virtues.

Two features of Edwards's position are especially significant. First, the epistemic virtues are not merely negative; they involve more than the exclusion of the passions and selfish partialities that subvert reason. Nor are the epistemic virtues confined to noncontroversial excellences such as the love of truth. They include properly ordered natural affections such as gratitude and a love of being in general that God infuses into the hearts of His elect. These affections not only cast out others that adversely affect reasoning; they also affect it themselves. Under their influence, we reason differently and more accurately.

The other significant feature is this. Two views should be distinguished. One is that there are circumstances in which it is legitimate for people's passions and affections to make up deficiencies in the evidence. Although the (objective) evidence is not sufficient to warrant belief, one is entitled to let one's passional nature tip the balance. The other is that a person's passional nature is sometimes needed to evaluate the evidence properly (to assess its force accurately). The first view is often attributed to James. Edwards holds the second.

Edwards's position differs significantly from the more familiar views of James, Kierkegaard, and others who appeal to passional factors. Edwards is a foundationalist and an evidentalist. A proper, and therefore rational, belief must be self-evident or based on adequate evidence. A properly held belief *in God* rests on evidence (the beauty of scripture, the effects of the Holy Spirit in our souls, apparent design, and so on).[69] But unlike most evidentialists, Edwards believes that passional factors are needed to appreciate the evidence's *force*. Only those with properly disposed hearts can read the evidence rightly.

Edwards's view thus also differs from Locke's. Fully rational judgments are not only determined by one's evidence and evidential standards; they are also determined by feelings and attitudes that express theological virtues.

But are not the promptings of true benevolence *themselves* evidence of a sort? And if so, is not the difference between Edwards and Locke illusory? I suggest that it is not.

The promptings of true benevolence in this context just *are* the assessments of the force of a body of evidence, *e,* made by a truly benevolent heart.[70] Suppose that one treats this assessment as a new piece of evidence, e^1. If one does, one must now assess *its* force (or the force of one's other evidence plus e^1). But this new assessment also reflects the state of one's heart. It, too, therefore, must be treated as a new piece of evidence, e^2, whose force (or the combined force of $e + e^1 + e^2$) must in turn be assessed. Hence, if one's assessment of the force of a body of evidence is itself part of one's evidence, then either the force of some of one's evidence is not assessed or one's evidence includes an infinite number of items.

Treating true benevolence's assessment of the force of the evidence as a piece of evidence is as misguided as treating an intellectually honest, critical, and fairminded historian's assessment of the strength of her argument as one of her premises. One's evidence must be distinguished from one's take on it.

It does not follow that true benevolence's take on the evidence is a "nonrational ground of belief" in Richard Swinburne's sense. A nonrational ground for belief that *p* is a reason for "believing it to be true other than that it [is] likely to be true." It might be good, for instance, to hold a certain belief although the evidence seems to count against it. (For example, respect for persons might entail a duty to think well of them in spite of appearances.) Or it might be prudentially worthwhile to hold a belief. But (Swinburne argues) even if you have a nonrational ground for believing *p*, you cannot believe *p* unless you believe that your evidence makes *p* probable. To get yourself to believe *p*, you must therefore get yourself to believe that your evidence supports *p*. Yet "to get yourself to believe that your evidence makes *p* probable" when it (now) seems to you that it does not involves "getting yourself to change your inductive standards by adopting standards which you now believe to be incorrect, or by getting yourself to forget about some of the unfavorable evidence, or by getting yourself to acquire new favorable evidence through looking only where favorable evidence is to be found and then forgetting the selective character of your investigation." It thus involves deliberately inducing beliefs that are irrational by your present standards.[71]

True benevolence's assessment of the evidence is not a nonrational ground for belief in this sense. It does not lead the saints to construct new inductive or deductive standards, forget about some of the evidence, or engage in selective investigation. Nor does it provide them with a *reason* for doing so. True benevolence is not a nonrational ground for belief in Swinburne's sense because it is not a *ground* for belief at all, although its presence *does* partially explain why the saints hold the beliefs they do. In the same way, a good scientist's impartiality, intellectual honesty, and desire for the truth help explain why she holds the beliefs she does and not the views of some less scrupulous or more credulous colleague. But they are not *grounds* for her belief.

The position Edwards represents must be distinguished, then, from other more familiar views. Whether it can be defended against charges of subjectivism, circularity, and relativism will be discussed in Chapters 4 and 5.

Notes

1. Jonathan Edwards's principal discussions of reason are located in the "Miscellanies" (a number of which can be found in *The Philosophy of Jonathan Edwards from His Private Notebooks,* ed. Harvey G. Townsend [Eugene, Ore.: University of Oregon Monographs, 1955], hereafter Misc. T; "A Divine and Supernatural Light" and "Miscellaneous Observations" (in *The Works of President Edwards* [New York: P. Franklin, 1968; reprint of the Leeds edition reissued with a two-volume supplement in Edinburgh, 1847], vol. VIII), hereafter DSL and Misc. Obs., respectively; "The Mind," "Subjects to Be Handled in the Treatise on the Mind," and "Of the Prejudices of Imagination" (in *Scientific and Philosophical Writings,* ed. Wallace E. Anderson [New Haven: Yale University Press, 1980], hereafter Mind, Subjects, and Prejudices, respectively; and *Original Sin* (Boston 1758; reprint, New Haven: Yale University Press, 1970), hereafter *OS.* Other relevant material can be found in *Religious* *Affections* (Boston 1746; reprint, New Haven: Yale University Press, 1959), hereafter *RA; The Nature of True Virtue* (Boston 1765; reprinted in *Ethical Writings,* ed. Paul Ramsey [New Haven: Yale University Press, 1989]), hereafter *TV;* and *History of the Work of Redemption* (Edinburgh, 1774; reprint, New Haven: Yale University Press, 1989), hereafter *HR.* The "Miscellaneous Observations" must be used with caution. It was originally published in 1793 and consists of material from the "Miscellanies." The editor (John Erskine) "took great liberties with the text, disregarded all chronological order, patched together widely separated excerpts, and added whatever connections or conjunctions seemed appropriate to him" (Townsend, *Philosophy of Edwards,* p. xi, n. 14).

2. John Morgan, *Godly Learning; Puritan Attitudes towards Reason, Learning and Education* (Cambridge: Cambridge University Press, 1986), p. 51.

3. The quotations from Bolton, Adams, Perkins, and Rous are found in ibid., pp. 51-53. The quotation from Sterry is found in Geoffrey F. Nuttall, *The Holy Spirit in Puritan Faith and Experience,* 2d ed. (Chicago: University of Chicago Press, 1992), p. 37.

4. Quoted in Morgan, *Godly Learning,* p. 59.

5. Quoted in Nuttall, *Holy Spirit,* p. 47.

6. In spite of their strictures on reason, Puritans insisted on a learned clergy, and Puritan divines commonly drew on the ancient philosophers, the schoolmen, Ramus, and so on.

7. At one point, Edwards glosses "inconsistent" and "incomprehensible" as (merely) "contrary to what would be expected" (Misc. 1340, T 232).

8. Consider, for example, the shift in interest from taxonomy and classification to developmental explanations that occurs between the eighteenth and nineteenth centuries or increasing refinements in sampling techniques.

9. See Basil Mitchell, *The Justification of Religious Belief* (London: Macmillan, 1973), chap. 7.

10. But *which* community? There is no agreement on paradigms. The situation in religion resembles the current state of the social sciences or the situation in the physical sciences in the sixteenth and early seventeenth centuries. (See Gary Gutting, "Paradigms and Hermeneutics: A Dialogue on Kuhn, Rorty, and the Social Sciences," *American Philosophical Quarterly* 21 [1984], 1-16.) Even in cases like these, however, a person is not likely to do good work if he or she stands aloof from *all* traditions or is hostile to *all* science. One should also consider the possibility (of which I am skeptical) that the world's religions are converging toward a single tradition or community that will incorporate earlier ones. (See John Hick and Wilfred

Cantwell Smith on this point.) Edwards assumes that the Christian tradition is paradigmatic. If it is, the analogy is strengthened.

11. Could not human beings *construct* the idea of God? Is it not probable that (as Hume, Feuerbach, and Freud argued) a weak, needy, and frightened humanity would invent ideas of supernatural beings? Edwards would undoubtedly agree with Calvin and Barth. Without supernatural assistance, the mind only manufactures idols—magnified images of itself, projections of its own hopes and fears. Edwards's criterion of idolatry would, of course, be the extent to which an idea of God conforms to Christian revelation. A nontheological (and possibly more persuasive) version of his argument might be this: Religious ideas cannot be adequately explained without appealing to religious experiences that are *sui generis* (Otto's numinous feelings, for example, or mystical experiences), or, more strongly, they cannot be adequately explained without appealing to *veridical* religious experiences.

12. Edwards does not clearly distinguish between evidence, argument, and rule of reason. The distinction is presumably this: Apparent memories are a type of evidence, justifying claims by appealing to memory is a type of argument, and the appropriate rule is "One's memories are normally reliable." Similarly, the contents of scripture are a type of evidence, justifying claims by appealing to scripture is a type of argument, and the appropriate rule is "Scripture is trustworthy."

13. Edwards says, for example, that "general propositions" such as "Memory is dependable" "can be known only by reason" (Misc. 1340, T 220). Unfortunately, he does not explain *how* reason knows them. Are there arguments? Are the rules expressions of something like Hume's natural beliefs or Reid's inborn belief dispositions? Does the answer differ from case to case? One test of a rule's rationality is whether the results of applying it agree with the results of applying other rules. A check on the credibility of sense experience, for example, is "the agreement of the testimonies of the senses with other criteria of truth" (Misc. Obs. 230).

14. Edwards does not discuss instances of apparent conflict—cases in which the results of appropriately applying a rule conflict with the results of appropriately applying others. For example, we sometimes discount memory when it conflicts with the testimony of others. Or testimony is rejected when it conflicts with our perceptual experience. We presumably use some (rough) hierarchy of rules to adjudicate conflicts of this kind. We also refine rules as a result of experience. We learn, for example, when memory is reliable and when it is not. Of special interest are cases in which scripture appears to conflict with the results of applying rules such as "The testimony of history and tradition is to be

depended on" (the question of the historicity of *Daniel* or *Esther,* for example) or the results of employing "strict metaphysical distinction and comparison." Edwards thinks that conflicts like these are only apparent and undoubtedly believes that "Scripture is reliable" takes precedence over other rules. Nevertheless, one wishes that he had discussed the issue more thoroughly.

15. These arguments were commonly employed in the eighteenth century. For one of the better examples, see Samuel Clarke's *A Discourse concerning the Unchangeable Obligations of Natural Religion and the Truth and Certainty of the Christian Revelation* (London, 1706), especially Propositions VII-XV.

16. That the evidence is intrinsically clear is confirmed by the fact that it seems clear when the scales of sin are removed from our eyes.

17. Edwards's discussions of the sense of the heart are located in *The Nature of True Virtue* and the "Miscellanies." For other relevant material, see *A Faithful Narrative of the Surprising Work of God, in the Conversion of Many Hundred Souls . . .* and *The Distinguishing Markds of a Work of the Spirit of God* (respectively, Boston, 1737; Boston 1741; both reprinted in *The Great Awakening,* ed. C. C. Goen [New Haven: Yale University Press, 1972]), hereafter *FN* and *DM,* respectively; "A Divine and Supernatural Light"; "The Mind"; and "Personal Narrative" (*Jonathan Edwards: Representative Selections,* ed. Clarence H. Faust and Thomas H. Johnson [New York: American Book Co., 1935]), hereafter PN.

18. Edwards believes that the immediate objects of mental acts are ideas. Like Berkeley, he tends to conflate ideas and their contents (what the ideas are ideas *of*).

19. Why regard these as objects of a sense or feeling of the heart? Presumably because (for example) a perception of beauty or importance involves a perception of the nonevaluative features on which beauty or importance depend, or because one cannot fully grasp or understand these nonevaluative properties without perceiving their beauty or importance, or both.

20. Edwards clearly thinks that there are qualitative differences between pleasures. The pleasure that the natural man takes in secondary beauty (i.e., in "regularity, order, uniformity, symmetry, proportion, harmony, etc." [*TV* 561-62]) is qualitatively different from the spiritual person's delight in holiness.

21. Locke's mixed modes are a species of complex ideas. Roughly, a mixed mode is an idea of a set of properties that cannot subsist by itself. (Ideas of substances, therefore, are not mixed modes.)

22. This is not absolutely decisive. In Locke's view, "red" can be used to refer not only to a simple sensation but also to a power of producing this

sensation that certain objects possess in virtue of their primary qualities; that is, "red" can be used to express a mixed mode as well as a simple idea. I will argue that Edwards's use of "beauty" exhibits a similar ambiguity. Nevertheless, it is reasonably clear that Locke believed that, in its primary sense, "red" denotes a simple idea and that Edwards thought the same of "beauty."

23. See Locke, *Human Understanding* (hereafter *HU*) 2.8. See also Hutcheson who says that moral approbation (i.e., the disinterested delight in morally good actions and dispositions) "cannot be supposed an image of anything external, more than the pleasures of harmony, of taste, of smell" (*Illustrations on the Moral Sense* [Cambridge: Harvard University Press, 1971], p. 164, hereafter *Illustrations*).

24. This point is inconclusive, however, because Edwards sometimes departs from Locke. For example, he asserts that beauty is a simple idea although Locke thought it was a mixed mode (*HU* 2.12.51).

25. Edwards was influenced by Henry More (who self-consciously combined Platonism and Cartesianism). He was also familiar with Ralph Cudworth and John Smith and quotes both with approval.

26. Of course, Edwards *might* have believed that the relevant relational terms ("consents," "is equal to," "agrees with," "harmonizes with," etc.) stand for simple ideas, but he never says this, and although Locke thinks that the ideas of relations "*terminate* in simple ideas" (arise from the comparison of simple ideas), he does not seem to think that relations themselves are simple ideas (*HU* 2.25.9-10; 2.28.18-20).

27. Does the idea of beauty not only "represent" but also "resemble" its object, as Locke's ideas of extension, figure and motion "resemble" the objective configurations that cause them? Edwards never explicitly says it does. (That the idea is a "perception" of "something without" only distinguishes it from ideas of tertiary qualities.) In calling it "knowledge," however, and in insisting that we can have no true idea of its object without it, Edwards implies that the idea *accurately* represents (some aspect of) its object. This suggests that the idea of beauty should be assimilated to Locke's ideas of primary qualities.

28. It is not clear that the mind's immediate objects are ideas, how they represent or resemble their objects, and so on.

29. At one point, Edwards asks, "concerning speculative understanding and sense of heart; whether any difference between the sense of the heart and the will or inclination" (Subjects 14).

30. Cf. *RA* 275. It involves a new "sort of *understanding* or *knowledge* . . . [viz.] that *knowledge* of divine things from whence all truly gracious affections do proceed" (my emphasis).

31. The quotations are from Nuttall, *Holy Spirit*, pp. 39, 139.

32. Locke was a major influence. Hutcheson's *Inquiry into the Original of our Ideas of Beauty and Virtue* (London: 1725; hereafter *Inquiry*) is referred to in Edwards's "Catalogue of Books" on p. 8 and p. 22. On p. 22, Edwards writes, "Hutcheson's Essay on the Passions cited in his Enquiry into the Original of our Ideas of Beauty and Virtue," which implies that he had read the *Inquiry* by that time. (Thomas H. Johnson ["Jonathan Edwards's Background of Reading," *Publications of the Colonial Society of Massachusetts* 28 (1930-33), 194-222] estimates that pages 15-43 date from 1746 to 1757.) Hutcheson is mentioned three times in *True Virtue,* and quotations from the *Inquiry* occur in *Original Sin* on pages 225 and 226. Hutcheson's *An Essay on the Nature and Conduct of the Passions and Affections* and *Illustrations on the Moral Sense* (two essays) appeared in 1728 (three years after the first edition of the *Inquiry*). This work is entered in the "Catalogue" on pages 22 and 32. In the "Book of Controversies," the *Nature and Conduct of the Passions* "is quoted, and this passage is incorporated into *Original Sin* but credited to Turnbull" (Clyde A. Holbrook, "Introduction," *OS* 74-75). The implication is that Edwards was familiar with the two essays. Whether he was significantly influenced by Hutcheson, though, is unclear.

33. Cf. *Religious Affections,* 281-82, where Edwards speaks of the immediacy with which this new sense judges of the spiritual beauty of actions. See also *The Nature of True Virtue,* pp. 619-20.

34. "If we take *reason* strictly—not for the faculty of mental perception in general [which would include sense perception], but for ratiocination . . . the perceiving of spiritual beauty and excellency no more belongs to reason, than it belongs to the sense of feeling to perceive colors. . . . Reason's work is to perceive truth and not excellency" (DSL 18).

35. See, for example, the correspondence between Hutcheson and Gilbert Burnet.

36. Edwards clearly thinks that at least some moral truths are necessary. See *Freedom of the Will* (Boston, 1754; reprint, New Haven: Yale University Press, 1957), p. 153. Edwards's example is, "It is . . . fit and suitable, that men should do to others, as they would that they should do to them." It is worth observing that Locke, too, thinks that moral truths are necessary (*HU* 3.11.15-18; 4.3.18-20; and 4.4.7-10.)

37. The quotations are from Smith's "Of the True Way or Method of Attaining to Divine Knowledge," in

Select Discourses (New York: Garland, 1978). (I have modernized the capitalization and spelling.) In his introduction to *Religious Affections,* John E. Smith denies that Smith's spiritual sensation is an intellectual intuition (*RA* 66). Quotations like the last, however, and the Platonic tenor of the discourse as a whole, seem to support my interpretation.

38. "Intellectual life, as [the Platonists] phrase it" is a nondiscursive "knowledge . . . [that] is always pregnant with divine virtue, which ariseth out of an happy union of souls with God, and is nothing else but a living imitation of a Godlike perfection drawn out by a strong fervent love of it. This divine knowledge . . . makes us amorous of divine beauty . . . and this divine love and purity, reciprocally exalts divine knowledge" (Smith, *Select Discourses,* p. 20).

39. For one thing (as John E. Smith and others have pointed out), the line between will and understanding is more flexible in Edwards than in Locke or Hutcheson.

40. Quoted in Nuttall, *Holy Spirit,* pp. 23, 39.

41. Presumably the argument is: (I) Gospel doctrines exhibit a divine excellency or beauty. Therefore, (2) Gospel doctrines are true. (2) follows from (I) *if* doctrines that exhibit this supernatural radiance or splendor have a supernatural author. (On this point, see DSL 10; Misc. 256, T 249; and Misc. 782, T 126.) How is this generalization related to the argument? If the inference involves only one step, it cannot be functioning as a premise. Perhaps, then, the generalization is an inference rule. Or perhaps Edwards thinks of it as a necessary truth. (If it is, then [1] entails [2]. Or perhaps it is simply an inductive generalization from a set of "natural inferences"—judgments that the redeemed find themselves spontaneously making in the presence of the gospel and that are trustworthy given that their new faculties are God-given. (If the third alternative is correct, the generalization plays *no* role in the argument. The second and third interpretations seem most likely.)

42. A superficial reading of some passages might suggest that Edwards thinks that our knowledge of divine reality is immediate. Thus Miscellanies 201 (T 246-47) and 408 (T 249-50) assert that ideas that are clear and lively and cohere with each other and with other ideas are quite properly regarded as real or true. Those with converted hearts find the ideas of religion (scripture) clear, lively, internally coherent, and in harmony with their other ideas. They, therefore, quite properly take them to be real or true. But this "appearing real . . . cannot be drawn out into formal arguments." It depends on "ten thousand little relations and mutual agreements that are ineffable" "and is a sort of seeing rather than reasoning the truth of religion." But Edwards is not clearly denying that the conviction of reality is inferential. (He may simply be insisting on its psychological immediacy and coerciveness and on the fact that it does not rest on *formal* argument.) In any case, his normal view is that presented in "Divine and Supernatural Light" and *Religious Affections,* namely, that the reality of divine things is inferred by one step from their spiritual beauty and excellency.

43. Paul Ricoeur, "Philosophy and Religious Language," *Journal of Religion* 54 (1974), 71-85.

44. Cf., for example, Ronald J. Butler, "Natural Belief and the Enigma of Hume," *Archiv für Geschichte der Philosophie* 42 (1960), 73-100, or John Hick, "A New Form of Theistic Argument," *Proceedings of the XIV. International Congress of Philosophy* 5 (1970), 336-41. See also J. C. A. Gaskin, *Hume's Philosophy of Religion* (London Barnes and Noble, 1978), chap. 8.

45. Jonathan Edwards, "Of Atoms" (*Scientific and Philosophical Writings,* p. 215). The quotations are from an argument "proving" that God is the only substance underlying corporeal properties. Edwards clearly thinks, however, that similar considerations show that God is also the only substance underlying mental qualities.

46. Edwards also thinks that God (who is "in effect being in general") is triune and thus inherently social.

47. It will be more difficult for a Christian to cast aspersions on (e.g.) a Vaisnava's religious belief-producing mechanism. Vaisnavism is a theistic grace religion that values love. To discriminate between the Christian's and the Vaisnava's intuitions, one must either (1) distinguish between the quality of the Christian's and the Vaisnava's benevolence, or (2) appeal to cultural or (less plausibly) psychological or moral factors that impede the proper operations of the Vaisnava's spiritual faculties. The Christian might, however, concede that some true beauty *is* perceived in the *Bhagavad-Gītā* and the theistic Upanishads. For he or she may think that these texts, too, are revelations though not as perfect as the Christian revelation. Cf. Clement of Alexandria's claim that philosophy may have been "given to the Greeks directly; for it was a 'schoolmaster,' to bring Hellenism to Christ, as the Law was for the Hebrews" (Henry Bettenson, *The Early Christian Fathers* [London: Oxford University Press, 1963], p. 232).

48. In *Freedom of the Will* Edwards asserts that propositions are self-evident when they express necessary truths or things present to (immediately perceived by) the mind. Examples are mathematical propositions, analytic truths, metaphysical principles, true moral statements, and reports of present ideas and sensations (see pp. 153, 181-82, and 259).

49. Although Edwards's identification with this tradition is not entirely straightforward. Edwards's sense of the heart, for example, is a *cognitive* faculty whereas (e.g.) Hutcheson's is not. Furthermore, even though Edwards normally assigns the sense of the heart to the will (i.e., to our affective nature), he sometimes assigns it to the understanding. See, for example, *RA* 206.

50. The saints are not wholly passive with respect to the reception of this new simple idea, for they can increase its clarity and intensity. They can do so, however, only "by the practice of virtue and holiness—for we cannot have the idea without the adapted disposition of mind" (Misc. 123, T 246).

51. Insofar as special grace simply strengthens natural principles, its effects are the same as those of common grace.

52. The exceptions will become clear as we proceed.

53. For a fuller treatment of these points, see my "Original Sin," in *Philosophy and the Christian Faith*, ed. Thomas V. Morris (Notre Dame, Ind.: University of Notre Dame Press, 1988).

54. Cf. Plato in *Phaedo* and elsewhere. As noted, there is an important Platonic strand in Puritanism.

55. "Hostility" may be too strong. But we do have a natural tendency to *resist* demands that cross our self-love and love of temporal goods by diverting our attention to other things, for example, or by rationalizing.

56. William James, *The Principles of Psychology,* vol. 2 (Cambridge: Harvard University Press, 1981), p. 924 (James's emphases).

57. William James, *The Varieties of Religious Experience* (New York: Modern Library, c. 1902), p. 500, n.

58. See Miscellany 353 (T 110-11) for an instance in which a natural sentiment legitimately affects the reasoning process. Our sense of justice (rightly) leads us to suppose that the world is governed by it.

59. This need not involve an infusion of supernatural principles. A love of God for His holiness is saving and truly supernatural. A love of God based on disinterested admiration of His greatness and on gratitude for His temporal benefits is not.

60. Natural goods and evils are those that can be appreciated without the help of infused supernatural principles (i.e., without a love of being in general and the sense of divine beauty that is rooted in it).

61. There is no indication of what other "ways" Edwards had in mind—if any.

62. Why must the parts, effects, and so on be sensible? Presumably, because sensible ideas are easier to excite and because sensible things are the kind "we are mainly concerned with" in ordinary life (T 177).

63. Cf. Locke's chapters on the inperfection and abuse of words (*HU* 3.9-11). In 11.8-9, Locke tells us to avoid terms that do not stand for clear and distinct, or determinate, ideas.

64. Although Edwards overstates his case, there is a measure of truth in it. The idea of an idea is not another instance of it but does include it. The ideas of fear and love are not fear and love, but an experience of these emotions may be needed to acquire them or to have the same ideas of fear and love that others do. Perhaps, too, ideas of this sort only become lively and vivid when we recall the relevant experiences, that is, when how they "feel" comes back to us.

65. Although "apprehension" or "an ideal view or contemplation of the thing thought of" (i.e., having an actual idea of it) are closely connected with a sense of the heart, they are not identical with it. The former is contrasted with "mere cogitation," "which is a kind of mental reading wherein we don't look on the things themselves but only on those signs of them that are before our eyes." The latter is contrasted with "mere speculation or understanding of the head," which includes "all that understanding that is without any proper ideal apprehension or view" and all understanding that does not "consist in or imply some motion of the will," that is, that does not involve the heart (Misc. 782, T 118-19). These distinctions cut across each other. A sense of the heart is not needed to "apprehend" (take "an ideal view" of) mathematical objects.

66. Sang Hyun Lee, *The Philosophical Theology of Jonathan Edwards* (Princeton: Princeton University Press, 1988). Whether this interpretation is compatible with the simplicity of the idea of true beauty is a moot point. On my account (second section), the idea of true beauty is ontologically distinct from the order or harmony that underlies the disposition to excite it in suitably disposed subjects.

67. Although, if I understand Edwards correctly, our bondage to the senses and self-interest can be fully eliminated only by God's infusing true virtue, that is, by His infusing a supernatural principle. Without a supernatural principle to govern them, our natural principles fall into disorder. "Man's nature, being left to itself, forsaken of the spirit of God . . . of itself became exceedingly corrupt" (*OS* 279). "The absence of positive good principles [holiness or true virtue] . . . leaving the common natural principles of self-love, natural appetite, etc. (which were in man in innocence) . . . will certainly be followed with corruption" (*OS* 381).

68. *HU,* "Introduction," section 3.

69. One must remember, however, that the most compelling evidence is the divine beauty or splendor that the elect see in the Gospel, in Christ, in the saints, and so on. (The belief that these are truly beautiful is properly basic.)

70. The assessments made by a truly benevolent heart must be distinguished from its perception of true beauty. The latter *is* a new piece of evidence.

71. Although they will not *seem* irrational once you have acquired them, and although (after you have acquired them) they will be rationally held in the sense that they follow from the evidence you will then have by the inductive standards you will then hold. (For Swinburne's discussion, see *Faith and Reason* [Oxford: Clarendon, 1981], pp. 82-92.)

Christopher Grasso (essay date 1996)

SOURCE: "Misrepresentations Corrected: Jonathan Edwards and the Regulation of Religious Discourse," in *Jonathan Edwards's Writings: Text, Context, Interpretation,* edited by Stephen J. Stein, Indiana University Press, 1996, pp. 19-38.

[In the following essay, Grasso analyzes the ways in which Edwards tried unsuccessfully to regulate the meaning of specific words within the rhetoric of church membership and communion eligibility vows at the church in Northampton, Massachusetts. The subsequent conflict with long-time church members culminated in his dismissal as pastor of the congregation.]

"The great thing which I have scrupled," Jonathan Edwards declared in the preface to his **Farewell Sermon** (1751), was that when people came to be admitted to communion, they publicly assented only to "a Form of Words . . . without pretending thereby to mean any such Thing as a hearty Consent to the Terms of the Gospel Covenant."[1] By common custom and established principle, a public profession of faith in Northampton had come to rest on a "diverse use" of words and signs. "People have in effect agreed among themselves," he complained in **An Humble Inquiry,** that persons who use the words need not intend their proper meaning, "and others need not understand them so."[2] Professing Christianity and "owning" the church covenant had become empty formalities for many young couples who wanted to have their babies baptized. He also argued that when families in Northampton and inhabitants of New England called themselves "Christians," they merely flattered themselves with a name while growing fat off the land and resting content with the hollow forms of faith. Edwards asserted his authority as preacher of the Word and teacher of words to bring practice and profession closer to the gospel truth. He tried to discipline his congregation by policing the meanings of words, sacramental symbols, and other signs within Northampton.

The communion controversy in Northampton and Edwards's subsequent dismissal is a familiar story in the annals of American religious history; the tale of the great theologian's being rejected by his own flock belongs, according to Perry Miller, "to the symbolism of America."[3] Miller told the story as the triumph of the merchant ethic over Christian virtue. Other scholars, looking more closely at Northampton than at the archetypal forces of American mythology, have tried to reveal the personal, social, and political tensions woven through the town's debate over church polity and practice.[4] Less attention has been given to the published arguments the controversy generated. But the rhetoric of the communion controversy reveals the ways that communal cohesiveness and corporate identity were rooted in public religious discourse; it shows questions arising about how public language was meaningful and who had the authority to regulate those meanings.

Edwards attempted to regulate public religious discourse—to control the meaning of signs *in* a community and to redefine the language *of* Christian community. First, he insisted that the minister, not the parishioners, set the terms of debate. Second, he sought to clear away the ambiguity and confusion arising from a diverse use of signs, some of which can be found in his own earlier preaching. Third, Edwards's definition of "visible sainthood" involved spelling out not just *what* this term should mean but also *how* terms in religious discourse should signify meaning. His disagreements with his cousin Solomon Williams and the Separatist position articulated by Ebenezer Frothingham reveal how each writer's position was based upon different epistemologies and different conceptions of signification.[5] Williams, writing from Lebanon, Connecticut, for the Stoddardean opposition, attacked Edwards's scriptural argument for restricted communion and his epistemological explanation of Christian profession. Frothingham, a Middletown Separatist, embraced Edwards's stricter view of the church as a gathered communion of saints, but found his arguments mystifying and contradictory.

Fourth and finally, Edwards wanted to restrict the rhetorical uses of flattering titles like "God's Covenant People" for all nominally Christian New Englanders, even when such language could be doctrinally justified. This is related to a rhetorical strategy that sought to accent the difference between nature and grace, and is connected to the question of Edwards and the national covenant. Clerical rhetoric during the Seven Years War (including Edwards's own) once again exploited the systematic equivocations at the heart of New England's system of interlocking covenants.

More than a sacramental controversy, therefore, the dispute Edwards set in motion made New Englanders question what it meant to call themselves "God's People." The issue involves broader questions of rhetorical emphasis as much as the narrower points of ecclesiastical doctrine, and understanding that rhetoric is essential to finding Edwards's place between his Puritan predecessors and the New Divinity theologians who followed him. The language of corporate identity changed in Edwards's preaching, as it would change throughout mid-eighteenth-century New England.[6] Arguments articulated during and after the communion controversy help reveal what Edwards perpetuated and what he discarded in the image of New England as "God's New Israel," as well as what he contributed to the myth of America as a "Redeemer Nation."

The Language of the Church

Edwards would grant people the liberty of conscience. But he knew that a collection of individuals following the dictates of their private judgments did not make a community. He believed that the church's public rituals should not be a marketplace for people to come and choose what they needed or wanted, but a communal expression of a single commonly understood idea. Yet the value of religious words and signs in New England seemed to depreciate as fast as the public bills of credit.

Edwards did not want to change what people said, but what they meant. He would be content with a simple statement, similar to those already used by candidates for church membership:

> I hope, I do truly find a Heart to give myself wholly to God, according to the Tenor of that Covenant of Grace which was seal'd in my Baptism, and to walk in a way of that Obedience to all the Commandments of God, which the Covenant of Grace requires, as long as I shall live.[7]

But what did these words mean? In Northampton, Edwards complained, they meant some indeterminate degree of "a common faith and moral sincerity short of true Godliness." A candidate, awakened but unconverted, could utter these words to express that she wanted to obey God's commandments and that she hoped someday to have a "heart"—that is, a predominant inclination—to give herself wholly to the Lord. The candidate *should* be professing, Edwards argued, that she believes she *presently* finds such a heart within herself, and hopes she is right. In Edwards's scheme, people with merely awakened consciences but not true religious affections need not apply; their so-called desire to obey God did not flow from their heart's love to God, but merely from their natural fear of hell.

The Northampton brethren interpreted Edwards's break from local church practices as a bid for ministerial power over the congregation, and they were right. But it was not, as some murmured, that he wanted to set himself up as the exclusive judge of other people's religious experiences, for he continued to maintain that even the most experienced eye could be deceived in such matters. Nor did he claim the sole right to measure a candidate's behavior against his profession, for when a minister did so, he acted publicly and only as an officer of the whole church. But Edwards did insist "that it belonged to me as a Pastor, before a Profession was accepted, to have Full Liberty to instruct the Candidate in the Meaning of the Terms of it, and in the Nature of the Things proposed to be professed."[8]

When he first brought his case before his congregation in a 1750 sermon on Ezekiel 44:9, Edwards made his arguments by establishing what basic terms like *professing* Christianity, *owning* the covenant, and *visible* sainthood should mean.[9] His 1750 demand for "a higher sense" of these terms was part of an effort to stem the erosion of meaning that had continued under his own ministry as scriptural words and phrases had been applied like rhetorical tags to a variety of circumstances. He was not just renouncing the doctrine of his grandfather and predecessor Solomon Stoddard, who had allowed striving sinners to come to the Lord's Table in the hope that they might be converted there. He was also renouncing the rhetorical imprecision of his own earlier preaching, which had moved among the "various senses" in which the covenant was offered and owned, and had acknowledged the different "degrees" of Christian profession.[10]

He had explained in 1737 that we can recognize a covenant people as such because they have access to the scriptures, they visibly take hold of the covenant in their profession, and they receive special mercies and judgments in God's providence.[11] But all covenanted nations were not equally favored. Edwards's fast and thanksgiving sermons, from a very early effort in the late 1720s to some of his laments during the French wars through the 1740s, describe how the English nation had been raised up above all other covenanted peoples to enjoy the peculiar blessings of religious liberty. God had distinguished "the Land" (New England) even above the rest of the nation; while England was overrun with deists and skeptics, New England had trained Protestant preachers and built churches in every village. New England, Edwards wrote, more closely paralleled God's covenant people Israel as "perhaps no People now on the face of the Earth."[12]

Every community where the Word was preached and acknowledged could call itself a "covenant people" or a "professing society." But Edwards explained that God distinguished a community as a covenant people not just by revealing the gospel light to them but by, in greater or lesser degrees, pouring out his Spirit among them and blessing their religious efforts.[13] Similarly, the community's profession in response to God's offer and blessings had varying degrees. A people made "a higher profession" when they acknowledged a greater degree of God's presence or mercies, or "when there is a far Greater Number among them that do make a Profession of special Experiences & of Extraordinary Light."[14]

A year after Northampton's 1735 revival, Edwards delivered a remarkable sermon that raised the town above all New England "as a city set on a hill."[15] He was not just a preacher tailoring a time-worn simile to his own locale. The religious excitement and "surprising conversions" in Northampton manifested an outpouring of the Spirit that had up to that point surpassed any local revival in living memory. The eyes of New England were therefore upon Northampton; but also "in new york . . . the Jerseys . . . upon Long Island . . . the Highlands on Hudson's River" and even in London eyes were turning toward God's People in Northampton.[16] The town now had to honor its high profession with godly practice, for the stakes had been raised.

But the "high profession" refers here to those reports of religious experiences being spread abroad, most notably by Edwards himself, first in a letter that Boston's Benjamin Colman summarized for his London correspondents, then in the famous *Faithful Narrative*.[17] In 1737, Edwards urged that the townspeople's profession become more formal and explicit in a reaffirmation of their obligations under the covenant of grace.[18] As the town's new church was raised, he called for a "Joint Resolution" made by the civil magistrate and the ministers of the Gospel, "the Leading men amongst a People and those that are Led by them," the rich and the poor, the old and the young.[19] Like the High Priest Jehoiada in Second Chronicles, Edwards called his people to bind themselves to God and to one another under God's covenant. He urged them to make their identity as God's People manifest in clear words and plain practices in their business and public affairs.[20]

At the height of the Awakening in March 1742, Edwards again called on the people of Northampton to commit themselves to be God's People. This time it was no mere public resolution; he asked every person in the congregation over fourteen years old to stand up, solemnly "own" the covenant, and vow to seek and serve God. Each congregant was to swear adherence to a sixteen-paragraph summary of proper Christian behavior, committing all to Christ and promising to treat neighbors in a spirit of meekness and charity.[21] This was a solemn oath to God, Edwards reminded his people a year later; it was an "extraordinary explicit vow" that was greater than an "ordinary implicit" one in that it called upon God to confirm the truth of what was said.[22] "Take heed," Edwards warned, "words are gone out of your mouths and you can not go back."[23] He told backsliders in 1747 that "their own former voice" would witness against them on Judgment Day, "so they will be sentenced out of their own mouths."[24]

In 1745 and again in 1747, Edwards explained that the 1742 covenant was more explicit but "not essentially different" from what parents dedicated their children to in baptism.[25] It was a fuller expression of what people implicitly acknowledged by attending church on the sabbath, and what their actions signified and renewed at the Lord's Table. By 1749, Edwards was arguing that any "implicit" professions such as joining public prayers and keeping the sabbath *only* take on meaning *if* they are rooted in "a declarative explicit convenanting" that all baptized true believers must make upon reaching adulthood. Eating and drinking at the Lord's Supper are only "speaking Signs" that symbolically reiterate a meaning that must already be fixed by the communicant's words.[26] Solomon Williams argued that Edwards's call for a personal explicit profession as a requirement for admission had no scriptural basis and no precedent in ecclesiastical history.[27] Edwards answered that actions, by themselves, were not properly a profession at all.[28] "[T]he Reason of Mankind teaches them the Need of joining *Words & Actions* together in publick Manifestations of the Mind, in Cases of Importance: *Speech* being the great and peculiar Talent, which God has given to Mankind, as the special Means and Instrument of the Manifestation of their Minds one to another."[29]

Edwards's use of the term *profession,* therefore, had narrowed, its meaning refined from a vague or implicit acknowledgment of God's gospel offer to the explicit, personal oath of the individual Christian. *What* Edwards expected people to profess (and not just *how* they professed) underwent a similar redefinition. What did it mean to visibly "own" the covenant? Edwards's early position resembled his cousin Solomon's. The candidate must signify his belief that the doctrines of the Gospel are true, submit himself to the terms of Christ's covenant, and endeavor to obey all the moral rules of the Gospel. No one with this belief and resolve can know for sure that he is not regenerated, and the church must give him the benefit of the doubt.[30]

Edwards's "new scruples" about the Stoddardean Lord's Supper and full membership in the visible church began appearing in his private notebooks as early as 1728.[31] His first corollary to a 1736 treatment of the covenant of grace was that "the revelation and offer of the gospel is not properly called a covenant till it is consented to," and as in the *Humble Inquiry* thirteen years later, he compared this consent to a woman's acceptance of an offer of marriage.[32] But we need to look beyond the gloss that Edwards's private writings give to his pulpit utterances, for if some sermon passages seem to tighten the requirements for owning the covenant, others leave room for a broader Stoddardean interpretation.

In his 1737 fast sermon on 2 Chronicles 23:16, for example, Edwards told his congregation what was stipulated on their part in being God's People. It is not just "an acknowledgment of the mouth," a professing of Christ in name only, for owning the covenant while having "an inward prevailing opposition" to God's rule is no real *consent* to it at all.[33] Only converts could so renounce the world and embrace Christ as a spouse. But this is the same sermon in which Edwards also speaks more broadly of the people's consent to the covenant as a public resolution, of at least visibly "taking hold" of the covenant, of "each one contribut[ing] what in him lies towards it that we may be the Lords People."[34] Could not the unconverted, therefore, in some sense own the covenant as well?

For loyal Stoddardean Solomon Williams, the answer was yes. The unregenerate could own the covenant and be counted among God's People because to do so meant to consent *to the terms* of Christ's offer.[35] They need not profess saving faith, since the term *belief* in the New Testament can signify "no more than the Assent of the Understanding" or "a Conviction of the Judgment and Conscience, that Jesus was the Messiah, or that the Gospel was true."[36] The unconverted "do enter into Covenant with God, and with all the Earnestness and Sincerity of soul they possibly can, do engage to keep Covenant."[37] They submit to the rules and ordinances of Christ, and vow to obey him to the utmost of their natural and legal—but not gracious—powers.

In his 1750 pulpit defense of his new position, Edwards made a clean break from both Stoddardeanism and the ambiguities of his own earlier preaching. "I cant understand that there is any such notion of owning the Covenant any where in the Christian world but in this Corner of it here in New England," he announced.[38] He then looked behind Stoddard to the Synod of 1662 and the New England forefathers for an earlier custom. "But now the Great part of the Country has forgotten the meaning of their forefathers and have gradually brought in a notion of owning the Covenant of Grace without pretending to profess a compliance."[39] Owning the covenant means not only acknowledging its terms but complying with them, he argued. Christ offers salvation for saving faith; the unconverted who offer only the promise of outward obedience are in no sense parties to the covenant.[40]

But Solomon Williams answered that this notion of covenanting confuses entering a covenant with fulfilling one, and destroys the whole concept of visible sainthood. Williams, Edwards, and even Separatist Ebenezer Frothingham agreed that only visible saints should be allowed to own the covenant and sit at the Lord's Table—but the three completely disagreed about what the term *visible sainthood* meant. Their definitions reveal the very different epistemologies that helped shape their visions of the church.

For Williams, visible saints are Christians according to all that is visible: profession of the gospel truth and good behavior. Arguing from Stoddard's skepticism about the ability of men to distinguish the truly gracious from the morally sincere, Williams described visible sainthood as a larger category that included real saints. Not all who are visible saints on earth will turn out to be real saints on Judgment Day, but until then the church has no business trying to search hearts and separate sheep from goats. At the other extreme, Frothingham maintained that a true Christian could *certainly* discern the presence of sanctifying grace in someone else. The Holy Spirit makes manifest, or visible, the godliness of saints to each other: "the Beams or Rays of Divine Light shining into the soul" enlighten the understanding and guide a Christian's judgment of his neighbor.[41]

Edwards tried to take the middle ground between Stoddardean uncertainty and Separatist certainty. For him, visibility was neither a category distinct from the real nor a supernatural manifestation of the real, but a *sign* that referred to the real the way a properly used word refers to the essence of the thing signified. He contended that there must be a stronger relation between the visible and the real—between what man sees and what God sees—than Stoddardeanism recognized. For both Edwards and the Separatists, the reality at the heart of public worship was the "peculiar love" Christians had for one another.[42] This affection "must have some Apprehension of the Understanding, some Judgment of the Mind, for its Foundations."[43] Perhaps Williams's lukewarm "benefit of the doubt" could be extended to all moral people who called

themselves Christians, but for Edwards the "mind must first Judge some Amiableness in the Object" before affections are bestowed. Edwards wanted something to tip the scales of uncertainty in a positive direction, some sign that gave the church probable grounds for judging a candidate a real saint before calling him a visible saint.[44]

Frothingham recommended Edwards's **Humble Inquiry** as an improvement over Stoddardeanism, but complained that Edwards "writes in a misterious Manner, backwards and forwards, about this visibility."[45] While Stoddard extended charity to all because he could obtain no reliable knowledge about their souls, and Edwards limited visible sainthood because he could gain probable knowledge of grace in others, Frothingham insisted that the church was a communion of real saints who were certain of each other's godliness. If I ask for a sheep, Frothingham wrote, and someone brings me either a sheep or a goat, "is the Sheep visible, or is it not?" The answer was either yes or no, not a degree of probability. "[T]herefore to have a Thing visible that is requested amounts to a certain Knowledge of the thing thus presented."[46] However, what was presented had to be more than "a bare profession of Godliness" and good behavior. Candidates for admission in a Separatist church had to describe their experiences of God's grace upon their hearts, and tell the story of their conversion to Christ.

Edwards had had his fill of people publicly describing their trembling, trances, and visions, and he took great pains to distance himself from Separatist enthusiasm, denouncing those "slanderous" reports that said he "had fallen in with those Wild People."[47] The Stoddardean church did not do enough institutionally to recognize conversions, but the Separatist church placed too much emphasis on personal experience, and fostered spiritual pride. He argued that the pastor should be the one to decide when a particular conversion narrative might edify the whole congregation. Regular professions should not describe the details of conversion. The candidate's words and deeds, in fact, need not even signify that he is assured of his own conversion. But they do need to signify that he has experienced the essence of Christian piety: believing with his heart, loving God with all his soul, and loving his neighbor as himself. The simple language of the kind of profession Edwards would accept did not describe how the person came to be "born again;" it *referred* to the experience of godliness as an unspoken context and necessary precondition for the candidate's appearance before the church. Edwards did not want the focus to be on the subjective sensations of fear or joy but on "the Supreme holy Beauty, and Comliness of divine Things, as they are in themselves, or in their own Nature"—a beauty that human signs can only gesture toward.[48]

When Williams read Edwards's discussion of an individual's examination of his own heart prior to profession, he thought that he had found the fatal flaw to the whole scheme. If coming to the Lord's Supper without saving grace is a damning sin (as Edwards claimed), how could anything short of certainty about conversion induce a person to come? A man believes the gospel and sincerely desires to do his duty before Christ. But he hesitates. What if this belief and sincerity, which he knows he has, is "no more than moral Sincerity, the effect of common Grace and Illumination?"[49] Common and saving grace are often hard to distinguish, and all but those wild Separates acknowledge that assurance is hard to come by. On the other hand, any sane person with a healthy conscience *must* know whether he is being morally sincere or not. Such an awareness is essential to moral agency, and distinguishes the man from his sheep and goats. Therefore, the awakened person who still doubts whether he has saving grace should be allowed to make "such a Profession as he finds he can truly make."[50] Williams's church rested on the rock of the awakened conscience.

But in the next step, as this morally sincere candidate offers himself to the church, Williams went beyond Stoddard. Williams argued that the church, listening to the candidate's profession of belief and sincerity, must take his words in their highest sense, as a profession of saving grace. Whether the candidate thinks he is converted or not is beside the point, since he may be mistaken either way. The church, "without any metaphysical Speculations or abstruse Reasonings, upon the Nature of *Visibilities* and *Realities,*" should treat the professor *as if* he were converted.[51]

Edwards found this more disturbing than anything in the bland rebuttal he had heard preached from his own pulpit by Jonathan Ashley of Deerfield in February 1750.[52] Ashley welcomed the merely moral to the Lord's Table, but at least did not then pretend that they were regenerate. After Williams set forth his position as an argument from "common sense," Edwards dismantled it with an argument based on three propositions about signification, summed up in a footnote citing Paul in 1 Corinthians 14:7, and then Locke's *Essay:* "He that uses Words of any Language without Distinct Ideas in his Mind . . . only makes a Noise without any Sense or Signification."[53] When a man says he has a king in his room, we do not know if he means George II or a chess piece. If he says he has metal in his pocket, we are not obliged by "charity" to assume it is gold and not brass. If a professor uses words allowed to signify either moral sincerity or real piety, he makes "no profession at all of *Gospel Holiness.*"[54]

Like Locke, Edwards knew that language becomes the "common Tye of Society" if the signs a person uses are held in common.[55] Locke distinguished between "ordinary" discourse, in which meanings established by "common use" and "tacit consent" usually served well enough, and "philosophical" discourse, which was more in need of an "Under-Labourer" in "The Commonwealth of Learning" who could point out abuses and demand more precision in the use of words.[56] Edwards, too, in his treatises on the will, true virtue, and original sin, tried to reform the vocabulary of the Commonwealth of Learning, aiming especially at points where ordinary and philosophical usage be-

came confused. But before he left Northampton for the Stockbridge settlement where he would write those treatises, he was more immediately concerned with reforming a different community of discourse. He tried to correct the damage that common usage and tacit consent had done to terms like *professing* Christianity, *owning* the covenant, and *visible* sainthood.

THE NEW ENGLISH ISRAEL

Scholars have long appreciated the central place Edwards and his followers gave to the *individual's* relationship to God in the covenant of grace.[57] The public or national covenant, however, conspicuously absent from Edwards's published writings, was thought to have been repudiated or replaced by new forms of Christian union achieved through revivalism or concerts of prayer.[58] At any rate, New Divinity ministers, others said, were too caught up with metaphysics and the millennium to be distracted by the mundane social and political concerns that Puritan covenant sermons had so often addressed.[59]

Three recent studies of Edwards and New Divinity manuscript sermons have reassessed the importance of the public or national covenant in Edwardsian preaching. Harry Stout's initial investigation of Edwards's occasional sermons found plenty of references to the national covenant, and contended that the formula Edwards inherited had become a "taken-for-granted reality."[60] Stout further argued that neither Edwards nor any other eighteenth-century established minister denied "New England's attendant identity as a special people with a messianic destiny."[61] Mark Valeri's essay on Edwards's New Divinity followers and the American Revolution, however, suggested instead that Edwards's references to New England's covenant were "somewhat untypical" of his preaching.[62] More importantly, Valeri argued that after 1750 Edwards, Bellamy, and Samuel Hopkins replaced covenantal terminology with the language of moral law, and spoke of a God who did not give special treatment to an elect nation but ruled all through "impartial, universal moral standards."[63] Another study of Edwards's manuscript sermons detached the question of the prominence of covenant discourse per se from its ideological implications. Yes, Edwards preached about the national covenant, Gerald McDermott wrote, but he did so as a "pessimistic" critic and not as an endorser of New England's special errand or America's manifest destiny.[64] All three of these studies point toward the need to put Edwards's covenantal preaching in the context of both the Stoddardean church he inherited and the post-Awakening evangelical union he championed. Changes in emphasis and relative importance are revealed only when the national covenant is seen within a larger understanding of Edwards's language of corporate identity—a language which changed as Edwards's focus shifted from Northampton and New England to the revival movement within international Protestantism.

As we have seen, covenantalism was neither taken for granted nor untypical; it was an integral part of Edwards's pulpit language of corporate identity before 1750. Certainly Edwards's early preaching recognized New England's high spiritual privileges, if not with grandiose claims for New England's national election. But to castigate Northampton for its spiritual and moral declension after the 1735 revival and the 1740 Awakening, Edwards pointed to the outpourings of the Spirit that they had all so recently witnessed rather than to an "inheritance" from the New England founders or the town's pious forefathers.[65] During the communion controversy, even as Edwards discussed Israel's covenanting in Deuteronomy, he emphasized the *experience* of the people's religious revival rather than the legal *fact* of their covenantal status.

Some historians have contrasted the covenant preaching of Puritan fast-day Jeremiahs with the "New Light" calls for revival and evangelical union. Covenantal jeremiads, Alan Heimert wrote, had become conservative, backward-looking instruments of social control, trying to impose order "mechanically" through institutional discipline and calls for obedience. "New Lights" called instead for an "affectionate union" of Christian brethren in Christ, looking ahead to the millennial age.[66] In 1747, Edwards published *An Humble Attempt to Promote Explicit Agreement and Visible Union of God's People* and compared the two forms of public worship. A fast day proclaimed by the civil government of a Christian society and a concert of prayer promoted by private Christians differed only in "circumstances," he argued.[67] The union of Christians in either case depended upon joining for prayer at a fixed *time* rather than gathering in a single *place*. Although the precedent Edwards cites for the concert of prayer had been proposed for the *national* deliverance of Great Britain in 1712, the concert he promoted was to be "an *union* of Christians of distant places," from many different cities, countries, and nations.[68] Although the plan was proposed by pro-revival ministers in Scotland and encouraged by private praying societies that had sprung up during the Awakening, Edwards offered the plan as an attempt to heal the divisions the Awakening had spawned.[69] Nevertheless, the concert, which people joined voluntarily, much more than New England's public covenant, which fell to them because of where they lived, matched the transatlantic vision and personal appeal of midcentury Protestant revivalism.

Edwards in the 1740s also reordered the relationship between the national covenant and the covenant of grace. Seventeenth-century Congregationalists spoke of the covenant of grace for individual saints, church covenants for those who professed to be saints (and, in some sense, for their children), and the national covenant for a whole people who acknowledged Christianity as the established religion. Northampton's Solomon Stoddard had, in effect, conflated these covenants, speaking instead of the internal (individual) and external (corporate) aspects or articles of the covenant of grace, and placing public worship and especially the Lord's Supper as the central ritual for them all. Stoddard's model was the Old Testament "Jewish church," rather than the early Christian congregations that

were set up before Christianity had been instituted as a national religion.[70] Edwards separated what Stoddardean practice had joined.

When Edwards defended his position on church membership before his congregation in 1750, he closed his argument by quickly dismissing any objections arising from a comparison to Israel's covenanting in the Old Testament.[71] But the senses in which the Jews—and like them, New Englanders—were "God's People" would loom larger in subsequent debates. Like Stoddard, Solomon Williams spoke of people keeping the external, public covenant by their natural powers and keeping the internal covenant by saving grace.[72] Edwards argued that outward covenanting must express an inward covenanting or it signifies nothing.[73] But did not Edwards himself preach that God makes a public covenant with a professing people, a covenant that does not require true piety but only religion and virtue in outward exercise and things visible? True, he had explained that this public or national covenant was one that God made with whole societies and not with particular persons; but then are not particular persons, as members of society and in respect to things external and temporal, *in* covenant, just as the Jews were?[74] The Jews, Williams wrote, gracious and moral alike, covenanted with their God, and "were alike called *the People of God, A chosen Generation, a royal Priesthood, an holy Nation, a peculiar People.*"[75]

Edwards argued "that such Appellations as God's *People*, God's *Israel*, and some other such Phrases, are used and applied in the Scripture with considerable *Diversity* of Intention."[76] There were appendages to Abraham's Covenant of Grace, promises to his family and bloodline that ceased with the Gospel dispensation. Sometimes "God's People" referred to all Jews in this carnal aspect of the covenant, which did not literally apply to Christians. But Williams dismissed this as more blather about names and words. Christians are in covenant just as the Jews were, he contended.[77] All Christian Gentiles are grafted onto the root of Abraham, so God's promise extends to them and their seed—meaning that all the children of Christian parents are born into a state of "federal holiness," and are (at least externally) in the covenant with their parents.

Edwards at first seemed to concede the narrow doctrinal point to Williams, though he in no way surrendered the larger issue. He turned to "the Ambiguity of the Phrase, *Being in Covenant,*" and noted that it "signifies two distinct Things: either (1.) *Being under the Obligations* [and] *Bonds of the Covenant;* or (2.) *A being conformed to the Covenant, and complying with the Terms of it.*"[78] Many ungodly Jews and New Englanders can be said to be some of God's Covenant People in the first, weaker sense of that expression, he admitted. But—and here Edwards reduced Williams' federal theology to an empty husk—being People under Obligations of the Covenant is hardly a special privilege, for "so are all Mankind" in covenant in this sense. Unconverted New Englanders are "God's Covenant People" in no greater sense than are *"Mahometans, or Heathens."*[79]

Thus Williams's "external covenant" seemed to be extended as the Moral Law of all mankind, and the title "God's People" became an empty phrase on the lips of the ungodly. Williams was horrified. Edwards's scheme denied morally sincere New Englanders under "the good Impressions of Convictions and Awakenings" their place alongside the truly godly; it classed them with the heathens and would perplex their tender consciences.[80] But that was precisely Edwards's point. Awakened sinners "are very ready to flatter themselves that they are willing to accept Christ," Edwards asserted, but they need to be driven to their knees. They need to see that they have not "the least spark of Love to God." Devils are even more convinced of the truth of the gospel; sinners roasting in hell have their consciences far more awakened than they ever had in this world.[81] Edwards warned that Williams's book might lead people to suppose that the Christless could be friends to Christ, when actually they were enemies who bore greater guilt than the heathens who had neither bibles nor preachers.[82]

Although the unregenerate living in a Christian nation could call themselves "God's People" in a very weak sense, Edwards wanted to strip them of their titles. "Now why is it looked upon so dreadful, to have great Numbers going without the *Name* and honourable *Badge* of Christianity[?]" Too many are "contented with the *Sign,* exclusive of the *Thing* signified!" They overvalue common grace and moral sincerity. "[T]his, I can't but think, naturally tends to sooth and flatter the Pride of vain Man."[83]

Here lies the crux of Edward's rhetorical strategy, which his New Divinity followers would accentuate and develop. Names and "appellations" that flattered graceless men, even if there was some scriptural precedent for their use, were to be applied with great care or avoided. The verbal badges of Christianity must conform to doctrine and cut through the rhetorical fog obscuring the chasm between nature and grace. Edwards tried to sift through the ambiguities of being "in" or "under" the covenant; later Edwardsians such as Nathanael Emmons simply defined a covenant as a mutual contract requiring the personal consent of all parties, and declared all other uses of the term, even in scripture, to be figurative rather than literal. "If faith is the condition of the covenant of grace," Emmons wrote, "there can be no medium between being completely in and completely out of it."[84]

From what has been discussed here, it would seem that Stout and McDermott's arguments about the importance of the national covenant for Edwards might be more suited to Edwards before the communion controversy. Valeri's stress on God's impartial moral government of nations, coupled with Heimert's emphasis on the "affectionate union" of Christians within the international visible church, might be more appropriate for the later Edwards. But there are problems with this conclusion. Edwards's shift toward moral law terminology can be seen in his private notebooks, implied in some of his sketchy outlines to sermons preached to the Stockbridge Indians, and inferred, perhaps, from his endorsement of Bellamy's *True Religion Delineated* in 1750.[85] However, in the 1750s, Edwards repreached several sermons written in the 1740s or earlier. In 1755, he again explained that "God in a national Covenant promises prosperity to External duties."[86] In 1754 and again in 1757, he described the great difference between these externally covenanted "People of God" and others: though under the same moral law, God's People received more special favors and mercies.[87] How could he give such titles to those he so strenuously argued did not deserve them—to those inhabitants of a nation who did not *experience* union through *religious* affections? How could he now hand out the badges of Christianity?

One answer lies in the difference between doctrine and rhetorical strategy. After careful study of the scriptures, Edwards had determined what God's will was with regard to admitting people to full communion in the church. He sacrificed his pulpit to this doctrine. He never completely abandoned the idea of a national covenant, although he argued that it could be neither sealed by church ordinances nor inflated with pretensions of unique national election. He had strongly objected to the diverse use of signs that had become a local habit and to the common custom that gave distinguishing names and titles to the whole body public. But correcting those who abused the idea of a national covenant or obscured the distinguishing marks of godliness became less important when faced not by hypocrites sitting at the Lord's Table but by French and Indian minions of Antichrist who threatened to wipe Protestant churches off the continent. The rhetorical context had changed, not his doctrinal commitments.

It is not that Edwards, having moved to the Stockbridge frontier, had decided that a little flattering exhortation might help rouse the militia. Just the opposite: he blamed Braddock's defeat in 1755 upon those who had trusted their own power rather than committing all to God's hands. Still, he called the soldiers who marched off to war "God's People," and did so because they fought *for* Christ's church (though many of them may not have been fully *in* Christ's church) against its openly professed enemies. They were God's covenant people in this weaker sense because they lived in a land of family bibles and learned preachers who *offered* the covenant, rather than in a nation of priestly inquisitors with Latin bibles under lock and key.[88]

If, during the communion controversy, it had been Edwards's burden to clarify the ambiguities of New England's covenant discourse for the sake of the church, during the Seven Years War he would exploit those ambiguities once again as he exhorted the defenders of Protestant civilization in the New World. Just as the sacramental controversy had drawn attention to the language that distinguished (or failed to distinguish) between the church and society at large, the war weakened that rhetorical boundary line. Edwards did not live to see Quebec fall; Williams did, and chose the text for his thanksgiving sermon carefully.[89] In Exodus 15:2 Moses and the Israelites sing God's praises just after Pharaoh's army had been drowned in the Red Sea. "God had not yet explicitly taken them into Covenant with himself, as he did a little after this at *Mount Sinai,*" Williams explained.[90] But the Israelites could look back to the covenant God had made with their fathers, Abraham, Isaac, and Jacob, and the promises extending to their seed. This generation of Israelites, then, prefigured baptized but unconverted Christians: they lived under the *promises* of their fathers' covenant and had to engage those promises by honoring God and preparing "an habitation" for him. Williams applied this text "to *New-England,* and the rest of the *British subjects* in America." You too, he told his congregation, had pious and holy fathers in covenant.[91] You too have been saved from your enemies. As a vast British Empire in America opened for settlement, "every *English American*" ought to prepare his soul as God's habitation and resolve to cleave to God as the New England forefathers had. Williams also joined many others in calling for the country as a whole to prepare a habitation for Christ's church on the frontier by sending missionaries to Christianize the Indians. While Edwards's New Divinity disciples were abandoning the idea of the public covenant, others, like Solomon Williams, were recasting the rhetoric to fit new situations. Williams combined preparationism, Stoddardean institution building, and a dawning vision of the westward course of Anglo-American civilization.[92]

Edwards's attempt to regulate religious discourse involved fixing the meaning of particular words used in public professions, controlling how religious signs in general ought to refer to divine realities and signify commonly understood ideas, and placing this regulatory power firmly in the hands of ministers rather than parishioners. His own earlier preaching contained some of the "diverse use" of signs in regard to covenants and profession that he objected to during the communion controversy. His preaching during the Seven Years War employed the kind of ambiguous terminology for the imperial context that he had condemned in connection with the local church. Yet his New Divinity followers embraced his effort to bring moral order to a changing world by controlling the terms of public religious discourse. By asserting the authority to regulate an increasingly diverse use of signs, Edwardsians fueled antagonisms between laity and clergy. Like Edwards, of course, they believed that they were only trying to correct the ways that discourse had come to misrepresent the Word.

Notes

1. Jonathan Edwards, *A Farewell Sermon* (Boston, 1751), iii.

2. Jonathan Edwards, *An Humble Inquiry* (Boston, 1749), 15-16. "And therefore whatever some of these words and signs may *in themselves* most properly and naturally import, they entirely cease to be significations of any such thing among people accustomed to understand them otherwise."

3. Perry Miller, *Jonathan Edwards* (Amherst, 1981; originally published 1949), 211.

4. Patricia J. Tracy, *Jonathan Edwards, Pastor: Religion and Society in Eighteenth-Century Northampton* (New York, 1980); Gregory H. Nobles, *Divisions throughout the Whole: Politics and Society in Hampshire County, Massachusetts, 1740-1775* (Cambridge, 1983).

5. Solomon Williams, *The True State of the Question* (Boston, 1751); Ebenezer Frothingham, *The Articles of Faith and Practice* (Newport, 1750). Hereafter, references to the "Discourse" following the "Articles" and "Covenant" will be referred to as Frothingham's *Discourse.*

6. Mark A. Noll has discussed the social, economic, and cultural conditions that may have made mid-eighteenth-century New England less receptive to the rhetoric of the national covenant. Noll, "Jonathan Edwards and the Transition from Clerical to Political Leadership in New England's Intellectual History," paper presented at the Writings of Jonathan Edwards: Text and Context, Text and Interpretation conference, Bloomington, Indiana, June 2-4, 1994.

7. Jonathan Edwards, letter to Peter Clark, May 7, 1750, quoted by Edwards in *Misrepresentations Corrected and Truth Vindicated* (Boston, 1752), 13.

8. Edwards, *Farewell Sermon,* vi.

9. Jonathan Edwards, MS Sermon on Ezekiel 44:9 [booklet one], delivered Feb. 15-March 22, 1750, Beinecke Rare Book and Manuscript Library, Yale University, New Haven. All manuscript sermons cited hereafter are from the Beinecke collection. For a brief discussion of this text, see Editor's Introduction, *The Works of Jonathan Edwards, 12, Ecclesiastical Writings,* ed. David Hall (New Haven, 1994), 88.

10. In a November 1746 lecture to young people, Edwards had tried to explain the various senses and different degrees behind a commonly used title like "God's Children." Spoken to the people of Israel in Isaiah 1:2, the words could also denote all mankind, since man was created in God's image, or refer to all who have been raised in "the House of God" among Christians. In a higher sense, the term could be limited to the saints, those "acknowledged as true born Children & not bastards" in God's family.

11. MS fast sermon on 2 Chronicles 23:16, March 1737, leaves 3r.-4v.

12. Ibid., leaf 13r. See also MS sermon fragment C, c. 1727.

13. MS fast sermon on 2 Chronicles 23:16, March 1737, leaves 3n.-4v. By "religious efforts" I mean the instituted "means of grace," i.e., prayer, preaching,

and public worship. Under God's blessing, preaching successfully awakens and converts sinners and enlivens saints, prayers are answered, and public worship becomes a joyous communion with God.

14. MS sermon on Matthew 5:14, July 1736, leaf 4v.

15. MS sermon on Matthew 5:14, July 1736.

16. Ibid., 18r.

17. See C. C. Goen, Editor's Introduction, *The Works of Jonathan Edwards, 4, The Great Awakening,* ed. Goen (New Haven, 1972), 32-46.

18. MS fast sermon on 2 Chronicles 23:16, March 1737. Here Edwards again notes that Northampton has been exceedingly exalted "as a most honourable People in the Esteem & Eye of the world" (17v.), and "no Town this day on the Face of the Earth" was more obliged "Jointly & with one Consent to Resolve upon it that we will be the Lords People" (16r.).

19. Ibid., 8v.

20. Ibid., 7v., 9v.

21. Edwards included a copy of the 1742 covenant in his December 12, 1743, letter to Thomas Prince, who published it in the *Christian History,* 1 (January 14, 21, and 28, 1744): 367-81, reprinted in *The Great Awakening,* 550-54. The sermon Edwards preached for the occasion drew its doctrine from Joshua 24: 15-27: "A visible people of God on some occasions are called plainly and publicly to renew their covenant with God."

22. MS sermon on Ecclesiastes 5:4-6, October 1743, ll. 12v., 14v.

23. Ibid., 14v.

24. MS quarterly lecture on Joshua 24:21-22, August 1747, l. 5r.

25. MS sermon on Ps. 111:5, August 1745, l. 6r., and MS quarterly lecture on Joshua 24:21-22, August 1747, l. 6r.

26. Edwards, *Humble Inquiry,* 16, 76.

27. Solomon Williams, *The True State of the Question* (Boston, 1751), 20, 60.

28. Edwards, *Misrepresentations Corrected,* 80.

29. Ibid., 148.

30. See Jonathan Edwards, "Miscellanies," no. 338. For passages in Williams's *True State of the Question* related to owning the covenant, see pp. iv, 5, 8, 9, 11, 24, 28, 53, 81, 83, 111, 112, 122, 125, 130, 133, 134.

31. See Edwards, "Miscellanies," nos. 389, 393, 394. I am indebted to Kenneth P. Minkema for this reference. Thomas A. Schafer, as cited by Tracy in

Jonathan Edwards, Pastor, 258, n. 1, points to an important discussion in "Miscellanies" no. 689, written in early 1736.

32. "Miscellanies" no. 617.

33. Edwards, MS fast sermon on 2 Chronicles 23:16 (1737), ll. 4v.-6v.

34. Ibid., 22r.

35. Williams, *The True State of the Question,* iv, 8-9.

36. Ibid., 53, 10.

37. Ibid., 134.

38. Edwards, MS sermon on Ezekiel 44:9 (1750), l. 17r.

39. Ibid., 17v.

40. Ibid., 18r.

41. Frothingham, *Discourse* (1750), 47; see also p. 37.

42. Edwards, *Humble Inquiry,* 71.

43. Ibid., 73.

44. Edwards, *Misrepresentations Corrected,* 10.

45. Frothingham, *Discourse,* 39.

46. Ibid.

47. Edwards, *A Farewell Sermon,* i-ii. See also the preface to *Humble Inquiry.*

48. Jonathan Edwards, *True Grace Distinguished from the Experience of Devils* (New York, 1753), 34.

49. Williams, *The True State of the Question,* 111.

50. Ibid.

51. Ibid., 11-14.

52. Jonathan Ashley, *An Humble Attempt to Give a Clear Account from Scripture* (Boston, 1753). These two sermons were first preached in Northampton, February 10, 1750.

53. The quotation from Locke is in Edwards's (7th) edition of Locke's *Essay concerning Human Understanding,* vol. 2, p. 103.

54. Edwards, *Misrepresentations Corrected,* 40-41.

55. John Locke, *An Essay concerning Human Understanding,* ed. Peter H. Nidditch (Oxford, 1975), Book III, chap. I, p. 402.

56. Ibid., 10, 476, 501.

57. Perry Miller incorrectly thought that Edwards had outgrown covenant theology altogether. See Conrad Cherry, *The Theology of Jonathan Edwards: A Reappraisal* (Garden City, N.Y., 1966), and Carl Bogue, *Jonathan Edwards and the Covenant of Grace* (Cherry Hill, N.J., 1975).

58. Alan Heimert, *Religion and the American Mind: From the Great Awakening to the Revolution* (Cambridge, Mass., 1966), 126. Harry S. Stout pointed to this interpretation as one of the few areas that had *not* been revised by post-Miller scholarship. See Stout, "The Puritans and Edwards," in Nathan

O. Hatch and Harry S. Stout, eds., *Jonathan Edwards and the American Experience* (New York, 1988), 143.

59. Mark Valeri, "The New Divinity and the Revolution," *William and Mary Quarterly,* 3d Ser., XLVI (October 1989): 743, n. 4, notes that this older view can be seen in Edmund S. Morgan, "The American Revolution Considered as an Intellectual Movement," in Arthur M. Schlesinger, Jr., and Morton White, eds., *Paths of American Thought* (Boston, 1963), 11-33.

60. Stout, 157.

61. Ibid.

62. Valeri, 751, n. 18.

63. Ibid., 745. Valeri follows Norman Fiering, *Jonathan Edwards's Moral Thought and Its British Context* (Chapel Hill, 1981), in arguing that the moral philosophy of Francis Hutcheson had a great impact on Edwards. This interpretation has been challenged by Paul Ramsey in Appendix II, *The Works of Jonathan Edwards, 8, Ethical Writings* (New Haven, 1989), 692-93, n. 1.

64. Gerald McDermott, "Jonathan Edwards, The City on a Hill, and the Redeemer Nation: A Reappraisal," *Journal of Presbyterian History* (Spring 1991). See also McDermott, *One Holy and Happy Society: The Public Theology of Jonathan Edwards* (University Park, Penn., 1992).

65. Contrast, for example, William Williams, *The Duty and Interest of a People* (Boston, 1736), which was published with Edwards's account of the 1735 Northampton revival.

66. Heimert, 95, 100, 120, 157, 402, 425, and 470. See also Perry Miller, "From the Covenant to the Revival," *Nature's Nation* (Cambridge, Mass., 1967), 90-120.

67. Edwards, *Humble Attempt,* in *The Works of Jonathan Edwards, 5, Apocalyptic Writings,* ed. Stephen J. Stein (New Haven, 1977), 372-73, 428. Heimert, 115, claims that "the crucial premises of Calvinist rhetoric [of union] were disclosed in Edwards's argument for a concert of prayer."

68. Edwards, *Humble Attempt,* 430; see also 317, 371.

69. Ibid., 360-61, and 434.

70. See, for example, Solomon Stoddard, *An Appeal to the Learned* (Boston, 1709), 55, 68-69, 82. Like Stoddard, Congregationalists recognized that their individual, church, and national covenants were in fact merely the different aspects of the single covenant of grace. But their *practice,* as well as their rhetoric, often emphasized the *differences* between inhabitants in New England, members of particular churches, and saints qualified to attend the Lord's Supper. See Samuel Willard, *Covenant-Keeping the Way to Blessedness* (Boston,

1682), especially 26-28, 68-74, and 96-101. It is a mistake to assume that the individual and corporate aspects of covenanting created radically distinct covenants with incommensurate aims and logics; but one may err at the other extreme by arguing that "the boundaries between self and society" were always blurred by the "bipolar thrust" of a single unified doctrine (Theodore Dwight Bozeman, "Federal Theology and the 'National Covenant': An Elizabethan Presbyterian Case Study," *Church History* 61 [December 1992]: 394-407).

71. MS sermon on Ezekiel 44:9 (1750) l. 20r. Hypocrites though many of the Jews were, Edwards argues, they still promised to abide by the covenant with all their hearts and souls. Moses Mather argued in 1772, referring to Edwards's published writings, that "when the late President *Edwards* wrote upon this controversy, he kept this general [external] dispensation of the covenant of grace, out of both his own, and the reader's view, and predicated his arguments only upon the covenant of grace, taken in its most limited tenor." Mather, *A Brief View of the Manner in Which the Controversy about the Visible Church, Has Been Conducted, in the Present Day* (New Haven, 1772), 6.

72. Williams, in *The True State of the Question,* 129, quotes a passage from Stoddard's *Appeal to the Learned,* 84, and then amplifies it with his own remarks, 129-30. Technically, Williams acknowledged only a single covenant of grace that was exhibited in two ways: internally to those who are converted and externally to those who profess and enjoy church ordinances (23).

73. Edwards, *Misrepresentations Corrected,* 89.

74. Edwards, MS sermon on Leviticus 26:3-13, February 28, 1745, and MS sermon on Joshua 7:12, Fast on the Occasion of the war with France, June 28, 1744, and March 1755.

75. Williams, 9.

76. Edwards, *Humble Inquiry,* 84.

77. Williams, 87.

78. Edwards, *Misrepresentations Corrected,* 151.

79. Ibid., 152.

80. Williams, 133.

81. See Edwards, *True Grace Distinguished from the Experience of Devils* (1753). See also Edwards, *The Nature of True Virtue,* chap. 5, and Ramsey's discussion of the development of Edwards's concept of natural conscience in "Appendix II: Jonathan Edwards on Moral Sense, and the Sentimentalists," both in *The Works of Jonathan Edwards, 8, Ethical Writings,* 689-705.

82. Edwards, *Misrepresentations Corrected,* 169-71. Like the Pharisees of Christ's day, nominal Christians were at once closest to the kingdom of

God and farthest from it. They enjoy the greatest of God's blessings, yet by so misimproving their privileges, they become more vile than heathens. Instead of taking pride in being members of God's privileged people, they should be confronting their own sin in fear and trembling. Nathaniel Appleton discusses this close-and-yet-far relationship in *Some Unregenerate Persons Not so Far from the Kingdom of God as Others* (Boston, 1763). Appleton, however, unlike Edwards, argues that someone with a good understanding of doctrine *is* closer to the kingdom.

83. Edwards, *Humble Inquiry,* 128-29.

84. Nathanael Emmons (1745-1840), *A Dissertation on the Scriptural Qualifications for Admission and Access to the Christian Sacraments* (Worcester, Mass., 1793), 45. See also Emmons, *A Candid Reply to the Reverend Dr. Hemmenway's Remarks* (Worcester, Mass., 1795). Emmons studied under John Smalley (1738-1808), who in turn had been Bellamy's student.

85. Edwards, "Miscellanies," no. 1338, probably written after 1755 (see Ramsey, 692); MS sermon on Luke 16:19, June 1753.

86. Edwards, MS sermon on Joshua 7:12, "Fast on occasion of the war with France," June 28, 1744, preached again March 1755.

87. Edwards, MS sermon on Exodus 33:19, "Thanksgiving for victory over the Rebels," August 1746, preached again November 1754; MS sermon on 1 Kings 8:44-45, "Fast for success in Cape Breton expedition," April 4, 1745, preached again July 1755; MS Thanksgiving sermon on Jeremiah 51:5, December 5, 1745, preached again November 1757.

88. Cf. William Hobby's *Happiness of a People, Having God for Their Ally . . . on Occasion of an Expedition Design'd against Canada* (Boston, 1758).

89. Solomon Williams, *The Relations of God's People to Him* (New London, 1760). Cf. Eli Forbes, *God the Strength and Salvation of his People* (Boston, 1761), a sermon preached the following year on the same text (Exodus 15:2). Neither Forbes nor David Hall's *Israel's Triumph* (Boston, 1761), on Exodus 15:1, focuses on *how* the colonies "resemble" the tribes of Israel, as Williams does.

90. Williams, *Relations of God's People,* 10.

91. Ibid., 10-11.

92. This was Williams's version of what historian Nathan Hatch has termed the "civil millennialism" taking root after the wars with France. See Nathan O. Hatch, *The Sacred Cause of Liberty: Republican Thought and the Millennium in Revolutionary New England* (New Haven, 1977), chap. 1.

Kenneth P. Minkema (essay date 1996)

SOURCE: "The Other Unfinished 'Great Work': Jonathan Edwards, Messianic Prophecy, and 'The Harmony of the Old and New Testament,'" in *Jonathan Edwards's Writings: Text, Context, Interpretation,* edited by Stephen J. Stein, Indiana University Press, 1996, pp. 52-65.

[In the following essay, Minkema traces what is known of one of Edwards's last—and unfinished—major projects, a little-studied work that Edwards had titled "The Harmony of the Old and New Testament." Minkema notes that the more than 500 pages of work that survive indicate that Edwards had embarked on new territory in Reformed thinking with his proposed arguments about the unity of Scripture, creation, and rational thought.]

In his famous letter of October 19, 1757, to the trustees of the College of New Jersey, Jonathan Edwards outlined his reasons why he should *not* accept their offer of the presidency. Besides his delicate constitution, Edwards cited his "course of employ in my study," which he feared would be permanently interrupted in governing a college. Too often he had been forced to put aside favorite projects—by the revivals of the 1730s and 1740s, by the communion controversy that ended in his dismissal from Northampton in 1750; now he wished to spend as much time as possible in his beloved study, before his giant "scrutore."

Edwards did not live to see any more of his books in print, but his unpublished writings reveal that, like another great philosopher before him, Isaac Newton, Edwards in his mature years found a rejuvenated interest in his lifelong love, the Bible, and became absorbed in the esoteric realm of precise scriptural exegesis. John F. Wilson writes that, shortly before his death, "Edwards was at a transitional point in his career as a theologian, preparing to return to exposition of strictly biblical themes but in a more rationalistic manner."[1] Many of his late **"Miscellanies"** and other manuscript notebooks, devoted to defending the truth of the Christian revelation, represent a much larger, though largely unappreciated, vein in Edwards's thought.[2]

Most significant among Edwards's later projects is a virtually unknown treatise—described thus far only by Stephen J. Stein—that explicates the messianic focus of biblical prophecy, where "prophecy" for Edwards comprehends promises concerning the Messiah already fulfilled and yet to come.[3] In its parts and method, as in the writers and trends it was addressing, the work was to be Edwards's contribution to the transatlantic debate over biblical messianic prophecy and the trustworthiness of the Bible.

Here we shall begin by briefly considering the place of this treatise within Edwards's larger corpus and by sketching its relation to the history of Christian scriptural exegesis. Though Edwards does not specifically name any of his opponents in the treatise, it is a polemical work; the second section therefore identifies authors and trends that Edwards was criticizing, particularly Deists, or "free thinkers," as well as those writers who eschewed a historical and literal interpretation of Scripture. And the concluding section reconstructs the structure and method of its component parts, focusing in turn on the themes of prophecy and fulfillment, typology, and harmonization. In combining his copious observations on these themes, Edwards wished to demonstrate not only the authenticity and unity of the Scriptures but also that biblical prophecies, types, and harmonies find their ultimate meaning in the person of the incarnate Logos as Messiah.

In his letter to the trustees, Edwards describes this treatise as one of two "great works" currently occupying his attention. The first, *A History of the Work of Redemption,* is well known among scholars of colonial America. Edwards then goes on to describe the other work at some length:

> I have also for my own profit and entertainment, done much towards another great work, which I call *the Harmony of the old and new Testament* in three Parts—The first considering the prophecies of the Messiah, his Redemption and Kingdom; the Evidences of their Referrences to the Messiah &c. comparing them all one with another, demonstrating their agreement and true scope and sense; also considering all the various particulars wherein these prophecies have their exact fulfillment; shewing the universal, precise, and admirable correspondence between predictions and events. The second Part: Considering the Types of the old testament, shewing the evidence of their being intended as representations of the great things of the gospel of Christ: and the agreement of the type with the antitype.—The third and great Part, considering the harmony of the old and new testament, as to doctrine and precept.—In the course of this work, I find there will be occasion for an explanation of a very great part of the holy scripture; which may, in such a view be explained in a method, which to me seems the most entertaining and profitable, best tending to lead the mind to a view of the true spirit, design, life and soul of the scriptures, as well as to their proper use and improvement.[4]

If size is any indication, **"The Harmony of the Old and New Testament"** was truly a major effort for Edwards, over 500 pages in manuscript. More important than sheer length, however, was the prodigious amount of labor that went into the work, which represents Edwards's accumulated knowledge on the subject. Alongside his repository of scriptural commentary consisting of **"Notes on the Scripture"** and the **"Blank (or Interleaved) Bible," "The Harmony of the Old and New Testament"** is the result of decades of close biblical study and reflection. But where the **"Blank Bible"** follows canonical order, the **"Harmony"** arranges biblical exegesis according to a preconceived method.

The interpretive methods Edwards planned to utilize in **"The Harmony of the Old and New Testament"** were as old as Christianity itself. The disciplines of delineating the fulfillment of prophecy, of finding typological links between the testaments, and of harmonizing the holy texts

began in the second century after Christ. Some early commentators argued that the testaments were irreparably contradictory, while others held that prophecy and fulfillment were important links between the testaments that confirmed their divine origins.[5] Over the centuries, Christian exegetes came to rely increasingly on symbolism and allegory to demonstrate the unity of the testaments. But there were some who were hesitant about allegorization, chief among them Augustine, who attached increasing importance to the historical sense of Scripture, which included the prophetic and typological dimensions. During the Reformation, John Calvin reemphasized the parity of the testaments rather than follow other Protestant leaders such as Martin Luther in relegating the Old Testament to an inferior status.[6] Together the Augustinian sense of Scripture and the Calvinist view of the inner relationship of the Bible were part of the English dissenting tradition that Edwards inherited.

Surprisingly, similar issues still prevailed in the eighteenth as in the fifth century, though now filtered through the Reformation and under vastly different historical circumstances. In biblical interpretation as in doctrine, the first half of the eighteenth century was the Age of Rationalism and the Age of Deism. It was largely agreed that revelation was agreeable to reason, yet orthodox and liberal exegetes came to very different conclusions about the truth of traditional Christian doctrines, the reliability of the Christian Bible, and the nature and meaning of its central figure, Jesus of Nazareth.

In his classic study, *The Eclipse of the Biblical Narrative,* Hans Frei traces the changes that occurred in biblical hermeneutics during the eighteenth century, culminating in the modern higher critical approach. During the "precritical" period, Frei states, figural interpretation confirmed that the meaning of the biblical texts and the story they told were one. However, as a result of Deist challenges and rationalist adjustments, a wedge was driven between meaning and story, between the biblical world and the real historical world, so that the author's intention and the meaning of what the author wrote became different things. Orthodox exegetes like Edwards, while wholly sharing in the assumption that religion was in accord with reason, sought for ways to affirm the intended meanings of the texts *and* their historical reality by demonstrating the overall integrity of the Scriptures.[7]

It is this larger struggle against Deism or free thought, along with an antihistorical approach to Scripture, a struggle that occupied some of the best minds of England—including Addison, Berkeley, and Butler—that the **"Harmony"** addresses. The **"Harmony,"** a lone voice from the colonial wilderness, was to join all of the traditional Protestant strands of scriptural interpretation into a synthetic proof of the unity and factuality of the Bible. Like Calvin, the hermeneutic linchpin for Edwards was Jesus Christ as Messiah, whose coming to earth and the particularities of whose life, death, and resurrection were foretold of old. The christocentric meaning of creation is illustrated in **"Miscellanies"** no. 837, where Edwards writes:

> The whole of Christian divinity depends on divine revelation, for though there are many truths concerning God and our duty to him that are evident by the light of nature, yet no one truth is taught by the light of nature in that manner in which it is necessary for us to know it: for the knowledge of no truth in divinity is of any significance to us, any otherwise than it some way or other belongs to the gospel scheme, or has relation to Christ the Mediator. It signifies nothing for us to know anything of any one of God's perfections, unless we know them as manifested in Christ.[8]

In response to those who argued that the "light of nature" alone was sufficient to teach morality and virtue, Edwards insisted that an experience of the excellency of Christ was essential. Only in Christ could the unity of Scripture be understood and the higher unity of all creation be achieved.

As a number of historians have pointed out, the modern critique of the Christian revelation began in 1695 with John Locke's *Reasonableness of Christianity*.[9] Locke reacted against the creedal and confessional strife of the Interregnum by attempting to boil down Christianity to what he saw as the fundamental, reasonable teachings on which all Christians could agree. During the following seven decades or so, authors followed Locke's lead with efforts to prove or disprove that Scripture was within the bounds of reason and empirical evidence. These included Edwards, who, though he emulated Locke's methodology, was intent on demonstrating that revealed religion was not merely a "republication" of natural religion.

Along with Enlightenment notions of toleration and reason, new attitudes toward religion were shaped by the Scientific Revolution. Many theologians sought to incorporate Isaac Newton's mechanical philosophy into their approach, including Edwards, who wrote that God had sent Newton "to make way for the universal setting up of Christ's kingdom."[10] But advocates of natural religion such as Samuel Clarke used Newton's writings to support their criticisms of revealed religion.[11] Human observation and reason alone, they argued, could prove the existence and wisdom of God and the superiority of natural law. The new authority given to scientific method threatened to deprive orthodox exegetes of their traditional appeals to biblical evidence and metaphysical argumentation, which were both subject to increasing ridicule.[12]

Some of Locke's and Newton's professed disciples took their ideas further than the masters themselves would have gone. Among them was John Toland, who in 1696 published *Christianity Not Mysterious*. If, Toland concluded, reason was the standard to which everything, especially revelation, was to be subjected, then many things in Scripture were suspect, including the credibility of inspiration, the reliability of the biblical narrative, its prophetic content, and its accounts of miracles—all subjects which Ed-

wards defended extensively in his private notebooks.[13] Scripture was attacked in several notorious books, with Matthew Tindal's *Christianity as Old as Creation* (1730) leading the way. Christianity, Tindal held, was "as old as creation" only insofar as it mirrored natural reason. On this basis, he dismissed much of the Old Testament and prompted a torrent of criticism, including some from Edwards.[14] In an essay toward a treatise on the mysteries of religion aimed at Tindal and his allies, Edwards attempts to explain the proper relation between reason and revelation:

> Multitudes of the free thinkers of late ages deceive themselves through the ambiguous or equivocal use of the word REASON. They argue as though we must make reason the highest rule to judge of all things, even the doctrines of revelation, because reason is that by which we must judge of revelation itself—'tis the rule by which the judgment of the truth of a revelation depends, and therefore undoubtedly must be that by which particular doctrines of it must be judged—not considering that the word *reason* is here used in two senses: in the former case, viz. in our judging of a supposed revelation, the word means the *faculty* of reason taken in the whole extent of its exercise; in the other case, 'tis the *opinion* of our reason or some particular opinions that have appeared rational to us. Now there is a great difference between these two.

Edwards goes on to assert that "divine testimony" is necessary and cannot be "contradistinguished" from other equally valid forms of evidence or argument. Resorting to one of his favorite tactics, he claims that making reason a higher rule than revelation is "making sounds without understanding or fixing any distinct meaning."[15]

Beside the Deist threat, the Bible was also being attacked by those who opposed an Augustinian or historical interpretation of Scripture. These "antihistoricists" comprehended a wide range of writers who argued that the Bible could not be taken as an accurate account of events, that its books—most prominently the Pentateuch[16]—were not written by the attributed authors, and that an historical approach to Scripture led on the one hand to Puritan dogmatism and on the other to enthusiasm. While there was no concerted effort during Edwards's life to reintroduce the extravagant allegorizing that had characterized the works of the metaphysical preachers such as Lancelot Andrewes and John Donne, there were those, including Collins and the French Catholic priest Richard Simon, who favored it over the literal-historical hermeneutic that had prevailed during the Puritan era. Most prominent among those who did call for a return to an allegorical approach was the English theologian Conyers Middleton, who found that efforts to defend Christianity through a literal exposition of the Bible only created embarrassing "difficulties."[17]

Though the **"Harmony"** was to be a work of apologetic theology par excellence against such antihistorical writers, it contains hardly any polemical statements. We must go to Edwards's other notebooks to find his unabashed, unedited condemnations of the antihistoricists and their treatment of Scripture. He bristled at his opponents' claims that many biblical passages could not be understood by uneducated readers and that only those versed in the original languages could hope to interpret the sacred texts correctly. In one series of notebooks, Edwards castigates the new critics' approach and "their MAGISTERIAL, CONTEMPTUOUS, SOVEREIGN, ASSURED, SUPERCILIOUS, OVERBEARING, INSULTING, OVERLOOKING AIRS." In contrast, he defends the accessibility of the Scripture to all believers, both learned and unlearned:

> SCRIPTURE EXPRESSIONS are everywhere exceeding contrary to their scheme, according to all use of language in the world these days. But then they have their refuge here: they say the ancient figures of speech are exceeding diverse from ours, and that we in this distant age can't judge at all of the true force of expressions used so long ago but by a skill in antiquity, and being versed in ancient history, and critically skilled in ancient languages—never considering that the Scriptures are written for us in these ages, on whom the ends of the world are come, yea, were designed chiefly for the latter age of the world, in which they shall have their chief and, comparatively, almost all their effect, and they were written for God's people in these ages, when at least 99 out of an hundred must be supposed incapable of such knowledge.

Edwards goes on to condemn "their vast pretenses to an accurate and clear view of the SCOPE and DESIGN of the sacred penmen and a critical knowledge of the ORIGINALS," concluding, "'Tis easy to refine and criticize a book to death."[18] Though Edwards was firmly against lay interpretation of Scripture, neither could he brook the elitist, exclusionary view of his opponents.

Such were the forces against which Edwards set himself when he laid out the tripartite structure of the **"Harmony."** With this background, we can better understand the purpose behind the treatise as a whole as well as its separate parts.

Following Edwards's synopsis in his letter to the trustees, the components of the **"Harmony"**'s first section are entitled "Prophecies of the Messiah" and "Fulfillment of the Prophecies of Messiah." "Prophecies" comprises a series of **"Miscellanies"** entries, nos. 891, 922, and (by far the longest) 1067, while **"Fulfillment"** is no. 1068.[19] As arrangements of the texts pertaining to the coming of Christ, Edwards's "Prophecies" and "Fulfillment" are strikingly reminiscent of Handel's *Messiah* (1742), which reflected the contemporary debate over Scripture. The librettos of "Prophecies" and "Fulfillment" both feature numbered sections (101 and 181 respectively), with each section considering a different passage. Throughout, Edwards engages in detailed textual study, dissecting the words of the text, exhaustively citing related texts, and gathering evidence from both ancient and modern authorities, from Josephus, Tacitus, and Cyrus to Jacques Basnage, Hugo Grotius, and Johann Stapfer. Like many other authors of his time, Edwards found these sources useful in marshaling

confirmation for events related in the Bible and in searching into the actual or multivalent meanings of Hebrew and Greek words.

The "Prophecies" considers significant Old Testament passages describing the Messiah. Section 91, for example, considers Dan. 9:24-27, which Edwards believed to be "a great prophecy of the messiah . . . one of the most remarkable and plain of all in the Old Testament."[20] In this lengthy and detailed article, Edwards seeks to show that the "Great King" often promised in prophecy is the same as the Messiah, or Anointed One, mentioned by Daniel. The "Fulfillment" explicates the Messiah's time of coming, his descent, his manner of person, the benefits of his death, and the many things relating to his church, his kingdom, his judgment, and the fate of his enemies. Section 3 takes up the same passage in Daniel, contending that the things prophesied in the Old Testament are literally embodied in the person of Jesus and contain mystical meanings for the church of God.[21]

For the revisionists with whom Edwards was so dissatisfied, among the most "irrational" elements of Christianity were the prophecies and their interpretation—topics very close to Edwards's heart. Controversial books that criticized the canon of Scripture included Thomas Woolston's *Six Discourses on Miracles* (1727) and William Whiston's *Essay towards Restoring the True Text of the Old Testament* (1722). While Whiston's method of "restoring" the original text was viewed by nearly everyone as eccentric, Collins and Woolston agreed with Whiston that the Old Testament texts were corrupt and untrustworthy, which rendered their literal interpretation irrelevant, even dangerous.[22]

Another seminal book was Anthony Collins's *Discourse of the Grounds and Reasons of the Christian Religion* (1724). Edwards's Catalogue" of his reading shows his immersion in the avalanche of apologetic literature that surrounded Collins's work. Among other volumes he cites Edward Chandler's *Defence of Christianity, from the Prophecies of the Old Testament* (1725), which linked prophecy and types in much the same way Edwards does; Thomas Sherlock's *Use and Intent of Prophecy* (1725), which he frequently cited to affirm the fulfillment of the prophecies in Christ; and Arthur Ashley Sykes's *Essay upon the Truth of the Christian Religion* (1725), which maintained that Christianity had its "real foundation" in the Old Testament and that Christ's claim to fulfill prophecy was among several proofs of the authenticity of Scripture.[23]

Literary scholars in particular will recognize Edwards's description of the second part of **"Harmony,"** "considering the Types of the old testament," as **"Types of the Messiah,"** which in the **"Miscellanies"** follows **"Fulfillment"** as no. 1069. This entry was first published by Sereno Dwight in his 1829 edition, without any indication that it was part of a larger work.[24] Only when viewed in the light of Edwards's letter to the trustees, however, do we understand the essay's true place and full function.

Edwards's aim in **"Types of the Messiah"** is to show that the Old and New Testaments cannot be understood apart from each other; the former prophetically and typologically anticipates the latter and the latter interprets the former. For Edwards, all of the things of the Old Testament are typical; it was, he says, "a typical world." Of utmost importance for understanding God's plan is that the Old Testament "abundantly prefigured and typified . . . the Messiah and things appertaining to his kingdom." "The introducing of the Messiah and his kingdom and salvation," Edwards continues, "is plainly spoken of in the Old Testament as the great event which was the substance, main drift and end of all the prophecies of the Old Testament, to reveal which chiefly it was that the Spirit of prophecy was given."[25]

Alongside messianic prophecy and fulfillment, typology became for Edwards one of the primary means of comprehending "the Messiah and things appertaining to his kingdom." Here Edwards was joining the argument against critics like Collins, Tindal, Woolston, and Simon in advocating the inseparable link between the testaments. Numerous works arose from the conservative camp that emphasized this "connection," among them Humphrey Prideaux's *Old and New Testament Connected* (1716), William Harris's *Practical Discourse on the Principal Representations of the Messiah throughout the Old Testament* (1724), and most importantly for Edwards, Samuel Clarke's *Discourse concerning the Connexion of the Prophecies in the Old Testament, and the Application of Them to Christ* (1723).[26] Eclectically pulling arguments and illustrations from Nonconformist typologists as well as from the more philosophical Clarke, Edwards ends his lengthy consideration of the Old Testament types of the Messiah with a corollary that sums up for him the meanings of the types:

Seeing it is thus abundantly evident by the Old Testament itself that the things of the Old Testament were typical of the Messiah and things appertaining to him, hence a great and most convincing argument may be drawn that Jesus is the Messiah, seeing there is so wonderful a correspondence and evident, manifold and great agreement between him and his gospel and these types of the Old Testament.[27]

It is in this light as well that we can more fully understand Edwards's theoretical statements about typology in **"Types of the Messiah,"** which were aimed at the natural religionists and anti-historicists. Edwards affirms an Augustinian approach to Scripture when he says that "the material and natural world is typical of the moral, spiritual and intelligent world, or the City of God."[28] In posing an objection concerning "the abuse that will be made of this doctrine of types," Edwards replies:

We have as good warrant from the Word of God to suppose the whole ceremonial law to be given in order to a figurative representing and signifying spiritual and evangelical things to mankind, as we have to suppose that prophetical representations are to represent and signify the events designed by them, and therefore as good reason to endeavor to interpret them.[29]

That Edwards had these same commentators in mind for his expanded theory of typology is also clear from his thesis in the **"Types"** notebook: "To show how there is a medium between those that cry down all types, and those that are for turning all into nothing but allegory and not having it to be true history; and also the way of the rabbis that find so many mysteries in letters, etc."[30]

Edwards's thesis as stated in the **"Types"** notebook does not apply to the entire **"Harmony"** project but rather to one discrete section of it. Nonetheless, his statement does point to his new way of viewing typology. Edwards, who saw all of creation as the "shadows of beings," found direct correspondences with divine things in history, nature, and human experience as well as in Scripture. To draw merely moralistic lessons from Scripture and observable phenomena, as did the antihistoricists, did not go far enough for Edwards; on the other hand, cabalistic claims concerning "mysteries in letters" went too far in his estimation. Where his fellow ministers in the dissenting and Reformed camps largely refused to venture outside of the Bible itself for types and antitypes, Edwards advocated stepping beyond the written Word for representations of divine things. "It would be on some accounts as unreasonable to say that we must interpret no more of them than the Scripture has interpreted for us, and than we are told the meaning of in the New Testament, as it would be to say that we must interpret prophecy, or prophetical visions and types, no further than the Scripture has interpreted it to our hand."[31]

With Edwards's thesis for the **"Types"** too, it becomes clear that **"Images of Divine Things"** and the notebook on **"Types,"** which contain the more innovative elements of Edwards's typology, were actually grist for the **"Harmony"** mill. In these notebooks he criticizes natural religionists for limiting the meaning of the created world by making it an end in itself rather than a source of references to divine truths. Throughout **"Images"** Edwards insists, as for example in no. 8, that "there is a great and remarkable analogy in God's works," and that "the whole outward creation . . . is so made as to represent spiritual things." And in **"Miscellanies"** no. 760, Edwards reiterates the christocentric focus of the realm of the types when he writes:

Things that appear minute in comparison with the work of creation are much insisted on in Scripture, for they become great by their relation to Christ and his redemption, of which creation was but a shadow. And the history of Scripture, which gives an account of the works of providence, are all taken up in the history of Christ and his church; for all God's works of providence are to be reduced to his providence towards Christ and his church.

Thus the **"Images"** and **"Types"** notebooks, with their shared ascription of the meaning of signs to things relating to the Messiah, unexpectedly find their home in a treatise about biblical prophecy.

While the previous sections of the treatise have survived intact, the final one, "considering the harmony of the old and new testament," is fragmentary. Only one quarto-sized notebook (not a part of the **"Miscellanies"**) has survived, entitled **"The Harmony of the Genius, Spirit, Doctrines and Rules of the Old Testament and the New."**[32] Since this notebook deals with Genesis through Psalms, we can only speculate that there were further notebooks toward this "great," or largest part of the treatise, taking us from Proverbs onward, that are no longer extant.

Edwards begins here by grouping Old Testament texts under the "signs of godliness," a rubric that underlies his revival works. These signs include faith in God, the Messiah, and a future state; love to enemies, humility, and selling all for Christ; sympathy for others, not being anxious, and not laying up earthly treasures. He then abandons this method and begins to go canonically through the Old Testament, noting how passages "harmonize with doctrines, precepts, etc. of the New." For instance, Edwards couples God's command to Abram to leave his home (Gen. 12:1-4) with Jesus' injunction that the Christian is to "forsake father and mother, brethren and sisters, and all that he hath" (Luke 14:26). Thus this biblical exercise becomes for Edwards a means of illustrating the central features of his theology, particularly his interest in Christian behavior as the primary "mark" or "sign" of true sainthood.

Just as in typology Edwards was forging a new way of viewing types, so in harmonizing the testaments he was also at the forefront of Reformed hermeneutics. Here Edwards could draw on a long tradition of Protestant writers who "harmonized" scriptural accounts, particularly the four gospels; but his aim was much more ambitious, comprehending the entire Bible and employing a unique organizing principle. This principle was what Stephen J. Stein has called the "spiritual" or "spirit-given" sense, the meaning available only to the regenerate by indwelling grace.[33] Through the spiritual sense, Edwards linked all the meanings of biblical texts through an "analogy of faith" by conforming them to the saving doctrines of Christianity, stressing, as Frei puts it, "the similarity of the effect all the parts of the Bible have on the devoutly inquiring mind."[34] The important point for Edwards was not the direct inspiration or literal wording of the Bible, but rather its *matter* or subjects and their agreement; the congruity of the whole was more important than the sum of its parts. Here Edwards was a leader, with German theologians such as Matthaus Pfaff, Johann Jacob Rambach, and Sigmund Jacob Baumgarten, in forging what Emanuel Hirsch has called the transition from "Bible faith" to "revelation faith."[35] It is yet another testimony to Edwards's genius that he developed this approach, emphasizing the unity and harmony of the testaments and the spiritual sense, virtually on his own.[36]

Yet we cannot ignore that "harmony" was a packed word for Edwards; it connoted for him an element of the excellency of the saint as well as Scripture, and so was integral to his philosophical theology. Moving from the testimony of prophecy and the created world, Edwards in this final section is considering not just the harmony of Scripture per se but also describing the necessary harmony, congruity, and correspondence of perceiving minds to Christ. The similarity and consent of God's Word to itself finds its analog in the similarity and consent of the soul to Christ. "The more the consent is, and the more extensive," Edwards wrote in **"The Mind"** no. 1, "the greater is the excellency."[37] So in the section on **"Harmony,"** Edwards's emphasis is on following what he calls "the way of universal holiness." The extent of consent applied as much among God's means of revealing his will—Scripture, nature, and the Spirit—as to the soul's accepting the revelation.

As a whole, **"The Harmony of the Old and New Testament"** was to combine the various sorts of internal and external proofs available to Edwards—prophecy and fulfillment, typology, and harmonization—into one work. Scripture, creation, and rational being, Edwards wished to argue, together found their ultimate meaning and unity in the person of Christ. Whether Edwards saw any problem with reconciling his traditional treatment of prophecy with his revisionist approaches to typology and harmonization is not clear. Two things, however, are clear: that at the end of his life Edwards had embarked on a new direction into biblical exposition; and that his unifying concept was Jesus Christ as the reference point of all promises, whether they had already been fulfilled through the incarnation of the Logos or were yet to be accomplished through the ongoing work of redemption.

Notes

1. *The Works of Jonathan Edwards, 9, A History of the Work of Redemption,* ed. John F. Wilson (New Haven, 1989), p. 554.

2. Among Edwards's late notebooks is "Subjects of Inquiry" (Beinecke Rare Book and Manuscript Library, Yale University, Edwards Papers, Box 21, f. 1251), which contains memoranda in which he directs himself to read through the Old Testament, the Evangelists, and the Epistles for confirmation of prophecies; his late "Miscellanies" contain a disproportionate amount of entries on such topics as Revealed Religion, the Necessity of Revelation, the Spirit of Prophecy, and the Prophecies of the Old Testament; and to facilitate his understanding of the Old Testament, Edwards was even attempting to improve his Hebrew. For example, he tells the trustees that he cannot teach languages, "unless it be the hebrew tongue, which I should be willing to improve my self in, by instructing others" (Samuel Hopkins, *The Life and Character of . . . Jonathan Edwards* [Boston, 1765], p. 78). In "Subjects of Inquiry," Edwards notes to himself that he should read the Scripture through and make a list of Hebrew words, which resulted in the notebook "Hebrew Idioms" (Box 16, f. 1211).

3. Stephen J. Stein, "Spirit and the Word: Jonathan Edwards and Scriptural Exegesis," in Nathan O. Hatch and Harry S. Stout, eds., *Jonathan Edwards and the American Experience* (New York, 1988), pp. 118-28.

4. Hopkins, *Life,* pp. 77-78. "Harmony" was to deal with the period up through the early church, while the *History* was to take the story of redemption to the end of time. In this way, they were related. Nevertheless, at the time of his letter, the *History* still lay at loose ends in several books of notes, in scattered "Miscellanies," and in the unrevised sermon series preached nearly two decades earlier, while the first two parts of the "Harmony" had been drawn up into nearly final form and the third section was well under way. The manuscript evidence suggests that the *History* may have reached publication first because of the interests of Edwards's disciples rather than because of any stated preference of his own.

5. *The Cambridge History of the Bible,* vol. 1, *From the Beginnings to Jerome,* ed. P. R. Ackroyd and C. F. Evans (New York, 1963), pp. 76, 258, 276, 330-31, 486.

6. Ibid., pp. 552-54; *Cambridge History of the Bible,* vol. 3, *The West from the Reformation to the Present Day,* ed. S. L. Greenslade, pp. 16-17.

7. Hans Frei, *The Eclipse of Biblical Narrative: A Study in Eighteenth and Nineteenth Century Hermeneutics* (New Haven, 1974), pp. 1-16.

8. Quotations from the "Miscellanies" are taken from Thomas A. Schafer's transcript on deposit at the Beinecke Library. On the christocentrism of the "Harmony," see Stein, "Spirit and the Word," pp. 124-27.

9. Mark Pattison, "Tendencies of Religious Thought in England, 1688-1750," *Essays and Reviews* (London, 1860), pp. 259-60; Leslie Stephen, *History of English Thought in the Eighteenth Century,* vol. 1 (London, 1876; rep. 1927), 91-96; Gerald R. Cragg, *Reason and Authority in the Eighteenth Century* (Cambridge, 1964), pp. 13-14; John Redwood, *Reason, Ridicule and Religion: The Age of Enlightenment in England, 1660-1750* (Cambridge, Mass., 1976), pp. 101-3.

10. Beinecke Library, Edwards Papers, Box 16, f. 1212, "Work of Redemption" Book I, p. 5.

11. J. P. Ferguson, *An Eighteenth-Century Heretic: Dr. Samuel Clarke* (Kineton, 1976), pp. 106-18, 210-25; Cragg, *Reason and Authority,* p. 50.

12. Cragg, *Reason and Authority,* pp. 13, 16-18, 46; Redwood, *Reason, Ridicule and Religion,* pp. 94-95; John Gascoigne, *Cambridge in the Age of the Enlightenment: Science, Religion and Politics from the Restoration to the French Revolution* (Cambridge, 1989), pp. 115-23, 164.

13. Among Edwards's notebooks is one defending the authenticity of the Pentateuch as a work of Moses (Beinecke Library, Edwards Papers, Box 15, f. 1204; see also notes on the Books of Moses, Box 15, f. 1204a), an extension of "Notes on the Scripture," no. 415. On Christ's miracles, see "Miscellanies" nos. 1306, 1311, 1319, and the sermon on John 10:37 f. (Jan. 1740). See also "On the Christian Religion" (Box 21, f. 1257), which contains materials relating to all of these topics.

14. Redwood, *Reason, Ridicule and Religion,* pp. 134-55.

15. Beinecke Library, Edwards Papers, Box 15, f. 1203, "Controversies" Notebook, pp. 190, 193. The "Controversies" essay on mysteries is linked by Edwards to "Miscellanies" no. 1340, entitled "Reason and Revelation," which is a direct response to Tindal's *Christianity as Old as Creation.*

16. See Edwards's manuscript notebook on Moses's authorship of the Pentateuch (Beinecke Library, Box 15, f. 1204), where he collected evidence that these books could not have been forged. The most famous work defending the Pentateuch as a work of Moses was William Warburton's *Divine Legation of Moses Demonstrated, On the Principles of a Religious Deist* (2 vols. London, 1737-38), which was listed by Edwards in his "Catalogue" of reading and used by him in teaching at Stockbridge. But Edwards's approval of the book was not without exceptions; his small manuscript entitled "Places of the Old Testament that Intimate a Future State" (Edwards Collection, ND5[xi]4-5, the Franklin Trask Library, Andover Newton Theological School, Newton Center, Massachusetts) may have been in response to Warburton's argument that the Old Testament did not contain proof of an afterlife.

17. Frei, *Eclipse,* pp. 120-22; W. Fraser Mitchell, *English Pulpit Oratory from Andrewes to Tillotson: A Study of Its Literary Aspects* (London, 1932), pp. 148-49; *The Works of Jonathan Edwards, 11, Typological Writings,* ed. Wallace E. Anderson and Mason I. Lowance, Jr. (New Haven, 1993), pp. 20-24. On Father Simon, see Dean Freiday, *The Bible: Its Criticism, Interpretation and Use in Seventeenth and Eighteenth Century England* (Pittsburgh, 1979), pp. 105-6.

18. Beinecke Library, Edwards Papers, Box 15, f. 1207, "Efficacious Grace," Book II, pp. 62-63.

19. "Miscellanies," Book 6, containing nos. 1067 and 1068, is at the Trask Library (ND6A-C); the remainder of the "Miscellanies" are at the Beinecke Library. The length of these entries is unparalleled among Edwards's unpublished writings: "Prophecies" and "Fulfillment" together amount to nearly 300 neatly written folio pages bound in their own cover. Each even has its own "table," or index.

20. See, for example, the early note in the Blank Bible (Beinecke Library, Edwards Papers, Box 17, f. 1216) on Dan. 9:23-24, which Edwards states is the angel's answer to Daniel's prayer concerning the Messiah.

21. On the mystical meaning, see Stephen J. Stein, "The Quest for the Spiritual Sense: The Biblical Hermeneutic of Jonathan Edwards," *Harvard Theological Review* 70 (1977): 99-113.

22. Stephen, *History of English Thought,* vol. 1, 210 ff., 228; Frei, *Eclipse,* pp. 68-70.

23. Edwards's manuscript "Catalogue" of reading (Beinecke Library, Edwards papers, Box 15, f. 1202) contains numerous titles relating to miracles (Sherlock), harmony of the evangelists (Lightfoot, Cradock, Fisher), Deism (Leland, Skelton), Scripture chronology (Hoar, Bedford, Lardner), and other current issues that show his involvement in the debate over Scripture.

24. Sereno E. Dwight, ed., *The Works of President Edwards,* vol. 9 (New York, 1829-30), pp. 9-111. The Yale Edwards Edition does only a little better, for though the connection of the piece to the larger project is made clear in the introduction to vol. 11, *Typological Writings* (pp. 12-13), the tradition of separate publication begun with Dwight is perpetuated.

25. *Works of Jonathan Edwards, 11,* pp. 202, 203.

26. Answering Collins on the nonliteral meaning of prophecies of the Messiah, Clarke cites typology as an important buttress for the claim of Jesus's messiahship: "The Correspondences of *Types* and *Antitypes,* though they are not themselves proper *Proofs* of the Truth of a doctrine, yet they may be very reasonable *Confirmations* of the *Foreknowledge* of God; of the uniform View of Providence under *different Dispensations,* of the *Analogy, Harmony, and Agreement* between the *Old Testament* and *the New.*" Samuel Clarke, *A Discourse concerning the Connexion of the Prophecies in the Old Testament, and the Application of Them to Christ* (London, 1729), p. 32.

27. *Works of Jonathan Edwards, 11,* p. 321.

28. Ibid., p. 191.

29. Ibid., pp. 321, 323-24.

30. Ibid., *11,* p. 151. Although his "Catalogue" of reading contains several items relating to rabbinic learning and cabal, Edwards most likely understood "the way of the rabbis" through Christian expositors such as the Cambridge Platonists rather than through primary sources.

31. *Works of Jonathan Edwards, 11,* pp. 147-48.

32. Beinecke Library, Edwards Papers, f. 33.

33. See Stein, "Quest for the Spiritual Sense," pp. 106-7, and "The Spirit and the Word," p. 123.

34. Frei, *Eclipse,* p. 92.

35. Ibid., p. 91.

36. See W. R. Ward, *The Protestant Evangelical Awakening* (Cambridge, 1992), chap. 1, which discusses the Pietist influence in the American colonies through immigration.

37. See "The Mind" no. 1, in *The Works of Jonathan Edwards, 6, Scientific and Philosophical Writings,* ed. Wallace E. Anderson (New Haven, 1980), pp. 332-38. See also the manuscript entitled "Christ's Example" (Beinecke Library, Edwards Papers, Box 21, f. 1259), which details the ways in which the believer should conform to Christ.

Wayne Proudfoot (essay date 1996)

SOURCE: "Perception and Love in *Religious Affections,*" in *Jonathan Edwards's Writings: Text, Context, Interpretation,* edited by Stephen J. Stein, Indiana University Press, 1996, pp. 122-36.

[In the following essay, Proudfoot examines Edwards's description of religious experience in Religious Affections, *in order to demonstrate the sophistication of Edward's analysis and argument as compared to that of William James in his* Varieties of Religious Experience.*]*

Recent philosophical analysts of religious experience have portrayed it as a kind of intuition or perception.[1] This is in part the influence of William James's *Varieties of Religious Experience.*[2] Though *Varieties* includes much more, James throughout identifies religious experience with a sense or feeling, and when he comes to assess its noetic value he focuses on the analogy with ordinary sense perception.

At first glance Jonathan Edward's **Treatise concerning Religious Affections** appears to be a distinguished predecessor in the same tradition. James cites Edwards approvingly at crucial points in his argument.[3] Though the term "religious experience" is somewhat anachronistic when applied to **Religious Affections,** Edwards has provided a rich and subtle account of experiential religion. His striking use of Lockean language to describe "some new sensation or perception of the mind, . . . or . . . what some metaphysicians call a new simple idea," and his analogy with the taste of honey, are among the best-known passages in the book.[4]

Closer inspection reveals, however, that the parallel with James and the use of Locke are misleading. The new sensation, and the analogy with the deliverances of the other senses, plays no epistemic role in Edwards's criteria for distinguishing genuine from spurious affections. Despite the fact that Perry Miller's characterization of Edwards as an enthusiastic Lockean has been discredited, the references to sense and taste continue to influence readers in ways that can detract from the main argument of the book. Edwards is well aware that sincere first-person reports of a new sensation or perception carry no guarantee that affections are "truly spiritual and gracious" (197). To discriminate genuine from spurious affections, Edwards turns away from the analogy with sense perception and toward the practice of moral appraisal. This turn leads to a more sophisticated understanding of self-examination and of experience than can be found in *Varieties.*

I want to examine the argument in *Religious Affections* in order to call attention to the sophistication Edwards brings to the description and examination of religious experience. By attending to the practice of moral inquiry and to the ways in which we attribute character traits to others and to ourselves, Edwards captures and contributes to the complex and reflexive self-consciousness that is constitutive of much religious experience. The reflexive character of this experience, with its attention to ubiquitous forms of self-deception and subtle changes in the moral will, is left unexplored by those who portray the experience chiefly as intuition or perception. At the outset and at the conclusion, I will contrast Edwards's approach with that of James's in *Varieties* in order to cast Edwards's contribution into greater relief. I have tried to lift the structure of Edwards's argument out of its theological context, not to claim that for him it was or could be independent of that context but to demonstrate its sophistication.

PERCEPTION AND LOVE

Edwards and James both examine both the perceptual and moral components of religious experience. Each builds his account chiefly around two aspects of that experience, the new sense or insight and the virtues of the saint or the fruits of the religious life. Both reflect at length on methods for assessing claims made on behalf of and by appeal to religious experience.

Given their very different contexts, it is not surprising that the claims they consider differ greatly. Edwards was a theologian, preacher, and pastor in the midst of a period of revivals of religion during which he had been attacked by both liberal rationalists and radical evangelicals. *Religious Affections* is the culmination of a series of polemical writings in which he addressed both groups, though the chief adversaries against whom this text is directed are the radical evangelicals.[5] Edwards was convinced that the Holy Spirit was at work in these events and tried to identify criteria that would distinguish genuine spiritual affections from spurious ones, those that are the result of divine operation from the raised affect and excitement that are artifacts of the revival and of other natural causes.

James wrote as a psychologist, a philosopher, and a member of a university faculty. He collected autobiographical accounts of religious experiences from classical religious literature, contemporary pamphlets, journalism, and other documents of personal testimony. As a philosopher, he wanted to determine to what extent such testimonies provide evidence for belief in an unseen order, a More that is continuous with the moral life and is not exhausted by natural causes. While Edwards was convinced that the divine was at work and tried to identify its effects, James asked whether the religious dimension of human experience could be accounted for by natural explanations alone.

It might appear that the distinction between Edwards's task as a theologian and James's as a psychologist and philosopher is sufficient to account for the differences in their approaches to religious experience. Edwards's initial appeal is to Scripture, and to what that can tell us about the operations of the Spirit of God. This is almost always followed by consideration of what reason can tell us on the particular topic at hand. James says that he approaches his subject as a psychologist and rejects any appeal to authority or tradition. But much of both treatises is occupied with what we might call philosophy of mind. Both authors reflect carefully and subtly on perception, moral appraisal, and varied components of the religious life. The sophistication in *Religious Affections* to which I want to call attention is in this reflection and analysis.

Both authors examine the moral life and the revelatory quality of religious experience. James inquires whether religious practice, or the life of the saint, contributes to or detracts from human flourishing. But the noetic quality of religious experience, its claim to truth or insight, rests for him on a sense that is analogous to our other senses. He considers this noetic component and assesses its epistemic value in the chapter on mysticism. As a sense analogous to the five senses, it cannot be impugned. Its deliverances are on as firm a foundation as our other knowledge. But, as is the case with those other senses, its results must be tested against our prior beliefs. If I seem to see something that I believe to be impossible or untrue, I may doubt the evidence of my own senses. Further inquiry will be required to resolve the matter.

Edwards takes quite a different tack. He does attribute to the saint a new sensation and perception that is wholly unlike anything available to natural men or women. "And if there be in the soul a new sort of exercises which it is conscious of, . . . then it follows that the mind has an entirely new kind of perception or sensation; . . . and something is perceived by a true saint, in the exercise of this new sense of mind, in spiritual and divine things, as entirely diverse from anything that is perceived in them, by natural men, as the sweet taste of honey is diverse from the ideas men get of honey by only looking on it, and feeling of it" (205-6). But this new sense serves no epistemic function. Religious affections comprise both love and joy, and it is love that is the source of both perception and practice. In order to distinguish genuine love from spurious, Edwards attends not to sense or perception but to practice. *Religious Affections* is a treatise about love and the assessment of loves. With talk of love, we are in the domain of the moral life, of will and inclination. The affections are "the more vigorous and sensible exercises of the inclination and will of the soul" (96). By locating religious affections in this domain, Edwards can avail himself of the complex and subtle language of character and moral assessment.

TESTING THE SPIRITS

Edwards opens *Religious Affections* with reference to the trials of the faith of the early Christians. Spirits are tested by trials, as gold is tried by fire. But spiritual trials not only reveal; they also purify and enhance. "True virtue never appears so lovely, as when it is most oppressed: and the divine excellency of real Christianity, is never exhibited with such advantage, as when under the greatest trials . . ." (93). Conditions of oppression and hardship enable us to distinguish those who give lip service to the gospel from those whose virtues or faith can stand the test. Later he draws a parallel with testing in science. "As that is called experimental philosophy, which brings opinions and notions to the test of fact; so is that properly called experimental religion, which brings religious affections and intentions, to the like test" (452).

Edwards's publications on the revival show a development from the relatively uncritical enthusiasm exhibited in *Faithful Narrative* (1737), with its citation of numerical evidence ("more than 300 souls") and naive descriptions of dramatic changes in behavior, to their culmination in the substantial and critical treatise *Religious Affections* (1746). *Distinguishing Marks* (1741) is a proposal for testing the spirits, and *Some Thoughts* (1742) a reflection on the multiple causes of a single effect and a redirection of attention toward spiritual growth.[6]

Even in *Faithful Narrative,* Edwards acknowledges some skepticism about the conversions he reports. He assures the reader that the people of Northampton and the surrounding county are free "from error and variety of sects and opinions" that might lead to enthusiasm, and that the revival appears to be not subjective experience alone "but the influence of God's Spirit with their experience, that attains the effect. . . ."[7] In *Distinguishing Marks,* Edwards takes as his text the New Testament injunction to test the spirits and offers five marks, of which the fifth is the most eminent: it operates as a spirit of love, not self-love but true benevolence.[8] This is the only mark the devil cannot counterfeit. The next year, in *Some Thoughts,* Edwards notes that a revival ought not to be dismissed because of its excesses or of the role of psychological and social causes in bringing it about. An effect may differ in kind from the occasional causes that contributed to its occurrence. He also includes a case study that is more extensive than those in *Faithful Narrative,* focusing now not on external behavior but on an inner life of moral and spiritual growth.[9]

In the preface to *Religious Affections,* Edwards states that this treatise differs from its predecessors in that he was formerly concerned "to show the distinguishing marks of a work of the Spirit of God, including both its common, and saving operations; but what I aim at now, is to show the

nature and signs of the gracious operations of God's Spirit, by which they are to be distinguished from all things whatsoever that the minds of men are the subjects of, which are not of a saving nature" (89). True virtue, love of God, and holy affections are consequent upon the gracious operations of the Spirit.

The first part of *Religious Affections* is prefaced with a text from 1 Peter, set by Edwards in the context of the trials of the early Christians, and characterizing true religion as love and joy: "Whom having not seen, ye love: in whom, though now ye see him not, yet believing, ye rejoice with joy unspeakable, and full of glory" (1 Peter 1:8, 93). Love and joy, but especially love, are the objects of Edwards's scrutiny. His problem is that of how to distinguish genuine spiritual love and joy, which have God for their object, from natural affections that might appear to be indiscernible from them, but upon analysis reduce to love of self and joy in one's experiences for their own sake.

UNDERSTANDING AND WILL

The soul, Edwards writes, has been endowed by God with two faculties, the understanding, by which it discerns and judges, and the will, by which it is inclined or disinclined. Affections are "the more vigorous and sensible exercises of the inclination and will" (96). By employing this distinction between the two faculties, Edwards makes available for his analysis the language of belief and desire. Affections are a form of desire, or love. Love is not independent of belief. Love that is premised upon false beliefs about the lover, that does not perceive her as she really is, is inferior love. But love and desire are not reducible to belief.

This language of belief and desire structures our interpretations of other persons, our attempts to understand them, attributions of character traits, and moral appraisal. From my observation of someone's behavior in a variety of situations, I attribute to him a set of beliefs and desires. If a person moves a dial on a thermostat, I understand what she is doing by attributing to her a desire for more heat and a belief that this action will bring that about. When Edwards constructs a sermon around a powerful image, I attribute to him the desire to move his congregation and a belief that this rhetorical device will contribute to that end. This attribution of beliefs and desire by inference from behavior and context is at the heart of our understanding and appraisal of the actions of others and, as Edwards makes clear, of ourselves as well.

The practice of moral appraisal includes resources for testing the spirits. Patterns and continuities in beliefs and desires are marked by ascribing traits of character. Character, whether virtuous or vicious, shows itself in a person's actions and attitudes. Someone may appear courageous, but a particular situation reveals him to be timid and cowardly. Kindness, humility, selfishness, and hypocrisy are all traits that are ascribed on the basis of observation of behavior and responses on different occasions, and especially under trying conditions. "Reason shows that men's deeds are better and more faithful interpreters of their minds, than their words. The common sense of all mankind, through all ages and nations, teaches 'em to judge of men's hearts chiefly by their practice . . ." (409-10). Edwards proposes to put religious affections to such a test.

Love is the chief of the affections, the fountain of all other affections. Edwards finds it evident from Scripture "that the essence of all true religion lies in holy love; and that in this divine affection, and an habitual disposition to it, and that light which is the foundation of it, and those things which are the fruit of it, consists the whole of religion" (107). In *Distinguishing Marks,* Edwards had said that love was the most eminent mark of the work of the spirit of God. Here, where the subject is restricted to gracious affections, love is no longer a mark of true religion, but is identical with it. The task, then, is to distinguish between genuine love and spurious, between love of God and self-love, between true virtue and counterfeit. It is the task of moral appraisal, and it is a task for which the language of understanding and will, or belief and desire, is well suited.

Symptoms and Criteria

The bulk of *Religious Affections* is devoted to commentary on twelve uncertain and twelve certain signs, those that are insufficient to identify gracious affections and those that are sufficient. In fact, Edwards uses the term "sign" very sparingly in his commentary on the sufficient characteristics.[10] There are no distinguishing marks of gracious affections if we mean by that something that can be empirically observed and that will clearly distinguish those affections that are genuine from those that are not. What are the marks of love? How do I know whether John loves Sarah, or even whether I am really in love? There is no decisive empirical evidence. Behavior that seems to express concern for the other and delight in her successes may or may not be an expression of genuine love. We must look at patterns of behavior, at responses to the presence and absence of the loved one, with particular attention to actions not governed by convention or determined by external circumstances. Even this evidence is not infallible.

The two sets of signs Edwards offers differ in kind, as symptoms differ from criteria.[11] The uncertain signs are symptoms. They can be observed empirically, but are insufficient to identify genuine religion. The certain signs are sufficient, but it is not possible to determine with certainty whether or not they obtain. Their identifying descriptions incorporate criteria that guarantee their success.[12] For example, an appearance of love is one of the insufficient signs, but a genuine loving disposition is sufficient.

Insufficient signs, which Edwards calls no certain signs, include intensity of affections, great bodily effects, fervent talk of religion, involuntary behavior, conformity to a cer-

tain pattern, attractiveness to the saints, and devotion to the external duties of religion. These are phenomena Edwards cited with enthusiasm in *Faithful Narrative* and include many that had been used in the Puritan tradition. A morphology of conversion had been employed, for instance, and testimonies and behavior of candidates were compared with that pattern to ensure that each component was included, and in the proper order.[13]

Edwards states his criterion for genuine religious affections in the first sufficient sign, and it is a causal one. "Affections that are truly spiritual and gracious, do arise from those influences and operations on the heart, which are spiritual, supernatural and divine" (197). If it holds, the affections are genuine. The Spirit of God "communicates himself in his own proper nature" to the saints, and "dwells in their souls" (200). But how are we to determine whether affections, my own or another's, arise from influences that are spiritual, supernatural and divine? This contrasts with the insufficient signs or symptoms, which are detectable by the observer.

The New Sense

Edwards introduces the new sense and the new simple idea in his commentary on the first sign, in which true religious affections are said to arise from spiritual, divine, and supernatural operations. He uses them chiefly to make the point that this is "an entirely new kind of perception or sensation" that differs completely from the deliverances of the natural senses (205). Like the taste of honey to one who has only seen honey, it is inaccessible to someone without the Spirit. The saint's idea of and delight in the loveliness of God "is peculiar and entirely diverse from anything that a natural man has, or can have any notion of" (208). It is qualitatively, not merely quantitatively, unlike anything that could result from natural causes or from common grace.

But the new sense does not play any role whatsoever in Edwards's inquiry into what distinguishes true religion from false. The saint does come to know divine things in a new way through this sense, but it is of no help for determining whether or not someone is a saint. How can this be? Edwards's chief reason is theological. Though the certain signs are infallible, no living saint can know his or her status with certainty, because of a twofold defect due to sin: a defect in the object, because grace may be feeble and mixed with corruption, and a defect in the eye, because these same factors cloud and distort perception (194-95).

As in other instances, though, Edwards's theological argument is supplemented by a consideration of the ways in which we do resolve doubts about such matters. Consider the epistemic status of sense impressions. Were a person who had never tasted honey to have a striking new taste of what she took to be honey, how would she know that this was genuine honey? She would know only by its provenance, and by criteria outside the initial tasting. Even more, a person captivated by what she takes to be a new sense of God's glory has no way of knowing whether this is the genuine work of the Spirit, or the result of natural causes. Persons with raised affections may sincerely report a new sense of the excellency of divine things, but this sense may be spurious, derived from self-love (252). Sincere first-person reports are not necessarily reliable.

The second sign addresses this point. "The first objective ground of gracious affections, is the transcendently excellent and amiable nature of divine things, as they are in themselves . . ." (240). The objective ground of a taste of honey must be authentic honey. A sense or taste of the divine must be objectively grounded in the divine nature, not in the illusions of self-love. The third sign is similar, but more specific. "Those affections that are truly holy, are primarily founded on the loveliness of the moral excellency of divine things" (253). Love is the chief and source of genuine religious affections, and the proper object of love is not natural beauty, but moral beauty, the beauty of moral agents, of beings with mind and will. That beauty is holiness.[14]

The fourth and fifth signs follow suit. "Gracious affections do arise from the mind's being enlightened, rightly and spiritually to understand or apprehend divine things" (266). "Truly gracious affections are attended with a reasonable and spiritual conviction of the judgment, of the reality and certainty of divine things" (291). This is like saying that true sentences must be grounded in reality rather than illusion, must derive from correct apprehension and must grasp the real with certainty. If the mind apprehends divine things, as opposed to misapprehending them, it has succeeded in grasping those things. But these considerations are of no help in deciding which sentences are true, or which claims to have apprehended divine things are valid.

CHARACTER AND VIRTUE

For signs 6-11, Edwards shifts into a new key. He identifies particular virtues as evidence of genuine religious affections. The Spirit of God dwells in the true saints, providing a new foundation for the exercise of the faculties of understanding and will, thus giving rise to a new sense and a new disposition (206). As we have seen, this new sense is of no help in testing the spirits, but we can look for evidence of the new loving disposition. Again there is no definitive mark. A person may appear to be humble, kind, or loving, while actually being motivated by self-love. But in ordinary moral inquiry, we are constantly called upon to make such judgments of character, and we make them by observing behavior over time and gradually coming to understand the particular structure of beliefs and desires that constitute that person.

The virtues and moral characteristics Edwards lists include humility, a loving spirit, a soft heart, beautiful and symmetrical affections, heightened spiritual appetite, and an abiding change of nature. In each case an adjective is included to assure that the virtue is genuine. For instance, gracious affections are attended with evangelical, as distinct from legal, humiliation. A change of nature is abiding rather than transient.

These are all thick terms of moral appraisal. While we can never be sure that our judgments applying them are correct, we make them all the time. We make them on the basis of our observation of moral practice. We attribute beliefs and desires to others on the basis of what they say and do, correcting for what we take to be disingenuous or self-deceptive and for exigencies of circumstance and constraints of convention. The moral distinctions available to us are subtle, and we are attentive to signs of illusion or self-deception. Edwards is able to bring all of this to bear on his analysis of religious affections.

Genuine religious affections are founded on love of God, and their false counterparts are founded on self-love. Much enthusiastic religion is the product of self-love. Hypocrites who are taken with the beauty of their own experiences engage in a kind of idolatry in which those experiences are loved for their own sakes (251). This provides Edwards with ample opportunity to call attention to self-deception. Liberation from love based on illusion comes from increased self-knowledge, from critically examining the illusions. Moral self-scrutiny exposes hypocrites. If they could see into their own hearts "it would knock their affections on the head; because their affections are built upon self, therefore self-knowledge would destroy them" (253).

The faith of the saints, on the other hand, is not only revealed but enhanced by increasing self-knowledge. In his discussion of humility, Edwards calls for relentless and recursive self-examination: "Let not the reader lightly pass over these things in application to himself. If you once have taken it in, that it is a bad sign for a person to be apt to think himself a better saint than others, there will arise a blinding prejudice in your own favor; and there will probably be need of a great strictness of self-examination, in order to determine whether it be so with you. If on the proposal of the question, you answer, 'No, it seems to me, none are so bad as I.' Don't let the matter pass off so; but examine again, whether or no you don't think yourself better than others on this very account, because you imagine you think so meanly of yourself. Haven't you a high opinion of this humility? And if you answer again, 'No; I have not a high opinion of my humility; it seems to me I am as proud as the devil'; yet examine again, whether self-conceit don't rise up under this cover; whether on this very account, that you think yourself as proud as the devil, you don't think yourself to be very humble" (336).

Moral self-scrutiny, proceeding from skepticism and doubt about the state of one's soul, is not only something that the faith of the saint can survive, but is essential to that faith, as it is to the examined moral life more generally.

PRACTICE

The criterion for gracious affections, as given in the first sign, is that they arise from spiritual, supernatural, and divine influences on the heart. We have seen that this condition is incorporated into the identifying description of each of the first eleven signs. The affections must be grounded on objective reality, proceed from a right apprehension, and must issue in true humility and a genuinely loving nature. But how can a person know whether or not these criteria are fulfilled? What evidence will enable him to distinguish apparent love from a loving nature? How does he test the genuineness of trust, humility, fear of God, gratitude, and an abiding change in nature? By attending to behavior, or practice.

When we say of someone that he or she is humble, selfish, courageous, or has undergone a change in character, the evidence we employ is practice. We observe how the person acts and responds over time and under a variety of conditions. This is the point of Edwards's twelfth sign: "Gracious and holy affections have their exercise and fruit in Christian practice" (383). While attributions of virtues and other traits of character are always under-determined by the evidence, this is the only evidence we have, and it is generally reliable. He recapitulates each of the first eleven signs, showing that they all culminate in Christian practice (392-97).

In all other matters, Edwards writes, we judge a person's heart chiefly by her practice, and we should do the same here (410). Words are not excluded; they are also a form of practice. But the mind is better known by deeds than by words. Voluntary actions, where a person was free to choose among alternatives, are more revealing than actions determined by external circumstances (426). Compliance with prescribed form is not sufficient; the person must understand what she is doing (416-17). Behavior under trying circumstances is particularly revealing (434). This is the proper evidence by which to make judgments of character and attributions of virtue. It is not merely a concession to our ignorance. God will employ this kind of evidence on the Day of Judgment (441).

Edwards goes further, and sees that the situation is not radically different in the first person case. Practice is the only evidence I have not only for judging others, but also for myself. It is "the chief of all the signs of grace, both as an evidence of the sincerity of professors unto others, and also to their own consciences" (406). It is, he says, "much to be preferred to the method of first convictions, enlightenings and comforts in conversion, or any immanent discoveries of grace whatsoever, that begin and end in contemplation" (426).

Am I really in love? I reflect on my behavior and my response to the presence or absence of the object of my affections. Am I humble or proud, selfish or considerate? In my own case, I have data not available to others. I can attend to private thoughts and associations, and to feelings and reactions that may be imperceptible to another. Edwards refers to these as acts and practices of the soul (422). To this extent, I am better placed to judge than others are. But self-interest may cloud my vision and influence my conclusions. A person is often not the best judge of whether he is jealous, angry, courteous, or kind. Reliable ascription of such traits requires a certain disinterestedness that one is seldom able to attain in his own case, and attention to patterns of behavior and their persistence over time. I may be the last to see that my behavior issues from self-love rather than from genuine regard for the other or from love for God.

Moral appraisal is no different, in principle, in the first-person and third-person cases. It requires an inference from practice to the attribution of particular virtues, vices, or other traits of character. Such inferences are always corrigible; they are underdetermined by the evidence. That, and the distorting effects of sin or self-love, lead Edwards to preface his commentary on the sufficient signs with the disclaimer that he cannot provide signs that will enable anyone with certainty to distinguish true affections from false in others, or for saints who are low in grace or hypocrites to judge accurately in their own cases (195-97). The signs are sufficient, but there is no algorithm for their application.

PROFESSION

In 1750 Edwards was dismissed from his church in Northampton as the result of controversy following his proposal to restrict church membership and communion to "such as are in profession, and in the eye of the church's Christian judgment, godly or gracious persons."[15] In *An Humble Inquiry,* published in 1749, he criticized the "halfway covenant" and Stoddardeanism, calling for "credible profession" and "a visibility to the eye of a Christian judgment" as qualifications for communion.[16] The emphasis here on profession might seem to differ from the position taken in *Religious Affections.*

In fact, Edwards's stand in the communion controversy does not conflict with, and is informed by, the argument in *Religious Affections.* He calls for profession of belief and visible evidence that it is grounded in the proper foundation, but he knows that there can be no certainty on this score. Edwards is suspicious of traditional narratives of spiritual experience. He criticizes those who attend to inessential articles "such as impressions on the imagination, instead of renewing influences on the heart; pangs of affection, instead of the habitual temper of the mind; a certain method and order of impressions and suggestions, instead of the nature of things experienced, etc."[17] Sincere profession and visible indications of character are far more reliable than these impressions.

Edwards does not say that only true saints, with genuine religious affections, can be admitted to membership in the church and to the sacrament of the Lord's Supper. "The question is not, whether Christ has made converting grace or piety *itself* the condition or rule of his people's admitting any to the privileges of members in full communion with them: there is no one qualification of mind, whatsoever, that Christ has properly made the term of this; not so much as a common belief that Jesus is the Messiah, or a belief in the being of a God. 'tis the credible *profession* and *visibility* of these things, that is the church's rule in this case."[18]

Neither the minister, other members of the church, nor the person herself can know with certainty who is a true saint. Edwards is concerned that prospective members have made lax and insincere professions of belief in order to gain membership in the church and to insure that their children will be baptized. He wants credible professions and visible evidence, but he knows that error can never be precluded. Edwards's insistence on sincere profession does not privilege the first-person perspective, but warns both professors and observers to attend to evidence regarding the fit or lack of it between statement and character.

COMPARISON WITH JAMES

James also examines both the perceptual component and the fruits of religious experience, what he calls the sense of immediate luminousness and the moral life of the saint. Unlike Edwards, however, he examines and evaluates each independently of one another. He cites *Religious Affections* in support of his claim that religious experience should be evaluated only by its fruits, not by its roots or causes.[19] James does not understand that Edwards turns to consequences as the only way we have of assessing whether or not affections arise from operations that are spiritual, supernatural, and divine.[20] In contrast, he wants to evaluate the consequences for their own sake, in order to discern whether they are beneficial or detrimental to human welfare. James proposes, then, to assess religious experience by attending to three components: the immediate feeling of luminousness, the moral helpfulness of the experience, and its philosophical reasonableness.[21] He does not explore the possibility of any internal relation between these, but considers each in turn.

After sketching a composite picture of saintliness ("the collective name for the ripe fruits of religion"), James examines what he takes to be its practical consequences: asceticism, strength of soul, purity, and charity.[22] In each case, he asks whether this ideal or character trait is conducive or detrimental to human flourishing. While deploring the ways in which asceticism and purity, for instance, can degenerate into paltry ideals when taken to extremes, his considered judgment is that, on the whole, "the saintly group of qualities is indispensable to the world's welfare."[23] The evaluation is frankly utilitarian, and benefits are assessed from the perspective of turn-of-the-century liberal values.[24] James does not consider self-deception, complexities of the moral will, or other perspectives on the inner moral life.

In the following chapter, under the heading "Mysticism," James focuses on the noetic quality in religious experience, the sense of intuition or insight into a higher truth. After another attempt at a composite sketch or core description, he asks how we should assess the validity of claims to such insight, and he answers in terms of the analogy with ordinary sense perception. Our "rational" beliefs are based on the same kind of evidence, he says, so we have no right to dismiss these claims out of hand. They are unassailable from without, though the most they can do for those of us who do not share the experiences is to establish a presumption. But they must be sifted and tested in the context of our other beliefs, just like the deliverances of the senses.[25] Their provenance alone should not be used either to dismiss them or to endow them with special authority.

These descriptions and evaluations of saintliness and the noetic sense in religious experience are completely independent of one another. From James's analysis, there is no reason to think that mystical intuition or insight might not equally well accompany distinctly unsaintly qualities, which are inimical to the world's welfare. In part, this is a consequence of James's methodological decision to keep completely separate the description and explanation of religious experience, on the one hand, and the evaluation of that experience on the other.[26] In part, it is a consequence of the attention to sense or perception on one hand, and benefits and deficits on the other, without any exploration of how they might be internally or grammatically related to one another.

The result is a sharp separation between explanation and evaluation, and another between the third-person perspective, from which James evaluates the moral qualities of the saint, and the first-person perspective, from which he evaluates the religious sense. As a consequence, he cannot portray moral and spiritual inquiry with the accuracy that Edwards achieves. In particular, he is not able to explore subtle forms of self-deception or the reflexive character of moral self-examination. Edwards makes the concept of love central and carefully considers the ways in which love is related to its object and its manifestations. In this way, he ensures that the internal relations between perception and action will be addressed.

By attending to the practice of moral inquiry and to the ways in which we attribute character traits to ourselves and to others, Edwards has brought a sophistication to the description and evaluation of religious experience that is lacking in much contemporary literature. The complexity of his analysis of self-knowledge, his exploration of subtle forms of self-deception and of the vagaries of the moral will, and his nuanced descriptions of the virtues of the saint are more akin to the thought of Augustine, Calvin, and Kierkegaard than they are to that of *Varieties.*

This difference is in part due to the fact that Edwards is a theologian and James a philosopher. But Edwards's descriptions of, and critical reflection upon, diverse practices of moral appraisal and self-examination are striking even apart from the theology in which they are embedded, and capture a dimension of religious experience that is missing from James's account.

Modern epistemology since Descartes has been hampered by overreliance on introspection and the first-person perspective. Edwards was right to see that the ways in which we come to know ourselves are not so different from the ways in which we come to know others. By shifting the focus of inquiry from scrutiny of first-person accounts of a new sense or perception of the divine that is not accessible for comparison or criticism to the practice of appraising character and identifying virtues, Edwards has provided a model for the proper study of religious experience.

Notes

1. See, for example, William Alston, *Perceiving God* (Ithaca, 1991).

2. William James, *The Varieties of Religious Experience,* in *The Works of William James* (Cambridge, 1985).

3. James used the Ellerby edition, which was popular in the nineteenth century: Jonathan Edwards, *A Treatise on Religious Affections,* abridged by W. Ellerby (New York, n.d.). See James, *Varieties,* p. 433. This edition is highly abridged, and lacks the philosophical and literary sophistication of the original text.

4. *The Works of Jonathan Edwards, 2, Religious Affections,* ed. John E. Smith (New Haven, 1959), p. 205. Parenthetical references in the text are to this volume.

5. For a good sketch of the polemical context of *Religious Affections,* along with attention to the theological dimension of the issues dealt with here, see Ava Chamberlain, "Self-Deception as a Theological Problem in Jonathan Edwards's *Treatise concerning Religious Affections,*" *Church History* 63 (1994): 541-56.

6. Edwards writes from within a tradition of Puritan and Reformed piety, with its attention to the need for constant introspection and to its fallibility. See Charles Hambrick-Stowe, *The Practice of Piety* (Chapel Hill, 1982), and Charles Cohen, *God's Caress* (New York, 1986).

7. *The Works of Jonathan Edwards, 4, The Great Awakening,* ed. C. C. Goen (New Haven, 1972), p. 144. Isaac Watts and John Guyse, editors of the first edition (London, 1737), assure readers that the sermons that occasioned the revival were "common plain Protestant doctrine of the Reformation," and that the revival was not a response to an earthquake or some other calamity; ibid., pp. 130-37. They also question the significance and appropriateness of Edwards's two case studies.

8. Ibid., pp. 255-59.

9. The case is that of his wife, Sarah Edwards, edited to serve his purposes. Ibid., pp. 331-42. For a discussion of the differences between Sarah's narrative and Jonathan's selective paraphrase of it, and a setting of her narrative in historical and social context, see Julie Elison, "The Sociology of 'Holy Indifference': Sarah Edwards' Narrative," *American Literature* 56 (1984): 479-95.

10. Edwards uses the term "sign" only in the introduction to Part III and in his commentary on the twelfth "sign."

11. For discussion of this distinction, see my "From Theology to a Science of Religion: Jonathan Edwards and William James on Religious Affections," *Harvard Theological Review* 82 (1989): 149-68.

12. The formulations of these signs contain what Gilbert Ryle called "achievement words." See Ryle, *The Concept of Mind* (London, 1949), pp. 149-53.

13. For a discussion of this morphology, see Edmund Morgan, *Visible Saints* (New Haven, 1963), pp. 66-73.

14. "The moral excellency of an intelligent being, when it is true and real, and not only external, or merely seeming and counterfeit, is holiness. Therefore holiness comprehends all the true moral excellency of intelligent beings: there is no other true virtue, but real holiness. Holiness comprehends all the true virtue of a good man . . ." (255).

15. *The Works of Jonathan Edwards, 12, Ecclesiastical Writings,* ed. David D. Hall (New Haven, 1994), p. 174. For a good discussion of the communion controversy and its context, see Hall's introduction, pp. 1-90.

16. Ibid., pp. 176-77.

17. Ibid., p. 310.

18. Ibid., p. 176.

19. James, *Varieties,* p. 25.

20. For a criticism of James's reading of Edwards, see my *Religious Experience,* pp. 166-67.

21. James, *Varieties,* p. 23.

22. Ibid., p. 221.

23. Ibid., p. 299.

24. Ibid., pp. 263-66.

25. Ibid., p. 338.

26. Ibid., p. 13. For a criticism of this separation, see my discussion of James in *Religious Experience,* pp. 156-79.

Ava Chamberlain (essay date 1997)

SOURCE: "The Grand Sower of the Seed: Jonathan Edwards's Critique of George Whitefield," *The New England Quarterly,* Vol. LXX, No. 3, September 1997, pp. 368-85.

[In the following essay, Chamberlain examines a series of sermons Edwards delivered in 1740 and suggests that they offer evidence that, despite his public commendation of his colleague, Edwards harbored a degree of professional jealousy toward evangelist George Whitefield, whose success at inspiring conversion among the Northampton church members rivaled that of Edwards himself.]

In anticipation of George Whitefield's upcoming tour of New England, on 12 February 1740 Jonathan Edwards wrote to offer his Northampton pulpit to the British evangelist. Whitefield must have received the invitation gladly, for the previous month he had declared in his *Journals* that Northampton was the only place in America, besides Pennsylvania, where "the work of conversion has . . . been carried on with so much power."[1] He arrived in the town on 17 October 1740, and during his four-day visit he preached four times in Edwards's meetinghouse, each time evoking a powerful, emotional response. Edwards's wife Sarah commented, "It is wonderful to see what a spell he casts over an audience. . . . I have seen upwards of a thousand people hang on his words with breathless silence, broken only by an occasional half-suppressed sob."[2] "Immediately after" Whitefield's visit, Jonathan Edwards noted, "the minds of the people in general appeared more engaged in religion, shewing a greater forwardness to make religion the subject of their conversation . . . and to embrace all opportunities to hear the Word preached."[3] In time, vigorously defending both man and movement, Edwards would credit the Grand Itinerant with a major role in the Northampton revival of 1740-42.

The very magnitude of Whitefield's triumph in Northampton has prompted some scholars to speculate that Edwards, despite his unwavering public commendation of Whitefield, privately resented his colleague.[4] Whitefield did succeed where Edwards apparently had failed. He moved Edwards's "sermon-proof" congregation to tears and precipitated in four days the revival that Edwards had been attempting to generate for five years. For a young and newly ordained minister so easily to upstage the internationally known author of *A Faithful Narrative* must have provoked in Edwards some feelings of wounded pride. But little evidence has been provided to support the interpretation.

There are indications of some minor discord between Edwards and Whitefield in the records of the pamphlet war Edwards conducted with Thomas Clap, rector of Yale College, in 1745.[5] In the course of the debate, Edwards disclosed a few details from conversations he had had with Whitefield during his visit to Northampton. Edwards "once purposely took an opportunity to talk with Mr. Whitefield alone about impulses" and "once talked with Mr. Whitefield (though not alone) about judging other persons to be unconverted," but Whitefield was neither inclined to debate these points with Edwards nor to change his views. At the time, Edwards did not publicize this personal slight. Not until five years later, in 1745—when it was quite commonplace, even expected, for moderate New Lights to

admit that certain "errors" had been committed in the early days of the Awakening—did he refer to the incident and remark that he "thought Mr. Whitefield liked me not so well, for my opposing these things: and though he treated me with great kindness, yet he never made so much of an intimate of me, as of some others."[6] Furthermore, in *Distinguishing Marks* Edwards admonished ministers "not to oppose [the revival], or say anything against it, or anything that has so much as an indirect tendency to bring it into discredit."[7] Even if he privately resented Whitefield's success or had theological disagreements with his means of achieving it, Edwards seemed firmly committed to a public display of "party unity."

Still, no one seems to have examined another important record of Edwards's views. In direct communication with those he cared most to reach, his congregation, Edwards must certainly have sought to convey his private thoughts in public form. Indeed, I believe such a record of his attitudes about Whitefield and the revival he spawned exists within Edwards's extant manuscript corpus in a sermon series he preached immediately after Whitefield's departure from Northampton. Treating the parable of the sower (Matt. 13:3-8), a traditional Puritan vehicle for discussing the work of the evangelist, the series contains nine distinct preaching units, all of which were delivered in November 1740.

. . . . .

Edwards derives the organization of the sermon series from the narrative structure of the parable itself. Beginning with Matt. 13:3, he considers each verse of the parable in scriptural order.[8] In the first sermon, which introduces the series as a whole, he draws from the text the observation that "those that God sends forth to preach the gospel may fitly be compared to husbandmen going forth to sow their seed." The "husbandman" uppermost in the minds of the people of Northampton was clearly Whitefield, and Edwards moves quickly to identify with him. He notes that both the minister who "comes to a people . . . as their settled pastor" and the itinerant who "is providentially sent among them" perform essentially the same work.[9] Indeed, throughout the series the figure represented by the husbandman in the parable slips back and forth between Whitefield and Edwards, with Whitefield predominating in its first several sermons and Edwards in its concluding units.

Edwards goes on to insist that the true husbandman, the sovereign lord of the harvest, is neither Whitefield nor himself but Christ. Christ owns the field and controls all the conditions—such as sun, rain, and soil—that affect the seed's ability to bear fruit. It is to Christ, Edwards declares, in again drawing attention away from Whitefield, "that a people should look when they have heard the word preached, especially after they have heard it powerfully preached, after God has sent a messenger with extraordinary fervency to deliver his message to them" (bk. 1, leaf 8).

But no matter how strenuously Edwards pushed Whitefield into the background, it was undeniable that the evangelist had profoundly moved the people of Northampton, and Edwards understood that he was expected to finish what Whitefield had begun. When Edwards first introduced his sower series, it was not at all certain that a revival would indeed take place. According to Edwards's later, 1743 account, not until "a month or six weeks" after Whitefield's visit was there "a great alteration in the town, both as to the revivals of professors, and awakenings of others."[10] Although Whitefield's success in the pulpit may have humiliated Edwards, had he failed to awaken Northampton thereafter, he would have suffered a public humiliation of much greater proportions.[11] Therefore, Edwards concludes his introductory sermon with an exhortation not to let "the seed that has now been sown, be rejected from our hearts as from frozen ground" (bk. 1, leaf 12).

The conflict between his desire for a revival in Northampton and his personal resentment of Whitefield's effect on the town is even more palpable in another sermon Edwards preached during or shortly after Whitefield's visit. Delivered to a "private meeting," probably one of the evening gatherings occasionally convened at his home, the brief address treats II Cor. 2:15-16.[12] Edwards invokes the example of the apostle Paul, "the most eminent minister of the gospel." Despite his eminence, however, Paul's "success was not alike in all places [or] amongst all sorts of people"; in fact, his "success [was] least [in places] where [there] had been great advantage long enjoyed." By implication, Whitefield, the most eminent contemporary evangelist, may also fail to awaken Northampton. Edwards carefully positions himself for that eventuality by maintaining that "the work that we do in preaching the gospel, whether it be effectual or no, is acceptable to God." Still, he also understood that his reputation would be enhanced if a revival were forthcoming, and so, in the sermon's application, he urges his listeners to make "a good improvement of the late labour of that servant of God, whom God has sent to us from afar."[13]

Edwards knew, too, that his own prestige would gain most if the results at Northampton exceeded those elsewhere. Noting "how remarkeably [Whitefield] has been blessed and succeeded in other places," Edwards challenged his auditors: "God expects a better reception and improvement of his means from us than others," he argued, "for we have received much more than others." "God and men," he emphasized, "expect more. His servant may well expect more. God's people abroad may well expect more."[14] Having himself felt challenged by Whitefield, Edwards was no doubt relieved to be able to report, scarcely two months after Whitefield's visit, that religion "has been gradually reviving and prevailing more and more, ever since you was here." Taking the next step in the dance of egos, Whitefield published the report in his own vehicle for self-promotion, the *Weekly History.*[15]

Edwards's exposition of the parable follows traditional patterns of interpretation insofar as he assumes that the various grounds in which the seed attempts to grow represent different means of receiving the Word. Within those confines, however, he is quite pointed about present concerns. The wayside hearers (Matt. 13:4) have hearts so hard that the Word cannot take root. In the previous sermon, Edwards had asserted that there "never was so dark a time in Northampton [as the present] since I dwelt in it" (bk. 1, leaves 10-11). The cause, he now explains, is that too many people attend church "only out of custom." Through repeated exposure to the gospel, their "hearts are like a path that is become hard by being often trodden." Despite their apparent adherence to the Christian faith, their hearts are "immensely harder than the hearts of idolaters, harlots, whoremongers, murderers, and sodomites." Indeed, Edwards declaims, he "had rather go into Sodom and preach to the men of Sodom, than preach to you," for in Sodom he would "have a great deal more hopes of success" than among the respectable, loyal, but unregenerate members of his Northampton church (bk. 2, leaves 2, 3, 11-12).

Were it not for God's assurance that He "can make the word pierce your hearts," Edwards would not "now think it worth my while to preach to you, or say anything more to you." Whitefield seemed not to have so completely despaired of this group of intractable sinners, and some among them had apparently responded to his preaching. Edwards, however, rushes to dispel such misunderstandings. In a clear reference to Whitefield's recent performance, he concedes that wayside hearers "are drawn to take some notice of what the minister says, either by the unusualness of the subject, or the unusual manner of treating it, or the loudness of his voice, or his extraordinary earnestness." But they attend to the preaching of the word only "as something new and strange and entertaining to a curious mind." Affections aroused by such superficial means, though, Edwards warns, ultimately produce not genuine convictions of conscience but greater hardness of heart (bk. 2, leaves 12, 8).

Having summarily dismissed, and insulted, the hard-hearted, in the final sermon of the series (Matt. 13:7), Edwards turns to another group of church members with whom he had a long, frustrating history: persons "so under the power of a carnal worldly spirit" that their hearts are "as ground that has never been plowed, and so is overgrown with thorns." Unlike the wayside hearers, these thorny-ground hearers "may seem to shew a considerable regard to the word preached for a while," but if God does not use the "plow of his law," the thorns will "at length prevail and choke the word, that it never brings forth any saving fruit" (bk. 6, leaves 1, 7-8).

By the end of November, when this sermon was preached, the longed-for revival was beginning to manifest itself in the town. Edwards's time frame accordingly expands to encompass not simply Whitefield's recent visit but the 1734-35 revival and its disappointing aftermath. When he says of the thorny-ground hearers that "you have heard a great deal to awaken you, and make you sensible of the miserable condition you are in, and the necessity you are in of an interest in Christ," the reference is ambiguous; images of either Whitefield or Edwards could have arisen in the congregants' minds. When Edwards states that they have "been preached to a long time; the sower has often sown the seed in the ground, but there never has been any fruit of it," however, he clearly intends that the membership reflect on his own, long-standing efforts (bk. 6, leaf 15).

Those Edwards labels thorny-ground hearers are persons who had pledged themselves to Christ in the earlier revival but had subsequently strayed. "When the extraordinary work of God that was here six years ago was a new thing," he notes, "you was affected. To hear the news of others' conversion moved you, and while all the conversation seemed to be about such things you continued under concerns." But, he reminds his congregation, "as worldly things became more the subject of conversation, your religious concern began to die away . . . till you had wholly lost your convictions." This previous experience prompts Edwards to question the staying power of the affections Whitefield had only recently generated among the same congregation. Those who "are now under some convictions and have lately begun to seek their salvation," he concludes, are again likely to lose their convictions as the revival fades. And even if those convictions are sustained, they are not likely to result in genuine conversion. "You may go on," Edwards mocks, "and seek salvation as you have done to the age of Methuselah, if you should live so long, and be never the nearer; but on the contrary, your heart all the while [will] grow harder and harder, and your case more and more deplorable" (bk. 6, leaves 11, 20, 14).

. . . . .

By using the experiences of a previous revival to discredit Whitefield's intense, but far from prolonged, effect on his congregation, Edwards clearly indicates that any revival to occur in Northampton will be on his, not Whitefield's, terms. Many members of Edwards's congregation who had participated in the 1734 awakening had failed to persevere in the religious life. As religious concern began to stir again in Northampton, he was determined to avoid the mistakes of the past. Almost as soon as Whitefield had left town, therefore, Edwards began to scrutinize the affections and convictions the evangelist had generated for signs of insincerity. Still, a wonderful opportunity had presented itself, for "at such times as this . . . a very earnest, constant seeking salvation is not want to be in vain" (bk. 6, leaf 20). And so Edwards created a crucial role for himself. Whitefield had lit fires indiscriminately in the bosoms of Edwards's parishioners. Only Edwards knew which bosoms provided a hearth in which those fires could produce heat and light and which were but a pile of straw that would burn out as quickly as it had been ignited.

Edwards devotes the majority of the sower series—three sermons preached in five separate units—to the stony-ground hearers (Matt. 13:5-6). Stony-ground hearers appear to be genuine Christians. They profess belief in the doctrines of the Reformed faith, have a wide range of religious affections, and report dramatic conversion experiences, but in reality their beliefs and experiences are false. Their "hearts are like a rock with a very thin covering of earth"; while the surface appears thoroughly plowed and prepared to receive and nourish the seed, underneath the ground remains impenetrable, an environment hostile to the Word. Therefore only with the stony-ground hearers does the problem of religious hypocrisy fully manifest itself. Both the wayside and the thorny-ground hearers have false convictions and affections, but their hearts do not appear essentially different from what they are. The wayside is "hard both above and beneath," while the thorny ground has "never . . . been plowed and fitted for the seed." By contrast, the hardness of the stony ground is "inward and hid," camouflaged not only by religious beliefs and affections but by an ability to live a moral life and to withstand some trials of faith. Consequently, their apparent faith misleads not only others but themselves to "mistake 'em for real saints, and sometimes for eminent saints" (bk. 3, leaves 2, 1; bk. 6, leaf 1; bk. 3, leaves 10, 11-12).

The extent to which Edwards considers the stony-ground hearers suggests that his principal concern in the sower series was religious hypocrisy. In the aftermath of the 1734-35 awakening, hypocrisy was rampant and Northampton a laboratory well suited to its study. A tireless investigator, Edwards observed the various manifestations of hypocrisy, formulated explanations of its root causes, and proposed solutions. Out of this course of inquiry, which received its final articulation in *Religious Affections,* he developed a sophisticated analysis of the psychology of religious conversion which included an intricate catalogue of the indicators of genuine religious affections.[16] When he sensed that Northampton was again entering a period of revival, he attempted to reduce the incidence of hypocrisy by applying this methodology to the affections generated by Whitefield's visit. Although we have glimpses of Edwards's religious psychology in the sermons on the wayside and the thorny-ground hearers, not until his discussion of the stony-ground hearers does he tackle the problem of hypocrisy scientifically.

The analysis of the structure of religious hypocrisy proposed in the sower series is not essentially different from that Edwards develops elsewhere, especially in *Religious Affections.* Unique to this series, though, is its focus on the minister's—specifically Whitefield's—method of preaching. From his treatment of the stony-ground hearers, it is clear that Edwards finds Whitefield's rhetorical style particularly fertile ground for hypocrisy. Hypocrites, he explains, assent to the truths of the gospel not because they have a "spiritual understanding" of "their divine authority and excellency" but "from the natural force of arguments and perswasions set before them." The preacher overpowers them with his "use of very plentiful arguments" which are "set forth in a very earnest and forceable manner." And they are impressed by "the air of sincerity and fervency that is in the preacher, his positiveness, and the authority with which he seems to speak" (bk. 3, leaves 3, 2, 3).

For example, hypocrites frequently experience a "joy in the hearing of the word preached." In *Religious Affections,* Edwards attributes this counterfeit affection to self-interest, and in the sower series he likewise states that "men may be very much raised with joy in things that they hear preached, from a mistaken notion that they have an interest in them" (bk. 3, leaves 4, 5).[17] In the sower series, however, he provides an additional cause for this false joy: "the manner of preaching." Describing what must have been a common reaction to Whitefield's performance in Northampton, Edwards states that people may experience joy when "exceedingly taken with the eloquence of the preacher" and when "pleased with the aptness of expression, and with the fervency, and liveliness, and beautiful gestures of the preacher." But affections grounded in superficial characteristics such as these are not gracious. Although hypocrites may be "greatly pleased and delighted with the preaching," they will have no genuine "joy in the things preached" because they are "destitute of any spiritual knowledge" and lack "any real insight into the glorious nature of the things of the gospel" (bk. 3, leaves 4, 8). Edwards therefore advises his congregation to be suspicious of their joyous responses to Whitefield's preaching, and he exhorts them to scrutinize their reactions carefully for any sign of hypocrisy. Although he apparently had no doubts about the orthodoxy of Whitefield's beliefs, Edwards viewed his "eloquence," "aptness of expression," and "beautiful gestures" as dangerous distractions, and he encourages his flock to separate the medium from the message, thereby discounting that aspect of Whitefield's homiletic style that was truly innovative and most directly responsible for his universal popularity.

In his discussion of the stony-ground hearers, Edwards specifically and repeatedly treats one of the most remarkable features of Whitefield's performance in Northampton. In his *Journals,* Whitefield notes with evident pride that each of his sermons drew tears from Edwards's congregation. At his first appearance, "both minister and people wept much." The following day, "[f]ew eyes were dry in the assembly." At the Sunday services, Whitefield reports that "good Mr. Edwards wept during the whole time of the exercise" and the "people were equally affected."[18] In his published account of the Northampton revival that followed Whitefield's visit, Edwards confirms—with apparent approbation—the force of Whitefield's sermonic style. "The congregation," Edwards observes, "was extraordinarily melted by every sermon; almost the whole assembly being in tears for a great part of sermon time."[19] But in the sower series tears emerge only in relation to religious hypocrisy. In fact, Edwards mentions shedding of tears no fewer than eleven times in the first sermon on the stony-ground hearers, and in each instance tears are considered suspicious. Just as hypocrites experience a counterfeit joy, so they also "may shed many tears" because they are "greatly affected with the manner of preaching." But tears are not a reliable indicator of grace, because "men may shed a great many tears and yet be wholly ignorant of this inward, refreshing, life-giving savor" that is the true foundation for genuine religious affections (bk. 3, leaves 5, 17). If not followed by a "lasting alteration in the frame of the heart," Edwards cautions the private meeting, tears are simply "hypocritical."[20]

If the affections are untrustworthy, then so must be the conversions attributed to Whitefield's preaching. To emphasize his point, Edwards devotes the entirety of the second sermon on the stony-ground hearers to the proposition that "sudden conversions are very often false." Of course they are not "alwaies false"; indeed, in "times of extraordinary pouring out of the Spirit," such as that Northampton was apparently entering, "'tis a common thing . . . for there to be sudden conversions." But at such times there are also "many false conversions." "Extraordinary spiritual showers from heaven," Edwards declares, "not only produce a great many true converts," they also are "the occasion of a great many hypocrites" (bk. 4, leaves, 1, 2, 3).

Although his advice is certainly sound, the vehemence of Edwards's denunciations is suspect. In the private meeting at his home he rails against those who were "talking much of the man [Whitefield], and setting forth the excellency of his manner of delivery, his fervency, affections, and the like."[21] And he remarks with evident dismay that some of his parishioners are "almost ready to follow the preacher to the ends of the earth." Unimpressed by Edwards's own eloquence, they are "ready to cry out concerning him, 'Never man spoke like this man!'" (bk. 3, leaves 5, 4). Edwards stresses that such excessive adoration of a minister is characteristic of hypocrites, and once again he uses his religious psychology to deflect attention away from Whitefield's manner of preaching and toward the gospel message. "Some men," he notes, "when they hear preaching concerning God and Christ, are filled with affections and admiration; but 'tis the preacher, and not God, that it terminates upon. They are filled with admiration of the minister, but are not filled with admiration of Jesus Christ" (bk. 3, leaf 14). In 1734 Northampton had overflowed with admiration for Edwards. In *A Faithful Narrative,* he reported with evident satisfaction that four-year-old Phebe Bartlet "manifested great love to her minister," and he described how, upon hearing of his return from a journey, she "told the children of it . . . repeating it over and over, 'Mr. Edwards is come home! Mr. Edwards is come home!'"[22] But this enthusiasm had faded, and Edwards now viewed the admiration his congregation—especially his own coterie of loyal supporters—manifested for Whitefield to be suspect. Conveniently slipping between the theological and the personal, he used his theoretical analysis to diminish the stature of a rival colleague.

In Edwards's religious psychology, perseverance is the ultimate arbiter between counterfeit and gracious affections. Accordingly, he argues in the third stony-ground sermon that a "religion that arises only from superficial impressions is wont to wither away . . . when it comes to be tried by the difficulties of religion." Even intense religious affections, he explains, are a deceptive and insufficient foundation for assurance, because it is always uncertain whether they are caused by a perception of divine excellency or by some epiphenomenal feature of the means of grace. The only reliable "distinguishing characteristick of the truly godly" is "that they should hold on their way, and that they should continue in Christ's word to the end" (bk. 5, leaves 1, 2).

This reliance on piety over time, frequently heralded by orthodox Puritan divines and defended by Edwards at length in *Religious Affections,* functioned in the sower series as a critique of Whitefield's evangelism. If perseverance triumphed over immediate experience in the theoretical context, then in the ecclesiastical context, settled ministry took precedence over itinerancy. As an itinerant minister, Whitefield simply scattered the seed and moved on. Only if properly cultivated throughout the growing season, however, would the seed eventually bear good fruit. But Whitefield did not assume this tedious job of cultivation. It was Edwards who nourished the tender shoots and shielded them from the heat of the noonday sun. During the debate over the Awakening in New England, Old Lights attacked itinerants for violating parish boundaries; by identifying perseverance as an assurance more reliable than immediate experience, Edwards questioned not the ecclesiastical regularity of an itinerant ministry but its evangelical efficacy.

Itinerancy also underlies a metaphor developed in the sermon on the wayside hearers. "The notice that we take," Edwards writes, "of persons passing by in the high way, is very transient; we do but salute them and then we have done with them." Similarly, the wayside hearers show "an outward transient respect [to the Word of God] as it passes by," but they experience no lasting benefit from it. "Christ only passes by them," Edwards states, "and never abides with them." Their hearts are "far from being the place of his abode. He never tarries there; . . . as soon as he is come, he is gone again." By contrast, the hearts of genuine saints become Christ's "habitation, his temple in which he makes his settled abode" (bk. 2, leaves 2, 1, 2).

This comparison between transience and permanence, although explicitly referring to different manners of hearing the Word, suggests different means of preaching it as well. As an itinerant minister, Whitefield makes his "habitation" with no particular congregation, and no town claims to be his "settled abode." Therefore his evangelism will, by implication, have no lasting effect. The people to whom he preaches will but "salute" him and "have done with" him. In reporting on the progress of the Northampton revival to Whitefield, Edwards employs, with perhaps unconscious irony, the very metaphor he used in the sower series to raise suspicions about itinerancy. He asks Whitefield to pray "that God would not be to us as a way-faring Man, that turns aside to tarry but for a Night." In other words, although Edwards reports to Whitefield that "God seems to have succeeded your Labours amongst us," he clearly

believes that the true means of success are within his command alone.[23] Under Whitefield's ministrations Northampton would experience at best a brief awakening tainted by hypocrisy; only by means of Edwards's careful guidance was genuine revival a possibility.

There are indications that the Northampton revival did take place on Edwards's, and not on Whitefield's, terms. By his own assessment, Edwards was able to avoid the mistakes that, out of ignorance, he had failed to forestall during the earlier awakening. During "the years 1740 and 1741," he reported, "the work seemed to be much more pure, having less of a corrupt mixture, than in the former great outpouring of the Spirit in 1735 and 1736." There was less confusion between counterfeit and gracious affections, more awareness of self-deception, "greater humility and self-distrust, and greater engagedness after holy living and perseverance."[24] Edwards's congregation had listened intently to his sermon series, and they had been guided beyond enlightenment to faithfulness.

Edwards reports in the narrative that the "revival at first appeared chiefly among professors, and those that had entertained the hope that they were in a state of grace." This group, the stony-ground hearers, Edwards fears are dangerously susceptible to hypocrisy, but he also is most optimistic about their future success. Accordingly, he devotes three sermons, over half the sower series, to their instruction and guidance, and they reward this attention with heightened religious interest throughout the course of the revival. Another group affected by the revival, Edwards states, were those "that had formerly been wrought upon," who "in the times of our declension had fallen into decays." In the series Edwards is pessimistic about the prospects of these thorny-ground hearers, but he does not totally dismiss them. In the narrative he reports that at the height of the revival they responded to his encouragements by experiencing "a very remarkable new work of the Spirit of God, as if they had been the subjects of a second conversion." Only the wayside hearers, those "that had enjoyed that former glorious opportunity without any appearance of saving benefit," were "almost wholly passed over and let alone."[25]

. . . . .

By means of the sower series, Edwards channeled the energy unleashed by Whitefield into a revival of his own making. Following the challenge posed by Whitefield's charismatic authority, he regained control of his congregation by the force of his intellect, by stifling the affections of some and encouraging others. Prior to Whitefield's visit to Northampton, Edwards may have been alerted to the potential dangers of the itinerant's preaching style by the public controversy that had marked his ministry from the outset. According to Harry S. Stout, Anglican ministers in London criticized Whitefield as early as 1739 for "theatricality in the pulpit." Commissary Alexander Garden of South Carolina, Stout later notes, believed that Whitefield "would equally have produced the same Effects, whether he had acted his Part in the Pulpit or on the Stage. . . . It was not the Matter but the Manner, not the Doctrines he delivered, but the Agreeableness of the Delivery," that explained the unprecedented crowds that flocked to hear him preach.[26] Sarah Edwards, in a letter describing Whitefield's visit to her brother James Pierrepont, was evidently aware of such charges and defended Whitefield against them. "A prejudiced person," she writes, "might say that this is all theatrical artifice and display; but not so will any one think who has seen and known him."[27] Jonathan Edwards also publicly defended the Grand Itinerant and considered him a colleague in the cause of evangelical religion. Nevertheless, the sower series reveals that Edwards harbored a deep ambivalence about Whitefield's ministry, which was rooted theologically in his conviction that Whitefield's theatrical preaching style dangerously encouraged religious hypocrisy and, personally, in feelings of professional rivalry.

Edwards was a revivalist, but he was also a Puritan. He identified the affections as essential to genuine piety, but he refused to accept the certainty of immediate experience. As a consequence, he developed a conversion psychology that was essentially a prophylactic against the hypocrisy he found endemic in religious life. Throughout his ministry Edwards repeated that message to his congregation, and in the sower series he uses George Whitefield as his foil. The admiration the congregation felt for Whitefield was, for Edwards, a prime illustration of the deceitful heart, and the tears they shed during his sermons an example of untrustworthy affections.

For all Edwards's efforts, however, Whitefield would ultimately prove the victor. Religious authority in American Protestantism was shifting. "Ordinary people" were being "empowered" to take "their deepest spiritual impulses at face value rather than subjecting them to the scrutiny of . . . respectable clergymen."[28] Edwards continued to operate within the older patriarchal model of ministerial authority and refused to adopt the newer charistmatic model, employed by Whitefield and his evangelical successors, in which "the power to speak was dispensed from beneath."[29] His insistence upon a piety vigilant to the ever-present possibility of self-deception, therefore, enhanced his own authority as a pastor at the expense of the individual religious authority of each member of his congregation. But Edwards's relentless admonitions that members of his congregation be suspicious of themselves finally made them increasingly suspicious of him. In the end, they rejected him, as much of the nation would reject, following the Revolution, the elegant but outmoded theology he represented.

Notes

1. "Jonathan Edwards's Letter of Invitation to George Whitefield," ed. Henry Abelove, *William and Mary Quarterly* 29 (1972): 487-89; *George Whitefield's Journals* (Edinburgh: Banner of Truth Trust, 1960), p. 386.

The literature on both Jonathan Edwards and George Whitefield is immense. Among the best, recent works are Allen C. Guelzo, *Edwards on the Will: A Century of American Theological Debate* (Middletown, Conn.: Wesleyan University Press, 1989); Frank Lambert, *"Pedlar in Divinity": George Whitefield and the Transatlantic Revivals* (Princeton: Princeton University Press, 1994); Sang Hyun Lee, *The Philosophical Theology of Jonathan Edwards* (Princeton: Princeton University Press, 1988); and Harry S. Stout, *The Divine Dramatist: George Whitefield and the Rise of Modern Evangelicalism* (Grand Rapids: Eerdmans Publishing Co., 1991).

2. Sarah Pierrepont Edwards to James Pierrepont, 24 October 1740, in Luke Tyerman's *The Life of the Rev. George Whitefield,* vol. 1 (New York: Anson D. F. Randolph & Co., 1877), p. 428. The original manuscript of the letter does not survive, and it is likely that it was edited for publication because its grammar, spelling, and punctuation are more regular and accurate than that found in Sarah Edwards's extant manuscript letters. However, there is no evidence indicating that she was not the original author of the letter.

3. Jonathan Edwards to Thomas Prince, 12 December 1743, in *The Works of Jonathan Edwards,* vol. 4: *The Great Awakening,* ed. C. C. Goen (New Haven: Yale University Press, 1972), p. 545.

4. Patricia J. Tracy interprets Whitefield's success in Northampton as an early sign of Edwards's growing disaffection from his congregation which would culminate some years later in his dismissal from his pastorate (*Jonathan Edwards, Pastor: Religion and Society in Eighteenth-Century Northampton* [New York: Hill and Wang, 1980], pp. 135-45).

5. The occasion of the debate was Clap's statement at the 1744 Harvard commencement that Edwards had told him "that Mr. Whitefield told me, that he had a design of turning out of their places, the greater part of the ministers in New England, and of supplying their pulpits with ministers from Great Britain and Ireland" (Jonathan Edwards, *Copies of Two Letters Cited by The Rev. Mr. Clap* [Boston, 1745], pp. 2-3).

6. Jonathan Edwards, *An Expostulary Letter from the Rev. Mr. Edwards* (Boston, 1745), p. 7.

7. Jonathan Edwards, *The Distinguishing Marks of a Work of the Spirit of God,* in *Works,* 4:275.

8. The sermon series is comprised of six separately-bound manuscript booklets located at the Beinecke Rare Book and Manuscript Library, Yale University, New Haven, Conn. The first two booklets are two distinct sermons on the two verses of Matt. 13:3-4; the third a two-unit sermon on Matt. 13:5; the fourth a single-unit sermon continuing the discussion of Matt. 13:5; the fifth a two-unit sermon on Matt. 13:6; and the final a

two-unit sermon on Matt. 13:7. The series does not contain a sermon on the final verse of the parable (Matt. 13:8), which describes the flourishing of the seed in good ground. The first two sermons were preached on a Sunday, at the morning and afternoon services. Given the structure of the series, it is likely that the three remaining two-unit sermons were preached on three of the remaining Sundays in November 1740, with unit 5 perhaps being delivered as a mid-week lecture.

9. Series on Matt. 13:3-7, booklet 1, leaves 1, 2. Edwards's manuscript sermons contain little punctuation, irregular capitalization, shorthand notations, and abbreviations. To facilitate comprehension, I have added punctuation, regularized capitalization, translated the shorthand, and completed the abbreviations. Further references to the sermon series will appear parenthetically in the text.

10. Edwards to Prince, 12 December 1743, *Works,* 4:545.

11. Edwards first articulated his anxiety in his letter of invitation to Whitefield. Speaking as much of Northampton as New England, he writes, "I am fearfull whether you will not be disappointed in New-England, and will have less Success here than in other Places: we who have dwelt in a Land that has been distinguished with Light, and have long enjoyed the Gospel, and have been glutted with it, and have despised it, are I fear more hardened than most of those places where you have preached hitherto" ("Edwards's Invitation to Whitefield," p. 488).

12. The manuscript, a one-unit sermon, written in an outlinish manner, is located at the Beinecke Rare Book and Manuscript Library, Yale University. It is dated October 1740 and contains a notation in the author's hand that it was delivered to a "private meeting." In the sermon, Edwards refers to Whitefield's "late labour" in Northampton (leaf 6). Therefore, he must have delivered it sometime between Whitefield's arrival on 17 October and the end of the month.

13. Sermon on II Cor. 2:15-16, leaves 1, 6.

14. Sermon on II Cor. 2:15-16, leaf 7.

15. Part of a letter sent to the Rev. Mr. Whitefield, from the Rev. Mr. Edwards of Northampton in New England, December 14, 1740," *Weekly History,* no. 9 (London), p. 2.

16. Edwards first delineated a comprehensive list of the signs of grace in the sermon series on the parable of the wise and foolish virgins, which he preached in the winter of 1737-38. See my "Brides of Christ and Signs of Grace: Edwards's Sermon Series on the Parable of the Wise and Foolish Virgins," in *Jonathan Edwards's Writings: Text, Context,*

Interpretation, ed. Stephen J. Stein (Bloomington: Indiana University Press, 1996), pp. 3-18.

17. Jonathan Edwards, *A Treatise Concerning Religious Affections,* in *The Works of Jonathan Edwards,* vol. 2: *Religious Affections,* ed. John E. Smith (New Haven: Yale University Press, 1959), pp. 249-50.

18. *Whitefield's Journals,* pp. 476-77.

19. Edwards to Prince, 12 December 1743, *Works,* 4:545.

20. Sermon on II Cor. 2:15-16, leaf 8.

21. Sermon on II Cor. 2:15-16, leaf 8.

22. Jonathan Edwards, *A Faithful Narrative of the Surprising Work of God,* in *Works,* 4:205.

23. Edwards, "Part of a letter to Whitefield," p. 2.

24. Edwards to Prince, 12 December 1743, *Works,* 4:555.

25. Edwards to Prince, 12 December 1743, *Works,* 4:545, 548.

26. Stout, *The Divine Dramatist,* pp. 83, 110.

27. Sarah Edwards to James Pierrepont, 24 October 1740, p. 428.

28. Nathan O. Hatch, *The Democratization of American Christianity* (New Haven: Yale University Press, 1989), p. 10.

29. Harry S. Stout, *The New England Soul: Preaching and Religious Culture in Colonial New England* (New York: Oxford University Press, 1986), p. 193.

Daniel Walker Howe (essay date 1997)

SOURCE: "Benjamin Franklin, Jonathan Edwards, and the Problem of Human Nature," in *Making the American Self: Jonathan Edwards to Abraham Lincoln,* Harvard University Press, 1997, pp. 21-47.

[In the following essay, Howe highlights the philosophical tenets of Benjamin Franklin and Jonathan Edwards and examines their divergent approaches to the problem of human nature. The critic notes that their writings indicate that, on numerous points, the two eighteenth-century intellectuals were in agreement as to the nature of a problem, but not in regard to the remedies necessary to address it.]

"Reason should govern Passion, but instead of that, you see, it is often subservient to it." So ran the conventional wisdom of the eighteenth century, in this case stated by Sir Richard Steele in *The Spectator.* Throughout the eighteenth century, the Western world typically thought of human nature in terms of a model of faculties or powers. The "active powers," which collectively composed the "will," supplied the motives prompting human action. The most common version of eighteenth-century faculty psychology arranged these powers in a hierarchical sequence. First in order of precedence came the rational faculties of the will: conscience (or the moral sense) and prudence (or self-interest). Below them were the emotional springs of action, called either by the approving term "affections" or the more derogatory word "passions," as the context might dictate. Still further down were mechanical impulses like reflexes, not subject to conscious control at all. The hierarchical structure of human nature, explained a later number of *The Spectator*, corresponded to humanity's intermediate position in the great chain of being, partly divine, partly animal.[1]

The model just described provided the basis for much of the philosophy, psychology, and literature of the eighteenth century. It was treated as the common sense of the matter by an age that idealized common sense. Embodied early in the century in such authoritative literary works as *The Spectator* and Alexander Pope's poetic *Essay on Man*, it was codified late in the century by the Scottish moral philosopher Thomas Reid. John Locke had worked within it, for the most part, in his writings on human understanding and education; Francis Hutcheson and David Hume challenged it by proposing to treat conscience as an emotional, rather than a rational, faculty.

Eighteenth-century faculty psychology was both descriptive and normative; that is, it was not only a psychology but also an ethic. By right, conscience should govern the commonwealth of the mind, but in practice, the passions were often too strong for it. As we have indicated, passion was considered the strongest faculty of the will, conscience the weakest, with prudential reason somewhere in between. The psychological fact, countless writers warned, was that the motivating power of the faculties varied in inverse proportion to their rightful precedence. This discrepancy between psychological fact and ethical imperative may be termed the problem of human nature. It is no exaggeration to call it *the* central problem of eighteenth-century moral philosophy.

The two greatest intellectuals of colonial British America were Benjamin Franklin and the Calvinist theologian Jonathan Edwards; each addressed, in his own way, the problem of human nature as their generation defined it. Both men were avid readers of *The Spectator* in their youth and were thoroughly conversant with its model of human nature.[2] Both were informed participants in the world of eighteenth-century moral philosophy; Franklin knew many of its leading figures personally. Franklin and Edwards were in agreement on the seriousness of the problem. "All things in the soul of man should be under the government of reason, which is the highest faculty," Edwards instructed his congregation; but "men's passions sometimes rise so high that they are, as it were, drunk with passion. Their passion deprives them very much of the use of reason." Franklin's *Poor Richard's Almanac* taught its readers the same lesson: "He is a governor that governs his passions, and is a servant that serves them." "If passion drives, let reason hold the reins."[3] While agreeing on the nature of the problem posed by their commu-

nity of discourse, Franklin and Edwards display for us, in the solutions they offered to it, differences of fundamental importance.

BENJAMIN FRANKLIN

Benjamin Franklin (1706-1790) is, of course, one of the most famous exemplars of self-construction who ever lived. He rose from obscurity to wealth, influence, and immense international popularity and fame. In old age he composed an *Autobiography* that is one of the classic "how-to" books, a manual full of lessons drawn from his own life—frequently from his own mistakes—on how to develop virtuous habits, how to fashion one's image, how to win friends and influence people. Franklin played many parts in the long drama of his career: businessman, scientist, lobbyist, legislator, colonial bureaucrat, republican diplomat, statesman, sage. The more we know about him, the more we are struck with the ironies of his self-created identities. Franklin boasted of his spartan thrift in youth, but relished the good life in maturity. A sophisticated cosmopolite, he cultivated an image of transparent simplicity. Full of advice on the importance of making friends, in real life he made plenty of enemies too.[4] As an American emissary in Paris, he found it convenient to be mistaken for a Quaker because of their reputation for honesty. He achieved a remarkable self-detachment, best manifested in his ability to laugh at himself. He made no secret of his sexual indiscretions. Franklin adopted so many different identities in the course of his elaborate self-constructions that some commentators have despised him as a hypocrite, while others have despaired of ever knowing who the real Franklin was; indeed, whether there was a real person at all or just a series of guises.[5]

Why did Franklin engage in this lifelong process of identity formation and urge it so upon others? Self-construction, as Franklin practiced it, was not undertaken merely for the sake of expediency but also as a matter of high principle. Why did he believe it was so important to recreate a self (or selves) by conscious plan? To answer that question, let us examine first his estimate of human nature, and then the various methods by which he sought to improve on that nature. In doing so, we shall take Franklin seriously, as a thinker concerned with serious issues. That he was also an ambitious man, capable of being manipulative, may be readily acknowledged.

"Men I find a sort of beings very badly constructed," Franklin wrote Joseph Priestley, his friend and fellow scientist, moral philosopher, and reformer. "They are generally more easily provoked than reconciled, more disposed to do mischief to each other than to make reparation, and much more easily deceived than undeceived." Franklin found human motivation a complex mixture, but he had no doubt that the baser impulses were the more powerful. For this reason, he felt Hobbes's depiction of the state of nature "somewhat nearer the truth than that which makes the state of nature a state of love."[6] Some of Franklin's satires on human motives have a bite worthy of Jonathan Swift.[7]

Characteristically, however, Franklin's low estimate of human nature did not lead him to express any personal *Angst*. In the Will he drew up in 1750, he thanked God for giving him "a mind with moderate passions."[8]

As a good eighteenth-century scientist, Franklin celebrated the rational order of the physical universe. (In a religious service he composed in 1728 he prescribed the reading of lessons; not from Scripture, however, but from John Ray's *The Wisdom of God in Creation* [1691] and other authoritative works of Enlightenment natural theology.)[9] Franklin took this rational order as a norm to apply to human affairs, both social and individual. In a properly ordered society, there would be no conflict between individual and community; each existed to serve the other. A person with a properly balanced individual nature would live a socially useful life. "Wise and good men are, in my opinion, the strength of the state," Franklin wrote the American philosopher Samuel Johnson; but neither is there any cause to doubt that he shared the assumption of the Declaration of Independence (which, of course, he helped Jefferson draft) that the state exists to serve wise and good men. The moral faculty, for Franklin, was the rational power that perceived the appropriateness and utility of actions in promoting both individual and collective happiness. "Virtue and sense are one," declared Poor Richard.[10] We may be confident that Franklin would have approved the teaching of his Scottish contemporary Francis Hutcheson: "That action is best which procures the greatest happiness for the greatest numbers."[11]

Just as external nature could be made to yield the secrets of its divine order to scientific research, so, Franklin was convinced, there could be a science of human nature, that is, of morality. Like all good science (in Franklin's view), moral science would have practical application to human affairs. This was by no means an eccentric opinion in the eighteenth century. Individual and social morality were governed by analogous principles: "No longer virtuous, no longer free, is a maxim as true with regard to a private person as a commonwealth." The danger to the individual posed by a usurping vice or passion was the same as that of a demagogue or tyrant to the state.[12]

The order of the external universe, though a model to be imitated, did not provide Franklin much encouragement for human moral strivings. The philosophical system that commended itself to Franklin's science and logic was deterministic deism. Yet deism, with its remote artificer-god, provided no basis for such human needs as prayer, special providence, or moral incentives. As he observed in his *Autobiography*, "I began to suspect that this doctrine, though it might be true, was not very useful." Having reached this conclusion, Franklin abandoned deist system-making and devoted himself instead to inquiries with practical application.[13] To his good friend George Whitefield he confided, "I rather suspect, from certain circumstances, that though the general government of the universe is well administered, our particular little affairs are perhaps below notice, and left to take the chance of human prudence or impru-

dence, as either may happen to be uppermost. It is, however, an uncomfortable thought, and I leave it." (After receiving the letter, the great evangelist wrote across the margin: "Uncomfortable indeed! And, blessed be God, unscriptural.")[14] Franklin's preoccupation with temporal goals, with human happiness rather than metaphysical values, should not be attributed to mere crassness of temperament. It followed from his conviction that the universe was ultimately indifferent, and that it was up to human beings to shape themselves and their destiny as best they could.

The most obvious alternative to deism was Christianity, in which Franklin had been reared by his Calvinist parents. The Christian religion seemed well suited to the needs of humanity, Franklin thought, provided it could be purged of intolerance and obsession with unanswerable theological conundrums. Like many subsequent Americans, he found refuge in the Anglican communion from the preoccupation with theology characteristic of the Reformed tradition. Anglicanism was traditionally concerned with issues of comprehensiveness and liturgy, both of which interested Franklin. It is a common mistake to suppose that Franklin involved himself with religion *solely* as a matter of social ethics; he also regarded worship and prayer as natural human impulses requiring expression. As the object of prayer, Franklin hypothesized a finite God, possessing passions, because he felt only such a divine being would be responsive to the worship of human beings.[15]

Like Locke, whom he followed in so many things, Franklin believed that the core of Christian belief consisted of a few short affirmations. Beyond that, religions justified themselves by their contribution to temporal human welfare, and should be judged accordingly. In a paper prepared in 1732, Franklin undertook to formulate a religious position that would be "a powerful regulator of our actions, give us peace and tranquillity within our own minds, and render us benevolent, useful, and beneficial to others."[16] He defended his Enlightenment version of Christianity against Calvinists on the one hand and deists on the other, and labored to see it taught in schools.[17]

In a vivid letter to an unknown deist, sometimes thought to be Thomas Paine, Franklin refused to discuss the truth of his correspondent's philosophy and strongly urged him not to publish it. Undermining respect for religion would not be socially beneficial, he explained.

> You yourself may find it easy to live a virtuous life without the assistance afforded by religion, you having a clear perception of the advantages of virtue and the disadvantages of vice, and possessing a strength of resolution sufficient to enable you to resist common temptations. But think how great a proportion of mankind consists of weak and ignorant men and women, and of inexperienced and inconsiderate youth of both sexes, who have need of the motives of religion to restrain them from vice, to support their virtue, and retain them in the practice of it till it becomes *habitual*, which is the great point for its security.[18]

It is clear in this passage that Franklin did not consider the Christian religion to be based on reason; on the contrary, he thought of Christian faith as an alternative to reason. ("The way to see Faith is to shut the eye of Reason," ran one of his aphorisms.) Encouraging religion was a concession to the strength of the nonrational component in human nature, especially appropriate for people in whom the rational faculty was undeveloped.[19]

Franklin's insistence upon discussing the issue entirely in terms of practical consequences became more and more typical of his attitude toward religion with the passage of time. In youth he had satirized Cotton Mather; later, however, he paid respectful homage to that Puritan patriarch for promoting philanthropic enterprises. "Opinions should be judged of by their influences and effects," he wrote to his parents.[20] A variety of different religions might all be deserving of support provided they all promoted socially beneficial virtues. Accordingly, Franklin contributed money to the Philadelphia congregations of several denominations (including the synagogue), while maintaining his family membership in Episcopal Christ Church.[21]

Organized religion was not the only form of association on behalf of virtue that Franklin endorsed. He formed a club in Philadelphia called the Junto, hoping that it would become the nucleus of an international United Party of Virtue. Junto members read and discussed good books, debated important topics, and enjoyed good fellowship. The association was envisioned as existing partly for self-improvement, partly for mutual aid of the members (in the form of business contacts as well as charity), and partly to exert virtuous leadership in the community. Had it developed in accordance with Franklin's vision, it might have become a kind of secular church of the Enlightenment. Only later did Franklin affiliate with an identifiable political party in Pennsylvania (the Quaker or Assembly party); during the years when the Junto was active, its founder probably thought of it as a nonpartisan political force sustaining reason and public virtue above the factionalism of ethnic or interest groups. Franklin apparently got the idea for the Junto from Mather's benevolent societies and the fictional club described in *The Spectator*. Evangelical Societies for the Reformation of Manners were common in early-eighteenth-century England and a favorite cause among Low Church Anglicans. However, the Masonic movement had already preempted the role Franklin envisioned for his order. When the Masons established a lodge in Philadelphia, Franklin joined it, and the Junto was gradually eclipsed.[22]

But Franklin's best known and most characteristic device for strengthening the conscience in its struggle to maintain supremacy over the baser motives was his invocation of prudential self-interest on the side of virtue. The prudential aphorisms of Poor Richard constituted Franklin's famous application of a general principle of eighteenth-century moral philosophy. According to this principle, conscience could compensate for its weakness by enlisting the motivating power of stronger faculties to do its bidding. For example, the love of fame—the "ruling passion of the noblest minds," according to Alexander Hamilton—could lead political men to serve the public interest when altruism alone might fail.[23] Franklin too relied on the love of fame this way; indeed, he regarded it as an enlightened form of prudence, akin to our concern with material well-being, rather than as a passion.

Even before Franklin, the Anglican Bishop Joseph Butler (1692-1752) had taught that the conscience could enlist the aid of prudence to help it control the passions.[24] By the latter part of the century this had become a standard technique for strengthening the motive to virtue in human behavior. Together, virtue and prudential self-interest made an effective combination in Franklin's scheme. The happiness of the greatest number, after all, was made up of many individual happinesses. If individuals could be persuaded to pursue their enlightened self-interest, this would be a large step in the right direction.[25] If they could be shown that their self-interest, properly understood, lay in hard work, honesty, thrift, and humility, the congruence between collective and individual welfare would be all the greater. Through publications like *Poor Richard's Almanac*, Franklin popularized *The Spectator's* gentlemanly precepts of self-construction among the common people of the colonies. To fashion the self the right way would help the average individual and society as well.

Franklin's invocation of prudence was part of a widespread upward revaluation of the faculty during the eighteenth century. At the beginning of the period, self-interest had generally been considered one of the passions, but by the end, moral philosophers had definitely promoted it to the rank of a rational faculty.[26] A key to this development lay in drawing a distinction between self-interest and pride. Pride, Franklin maintained, was very different from self-interest and could even blind a person to his true self-interest. While self-interest was rational, pride was a passion.[27]

Religion of course had its own form of prudential incentive: a heavenly reward. This incentive found a prominent advocate during the eighteenth century in Archdeacon William Paley (1743-1805), who made it central to his system of moral philosophy, called "theological utilitarianism." Franklin did not ignore this motive to virtue,[28] but he devoted much more attention to tangible temporal rewards. By doing so he included in his audience those for whom religion had lost its appeal. Virtue, he argued—in both his own voice and that of Poor Richard, his most famous *persona*—was a good bargain. A virtuous way of life—honest industry, rational foresight, restraint of the passions—was "the Way to Wealth."[29]

For a person who is usually associated with the work ethic, Franklin had surprisingly little to say about the intrinsic satisfactions of work. In fact, the joy of work for its own sake did not fit into his theoretical model of human motivation. He himself, after all, quit work at the age of forty-two, once he had acquired a sufficient fortune. The remainder of his life he devoted to science and public service—gentlemanly pursuits which, in the eighteenth century, did not count as work.

In 1730 Franklin printed in the *Philadelphia Gazette* two "Dialogues between Philocles and Horatio" treating the proper role of prudential self-interest. For a long time it was assumed that Franklin had composed the dialogues himself; thanks to Alfred Owen Aldridge, we now know that he reprinted them from the *London Journal* of the year before. But we may take it that Franklin did so because they set forth so well the view to which he subscribed. That Franklin picked up on the dialogues illustrates his involvement with the central issues of eighteenth-century moral philosophy. In the first dialogue, Philocles explains to the naive young Horatio that self-love has two versions: self-indulgence and enlightened self-interest. The former is short-term and passionate; the latter, long-term and rational. Horatio is persuaded to subordinate his passions to prudential reason for the sake of greater happiness. In the second dialogue, Philocles argues that the highest happiness lies in a life of benevolent virtue, the pleasure of which can never cloy. The conventional hierarchy of the faculties—moral sense, prudence, passion—has been legitimated. Nothing is said about the satisfactions of work.[30] Though Franklin devoted much of his energy to reinforcing the lesson of Philocles's first dialogue, he seldom recurred to the subject of the second, which would interest Jonathan Edwards.

A discipline closely related to moral philosophy in the eighteenth century was rhetoric. There was a widespread desire to reformulate the ancient rules of rhetoric so as to take advantage of the principles of eighteenth-century moral philosophy and, in particular, those of faculty psychology.[31] Franklin was a careful rhetorical craftsman, a pioneer in the all-important art of persuasive argumentation. Analyses of his writings on public issues and private morality reveal a strategy of invoking a mixture of various faculties on behalf of his case. Typically, his rhetorical stance is "to speak not simply as an individual promoting a private scheme, but rather as a representative of a group of rational, fair-minded, public-spirited men who strive to improve their community." While presenting himself as altruistic, Franklin addresses his audience's faculty of prudence and makes his appeal to their enlightened self-interest.[32] This is a rhetorical strategy that Publius, the pseudonymous author of *The Federalist Papers,* would bring to perfection.

Despite all the care with which he crafted his appeals, no one could be more aware than Franklin himself of the likelihood that they would fail. Human nature being what it was, exhortations to virtue, even when coupled with prudential incentives, were seldom efficacious. Poor Richard admitted that hardly anyone could really live by his precepts:

> Who is wise? He that learns from everyone.
> Who is powerful? He that governs his passions.
> Who is rich? He that is content.
> Who is that? Nobody.

At the conclusion of "The Way to Wealth," Franklin's valedictory summation of Poor Richard's precepts, he notes, "the people heard it, and approved the doctrine, and immediately practiced the contrary, just as if it had been a common sermon."[33]

The problem was one of human nature, not one of knowledge. "Men do not generally err in their conduct so much through ignorance of their duty, as through inattention to their own faults, or through strong passions or bad habits." More succinctly: "Inclination was sometimes too strong for Reason."[34] What was needed, Franklin recognized, was a practical regimen, an applied "science of virtue" or "art of virtue" (he used both terms). The importance of such a program he outlined in a dialogue he wrote for discussion at a meeting of the Junto. In it, Socrates persuades Crito that an applied science of virtue was the most important of all branches of learning.[35] As Franklin explained years later to his friend, the Scottish moral philosopher Lord Kames,

> Most people have naturally some virtues, but none have naturally all the virtues. To acquire those that are wanting, and secure what we acquire as well as those we have naturally, is the subject of an art. It is as properly an art as painting, navigation, or architecture. If a man would become a painter . . . he must be taught the principles of the art, be shown all the methods of working, and how to acquire the habits of using properly all the instruments. . . . My art of virtue has also its instruments and teaches the manner of using them.

Faith in Christ works as the requisite instrument for some people, Franklin acknowledged, though not for all. His own program would benefit everyone, including those with weak faith or none. The program involved systematic practice in a rotating sequence of individual virtues, and Franklin followed it himself over a period of many years.[36]

A modern scholar has noticed similarities between Franklin's program and the Puritan process called "preparation for grace."[37] But Franklin's "art of virtue" was intended to operate naturally, not supernaturally, and to be suitable for all, not only the elect. The virtue it produced was an end in itself, not a manifestation of divine grace—or even of good intentions. The goal, in fact, was for virtuous behavior to become automatic, a conditioned reflex.[38] Ideally, it should be like the "mechanical powers": those unthinking reactions not subject to conscious will, humbler than the passions but the strongest of all the springs of action, being irresistible. The perfect person was one whose "knee-jerk" reactions were morally correct. "The strongest of our natural passions are seldom perceived by us; a choleric man does not always discover when he is angry, nor an envious man when he is invidious." Unreflective habit, an even stronger force than passion, could master it where reflective reason might not.[39]

For Franklin, the passions were to be denied only to the extent that they sacrificed long-term or general welfare. Like work, self-denial was not an end in itself. The end was happiness, that is, individual and collective well-being. "A sound mind and a healthy body, a sufficiency of the necessaries and conveniences of life, together with the favor of God and the love of mankind," was Franklin's definition of happiness.[40] Self-denial, like work, was only justified in terms of its results. Franklin wrote an essay to prove the point in 1735. Acting contrary to one's inclinations was not the essence of virtue, he argued. "Temperance, justice, charity etc. are virtues, whether practiced with or against our inclinations." A person who automatically acted right was to be preferred to one who pondered over it. "The most perfect virtue is above all temptation." Worst of all, in Franklin's eyes, was asceticism practiced for its own sake. "He who does a foolish, indecent, or wicked thing, merely because 'tis contrary to his inclination (like some mad enthusiasts I have read of, who ran about naked, under the nation of taking up the Cross) is not practicing the reasonable science of virtue, but is a lunatic."[41] Like the authors of *Cato's Letters,* Franklin was not interested in denying or suppressing any aspect of human nature but only in controlling and manipulating them all in the interest of general happiness.

Clearly, Franklin was interested in virtuous behavior (that is, behavior productive of human happiness) regardless of the motive or source from which it stemmed. Christian love, voluntary associations like the Junto, prudential calculation, or ingrained habit—whatever worked would do. He concentrated his efforts on the young because it was during their time of life that habits, the most promising of the "instruments" of virtue, were most effectively formed.[42] In the last analysis, Franklin was more interested in "merit" than in "virtue." "True merit" he defined as "an inclination joined with an ability to serve mankind, one's country, friends, and family." Virtue might only be a matter of intention, but *merit* joined this with ability, a behavioral test that took account of acquired skills and habits.[43]

Franklin never wrote the definitive handbook he projected on "the art of virtue." Instead, he left his (incomplete) *Autobiography,* in which his own life story is related as a sequence of parables, each with its moral lesson. The book shows how to shape one's personality through fostering some impulses and restraining others. The rhetorical posture of the detached, self-controlled observer, like the postulated model of human faculties, is quintessential eighteenth-century moral philosophy and can be traced back to *The Spectator.* Overall, the lesson is that by shaping and controlling one's self, one can shape and control one's destiny, even in an uncaring world. Self-discipline is the key to success. The author Franklin is necessarily detached from the character Franklin in the book, since the character is meant to stand for Everyman, to be a model for universal imitation. (The postulated universal desire for success is part of the security for the system. A person who has constructed himself in accordance with Franklin's maxims will be of use to society because he will want a good reputation, and the way to gain that is by being useful to others.)

Franklin would have found the opposition between public and private virtue, supposedly characteristic of eighteenth-century American republicans, quite incomprehensible. For him, there was no conflict between virtue and commerce, or between the individual and the collective welfare. The prudential virtues that made one a good tradesman or a good housewife also characterized the good citizen.[44] Indeed, his *Autobiography* points out, the good reputation that one earns by private virtue can be put to use in politics. Far from there being a conflict between virtue and self-interest, self-interest should be a motive to virtue and virtue should be practically useful.[45]

It is a cliché, though not less true for being such, that Franklin was more interested in means than ends, in practice than theory. This does not mean he was unsophisticated; the choice was quite deliberate on his part. He accepted the prevailing model of the human faculties and addressed himself with shrewdness to the practical problems that model posed. He assumed that the autonomous, rational self would be socially useful and that society would appropriately reward, with fame, those who served it. He devoted little thought to the nature of virtue in and of itself. Once, when Franklin was planning the agenda for coming Junto meetings, he considered discussing "whether men ought to be denominated good or ill men from their actions or their inclinations." But then he crossed it off the list.[46] Very likely the question seemed too abstract to be interesting. It seemed quite otherwise to Jonathan Edwards.

JONATHAN EDWARDS

Precocious Yale student, village pastor, revival preacher, missionary to the Indians, and finally president of Princeton University (then called the College of New Jersey), Jonathan Edwards (1703-1758) is remembered as the last and greatest of American Puritan evangelists and theologians. For the past generation, scholars have been engaged in a process of recovering and appreciating his impressive intellectual accomplishments. Edwards's philosophy restated the Protestant faith for the age of the Enlightenment. Like Benjamin Franklin, he was deeply concerned with the problem of human nature and with identifying the proper remedy for its deficiencies.

Unlike the cosmopolitan Franklin, Edwards never travelled outside the American colonies and spent most of his life in tiny villages. Yet Edwards worked in a transatlantic intellectual context every bit as much as Franklin did. As Norman Fiering has demonstrated, "Edwards's treatises on the will, on the affections, and on virtue are not readily classifiable in twentieth-century categories, but they can be comfortably fitted into the context of eighteenth-century moral philosophy debates."[47] These debates were predicated on a common model of the human faculties. The influential scholar of Puritan thought, Perry Miller, misled many a subsequent inquirer with his careless assertion that Edwards and Locke both discarded the model of faculty psychology.[48] In fact, Edwards argued within the terms of the prevailing dual system of faculties: the understanding, which consisted of the powers of perception, and the will, which consisted of the powers motivating action. "Knowledge of ourselves consists chiefly in right apprehensions concerning those two chief faculties of our nature, the understanding and the will. Both are very important: yet the science of the latter must be confessed to be of greatest moment; inasmuch as all virtue and religion have their seat more immediately in the will, consisting more especially in right acts and habits of this faculty."[49]

Edwards's use of the model and vocabulary of faculty psychology was encouraged by his admiration for the Platonic tradition, particularly as exemplified in the writings of the Earl of Shaftesbury (1671—1713) and the seventeenth-century Cambridge Platonists. These thinkers had followed Plato in distinguishing within human nature various components competing with each other for supremacy. In a well-ordered personality, the one that would prevail was the quality of rational insight into the universal good; the other elements of the soul would be kept in their proper places. A well-ordered commonwealth followed the same principles.[50] "God has given . . . all the faculties and principles of the human soul," Edwards wrote, "that they might be subservient to man's chief end, . . . that is, the business of religion."[51] Such an affirmation was typical of Christian Platonism. Among the God-given faculties were the affections, both benevolent and malevolent, prudential reason, and even a natural conscience, which "doth naturally, or of itself, . . . give an apprehension of right and wrong."[52] The Platonic tradition would remain an important element in the project of self-construction as carried on by New Englanders for another century and more.

More of a problem for Edwards than Platonism was how to define his relationship to the moral philosophy of his own time. Most of early-modern moral philosophy was the creation of theological Arminians, Christian thinkers seeking to refute Hobbes on the one hand and Calvin on the other by establishing a natural basis for human moral values. They believed human beings had a meaningful power to choose between right and wrong. In addition to Locke, writers answering to this description included Francis Hutcheson (1694-1746), Thomas Reid (1710-1796), Joseph Butler (1692-1752), most of the literary circle around *The Spectator,* and even the Cambridge Platonists whom Edwards so admired. Edwards respected the achievement of these moralists and undertook to relate it to another great system of thought, Reformed theology. Unlike Franklin, who thought religion mostly nonrational, though potentially useful, Edwards believed the doctrines of religion eminently rational: "there is the most sweet harmony between Christianity and reason," he declared.[53]

Jonathan Edwards set out to show that the moral philosophy of his age did not really dictate an Arminian theology; it could be comprehended within a Calvinist system as well. Furthermore, he believed that the Calvinist system was not simply viable but preferable on logical, scriptural, and empirical grounds. In fact, Edwards looked to Re-

formed theology to solve the problem of human nature posed by eighteenth-century faculty psychology. Edwards produced in the end a dual system of morality, one natural and one divine. What he called natural morality was essentially the conventional moral philosophy of the eighteenth century, based on man's own unaided faculties. As a consequence of original sin, however, these faculties were corrupted by pride, which alienated humanity from God and prevented the individual from following the dictates of reason. Since this fallen human nature was hopelessly self-centered and incapable of true virtue, Edwards called a divine system of ethics into existence to rescue it.[54]

Nowhere is the contrast between Edwards and Franklin more striking than in their attitude toward what Edwards called "the great Christian doctrine of original sin." Although he shared Edwards's low estimate of human nature, Franklin despised the doctrine of original sin, declaring it had been "invented . . . by priests (whether Popish or Presbyterian I know not) to fright and scare an unthinking populace."[55] For Edwards, original sin was the fundamental truth of the human condition, around which he constructed his ingenious moral philosophy.

The problem, for Edwards as for Franklin and so many others, began with the weakness of the rational faculty in the human will. In the conventional model, conscience was a faculty of both the understanding and the will. As far as the perceptions of the understanding went, there was little difficulty: people were capable of *knowing* the right by means of their natural conscience. The problem lay in the will, in the helplessness of the conscience to *motivate* right action. The natural conscience was a rational power, which perceived moral obligations as part of the proper fitnesses of things. But it did not control the will. In its fallen state, the human will was incapable of transcending self-interest to achieve the austere altruism Edwards insisted was the one true virtue. Only God's grace could supply this.[56]

Edwards's decision to define conscience as a rational power was important. It meant that he was defending the conventional view, going back to Plato, that moral judgments were real judgments and not (as Hutcheson and Hume claimed) emotional reactions. But it also meant that conscience partook of the weakness of reason. Whether reason could motivate to action at all was the subject of a long-standing philosophical disagreement. The dominant school (sometimes called intellectualism), looking back to Aristotle and Aquinas, held that reason could motivate, even while deploring its weakness. A rival school of thought (voluntarism), led by Augustine, held that reason had no motivating power whatsoever.[57] Edwards associated himself with the latter position, which helped him in his theological argument against free will. (Our actions are prompted by our emotions; but we do not voluntarily choose our emotions; therefore we do not have free will.)[58]

It might seem that Edwards, in espousing voluntarism, was excluding the rational conscience altogether from the operation of the will and defining it as solely a faculty of the understanding. Such was not the case. In matters of practical morality Edwards still expected reason to regulate and legitimate the motives, though it could not itself be a motive. "All things in the soul of man should be under the government of reason, which is the highest faculty."[59] He accepted the conventional terminological distinction that a passion was a bad affection, one that had usurped the governing role of reason. The Christian life was a process of "ruling and suppressing the evil and unruly passions" while "exerting and following good affections." The degree of rational justification and order that natural emotions displayed provided Edwards with a basis for judging them. For example, anger was legitimate or not depending on whether it was rationally appropriate.[60]

Edwards, then, agreed with Franklin that there was such a thing as a natural morality, discoverable by human reason. "There are many in this world, who are wholly destitute of saving grace," he wrote, "but nevertheless have something of that which is called moral virtue."[61] In accordance with standard eighteenth-century moral philosophy, the natural conscience could invoke the aid of other faculties in the performance of its task; thus, Edwards explained, reason can ally with love "to keep men's irascible passions down in subjection, so that reason and love may have the regulation of them." Among the principles in human nature that Edwards recognized as potentially helpful to the natural conscience were prudential self-interest, benevolent affections, and the force of good habits.[62]

Edwards would have found nothing actually wrong with most of Franklin's homely devices for self-improvement, based as they were on nature and the general Providence of God that made provision for human welfare in this world. No more would he have objected to the Founders' constitutional provisions for checks and balances, which imaginatively used human wickedness to combat wickedness. ("Ambition must be made to counteract ambition," as Madison explained it, invoking the principle of countervailing passions.)[63] Such devices took human nature as they found it, and did the best that could be done with it. They tamed the effects of evil without actually eradicating it. But, of course, all that could be achieved in such a fashion was better behavior; the basic self-preoccupation that corrupted the human heart remained untouched. True virtue, Edwards insisted, was a matter of inward disposition, not outward behavior.

Both Edwards and Franklin carried on inward dialogues in the course of trying to master their own subordinate faculties. Like Franklin, Edwards addressed good resolutions to himself. "Resolved to do whatever I think to be my duty, and most for the good and advantage of mankind in general." "Resolved, to be continually endeavoring to find out some new contrivance and invention to promote the forementioned things." "Remember to Read Over These Resolutions Once a Week."[64] Some of Edwards's private resolutions are as candidly prudential as anything Franklin ever expressed. The cover-leaf memoranda Edwards wrote for his projected monumental work on natural philosophy, for example, include: "The world will expect more modesty because of my circumstances—in America, young, etc. Let there then be a superabundance of modesty [in the work], and though perhaps 'twill otherwise be needless, it will wonderfully make way for its reception in the world."[65] Not only self-exhortation but also self-evaluation characterized the inward dialogues of Edwards and Franklin. The two were working within a cultural inheritance of Puritan introspection that had produced innumerable diaries, conversion narratives, and similar documents. The traditional purpose of such efforts was to assess the quality of one's motives, in order to ascertain whether they were grace-given or self-seeking. Both Edwards and Franklin show finely honed skills at detecting the dangers of self-deception, particularly "how exceedingly affection or appetite blinds the mind and brings it into entire subjection."[66]

Franklin, as we have seen, expected that his practice of self-discipline would eventually lead to the formation of good habits that would render virtue automatic and unproblematic. He realized that pride could never really be overcome, but treated this as a minor exception to the rule.[67] Edwards worked just as hard at self-discipline and industriousness. ("By a sparingness in diet," he wrote in his diary while a student at Yale, "I shall doubtless be able to think more clearly, and shall gain time.")[68] But he harbored no expectation that self-discipline would ever come easily; it would always be a struggle requiring conscious effort. The residue of pride was no small matter for Edwards. Besides, any good behavior that came reflexively, without manifesting an intention, might be useful but could not be truly virtuous in his eyes.

At most, Edwards's self-imposed rules of discipline might manifest a grace already received or in some vague way prepare one to receive it. Whatever practical payoff they had in this life must be set against the unremitting toil they cost him. Edwards's life, like his writings, was organized methodically, even painfully. The evidence that has come down to us provides little indication that Edwards enjoyed relaxation as Franklin obviously did.[69] Expecting so little from his regimen, why did Edwards subject himself to it? One is driven to the conclusion that he found austerity and hard work satisfying in their own right. If so, Jonathan Edwards was a more thoroughgoing exemplar of the work ethic than Benjamin Franklin.

There is a striking contrast between Franklin and Edwards in their attitude toward the faculty of prudence, or self-interest. In theory, Edwards admitted that self-interest, if properly enlightened, could be a legitimate motive.[70] In practice, however, he very seldom urged prudential considerations upon his audiences except with regard to the hereafter. Imprecatory sermons like the famous **"Sinners in the Hands of an Angry God"** were addressed to the prudential self-interest of sinners to awaken them to a proper sense of their danger. Perhaps this would be of some help in preparing them for grace. However, Edwards pointed out elsewhere that fear of hell was only a "natural" and loveless motive, not to be equated with true virtue.[71]

According to Edwards, the self-preoccupation of human nature was the essence of its sinful alienation from God; "selfishness is a principle natural to us, and indeed all the corruption of nature does radically consist in it."[72] To exploit this ultimate vice, even for limited ends, must have been too distasteful for the evangelical philosopher. Instead, over and over again, he inveighed against it. "A Christian spirit is contrary to a selfish spirit." "Men are not to act as their own or for themselves singly, for they are not their own." "If you are selfish, and make yourself and your own private interest your idol, God will leave you to yourself, and let you promote your own interest as well as you can."[73]

Social ethics was really too important to be left to the second-best devices of natural morality; Edwards insisted upon applying the standards of divine morality in his social thought. He demanded the transcendence of self-interest and the attainment of altruism, both of which only come through divine grace. Only a religious awakening, therefore, could redeem secular society. Once a person had been converted, he would be "greatly concerned for the good of the public community to which he belongs, and particularly of the town where he dwells."[74] The specification of the town is significant; practically all of Edwards's own interest in what we would call politics was expressed at the town level.

Rejection of individualism was a prominent feature of Edwards's social thought and social ethics. In one of his rare references to an American identity, Edwards criticized the individualistic culture he and his neighbors shared: "We in this land are trained up from generation to generation in a too niggardly, selfish spirit and practice." When he persuaded his parishioners to subscribe to a town covenant in 1742, he made its central theme the renunciation of "private interest" (including its corollary, party spirit).[75] In his sermons on economic life, usually based on Old Testament texts that emphasized communal responsibility, Edwards repeatedly denounced individualism, market values, and laissez-faire.[76] Edwards stood closer to the classical republican tradition than to the liberal one, but his views on political and social morality owed more to biblical sources than to any secular philosophy. His teachings exemplified ideals of Christian communalism often expressed in the church-centered villages of colonial New England.[77]

For Jonathan Edwards, society was ideally an organic whole, in which persons treated each other as fellow members of the body of Christ. This is clearly set forth in his sermon cycle on I Corinthians 13, entitled **"Charity and Its Fruits,"** now available in the Yale edition of Edwards's works. The proper model for society he presented was not a contractual arrangement but the human family, with the

magistrates acting "as the fathers of the commonwealth." In a good society, Christians "will not desire that all should be upon a level; for they know it is best that some should be above others and should be honored and submitted to as such."[78] (When Tryon Edwards published the work in the nineteenth century, he inserted some extra sentences at this point to try to soften and explain away his ancestor's endorsement of social inequality.)[79]

Edwards clearly believed that social morality was important. As a manifestation of grace, social morality was more important than acts of worship: "moral duties, such as acts of righteousness, truth, meekness, forgiveness, and love toward our neighbors . . . are of much greater importance in the sight of God than all the externals of his worship."[80] Edwards practiced what he preached and stood up for his social vision regardless of its unpopularity with a majority of his congregation. However, the social morality that interested him was properly only a by-product of true virtue, the faith of the heart. This relationship is clearly evident in the biography Edwards prepared of a model Christian saint, David Brainerd.

Although the account is nominally Brainerd's own journal, we know from the evidence presented by Norman Pettit that Edwards extensively edited and rewrote it, making it conform with his own theories concerning the religious affections.[81] The didactic life story that Edwards presented could hardly contrast more sharply with that of Franklin's *Autobiography*. Where Franklin chose himself as the subject, Edwards selected another. Where Franklin's subject lived to achieve wealth and fame at a ripe old age, Edwards's subject endured unremitting physical and psychological affliction, worked hard for very modest results, and died young. Yet Edwards held David Brainerd up as an example to young Christians of what life was really all about.

Like Franklin and Edwards, Brainerd was constantly in dialogue with himself. This dialogue concerns his relationship with God, the purity of his own motives, and his struggle to attain mastery over his baser faculties. His emotional highs and lows are vividly recorded. For all Brainerd's obsessive concern with overcoming pride, the dialogue seems in its own way totally self-absorbed. A missionary to the Indians, Brainerd only rarely notices the Indians as individual personalities. Most of the time they are means to his ends, his service to them an act of determined self-abnegation.[82] Franklin had thought personal religious practice could be useful as a spur to a life of public service, but Brainerd leads his life of service as a means to his personal religious practice. Franklin imposed personal discipline on himself as a means to temporal success; Brainerd uses self-discipline as a means to evangelical humiliation. In the end, the meagre results Brainerd achieved in his mission were irrelevant to him and his editor; Edwards was interested in Brainerd's state of mind, not in what Franklin would call his merit.

In practice, Edwards showed scarcely any concern with working for a just society through the devices of natural morality that Franklin and the other framers of the Constitution employed. While there was nothing wrong with these devices in principle, neither did they seem very important. They did nothing to liberate humanity from its prison of self-centeredness. Edwards wanted to change hearts, to be an instrument of divine grace for individuals. When enough individuals were saved, the community would be saved by the manifestation of their grace. In the meantime, a person would be foolish to attach much importance to what Edwards called "this world of pride and malice and contention and perpetual jarring and strife, . . . where all are for themselves and self-interest governs." The world Edwards described was the same one Franklin knew, but their responses to it were different. "What man acting wisely and considerately would concern himself much about laying up a store in such a world as this?" demanded Edwards.[83] Franklin could have cheerfully responded, "I would."

For Edwards, society was too individualistic because the people who composed it were too selfish; the problem of society was rooted in the problem of human nature, most specifically, in the defective human will. "The ruin which the Fall brought upon the soul of man consists very much in that he lost his nobler and more extensive principles, and fell wholly under the government of self-love." To supply the motivating power toward virtue that fallen human nature lacked, Franklin and the Arminian moral philosophers invoked prudence, instinctive emotions, and unthinking habits. But Edwards pointed out that none of these was *truly* virtuous: they might shape outward behavior but they did not alter one's egocentric state of mind. Preoccupation with self was a kind of prison, from which only Christ offered hope of deliverance. "God hath in mercy to miserable man contrived in the work of redemption . . . to bring the soul of man out of its confinement and again to infuse those noble and divine principles by which it was governed at first [before the Fall.]"[84]

"There is a distinction to be made between some things which are truly virtuous, and others which only seem to be virtuous," wrote Edwards in what is probably his most famous philosophical distinction. "True virtue," as distinguished from the various halfway measures and imitations that Franklin and the Arminians discussed, Edwards defined as "benevolence to Being in general."[85] This was not part of fallen humanity's natural make-up; it could only be bestowed through God's saving grace. In His "ordinary method," to be sure, God would "give grace to those that are much concerned about it," those who had worked to attain "a preparatory conviction of sin." Ordinarily, "God makes use of . . . a good understanding, a rational brain, moral prudence, etc."[86] But of course there were many exceptions and "surprising" conversions. there was no secret sure method, no gradual progression up the ladder of love (as Plato had supposed). Grace was a matter of all or nothing, a blessing from God, which one could neither earn nor resist. When it came, it shed "a divine and supernatural light" upon experience.[87] Of course even a sanctified person would not be sinless. But he or she would have

been definitively liberated from the prison of self and weaned away from this world of selfishness. "By living a life of love, you will be in the way to heaven. As heaven is a world of love, so the way to heaven is the way of love."[88]

True virtue, "benevolence to Being in general," was an affection, that is, an emotion. Franklin had considered religious belief nonrational and morality rational. For Edwards, it was just the opposite: Christianity was rationally justifiable, but true virtue was an emotional quality. Being an emotion, the God-given power of true virtue conferred no additional knowledge about right and wrong; the natural conscience, if well informed, will "approve and condemn the same things that are approved and condemned by a spiritual sense."[89] The difference was in the beholder, not in the principles beheld. Being an emotion, true virtue was involuntary: one does not love or hate as a result of a deliberate decision. Most importantly, true virtue, being an affection or emotion, had what the merely speculative, natural conscience lacked: the power to motivate. True virtue "not only removes the hinderances of reason, but positively helps reason,"[90] empowering one to act rationally, that is, rightly. True virtue overcame the limitations of self and opened the door to the world of love. Divine grace solved the problem of human nature.

As Norman Fiering has brilliantly demonstrated, Edwards's theory of natural morality was rationalistic, but his theory of divine morality or "true virtue" was a form of ethical sentimentalism.[91] It was also a form of ethical aestheticism. Like a number of other moral philosophers of his time, Edwards sometimes used the term "moral sense" as a synonym for "conscience." For him, the moral sense meant the natural conscience. True virtue, on the other hand, was not a moral sense but a quality of moral *taste*. Just as some people had an aesthetic sensibility that enabled them to react immediately to beauty, he explained in his famous treatise on the religious affections, "so there is likewise such a thing as a divine taste, given and maintained by the Spirit of God, in the hearts of the saints, whereby they are in like manner led and guided in discerning and distinguishing the true spiritual and holy beauty of actions."[92] As our responses to natural beauty are immediate, disinterested, and involuntary, so are the responses of the truly virtuous person to moral beauty. "The soul [of the saint] distinguishes as a musical ear."[93] What interested Franklin about morality was its usefulness, but what interested Edwards about morality was its beauty. In the last analysis, for Edwards, beauty and morality were the same thing.[94]

Like Franklin, Edwards was much interested in natural science; he projected, though he never wrote, a comprehensive work on natural philosophy, as the physical sciences were then called. The differences between Franklin and Edwards, however, are as apparent in their approach to science as in their moral philosophies. Where Franklin was primarily an experimentalist, Edwards was primarily a theoretician. Franklin was interested in applied science;

Edwards, in pure science. Edwards's interest in science stemmed from his love of harmony, symmetry, and beauty. "Always a metaphysician and an artist," even in his scientific writings, "he wanted to fit all loose parts into a perfect whole," writes Paul Conkin. Scientist as well as logical determinist, Edwards wanted "to live in a universe in which nothing was left to chance."[95] Eventually, Edwards's scientific activities were crowded out of his life by his theological and evangelical efforts. From his point of view, the latter were more relevant to the needs of the human condition.

Edwards was always clear about his priorities. The work of Redemption was more important than either the study of the material universe or the promotion of social reform.

> The conversion of one soul, considered together with the source, foundation, and purchase of it, and also the benefit and eternal issue of it, is a more glorious work of God than the creation of the whole material universe. . . . More happiness and a greater benefit to man, is the fruit of each single drop of such a shower [of grace], than all the temporal good of the most happy revolution in a land or nation amounts to, or all that a people could gain by the conquest of the world.[96]

Edwards could not more eloquently have summed up his differences with Benjamin Franklin.

While Franklin and Edwards both addressed the problem of human nature as posed by eighteenth-century moral philosophy, in the end each of them transcended the conventional model of the faculties. That model was based on the assumption that rationality ought to govern human nature; its failure to do so was deplorable. Far from simply bemoaning the failure of rationality, however, Franklin and Edwards both found substitutes for it in the course of their quests for virtue. Franklin substituted habit; Edwards, a divinely disinterested benevolence. One came through practice and the other through grace. Each was, in its way, an answer to the problem of humanity's perverse irrationality.

For Franklin, the process of self-construction was secular, deliberate, and highly individualistic. For Edwards, self-construction was at best a preparation for a divine grace that would be necessary to fulfill the promise of rebirth; it was a preparation undertaken within the tutelage and discipline of a local church community. Franklin encouraged people to feel pride in their accomplishments, however partial; Edwards deplored human pride. Surprisingly, however, after their deaths the intellectual history of self-construction in America developed in the direction of synthesizing their approaches rather than leaving them as mutually exclusive alternatives.

EPILOGUE AND SYNTHESIS

Edwards's message urged people to let God take over their hearts, and all else would follow. Franklin's message was that God helps those who help themselves. There have always been many Christians in America who cannot help feeling that both are somehow true. In the light of the differences between Jonathan Edwards and Benjamin Franklin, it may seem remarkable that there should be an American tradition drawing upon both of their approaches to the problem of human nature. But such there is, and it goes all the way back to their contemporary, George Whitefield, the Christian evangelist from England who came to know and admire them both. Edwards and Whitefield had in common the desire to save souls; Franklin and Whitefield had in common a concern with social morality and organized social reform. Franklin welcomed Whitefield's energy, rhetorical power, and organizational skills in humanitarian causes.[97] The next several generations of evangelicals developed along the lines Whitefield pioneered and Franklin approved. In the nineteenth century, American evangelical Protestants created an impressive synthesis of the Edwardsian and Franklinian approaches to religion that had momentous historical consequences.

The Evangelical movement of the nineteenth century, international and ecumenical in scope, active in both political and private sectors, innovative in its use of the media of communication, became a major culture-shaping force for its age. Like latter-day Franklins, the evangelical Christians of the century after Franklin's death in 1790 were utilitarian, humanitarian, well organized, and not afraid to make big plans. But in the spirit of Edwards, they centered their personal lives upon an experienced relationship with Christ. As compared with *both* Franklin and Edwards, the evangelicals of the nineteenth century strike us as optimistic. They combined Edwards's faith in God's grace with a more positive estimate of human nature than that of either of the eighteenth-century thinkers we have been examining. When Jonathan Edwards's descendent Tryon Edwards edited **"Charity and Its Fruits"** in 1851, he found the conclusion of the seventh sermon, against selfishness, in need of revising. Edwards had ended on a note of pessimism regarding the likelihood of overcoming selfishness; his nineteenth-century successor added a more positive peroration, ending: "Let us strive to overcome it that we may grow in the grace of an unselfish spirit, and thus glorify God and do good to man."[98]

Edwards had thought Franklin's devices to improve natural morality valid but not very important. Franklin, however, felt the same way about Edwards's solution to the problem of human nature. "So Dr. Edwards assures us that a few people experience (now and then) a beatific vision of the divine," one can imagine Franklin complaining; "so what? The world needs solutions appropriate for everybody, not just for a few saints." The evangelicals of the nineteenth century shared Franklin's attitude on this matter. They preached *plenteous* grace, enough grace for all. And instead of relying on occasional "showers" of grace in periodic revivals, the nineteenth-century evangelicals so organized and institutionalized their revival as to make it a continuous downpour. By the same token, they organized the charitable fruits of grace on a scale Cotton Mather could never have imagined.

The nineteenth-century evangelicals still conceptualized human nature in terms of a faculty psychology, for they continued to use and adapt the intellectual constructs of eighteenth-century moral philosophy. By their time, these had been codified by the Scots Thomas Reid and Dugald Stewart and the Scottish-American John Witherspoon. The form of Scottish moral philosophy that the American evangelicals mainly used was actually closer to Franklin's than to Edwards's model, for the sentimentalist side of Edwards's ethical theory did not win broad acceptance, even within the Reformed community.

Within the framework of faculty psychology, Edwards's evangelical descendents even found an ingenious way of accepting the legitimacy of prudential self-love. The self-love of the regenerate was legitimate, Edwardsean theologians decided, because a person who was full of benevolence to Being in general would inevitably direct at least a little of this benevolence toward his or her own being. And the self-love of the unregenerate, while morally culpable, was still socially useful. Just as God had turned the wickedness of Pharaoh to the good of the Exodus or the wickedness of Judas to the good of Redemption, His Providence could make good come out of evil on an everyday basis. As Adam Smith himself pointed out, the self-interested labors of the baker provided society with its bread. The theology of Edwards thus made its peace with the utilitarian psychology of Benjamin Franklin.[99]

Some of the credit for adapting Edwards's legacy to a new age belongs to his disciple Samuel Hopkins (1721-1803). Hopkins taught that in the millennial time to come there would be a larger population and more virtue, so that God would in the end save many more people than were damned. He reconciled divine sovereignty with revival preaching and individual preparation by teaching that these were the "occasions" of grace, if not the "causes" of it. He completed the divorce of salvation from the fear of hell by teaching that after conversion a person should be so caught up by benevolence to Being as to be willing to be damned, if that was for the good of the whole. And through his courageous opposition to the New England slave trade, Hopkins pioneered the humanitarianism that would become such an admirable fruit of nineteenth-century evangelical piety.[100]

As mediated by Hopkins, Edwards became a heroic precursor and legitimator to the nineteenth-century evangelical humanitarian tradition. Joseph Tracy's magnificent centennial history of the revival of the 1740s (still indispensable for its lucid expositions of the context of events) typifies the respect that the Second Great Awakening felt toward the First.[101] Many a laborer in the vineyards of the Second Awakening drew inspiration and reassurance from **The Life of David Brainerd.** (Franklin's *Autobiography* was popular too in Victorian America, though not assembled and published in its present form until 1868.) The mantle of Edwards became a prize for which rival evangelical schools of thought grappled through prolonged theological debates. Meanwhile, religious liberals like Oliver Wendell Holmes the elder struggled to rid American culture of Edwards's towering presence.[102]

What happened in the nineteenth century was that evangelical Christians came to accept the importance of many of Franklin's concerns for temporal human welfare and incorporated them into their own version of the Edwardsian model of faith. Christian Sunday schools and Temperance organizations inculcated the habits of industriousness and sobriety that Franklin wanted encouraged. Edwards's concerns with church discipline and the social morality of the town were grandly generalized by his nineteenth-century admirers into a commitment to making the United States as a whole a Christian nation. His postmillennial speculations were likewise grandly elaborated by Lyman Beecher (1775-1863) and others as justification for social reform. This process reached a climax in the work of Charles Grandisson Finney (1792-1875), the central figure of the antebellum revival. Finney has been called a man with a "divided conscience": a utilitarian like Franklin, yet still committed to benevolent and religious motives like Edwards.[103]

Thus evangelical piety energized humanitarianism as deism never could—just as Franklin had expected. Franklin, who encouraged Whitefield's social enterprises, would have approved of the Evangelical United Front, perhaps viewing it as a Christian version of his United Party of Virtue. Since he looked upon all religions as means to temporal ends, we may surmise that Franklin would have thought the emancipation of the slaves alone sufficient justification for the religious faith of the Victorian era. Edwards, on the other hand, might well have worried about the strict doctrinal purity of many of those who so proudly claimed him. Philosophies that logic declares different, history may still reconcile.

Notes

1. *The Spectator,* no. 6 (March 8, 1711) and no. 408 (June 18, 1712), ed. Donald F. Bond (Oxford, 1965), I, 29; III, 524; Norman Fiering, "Will and Intellect in the New England Mind," *William and Mary Quarterly* 29 (Oct. 1972), 515-58; Daniel W. Howe, *The Unitarian Conscience,* rev. ed. (Middletown, Ct., 1988), 56-64; Arthur O. Lovejoy, *The Great Chain of Being* (Cambridge, Mass., 1936), chap. VI; Arthur O. Lovejoy, *Reflections on Human Nature* (Baltimore, 1961).

2. On Franklin, see Albert Furtwangler, *American Silhouettes: Rhetorical Identities of the Founders* (New Haven, 1987), 20-34; and Jeanette S. Lewis, "'A Turn of Thinking': The Long Shadow of *The Spectator* in Franklin's *Autobiography,*" *Early American Literature* 13 (Winter 1978-79), 268-77. On Edwards, see Norman Fiering, "The Transatlantic Republic of Letters," *William and Mary Quarterly* 33 (Oct. 1976), 642-60.

3. Jonathan Edwards, "Charity and Its Fruits" in *Ethical Writings,* ed. Paul Ramsey, *The Works of*

Jonathan Edwards (New Haven, 1959-), VIII, 277. Benjamin Franklin, "Poor Richard's Almanac" (1749 and 1750), in *The Papers of Benjamin Franklin,* ed. Leonard W. Labaree et al. (New Haven, 1959-), III, 340, 441. (I have modernized the spelling.)

4. See Robert Middlekauff, *Benjamin Franklin and His Enemies* (Berkeley, 1995).

5. A famous indictment of Franklin was handed down by D. H. Lawrence, *Studies in Classic American Literature* (London, 1924). More recent assessments of the problem of Franklin's identity are Mitchell R. Breitwieser, *Cotton Mather and Benjamin Franklin: The Price of Representative Personality* (Cambridge, Eng., 1984); and Ormond Seavey, *Becoming Benjamin Franklin: The Autobiography and the Life* (University Park, Penn., 1988).

6. Franklin to Joseph Priestley, June 7, 1782, *Works,* ed. Jared Sparks (Chicago, 1882), IX, 226. (I use Sparks's edition for the years that the Yale edition has not yet reached.) Franklin to James Logan [1737?], *Papers,* II, 185.

7. See David Larson, "Franklin on the Nature of Man and the Possibility of Virtue," *Early American Literature* 10 (Fall 1975), 111-20; and Ronald A. Bosco, "'He That Best Understands the World, Least Likes It': The Dark Side of Benjamin Franklin," *Pennsylvania Magazine of History and Biography* 111 (Oct. 1987), 525-54.

8. *Papers,* III, 481. Franklin repeated this passage *verbatim* when he revised his Will in 1757: *Papers,* VII, 204.

9. *Papers,* I, 105.

10. Franklin to Samuel Johnson, Aug. 23, 1750, *Papers,* IV, 41. "Poor Richard's Almanac" (1745), *Papers,* III, 6.

11. Francis Hutcheson, *An Inquiry into the Original of Our Ideas of Beauty and Virtue* (London, 1729), 180. On Franklin as a proto-utilitarian, see also Norman Fiering, "Benjamin Franklin and the Way to Virtue," *American Quarterly* 30 (Summer 1978), 199-223. The political dimension of Franklin's concept of virtue is discussed in Paul W. Conner, *Poor Richard's Politicks: Benjamin Franklin and His New American Order* (New York, 1965); and Drew R. McCoy, "Benjamin Franklin's Vision of a Republican Political Economy for America," *William and Mary Quarterly* 35 (Oct. 1978), 605-28.

12. "Poor Richard's Almanac" (1739), *Papers,* II, 223; cf. *ibid.,* IV, 86. See also Paul Conkin, "Benjamin Franklin: Science and Morals," in his *Puritans and Pragmatists* (Bloomington, 1976), esp. 87-89.

13. *The Autobiography of Benjamin Franklin,* ed. Leonard W. Labaree et al. (New Haven, 1964). An example of Franklin's early interest in deism, "A Dissertation on Liberty and Necessity" (1725),

Papers, I, 57-71, expounded a system which, although internally logical, was not in the slightest useful to mankind.

14. Franklin to George Whitefield, Sept. 2, 1769, *Papers,* XVI, 192.

15. For Franklin's interest in liturgics, see his revision of the Lord's Prayer (1768) and of the Anglican Book of Common Prayer (1773), *Papers,* XV, 299-303, and XX, 343-52. On prayer, see his "Articles of Belief and Acts of Religion" (1728), *Papers,* I, 101-09.

16. "On the Providence of God in the Government of the World" (1732), *Papers,* I, 264.

17. In a letter to his Calvinist sister Jane Mecom, Franklin invoked (for tactical reasons) the authority of Jonathan Edwards to score a point; *Papers,* II, 384f. "The Education of Youth" (1749), *Papers,* III, 413.

18. Franklin to unknown addressee [Dec. 13, 1757], *Papers,* VII, 294.

19. "Poor Richard's Almanac" (1758); *Papers,* VII, 353.

20. Franklin to Samuel Mather, May 12, 1784, *Writings,* IX, 208; Franklin to Josiah and Abiah Franklin, April 13, 1738, *Papers,* II, 203; *Papers,* III, 125.

21. On Franklin's religion, see Elizabeth Dunn, "From Bold Youth to Reflective Sage: A Re-evaluation of Benjamin Franklin's Religion," *Pennsylvania Magazine of History and Biography* 111 (Oct. 1987), 501-24; D. H. Meyer, "Franklin's Religion," in *Critical Essays on Benjamin Franklin,* ed. Melvin Buxbaum (Boston, 1987), 147-67; and Alfred O. Aldridge, *Benjamin Franklin and Nature's God* (Durham, N.C., 1967).

22. See Alfred Owen Aldridge, *Benjamin Franklin: Philosopher and Man* (Philadelphia, 1965), 39-46. On the Societies for the Reformation of Manners, see Shelley Burtt, *Virtue Transformed: Political Argument in England, 1688-1740* (Cambridge, Eng., 1992), 22-24. Franklin's own account of the Junto is given in his *Autobiography,* 162f.

23. Alexander Hamilton, in *The Federalist,* no. 72, ed. Jacob Cooke (Middletown, Ct., 1961), 488.

24. W. E. Gladstone, ed., *The Works of Joseph Butler* (Oxford, 1896), I, 97-98.

25. On the relationship between happiness and virtue in Franklin's thought, see Lorraine Smith Pangle and Thomas L. Pangle, *The Learning of Liberty: The Educational Ideals of the American Founders* (Lawrence, Kan., 1993), 265f.

26. On this process, see Albert O. Hirschman, *The Passions and the Interests: Political Arguments for Capitalism Before Its Triumph* (Princeton, 1977).

27. See, e.g., "Poor Richard's Almanac" (1744), *Papers,* II, 397; *Autobiography,* 160.

28. See *Papers*, VII, 89.

29. "Wealth" was a relative term for Franklin: "Who is rich? He that rejoices in his portion." "Poor Richard's Almanac" (1744), *Papers*, II, 395.

30. Since Jared Sparks supposed Franklin the author of the dialogues, he printed them in his edition of the *Works*, II, 46-57. Alfred Owen Aldridge, "Franklin's 'Shaftesburian' Dialogues Not Franklin's," *American Literature* 21 (May 1949), 151-59.

31. See Wilbur Samuel Howell, *Eighteenth-Century British Logic and Rhetoric* (Princeton, 1971); William Charvat, *Origins of American Critical Thought* (Philadelphia, 1936, reprinted 1961).

32. David M. Larson, "Benevolent Persuasion: The Art of Benjamin Franklin's Philanthropic Papers," *Pennsylvania Magazine of History and Biography* 110 (April 1986), 195-218, quotation from p. 216. See also Edward J. Gallagher, "The Rhetorical Strategy of Franklin's 'Way to Wealth,'" *Eighteenth-Century Studies* 6 (June 1973), 475-85.

33. "Poor Richard's Almanac" (1755 and 1758), *Papers*, V, 473 and VII, 350. See also Cameron Nickels, "Franklin's Poor Richard's Almanacs," in *The Oldest Revolutionary: Essays on Benjamin Franklin*, ed. J. A. Leo Lemay (Philadelphia, 1976), 77-89.

34. Franklin? "Letter from Father Abraham to His Beloved Son" (1758), *Papers*, VIII, 123f; Franklin, *Autobiography*, 148.

35. Franklin, "A Man of Sense," (1735), *Papers*, II, 15-19.

36. Franklin to Lord Kames, May 3, 1760, *Papers*, IX, 105. Franklin's famous description of the regimen and his practice of it is in *Autobiography*, 148-60.

37. David L. Parker, "From Sound Believer to Practical Preparationist: Some Puritan Harmonics in Franklin's *Autobiography*," in Lemay, ed., *Oldest Revolutionary*, 67-75.

38. See Fiering, "Franklin and the Way to Virtue."

39. Franklin? "Letter from Father Abraham" (1758), *Papers*, VIII, 127; *Autobiography*, 148.

40. The first part of the definition follows Locke. Franklin, *Papers*, I, 262.

41. Franklin, "Self-Denial Not the Essence of Virtue," (1735), *Papers*, II, 19-21; quotations from p. 21. Franklin was probably arguing against Bernard Mandeville, though the position that virtue implies self-denial is also associated with Kant.

42. Franklin to Samuel Johnson, Aug. 23, 1750, *Papers*, IV, 41.

43. Franklin, "Proposals Relating to the Education of Youth in Pennsylvania" (1749), *Papers*, III, 419. The Scottish moral philosopher Francis Hutcheson defined the "moral importance of any agent" as M = B x A, where B = benevolence and A = abilities. See his *Inquiry* (cited in n. 11), 185.

44. Franklin's position resembles that attributed to the English "Court Whigs" in Shelley Burtt, *Virtue Transformed*, 112.

45. See Albert J. Wurth, Jr., "The Franklin Persona: The Virtue of Practicality and the Practicality of Virtue," in *Virtue, Corruption, and Self-Interest: Political Values in the Eighteenth Century*, ed. Richard K. Matthews (Bethlehem, Penn., 1994), 76-102.

46. "Proposals and Queries to Be Asked the Junto" (1732), *Papers*, I, 263.

47. Norman Fiering, *Jonathan Edwards's Moral Thought and Its British Context* (Chapel Hill, N.C., 1981), 7. For Edwards's participation in transatlantic religious dialogue, see Harold P. Simonson, "Jonathan Edwards and his Scottish Connections" [British] *Journal of American Studies* 21 (Dec. 1987), 353-76.

48. Perry Miller, *Jonathan Edwards* (New York, 1949), pp. 180-84, 237, 252. Miller seems to have thought that if one rejected the existence of innate *ideas*, one had to reject the existence of innate *powers*, which is what the faculties were.

49. Jonathan Edwards, *The Freedom of the Will*, ed. Paul Ramsey, in *Works*, I, 133. On Edwards's use of faculty psychology, see William J. Scheick, *The Writings of Jonathan Edwards: Theme, Motif, and Style* (College Station: Texas, 1975).

50. *The Republic* IV.434D-441C.

51. Jonathan Edwards, *A Treatise Concerning Religious Affections*, ed. John Smith, in *Works*, II, 122. On Edwards's Platonism, see Paul Conkin, "Jonathan Edwards: Theology," in *Puritans and Pragmatists*.

52. Edwards, "A Divine and Supernatural Light" (1734), in Jonathan Edwards, *Representative Selections*, ed. Clarence Faust and Thomas Johnson (New York, 1935), 103.

53. Edwards, "Charity and Its Fruits," in Jonathan Edwards, *Ethical Writings*, ed. Paul Ramsey, in *Works*, VIII, 286f.

54. *Ibid.*, 252; Edwards, "Divine and Supernatural Light," *Selections*, 103.

55. Benjamin Franklin, "Defence of Rev. Mr. Hemphill" (1735), *Papers*, II, 114.

56. Edwards, *Religious Affections*, 206-07. See also Clyde Holbrook, *The Ethics of Jonathan Edwards: Morality and Aesthetics* (Ann Arbor, 1973), esp. pp. 56-71.

57. See Fiering, "Will and Intellect," and Fiering, *Edwards's Moral Thought*, 263-69.

58. "All acts of the will are acts of the affections." Edwards, "Some Thoughts Concerning the Revival of Religion in New England" (1742), in Jonathan

Edwards, *The Great Awakening,* ed. C. C. Goen, in *Works* IV, 297. Cf. Edwards, "The Mind," in Jonathan Edwards, *Scientific and Philosophical Writings,* ed. Wallace Anderson, in *Works,* VI, 388, which equates the affections with "lively exercises of the will."

59. Edwards, "Charity and Its Fruits," in *Ethical Writings,* 277.

60. Edwards, *Religious Affections,* 98, 350; "Charity and Its Fruits," in *Ethical Writings,* 277.

61. Edwards, *True Grace, Distinguished from the Experience of Devils* (1753), quoted in Fiering, *Edwards's Moral Thought,* p. 61.

62. Edwards, "Charity and Its Fruits," *Ethical Writings,* 278; Fiering, *Edwards's Moral Thought,* 92.

63. James Madison, in *The Federalist,* no. 72, p. 349.

64. These "Resolutions" are among many printed in Edwards, *Representative Selections,* 38.

65. "Natural Philosophy," in *Scientific and Philosophical Writings,* 193.

66. Edwards, "Journal" (1723), quoted in Fiering, *Edwards's Moral Thought,* 151.

67. Franklin, *Autobiography,* 159-60.

68. "Diary" in *Selections,* 51.

69. See Holbrook, *Ethics of Edwards,* 91.

70. Edwards, "Charity and Its Fruits," *Ethical Writings,* 254.

71. Edwards, *Ethical Writings,* 176.

72. *Ibid.,* 271. In Puritan moral theology, it was important to "wean" one's affections away from selfish and worldly things.

73. These quotations are from "Charity and Its Fruits," *ibid.,* 260, 276, and 269.

74. *Ibid.,* 260.

75. *Ibid.,* 271; Richard Bushman, ed., *The Great Awakening: Documents on the Revival of Religion 1740-1745* (New York, 1970), 166-68.

76. Mark Valeri, "The Economic Thought of Jonathan Edwards," *Church History* 60 (March 1991), 37-54. Patricia Tracy calls Edwards's outlook "Tory" (*Jonathan Edwards, Pastor* [New York, 1980], p. 149); perhaps a more accurate term would be "patriarchal."

77. See Barry Shain, *The Myth of American Individualism: The Protestant Origins of American Political Thought* (Princeton, 1994).

78. "Charity and Its Fruits," *Ethical Writings,* 242-79; quotations from pp. 261 and 242.

79. See Paul Ramsey's commentary, *ibid.,* 105-06 and 242n.

80. Edwards, "Some Thoughts," in *The Great Awakening,* 522. This was the passage that Franklin cited approvingly; see n. 17 above.

81. See "Introduction" to Jonathan Edwards, *The Life of David Brainerd,* ed. Norman Pettit, in *Works,* VII.

82. E.g., *ibid.,* 261. An interesting exception is Brainerd's encounter with an Indian medicine man who explained a little of the native religion to him (*ibid.,* 329-30).

83. The two quotations are from Edwards, "Charity and Its Fruits," *Ethical Writings,* 393-94.

84. *Ibid.,* 252-53; "Divine and Supernatural Light," 103.

85. Edwards, "The Nature of True Virtue," in *Ethical Writings,* 540.

86. Edwards, "Miscellanies," no. 116, in *The Philosophy of Jonathan Edwards,* Harvey G. Townsend, ed. (Eugene, Or., 1955), 109-110.

87. Edwards, "A Divine and Supernatural Light," *Representative Selections,* 102-11.

88. "Charity and Its Fruits," *Ethical Writings,* 396.

89. Edwards, "The Nature of True Virtue," *Ethical Writings,* 596.

90. Edwards, "Divine and Supernatural Light," *Representative Selections,* 108.

91. Fiering, *Edwards's Moral Thought,* 64-66, 87, 103-04, 119, 143.

92. Edwards, *A Treatise Concerning Religious Affections, Works,* II, 283.

93. Edwards, *Miscellanies,* no. 141, quoted in Fiering, *Edwards's Moral Thought,* 351.

94. Many writers have commented on Edwards's aesthetics. Besides Holbrook, *The Ethics of Edwards,* chap. 6, see esp. Roland DeLattre, *Beauty and Sensibility in the Thought of Jonathan Edwards* (New Haven, 1968).

95. Paul Conkin, "Jonathan Edwards," in *Puritans and Pragmatists* (cited in n. 12 above), 46. See also Wallace Anderson's superb introduction to Edwards's *Scientific and Philosophical Writings* (cited in n. 58), pp. 1-142.

96. "Some Thoughts Concerning the Present Revival of Religion," *The Great Awakening,* 344-45.

97. See David T. Morgan, "A Most Unlikely Friendship: Benjamin Franklin and George Whitefield," *The Historian* 47 (Feb. 1985), 208-18.

98. Edwards, *Ethical Writings,* 271n.

99. See James D. German, "The Social Utility of Wicked Self-Love: Calvinism, Capitalism, and Public Policy in Revolutionary New England," *Journal of American History* 82 (Dec. 1995), 965-98.

100. See Joseph Conforti, *Samuel Hopkins and the New Divinity Movement* (Grand Rapids, Mich., 1981). Still very useful is Alexander Allen, "The Transition in New England Theology," *Atlantic Monthly* 68 (Dec. 1891), 767-80.

101. Joseph Tracy, *The Great Awakening: A History of the Revival of Religion in the Time of Edwards and Whitefield* (Edinburgh, 1976; first published in 1842). I am here using the term Second Great Awakening, as historians sometimes do, to refer to the entire era of evangelical activity from 1800 to the Civil War.

102. See Joseph Conforti, *Jonathan Edwards, Religious Tradition, and American Culture* (Chapel Hill, N.C., 1995); Nathan Hatch and Harry Stout, eds., *Jonathan Edwards and the American Experience* (New York, 1988); Mark Noll, "The Contested Legacy of Jonathan Edwards in Antebellum Calvinism," *Canadian Review of American Studies* 19 (Summer 1988), 149-64; and Daniel B. Shea, "Jonathan Edwards: The First Two Hundred Years," [British] *Journal of American Studies* 14 (August 1980), 181-98.

103. James Moorhead, "Social Reform and the Divided Conscience of Antebellum Protestantism," *Church History* 48 (Dec. 1979), 416-30.

Susan Clair Imbarrato (essay date 1998)

SOURCE: "Declaring the Self in the Spiritual Sphere: Elizabeth Ashbridge and Jonathan Edwards," in *Declarations of Independency in Eighteenth-Century American Autobiography,* University of Tennessee Press, 1998, pp. 14-39.

[In the following essay, Imbarrato compares the voices and analyzes the gender differences between two autobiographical narratives from the 1740s period of the Great Awakening: a spiritual autobiography written by Elizabeth Ashbridge, Quaker daughter and wife, and Edwards's Personal Narrative.*]*

Reconstructing one's life prompts the autobiographer to suggest a certain overall plan or direction to this life. When this retelling is inspired by religious conversion, the author's secular life is recast within a newfound spiritual context to demonstrate how random events are part of a divine plan. The conversion experience initiates a revision of one's life whereby seemingly fragmented episodes suddenly assume a coherent narrative that finds the pilgrim emerging from a state of darkness, or spiritual ignorance, into a state of spiritual enlightenment. And unlike the secular autobiographer, who might claim credit for personal achievement, the spiritual autobiographer emphasizes the superiority of divine will over human willfulness.[1] Thus even though autobiography is a deliberate construction of self and has even been called a "creation myth written in the first person,"[2] the spiritual autobiographer does not indulge in first-person narrative as a means of self-promotion but, instead, employs this form to reevaluate his or her relationship with Divinity.[3] The conversion narrative is often dramatic, casting events and characters onto an exaggerated stage that contrasts a life before and after the transformation. In the eighteenth-century spiritual autobiographies of Jonathan Edwards and Elizabeth Sampson Ashbridge, conversion both challenges and inspires their faith. For the Puritan, Jonathan Edwards, the conversion experience affirms his religious commitment as a member of the elect. For the Quaker, Elizabeth Ashbridge, conversion allows her to break through doubt and embrace her true religion. Within this larger study of first-person narratives, the spiritual autobiography serves as the initial link from the practice of seventeenth-century self-examination to the act of eighteenth-century self-construction.

THE IMPLICATIONS OF GENDER IN THE SPIRITUAL AUTOBIOGRAPHY: INDIVIDUAL AUTHORITY AND PERCEPTIONS OF DIVINITY

The eighteenth-century attitude that character is a constructed image enhances subjectivity in the spiritual autobiography. If character can be cultivated and is not merely dictated from birth, so that nurture dominates nature, individual perspective gains credibility in all aspects of inquiry, secular and religious. The rise of evangelicalism complements this perspective by encouraging personal revelations and recognizing the individual church member as an important force in the congregation. The conversion experience has always been both a private and a public affair in that the community validates the individual experience.[4] The evangelical movement builds on this relationship by eliciting more individualistic expressions of the experience itself. The Edwards and Ashbridge narratives, both written in the 1740s during the renewed religious fervor in colonial America known as the Great Awakening,[5] demonstrate personal response through a more prominent sense of the individual voice.[6] Within this context, these narratives challenge earlier texts, such as St. Augustine's, in which "self-analysis is valued not for its own sake but as a means of exposing the fallibility of humanity and affirming the ultimate authority of a divine knowledge beyond the individual's grasp" (Felski 103). By bringing this "ultimate authority" to a personal level, Edwards and Ashbridge contradict this view. It is precisely because of their self-analysis that their spiritual autobiographies explore their personal relationships with Divinity.

Individual analysis is further supported by the Enlightenment's privileging of experiential knowledge, which encourages investigation of all matters, secular and divine. Gordon Wood points out that even God's authority "was not immune to challenge. In an enlightened age God could no longer be absolute and arbitrary" (158). This perspective may be less applicable to Edwards's Puritanism than it is to Ashbridge's Quakerism, but in each text, their depictions of Divinity as a stern yet sympathetic figure render God more approachable. Writing about the self in this investigative age enhances spiritual understanding and encourages subjectivity.

The congregationalist movement empowers the individual's voice by granting each member more say in church matters. The female's voice gains particular attention as she actively participates in the administration of the congregation. Although men generally hold leadership positions, women expand their roles beyond their expected demonstrations of piety. Amanda Porterfield considers the religious arena a means for "attaining status and exercising influence in a culture that prized humility." Following this model, submissiveness was not necessarily a sign of weakness but rather a "highly self-restrained and indirect means of exercising authority" (87).[7] Self-examination provides the female with a sanctioned privacy, which allows for self-directed thought and prayer. Spiritual identity thus expands the woman's otherwise limited sphere of authority. Laurel Thatcher Ulrich, for example, notes that within ministerial literature "women became legitimately visible in only three ways: they married, they gave birth, they died. In the written materials, dying is by far the best documented activity" ("Virtuous" 69). Despite this lack of attention, Ulrich notes that "[c]hurch membership was one of the few public distinctions available to women" (*Good Wives* 216). Nancy Cott elaborates on this argument, claiming that within Puritanism, "religious identity also allowed women to assert themselves, both in private and in public ways. . . . to rely on an authority beyond the world of men" (140).[8] And although this privacy is carefully circumscribed and the boundaries are clearly drawn, as the case against Anne Hutchinson confirms, the practice of self-examination itself can potentially encourage the female seeker.[9] When compared to a previous generation's social codes, moreover, the Great Awakening encourages each gender's individual response. Women can claim the sphere of personal contemplation through religious practice without drawing criticism for neglecting domestic responsibilities.[10] Men are free to explore doctrinal variations and establish new denominations.[11]

The woman's spiritual autobiography is often located in her domestic world, and thus it integrates personal, familial concerns more fully into the narrative than the male's. From a congregational perspective, the woman's domestic base as spiritual center is not necessarily a hindrance, as it too favors a more localized administration. The eighteenth-century spiritual autobiography, in fact, encourages her to draw upon her domestic identity to empower her spiritual voice.[12] So where the female is more domestically bound, and therefore less likely to have the luxury of retreat, she refigures the domestic sphere as a source of spiritual guidance and strength.

Although such gender-based differences separate Edwards and Ashbridge in terms of their public authority, their conversion experiences share common ground. In both accounts, they trace a spiritual path subject to perpetual self-examination, and they each acknowledge their spiritual

transgressions and praise spiritual conversion for keeping them from what Edwards calls "the ways of sin." With these strategies in mind, Elizabeth Ashbridge begins *Some Account of the Fore Part of the Life of Elizabeth Ashbridge . . . Written by her own Hand many years ago*: "My Life being attended with many uncommon Occurences, some of which I through disobedience brought upon myself, and others I believe were for my Good, I therefore thought proper to make some remarks on the Dealings of Divine Goodness to me . . . and most earnestly I desire that whosoever reads the following lines, may take warning and shun the Evils that I have thro' the Deceitfulness of Satan been drawn into" (147).[13] In admitting her own "disobedience" as both self-inflicted and divinely orchestrated, Ashbridge's text can serve a larger didactic purpose. Hope comes for those readers who are similarly strong-willed and who also "earnestly" desire guidance to overcome demonic forces. From this gesture of self-disclosure, Ashbridge's "uncommon" life unfolds.

Edwards's self-examination is conducted within a more traditional, nondomestic structure and takes on its own confessional voice inspired by the enthusiasm of the Great Awakening. In the ***Personal Narrative***,[14] Edwards's self-reflections express a vulnerability willing to admit transgressions as he retraces his spiritual path: "I had a variety of concerns and exercises about my soul, from my childhood; but I had two more remarkable seasons of awakening, before I met with that change, by which I was brought to those new dispositions, and that new sense of things, that I have since had. The first time was when I was a boy, some years before I went to college, at a time of remarkable awakening in my father's congregation. I was then very much affected for many months, and concerned about the things of religion, and my soul's salvation . . ."(81).[15] Edwards asserts the "I" within the spiritual realms in an attitude of repentance and exemplifies the narrative as a vehicle for self-understanding and a guide to spiritual reflection. Edwards introduces himself as a sensitive, thoughtful child whose spiritual state is a primary concern and uses an earthly, cyclical image, "seasons of awakening," to mark the stages of his spiritual development, which suggest a New Testament sense of renewal through faith.[16] Edwards places his revelations within the context of both his father's congregation and God's graces, which provide familiar, supportive surroundings for self-examination. This privileged social position lends his autobiographical voice an inherent authority. Above all, the ***Narrative*** marks his commitment to his spiritual salvation.

Each author thus affirms belief in a higher will and places his or her personal struggles within a larger context of fulfilling God's plan. In different ways, Ashbridge and Edwards are subject to regulation of the spiritual journey. Ashbridge must comply to social expectations as daughter, servant, and wife. As a minister, Edwards is beholden to public approval. For each, private contemplation reinforces community strength, especially in the congregational culture, in which, as Daniel Walker Howe explains, "society was ideally an organic whole, in which persons treated each other as fellow members of the body of Christ" (87). Given their common ground, Edwards and Ashbridge are each influenced by cultural expectations and each answers to divine law: Ashbridge must appease husband, family and God; Edwards answers to his congregation and to God.

Although their spiritual paths share common goals, their differences are marked primarily by their social positions as dictated by gender and class. Where Edwards is surrounded by encouraging role models, Ashbridge must construct her support system and explore her spiritual landscape alone, for as she narrates, "As I grew up, I took notice there were several different religious societies, wherefore I often went alone and wept; with desires that I might be directed to the right" (148). Contemplation is usually a private act, and seeking a spiritual community on her own signals both her autonomy and her isolation. Ashbridge thus introduces herself as an earnest, solitary seeker.[17] Upon arrival in colonial America from Ireland, she again seeks direction and finds the search difficult: "I used to Converse with People of all societies as Opportunity offer'd & like many others had got a Pretty Deal of Head Knowledge, & Several Societies thought me of their Opinions severally; But I joyned Strictly with none, resolving never to leave Searching till I had found the truth" (155). In her distinction between "Head Knowledge" and "truth," she indicates that she will not be persuaded by dogma alone, a difficult task considering the enthusiasm of the Great Awakening. And in noting her desire for "truth," Ashbridge uses a Quaker term which refers to an inner revelation directed by spirit. By doing so, she foreshadows her Quaker beliefs and marks "truth" as a key to inner knowledge. Ashbridge thus constructs the autobiography to underscore the suspense of her story, wherein a solitary, female seeker who is reticent to join a false society will be guided to the truth.

Another gender-based difference in their narratives derives from their identification with God as the Divine Father. In that Divinity is often perceived as a paternal figure in the Judeo-Christian tradition, the seeker's relationship to this figure is affected by his or her relationship to the father. And even though the male may identify with divine power more easily through the Christ image,[18] each gender to some extent bows to a higher authority as an obedient child complying to the Father's wishes. From the smallest social unit, the family, to the larger spiritual unit, the church, a father rules over a membership, and a father doles out judgment.[19] Divinity is subsequently imagined and portrayed in various forms ranging from legalistic portraits of a condemning God to a more forgiving, sympathetic figure. As eighteenth-century spiritual autobiographers who express their subservience in individuated voices, Edwards and Ashbridge honor Divinity while refiguring the more fearful aspects. True to the emotionalism of the Great Awakening, their conversions are ultimately inspired by a compassionate God.

Considering how theological images mirror paternal models, the female aspirant must readjust her relationship to this image in ways that her male counterpart may not. When she looks toward this image, the female seeker is confronted by expectations of her submission to male authority. For the male aspirant, such subordination is never as absolute, as he can still imagine himself in some form of authority in worldly affairs. Where Edwards assumes the lineage of a male tradition, Ashbridge seeks permission from the male authority figures in her life: her father, master, and husband.[20] Edwards impressively expands his ministry, but it is Ashbridge who offers a new template for female spiritual authority.

In Ashbridge's initial desire to become closer to God, she longs to be more in his image. At one point, she identifies so closely with the male that she regrets her own femaleness: "In my very Infancy, I had an awful regard for religion & a great love for religious people, particularly the Ministers, and sometimes wept with Sorrow, that I was not a boy that I might have been one; believing them all Good Men & so beloved of God" (148). Finding her female status a barrier, Ashbridge imagines that becoming a boy would enhance her spirituality. Eventually, Quakerism will fulfill her spiritual desire by allowing her to transfer her identification from a male-identified spiritual authority to a female one.

Edwards also shares his spiritual anxieties, but they are never drawn within the same sense of alienation; instead, his fears are expressed within the support of his male community. When he speaks of his first "awakening," it occurs in his "father's congregation," and when he grows "concerned about the things of religion," he is able to "spend much time in religious conversation with other boys" (81). His doubts and his joys occur in a more inviting, self-imposed solitude, as when he writes of "sweetly conversing with Christ, and wrapt and swallowed up in God" (84). Within this private sphere, he is inspired, and unlike Ashbridge, he has the added pleasure of sharing his experiences with his father: "I gave an account to my father of some things that had passed in my mind. I was pretty much affected by the discourse we had together . . ." (84). Edwards's meditations are thus validated by his community as he anticipates his pending ministry. Within this ongoing process of preparation, his spiritual path is carefully directed, and yet, as a Calvinist who never assumes his own worthiness, his obstacles are more internal than external: "I used to be continually examining myself, and studying and contriving for likely ways and means, how I should live holily, with far greater diligence and earnestness, than ever I pursued any thing in my life . . ." (86). Clearly there is more public pressure for Edwards, who must justify his position to God, his congregation, and himself. Given this capacity for self-criticism, his narrative demonstrates how self-examination forges spiritual rebirth. He concludes this statement with an admission that he pursued his examination "with too great a dependence on [his] own strength; which afterwards proved a great damage to [him]" (86). Edwards may be able to model his spiritual life upon male images of Divinity, but he must also avoid the temptations of adopting a "proud and self-righteous spirit" (95). The danger of too much self-authority keeps Edwards in line. He seeks an intimate, compassionate relationship with God that will guide and inspire.

Even within these Calvinistic restrictions on individual authority, Edwards can draw comparisons to the Divine Legislator in almost administrative ways that enhances his sense of authority. In one passage, he describes walking along the Hudson River with a Mr. Smith and explains how their conversations "used to turn much on the advancement of Christ's kingdom in the world, and the glorious things that God would accomplish for his church in the latter days" (88-89). Edwards is not, of course, presenting himself as God's equal, yet the comfortable manner in which these conversations take place suggests a contrast to a female Puritan, who might feel inspired but not instrumental in advancing such divine causes. As he watches over his own congregation, Edwards can more easily imagine himself as a student of Christ's. By contrast, the woman simply can not imagine herself directly in Christ's image, a barrier that limits her sense of authority.

For both genders, the image of the patriarch embodies mastery, and in each text the authors are interested in the self-improvement that comes from self-examination. Although Ashbridge initially judges herself against the pending approval and disapproval of male authority, she will forge a new spiritual self with a distinctively female identity. Where Ashbridge battles, Edwards is supported. Solitude is encouraged in Edwards's life, but Ashbridge must construct her own sanctuary. Edwards grows into his position of authority; Ashbridge recognizes her limitations.[21] These two narratives are not meant to represent all conversion narratives, nor are they presented here to epitomize the male or female account. Instead, the gender issues are raised as another way to understand the complicated act of surrender within a narrative that values individual experience.[22] For each author, the spiritual autobiography legitimizes subjectivity in the name of self-examination and develops self-awareness.

THE FEMALE'S QUEST: LITERARY SOURCES AND SPIRITUAL GUIDES

In Elizabeth Ashbridge's text, spiritual authority develops from confrontation and crisis, making hers the more flamboyant narrative. Although this style might be closer to the sentimental novel than to the traditional spiritual autobiography, her text breaks new ground in showing us the possibilities for female authority within the spiritual realm where all individuals are subject to divine rule. Although her choices may be limited, Ashbridge asserts some control over her life and inadvertently sets herself upon the spiritual path. Spiritual questing thus provides a sanctioned opportunity to exercise change, and the spiritual autobiography allows her to recast the apparent chaos of her journey into a unified narrative.

Literary outlets for women in early America were generally limited to the spiritual realm through the journal or poem. It is provocative, then, to wonder if Ashbridge may have found inspiration in the captivity narrative, a genre of colonial Puritan literature wherein female authorship is acceptable. Similar to the captivity narrative, Ashbridge's account integrates spiritual dilemmas with the physical and emotional demands of an external journey. Consistent with both the spiritual autobiography and the captivity narrative, Ashbridge demonstrates how physical hardship can be transcended by calling for divine intervention. A century earlier, *A True History of the Captivity and Restoration of Mrs. Mary Rowlandson* (1675) testifies that a woman can survive the rigors of a wilderness captivity primarily because of her strong faith. Although the captivity narrative limited personal discourse to religious concerns, it elicits the female reader's identification with the narrator's ordeal, offering her a potential role model and prompting her to ask, What would I have done in a similar situation?

The captivity narrator adopts a carefully constructed tone that avoids self-promotion by framing the experience within a spiritual context, one that dramatizes the need for reassurance and affirmation. Even when Rowlandson mourns her child's death, for example, she places her grief within the larger scriptural context. The captivity narrative also shows how self-examination provides strength while also reinforcing social conformity.[23] Rowlandson's dramatic experiences parallel Ashbridge's story as she must also overcome external obstacles and remain committed to her faith. Ashbridge's transformation from servant to wife to minister proves as dramatic as Rowlandson's release from captivity. And although Ashbridge follows in this tradition of spiritual autobiography, her text represents a significant shift, for her secular life plays a much more prominent part in her narrative. Self-examination allows each author a sense of order and control over her inner struggles, and each narrative reinforces the power of divine will over self-will.

While the seventeenth-century captivity narrative may have inspired Ashbridge in her spiritual conflicts, the eighteenth-century sentimental novel may have provided secular guidance. Novels such as Samuel Richardson's *Pamela* or *Clarissa,* for instance, portray young heroines who attempt to break free from oppressive circumstances and challenge male authority. As these heroines' virtues are tested, the audience debates the right to individual choice. Jay Fliegelman finds Clarissa "a martyred heroine who had led a revolutionary cause" and Pamela more virtuous than Mr. B when she "refuses the overtures of her master and fails to be blackmailed into reciprocating with sexual favors" (*Prodigals* 89, 100).[24] And while American society was certainly not completely egalitarian, one's choices seemed less determined by class structures than in England. Clarissa, for example, may not have suffered the degree of social condemnation in the more fluid colonial American society than she did in England. For both British and American females, the sentimental novel provides clear messages for the wayward female. For example, Susanna Rowson's *Charlotte Temple* and Mrs. Foster's *The Coquette* ask their audiences to ponder the alternatives to being seduced and abandoned if indeed a young woman should transgress the prescribed social roles of female sexuality. If such rules are transgressed, the woman would be accused of coquetry, whereas a man would garner the more exotic title of "rake," as his promiscuous actions are supposedly more understandable than the mistakes of a Charlotte Temple or an Eliza Wharton.

In this sentimental tradition, therefore, Ashbridge's *Account* echoes the passions of Clarissa Harlowe, who also disregards her father and confronts a seducer. The *Account* blends the drama of the novel with the humility of the confession as she relates her story with echoes of an Edenic fall from innocence brought on by her elopement: "From my Infancy till fourteen years of age I was as innocent as most Children, about which time my Sorrows began, and have continued for the most part of my life ever since; by giving way to foolish passion, in Setting my affections on a young man who Courted me without my Parents' consent; till I consented, and with sorrow of Heart may say, I suffered myself to be carried off in the night" (148). Childlike innocence is corrupted by the "foolish passion" of young love as Ashbridge struggles with the powers of female sexuality that precipitate her banishment. Not unlike her fictional counterparts, Ashbridge follows her romantic urgings and is cast into exile.

The woman generally sees herself more as a consequence of action rather than as an agent in sentimental fiction. Similarly, Ashbridge portrays herself reacting to various events and authorities. To begin, her elopement alienates her father, and upon her husband's early death, she leaves England for Dublin to live with relatives, hoping that her absence will "regain [her] Father's Affection." But the reconciliation is thwarted, as her father "continued Inflexible, & would not send for [her] again" (148). His disapproval is so potent that Ashbridge chooses to sail for America rather than face his condemnations: "My Father still keeping me at such a distance that I thought myself quite shut out of his Affections, I therefore Concluded since my Absence was so Agreeable, he should have it" (150). Exile from her parental home parallels her spiritual isolation, and her narrative becomes an attempted reconciliation between spiritual and secular forces. To initiate this process, this defiant young woman arrives in New York in "the 7 mo 1732 . . . a Stranger in a Strange Land" (151). Instead of this act liberating her, Ashbridge confronts an even more threatening oppression as an indentured servant, an unfortunate compromise which she committed to unknowingly while on board the ship, for as she explains, "I soon agreed with [a Gentlewoman] for my passage & being ignorant of the Nature of an Indenture soon became bound, tho' in a private manner, (for fear I should be found out) tho' this was repugnant to law" (150). Her choices may be limited, but the role of daughter or wife will soon seem preferable.

Despite her rebellion, Ashbridge survives the perils of servitude by establishing her own spiritual and ethical codes. From her initial state of spiritual depravity, Ashbridge questions the legitimacy of external authority, especially her master who "would seem to be a Very Religious Man, taking the Sacrament (so called) & used to Pray every Night in his family." She then notes that "when his Prayer Book was Lost," he ceased to pray, which appears hypocritical. This man's dependence upon external religious props to validate his faith provokes further criticism: "The Afforesaid Difference was of Such a kind that it made me Sick of his Religion; for tho' I had but little my Self yet I had an Idea what sort of People they should be that were so" (152). By rejecting his religion, she favors a more internalized source of spirituality and begins to define her own religious preferences. Here, she does so in opposition to her master—a remarkable display of independent thought. This overlapping of past and present within the narrative illustrates how Ashbridge constructs the text to demonstrate the complexities of her approaching consciousness by using her current spiritual perspectives to evaluate her past experiences. Criticizing her master's dependence upon his prayer book prefigures her acceptance of a Quaker doctrine that divinity is experienced inwardly and is not subject to external proof.[25] For now, she is responding intuitively to an inconsistency that undermines the master's authority, and following the sentimental style, the heroine has named her oppressor.

Ashbridge uses her first-person narrative to register her displeasure, but it is clear that she lacks authority to create change. Initially, she can only declare what she dislikes and has yet to define what she wants; at first, she rejects all religion and "was Ready to Conclude that there was no God" (152). From this flirtation with atheism, she begins to speculate that God is "a pure being" who would not bother to "hear the Prayers of Polluted Lips." Ashbridge as "narrator" then intrudes with this explanation: "But he that hath in an abundant manner shown mercy to me (as will be seen in the sequel) did not Long Suffer me to Doubt in this Matter, but in a moment, when my feet were near the Bottomless Pit, Pluckt me Back" (152). Noting her life's events in terms of a "sequel," the text's literary parallels are once again evident. This depiction of God as a more compassionate force allows the possibility of her salvation as she reluctantly takes up the spiritual path.

Along the way, Ashbridge is often harshly treated, and the narrative illustrates her vulnerability as both a woman and a seeker. One such incident echoes the master-servant scenario found in several popular novels of the time, such as *Pamela*. Ashbridge has been outlining the deterioration of her relationship with her master and admits that "[f]or a While at first [she] was Pretty well used," but then "the Scale turned" because of "a Difference" that passed between them. Upon declaring herself "Innocent," Ashbridge then catalogs the abuses of her "Inhuman" master: "He would not suffer me to have Clothes to be Decent in, having to go barefoot in his Service in the Snowey Weather & the Meanest drudgery, wherein I Suffered the Utmost Hardship that my Body was able to Bear, which, with the afforesaid Troubles, had like to have been my Ruin to all Eternity had not Almighty God in Mercy Interposed" (152). Although the account never clearly identifies the specific nature of these transgressions, Ashbridge attributes her endurance and strength to divine assistance. This passage not only underscores the moral poverty of her master but also emphasizes Ashbridge's vulnerability. In keeping with the sentimental style, Ashbridge's ordeal informs and instructs her female audience on the dangers of such servitude.[26] By transcending this experience and recreating it in the spiritual autobiography, Ashbridge reaffirms female strength in a genre that sanctions first-person narrative.

The spiritual autobiography also allows her to express doubts and share tribulations without appearing self-promoting, for as she relates a series of crisis, their resolution will signal that grace is working in her life. In so doing, she satisfies Nussbaum's definition of the conversion experience itself, wherein a "crisis brings transformation, a time when the individual becomes inevitably and incontrovertibly different from what s/he was" ("Heteroclites" 157). Before she can be transformed, Ashbridge must first overcome self-doubt. At one point, when she finds herself ready to relinquish all hope and contemplates suicide, she hears a voice that warns "there is a Hell beyond the grave." Suddenly aware of the consequences of damnation if divine punishment does exist, Ashbridge transcends her situation by imagining a female guide as an alternative authority figure:

> . . . I had a Dream, & tho' some make a ridicule of Dreams, yet this seemed a significant one to me & therefore shall mention it. I thought somebody knocked at the Door, by which when I had opened it there stood a Grave woman, holding in her right hand an oil lamp burning, who with a Solid Countenance fixed her Eyes upon me & said—"I am sent to tell thee that If thou'l return to the Lord thy God, who hath Created thee, he will have mercy on thee, & thy Lamp shall not be put out in obscure darkness;" upon which the Light flamed from the Lamp in an extraordinary Manner, & She left me and I awoke. (153)

Despite a nod to those who would invalidate dreams, Ashbridge overcomes doubts and explores the dream's power. With its Quaker-speaking guide, this vision of a solemn "Grave woman" calling the wayward pilgrim out from obscure darkness and toward a flaming light represents the spiritual quest as a movement away from ignorance and toward enlightenment. In turn, this woman awakens Ashbridge with the directness of a flaming light—a symbol of spiritual enlightenment—and places her on the threshold of a spiritual gateway. Although Ashbridge cannot pass over it, bound as she is by her own struggles, her ability to conjure this image speaks to her desire to break free. Just as the male pilgrim envisions a "city upon a hill" and can imagine himself its legislator, Ashbridge illuminates her path with a lamp from her own subconscious. By allowing this dream-vision a place in the narrative, Ashbridge fills her spiritual autobiography with her own iconography. The

dream marks a dramatic break in a narrative which has so far depicted Ashbridge steadily slipping into spiritual ruin.

This momentary vision fades, however, in keeping with the format of the spiritual autobiography, which alternates revelation with despair, and Ashbridge continues to test both her spiritual and secular worlds, for as she tells us, "But alas! I did not give up nor Comply with the heavenly Vision, as I think I may Call it" (153). Calling her dream a "heavenly Vision" illustrates how the Quakers "treated their dreams as divinely inspired visions and messages."[27] While the dream may reinforce Ashbridge's good fortune, her rejection marks her resistance. It follows then that her opposition almost leads to another crisis, or "Snare" as she calls it. This was a brief consideration of an acting and singing career in New York, which she cannot go through with for fear of "what [her] Father would say" (153). Incapable of either following the dream or dishonoring her father, she decides to remain a servant rather than return home to the father who has now forgiven her: "[M]y proud heart would not Consent to return in so mean a Condition; therefore I chose Bondage rather" (153). Again, her decisions identify some of the psychological barriers that Ashbridge must contest before she can begin to assert her own authority and embrace her spiritual path. Ultimately, her narrative introduces possibilities for female authors who will eventually transcend such limitations and write of their own female quests.[28] Until that time, a woman must negotiate within a power structure that assumes her subordination and resists her independence. Although the spiritual realm provides more chances for female leadership than the social sphere, the female aspirant of the eighteenth century is still beholden to the overriding expectations of social custom.

Amidst the spiritual autobiography's depiction of its author's struggles toward conversion, the narrative episodically charts numerous trails that test the aspirant's faith. For Ashbridge, the spiritual path is strewn with obstacles, and she must construct her own ethical codes as she struggles to overcome her own powerlessness. After confiding to another servant about their master's sexual advances two years earlier, for example, Ashbridge is called in to defend herself against a pending whipping. The master is clearly not interested in hearing Ashbridge's defense: "[He] ordered me to strip; at which my heart was ready to burst; for I could as freely have given up my Life as Suffer such Ignomiy" (152). Despite her lowly status, however, Ashbridge defies her master's authority and avoids his punishment. Casting herself as the suffering heroine whose virtue is tested by the morally corrupt master, Ashbridge affirms the higher code: "I then fixed my Eyes on the Barbarous man, & in a flood of Tears said: 'Sir, if you have no Pity on me, yet for my Father's Sake spare me from this Shame (for before this time he had heard of my Father &c. several ways) & if you think I deserve such punishment, do it your Self.' He then took a turn over the Room & bid the Whipper go about his business, and I came off without a blow . . ." (153). In what should have been a moment of humiliation, Ashbridge neutralizes her master's power by evoking her father's authority as she casts her fixed eyes upon the "Barbarous man" and makes an emotional plea. Although his barbarity is clearly drawn, she is still at his mercy, much as the heroine of the sentimental novel whose sense of virtue may be superior to her transgressor's. In both situations, the woman is left with little negotiating power. Ashbridge's defiance is thus placed within a broader, moral context, for she could not have confronted him solely on the basis of her own authority. Instead, she evokes a higher force, her father's authority, and challenges this "Barbarous man" to carry out the whipping himself. The confrontation halts his designs, and Ashbridge's narrative provides her female audience with a guide for negotiating such oppression by neutralizing her master's power and protecting her virtue—two admirable achievements for any eighteenth-century heroine.

The parallels between the novel and the spiritual autobiography are further drawn by a new series of events whereby she eventually buys off the rest of her indenture and supports herself "handsomely" by her needle until she remarries, an event noted with certain regret: "I had got released from one cruel Servitude & then not Contented got into another, and this for Life" (153-54). In equating marriage with servitude and reinforcing her depravity, Ashbridge portrays her life as increasingly oppressive, and after admitting this transgression, as she views it, she follows with this description of her husband, a man named Sullivan: "I married a young man that fell in Love with me for my Dancing, a Poor Motive for a man to Choose a Wife, or a Woman a Husband. But for my Part I fell in Love with nothing I saw in him" (154). While the frankness of her declaration lacks the passionate tone of earlier episodes, it carries a similar tone of desperation. The decision appears made out of an apathetic resignation, a condition in which the spiritually depraved dwell. The section ends with this final admission: "[I]t seems unaccountable that I who had refused several, both in this Country & Ireland, at Last married a man I had no Value for . . . I now saw my Self ruined" (154). This marriage choice only intensifies her depression. Not only is Sullivan without religion and prone to "the worst of Oaths" when drinking, but this union appears to be taking her "to destruction" unless she can "alter [her] Course of Life" (154). Ashbridge's external guides are few, and she has resisted the inner vision. To this point, her attention has been taken up by external affairs, and as she begins to embrace Quakerism, guidance will manifest in all aspects of her life.

THE FEMALE'S QUEST: FROM SERVITUDE TO SURRENDER

Spiritual and marital activities are not, however, mutually exclusive, and unlike Edwards's narrative, the secular world intrudes upon Ashbridge's spiritual quest, forcing her to choose between authorities rather than simply reaffirm her belief in God. From this perspective, Ashbridge explains the impossibility of setting her "Affections upon the Divine being & not Love [her] husband," so to make amends, she explains: "I Daily Desired with Tears that my Affections might be in a right manner set upon my husband, and can say in a little time my Love was Sincere to him" (154). Although this marriage appears to be a move toward "destruction," she "resolved to do [her] Duty to God" and prays to become a better wife and aspirant.[29] Notably, Edwards never appears to direct his prayers in a similar direction. Ashbridge, on the other hand, must establish her credibility within the domestic sphere before her spiritual search can resume. Her spiritual autobiography shows how Ashbridge is led to the Quakers, where she will be encouraged to follow an Inner Light, an apt symbol for the inherent subjectivity of her narrative. Through self-examination, Ashbridge will cultivate this light just as through self-reflection her narrative encourages her subjective voice.

Fortuitously, Quaker doctrine is grounded in William Penn's claim that "Sexes made no difference; since in Souls there is none: and they are the subjects of Friendship" (qtd. in Shea, "Introduction" 123). This premise renders it more responsive toward the needs of a female seeker such as Ashbridge who must reconcile domestic struggles with her spiritual longings.[30] Indifference toward gender is also reinforced by doctrine that finds that once a person chooses to be "convinced" of the truth, each individual is a potential vehicle for this light.[31] Daniel Shea explains that "the Quaker who felt himself prompted to speak in meeting did so, not as an individual subject to praise or blame, but as the medium of the Spirit" (*Spiritual* 12). This assertion that spirit holds no gendered preferences encourages women to become vehicles for spirit, and this emphasis upon truth as a guiding force expands the woman's role. Moreover, as the Quaker spiritual autobiography is only published upon one's death, the text is meant to be explicitly instructive. Ashbridge can thus speak beyond her time and potentially frame a shared female experience as a woman who navigates her domestic and spiritual worlds as she moves from servitude to surrender to ministry.

In her initial encounter with Quakerism, however, self-reliance proves too radical. Ashbridge goes to a Quaker meeting in Boston "not Expecting to find what [she] wanted, but out of Curiosity," and her curiosity is met by her incredulity as she describes her reaction: "[T]here was a Woman friend spoke, at which I was a Little surprised, for tho' I had heard of Women's preaching I had never heard one before. I looked on her with Pity for her Ignorance (as I thought) & Contempt of her Practise, saying to myself, 'I am sure you are a fool, for if ever I should turn Quaker, which will never be, I would not be a preacher'" (155). Even though Ashbridge is willing to attend Quaker meetings and hear their doctrines, she cannot yet accept the gender-breaking role of this woman preacher. Instead, Ashbridge actually pities this woman, an act which, of course, adds to the suspense and drama of her narrative while marking the range of Ashbridge's personal transformation. When confronted by this woman, Ashbridge berates a potential self-mirror and resists acknowledging the female preacher's authority. In Ashbridge's inability to imagine female authority, her anger seems infused with fear as this woman threatens Ashbridge's assumptions of social conduct and position. Before she can acknowledge this woman's authority, Ashbridge must relinquish preconceptions of external authority, and, as her narrative will ultimately demonstrate, honor a higher authority.

The Quakers' inclusion of the female minister complicates Ashbridge's relationship to authority. Having rejected the guide of the dream-vision, Ashbridge cannot imagine the actual manifestation of female authority before her. The initial shock of seeing a female preacher is quickly allayed when a man, whom she "could better Bear," takes over. Ashbridge is calmed by this more traditional figure and comments, "He spoke well & I thought raised sound Doctrine . . ." (155). This response echoes her earlier admission that she "wept with sorrow" while wishing she could be a man and thus a minister. Quaker doctrine may allow Ashbridge to fulfill this desire to be a minister, but she must first transcend her resistance. The journal thus complies with the classic conversion structure of resistance followed by realization in which pride is the determining factor that keeps the pilgrim from spiritual enlightenment. The retelling enables her to see the providential design of her life, and the autobiographical narrative provides her with the appropriate ordering device.

Captive to her spiritual ignorance, Ashbridge is not fully convinced that the Quakers are her answer, but her husband's resistance fuels her spiritual quest as she heads off to visit relatives in Pennsylvania. As an instructive text, the spiritual autobiography is meant to illustrate an aspirant's ignorance, which will dramatize the eventual conversion and realization of spiritual truth. Appropriately, then, upon Ashbridge's arrival she has this hostile reaction: "I met with no small Mortification upon hearing that my Relations were Quakers, & what was worst of all my Aunt a Preacher." Ashbridge is apparently willing to question some social institutions, such as her indictment of marriage, yet she hesitates to expand the boundaries of authority that would, again, allow her to accept a female preacher. Her hostility, however, is immediately tempered by the larger intentions of the narrative to illustrate how "God brings unforeseen things to Pass" (158). The narrative continues to weave its thread of text-as-symbol when Ashbridge inquisitively picks up her Aunt's book and proceeds to read "Saml. Crisp's Two Letters." She then stops after reading two pages because "Tears Issued from [her] Eyes."[32] Fearing discovery, Ashbridge brings the book outside "into the garden, sat Down, and the piece being Small, read it through before [she] went in" (158-59). Emotionally charged, she continues reading, but "Some Times was forced to Stop to Vent [her] Tears, [her] heart as it were uttering these involuntary Expressions" (159). Ashbridge's reaction marks the intensity of her prejudice toward the Quakers and the power of the text to evoke such response. Even though her Aunt had warned her that "'Cousin that is a Quakers' Book,'" Ashbridge defies authority by reading, and yet, ultimately, she realizes, by "going there [she] was brought to [her] Knowledge of his Truth" (158).

Spiritual surrender requires an internalization of spiritual knowledge. In moving toward this state, Ashbridge remains highly sensitive to external representations. This incident, in turn, mirrors the earlier condemnation of her master's dependence upon his prayer book as a religious prop, for now when Ashbridge holds such a "prop," she attests to some force in this Quaker book wherein her burning heart and tearing eyes evoke an image of spiritual passion. Walking "into the garden" offers Ashbridge some relief as she surrounds herself with nature and surrenders more completely to the text and her emotions. Providence has ordained that she relinquish discrimination against the Quakers and begin the self-examining process that will lead to her conversion. This episode also parallels her dream in that here words are made more tangible and Ashbridge reacts to them in her waking life just as powerfully as when she was awakened by the grave woman holding the flaming light. In the dream, the passive Ashbridge can only listen; now, she actively gives voice to her spiritual questing.

Clearly, she is willing to sacrifice anything for the approval of Divinity, but Ashbridge is not entering the same subordinate state that she experienced as servant and wife; instead, as a Quaker, her relationship with Divinity will elevate rather than diminish her self-worth. The book, in turn, substitutes for the traditional male mentor as it allows Ashbridge to fashion an internalized authority that will lead to her spiritual reinvention. Kevin J. Hayes marks this scene as a reaffirmation of the "essentially private nature of devotional reading," which emphasizes the value of the spiritual sphere for contemplation (49). Unlike Edwards, Ashbridge lacks role models who can offer instruction in negotiating her spiritual path, and as she persists in self-questioning, her doubt increases her isolation. Prior to her revelation in the garden, there were profound inner struggles. Ashbridge glimpses a vision of her own darkness while sitting by a fire on a stormy night surrounded by her husband and others:

> . . . there arose a Thunder Gust, & with the Noise that struck my Ear, a voice attended, even as the Sound of a mighty Trumpet, piercing thro' me with these words, "O! Eternity, Eternity, the Endless term of Long Eternity:" at which I was Exceedingly Surprized, sitting speechless as in a trance, and in a moment saw my Self in such a state as made me Despair of ever being in a happy one. I seemed to see a Long Roll wrote in Black Characters, at sight whereof I heard a Voice say to me, "this is thy Sins;" I then saw Sin to be Exceedingly Sinful. . . . (156)

Rapt in this view of two worlds, the awesome power of divine thunder and the distressing power of sin, Ashbridge's perceptions and sense of reality are challenged. This altered state goes unperceived by her company who think that her "[i]ndisposition proceeded only from a fright at the Thunder." And yet in this state of separation, she creates a sphere in which she reads the signs of nature, thunder, as a portent to her spiritual struggles. Although such readings are similar to Samuel Sewall's interpretations of natural phenomena, when Ashbridge sees the "Long Roll wrote in Black Characters," she decides that no matter how painful the struggle might become that she will alter this "fate." By contrast, Sewall may not have imagined this same assertion of individual direction. The scene leaves her profoundly changed, and "from that time for several months [she] was in utmost Despair." This disorientation ushers in a new phase of her transformation.

With renewed spiritual strength. Ashbridge continues to fight her domestic battles. Sullivan's displeasure increases, and Ashbridge moves further away from the original image of the dancing wife. Although she realizes how painful her radical change has been on her husband, she cannot alter her path: "My singing now was turned into mourning & my Dancing into Lamentations: my Nights and Days were one Continual Scene of Sorrows . . ." (156). More so than Edwards, Ashbridge dramatizes her situation in hopes of convincing a sympathetic audience that her commitment to spiritual salvation overrides her attempts to save a floundering marriage. The narrative's sentimental tone reinforces her anxiety as she adopts the voice of a struggling heroine. Ashbridge cannot assume the same level of authority as Edwards does in his text. The drama must then explain her self-assertion.

Confidence fluctuates, however, and Sullivan's desire that she fulfill her roles as entertainer and helpmate proves overwhelming. Ashbridge falls into a suicidal depression for the next two months wherein she is "Daily tempted to destroy [herself]." Only her surrender to divine will can alleviate this despair. As she lay awake beside her sleeping husband "bemoaning [her] Miserable Condition," she appeals to God, and finds immediate relief: "—In an Instant my heart was tendered, & I dissolved in a flow of tears, abhorring my Past Offences, & admiring the mercy of God" (157). She then looks upon Christ "with an Eye of Faith," and with new sight she writes, "[I] saw fulfilled what I believed when the Priest lent me his Book, (Viz.) that if ever my Prayers would be Acceptable I should be Enabled to pray without form & so used form no more" (157). By aspiring to "pray without form," she begins to internalize her spiritual relationship. Criticism of external forms suggests Ashbridge's cynicism of a nonbeliever, and as she grows closer to Quaker doctrine, she will accept new forms, albeit more internalized ones. The autobiography is constructed after she has reconciled these external and internal manifestations of spirituality so that "external" forms of her belief are permissible once they are inspired by a valid "inner voice." The narrative's perspective is, of course, one of the convert who attempts to recapture the emotional state of the aspirant, and as with Franklin, Ashbridge's narrative construction of identity can potentially remake the self.

Ashbridge's spiritual struggles must certainly be placed against the larger social and religious backdrop of the evangelical excitement of the Great Awakening, for as she restructures her relationship with Divinity, she is encouraged by the emphasis upon more immediate and individual relationships with God. In forging this new bond, Ashbridge experiences a series of spiritual crisis which render her helpless in order to prepare her for the new, postconversion life. By embracing "formlessness," Ashbridge will then be encouraged to cultivate an inner guide which is ultimately more individualistic than either the Catholic or Protestant alternatives, especially for a woman. In her new state she "seemed Like another Creature, and often went alone without fear, & tears abundantly flowed from [her] Eyes." Ashbridge relinquishes sterner, unapproachable images of Divinity and portrays a nurturing and merciful figure: "I heard a gracious Voice full of Love, saying, 'I will never Leave thee, nor forsake thee, only obey what I shall make known to thee.' I then entered Covenant saying: 'My soul Doth Magnify thee the God of mercy, if thou'l Vouchsafe thy Grace the rest of my Days shall be Devoted to thee, & if it be thy Will that I beg my Bread, I'll be content and Submit to thy Providence'" (158). With the voice of God perceived as a "voice full of Love," Ashbridge indicates a new confidence in her spiritual musings. Although she is inspired here, Ashbridge's spiritual rebirth is not instantaneous, for immediately after she feels drawn into a covenant with God, she writes of a sleepless night in which she encounters "the old Enemy." After raising doubt, this "Subtile Serpent transformed himself so hiddenly" that Ashbridge reverts to her earlier caution and tells us that she "so resolved to beware of the Deceiver, & for Some weeks Did not touch any of their Books" (159). Resolving not to "touch any of their Books" implies that she will avoid the impact of their teachings as the temptations of the "Subtile Serpent" force her to construct her own internal sense of authority. Contrary to Edwards, Ashbridge cannot openly claim her spiritual authority. Instead, she allows external authorities—books, father, husbands, ministers—to influence her direction. The process of conversion allows her internal voice to take on external form, much as the spiritual autobiography provides the physical structure for her internal musings.

This spiritual autobiography is further distinguished by the dramatic presence of Ashbridge's husband as antagonist, who considers his wife's foray into Quakerism a sickness that needs immediate attention. Dismissing her faith as an external construction, Sullivan is convinced that geography somehow determines spirituality, and he orchestrates their sudden departure from Pennsylvania to Staten Island. He feels justified in his fight as his once cheerful wife continues to transform into a plain and somber Quaker, and so Ashbridge submissively writes, that the "time of Removal came, & I must go" (162). Then, after traveling fifteen miles, Sullivan decides they are far enough away from Quaker influence and stops at a tavern where, in an apologetic tone, he explains to those present that his wife is a Quaker and that he sought a place "where there was none" (162). He then attempts to get his wife to dance and thereby reenter "normal" society. It is a tense scene that Ashbridge narrates: "He comes to me, takes me by the hand saying, 'come my Dear shake off that Gloom, & let's have a civil Dance; you would now and then when you was a good Churchwoman, & that's better than a Stiff

Quaker.' I trembling desired to be Excused; but he Insisted on it, and knowing his Temper to be exceedingly Cholerick, durst not say much, yet did not Consent. He then pluk'd me round the Room till Tears affected my Eyes, at sight whereof the Musician Stopt and said, 'I'll play no more, Let your wife alone,' of which I was Glad" (162). Sullivan's reference to a "Stiff Quaker" and his angry manner in which he "pluk'd" Ashbridge round the room shows his utter frustration and suggests a rape of her will. The musician who "Stopt and said, 'I'll play no more, Let your wife alone,'" counteracts this force and, although Ashbridge is still being saved by a man, she wins this battle by remaining true to her beliefs. Sullivan's desire for conformity contrasts Ashbridge's desires for spiritual truth.

Faced with Sullivan's persistent disapproval, Ashbridge finds herself in danger of aborting her quest altogether and succumbing to an unhappy marriage. When someone offers to "cure her of her Quakerism" by giving both she and Sullivan teaching positions in Freehold, East Jersey, this new development has an unexpected effect by inspiring Ashbridge to assert her will more fully. Consequently, Sullivan becomes even more aggressive and brandishes a pen knife, threatening, "'[I]f you offer to go to Meeting tomorrow, with this knife I'll cripple you, for you shall not be a Quaker'" (166). Despite Sullivan's protestations, however, he gradually acquiesces to his wife's determination: "One day he said, 'I'd go to Meeting, only I am afraid I shall hear you Clack, which I cannot bear.'" He then remarks, "'I'll no Longer hinder thee'" (168). In granting his permission, Sullivan frees Ashbridge to assume a more active role in meetings. Although they stay together, they stand as opposites; Sullivan falls further into spiritual darkness while Ashbridge moves closer toward the light, which allows her to withstand her husband's threats, drinking, and beatings. In a rather perverse way, therefore, Sullivan hastens her spiritual search by providing such an unappealing alternative.

Sullivan's agreement not to "hinder" his wife's ministry is somewhat anticlimactic, for, soon after, Sullivan enlists "as a Common soldier to Cuba anno 1740," and goes off to fight in a war wherein he refuses to take up arms and is arrested. Ashbridge sincerely bemoans his situation and includes an extensive description of his final days, which she concludes with: "They used him with much Cruelty to make him yield but Could not, by means whereof he was So Disabled that the General sent him to the Hospital at Chelsea, where in Nine Months time he Died & I hope made a Good End, for which I prayed both night & Day, till I heard of his Death" (170). Refusing to fight, the once-combative Sullivan seems to have resolved his battle with Quakerism by embracing pacifism. Upon acknowledging his death, Ashbridge writes that she is being prepared "for future Service" and having fulfilled her social duty as wife pursues her spiritual path with renewed intensity.[33]

Ashbridge's *Account* addresses the difficulties of a female spiritual quest complicated by paternal banishment, early widowhood, indentured servitude, and marriage. Embattled by men who try to repress her spirit, she remains steadfast in her quest and takes her place as a devoted follower after having challenged traditional notions of religious authority. The *Account,* rather traditionally, concludes with a final acknowledgment of God's power. "[M]ay thou O God be Glorifyed and I abased for it is thy own Works that praise thee, and of a Truth to the humble Soul that Makest every bitter thing Sweet.—The End.—" (170). The tensions between an external and internal authority have been played out on several levels in Ashbridge's life until she ultimately triumphs as pilgrim and minister. Her narrative testifies to the difficulty of the female's spiritual path amidst social prejudice toward female authority. And in writing her narrative, Ashbridge demonstrates how self-examination encourages this authority.

The Male's Quest: The Burden and Blessing of Spiritual Primogeniture

The spiritual quest is designed to curtail personal inclinations for the glory of spiritual commitment. Jonathan Edwards must also contend with the added pressures of an inherited spiritual legacy. Within this study of the developing subjectivity of the first-person narrative, Edwards moves us into altogether new territory. For Edwards, the narrative's innovation is not so much in the claiming of a spiritual identity or authority as it is in the expression and quality of this identity. Edwards converses with Divinity in a confidential, sometimes poetic voice about his trials along the spiritual journey.

In contrast to Ashbridge's more earthbound narrative, which includes domestic and everyday affairs, Edwards's autobiography dwells on more abstract and idealized planes, and one feels that he is not quite a mortal human being but, rather, a representative, emblematic figure. When Edwards strolls in his "father's pasture, for contemplation" or walks along the Hudson River, these scenes reaffirm a spiritual primogeniture as Timothy Edwards mentors his son. The young Edwards is clearly supported on his ministerial path. These avenues are unavailable to Ashbridge, and what is expected for Edwards is denied to Ashbridge. The assumption that Edwards will carry on the tradition, however, poses different problems. Ashbridge may lack confidence, but Edwards must make sure that his advantages do not keep him from submitting to God's will. Coming to spiritual surrender from a place of potential authority appears to be just as problematic for Edwards, who writes of "violent inward struggles." And where Ashbridge indicates a greater concern for pleasing others, Edwards asserts himself more autonomously. The aspiring minister conveys a stronger sense that his actions will have some influential effect.[34]

Even though Edwards projects self-confidence, his *Narrative* catalogs his numerous conflicts and doubts. During his final year at Yale, for example, Edwards experiences this affliction: "[I]t pleased God, to seize me with a pleurisy; in which he brought me nigh to the grave, and shook me over the pit of hell" (82). Edwards had been in a "very uneasy" state about his spiritual health, and so as God seizes and shakes him, it forces him to confront his own doubts and once again face his own worthlessness. This foreboding figure stands in contrast with other images of a more forgiving God, suggesting salvation through the redemption of a New Testament God is preferable to the condemnations of an Old Testament figure. Owen Watkins, in turn, identifies a pattern to the spiritual autobiography in which "conviction of sin, followed sometimes sooner, sometimes later, by an experience of forgiveness" (9). Through various episodes, Edwards graphically illustrates these fluctuations.

Edwards's struggles are often internal, and conflict centers around doctrine, for to doubt is to question the very core of his Puritanism. Edwards tell us the worst episode yet when he recounts: "From my childhood up, my mind had been full of objections against the doctrine of God's sovereignty, in choosing whom he would to eternal life, and rejecting whom he pleased; leaving them eternally to perish, and be everlastingly tormented in hell. It used to appear like a horrible doctrine to me" (83). To call divine sovereignty "horrible" is to question his own election. By challenging this fundamental belief, Edwards marks an important moment in the evolution of his faith. Before he surrenders to the ultimate will of divine power, he subjects this doctrine to his rational faculties. Edwards then recognizes that both reason and intuition inform his understanding of the doctrine of God's sovereignty. His understanding is ultimately a matter of faith: "But never could give an account, how, or by what means, I was convinced, not in the least imagining at the time, nor a long time after, that there was any extraordinary influence of God's Spirit in it; but only that now I saw further, and my reason apprehended the justice and reasonableness of it" (83). In reconciling his faith and reason, Edwards expresses humility without sacrificing individual expression. Although he questions, Edwards traces the process through which the doctrine eventually appears as "exceedingly pleasant, bright, and sweet," and he concludes with this dictum: "Absolute sovereignty is what I love to ascribe to God. But my first conviction was not so" (83). The assertion made, Edwards's narrative goes on to illustrate both his lingering rebellion and his eventual embrace of this doctrine.[35]

One manifestation of this struggle appears much later, when Edwards is a minister himself who preaches and abides by God's law. Although Edwards promoted and supported the Great Awakening's call to emotionalism, which encouraged individual responses to conversion, he was also subject to its challenges to the church's power structures. For example, in the Northampton Controversy in 1750, Edwards demanded that "all new communicants profess conversion" (Karlson and Crumpaker 13). Rather than comply, members questioned the omnipotence of such authority and voted to remove Edwards. True to the very

goals that Edwards promoted, the dissolution of his ministry prompted a more direct relationship between the devout and the divine, demoting the minister's role as absolute mediator. Ironically, Edwards was cast out by the rise in individual involvement that he helped create. Although his particular circumstance may have been extreme, Edwards neither denied the power of enthusiasm nor advocated a return to more subdued times. Instead, he offered a moderate expression, one which Michael Gilmore calls "the middle way," that attempted to balance radical factions between the "legalism of the established clergy and the otherworldliness and spiritual pride of the Separate zealots" (*Middle* 4). Establishing this balance between individual and institutional authority was key for maintaining church stability. Edwards offers an unusual example of maintaining this equilibrium.

THE MALE'S QUEST: FROM BATTLE TO SURRENDER

The public sphere may have ultimately been dissatisfying for Edwards, but as the ***Narrative*** frequently illustrates, solitude for spiritual contemplation is readily available. By assuming this privilege, Edwards can assert the "I" more definitively in his spiritual autobiography than the female, for he is less concerned with appeasing external authority or reinforcing servitude. Another manifestation of Edwards's independence is the confidence portrayed in his interactions with nature. As he walks along chanting his prayers, Edwards appears suspended in an almost romantic isolation as he brings the practice of self-examination out onto the colonial landscape. Edwards frequently places himself outside of the community for contemplation, which suggests a new relationship between individual and society.[36] Benefiting from his ministerial heritage, Edwards draws on his solitude for self-examination and frames the pilgrim's quest as an intimate conversation with God as he strolls through pasture and forest. Spiritual contemplation can clearly take precedence over his domestic concerns in a manner unavailable to his female counterpart. His solitary walks, in turn, fall outside of the Augustinian tradition by not addressing a future recipient of his spiritual legacy.[37] And where such removals would have been suspect to his seventeenth-century ancestors, they will seem commonplace to his nineteenth-century progeny. Edwards shows us where the personal narrative is going, for it will become an arena for philosophical and spiritual self-reflection as manifest in the Transcendentalists of the next century.

Edwards's romantic sense of his natural environment is the most distinguishing difference between the Ashbridge and the Edwards texts. In contrast to earlier, Puritan attitudes that nature was a force to be controlled or avoided, nature is often seen as a sympathetic presence in his narrative. When Jonathan Edwards takes his meditative walks through the woods, he replaces fearful images of nature as a foreboding wilderness with his "vision, or fixed ideas and imaginations, of being alone in the mountains, or some solitary wilderness, far from all mankind, sweetly conversing with Christ, and wrapt and swallowed up in

God" (84). The witch-infested forests of Cotton Mather have become a contemplative landscape, and a fiery God has taken on a more compassionate nature. Although Ashbridge's text rarely ventures into Edwards-like pastures, she too uses the woods to vent her sorrows: "I used to Walk much alone in the Wood, where no Eye saw nor Ear heard, & there Lament my miserable Condition, & have often gone from Morning till Night and have not broke my Fast" (161). In each case, the woods are valued for their restorative powers, marking a departure from earlier visions of the "desolate and howling wilderness." This comforting image further suggests an increasing familiarity with the colonial landscape, which encourages a larger projection of the self onto this natural stage.

Nature and contemplation allow Edwards to fulfill his desire to be "far from all mankind." After reading from the "book of Canticles," Edwards writes of an "inward sweetness, that would carry me away, in my contemplations" (84). In his own willingness to be carried away, Edwards invites his congregation to experience being "wrap and swallowed up in God" (84).[38] Finding himself moved by his father's discourse, the young Jonathan Edwards walks "abroad alone, in a solitary place in [his] father's pasture, for contemplation." He then has this revelation: "[L]ooking upon the sky and clouds, there came into my mind, a sweet sense of the glorious *majesty* and *grace* of God, as I know not how to express.—I seemed to see them both in a sweet conjunction; majesty and meekness joined together: it was a sweet, and gentle, and holy mystery; and also a majestic meekness; an awful sweetness; a high, and great, and holy gentleness" (84-85). The sensual quality with its sweet and gentle images finds Edwards cradled in nature. His prose here certainly warrants Emory Elliott's description of Edwards as "an artist of language" ("New England Puritan" 301). In his pairing of polemical images, Edwards exaggerates the "sweet conjunction" of sensual elements that carry an "awful sweetness" which can either uplift or humble him. The alternate rhythm of these images suggests the regenerative, sexual potential of nature in which opposite energies move toward consummation. Edwards thus celebrates God's power by allowing himself to be immersed in the contemplative powers of nature.

It has always seemed curious that Edwards could author both the **Personal Narrative** and the prototypical fire and brimstone sermon, **"Sinners in the Hands of An Angry God"** (1741), curious because equally strong images of nature are used to create entirely different effects. The benevolent images of God and nature in the **Personal Narrative** are replaced by fear and damnation in **"Sinners"** which he delivered as a visiting minister in Enfield. Natural forces are associated with horrific images, such as the "lake of burning brimstone," as Edwards warns his congregation: "There are black clouds of God's wrath now hanging directly over your heads, full of the dreadful storm, and big with thunder; and were it not for the restraining hand of God, it would immediately burst forth upon you. The sovereign pleasure of God, for the present, stays his rough wind; otherwise it would come with fury, and your destruction would come like a whirlwind, and you would be like the chaff of the summer threshing floor" (158). This passage emphasizes the darker forces in a relentless catalog of the potential dread awaiting the unfaithful. God is filled with fury as the howling wilderness and Ednic garden collide, and Edwards reinforces traditional Calvinist images of a wrathful God and a fearful, submissive congregation as he urges public confessions of faith. In some ways, the contrast between these two works foreshadows the ranges of Romanticism, with its dark and light manifestations.

Where **"Sinners"** diminishes the individual's power, the *Narrative* encourages the individual's search for spiritual knowledge. Edwards muses upon his soul in a romantic style as he testifies that his "sense of divine things gradually increased, and became more and more lively and had more of that inward sweetness." In fact, Edwards's entire sensory field is transformed and the "appearance of every thing was altered." The interaction suggests that as Edwards is filled with God's beauty, everything around him becomes beautiful: "[T]here seemed to be, as it were, a calm, sweet, cast, or appearance of divine glory, in almost every thing. God's excellency, his wisdom, his purity and love, seemed to appear in every thing; in the sun, moon and stars; in the clouds and blue sky; in the grass, flowers, trees; in the water and all nature; which used greatly to fix my mind" (85). Edwards internalizes this power. His spiritual vision then illuminates and animates the physical world. For Edwards, conversion is an intensification of his innate spiritual sensibility. Edwards honors God's presence and feels profoundly connected to the whole of creation in this moment of surrender.

From these passages, the *Narrative* most fully anticipates Romantic associations between nature, contemplation, and Divinity. Ultimately, these associations will give the individual more confidence as nature supports spiritual growth and encourages self-reflection. Nature reveals a "glorious majesty" to Edwards, and he feels closer to God's graces. Majesty couples with meekness, and Edwards is inspired by an external world that nurtures his spiritual questing.

His predecessors would have considered Edwards's haunts a forbidden wilderness, and yet he feels uplifted rather than frightened. Edwards subsequently reinterprets nature. For, unlike Sewall who marks thunder and lightning as images of God's displeasure, Edwards claims that "I felt God, if I may so speak, at the first appearance of a thunderstorm . . ." (85). God's power inspires Edwards to share in the glory and become uplifted. Delighting in this display, Edwards then explains how he "used to take the opportunity, at such times, to fix [himself] in order to view the clouds, and see the lightnings play, and hear the majestic and awful voice of God's thunder. . . ." While enraptured by this view, Edwards would "sing, or chant forth [his] meditations; or, to speak [his] thoughts in soliloquies, with a singing voice" (85). This reaction complements God's power, and as Paul David Johnson sees it, "[Edwards's] singing re-creates the expansiveness of divine immensity within him and, in repetition, creates infinity" (279). Edwards is inspired by the forces of nature, and, unlike Sewall, he is not diminished by this power; instead, nature elevates and empowers him. In his willingness to embrace nature, Edwards alter his temporal relationship with his surroundings. His lyrical descriptions of forest and sky focus more upon the present moment. By slowing down the time frame and isolating the moment, Edwards marks time in a more personal way, exclusive of a larger social context. This gesture enables him to have more control over the moment, a quality that can potentially enhance his projection of self into the narrative.

Edwards's pose of the contemplative pilgrim surrounded by nature portrays an interactive relationship between the seeker, Divinity, and nature. His harmonious imagery mirrors his spiritual world and expands into his physical sphere, a privilege that Ashbridge the minister might have also enjoyed. Edwards brings the aspirant out onto the landscape and asserts the self in new ways through a most traditional form. Metaphorically, conversion is an affirmation of subjectivity; it is the individual's most personal articulation of spirituality.

The spiritual autobiographies of Elizabeth Ashbridge and Jonathan Edwards are written in a spiritually revolutionary time when authority is questioned and gender roles are challenged. Reaching toward synthesis of some kind, the gender roles represented in these narratives illustrate an attempt to integrate opposite poles. Edwards reveals a softer, contemplative voice, while Ashbridge speaks with conviction, declaring her spiritual quest valid and important. Daring to explore these realms, the consequences are often complicated. Edwards suffers a fall from church power, and Ashbridge must deal with an abusive husband. For each, the individual's responsibility is to balance faith in external authority, God, with trust in internal authority, an inner voice. Where Ashbridge is rescued, "Pluckt me Back," Edwards is potentially abandoned, "shook me over the pit of hell." In each case, these encounters cause them to renew their quests. Edwards strengthens his commitment: "My concern now wrought more, by inward struggles, and conflicts, and self-reflections. I made seeking my salvation, the main business of my life" (82); Ashbridge withstands her master and husband and embraces Divinity in preparation for the ministry: "which I did with all my whole heart & hope ever shall while I have a being" (168). They present a more intimate relationship between aspirant and Divinity, which encourages individual emotional responses to spiritual matters.

This respect for the individual voice allows them to write about their spiritual paths with greater subjectivity. Edwards and Ashbridge acknowledge both personal and social authority within the religious sphere. The Transcendental movement of the nineteenth century will build upon these individual responses to Divinity and further articulate the relationship between nature and spiritual contemplation. This trend toward a greater respect for the individual's voice in the spiritual realm begins with the eighteenth-century spiritual autobiography. Even though the spiritual path remains demanding, Edwards and Ashbridge have more choice to act as individuals. For the male, Edwards inspires a closer association with nature and portrays a more contemplative, solitary figure. For the female, Ashbridge entertains new arenas altogether as she asserts her spiritual direction at the risk of displeasing male authority. The spiritual autobiography sanctions the first-person narrative as a legitimate vehicle for self-construction borne from self-examination.

Notes

1. Owen C. Watkins confirms that spiritual autobiographies were not written because the writers thought their lives were "'exemplary ones.'" . . . They hoped through the record of their own experience to offer experimental proof of some of the eternal truths of Christianity." See *The Puritan Experience: Studies in Spiritual Autobiography* (New York: Schocken, 1972), 1.

2. See Daniel Shea, *Spiritual Autobiography in Early America* (Princeton: Princeton Univ. Press, 1988), xvii.

3. Charles Lloyd Cohen explains that conversion "begins with the soul's initial conviction of sin, an event that usually took place before an individual reached twenty-five." See *God's Caress: The Psychology of Puritan Religious Experience* (New York: Oxford Univ. Press, 1986), 202.

4. Patricia Caldwell notes that in the Cambridge Platform of 1648, the conversion narrative was "'personall' because it represented the speaker's own inner experience [and] 'publick' because it was required of all who would become church members in full communion . . . and had to be delivered before and voted upon by an entire membership." See *Puritan Conversion Narrative,* 46.

5. Alfred Owen Aldridge marks differences in dates for the Great Awakening from New England to Georgia as either 1739-44 or 1734-49. See "Enlightenment and Awakening in Edwards and Franklin," in *Benjamin Franklin, Jonathan Edwards, and the Representation of American Culture,* ed. Barbara B. Oberg and Harry S. Stout (New York: Oxford Univ. Press, 1993), 27.

6. Susan Juster finds that evangelicals "stressed the primacy of personal, experiential religion in which the relationship of man to God was central." See "In a 'Different Voice': Male and Female Narratives of Religious Conversion in Post-Revolutionary America," *American Quarterly* 41 (1989): 37.

7. Although displays of female piety are often assumed to reflect a passive female subordination, Ann Taves finds that "it meant determining what response (whether active or passive) God would have the believer make to the affliction." Taves also explains the conversion experience itself as "the process

whereby the 'natural' self was brought into a proper, that is, a subordinate and dependent, relationship with God," which then she marks as a "paradoxical relationship between explicit self-denial and implicit self-assertion or individualism." See "Self and God in the Early Published Memoirs of New England Women," in *American Women's Autobiography: Fea(s)ts of Memory,* ed. Margo Culley (Madison: Univ. of Wisconsin Press, 1992) 61, 59.

8. Cott finds that this private sphere of faith "allowed women a sort of holy selfishness, or self-absorption, the result of self-examination intrinsic to the Calvinist tradition." See *The Bonds of Womanhood: "Woman's Sphere" in New England, 1780-1835* (New Haven: Yale Univ. Press, 1977), 140.

9. Amanda Porterfield's extensive discussion of Hutchinson's ordeal confirms that "Hutchinson's acceptance of the conventions of her town was the means by which she attained religious authority. She relied on the convention of female submissiveness to God to obtain social authority, and defended herself before the General Court for holding religious meetings outside of church with the argument that those meetings were designed only for women and never presumed to encroach on male authority." See *Female Piety in Puritan New England: The Emergence of Religious Humanism* (New York: Oxford Univ. Press, 1992), 101.

10. Although women's authority is primarily recognized through her domestic roles, Daniel Shea finds that the domestic role is not necessarily an oppressive one, especially in the case of the Ashbridge narrative, wherein he finds a "committed refusal to accept any voice as her own which she has not encountered as central to her own interiority." See the introduction to *Some Account of the Fore Part of the Life of Elizabeth Ashbridge,* by Elizabeth Ashbridge, in Andrews, *Journeys in New Worlds,* 121.

11. Certainly her male counterparts, George Fox, Jonathan Edwards, or John Woolman, struggle against potential political and religious persecution, but they are not expected to justify their absence from the domestic sphere.

12. In Mary G. Mason's discussion of Anne Bradstreet's poetry, she notes how Bradstreet integrated the domestic and the spiritual by observing "a unique harmonizing of the divine, the secular, and the personal, a unifying of a public and a private consciousness." See "The Other Voice: Autobiographies of Women Writers," in *Autobiography: Essays Theoretical and Critical,* ed. James Olney (Princeton: Princeton Univ. Press, 1980), 211.

13. All quotations from Ashbridge are from *Some Account of the Fore Part of the Life of Elizabeth Ashbridge,* ed. with introduction by Daniel B. Shea, in Andrews, *Journeys in New Worlds,* 117-80. Used by permission. This text is, in turn, based upon 1774 manuscript copies from the Woodbrooke Quaker Study Center, Birmingham, England, BN 1172.

14. According to David Levin, the *Personal Narrative* was "written within a year or two after the winter of 1739, apparently in hope of guiding people who were trying to distinguish the signs of grace in a new outpouring of the divine spirit. . . ." See *The Puritan in the Enlightenment: Franklin and Edwards* (New York: Rand McNally, 1963), 3.

15. All quotations from Edwards's *Personal Narrative,* and other works are from *Jonathan Edwards: Basic Writings,* ed. Ola Elizabeth Winslow (New York: Meridian, 1966), 81-96.

16. David Levin reminds us, "Edwards believes that his new insight and judgment are caused by grace, the new sense that not only sustains his conviction of God's sovereignty and justice but converts it into 'a *delightful* conviction.'" See "Reason, Rhythm, and Style," in Oberg and Stout, *Benjamin Franklin,* 177-78.

17. Felicity Nussbaum notes that women's autobiographical writing "testifies to the absence of the female 'self' from theological and philosophical formulations of identity in the period. . . . For the Prodigal Son, it is separation from family and the fall into sin that enables him to achieve independence, as well as return to the father's fold. In contrast, the female autobiographers in their writing, subvert the idea of permanent regret or change which follows the fall." See Nussbaum, "Heteroclites: The Gender of Character in the Scandalous Memoirs," in Nussbaum and Brown, *New Eighteenth Century,* 157.

18. In the introduction to Esther Edwards Burr's journal, Carol F. Karlson and Laurie Crumpaker mark similar gender issues regarding conversion and observe that "for men to question their vocations in life was to question God, but for women to question theirs was to question the authority of both God and men." See *Journal of Esther Edwards Burr,* 10.

19. Philip Greven finds: "Evangelical family government was authoritarian and rigorously repressive. Parental authority was absolute, and exercised without check or control by anyone else within the household. Obedience and submission were the only acceptable responses for children." See *The Protestant Temperament: Patterns of Child-Rearing, Religious Experience, and the Self in Early America* (New York: Knopf, 1977), 32.

20. Ashbridge was married three times. She eloped, as Emory Elliott notes, when she was fourteen with "a poor stocking-weaver" ("New England Puritan" 291). This marriage lasts but a brief five months, ending upon her husband's death. Her second husband, Sullivan, whose story is included in her spiritual autobiography, dies in Cuba while

protesting his part in the military. She met her third husband, Aaron Ashbridge, while in the Quaker ministry. For a more detailed biography, see Daniel Shea's *Introduction,* 119-41.

21. Lois J. Fowler and David H. Fowler confirm that for women as autobiographers, "the selves they put forward are inevitably shaped . . . by their need to conform to—or rebel against—a society largely defined by the values of a sex that is not their own," and that "[m]en do not face that challenge." See *Revelations of Self: American Women in Autobiography* (Albany: SUNY Press, 1990), xxiii.

22. Virginia Brereton compares male and female narratives and finds that "women's narratives reveal more struggle, more painful self-examination, more intensity, more agonizing about 'sins' that a later age would consider harmless. . . ." She then observes that men's conversions are "more matter-of-fact," and that "men were often reluctant even to begin the process, but once on their way they often seemed to accomplish it with less fuss." See *From Sin to Salvation: Stories of Women's Conversions, 1800 to the Present* (Bloomington: Indiana Univ. Press, 1991), 38.

23. Richard Slotkin points out that the captivity narratives were the "root of a growing American mythology in which self-transcendence through acculturation and acculturation through acts of violence were the basic themes." See *Regeneration Through Violence,* 102. The captivity narrative also serves as an inspiration for historical fiction, as in Catharine Maria Sedgwick's novel *Hope Leslie,* written in 1827 and set in the seventeenth century, which challenges notions of female authority in both her white and Native American female characters.

24. In addition, Helena M. Wall sees these novels as a larger eighteenth-century challenge to authority in that they "justified filial disobedience in response to parental tyranny. The political echoes were unmistakable: John Adams himself said, 'The people are Clarissa.'" See *Fierce Communion,* 133.

25. See Jerry Frost, *The Quaker Family in Colonial America: A Portrait of the Society of Friends* (New York: St. Martin's Press, 1973), 25.

26. The difficulty of the female's path toward individuation is confirmed by Felicity Nussbaum when she remarks that for eighteenth-century woman, "'character' or selfhood was guaranteed only if the 'I' could recreate itself in the images created by man and God." See "Heteroclites," 157.

27. That is, according to Jack D. Marietta, who qualifies this belief by explaining that although "Friends did not tolerate any form of occult divination or prophecy, they labored over the Christian interpretation of their own dreams and visions." See *The Reformation of American Quakerism, 1748-1783* (Philadelphia: Univ. of Pennsylvania

Press, 1984), 94. Daniel Shea also notes that as the dream is retold, the narration "establishes a meeting ground of the personal and impersonal" which reinforces the notion of the Quaker as a vehicle for spirit and not the author of the revelation itself. See *Spiritual Autobiography,* 14.

Patricia Caldwell, in turn, offers the contrast from the Puritan's perspective that "dreams are not traditionally part of the *ordo salutis* and that a deep suspicion of 'revelations and dreames' is firmly established in Puritan psychological theory." This is an important reminder, for it provides further contrast between the Quakers and the Puritans. See *Puritan Conversion Narrative,* 16.

28. Margaret Fuller comes to mind as a pioneer in gyno-centered spirituality when she proclaims, "I believe that, at present, women are the best helpers of one another. Let them think; let them act; till they know what they need." See *Woman in the Nineteenth Century* (1855; reprint, New York: Norton, 1971), 172.

29. In Barbara E. Lacey's discussion of Hannah Heaton's journal, Heaton's marriage to an unconverted husband poses similar problems: "[Hannah] wanted their relationship to be based on equality. She referred to 'userped authority' on an occasion when Theophilus kept her from attending a religious meeting. Further, he threw her diary into the mud, hid her spectacles so she could not spend time in pious reading, and expressed suspicions about her fidelity when she spent long hours away from home with the Separates. . . . She has spent a lifetime asserting her spiritual independence, yet also hoped for close companionship with her husband—goals whose irreconcilability was painful for her." See Lacey, "World of Hannah Heaton," 294-95.

30. For an extended discussion of Quaker gender relations, see David Hackett Fischer, *Albion's Seed: Four British Folkways in America* (New York: Oxford Univ. Press, 1989), 490-98.

31. Spiritual rebirth is thus applied equally to women and men, so that, as Jack Marietta notes, "Judeo-Christian disabilities upon women, supported by Scripture, were annulled by revelations tendered to all by the Inner Light." See *Reformation of American Quakerism,* 29. According to this understanding, women were not solely destined to suffering.

32. For an insightful discussion of women's devotional reading and Ashbridge's encounter with the Samuel Crisp letters, see Kevin J. Hayes, *A Colonial Woman's Bookshelf* (Knoxville: Univ. of Tennessee Press, 1996), 45-50.

33. Phebe Davidson finds that Ashbridge's stopping here makes "good storytelling sense" and gives her a "narrative design that makes her ultimate triumph

over the bad marriage the mundane balance for her spiritual salvation." See *Religious Impulse in Selected Autobiographies of American Women (c. 1630-1893): Uses of the Spirit* (Lewiston, N.Y.: Edwin Mellen, 1993), 60.

34. Regarding this stance, Richard Hofstadter comments: "Edwards preached with growing confidence and assertion, reinterpreting the older theology in the light of ideas taken from Locke and Newton." See *America at 1750: A Social Portrait* (New York: Knopf, 1971), 237.

35. David Levin comments that although Edwards is part of the evangelical movement, his Calvinism suggests a return to an earlier Puritan era, which causes him to reject "the idea of a self-determining will as absurd and self-contradictory." See *Puritan in the Enlightenment,* 34. Perry Miller supports this opinion through contrast: "[Edwards] was not Thomas Jefferson: he did not preach democracy, and he had no interest whatsoever in any social revolution." See *Errand into the Wilderness* (Cambridge: Harvard Univ. Press, 1956), 162.

36. For Richard Slotkin this relationship "attempted to make a philosophic reconciliation between Lockean sensationalism and Calvinist orthodoxy, and his recollection of his own conversion experience emphasized the operation of the frontier landscape on his mind, couching Lockean theory in imagery appropriate to an American experience." See *Regeneration Through Violence,* 201. Bruce Kuklick reinforces that "[f]or Edwards the self is not an entity, something that stands behind appearances as their cause. Rather, the self is a construct—the structure of the series of an individual's momentary engagements with the world." See "The Two Cultures in Eighteenth-Century America," in Oberg and Stout, *Benjamin Franklin,* 106.

37. Daniel Shea concurs that the *Narrative's* "most striking characteristic is its apparent solitariness. It is not addressed to posterity in general or to Jonathan Edwards, Jr., in particular, and it is silent as to its purposes and the occasion of its composition." See *Spiritual Autobiography,* 182-83.

38. Karlsen and Crumpaker describe the profound influence of the revivals that Esther Edwards Burr's father led in New England: "[Esther] developed what was to be a lifelong conviction that the only true religion was indeed heartfelt, nothing short of a total and joyous submission to the will of God" (9). Hofstadter adds that for Edwards, "there could be no true religion without a profound stirring of the affections." See *America at 1750,* 239.

FURTHER READING

Bibliographies

Lesser, M. X. *Jonathan Edwards: A Reference Guide.* Boston: G. K. Hall & Co., 1981, 421 p.

Comprehensive bibliography of writings about Edwards, from early eighteenth-century reactions to late 1970s scholarly studies. Lesser precedes his bibliography with a useful overview of the major critical commentary.

Lesser, M. X. *Jonathan Edwards: An Annotated Bibliography, 1979-1993.* Westport, Conn.: Greenwood Press, 1994, 189 p.

Annotated list of writings about Edwards published between 1979 and 1993, a continuation of his 1981 bibliography. Lesser includes a chronology of Jonathan Edwards's works by short and long title, and in a comprehensive introduction, he provides a detailed overview of the growth and direction of Edwards between 1979 and 1993.

Biographies

Morris, William Sparkes. *The Young Jonathan Edwards: A Reconstruction.* New York: Carlson Publishing, 1991, 688 p.

Portrays Jonathan Edwards as a creative thinker and unique philosopher/theologian notable in part for synthesizing a Calvinist interpretation of Christianity with the secular thought of Locke, Descartes, and Newton. The volume includes a critical bibliography.

Murray, Iain H. *Jonathan Edwards: A New Biography.* Edinburgh: The Banner of Truth Trust, 1987, 503 p.

A compilation of short biographical essays previously published in the periodical *The Banner of Truth* between 1974 and 1986. Murray includes illustrations and the text of a letter written by Sarah Edwards.

Tracy, Patricia J. *Jonathan Edwards, Pastor: Religion and Society in Eighteenth Century Northampton.* New York: Hill and Wang, 1980, 270 p.

Examines the life and work of Jonathan Edwards as pastor of the Northampton church. Tracy discusses Edwards's failings as a pastor within the context of his upbringing, the lack of pastoral training in his education, and the changing social values and church practices of the Northampton community and congregation.

Criticism

Bell, Richard H. "On Trusting One's Own Heart: Scepticism in Jonathan Edwards and Søren Kirkegaard." *History of European Ideas,* 12, No. 1: 105-116.

Compares ideas from Edwards's *Religious Affections* with Søren Kirkegaard's *On Authority and Revelation,* drawing conclusions about various ways of talking about and interpreting religious experience.

Chai, Leon. *Jonathan Edwards and the Limits of Enlightenment Philosophy.* New York: Oxford University Press, 1998, 164 p.

Traces the major philosophical themes of the Enlightenment and discusses their influence on the philosophy of Jonathan Edwards.

Daniel, Stephen H. *The Philosophy of Jonathan Edwards: A Study in Divine Semiotics.* Bloomington, Ind.: Indiana University Press, 1994, 207 p.

Philosophical approach to analyzing Edwards's doctrines. Daniel challenges assumptions previously made and traces the philosophical insights of Edwards that, according to Daniel, place Edwards among early modern thinkers.

Guelzo, Allen C. *Edwards on the Will: A Century of American Theological Debate.* Middletown, Conn.: Wesleyan University Press, 1989, 349 p.

Traces one hundred years of Edwardsean influence on American religious thought and practice. Includes illustrations and a critical bibliography.

Guelzo, Allen C. and Sang Hyun Lee. *Edwards in Our Time: Jonathan Edwards and Contemporary Theological Issues.* Grand Rapids, Mich.: W. B. Eerdmans, 1999, 208 p.

Essays trace the influence of Edwards's philosophy and theology on late twentieth-century religious thought and practice.

Knight, Janice. "Learning the Language of God: Jonathan Edwards and the Typology of Nature." *William and Mary Quarterly* XLVIII, No. 4 (October 1991): 531-51.

Focus is on Jonathan Edwards's embrace of nature as a communication of God's divinity.

Lee, Sang Hyun. *The Philosophical Theology of Jonathan Edwards.* Princeton, N. J.: Princeton University Press, 1988, 248 p.

Traces various influences on the development of Edwards's thought and outlines his philosophical theology, particularly as it relates to habit, aesthetics, and destiny.

Munk, Linda. "Jonathan Edwards and the Angel of the Lord: *A History of the Work of Redemption.*" In *The Devil's Mousetrap: Redemption and Colonial American Literature,* pp. 24-46. New York: Oxford University Press, 1997.

Examines the Calvinist treatment of angels and the being of Jesus in Edwards's *A History of the Work of Redemption.*

Pettit, Norman, ed. *Jonathan Edwards, The Life of David Brainerd.* New Haven, Conn.: Yale University Press, 1985, 620 p.

Editor's introduction provides historical background of this work, plus references for names that appear in Brainerd's diary and a publication history of the diary. Pettit discusses the place of this work in Edwards's life and thought.

Proudfoot, Wayne. "From Theology to a Science of Religions: Jonathan Edwards and William James on Religious Affections." *Harvard Theological Review* 82, No. 2, 1989: 149-68.

Proudfoot compares and contrasts the writings of Jonathan Edwards and William James on the topic of the experience and role of religion in society.

Steele, Richard B. *"Gracious Affection" and "True Virtue" According to Jonathan Edwards and John Wesley.* Metuchen, N.J.: Scarecrow Press, 1994, 423 p.

A comparison of Jonathan Edwards and John Wesley examining the historical and literary relationships between the two eighteenth-century theologians separated by the Atlantic Ocean and doctrinal differences.

Stein, Stephen J. *Jonathan Edwards's Writings: Text, Context, Interpretation.* Bloomington, Ind.: Indiana University Press, 219 p.

Collection of critical papers on the work of Jonathan Edwards presented at a June, 1994, conference at Indiana University, Bloomington, Indiana. Includes bibliographic references.

Additional coverage of Edwards's life and career is contained in the following sources published by the Gale Group: *Dictionary of Literary Biography,* **Vol. 24;** *DISCovering Authors; DISCovering Authors: Canadian; DISCovering Authors: Modules*—**Most-Studied Authors Module.**

Pierre Gassendi
1592-1655

(Born Pierre Gassend) French philosopher, astronomer, historian, and priest.

INTRODUCTION

Pierre Gassendi's place in the history of science and philosophy is still being written and revised. Gassendi was well known to his contemporaries in his native France and in England as a formidable scholar, the foremost proponent of the Epicurean revival, and an estimable astronomer. However, Gassendi's dense Latin prose, his wearisome prolixity, and his apparent (and perhaps temporary) loss to René Descartes of one of the great battles of Western philosophy condemned him to obscurity from the eighteenth century to the late twentieth century. As the importance of atomism and neo-Epicureanism to the development of modern science becomes clearer, however, Gassendi's stature amongst such notable seventeenth-century thinkers as Thomas Hobbes, John Locke, Robert Boyle, Isaac Newton, and even his adversary Descartes, has risen. A leading exponent of French empiricism, Gassendi advocated a skepticism which held that knowledge could be received only through the senses; experiment and observation, rather than pure ratiocination, were the requirements of his natural philosophy. Gassendi's materialism and connection to Epicurus opened him to groundless charges of libertinism and atheism; ironically, the focus of the French priest's life's work was to reconcile Epicureanism with Christianity.

BIOGRAPHICAL INFORMATION

Pierre Gassend was born January 22, 1592, in the small village of Champtercier, in the Provencal region of France. (Gassendi is the Italianized version, the final "i" a mark of honor added due to his scholarly reputation.) His schooling began under his uncle Thomas Fabry, until at the age of seven he was sent to the larger town of Digne to study Latin and arithmetic. At 14 he returned to Champtercier for two years before going to the University of Aix, where he studied philosophy and theology. In 1614 he received his doctorate in theology from the University of Avignon, and in 1616 he celebrated his first Catholic Mass as an ordained priest. It was also in 1616 that Gassendi met his great mentor, Nicolas-Claude Fabri de Peiresc, with whom he maintained a close friendship and extensive correspondence until Peiresc's death in 1637. In 1617 Gassendi took the Chair of Philosophy at the University of Aix. During his six years teaching philosophy (primarily Aristotelian),

Gassendi also taught his students his own arguments contrary to the Aristotelian doctrines that dominated early seventeenth-century thought. When, in 1622, Jesuits took over the University and Gassendi was compelled to leave teaching, friends encouraged him to make public his lectures, which constitute his first work, Book I of *Exercitationes Paradoxicae adversus Aristoteleos,* published in 1624 (planned later books were not completed).

Gassendi traveled to Paris in 1625, beginning a friendship with Père Marin Mersenne, who would later be instrumental in the great debates between Gassendi and Descartes. During this year, Gassendi also made connections with Elie Diodati and Galileo as he pursued his interest in observational astronomy, an interest that helped provide the foundation for his philosophical skepticism, which held that knowledge apprehended through the senses was uncertain at best. Meanwhile, his attacks on Aristotle finding only a mixed reception, Gassendi turned his attention to Epicurus, beginning an explication of his philosophy and a short *Life of Epicurus* for its preface. He proceeded slowly with this work, continuing to maintain his interest in astronomy as well. Interrupted by serious illness and the death of his mentor, Peiresc, Gassendi abandoned the work in 1637 for four years. Instead, he wrote his *Life of Peiresc* (1641) and, at the request of Mersenne, reviewed Descartes' *Meditations,* preparing a set of *Objections* (1641). Descartes' *Responses* were contemptuous, and Gassendi replied with *Instantiae* (first circulated in Paris in 1642), creating a public battle between the two philosophers. Gassendi also maintained at this time a heated debate with the astrologer Jean-Baptiste Morin, whose insistence that the earth was the center of the universe spurred Gassendi to develop further the views of Copernicus and Galileo.

In 1645 Gassendi returned to teaching as the Chair of Astronomy at the College Royal de France in Paris, during which time he published his coursework as *Institutio astronomica* (1647). He was compelled to leave due to failing health, returning to Provence in 1648, a year after his *De vita et moribus Epicuri libri octo (Life of Epicurus)* finally appeared. Gassendi had not approved of this publication, which barely scratched the surface of what Gassendi had hoped to achieve in reviving Epicurus. Encouraged by friends, Gassendi released much of his later work on Epicurus attached as an appendix to his translation of the Tenth Book of Diogenes Laertius' *De Clarorum Philosophorum Vitis.*In 1649 his massive *Animadversiones in Decimum Librum Diogenes Laertii* was published, but despite its positive reception, Gassendi was again displeased with its over-hasty release. The *Animadversiones* is the only work not reproduced in its original form in Gassendi's *Opera omnia.*

In 1653 Gassendi returned to Paris, telling a friend in a letter that in leaving Provence he had been delivered "from the jaws of Hell," so ill had he been feeling. While in Paris Gassendi busied himself with a new edition of his *Animadversiones,* which would be published posthumously as his *Syntagma philosophicum.* He also wrote biographies of several astronomers, including Copernicus and Tycho Brahe, and published works on coinage, music, and the history of the diocese of Digne. Beginning in August 1654, however, Gassendi suffered from more severe and more frequent bouts of illness; he was not able to fulfill his plans for his *Syntagma philosophicum,* which his editors completed in 1658. He died in Paris on October 24, 1655. Prior to his death, Gassendi had selected those texts he wanted included in his complete works and arranged for their publication in Lyon; they were published as his *Opera omnia* in 1658.

MAJOR WORKS

Gassendi's chief importance in the history of science and philosophy has been in his conflict with Descartes and, especially, in his revival of Epicurean philosophy. His first work, *Exercitationes Paradoxicae adversus Aristoteleos,* demonstrates the frustration with the state of seventeenth-century philosophy that would characterize much of his work. To many of his contemporaries, his attack on Aristotelian philosophy was tantamount to an attack on the seventeenth-century worldview, but he was not yet prepared to offer an alternative, as he eventually would in his exposition of Epicurus. Gassendi did, however, promote a positive skepticism that offers intellectual freedom and advocates experimental knowledge, while denying the possibility of complete and certain knowledge. That possibility was a major part of Gassendi's debate with Descartes, who held in his *Meditations* that things could be known purely via the mind, while Gassendi maintained that knowledge could be obtained only through the senses and was thus necessarily incomplete and uncertain. Throughout Gassendi's *Objections,* Descartes' *Replies,* and Gassendi's lengthy *Instantiae,* the two refer to each other as "Mind" and "Flesh" as an indication of their contempt for the other's position, and as a reflection of the core difference in their epistemology. Yet although Gassendi was best known through the twentieth century for his skirmish with the man who became one of the most important philosophers in the history of Western thought, during his lifetime battling with Descartes was not one of his major concerns.

Throughout the later part of his career especially, vindicating and "Christianizing" Epicureanism as a viable philosophy was the most prominent theme in his work. In particular, Gassendi needed to counter the popular belief that Epicureanism could be equated with libertinism and athe-

ism in order to achieve his goal, and this was part of the work of his *De Vita et Moribus Epicuri.* Begun in 1626 as an extension of his attack on the Aristotelians, Gassendi revised it significantly to make it an account of Epicurean philosophy and a careful defense of Epicurus from the misrepresentations of the Stoics, early Christian writers, and others who accused him of sensualism or impiety. Gassendi initially intended for *De Vita et Moribus* to precede a more thorough exposition of Epicurean philosophy, but his original plans were never realized. He published much of his subsequent work on Epicurus with *Animadversiones in Decimum Librum Diogenis Laertii,* in an appendix titled *Philosophiae Epicuri Syntagma,* but with his last major work, *Syntagma Philosophicum,* Gassendi shifted his focus from explicating the doctrines of Epicurus to expounding his own philosophy. Divided into three sections—*Logic, Physics,* and *Ethics*—and preceded by a short book on the nature of philosophy, the *Syntagma* promotes the atomism, skepticism, and materialism Gassendi found in Epicurus and develops it in a seventeenth-century context. The *Syntagma* was published as the first two volumes of the massive six-volume *Opera omnia* in 1658, not fully completed by Gassendi, but still offering the most fully realized explication of his neo-Epicurean philosophy.

CRITICAL RECEPTION

Even Descartes, who could not contain his frustration with what he considered Gassendi's inability to comprehend his *Meditations,* had great respect for Gassendi as a scholar. Gassendi's reputation in England was considerable; along with Descartes, he was considered a model for the New Science practiced by the Royal Society. The question of his influence on English thought has been complicated by the vexing practice held by early modern authors of not citing their sources; however, modern studies have convincingly demonstrated the indebtedness of Boyle, Newton, and Locke to Gassendi's work. Olivier Bloch and Richard Kroll, among other modern critics, have endeavored to promote Gassendi's importance to English neo-Epicureanism in both scientific and social circles. In particular, Locke's relationship to Gassendi has been the topic of long-standing critical debate. Kroll suggests that Gassendi was merely one influence among many, while Fred S. and Emily Michael argue that Gassendi's theory of ideas was clearly the foundation for Locke's *Essay Concerning Human Understanding.* Gassendi's alleged libertinism has also attracted the attention of scholars; Richard H. Popkin distinguishes Gassendi's skepticism from the charges of dissolution, while Lisa T. Sarasohn suggests that Gassendi's emphasis on pleasure was a part of the voluntarism that distinguished him from his fellow materialist Thomas Hobbes. The great battle between Cartesian certainty and Gassendist skepticism remains a major focus of the scholarship: Thomas M. Lennon, among others, suggests that Gassendi has long been judged unfairly as a result of Descartes' scorn.

PRINCIPAL WORKS

Exercitationes Paradoxicae adversus Aristoteleos (philosophy) 1624

Parhelia sive soles quator spurii, qui circa verum appaverunt Romae anno MDCXXIX, de XX (philosophy) 1630

Petri Gassendi Theologi Epistolica Exercitatio, in quo Principes Philosophiae Roberti Fluddi Medici relegantur et ad recentes illius libros adversus R.P.F. Marinum Mersennum, Ordenes Minimorum Sancti Francisci de Paula sareptos responditur (philosophy) 1630

De Mercurio in Sole viso et Venere invisa Parisiis anno (1631) (philosophy) 1632

Instructions de M. Gassend au R. P. Ephrem de Nevers Capucin et a Frere Alexandre d'Angoullesme pour les observations celestes (philosophy) 1636

De apparente magnitudine solis humilis et sublimis (philosophy) 1636; reprinted in

Epistolae quatuor 1642

De Nicolai Claudii Fabrici de Peiresc, Senatoris Aquisextiensis, Vita [*Life of Peiresc*] (biography) 1641

Objectiones quintae Petri Gassendi diniensis ecclesiae praepositi et acutissimi philosophi [*Objections*] (philosophy) 1641

De Motu impresso a Motore translato (philosophy) 1642

De apparente magnitudine solis humilis et sublimis, Epistolae quatuor (philosophy) 1642

Novum stellae circa Jovem visa, et de eisdem P. Gassendi judicium (philosophy) 1643

Disquisitio metaphysica adversus Cartesium (philosophy) 1644

Institutio astronomica (philosophy) 1647

De vita et moribus Epicuri libri octo [*Life of Epicurus*] (philosophy and biography) 1647

Animadversiones in Decimum Librum Diogenis Laertii (philosophy) 1649

Philosophiae Epicuri Syntagma (philosophy) 1649; printed as an appendix to *Animadversiones in Decimum Librum Diogenis Laertii*

Tychonis Brahei, equitis Dani, astronomorum coryphaei . . . Nicolai Copernici, Georgii Puerbachi et Joannis Regiomantani, astronomorum celebrum vita [*Lives of Tycho Brahe, Nicolas Copernicus, et al.*] (history and biography) 1654

†*The Mirrour of True Nobility and Gentility, Being the Life of The Renowned Nicolaus Claudius Fabricius Lord of Peiresk, Senator of the Parliament at Aix* (philosophy) 1657

Syntagma Philosophicum (philosophy) 1658

Opera omnia (philosophy) 1658

§*The Vanity of Judiciary Astrology or Divination by the Stars Lately Written in Latin, by that Great Scholar and Mathematician, the Illustrious Petrus Gassendus* (philosophy) 1659

The Selected Works of Pierre Gassendi [translation by Craig B. Brush] (philosophy) 1972

Institutio Logica: A Critical Edition with Introduction and English Translation [edited by Howard Jones] (philosophy) 1981

*This work, published by Gassendi's (and Descartes') friend Samuel Sorbiere, contains Gassendi's *Objections*, Descartes' *Responses*, and Gassendi's *Instantiae*. The *Instantiae*, Gassendi's reply to Descartes' *Responses*, were circulated among Gassendi's friends in 1642, but not published until Sorbiere obtained his permission to print this edition.

†This work is a translation of *Life of Peiresc*.

§This work is a translation of part of the *Syntagma Philosophicum*.

CRITICISM

William Rand (essay date 1657)

SOURCE: "To the ingenious and learned Gentleman, the worshipful John Evelyn Esquire," in *The Mirrour of True Nobility & Gentility: Being the Life of the Renowned Nicolaus Claudius Fabricius Lord of Peiresk, Senator of the Parliament at Aix,* by Pierre Gassendi, translated by William Rand, J. Streater, 1657, n.p.

[*Dr. William Rand translated Gassendi's early* Life of Peiresc *into English as* The Mirrour of True Nobility and Gentility. *In this excerpt from the work's dedicatory epistle addressed to the diarist John Evelyn, Rand reveals his admiration for Gassendi's original text and for Gassendi himself.*]

To the ingenious and learned Gentleman, the worshipful John Evelyn *Esquire.*

Worthy Sir,

Much about ten years are fled, since my learned friend Dr. *Benjamin Worsley* brought me first acquainted with the name and fame of *Peireskius,* and knowing that I delighted to busie my self in that kind, wished that I would render his history into English. And not long after, my good friend Squire *Harlib* seconded his Motion, and put the Latine Book into my hand, to take home with me and peruse and consider of. Which I did; but finding it so knottie a piece, both in respect of the matter, and the presse and elegantly concise style, of the learned and judicious *Gassendus,* I had not the courage to venture upon it; but restored my friend his Book, without any more adoe. Since which time having (during our intestine broiles in *England*) spent an ordinary Apprenticeship in Contemplation of the Belgic Provinces of Holland, Utrecht, Brabant, Flanders, and their many fair Cities and Universities, of which that of Lovaine seems likest ours, as much resembling Cambridge, in many respects: not long after my return, I was a fresh importuned by another friend, to let our Countreymen understand the Life of the renowned *Peireskius.* Which at last, though with very much diffidence, I did undertake and accomplish; and how I have therein acquitted my self, you are best able to judge; who besides your parts of wit and learning, know by experience the labour and care belonging to such works, and are best qualified to excuse an over-sight or mistake. You know that *Gassendus* a general Scholar, and one of the greatest wits in Europe, and a perfect Master of the Roman Language, comparable to any of the ancients, could not have taken in hand an Argument, that would have more effectually called forth, and employed the utmost of all his Activities, than to write the Life of this rare French Gentleman, whose sprightful curiosity left nothing unsearcht into, in the vast and all-comprehending Dominions of Nature and Art.

J. S. Spink (essay date 1960)

SOURCE: "Gassendi's Account of the Nature of Things," in *French Free-Thought from Gassendi to Voltaire,* Athlone Press, 1960, pp. 85-102.

[In the excerpt below, Spink considers Gassendi's adaptations of Epicurus, comparing Gassendi's work with Lucretius' De Rerum Natura. *The critic also examines Gassendi's* Syntagma philosophicum, *finding Gassendi singular among his French contemporaries as a proponent of atomism.]*

It is difficult to determine which of several possible reasons attracted Gassendi to Epicurus in the first place in 1626. He had just given up, or was in process of giving up his plan for publishing a series of direct attacks on the old school in continuation of his *Exercitationes paradoxicae.* Doubtless it was prudence which caused him to do so; not that he felt menaced by the campaign of his friend Mersenne against the sceptics and deists; more probably he realized that attempts of the type of the *Exercitationes paradoxicae* were neither new nor effective. The old guard was strongly entrenched, especially in Paris, and was merely irritated without being shaken by such skirmishing. Was he attracted by the idea of rehabilitating Epicurus as a means of decrying Aristotle without openly flouting the authority of his elders? Very possibly. He at any rate intended his *Epicurus* to be a sequel to his *Exercitationes paradoxicae,*[1] and such an indirect approach was entirely suited to his cautious temperament. He had no desire to stir up a hornets' nest, but at the same time his lively intelligence must have been tempted by the prospect of justifying, with sound evidence in hand, a man so universally condemned by the unintelligent as was Epicurus: here was a 'paradox' he could victoriously force upon the adversary! Did the success of others with whom he was in contact, Galileo, Mersenne, Beeckmann, Descartes, who were achieving results by reducing the problems of physics to those of mechanics, encourage him to develop his study of a mechanistic philosophy? Was he attracted by Epicurus's method as a means of overcoming his own natural scepticism? All these factors may have weighed with him. In 1628 he was still asserting, to both Peiresc and Mersenne, that he was of a sceptical turn of mind, but on one of these occasions he was referring to astrology and so probably meant no more than that he was intellectually cautious to a fault and found it difficult to convince himself rationally of the truth of any proposition. Such a scepticism would not be the same as Pyrrhonic doubt, content with an exact equilibrium of pro and con; it would rather

be an inhibiting excess of caution, to be overcome by intellectual effort and courage. In Epicurus's 'Canons' lay a means of acquiring a reasonable degree of certainty, or at least the means of making possible an advance in philosophic inquiry beyond one's starting point. This is the attitude which Gassendi eventually reached, as is amply shown by the *Syntagma philosophicum*; it is the attitude of mind which has since become general in the scientific world, where theories which no one would claim as ultimate are nevertheless used as working hypotheses.

Gassendi's friends were from the first acquainted with his plans and Beeckmann, going straight to the heart of things, was anxious that he should tackle at once the problem of how sensitive organisms can be formed from insensitive atoms.[2] Neither of the two philosophers was worried by the religious significance of such an inquiry; at least neither mentioned it. It was indeed to Mersenne, the author of *l'Impiété des déistes,* that Beeckmann addressed his inquiry. Both he and Gassendi were prepared to take elasticity in bodies as the starting point in an attempt to proceed from the insensitive to the sensitive.

Gassendi's plan grew in scope as he worked upon it. By 1631 he intended to put into his book all that could be learned on the life and thought of Epicurus; he was planning a work of scholarship rather than of science. The first part was to be a life of the philosopher and a defence of his character. This was to be followed by the Physics of Epicurus. The Physics was to contain first an account of Epicurus's views on the nature of things in general: the atoms and their properties, motion, space, the existence of God, the existence (or rather non-existence) of demons. The second part of the Physics was to deal with the origin and structure of the world, the existence or non-existence of a Providence, the end of the world and the existence of innumerable other worlds. The third part was to deal with the heavens, the stars, their motion and whether they exercise an influence on human affairs. And the last book was to deal with the Earth, with animate and inanimate beings on the Earth, the generation, nutrition and reproduction of animals, the senses; the soul or mind, its seat and functions, the appetites, animal motions, sleep, health and sickness and the immortality of the soul. A final section, on Epicurean moral philosophy, was not yet planned.

The various chapters were sent round to Gassendi's friends in manuscript form as they were written, and were read and argued about in an active philosophical correspondence. The work progressed slowly because of interruptions, occasioned by Gassendi's ecclesiastical duties and his numerous journeys. Sometimes the interruptions were of long duration, from 1637 to 1641 for example. In 1647 Gassendi allowed the first part to appear under the title *De vita et moribus Epicuri libri octo*[3] and in 1649 he edited with long philological and philosophical commentaries drawn from his voluminous notes the tenth book of Diogenes Laertius, which deals with Epicurus. His systematic treatment of the subject was as yet known only to the friends to whom he had communicated his manuscript or summaries of it.

A certain amount of opposition and doubt was expressed by his friends. In 1632 Campanella wrote to him announcing his *Atheismus triumphatus,* which sets Campanella's own picture of a world permeated with intelligence beside that described by Lucretius from which design and purpose are excluded. Gassendi replied that there were indeed aspects of Epicurus's philosophy which he would have to refute, but that he should not for that reason fail to give a complete and impartial account of it. Mersenne did not think atomism could be made acceptable to religion, nor could he accept as conceivable an atom extended in space and at the same time indivisible.[4] He had however already expressed his approval of Gassendi's *Apology,* which he had read in manuscript.[5]

Chapelain was worried both by the general idea of a defence of Epicurus[6] and by what seemed to him a contradiction affecting the whole system. If the atoms were to replace the old idea of matter, how could they at the same time be the cause of motion? 'Matter' was something essentially inert. Gassendi replied that the atoms are always in motion, that motion is one of their properties: his conception of the atoms was essentially 'dynamic', though he did not use the term. While making motion essential to the atoms, he was however careful to point out to Chapelain that he considered Epicurus to be in error for having assumed the existence of eternal atoms eternally in motion. God created the atoms and directed their motion according to his own design; all their movements are therefore the expression of God's providence.

Indefatigably Gassendi strove in his correspondence to show his friends how the difficulties of Epicurus's system could be removed. Epicurus assumes an infinite number of atoms in an infinite space. If that were so, God's providence would not be necessary in order to explain the present appearance of things, as an infinite number of atoms, moving eternally in an infinite space would at some time or other, in some place or other, actualize every possible combination of themselves and there would be no problem to solve in explaining why the present constitution of things as we see them has come about: it would merely be one of an endless series of possible combinations of atoms. Gassendi's reply was that God alone is absolutely infinite; Epicurus was therefore wrong in postulating an infinite number of atoms.[7]

In order to put his answer to Epicurus on a rational basis, he had to be prepared to prove at least the existence of God, and not be content with the authority of religion as sufficient grounds for affirming it, and indeed, in the years following 1631 he showed himself more and more ready to admit the importance of reasoned argument as against unquestioning faith. In 1636 he was prepared to prove the existence of God, God's providence and the immortality

of the soul by reason,[8] and in 1642, in his controversy with Descartes, he had his own proofs to offer as an alternative to his adversary's.

So far, such objections as had been made against Gassendi's Epicureanism had been made by personal friends. Descartes indulged in harder hitting, but had no desire to cause his adversary any trouble with the religious authorities; the argument between him and Gassendi was purely philosophical. That was not the case with J.-B. Morin, who declared publicly that Gassendi was fit to be burnt at the stake. Morin was a teacher of the old school and an astrologer. He took up the cudgels for Aristotle against Etienne de Claves in 1624 and in 1643 published a refutation of Copernicus. A reply by Gassendi in the same year, published without the author's consent in 1649, started a violent quarrel between the two and it was in Morin's *Dissertatio de atomis et vacuo contra Gassendi philosophiam Epicuream* in 1650 that the menace of the stake occurred. Bernier continued the argument and succeeded in presenting Morin in a ridiculous light.[9] No one in authority took any notice of Morin as far as one can make out, and it was not until long after Gassendi's death in 1655 that it was again suggested that Gassendi's teaching was dangerous for the faith, by the Cartesian theologian Antoine Arnauld. By that time (1692)[10] the atmosphere had changed and Cartesian habits of thought had made possible interpretations of Gassendi's ideas which Gassendi probably never even dreamed of. Gassendi's Epicureanism was framed at a time when scholastic theology was scarcely challenged and was taken for granted in its own domain; it was Cartesianism itself, with its ruthless simplification of current ideas, which was to cut away that framework and leave the picture almost as Epicurus had originally painted it.

Apart from Lucretius himself, whose *De rerum natura* was always readily available and widely read, Gassendi seems to have had few competitors as an exponent of Epicurean atomism. Descartes was developing a corpuscular physics, but his particles of the first, second and third elements were not atoms; they were mere parts of a continuum and were divisible to infinity. It is true that at Pavia, a Frenchman by birth, Jean Chrysostome Magnen, was professing an atomic theory taken from Democritus, and that his lectures were published, but there is no evidence of his having had many readers in France.[11] One can also mention an abortive effort of two Frenchmen, Jean Bitaud and Etienne de Claves to defend in public a certain number of theses (one of them being a clear statement of atomism) in Paris in 1624. The Parlement intervened at the request of the Sorbonne and drove the two disputants out of the confines of its jurisdiction. It was on this occasion that attacks on the 'ancient and approved author'—meaning Aristotle— were forbidden on pain of death; the Aristotelian professors of the University of Paris had claimed and obtained the protection of the civil authorities. As for Bitaud's and Claves's claim that 'all things are composed of indivisible atoms' it was condemned by the Sorbonne as 'false, audacious and contrary to the faith'. Their statement of the principle is dogmatic enough, but they do not seem to have developed it systematically. They were interested in chemistry and not mechanics, to the point of being suspected by Peiresc of seeking in chemistry the revelation of all nature's secrets, and though they were sufficiently scientific in their attitude for us to call them 'chemists' rather than 'alchemists', they were not, of course, in a position to make a systematic application of the atomic theory to chemistry; they were still at grips with the five 'elements': water, earth, salt, sulphur and mercury, which were for them the component parts of all 'mixed' substances (theses nos. IV to X). However one looks upon it, they cannot be thought of as serious rivals of Gassendi, who, be it said by the way, seems not to have been in contact with them.

When Gassendi died on 9 November 1655 he was still engaged in putting his notes in order under the title *Syntagma philosophicum.* In 1658 the work was published by his literary executors in two volumes at the head of his complete works. Such parts as were still not written up in their final form were printed from earlier drafts dating from 1636-45. The *Syntagma* is the most complete and systematic exposition which Gassendi made of his teaching, and while it follows more or less the author's original plan (1631) for an account of Epicurus's opinions, it does not limit itself to them, but on the other hand discusses other ancient and contemporary theories relating to each question under discussion. It is indeed an account of Epicurean atomism presented in the light of seventeenth-century speculation.

The *Syntagma* begins with a discussion of philosophical method and continues through 'physics' (physics, biology and psychology) to morals. The first part, the *Institutio logica* tries to overcome the sort of scepticism which makes philosophy impossible and replace it by a 'prudent confidence' in being able to attain to truth, holding the balance evenly between reason and experience, accepting the axioms and the law of contradiction as limits beyond which the necessity of proving first principles need not be pushed and contending that to know the properties or operations of a thing is to know the thing itself. Our ideas come to us through our senses; there are no innate ideas. All the ideas we receive through our senses are singular or particular, not general; it is the mind that makes general ideas out of singular or particular ideas. But ideas can also be communicated to us by other people, so that we can say that our ideas come to us from two sources, (1) our own experience, and (2) another's teaching. A good philosophical method consists in discovering hidden relations between things, in interpreting these relations correctly and in expounding their explanation clearly.

The second part of the *Syntagma,* that is to say the *Physica,* begins with a discussion of the nature of things followed by a discussion of the causes of things. In discussing the nature of things, Gassendi deals first with the four categories of being which he calls space, time, substance and accident. Space and time are not primary substances, nor are they ideas, nor are they modes of a primary substance, nor are they mere fictions: they are categories of being. One

can summarize the foregoing by saying that according to Gassendi the things which are and which we can know by experience are accidents of a primary substance existing in temporal and spatial relations with each other. Accident alone, substance alone, time alone, space alone cannot be objects of experimental knowledge; they can only be known as part of a complex of all four. The term 'substance' then disappears from Gassendi's discussions and is replaced by the term 'matter'. 'Matter' is that which is permanent under the ceaseless change and variety we see in things; it is the matrix from which all things come and to which they all return. It is not merely an indeterminate something, capable of receiving forms and qualities, as was taught in the schools. Such a being would be nothing and nothing could come from it. No purpose is served, on the other hand, by imagining four primary elements, fire, air, water and earth, because the immense variety we see in nature cannot be explained by combinations of only four elements. The most satisfactory theory is that of the atomists Democritus, Epicurus and Lucretius. The atoms can be imagined by analogy with the motes one sees in a ray of sunlight. From their innumerable combinations come all things with all their properties, which are the properties of matter. We cannot see the atoms, but we can determine their characteristics by reasoning. They must be indestructible, indivisible, solid; they must have size, however minute they be. Their essence cannot be mere extension, as Descartes says, otherwise nothing could be produced from them. They must be indivisible, because if matter was infinitely divisible there would be as many parts in a grain of sand as in a mountain. They must be very (though not infinitely) varied in shape in order to explain the great variety we see in things, and there must be a finite number of atoms and not an infinite number of each shape as Lucretius says. The atoms must have weight and they must have a tendency to movement or action by their nature. Repose is a mere illusion; everything is constantly changing, although some things change very slowly. Where the atoms are not, there is vacuum, otherwise movement would be impossible, as can be shown by reasoning and proved by experiments such as the dissolution of salt in water or the compression of air.

After discussing the *nature* of things, Gassendi deals with the *causes* of things. He distinguishes the first cause and the secondary causes. The first cause of all things is God and the existence of God must therefore be established first and foremost. For Gassendi the existence of God is proved by our having the idea of him in our minds and by the evidence of harmony and order in the universe. Of these two proofs the first is drawn from the second, so that the one great proof of the existence of God is the evidence of harmony and order in the universe. Lucretius is wrong therefore in giving fear as the source of our idea of God; we do not fear God in times of danger, we turn to him for help. The idea of God is not an innate idea, but on the other hand it does not come entirely from experience. There is in the mind a predisposition to know God, so that we readily believe what we are told about him, and form the idea of him spontaneously when we behold the harmony of nature and its laws. To say with Lucretius that the world needs no cause is unreasonable. A prosperous state presupposes a good ruler, a magnificent palace presupposes a clever architect; by analogy the world presupposes God. God must be distinct from the world and must exist *necessarily* or by himself. We cannot conceive his nature because our senses give us no help: he can be thought of as the reason for all things and as perfection, but no relative quality can be attributed to him. He must be intelligent because he is the cause of an intelligible effect; he can have nothing in common with matter because matter is limited, composite, divisible, changeable, corruptible. He is known by the intellect and not by the imagination, and as our language is never devoid of imaginative content it can never correspond with his nature. Considered in himself, or as a substance, his attributes are unity, eternity, immensity (understood as a quality and not as an extent of space). Considered as the intelligent cause of all things he is omniscient, omnipotent, good, free, wise and blessed. In the world his intelligence and activity are seen, for example, in the regularity of the crystals of which minerals are composed, in the wonders of the bodies of animals, in the return of the seasons. It is not reasonable to attribute these marvels to chance. Creation is incomprehensible, but is a fact none the less. Before the creation God was an active intelligence contemplating his own perfections; in the creation his goodness radiated outside himself for his own glory alone. Nothing thereby was added to his being because he is sufficient unto himself: creation is the expression of God's goodness. Lucretius was so preoccupied with the sight of evil, that he failed to understand that life is good (or rather a good, not an evil) and that it is better to be, than not to be, alive.

Providence in general is not inconceivable because for God to care for his creation is surely a perfection in him. Without it he would not be all perfect. Also, as action is more perfect than contemplation, he would not be all perfect if he were not active. *A posteriori* his providence can be proved by the order and harmony of the universe. Chance is no explanation of order and harmony. The idea of chance is merely an expression of our ignorance. God has a special providence for man, the most perfect of his creations. To say with Lucretius that God's felicity would be deranged thereby is sheer anthropomorphism, and to ask why there are dangerous animals in the world, and why the virtuous suffer, is to fail to see that God allows the causes he has created to act independently of himself. He allows man the liberty to do evil, but he gives him the strength to do good, and the fact that the virtuous suffer is a proof of the immortality of man's soul because the balance must be redressed in a future life.

The secondary causes of things can be reduced to one, that is to say motion. Motion according to Lucretius is the passage of a body from one place to another. The principle of motion is the atoms themselves which are naturally active and always active. When they meet an obstacle their effort is not destroyed, it continues to be exercised. Differences of movement are explainable by the different shapes of the atoms, for their motion is more or less hindered by their shape. The principle of motion is in bodies. There is no point in making a distinction between motion and what moves, as the Aristotelians do, nor is Aristotle's way of explaining motion by the desire of the world to turn towards God any more than the product of his imagination. The principle of motion is in bodies and especially in the most active of the atoms, the 'flower of matter' so to speak, the part that is usually called 'form' in the schools. Gravity is a movement of one body towards another body to be understood by analogy with the action of the magnet. One must suppose an emanation of particles (species) from one body (the earth, say) which operate on another body (a stone, say) either by squeezing from the sides, as Descartes suggests, or (and this Gassendi would prefer to believe) one can imagine a sort of feeling in the stone in response to an impression carried to it by the emanation of species from the earth, the species themselves being very fine and subtle atoms such as the sentient faculties are made of. This hylopsychistic theory Gassendi develops at length and with obvious affection. It is the first of a whole series of explanations in which he gives preference to hylopsychistic over mechanistic theories, throughout the whole of his physics and biology. The similarity with Maignan is too obvious to need to be stressed. The principle of latent sensitivity diffused throughout the whole of nature and differing only in degree from our own, is essential to the teaching of both authors, and in this respect they carry on the traditions of the philosophers of the Italian renaissance, and especially Telesio, just as Bacon had done in England. Later in this same book (book V of Section I), Gassendi compares the earth with a living creature calling back to itself the parts that become detached from it, as though by a vague sense of self-preservation, and here again his acquaintance Campanella, who had brought with him into France the ideas of sixteenth-century Italy, would certainly have approved, had he lived to read the **Syntagma,** though he was at variance with Gassendi on most other questions and particularly that of the atoms themselves. Gassendi develops the theory tentatively and as a hypothesis, but there can be no doubt that he was attracted by it, and it is indeed an attractive notion, although science has resolutely turned its back upon it ever since the seventeenth century.

Qualities can be reduced to the arrangement of the parts of a thing. 'Form' is a useless word if it does not have the same meaning. All qualitative differences are differences of quantity or arrangement. The secondary qualities, such as heat and cold or colours, are not in things nor in us: for secondary qualities to exist, species must pass from the thing into a sense organ and be perceived.

Motive force is the resultant of all the movements of the atoms in a body. The more active atoms drag along the more sluggish and force them into positions suitable to their own rapid movement. The more sluggish atoms become fixed in such positions and thus certain movements of the body become 'habitual'.

The generation or coming into being of things is not caused, as the Aristotelians say, by a 'form' coming into 'matter', nor, on the other hand, is the problem of generation a false problem, as Epicurus says. According to Epicurus there is no idea of the whole anterior to the idea of the parts and it is obvious that the whole will act in conformity with the arrangement and movement of the atoms which compose it. Gassendi rejects the idea that the whole is merely the sum of the parts, and is not impressed by Lucretius's examples of eyes without sight, genital organs in a sterile mule, rudimentary teats in the male or by the fact that one organ can perform the functions of another organ. He has no doubts about the evidence of design or purpose in the world. He is not put off by the existence of monstrosities and thinks they are greatly exaggerated anyway and are merely relative imperfections about which our limited intelligence has no right to judge. Design is for him perfectly apparent in everything and if some organs exist before their functions, they do not exist before the *idea* of their functions in the mind of the creator. His application of the idea of design leads in the direction of hylopsychism rather than of mechanism. Everything that exists develops from a kind of semen. Gassendi not only rejects the idea of plants and animals being produced by spontaneous generation from 'dead' matter, he suggests that God arranged the atoms at the beginning in the form of 'seeds' and that metals, plants and animals grow by means of atoms collecting round the original semen under the influence of formative principles which he compares with little prudent and industrious artisans. Or God may have placed the atoms originally in such a position that the 'seeds' would be formed by the atoms' own natural motion. None of this is dogmatically stated and Gassendi frankly admits his ignorance on the subject, but his hypothesis carries him the whole way towards universal animism.

The third section of the *Physica* begins with a long historical account of the doctrine of the *Anima Mundi,* which Gassendi finally rejects, except as a way of referring figuratively to God, or of referring to the heat of the sun, or of expressing the principle of unity of the whole world, and provided that no similarity is implied between such a Soul of the World and the souls of beasts and men. The use of the term in the last of these three senses Gassendi himself finds attractive, and he is prepared to say that the world has a soul *sui generis,* as one might say that minerals have a soul *sui generis,* suited, that is to say, to their peculiar operations. Next comes a review of the opinions expressed by the ancients for and against the eternity of the world, and in this dispute Gassendi sides first with the ancient Atomists against the ancient Academicians, preferring, that is to say, the theory of a world formed from eternal matter to the theory of an eternal world, but then he sides with the Church against the ancient Atomists and decides in favour of the creation of the world from nothing. His descriptions of minerals need not detain us, nor what he has to say about rain, thunder, the rainbow and other 'meteors', but then he returns to the need for a 'formative' or 'seminal' agent in stones, especially precious stones and

the magnet, and the magnet becomes the subject of a discussion concerning a sort of sensation in metals, with references taking us back to Cardano and Pliny. Cardano wrote of iron's 'appetite' for the magnet, and Pliny of the magnet's 'sense' by which it perceives the iron and the 'hands' by which it draws the iron towards itself. Of the plants Gassendi uses the word 'soul' because their *functions* allow of its use. Their roots find food, their leaves turn to the light; creepers wind round sticks, the sensitive plant reacts to touch. There is a corporeal soul in plants, like a spirit or flame, very active and industrious and spread out throughout the plant. This spirit wilts if it is deprived of food; it is exhaled if it becomes too hot; it governs the growth of the plant. But again Gassendi proceeds warily and admits that we can only stammer (*balbutiendo solum et quatenus licet*) in dealing with these matters, and Bernier adds in his analysis[12] that Gassendi is far from having given a clear idea of the soul of plants, although he has penetrated deeper into the subject than any other natural philosopher.

Gassendi's section on animals begins with a classification followed by a discussion on the nature of the soul in animals. He gives first an account of the opinions of the ancient philosophers, then examines the solutions worthy of consideration and finally gives his own opinion. The soul of animals is known by the understanding, in an abstract manner, from its functions. It must be a real principle and not just a proportion or symmetry of the parts of the body, for in such a proportion or symmetry there would be no source of activity. It must be a contexture of very fine and mobile particles like those of heat, moving in the cavities and passages of the body. Heat is its instrument and it is inseparable from heat; it is of an igneous nature. It comes into the body in the semen.

The following sections on the formation of the foetus, nutrition and the circulation of the blood show Gassendi abreast of contemporary theory, but he was not leading the way by any means and was prepared to believe stories of men with goats' heads and the like due to cross-breeding.

In discussing sensation he begins again from the magnet and the piece of iron. Iron perceives the magnet and a stone does not; a goat perceives a branch of an ash tree and a fox does not. It can be said that iron has a 'phantasm' or 'imagination' of the magnet as something which suits it, provided that too much meaning is not read into the terms 'phantasm' and 'imagination', but only such as is fitting to the operations of iron and the magnet.

Sensation is not merely passive: it is an 'immanent' not a 'transitive' motion and consists of the self-motion of the atoms. It does not consist merely in receiving the species emanating from an object but also in apprehending them and striving towards their source. The species press upon the sense organ and their pressure is transmitted to the brain, but the sensation is in the organ as well as in the brain, an opinion Gassendi affirms while being well aware of what is said of people who lose a limb and can still imagine pain in it. The sensitive part of the soul is composed of very fine particles and is divided into parts corresponding to the various senses, the atoms of each part being variously shaped and variously mobile so that they move through different passages in the body according to their shape and mobility. Lucretius teaches that insensitive atoms combine to form sensitive things, and points to the worms which appear in dunghills and the grass which is assimilated to the substance of the cow as experimental proof, and Gassendi here seems prepared to go all the way with him and find the source of sensation in a certain ordering of the atoms. But he attempts to make sensibility fade off into insensibility by minute stages and would like to see in the way the flames devour a piece of wood a sort of rudimentary feeling of hunger. Similarly, he argues, the roots of a plant must have something like taste and the rain must give a sort of pleasure to plants. The sensitive plant has a sort of touch and oysters and worms slightly more. But though one can distinguish these rudimentary forms of sensation as various degrees of the same power, yet the original problem of how insensible atoms begin to feel remains and is above human understanding. For that matter, it is equally difficult to explain how atoms, which are not hot, make hot things, and how atoms, which are not white, make white things. We must conclude that a body composed of atoms has properties which the individual atoms do not have.

When he comes to discuss the Internal Sense, Gassendi is willing to start from a scholastic distinction between the Imagination, attributed to both beast and man alike, and the Understanding, reserved for man alone, but he is careful to say that, apart from what religion teaches, very little is certain concerning this distinction. He refuses to follow the schoolmen when they divide up the Internal Sense into various faculties, such as those of judging, cogitating, remembering, and is content with a *sensus communis,* in the brain, to which all the sense organs are connected by the nerves. The differences between sensation and imagination are, firstly, that the object of sensation must be present, whereas the object of imagination may be absent, and, secondly, that sensation implies no comparison between impressions, whereas imagination does. These are not however essential differences. When the impression is made by an absent object, it is made by means of a trace left previously by the spirits on the soft substance of the brain. Sometimes these traces, or 'vestiges', become confused, so that one can imagine eyes in the middle of a man's shoulders, for instance, but no new factor is involved in such fantasies. The Internal Sense can put together two images and can perceive their suitability or unsuitability to each other. In the beasts this process is implicit; in man it is explicit, because man enjoys the power of reflection and the use of language. A beast's imagination contains no universal ideas, but merely a collection of particular apprehensions. A beast has no apprehension representing *all* men, but it has a collective apprehension representing *many* men and this collective apprehension representing many men, is distinct from one representing, say, many sticks. In a dog's imagination a particular apprehension

representing a particular man can appear beside the collective apprehension representing many men and suffice for a *judgment*. A dog has no abstract ideas and no use of speech, so he cannot think or say, 'This man is my master', but he can put together the concrete apprehensions *man—master* and the verb *to be* seems to be potentially present. Brutes can therefore reason in a certain manner called 'sensitive reasoning', which is used by men also in certain cases, though man is also capable of intellectual reasoning. Brutes can make inferences: a dog runs away when he sees a man pick up a stone, a fox turns back when he hears water running under the ice; a swallow wets its wings in order to mould the clay of its nest; an ass suffers blows rather than be driven over a cliff. The brute is not only able to unite and separate simple apprehensions according to their suitability or unsuitability to each other; it can also link each one with a third or separate each one from a third, and this is argumentation.

The brute's Imagination can be said to exist from the moment it receives its first sense impressions. These first sense impressions are those of pleasure and pain, from which the brute proceeds by experience to the knowledge of the useful and the noxious. The brute also learns by example and from the teaching of its parents, as when the parent birds teach their young to fear and flee from men. And knowledge is also transmitted to them by the semen, as in the case of the silkworm which knows how to spin its cocoon without instruction.

In man the Intellect (or Understanding or Rational Soul) is incorporeal and is created by God. The Intellect differs from the Imagination in that man knows things by reasoning, such as the size of the sun, which it would be impossible to know by imagination. The Intellect differs too in that it knows itself and is conscious that it knows what it knows. It differs thirdly in that it has abstract ideas as its object; the Imagination can contain a collective apprehension such as *man,* but it cannot contain an abstract and universal idea such as *humanity.* And fourthly it differs in that it comprehends not only corporeal things (which it is able to do by virtue of being a superior faculty to the Imagination and so possessed of all the powers of the Imagination 'eminently') but also incorporeal things. It knows incorporeal things *positively,* only with the aid of corporeal images, it is true, but it knows them *negatively,* by reasoning as (being *in*corporeal) and *abstractedly.* At any rate it knows them sufficiently to be sure of their existence. The imagination represents something corporeal, the intellect *understands* something incorporeal. But the intellect, when associated with the body, proceeds only by stages, from experience. Separate from the body it comprehends immediately by intuition, but when it is associated with the body it cannot function without the brain; that is why illness destroys knowledge by obliterating the traces in the brain left by previous experience. The intellect agrees with the axioms as soon as it is acquainted with them, not because of any immediate connection between the intellect and the truth, but because the axioms are in accordance with any man's previous experience. It understands general ideas by means of the particular apprehensions of the Imagination. The best method of reasoning, in the search for new truths, is the 'analytical' method, which starts from experience and proceeds from effects to causes, although it may well be true that the 'synthetic' method, typified by the syllogisms of scholastic logic, provides a useful means of demonstrating truths already attained.

The Intellect is the same in all men by nature, but differences and inequalities arise from different temperaments and especially different temperaments of the brain. The temperament of the brain which is most favourable to the Intellect is one which is neither too hot nor too cold, neither too dry nor too humid, but on the hot, dry side rather than the cold, humid side, not too rare nor too dense, but on the rare rather than the dense side.

The Will or 'Reasonable Appetite', whose seat is the same as that of the Intellect and the Imagination, differs from the 'Sensitive Appetite', or Passion, as the Intellect differs from the Imagination. The Will uses the Passions as the Intellect uses the Imagination. Passion is an agitation of the soul caused by the anticipation of something advantageous or noxious, but the Will can love and pursue the good for its own sake.

Morals is the science, or rather the art, of living according to virtue and of turning other men's will towards the virtuous. Pleasure and pain are the sources of men's actions, even though at first sight this does not seem to be so, as when men sacrifice themselves for their children or for their country. Everybody's aim is supreme happiness, and though supreme happiness cannot be attained on earth, a relative felicity can be achieved. According to some (Anaxagoras, Pythagoras, Plato) it is to be found in knowledge, which frees us from passion. According to others (Zeno and the Stoics) it is to be achieved by virtue. According to Aristippus and the Cyrenaics it is to be found in the fleeting pleasures of the body, and Epicurus is often accused of holding the same opinion, but such an accusation comes from ignorance and prejudice. Epicurus begins from the fact that every living thing seeks pleasure and flees from pain. Pleasure can be pleasure of the body or pleasure of the mind and pleasure of the mind is superior to pleasure of the body. Tranquillity of mind and health of body are the highest pleasures each of its own kind, and the Epicurean term *voluptas* means only absence of agitation in the mind and absence of pain in the body. The way to it is through virtue.

For Gassendi this means firstly meditation upon the nature of God so as to become enamoured of his perfections and to seek to please him, and meditation upon death so that death becomes, not a source of fear, but an anticipation of greater happiness. Secondly it means the making full use of the present, because constant temporizing results in making of oneself the slave of the future. Thirdly it means the schooling of oneself in wisdom, which alone can give us the true discernment of what is good for us, in forti-

tude, which removes the fear of death and enables us to brave misfortune, in justice, without which quiet of mind is impossible. These precepts Gassendi draws from Epicurus, making only the changes necessary to adapt them to his Christian point of view. For instance, when he speaks of the nature of God, or rather the gods, Epicurus is concerned only with getting rid of a source of fear and disquiet of mind, whereas Gassendi discourses on the positive idea of God's perfections. But Gassendi claims Aristotle also as his ally and quotes the Aristotelian definition of virtue: the elective habit of choosing the happy mean determined by reason and prudence.

Gassendi's attitude is that of a teacher whose business it is to show his disciples how to live in society, and especially the aristocratic society of his time, in a post of command. The virtues he demands are fortitude (which includes firmness of mind and constancy), temperance (which includes modesty, chastity, long-sufferance, clemency and humility), and justice. Justice is based on Right, and Right is derived from social utility. Without society there is no law and no right. Right presupposes a contract, but is 'natural' in the sense that it is natural to seek the best way of safeguarding one's interest.

Without freedom of the will there is neither virtue nor vice. But free will does not mean unmotivated choice. As long as the understanding fails to discern the truth, the will hesitates, and similarly the will suspends its action while the understanding considers first one side and then the other of a question. Freedom of the will *is* this capacity to suspend its action. Once the evidence is clear, the will acts in accordance with it. It is not possible to know the good (the advantageous) and not pursue it, but one's knowledge of the good may be destroyed by drunkenness or passion. In that case, however, one's responsibility for one's actions is not removed, as one is at liberty not to get drunk and not to give way to passion. The complete determinism of Democritus has the advantage, as against the doctrine of free will, of emphasizing the order and connectedness of all the facts of nature, but this system cannot account for man's consciousness of his own liberty. Epicurus attempts to explain why he is free to move backwards and forwards at the bidding of his will by supposing that atoms sometimes follow a curved path instead of a straight one, but such a curved path would be just as much determined by fate as a straight one. And there Gassendi leaves the matter; he is content to accept the regularity of nature's operations on the one hand and the existence of free agents on the other. He was not faced, as Leibniz was to be faced, by the knowledge that no energy is ever lost and no energy is ever gained in any operation of nature and was not therefore obliged, as was his successor, to imagine two entirely separate explanations for each event that happens in the world, the one in terms of beginnings and the other in terms of ends, the one in terms of efficient causes and the other in terms of final causes, the one entirely mechanistic, and the other entirely teleological. Gassendi's world was still *one* world and for him the world has only *one* face and that face turned towards man. For him as for Maignan the material and the psychical are mingled intimately together except at the very bottom and the very top of the scale of creation.

Notes

1. 'Ego tanto viro paravi Apologiam, destinato ipsius doctrinae volumine integro, quod Paradoxicarum Exercitationum adversus Aristoteleos volumini, cujus ideam, primumque librum feci jam juris publici, attexatur.' (Letter to Du Puy, *Opera*, vi, p. 11; cf. B. Rochot, *Les Travaux de Gassendi sur Epicure et sur l'atomisme*, Paris, 1944, p. 31). Gassendi's close friend Peiresc (H. Fabri de) said explicitly (according to Morhof's *Polyhistor philosophicus*, l. 1, cap. xii, § 3) that the work on Epicurus was a continuation of the campaign: 'Caeteros 5 libros, nimirium in libros Physicorum, de corpore simplici, de mixtis, in Metaphysicam et moralem Aristotelis Philosophiam, teste Honorato Fabri, ex concilio amicorum suppressit. Quam telam suam cum non posset absolvere, et vituperare Aristotelem amplius sine dedecore, ad alterum extremum delapsus, Epicurum laudare, ejusque Philosophiam illustrare coepit.' (Lübeck, 1708, 1714, ii, p. 68; cf. Rochot, op. cit., p. 28.)

2. Rochot, ibid., p. 38.

3. Published at Lyons. Cf. below, p. 138. [Not excerpted.]

4. Mersenne to Gassendi, 1 Jan. 1636.

5. In his *Preludes*, 1634, p. 66, see R. Lenoble, *Mersenne*, Paris, 1943, pp. 419-20, and Rochot, op. cit., p. 74 n.

6. To Gassendi, 7 Dec. 1640, Rochot, op. cit., p. 104.

7. To the comte d'Alais, 24 Oct., 31 Oct., 7 Nov., 14 Nov. 1742; cf. Rochot, op. cit., pp. 95-6. Gassendi considered it possible to accept 'imaginary' infinite space(s), but not an infinite number of atoms: 'Si quidem et nostri [i.e. theologians] plerumque admittunt esse ultra Mundum infinita spatia quae *Imaginaria* appellant, et in quibus fatentur Deum posse condere innumeros Mundos: non perinde tamen tolerari potest infinitudo corporum.' (To the comte d'Alais, 7 Nov. 1642, *Opera*, vi, p. 158.)

8. Cf. R. Pintard, *Le Libertinage érudit*, p. 498.

9. Cf. R. Pintard, op. cit., p. 386; B. Rochot, op. cit., p. 16.

10. Cf. above, p. 16. [Not excerpted.]

11. J. C. Magnen was born at Luxeuil and studied at Dôle. He became professor of medicine and philosophy at the university of Pavia. He published his *Democritus reviviscens sive de Atomis. Addita est vita Democriti* at Pavia in 1646 (Leyden, 1648; The Hague, 1658; London, 1688).

12. *Abrégé de la philosophie de M. Gassendi,* Lyons, 1678, V, p. 395.

Olivier René Bloch (essay date 1973)

SOURCE: "Gassendi and the Transition from the Middle Ages to the Classical Era," in *Yale French Studies,* No. 49, 1973, pp. 43-55.

[In the following essay, Bloch discusses Gassendi as a transitional figure in the development of modern thought, focusing on his materialism and his epistemology. Bloch argues for the unrecognized importance of Gassendi both to British materialist thought, from John Locke to Immanuel Kant, and to political philosophy through modern times. This essay was translated by T. J. Reiss.]

"In the *English* materialists, nominalism is an all-important element and broadly speaking it constitutes the *first expression* of materialism." The philosopher Pierre Gassendi (1592-1655) was the compatriot and contemporary of Descartes. Yet this remark of Marx in the *Holy Family* concerning the birth of modern materialism from the womb of medieval theology may equally well be applied to him.[1] The very real role played by him in the history of ideas is due no doubt less to his work's immediate public than to the loud echo it provoked in the English scholars and philosophers of the second half of the seventeenth century. In a way they acted as the intermediaries who transmitted his message to the thought of the eighteenth century; such that I feel we may speak of a veritable fusion, beginning in the years 1660-70, of Gassendism with the British philosophical tradition.[2] His role and message, in any case, move towards materialism, a materialism of which his attempted restoration of Epicurean atomism certainly served as a basis, though perhaps more in the sense of a point of reference than in that of a foundation. And it is certain that in his case the "first expression" of this materialism was the acceptance in his early *Exercitationes Paradoxicae* of the essential theses of medieval nominalism.[3]

We may thus see in Gassendi the last link binding the materialism, or rather the prematerialism, of the Middle Ages with the thought of the classical era, in so far as its materialist aspects are concerned, whatever may be the diversity, contradictions and ambiguities of that thought in other ways, like that of Gassendi himself. Taking up once again some of the conclusions to which I have previously come,[4] I would like to demonstrate here this transitional function of Gassendist thought as it applies to certain aspects of his conception of nature, his theory of knowledge, and his views on society.

If we are going to talk about Gassendi's world view, it is *view* that must first of all be emphasized. The importance of the theme of visuality in the seventeenth century is well known: if we want to use a term made fashionable by one of those who have recently brought out its importance,[5] it is an integral part of the substitution of a classical *episteme* for the medieval and Renaissance *episteme* of word and sign. In the seventeenth century this theme of visuality is vastly over-determined. It institutes, in a way, a structure in which come together significations of a technical, methodological and scientific, epistemological, and ideological kind. For the first, we need but think of the perfecting and use of optical instruments; for the second, those concerning for instance the role and import of celestial observations; for the third, the notion of vision as the model of knowledge; and, finally, the substitution of a universe which reveals itself to man through the transparency of his gaze for a world which was the mediator of the divine word. It is a structure elaborated via a return to the thought of antiquity—Platonism and the view of essences, Epicureanism and the primacy of sensuous vision.

There is no doubt that Gassendi is at once a privileged witness to and a founder of the polysemous structure thus elaborated. The theme of visuality runs through his work and thought in all its dimensions and its ambiguities: from the astronomical observations that he was making and recording without interruption from 1618 to his last days,[6] and the anatomical ones undertaken with his friend Peiresc in 1634-35 in a study of the eye, together with the psycho-physiological, methodological and epistemological reflections that both inspired in him,[7] to the theological position he takes, particularly during the polemic with Descartes of 1641-42,[8] and in the posthumous *Syntagma Philosophicum*,[9] of assigning to metaphysics the mission of comtemplating divine finality at work in the universe. Between these two poles, the same theme is revealed in the epistemological critique, stemming from his initial nominalism and reinforced by the contribution of the Epicurean theory of knowledge, that he never ceased making of the idea of intellectual intuition which constitutes one of the axes of the *Disquisitio Metaphysica*: if it is true that knowledge has no other function but that of representing reality, then man has no other material for such a representation than the visual sense, and intellectual processes, presupposed by the latter in any case if it is to have any objective value, can only serve to extend this sight by applying discursive operations to its decipherment.[10]

In Gassendi, as his contemporaries, this visualization of object, situation, and processes of knowledge is one with a mechanistic representation of the universe, in the sense according to which it is considered as a complex of displacements of matter in space; which first of all supposes a new conception of the latter and, correlatively, of time. It is indeed such a conception that Gassendi strove to evolve, or rather, it was he who was the first to express, in formulae of a striking clarity, the characteristics which constitute the classical notions of space and time.[11] Space, and entity at once immobile, homogeneous, infinite and infinitely divisible, indifferent of all content, freed of the traditional ontological categories of substance and accident, is conceived as a kind of object/medium of an ideal visualization of the sensible, which is achieved only by its negating itself in its abstraction as a limit case: it is a seeing which is view of nothing, of a nothing which is object, and site of all viewing of objects. At the same time it serves as the model for the new representation of time, which is conceived and defined from now on—by virtue of its "parallelism" with space—as an infinite, continuous, invariable flow, indiffer-

ent of events, the frame of succession in the same way as space is the condition of localization.

Linked with the "geometrization of space" which is responsible for the transition from the "closed world" to the "infinite universe,"[12] these notions, which are none other than the presuppositions of classical mechanics, were in fact constructed by Gassendi from his contact with the work of Galileo, of whom, like his friend Mersenne, he made himself the vulgarizer and propagandist in several minor writings of the 1640s.[13] Indeed, the comparison of published and unpublished texts reveals that it is in these very years that he perfected the central element—and the one most difficult to establish—of this conceptual edifice: the strict parallelism of time and space for which he was obliged, whether he would or no, to break with the Epicurean thesis which held time to be the "accident of accidents." And, together with the representation of matter provided by the atomism of antiquity and with that dynamism, drawn from, though doubtless surpassing, Epicurus—Democritus, rather—which he posited in the thesis regarding the "active matter" and the "innate mobility" of the atom,[14] it is these notions which for him condition the principles of mechanics: the principle of inertia of which he was the first, as we know, to publish a correct statement,[15] principles of conservation which he tried, in a very concise if not quite precise formulation, to deduce from the "mobility" of the atom.[16]

It may be that this visualization of science and the world helped him to extend this mechanism to chemistry for which, taking seriously methodological and experimental elements which were as much hidden as revealed in the researches of the "chymistes" of his age, he proposed an atomistic and "molecular" interpretation.[17] Even more likely is it at work in the cosmological descriptions in which, despite the restrictions he imposed—partly out of prudence, but just as certainly from a real concern for orthodoxy—upon his scientific and philosophical tendencies in this area, he maintained as far as possible the Copernico-Galilean heliocentric theory, and in which, despite his theological creationism and finitism, he revealed his partiality for Bruno's thesis of the infinity of worlds, and narrowly managed to repress the temptation of proposing a materialist cosmogonic model.[18]

In brief, if we but take the trouble of freeing them from the mass of erudition in which they are enveloped, Gassendi's work in the realm of physical thought provides quite an imposing array of astonishingly modern ideas which lead essentially in the direction of scientific materialism, such as it was in his time, and many of which form an integral part of the seventeenth- and eighteenth-century world view. This is particularly striking in the case of his ideas on space and time, where it is clear that the Gassendist formulae, prior even to his publication of them, were a direct inspiration to Pascal in his writings on the vacuum,[19] and will be taken up again in very similar terms by Newton in the celebrated opening pages of the *Principia Mathematica*. And yet to a very great extent Gassendi worked out these novel expositions *on the basis of the past*: the distant past represented by the atomism of antiquity and the past of the Renaissance, whose "humanistic" concerns permitted the reintroduction of this atomism in the presence of the new science; the past of the Middle Ages, whose theological notions of "imaginary" spaces and times and, more precisely perhaps, the nominalist theologians' arguments,[20] provided a primary support for the new concepts he was proposing; and the more recent past of the Italian naturalism of *novatores* like Patrizzi and Telesio, of whose speculations he certainly made use, correcting and surpassing them, fertilizing them through contact with scientific development.[21]

This process of transmutation by means of which old-style thinking and data come to furnish the bases of the philosophy of modern times is no doubt even more apparent, or at least, other things equal, better known, in the Gassendist concept of knowledge. Because it is better known, but also because there is less originality evident in it, we need not discuss this point at any great length. I will limit myself to a few reminders and comments.

There is no doubt that nominalism is a feature common to all the important philosophies of the seventeenth century: with greater or less explicitness, with more or less divergence of meaning and intention, Descartes is as much of a nominalist as Hobbes, Spinoza as Locke. But their common refusal to attribute the value of real essence to general concepts formed by the understanding through the abstraction of individual characteristics, appears within their systems without direct reference to medieval nominalism. Gassendi, on the other hand, as I indicated at the beginning, refers explicitly to it in 1624 in Book II of his *Exercitationes Paradoxicae* in order to maintain that universals exist only in the understanding, that only individual cases are real, that concept and essence have no common measure.[22] But for the name alone, it is this same nominalism that he will oppose to Cartesian metaphysics: if, as far as the reality of all things is concerned, existence and essence are one, then we must beware of confusing this undivided and individual reality with existence as an idea or with essence as an idea. For this last is nothing but the universal concept which, for lack of intellectual intuition, is forged out of experience by the human mind and which, as such, is no more than a relative instrument inadequate to the profound nature of things. It is from this confusion that is born the illusion of "eternal essences" to which existence is supposed to be added as a real "property" and as a "predicate" of judgment, an illusion on which rests the ontological proof of God's existence in Descartes' Fifth Meditation.[23] While Gassendi, then, links himself from the outset with medieval nominalism, and while, in a more general sense, he draws on the scholastic sensualist tradition according to which the understanding cannot think without an image, both this nominalism and sensualism eventually meet in him with the more distant past represented in the Epicurean doctrine which he first sought to restore then to defend, but only from 1626 on. The unpublished version of the *Logique* of what was to become the

Syntagma Philosophicum reveals furthermore that it is his initial nominalism which forms the link between the "skeptic" critique developed in the *Exercitationes Paradoxicae* and the Epicurean gnoseology which serves henceforth as Gassendi's inspiration, though he never adopted it unequivocally.[24] It is this encounter and inspiration indeed that led him to the constitution of a relatively original empiricism, which gains in coherence at the time of the polemic with Descartes, and whose structure seems quite close to that of Locke's. The latter certainly draws on Gassendi, and not only through such intermediaries as Boyle, Charleton or Bernier, but also doubtless as a result of a direct acquaintance with his writings:[25] the critique of the notions of essence, substance, or infinity, the rejection of intellectual intuition and Cartesian innateness, the construction of a system of knowledge on the basis of sensation and reflection, all these major themes of the *Essay Concerning Human Understanding* are often more than merely prefigured during the polemics of the *Disquisitio Metaphysica,* then later in the *Logique* of the *Syntagma Philosophicum* and the Books on "Imagination" and "Entendement,"[26] and even before in many a passage of the *Exercitationes Paradoxicae.* By means of this intermediary, Gassendi's empiricism, itself due to the inspiration of the Middle Ages and antiquity, acts to a considerable degree as the remote source of the dominating stream of thought throughout the eighteenth century which took Locke's *Essay* as its breviary, up to and including the issue it finds in Kantian philosophy.

While these facts are relatively well known, Gassendi's ideas concerning the social world and political order are much less so. We may almost say that they are not known at all. However apparently minor may be their place in his work, and however doubtful their coherence, certain of their aspects seem to me of great interest, taking into consideration their historical significance and the very real role they may perhaps have played in the history of juridico-political ideas. There may therefore be some point in emphasizing them here somewhat.

As often in the *Syntagma Philosophicum,* Gassendi presents these ideas in a traditional framework: the treatment of questions of political Prudence and Justice, of Right and Laws,[27] the classic theme of the theological treatise, to which indeed, if we are to believe his secretary and biographer La Poterie, he had intended to devote his first theological teaching as early as 1616. In the case of the chapter of the *Syntagma* entitled *De Justitia, Jure ac Legibus,* it is furthermore at the moment of a commentary on Epicurean doctrine and texts (the *Principal Doctrines* of Epicurus, the fifth canto of Lucretius' poem, and a long fragment of Hermarchus cited in Porphyry's *De Abstinentia*) that the most striking concepts appear. But it is quite clearly Hobbes' doctrine of the *De Cive,* whose name is never mentioned, that forms the center of Gassendi's reflections in these pages. It is this that is paraphrased and indeed criticized there on the basis of positions inherited from the sixteenth century, not to mention the medieval traditions. At the same time this reflection and criticism take their place, *de facto,* in the history of theories concerning the social contract and natural right.

Like Hobbes and Lucretius, but also such theologians as Mariana for example,[28] Gassendi in fact connects the problem of Right with that of society's origin, as though to its source. He thus refers it back to the state of nature taken as preceding it and to the process by which men are supposed to have passed from one to the other for reasons of utility.[29] But when he comes to give his own opinion, he in fact opposes to the Hobbesian theory a kind of dualistic one resting on a distinction between the point of view of man considered in himself, singly and "absolutely," and that of man considered in his relationship with others.[30] The first corresponds to a state of pure nature, basis of a "primary" natural Right, a state and a Right of which Gassendi draws a picture no different from Hobbes': a state of struggle and warfare in which there is a confrontation resulting from everyone's equal claim over all things, and where each man's right is none other than his strength. But according to Gassendi, this state is joined from the start with a state of nature which, though no less natural, is "as though modified," and predisposes man naturally to the social condition as it establishes a "secondary" natural Right of a contractual kind. It is nature itself that, having already and always placed in man the desire to escape from the state of "pure" nature, grants him the capacity to conclude agreements with others for that end. Man is possessed, in short, of a social predisposition no less fundamental than the individual's tendency towards the satisfaction of his egoistic needs by any means whatever. On the other hand, in so far as the first agreements themselves are concerned, Gassendi substitutes for the single pact by which, for Hobbes, all by common accord place the totality of their rights and powers in the hands of a third party and thus by a single act constitute at once society and absolute power, a series of three basic contracts: the first, veritable birth certificate of the social condition, by which each individual renounces his right over all things so as to retain it only over a few, institutes property therefore; the second, according to which each gives over to the collectivity his power of "vengeance" (*vindicandi facultatem*), constitutes sovereignty, laws and penal justice; the third, finally, which for reasons of convenience confers on one or more leaders the exercise of the sovereign power thus constituted, is properly speaking the foundation of the State.[31] The separation of these contracts, particularly that of the last two, has the explicit effect of rendering conditional in theory the transfer of collective sovereignty to the chosen leaders whose power is supposed to respect previously established laws or modify them only with the at least tacit consent of the collectivity.[32]

By conferring on "nature" itself the principle of sociability which for Hobbes was only the calculation of a reason which, in order to survive, is obliged to denature nature, by splitting into successive contracts the single pact which in Hobbes is the result of this calculation, there is no doubt that Gassendi is interpreting and correcting the Hobbesian doctrine in the light of a return to the traditions of antiquity and the Scholastics, and to the contractualist theories that had been born or reborn as a result of the politico-religious struggles of the sixteenth century. In doing so he reveals, it seems to me, the "feudal" orientation of his political leanings. In the context of the first half of the seventeenth century, and particularly of the 1640s in France, the presentation of the act which constitutes the State's power as a *last* act, incapable of annulling those which precede it, as an act of delegation of power rather than of transfer, presupposing laws antedating it and of which it is not the basis, such a presentation is very likely to be used to justify the feudal claim to oppose the progress of absolute monarchy with the "fundamental laws of the kingdom," in other words with the prerogatives of constituted bodies and the privileges of the feudal orders. At the same time, the placing of this claim within a contractualist theory inspired by Hobbes, the correction thus imposed of the views of the author of the *De Cive* by the appeal to "nature," in short the critical conceptualization of a political concern, result in the production of a schema which at the very least prefigures the classical theory of contract of the school of Natural Right and the liberal doctrine of the State as they will appear in the second half of the century.

Indeed, despite the antecedents which have been claimed for it, to my knowledge it is only in Pufendorff that the first explicit formulation of the double contract is to be found, generally held to be typical of the traditional conception of the State and society held by the school of Natural Right.[33] While the "contract of submission" by which the subjects promise obedience to the monarch in exchange for protection is clearly expressed during the sixteenth century in the libels of the protestant monarchomachs, followed by those of the Ligue, while the "contract of association" by which individuals decide to become a society can be connected with such traditional— and vague—formulations as those found in Cicero, and while it is also true that the Hobbesian concept aims at placing in a single contract the origins of society and State, I do not think that the explicit statement of two successive contracts instituting first the one then the other can be found before the end of the seventeenth century. On the other hand, nothing seems nearer to it than the Gassendist distinction between the three contracts which establish in succession the right of property simultaneously with the social condition, then sovereignty and laws, and only afterwards the State. And it may be asked, though I do not for the moment see a way to answer the question, whether the indications contained in the *Syntagma* could have been used by the theorists of Natural Right, and if so how.[34] Furthermore, the liberal theory of the State in the form whose foundations are laid by Locke rests precisely for him upon the preexistence to the State of rights which already have a value in the state of nature, and in particular of the right of property, such that, far from being endowed with an absolute power, the State has as its first function that of making sure these rights are respected. Now, whatever may have been Gassendi's no doubt very different intentions, and however much his affirmation of the monarch's or the "magistrates'" obligation to respect preexisting laws may have remained a matter of theory, the schema he proposes arrives expressly at the same conclusion. In this case the certainty we have otherwise of Locke's knowledge in other areas of Gassendist ideas and texts may lead us to suppose that here, too, the views of the *Syntagma*'s author may not have left him indifferent.

We can discover here again then, in so far at least as the question of the foundations of political right is concerned, a process analogous to that which I have tried to describe in the area of the theory of knowledge and the conception of the world. Using old theoretical bases, retrograde political concerns even, to approach the problem of the politics and political doctrine of his age, Gassendi manages in a sense to open the way to the theses which will be fundamental to the thinking of the following century.

The ambiguity which characterizes the content of Gassendist thought is thus joined by that of his historical situation. While Gassendi seems at once a materialist thinker and one eager to remain within the bounds of orthodoxy, he also stands out as one of the last—the last?—thinkers of the Middle Ages and Renaissance, as well as one of the first classical thinkers. As I have tried to show, this pivotal position, this privileged transitional moment reveals itself characteristically in the application of the same thought process to the most varied objects. It is a process which, starting with old schemas and concepts drawn at one from Greco-Latin antiquity, from scholastic traditions, and from the humanism of the Renaissance, ends with the formulation of theses and themes which inaugurate the science, gnoseology, and even political thought, of modern times.

Notes

1. *Marx-Engels Gesamtausgabe* (Frankfurt, 1927-35), Part. I, vol. III, p. 304.

2. We may note that in the above-quoted text, Marx, for his part, linked Gassendi with Hobbes in materialism's opposition to Cartesian metaphysics (*op. cit.,* p. 302).

3. *Exercitationes Paradoxicae adversus Aristoteleos,* in Pierre Gassendi, *Opera Omnia* (Lyon 1658), III, pp. 95-210. Saving indication to the contrary, all future references here will be by volume and page to this posthumous edition.

4. O. R. Bloch, *La Philosophie de Gassendi: Nominalisme, matérialisme et métaphysique* (The Hague, 1971).

5. Michel Foucault, *Les Mots et les choses* (Paris, 1966).

6. *Commentarii de Rebus Caelestibus,* IV, pp. 75-498.

7. See for example the *De Apparente Magnitudine Solis Humilis et Sublimis,* III, pp. 420-77.

8. *Disquisitio Metaphysica seu Dubitationes et Instantiae adversus Renati Cartesii Metaphysicam, et Responsa,* III, pp. 269-410.

9. This essential work occupies in their entirety the first and second volumes of the Lyon edition cited in note 3. The text of volume I goes back to 1649-55, that of volume II to 1644-45 (or perhaps 1646). It was preceded by a work of quite different appearance but whose content is essentially identical, the *Animadversiones in Decimum Librum Diogenis Laertii,* which was published at Lyon in 1649. Manuscripts of almost the whole of a previous version, entitled *De Vita et Doctrina Epicuri,* exist in the libraries of Tours, Carpentras and Florence. It is the end of this version which, for lack of anything more recent, was reproduced as the second volume of the printed *Syntagma,* while the beginning, which dates from 1633-34, had already been published as early as 1647, also at Lyon, with the title *De Vita et Moribus Epicuri* (the manuscript of which has not survived). The remainder, written between 1636 and 1643 (with a long interruption between 1637 and 1641), remains unpublished.

10. On this point, see my article, "Gassendi critique de Descartes," *Revue Philosophique* (1966), pp. 217-36.

11. See, in the *Syntagma Philosophicum,* the Book *De Loco et Tempore* (I, pp. 179-228), and earlier the substantially identical development in the *Animadversiones* (pp. 605-30).

12. See Alexandre Koyré, *From the Closed World to the Infinite Universe* (Baltimore, 1957).

13. See the *De Motu impresso a Motore translato* (III, p. 478-563) and the *De Proportione qua Gravia decidentia accelerantur* (III, pp. 564-650).

14. See, particularly, I, pp. 335b-336a.

15. In Letter I (dated November 20, 1640) of the *De Motu impresso,* published in 1642 (see III, pp. 489a-b and 495b-496b).

16. I, p. 343b.

17. Particularly, I, pp. 243b-245b and 472a.

18. For the first, see especially, I, pp. 667b-669a; for the second, see I, pp. 480b-486b—particularly if this passage is read in the light of the earlier unpublished version.

19. See the letter to Le Pailleur of February or March 1648, in the Brunschvicg and Boutroux edition (Paris, 1908), II, p. 188.

20. Alexandre Koyré, "Vide et espace infinis au 14e siècle," in *Etudes d'histoire de la pensée philosophique* (Paris, 1961), pp. 33-84. The matter was also treated in Paul Vignaux's lecture given at the XXVIIIe Semaine de Synthèse in Paris in 1967, though to my knowledge this remains unpublished as yet.

21. I, pp. 245b-246b.

22. III, pp. 159a ff.

23. See, particularly, III, pp. 374b-383a.

24. See above, note 9: the *"Logique"* of the *De Vita et Doctrina Epicuri* was written in 1636; a manuscript of it (not an autograph one) is to be found in the Bibliothèque de Carpentras.

25. Valuable indications on this point are to be found in Locke's manuscript notebooks, especially those of the Lovelace Collection owned by the Bodleian Library, and in the *Medical Commonplace Book* preserved in the British Museum.

26. I, pp. 31-124; II, pp. 398-468.

27. II, pp. 754b-765a; II, pp. 783a-808a.

28. Juan Mariana, *De Rege et Regis Institutione Libri III* (Toledo, 1599).

29. II, pp. 787b ff.

30. II, pp. 794a ff.

31. II, pp. 795b-796a.

32. II, p. 796a. This explicitness is true at least of the development I am resuming here, but the parallel development of the *Prudentia* (II, pp. 755a-b) seems to lean in the opposite direction, though it is true that it is less explicit. It must needs be said that the *De Prudentia* is strongly marked by the influence of Jean Bodin, which helps to explain the contradiction.

33. Samuel Pufendorff, *De Jure Naturae et Gentium Libri octo* (Lund, 1672), Book VII, Ch. II.

34. Despite the personal relations between him and Gassendi, I think we must set aside any mediation on the part of Grotius here, for his ideas, on this subject, are not relevant.

Richard H. Popkin (essay date 1979)

SOURCE: "The Libertines Érudits," in *The History of Scepticism from Erasmus to Spinoza,"* University of California Press, 1979, pp. 87-109.

[In this excerpt, Popkin considers the work of Gassendi in the context of the so-called French libertines of the seventeenth century. The critic debunks the myth of the libertine philosopher as a dissolute atheist, finding instead that although Gassendi was a skeptic, his motives were of an anti-Aristotelian and not an anti-Christian bent.]

Gassendi (or perhaps Gassend)[1] was one of the prodigies of the early seventeenth century. He was born in 1592 in Provence, went to college at Digne, and by the age of 16 was lecturing there. After studying theology at Aix-en-Provence, he taught theology at Digne in 1612. When he received his doctorate in theology, he became a lecturer in philosophy at Aix, and then canon of Grenoble. Quite early in life, Gassendi began his extensive scientific researches, assisted and encouraged by some of the leading intellectuals of Aix, like Peiresc. The philosophy course that he taught led Gassendi to compile his extended cri-

tique of Aristotelianism, the first part of which appeared as his earliest publication in 1624, the *Exercitationes Paradoxicae adversus Aristoteleos.* This was followed by several scientific and philosophical works, which gained Gassendi the greatest renown in the intellectual world and brought him into contact with the man who was to be his life-long friend, Father Marin Mersenne. In 1633, Gassendi was appointed Provost of the Cathedral of Digne, and in 1645, Professor of Mathematics at the Collège Royal in Paris. Gassendi retired in 1648, and died in 1655.[2]

In spite of his tremendous role in the formation of 'the new science' and 'the new philosophy', Gassendi's fame has survived mainly for his criticisms of Descartes' *Meditations,* and not for his own theories, which throughout the seventeenth century had rivalled those of his opponent. He is also remembered for the part he played in reviving the atomic theory of Epicurus. But by and large, until quite recently, Gassendi's status as an independent thinker has been most neglected. Perhaps this is due in part to Descartes' judgment of him, and in part to the fact that he usually presented his ideas in extremely lengthy Latin tomes, which are only now being translated into French.[3]

But Gassendi, in his life time, had an extremely important intellectual career, whose development, perhaps more than that of René Descartes, indicates and illustrates 'the making of the modern mind.' Gassendi started out his philosophical journey as a sceptic, apparently heavily influenced by his reading of the edition of Sextus brought out in 1621, as well as by the works of Montaigne and Charron. This phase of 'scientific Pyrrhonism' served as the basis for Gassendi's attacks on Aristotle as well as on the contemporary pseudo-scientists, and made Gassendi one of the leaders of the Tétrade. However, he found the negative and defeatist attitude of humanistic scepticism unsatisfactory, especially in terms of his knowledge of, and interest in, the 'new science'. He announced then that he was seeking a *via media* between Pyrrhonism and Dogmatism. He found this in his tentative, hypothetical formulation of Epicurean atomism, a formulation which, in many respects, comes close to the empiricism of modern British philosophy. In this chapter we shall deal with the sceptical views of Gassendi's early writings, and in a later chapter shall discuss his 'tentative Epicureanism' or 'mitigated scepticism'.

Bayle, in his article on Pyrrho, credited Gassendi with having introduced Sextus Empiricus into modern thought, and thereby having opened our eyes to the fact that 'the qualities of bodies that strike our senses are only appearances,'[4] This attack upon the attempts to build up necessary and certain sciences of Nature from our sense experience is the starting point of Gassendi's thought. As early as 1621, he announced his admiration for the old and the new Pyrrhonism.[5] In his lectures on Aristotle at Aix, he began employing the sceptical arsenal to demolish the claims of the dogmatists, and especially those of Aristotle. The *Exercitationes Paradoxicae adversus Aristoteleos,* of 1624, represent the first installment of this sceptical onslaught against those who claim to have knowledge of the nature of things, and who fail to see that all that we ever actually do or can know are appearances. (The book was planned as having seven parts, of which only two ever appeared. It is possible that Gassendi stopped work on it after he heard of the attacks by some of the entrenched philosophers on a few of the anti-Aristotelians in Paris, in 1624-5.)[6] In it, Gassendi asserted bluntly that he much preferred the *acatalepsia* of the Academics and Pyrrhonians to the arrogance of the Dogmatists.[7]

From the outset, Gassendi proclaimed himself a disciple of Sextus, and for him, this involved two main elements, a doubt of all claims to knowledge about the real world, and an acceptance of the world of experience or appearance as the sole basis for our natural knowledge.[8] After presenting his sceptical attitude in the preface, Gassendi criticized the insistence of the Aristotelians on their way of philosophizing. Instead, he called for complete intellectual freedom, including a recognition that Aristotle's doctrines do not deserve any special or privileged position. The Aristotelians have (he said) become merely frivolous diputers instead of searchers after truth. They argue about verbal problems instead of studying experience. They submit servilely to the word of the Philosopher or his interpreters rather than thinking for themselves; a submission one owes to God, but not to a philosopher. Aristotle's views are not so wonderful that they deserve all this respect. To show this Gassendi tried to point out all the errors and doubts that existed in Aristotle's theories.[9]

The second book of the *Exercitationes,* not published till later,[10] contains the heart of the sceptical criticism of Aristotelianism, and of dogmatic philosophy in general. The attempt to discover scientific knowledge, in Aristotle's sense, is doomed to failure because the principles and the definitions can only be gained through experience. The only clear information we have is what we perceive. In order to arrive at real or essential definitions of objects we need some basic concepts by which to understand things, but we actually know only the sensible object. From experience, we cannot induce general propositions or principles, because it is always possible that a negative instance may turn up later. (Although Gassendi was acquainted with Bacon's work, this problem, as well as most of Gassendi's views here, is more likely derived from Sextus' discussions of logic.)[11] Even if we knew some definitions and principles, we could gain no scientific knowledge by means of syllogistic reasoning, since, as the Pyrrhonists had shown, the premises of the syllogism are only true if the conclusion is antecedently known to be true. The conclusion is either part of the evidence for the premises, in which case the syllogism is a circular argument, or the syllogism is inconclusive since one does not know if the premises are true (the problem later raised by J. S. Mill.)[12]

The high point of Gassendi's Pyrrhonian attack occurs in the last chapter, entitled, 'That there is no science, and especially no Aristotelian science.' Here, the tropes of the ancient Pyrrhonists, of Sextus, Agrippa, Aenesidemus and others, were employed in order to show that our knowledge is always restricted to the appearances of things, and can never deal with their real, hidden inner natures. We can tell how things seem to us, but not how they are in themselves. Thus, for example, we know from our experience that honey seems sweet. But we cannot discover if it is *really sweet.*[13] The distinction Gassendi made between apparent qualities, how things seem or appear to us, and real qualities, what properties the object actually has, is one of the earliest clear formulations of the primary-secondary quality distinction in modern philosophy.[14]

Since we can know nothing 'by nature and in itself, and as a result of basic, necessary and infallible causes',[15] no science, in the sense of necessary knowledge about the real world, is possible. All that we can know about nature is how it appears to us, and, as the sceptical arguments show, we can neither judge nor infer the real natures of things which cause or produce the appearances. Variations in sense experience prevent us from being able to define or describe the real objects on the basis of what we perceive. Due to the lack of indicative signs, that is, necessary true inferences from experience to reality, and due to the defects of syllogistic reasoning, we have no way of reasoning from our experience to its causes, or from its causes to their effects. We cannot even establish a criterion of true knowledge, so we cannot tell what would constitute a science. All that we can conclude is nothing can be known.[16]

In all this, Gassendi was challenging neither Divine Truth, which he accepted primarily on a fideistic basis, nor common-sense information, the world of appearances.[17] Rather, he was attacking any attempt, be it Aristotle's or anyone else's, to construct a necessary science of nature, a science which would transcend appearances and explain them in terms of some nonevident causes. In experience, and in experience alone (he said), lay the sole natural knowledge that men could attain. Everything else, whether it be metaphysical or mathematical foundations or interpretations of our sense information, is only useless conjecture. As Gassendi's disciple, Samuel Sorbière, said of him 'This learned man does not assert anything very affirmatively; and following the maxims of his profound wisdom, he does not depart from the Epoche, which protects him from the imprudence and presumption to which all the other philosophers have fallen.'[18]

The early Gassendi was concerned primarily with the destructive side of the sceptical critique of scientific knowledge, attacking any who sought to discover necessary, certain knowledge of things. If such knowledge must be demonstrable from certain premises, or be self-evident, and yet must also deal with something other than appearances, then all that can be concluded is 'nothing can be known'. Starting his attack with Aristotle, Gassendi quickly broadened it to include the Renaissance naturalists, the Platonists, and any philosophers whatever who claimed to know the true nature of things.[19]

On the other hand, while Gassendi called himself a disciple of Sextus, he included in his discipleship an unquestioned acceptance of experience as the source of all knowledge. And, as one of the major figures in the scientific revolution, Gassendi sought to extend man's knowledge through careful examination of nature. In the fields of astronomy and physiology, he made important contributions, describing and discovering facets of the natural world.[20] Later he made perhaps his greatest contribution to modern science by developing the atomic theory of Epicurus as an hypothesis, or mechanical model, for relating appearances and predicting future phenomena.[21] The positive side of Gassendi's thought led him to an attempt to mitigate his initial Pyrrhonism into a type of 'constructive scepticism' and to develop a theory which would lie between complete scepticism and dogmatism.[22] This later view, fully developed in his **Syntagma,** as well as the theory of knowledge of his friend Mersenne, constitutes, perhaps, the formulation, for the first time, of what may be called the 'scientific outlook'. This view will be examined later, and it will be shown to be perhaps the most fruitful result of the impact of Pyrrhonism on modern philosophy.

In evaluating Gassendi, two questions have been debated by many commentators; first, was Gassendi really a sceptic? and second, was Gassendi a *libertin*? The problem of the first of these revolves around what is meant by a sceptic. If a sceptic is supposed to be someone who doubts everything, and denies that we have, or can have, any knowledge, then Gassendi definitely was not a sceptic, especially in his later writings, where he specifically denied these views, and criticized the ancient sceptics.[23] However, there is a more fundamental sense of sceptic, that is, one who doubts that necessary and sufficient grounds or reasons can be given for our knowledge or beliefs; or one who doubts that adequate evidence can be given to show that under no conditions can our knowledge or beliefs be false or illusory or dubious. In this sense, I believe, Gassendi remained a sceptic all of his life. In the chapter dealing with the 'constructive scepticism' of Mersenne and Gassendi, I shall try to show that though both thinkers attack, and claim to answer scepticism, their positive views actually constitute a type of epistemological Pyrrhonism, much like that of David Hume. As the Jesuit writer, Gabriel Daniel, said of Gassendi, 'He seems to be a little Pyrrhonian in science, which, in my view, is not at all bad for a philosopher.'[24]

The other question, about Gassendi's *libertinism,* is more difficult to decide. Gassendi was a priest, who performed his religious duties to the satisfaction of his superiors. He was a fideist, by and large, offering theological views like those of Montaigne and Charron.[25] He was also a member of the Tétrade along with such suspect figures as Naudé, Patin, and La Mothe Le Vayer and went to their *débauches pyrrhoniennes.* He was a friend of some very immoral *libertins* like Lullier and Bouchard.[26] His religious friends found him a most sincere Christian. In view of this apparently conflicting information, French commentators have debated 'le cas Gassendi'. Pintard has recently marshalled the evidence that suggests Gassendi was really a *libertin* at heart.[27] On the other side, Rochot has argued that none of the evidence against Gassendi actually proves his libertinism, and that there is overwhelming evidence to the contrary.[28]

In previous discussions of the question of the sincerity of the other so-called *libertins érudits,* I have tried to show that there is a problem in estimating the actual views of the Christian Pyrrhonists. The majority of reasons for classifying them as either dangerous or exemplary unbelievers are based upon traditional evaluations and guilt-by-association. The traditional estimates were formed by and large by either extremely intense religious thinkers such as Pascal and Arnauld, or extremely anti-religious writers like Voltaire. The information about the lives and views of all the so-called *libertins érudits* is compatible, both philosophically and psychologically with either an interpretation of sincerity or insincerity. But, in the case of Gassendi, it most strains the limits of one's credulity, to consider him as completely insincere. If, as I have previously suggested, it is possible that Naudé, Patin and La Mothe Le Vayer might have been true Christian fideists in the style of Montaigne and Charron, then it is even more possible and likely that Gassendi was, in view of his religious life, the testimonials of his religious friends and friendships, etc. As the Abbé Lenoble has put the problem,

> If one wishes at all costs to penetrate to the inner core of Gassendi in order to determine the reality of his faith and the extent of his 'libertinage' (in which I do not believe), it is necessary to analyze closely the letters of Launoy and Boulliau. Both speak of a profoundly Christian end of his life, and without any anxiety of a repentant libertine. But then how does one judge (again!) the secret heart of these two witnesses?

If one suspects the two witnesses, as well as Gassendi, of lying, 'One here, I believe, runs into a psychological impossibility, unless it is supposed that the two (it would be necessary then to say three) cronies possessed an exceptional cynicism, of which we have, no proof, this time.'[29]

The long tradition of assuming that there must have been duplicity in the writings and actions of the *libertins érudits* depends, it seems to me, on the supposition that no other explanation of their views can be offered. But, as I have tried to indicate, another possibility exists, namely that men like Naudé, La Mothe Le Vayer and Gassendi were sincere Christians (though, perhaps, not particularly fervent ones). In the absence of completely decisive evidence as to the real intentions of these men, why should we assume the worst (or the best?), that they were engaged in a conspiracy against Christendom. The overwhelming number of their intimates and contemporaries found no signs of insincerity. And one of the basic sources of the suspicion of *libertinage* in each case has been the friendship with the others; Naudé was a friend of La Mothe Le Vayer and Gassendi; Gassendi was a friend of Naudé and La Mothe Le Vayer, etc. If we knew definitely (a) that at least one of these men was a genuine *libertin* trying to undermine Christendom, and (b) that the others accepted his friendship because of (a), then the argument of guilt-by-association might be significant. But since it is possible that each of the men in question was a sincere fideist, and quite probable that Gassendi was, then nothing is indicated by the fact that these men, all to some extent involved in the affairs of the Church or the Christian State, with similar avowed sceptical views and fideistic theologies, were close friends. (One might mention that they were all, apparently, intimates of Father Mersenne, who has not, to my knowledge, ever been accused of libertinage.) If one considers the *liberitns érudits* without any preconceptions as to their intent, can we decide positively either from their views, or their careers, or the circle of religious and irreligious figures within which they moved, whether they were the center of a campaign against Christianity, or part of a sincere movement within the Counter-Reformation aimed at undermining Protestantism through the advocacy of fideism?

To return to the historical material, the last of this group of sceptical thinkers of the early seventeenth century whom we shall mention here is Gassendi's and La Mothe Le Vayer's disciple, Samuel Sorbière. He was not an original thinker, but more a parrot of the most Pyrrhonian side of his mentors. Perhaps, in the context of the history of French scepticism, what is different or novel about Sorbière, is that he was both a philosophical sceptic and a Protestant.[30] However, he overcame this peculiarity later in life by becoming a Catholic. Much of Sorbière's success in publication came from printing other people's works, like those of Hobbes and Gassendi. And, for the sceptical cause, he attempted a French translation of Sextus Empiricus which was never completed.[31]

In the two letters of Sorbière which contain the surviving fragments of his translation of Sextus's *Hypotyposes,* he indicated that he had started this task on leaving college in order to cultivate his knowledge of Greek, and to learn a type of philosophy he had not been taught.[32] He evidently became a complete admirer and advocate of Pyrrhonism and, hence, a disciple of the 'nouveaux pyrrhoniens'. With almost a fanatic consistency, he continued throughout his life to advocate a complete scepticism with regard to all matters that went beyond appearances, and to phrase his observations so that he could not be accused of transgressing the doubts of the sceptics. In a *Discours sceptique* about the circulation of the blood, Sorbière said, 'Permit me then, Monsieur . . . to remain in suspense of judgment regarding scientific matters. On others, that divine revelation convinces us of or that duty orders us to, you will find me more affirmative. These latter are not in the province or jurisdiction of my scepticism.'[33] Only when he was shown that the circulation of the blood was an empirical theory, and not a judgment of what existed beyond experience, was he willing to accept it. In his account of his voyage to England, Sorbière carefully stated that he was only recounting 'what appeared to him, and not what is perhaps actually in the reality of things.'[34] Bishop Sprat, in his rejoinder for the Royal Society against some of Sor-

bière's nasty comments, chided him for not maintaining his suspense of judgment on such questions as whether English cookery was bad.[35]

Sorbière appears to have been a man quite well versed in the intellectual movements of his time, seeing them all in terms of a constant Pyrrhonian attitude. With such an outlook, he could only see as meaningful questions those that related to matters of appearance. The rest were only the vain presumptions of the Dogmatists. Sorbière was not a theoretician of the 'nouveau Pyrrhonisme', but rather represented the next generation which absorbed its conclusions and applied them almost automatically to whatever problems it was confronted with.

The French sceptics of the first half of the seventeenth century confronted the new, optimistic age in which they lived and prospered with a complete *crise pyrrhonienne.* As the avant-garde intellectuals of their day they led the attack on the outmoded dogmatism of the scholastics, on the new dogmatism of the astrologers and alchemists, on the glorious claims of the mathematicians and the scientists, on the fanatic enthusiasm of the Calvinists, and, in general, on any type of dogmatic theory. Some, like La Mothe Le Vayer, heaped up information from the classical world and the New World and, of course, from 'the divine Sextus', to undermine the moral sciences. La Peyrère was casting doubts on some of the basic claims of the Bible. Others, like Marandé and Gassendi, used the Pyrrhonian doubts and new information to undermine the natural sciences.

The Reformation had produced a *crise pyrrhonienne* in religious knowledge in the quest for absolute assurance about religious truths. The new Pyrrhonism had begun as a means of defending Catholicism by destroying all rational grounds for religious certainty. From Montaigne and Charron, down to the Tétrade, an abyss of doubts had been revealed, undercutting not only the grounds of religious knowledge, but of all natural knowledge as well. As the Scientific Reformation began, and the system of Aristotle was challenged, the sceptical attack quickly broadened the problem to an assault on the bases of all knowledge. In two orders of human knowledge, revealed and natural, the very foundations were taken away.

Not only had the old problem of the criterion been raised in theology setting men off to justify a 'rule of faith', but the same difficulty had occurred in natural knowledge, forcing men to search for some 'rule of truth.' The 'new science' of Copernicus, Kepler, Galileo and Gassendi has 'cast all in doubt'. The discoveries in the New World and in the classical world had given other grounds for scepticism. And the 'nouveaux pyrrhoniens' showed man's inability to justify the science of Aristotle, of the Renaissance naturalists, of the moralists, and of the new scientists as well. The cumulative attacks of humanistic Pyrrhonists from Montaigne to La Mothe Le Vayer, and of the scientific Pyrrhonists like Gassendi and Marandé, left the quest for guaranteed knowledge about the 'real' world without a method, a criterion, or a basis. No type of rational inquiry into the truth of things seemed possible, since for any theory, or any dogma, a battery of apparently irrefutable arguments could be put up in opposition. The *crise pyrrhonienne* had overwhelmed man's quest for certainty in both religious and scientific knowledge.

Notes

1. The problem of the true name of the philosopher is discussed by Bernard Rochot in some introductory comments to his paper on 'La Vie, le caractère et la formation intellectuelle', in the Centre International de Synthèse volume, *Pierre Gassendi, 1592-1655, sa vie et son oeuvre* (Paris 1955), pp. 11-12.

2. For information about Gassendi's life, see Rochot, 'La Vie, le caractère'; and René Pintard, *Le Libertinage érudit dans la première moité du XVIIᵉ* (Paris 1943) Tome I, pp. 147-56.

3. Professor Rochot had undertaken this task. Since his unfortunate demise, this project has been halted. An English translation of a representative sample of Gassendi's work has been published by Craig Brush, *The Selected Works of Pierre Gassendi* (New York 1972).

4. Bayle's *Dictionaire,* art. 'Pyrrhon', Rem. B.

5. Cf. Gassendi's letter to Henricus Fabri Pybracii, April 1621, in Petrus Gassendi, *Opera Omnia* (Lyon 1658), Vol. VI, pp. 1-2.

6. This matter is discussed in Rochot's *Les Travaux de Gassendi sur Épicure et sur l'Atomisme, 1619-1658* (Paris 1944), chap. 1, and in his article 'La Vie, le caractère', pp. 18-20; and in Gaston Sortais' *La Philosophie moderne depuis Bacon jusqu' à Leibniz* (Paris 1922), Tome II, pp. 32-36.

7. Gassendi, *Exercitationes Paradoxicae Adversus Aristoteleos,* in *Opera,* Vol. III, Praefatio, p. 99.

8. Cf. Gassendi's letter to Henricus Fabri Pybracii, April 1621, in *Opera,* Vol. VI, p. 1; the Praefatio to *Exercitationes Paradoxicae,* in *Opera,* Vol. III, pp. 98-104; and Gassendi's letter of 15 Juin 1629, in *Lettres de Peiresc,* Tome IV, publiées par Philippe Tamizey de Larroque (Paris 1893), in *Collection de Documents inédits sur l'histoire de France, publiées par les soins du Ministre de l'Instruction Publique. Mélanges Historiques,* Tome I (Paris 1873), p. 196n.

9. Gassendi, *Exercitationes Paradoxicae,* Lib. I, in *Opera,* Vol. III, pp. 105-48. A summary of this is given in Sortais, *La Philosophie moderne,* Tome II, pp. 28-30.

10. Sortais, *op. cit.,* Tome II, pp. 23-4 and 32; and Rochot, *Les Travaux de Gassendi sur Épicure et sur l'atomisme 1619-1658 (Paris, 1944)* pp. 9-22, where the reasons for the delayed publication are discussed.

11. Cf. Sextus Empiricus, *Outlines of Pyrrhonism,* II, sec. 204.

12. Gassendi, *Exercitationes Paradoxicae,* II, in *Opera,* Vol. III, pp. 187-91. See also F. X. Kiefl, 'Gassendi's Skepticismus und seine Stellung zum Materialismus', *Philosophiches Jahrbuch der Görres-Gesellschaft,* VI (1893), pp. 27-34.

13. Gassendi, *Exercitationes Paradoxicae,* lib. II, Exer, vi, *Opera,* Vol. III, pp. 192-210.

14. Cf. Kiefl, 'Gassendi's Skepticismus', pp. 301-5.

15. Gassendi, *Exercitationes Paradoxicae,* Lib. II, *Opera,* Vol. III, p. 192.

16. *Ibid.,* Lib. II, Exer. vi.

17. *Ibid.,* Lib. II, Exer. vi, p. 192.

18. Quoted from the manuscript of Sorbière's *Discours de M. Sorbière sur la Comète,* in Gerhard Hess, 'Pierre Gassend. Der französische Späthumanismus und das Problem von Wissen und Glauben', in *Berliner Beiträge zur Romanischen Philologie,* Band IX, Heft 3/4 (1939), p. 77.

19. See, for instance, Gassendi's work against the Rosicrucian, Robert Fludd, *Examen Philosophiae Roberti Fluddi,* the answer to Herbert of Cherbury, 'Ad Librum, D. Edoardi Herberti Angli, de Veritate', and the *Disquisitio Metaphysica seu Dubitationes, et Instanciae adversus Renati Cartesii Metaphysicam,* all in Vol. III of *Opera.*

20. On Gassendi's scientific achievements, see Alexandre Koyré's paper, 'Le Savant', in the *Synthèse* volume, *Pierre Gassendi,* pp. 59-70; and Rochot, 'Gassendi et le Syntagma Philosophicum', in *Revue de Synthèse,* LXVII (1950), pp. 72-77, and Rochot, *Les Travaux de Gassendi.*

21. Cf. Rochot's paper, *Le philosophe,* in *Synthèse* volume, *Pierre Gassendi,* pp. 74-94 and 104-6, and Rochot, *Les Travaux de Gassendi,* passim.

22. 'Media quadam via inter Scepticos & Dogmaticos videtur tenenda', Gassendi, *Syntagma philosophicum, Logica,* Lib. II, chap. V, in *Opera,* Vol. I, p. 79.

23. Cf. Gassendi's discussion of scepticism and knowledge in the second book of the *Syntagma philosophicum, Logica,* in *Opera,* Vol. I, pp. 69ff.; Henri Berr, *An Jure inter Scepticos Gassendus Numeratus Fuerit* (Paris 1898). This work has recently been translated into French by B. Rochot, with the title *Du Scepticisme de Gassendi,* (Paris 1960). Kiefl, 'Gassendi's Skepticismus', pp. 311 and 361-2; Rochot, 'Gassendi et le Syntagma Philosophicum', pp. 76-7; *Les Travaux de Gassendi,* pp. 79-80; 'Le philosphe', pp. 78ff; and Sortais, *La Philosophie moderne,* Vol. II, pp. 252-7. The most complete study now available of Gassendi's thought is Olivier R. Bloch, *La Philosophie de Gassendi* (The Hague 1971). Also see Tullio Gregory, *Scetticismo ed empirismo: studi su Gassendi,* (Bari 1961). Bloch tries to modify and expand some of Gregory's and my interpretations.

24. Gabriel Daniel, *Voyage du Monde de Descartes,* as quoted in Sortais, *op. cit.,* Vol. II, p. 257 n.1.

25. Cf. Rochot, 'Le philosophe' in *Pierre Gassendi,* pp. 98-9 and 102-3 (on p. 81-2, Rochot indicates that Gassendi had some empirical leanings in theology). See also Hess's chapter on 'Wissen und Glauben' in 'Pierre Gassend', pp. 108-58.

26. On Gassendi's friendship with Lullier and Bouchard, see Rochot 'La Vie et le caractère' in *Pierre Gassendi,* pp. 26-32; Gassendi, *Lettres familières à François Lullier pendant l'hiver 1632-33, avec introduction, notes et index par Bernard Rochot* (Paris 1944); and Pintard, *Le libertinage érudit,* pp. 191-5 and 200-3.

27. Pintard, *Le libertinage érudit,* esp. pp. 147-56 and 486-502, and also the various links between Gassendi and the *libertins* that are discussed throughout the book; and Pintard, 'Modernisme, Humanisme, Libertinage, Petite suite sur le "cas Gassendi",' in *Revuew d'Histoire Littéraire de la France,* 48 Année (1948), pp. 1-52.

28. Rochot, *Travaux de Gassendi,* pp. 137-9 and 192-4; 'Le Cas Gassendi', in *Revue d'Histoire Littéraire de la France,* 47 Année (1947), pp. 289-313; and 'La vie et le caractère', pp. 23-54. See also Henri Gouhier's excellent discussion of 'le cas Gassendi' in his review of Pintard's *Le libertinage érudit* and *La Mothe le Vayer, Gassendi, Guy Patin,* in *Revue Philosophique de la France et de l'Etranger,* CXXXIV (Jan-Juin 1944), pp. 56-60.

29. Robert Lenoble, 'Histoire et Physique. A propos des conseils de Mersenne aux historiens et de l'intervention de Jean de Launoy dans la querelle gassendiste', *Revue d'Histoire des Sciences,* VI (1953), p. 125, n. 1.

30. So was Élie Diodati, the least philosophical member of the Tétrade. Cf. Pintard, *Le Libertinage érudit,* pp. 129-31.

31. On Sorbière, see André Morize, 'Samuel Sorbière (1610-70)', in *Zeitschrift für französische Sprache und Litteratur,* XXXIII (1908), pp. 214-65; Pintard, *Le Libertinage érudit,* pp. 334-45; Popkin, 'Samuel Sorbière's Translation of Sextus Empiricus', pp. 617-8; and Sortais, *La philosophie moderne,* II, pp. 192-228.

32. Samuel Sorbière, *Lettres et Discours de M. de Sorbiere sur diverses matieres curieuses* (Paris 1660), letter to Du Bosc, pp. 151-2.

33. Sorbière, *Discours sceptique sur le passage du chyle, & le mouvement du coeur* (Leyden 1648), pp. 153-4. This passage is cited in Sortais, *La philosophie moderne,* II, p. 194.

34. Quoted in Vincent Guilloton, 'Autour de la Relation du Voyage de Samuel Sorbière en Angleterre 1663-1664', in *Smith College Studies in Modern Languages,* XI, no. 4 (July 1930), p. 21.

35. Thomas Sprat, *Observations on Monsieur de Sorbier's Voyage into England* (London 1665), pp. 275-6. 'But yet I must tell him, that perhaps this Rigid condemning of the *English* Cookery, did not so well suit his belov'd Title of *Sceptick.* According to the lawes of that profession, he should first have long debated whether there be any tast, or no; whether the steam of a pot be only a fancy, or a reall thing; whether the Kitchin fire has indeed the good qualities of rosting, and Boiling, or whether it be only an appearance. This had bin a dispute more becomming a *Sceptick,* then thus to conclude Dogmatically on all the *Intrigues of Haut gousts*; and to raise an endlesse speculative quarrel between those that had bin hitherto peaceful and practical *Sects,* the *Hasche's* and the *Surloiners.*'

Lynn Sumida Joy (essay date 1987)

SOURCE: "Gassendi's Life of Peiresc: The Humanist's Unattainable Goal of Writing a Universal History," in *Gassendi the Atomist: Advocate of History in an Age of Science,* Cambridge University Press, 1987, pp. 41-65.

[In this excerpt, Joy considers Gassendi as a historian, using an examination of his early Life of Peiresc *to demonstrate the development of his historiography. Finally, Joy proposes, Gassendi's recognition of the futility of Peiresc's "universal history" fueled his later development and expansion of Epicurean philosophy.]*

Gassendi's residence in Paris and his Dutch travels in the late 1620s were significant not only because they resulted in his decision to expand the scope of the Epicurean project. They also constituted a key period in his development as a historian of philosophy. For just as his earlier encounters with Mersenne had forced him to rethink the consequences of his use of skepticism as a weapon against Aristotle, his new encounters with influential humanists forced him to recognize the importance of other aspects of humanism, especially those aspects involving the creation and use of scholarly libraries. In Paris Gassendi himself succumbed to the attraction of days of endless research in an impressive repository of books and documents, the library of the historian Jacques-Auguste de Thou, which was administered since De Thou's death in 1617 by Pierre and Jacques Dupuy. Mindful of the open-endedness of research in a library containing over 8,000 volumes of printed books and over 1,000 manuscripts—research in which the determinate goal of refuting Aristotle may easily have been subsumed in the investigation of other philosophical systems—Gassendi began to recognize a tacit assumption underlying the humanists' devotion to scholarship.[1] He recognized the tendency of his scholarly friends to assume, on the basis of their research in such libraries, that the whole spectrum of past human cultures could be assembled and analyzed if only scholars would work assiduously enough toward that end. This assumption may even have heightened his own interest in reconstructing the philosophy of Epicurus. For if one were seeking to demonstrate the superiority of Epicurean principles over Peripatetic principles, then a historical delineation of the advantages and disadvantages of each school's views over the course of the history of philosophy might provide an unimpeachable way of establishing that superiority. Gassendi might further compare the views of the Epicurean school with those of other ancient philosophical schools in order to show why Epicureanism was the preferable philosophy.

He at no time articulated in writing this strategy which ultimately shaped his Epicurean studies. However, his development as a scholar was influenced by several possible sources of such a strategy. His exposure to one source had already occurred while he was a professor at Aix. In the early 1620s, when he had been engaged in criticizing his university's Aristotelian curriculum, he had read a wide range of recent Latin authors, several of whom had employed a notably historical method in expounding their philosophical views. Among these recent authors were Justus Lipsius, the reviver of Stoicism, and Francesco Patrizi, the Platonist critic of Aristotle.[2] Although Lipsius and Patrizi had advanced widely divergent philosophical principles, they had employed similar historical methods of exposition when presenting their respective views. Patrizi had structured his *Discussiones Peripateticae* (1581) in such a way that he first defined the Aristotelian philosophical tradition by giving a detailed account of Aristotle's life, his character, his writings, and his method of philosophizing as well as an account of his students, disciples, expositors, interpreters, and sects.[3] In Parts 1 and 3 of his *Discussiones,* Patrizi had then placed Aristotle's principles within the context of Greek philosophy as a whole by pinpointing the areas of agreement and disagreement among Aristotle and many other ancient philosophers including Plato. Only in Part IV, after having carefully established a historical context, did Patrizi finally offer his own criticisms of various Aristotelian doctrines. This comprehensive historical treatment of Aristotle's views was considered by Patrizi to be a necessary part of his refutation of them. Lipsius had adopted a similar historical approach in his *Manuductionis ad Stoicam philosophiam libri tres* (1604), which he had composed in order to restore to prominence, not to combat, an ancient philosophical school.[4] Lipsius' revival of Seneca's Stoicism in the *Manuductio* consisted of three books, in the first of which he described the origins of philosophy among the barbarians, the Italians (Pythagoreans), and the Greeks (whom he divided into poets, Ionians, and Eleatics). Lipsius explained that Stoicism had developed as an offshoot of the Cynic school, which had itself been an offshoot of the Ionian tradition. Just as Patrizi had done in the case of the Aristotelians, he summarized the important statements made by numerous ancient authors both for and against Stoic principles, and he gave a brief defense of Seneca's character and writings.[5] This was followed, in Books II and III, by a discussion of how to classify the different parts of philoso-

phy and also by a comparison of Stoic ethical doctrines with those of their ancient rivals, including the Academic skeptics.

Gassendi's awareness of the historical style of exposition in philosophy was further enhanced by his friend and patron in Provence, Nicolas-Claude Fabri de Peiresc. The long-term effects of their relationship will be examined later in this chapter, but it is worth noting now that Peiresc's encouragement of Gassendi's Epicurean researches had a profound effect on the latter's career. His encouragement did not simply take the form of an interest in overthrowing the hegemony of the various Aristotelian sects in philosophy. Peiresc also anticipated that a significant increase in the knowledge of ancient cultures in general would result from Gassendi's successful rehabilitation of Epicurus' reputation and principles.[6] Thus he helped Gassendi to understand his own aims by emphasizing Gassendi's potential contributions not just to philosophy or physics but to the humanists' larger goal of reconstructing the history of the ancient world.

Gassendi's stay in Paris from 1628 to 1632 exposed him to still other ways of understanding the relations between historical studies and philosophical inquiry. During this stay, he composed parts of his life of Epicurus, which later appeared in print as *De vita et moribus Epicuri libri octo* (1647). He also probably finished a Latin translation of three of Epicurus' texts which was published as part of his *Animadversiones in decimum librum Diogenis Laertii* (1649), and he started, although he did not immediately complete, the lengthy commentary that accompanied this translation in the *Animadversiones.*[7] In the research associated with these works and in conversations with Parisian humanists, Gassendi acquired an increasing familiarity with the variety of scholarly techniques that were being utilized by the humanists in the writing of their histories of empires, histories of great men, and histories of such subjects as Roman law and natural magic. He became in effect a fellow traveler in several circles of historians who adhered to a common humanist goal, the development of the historiographical disciplines, but who did not always agree about the kind of history which should be the end-product of work in these disciplines. Thus to say that he had become a student of the *discipline* of history would be highly misleading, for history writing in the early seventeenth century comprised a cluster of disparate activities which were themselves undergoing significant changes in definition and scope.[8]

In particular, Gassendi formed lifelong friendships with Gabriel Naudé and François de la Mothe le Vayer, whose careers as humanists and historiographers he was now well placed to observe. Naudé had served as librarian to Henri de Mesme, president of the Parlement of Paris, and had recently published his widely read summary of how to create a first-rate scholarly library, *Advis pour dresser une bibliothèque* (1627). Over the course of his friendship with Gassendi, Naudé would administer, augment, and in some cases found libraries for a formidable host of patrons: the

Italian Cardinal De Bagni, the French Cardinals Richelieu and Mazarin, and Queen Christina of Sweden.[9] Besides being one of the most assiduous book buyers on the Continent, he edited or brought to publication works by no less than twenty-five authors, including many Italians such as Leonardo Bruni, Tommaso Campanella, Hieronymo Cardano, Augustino Nifo, and French writers such as Jean Riolan and Gassendi.[10] Naudé was also notable because of his familiarity with numerous sixteenth- and seventeenth-century writers of handbooks on the methods of writing history.[11] Among these was the same Francesco Patrizi who was already known to Gassendi as an opponent of Aristotle's philosophy. Had it not been for Naudé's and, later, La Mothe le Vayer's repeated references to Patrizi's writings, it seems unlikely that Gassendi would have known about the Italian philosopher's *De legendae scribendaequae [sic] historiae ratione dialogi decem* (Italian first edn, 1560).[12] Naudé himself wrote several controversial histories, one of which stressed the importance of understanding the principles of history writing if one were a monarch who used histories as aids in the analysis of contemporary politics. In another of his books, he advanced a cyclical theory of history, according to which he concluded that Rome would not always be the seat of St Peter or Paris, the seat of the kings of France. His cyclical theory was applied by him even to the fortunes of the sciences which, he said, would exhibit the advances and declines inherent in historical change.[13] They were no less affected by historical change than were the fortunes of French kings.

La Mothe le Vayer's career also proved instructive to Gassendi. La Mothe le Vayer was an ambitious private scholar who, for nearly twenty years, enjoyed the generous patronage of the King's minister, Cardinal Richelieu. Following Richelieu's death in 1642, he was moreover considered as a strong candidate for the positions of tutor to young Louis XIV and tutor to Philippe, Duc d'Anjou.[14] He failed to get the former post, owing to opposition from the Queen, but he was appointed to the latter and hence was able to put into practice the pedagogical precepts which he had advocated several years earlier in his *L'Instruction de Monseigneur le Dauphin*. His numerous other writings included a *Discours de l'histoire* (1638) and an evaluation of the methods of the ancient Greek and Latin historians in *Jugement sur les anciens et principaux historiens Grecs et Latins* (1646).

Gassendi was also befriended in Paris by the wealthy lawyer and Epicurean, François Luillier. Luillier not only exhibited great generosity as a patron, but he showed genuine enthusiasm for Gassendi's Epicurean ideas as well. It was he who organized and accompanied Gassendi on a stimulating trip to the Netherlands in 1628-9. During these travels, Gassendi became acquainted with many of the leading Dutch scholars, including two notable specialists in the discipline of chronology, Gerardus Joannes Vossius (1577-1649) of Leiden and Eerryk van de Putte (1574-1636) of Louvain. In Dordrecht he also met Isaac Beeckman, the physicist who most probably persuaded him to

undertake the reconstruction of Epicurus' physics as part of his work vindicating the beliefs and practices of the philosopher of the Garden.[15]

It is not surprising that Gassendi's involvement in the activities of the international community of humanist historiographers helped to bring about his ultimate decision to shelve his anti-Aristotelian project and to focus his efforts instead on the reform of philosophy through the rehabilitation of Epicurean atomism. He had, whether in Paris, in the Netherlands, or in Provence, gained access to the best printed texts and manuscript sources for the study of Epicurus' philosophy. He further enjoyed, at a letter's notice, the combined wisdom of a variety of learned friends. Observing their expertise in philology, chronology, geography, epigraphy, and numismatics, he became increasingly conscious of the ways in which contemporary philosophers depended upon the techniques of the historiographers. Gassendi himself may even have perused the widely available handbooks on historical method, in which scholars sought to define the aims of ancient Greek and Latin as well as modern historical narratives ranging from biography to universal history. These narratives together with the specialized studies produced by philologists, chronologers, geographers, epigraphers, and numismatists dominated European intellectual life at the beginning of the seventeenth century.

Historiographers were often in positions which allowed them to determine the meanings of the words that philosophers used. They edited the texts that philosophers studied. They provided what limited biographical information was available concerning past philosophers, and they also summarized the agreements and disagreements which had occurred among the ancient philosophical schools. Gassendi, for example, became well acquainted during his studies of Epicurus' Greek texts with the multiple talents of the formidable Estienne family. In five generations, this family of scholars had produced by birth or marriage several notable printers and philologists whose works were respected throughout Europe: Josse Badius Ascensius (d. 1535), Robert Estienne (1503-59), Henri Estienne (1528-98), Isaac Casaubon (1559-1614), and Meric Casaubon (1599-1671).[16] Of particular interest to Gassendi was Henri Estienne, whose works included not only the standard Greek edition of Plato (1578) and the *Thesaurus Graecae linguae* (1572) but also a major annotated edition (1570) of the Greek text of Diogenes Laertius' *Lives and Opinions of Eminent Philosophers*.[17] Book X of Diogenes Laertius contained both the biographical sketch of Epicurus and the three longest pieces of Epicurus' extant writings which Gassendi used to reconstruct his philosophy. Gassendi was similarly indebted to Henri's son-in-law, Isaac Casaubon, for his reprinting (1594) of Estienne's edition of Diogenes Laertius together with additional notes which Gassendi consulted when preparing his own **Animadversiones**. Humanists like the Estiennes were historiographers in the most fundamental sense of performing the tasks, such as the writing of dictionaries and the translation of key texts, which gave philosophers their principal access to classical

Greek, Hellenistic, and Latin thinkers. Narrative historians they were not, yet their achievements in reconstituting and transmitting the languages, laws, and beliefs of past cultures were a sine qua non for all other research concerning those cultures.

As a philosopher who sought to master the philological skills so amply deployed by the Estiennes, Gassendi polished his own humbler knowledge of the Greek language in order to interpret for himself the puzzling Epicurean texts which had been preserved by Diogenes Laertius. He embarked on an ambitious reading program in which he prescribed for himself the laborious study of all forms of Greek literature as well as the study of philosophy and history.[18] Whether this strenuous reading improved his translation of Epicurus' texts is difficult to judge, but it undoubtedly slowed him down. After laboring intensively on his Latin translation of Book X of Diogenes Laertius during several periods in the years 1629-31, he worked by fits and starts until 1645 on the philological commentary which eventually accompanied it in his *Animadversiones.* However, Gassendi conceived of the commentary not simply as a philological tool, in which he would provide information about the manuscripts he had consulted in establishing the Greek text and notes about his Latin renderings of certain Greek words. He also planned to explicate Epicurus' substantive views. And, as if these two aims were not enough, he added a third, that of discussing the modern debates and experiments in natural philosophy which were related to several of the topics covered by Epicurus' physics. Hence the range of possible reasons for postponing the completion of his commentary was expanded to include, besides his ecclesiastical duties as dean of the cathedral at Digne, a potentially endless regress of efforts to polish his Greek, to analyze philosophical arguments, and to study contemporary scientific experiments. This combination of rigor and folly was not surprising in a young man who had been and would continue to be closely associated with Peiresc. For Gassendi's Provençal patron was notorious for his own encyclopedic interests and prodigious efforts to master every humanist discipline.

Naudé in Paris recognized, as early as 1630, comparable tendencies in Gassendi.[19] He thus tried to warn his new friend of the practical pitfalls which could result from too demanding an attempt to fulfill one's scholarly goals. A humanist himself, Naudé never advocated abandoning the larger goal of humanist scholarship, that of deciphering the meaning of human history through the reconstruction of all important past cultures. However, he did exert a counter-weight to Peiresc's influence by telling Gassendi in no uncertain terms that he must buckle down and find an intellectual focus, preferably in his Epicurean researches, if he wanted to realize a productive scholarly career. The larger goal of the humanists, in Naudé's estimation, was one that no single individual should set himself to achieve. It was one whose fulfillment would depend on the joint labor of scores of specialists. Although Naudé himself published books designed to synthesize the works of the specialists, the pragmatic aims and eclectic form of

his writings suggest that he believed that the narrative history of any subject should be written quickly and provisionally.[20] Such a history could later be corrected or amended, and its utility even in a rough, imperfect state was preferable to the perfect, nonexistent work of scholars whose standards of rigor and universality led them to entertain unrealistic views concerning methods for digesting the burgeoning mass of texts and artifacts which were being collected in France from sources all over the world.

Naudé was alarmed to learn in the fall of 1630 that Gassendi planned to accompany the Comte de Marcheville on his impending trip to Constantinople on behalf of the French government. Naudé knew of the valuable astronomical observations and natural history investigations which Gassendi would be able to make while traveling with Marcheville in the Ottoman Empire. But even the possibility of sojourns in places like Alexandria compared poorly, he thought, with the opportunities for research on Epicurus' writings now available to Gassendi in Paris.[21] It was true that in Alexandria Gassendi could obtain astronomical observations which might allow him better to comprehend the works of Ptolemy, the great astronomer of that city. Nonetheless astronomical observations could be conducted anywhere in the world simply through the use of an astrolabe, a telescope, and a gnomon. By contrast, Naudé argued, nowhere in the world would Gassendi be as well situated to consult other scholars and to obtain the printed and manuscript sources necessary for his Epicurean researches as in Paris.

In making his plea for the abandonment of this trip, which was finally canceled by Gassendi, Naudé offered some additional timely advice. Gassendi must take less seriously the ambitious program of literary studies which he had begun in order to perfect his Greek. Naudé cautioned him about the mistake of assuming that an understanding of the recondite language of comic poets like Aristophanes or tragedians such as Lycophron would improve his reading of Greek philosophy. Underscoring this point, Naudé asked, "What did St Thomas and Nifo and Pomponazzi not perform in philosophy without its aid, [and] what in mathematics did Peurbach, Tycho, and Copernicus not accomplish [while] deprived for the most part of the assistance of the same?"[22] He explained that philosophy and the other scholarly disciplines had suffered a serious setback in recent times because of the inflated and immoderate use of the Greek language by contemporary scholars.[23] It was true that philosophers and mathematicians in the past who had *totally* lacked a facility in Greek may have suffered from the want of such erudition. However, this was no reason for contemporary scholars to engage in the excessive study of esoteric forms of Greek literature. Gassendi, he concluded, should see at once that his own possession of even an ordinary reading knowledge of Greek would easily enable him to expound the best Greek historians, orators, and philosophers.[24] With just his present command of the language, Gassendi could develop an exemplary scholarly career through his rehabilitation of the reputation, texts, and principles of Epicurus.

Naudé's remarks revealed both concern for his friend's welfare and a shrewd assessment of the present state of affairs among the historiographical disciplines. In his opinion, Gassendi was incurring definite risks in his attempt to master the wide range of humanist historical techniques. For the study of history was itself undergoing a period of crisis and reorganization, and, in emulating the practices of contemporary historiographers, Gassendi himself was becoming a participant in the crisis. This crisis had partly come about because scholars were now better equipped than ever to investigate the past cultures of Greece, Rome, or indeed any other society whose remains could be analyzed by means of philology, geography, chronology, epigraphy, and numismatics. The pursuit of rigorous techniques for the study of the Greek language in all its forms was just one example of the contemporary scholar's increased mastery. However, at least two circumstances threatened to render the techniques of the humanists ineffective and sterile. One of these had already been noted by Naudé when he urged Gassendi to rely on his ordinary reading knowledge of Greek in expounding Epicurus' philosophy. Gassendi, he had advised, should not aspire to acquire a perfect knowledge of that language, for that would be to specialize unnecessarily and to put such constraints on his writing that he might never complete his planned work. Too many humanists, Naudé thought, could no longer distinguish the forest from the trees, and they had allowed their methods of scholarship to become ends in themselves.

The second circumstance which threatened to render humanist techniques ineffective was a circumstance that Naudé himself had helped to create, and, not surprisingly, he was less perceptive about its contribution to the present crisis. By the mid seventeenth century, humanist patrons and their librarians had greatly expanded the supply of texts and artifacts which were available for scholarly research. However, their success as procurers and collectors had made the tasks of scholars in the historical disciplines increasingly difficult, if not impossible. There were simply too many texts! Naudé, for instance, built up the Bibliothèque Mazarine from a good private collection of some 6,000 volumes in 1643 to a collection of 45,000 volumes, which was open to the public, by 1647.[25] In the great gallery and six adjoining stack rooms of the Hôtel de Tubeuf on the Rue de Richelieu, he eventually administered this matchless collection, which covered *all* of the following subjects: philosophy, jurisprudence, theology, civil and customary law, chemistry, astronomy, natural history, bibles in all languages, the Koran, the Talmud, Latin and Oriental manuscripts, canon law, politics, light literature, and a special section devoted to Protestant, Jansenist, and other heretical writings. Thus while Naudé disapproved of the counterproductive results of excessive rigor in philology, he nonetheless introduced his own form of rigor at another stage in the humanist research process. His idea of rigor was to build libraries which would serve as repositories of universal knowledge. He did not expect any one scholar to master the whole of such a library. But the fact that a scholar's work had been researched in a first-rate

scholarly library was rigor enough for Naudé since it indicated that the author of the work had consulted a significant number of the available extant sources relevant to his topic.

Concomitant with the growth of such libraries was the widespread acceptance of the assumption that humanist methods could be detached from their original aims of recovering the classical cultures of Greece and Rome and could be applied to any and all cultures. These methods were now being routinely employed in the reconstruction of a variety of cultures, especially those of the Near East whose Egyptian, Hebrew, Samaritan, Arabic, Syriac, Turkish, Persian, and Indian texts were the subject of growing interest not only among scholars studying their histories but among buyers and collectors, too. As early as 1593, the philogist Joseph Scaliger (1540-1609) had conceived the project of analyzing the Samaritan Pentateuch as part of his Semitic studies.[26] When his efforts to obtain a copy of that work through his usual agent in Marseille failed after a fifteen-year wait, Scaliger enlisted the aid of Peiresc and his agents in Egypt.[27] The latter finally succeeded in procuring a copy of the work, but it was lost to pirates at sea and never reached Scaliger in Leiden. Nonetheless two letters from the Samaritan priests at Sichem—written in response to an earlier communication from Scaliger and containing accounts of the Samaritans' observation of the Sabbath and their beliefs about the Messiah—were recovered from another source. These were eventually published after Scaliger's death, and thus his hopes of bringing the Samaritans' religion to light were at least partly achieved.[28]

Since the mid sixteenth century, moreover, the humanists' critical method of explicating texts and evaluating the manuscript sources had begun to be utilized in the writing of the history of France itself. Historians of France adopted the methods of the humanists because of their dissatisfaction with the prevalent forms of chronicle writing employed in the treatment of France and also because of their desire to reform Greek and Latin classical models of narrative history. Estienne Pasquier (1529-1615), for example, had produced studies of France as a historical civilization which borrowed heavily from the techniques of humanist legal scholars like the influential Jacques Cujas (1522-90) and François Baudouin (1520-73).[29] Pasquier, who studied law under both Cujas and Baudouin, published in 1560 the first edition of his *Les Recherches de la France*. This work, which was based on his analyses of French law and government and the French language and its literature, has been characterized by one recent scholar as a compendium of monographs on all facets of French culture.[30] Another calls it "a collection of essays whose arrangement is neither entirely topical nor quite chronological."[31] Its purpose is to define French civilization by contrasting it with Roman civilization. Although not a unified narrative, Pasquier's *Recherches* was exceptionally effective in establishing the origins of French society during Julius Caesar's wars in Gaul and in explaining the medieval history of France with essays such as the three that he devoted to the Hundred Years War.

What did the detachment of the methods of the humanist disciplines from their original ends and their reapplication to French and various Near Eastern cultures signify about the new aims of the historiographers who befriended Gassendi in France, in Italy, and in the Netherlands? Why was this shift in cultural subject matters tolerated? Furthermore, why did the tension between gifted practitioners of the highly technical individual disciplines such as Scaliger and the generalist builders of libraries such as Naudé not produce a fragmentation of the humanist community? Did humanism still have a coherent and convincing rationale as a set of related scholarly methods and as a shaper of intellectual careers? Was it still a viable means for defining and deciding one's substantive beliefs about law, religion, and politics?

Several illuminating answers to these questions emerge from a consideration of the next important stage in Gassendi's Epicurean researches, his residence with Peiresc in Aix from 1636 to 1637 and the composition of his *Viri illustris Nicolai Claudii Fabricii de Peiresc . . . vita* from 1637 to 1639. Peiresc's remarkable career had exemplified the flexibility and continuing effectiveness of the humanist disciplines in France. A skilled practitioner of numismatics and epigraphy, for example, Peiresc showed how the study of coins and inscriptions could be used to reconstruct not only Greek and Roman history but also the history of other civilizations.[32] He further sought to improve the humanist disciplines by deploying them as mutual checks upon each other's accuracy. In Peiresc's hands, numismatics and epigraphy became methods for testing the accuracy of the philological (i.e., manuscript) evidence on any subject which was commemorated by artifacts and buildings as well as by written records.[33] Similarly, he employed the disciplines of chronology and geography to assess the accuracy of the extant narrative histories written by both ancient and recent historians. Peiresc was able therefore to win the respect of specialists and generalists alike, managing on different occasions to be as rigorous a specialist as Scaliger and as encyclopedic a generalist as Naudé.

Although Gassendi's new contacts with historiographers in Paris and the Netherlands had introduced him to conceptions of historical studies which did not always agree with Peiresc's all-encompassing conception, he still remained powerfully influenced by his friend in Aix. On returning from Paris to Digne in 1632, Gassendi found that his duties as dean of the cathedral and his commitments to complete other philosophical and astronomical projects effectively halted all progress on his Epicurean writings. At Peiresc's urging, however, he made major efforts in 1634 and again in 1636 to finish his life of Epicurus and to resume full-time work on his commentary on Book X of Diogenes Laertius.[34] During this period Gassendi was a frequent houseguest of Peiresc in Aix, and it was while residing with him that he finally focused his undivided attention on Epicurus. He was preparing new sections of the commentary explaining Epicurus' physical principles when, in June 1637, Peiresc painfully succumbed to the kidney stones which had plagued him for many years.[35]

For Gassendi this death was a devastating experience, one which profoundly affected his intellectual progress. As was noted by Rochot, he wrote no letters to his usually wide circle of correspondents for nearly two years afterwards.[36] What absorbed him instead was the composition of his biography of Peiresc. In composing this beautifully detailed work, he articulated for the first time his own opinions concerning the problems of method which were facing the humanist historiographers. His reflections on Peiresc's career forced him to ask whether Peiresc had in fact pursued a viable conception of history and whether the attempt by Peiresc to preserve the unity of the humanist community—in the face of emerging divisions caused by the increasing specialization of techniques and the increasing scope and number of the available texts—had been a successful one. Gassendi had at last reached the stage of his own career when his general interest in mastering the historian's methods for the purpose of achieving the reform of philosophy led him to confront specific historiographical questions. He had ceased to be just a fellow traveler and now regarded the humanists' dilemmas as his own.

In describing Peiresc's life, Gassendi identified its major events by asking whether they had been significant contributions to Peiresc's development as a humanist scholar. He thus set aside the standard contemporary practice of writing biographies chiefly about the public achievements of political rulers or military leaders.[37] Of course Peiresc did to some degree possess a public identity, since he had represented the fourth generation of his family to serve as counselor to the King in the Parlement of Aix. Like previous generations of the Fabrii or Fabricii family, which had been transplanted from Pisa to Provence in the mid thirteenth century as a result of its participation in the first Crusade of St Louis, he had been exceptionally scrupulous in the performance of his duties to the Catholic Church and the French Crown.[38] Still these did not constitute the truly significant parts of his life, on Gassendi's view. They were eclipsed by Peiresc's activities as a scholar, which were by definition those of a private person, since they did not directly affect the maintenance of public life in Provence. To explain fully the accomplishments of a private person, Gassendi extended the scope of the standard humanist biography to include a description of the intimate thoughts and habits of his friend. He looked, as he said, at "what lies hid under the skin and in the heart."[39]

Gassendi conceived of his biography as an account of the *res gestae* of a prince of learning. Although he violated certain precepts which had been recommended by the sixteenth-century handbooks on historical method, regarding the type of subject and style suitable to a biography, he did so in order to extol the virtues of a private man *as if* they were comparable to those of the kings and princes who were thought to be more appropriate subjects of biographical studies by the authors of these handbooks.[40] Peiresc's scholarship constituted, in Gassendi's estimation, a series of great deeds:

But if some shall expect deeds more illustrious and honorable than [those] we are about to recall, they ought to know that every man cannot be a Scipio or a Maximus, whose battles and triumphs should be recorded. Those men deserve abundantly to be commended who, although fortune has not raised them to the greatest wealth and dignities, yet they display greater minds, are of a more generous virtue, and undertake far greater designs than anyone could expect from men of their condition. Such was Peiresc, who will be presented as only a man of Senatorial rank and order, and who nevertheless so carried himself as to transcend any encomium and even any panegyric.[41]

Gassendi spoke modestly about the style of his biography. He would simply write, he said, "such commentaries as I shall only digest as loose materials in the order of years, as in the manner of annals."[42] Yet his annals were studded with detailed information about every aspect of his subject's personal and intellectual life. A firsthand knowledge of Peiresc's private affairs and unlimited access to his letters and memorabilia after his death turned the simple task of narration into a formidable one, as Gassendi himself confessed in the dedicatory epistle:

> For he loved me so much that it is easier for me to conceive it in my mind than to express it in words. It may suffice to say that I regard it as a great happiness that he prized me so dearly, and that it was his pleasure to have me so frequently with him and to make me privy to the intentions of all [his] plans and, besides other matters, to utter his last words and breathe out his very soul itself upon my bosom.[43]

Although Gassendi wrote the first five books of his *Vita Peireskii* in the form of annals, his method of organizing the biography as a whole was far more sophisticated than the mere chronicling of successive events. This was because, in the sixth and final book, he provided a summary of the kind of man Peiresc had been, analyzing his physical constitution and bodily habits and also the disposition of his mind as it was reflected in his moral character and scholarship. This account of the kind of man it had taken to conceive and perform the actions described in Books I to V enabled Gassendi to explain how these notable actions had been brought about by the conjunction of Peiresc's abilities with the circumstances prevailing in the life of the humanist community in Europe at the turn of the seventeenth century. By offering such causal explanations of the achievements of a prince of learning, Gassendi thus fulfilled a crucial requirement which had been set by sixteenth-century historical methodologists such as Patrizi. The histories of great men must explain the causes of their actions, for only through the proper identification of the causes can the true nature of the actions themselves be specified.[44]

Gassendi's sensitivity to questions of historical method was most striking of all in the actual content of his portrayal of Peiresc. Modern readers may view this portrayal as an uncritical panegyric written by one friend about another or as a determined attempt by Gassendi to recount the praiseworthy details of his mentor's life. So it seems, because what other reason could there be for recounting Peiresc's universal interests and proficiencies? In reality, however, his *Vita Peireskii* reveals Gassendi's ambivalence toward his friend's fundamental belief in the unlimited possibilities of humanist learning, and his encomium is tempered by a sense that Peiresc's career as a humanist had been a unique one which could not be replicated by most scholars. Gassendi's principal reason for writing the biography was to preserve the record of an outstanding humanist's career which might not otherwise be remembered on account of its unusual nature. Perhaps the most unusual feature of Peiresc's career was the fact that he never published any of the works which his extensive researches were meant to embody.[45] There was thus no public record of his achievements or his views concerning the humanist disciplines in which he excelled. All that remained were numerous letters, notes, and collections of documents. Gassendi's ambivalence about Peiresc's beliefs principally concerned his mentor's conception of universal history. It was this conception which seemed to him to underlie both Peiresc's view of the kinds of knowledge which humanists ought to seek and Peiresc's own scholarly interests. In his biography, Gassendi struggled to define universal history first by suggesting its relationship to Peiresc's legal career as a counselor in the Parlement of Aix:

> For he studied jurisprudence according to the liberal method of Cujas, which from the very sources of the law rather than from the rivulets of the doctors [of law] reveals the excellence of the laws. It was this that chiefly made him take pleasure in the study of antiquity . . . And in addition to the Pandects manuscripts which he had, he sought even other codices because certain passages in the published books demanded clarification from them.[46]

However, the study of antiquity for the specific purpose of enhancing his legal education comprised just one part of Peiresc's conception of history. Gassendi further explained:

> What I said formerly . . . about his study of antiquity especially comprehends universal history, which he so conceived and retained in his mind that it might have appeared that he had lived in all places and times. Indeed he always held it as a maxim that history most of all serves not only to elucidate the study of the law but to order [one's] life and to bestow on the mind a certain rare and noble delight. For he counted it in some ways more effective than philosophy since the latter instructs men with words, but the former rouses them with examples . . . He always sought the historians of all nations, and not only did he value the very ancient [historians], but he also esteemed most dearly those who either were of our own nation or had to do with it . . . Thus he wished to know of whatever was recorded in memorials not only regarding the affairs of Provence or France in particular but also regarding [the affairs] of the Italians, Spaniards, Germans, English, Hungarians, and all those with whom [our nation had] commerce or quarrel.[47]

Peiresc's assumption that no nation, whether past or present, should be ignored by the historian and his confidence that universal history would instruct men in how to order their lives through examples drawn from the whole of human history saddled historians with several unattainable goals. To attain them, historians would have been required to develop criteria of rationality capable of serving as the basis for the comparative study of all human cultures. They would actually have had to digest the bewildering diversity of texts and artifacts which were being amassed in their scholarly libraries. Peiresc considered himself a citizen of the world, a scholar whose intellectual prerogative was to become a member of all nations and an exponent of all cultures. It was the exercise of this prerogative which caused him to entertain a conception of history involving an unavoidable double standard. He wanted historians strictly to observe the laws of their own country while at the same time they were engaging in the sympathetic study of other nations' laws and customs. He asked historians to "lay aside that prejudice which makes the vulgar [sort of person] count as the law of nature whatever is customary to them . . . [and] to be equally inclined toward all men . . ."[48] But he also demanded that they defend the laws of France.

Peiresc could see no irresolvable moral problems arising from this double standard. He firmly held that once the perspective of universal history was adopted, the "greatest tranquillity" and "greatest good" would somehow be discoverable by historians sifting through the alternative prescriptions given by diverse cultures. However, Gassendi was considerably more realistic than Peiresc about the amount of intellectual labor which would be needed to reconcile conflicting moral systems, and he seriously doubted the feasibility of Peiresc's conception of universal history. Could such a history actually be written? He pointed out in no uncertain terms that Peiresc himself had proven incapable of completing for publication any of the individual projects which he had planned and which might have served as the first steps toward a universal history:

> It cannot be denied that for a long time he had given great hope of bringing to light the antiquities of Provence and of publishing observations about coins and other choice monuments of antiquity; that he had had a consuming desire to publish commentaries concerning the Medicean stars and the calendar of Constantine; that he had wanted to publish a complete work dealing with weights and measures in jurisprudence; [and] that he had attempted many other subjects. For, as there was no kind of praiseworthy knowledge which he did not comprehend by means of his wide-ranging and curious mind, there was almost nothing concerning which he did not intend to write in a scholarly manner. Nevertheless he in fact did none of the writing which he undertook except that . . . which he inserted in his letters . . . This excellent man, who—however many monuments he obtained on any subject—never thought they were sufficient, gathered a variety [of them] all his life . . . But because the more he obtained, the more he thought was wanting, he digested nothing in the end, nor did he even begin [to digest anything].[49]

What Gassendi discerned with great clarity was the connection between the unattainable nature of Peiresc's goals and his heroic efforts to master the full range of humanist disciplines. Although he praised Peiresc's proficiency in so many disciplines, he recognized that these multiple interests and skills did not add up to a coherent intellectual project. Their very diversity helped to mask the ambiguities left unresolved in Peiresc's conception of universal history. Conversely, the ambiguities of this conception of history had concealed from Peiresc the gravity of the problems facing the humanist disciplines. He had taken too lightly the divisiveness which had been caused by the specialization of techniques and the increasing number of subjects treated according to these techniques. He had assumed that such problems were only the growing pains that must reasonably be expected in a project as vast as the writing of universal history. In Book VI of his biography, Gassendi marveled at his friend's strategies for managing these metaphorical growing pains just as he had marveled in real life at Peiresc's courage in dealing with the pains of his chronic kidney stone condition. Among the examples of these strategies mentioned by Gassendi were Peiresc's frequent consultation of the works of foreign historians to verify the events reported in French history books.[50] He had used Arabic accounts of the campaigns of the French kings in Syria to supplement the accounts of French writers. By thus enlarging the fund of evidence, Peiresc had hoped to improve the accuracy as well as the scope of his narratives. Furthermore, by consulting not only the evidence in books and manuscripts but also charters, letters, seals, coats of arms, inscriptions, coins, and other such things, he had sought to "clear up most of the obscure passages of [past] authors that were intelligible by no other means."[51]

Gassendi also observed that Peiresc had easily moved from this verification of the written accounts of historical events to the empirical study of nature. In pursuing his interest in natural philosophy, he had had no patience with "those logical and metaphysical subtleties which held nothing of profit and were established only by fostering clamorous disputes."[52] He preferred the careful observation of minerals, stones, plants, and animals to the study of Aristotelian natural philosophy, which he thought was "based more on tricks of the wit than on experiments of nature." Even his investigations in the mathematical disciplines were considered by Peiresc to be related to the attainment of certain humanist goals. As Gassendi explained:

> Moreover, he chiefly loved astronomy because a man born for contemplation could behold nothing greater, more sublime and excellent than those bright [celestial] regions. Next to that he loved geography, because it and chronology especially illuminate history and are responsible for [the fact that] noble and otherwise learned men do not behave themselves like children but instead are furnished with a grasp of the whole world and even the whole of time. And next to that he loved optics because the causes of so many things which appear to the eyes are explained by it. . . . [53]

Peiresc's strategies for managing the growing pains experienced by practitioners of the humanist disciplines further dealt with the actual physical processes for handling books and artifacts. He had not been content simply to suggest how scholars should interpret their evidence. He also took great care to specify how exactly the evidence required in the writing of universal history should be organized and stored. Gassendi had admired his friend's rigorous personal habits, which had made him highly efficient in obtaining, copying, and disseminating scholarly information. However, he suspected that these habits may also have concealed from Peiresc the impossibility of digesting all the information he was so adroit in collecting. These habits included the year-round purchase of printed books, not only through periodic book marts such as Frankfurt's, but through the efforts of his friends in Rome, Venice, Paris, Amsterdam, Antwerp, London, Lyons, and elsewhere.[54] Peiresc had kept constant watch over the catalogues of the major research libraries of Europe. If he could not purchase a manuscript that he needed he would borrow it from the relevant library. His personal scribes, like the gifted François Parrot, stood ready to reproduce any text at his request whether in the vernacular languages or in Latin, Greek, Arabic, Turkish, or any other language.[55] Peiresc even had employed in his home a personal bookbinder whose job it was to bind newly purchased texts and to repair any worn or damaged books which he had borrowed from fellow scholars. Often these scholars discovered much to their surprise that books which they loaned Peiresc were returned to them in better condition than they were in when he had borrowed them. But his acquisitive practices were not merely designed to enhance his own scholarship and to enlarge his personal library. As Gassendi noted, " . . . he sought books not only for himself but for anyone who might have needed them. He loaned countless numbers which were never restored [to him]; he also gave away countless numbers. . . ."[56]

During his last years Peiresc's intellectual activities were confined to the maintenance of his massive correspondence with other scholars. He worked long hours in his library, yet he had effectively stopped reading books himself except to gather the materials for his letters.[57] He had reached that stage of his career when, acutely conscious of the fact that he would never publish any works embodying his conception of universal history, he tried as much as possible to insert the sum of his knowledge into his correspondence. There at least his scholarly expertise might assist other writers in the production of their works, and it would not be lost forever. Gassendi spoke with mixed admiration and regret when he described Peiresc's preoccupation with letter writing and with the clerical procedures which he adamantly followed to insure the efficiency of his communications.[58] All of his letters were written in duplicate. He kept his scribe's copy of each letter to remind him of exactly what he had previously said in any exchange with another scholar. All of these copies and all of the incoming letters which he received were bound into fascicles according to their author, place of origin, or date of composition. Every incoming letter was marked with the name of its author, its date, and its place of origin. Both incoming and outgoing letters had their significant sentences underlined, and the topics of these sentences were recorded in an index appended to each letter. Peiresc had organized all of his research notes with similar meticulous care.

Admirable as these clerical procedures were, Gassendi saw in them still another instance of virtues which, pursued to excess, had hampered Peiresc's intellectual productivity and blinded him to the changing realities of scholarly life. Peiresc, he reluctantly acknowledged, had been moderate in all other things, but he had been notably immoderate in his desire for knowledge. He had in his excessive zeal turned scholarly virtues into vices. He was paralyzed by detail. Occasionally he seemed overly credulous when evaluating documents or listening to the testimony of witnesses.[59] He never completed any of the histories which he had planned to write. What he left behind at his death in 1637 was a massive collection of letters and manuscript notes on every conceivable subject which, when bound by later scholars, amounted to 132 volumes—according to the 1739 catalogue of Montfaucon—and which contained enough letters alone to fill the anticipated ten or eleven volumes of Tamizey de Larroque's modern edition of his correspondence (only seven of which reached publication).[60] He also bequethed to his friends and family assorted paintings, instruments, and artifacts as well as a library of printed books that numbered about 5,000 volumes.[61]

Gassendi's shrewd assessment of the successes and failures of his friend from Aix gave seventeenth-century readers an insider's view of the complex relations which had gradually been established between the humanist disciplines (including philology, chronology, geography, numismatics, and epigraphy), on the one hand, and a major form of classical as well as contemporary historiography known as universal history, on the other. Because of the complexity of these relations, there was no straightforward way of defining what it meant to be a humanist historiographer. The subject matter of such a scholar's work might vary enormously, depending on whether he had specialized in a discipline like philology, where texts in a particular language were studied for their own sake, or whether he had undertaken philological investigations merely as a preparation for the more general task of writing a universal history of the entire world or a universal history of the civilization whose language he had mastered. Moreover, the attitudes that humanist historiographers took toward their subjects could range from a strong sense of identification with the past cultures they chose to study to a strong sense of detachment from these cultures. Some scholars felt an intense personal involvement in the perpetuation of classical Greek thought, for example, while others exhibited a more historicist view, regarding classical Greece as one of several past civilizations which might be emulated by moderns but could not be relived by them.[62] In Peiresc's France, practitioners of the humanist disciplines were either historians themselves or were closely related to writers of history by social, educational, and family ties. To such a variegated community of humanist scholars, Peiresc's assumption that diverse scholarly interests could contribute to a common fund of historical knowledge from which a universal history might be written had a genuine appeal.[63] In his biography Gassendi was thus able to show how this community's social ties and its somewhat ambiguous interest in universal history had combined to provide its members with a rationale for understanding the relationships between their individual researches and their common historical aims. He described, for instance, how Peiresc had acquired an important part of his humanist training in Italy at the turn of the seventeenth century.[64] As a young student in Padua, Peiresc had become the protégé of Giovanni Vincenzio Pinelli, a model patron through whose influence he had entered a circle of scholars which included, in Italy, Cardinal Caesar Baronius (author of the *Annales ecclesiastici*), Paolo Sarpi (author of the *Istoria del Concilio tridentino,* which contained an influential refutation of Baronius' *Annales*), Cardinal Robert Bellarmine, Galileo, the Contarini family of Venice, and also the visiting Dutch chronologer Eerryk van de Putte. Outside Italy, Pinelli's influence had brought the young Peiresc into contact with scholars such as Lipsius, Joseph Scaliger, Casaubon, the De Thou family of Paris, and the Pithou family of Troyes. Gassendi of course recognized that Peiresc had modeled himself after Pinelli and had devised for *his* protégé—Gassendi—a similar set of introductions to many of these scholars. In the case of those who were no longer living, Peiresc had introduced Gassendi to their writings. However, Gassendi was led by his analysis of his mentor's failures to ask two disturbing questions concerning the practices of these scholars. Were they, like Peiresc, pursuing an ambiguous, counterproductive conception of history? Could they and their successors continue to call themselves a community in the face of the emerging divisions which had been caused by the increasing specialization of techniques and the greater scope and number of the texts being studied?

It would exceed the limits of the present study of Gassendi to try to offer a complete account of the genre of history writing called "universal history" as it was practiced throughout Europe during the sixteenth and seventeenth centuries.[65] The foregoing discussion has featured only a selective sampling of the individuals who comprised the ranks of humanists and historiographers of the period. I do, however, want to suggest that Gassendi had acquired by the early 1640s a fairly sophisticated knowledge of the conception of universal history as it was articulated by his wide circle of acquaintances. The example of Peiresc had taught him that universal history could function as a conceptual catchall which merely associated under a convenient label the interests of very different scholars or it could function, as Peiresc had hoped, as a synthetic concept which would unify the respective works of the specialized humanist disciplines into a single, coherent account of human history. But Peiresc's failure to produce any part of such a universal history had led Gassendi to entertain reservations about the feasibility of this genre.

He acknowledged the effectiveness of Peiresc's conception as a catchall capable of strengthening existing social ties within the humanist community. Concerning its potential as a genuinely synthetic concept, however, he was less optimistic. When Gassendi further considered what his other humanist friends had to say about their own projects for writing universal histories, he could not have been very encouraged.

The pronouncements of historians such as La Mothe le Vayer and Naudé certainly did little to clarify Peiresc's conception. Their views merely made the notion of universal history more confusing since they attempted to articulate this notion both in terms of classical Greek and Latin examples of universal history and in terms of more recent French and Italian models of the genre. La Mothe le Vayer developed a keen interest in the methodology of history during the 1630s and 1640s despite having begun his career as a writer of philosophical dialogues. This new interest, he explained, was the result of a friend's suggestion that he should switch fields, from philosophy to the writing of histories.[66] His friend had especially encouraged him to compose the type of history commonly known as "a history of one's time." La Mothe le Vayer had initially refused to make such a switch on the grounds that a project so vast would require skills which he did not possess. However, this episode did start him thinking about methodologies of history. He was of course familiar with the controversial *Historia sui temporis* (1603-17) of Jacques-Auguste de Thou, a work which was well known to scholars as a model of the kind of history named in its title despite the fact that it had been listed on the Catholic Church's Index of Prohibited Books in 1609.[67] But it was the ancient Greek and Latin historians who most engaged La Mothe le Vayer's attention, and in 1646 he published his *Jugement sur les anciens et principaux historiens Grecs et Latins,* a study summarizing their achievements. He later conceived a serious ambition to write a history of his own time and drafted his *Préface pour un ouvrage historique* in anticipation of the substantive work which he hoped would follow.

Because La Mothe le Vayer never actually produced the substantive history that he had promised to write, the best evidence concerning his ideas about history is limited to the methodological discussions of his *Préface* and his book on the ancient historians.[68] Both of these leave little doubt that the genre of history he endorsed was universal history. In *Jugement sur les anciens et principaux historiens Grecs et Latins,* for instance, he made it a rule only to survey the works of those ancient authors whom he believed to have been writers of universal histories.[69] Of the twenty-four authors included in his study, he reserved the highest praise for the Greek historian Polybius, whose narrative of Rome's rise to world power during the third and second centuries BC seemed to La Mothe le Vayer perfectly to exemplify the genre of universal history. Most notably, La Mothe le Vayer omitted from his study any treatment of two widely read Greek historians, Plutarch and Diogenes Laertius, on the grounds that, as writers of biographies, they did not "comprehend much more than the simple narration of a life."[70] Still he did not exclude all biographers, for among the Latin writers he treated were Suetonius and Quintus Curtius. He included Quintus Curtius because he judged the latter's life of Alexander the Great as having been essentially a much larger history of the transformation of the Persian Empire into the Macedonian Empire. As such Quintus Curtius counted as a writer of universal history.

The conception of universal history which La Mothe le Vayer articulated resembled Peiresc's conception in several respects. He shared Peiresc's assumption that a universal history must tell an all-encompassing story which involves as many societies as possible. In praising the ancient historian Polybius, he accordingly endorsed Polybius' explanation of why his history of Rome had been a universal history. From Polybius' history, the reader could apprehend the destinies of all nations because, during the period which it described, almost all nations had had to contend with the Romans.[71] Secondly, La Mothe le Vayer shared Peiresc's belief that history competed favorably with philosophy in furnishing moral instruction, especially to political leaders. He maintained that history could surpass the pedagogical efficacy of philosophy by its teaching through actions and examples rather than through words and principles. History, he said, should be regarded as "the metropolitan of philosophy."[72] Statements such as these revealed the extent to which seventeenth-century historiographers continued to depend on the ancient Greek and Latin exponents of universal history. For it was again from Polybius that many of them borrowed the argument that history, defined as *magistra vitae,* was simply philosophy teaching by example.[73] Not surprisingly, Polybius' ΙΣΤΟΡΙΑΙ [*Histories*] were widely read in France at this time, particularly in Isaac Casaubon's Latin translation (1609) of the Greek text.

Despite the ancient precedents for such a conception of universal history, it seemed to Gassendi unlikely that these precedents were adequate models for the sort of histories which contemporary historiographers aspired to compose. Most of them gave no clues about how contemporary writers should synthesize the proliferating studies of past cultures now being produced. It was one thing to write a history of Rome, but it was quite another to write histories of all the empires that ever existed and to digest the evidence for these histories from sources written in every conceivable classical and vernacular language. Analytic problems involving questions such as historical relativity and narrative order needed to be solved, together with more practical problems such as the division of labor among specialists handling similar or related subjects. La Mothe le Vayer's and Peiresc's humanist scholarship crucially distinguished their problem situation from the problem situation of the ancient historians. Their friend Naudé perhaps best characterized this distinction when he remarked that, for the *érudit,* history was the pre-eminent subject of scholarship not only because it served as a witness of past times and as a teacher by example but because it represented the knowledge which had been accumulated and collected from all parts of the world.[74] The seventeenth-century *érudits'* historical researches had become so prolific as to defy assimilation in any single model of history. Naudé also pointed out that, while the study of the ancient authors' rules for writing different genres of history should remain an indispensable part of the historian's training modern historians could not agree on which of the ancient rules should be followed in contemporary works. Although eminent sixteenth-century methodologists of history like Jean Bodin and Francesco Patrizi had drawn some of their ideas from the ancients, it would be misleading to think that their study of the ancients had led to any consensus among them about how best to interpret historical evidence and how best to compose an actual history.[75] The ancients were still to be emulated, but one should not expect that this would solve contemporary problems of method.

It became clear to Gassendi after the death of Peiresc that Naudé had been right. The classical Greek and Latin models of universal history and even the sixteenth-century emendations of these models did not appear to be adequate to the task of defining a genre of history in which the *érudits* could digest all the knowledge of past cultures that had been unearthed in their researches. Peiresc's conception of universal history had proven to be too loosely defined to guide him in the actual writing of the works which he had hoped would embody the information he had collected in his philological, geographical, chronological, numismatic, and epigraphic investigations. Perhaps Gassendi realized that *no* form of history could have done what Peiresc had expected of universal history. In any case, during the years following the completion of his **Vita Peireskii,** Gassendi puzzled over the dilemmas of the humanist historiographers. These would now be *his* dilemmas if he continued to pursue his historical researches on the philosophy of Epicurus. For, by the early 1640s, he had become a true *érudit,* one who regarded the skills inculcated by the humanist disciplines as something more than mere exegetical tools to assist him in becoming a better philosopher. He was even open to the suggestion that the relationship between historians and philosophers, hitherto a one-way exchange from the former to the latter, might become a profitable two-way exchange. Not only should philosophers continue to rely on the humanist historiographers for texts and translations, but the community of historians should in turn consult the philosophers to develop more effective ways of interpreting the histories of past cultures. Gassendi himself refused to characterize the relationship between history and philosophy by reiterating, as his friend La Mothe le Vayer had done, the ancient exemplar theory of history. La Mothe le Vayer's endorsement of this theory's maxim—that history and philosophy both aim at moral instruction, but history teaches by example whereas philosophy teaches by reasoning from general principles—fell far short of what Gassendi had in mind. He now realized that his own Epicurean researches were pointing the way toward a different understanding of the relationship between history and philosophy. The Epicurean texts on which he had been working were taken from Diogenes Laertius' *Lives and Opinions of Eminent Philosophers,* itself a notable model of Greek history writing. In extolling the virtues of the ancient historians, La Mothe le Vayer had deliberately ignored this Greek model on account of his preference for more universal works. Gassendi, by contrast, considered Diogenes Laertius to be one of the few ancient authors who could offer contemporary historians at least a good provisional model for writing the history of past cultures. This was because Diogenes Laertius' historical subject had been, not wars or politics, but ancient philosophy. And it was in writing the history *of philosophy* that Diogenes had already encountered the fundamental problem of writing a history of past cultures: the problem of how to treat in a coherent narrative a wide variety of incommensurable systems of belief. But Gassendi thought that contemporary philosophers, too, would benefit from this emphasis on the history of philosophy because the increased deployment of historical arguments in philosophy might provide acceptable solutions to the problems of justification which stymied so many of his contemporaries whenever they attempted to refute the doctrines of the Aristotelians.

The making of Gassendi the *érudit* therefore ended by rekindling his earliest ambition to achieve the reform of philosophy. However, the complex form in which Gassendi now conceived this ambition requires careful elaboration. Since his exposition of Epicurus' principles would become the basis for his writing of a larger history of philosophy, we need to ask what exactly constituted the relationship between these two activities.

Notes

1. Concerning the holdings of De Thou's library, see Mark Pattison, *Isaac Casaubon, 1559-1614* (Oxford, 1892), p. 120.

2. According to the eulogy of him written by Jacques-Auguste de Thou, Francesco Patrizi taught Plato's philosophy at the University of Ferrara for seventeen years. His criticism of Aristotle and his idiosyncratic interpretations of other ancient philosophers made him many enemies, and his *Nova de universis philosophia . . .* (Ferrara, 1591) was placed on the Index of Prohibited Books. See De Thou, *Histoire universelle de Jacque-Auguste [sic] de Thou depuis 1543 jusqu'en 1607,* French trans. of the London Latin text which was edited by Thomas Carte (16 vols., London, 1734), vol. 13, p. 189. On Gassendi's familiarity with Patrizi's *Discussiones Peripateticae,* see my Chapter 2, pp. 32-3 and n. 32. Justus Lipsius (1547-1606) was professor of history and Latin literature at Louvain and, prior to that, at Leiden. On Gassendi's familiarity with Lipsius' writings, see Gassendi to Pibrac, April 8, 1621, in Gassendi, *Opera,* vol. 6, p. 2A.

3. Patrizi, *Discussiones Peripateticae,* pp. 2-175 (pt 1), 176-287 (pt 2), 288-361 (pt 3), 362-479 (pt 4).

4. Justus Lipsius, *Manuductionis ad Stoicam philosophiam libri tres . . .* (Antwerp, 1604), pp. 48-53.

5. *Ibid.,* pp. 27, 42-6 on the Ionian and Cynic origins of Stoicism, 57-61 on Seneca's character.

6. The correspondence during this period between Peiresc and Gassendi contains references to a wide range of historical projects in which Peiresc was assisting other scholars who were investigating such ancient texts as the Samaritan Pentateuch and various Arab books. Gassendi's research on the Greek text of Diogenes Laertius' *Lives and Opinions of Eminent Philosophers* was just one of the many historical projects that Peiresc helped to sponsor. See Gassendi to Peiresc, August 28, 1629, pp. 206-9; Peiresc to Gassendi, January 18, 1630, p. 239; and Peiresc to Gassendi, November 18, 1632, pp. 262-6, in Nicolas-Claude Fabri de Peiresc, *Lettres de Peiresc,* ed. Philippe Tamizey de Larroque (7 vols. Paris, 1888-98), vol. 4.

7. See Gassendi's letters to Peiresc of September 11, 1629 and April 28, 1631, and several relevant ones written between these two dates in *Lettres de Peiresc,* vol. 4, pp. 217, 249-52. Rochot summarizes the information about Gassendi's work on the translation and commentary which is contained in these letters. See Bernard Rochot, *Les travaux de Gassendi sur Epicure et sur l'atomisme, 1619-1658* (Paris, 1944), pp. 41-8.

8. See Chapter 1, n. 7. [Not excerpted.]

9. James V. Rice, *Gabriel Naudé, 1600-1653* (Baltimore, 1939), pp. 14-17, 22-5, 41-3.

10. Kristeller, "Gabriel Naudé as an Editor," *Renaissance Quarterly* 32 (1979), esp. 61-8.

11. On Naudé's references to Patrizi and other writers of handbooks on history, see Gabriel Naudé, *Bibliographia politica* (Venice, 1633), pp. 102-6. Naudé also mentions Patrizi in: Gabriel Naudé, *Advis pour dresser une bibliothèque . . .* (Paris, 1627), 2nd edn (Paris, 1644), pp. 41, 90; Gabriel Naudé, *Syntagmata de militari studio* (Rome, 1637), p. 18.

12. La Mothe le Vayer commented on Patrizi's dialogues on the method of reading and writing history in his *Jugement sur les anciens et principaux historiens Grecs et Latins, dont il nous reste quelques ouvrages* (Paris, 1646), in *Oeuvres de François de la Mothe le Vayer,* reprint of Paris, 1669 edn (7 vols. in 14 pts, but lacking vol. 15 of the 1669 edn, Dresden, 1756-9), vol. 4, pt 2, pp. 44-5; and in his "Préface pour un ouvrage historique" (undated), in *Oeuvres de François de la Mothe le Vayer,* vol. 4, pt 2, p. 286. For a modern scholar's evaluation of Patrizi's contributions to sixteenth-century historiography, see William J.

Bouwsma, "Three Types of Historiography in Post-Renaissance Italy," *History and Theory* 4 (1965), 303-14, esp. 310.

13. Naudé discussed history as an aid to politics in his *Bibliographia politica*, pp. 102-6. His cyclical theory regarding kingdoms appeared in Gabriel Naudé, *Considérations politiques sur les coups d'estat* (Paris, 1639; Rome, 1679), p. 228. For his theory's application to the sciences as well as to politics, see Gabriel Naudé, *Addition à l'histoire de Louis XI* (Paris, 1630), pp. 132-5.

14. Mr le Ch . . . C . . . D.M . . . "Abrégé de la vie de Monsieur de la Mothe le Vayer . . ." in *Oeuvres de François de la Mothe le Vayer,* vol. 1, pt 1, pp. 21-60, esp. 39.

15. Gassendi lists the Dutch scholars whom he met in a letter to Peiresc of July 21, 1629 in *Lettres de Peiresc,* vol. 4, pp. 198-202. Concerning Gassendi's meeting with Beeckman, see my Chapter 2, n. 50. [Not excerpted.]

16. On the family as a whole but focusing on Henri Estienne, see Mark Pattison, "Classical Learning in France: The Great Printers Stephens," *Quarterly Review* 117 (Jan.-Apr., 1865), 323-64, esp. 326 on Badius. Regarding Badius, who was Robert Estienne's father-in-law and the publisher of most of Guillaume Budé's works, see David O. McNeil, *Guillaume Budé and Humanism in the Reign of Francis I* (Geneva, 1975), pp. 15, 27, 71-6, esp. 72 n. 68. For other individual family members, see Elizabeth Armstrong, *Robert Estienne, Royal Printer* (Cambridge, 1954) and Mark Pattison, *Isaac Casaubon.*

17. For a full account of the editions of Diogenes Laertius which were available to Gassendi, see Chapter 4, pp. 74-5.

18. See Naudé's warning about the possible ill effects of this reading program in Naudé to Gassendi, October 31, 1630, in Gassendi, *Opera,* vol. 6, p. 399.

19. *Ibid.,* pp. 396-9.

20. For instance, Naude's *Apologie pour tous les grands personnages qui ont esté faussement soupçonnez de magie* (Paris, 1625), *Addition à l'histoire de Louis XI,* and *Considérations politiques sur les coups d'estat* were all eclectic works which borrowed principles as well as examples from the writings of others such as the skeptic Pierre Charron. All of these works were, moreover, designed to correct or enhance the previous interpretations of important persons or events which had been attempted by scholars before Naudé.

21. Naudé to Gassendi, October 31, 1630, in Gassendi, *Opera,* vol. 6, pp. 397-8.

22. *Ibid.,* p. 399.

23. *Ibid.,* p. 399.

24. *Ibid.,* p. 399.

25. Jack A. Clarke, *Gabriel Naudé, 1600-1653* (Hamden, Conn., 1970), pp. 62-82, esp. 79-80; Rice, *Gabriel Naudé,* pp. 24-5.

26. *Vita Peireskii,* p. 270B.

27. *Ibid.,* p. 270B. On Scaliger's friendship and prior encounters with Peiresc, see also pp. 254B, 258A, 259A, 264B-265A.

28. Several excellent accounts of the different facets of Scaliger's work may be found in: Jacob Bernays, *Joseph Justus Scaliger* (Berlin, 1855) on Scaliger's Semitic studies; Grafton, "Joseph Scaliger and Historical Chronology: the Rise and Fall of a Discipline," *History and Theory* 14 (1975), 156-85, on his chronologies; Grafton, *Joseph Scaliger. A study in the History of Classical Scholarship* (Oxford, 1983) on his conception of philology.

29. See the discussions of Pasquier in George Huppert, *The Idea of Perfect History. Historical Erudition and Historial Philosophy in Renaissance France* (Urbana, 1970), pp. 32-71; Donald R. Kelley, *Foundations of Modern Historical Scholarship. Language, Law and History in the French Renaissance* (New York and London, 1970), pp. 271-300.

30. Kelley, *Foundations of Modern Historical Scholarship,* pp. 271-2.

31. Huppert, *The Idea of Perfect History,* pp. 63-5.

32. *Vita Peireskii,* p. 253A.

33. *Ibid.,* pp. 342A-B, 344A.

34. See the following correspondence cited by Howard Jones in *Pierre Gassendi, 1592-1655. An Intellectual Biography* (Nieuwkoop, 1981), pp. 49-50; Gassendi to Peiresc, January 13, 1634, and Peiresc to Gassendi, February 1, 1634 and February 3, 1634, in *Lettres de Peiresc,* vol. 4, pp. 414-15, 428, 444; Peiresc to Dupuy, November 25, 1636, in *Lettres de Peiresc,* vol. 3, p. 611.

35. *Vita Peireskii,* pp. 347B-348A.

36. Rochot, *Les travaux de Gassendi,* pp. 82-3.

37. Gassendi was very conscious of the fact that, in his biography of Peiresc, he was treating Peiresc's private achievements as a scholar as if they had been the *res gestae* of a prince. See his dedicatory remarks to Louis-Emmanuel de Valois in *Vita Peireskii,* esp. pp. 240, 242. Whether a historian should commemorate a person's private actions, as opposed to those public actions which have consequences for the well-being of the political state, was a lively subject of debate in late sixteenth-century handbooks on methods of writing history, such as Francesco Patrizi's *De legendae scribendaequae [sic] historiae ratione dialogi decem . . .* Italian edn (Venice, 1560), Latin edn (Basle, 1570), pp. 6-7, 64-73. A useful discussion of the

classical Greek and Latin traditions which led to the sixteenth-century exemplar theory of history's focus on the actions of great men and political states appears in George H. Nadel, "Philosophy of History before Historicism," *History and Theory* 3 (1964), 291-315.

38. *Vita Peireskii,* p. 337B.

39. The phrase I have quoted is from the following passage of *Vita Peireskii,* p. 241: " . . . Unde quidnam intus, et sub cute lateat, internosse per-arduum sit; quae vero procul ab arbitris, et sine famae captatione, atque idcirco sine fuco, ereptaque persona fiunt, ea demum hominem ostendunt; quod discernere est operae-pretium." Unless otherwise noted, all English translations of Latin and French quotations in this book are my own. In translating excerpts from *Vita Peireskii,* I have generally followed, although with my own revisions, William Rand's translation, *The Mirrour of True Nobility and Gentility. Being the Life of the Renowned Nicolaus Claudius Fabricius, Lord of Peiresk . . .* (London, 1657).

40. See above, Chapter 3, n. 37. [Not excerpted.] The popularity of both the subject of his biography and his method of composing it is evident in the number of editions of Gassendi's *Vita Peireskii* that were published within a short period of time. There were five Latin editions—1641, 1647, 1651, 1655, and 1656—followed by Rand's English translation of 1657.

41. *Vita Peireskii,* p. 242: "Sin vero nonnulli requirent illustriora quaedam, et ampliora facta, quam commemoraturi simus; norint oportet non omneis posse Scipiones esse, aut Maximos, ut bella, triumphosque recordari valeant. Abunde illi merentur laudem, quos cum Fortuna ad summas opes, atque dignitates non evexerit; majores tamen animos gerunt, generosiore virtute sunt, ac moliuntur grandiora longe, quam pro conditione sperare quis possit. Talis porro Peireskius fuit, quem exhibituri non sumus, nisi ut Virum, qui fuerit gradus, censusque Senatorii; et qui sese tamen ita gesserit, ut se fecerit quolibet encomio, ac panegyri superiorem."

42. The phrase I have quoted is from this sentence of *Vita Peireskii,* p. 241: "Alii, si videbitur, comptiore calamo expolient, ac historiae forma donabunt quos ipse commentarios, ceu rudera quaedam, digessero solum, veluti annaleis, in temporum seriem."

43. *Vita Peireskii,* p. 240: "Nam me quidem quantum amarit, promptius est animo sentire, quam verbis exprimere; satisque est dicere me foelicitati vertere magnae, quod me tam carum habuerit, quod tam frequentem sibi adesse, consiliorumque animi omnium esse conscium voluerit; quod in meum sinum ut caetera, sic extrema verba, animamque ipsam tandem exhalarit."

44. Patrizi, *De legendae scribendaequae [sic] historiae ratione dialogi decem,* pp. 155-61.

45. See Chapter 3, p. 59.

46. *Vita Peireskii,* p. 341B: "Jurisprudentiam nempe excoluit Cujaciana illa, ac liberali methodo, quae ex ipsis fontibus Juris, potiusquam ex Doctorum rivulis, Legum nitorem conspicuum facit. Heinc vero praecipue amavit antiquitatis studium; . . . et praeter Pandectas MSS. quos habuit, requisivit etiam alios Codices, quod quaedam editorum loca expeterent ab ipsis lucem."

47. *Ibid.,* pp. 341B-342A: "Quod dixi porro obiter circa antiquitatis studium, complectitur id maxime universam Historiam, quam sic animo informaverat, tenebatque, ut videri posset omnibus et locis, et temporibus interfuisse. Defixum quippe hoc semper habuit, conferre maxime historiam non illustrando modo Juris studio, sed componendae etiam vitae, animoque eximia quadam atque liberali delectatione afficiendo. Censebat enim quodammodo efficaciorem Philosophia, quod haec quidem verbis homines erudiat, sed illa exemplis accendat . . . Conquisivit proinde semper nationum omnium Historicos, et cum per-antiquos haberet per-caros, tum eos duxit carissimos, qui vel nostrae gentis essent, vel quomodocunque ad eam attinerent . . . Ita callere ipse voluit quicquid monumentis esset proditum, non de rebus modo ad Provinciam, Galliamve speciatim pertinentibus; sed etiam de iis, quae ad Italos, Hispanos, Germanos, Anglos, Hungaros spectarent, universeque ad illos omneis, quibuscum hominibus nostris commercium, aut dissidium fuit."

48. The phrases I have quoted are from the following passage of *Vita Peireskii,* p. 343B: "Heinc enim putabat hominem ingenuum exuere posse praeoccupationem, qua vulgus legem naturae putat, quicquid sibi in usu est . . . Tum posse illum animum suum supra vulgarem conditionem evehere, et defensurum quidem sua, sed aequum tamen se praebiturum adversus omneis homines . . . et, ut paucis dicam, ea exstiturum temperatione animi, ut maximam tranquillitatem, maximumque adeo bonum consequatur."

49. *Vita Peireskii,* p. 344B: "Et sane haud negandum quidem, quin dudum spem multam fecisset edendi in lucem Antiquitates Provinciae, evulgandique observationes in numismata, selectaque alia priscarum rerum monumenta: quin flagrasset pridem desiderio emittendi Commentarios de Mediceis Sideribus, et Kalendario Constantiniano; quin voluisset perfectum opus de ponderibus, et mensuris publici Juris facere; quin multa quoque alia argumenta non affectasset: quoniam, ut nullum fuit genus laudabilis eruditionis, quod animi sui amplitudine, curiositateque non fuerit complexus; ita nihil propemodum fuit, de quo aliquid scribere pererudite non destinarit. Veruntamen nihil demum fuit, cuius scriptionem fuerit aggressus; si ea

excipias, quae, ut iam innui, in Epistolas transsumpta inservit . . . Is nempe optimus Vir fuit, qui factum satis nunquam putarit, quantumcunque monumentorum aliqua de re obtinuisset: adeo ut toto quidem aevo congesserit varia de argumento quolibet; sed, quia quo plura nanciscebatur, eo sibi plura deesse censebat, nihil tandem digesserit, imo ne inchoarit quidem."

50. *Ibid.*, p. 342A.

51. *Ibid.*, p. 342B: " . . . Adeo ut innotuerint demum pleraque Auctorum obscura, nec alia ratione intellecta loca."

52. The phrases I have quoted are from the following sentences of *Vita Peireskii*, p. 343A: (a) "Ex his fere elicitur non placuisse ipsi Dialecticas illas, Metaphysicasve argutias, quae nihil bonae frugis haberent, et fovendis solum clamosissimis contentionibus essent comparatae." (b) "Displicebat profecto illi quae Physica vulgo docetur in Scholis, tanquam nimis umbratica, et ingeniorum potius technis, quam experimentis naturae innixa."

53. Note that, in the quoted passage from *Vita Peireskii*, p. 344A, Gassendi says that Peiresc regarded geography and chronology as mathematical as well as historical disciplines: "Adamavit autem praesertim Astronomiam, quod homo natus ad contemplandum, nihil possit majus, sublimius, excellentius, illustribus illis plagis inspectare. Deinde Geographiam, quod illa, una cum Chronologia, Historiam maxime collustrent, praestentque ne Viri ingenui, ac aliunde literati, gerant sese pro pueris; quin potius in totius Orbis, atque temporis quasi possessionem mittantur. Postea Opticen, quod per illam explicentur causae tam multarum rerum, quae apparent oculis . . ."

54. *Vita Peireskii*, pp. 339B-340A.

55. *Ibid.*, p. 341A.

56. *Ibid.*, p. 340A: " . . . Quaesiisse eum libros non sibi solum sed etiam quibusve opus illis foret. Innumeros vero commodato dedit, qui restituti nunquam sunt; innumeros quoque donavit . . ." Modern scholars have estimated that, at the time of his death, Peiresc's library contained, among other items, about 5,000 printed books. See: Henri Auguste Omont, "Les manuscrits et livres annotés de Fabri de Peiresc," *Annales du Midi* 1 (1880), 316-39, esp. 317; Francis W. Gravit, *The Peiresc Papers* (Ann Arbor, 1950), p. 1.

57. *Vita Peireskii*, p. 341A.

58. *Ibid.*, pp. 339A-340B.

59. *Ibid.*, p. 338B. Peiresc's credulousness was also noted in Gabriel Naudé, *Jugement de tout ce que a esté imprimé contre le Cardinal Marzarin* . . . (Paris, 1649), p. 667.

60. Dom Bernard de Montfaucon, *Bibliotheca bibliothecarum manuscriptorum nova* (2 vols. Paris, 1739), vol. 1, pp. 1181-9. Montfaucon was the second important cataloguer of Peiresc's manuscripts. The first was Pierre Dupuy, whose original catalogue was revised and published by François Henry in an appendix to an edition (The Hague, 1655) of *Vita Peireskii*. For a description of all of the modern collections of Peiresc's papers, especially the main body of them in the Bibliothèque Inguimbertine at Carpentras, see: Gravit, *The Peiresc Papers*, pp. 7-57; Omont, "Les manuscrits et livres annotés de Fabri de Peiresc," pp. 319-36.

61. *Vita Peireskii*, pp. 346B-347A. See also: Omont, "Les manuscrits et livres annotés de Fabri de Peiresc," p. 317; Gravit, *The Peiresc Papers*, p. 1. An unedited version of Peiresc's will has been published by Philippe Tamizey de Larroque in his "Le testament de Peiresc," *Annales du Midi* 1 (1889), 35-46. According to the will, Gassendi received all of Peiresc's mathematical books and instruments plus 100 other books on whatever subjects he desired. This version of the will has been reprinted in a volume which also contains and bears the title of Léopold Delisle's *Un grand amateur français du dix-septième siècle, Fabri de Peiresc* (Toulouse, 1889).

62. This contrast between devoted Hellenists and contemporary historians who adopted a more historicist approach was clearly recognizable among French humanists during the sixteenth century and continued to be so during the early seventeenth century. Striking examples of sixteenth-century works that illustrated this contrast were, on the one hand, Guillaume Bude's *Commentarii linguae graecae* (Paris, 1529) and Henri Estienne's *Thesaurus Graecae linguae* (Geneva, 1572) and, on the other hand, Henri Lancelot-Voisin de la Popelinière's *L'histoire des histoires* (Paris, 1599). On Budé, see Kelley, *Foundations of Modern Historical Scholarship*, esp. pp. 64-6. On La Popelinière, see Huppert, *The Idea of Perfect History*, esp. pp. 139-44 concerning La Popelinière's distinction between "general history" and the older Christian idea of universal history, and pp. 161-6 on La Popelinière's historicism.

63. In the close ties maintained between French historiographers and other varieties of French humanists, France differed notably from Italy, where the historians and the antiquarians operated to a large extent independently of each other. France also differed from Italy because, in Italy, the writers of universal history were isolated from the intellectual transactions of other humanists. For a description of these two features of Italian humanism, see Eric Cochrane, *Historians and Historiography in the Italian Renaissance* (Chicago and London, 1981), esp. pp. 382-9, 435-44. For further discussion of the patronage ties which helped to bind together the French historiographical community, see Orest

Ranum, *Artisans of Glory. Writers and Historical Thought in Seventeenth-Century France* (Chapel Hill, 1980), pp. 26-102.

64. *Vita Peireskii,* pp. 248A-255B. For a modern account of Peiresc's dealings with Italian scholars, see Cecilia Rizza, *Peiresc e l'Italia,* with a preface by Raymond Lebègue (Turin, 1965).

65. There are useful short discussions of universal history in many of the works cited above, in Chapter 1, n. 7. See especially some of the passages from: Cochrane, *Historians in the Italian Renaissance;* Huppert, *The Idea of Perfect History;* Kelley, *Foundations of Modern Historical Scholarship.* See also F. Smith Fussner, *The Historical Revolution. English Historical Writing and Thought, 1580-1640* (London, 1962), pp. 163-75, 191-210.

66. François de la Mothe le Vayer, *Discours de l'histoire* (Paris, 1638), in *Oeuvres de François de la Mothe le Vayer,* vol. 4, pt 1, pp. 280-4.

67. Samuel Kinser, *The Works of Jacques-Auguste de Thou* (The Hague, 1966), p. 1.

68. The fact that La Mothe le Vayer never completed this history of his own time was noted by Michel Groell, printer of the 1756 edn of his *Oeuvres,* in an advertisement at the beginning of vol. 4, pt 2.

69. La Mothe le Vayer, *Jugement sur les anciens et principaux historiens Grecs et Latins,* pp. [1-3] of his unnumbered preface and pp. 32-4 on Polybius, in *Oeuvres de François de la Mothe le Vayer,* vol. 4, pt 2.

70. *Ibid.,* p. [2] of unnumbered preface: "En effet, une vraie et legitime Histoire embrasse bien plus que la simple narration d'une vie de qui que ce soit . . ."

71. *Ibid.,* pp. 33-4.

72. *Ibid.,* pp. 32, 44-5; La Mothe le Vayer, *Discours de l'histoire,* in *Oeuvres,* vol. 4, pt 1, pp. 281-3.

73. For an account of Polybius as a source for the concept of history as philosophy teaching by example, and an account of his influence on the sixteenth-century historiographer Jean Bodin and the seventeenth-century historiographer Gerardus Vossius, see Nadel, "Philosophy of History before Historicism," *History and Theory* 3 (1964), esp. 295, 300-1, 305-8.

74. Naudé, *Bibliographia politica,* p. 103.

75. *Ibid.,* pp. 103-4.

David K. Glidden (essay date 1988)

SOURCE: "Hellenistic Background for Gassendi's Theory of Ideas," in *Journal of the History of Ideas,* Vol. XLIX, No. 3, July-Sept., 1988, pp. 405-24.

[In this essay, Glidden demonstrates how Gassendi's reading of Epicurus—transmitted via Thomas Stanley's translation of Philosophiae Epicuri Syntagma—*influenced the development of Epicureanism in England. The critic also argues that Gassendi's interpretation of Epicurean philosophy is influenced by his reading of the Stoics.]*

Renaissance humanism is characterized by a revival of interest in ancient Greek and Latin writings. At the same time, the uses to which these ancient texts were put were typically contemporary, as Renaissance authors borrowed eclectically from their favorite ancients to make their modern claims. Montaigne wrote this way, but so did many others, many of whom did not feel obliged to cite their sources. For one thing, the audience they were writing for did not need to be informed of these allusions. These who knew their Cicero or Sextus did not require the pedantry of citation or quotation. Those who were unread in the classics could follow the argument all the same. And so Descartes could begin the first of his *Meditations* with allusions to well known Pyrrhonist arguments, without mentioning them by name.

Unacknowledged borrowings extended to other materials as well. This is especially evident in the use of translated materials not only from ancient Greek to modern Latin but also from modern Latin to the vernacular. Just as Gassendi translated Greek philosophy into the body of his Latin texts, so Gassendi's Latin was translated by English authors, without much effort being made to make this plain. Walter Charleton's *Physiologia Epicuro-Gassendo-Chaltoniana* (1654) was largely a translation from Gassendi's work, complete with Gassendi's borrowings from Epicurus. Since translated material could be expropriated this way, it is hardly surprising that philosophical themes and arguments would also make the rounds as commonplaces.

The transmission of Epicureanism into seventeenth-century England is a matter of importance. It is not merely that, as a matter of antiquarian interest, Boyle's corpuscularianism owes something to the ancient Epicureans in general.[1] It is rather that seventeenth-century science, which made such corpuscularianism plausible, is deeply indebted to what was understood at the time to be the empiricism of Epicurus. Establishing precise connections, beyond similarity of content, is an altogether different matter, since authors disdainful of citation were no more enthusiastic to confess the history of their own ideas. But here the expropriation by translation provides a useful tool in detecting the history of such transmission all the same, especially in the selection of lifted materials and their new employment.

It has recently been argued that "The Doctrine of Epicurus," which is part XIII of Thomas Stanley's *History of Philosophy* (1660), was an important vehicle for this transmission, written as it was by a charter member of the Royal Society, an acquaintance of Locke and Boyle. Locke himself owned Stanley's *History.*[2] It is an even more compelling connection when we note that "The Doctrine of Epicurus" contained in Stanley's *History* is a literal translation of Gassendi's *Philosophiae epicuri syntagma* (1658), which in turn is largely a compilation of ancient texts that Gassendi had translated.

Gassendi actually listed many of his ancient sources in marginal notes alongside the columns of his text, while Stanley obligingly added more citations in his own notes, without finding it necessary to acknowledge Gassendi's role in their transmission.[3] So this translation from ancient Greek to Gassendi's Latin to Stanley's English might well seem to be a path Epicurean empiricism had taken in getting from ancient Greece to modern England. Since the translations were competent, little seems to have been lost in their transmission, except of course for the control initiated by Gassendi's selectivity and presentation.

I. In that part of his *Syntagma Philosophicum* entitled *De Logicae Fine* (1658) Gassendi wrote: "It can be known certainly that Epicurus did not believe in only one criterion, that is, sense perception, but he called in two besides, namely 'anticipation' and 'feeling,' of which 'anticipation' pertains to the intellect."[4] Gassendi had arrived at this interpretation of Epicurus as a consequence of reading ancient sources. And Gassendi warns us that his documentation is the best he could provide, collected from Diogenes Laertius, Sextus Empiricus, and others, such as Cicero and Plutarch.[5] The only primary texts available to Gassendi would have been the letters and sayings of Epicurus preserved in Book X of Diogenes Laertius. There was also the *De rerum natura* of Lucretius, whose manuscript had been rediscovered in the fifteenth century and printed in a notable edition by Lambinus in 1563. While Gassendi made much use of these primary materials in the course of his presentation, paraphrasing passages from Epicurus and Lucretius in the body of his text, he also adopted the overview of Epicureanism provided by Diogenes and to some extent attested to by Sextus.

Diogenes Laertius had stated, in a book which Gassendi had previously translated and annotated, that there were three Epicurean κριτηρια for settling disputes: αισθησεις, προληψεις, and παθη—that is to say, sense perceptions, pattern recognitions, as I translate προληψεις, and feelings.[6] There is no explicit statement to this effect in the extant Epicurean corpus. In the Epicurean letters which accompany Diogenes' summation, Epicurus's numerous and formulaic references to the means for determining the truth are to sense perception and feelings alone.[7] The word προληψις does not occur in the canonical section of the *Letter to Herodotus,* where the sensory foundations of knowledge are referred to, although the term does occur later in the letter[8] as well as in the *Letter to Menoeceus,* both times in an epistemic context.[9] There is no explicit discussion of προληψις in Lucretius, where the criteria for knowledge are presented uniformly as perceptual.[10] Furthermore, παθη, or feelings, play a prominent evidentiary role in Epicurus's letters and also in Lucretius,[11] although Diogenes relegates them solely to the realm of eth-

ics, leaving, according to Diogenes, only two effective criteria for determining the truth: perception and pattern recognition.[12]

Gassendi follows Diogenes' lead, accepting two epistemic criteria: perception and προληψις, translating the latter as "anticipatio" or "praenotio" following Cicero,[13] and relegating feelings to the realm of ethics.[14] At the same time Gassendi gives considerable emphasis to προληψις as a separate criterion of its own. In doing so Gassendi overrides the agreement of Cicero and Sextus Empiricus, for example, who insisted that the only measure of reality for the Epicureans was the senses.[15] As Gassendi presents the Epicurean *Canon,* the pattern recognition of προληψις is a separate act of intellection, not an act of sensation, thereby adding a rational criterion to a sensory one. In this way the criteria for knowledge contain a purely conceptual component in their very foundation, empiricism notwithstanding. Gassendi presents this as his interpretation of Epicurus.[16] It is also his own view.

In the *Syntagma philosophicum* of 1658, a different *Syntagma* from the *Philosophiae epicuri syntagma* which Stanley used in his *History of Philosophy,* Gassendi presents an abbreviated version of that other work. Gassendi concedes that the Epicureans rejected the "logic" of the Stoics. Gassendi's concession is taken directly from Diogenes, who wrote that the Epicureans rejected "dialectic logic" as superfluous because they thought it sufficient for philosophers of nature just to make use of the sounds we make for things—τους τγν πραγματγν φθογγους, echoing the words of the *Letter to Herodotus.*[17]

But unlike his ancient sources, Gassendi worries over the claim whether to forswear for the Epicureans any logic whatsoever, concluding that it must have been only Stoic dialectic which they had rejected.[18] Gassendi examines the Epicurean foundations of knowledge as "dialectica" just the same, logic under a different name. Gassendi makes explicit what Diogenes assumes in practice, operating on the assumption that the Epicureans conducted philosophy along the same lines as their own contemporaries, the Stoics, had established—not of course exactly following in their footsteps but observing the general distinction between Logic, Natural Philosophy, and Ethics all the same—a distinction which Diogenes tells us the Stoics had invented.[19] Following Diogenes, Gassendi could read the Epicureans as asking many of the same questions that the Stoics had addressed, despite their different answers. So Gassendi in his *Philosophiae epicuri syntagma* presents Epicurean doctrine according to the three Stoic divisions of philosophy, which Stanley dutifully repeats, "The First Part of Philosophy" being the *Canonica.*

In his abbreviated chapter on Epicurean logic, found in the *Syntagma philosophicum,* Gassendi follows up his discussion of the question of Epicurean logic with the observation that Epicurus first of all supposes that every question can be examined either *de re* or *de voce.*[20] This statement is ostensibly lifted from Diogenes' summation of Epicureanism: "Of inquiries, some concern things, others mere speech."[21] Gassendi adds that the former division is concerned with the way things are, while the latter is devoted to the meaning or significance we give to things. This seems to be Gassendi's interpretive intervention, for when he turns to the *de voce* question to provide the last two canons in his presentation of Epicurean dialectic, Gassendi acknowledges that he has gathered these together "ex fragmentis," and what he has gathered together appear to be Epicurus's own remarks in the *Letter to Herodotus,* repeated by Lucretius, concerning the importance of straightforward language.[22]

The use and abuse of words was a favorite Epicurean theme, but the sources of this abuse were always said to be the same: failing to index or label real facts or features in the world and as a consequence failing to provide any real reference for the words we use. When sounds we make fail to point to real things that underlie those utterances (τγν υποτεταγμενγν ταις φγναις πραγματγν),[23] they become noise instead of words. This is the point of Diogenes' division between *de re* and *de voce,* contrasting genuine inquiry into reality over against the empty sounds of bare speech (περι ψιλην την φγνην), which would afford nothing but an idle inquiry when there is nothing in the world for those empty sounds to name. Ignoring the force of Diogenes' ψιλην, Gassendi takes this latter sort of inquiry seriously, as the subject matter of Epicurean logic.

Gassendi takes Epicurus's reference to the things our utterances signal as a reference to the immediate signification we give to what we say, the thoughts or ideas in our minds first signified by speech. "Res subiectas vocibus, seu quid voces significent" is the way Gassendi translates the relevant passage in the *Letter to Herodotus.*[24] Gassendi interprets the things which underlie our utterances as the meanings of our terms, the notion or primary signification of our speech (*vocis notionem, significationemve primariam*), understanding Epicurus's Greek that way: το πργτον ηννοημα καθ ηκαςτον φφογγον βλεπεςθαι.[25] Gassendi takes Epicurus's "empty utterances" (κενους φθογγους) to refer to meaningless utterances, sounds which lack thoughts or ideas to back them up.

Gassendi thereby finds a place in Epicurean theory for a purely conceptual criterion of meaning over and above the empiricism Gassendi's sources had insisted on. To defend this interpretation Gassendi draws upon a distinction between *de re* and *de voce* which he found in Book X of Diogenes Laertius, using this distinction to distinguish a theory of meaning from a theory of evidence. It is worth noting that this may not have been the distinction Diogenes intended. It is rather in Book VII of his *Lives* where Diogenes draws that sort of distinction, but there he attributes it to the Stoics, not the Epicureans.[26]

II. In his *Philosophiae epicuri syntagma,* which Stanley appropriated for his *History,* Gassendi first explores the nature of truth before turning separately to the three criteria listed by Diogenes. Anticipating this discussion Gassendi establishes a distinction between the senses and the mind on the one hand, and our feelings on the other: "But forasmuch as natural things affect the *Sense* or *Intellect,* and moral things the *Appetite* or *Will;* for this reason, Criteria are to be taken from both these."[27] This allows for a division between moral and epistemic criteria.

Gassendi then segregates the role of the mind, or intellect, from that of the senses:

> From the *Sense,* nothing can be taken more than its Function, Sensation, which likewise is called Sense.
>
> From the *Intellect,* forasmuch as besides the Function which it hath, whil'st like the Sense it contemplateth the thing, as if it were present and apparent, (whence the perception of a things appearing [*perceptio apparentiae*], which appeareth to be as well to the Intellect, as to the Sense, is called a Phantasie, or Appearance); forasmuch, I say, as besides this Function, it is proper to the Intellect to ratiocinate or discourse; there is therefore required a Praenotion or Anticipation, by looking upon which, something may be inferred.[28]

The interpretation presented in these lines and dutifully translated by Stanley establishes the grounds for there being a separate, rational Epicurean criterion, in addition to a sensory one. Even if the mind could act as if it too were a sense organ in regarding the appearances presented before it, Gassendi argues that the mind must also manufacture concepts, or praenotions, as the vehicles for thought. Although this is presented as Epicurus's view, Gassendi in this instance is not quoting some ancient source but instead presenting his own interpretation of the philosophic necessity he believed Epicurus was responding to. It is also Gassendi's preferred view.

The Epicureans were notorious for saying that the mind could itself function as a sense organ, thereby accounting for dreams, mental visions, hallucinations, and the like, all of which might be thought to undermine the infallibility of our sense perceptions. To protect the authority of perception, the Epicureans insisted that there was nothing we could imagine or experience in this way which was not itself simply the impact of something from the outside, something we did recognize even though we might go on to make false claims about it.[29] Imagination was simply another form of direct perception attentive to external appearances, rather than something made up in the mind.

Gassendi acknowledges that doctrine by admitting that the mind could experience appearances too, and that all such appearances are true.[30] But Gassendi goes on to insist that because the Intellect can reason and speak, there must be required a separate conceptual criterion, separate from these imaging appearances. The specific content of this criterion Gassendi calls Praenotion or Anticipation, after the Epicurean προληψις. This is the criterion for inquiries *de voce* and the foundation for what Gassendi takes to be the Epicurean theory of significance and meaning.

As far as the senses are concerned, Gassendi's presentation is accurate, that the senses of themselves make no claims on the world and are never false, that the senses do not interpret the world but instead present it to us, as it appears to be: "Now where there is a bare apprehension, not pronouncing any thing, there is no error or falsehood."[31] Gassendi is also quite clear that the appearances presented to the senses and the mind are not interpreted at all but are rather just the way the world looks as it presents itself before us, constructed as we are and as the world is.[32] The sense organs provide purely mechanical transcriptions of the way the world looks to us to be.

Gassendi also appreciates how such a mechanical transcription limits the ability of the senses for getting at the truth, conceding that not all appearances are evident, even though all of them are true: "Evidence of Sense, I here call that kind of Sensation, or Appearance, which, all things obstructive to Judgment being removed, as distance, motion, indisposition of the Medium, and the like; cannot be contradicted. Whence to the Question, Whether a thing be such as it appears? We ought not to give a sudden Answer."[33] But the source for Gassendi's statement here is taken from Cicero, in a passage where the Epicureans are being criticized from a Stoic point of view.

Gassendi understands the Epicurean contention, shared by the Stoics, that if there is to be any knowledge of reality at all, it is a knowledge that comes to us through the direct contact our senses have with the outside world, even though that knowledge may in turn be limited by the circumstances of perception. But it was Stoic philosophy which called attention to the limiting circumstances of perceiving, and Gassendi quotes them on this, in describing the Epicureans. It is not just that Gassendi employs Stoic categories of analysis found in ancient sources on Epicurus, but as he goes along Gassendi is apparently making improvements upon the Epicurean philosophy, improvements borrowed from the Stoics. Gassendi goes to explicitly Stoic sources and uses them to expound on Epicurus.

After examining the Epicurean sensory criterion, Gassendi next turns to the criterion of the intellect. Consider, for example, the first of Gassendi's four "Canons of Praenotion or Anticipation":

> (a) *All Anticipation or Praenotion, which is in the Mind, depends on the Senses, either by Incursion, or Proportion, or Similitude, or Composition,* I mean, that the Notion (or Idea, and Form as it were, which being anticipated is called Praenotion) is begotten in the Mind by *Incursion* (or Incidence,) when the thing incurreth into the Sense directly and by itself, as a man just before our eyes. By *Proportion,* when the Praenotion is amplified or extenuated. . . . By *Similitude,* when according to a thing first perceived by the Sense, we fancy another like it. . . . Lastly, by *Composition,* when we put as it were into one the distinct Notions which we have of two or more things, as when we so unite the Notions of a Horse and a Man, as that the Notion of a Centaur ariseth out them, but (b) *not without some assistence of Ratiocination.*[34]

Stanley reorganizes the text by adding the markers (a) and (b) and the final italics, so that the final qualification is conjoined with the first, requiring that "Praenotion" explicitly depends on both the senses and ratiocination. As we have seen, Stanley's emphasis is perfectly consistent with Gassendi's own initial statement, that προλήψεις are separate acts of Intellection, though subsequent to perception and imagination.

The passage which Stanley translates from Gassendi is in turn taken from Diogenes Laertius, but it is not taken from Book X but rather from Book VII, where it explicitly describes the Stoic theory of ideas, and how those ideas are constructed in the intellect.[35] Once again, Gassendi goes to Stoic sources to explicate Epicurus. But this presents an immediate conflict with what Gassendi himself admits is the Epicurean doctrine of mental apparitions, where the appearance of a Centaur, say, is not for the Epicureans an intellectual composition invented by the mind but an externally constructed atomic ειδγλον, or physical image, impressed directly on the mind. Such "mental" presentations are for the Epicureans as rigidly segregated from mental constructions as αιςθησις is distinct from δοξα.[36]

Gassendi identifies Epicurean πρόληψις as if it were generically a kind of mental notion, εννοια, or idea. This is explicit doctrine of the Stoics, who typically regarded praenotions and general notions as alike in character, προλήψεις and κοιναι εννοιαι, regarding them all as rational constructions, as opposed to solely something sensory.[37] And so the Stoics insisted that only creatures with an intellect could enjoy προλήψεις too, along with the entire mosaic of mental creativity, while the Epicureans allowed προλήψεις to deer, dogs, and parrots as well as generals, restricting rationality to matters of opinion.[38]

In Book X of his discussion of Epicureanism Diogenes does discuss how Epicurean concepts, or επινοιαι, are generated from φαινομενα, and he alludes to this same fourfold process of construction which Diogenes had previously elaborated upon in his discussion of the Stoics, but here Diogenes insists that all such conceptual constructions arise just from sense perception (απο τγν αιςθησεγν γεγονασι) with no mention made of ratiocination.[39] The coincidence of presentation between Books VII and X of Diogenes Laertius extends only to the generation of ideas and their composition and not to Epicurean προλήψεις, except that Gassendi wants to understand Epicurean προλήψεις as ideas, and so he completes the identification. Stanley emphasizes this interpretation in italics, that according to Gassendi the Epicurean intellectual criterion is effected by ratiocination and not just by sensation.

The Epicureans had argued that when the organism has sufficient experience to recognize the same appearance over and over again, it comes to recognize patterns in the world, and so it can recognize a horse when it sees one or a horse can recognize a man. And Lucretius reports that in this same way we can learn to recognize pestilence or peace. Epicurean προλήψεις display habituated perceptions of φαινομενα extended over time.[40] Here there would be no need for ratiocination. Instead there is merely the reflexive recognition of repeated patterns of appearance, τουτεστι μνημην του πολλακις εξγθεν φανεντος, as Diogenes put the point.[41] As we have seen, Gassendi explicitly rejects this interpretation of προληψις as appearance, in favor of the Stoic understanding of προληψις as conceptual.

Gassendi took it upon himself to borrow Diogenes' account of the Stoics to explicate Epicurus. It served his own philosophical purposes to do so. This becomes evident as we examine Gassendi's second canon of interpretation concerning what Epicurean προληψις is supposed to be: *"Anticipation is the very Notion, and (as it were) Definition of the Thing; without which, we cannot Enquire, Doubt, Think, nor so much as Name any Thing."*[42] That προληψις is the *sine qua non* for enquiry, thought, and language is well attested from other sources besides Diogenes. The question is how it plays that role. This is the role Gassendi sees:

> Hence it comes to pass, that, if it be demanded what any thing is, we define or describe it in such manner as it is, according to the Anticipation thereof which we have in our Mind. Neither do we thus only, being demanded what some singular thing is, as what *Plato* is, but also what an Universal is, as Man, not this or that, but considered in general; this is brought to pass according as the Mind, having seen many Singulars, and set apart their several Differences, formeth and imprinteth in herself the Anticipation of that which is common to them all, as an Universal Notion; reflecting upon which, we say, Man (for example) is something animate, and endued with such a Form.[43]

According to Gassendi, Epicurean προληψεις provide the meanings of our general terms, and the role Intellection plays in the formation of προληψεις is that, upon the presentation of many single appearances, it sets apart their several differences. This is just one method of conceptual formation, the method of Incursion, but it is this method that establishes what our words for kinds or species signify.

Recognizing Plato when you see him may require an Anticipation too, but apprehension of a man as such, or anything requiring a general idea for its recognition, insists upon it. And since this Anticipation is a rational construction, it is open to explication by definition. In this way the conceptual definitions of our general ideas are established as the foundations for our knowledge. Now the Epicureans were famous for insisting that definitions were superfluous, since all that any organism needed was to see the patterns in the world and respond to them directly. Rather, it was the Stoics who insisted on definitions as the foundations for conceptual understanding. Once again, Gassendi prefers the Stoic point of view, even as an explication of Epicurus.

Gassendi also wants to insist, as the Stoics had before him, that these conceptual creations, mental contents as they are, are no less authoritative than the raw evidence of our senses:

> But it is not necessary to confirm all things with exquisite Reasons or Arguments, and scrupulous forms of Reasoning, which are cried up by the Dialectics; For there is this difference betwixt an Argument and the Conclusion of the Reason, and between a slender Animadversion and an Admonition; that in one, some occult, and (as it were,) involved things are unfolded and opened; in the other, things ready and open are judged. But where there are such Anticipations as ought to be, then what will follow or not follow from them, or what agrees or disagrees with them, is perspicuously discerned, and naturally inferred, without any Artifice, or Dialectic Construction; wherefore we need only take care, that the Anticipation which we have of Things be clear and distinct.[44]

Although they are rational representations responding to the senses, Anticipations are said to enjoy the authority of general truths because they are rationally perspicuous to the Intellect. These same Anticipations provide the vocabulary of thought and the general ideas "from which we infer Something, and thinking upon which we make Sumptions or Propositions, which are Maxims or Principles, by which that which is inferred or concluded is conceived to be demonstrated."[45] So Gassendi argues on behalf of his Stoicized Epicureans that we suppose "the Anticipation of Vacuum" on the basis of "the Anticipation of a manifest thing" (Motion). Yet, in fact, for the Epicureans there could be no "Anticipation" of a vacuum, since a vacuum is something that we cannot directly experience.

The difficulty with Gassendi's interpretation is that not all Anticipations will then be true when they fail to be clear and distinct, when they are not "perspicuous and manifest," when they are not such as they "ought to be." Yet Epicurean προληψεις were supposed to be a constant criterion of truth in explicit contrast to whatever conceptions or opinions we might form consequent upon experience. Once these προληψεις are interpreted as intellectual creations, their authority comes into question. By converting Epicurean προληψεις over to their Stoic counterparts, Gassendi has undermined their infallibility.

Gassendi compares Epicurean προληψεις with general ideas. In doing so Anticipations become conceptual foundations for knowledge, the vocabulary for our propositions. The senses are relegated to mechanical harbingers of consequent mental apprehensions. Yet only some of these ensuing mental conceptions will be truly manifest and evident. In this way Gassendi's presentation of Epicureanism is modified by a Stoic epistemology still wedded to Epicurean atomism. To some extent Gassendi may have taken this path because he was led to do so by his sources. But there was another path he could have chosen, and that he did not choose it suggests his own commitment to this doctrine, which he himself defends. It must not be forgotten that Renaissance humanists made use of ancient sources for their own contemporary purposes.

III. Gassendi's four-part *Institutio logica* was published in 1658 as part of his *Syntagma philosophicum.* It is the initial portion of the *Institutio logica* concerning the origin and nature of ideas that is of interest to us here. Subsequent divisions addressing the nature of propositions, syllogistic argument, and rational signification all presuppose ideas as the vocabulary of thought. Gassendi employs a wide variety of ancient sources in formulating his general views. Yet it is Gassendi's understanding of the second of the Epicurean Canons of Criteria, which Gassendi had termed "the Canons of Praenotion or Anticipation," that proves especially formative for his theory of ideas, although he does not mention Epicurus by name. Of course I am not claiming that Gassendi's *Logic* as a whole is singularly Epicurean, but I am suggesting that Gassendi's theory of ideas specifically owes a special debt to his understanding of Epicurus.

The first division of Gassendi's logic is entitled: "De simplici rerum imaginatione," and Gassendi begins by explaining what this means:

> We are here using the word "Imagination" for Thought, or that action of the Mind which terminates in an image of the thing thought [*rei cogitatae imaginem*] passing in front of the Mind. This must be noted because the expression is sometimes used for the imaginative faculty, which many people call also by the Greek word Phantasia and assign to the lower part of the Soul, which is common in Man and Brutes; for indeed, at this level, Brutes also imagine.[46]

This is similar to a point Gassendi had made on behalf of the Epicureans, insisting as he had that Epicurean Praenotions and Anticipations were not part of animal imagination but the work of the intellect instead. In this way Gassendi separated man from brutes precisely at the point of conceiving in our minds what it is we are experiencing through our senses, exactly as the Stoics had.

Gassendi wants to insist that such a presence in the intellect of the thing one is thinking of has authority as something rationally apprehended: "that image which is passing before the mind, indeed is almost thrust before it when we think [*veluti obiicitur*]."[47] Gassendi argues that it makes no difference what we call this image—"Conceptio, Apprehensio, Intellectio, Imago, Idea, Species, Notio, Praenotio, Anticipatio, seu anticipata notio (prout nempe fuit prius acquisita); Conceptus, Phantasma"—since it is the very same ratiocination we are referring to.[48] But for the sake of convenience and of clarity Gassendi decides upon "Idea" as his term. These are the foundations of knowledge for Gassendi, what we might call simple ideas, or common notions and cognitive impression, as the Stoics had once called them: κοιναι εννοιαι and φαντασιακαταληπτικν.

Gassendi's separation of intellect from sense makes something of a mystery how one contributes to the other. If sensations and sensory images directly presented to the mind are not themselves ideas, it is hard to understand how the senses make their contribution to our understanding. Gassendi addresses this issue in the first three canons of his presentation. First of all, the simple concept of a thing requires repeated experience, enough to enable us even just to recognize a particular man when we see him again.[49] This requires repeated patterns of sensation. Secondly, the kinds of ideas we are capable of owe something to the kinds of sense organs we are equipped with. As Gassendi puts it, a man born blind cannot conceive of color, but how it is he does conceive of color once he has the sight to do so is left by Gassendi unexplained and inexplicable.[50]

Finally, to those who object that some of our simple ideas are too incredible and fantastic to owe their origins to the senses, Gassendi responds with the very same fourfold construction of ideas which he had explicitly attributed to the Epicureans but had taken from the Stoics. Here Gassendi lays greater emphasis on the method of incursion or incidence (περιπτγσις) as our means for acquiring our most ordinary ideas of horses, plants and flowers, the sun and moon, and men: "There are then Ideas which are said to cross over by impressions through the Senses, and are impressed upon the Mind, which are ideas of things which themselves strike upon the Senses."[51] Our other ideas are made up from these, constructed in those other ways. Consequently, Gassendi's separation of the intellect from sense must not be taken to resemble Descartes's separation of the mind from the body. For Gassendi, the intellect is entirely dependent on the senses for the origins of its ideas. It is just that the intellect interprets what the senses have presented to it.

Gassendi's Ideas are not mental objects of awareness, despite his describing them as images.[52] Gassendi's Ideas do not veil our understanding of the world by substituting for it as the reference of our thought. Rather, they are acts of native intellection directed at the world, consequent upon the world's own effects upon us. It is not that Gassendi's Ideas come to take the place of things; instead such ideas are ways we have of making sense of the reality we experience with our senses. Ideas are vehicles of signification, which explains their role in formulating propositions. They are mental interpretants of the causes of our physiological experience. My idea of the sun is not the sun that so affects my eyes, but it is of that sun nevertheless, as my mind conceives it, responding to the sun's own physical impressions on my sense organs.

The source of this representation may be thrust upon the intellect, but its representation is an act of intellection all the same, something animals are quite incapable of. In this way, what Gassendi thought the Epicureans had meant by their προληψεις become our first ideas and indeed the very foundations for all our knowledge, leaving to physical sensations the ancillary role as necessary but not sufficient prerequisites for rational recognition.[53] As a consequence of intellectualizing these acts of recognition, not all our simple ideas of intellection will prove true, as when we think of Pegasus for instance.[54] But our most ordinary ideas will be nothing more significant than rational recognitions of what it is that is effecting our bodily sensations.

Gassendi presents the fourth Canon of his logic, which he then elaborates upon as follows:

> *Every Idea which crosses over through the Senses is singular; it is the Mind which forms a general idea out of similar singular ones.* Since all the things which are in the World and which are able to strike upon the Senses are singulars, like Socrates, Bucephalus, this stone, this piece of grass, and the other things one can point to with a finger (and of course there are not sufficient proper names to enable every individual thing to be designated), the ideas which cross over from them into the Mind and stick there can only be singular.[55]

Even singular ideas, once they have made it into the mind, are ideas or anticipations, just as Gassendi said they were in his parallel discussion of Epicurean προληψις. All the same, there is a difference between a singular idea and a general one. In discussing Epicurus, Gassendi had maintained that general Anticipations, or Universal Notions, are "brought to pass according as the Mind, having seen many Singulars, and set apart their several Differences, formeth and imprinteth in herself the Anticipation of that which is common to them all, as an Universal Notion." Here Gassendi elaborates on this very same procedure, eliding the transition between single real things and our corresponding singular ideas just as he previously had done, leaving to the method of incursion the authority to effect the transition from singular impressions made upon our sense organs to simple recognitions of the specific objects causing them.

This elision is somewhat awkward, since the Epicureans, I take it, had insisted that individual appearances were presented to us through physical impressions made upon our sense organs and responded to directly by the material mechanism of the mind. There was not an additional epistemic transition from singular real things to our conceptual recognitions of them over and above the physical transition from object to the eye. By contrast Gassendi needs this second sort of transition, too, while relying on the first to do the work of both. Ideas strictly cannot cross over from the world to our intellect, since they are creatures of the intellect all along.

On the one hand, Gassendi wants to claim that ideas directly impress themselves upon us as they cross over from the world. On the other hand, Gassendi wants to insist that strictly speaking there are no ideas of sensation; there are only ideas of intellection consequent upon our physical sensations. The former claim was strict Epicurean doctrine, except that it was not a theory of ideas rather than a description of our physiology. The latter was established Stoic doctrine and vulnerable to well-known skeptical objections denying that the world need be anything like our

ideas of it, even at the level of individual experiences. Epicurean doctrine was seen by ancient skeptics to be invulnerable to that specific criticism, and it was natural of Gassendi to embrace Epicurean mechanism. Yet Gassendi insisted upon the role of Stoic common notions, too, once he understood Epicurus along those same lines.

Although attentive observation and reliance on firsthand experience, in preference to what others say or write, can help perfect the ideas we do have, all our ideas are alike in character as rational representations of our experience.[56] And ideas can arise from conversation and written definitions just as they can from direct experience, the only difference being that ideas which arise by incidence, where a thing has made its impression on our senses, are really of that thing itself, whereas ideas which are formed another way are not so much of that very thing itself, but rather the accommodation of some other idea we have within us to signify the other thing in question.[57] Such an approach to knowledge trades off empirical exactitude for rational understanding, but it by no means makes all our ideas merely fanciful creations.

According to Gassendi there are two complementary methods for formulating general ideas out of singular ones (*uno aggregando, alio abstrahendo*).[58] The first involves discernment of collective similarity, the second sets aside individual differences by abstraction. The former method of collection might at first appear to be closer to the original intent of Epicurean προληψις as a purely sensory apprehension of the mind (επιβολη της διανοιας), where the mind becomes physically accustomed to sufficiently similar appearances over time to be able to recognize them as the kinds of things they are, in just the way a cat comes to recognize a mouse. The mind would collect and set aside similar experiences without applying to them any protocol of similitude of its own invention. Nature would do the sorting and the organism would be responsive to it.

Such a simple method of assimilation would be insufficient for Gassendi's purposes, since he requires that the method of collection be an intellectual operation employing some rationally articulated protocol, so that the mind can continue to take an active role in subsequently collecting these collections together, reaching ever higher levels of generality: in going from the general idea of "man" to that of "animal" or "substance," for example.[59] Consequently, general ideas formulated in this way, just by being collected together by the mind, suffer varying degrees of perfection and completeness, the more neatly they portray what it is the separate singulars have in common (*repraesentat purius id in quo singularia conveniunt*). It is now the custom, Gassendi points out, to allow the idea of mankind to encompass Americans as well as Europeans. This example in turn suggests how the protocol of similitude is itself susceptible to change, due to new discoveries and differences in historical discernment.[60] In simply recognizing similarities and formulating general ideas to encompass them, the mind makes its own decisions and must answer for them to other minds.

The further method of abstraction operates upon such collections and gives them greater definition, as it goes through the ideas individually to determine what it is precisely that the members have in common, while setting aside their separate differences.[61] In this way generality and universality are achieved by taking features away from singular ideas, resulting in the general idea of a man, for instance, who is neither young nor old nor middle-aged, something impossible to imagine but necessary for rational discrimination and definition.[62] There seems to be this difference between the method of assimilation and the method of abstraction: the latter is a more self-conscious and articulating process, requiring increasing intervention by the mind as it maps out its own path of similarity and difference, rather than responding to a pattern it can recognize as more or less presented to it by the senses.

Abstraction is a method of selective definition conducted at any level of generality, as the mind identifies a thing for the kind of thing it is by rationally deciding upon the nature of that thing, fleshing out the definition of the matching notion. But this too is required of our idea of Socrates and its definition just as it is of "man."[63] Furthermore, relations among ideas affect our individual understanding of them, be they singular or general.[64] At its very onset, each of our ideas, singular or general, is delineated by reason, whose definition of the thing can be articulated, be it Socrates or substance. The more rationally comprehensive such a classification scheme becomes, the more vulnerable it is to losing touch with nature's very own organization.[65]

There are then various sources of vulnerability affecting our ideas that Gassendi recognizes. There is the question of our own rational satisfaction with our way of estimating our experience. There is also the need to isolate our ideas from temperament and prejudice and failure of articulation, so that our ideas remain cool and collected, measured responses to experience.[66] To defend against these vulnerabilities, Gassendi's theory of ideas requires a complex epistemology, one which must take into careful consideration failures of rationality over and above any lack of physiological experience, which itself amounts to a relatively minor factor in the epistemic scheme of things. Although Gassendi establishes this epistemology on the basis of experience, what he means by experience as an intellectualized reaction requires an elaborate defence and as a consequence is only capable of a moderate success and a modest knowledge. In this way Gassendi's epistemology is not beyond the reach of skepticism.

It is historically interesting in this respect that, although Gassendi would appear to present himself as following the path of the Epicureans, the epistemology of ideas that he practices is largely Stoic in its character and origins, and well known for its vulnerability to skepticism. Whereas for the Epicureans problems with our organs and the limits of their vision provided the primary limitations upon the reach of our experience, Gassendi's theory must take those physical limitations in stride as it delves into the psychological sources of our errors and the logic of such mistakes. Whereas for the Epicureans successful sensory apprehension of the way the world looks is guaranteed by the very mechanism of perception, for Gassendi the epistemic character of human experience is never beyond interpretation.

IV. A philosophical system that begins with ideas for its foundations in the end depends entirely upon the agreement or disagreement of those ideas with each other. The relation between conceptual schemata and the world those schemata are about might then appear to be problematic, if only temporarily so, requiring elaborated protocols for authenticating that relation. What it is those protocols would regulate is the particular way in which a coherent set of ideas conceives of reality so as to suit and signify the way the world really is.

By contrast, a philosophical system that depends on perceptual recognitions merely as acts of interaction between one physical reality and another is not much of an epistemology at all. On such a view, animals equipped with sensory organs mechanically discriminate among the causes of their physiological sensations, without the need to think about it. The mechanism of such a system presupposes a thorough-going materialism, to accommodate the connections between what affects those organisms and what those organisms then respond to. This sort of mechanism makes reason seem superfluous.

Proponents of a mechanistic physiology have always met with some resistance. What the horsefly sees as it flies around my head has, for example, been commonly described in epistemic rather than mechanical terms. And so we say without reflection that the horsefly sees my head, that it has some conception of my head, thanks to using its eyes the way it does. Although such an attribution to flies is somewhat gratuitous, over the centuries there has always been some recognized level of organic sophistication, in which it is readily agreed that the creature in question formulates organizing conceptions of its own in response to physiological stimulation. So we say that the dog recognizes his master, although we might not want to say that an amoeba sees the light, no matter how it might respond.

In the seventeenth century it was common for advocates of a mechanical philosophy, from Descartes and Gassendi to Robert Boyle, to fathom animal perception, such as how dogs recognize their masters, as a purely mechanical affair. This allowed for one sort of pattern recognition which was purely automatic, in contrast with another sort of recognition that was intellectually organized and complete with ideas and conceptions. Animals might respond to repeated patterns of experience, without requiring general ideas to do so, or any ideas at all. Yet such bestial pattern recognition contrasted sharply with intelligent perception. In the history of the period the former was just a form of mechanism, while the latter required the presence of a mind to respond mentally to the mechanics of the body.[67]

Epicurean materialism made no separation between its theory of knowledge and its physics. Gassendi made a place for one, following Diogenes Laertius and the Stoics. We can understand how this might have seemed to Gassendi a charitable interpretation, to comprehend Epicurean προληψεις as part of human rationality. Otherwise, lacking any theory of conceptually organized experience to account for the ways in which we conceive of the world, the Epicurean senses would appear to establish only a causal link between the world and our organs without going on to establish our conceptions of the ways things are. If Epicurean προληψεις were just a part of the mechanism of physiological discrimination, it would appear to prove inadequate to formulate the foundations for our knowledge, once those foundations were required to be the rational representations of human beings and not beast machines. For this reason, Gassendi emphasizes that there must be two epistemic criteria for the Epicureans: sensation and intellection.

The scholarly Gassendi was an appreciative reader of the ancients and extended his appreciation especially to Epicurus, whose physics was of such interest to him but whose reduction of the mind to matter was at the time anathema. Borrowing heavily from the Stoics, Gassendi attributes to the Epicureans an additional, ratiocinative foundation for their knowledge, a theory of ideas with empirical authority. The generality of such ideas, as forms conceived in the mind and said of the world, provides for the universality of knowledge. And Gassendi adopts this same theory of ideas in his own **Logic.**

Mechanically speaking, our human bodies are in contact with the world that surrounds us. Epicurean atomism proved to Gassendi to be the most convenient way in which to describe the nature of that contact. As human beings, we are also in a position to have knowledge of that world as it brushes up against our senses whenever we experience it. Yet the nature of that experience must enable us not merely to respond to whatever is affecting us but to conceive of it as well. So, following his reading of Epicurus, Gassendi insisted upon the mind's own appreciation of that experience, as the mind intervenes to organize and recognize the world presented to it.

The theory that he came up with was flawed and fragile in character, since ideas themselves could not themselves be mechanically transmitted from the outside into us. The method of incursion for the formulation of our most basic ideas proved susceptible to skepticism exactly at the point of transition from the mechanism to the mind, for there was no reason to be sure that the mind's reactive interpretation of a pattern impressed upon the bodily sense organs would be true to nature's intrinsic order.

The philosophical construction of an empiricism resting on ideas is the story of seventeenth-century philosophy. Here I have only sketched out Gassendi's contribution to such a theory of empirical ideas by discussing its Hellenistic heritage. It is no coincidence that, given such a heritage, skep-

ticism should be such a constant worry in the period. Yet the alternative was unthinkable; namely, pure mechanism stripped of all conceptions. Even though he was happy to criticize Descartes's mentalism from an Epicurean point of view, Gassendi's own theory of ideas was just as hostile to the mechanistic reduction of mind to matter.

Notes

1. See for example, C. T. Harrison: "Bacon, Hobbes, Boyle, and the Ancient Atomists," *Harvard Studies and Notes in Philology and Literature,* 15 (1933), 191-218 and "The Ancient Atomists and English Literature of the Seventeenth Century," *Harvard Studies in Classical Philology,* 45 (1934), 1-79; also R. H. Kargon, "Walter Charleton, Robert Boyle and the Acceptance of Epicurean Atomism in England," *Isis,* 55 (1964), 184-92, and *Atomism in England from Hariot to Newton* (Oxford, 1966).

2. Cf. R. W. F. Kroll, "The Question of Locke's Relation to Gassendi," *JHI,* 45 (1984), 346-52. Gassendi's 1658 edition of his *Philosophiae epicuri syntagma* was reprinted from his earlier *Animadversiones in decimum librum Diogenis Laertii* of 1649, which was in turn derived from his *De vita et doctrina epicuri,* composed between 1633 and 1645. All subsequent citations to Gassendi's *Philosophiae epicuri syntagma* will be to the 1658 Lyon edition, abbreviated as *ES.* Cf. H. Jones *Pierre Gassendi's Institutio Logica* (Assen, 1981), vii-lxviii; also B. Rochot, *Les Travaux de Gassendi sur Épicure et sur l'atomisme 1619-1658* (Paris, 1944).

3. See Stanley's reference to Gassendi in his marginal note (a) in Part XIII, Chapter 2, Canon 1 of his *History of Philosophy* (London, 1701), 549. This will be the edition I shall be citing from, subsequently abbreviated as *HP.* Stanley's section on Epicurus was first published as the third volume of his *History,* in 1660.

4. This is a correction of an unfortunate error in C. B. Brush's translation in *The Selected Works of Pierre Gassendi* (New York, 1972), 317. The reference is to Gassendi *Syntagma philosophicum, De logicae fine (liber alter)* (Lyon, 1658), 76 (ch. 4), abbreviated as *SP.*

5. *SP,* 52, cf. *ES,* 1-2.

6. Cf. Diogenes Laertius [D.L.], X, 31.

7. See, for example, sections 38, 55, and 82 of the *Letter to Herodotus* as well as *R.S.,* XXIV, preserved in section 147 of D.L., X.

8. D.L., X, 72.

9. D.L., X, 123-24, discussed at length in Cicero, *De natura deorum,* I.

10. Cf. Lucretius, IV, 469-521.

11. For the passages in Epicurean writings concerning the evidence of feelings see the discussion in D. K.

Glidden: "Epicurus on Self-Perception," *American Philosophical Quarterly,* 16 (1979), 297-306, and "*Sensus* and Sense-Perception in the *De rerum natura,*" *California Studies in Classical Antiquity,* 12 (1980), 155-81.

12. D.L., X, 32-34. In this context see Diogenes' explicit attribution of a twofold epistemic criterion to the Stoic Chrysippus at VII, 54: κριτηρια θησιν ειναι αισθησιν και προληψιν.

13. *Gassendi SP,* 52-56, and *ES,* 4-10. Cf. Cicero, *De natura deorum,* I, 44.

14. Cf. *SP,* 52-53, and *ES,* 5.

15. Cf. Cicero, *Academica,* II, 142, with II, 19, 79, 82, which suggests that what gives authority to Epicurean παθη and προληψεις is the general infallibility of the senses. This becomes especially clear in Sextus's presentation of Epicurean epistemology at *M,* 7, 203-16, which may have been taken from Antiochus's *Canonica,* one of Cicero's sources.

16. Most scholars accept Gassendi's interpretation of Epicurus. See, for example, A. A. Long, "Aisthesis, Prolepsis and Linguistic Theory in Epicurus," *Bulletin of the Institute of Classical Studies,* 18 (1971), 114-33; A. Manuwald, *Die Prolepsislehre Epikurs* (Bonn, 1972); G. Striker, "Kriterion tes aletheias," *Nachrichten der Akademie der Wissenschaften in Göttingen,* II (1974), 47-110; E. Asmis, *Epicurus' Scientific Method* (Ithaca, 1984), 19-80. I do not: Cf. D. K. Glidden, "Epicurean Prolepsis," *Oxford Studies in Ancient Philosophy,* 3 (1985), 175-217.

17. *SP,* 52, and D. L., X, 30-31.

18. *SP,* 52. The status of an Epicurean logic is not discussed in the earlier *ES* and consequently not translated by Stanley. Instead, *ES* simply cites the claim of Diogenes about there not being a third part of philosophy, dialectic, and leaves it at that (4), and that is what Stanley translates (548), even though Stanley follows Gassendi's presentation of Epicurean doctrine in terms of the three divisions of philosophy, treating Epicurean dialectic as a separate division.

19. D.L., VII, 39, attributes the invention of this trichotomy to the Stoic Zeno of Citium.

20. *SP,* 52-53; cf. *ES,* 4, Stanley, *HP,* 549.

21. D.L., X, 34.

22. *SP,* 52, 55; *ES,* 4, 10. See, for example, *Letter to Herodotus* at D.L., X, 37, discussed at length in *Peri physeos,* XXVIII, as well as in Lucretius, V, 1028-90. Cf. also Sextus, *M,* 8, 11-13, 258; also Plutarch, *Adv. Col.,* 1119f-20a.

23. Cf. *Letter to Herodotus* (D.L., 37) with D.L., X, 31, and Sextus, *P,* 2, 211-12.

24. *ES,* 10.

25. *Letter to Herodotus* (D.L., X, 37). Gassendi understands το πρωτον ηννοημα as a conception of our consciousness rather than an act of recognition, what the mind conceives rather than what is deposited upon it by the senses. Asmis, *op. cit.,* 19-34, largely accepts Gassendi's interpretation. But the Greek ηννοημα is a *hapax legomenon* in Epicurus and, for that matter, is found uncontestably only once in Aristotle. Yet it seems to mean the same in both authors, designating something brought to mind (i.e., noticed by the mind) as opposed to something conceived of in the mind of its own invention. So the charge to look at the principle ηννοημα in one's mind is not a request for introspection but a demanded act of attention, in this case directed at one's perception of the world, as I understand the passage. Cf. D.K. Glidden, "Epicurean Semantics," in ΣΥΖΗΤΗΣΙΣ: *Studi sull' epicureismo greco e romano offerti a Marcello Gigante* (Naples, 1983), 185-226.

26. Cf. D.L., VII, 41-44, as for example 42: και το ορικον δε ομοιγς προς επιγνγσιν της αληθειας δια γαρ τγν εννοιγν τα πραγματα λαμβανεται.

27. Stanley translation (*HP,* 549) of *ES,* 5.

28. *Ibid.*

29. Epicurus's technical term for this direct mental perception was επιβολη της διανοιας, as at *Herodotus,* 38, and *R.S.* XXIV. It is discussed at length by Lucretius, IV, 722-826, 962-1010, 1030-36; Cicero, *De natura deorum,* I, 49, 75-76, 82-83, 105-114; Diogenes of Oenoanda, frg. 6, new frgs. 5-6.

30. Cf. *ES,* 4, as well as chapter xviii of part 2 (*de natura*) of his presentation, translated by Stanley in *HP,* 589-90.

31. Stanley translation (*HP,* 550) of *ES,* 5.

32. Cf. D.K. Glidden, "The Epicurean Theory of Knowledge" (Princeton Univ. Ph.D. Diss., 1971); G. Striker, "Epicurus on the Truth of Sense Impressions," *Archiv für Geschichte der Philosophie,* 59 (1977), 125-42; C. C. W. Taylor, "All Perceptions Are True," in *Doubt and Dogmatism,* ed. M. Schofield, M. Burnyeat, and J. Barnes (Oxford, 1980), 105-24.

33. Stanley translation (*HP,* 551) of *ES,* 7. Cf. Cicero, *Academica,* II, 7.19.

34. Stanley translation (*HP,* 552) of *ES,* 8.

35. D.L., VII, 52-53. Cf. Cicero, *Academica,* II, 30, *De finibus,* III, 33; Sextus, *M,* 9.393, 11.250.

36. Cf. Lucretius, IV, 739-44, quoted by Gassendi in *ES* and translated by Stanley, *HP,* 589.

37. Cf. M. Frede, "Stoics and Skeptics on Clear and Distinct Impressions," in *The Skeptical Tradition,* ed. M. Burnyeat (Berkeley, 1983), 65-94.

38. Cf. Lucretius, IV, 962-1036.

39. D.L., X, 32: The sentence referring to the construction of Epicurean επινοιαι may even be an interpolation, since it interrupts the flow of argument which resumes with the ensuing sentence.

40. Asmis's account, *op. cit.* 19-80, is compatible with my own account on this point: cf. "Epicurean Prolepsis," cited in n. 16 above.

41. D.L., X, 33, although the value of this testimony is somewhat tainted by Diogenes's use of a string of well-known Stoic expressions with which to describe the Epicurean doctrine further. This particular phrase also has a long history, going back to ancient medicine and Aristotle.

42. Stanley translation (*HP,* 553) of *ES,* 8.

43. *Ibid.*

44. Stanley translation (*HP,* 553) of *ES,* 9.

45. *Ibid.*

46. Gassendi, *Institutio logica* (*IS*) Part 1, 3, from the Jones 1981 edition, cited in note 2 above, with some changes, from Jones's translation.

47. *Ibid.,* 3-4.

48. *Loc. cit.*

49. *Ibid.,* 4.

50. *Loc. cit.*

51. *Ibid.,* 5.

52. Cf. O. R. Bloch, *La Philosophie de Gassendi: Nominalisme, matérialisme et métaphysique* (The Hague, 1971), 7-29, 77-147; F. Duchesneau, *L'Empirisme de Locke* (The Hague, 1973), 92-119. I find it more illuminating to compare Gassendi's theory of Ideas with the Hellenistic debates between the Skeptics and the Stoics. That debate was never a phenomenalist one, and it is the one Gassendi studied closely. Cf. L. S. Joy, *Gassendi the Atomist* (Cambridge, 1987), 165-74.

53. *IS,* 4-20.

54. *Ibid.,* 4.

55. *Ibid.,* 6.

56. *Ibid.,* 11-12.

57. *Ibid.,* 12.

58. *Ibid.,* 6.

59. *Ibid.,* 6-7, 10-11.

60. *Ibid.,* 10-11.

61. *Ibid.,* 6-11.

62. *Ibid.,* 6, 12.

63. *Ibid.,* 15-16.

64. *Ibid.,* 18-19.

65. *Ibid.,* 7-9, 16-19.

66. *Ibid.,* 12-14.

67. See, for example, M. Boas, "The Establishment of the Mechanical Philosophy," *Osiris,* 10 (1953), 413-541.

Fred S. and Emily Michael (essay date 1990)

SOURCE: "The Theory of Ideas in Gassendi and Locke," in *Journal of the History of Ideas,* Vol. LI, No. 3, July-Sept., 1990, pp. 379-99.

[In this essay, the Michaels argue strongly for Gassendi's considerable influence on John Locke, discussing possible sources for Locke's knowledge of Gassendi and comparing passages from Gassendi's Syntagma Philosophicum *and* Exercitationes Paradoxicae adversus Aristoteleos *with Locke's* Essays on the Law of Nature *and* Essay Concerning Human Understanding.*]*

There has recently been controversy over whether Gassendi should be considered the source of modern empiricism.[1] Present day interest in Gassendi's influence on Locke perhaps dates from the observation of R. I. Aaron in his book on Locke, first published in 1937, that "The influence of Gassendi upon Locke, and indeed, upon English thought in general at this period has been strangely neglected."[2] David Fate Norton in his paper "The Myth of 'British Empiricism'" goes substantially further than Aaron, asserting not only that Gassendi influenced Locke but that Gassendi, not Locke, is the founder of modern empiricism.[3] Richard Kroll questions the grounds for Norton's claim but concludes that there is evidence supporting an influence of Gassendi upon Locke.[4]

While Locke did have contact with Gassendists in France, notably François Bernier, and owned a copy of Bernier's *Abregé de la Philosophie de Gassendi,* Kroll denies that this could be the source of Gassendist influence on Locke's essay; for as Kroll points out, much of the substance of Locke's *Essay* was in draft form in 1671. At this time Locke had not met Bernier and Bernier had not yet published his translation of Gassendi.[5] The source of Gassendist influence on the early drafts of Locke's *Essay,* Kroll suggests, is the translation of Gassendi's **Philosophiae Epicuri Syntagma** published in Thomas Stanley's *The History of Philosophy,* a work found in Locke's library.[6]

Kroll criticizes Norton for making use of a somewhat ahistorical "morphological" method, relying mainly on internal evidence, evidence of similarities in doctrine between Gassendi and Locke, to support the view that Gassendi influenced Locke.[7] It does not follow from the fact that certain of Locke's views are similar to views of Gassendi, Kroll argues, that Locke's views derive from Gassendi: there might have been other sources for these views. As far as we can make out, this is Kroll's only justification for doubting the value of morphological evidence. Kroll appears to agree with Yolton that Locke was indebted to a variety of sources. As Yolton says: "It would be difficult to say where . . . are the direct influences on Locke's *Essay Concerning Human Understanding;* but it is easy to find in Descartes, Malebranche, the logicians of the Port Royal school, Gassendi, Boyle, and Burthogge, and many lesser men in seventeenth-century England almost all of the important epistemological principles later worked into the fabric of Locke's book."[8] But the possible sources are far fewer if we restrict our attention to those works which could have influenced the two 1671 drafts of the *Essay;* apart from the unspecified "lesser men," there remain only Descartes, the Port Royal logicians, Boyle, and Gassendi. Of these, Boyle and the Port Royal Logicians are among the sources from which Locke could have obtained an indirect knowledge of Gassendist views; they are not sources of Locke's early views in their own right.

While Boyle was an experimentalist of genius, he was no innovator in epistemology, and epistemology was not one of his major concerns. Also, while he acknowledges a debt to Descartes as well as Gassendi in physics, in epistemological doctrine he is far closer to Gassendi than to Descartes. What we find of empiricist epistemological doctrine in Boyle is very likely to have come from Gassendi.[9] With the Port Royal Logicians the situation is reversed. They follow Descartes on the whole and are hostile to Gassendi. Yet the authors of the Port Royal Logic had Gassendi very much in mind. In many respects, Gassendi's *Institutio Logica* was a model for the Port Royal Logic, and it appears to be the only epistemologically based logic prior to the Port Royal Logic. It is the first logic in the four parts made standard by the Port Royal Logic: the first part is concerned with ideas, the second with judgment, the third with reasoning, and the fourth with order. Even the title of the Port Royal Logic, *L'Art de Penser,* which in Latin is *Ars Cogitandi,* appears to derive from Gassendi's Logic. In the preface to his Logic Gassendi defines logic as *ars bene cogitandi,* the art of thinking well. The Port Royal Logic objects to this definition on the grounds that it takes no art to think poorly and defines logic as the art of thinking; from this definition the Port Royal Logic gets its title. But if Gassendi's Logic and the Port Royal Logic are similar in structure and approach, they are rivals in doctrine. The authors of the Port Royal Logic are rarely in agreement with Gassendi on epistemological doctrine, but they do present the main principles of Gassendi's empiricist epistemology, if only to identify them as dangerous, even ridiculous errors which should carefully be avoided. Owing to its phenomenal success, the Port Royal Logic may have been—rather ironically, in view of the hostility of the authors of the Port Royal Logic to Gassendi—the most long-lived source of information about Gassendi's views.[10] At any rate the empiricist doctrine presented but not endorsed in the Port Royal Logic and the empiricist epistemology implicit in Boyle's work do seem, for the most part, to have been derived from Gassendi.

Only two of the figures identified in Yolton's list, then, could be ultimate sources of the early drafts of Locke's Essay: Descartes and Gassendi. Under these circumstances, morphological evidence supporting the influence of Gas-

sendi on the early drafts of Locke's *Essay* seems far more significant than Kroll appears to recognize.

Yet Kroll is quite correct in his belief that the evidence Norton cites in order to show Gassendi's influence on Locke is far from conclusive. Of the three features common to Locke and Gassendi mentioned by Norton, antidogmatism, the view that all knowledge has its origin in sensation, and the view that we have no knowledge of the real essence of things,[11] Locke could have derived at least the first two from many sources other than Gassendi. But it is probably a mistake to see the brief account in Norton's paper of what is known of Gassendi and of his relationship to Locke as anything more than an attempt to draw attention to an unduly neglected figure; and Norton's statement that Gassendi was the founder of modern empiricism seems most suitably taken not as something Norton thinks he has established but as something which, in Norton's view, those familiar with Gassendi's work can see to be true. To see if he is right, we have to look not at what Norton says of Gassendi but at what Gassendi himself says. We will try in this paper to show that Norton's claim is correct: Gassendi had a significant influence upon Locke; and Gassendi, not Locke, was the founder of modern empiricism.

Kroll's account is valuable in its attempt to pursue Aaron's suggestion of a Gassendist influence on the early drafts of the *Essay.* This is important in implying that Locke knew Gassendi's views much earlier than has generally been conceded. Apart from this historical point, if we pay special attention to the early drafts of the *Essay,* we simplify the problem of tracing the influence of Gassendi upon Locke for two reasons. First, it is reasonable to expect these drafts to be relatively derivative; for at the time Locke wrote them, he tells us, he had not thought much about epistemological questions. Second, since there were not many sources from which Locke could have acquired a knowledge of epistemological doctrine at the time he was writing the early drafts, the influences on these drafts should be relatively easy to detect. There are, however, problems with Kroll's suggestion that Gassendi's *Epicurean Syntagma,* as translated by Stanley, was the source of Locke's knowledge of Gassendi.

First, the edition of Stanley's *History* in Locke's library was published in 1687.[12] Kroll thinks it likely that Locke had read the first edition of this work by 1671. This is certainly possible, but it is no less possible that Locke had read the *Epicurean Syntagma* in the original Latin. Kroll doubts this on the grounds that Stanley's translation appeared only a year after the publication of the original and that the Latin of the original is "proverbially tortuous." Now as a matter of fact Kroll is mistaken in believing that the *Epicurean Syntagma* first appears in Gassendi's complete works published in 1658. It was first published in 1649 as an appendix to the second part of Gassendi's mammoth *Animadversiones in Decimum Librum Diogenis Laertii.*[13] At any rate, all that is at issue is whether Locke had read the work by .1671 and whether, by that date, he could have read it in the original Latin or in Stanley's translation. In fact a knowledge of the Epicurean canons which Kroll contends influenced Locke need not even have come from the *Epicurean Syntagma*; much the same text is also found in the survey of the history of logic beginning Gassendi's massive *Syntagma Philosophicum* in a section surveying the logic of Epicurus,[14] and its doctrine is worked into the body of the *Institutio Logica,* the final segment of the logic of the *Syntagma Philosophicum.* Finally, that the difficulty of the Latin of the *Epicurean Syntagma* would be enough to deter a seventeenth century thinker literate in Latin, as Locke certainly was, seems hardly conceivable.[15] We may conclude that Kroll gives us no reason to believe that Locke's knowledge of Gassendi came from Stanley's translation of the *Epicurean Syntagma.*

The more basic question, however, is whether Kroll provides evidence that Locke was familiar with the epistemological doctrines of the *Epicurean Syntagma,* and to this question the answer seems to be yes. Does this establish that Gassendi had an influence on Locke? Unfortunately, not. This is because of a second, more serious, problem with Kroll's account: the *Epicurean Syntagma* contains the views not of Gassendi but of Epicurus.[16] Stanley's *The History of Philosophy* deals only with the sects of ancient philosophy, and Gassendi's *Epicurean Syntagma* is included just because it is an accurate account of the philosophy of Epicurus.[17] The *Syntagma* is a handbook of the philosophy of Epicurus as reconstructed by Gassendi. Gassendi's own views diverge in various ways from the views of Epicurus expounded in his handbook. Now the canons of sense which Kroll believes influenced Locke are Epicurean. To be sure, Gassendi does accept these and in fact builds upon them. But if this were the limit of Gassendi's influence on Locke, then it would be more accurate to describe Epicurus rather than Gassendi as a significant influence on Locke's epistemology. Kroll provides us with morphological evidence indicating the influence of Epicurean doctrine on Locke's early epistemology. We have no wish to dispute the value of this; it is certainly of interest. The problem is that it establishes nothing about the influence of Gassendi's own views on Locke. If we wish to investigate this influence, we must look beyond the *Epicurean Syntagma.*

The principle source of evidence of Locke's knowledge of Gassendi is Locke's notebooks. Gassendi appears to be mentioned explicitly only once in the whole of Locke's published writings, in Locke's Third Letter to Stillingfleet, and we are aware of no references to Gassendi in Locke's correspondence. But it was not Locke's practice to acknowledge sources; like many others in the late seventeenth century, Locke gives few explicit indications of where his intellectual debts lie. In Locke's library there were two books of Gassendi, Bernier's *Abregé* and Gassendi's *Life of Peiresc,* while Gassendi's objections to Descartes's *Meditations* are to be found in the copy of the *Opera Philosophica* of Descartes owned by Locke;[18] but neither these nor any other works of Gassendi are in the list Locke made in 1681 of the books he had at Oxford. To put this in perspective, only one work of Descartes is on this list, a volume of Descartes's letters.[19] On the whole, what we know of Locke's library in 1681, the earliest date for which there is any list at all, tells us little about Locke's philosophical background. Locke's notebooks however are much more revealing. From time to time in the notebooks of the Lovelace Collection, according to Aaron, Locke quotes Gassendi's opinion of various other thinkers.[20] Von Leyden informs us that there are quotations from Gassendi's *Life of Peiresc* in Locke's notebook of 1664-66, and from the physics of the *Syntagma Philosophicum* in the notebook of 1667.[21] Cranston claims that Locke had read Gassendi's *Disquisitio Metaphysica,* which contains a lengthy elaboration of Gassendi's objections to Descartes,[22] presumably, Locke's notebooks are Cranston's source. Most interesting are the reports of Antoine Adam and Olivier Bloch: Adam tells us that in Locke's *Medical Commonplace Book,* where Locke indicates what he studied during 1659-60, there are notes on Gassendi,[23] while Bloch has found in Locke's *Medical Commonplace Book,* for the years 1659-66, an extract on *place* from the Physics of Gassendi's *Syntagma Philosophicum.*[24] Now the *Syntagma Philosophicum* was available only in the six volumes of Gassendi's *Opera omnia,* published in 1658, suggesting that at a very early period, Locke had some familiarity with the contents of these volumes. Other indications that Locke was familiar with Gassendi's views at an early date are provided by Locke's close association during the 1660s with Boyle and by the fact that during the 1660s Gassendi's influence was at its height. Such are the grounds we have for believing that Locke had an early knowledge of some of Gassendi's views.

There may be very early indications of influence by Gassendi on Locke's epistemological views in Locke's *Essays on the Law of Nature* of 1664. In the fourth essay we find:

> . . . [O]nly these two faculties [reason and sense-perception] appear to teach and educate the minds of men and to provide what is characteristic of the light of nature, namely that things otherwise wholly unknown and hidden in darkness should be able to come before the mind. . . . As long as these two faculties serve one another, sensation furnishing reason with the ideas of particular sense-objects and supplying the subject-matter of discourse, reason on the other hand guiding the faculty of sense and arranging together the images of things derived from sense perceptions, thence forming others and composing new ones, there is nothing so obscure, so concealed, so removed from any meaning that the mind, capable of everything, could not apprehend it by reflection and reasoning. . . . But if you take away one of the two, the other is certainly of no avail, for without reason, though actuated by our senses, we scarce rise to the standard of nature found in beasts. . . . On the other hand, without the help and assistance of the senses, reason can achieve nothing more than a labourer can working in darkness behind shuttered windows . . . reason is here taken to mean the discursive faculty of the mind, which advances from things known

to things unknown and argues from one thing to an-other in a definite and fixed order of propositions.[25]

Von Leyden attributes this passage to the influence of Culverwell.[26] While Von Leyden does acknowledge that Gassendi had a significant influence on Locke, he does not think that this influence can be found as early as 1664. In the passage from Culverwell's *Discourse of the Light of Nature,* to which Von Leyden refers us, Culverwell writes:

> He [Aristotle] shows you . . . an *abrasa tabula,* a vir-gin soul espousing itself to the body, in a most entire, affectionate, and conjugal union, and by the blessing of heaven upon this loving pair, he did not doubt of a no-tional offspring and posterity; this makes him set open the windows of sense to welcome and entertain the first dawnings, the early glimmerings of morning light. . . . Many sparks and appearances fly from variety of ob-jects to the understanding; The mind . . . catches them all and cherishes them and blows them; and thus the candle of knowledge is lighted. As he [Aristotle] could perceive no connate colours, no pictures or portraitures in his external eye: so neither could he find any signa-tures in his mind till some outward objects had made some impression upon . . . his soft and pliable under-standing impartially prepared for every seal. . . . The mind . . . doth strongly evince that the true rise of knowledge is from the observing and comparing of ob-jects, and from thence extracting the quintessence of some such principles as are worthy of all acceptation; that have so much of certainty in them that they are near to a tautology and identity, for this first principles are.[27]

There is in Culverwell's account of Aristotle's position the same implied empiricism as in the passages from Locke, and both Culverwell and Locke use the metaphor of the "windows of sense." But the passage from Locke concerns chiefly the cooperation of sense and reason, and reason is characterized by Locke as a power by which what is not known by sense is inferred from what is. None of this is found in Culverwell, but it is found in Gassendi. In his *Institutio Logica,* Part IV, Canon IV, Gassendi writes:

> *The Method of Judgment involves the use of a double criterion or instrument of assessment, the senses and reason.*
>
> Since all things are either presented directly to the senses or are perceived by reason alone (remembering, of course, that in every case it is the senses which ulti-mately provide the material . . . , whenever there is a question about something which can be verified by the senses . . . we must refer the matter to the senses and rely upon the evidence which they supply. . . .
>
> When the question concerns a matter which can be re-solved by the understanding alone, then we are re-quired to refer to reason, which has the power to infer from something perceived by the senses some further thing which the senses do not perceive; for example, *"whether or not there are pores in the skin."* That pores do, in fact, exist (however much they may escape the senses) is proved from the consideration that if they did not, there would be no possibility for the sweat

which we perceive on the outer surface of the skin to have made its way there from the inside. Similarly, on the question *"whether there is a void,"* Epicurus infers that there is from the consideration that if there were no void there would be no motion, which the senses do, in fact, perceive.[28]

The evident similarity of this with the passage from Locke's *Essays on the Law of Nature* gives us some rea-son to believe that Gassendi's views had an early influ-ence upon Locke.

In considering the extent to which Gassendi's influence is perceptible in Locke's epistemology, we will restrict our attention to works of Gassendi that have significant episte-mological content. Of these works we may exclude the **Epicurean Syntagma,** as it contains the views of Epicu-rus, not Gassendi. If we concentrate on the content and not on the structure of the **Animadversiones,** it is basically an early version of the **Syntagma Philosophicum** and so need not be given independent consideration. Gassendi's basic epistemological principles can be found in his anti-Cartesian **Disquisitio Metaphysica,** but this work contains no organized presentation of Gassendi's epistemology. Gassendi's purpose in this work was to show what is wrong with the views of Descartes, not to elaborate his own views. For an organized presentation of Gassendi's own epistemological views, we must look elsewhere. Kroll rejects the view that Gassendi's anti-Aristotelian work, the **Exercitationes paradoxicae adversus Aristoteleos,** was in-fluential on Locke, on the grounds that "by the mid-seventeenth century, attacks on Aristotle were entirely commonplace."[29] But not all attacks on Aristotle are alike, and there are distinctive features of Gassendi's critique also found in Locke. Consider, for instance, the views of Gassendi and Locke with respect to scientific knowledge conceived as Aristotle conceives it, as a knowledge of real essences, real forms, real differences.

With respect to real essences there are, Locke says in the *Essay,* two opinions:

> The one is of those who, using the word essence for they know not what, suppose a certain number of those essences, according to which all natural things are made, and wherein they do exactly every one of them partake, and so become of this or that species. The other and more rational opinion is of those who look upon all natural things to have a real, but unknown, constitution of their insensible parts; from which flow those sensible qualities which serve us to distinguish them one from another, according as we have occasion to rank them into sorts, under common denominations (*Essay,* III.III.17).

It is plain that Locke already accepted the second view in 1671, when he wrote, in Draft B of the *Essay,*[30] that the opinion that "the specific constitution and difference of things have depended on a *form*" impedes "a laborious and exact scrutiny into the nature of things, and a search-ing out of all their qualities and properties" (Section 72). Such a form, Locke asserts, can be known only by its sensible properties, "by the sensible simple ideas that are supposed to flow from it" (Section 72). Also: " . . . [M]en have been taught that the several species of things have had distinct essences, the knowledge of which was necessary for the clear knowledge of this or that species. And so men have been led into a fruitless enquiry after the essences of things thereby to find their distinct species" (Section 73).

In the second book of the **Exercitationes** Gassendi argues similarly that an ontology of matter, form, and privation tells us nothing about the essence of even the least of natural things, such as a flea. To know the essence of a flea, it is not enough to know that it is composed of matter and form; we must be able to answer questions such as

> . . . just what sort of matter this was, what dispositions it required to receive that form, for what reason it was distributed so that this part of it went into the proboscis, that part into its feet, another into its hair and scales, and the others into the remainder of its body, what was the active force and how was it brought to bear when it formed both the entire body and its very different parts in this order, this shape, this texture, this size, this colour.

> Again, just what would the nature of this form be, what its origin, by what force is it stimulated to action, how is its perceptive and sentient faculty forged, how does it penetrate such tiny body tissues, which of the organs does it use, how does it make use of such organs By what power does the flea bite you so sharply to ingest his nourishment from you, how does he digest it and assimilate part of it in various passages, and transform part of it into spirits which conserve him and impart life to his entire body, and eliminate its superfluous parts through his different winding intestines? Where does the power to jump so swiftly dwell in him? . . . What does he think when he does not want to be caught? What qualities result from that form deep within him and how? When his little body is crushed, what becomes of that form? And a hundred other questions like that.[31]

It is plain from this that in the **Exercitationes** Gassendi maintains, like Locke, the second, "more rational" opinion about real essences; and he seems to have been the first in the seventeenth century to take this position. But the **Exercitationes,** although it may be the source of Locke's position on real essences, does not seem otherwise to be an important source of Locke's views.

That leaves the **Syntagma Philosophicum.** Epistemological matters are dealt with in two parts of this work: in the **Institutio Logica,** particularly the first part, and in that part of the *Physics* concerned with animal functions. In the latter Gassendi develops a faculty psychology, a psychology in which there is a hierarchical arrangement of the powers of the soul: sensation, imagination and intellection. At the lowest level is sensation, by means of which the soul is aware of the external world; above this is the imagination, which, among other functions, serves as the common sense and which acts on and judges data derived

from sensation; at the summit is the intellect, which in turn acts upon and judges the products of imaginative activity. While the senses and the imagination operate through organs of the body, the intellect, Gassendi argues, carries out functions (e.g., reflection upon itself and formation of universal concepts) which no corporeal organ can perform; it is immaterial and, consequently, immortal.

Concerning matters such as these, Locke remarks:

> I shall not at present meddle with the physical consideration of the mind; or trouble myself to examine wherein its essence consists; or by what motions of our spirits or alterations of our bodies we come to have any *sensation* by our organs, or any *ideas* in our understandings; and whether these ideas do in their formation, any or all of them, depend on matter or not. These are speculations which, however curious and entertaining, I shall decline as lying out of my way in the design I am now upon. It shall suffice to my present purpose, to consider the discerning faculties of a man, as they are employed about the objects which they have to do with (*Essay,* Introduction; Draft B, section 2).

Those who engage in speculations about the nature of the soul and so on, Voltaire says, write the romance of the soul; Locke gives its history.[32] Was this the way Locke saw the matter? Did he consider questions such as those about the nature of the mind as illegitimate in some way or as too speculative? Locke says no such thing, only that questions such as these are outside the scope of his project. What did he consider his project to be? In the last chapter of the *Essay* Locke makes clear that he considers the *Essay* to be a work in semiotic or logic. It is true that there are logics in which questions such as those about nature of the mind, about how we acquire ideas and the like, are considered; the *Port Royal Logic* is an example. But certainly Gassendi did not consider such questions as proper to logic. Gassendi praises Ramus's logic chiefly because it is pure logic; it contains nothing but logic.[33] Questions of the sort Locke declines to consider are no more discussed by Gassendi in his **Institutio Logica** than by Locke in his *Essay.* They are considered both by Gassendi and by Locke to be questions of physics. It is in the Physics of the **Syntagma** that questions about the nature of the mind are discussed, and properly so, according to Locke, who characterizes physics as:

> The knowledge of things as they are in their own proper beings, then constitution, properties, and operations; whereby I mean not only matter and body, but spirits also, which have their proper natures, constitutions, and operations, as well as bodies. . . . The end of this is bare speculative truth: and whatsoever can afford the mind of man any such falls under this branch, whether it be God himself, angels, spirits, bodies; or any of their affections, as number and figure, etc. (*Essay,* IV.XXI.2).

Locke is in effect following Gassendi's practice in not considering questions about the nature of the mind and how it relates to the body in the *Essay* or the early drafts.

Now if Locke saw the *Essay* and the early drafts of it as logic, then its antecedents are likely to be other works in logic, at any rate logic as seen by Locke. Most works in logic prior to 1671 were Aristotelian or Ramist or involved some compromise between the two approaches. Locke's epistemological writings have little in common with any of these. Aside from these, the most notable works in logic were Gassendi's *Institutio Logica* and the *Port Royal Logic*. Gassendi's *Institutio Logica* contains the first systematic treatment of the modern theory of ideas. While Descartes certainly preceded Gassendi in his treatment of ideas, he did not treat them in a systematic manner; for him, they were only of incidental interst, not of concern for their own sake. Gassendi's treatment of ideas was quickly followed by that in the *Port Royal Logic*. The Port Royal theory of ideas is a systemization of the Cartesian theory and is embedded in a Cartesian conception of the nature of the mind and of mental operations. The Gassendist and Cartesian approaches to the theory of ideas were on the whole rivals, and it will be seen that, in this rivalry, Locke was firmly on the Gassendist side. Referring the reader to Gassendi's *Institutio Logica,* Aaron remarks: "The measure of Locke's debt to Gassendi will probably surprise him."[34] In order to determine the extent of this debt, we must examine in some detail the theory of ideas in the first part of the *Institutio Logica.*

Kroll suggests that an important influence on Locke's epistemology was the Canonic of Gassendi's *Epicurean Syntagma.* Now as has already been mentioned, the canons of the *Epicurean Syntagma* represent the views not of Gassendi himself but of Epicurus as formulated by Gassendi. Nonetheless, Gassendi does accept them at least in spirit, and their influence is unmistakably reflected in the *Institutio Logica.* These canons are the principle source of Gassendi's empiricist epistemology. In the Epicurean Canonic there are two groups of epistemological canons, the canons of sense and the canons of the *anticipatio.*[35] There are four canons of sense: (1) Sense is never mistaken; and therefore every sensation and every perception of a phantasy or appearance is true. (2) Opinion follows from sense, and is something added to sense, capable of truth and falsity. (3) That opinion is true which is supported, or not opposed, by the evidence of sense. (4) That opinion is false which is opposed, or not supported, by the evidence of sense. Canons 3 and 4 are intended to provide not a definition of truth, which for Gassendi is correspondence, but a criterion of truth. A more precise formulation of the intent of Canon 3 might be: that opinion is true which the evidence of sense supports either directly (e.g., that sugar is soluble in water) or indirectly (e.g., that there are pores in the skin, that there are atoms). Canon 4 can be similarly reformulated. Correspondence with sense is then, according to Canon 3, the criterion of truth. Gassendi's own view is slightly different. For him, the criterion of truth is correspondence with sense assisted by reason.

In addition to the canons of sense, there are, in the Epicurean canonic, four canons of the *anticipatio:* (1) Every anticipation or prenotion in the mind depends on the senses and does this by incursion, proportion, similitude, or composition. (2) The anticipation is the very notion or definition of a thing, without which we may not enquire about, doubt, believe, nor even name anything. (3) Anticipation is what is basic in all reasoning, as that which we consider when we infer that one thing is the same as another or different, conjoined with another or disjoined from it. (4) From the anticipation of that which is evident, that which is not evident ought to be demonstrated. We have already encountered the fourth of these canons in our consideration of the *Institutio Logica,* Part IV, Canon 4, concerned with the cooperation of the senses and reason, where reason is said to be the power to demonstrate, from something evident, something which is not. The remaining these canons of the *anticipatio* form the basis of the theory of ideas in the *Institutio Logica,* Part I.

Part I of the *Institutio Logica* is called "Of the Simple Imagination of Things" and is concerned with the simple apprehension of things (apprehension of things without affirming or denying anything of them) by means of images.[36] These Gassendi calls ideas, he tells us, because "idea" had become a familiar term. Ideas, for Gassendi, then are just images. Part I of the *Institutio Logica* is Gassendi's theory of ideas and consists of eighteen canons, which can conveniently be divided into five groups. The canons of the first group are the most important.

The first canon asserts that the simple imagination of a thing is the same as the idea we have of it. A clear and distinct idea Gassendi describes as a strong and vivacious image, such as we have of a man we have seen often and recently, and to whom we have paid particular attention as compared with the image of a man we have seen once only, in passing. This makes it plain that clearness and distinctness is not for Gassendi, as it is for Cartesians, a criterion of truth. An idea or image which is clear and distinct simply is one likely to represent its object more adequately than one which is not.

The second canon, which can be seen to derive from the first canon of the anticipatio, formulates a fundamental empiricist principle: Every idea in the mind derives its origin from the senses. Gassendi elaborates as follows:

> This indeed is the reason why a man born blind has no idea of colour. He lacks the sense of vision by which he might obtain it. It is also why a man born deaf has no idea of sound, for he is without the sense of hearing, the power by which he might acquire it. So therefore, supposing this were possible, a man who lived without any senses . . . would have no idea of anything and therefore would imagine nothing.

It is this then that the celebrated saying, *There is nothing in the intellect which was not first in sense,* means. This is also what is meant by the claim that the intellect, or mind, is a *tabula rasa,* on which nothing has been engraved or depicted.[37]

Gassendi then holds that mind is a *tabula rasa*. This was a commonly held view, as Gassendi points out; but though not original, the argument he uses to support it appears to be.

Concerning innate ideas, Gassendi remarks only that those who say that there are ideas that are naturally imprinted, or innate, not acquired by sense, do not prove this claim.

For further discussion of whether there are innate ideas or principles innately known to be true, we must consult other works of Gassendi. In the *Disquisitio Metaphysica,* Gassendi tries to show that ideas claimed by Descartes to be innate (e.g., the idea of "thing") could not have been acquired without the assistance of sensation.[38] In the chapter on the intellect in the *Physics* of the *Syntagma* Gassendi argues that not even first principles are known innately to be true; we discover the truth of even the most general and indubitable principles, such as *the whole is greater than the part,* by induction from experience. His argument is as follows: "When we first hear this principle and understand what "whole," "part," and "greater than" mean, there occur to us instantaneously, as it were, several examples of this sort, the house is greater than the roof, the man than his head, the tree than the branch, the book than the page; and at once it comes into the mind confusedly that all that we ever have seen, or ever could see, is like this, as a result of which without delay we admit the principle to be true."[39] This argument is given in the *Port Royal Logic* (Part IV, Chapter VI), where it is said to be as false as the doctrine that all of our knowledge comes from the senses. But although it is quite clear that Gassendi rejects innate ideas, there is nowhere in Gassendi's work a polemic against innate ideas like that in Book I of Locke's *Essay.*

The third canon of *Institutio Logica,* I, asserts that every idea either passes through sense or is formed from those which pass through sense. In addition to the ideas we have of the things we sense, as in the first canon of the *Anticipatio,* there are said to be ideas formed by increase and diminution, as when from the idea of a person of normal size, we form the idea of a pygmy or giant; by composition, as when from the ideas of gold and a mountain we form the idea of a golden mountain; and by comparison or analogy, as when by analogy with a city we have seen we form the idea of one we have not. Ideas of incorporeals, such as God, according to Gassendi, are always analogical. Thus we form the idea of God from the image of some such thing as a grand old man or a blinding light.

There now follow a group of three canons concerned with the formation of general ideas. Everything that exists and all that we sense is singular, Gassendi holds; it is the mind which out of similar singular ideas forms general ones (Canon IV). The mind can form general ideas in two ways. One way is by joining similar singular ideas together and forming the idea of the collection to which each of these singular ideas belong. Thus, from the ideas of Socrates, Plato, Aristotle, and like individuals, we can form the idea,

"man," a general or universal idea, since it applies to all of the individuals in the collection. The second way is by abstraction, by which we determine what features a group of similar singular ideas have in common and, disregarding differences between them, form a separate idea of the common features. This idea is general, since it represents the features which a group of singular ideas share. Thus, when the mind notes that ideas such as those of Socrates, Plato, and Aristotle have in common that they all represent two-legged animals with head erect, capable of reason, laughter, discipline, and so forth, it forms the idea of a creature with these features, disregarding features which do not apply to all, such as that one (Socrates) is the son of Sophroniscus, while another (Plato) is the son of Ariston, that one is tall, another short; the idea of a creature with the common features is the general idea of man, obtained by abstraction. Irrational animals, Gassendi believes, can form ideas of collections of things; they cannot, however, form general ideas by abstraction.

By collection and abstraction from general ideas, ideas more general are formed (Canon V). By joining together the collections (or general ideas) of men, lions, goats, and so on, we get the collection (or idea), "animals." Joining this to the collection, "plants," gives the more general collection, "living things," to which (if we add the collection "inanimate things") we get the still more general collection, "corporeal things." Adding to this "incorporeal things" gives "substances," which (when attributes" is added) gives the most general collection, "beings."

By abstraction, once we have determined the features common to "man," to "lion," and so forth, noting that "man," "lion," and the other animals have in common that all are animate creatures that have the power of sensation, we obtain the general idea, "animal." Animals and plants are alike animate bodies, and so we get the general idea of living beings. Living beings and non-living beings are both bodily; abstracting this feature gives us the notion of corporeal substance. Continuing this process of abstraction, we can form the idea of substance and finally of being. A classification scheme, such as the Tree of Porphyry, which arranges ideas in a sequence from the most specific to the most general, is useful (Canon VI), since it helps us learn to classify things, to form clear ideas of things, and to gain clarity in definition, division, and description.

That there are two ways of forming general ideas, by collection and abstraction, implies, although Gassendi does not say this explicitly, that general ideas have a double signification. A general idea signifies the collection of objects represented by the idea and also the collection of all the properties these objects have in common, considered in abstraction; the former comes to be called in the *Port Royal Logic* (Part I, Chapter VI) the extension, the latter the comprehension of ideas or terms. Although the *Port Royal Logic* is generally credited with introducing the distinction between extension and comprehension, it is quite clearly implied in what Gassendi says about the two ways of forming general ideas.

After this is a set of four canons concerned with the perfection of ideas. A singular idea is said to be the more perfect, the more parts of a thing, and the more of its attributes the idea represents (Canon VII). The sciences, since they reveal to us attributes of a thing about which we would otherwise be unaware, enable us to have more perfect ideas of them. A general idea is more perfect the more it is complete and the more purely it represents what singulars have in common (Canon VIII). A general idea obtained by collection is the more perfect, the more members of the collection we know. A general idea obtained by abstraction is perfect to the extent that its features are shared by the individuals it represents. Gassendi adds: "It is truly difficult, not to say impossible, so purely to imagine man in common, that he is not large, small nor of moderate size; that he is not old, young, nor of an age in between; that he is not white, black, nor of some other particular colour: but one should at least keep it in mind that the man we wish considered generally, ought to be free of all these distinctions."[40] That is, even general ideas are singulars; but if the image of a man is used to represent man in general, it ought, as far as possible, to be that of a typical man. Finally, Gassendi claims, an idea obtained by personal experience is more perfect than one formed from somebody else's report (Canons IX and X).

The next four canons consider how we can be misled in forming ideas and how error can be avoided. The senses can deceive (Canon XI), as when a straight stick partially immersed in water appears bent. But when we are aware that some appearance may be deceptive, we can check to see if it is and so avoid being misled. We can, for example, find out if the stick immersed in water is really bent by taking it out of the water, and we can find out if something which appears to be gold really is gold by using a touchstone. We should also take care not to be mislead by temperament, state of mind, custom, or prejudice (Canon XII); by the false reports of others (Canon XIII); by ambiguous or figurative language (Canon XIV).

The last four canons of *Institutio Logica,* I, elaborate the second and third canons of the *anticipatio* and concern how definition, division, and our knowledge of relations depend upon ideas and how ideas are the basis of all we know.

The idea of a thing is what is formulated in its definition (Canon XV). We define a thing according to the idea we have of it, and the more perfectly the idea we have represents it, the more accurate our definition will be. What is defined is a species (individuals are the lowest species), and it is defined in terms of *genus* and *differentia.* The idea of a thing also brings about the division of that thing into species, parts, and attributes (Canon XVI). The more perfect the idea we have of a thing, the more perfectly the division of genus into species, whole into parts, and subject into attributes can be brought about. The idea of a thing also makes intelligible its relation to other things (Canon XVII). We can conceive a thing not just as it is in itself but in relative terms as well, as when Socrates is conceived as the son of Sophroniscus or as the wisest of men. Finally, the more things of which a person has ideas and the more perfect the ideas he has of them, the more powerful his knowledge is (Canon XVIII).

While certain similarities between this account of ideas and Locke's are easy to see, the extent to which Locke adopts Gassendi's account of ideas is not at first sight evident. The similarities between Locke and Gassendi are overshadowed by one very noticeable difference; there is no sign in the *Institutio Logica* of the most characteristic feature of Locke's account of ideas, the system of classifying ideas, found in the 1671 drafts as well as the *Essay.* But if we supplement Gassendi's account of ideas by Locke's classification, the result closely approximates the theory of ideas in the *Essay.* In fact, virtually the whole content of the account of ideas in *Institutio Logica,* I, is incorporated somewhere in Locke's *Essay* or in the early drafts.

Repeatedly, in both 1671 drafts of the Essay (Draft A and Draft B), ideas are said to be images of things (as in *Institutio Logica,* I, Canon I). But this Gassendist usage is not found in the *Essay,* where ideas are said to be perceptions, not images. Locke discusses the clearness and distinctness of ideas only in the *Essay;* his view is like that of Gassendi (Canon I). "Our simple ideas are *clear,*" Locke says, "when they are such as the objects from whence they were taken did or might, in a well ordered sensation or perception, present them." So long as they retain "their original exactness," they are clear; they are obscure when they have been "as it were, faded or tarnished, by time" (II.XXIX.2).

Locke certainly maintains that all our ideas derive from sense (as in *Institutio Logica,* I, Canon II). Gassendi's argument in favor of this is found in an expanded version in Draft B, section 66. Not only can a blind man have no idea of color and a person who has never tasted pineapple have no idea of its taste, but Locke observes, "Could we suppose a man to exist and live for sixty years without sight or feeling, he would have no other ideas of tangible qualities than he has of colours." Thus, as Gassendi maintains, an individual with no senses could have no ideas either. Much of the material of Draft B, section 66 is incorporated into the *Essay* (III.IV.11-14), but its form is so altered that its connection with Gassendi's argument is no longer recognizable. Gassendi's argument that so-called self-evident truths, such as *the whole is greater than the part,* are derived by induction from experience, is found in a qualified form in Draft A, section 11, where Locke attributes our knowledge of them to the "constant observation of our senses." "I think I may say that the whole of them and all whereby they gain such an assent (farther than those that are barely about the signification of words) is only by the testimony and assurance of our senses (and if our senses could bring but any one instance contrary to any of these axioms, the force and certainty of that axiom would presently fail)." This changes in Draft B. What was attributed in Draft A to "constant observation of our senses" is said in Draft B to be "borrowed from number, the evidence whereof, if not solely got, most satisfactorily arises from the clear and distinct notions we have of numbers, and equal or unequal in them" (section 51). In the *Essay* principles such as *the whole is greater than the part* are characterized as "bare verbal propositions" (IV.VIII.11). Knowledge does not begin with such principles but "began in the mind and was founded on particulars" (IV.XII.3).

Concerning the formation of ideas, which Gassendi says is by increase or diminution, composition, and comparison, or analogy, Locke says in Draft A that this is by "comparing, uniting, compounding, enlarging" (section 2). In Draft B the understanding is said to have the power to "join together, enlarge, compare one (idea) with another" (section 20). In the *Essay* this is simplified to comparison and composition; enlargement and diminution are understood to fall under composition (II.XI.4,6). For Locke the idea we have of God is not purely corporeal, as it is for Gassendi; but is a composition which includes such "incorporeal" ideas as "thinking, knowing, willing, existence without beginning, power of motion" (Draft A, section 2).

Locke, like Gassendi, maintains that all that exists is particular but that we can form general ideas. About the formation of general ideas, Locke says nothing in Draft A; he treats the matter implicitly in Draft B and discusses it explicitly only in the *Essay*. About Gassendi's two ways of forming general ideas, by collection and by abstraction, Locke denies that the idea of a collection is a general idea. General words, he holds "do not signify a plurality; for *man* and *men* would then signify the same" (*Essay*, III.III.12). In Locke's view there is only one way of forming general ideas, and that is by abstraction. Now, Locke's account of how ideas are formed by abstraction, is exactly like Gassendi's. To form the general idea *man,* for instance, we leave out of the ideas of particular men "that which is peculiar to each, and retain only what is common to all" (*Essay*, III.III.7; see also Draft A, section 83a). Contrast this with the account of abstraction in the *Port Royal Logic* (Part I, Chapter V), which involves no comparison of particulars but consists rather in attending to some of the attributes of a thing, disregarding others. Ascent to ideas of greater generality is explained by Locke just as Gassendi explains this; and Locke, like Gassendi, illustrates this ascent using the Tree of Porphyry (*Essay*, III.III.8 and 9; see also Draft B, section 83a, 84a). Finally, Locke maintains, just as Gassendi does, that irrational animals, although they can form ideas and even have some capacity to reason, are devoid of any power to abstract (*Essay*, II.XI.11).

Locke speaks about the perfections of ideas in Drafts A and B much as Gassendi does; in the *Essay,* however, he seems to abandon this terminology. It should be noted that Locke speaks only of the perfection of *general* ideas. For an idea to be perfect, it must be both distinct and complete. A complex idea is distinct when it contains a collection of simple ideas adequate to distinguish it from any other idea, "a collection of simple ideas as they are really and constantly in any one sort of things, and belong not to any other (sort of thing)"; a complex idea of some sort of thing is perfect if it is distinct and, further, contains a complete enumeration of "all the simple ideas which are in . . . (that) sort of things" (Draft B, sections 86a, 87a). This corresponds exactly to Canon VIII of *Institutio Logica,* I.

The problem of error and how it can be avoided is treated by Locke principally in Book IV, chapter XX of the *Essay* and foreshadowed in Draft A, section 42. Locke does not seem ever to take skeptical doubts seriously, and so there is no consideration of how sense experience may deceive us, as there is in *Institutio Logica,* I, Canon XI. The other important sources of error, considered by Gassendi in Canons XII and XIII (prejudices of various kinds, reliance on authority), are what Locke in the *Essay,* IV.XX.7, calls *wrong measures probability.* These are: (1) *Propositions that are not in themselves certain and evident but doubtful and false, taken up for principles,* (2) *Received hypotheses,* (3) *Predominant passions or inclinations,* and (4) *Authority.* Error can also arise, Gassendi holds (Canon XIV), from ambiguous or figurative language. This is considered by Locke in the *Essay,* III.IX.4 and III.X.34.

On the subject of error it should be noted that Locke holds the doctrine implied in the first two Epicurean Canons. No sensation, idea, simple apprehension, can be mistaken. Only where there is judgment is there truth or falsity. " . . . the ideas in our minds, being only so many perceptions or appearances there, none of them are false. . . . For truth and falsity lying always in some affirmation or negation, mental or verbal, our ideas are not capable, any of them, of being false, till the mind passes some judgment on them; that is, affirms or denies something of them" (*Essay,* II.XXXII.3; see also Draft A, section 8 and Draft B, section 92).

Where Gassendi says that the idea of a thing is what is put forth in its definition (Canon XV), Locke describes the definition of a thing as an enumeration of all the simple ideas out of which the complex idea of it is made (Draft A, section 1; Draft B, section 67). Concerning the definition of a thing in terms of *genus* and *differentia,* Locke remarks that it " . . . is not out of necessity, but only to save the labour of enumerating the several simple ideas which the next general word or *genus* stands for. . . . For, definition being nothing but making another understand by words what idea the term defined stands for, a definition is best made by enumerating those simple ideas that are combined in the signification of the term defined" (*Essay,* III.III.10). From this it is plain that the definition of a term when "best made" as Locke puts it would, as Gassendi says, determine its division into species, parts, and attributes (Canon XVI). Also, Locke notes, as does Gassendi (Canon XVII), that a thing may be thought of, not absolutely, but as it relates to other things; thus Caius can be thought of not just as a man, but as husband of Sempronia (*Essay,* II.XXV.1; see also Draft A, section 18 and Draft B, section 98). Finally, just as Gassendi says that our knowledge of things is the greater, the more perfect the ideas we have of them and the more things of which we have ideas (Canon XVIII), so Locke claims that our knowledge is enlarged by getting "clear, distinct and constant ideas of the things we would consider and know" (*Essay,* Ist Ed, IV.XII.14), and we may surely add to this that the more things of which we have such knowledge, the greater our knowledge is.

Gassendi's theory of ideas is found virtually intact even in the earliest versions of Locke's theory of ideas. The extent to which Locke builds on Gassendi's theory is somewhat obscured in the *Essay* due to its very elaborate treatment of ideas and the diffuseness of its text. Yet a comparison of the two theories leaves little room to doubt that Gassendi's theory was Locke's starting point.

There is much more to say about the relation of Locke's views to those of Gassendi. We have been concerned in this paper principally with Locke's debt to Gassendi's theory of ideas, but Locke's debt to Gassendi goes well beyond this. Other areas in which Locke adopts Gassendist views are specified by Leibniz at the beginning of his *New Essays on Human Understanding,* where he says of Locke: "This author largely accepts the system of Gassendi, which is at bottom, that of Democritus; he is for the void and for atoms; he believes that matter might think; that there are no innate ideas; that the mind is a *tabula rasa,* and that we do not always think; and he appears inclined to approve most of the objections Gassendi brought against Descartes."[41] To this it should be added that Locke also accepts Gassendist views on space, time, and infinity.[42]

Yet by no means is Locke a disciple of Gassendi; not only does Locke develop the theory of ideas far further than Gassendi does, in important respects his epistemology is at odds with that of Gassendi. In a full scale study of the relation between Gassendi and Locke, this would have to be spelled out. But it is enough for the present to have shown that Norton is correct in claiming that the modern theory of ideas originates with Gassendi.

Notes

1. We gratefully acknowledge that research for this paper was partially funded by a fellowship from the National Endowment for the Humanities.

2. Richard I. Aaron, *John Locke* (3rd Edition; Oxford, 1971), 31.

3. David Fate Norton, "The Myth of British Empiricism," *History of European Ideas,* 1 (1981), 336.

4. Richard W. F. Kroll, "The Question of Locke's Relation to Gassendi," *JHI,* 45 (1984), 339-59.

5. *Ibid,* 341.

6. *Ibid,* 347, 352-59.

7. *Ibid,* 340.

8. John W. Yolton, "Locke and the Seventeenth Century Logic of Ideas," *JHI,* 16 (1955), 431.

9. As early as 1647, in a letter to Samuel Hartlib, Boyle describes Gassendi as "a great favourite of mine" (Robert Boyle, *The Works,* ed. T. Birch [London, 1772], xli). Some light is cast on Boyle's denial that he had read Gassendi "properly" (*cf.* Kroll, 345), by a remark of Boyle at the beginning of his 1661 *Certain Physiological Essays.* With respect to the *Epicurean Syntagma,* Descartes's *Principles of Philosophy* and Bacon's *Novum Organum,* Boyle says: "I purposely refrained, though not altogether from transiently consulting about a few particulars, yet from seriously and orderly reading over those excellent . . . books . . . that I might not be prepossessed with any theory or principles" (*Works,* I, 302). Boyle is not denying that he is *familiar* with these works; what he is denying is that he has *studied* them. In Boyle's works on the whole, there appear to be only occasional remarks having epistemological import.

10. *The Port Royal Logic* was first published as *La Logique or L'Art de Penser* (Paris, 1662). Gassendi's empiricist theory of ideas is discussed (and dismissed) in Part I, Chapter 1. The structural similarity between Gassendi's *Institutio Logica* and *The Port Royal Logic* is somewhat obscured by additions to the text in later editions of the latter work. The objection to defining logic as "the art of thinking well" is in the second Discours, first published in the 2nd edition (1664). References to the *Port Royal Logic* will be to the "definitive" fifth edition (1683).

11. Cf. Norton, 335.

12. See John Harrison and Peter Laslett, *The Library of John Locke* (Oxford, 1965), item #2755.

13. The pagination of the *Epicurean Syntagma* is distinct from that of the rest of volume II of the *Animadversiones.* The situation is fully described in the Centre International de Synthèse, *Pierre Gassendi 1592-1655: Sa Vie Et Son Oeuvre* (Paris, 1966), 187-88. The *Epicurean Syntagma* should not be confused with the *Syntagma Philosophicum,* which is Gassendi's most important philosophical work and occupies two of the six volumes of the *Opera Omnia* (Lyon, 1658). The *Syntagma Philosophicum* itself is essentially a revised version of the three-volume *Animadversiones in Decimum Librum Diogenis Laertii* (Lyon, 1649). The main difference between the *Animadversiones* and the *Syntagma* is that the text is reorganized and the *Syntagma* contains a newly written section on logic, which replaces the section on Canonic in the *Animadversiones.* Only two sections of the *Animadversions* are reprinted in the *Opera Omnia:* the *Epicurean Syntagma* and *Diogenes Laertii Liber Decimus,* which contains the text of Diogenes Laertius Book X, a translation of the text, together

with some interpretive comments and philological notes extracted from the *Animadversiones.*

14. Gassendi, *Opera Omnia,* I, 52-56.

15. Virtually every educated person in Western Europe had a thorough knowledge of Latin during the seventeenth century. University instruction was in Latin and works of interest to scholars, if not written in Latin, were quickly translated into Latin so as to be generally available to the scholarly community. More than a third of the titles in Locke's library were in Latin, according to Harrison and Laslett, 19.

16. The Centre International de Synthèse volume on Gassendi has the following comment (188): "This Epicurean breviary contains hardly a word of Gassendi himself: it is a collection of texts translated from the Greek, of verses of Lucretius put into prose, of extracts from Cicero, etc."

17. There is a real question about how widely known it was that the section on Epicurus in Stanley's *History* is a translation of Gassendi's *Epicurean Syntagma,* since the only indication of this are two words near the end of the section on Epicurus: "Hitherto *Gassendus.*" See Thomas Stanley, *The History of Philosophy,* 2nd ed. (London, 1687), 935.

18. Harrison and Laslett, items #283, #1211, #603.

19. *Ibid,* item #604; also 270.

20. Aaron, 35, n. 1.

21. John Locke, *Essays on the Law of Nature,* ed. by W. von Leyden (Oxford, 1954), 59, n. 1.

22. Maurice Cranston, *John Locke: A Biography* (London, 1957), 102.

23. Centre International de Synthese, *op. cit.,* 159.

24. Olivier Bloch, *La Philosophie de Gassendi* (The Hague, 1971), 198.

25. Von Leyden, *op. cit.,* 147, 149.

26. *Ibid,* 41, 149.

27. Nathaniel Culverwell, *An Elegant and Learned Discourse of the Light of Nature* (London, 1652), 90-92.

28. Howard Jones, *Pierre Gassendi's Institutio Logica (1658)* (Assen, 1981), 160.

29. Kroll, 342.

30. What is now known as Draft B of the *Essay* is John Locke, *An Essay Concerning the Understanding, Knowledge, Opinion and Assent,* ed. Benjamin Rand (Cambridge, Mass., 1931). Draft A is *An Early Draft of Locke's Essay,* ed. R. I. Aaron and Jocelyn Gibb (Oxford, 1936).

31. *The Selected Works of Pierre Gassendi,* ed. and tr. Craig B. Brush (New York, 1972), 98-99.

32. See Letter 13 of Voltaire's *Lettres anglaises.*

33. Gassendi, *Opera omnia,* I, 89b.

34. Aaron, 32.

35. These are given in the *Opera omnia,* I, 52-56, and also in III, 4-10. They are newly translated in this paper.

36. The text of the *Institutio Logica,* Part I is in the *Opera omnia,* I, 92-99. A new edition of the *Institutio Logica* together with an English translation is in Jones, *op. cit.;* text of Part I (3-20), translation on 83-101. The translation of all passages cited in this paper is ours.

37. Jones, 4.

38. See *Opera Omnia,* III, 318-20.

39. *Opera Omnia,* II, 458a; a condensed version of this argument is found in the *Institutio Logica,* III, Canon XVI. Jones, 61, 146.

40. Jones, 11. This passage calls attention to a problem with Gassendi's use of "idea." While ideas may be general, images cannot be. Yet ideas, for Gassendi, are images. Gassendi really shouldn't speak of general ideas here at all, but instead of general notions or conceptions, as he does elsewhere (e.g. *Opera omnia,* II, 441).

41. Leibniz, *Nouveaux essais sur l'entendement humain* (Paris, 1966), 55-56.

42. See Bloch, *op. cit.* ch. 6.

Richard F. W. Kroll (essay date 1991)

SOURCE: "'Living and Speaking Statues': Domesticating Epicurus," in *The Material World: Literate Culture in the Restoration and Early Eighteenth Century,* Johns Hopkins University Press, 1991, pp. 140-79.

[In this excerpt from his study of literature and culture in Restoration England, Kroll argues for Gassendi's importance to the importation of Epicureanism into England. Emphasizing motifs of circulation, the critic demonstrates the influence of not only Gassendi's written works, but also the symbolic figure of Gassendi himself.]

> If Galilaeus with his new found glass,
> Former Invention doth so far surpass,
> By bringing distant bodies to our sight,
> And make it judge their shape by neerer light,
> How much have you oblig'd us? In whose mind
> Y'have coucht that Cataract wch made us blind,
> And given our soul and optick can descrie
> Not things alone, but where their causes lie?
> *Lucretius* Englished, Natures great *Code*
> And *Digest* too, where her deep Laws so show'd,
> That what we thought mysteriously perplext
> Translated thus, both *Comment* is and *Text*
>
> Sir Richard Browne, "On My Son *Evelyns* Translation
> of the First Book of Lucretius" (1656)

Cartesius reckoned to see before he died the sentiments of all philosophers, like so many lesser stars in his romantic system, wrapped and drawn within his own vortex.

Jonathan Swift, *The Tale of a Tub* (1710)

TRANSLATING AND DOMESTICATING EPICURUS

In 1656 John Evelyn published the first English translation of Lucretius.[1] His "Animadversions upon the First Book of T. Lucretius Carus De Rerum Natura" (appended to that pioneering translation) refers Evelyn's reader by a marginal gloss to Gassendi's life of Epicurus (***De Vita et Moribus Epicuri*** [1647]). Paraphrasing Diogenes Laertius, Evelyn writes that Epicurus "was a person of super-excellent candor and integrity, as testified by his Countrey in general; the costly *Statues,* and glorious *Inscriptions* erected to his memory; his many Friends and Disciples; and lastly, that *promiscua erga omnis benevolentia;* nay, and (what the Reader little expected) even his *Religion* and *Charity.*"[2]

Evelyn reminds us that Epicureanism sustained itself after the death of its master by referring to the memorial inscriptions dedicated to Epicurus. And Gassendi's and Bougerel's textualization of the self continues that tradition. Similarly, Evelyn could well be commenting on his own text, which serves as a kind of epitaph for Gassendi. Indeed—anticipating Bougerel—Evelyn concludes his translation with a printed fascimile of Gassendi's epitaph (p. 136). Evelyn's famous translation of Lucretius appeared less than a year after Gassendi's death in 1655: even the title of the "Animadversions" fortuitously echoes the title of one of Gassendi's two most important neo-Epicurean works.[3] The gesture toward Gassendi's ***Animadversiones in Decimum Librum Diogenes Laertii*** (originally published in 1649 and only fragmentarily reproduced in the 1658 ***Opera Omnia***) seeks to remind us not only of Gassendi's revision of Epicurus but also of his more comprehensive schemes to construct his own ***Syntagma.***[4] Thus by translating book one of *De Rerum Natura* with its speculative physics, Evelyn not only propagates Lucretius's sublime understanding of "the Principles of things"[5] but also reminds his compatriots of Gassendi's neo-Epicurean cosmology.

In 1657, only a year after Evelyn's translation of Lucretius, William Rand translated Gassendi's important ***Viri Illustris Nicolai Claudii Fabricii de Peiresc,*** his life of Peiresc issued in English as *The Mirrour of True Nobility and Gentility.* Rand's dedication celebrates Evelyn, whom Rand associates with Gassendi's neo-Epicurean ethos. And just as Gassendi saw in Peiresc an anticipation of the ideal Epicurean gentleman and scholar, so Rand depicts Evelyn as an English version of the same *"Peireskian Vertues."*[6] Rand concludes his dedication to Evelyn by celebrating Mary Evelyn. In the hope that the Evelyns' offspring will generate a newly reformed English gentry, Rand beseeches "Almighty God to make you the happy and joyful Parents of many faire, wise, and well-bred Children, that may tread in their Parents steps, and as living and speaking Statues, effectually present your names and vertues to succeeding Generations."[7]

Evelyn and Rand evidently conceive of the transmission of culture (here spoken of as "vertue") as a process by which an image becomes over time a kind of archaeological counter or coin, which it is the purpose of texts—such as Peiresc's antiquarian endeavors—to secure against dissolution. This view applies equally to Epicurean inscriptions, Peiresc's biography, Gassendi's epitaph, or Evelyn's children, whom Rand imagines as "speaking Statues" conveying Evelyn's virtues to later generations. Accordingly, Rand carefully links Gassendi's deliberations on history to Peiresc's fascination with its concrete (as opposed to merely verbal) remnants: whereas "Philosophy instructs men indeed with words, . . . History inflames them with examples."[8] And the exemplary force of historical knowledge is only fully realized by an essential supplement to textual evidences, what Peiresc saw as the "incorrupted witnesses of antiquity"—namely, "Charters, Letters, Seales, Coates of Arms, Inscriptions, Coins and other such like things."[9] The attitude is perfectly captured in the specular image of Peiresc "looking through certain spectacles of Augmenting glasses upon Papers and Coins, whose letters were exceedingly small, and half eaten away."[10] Just as this biography is intended, for the similarly attentive reader, as a "Mirrour of True Nobility & Gentility," so "by Statues and Coins" (Peiresc would retort to his detractors) "we may know what was the Countenance and habit of renowned men and illustrious women, whose actions we delight to hear related."[11] Antiquarian ideals such as Peiresc's predicate Rand's striking invocation of a statuary trope to prophesy Evelyn's propagation of knowledge and virtue.

Evelyn's and Rand's two translations indicate the extent to which Gassendi played a catalytic role in the development of a specifically English neo-Epicureanism. This role has been misunderstood, because, as I have already argued, Gassendi has usually been treated *either* as a contributor to mid-seventeenth-century European atomism (taken as the most marketable product of the neo-Epicurean revival) *or* as a figure in the development of European libertinism and free thought. By restricting its field of focus, either genealogy unnecessarily distorts the historical picture. If we separate Gassendi's physics from his larger cultural program, we fragment the coherence of his writings and in so doing allow more powerful claims to 'scientific' influence on British natural philosophy to dominate the discussion. Descartes's enormous modern reputation, for one, is always in danger of blocking our vision.[12]

More importantly perhaps, neoclassical thinkers often sought to absorb and domesticate their intellectual debts silently. Consequently, to measure the effect of a given cultural figure, we must examine methodological rather than purely thematic issues. For example, without explicitly referring to him, Dryden's epistle to Charleton uses Epicurus to exorcize Aristotle from its new discursive polity: Epicurus authorizes the contingent modes of apprehension the poem enacts, which themselves connote an epistemology that resists Aristotle's.

An equally frequent and misleading habit is the tendency of seventeenth-century writers to refer to figures of intellectual authority for purely polemical purposes. For example, if we examine the figure of Descartes in the *Vanity of Dogmatizing* for the epistemological and methodological role he plays in Glanvill's text, we discover that he acts out a part that in its details is closer to the 'actual' Gassendi than the 'actual' Descartes. By invoking Descartes, Glanvill evidently lends a certain philosophical grandeur to his text, and he neatly avoids the difficulties of consorting too openly with Epicureanism, which others might associate with the abominable Hobbes. I have been arguing so far that a particular method betokens an ideology, an entire approach to personal and public knowledge, which encompasses natural philosophy, theology, criticism, and literature. Consequently, we now discover philosophical debts not primarily by hunting out explicit allusions, but by calibrating the ways in which epistemology and method are understood, used, and represented.

Thus I argue that Gassendi's peculiar methodical appropriation and domestication of Epicurus set the stage for an entirely critical and uniquely English reappropriation of Gassendi and Epicurus. Speaking of himself as the "interpreter" of Lucretius,[13] and conscious of the "latitude" his interpretive method permits,[14] Evelyn gauges his own cultural distance both from Lucretius the ancient and Gassendi the modern, while still offering an entirely exemplary vehicle—his translation of Lucretius—to make both authors available to his reader. Rand similarly encourages a series of contingent negotiations among the figures of Peiresc, Gassendi, and Evelyn. Like the "living and speaking statues" by which he describes Evelyn's children, Rand's *Mirrour of True Nobility and Gentility* recognizes both the continuities and the disruptions involved in the transmission of culture, because it occurs like a series of translations on translations, mediated texts succeeding mediated texts. (And by reminding us of Evelyn's earlier translation of Lucretius, Rand simply amplifies this recognition.)

Gassendi is not a figure without whom the English neo-Epicurean revival is inconceivable. But it is clear that his presence on the European intellectual scene helped to organize and catalyze it: in short, his neo-Epicureanism establishes a precedent for the whole neoclassical move. Both French and English culture possessed the same classical texts, and Boyle's early and seminal manuscripts on atomism contain no explicit references to Gassendi.[15] But the onset of translations of Lucretius from the mid-1650s on testifies strikingly to a new sense of the applicability of the Epicurean model to this particular crisis in English history.[16] Here was a crisis that required a critical reflection on the founding premises of culture, and such criticism was in part enabled by Gassendi.

The determination to nationalize and domesticate English cultural resources, which fluctuates between desire and resistance, has also made it difficult to measure the influence of earlier sources on the Restoration. For example, the precise impact of Bacon or Descartes on Restoration culture is still inadequately understood.[17] Bacon's hugely exaggerated reputation as the founder of English science derives in large part from the Restoration anxiety to preserve the native quality of its intellectual debts. Bacon frequently appears in Restoration texts, but his role—like his presence in the title page of Thomas Sprat's *The History of the Royal Society*—is more polemical than methodological.[18] The appeal to Bacon serves a double purpose. On the one hand, it Anglicizes the institution and practice of natural philosophy. Thus Bacon's atomistic theories were republished at midcentury in order to provide an English claim to a movement whose sources were primarily Continental.[19] On the other hand, Bacon provides an intellectual authority from some antique past divorced from associations with the late civil upheaval.[20] A large number of scholars agree that, apart from a generic emphasis on experimentation, Bacon provided no adequate methodological tool or model for the practice of Restoration natural philosophy.[21] It is therefore misleading to revitalize R. F. Jones's highly positivistic appreciation of Bacon first to argue some founding distinction between the "mechanical" (or "corpuscular") philosophy and the "experimental," and second to apply the ideal of "experiment, observation and natural histories" to Locke's philosophical practice, as if Locke had more in common with Baconian experimentalism than with atomism.[22] Locke's understanding of method (and thus of history, however defined) could not operate further from Baconian inductivism: Locke believes that without hypothetical modeling (very like that described by Gassendi), particulars will never form themselves into universal propositions.[23] In his discussion of philosophical style, which has profoundly methodological implications, even Sprat evidently views Bacon as stylistically archaic: it is Hobbes, as Sprat describes him, who echoes the prescription for philosophical prose laid down in *The History of the Royal Society.*[24]

The English pretense to fabricate a cultural norm without the assistance of Continental philosophy is demonstrated in a notorious debate between Sprat and Sorbière. In 1664, Sorbière, long Gassendi's disciple and an individual highly qualified to comment on the European intellectual scene, published his *Relation d'un Voyage en Angleterre.*[25] To this tendentious but nonetheless detailed and informative report, Sprat issued a shrill and frequently *ad hominem* reply, his *Observations on Monsieur de Sorbier's Voyage into England* (1665), dedicated to Christopher Wren. Like his belief that the English are innately xenophobic, some of Sorbière's observations are indeed impressionistic and offensive, and they belie his general acuity. But many of the judgments to which Sprat most objects are highly suggestive, such as Sorbière's view that there is widespread resistance to Anglican hegemony.[26] Sorbière's attitudes provide an occasion for Sprat to demonstrate a meanness of temper, a mediocrity of mind, and a deeply suppressed fear that Sorbière's views might have foundation. If Sorbière indulges Catholic prejudice, Sprat vents a strident anti-Catholicism, and he equally stridently declaims that nothing is rotten in the state of England. The Anglican Church and the Stuart State, he writes, receive the full support of the people.[27]

Interestingly, Sorbière records a visit to the Royal Society, in which he is first and foremost struck by the prevailing ideals of intellectual moderation and cooperation, to which he refers at least twice.[28] He emphasizes that such a moderate intellectual climate prohibits any uniform adherence to a single intellectual source of authority; but he nevertheless notices a distinction between the "simple Mathematiciens" and "less literateurs," the former group inclined toward Descartes, the latter toward Gassendi.[29]

Whatever Sorbière meant by his distinction between simple mathematicians and "literateurs," it is possible to imagine a working methodological difference between the mathematical and experimental traditions within the Royal Society, which was later epitomized in the difference between Newton's *Principia* and *Optics*. Sorbière presents two native groups of figures to represent this difference: he describes meeting John Wallis (he also mentions Wallis's mathematical dispute with Hobbes) and also "les immortels ouvrages" of Boyle, Willis, Glissonius, and Charleton, referring especially to Boyle's air pump, on which he has performed "une infinite d'experiences."[30] It is entirely likely that (even if they allowed the distinction) neither group would have admitted an allegiance either to Descartes or Gassendi. Sorbière notes precisely this resistance to factionalism, which Sprat's outrage fully confirms, but he nevertheless arguably intuits something about the different styles of philosophic practice available to the Royal Society.

Sprat, however, displays nothing but impatience with Sorbière, whose qualified judgments he caricatures as absolutes, which in turn predicate his own absolute (and absurd) declaration that "neither of these two men [Descartes and Gassendi] bear any sway amongst them [the Royal Society]: they are never nam'd there as Dictators over men's Reasons; nor is there any extraordinary reference to their judgments."[31]

Sprat's double polemic against foreign intellectual 'dictatorship' and the memories of domestic strife discloses two motives for the English determination to translate and domesticate its sources, for which Bacon is the perfect instrument. Bacon swells the native strain and lends an image of primitive purity that releases the Restoration from obligations to more recent and painful events.

The appeal to an ancient past can also help avoid those charges of atheism or heterodoxy to which the age was highly attuned, and thus Bacon and similar figures could stand in for more immediately valuable but problematic sources, such as Epicurus. To recognize this strategy of camouflage is not only to recognize that the appeal to certain older figures of authority was frequently more strategic than truly methodological, but also that it reveals the extent to which the Restoration desired to appropriate the methodical power of texts, such as Epicurus's, that could be seen as subversive. Nevertheless, it is important to recognize that modern interpreters have sometimes exaggerated the degree to which such texts were, or were taken to be, subversive. Hence, contrary to a comfortable historiographical myth for which Thomas F. Mayo is primarily responsible, Epicurus was not the object of attack by all outside the decadent "Restoration world of fashion,"[32] though there were grounds for concern. At one level, the neo-Epicurean movement merely revitalized a familiar Renaissance problem of how an officially Christian culture could adopt or accommodate pagan authors. And at another level, Epicurus's distinctive theology did indeed raise particular difficulties: Epicurus is sometimes associated with Hobbes's putative materialism and atheism.

The calculus of responses to Epicurus in the early Restoration (and immediately before) will remain elusive unless we permit a kind of circular device, which earlier chapters have urged. That is, neo-Epicureanism was already understood as a highly sophisticated cultural organism. By 1660, it had long been the object of careful modifications in the direction of Christian orthodoxy. Epicurean theology creates the greatest difficulties, but these had been variously pruned by Erasmus, Valla, Gassendi, Charleton, and others. Thus to many during the Restoration, neo-Epicureanism denoted not only an extraordinarily powerful physical hypothesis but also a probabilist epistemology, imparting a specific cognitive principle, an hypothetical method, and an irenist and apparently latitudinarian ethic.

Baxter's hostile but still comprehensive grasp of the new "somatism" reflects the extent to which by the mid-1660s Gassendi was known even to his detractors. Moreover, English publications represent a very significant percentage of European editions of Gassendi from the 1650s on, beginning with the **Institutio Astronomica,** published at least as early as 1653, and frequently reprinted into the early eighteenth century.[33] Descartes was published no more frequently in England after 1640,[34] but the number of Gassendi's books (unimpressive even by late-seventeenth-century standards) is less significant than the overall intellectual profile of Gassendi it presents. English readers would encountered a sceptic attacking hermetic forms of knowledge, a practicing astronomer, a biographer, a historian of ancient philosophy, and a powerful theorist of method, which provides the rationale for all other intellectual practices. Indeed, in the 1660s, in an apparently unusual departure from Continental modes of publishing Gassendi's works, there were two editions of the relatively youthful **Philosophiae Epicuri Syntagma,** issued in tandem with that fruit of Gassendi's most mature deliberations, the **Institutio Logica.** In consequence, access to Gassendi's recuperation of Epicurus entailed its most syntagmatic and revolutionary distillation: Gassendi's meditations on knowledge and method. Perhaps significantly, the first of these editions appeared in 1660.

If Epicurus and Epicureanism were attacked, C. T. Harrison, in a judicious essay published the same year as Mayo's book, demonstrates the range of responses manifested by seventeenth-century English writers.[35] Harrison describes some unambiguous attacks on Epicureanism after midcentury by such figures as Samuel Parker and Henry Stubbe. But for the most part, resistance to Epicurus is limited to isolated implications of his philosophy and (as with John Pearson) heavily qualified by a solid knowledge of Epicurean texts and respect for Gassendi's work.[36] Taking the picture as a whole, Harrison's painstaking account creates the impression that, even for many of its critics, the Epicurean myth had already deeply permeated some English cultural assumptions. Although Kargon credits Charleton with the acceptance of atomism after midcentury, Harrison mentions a host of reputable and influential thinkers, for whom Epicureanism represents an established if involved fact, among them John Pearson, Edward Stillingflect, John Tillotson, Henry More, Ralph Cudworth, John Wilkins, Thomas Sprat, Robert Hooke, John Ray, Gilbert Burnet, Aphra Behn, Jeremy Taylor, William Temple, and Isaac Newton.[37]

With many of these figures, the use of an etiological myth proved useful. First, Democritus could serve as a figure for a version of the *prisca theologia* in which the more ancient and primitive philosopher acts as proxy for Epicurus, whose more elaborate formulations invited more detailed charges of paganism.[38] (This is not to say that Democritus entirely escaped charges of materialism.) A second and even more neutral device was sometimes to refer to Epicurean physics as the "corpuscular philosophy," which was also a way to refer loosely to all atomic theories of matter. Nevertheless, in Boyle's case "corpuscularianism" also denotes an entire probabilist method bolstering a calculated irenist ethic. There is no question that Boyle must have learned both from Gassendi's and Descartes's physics, but what is often interpreted as Boyle's refusal to swear allegiance to Epicureanism as a system (and hence as a proof he was no Epicurean)[39] constitutes part of a distinctive view of hypothetical knowledge that Epicureanism propounds.[40] M. A. Stewart thus quite properly chides Richard Westfall and R. H. Kargon for their assumptions that the young Boyle wished to escape the embarrassments of Epicureanism.[41] (Ironically, the Boyle manuscripts that Westfall publishes in company with his contention constitute an extended series of deliberations on method that a neo-Epicurean would instantly recognize.)[42] What Sorbière noticed on his visit to the Royal Society was exactly that irenist, moderate, exemplary, and hypothetical ethic of intellectual conduct which reminds him of Gassendi, and which paradoxically encourages Sprat to conflate his Francophobia with a resistance to intellectual tyranny, a resistance that Gassendi himself actually symbolizes. If his very successful *Plague of Athens* (1659) is any indication, Sprat was not averse to associations with Epicureanism as such; his translation not only celebrates the famous closing passage of *De Rerum Natura* in its choice of subject but also adopts its resonances more than those of Thucydides, to whom Sprat also genuflects.

The third device by which Epicurus could be adapted to orthodox Christianity was to construct a Christian, rather than a pagan, etiology for the atomic hypothesis. It is well known that Cudworth's *True Intellectual System of the Universe* (1678) wishes to save atomism as "unquestionably true"[43] and does so by ascribing its invention to Moses, and its gradual corruption and increasingly materialist emphasis to Pythagoras, Empedocles, and Anaxagoras, then Democritus, Leucippus, and, finally, Epicurus.[44] Apparently, Cudworth had conceived his project by May 1671, when it received Samuel Parker's imprimatur,[45] in which case Cudworth is registering the substantial success of the neo-Epicurean scheme by that date, the same year in which Locke completed Drafts A and B of his *Essay.*

An earlier work by a younger man, Theophilus Gale, Boyle's and Temple's close contemporary, commenced publication in 1669. All four parts of *The Court of the Gentiles* remained incomplete until 1677, but part one, which was reissued in 1672, provides another view of the effect of the neo-Epicurean revival by the end of the 1660s. Like Cudworth (who clearly aided Gale in his project[46]), Gale seeks to Christianize the substance of ancient cosmology by claiming priority for an Hebraic, if not expressly Mosaic, dispensation. Insofar as their respective aims coincide, Cudworth and Gale may at first appear to share an affiliation with a vestigial Renaissance hermeticism, detecting in ancient wisdom the traces of divine footsteps outside the circle of revealed religion;[47] but unlike Cudworth, Gale reveals how much Restoration historiographic method secretly owes to a neo-Epicureanism that it is his purpose in part to confine.

Cudworth lies on the far side of an epistemological watershed from Gale: though willing to entertain atomism as a model strictly for physics, Cudworth steadfastly refuses uniformly to apply the phenomenalism it entails.[48] He is dismayed by the notion that questions of faith may have to subject themselves to the same criteria of evidence as secular history,[49] and the final pages of the *True Intellectual System* elaborate a rejection of all notions of artificial justice and thus of contractual societies. Both positions depend on momentary but crucial suspensions of sceptical judgment, betokening on the one hand a belief in the accessibility of certain noumenal essences, and on the other an argument increasingly at odds with the age—namely, the view that because political obligation enjoys its own actual, ontic being, "private judgment of good and evil . . . is absolutely inconsistent with civil sovereignty."[50] Appropriately, Cudworth manifests more patience with the Stoics than the Epicureans.[51]

By contrast, Gale rigorously grounds his massive project on precisely those inferential and analogical foundations that neo-Epicurean methodology had sought to advertise. If his intentions appear to us strange and remote, his method is recognizably less so. By examining and presenting only those (phenomenal) records available to us, Gale seeks to show that it is "very probable"[52] that pagan mythologies embed "*traces* and *footsteps* . . . of *Jewish,* and *sacred Dogmes.*"[53] Thus he writes (citing Chillingworth):

> From so great a *Concurrence* and *Combination* of *Evidences,* both *Artificial* and *Inartificial,* we take it for granted, that the main conclusion will appear more than conjectural, to any judicious Reader. Or suppose we arrive only to some *moral certaintie* or strong *probabilitie,* touching the *veritie* of the *Assertion;* yet this may not be neglected: for the least *Apex* of truth, in *matters* of great moment, is not a little to be valued. Besides, we may expect no greater certaintie touching any subject, than its *Ground* or *Foundation* will afford.[54]

Even as early as the late 1660s, Gale's case shows us how far in some instances an anti-Epicurean (or antimaterialist) polemic could marshal expository devices that it owes in part to the neo-Epicurean contribution to method. Admittedly, Gale's references to Chillingworth and other "*Modern Criticks,*" such as "*Ludovicus Vives, Stenchus Eugobinus, Julius* and *Joseph Scaliger, Serranus, Heinsius, Selden, Preston, Parker, Jackson, Hammond, Cudworth, Stillingfleet, Usher, Bochart, Vossius* and *Grotius,*" testify that certain approaches to criticism had long been possible.[55] But Gale's appropriations of comparative and contingent method are typical of the later seventeenth century. The same point could be made of Glanvill's approach to witchcraft.[56]

Richard Bentley dutifully attacked Epicurean and Hobbesian materialism in the first Boyle lectures of 1692.[57] But these demonstrate how, by the end of the century, the role of Epicurean atomism in Boyle's cosmology was widely understood. Bentley therefore selects for criticism only those distinctly pagan and unorthodox features of Epicurean thought which contradict the truths of the Christian faith. By contrast, Bentley reminds his audience that "the Mechanical or Corpuscular Philosopy, though peradventure the oldest as well as the best in the world, had lain buried for many Ages in contempt and oblivion; till now it was happily restor'd and cultivated anew by some excellent Wits of the present Age. But it principally owes its reestablishment and lustre, to Mr. *Boyle.*"[58] Bentley asserts that select doses of Epicureanism may serve as an antidote to more dangerous forms of atheism, because they contribute to a proper understanding of the true nature of matter, which cannot think. Such a cosmology, he writes, "being part of the *Epicurean* and *Democritean* Philosophy is providentially one of the best Antidotes against other impious Opinions: as the oil of Scorpions is said to be against the poison of their stings."[59] Epicureanism as such was ceasing to become quite the loaded subject it once had been. Mayo interprets the apparent decline in Epicurean texts published in the first quarter of the eighteenth century as a decline of interest in Epicureanism,[60] but it is possible to take the same phenomenon to indicate a less intense anxiety about its implications. Thus, when Thomas Creech published the first complete English translation of Lucretius in 1682, he had to deflect potential attacks by elaborate and defensive annotations. But in the 1715 edi-

tion of Creech's translation, the annotator (who is not the translator) clearly no longer feels impelled so vigorously to vilify Lucretius's pagan attitudes, though he carefully signals his own orthodoxy, especially in his preface.[61]

In view, then, of what seems a predominantly silent absorption of neo-Epicurean method and hermeneutic (going well beyond atomistic physics), Gassendi's specific contribution to English culture has understandably remained somewhat of a mystery. On the one hand, critics have tended to rely on broad analogies between Gassendi's formulations and a defined version of English 'empiricism.'[62] On the other hand, finding such correspondences insufficiently compelling, and unable to forge more concrete connections between Gassendi and the English, Lynn Joy fails to admit any valuable link.[63] I have already disputed Joy's contention that Gassendi's historiography decisively separates him from the late seventeenth century; but she also contends that we possess no adequate textual evidence for Gassendi's influence on the Restoration.

I believe, however, that there is more evidence than most earlier scholars (except perhaps Kargon) have generally recognized.[64] First, we have presumptive evidence both in the contemporary English publications of Gassendi's works, and even more so in Charleton's imaginative, compelling, and stylish naturalization of Gassendism in a body of work initiated by *The Darkness of Atheism Dispelled by the Light of Nature* (1652) and continuing with his *Physiologia Epicuro-Gassendo-Charletoniana* (1654), *Epicurus's Morals* (1656), and *The Immortality of the Human Soul, Demonstrated by the Light of Nature* (1657). The immense range of Charleton's interests can be seen as integral to his "physio-theologicall" habilitation of Epicureanism in general and Gassendi in particular. Charleton's authorial career had begun in 1650 with two translations of Jean Baptiste van Helmont's works, representing an earlier tradition of natural philosophy.[65] Nor, I would argue, are Charleton's adaptations of Gassendi anything short of original, a claim that even Kargon has resisted.[66]

Second, Thomas Stanley's influential *The History of Philosophy* (1655-60), in its section devoted to Epicurus, incorporates translated portions of Gassendi's **De Vita et Moribus Epicuri,** some passages from book ten of Diogenes Laertius, and the complete text of Gassendi's **Philosophiae Epicuri Syntagma.**[67] Stanley, a charter member of the Royal Society, was reckoned—along with Richard Crashaw—one of the two finest translators of mid-seventeenth-century England, and he proved an exceedingly successful poet. Stanley's edition and translation of Aeschylus (1664), with which John Pearson may have assisted, gained him lasting fame,[68] and his *The History of Philosophy* proved to be something of a publishing wonder. First issued serially between 1655 and 1662, it was reissued complete either seven or eight times before 1743, both in England and on the Continent. Sections of Stanley's *The History of Philosophy* also appeared in four separate books before 1701 in the guise of *The History of Chaldaic Philosophy* and *The Life of Socrates.*[69] Jean Le

Clerc included Stanley in his *Opera Philosophica* of 1704. *The History of Philosophy* appears in the listings for Evelyn's, Locke's, and Newton's libraries.[70] Cope shows how heavily Glanvill also drew upon this source.[71] The section of *The History of Philosophy* devoted in part to Epicurus (originally in volume three) was issued in 1660, but the title page of the "Fifth Part" of Stanley's work claims that it was printed for Humphrey Moseley and Thomas Dring in 1659; that is, only a year after the appearance of Gassendi's Lyons edition of the *Opera Omnia.*

Furthermore, not only does Stanley indicate a primary debt to Gassendi's historiographical approach in his dedication to John Marsham, his uncle,[72] but the work constantly reminds us of the special values of embedding all philosophical knowledge in biography and history. Stanley's preface applies the lessons of history to painting, because both vindicate the cognitive priority of the particular, such that "he who rests satisfied with the general Relation of Affairs, (not fixing upon some eminent Actor in that Story) loseth its greatest benefit; because what is most particular, by its nearer affinity with us, hath greatest influence upon us."[73] The epigraphs to volume three, taken respectively from Bacon's *Advancement of Learning* and Montaigne's *Essais,* not only amplify the theme but also do so just as the reader approaches the Hellenistic philosophers, culminating—as in book ten of Diogenes Laertius—in the lengthy section devoted to Epicurus.

Joy rightly objects that Stanley's *The History of Philosophy* provides no final proof of a true English appreciation of Gassendi, because she argues that the *Animadversiones* and the large *Syntagma* represent the core of Gassendi's real contribution to mid-seventeenth-century natural philosophy. But the objection ignores several important facts: the small *Philosophiae Epicuri Syntagma,* translated in 1659 by Stanley, was not only supplemented by other English publications of Gassendi's *oeuvre* but also by three reprintings (1660, 1668, and 1718), the last two offered first as a presentation of the *Institutio Logica* and only subsequently of the small *Syntagma.*[74]

Moreover, Evelyn, whom Margaret C. Jacob treats as "a veritable weather vane of latitudinarian sentiment on political matters,"[75] and who was a close friend of Taylor and later of Boyle, whose executor he became,[76] assumes that the English readership of his Lucretius is fully and intimately conversant with Gassendi's work, including explicitly the *Animadversiones.* Again, it is arguable that Stanley assumed some similar fund of associations or knowledge on his readers' part, because the Latin Leipzig edition of his *The History of Philosophy* (1711) supplies marginalia to the now more pointedly renamed *Philosophiae Epicuri,* which not only more carefully elaborate the classical sources than Stanley's original translation but also supply almost seventy running references to both volumes of Gassendi's 1649 *Animadversiones.*[77]

Despite the imputation of atheism, which neo-Epicureanism never entirely managed to elude, it is re-markable what kinds of texts register Gassendi's impact. On the Continent, Leibniz's *Nouveau Essais* pays homage to Gassendi as a significant feature of the intellectual landscape. Vico's *Autobiography* also testifies to the pervasiveness of Gassendism in late-seventeenth-century Europe. Vico records the moment at which he is forced, by its success, to encounter Gassendi's neo-Epicureanism. Only after reading Lucretius does Vico feel authorized to criticize the grounds of Gassendi's metaphysic, a process that anticipates his investigation and subsequent rejection of Cartesianism.[78] Closer to home and much earlier in the Restoration, Glanvill's *Vanity of Dogmatizing* (1661) and *Plus Ultra* (1668) both display a knowledge and approval of Gassendism, as does Boyle's *Works,* whose index devotes only slightly less attention to Gassendi than Descartes. For example, Boyle recommends Gassendi's *Institutio Astronomica* as the best single exposition of "the *Copernican Hypothesis.*"[79] Boyle's *Examen of Mr. T. Hobbes His Dialogus Physicus de Natura Aeris* (1662) explicitly commends Gassendi's atomism but attacks Hobbes's unfortunate materialism.[80] Here Gassendi stands as the foremost among "many other Atomists (besides other Naturalists) ancient and modern [who] expressly teach the sun-beams to consist of fiery corpuscles, trajected through the air, and capable of passing through glass," a view Boyle first associates with "the Epicurean hypothesis."[81]

Finally, as if to register and seal the orthodoxy of these earlier Restoration figures, Edward Phillips (a contemporary of Dryden and Locke) introduces Stanley and Gassendi into his *Life of Milton* (1694), still the most reliable early biography of his famous uncle. Gassendi appears as the last of a distinguished line of biographers stretching from Plutarch through Diogenes Laertius, Cornelius Nepos, Machiavelli, Fulke Greville, Thomas Stanley, and Isaac Walton. The "great Gassendus" occupies his position as "the worthy celebrator" of "the noble philosopher Epicurus" and Peiresc, in order to empower Phillips's own celebration of the greatest Christian poet in English.

THE ENGLISH IN PARIS: GASSENDI VERSUS DESCARTES

In the 1640s and 1650s there were some very different and much more personal contacts between Gassendi and important representatives of English society. Kargon admirably describes the émigré group in Paris circulating around Sir Charles Cavendish and Lady Margaret Cavendish, and known as the Newcastle circle. The group, which included Digby, Hobbes, and Pell, regularly communicated with the greatest representatives of French intellectual life—Marin Mersenne, Gassendi, and Descartes—as well as figures such as Pierre de Fermat, Gilles Personne de Roberval, and Sorbière. Kargon treats the Newcastle circle as a decisive vehicle for importing the new mechanical philosophy directly into England, a judgment with which Robert G. Frank concurs.[82] But because he is chiefly interested in the history of atomism, Kargon focuses equally on the physical theories of Descartes and Gassendi, a strategy that appears to lend them equivalent authority in the midcentury development of English atomism.

For his picture of this Paris circle, Kargon draws on the well-known correspondence between Sir Charles Cavendish and Dr. John Pell, partly published in an influential article by Helen Hervey.[83] Hervey's purpose is to illuminate the contacts between Hobbes and Descartes. But the value of the correspondence is that it provides an almost phenomenological report from the scene and, taken as a whole, more accurately reports on English attitudes toward Gassendi and Descartes, with somewhat less focus on Hobbes. Although Hobbes is an assumed member of the group, we can witness in this correspondence, with chiefly covers the years from 1644 to 1646, the formation of a series of personal and intellectual prejudices, which finds Gassendi more persuasive than Descartes as a mentor for English cultural motives. By examining another epistolary exchange, we shall also see how these attitudes are shared both by the royalist émigrés and the Dury and Hartlib circle at home, of whom the young Boyle was an impressionable member.[84]

The Paris group evidently fosters frequent and intimate contact among its members: in November 1645 William Petty thanks Pell for the ease with which his letters of introduction to Hobbes have also introduced him to Sir Charles Cavendish, Sir William Cavendish, and Mersenne.[85] Furthermore, Hobbes has happily provided Petty with access to the latest French mathematics. Consequently, in part owing to his decidedly generous intellectual disposition, Sir Charles evinces a concern to heal the obvious friction between Hobbes and Descartes. He feels indebted to Descartes for unnamed favors and finds Cartesianism "most ingenious."[86] But Sir Charles's concern seems, from the evidence, the response to a more widespread irritation with Descartes. Pell reports that Descartes is difficult to handle on intellectual matters ("I perceive he demonstrates not willingly").[87] Overall, we receive the impression that Descartes is exacting, prickly, and dogmatic.

By contrast with Descartes, Gassendi is a welcome and intimate member of the social and intellectual scene. It is true that Gassendi and Hobbes were allied in rebutting Descartes's *Meditations;* but again, the sense of the preference for Gassendi seems to stem from his general ethical and intellectual *modus operandi.* Thus, in September 1644, Pell doubts that Hobbes and Gassendi can reconcile with Descartes.[88] Despite his "esteem" for Descartes's "last newe booke of philosophie," Sir Charles Cavendish admits that "I am of your opinion that Gassendus and De Cartes are of different dispositions," adding that "Mr. Hobbes joins with Gassendes in his dislike of De Cartes his writings."[89] He volunteers in the same passage that Hobbes "is joined in a greate friendship with Gassendes."[90] In the letters written between August 1644 and October 1646, Gassendi circulates almost as frequently and certainly more fluently than either Hobbes or Descartes, to such an extent that, after a noticeable absence, he reappears in a telling aside. Sir Charles Cavendish has been tempted by Athana-

sius Kircher's "book . . . of light and shadow," but because "Monsieur Gassendes doth not much commend it . . . I have no encouragement to buy or to read it."[91] Gassendi's authority is perhaps subtle, but it is real.

It is possible to cull from these exchanges solely the whims of personal prejudice, an early but familiar version of academic politics. But the grouping of alliances seems as consistently intellectual as social: Pell carefully selects the word "genius" to describe the difference between Gassendi's (thus Hobbes's) and Descartes's ethic.[92] Sir Charles Cavendish knows that the degree of difficulty between Hobbes and Descartes is in direct proportion to their philosophical differences. Like Gassendi's, Hobbes's physical theories are much more Democritean than Descartes's—one cause for the failure of their meeting.[93]

The intellectual content of such enmities and alliances is vividly illustrated by two features of the correspondence. The first concerns the theme of Descartes's intellectual envy, which Pell introduces in a letter dated August 1644, and which informs my epigraph from Swift. Descartes has attacked "Monsieur Hardy" for buying an expensive "Arabicke manuscript of Apollonius."[94] Searching to explain this behavior, Hardy interprets it "as a signe of envy in Des Cartes, as being unwilling that we should esteeme the ancients, or admire any man but himself for the doctrine of lignes courbes."[95] Not only does Descartes later refuse fully to cooperate in conversation with Pell by offering mathematical demonstrations, but his attitude informs a singular approach to the ancients, of whom "he magnifies none but Archimedes," though he "hath a high opinion of Euclid and Apollonius for writing so largely y^t which he conceives may be put into so little roome."[96] In sum, Descartes refuses to credit the ancients with their own historical life apart from his most immediate intellectual desires, because he resents the philosophical space that historical baggage occupies. History mediates and frustrates the search for absolute philosophical categories. Predictably, "he suspects Diophantus might be excellent in the books wch are lost," because that permanently muted knowledge suits his own intellectual supremacy.[97] Of course, the moderns fare no better: Pell would be embarrassed to repeat what Descartes has said about Vieta, Fermat, Roberval, and Golius, and he has been too wise even to mention Hobbes.[98] The same month (March 1646), Sir Charles Cavendish (ultimately in vain) encourages Pell to publish his own works, despite Descartes's persuasions to the contrary.[99]

The second feature of the correspondence that lends an intellectual weight to its social preferences is the writers' fascination with the latest philosophical publications. Many of Sir Charles Cavendish's letters to Pell begin with either requests or thanks for some new tract or book. Cavendish's letters of 1644 engage, for example, with the publication and reception of Descartes's *Principles of Philosophy.* Although Cavendish discovers he likes the work, Pell reports that Gassendi remains unconvinced (August 1644), whereas Cavendish predicts that Hobbes will not like it either, a suspicion that proves correct (October 1644). The letter of October 1644 reveals that Hobbes, who had already read and dismissed the manuscript of Descartes's *Principles of Philosophy,* has received support for his intellectual judgment from a friend who also has seen it. It is possible that this friend is Gassendi, who immediately provides the next topic: Hobbes has seen an impressive manuscript of Gassendi's, and he judges it to be "as big as Aristotle's philosophie, but much truer and excellent Latin," which Kargon concludes to be a draft of the *Animadversiones.* Cavendish requests Gassendi's *Disquisitio Metaphysica,* his rebuttals of Descartes, about which he has been inquiring for a month. In December, Cavendish gratefully records its arrival.

Now writing in 1648, Sir Charles Cavendish again indulges his interest in Gassendi. Cavendish believes that *De Vita et Moribus Epicuri* (1647) and the *Animadversiones* compose an integral project, because he reports that "Gassendus . . . proceeds with his Epicurean phylosophie, the halfe of which; I doubt is not yet printed" (August 1648). In early 1649, Descartes's *The Passions of the Soul* has appeared, but Cavendish is anxious by March to obtain a copy of Gassendi's *Animadversiones* ("Mr: Gassendes his Epicurean philosophie"). In May Pell announces its long-awaited publication, describing its cost and size. He has, he says, met Sorbière, who supervised the publication of Gassendi's *Disquisitio Metaphysica* and translated Hobbes's *De Cive* into French. Sorbière also mentions that the *Animadversiones* have sold so well that a second printing is contemplated. A year later (June 1650), Cavendish has finally received his own copy of the *Animadversiones.* Significantly, especially in light of their mathematical biases, Cavendish and Pell think of Gassendi's work not even primarily as a treatise on physics, but as the exposition of an organic and refined philosophical scheme. It is therefore no accident that Cavendish retails Hobbes's remark that the *Animadversiones* will effectively displace Aristotle in scope, penetration, and style.

HARTLIB, GASSENDI, THE AIR PUMP, AND BOYLE

The Newcastle circle also anticipates the neo-Epicurean strain in Restoration culture because it was indirectly linked with a significant group of individuals in England, which did not share its party political affiliations. Through Petty, both Hartlib and Boyle seem to have learned of Gassendi's *Animadversiones* at a point in Boyle's career that has remained somewhat of a mystery. Steven Shapin and Simon Schaffer have argued that Boyle's belief in the vacuum (defended by experiments with his air pump) served an ideological debate with Hobbes, on the grounds that his plenism was the physical equivalent to his political absolutism. But these were the actions of a mature Boyle, and Shapin and Schaffer's book does not connect this ethical use of a physical hypothesis with Epicureanism as a cultural organism, which specifically encourages a cohesive link between method, the void, and an ethical voluntarism. The void, in short, represents the possibility of movement and negotiation among the constituents of

matter or society, and thus it encourages the notion that, on the one hand, the discrete particles in this economy must retain their integrity and, on the other, that we must discover a literary technology that promotes the dual possibility of integrity and assent. I have also argued that the integrity of the atomic particle encourages a view of the example that resists reduction and that therefore encourages the movements of assent or dissent. Like Evelyn, Boyle seems to seek an idea of the exemplary suited to new ethical and cognitive requirements, and to intuit very early on that the rhetoric of the dialogue and the epistle seems to offer the desired effect.

By attending to the rather fragmentary correspondence between Hartlib and Boyle, I want first to suggest that, before he could explore Gassendi in full, the young Boyle already associates a certain literate method with a distinct ethic, that he knew of the *Animadversiones* before they were published, and that his early interest in atomism must therefore have occurred in an atmosphere which treats that physical hypothesis as part of an entire methodological and ethical program.

In a letter to Hartlib dated 8 May 1647, Boyle indicates that "*Gassendus* [is] a great favourite of mine."[100] But at this point relatively little of Gassendi's important work had been published. Boyle's full appreciation of Gassendi almost certainly had to wait a year or more, because the *Animadversiones* was published in 1649. It is Hartlib's contact with Petty in particular that first connects Boyle to the Newcastle circle. Hartlib introduces Petty to Boyle in a letter dated 16 November 1647: Petty, it transpires, is "a perfect *Frenchman,* and a good linguist in other vulgar languages besides *Latin* and *Greek,* a most rare and exact anatomist, and excelling in all mathematical and mechanical learning, of a sweet natural disposition and moral comportment."[101]

In May 1648, in a pivotal letter Hartlib writes again to the youthful Boyle (he is only twenty-one). Here Hartlib acts as purveyor of intellectual goods: his main purpose is to enclose an extract of a letter from Sir Charles Cavendish to Petty, which Hartlib has received through Benjamin Worsley (the surveyor general under whom Petty was to work in Ireland after 1652). Clearly, Hartlib's general motive for copying the extract is his detailed interest in intellectual affairs on the Continent. But the more specific motive is captured by the letter's suggestive conjunction between Gassendi and the air pump, which was to play such an iconic role in Boyle's career. Gassendi "hath now" his "Philosophy of Epicurus" in "the press at *Lyons*"; the existence of the *Animadversiones* (to which Cavendish refers) thus seems already to have been introduced to English intellectual circles by mid-1648.

Gassendi's text seems to fit with Hartlib's and Boyle's correspondence in several ways. Because Gassendi seeks, like Epicurus, to fuse all intellectual issues with ethical ones, the reference to his *Animadversiones* could mirror Hartlib's evident concern to treat Petty's intellectual credentials and certain social and moral values as one. Petty meets Hartlib's criteria for reforming and harmonizing philosophical enquiry and political conduct, a project that deeply influenced Boyle, even before he could articulate it by reference to the embryonic neo-Epicurean revival.

Before Boyle could have known of Gassendi's *Animadversiones,* Boyle's series of letters to Hartlib and Dury of 1647 discuss Dury's and Hartlib's utopian projects, themselves of course responses to the unsettled times. But, more interestingly, Boyle's letters seem to anticipate the neo-Epicurean texts we have examined, because they are highly self-conscious dramatizations of a mode of intellectual and ethical behavior that display a moderate and irenist ethic. The point here is that Boyle seems to seek a rhetoric that in its method will itself enact the contingent epistemology that—as a response to the civil war—would make forms of social negotiation necessary and desirable. Indeed, the first letter (19 March 1647), which mentions two of Hartlib's utopian tracts, as well as suggestions for a universal character, begins with an invocation to the epistolary muse. "I need a great deal of rhetoric to express to you, how great a satisfaction I received in the favor of your letter," Boyle writes, "both for the sake of the theme, and more for that of the author."[102] Boyle believes that rhetoric is the contingent instrument for lending ideas phenomenal weight within the social and intellectual arena. In the final letter in the series, he determines not to neglect "improving my rhetoric to the uttermost," in order to assist Dury's logical schemes (themselves integral to the social program) "by exemplifying his rules, to clothe with flesh and skin his excellent skeleton of the Art of Reasoning."[103] Here Boyle clearly speaks in terms of incarnating knowledge, of rendering it somatic in order to propagate it.

Other very closely related metaphors for incarnating and textualizing knowledge in order to render it socially negotiable also appear in these letters from Boyle. The first occurs in the title of Hartlib's now lost *Imago Societatis.* Like Hartlib's description of Macaria (1641), this tract seeks to propose a society that exemplifies a Christian reformation of education and politics. The subtitle to Hartlib's *Macaria* conceives of its polity as "an example to other nations," which mirrors the theology of 1 Pet. 1:9: "But ye are a chosen generation, a royal priesthood, an holy nation, a peculiar people; that ye should show forth the praises of him who hath called you out of darkness into his marvellous light." However, the imaging or "showing forth" of the new nation exploits the device of the dialogue ("between a scholar and a traveller"), which enjoys more classical than biblical antecedents and, like rhetoric in general, presumes the merely contingent negotiations of knowledge. That is, "showing forth" can be seen as an incarnation of knowledge, which is made possible by the enactments of dialogue. And, curiously, as Boyle reports his response to having read "your *Imago Societatis* with a great deal of delight," he himself has "lately traced a little dialogue in my thoughts."[104] A few lines later, he expresses his hope for Mr. Hall's "Divine Emblems," which itself

distills Boyle's interest in the ideal exemplary image, whose power he describes as "probable."[105]

The letter of May 1647 in which Boyle mentions his special regard for Gassendi is devoted to a discussion of the *"Invisible College,"* and it is explicitly in this relation that Gassendi appears.[106] The letter is also deeply concerned with the question of exemplarity. Having introduced the topic of Hartlib's invisible college, Boyle pauses to thank Hartlib for his letters and reaches for a doubly numismatic and plastic metaphor: "And truly, Sir, for my particular, had you been to coin and shape news, not so much to inform, as to delight me, you should scarce have made choice of any, that were more welcome."[107] Although ostensibly serving private communication, the epistolary manner, Boyle tells us, achieves a kind of public value and a capacity for circulation and exchange, like a coin or statue; it then gathers the power to instruct and delight. Like the epistolary mode, the invisible college will become a discrete concrete example to the nation. And, like his role in the Newcastle circle, it is possible that Gassendi could already represent to Boyle the advancement of knowledge in association with an ideal of essentially private, cooperative, and even redemptive social behavior, which as we have seen, is dear both to Sir Charles Cavendish and Hartlib.[108]

The degree to which Gassendi's eno-Epicureanism could specifically provide a vocabulary for that ideology was a mere potential in 1647: Boyle's letter of May was written three months before Gassendi's *De Vita et Moribus Epicuri* received royal approval,[109] and two years before the *Animadversiones* appeared. But by 1648, things have changed. Petty arrives on the scene, importing his knowledge of Continental affairs, and Hartlib, in two letters to Boyle, can now convey more details of Gassendi's neo-Epicurean project.

The letter that Hartlib copies for Boyle in May 1648, and that I introduced above, fortuitously realizes some of the terms of Gassendi's neo-Epicureanism, now a matter of public record. For just as Petty represents to Hartlib an ideal combination of philosopher and moral agent, so Gassendi embodies a strikingly similar complex of values, and thus he serves to link Sir Charles Cavendish and Petty, the society they create, and Hartlib's friendship with Boyle. Cavendish refers to Gassendi as "your worthy friend and mine,"[110] thereby uniting an ideal of intellectual inquiry with the exemplum of friendship, a virtue appropriately textualized in the intimacies of the private letter. For all his personal feelings for Descartes, Cavendish never accords him the particular value that Gassendi not only assumes here but also had himself described in his *De Vita et Moribus Epicuri.*

We also saw that Cavendish—in the same letter that Hartlib copies for Boyle—discusses Gassendi's *Animadversiones* and enumerates the details of the air pump. The conjunction is significant, because the air pump represents "an experiment how to show . . . that there is or may be a vacuum."[111] In contrast to Cartesian or Hobbesian plenism, the existence of a vacuum establishes one of the premises of neo-Epicurean physics, of which the *Animadversiones* is a revolutionary vehicle. And by virtue of the characteristically isonomic Epicurean device, the vacuum (like the atomic swerve that Gassendi revised out of the physics) represents not only the physical space in and through which atoms can move but also its ethical corollary, the desideratum of social and intellectual accommodation and choice. If Shapin and Schaffer are correct, it is precisely this corollary that Boyle was later to implement, with devastating effect, against Hobbes's physics.

If Hartlib's letters of 1647 and 1648 represent any development in Boyle's early and express enthusiasm for Gassendi, then we might ask how Gassendi's neo-Epicureanism was to achieve through Boyle a revolutionary effect on English culture—that is, how closely can we link Boyle's enormously influential adoption of corpuscularian physics to a knowledge of Gassendi at midcentury? Richard Westfall believes that Boyle's earliest extant manuscripts concerning "Ye Atomicall Philosophy" were written by 1653. Westfall argues that they postdate 1649, when, he tells us, Gassendi published his *Philosophiae Epicuri Syntagma.* By implying that the Epicurean *Syntagma* alone was published in 1649, Westfall conveniently supports his assumption that Boyle was embarrassed by his own putatively illicit interest in Epicureanism, because the small *Syntagma* does not present Gassendi's revisions of Epicureanism. However, M. A. Stewart's challenge to Westfall is supported by the fact that the *Philosophiae Epicuri Syntagma* originally appeared in 1649 as a condensed appendix to volume two of the much more comprehensive *Animadversiones,* and Boyle's access to the Epicurean *Syntagma* could only occur by his knowing of the entire *Animadversiones.* The implications for our view of the early Boyle are at least twofold. First, if—as is highly probable, and in practice Westfall and Kargon must assume—Boyle had read the *Animadversiones* in 1649, Boyle's understanding of Gassendi would then extend well beyond the biography and redaction of Epicurus. Second, because Gassendi's adaptation and modification of Epicureanism sought to transpose pagan requirements into Christian ones; because both the ancient and the modern forms of Epicureanism provide perfect equivalents to Boyle's early union of method, physics, and ethics; and because the figure of Gassendi evidently circulated as easily in the Hartlib as the Newcastle circle, there seems little reason to see in Boyle an urgency to reject associations with Epicureanism. Thus, writing about Boyle's physics to Spinoza in 1663, Henry Oldenburg is wonderfully unembarrassed by the current status of "Epicurean" physics. He reports that Boyle wishes to adopt it in order to displace "the chemists and the schoolmen" and then to reform it on experimental grounds, themselves reflecting—as Boyle himself at one point writes—neo-Epicurean method: "Our Boyle is one of those who are distrustful enough of their reasoning to wish that phenomena should agree with it."[112]

JOHN EVELYN: THE NEO-EPICUREAN NATURALIZED

John Evelyn's career epitomizes the matrix of cultural and philosophical attitudes that neo-Epicureanism came to symbolize in the Restoration. Evelyn served as an important vehicle for translating French cultural attitudes into English ones during the Interregnum; he was closely in touch with the developing interest in natural philosophy, both in the royalist and Cromwellian camps; and he developed a vocabulary of cultural knowledge, which owes something to the Epicurean *Suggrammata* and to Gassendi's ideal of biographical and historical modes of reading. The probable occasion of Evelyn's contact with Gassendism, if not Gassendi—his trip to Europe in the 1640s—itself manifests the distinctive combination of royalist, Anglican, and irenist commitments, which was to form Evelyn's entire reputation. E. S. de Beer records that Evelyn left England in 1643, unwilling to swear allegiance to Parliament. In 1646 he established contact with the group of émigrés in Paris, which worshipped at the chapel of Sir Richard Browne, the king's emissary to the French court. Browne had instituted his chapel—significantly—as a visible reminder of his devotion to a uniquely Anglican polity, which increasingly dissociated itself from the courtly and predominantly Catholic circle gathered around Queen Henrietta Maria.[113] Evelyn married Browne's daughter, Mary, who was to design the frontispiece to the *Essay on the First Book of T. Lucretius Carus De Rerum Natura; Interpreted and Made English Verse* and whose virtues Rand celebrates in his translation of Gassendi's life of Peiresc. Additionally, in 1656, Browne cemented a public and literary relationship with his son-in-law by dedicating a poem to Evelyn's Lucretius.

Evelyn's return to England in 1652 marks the point at which Evelyn began systematically to cultivate himself as a palpable example of that confluence of private and public virtue for which he became famous, and which Taylor distills in a reference to Tusculanum.[114] Circero's *Tusculanian Disputations* enacts a search for, and the methods appropriate to, a probabilist epistemology by dramatizing a series of dialogues conducted in Cicero's seaside villa at Tusculanum, itself symbolizing a studied perspective on the turbulence of public life in Rome.[115] Evelyn's posture of moderation and virtue permitted him to reconcile a fervent Anglican and royalist temperament with an astonishingly wide range of acquaintance.[116] Evelyn articulated his cultural and personal projects by several means. First, especially in the form of letters, he developed a marked and novel ideal of intimate friendship.[117] Second, with an almost mystical enthusiasm, he appropriated and elaborated the image of hortulan retirement in a number of concrete forms: his renowned garden at Sayes Court (Evelyn's aforementioned Tusculanum and, in Taylor's words, his "Terrestrial Paradise"); his extensive writings about horticulture; and his equally extensive collection of books on the subject. Third, Evelyn patiently explored and articulated the nature of the exemplary phenomenal image, a fascination that unites his concern over the minutiae of printing with his antiquarian and numismatic interests.

The correspondence of Taylor and Evelyn breathes the atmosphere of a cultivated, intense, and intimate friendship of the kind Taylor describes in his *Discourse of the Nature, Offices and Measures of Friendship* (1657).[118] Not unlike Boyle, Taylor and Evelyn stretch the capacities of their epistolary styles to manufacture an original and urgent language of friendship. A deeply moving exchange between them occurs at the loss of Evelyn's young son in February 1657/58; but we also catch something of the artificiality of the pose, an emblem of the discourse under construction, as it were, in a letter from Taylor to Evelyn dated May 1657, written during the composition of Taylor's *Discourse:* "I only can love you, and honour you, and pray for you; and in all this I can not say but that I am behind hand with you, for I have found so great effluxes of all your worthinesses and charities, that I am a debtor for your prayers, for the comfort of your letters, for the charity of your hand, and the affections of your heart."[119] The spatial trope, by placing the author temporarily *behind,* implicitly at a competitive disadvantage to his addressee, predicates the quality of the prose, which seeks by a flurry of activity, accumulating clauses, to close the distance. What is artificial, however, is no less felt. On completing his *Discourse* (June 1657), Taylor proclaims Evelyn the concrete realization of the ideas it describes. "Sir, your kind letter hath so abundantly rewarded and crowned my innocent endeavors in my description of Friendship," Taylor begins,

> that I perceive there is a friendship beyond what I have fancied, and a real, material worthiness beyond the heights of the most perfect ideas: and I know now where to make my book perfect, and by an appendix to outdo the first essay: for when anything shall be observed to be wanting in my character, I can tell them where to see the substance, much more beauteous than the picture, and by sending the readers of my book to be spectators of your life and worthiness, they shall see what I would fain have taught them, by what you really are.[120]

In Taylor's allegory, true perfection resides not in the implicitly Neoplatonic perfection of ideas, abstracted ("beyond the heights") from the mundane, or so much in the *particular,* as in the "material," substantial, or "real." And Evelyn consciously strove to articulate this incarnated perfection in his Kentish garden, and, by extension, in his numerous schemes for improving the forestry, ecology, horticulture, and habitable spaces of England.[121] Evelyn strives comprehensively to embody and enact the conditions for a new variety of citizen, for which private friendship is a prolegomenon. Sayes Court, as an image of that desired culture, attracted precisely such spectators of Evelyn's art as Taylor imagines, in the form of Cromwellian and Stuart grandees.[122] Executing Taylor's prescriptions for friendship in his *Discourse,* Evelyn subtly revises his polity away from the Ciceronian and Plutarchan models of social intercourse to embrace female company. Addressing the question of "how friendships are to be conducted,"[123] the *Discourse,* an epistle addressed to Mrs. Katherine Philips, inveighs against "the morosity of those cynics, who would not admit your sex into the communities of a noble friendship."[124] Like the Epicurean community, which in this respect was unique within classical culture, both Evelyn and Mrs. Philips conscript their spouses into a mythology of friendship, which seeks at once to reform the conventional terms of marriage and to embrace other individuals. They share Taylor, the "Palaemon" to Mrs. Philips's "Orinda."

Mary Evelyn is a silent partner in this discussion of friendship, but her engagement within the hortulan virtues of Sayes Court has a striking parallel in a different textual space of her own making, namely the frontispiece to John Evelyn's *Essay upon Lucretius* (p. 168). (Rand was later to refer to John and Mary Evelyn as "true yoakfellowes."[125]) It should first be noted that Mary Evelyn inherited the main features of her design from Michel de Marolles's translation of Lucretius (1650), the first full translation into French. Marolles's frontispiece in turn owes something to Jan Jansson's Amsterdam edition of 1620, which Cosmo Alexander Gordon believes to be "the earliest printed illustration" of *De Rerum Natura.*[126] Mary Evelyn's appropriation of Marolles's frontispiece should be read in at least two directions: it comments on the general project, shared by Marolles and John Evelyn, of translating Lucretius into vernacular languages; it also comments on the specifically English desire to import and so domesticate French cultural artifacts at this historical juncture. The one commentary occurs in Marolles's original, in which the conventional iconology of the four elements is subtly altered; the other occurs in Mary Evelyn's equally delicate adjustments to that original. The four main figures represent earth, water, fire, and air.[127] But by a series of intricate iconological adjustments, the design subtly revises the political connotations of its emblems by Christianizing, feminizing, and particularizing their cultural associations. The most obvious and important fact is that it is Evelyn's wife who supervises the reader's entrance upon her husband's translation, a fact engraved on the lip of Neptune's urn. Mary's name thus publicly cooperates in a cameo of cultural reinterpretation with her husband ("J.E.") and Wenceslaus Hollar, the period's most distinguished engraver and illustrator. Second, the design balances the presence of three male figures (Neptune, Vulcan, and John Evelyn) with three female figures by adding the presiding allegorical figure of *begnignita,* or *sostanza:* Cesare Ripa's *Iconologia* allegorizes both virtues with a woman whose breasts, like Ceres' fruit, represent abundance. At the same time, Mary Evelyn has also differentiated the sexes by substituting Vulcan for the more habitual female representation of fire. The Vulcanic hammer can now economically allude to Lucretius's mechanistic universe.

The frame accordingly achieves a temporary balance between its representations of gender; however, on closer examination, the rhetorical weight shifts from the masculine left to the feminine right. The conventional grammar of reading pictures favors the move, but, as if to assist it, the rather bland allegorical figures of Neptune and Vulcan stolidly clutching trident and hammer, respectively, lose something by comparison to the more fertile, lavish, and polyvalent female figures. (The action is articulated by the sweeping gesture of the gown on the top of the frontispiece, which directs the eye in a circular movement toward the right.) The seated Ceres, for example, concentrates several associated iconological possibilities. Her coronet is borrowed from Cybele, founder of civilizations, while Ceres herself inherits from medieval iconology the image of the nourshing church, apparently the central edifice on the coronet. Ceres shares with Minerva the serpent, representing, in this connection, prudence and logic. Hence Ceres not only plays a part in the generic allegory of the four elements by symbolizing earthly plenitude but also infuses a Christian tonality into the Lucretian fascination with the founding elements of human civilization, as well as the cosmos.

The act of feminizing and Christianizing is, however, by no means unambiguous. Just as the Christianized possibilities of the frontispiece exploit a pagan mythology, such that the pagan image only hazily predicates a submerged Christian icon, so the cultural resonance of translating Lucretius in the mid-seventeenth century is at least double-edged. By presenting the lion peeping from beneath Ceres/Cybele's gown, it is almost as if the frontispiece dramatizes this peculiarly destabilized hermeneutic: the classical iconology surrounding Cybele usually requires two lions, the transfigured forms of Atalanta and Hippomenes,[128] but the single lion here, though admitting that pagan tradition, invokes the Christian iconology by which a lion could represent either Christ or Satan. The lion rises as a warning to the Christian about to engage Lucretius's pagan masterpiece.

The figures in the frontispiece do not behave in a uniformly allegorical manner. The tension within the frame questions the nature and role of allegorical interpretation itself and, in so doing, revises the epistemological and political terms under which representation operates. John Evelyn's portrait directly faces a figure ambiguously representing air, and only by default: apart from occupying the conventional space given to the fourth element, she has been denuded of Juno's emblems—the peacock, or an anvil on each foot signifying her punishment for disobeying Jupiter.[129] The political premises of the frontispiece preclude such images of female subservience. The absence of such iconological cues, as well as this most realistic and Christianized allegorical figure of all, invites the consideration that the image setting itself against Junoesque vanity and submission may stand for Mary Evelyn herself. The postulate encourages the historical and concrete to emerge from and even escape general and abstract knowledge. It inscribes a moment of translation. The figure of Mary Evelyn can be felt to resist the weight of inherited, reflex modes of interpretation constituted by male, classical, and pagan influences, yet she also approaches and greets her husband.

Where the top and right frames of the frontispieces succor the feminine, its bottom frame curiously mingles male and female. Technically, the snake is Ceres' possession; the urn, Neptune's. But here their juxtaposition confuses such identities. First, Mary Evelyn's name marks the gushing urn: the rim identifies her genius within the frame, and the action of the water mirrors the fruit spilling onto Ceres' gown and the milk of abundance raining down from the officiating figure of sustenance. The snake and the urn, moreover, move away from their proper points of origin, causing them to mingle, so the womblike urn is about to swallow the snake. The water gushing from the urn's mouth further mixes male and female polarities, because it seems to drench both Ceres' and Neptune's feet. The feminized terms of the emblem absorb rather than exclude the masculine.

Hence by juggling the tropes of an emblem that, like *De Rerum Natura* itself, raises the most elemental questions about civilization and the cosmos, Mary Evelyn's frontispiece effectually contributes to the wider debate to which neo-Epicurenism was also tributary. In short, the frontispiece constitutes its own discursive space, which, by alluding to and revising the presumptions of iconological reading, establishes its own delicate critique of interpretive authority and behavior. The polity of the Epicurean garden, made real in Sayes Court and in John Evelyn's conduct of friendship, can foster Mary Evelyn's subtle but ambitious claims for the role of women and for cooperation between the sexes within her own design for a new social order.[130]

The ambiguous emblem of the lion curiously focuses something of Evelyn's own ambivalence about his *Essay on Lucretius*. He expresses his hesitation about his project in terms of his frustrations with a sloppily printed edition—something that later irritated him about the printing of his *Numismata*.[131] But in response to Taylor's much more uncomplicated admiration for the translation, Evelyn also rather vaguely fears that he might indeed have loosed a lion on an unsuspecting public. A penciled gloss appended to a letter from Taylor in 1656 reads: "I would be none of yᵉ Ingeniosi malo publico."[132] Years later, in his guardedness about popular misconceptions of Epicureanism, Evelyn tells William Wotton that his recently dead friend Boyle "was a *Corpuscularian* without Epicurus."[133]

Curiously, however, it is in the context of the elaborately constructed letters of friendship between Evelyn and Taylor that we detect not only the fascination Lucretius could exercise for Taylor's immaculate orthodoxy but also the terms in which Lucretius's pagan theology was debated and revised. Like John Wilkins, Taylor is deeply impressed by Evelyn's translation, and he urges Evelyn more than once to finish the final four books of *De Rerum Natura*. Taylor's initial enthusiasm is somewhat tempered by his advice that Evelyn should strategically distance himself from Lucretius's theological views,[134] subsequently, the friends discuss the immortality of the soul,[135] only some time after Evelyn has written that "my animadversiones

. . . will I hope provide against all . . . ill consequences, and totally acquit me either of glory or impiety."[136] None of these gestures even hints at rejecting neo-Epicureanism *tout court.*

Evelyn might attempt to preserve Boyle from Epicurean heterodoxy. But if we step back from the minutiae of Evelyn's response to *De Rerum Natura,* and particularly if we register his *obiter dicta,* we see how profoundly he associates neo-Epicureanism with the new philosophy, especially the community it signifies. Returning to his diary entry for 12 May 1656, which records the initial publication of the *Essay on Lucretius,* Evelyn retrospectively comments that "little of the Epicurean Philosophy was known then amongst us." The temporal logic here is critical. For if Evelyn's correspondence—treated as a coherent allegory of English culture between 1647 and 1704—describes a triumph of knowledge, it occurs in the form not of atheism or materialism, but of "the new philosophy," which, he declares in 1703, "has since obtained."[137] At this point, Wotton is researching the life of Boyle, a project to which Evelyn attaches absolute significance; it is uniquely biography which can preserve that fragile relation between natural philosophy and culture, for which neo-Epicureanism is a perfect figure. For Evelyn, Gassendi's life of Peiresc has achieved the task definitively by transmitting the memory of "that illustrious and incomparable virtuoso."[138] Whereas Peiresc exemplifies a mode of knowledge for which Gassendi has invented the perfect literary vehicle, Wotton's biography can now make of Boyle an ideal example for future generations. By the end of Evelyn's life, Boyle's name evokes in him such powerful resonances for a peculiar set of philosophical and cultural values that Evelyn finally indulges in a fanciful and elaborate myth that will permanently link the Boyles with the Evelyn family name.[139]

The impulse behind Evelyn's mythologizing of Boyle derives from his earliest dealings with him. Like his visit to the Oxford philosophical group in July 1654, prompted by "my excellent & deare Friend *Dr. Wilkins,*"[140] Evelyn's relationship with Boyle extends the ideals of intimate friendship to more public models of social exchange. Evelyn lends his own diary and correspondence the weight of a developing but coherent narrative in a series of retrospective comments, which by hindsight realigns the allegory of events as they were originally recorded. The result is a vision of the gradual expansion of his private ideals into the cultural and political landscape. Evelyn editorializes his visit to Oxford in 1654 by later inserting the comment that Wilkins is "now Bishop of *Chester,*" an institutional turn taken by other members of the Oxford group, and that Evelyn describes in a letter of 1703.[141] Evelyn himself accentuates the activity of a historical narrative in which an ever-widening circle of friends seems to have begun—like Evelyn tending his garden—at some intellectual and geographical fixed point. The general concern with the transmission and propagation of cultural knowledge also discovers a convenient metaphor in the figure of the expansion of knowledge by an ever-widening series of concentric circles.

Of this activity, Boyle is a persistent feature. In 1659 Evelyn writes to Boyle about "our common and good friend Mr. Hartlib"[142] and alludes to a work "concerning the ornaments of gardens, which I have requested him to communicate to you."[143] Evelyn's assumption of an *imago societatis* later finds unpremeditated reinforcement in 1665, when Evelyn rejoices in the prospect of Wilkins, Petty, and Hooke living together at "my Lord Geo. Barclay's at Durdans near my brother" and discussing all kinds of schemes, which excite in Evelyn the reflection that "I know not of such another happy conversation of Virtuosi in England."[144] Evelyn's enthusiasm is to be expected not only on account of his hortulan and familial *imaginatio* but also because such a conversational and harmonious society is the subject of an elaborate proposal he presents to Boyle in 1659, less than a month after he hopes Hartlib will have conveyed Evelyn's work on gardens. The letter lays bare the motives that combine the interests of friendship, hortulan virtue, and social exemplification united under a single rubric—the determination to resist cultural and political instability ("that fond morigeration to the mistaken customs of the age").[145] Prevented by his family ("an aggregate person") from offering himself as the founder of his proposed community, Evelyn finds in Boyle the embodiment and seminal figure of his design.[146] A plot of "thirty or forty acres of land, in some healthy place, not above twenty-five miles from London"[147] will provide space for the cultivation of true religion and "experimental knowledge,"[148] while a kind of sabbatical system will infuse into the larger body politic those virtues cultivated in Tusculan retirement. Evelyn's precise spatial descriptions emphasize how this society may fill the gap or interruption in culture that he characterizes as "this sad *Catalysis.*" Evelyn describes his general aim:

> In order to this, I propound, that because we are not to hope for a mathematical college, much less, a Solomon's house, hardly a friend in this sad *Catalysis,* and *inter hos armorum strepitus,* a period so uncharitable and perverse; why might not some gentlemen, whose geniuses are greatly suitable, and who desire nothing more than to give a good example, preserve science, and cultivate themselves, join together in society, and resolve upon some orders and oeconomy, to be mutually observed, such as shall best become the end of their union, if, I cannot say, without a kind of singularity, because the thing is new: yet such, at least, as shall be free from pedantry, and all affectation?[149]

The spatializing of knowledge that actuates a coherent cultural image implies specular activity at two levels. Each participant, cultivating an individual garden within the boundaries of the smaller world, sees in each cohabitant a reflection of the ideals that the community desires. Similarly, the community serves as a complete example to official culture, signaled by the relative proximity of London—a Rome to Horace's Sabine farm. Knowledge of the example is enacted in terms primarily of *circulation*—the circulation of virtuous examples within the community's confines, as well as the recycling of continuously refurbished images to and from the wider society. It should not surprise us, then, that Evelyn's antiquarianism should lead him to a fascination with numismatics—material images confronting us from the past—or that Gassendi's biography of Peiresc should represent both sets of values to Evelyn.

A number of letters from the 1680s and 1690s develop Evelyn's elaborate conception of the use and function of medals as cultural artifacts. Medals assume a peculiar value, which they share with pictures, title pages, and illustrations, but to which they literally lend unusual weight and compression. Evelyn's discussion of these images from the past occurs within a heightened consciousness of their historical and epistemological status. Such images "transmit anything valuable to posterity"[150] only by a lucky chance, a happy union of fragmentary evidences. But Evelyn wants to regularize conditions of misfortune, malice, and accident by prescribing methods for collecting and maintaining books, pictures, and medals. His most extended deliberations on the topic occur in a letter to Samuel Pepys, dated 12 August 1689, in which he repeatedly indicts the "sad dispersions" of great repositories of culture—such as King Charles I's, Prince Henry's, and the Earl of Clarendon's collections—in the recent past and especially during "the late fanatic war."[151] Clarendon provides the most public and magnificent ideal of the collector, to whom (in Evelyn's epistolary drama) Pepys plays the most appropriate, if more modest and private, late Restoration equivalent. Moreover, whereas Clarendon's art collection is dispersed, his palace demolished,[152] and his political career wrecked,[153] Evelyn places hope in Pepys's library as a more secure and long-lasting repository of cultural images. Evelyn conveys his determination to repair the damage done to the great art collections and libraries during the civil wars in a generational metaphor of the kind that opens Dryden's "Astrea Redux." A younger generation must assume the responsibility for reassembling and reanimating a culture that has suffered a series of lacunae not only by war and fire[154] but also by the negligence and greed of prodigal children, even though Clarendon provides an exception.[155]

The responsibility of a younger generation to an older one is reflected in a parallel responsibility of the English to themselves. Again, Clarendon provides the perfect vehicle for Evelyn's argument, because his criticisms of "the open and avowed luxury and profaneness which succeeded, [in the Stuart court] *à la mode de France*"[156] motivated his disgrace and exile to that country. Like the frequent sale of great English collections on the Continent, it is all too easy for a culture intent on dismembering itself to export or otherwise to dispose of those "effigies" (to adopt Evelyn's term) that it finds inconvenient. Evelyn wants to control and regulate the wholesale exportation of cultural artifacts to France, as well as indict the indiscriminate taste for foreign, especially Italian, painting, in order to reinvent

and propagate a native virtue and integrity. Thus he unequivocally defends his panegyric to Clarendon (an encapsulation of Clarendon's historic value) in the dedication to his translation of Gabriel Naudé's *Advis pour Dresser une Bibliothèque* (1627; trans. 1661).[157]

The determination to compete with the institutions of French culture (in particular) is both domesticated and cleansed of any associations with pomp and grandeur by a dual metaphor of circulation juxtaposed with a highly specialized conception of space. The circulatory and spatial assumptions driving Evelyn's argument meet in an image of the Thames flowing by Lambeth Palace: like the commerce the Thames allows, the formerly plundered palace can become one of several new loci of cultural wealth, realized most profoundly in terms of books, pictures, and medals. Like Harvey's circulation of the blood, an English discovery that Evelyn remembers here, the circulation of artifacts will restrengthen the sinews of the body politic.[158] And like the library of Lambeth Palace, the new spaces Evelyn imagines as repositories of knowledge (from the virtuoso's cabinet to the Wren library at Cambridge[159]) both copy and revise French models, especially the Académie Française. However, whereas Cardinal Mazarin's library and the Académie connote an almost stifling grandeur and a vision of the state control of culture, Evelyn desires a public effect to be achieved by more local and domestic means. The linguistic functions of the Académie are, in Evelyn's imagination, transferred to a group—such as the "three or four meetings . . . begun at Gray's Inn, by Mr. Cowley, Dr. Sprat, Mr. Waller, the Duke of Buckingham, Matt. Clifford, Mr. Dryden, and some other promoters" of wit[160]—which is "brought together into conversation" in "one competent room in [a] gentleman's house."[161]

Evelyn is profoundly concerned with the ontic and epistemological status of the artifacts that will compose the counters or currency of his new cultural economy. Evelyn's hostility to art collectors' undiscriminating preference for Italian mythological paintings denotes a wider resistance to the speechless and "dusky lumber" of history.[162] Part of Evelyn's argument is that such representations are not historical enough in nature; because the "real image"[163] or "instructive types"[164] only achieve power by marking their space in some larger cultural grammar, they must be framed in some way by the contexts and aims of history. This is the purpose of Evelyn's confessedly "promiscuous" but equally prescriptive catalogue of famous individuals, who represent, singly or together, for good or for ill, examples for the kind of society he postulates. As we might expect from the striking mutuality of John and Mary Evelyn's personal and intellectual relationship—Mary evidently accompanied John as an intellectual peer on that famous visit to Oxford in 1654—John Evelyn calculatedly includes women in his ideal society.[165] Indeed, the most vivid individual heading his vast list of historical figures is Helen Cornaro, who, as a member of "one of the most illustrious families of Venice," refused all offers of marriage and preferred to cultivate a "universal knowledge and erudition," and died a celebrated public figure.[166] Evelyn, of course, mentions Katherine Philips and Princess Elizabeth of Bohemia.[167]

Evelyn believes that the meaning and eloquence of such portraits derive exclusively from an implicit or explicit context—manufactured from received knowledge or embedded in the image—which explicates their moral and cultural significance. That is, the portrait's significance lies less in its status as a fragment, a piece of isolated historical lumber cast up on the shores of the modern consciousness, than as a synecdoche, a concreted and objectified sign of a history whose movements and motives remain largely unreified and whose true process remains largely inaccessible. Moreover, because writing and inscriptions compose another, larger body of the actual history we inherit, no single historical image more perfectly encapsulates, embodies, and condenses historical significance than the medal, whose emblematic constitution fuses the pictorial and linguistic. Writing under the shadow of Ezekiel Spanheim's revolutionary contributions to numismatics, Evelyn treats the medal as a plastic example of the wider hermeneutical problems attendant on history, for which the Cotton manuscripts also serve as a figure.[168] But medals, though distinct, are also obviously associated with coins—they share a common origin at the mint—and in 1696 Evelyn links their peculiar weight as cultural currency (with its attendant metaphors of circulation and potential inflation) to the current debate on the coinage.[169] By implication, Evelyn's activity of "gathering up all. . . . Medals as I could anywhere find had been struck before and since the Conquest . . . relating to any part of good history"[170] seeks at a cultural level to resist the decline of value in "this mercantile nation" by "clipping, debasing, and all other unrighteous ways of perverting the species."[171]

Medals, then, bear a special cultural burden, because "we are not only informed whose real image and superscription they bear, but have discovered to us, in their reverses, what heroical exploits they performed; their famous temples, basilicae, thermae, amphitheatres, aquaducts, circuses, naumachias, bridges, triumphal arches, columns, historical and other pompous structures and erections."[172] Like the Epicurean icon, the medal provides a peculiar arena for the play of instructive images and discourses, which resists the entropy of history.

Evelyn's own strategy of resistance and gathering is captured in his last major publication, the *Numismata* (1697). Like the museum, the library, and the cabinet, the book now establishes a space for the selection, concentration, and ordering of cultural artifacts (p. 176). And curiously, like the medals that the facticity of the book imitates, the book is itself—as Evelyn is painfully conscious—subject to a process of clipping and debasing. What created in Evelyn the most intense anxiety during the publication of his *Essay on Lucretius* and equally his *Numismata* (almost exactly forty years later) are the errors created for posterity by his printer's negligence. Sir Geoffrey Keynes writes that the publication of *Numismata* "brought no satisfaction

to its author, for he was deeply mortified to find that, in spite of the trouble he had taken, it was full of errors and misprints."[173] By the intervention of Richard Bentley and Benjamin Tooke, Evelyn was dissuaded from inveighing against these errors in his preface, and he compiled instead "an immense list of *Emendata*."[174]

Evelyn's response is less explicable as an obsession with tidiness or accuracy as such than as a response to his own aesthetic of cultural imagery. So, again in that historic letter to Pepys, he advises Pepys that because oil paintings are expensive, clumsy, and sporadic vehicles of historical knowledge, a cheaper and more useful device would be to convert his library into a kind of cultural gallery, where, like medals, books enclose the pictorial and verbal. Evelyn advises Pepys "to add to your title-pages, in a distinct volume, the heads and effigies of such [historical figures] as I have enumerated, and of as many others as either this or any other age have been famous for arms and arts, in *taille douce,* and with very tolerable expense to be procured amongst the printsellers."[175] As William Rand recognizes in his translation of Gassendi's life of Peiresc, it is finally in the book itself that the life, the image of the life, can be textualized and—like Epicurus's *suggrammata,* Gassendi's biography of Nicolas-Claude Fabride Peiresc, Bougerel's biography of Gassendi, and Evelyn's own children—can become a kind of statue "living and speaking" to posterity. Similarly, just as Sir William Temple imagines the inhabitants of his ideal Epicurean garden contemplating, within its space, the statues that punctuate it, so Evelyn imagines Pepys standing within the virtuoso's cabinet, turning to his books to contemplate "the effigies of those who have made such a noise and bustle in the world, either by their madness and folly, or a more conspicuous figure by their wit and learning."[176]

If we began the story of neo-Epicureanism by meditating on the relationship between Epicurus's physics, cognitive mechanism, and his own contingent and mediated view of the propagation of the self in the *suggrammata,* Evelyn now imagines an entire culture, which those series of imaginative relations define. Like the woman in Le Clerc's *Ars Critica,* Pepys is finally handed to us as an image of the neoclassical reader contemplating the necessarily phenomenal, though atomized, remains of a history he must strenuously and methodically reassemble.

Notes

1. Lucy Hutchinson had already completed a translation of Lucretius in manuscript (see BM Add. MS 19.333). She refers to making the translation while attending to her young children, which probably places the translation in the 1640s, taking a cue from her *Memoirs of the Life of Colonel Hutchinson,* ed. James Sutherland (London: Oxford Univ. Press, 1973), 33-34.

2. John Evelyn, *An Essay on the First Book of T. Lucretius Carus De Rerum Natura Interpreted and Made English Verse* (London, 1656), 109. Sixteen

hundred and fifty-six was a year of wonders, in that it also saw the publication of Walter Charleton's *Epicurus's Morals,* following the publication of his *Physiologia Epicuro-Gassendo-Charletoniana* (London, 1654).

3. I adopt Joy's argument that Gassendi's *Animadversiones,* never printed entire in the *Opera Omnia,* represents Gassendi's most synthetic philosophical oeuvre prior to the publication of the large *Syntagma Philosophicum* (1658), which Evelyn could not have known in 1656. Although she refers to Evelyn's translation of Lucretius, Joy does not seem to notice that it adumbrates a comprehensive grasp of Gassendi's published work and therefore indicates a knowledge of Gassendi in circles that were profoundly to influence Restoration culture. Evelyn cites many of Gassendi's works, including the *Animadversiones* in his *Essay* at 109; 110; 123; 131; 135; 136; 138 *[Animadversiones];* 147; 169; 172 *[Animadversiones].* See Lynn Sumida Joy, *Gassendi the Atomist: Advocate of History in an Age of Science* (Cambridge: Cambridge Univ. Press, 1987), 70. The specificity of relations between Gassendi and English cultural figures is suggested by the striking fact that the figure of Epicurus on the title page of Gassendi's *De Vita et Moribus Epicuri* (1647) and his *Animadversiones* (1649) is virtually identical to the frontispiece of Walter Charleton's *Epicurus' Morals* (1656) (see pp. 153-54 above). The image of Epicurus is almost literally and physically the vehicle of cultural transmission.

4. Writing to Jeremy Taylor on 27 April 1656, Evelyn says that "my Essay upon Lucretius, which I told you was engaged, is now printing, and (as I understand) near finished: my animadversions upon it will I hope provide against all the ill consequences, and totally acquit me either of glory or impiety" (*Diary and Correspondence of John Evelyn, F.R.S.,* 4 vols. [London: Bohn, 1859], 3:73). References to Evelyn's letters are to this edition and will appear as *Corres.*

5. Evelyn, *Essay,* Sig. A6^v.

6. William Rand, trans., *The Mirrour of True Nobility and Gentility. Being the Life of the Renowned Nicolaus Claudius Fabricius Lord of Peiresk, Senator of the Parliament at Aix. Written by the Learned Petrus Gassendus . . .* (London, 1657), Sig. A3^v.

7. Ibid., Sig. A6^r.

8. Ibid., 6:202. The book has odd pagination, so my references may appear slightly misleading.

9. Ibid., 6:203.

10. Ibid., 6:204.

11. Ibid.

12. A classic case occurs in Marie Boas's monograph "The Establishment of the Mechanical Philosophy," *Osiris* 10 (1952): 412-541, a canonical text in the historiography of midcentury natural philosophy. For Boas, Bacon and Descartes are the two "heroes" of the story. I am proposing that, in contrast to the attention lavished on these two hugely authoritative figures, we also admire less epic—and perhaps more enduring—values for the narrative of cultural history.

13. Evelyn, *Essay,* Sig. A3^r.

14. Ibid., Sig. A5^r.

15. See Richard Westfall, "Some Unpublished Boyle Papers Relating to Scientific Method," *Annals of Science* 12 (1956): 63-73; 103-17.

16. I refer to Evelyn's *Essay on . . . Lucretius* (1656) and to Thomas Creech's translation of *De Rerum Natura,* which appeared first in 1682, but reappeared regularly thereafter. The "third edition" of Creech's translation, published in 1683, includes a series of poems to Creech by such authors as Evelyn, Nahum Tate, Thomas Otway, Aphra Behn, and E[dmund] W[aller]. Dryden translated parts of Lucretius in *Sylvae* (1685).

17. A careful assessment of relations between Descartes and More is to be found in Alan Gabbey, "Philosophia Cartesiana Triumphata: Henry More (1646-1671)," in *Problems of Cartesianism,* ed. Thomas H. Lennon et al. (Kingston, Montreal: McGill-Queen's Univ. Press, 1982), 171-250.

18. See, for example, Joseph Glanvill, *The Vanity of Dogmatizing* (London, 1661), 146, and the commentary on Sprat in Charles Webster, "The Origins of the Royal Society," *History of Science* 6 (1967): 116-19.

19. R. H. Kargon describes how William Boswell, who inherited Bacon's manuscripts and in response to the emergence of the mechanical hypothesis, arranged to have his atomistic works, *inter alia,* published in 1653, under the title *Scripta in Naturalia et Universalia Philosophia* (*Atomism in England from Hariot to Newton* [Oxford: Clarendon Press, 1966], 52).

20. Brian Vickers, for example, shows that the polemics surrounding the nature of language in the Restoration had less to do with substance than the institutional position of the combatants: the appropriation of Bacon was primarily symbolic ("The Royal Society and English Prose Style: A Reassessment," in *Rhetoric and the Pursuit of Truth: Language Change in the Seventeenth and Eighteenth Centuries* [Los Angeles: William Andrews Clark Memorial Library, 1985], 3-76).

21. See, variously, Robert G. Frank, *Harvey and the Oxford Physiologists: A Study of Scientific Ideas* (Berkeley: Univ. of California Press, 1980), chap. 4;

A. R. Hall, *The Scientific Revolution, 1500-1800: The Formation of the Modern Scientific Attitude*, 2d ed. (Boston: Beacon Press, 1962), 166-68; Michael Hunter, *Science and Society in Restoration England* (Cambridge: Cambridge Univ. Press, 1981), passim; M. M. Slaughter, *Universal Languages and Scientific Taxonomy in the Seventeenth Century* (Cambridge: Cambridge Univ. Press, 1982), 90-100; and Richard S. Westfall, *The Construction of Modern Science: Mechanisms and Mechanics* (1971; reprint, Cambridge: Cambridge Univ. Press, 1977), 114.

22. See, for example, John W. Yolton, *Locke and the Compass of Human Understanding* (Cambridge: Cambridge Univ. Press, 1970), 7, which stresses Locke's Baconianism.

23. This is the distinction that Evelyn communicates between Boyle's critical method and Bacon's less discriminate inductivism. See *Corres.*, 3:348: Talking of Boyle, Evelyn writes that "never did stubborn matter come under his inquisition but he extorted a confession of all that lay in her most intimate recesses; and what he discovered he as faithfully registered, and frankly communicated; in this exceeding my Lord Verulam, who (though never to be mentioned without honour and admiration) was used to tell all that came to hand without much examination."

24. See Thomas Sprat, *Observations on Monsieur Sorbière's Voyage into England* (London, 1665), 233-34: "I scarce know two men in the World, that have more different colors of Speech, than these two great Witts: the Lord *Bacon* short, allusive, and abounding with Metaphors: Mr. *Hobbs* round, close, sparing of similitudes: but ever extraordinary decent in them. The one's way of reas'ning, proceeds on particulars, and pleasant images, only suggesting new ways of experimenting, without any pretence to the *Mathematicks*. The other's bold, resolv'd, setled upon general conclusions, and in them, if we will believe his *Friend, Dogmatical*."

25. Samuel Sorbière, *Relation d'un Voyage en Angleterre, Ou sont Touchées Plusieurs Choses, qui Regardent l'Estat des Sciences, et de la Religion, et Autres Matières Curieuses* (Paris, 1664).

26. Sprat, *Observations*, 110-11.

27. Ibid., 180.

28. Sorbière, *Relation*, 91; 93.

29. Ibid., 92.

30. Ibid., 94; 82-83.

31. Sprat, *Observations*, 241-42.

32. See Thomas Franklin Mayo, *Epicurus in England, 1650-1725* (Dallas: Southwest Press, 1934), 170.

33. The *National Union Catalogue* and *Short Title Catalogue* record the following publications for Gassendi: *Institutio Astronomica* (1653; anr. ed., 1653; 1674; 1675; 1683; 1702); *Institutio Logica et Philosophiae Epicuri Syntagma* (1660; 1668); *The Mirrour of True Nobility and Gentility* (1657); *Three Discourses of Happiness, Virtue, and Liberty* (1699); and *The Vanity of Judiciary Astrology* (1659; anr. ed., 1659). I have also shown that the section on Epicurus in volume three of Thomas Stanley's popular *History of Philosophy* (1655-62; vol. 3: 1659) is a translation of Gassendi's *Philosophiae Epicuri Syntagma*. And, finally, Walter Charleton's *Physiologia Epicuro-Gassendo-Charletoniana* (1654) is often treated as a redaction of Gassendist views.

34. The *Short Title Catalogue* and the *Gallery of Ghosts* record the following titles for Descartes: *A Discourse of Method* (1649); *Renati Descartes Epistolae* (1668; 1683); *Ethice* (1685); *Renatus Descartes Excellent Compendium of Music* (1653); *Exercitationes* (1685); *R. des Cartes Meditationes* (1664; anr. ed., 1664); *The Passions of the Soule* (1650); *Principia Philosophiae* (1664); *Six Metaphysical Meditations* (1680); *Specrmene Philosophiae* (1667); and *The Use of the Geometrical Playing Cards* (1697).

35. See C. T. Harrison, "The Ancient Atomists and English Literature of the Seventeenth Century," *Harvard Studies in Classical Philology* 45 (1934): 1-79; and "Bacon, Hobbes, Boyle, and the Ancient Atomists," *Harvard University Studies and Notes in Philology and Literature* 15 (1933): 191-218.

36. Harrison, "Ancient Atomists," 23.

37. Kargon, *Atomism in England*, chap. 8; Harrison, "Ancient Atomists," 56ff. A particularly vivid example of the degree to which influential writers were acquainted with neo-Epicureanism is Edward Stillingfleet's *Origines Sacrae: Or a Rational Account of the Grounds of the Christian Faith* (1662; 3d ed., Cambridge, 1701). Already in 1662, Stillingfleet records "the *Atomical* or *Epicurean Hypothesis*" as "that which makes most noise in the World" (301), and, though he attacks its materialist implications, he actually seeks to subordinate the atomic hypothesis to providence. One device Stillingfleet uses is to attack the potential dogmatism of Epicurean physics by resorting to Epicurus's own probabilistic criteria for knowledge in his canon (303). Stillingfleet displays a considerable acquaintance with Gassendi's *Opera Omnia* (e.g., 307; 309).

38. Cudworth pushes Greek atomism back to Empedocles, Pythagoras, and Anaxagoras, accusing Democritus and Leucippus of being "the first atheizers of this ancient Atomic physiology" (*The True Intellectual System of the Universe*, ed. Thomas Birch, 4 vols. [London: R. Priestley, 1820], 1:53); and John Smith, attacking Epicurus in great

detail, reminds his readers that Democritus was "the first Author" of the atomic thesis (*Select Discourses* [London, 1660], 47).

39. See for example, Kargon's comment on *The Origin of Forms and Qualities* in *Atomism in England*, 99.

40. Slaughter writes, however, that "for the most part, the early Royal Society was firm in asserting its opposition to hypothetical physics. . . . The 'empirics' rejected all theories and asserted the primacy of natural history—of the minute observation of phenomena and the recording of data" (*Universal Languages*, 190). She sees Locke as a hypotheticalist and Boyle and Hooke as "empirics." These dichotomies seem too absolute.

41. M. A. Stewart, ed. and intro., *Selected Philosophical Papers of Robert Boyle* (Manchester: Manchester Univ. Press, 1979), xxx.

42. Richard S. Westfall, "Some Unpublished Boyle Papers Relating to Scientific Method," *Annals of Science* 12 (1956): 63-73; 103-17.

43. Cudworth, *True Intellectual System*, 1:53.

44. Danton B. Sailor, "Moses and Atomism," *Journal of the History of Ideas* 25 (1964): 3-16; see also E. A. Burtt, *The Metaphysical Foundations of Modern Science: The Scientific Thinking of Copernicus, Galileo, Newton, and Their Contemporaries* (1924; reprint, Atlantic Highlands, N.J.: Humanities Press, 1980), 149.

45. Cudworth, *True Intellectual System*, 1:20.

46. Ibid., 2:123.

47. Cudworth must be one of the last people to have defended the authenticity of the hermetic corpus against Isaac Casaubon's devastating criticisms of it (*True Intellectual System*, 2:124-30). For Isaac Casaubon's effect on hermeticism, see Anthony Grafton, "Protestant versus Prophet: Isaac Casaubon on Hermes Trismegistus," *Journal of the Warburg and Courtauld Institutes* 46 (1983): 78-93; Grafton is elaborating in part the suggestion of Frances A. Yates, *Giordano Bruno and the Hermetic Tradition* (New York: Vintage, 1964), 423-37.

48. Henry More also shares something of this peculiar midcentury ambivalence toward atomism and method. For a discussion of the difference between More and Stillingfleet on these and related issues, see Alison Coudert, "Limits of Latitudinarianism: Henry More's Reaction to the Kabbala and Quakerism"; and Sarah Hutton, "Neoplatonism and Latitudinarianism: Henry More, Edward Stillingfleet and the Decline of *Moses Atticus*," in *Philosophy, Science, and Religion in England, 1640-1700* (Cambridge: Cambridge Univ. Press, 1991), ed. Richard W. F. Kroll et al. John Tulloch provides a critique of Cudworth's uncritical method: see *Rational Theology and Christian Philosophy in England in the Seventeenth Century*, 2 vols.

(Edinburgh: Blackwood, 1872), 2:479-80; and Joseph M. Levine refers to More's "hopelessly unhistorical" use of the ancient wisdom ("Latitudinarians, Neoplatonists, and the Ancient Wisdom," in *Philosophy, Science, and Religion*).

49. *True Intellectual System*, 2:64.

50. Ibid., 4:211.

51. Ibid., 2:328.

52. Theophilus Gale, *The Court of the Gentiles: Or A Discourse Touching the Original of Human Literature, both Philologie and Philosophie, from the Scriptures, and Jewish Church* (London, 1669), Sig. $\pi3^r$; italics reversed.

53. Ibid., Sig $\pi2^v$.

54. Ibid., Sig. $\pi3^r$; italics reversed.

55. Ibid., 14.

56. See Thomas Harmon Jobe, "The Devil in Restoration Science," *Isis* 72 (1981): 343-56.

57. Richard Bentley, *The Folly and Unreasonableness of Atheism* (1692; 5th ed. entitled *Eight Sermons Preach'd at the Honourable Robert Boyle's Lecture* [London, 1724]).

58. Ibid., 125.

59. Ibid., 61.

60. Mayo, *Epicurus in England*, 191-92.

61. Thomas Creech, trans., *T. Lucretius Carus, Of the Nature of Things* (London, 1715). Creech died in 1700. Cosmo Alexander Gordon points out that the '1715' edition is a state of the 1714 edition (*A Bibliography of Lucretius* [London: Hart-Davis, 1962], 178-79). He also suggest that the additional reflections are by John Digby, the translator of *Epicurus' Morals* (ibid., 171).

62. See chapter four above, n.6.

63. Joy, *Gassendi the Atomist*, chap. 9.

64. See Kargon, *Atomism in England*, chaps. 8 and 9.

65. J. B. van Helmont, *Deliramenta Catarrhi*, trans. Walter Charleton (London, 1650); *A Ternary of Paradoxes*, trans. Walter Charleton (London, 1650).

66. Kargon, *Atomism in England*, 86.

67. See Richard W. F. Kroll, "The Question of Locke's Relation to Gassendi," *Journal of the History of Ideas* 45 (1984): 339-59. Although I demonstrate this fact, I mistake the 'small' *Syntagma* (1649)—which Stanley translated—for Gassendi's 'large,' final *Syntagma Philosophicum* (1658).

68. See "An Account of the Life and Writings of *Thomas Stanley, Esq.*," in Thomas Stanley, *The History of Philosophy*, 3d ed. (London, 1701), Sig. d1^v.

69. The *National Union Catalogue* records the following: *The History of Chaldaic Philosophy* (1662; 1687; 1701); and *The Life of Socrates* (1701).

70. See *The Evelyn Library*, 4 vols. (London: Christie's, 1977-78), 3, item #1409; John Harrison and Peter Laslett, eds., *The Library of John Locke*, 2d ed. (Oxford: Clarendon Press, 1971), item ##758; 2755; John Harrison, ed., *The Library of Isaac Newton* (Cambridge: Cambridge Univ. Press, 1978), item ##1551-1552.

71. Jackson I. Cope, *Joseph Glanvill: Anglican Apologist* (Saint Louis: Washington Univ. Studies, 1956), 133-39.

72. Stanley writes that "the Learned *Gassendus* was my precedent" (*The History of Philosophy*, Sig. $\pi 2^r$).

73. Ibid., Sig. $\pi 2^v$ (italics reversed).

74. Additionally, Bernier's important *Abrégé de la Philosophie de Mr. Gassendi* (Paris, 1674) was issued five times in the first ten years of its existence.

75. Margaret C. Jacob, *The Newtonians and the English Revolution, 1689-1720* (Ithaca: Cornell University Press, 1976), 33.

76. For details of Evelyn's life, see the introduction to E. S. de Beer, ed., *The Diary of John Evelyn*, 6 vols. (Oxford: Clarendon Press, 1955), 1:1-43.

77. Thomas Stanley, *Historia Philosophiae* (Leipzig, 1711). In the section devoted to Epicurus (pt. 12, 924-1110), there are sixty-seven references to the *Animadversiones* in the marginalia, almost exactly half of them in the section on ethics.

78. *The Autobiography of Giambattista Vico*, ed. Max Harold Fisch and Thomas Goddard Bergin (1944; reprint, Ithaca: Cornell Univ. Press, 1963), 126; 128.

79. *The Works of the Honourable Robert Boyle*, ed. Thomas Birch, 2d ed., 6 vols. (London, 1772), 6:724.

80. Ibid., 1:194.

81. Ibid., 1:222.

82. Kargon, *Atomism in England*, 63; and Frank, *Harvey and the Oxford Physiologists*, 90-93.

83. Helen Hervey, "Hobbes and Descartes in the Light of Some Unpublished Letters of the Correspondence between Sir Charles Cavendish and Dr. John Pell," *Osiris*, 10 (1952): 67-90.

84. In the dedication to *The Mirrour of True Nobility and Gentility*, Rand mentions his friendship with Hartlib *("Harlib")*, who had ten years previously recommended Gassendi's life of Peiresc to him (Sig. A3^r).

85. Robert Vaughan, D.D., ed., *The Protectorate of Oliver Cromwell, and the State of Europe during the Early Part of the Reign of Louis XIV*, 2 vols. (London: Henry Colburn, 1838), 2:367-68.

86. Ibid., 2:370.

87. Hervey, "Hobbes and Descartes," 78.

88. Ibid., 73.

89. James Orchard Halliwell-Phillips, *A Collection of Letters Illustrative of the Progress of Science in England, from the Reign of Queen Elizabeth to that of Charles the Second* (London: London Historical Society of Science, 1841), 86.

90. Ibid., 87.

91. Vaughan, *Protectorate*, 2:371-72.

92. Hervey, "Hobbes and Descartes," 73.

93. Ibid., 85.

94. Halliwell-Phillips, *Collection of Letters*, 80.

95. Ibid.

96. Hervey, "Hobbes and Descartes," 78.

97. Ibid.

98. Ibid.

99. Ibid., 80.

100. Boyle, *Works*, 1:xli.

101. Ibid., 6:76.

102. Ibid., 1:xxxvii.

103. Ibid., 1:xli.

104. Ibid., 1:xxxviii.

105. Ibid., 1:xxxix.

106. Ibid., 1:xl.

107. Ibid. This metaphor of coinage also occurs in Rand's translation of Gassendi's life of Peiresc.

108. On the role of corresponding societies and learned colleges, see Charles Webster, ed., *Samuel Hartlib and the Advancement of Learning* (Cambridge: Cambridge Univ. Press, 1970), 30.

109. Gassendi, *De Vita et Moribus Epicuri* (Lyon, 1647), Sigs. II2^v-II3^r. It was approved on 5 August 1647.

110. Boyle, *Works*, 6:77.

111. Ibid.

112. *The Correspondence of Henry Oldenburg*, ed. A. Rupert Hall and Marie Boas Hall, 9 vols. (Madison: Univ. of Wisconsin Press, 1965-73), 2:42. In *Some Considerations touching the Usefulness of Experimental Natural Philosophy*, Boyle writes in praise of Epicurus: "And as confident as those we speak of use to be, of knowing the true and adequate causes of things, yet *Epicurus* himself, as appears by ancient testimony, and by his own writings, was more modest, not only contenting himself, on many occasions, to propose several possible ways, whereby a phaenomenon may be accounted for, but sometimes seeming to dislike the

so pitching upon any one explication, as to exclude and reject all others: and some modern philosophers, that much favour his doctrine, do likewise imitate his example, in pretending to assign not precisely the true, but possible causes of the phaenomenon they endeavour to explain" (*Works*, 2:45).

113. See E. S. de Beer, introduction to *The Diary of John Evelyn*, 1:10. And also Evelyn's own dedication to Sir Richard Browne in *Publick Employment and an Active Life Prefer'd to Solitude* (London, 1667), Sigs. A4ᵛ-A5ʳ: "I might here mention the constant *Asylum* which the Persecuted *Clergy* found within your *walls* upon all occasions. . . . When your *Chappel* was the *Church* of *England* in her most *glorious estate*." For a description of the state of the church in exile during the Interregnum, see R. S. Bosher, *The Making of the Restoration Settlement: The Influence of the Laudians, 1649-1662* (Westminster: Dacre Press, 1951), chap. 2.

114. Taylor to Evelyn, 16 April 1656, *Corres.*, 3:71. See also Seth Lerer, *Boethius and Dialogue: Literary Method in the Consolation of Philosophy* (Princeton: Princeton Univ. Press, 1985), 32ff., for a commentary on the epistemological and literary significance of the Ciceronian dialogue.

115. Like *De Rerum Natura*, the *Tusculanian Disputations* occur in five movements.

116. For example, Evelyn's correspondents include Wilkins, Sprat, Boyle, Hartlib, Jeremy Taylor, Pepys, Clifford, Creech, Meric Casaubon, Lady Margaret Cavendish, Wotton, Sir Thomas Browne, and Glanvill.

117. Charleton predicts a relationship between reading and friendship in *Epicurus's Morals*, when he writes to his reader that "if the Rule hold, that Similitude of Opinions, is an argument of Similitude in Affections, and Similitude of Affections the ground of Love and friendship, certainly I am not altogether destitute of support for my conjectures, and consequently that you will soone admitt him [Epicurus] into your bosome" (Sig. A4ʳ).

118. On the Taylor-Evelyn friendship, see Tulloch, *Rational Theology*, 1:366-67. Jeremy Taylor's *A Discourse of the Nature, Offices and Measures of Friendship with Rules of Conducting it. Written in answer to a Letter from the Most Ingenious and Vertuous M.[rs] K.[atharine] P.[hilips]* (London, 1657; reprint, London: Chapman and Hall, 1920) includes an appendix consisting of two exemplary letters.

119. Taylor to Evelyn, *Corres.*, 3:94.

120. Ibid., 3:97.

121. Evelyn records in his diary that he began planting for his garden on 17 January 1653: "This was the beginning of all the succeeding *Gardens, Walkes, Groves, Enclosures & Plantations* there." See John Evelyn, *Diary*, ed. E. S. De Beer, 6 vols. (London: Oxford Univ. Press, 1955), 3:80.

122. In his diary, Evelyn records a number of visits to Sayes Court, mostly by royalists, including King Charles II himself. But the entry for 1 May 1657 reads: "There had ben at my house this afternoone *Laurence* president of *Olivers* Council, & some other of his Court Lords to see my Garden and plantations."

123. Taylor, *Discourse*, 58.

124. Ibid., 59.

125. Rand, *Mirrour of True Nobility and Gentility*, Sig. A6ʳ.

126. For bibliographic commentary, as well as illustrations of the Jansson and Marolles frontispieces, see Cosmo Alexander Gordon, *A Bibliography of Lucretius* (London: Hart-Davis, 1962), 135-36; 154-55; and 172-75.

127. Thomas P. Roche, Jr., has suggested in conversation that Mary Evelyn's early training in Renaissance iconology could have come to her in France, through the second school of Fontainebleau.

128. For a reading of this icon, see Thomas P. Roche, Jr., *The Kindly Flame: A Study of the Third and Fourth Books of Spencer's "Faerie Queene"* (Princeton: Princeton Univ. Press, 1964), 23-26.

129. Interestingly, Evelyn himself describes the revision or rendering orthodox of cultural figures in terms of the activity of denuding a female image (Evelyn to Taylor, 27 April 1656, *Corres.*, 3:73-74).

130. Evelyn was himself to design the famous frontispiece to Sprat's *History of the Royal Society*.

131. See John Wilkins to Evelyn, 16 August 1656, *Corres.*, 3:76; and Evelyn to Meric Casaubon, 15 July 1674, *Corres.*, 3:246-47.

132. Taylor to Evelyn, 9 October 1656, *Corres.*, 3:78n.

133. Evelyn to William Wotton, 30 March 1696, *Corres.*, 3:349.

134. Taylor to Evelyn, 9 October 1656, *Corres.*, 3:72.

135. Taylor to Evelyn, 29 August 1657, *Corres.*, 3:98ff.

136. Taylor to Evelyn, 9 October 1656, *Corres.*, 3:73.

137. Evelyn to Wotton, 12 September 1703, *Corres.*, 3:391.

138. Evelyn to Mr. Maddox, 10 January 1656-7, *Corres.*, 3:85; see also Evelyn to Wotton, 30 March 1696, *Corres.*, 3:346.

139. Evelyn to Wotton, 12 September 1703, *Corres.*, 3:395-96. The myth demonstrates by an almost parabolic narrative that the two families are allied by blood.

140. *Diary*, 10 July 1654.

141. See Evelyn to Wotton, 12 September 1703, *Corres.,* 3:391.

142. Evelyn to Robert Boyle, 9 August 1659, *Corres.,* 3:114.

143. Ibid., 3:115.

144. Evelyn to Lord Viscount Cornbury, 9 September 1665, *Corres.,* 3:167. Later, we discover in a letter to Pepys that Durdans is also one of those loci in which cultural artifacts are being gathered.

145. Evelyn to Boyle, 3 September 1659, *Corres.,* 3:116.

146. Ibid., 3:117.

147. Ibid.

148. Ibid., 3:119.

149. Ibid., 116.

150. Evelyn to Samuel Pepys, 12 August 1689, *Corres.,* 3:295.

151. Ibid., 3:304; 308.

152. Ibid., 3:295.

153. Ibid., 3:302.

154. Evelyn mentions that Prince Henry's collection of ten thousand medals was dispersed by the Civil War (ibid., 3:305-6); he also fears that Ashmole's collection may have been destroyed by fire (ibid., 3:299).

155. Ibid., 3:300.

156. Ibid., 3:302.

157. See Evelyn, *Instructions concerning Erecting of a Library* (London, 1661); and *Corres.,* 3:303: "Yes, he was a great lover at least of books, and furnished a very ample library, writ himself an elegant style, favoured and promoted the design of the Royal Society; and it was for this, and in particular, for his being very kind to me both abroad and at home, that I sent *Naudaeus* to him in a dedicatory address, of which I am not so much ashamed as of the translation."

158. Evelyn uses an extended image of dismemberment (*Corres.,* 3:309) and also refers to the new mode of writing as embodying "nervous, natural strength, and beauty, genuine and of our own growth" (ibid., 3:311).

159. Evelyn refers to Wren's "sumptuous structure" (*Corres.,* 3:306).

160. *Corres.,* 3:311.

161. Ibid., 3:310.

162. Ibid., 3:297.

163. Ibid.

164. Ibid., 3:304.

165. For example, Evelyn refers us to "sundry more of that fair sex who ruled the world" (ibid., 3:298).

166. *Corres.,* 3:298.

167. Ibid., 3:296.

168. Ibid., 3:299.

169. Evelyn to Lord Godolphin, 16 June 1696, *Corres.,* 3:354ff.

170. Ibid., 3:354.

171. Ibid., 3:355.

172. Evelyn to Pepys, 12 August 1689, *Corres.,* 3:297.

173. Sir Geoffrey Keynes, *John Evelyn: A Study in Bibliophily with a Bibliography of His Writing* (Oxford: Clarendon Press, 1968), 231.

174. Ibid.

175. Evelyn to Pepys, 12 August 1689, *Corres.,* 3:303-4.

176. Ibid., 3:304.

Thomas M. Lennon (essay date 1993)

SOURCE: "Mind Versus Flesh," in *The Battle of the Gods and Giants: The Legacies of Descartes and Gassendi, 1655-1715,* Princeton University Press, 1993, pp. 106-37.

[In this excerpt, Lennon considers in depth Gassendi's Objections *to René Descartes'* Meditations. *Focusing on the problem of representation, Lennon defends Gassendi from the charge, put forth by both Descartes and later critics, that he simply did not understand the nature of Descartes' method. Nevertheless, as Lennon argues throughout his book, the materialism that provided the foundation for Gassendi's critiques eventually could not compete with the dominance of Cartesian philosophy.]*

Mind Versus Flesh

Early on Descartes had taken Gassendi to be, if not an authority, then at least someone to be regarded seriously in optics, astronomy, and other matters.[1] With Gassendi's **Objections,** however, Descartes's attitude changes dramatically. On June 23, 1641, he returned to Mersenne Gassendi's objections along with the advice to have them printed without showing them to Gassendi, who when he saw how bad his objections were would want them "suppressed." Descartes meanwhile was loathe to see his time in replying wasted or the possibility realized that some would think that it was he who, unable to answer the objections, had them suppressed. He concludes the letter: "you will see that I have done all I could to treat Gassendi honorably and gently; but he gave me so many occasions to despise him and to show he has no common sense and can in no way reason, that I would have done too much less than my duty had I said less, and I assure you I could have said much more."[2]

A month later Descartes again wrote to Mersenne, saying that Gassendi had no grounds for complaint at his treatment, for he gave only equal in kind despite what he had always heard, namely, that the first blow is worth two and that thus to be really equal the reply should have been doubled. "But perhaps he was affected by my replies because he recognized their truth, while I was not for an entirely different reason; if so, it is not my fault."[3] Two years later Descartes could still muster respect for Gassendi's empirical astronomy,[4] but by then he could tell just from the index of Gassendi's letters that they contained nothing he needed to read.[5] The literature has tended to fault Gassendi for failing really to engage Descartes's views; the converse seems no less true. For the most part Descartes treated his would-be adversary as beyond contempt. Discussing why criticism of his work is no burden Descartes wrote that Gassendi's *Instantia* did not displease him as much as he was pleased by Mesland's judgment that there was nothing in the work not easily answered.[6]

As for Gassendi's attitudes, there are two versions of the story. One has it that he was no less than livid with Descartes and no less than he in his acrimony and petulance. But this version is based on the testimony of Jean-Baptiste Morin, an eccentric to say the least, who on other grounds was concerned to besmirch the reputation of Gassendi. Thus, for example, Descartes's calling Gassendi "Flesh" in his *Replies* would be understood only as justified retaliation for having been referred to as "Mind" in the *Objections.* More credible is the account of Bernier, who portrays a rather more detached, long-suffering response from his teacher. In any case, the personal differences between the great antagonists were finally repaired in 1648 following a dinner arranged for them by the Abbé d'Estrées. As it happened, Gassendi was unable to attend because of illness; but after the dinner, the assembled party visited Gassendi, who was embraced by Descartes.[7]

Gassendi's *Objections* may well be regarded as unique.[8] Among other objectors, Arnauld, who really asks only for clarifications, and the Scholastic theologians share important metaphysical presuppositions with Descartes. Hobbes does not engage Descartes so much as merely juxtapose his own views to those of Descartes, with Descartes replying in kind. In the case of Gassendi, however, we find an elaborated and systematic metaphysical confrontation. The length of his exchanges with Descartes thus reflects their relative importance. The *Fifth Objections* (1641) are more than twice as long as any other set, and if Descartes thought them "not the most important"[9] he nonetheless replied to them at greatest length. Within a year Gassendi had responded with his *Rebuttals* (*Instantiae*: literally, follows-up) which with the *Fifth Objections* and *Replies* were published in 1644 under the general title of *Disquisitio metaphysica,* totaling some 150 pages *in folio* of the *Opera omnia.*

At the core of Gassendi's critique of Descartes is the notion of representation. There are arguments from Gassendi against Descartes, as there were later to be from Locke and Foucher against Malebranche,[10] to the effect that an idea to represent a square would have to be square. At one point, for example, Gassendi poses the following dilemma, designed to argue that the mind of which Descartes claims to have an idea is essentially extended. Only if an idea has extension can it represent extension; only if it has shape and location can it represent what has shape and location, for an idea must be like what it represents. But only if an idea has no extension, shape, or location can it be joined to the essentially unextended, unshaped, unlocated thing that the mind is alleged to be, for the essence of the mind is supposed to be thought, which excludes properties of extension.[11]

The dilemma may be released, as Gassendi urges, by denying that the self is an essentially unextended, unshaped, unlocated thing. But this does not explain how Gassendi, or any imagist, deals with the first horn of the dilemma. There seem to me three possible answers to the problem of imagist ideas representing extension. Historically they overlap. One is the skeptical answer, to which Gassendi is certainly inclined, namely, that the idea of a square, for example, just does not represent at all; we do not know the real. But this response by itself is insufficient. Even if the idea does not represent a real square, it is a different idea from the idea of a circle, and it is not clear that the problem of distinguishing them is any more tractable than the problem of how an unextended idea can represent an extended thing. In fact, it might be argued, these are versions of the same problem. It is not surprising, then, that the skeptical answer is to be found combined with others among the philosophically more astute.

A second possible answer, one emphasized by Locke, is to give an account of resemblance that would allow the unextended to resemble and thus to represent the extended. I do not have in mind here the realist account in terms of the same thing existing in different ways—a mental, nonspatial square being qualitatively identical to, and thus representing, a material, spatial square. Many agree that this is the account advanced by the orthodox Cartesians. . . . It is also the account advanced by Leibniz, according to whom even ideas of secondary qualities resemble. The idea of pain resembles, although confusedly, a certain motion in the body, for example.[12] There are many reasons, however, why this account is inimical to the tradition whose view of ideas I am discussing here. The one of immediate relevance is that this realist account is incompatible with the skeptical answer above, for it grounds knowledge of the real. Far from cutting us off from the real, this account of ideas gives us immediate access to it. As Arnauld put it, the idea is the thing itself insofar as it exists in the mind.[13]

Instead, the possible answer I have in mind would have it that an unextended idea resembles an extended thing just in case it stands in a certain causal relation to it. Thus we may call it the causal answer. Later there will be a more appropriate occasion to develop Locke's version of this answer. The gist of it is that the idea of a square, and of primary qualities generally, resembles and thus represents its object in that given the corpuscularian hypothesis, the object could produce only that idea. The reality, inseparability, and resemblance to ideas of primary qualities come to the same thing. Given the corpuscularian hypothesis, the world must have certain features in order to appear to us as it does. Secondary qualities, on the other hand, are imputed, separable, and fail to resemble. Even given a fully articulated corpuscularian account, there is no reason why the motion that in fact produces the idea of pain should not produce the idea of redness. That it does not is attributable to the biological utility of the former arrangement. Still, even ideas of secondary qualities are said by Locke to represent and may be said to represent their (partial, remote) causes. However contingent it might be, the fact of the matter is that lemons taste tart and pineapples sweet. And we perceive them in this way at least partly because of their fine structure, between which and our perceptions there is a regular, if mechanistically inexplicable, correlation. Thus, Gassendi's dilemma is generally resolved by denying the crucial premise of the first horn. Representation does not depend on resemblance in the sense that representing idea and represented object both have the same property, but rather on the causal connection between them. The historical irony is that Locke's actual version of the causal answer allows for resemblance in a way that construes ideas as extended and the thing represented as unextended. . . . The short of it is that (1) ideas are impressions of which we are aware, that is, corporeal states or motions, and are thus extended, and (2) extension is relational and thus only phenomenal, and hence the noumenal object represented by an idea is unextended.

Ideas are also extended according to the third answer, the materialist answer. According to it, the idea of a square represents a square because it actually is square. This is to embrace the first horn, suitably interpreted, as it is for Locke in the causal answer just given. The historical plausibility of my thesis here will be enhanced by noting that, although essentially materialistic, this tack was taken by Berkeley. Consider, for example, his argument with respect to the intense degree of heat as pain, the very first argument of the *Three Dialogues*. No unperceiving thing is capable of pain; a material substance is unperceiving, hence incapable of pain; but the intense degree of heat is pain, thus material substance is incapable of, that is, cannot have as a property, the intense degree of heat. And, of course, what is true of the intense degree of heat, we later learn, is true of all properties. Given his own analysis of objects as bundles of ideas or sensations, Berkeley is not entitled to the first premise, and he effectively rejects it. More generally, ideas and only ideas have the properties they appear to have, so that when Berkeley takes representation to depend on resemblance in the sense that representing idea and represented object both have the same property, representationalism comes under attack. As Berkeley insists repeatedly, an idea can resemble only another idea. The moral of the story is that the essential element in this approach to ideas is not the invitation to materialism, but the construal of ideas as images. Just how Berkeley distinguishes his view from the materialists is a question beyond the scope of my story. Here it will suffice to show

how the imagist conception of ideas ties together the three answers to Gassendi's dilemma.

Taken no further, the dilemma Gassendi poses for Descartes remains at a superficial level. A deeper concern is the whole notion of representation that Descartes employs in extrapolating from ideas to things, or more precisely, from the realm of thought to that of essences. According to one particularly relevant interpretation, the key to Descartes's theory of ideas is his analytic geometry, which provides the model for representation: An idea represents in the way in which the algebraic equation for a curve expresses that curve by giving a rule for the deduction of all its properties.[14] I am not quite convinced that this Leibnizean reading can be wrung from the Cartesian texts. At a minimum, however, it is true that for Descartes an idea is an intelligible rather than sensible representation. As opposed to Gassendist images, which are particular, it is universal. Gassendi has been charged by later commentators with having failed to see how different a theory of ideas he was dealing with, or worse, with having just failed to understand it. But of this Gassendi is innocent, for he correctly saw that Cartesian knowledge would be abstract in just the pejorative sense in which Descartes had castigated Aristotelian-Scholastic knowledge as abstract (and in which Bernier, as we have just seen, was to castigate Gassendi's conception of time). Were there Cartesian ideas, Gassendi argued, they might lead to what is true of a thing, but failing to be an image of it, they would not provide *real* knowledge of it. How so?

Gassendi does not object to Descartes's conclusions, at least not to his principal ones concerning the existence of God and the immortality of the soul.[15] Instead, in a way that adumbrates Locke's reaction to Cartesianism, he attacks the arguments for Descartes's conclusions, and especially the *kind* of argument they exemplify. Thus, for example, we find Gassendi taxing Descartes for claiming that his metaphysical demonstrations are more certain than those of mathematics when they do not even get general assent. The following is paradigmatic of the offending sort of argument:

> 1. Things I consider as conceptually distinct are really distinct.
>
> 2. I consider thinking substance and corporeal substance as conceptually distinct. Therefore,
>
> 3. Thinking substance and corporeal substance are really distinct.[16]

The first premise expresses a necessary connection between concepts that is apprehended by a metaphysical or intellectual intuition; the second expresses an instantiation of the same concepts apprehended by the same intuition. Now, to be sure, Descartes rejects this syllogized version of his reasoning that Gassendi attributes to him.[17] For Descartes, the conclusion of what is really an intellectual induction is the first premise, drawn on the basis of the second premise and the conclusion. But it is precisely this induction and the intuition on which it rests that Gassendi rejects and that lies at the heart of his critique of Descartes.[18] For Gassendi, as for Locke, experience is the only source of knowledge. For Locke, as for Gassendi, we have no intellectual intuition and thus his rejection of the innate ideas claimed by Descartes and others is of a piece with his rejection of the ideas Malebranche claimed to see in God. Gassendi shows the way, effectively by rejecting the nonsensuous half of *Republic's* Divided Line.

Consider his reaction to the Cartesian method of doubt, a topic on which as a skeptic he is especially sensitive. In the **Disquisitio**[19] he argues that contrary to what is claimed for this method, it is impossible to free the mind from its prejudices. The attempt to do so is, we might say, (1) psychologically, (2) methodologically, and (3) epistemologically futile. Let us consider each of these aspects, which are important even quite apart from the issue of intellectual intuition.

(1) The *psychological futility* of Cartesian doubt is of a piece with a skeptical position advanced since antiquity. Gassendi's point is that we just cannot avoid making judgments that we are accustomed to making such as that the intersection of two lines produces angles equal to two right angles or that a certain round object shines. And his point perfectly accords with the recommendation of traditional skeptics that we suspend judgment whenever it is possible to do so. For it is possible to suspend judgment in their view only with respect to metaphysical issues, that is, the essences of things. In all other cases, that is, in sense perceptions, nature breaks the skeptic by constraining assent.

Gassendi is often portrayed as having missed, not just Descartes's theory of ideas, but more especially the nature of his method of doubt. Gassendi failed to distinguish, so the story goes, between the intrinsic doubt of convinced skeptics and the instrumental doubt Descartes uses against them, between real and practical doubt on the one hand, and the merely theoretical doubt advocated by Descartes on the other. Descartes did not really doubt he had a body, but only feigned such doubt in order better to support his belief that he did. But in fact Gassendi shows remarkable sophistication in replying to this charge of oversight as it was first raised by Descartes himself. To be sure, "the distinction 'between the acts of daily life and the inquiry after truth' is totally justified."[20] The skeptics reject indifference in questions of daily life (and, we might add, in precisely the same conservative way Descartes did with his provisional morality).[21] With respect to the inquiry after truth they distinguish between *phainomena,* "things which appear to the senses," which they accept, and *noumena,* "the things which are understood by the mind," which they do not.[22] Thus the dogmatist Descartes gets it exactly the wrong way round. This assertion is no argument, but it at least shows that Gassendi understands perfectly well what is at issue.

(2) Gassendi's charge under the rubric of what I have called the *methodological futility* of Cartesian doubt is rather ill-defined.

Secondly, even if I granted that the mind is liberated and is like a *tabula rasa* on which no judgment has been traced, you assume that "it can deduce some conclusions from principles";[23] but this too appears to be impossible. Clearly if it has no preconceived notions [*praejudicia*], then it does not have any principles; for principles, as they are here understood, are statements [*enunciationes*]; and statements are kinds of judgments in which something is either affirmed or denied. Hence these principles will be judgments, and inasmuch as they are conceived in advance, they are preconceived notions. Therefore, if the mind has no preconceived notion in it, neither will it have any principles from which it may deduce something . . . since no new evidence appears which convinces us that any different relationship than the one above is to be enunciated, it follows that the statements about reality will be neither new statements, nor opposite ones, but the same ones as before, and so the same preconceived notions will crop up again.[24]

Essentially he seems to be saying that even if the doubt Descartes recommends were possible, it could not yield the result he thinks. Gassendi claims that nothing really new emerges from the method of doubt as a deconstruction of all the propositions we have held; that is, having broken down these propositions (enunciationes) into their constituent elements, we then put them together again in exactly the same way. Now, of course we know that the Cartesian restoration of the house of belief may look room-for-room identical; but its novelty is the supposed foundation on which it rests. And it may be to this very supposition that Gassendi objects.

In addition, Gassendi may be arguing "holistic empiricism." Though the mind is initially a *tabula rasa,* and though all knowledge is empirically derived, we need principles to derive principles. We may have here, from the principal source of seventeenth-century empiricism, a prototype of more recent arguments against concept empiricism. Epistemologically, it takes a pair of tongs to make a pair of tongs.

Finally, Gassendi may partially misunderstand Descartes, whose principles are not statements, that is, things *we* put together, but common notions or innate ideas, that is, structures that are *given*. This is the realism to which Descartes, whatever the details of his theory of innate ideas, is clearly committed. In these terms, however, the issue is the very fundamental one we have been discussing of whether we have the intellectual intuition to apprehend these structures that give us the essence of things.

(3) Under the heading of the *epistemological futility* of Cartesian doubt, Gassendi reiterates a point from above and focuses it on a familiar anti-Cartesian theme, namely, that the precious criterion of clarity and distinctness is a psychological phenomenon only.

Thirdly, granted that the mind may retain some principles from which it may draw conclusions, you assume that they are "not obscure and uncertain, but very evident and certain." But, finally, this too is impossible, namely that there should be different principles from the ones that already were, that is to say some that are self-evident and certain, and the majority obscure and uncertain . . . after this liberation from preconceived notions, it remains equally inclined to assent to false principles as to true ones in the event that the former should turn up first and appear to be fact; and you cannot induce any reason why in this state of equal inclination false principles must come to the mind seeming only apparent and obscure and therefore uncertain rather than seeming evident and therefore certain. For the mind will be as it were at a crossroads, and it will be a matter of chance whether one set of principles offers itself, or another, and whether it accedes to the first, to the ones that make a stronger impression by the mere fact that they appear to be real, rather than to the others.[25]

For Gassendi, the conviction reached by the Cartesian method of doubt is only psychological, with no guarantee of objective validity for either his concepts or his reasoning. For all we know, clarity and distinctness may be reliable, but how do we even know, asks Gassendi, which ideas are clear and distinct?

Gassendi's answer to the skeptical challenge he poses is a naturalistic empiricism. Thought has an empirically derived structure. It consists solely of material images produced in the brain, stored in the memory, and processed by analogy, composition, division, augmentation, and division.[26] The argument for the central role of these images and against the Cartesian intellectual intuition of essences is one found often enough in the materialist tradition. People affected by drugs or dreaming are furthest removed from the senses and least dependent on corporeal memory, but they are also least capable of thought.[27] Locke was to raise the same consideration as part of his argument against the Cartesian thesis that the soul always thinks: "This I would willingly be satisfied in, Whether the Soul, when it thinks thus apart [i.e., when we are asleep], and as it were separate from the Body, acts less rationally than when conjointly with it, or no: If its separate Thoughts be less rational, then these Men must say, That the Soul owes the perfection of rational thinking to the Body: If it does not, 'tis a wonder that our Dreams should be, for the most part, so frivolous and irrational; and that the Soul should retain none of its more rational Soliloquies and Meditations."[28] The rest of Locke's argument will be discussed below.

Whatever Gassendi's arguments against Cartesian intuition, the question might plausibly be raised as to why images would be epistemologically inadequate to the Cartesian task. However ideas are produced, why do they not give us the essences of things? The crucial consideration here is Gassendi's nominalism, found explicitly in his first work, the *Exercitationes* of 1624,[29] and controlling his thought thereafter. In stating it, Gassendi is as blunt as Locke was to be in stating his: "nothing can be found that is not a unique thing."[30] Nor at this level of philosophical analysis can there be much by way of argument apart from an appeal to parsimony. To invoke or ignore universals is

the first step of a research program for which the confirmation or disconfirmation is very remote. The upshot, in any case, is that ideas qua images are particulars and contain no essences. They can contain only what by experience and reasoning we put into them. Gassendi clearly saw the importance of this difference from Descartes, which is worth pursuing textually in some detail.

Descartes in *Meditations* 3 had argued that the idea of God must be innate since (1) it is not derived from the senses; (2) "nor is it likewise a fiction of my mind for it is not in my power to take from or add anything to it."[31] Gassendi objected to this, claiming that in fact the idea of God was partly derived from the senses and partly composed by the mind, for obviously an idea can be added to. Indeed, this is precisely what we do in coming to know God more fully.[32] Locke gives a similar account of our idea of God. The mind "enlarges upon" ideas of existence and duration, knowledge and power, which are ultimately derived from experience, making them "boundless," that is, (potentially) infinite.[33]

In his response to Gassendi, Descartes invoked "the common philosophical maxim that the essences of things are indivisible. An idea represents the essence of the thing, and if anything is added to it or subtracted from the essence, then the idea automatically becomes the idea of something else."[34] To rebut Descartes's response, Gassendi turns against him another of his own responses. Recall the moral of the piece of wax story from *Meditations* 2. We know the piece of wax, not through the senses, nor through the imagination, but by the mind alone (*mentis inspectio*). Gassendi reads this to mean that we are supposed to know the wax itself, the substance of the wax or its essence, and objects that all that we know of it are its accidents, that in fact we cannot conceive of the wax apart from any extension, figure, and color.[35] Similarly, we do not know that the self is essentially thinking, only that it as a matter of fact thinks. In his reply, Descartes seems to give up the game: "I wanted to show how the substance of wax is revealed by means of its accidents. . . . I have never thought that anything more is required to reveal a substance than its various attributes, thus the more attributes of a given substance we know, the more perfectly we understand its nature. Now we can distinguish many different attributes in the wax. . . . And there are correspondingly many attributes in the mind."[36] This seems to mean both that ideas can be enlarged upon, that the essences of things are not indivisible, and that our knowledge is limited to the accumulation of accidents or appearances. And Gassendi is quick to exploit this opening to full advantage.[37]

The opening seized by Gassendi is only an apparent one, however, for Descartes's substance-attribute language cannot be understood in the Aristotelian terms Gassendi clearly assumes. Instead, individual things like the piece of wax are modes of extension in the sense of being instantiations of it, that is, ways that extension can exist (thus the French *façon d'être* as the translation of *modus*). And the better we know extension, the one essence of the material world, the better we know individually extended things like the piece of wax. The connection between extension (*extensio* or *res extensa*) and extended things (*extensa*) is the connection between the axioms and the theorems of geometry; it is the deductive connection that replaces the connection of inherence in the Aristotelian substance ontology.[38] Thus can Descartes claim in response to Gassendi's original objection that by coming to know God better we alter our idea of Him: "once the idea of the true God has been conceived, although we may detect additional perfections in him which we had not yet noticed, this does not mean that we have augmented the idea of God; we have simply made it more distinct and explicit, since, so long as we suppose that our original idea was a true one, it must have contained all these perfections."[39] The process of making explicit what is only implicit in an idea is that of deduction, the possibility for which . . . qualifies the idea as both innate and distinct.

Gassendi just denies that there are such ideas:

> As for you, when you say that "the idea represents the essence of a thing," it seems that I may infer not incorrectly that if there are any things whose essence you do not know, you do not have an idea of them. Therefore I ask you: do you know the essence of the sun, of the moon, or of some other star? I suspect that you will not say that you do. For what do you know about them besides their size, shape, movement, distance, light, brightness, heat, their power to generate growth, to warm, to move, and other such things, if there are any. But the very essence, the nature, the inner substance which lies underneath these is totally hidden from you.[40]

To be sure, there are ideas, but from the nominalist point of view they are of a very different sort.

> Actually, you do have ideas of things, but not the kind you claim to have. In fact ideas of things exist only to the degree that we know them. And since we know their accidents with a distinct knowledge, but not their essences, which we divine as it were or conceive indistinctly as lurking under them, therefore, there is a distinct idea of their accidents, but not of their essences, which we comprehend indistinctly underneath them. From which it results that the clearer and more precise idea we have of something, the clearer and more precisely we know several of its accidents. Since experience shows that the ideas in our minds are like images of things, and the images are not of a thing's essence, but of its accidents, it follows that just as the image of a certain man reproduced in a picture is all the more perfect if the symmetry, the arrangement, and the representation of a great number of parts is more elaborately worked out, and each of the individual traits which are in the separate parts is more carefully reproduced, so the idea of any thing becomes all the more perfect if it portrays more of its accidents, or more of the things surrounding it, as it were, in a more ordered fashion, with greater skill, and more lifelike.[41]

GASSENDIST THEORIES OF SPACE: APOTHEOSIS AND ANNIHILATION

Gassendi's account of space and time begins with an attack on the received view that all being is divided into substance and accident.[42] Although it is primarily Aristotle who receives Gassendi's attention, Pythagoras, Epicurus, Lucretius, and others[43] are noted as well, since Gassendi is concerned with a range of views based on the principle that all being is either in itself or in another.[44] With the additional premise that all being is either corporeal or incorporeal, space and time could plausibly be regarded on the Aristotelian view only as corporeal accidents, so that if there were no bodies there would be no space or time. Gassendi's contention is that even without body there would be unchanging place and flowing time,[45] and that therefore a category beyond substance and accident must be admitted.

Space (*locus*, i.e., unspecified place) is a "quantity or some sort of extension,"[46] an incorporeal tridimensionality: "the length, width, and depth of the walls of some water contained in a vase would be corporeal; but the length, width and depth of the walls of the vase if the water and every other body were excluded from it would be spatial."[47] Note that the corporeal quantity is not the water itself, but its dimensions. One wonders how these corporeal dimensions differ from the incorporeal dimensions of the space it occupies. The distinction itself that Gassendi wants to draw is clear enough, and we shall turn to it at length below. What is unclear is the motivation for the distinction. A thing might be said to be extended either because it is in space, in which case corporeal extension is superfluous, or because it has corporeal extension, in which case its space is superfluous. Gassendi's text thus suggests two, more parsimonious views, each of which was later picked up and developed by his followers.

One view tended to emphasize space and time as conditions for existence—affections as Gassendi called them[48]—and then to use some quality other than extension such as solidity or impenetrability to distinguish body from space. This is the active view of space[49] that dominates the Neo-Platonic tradition and to which Gassendi himself clearly is inclined. There are strategic reasons that make this route attractive to him, but quite independently of these he subscribes to a localization pattern. "There is no substance and no accident for which it is not appropriate to say that it exists somewhere, or in some place, and exists sometime, or at some moment."[50] Cureau is an obvious proponent of this view, and Launay notably arrives at it. In order to secure divine immutability, argues Launay, God must be conceived as in space; besides which, "it is impossible for the human mind to conceive a being that exists and that is not in any place; for everything that is in itself necessarily is someplace."[51]

The other view suggested by Gassendi's text tended to reject spatial dimensions as primitive and instead to derive them from corporeal dimensions. This represents the passive view of space that traces to Democritus.[52] Bernier, for example, may have been led to it by considerations such as those just raised. Why must a body be in space in order to exist, he asked, when space is not its "productive cause" and is "of an entirely different nature"? If space can exist without body, why should body not be able to exist without space?[53] If a body has corporeal dimensions different from spatial dimensions, he may be arguing, there is nothing to preclude that a body should exist and yet not be in space. We shall return to both of these tendencies, and the views they embrace, below.

Meanwhile, because these Gassendist views on space are sometimes difficult to sort out, a roadmap through the two tendencies may be of use here before journeying through them. Both tendencies were initially driven by a theological problem that had already been raised by Gassendi himself, namely, that if space is uncreated and independent of God, as it is on his view, then God is not the author of all things. Each is inclined to its own solution. Launay's solution, on the one hand, was obvious. Roughly put, spatiality is a feature of God, not something different from, and rivaling Him. This view may be called the apotheosis of space. In this, Launay was preceded, if not influenced, by Cureau. With Bernier, on the other hand, the tendency was to minimize, and finally to eliminate altogether, the ontological status of space and thus any theological problem it posed. This view may be called—literally, as we shall see—the annihilation of space. An additional contribution of the proponents of either the apotheosis or the annihilation of space was to advance the dialectic beyond anything in Gassendi's text. They each did so in two ways: (1) by giving far greater emphasis to the importance of views on space, and (2) by applying the theological objection to the Cartesians' views on space. In this, both Launay and Bernier were preceded, if not influenced, by Charleton. Bernier's views in particular were anticipated by La Grange's *novantique* criticism of the Cartesian views of Rohault. In turn, Bernier was attacked in Régis's defense of those same Cartesian views. To conclude this section, finally, two reflections will be offered in an effort to establish the contest for the historical and philosophical importance of these views on space. It is important to begin sorting out who may have influenced whom on space as absolute or relative, and to indicate that the stakes concerned no less than the principle of sufficient reason itself. But first, Gassendi's view and his attempt to answer the theological objection to it must be investigated.

GASSENDI'S VIEW AND THE OBJECTION TO IT

To distinguish corporeal and incorporeal extension, Gassendi asks us to imagine that God has annihilated everything below the Aristotelian lunar sphere, the result of which would be the preservation of its original dimensions without any corporeality. For example, a point on the sphere would be a certain distance from the one opposite it, namely, the diameter of the sphere. He next imagines that God creates and then destroys an infinitely large world. The space that remains—in truth, actual space—would have three properties: (1) immensity—space is without limit, although the world occupies only a part of it; (2) immobility—the world or any part of it may be moved without the space it occupies; (3) incorporeality—the space occupied by an object offers no resistance to bodies penetrating it or abiding with it (*corporeis penetranteis . . . compatienties*). This way of expressing its incorporeality distinguishes space from incorporeal entities such as God, intelligences, and the human mind, the last of which, at least, is a "real and genuine substance with a real and genuine nature."

With the characteristics he has given it, Gassendi's space is indeed liable to the theological objection that it is a thing uncreated and independent of God with the result that He is not the author of all things. To this Gassendi had three kinds of reply. One was to minimize the ontological status of space. As opposed to positive incorporeal things like minds, space cannot act or be acted upon and is characterized only by its penetrability. One wonders how Gassendi can have it both ways. Indeed, the tendency among those who like Cureau and Launay made space and time conditions for existence was to resolve the problem by making space and time properties of God.

A second reply from Gassendi was the argument that he meant by space nothing more than what was admitted as the imaginary spaces by the "majority of sacred doctors," who are undeterred by the objection, "alleging that it is nothing positive, neither a substance nor an accident, under which heading all things created by God are subsumed."[54] These spaces are called imaginary, he insists, not because they depend on the imagination as do chimeras, but because we imagine their dimensions as we do the dimensions of bodies falling under the senses. The way in which these imaginary spaces are apprehended is crucial to their status, but it is just this that Gassendi left unclear. Nor was it made any clearer by Bernier, who at first gave as the reason these spaces are called imaginary that we are unable to conceive of them according to their whole immensity.[55] Later he gave as the reason that we conceive their extension or dimensions in the fashion of corporeal dimensions.[56] But then he tried to reply to the Cartesian argument, to which we shall return below, that if there were nothing between the walls of an empty room they would touch.[57] Here, Bernier interpolates a remark not to be found in Gassendi, namely, that indeed there is nothing between them, that is, "nothing corporeal, nothing that falls under the senses." So either Bernier contradicts himself, or imaginary space is somehow imaginable but not perceptible.[58] Nor had Charleton offered any improvement: "not that they are merely *Phantastical,* as Chimaera's; but that our imagination can and doth apprehend them to have Dimension, which hold an analogy to the Dimensions of Corporeal substances, that fall under the perception and commensuration of the sense."[59] All of this sounds suspiciously like an important Cartesian view to which we shall also return, at great length, below. Descartes, Malebranche, and others held that we can perceive, not just extended things, but extension in general and that we can do so independently of any sense perception of it. As we shall see here, this is why Bernier came finally to reject the notion.

John Sergeant also rejected it, but for a different reason. He thought that the notion of real imaginary space was either incoherent or contradictory and that what its proponents were talking about existed only in the imagination. In his view they ought to have said that it is the imagination that is infinitely extended beyond the world; "but this is so notorious a Banger, that they say not this neither."[60] That is, if imaginary space is real, the mind is extended. This is not the last of the bangers over the mind's location with respect to its object that will be encountered. The imagination does extend beyond the world in the same sense, according to some, that things beyond the world are in the mind. Indeed, . . . [Arnauld argues] that Malebranche makes both God and the individual mind materially extended in order to explain perception of things at a distance. We shall also then see that the question of perception at a distance distinguishes the theories of ideas of the gods (Malebranche) and giants (Locke).

In a third reply to the theological objection, Gassendi argues that space as he conceives it with its three characteristics poses less of a threat than those essences admitted as eternal, uncreated, and independent of God and that are the eminence (*praecipuum*) of substances and accidents. This is the problem in spades that Gassendi saw in allowing space as an element of things, for a doctrine of independent essences puts the intelligible component of things beyond divine control. As Charleton put it, "To hold [an essence] uncreat and independent, is obliquely to infer God to be no more than an *Adopted Father* to Nature, a *titular* Creator, and Author of only the material, grosser and unattractive part of the World."[61] Gassendi does not have this problem since he denies the distinction between essence and existence, as much for created things as for God, with the result that no essence is eternal except God's, which is eternal but not essentially so. Thus God according to Gassendi is freer and more powerful even than according to Descartes. For the latter, all truth, including eternal truths, even such as 3 + 2 = 5, depend on the divine will; but the Cartesian God is constrained by His own immutability. While He could have willed that 3 + 2 be other than 5, once having willed so He cannot will otherwise. Whether immutability is sufficient to the constraining task that Descartes sees for it is a question to be considered in chapter 4. Meanwhile, we can say that the Gassendist deity is under no such constraint.[62]

APOTHEOSIS

The simplest way of resolving the problem of space as a competing divinity is the way taken by many of those for whom an eternal essence loomed as a competing divinity, namely, by making it an aspect of the single divinity. To this solution Gassendi himself showed more than passing partiality. The localization pattern found in Cureau, however problematic, certainly suggests it. Launay commits himself to the view, though not without a certain ambivalence. He follows Gassendi's characterization of place (*lieu, locus*) as an incorporeal tridimensionality allowing penetration by bodies, and then immediately describes it as nothing other than the virtual or eminent (*eminentielles*) parts of God's immensity.[63] He realizes that "to admit real

spaces" [*espaces*] that preceded the world and that will follow it as an uncreated being if it is annihilated is a "difficulty" (*inconvenient*)—presumably the theological difficulty above—but he immediately replies to it that spaces so conceived accord quite well with God's immensity.[64] The way such spaces accord with divine immensity, it would seem, is that they just *are* the divine immensity, that is, space is actually a feature of God and the virtual or eminential parts of it that are distinguished by their capacity to receive different bodies are what he calls place. Here Launay uses an image that dates to a pseudo-Hermetic text of the twelfth century, the *Book of Twenty-four Philosophers:* God is a sphere whose center is everywhere and whose circumference is nowhere.[65]

However unclear this conclusion might be throughout Launay's essay on space, none other is possible by the end. Launay repeats the argument that God could create innumerable worlds or enlarge this one and that, to place these worlds, ultramundane spaces must be admitted.[66] These spaces must be infinite, otherwise we would be unable to conceive or represent the divine immensity (p. 102). But Lauany slides from its conception or representation to immensity itself. We must be careful not to make God material, he says, but there is no danger in making God spiritually extended (p. 203). This gives us the significance of the problem in seeking whose solution Launay had "stirred all the dust in the colleges," namely, how to make place immobile, as it must be in order to mark the beginning and end of locomotion; for otherwise a thing could change place without moving or move without changing place (p. 80 *passim*). His answer was divine immobility: Because God is by His nature incapable of change and hence immobile, space as a system of virtual places is immobile (pp. 80-81). Conversely, this conception of space shows how God is immobile and unchanging even if He should move the world or create others elsewhere—unlike "our adversaries" (unnamed) who are forced to say that God must move in these instances as the soul moves when the body does (p. 103).

At this point, however, it is not clear whether for Launay God *is* space or is *in* (all of) space. Despite his clear adherence to the localization pattern, Launay's conception of space effectively undermines the active, absolutist alternative, for in the final analysis Launay must deny that space is independent of the things it contains. As for Gassendi, so for Launay, not only are matter and space different, but corporeal and incorporeal dimensions are different. They are specifically different kinds of being, as he says: "Extension is the genus of occupied [*plein*] and void place," the specific difference between them being, as Lucretius pointed out, tangibility (p. 97). Thus, Launay may be able consistently to maintain that time (or the virtual parts of God's eternity) endows things with their duration and continuation in existence, but not that space grounds their extension. If anything, corporeal extension is prior to incorporeal. As we have seen, Launay thinks that without an infinite incorporeal extension there can be no account of immensity; similarly, without it there would be no account of "the sphere of activity of an angel or a rational soul, which act only in determinate spaces because their power is limited. To make one thing coexist with another, to render it closely present to all the parts of an extended body without giving it extension is a thing inconceivable and impossible."[67] Two lines of argument thus converge in the conception of immensity. God to act everywhere must be everywhere; and since He is everywhere He is immobile (there is nowhere else for Him to go) and thus the reference with respect to which other things move. But this is to give up the absolutist conception of space, not just in the trivial sense that space as a feature of God is no longer an independent being *suo modo*. For God is *in* space in the sense that He stands in all possible spatial relations. He is to the left of everything and to the right of everything, and He *is* space in the sense that with respect to those relations all other spatial relations can be defined. There is no space apart from things in spatial relations. On this reconstruction of Launay's position, then, he eliminates Gassendi's extra set of dimensions in favor of a relational theory of space. Indeed, . . . the only difference between it and Malebranche's relational theory is the difference between real and intelligible extension. This is the enormous difference, however, that places them on opposite sides of the *grande bataille*. However eclectic he may be, Launay does not for a moment flirt with the Cartesian theory that makes extension the essence of matter.

A striking feature of Launay's treatment of space is his unabashed application to the Cartesians of arguments that he takes from Gassendi and elaborates. For, in identifying space, matter, and extension and thus eliminating the void, the Cartesians hold a view that is "much bolder and more dangerous than that of the Peripatetics, who at least do not claim that the void is inconceivable," which amounts to denying divine omnipotence. Affirming omnipotence gives Launay his principal argument, which takes two forms. First, God can destroy all that He has created (pp. 76-78); He can also destroy a part of what He has created, such as the contents of some container whose walls He keeps immobile. *Ex hypothesi* there will not be body between the walls of the container, yet there will be extension between them because they are immobile and would touch only if they moved. Even if as a result of God's act they did move, they could do so only over time, and since God could destroy the contents instantaneously, there would be at least an interval during which there would be extension without body. This form of Launay's argument of course does not really address the Cartesians, for whom the void is not just a physical, but a conceptual impossibility.

A second form of the argument is better in this regard since it involves or at least adumbrates the independence principle that was to figure so importantly in the vacuum-plenum debates. The principle, to be found already in Descartes's *Principles*,[68] is that what is conceivable apart is really distinct as an individual. As we shall see, just what is conceivable apart, with respect to space and its contents and to many other issues, was very much a matter of debate. For the present argument, at any rate, we are again

asked to consider an emptied container, for example, a triangular room. Its inner surface "is distinguished only by the mind from the exterior (surface), with which it makes the same body,"[69] and must therefore have the same shape that the exterior surface has. But in order for the inner surface of the room to be triangular, there must be some extension between its sides. That is, the triangle requires the void in order to be preserved as the individual that it is. Perhaps another way we can put this issue for the Cartesians is that if God were to destroy a part of extension as Launay supposes, He would falsify geometry, for the perpendicular drawn from the base to the apex would not have the extension required by Euclid, but none at all. Thus, those Cartesians who save omnipotence in Launay's sense do so only by making geometry depend on the divine will, for if the altitude of a given triangle is equal to its area divided by half its base, this is only because God wills to create the space between its apex and base, that is, to create that particular triangle.

That a ground for geometry is the interesting issue here is suggested by a pair of arguments Launay raises that Bernier later picked up in the *Abrégé*. This time God is supposed to create three contiguous worlds in a row and then to annihilate the one in the middle while keeping the two others immobile. The Cartesians would have to say that though they are at a distance these worlds touch and moreover that God could re-create the world between them without moving them. Second, if God were to create a pile of spherical worlds, the Cartesians would have to say that they all touch each other not just at one point, but at all points in the way a pile of cubes would, which "seems to me so contrary to common sense and the demonstrations of mathematics" that the void must be admitted (pp. 101-2). Even these arguments do not get at the core conceptual issue, however, since they assume what for Descartes is unintelligible, namely, that God could create only three extended objects. . . . [For] Descartes there is only one really extended object—what he called *res extensa*. It is infinite, and cannot be conceived otherwise without doing violence to geometry. For Descartes, the globes Launay is talking about are, if anything, phenomenal entities that depend on *res extensa* for their essence. With respect to them the relevant question is whether they could be conceived without any extension at all or whether they must have an extension that satisfied just the Euclidean requirements that Launay cites. That is, the issue is whether things have essences (of a certain sort) as the Cartesians held, or are bare as the Gassendists held. As we shall see, here and in the next section, Bernier offered arguments that relate more obviously to this issue.

ANNIHILATION

Bernier's account of Gassendi's views on space is problematic in the extreme. There are three versions (the proto-*Abrégé*, *Abrégé* 1, *Abrégé* 2) and there are significant differences among them as to the material from the **Syntagma** that Bernier chooses to include or omit, the ordering and emphasis of the material, and the material of his own that he interpolates. Although it is impossible to spell out the historical details, it seems clear that Bernier was responding to Cartesian arguments on the topic whose general thrust can be made out. These arguments may well have had the additional result of changing Bernier's own views. Whatever its source, in at least one case the change in Bernier's own views altered the way in which he presented Gassendi's. Whether driven to it by the Cartesians or not, Bernier came to a view of space that was more Gassendist than Gassendi's own view.

The most obvious departure is the emphasis given the topic of space by its placement at the very outset of the proto-*Abrégé* and *Abrégé* 1. For Bernier space is of primary importance. "The first thing we must do in turning our eyes toward the universe is to conceive a vast and immense space, infinitely extended everywhere in length, depth and breadth, the field[70] of the Almighty's works and the general place of all that is or may be produced."[71] Gassendi's treatment of space, however, had occurred only in the second of the seven books that comprise the first of three parts of the physics, which occurs between the logic and the ethics; that is, it is rather buried away.[72]

Indeed, Gassendi seemed not to have recognized the significance of his views on space. The *Animadversiones* initially plumps for the void on the basis of physical arguments concerning motion, rarefaction and condensation, and saturation, but connects it to an analysis of space only by way of a worry about the substance-accident dichotomy (pp. 169-77). The account of space, which is actually quite close to what later appeared in the *Syntagma,* figures only as a digression, as Gassendi calls it, from the discussion of time, which space is used to explain since it is a parallel concept (pp. 610-22). Indeed, the account of space is separated from the discussion of atoms and the void by over four hundred pages of text. It was Charleton, six years before the *Syntagma,* who picked out this material and coupled it with the earlier topics and other related material in the first book of his *Physiologia.* This chapter follows the material in the *Animadversiones* fairly closely, consisting of translation, paraphrase, and summary. Occasionally Gassendi does not quite get the argument right, as when he seems to think that it follows from the possibility of God's annihilating and then re-creating the world that the space in which He does so must be immense (p. 67). The crucial premise of the argument, made explicit by Gassendi but ignored by Charleton, is that the world God might create could be infinitely larger than the present one He might annihilate (p. 615). But generally, Charleton's espousal of the Gassendist cause, although ruinous in other respects, undeniably advanced it in the case of the analysis of space. For one thing, Charleton included Descartes in his rebuttal of an argument that Gassendi had attributed only to the Aristotelians, namely, that the sides of a container whose contents have been annihilated must touch since there is nothing between them.

The principal thrust of Charleton's argument for the void is that all the arguments against it fail. The argument in particular from Descartes, White, and the other Aristotelians fails because the substance-accident dichotomy is gratuitously restrictive. "When any Cholerick Bravo of the *Stagirites* Faction shall draw upon us with this Argument . . . we need no other buckler than to except Place and Time."

Gassendi's arguments in the *Syntagma* on behalf of the void are aimed directly against the Aristotelians and, if at all, only indirectly against Descartes to the extent that the identification of matter and space, and thus the elimination of the void, relies on an ontology of substance and accident. Like Charleton, Bernier picks up these arguments and turns them specifically against the Cartesians, elaborating them beyond any warrant in Gassendi's text. The clearest example of this is the argument with which he closes the chapter on space: "I might add that those who are unwilling to recognize space in the way in which we allow it seem reduced to an extreme predicament, which is to allow a body of infinite extent that is perhaps eternal, independent and incapable of being destroyed—space, body and extension being the same thing in their view—which is no cause for concern on our view because on it space is neither substance, nor accident, nor anything capable of action or passion . . . and is but a pure capacity for receiving bodies. But I would be ashamed to pause further on this."[73]

Four years later, in 1678, Bernier's shame had vanished and, even if he does not name them as such, he directly attacks the Cartesians. Those who confuse space and body are reduced to the extreme predicaments of "allowing a corporeal substance that fills all possible spaces, or rather, which is itself space and which is consequently of infinite extension, and of maintaining (for fear of being obliged to allow any void) that God with all His power would be unable to destroy or annihilate the least part of that substance and that it is therefore independent of God."[74] But even this he thinks gives them too much attention. By 1684, however, a separate section is devoted to the predicaments of these "moderns" as he calls them. Not only are they taxed with the above theological objection, but Gassendi's objection that the Aristotelians reject the void only by relying on an ontology of substance and accident is now directed against the Cartesians as a great predicament in physics. If God were to empty a room of its contents while preventing both anything else from entering and its walls from moving, they would say that since there was nothing between them the walls would touch.[75]

An additional feature of Bernier's treatment of the above argument shows him to have been involved in the polemics of the period. In all three versions of the theory of space, he argues that the existence or the mode of existence of one body cannot "absolutely" depend on the existence of another body, that the shape of the room cannot depend on air or anything else that it may contain. The result is that God might begin by producing the air that the room will contain and then the room; but He might equally well produce the room first and then the air it contains.[76]

This of course is the independence principle invoked by the Cartesians, among others, that we soon shall see Cordemoy to have used against them in just this way on behalf of atomism.

An important question is raised by Bernier's attack on the Cartesians. How is it that he thinks the Gassendist theory can avoid the difficulties he aims against the Cartesians? For although the Cartesian extension is corporeal, it does not satisfy the Gassendist condition for being something positive, namely, that it have the power of acting.[77] On the contrary, active matter of the Gassendist sort ought not to have been and was not intelligible to any Cartesian. Indeed, as I shall try to show, for Descartes and some of his followers, the matter identical to extension is incapable even of real motion. Even for those like Malebranche who thought matter capable of real motion, matter had no dynamical properties. It was this conception of matter that figured so prominently in arguments for occasionalism, for example. The most basic dynamical property of impenetrability was necessitated for the Gassendists because they distinguished matter from extension. Bernier's argument, therefore, that the Cartesians introduce a "positive nature capable of acting" because it cannot be destroyed by God[78] either is no objection at all or tells at least as well against the Gassendist theory. In addition, by appealing to the independence principle, Bernier threatens to make not just space independent but bodies as well. If the room and the air it contains can exist apart because they are individuals, then they can exist apart from God. To this the alternative seems to be Spinozism: They are not individuals because they cannot exist independently of God, of whom they must be a feature or a part. Why would Bernier subject Gassendi to the contagion of these issues?

At first Bernier seems to ignore, or at least minimize these difficulties. The proto-*Abrégé,* for example, does not raise the theological difficulty at all as far as Gassendist space is concerned. Instead, Bernier there advances two arguments that space need not be created. One is an argument from the pseudo-Archytas modified to read that everything must be created in some place, but that place cannot be created in some other place since this would open an infinite regress.[79] The other is the argument that if the earth were withdrawn from the place it occupies, there would be no need to create that space in order to replace the earth, and thus there was no need to create its space in order originally to create the earth. (Neither argument figures as such in *Abrégé* 1 or *Abrégé* 2.) In *Abrégé* 2, however, the objection is raised in no uncertain terms. Bernier at length applies Gassendi's worry with respect to eternal essences directly to the Cartesians. On behalf of Gassendi's theory, meanwhile, he is content merely to counter with the reply that space thus conceived is no more problematic than the sacred doctors' imaginary spaces.

A clue to the evolution of Bernier's reaction to this problem is his growing reservation over Gassendi's theory of space. Consider the characterization of the void as imaginary space, which differs markedly in *Abrégé* 1 and *Abrégé* 2. To be sure, both make the point that it is so characterized by the theologians not because it is chimerical, depending only on the imagination, but because we imagine its extension or incorporeal dimensions "after the fashion of corporeal dimensions." But, following an ambiguity of emphasis in Gassendi's text, *Abrégé* 1 makes the point in order to emphasize the existence of this space lest having been distinguished from incorporeal *substance* it be thought of as nothing at all. *Abrégé* 2 makes the point in the course of an apology for Gassendist space vis-à-vis Omnipotence; all that is admitted is what the theologians meant by imaginary space, which was uncreated and independent of God and which they yet allowed as orthodox. The change seems explained by the threat expressed in *Abrégé* 1 to the reality of space, which by 1682 becomes the full-blown doubt that space seems properly to be "a pure nothing": "only with difficulty could a being other than God be admitted which is eternal, immense, independent, indestructible . . . penetrable, and immobile, which are nonetheless the properties [that had been] attributed to space."[80] What I am suggesting, then, is that Bernier felt free to attack the Cartesians on a point on which Gassendi's theory was no less vulnerable since he himself was hesitating about just that problematic aspect of it.

Indeed, Bernier's reservation becomes a penetrating nominalist critique of Gassendist space. In addition to the theological difficulty, it is objected that space (1) is incorporeal yet has parts; (2) is imperceptible hence should not be admitted except for very strong reasons; and (3) when imagined as empty is not imagined as a being, whether corporeal or incorporeal.[81] The criticism is sharpened in *Doubts* 2, where such a space is described as the chimera of those who delight in deceiving themselves, and where the characterization of space as a being "in its own fashion" is ridiculed as both obscure and useless against the above objections. The root difficulty, clearly expressed in both sets of doubts, is that the Gassendist space is an abstract entity. To the argument that between the walls of an empty container there must be some distance Bernier now replies that if that distance is "a certain line, or spatial, invisible and incorporeal length which makes the walls distant from each other, it is a pure fiction"—to be distant they need only not touch.[82] What is true of equality is true of distance; "they are abstract terms, which like all others of this sort, lead us to error if we conceive something abstract or separated from the concrete" (pp. 387-88).[83] For two things to be equal there need not be some "distinct entity which is the equality" to make them equal. They need only each have a certain size. And when one measures the distance between two things, there is no *thing* that is being measured any more than there is a capacity in an empty room that can receive things. Space in fact is nothing at all: "I maintain that [these allegedly infinite, etc.] spaces are not, do not exist, are not a being, are not a thing" (p. 386). Empty space is best referred to by a negative judgment (p. 385). For example, nothing is in this room, where 'nothing' functions as a "particle" (p. 392) or syncategorematic term, just as there need be no thing called "darkness" spread out in a room in order for it to be dark—there just need be no light in it.

It was not likely that this radically nominalized space, despite its drawing near a relational view, would be found congenial by the Cartesians, who in one way or another take a position of extreme realism with respect to space. Nor was it. Régis for one agreed that the void as a room from which God has removed the air should be conceived by the same kind of negative judgment by which the dark is conceived; but just as the dark is a lack of light in air capable of being illuminated, so the void is a lack of air in a room capable of having it, and since the void has some quantity it is some matter or other.[84] Régis goes on to argue against "others" (presumably, than Bernier) who nonetheless seem to hold his view of the void. They maintain that since space as a mere negation or privation would presuppose some subject, it might be viewed as pure non-being (*pur néant*). Régis's main argument that pure nonbeing has no properties, while the void has extension, fails against Bernier, for whom nothing *has* extension. There are things that are extended and qualified in other ways, but apart from which there is no extension or anything else. The distance between two things is not itself a thing but a property of the things distant that is not different from them. Thus, Régis just begs his realism against Bernier, just as he begs the question against Gassendi who rejects the substance ontology.

Bernier's conception of space as a pure nothing was anticipated by La Grange, who in his criticism of the Cartesians departed from Aristotle to allow not only the absolute but the natural possibility of the void.[85] In particular he is concerned with the views of Rohault, the natural sense of whose expression of them, according to La Grange, is that matter is infinite, uncreated, and independent of God. But he is also concerned with Descartes's view, which he sees as in effect coming to the same thing, namely, that a plurality of worlds is impossible because there is no place for another beyond the actual one (chap. 28). To combat both Rohault and Descartes, he thinks that either real, extraterrestrial space must be denied, which is not easy, or space though real (*veritable*) must not be something positive (*rien de positif*) or have real extension. The latter is supposed to become plausible when we realize that there is no space between things that touch, but that there is between those that do not because a third thing can be placed between them. "Thus space, properly speaking, is a certain capacity for receiving a body because there is no space in which a body cannot be put" (p. 403). So far this sounds like the Gassendist passive container. Indeed, the space now occupied by the world was the same before the world was created, and is neither substance nor accident. But it is not a being suo modo—"it is not a being at all. It is nothing [*ce n'est rien*]" (p. 404). The line he takes in explaining this view, however, is not at all as clear as Bernier's. Like Bernier, his inclination is to talk of space in terms of relations of distance. Thus he supposes that beyond the created world God could create a stone at a certain distance from it and then, without any

real extension between them, alter that distance, and so on. But he gives distance a status Bernier clearly wants to deny it. Although space is nothing, "this nothing is real in its fashion, i.e. it is something that is such as it is imagined to be and thus is not imaginary." (And therefore those who call it imaginary space are badly mistaken.) If we were to imagine real extension where there is none, he explains, it would be imaginary. But space is imagined as it is, that is, not as a being but nonetheless real. He sees two senses of the term 'real': real in the nature of things and real in representation. Space is real only in the latter sense, or can be as when we conceive space between two things that are not in contact. (By contrast, the space imagined between things that are in contact is imaginary.) Space thus conceived as nothing can be uncreated, infinite, indestructible, and immobile (pp. 407-8).

La Grange's rather Hobbist theory of space perhaps gives us a reading of another of Bernier's texts of obvious relevance to his account of space, namely, his chapter on place. The basic structure of the chapter remains unchanged throughout the three *Abrégés*. The problem Bernier deals with, as well as his eventual solution to it, is at least partly linguistic. Place must be immobile otherwise a thing might move without changing place or change place without moving. Thus the place of a thing cannot be the immediate surface of what surrounds it. This Aristotelian view has the additional inconveniences that a tower in the wind, for example, must move, and that the universe as a whole has no place. Place, then, is just occupied space, which when unoccupied is the void. Thus the basic structure of the three *Abrégés*. The tone and detail of the arguments, however, differ markedly. *Abrégé* 2, for example, compresses the material, treats it rather less enthusiastically, and suppresses two rebuttals appended to the earlier editions. One rebuttal replies to the Aristotelian argument that place is not a volume occupied by a body because, as the body itself has volume, two volumes would then occupy the same place. The other replies to the argument that space must be regarded as material since it is a divisible quantity. Both arguments are rebutted with the distinction between divisible corporeal and indivisible incorporeal extension. Once again, these changes in *Abrégé* 2 are explained by Bernier's *Doubts*.

In his *Doubts* Bernier is prepared to endorse the Aristotelian view of place as more plausible than Gassendi's view, at least to the extent that it reflects the commonsense conception of place and melds with his own nominalist conception of space. Place as the surface of a surrounding body seems clearly known, he thinks, by everyone, including children and even animals (a room is the place of a bed, a trunk the place of some gold, etc.). To the objection that such a view leaves the world without a place, Bernier with Aristotle grants the objection as harmless and then argues that the space in which we make distinctions beyond the world is *only* imaginary. It is a pure fiction that is regarded as real, seemingly in La Grange's sense, only because it is formed through constant experience of things that really are in place. The reality is only in the representation. Properly speaking, the void itself is (a place where there is) nothing. Thus neither this world nor some world God might create beyond it are contained *in* the void.[86]

Part of Bernier's worry over place is merely linguistic insofar as the representation or description of motion as change of place is concerned. But part of it would seem to hinge on the deep ontological question of the status required by what is described. And it is here that Bernier's nominalism becomes obvious and perhaps obviously problematic. He tells us that it came to him while thinking about modes that most if not all of them are indefinable, being themselves what enter into definitions of things. What Bernier has to say suggests that modes are known only on the basis of acquaintance: (1) modes are clear and evident by themselves and one need only have eyes to see what they are (p. 408); (2) this is plausibly true of some (e.g., pain) but perhaps not all (e.g., action) of Bernier's examples (p. 407); (3) modes are primitives that cannot be defined without circularity or synonymy (p. 406). Consequently, motion and rest, qua modes of bodies, cannot be defined and are known perfectly and definitively in the fashion of Diogenes. The upshot is that the basic objection to the Aristotelian view of place, viz. that it allows a thing to move without changing place and to change place without moving, is overcome, for it is based on a definition of motion as "a successive application of a body to the parts of the bodies surrounding it" (pp. 401, 410). In fact, only to allow the possibility of motion as "the passage of a body from one place to another" did Gassendi, following the ancients, admit space—that strange entity now viewed by Bernier as virtually contradictory—"a being which [though] incorporeal has parts . . . which subsists in itself and is not a substance, a being which is everywhere and is nowhere" (pp. 410-11). Better, then, to accept the commonsense view of place and refuse all definitions of motion and all the paradoxes with them.

Bernier thus in a sense avoids difficulties at the linguistic level, but it is not clear just what else he has done. It is one thing to deny to space any independent ontological status. It is quite another to provide an account that without it nonetheless grounds everything that Bernier must regard as true of material things and their motion. After all, the void was admitted, not to provide a definition of motion *in vacuo*, as it were, but, for among other reasons, to avoid the difficulty of the plenum vis-à-vis motion. For Bernier to reject the void and regard motion as a primitive is, at least historically, an unusual procedure. For he not only regards the space in terms of which motion is conceived as merely imaginary, but he rejects every definition of it because "definitions explain the nature of the thing" defined. Those who define motion treat it as a thing that is passed from one moving thing to another, a mistake that he thinks lies at the root of their mistaken view about collision and conservation of motion and of the difficulties they see in projectile motion. Although he never quite puts it in these terms, Bernier's procedure is to move the problems from the level of things to the level of how we talk about them. The procedure may be fair enough, except

that the move as effected by Bernier converts nominalism from an ontological view into a lexicographical one. Even if, as some have come to believe in recent years, the world is the language we use to describe it, there is still a difference between physical or metaphysical problems and merely linguistic ones. It is one thing to say there is nothing to talk about; it is another to refuse to talk about it.

FURTHER REFLECTIONS

I shall conclude this section with two further reflections. One has to do with the principle of sufficient reason, which in the end will restore the larger context for the philosophical significance of these Gassendist analyses of space. The other, with which I shall begin, concerns the question of historical influences. Toward the end of his chapter on space[87] Gassendi has an argument for the existence of space *suo modo* that may be important in sorting out who was influenced by whom on the question of space. The argument is intended to rebut the view that all being must be substance or accident and that space, since it is dependent on what is in it, must be an accident—a thing can change place as it can change color; hence place like color is an accident of it. Gassendi responds that though place can join and separate from (*accedat, & abscedat*) the thing located without the destruction of that thing, and hence may seem to be an accident of it, place in fact does not approach or recede (*neque accedere, neque abscedere*) but is immobile; it is the thing located that moves. That is, what remains through change in the case of motion is space, not the thing in it which ex hypothesi has changed place. Thus, once again it is the absolute impassivity of space that emerges as crucial in Gassendi's analysis. In this instance, however, either Gassendi just begs the question on behalf of an independent space or what he says is true of all qualities. When a thing changes color, *it* changes, not its *color:* The apple, not greenness, becomes red. Thus, he says that, if anything, substance should be attributed to space insofar as it is successively occupied by bodies (presumably as a thing successively can have different colors). But space cannot be a substance either, "which ordinarily is understood not only as what exists through itself, but also and especially as something corporeal and material, or what has the faculty of acting and abiding, which surely are incompatible with place."

The proto-*Abrégé* and *Abrégé* 2 ignore this argument altogether. *Abrégé* 1 perhaps hints at it, arguing that place has properties not generally attributed to substances: immobility, incorporeality, and inability to act.[88] It is tempting to attribute Bernier's lack of attention to the argument to his own disenchantment with the conception of space as a separate being.[89] Whatever the explanation, Bernier cannot have been anyone's source for the argument. Launay has a version of the argument, but one that is even less successful than Gassendi's in motivating the rebuttal: "If our adversaries say that place [*lieu*] is an accident, because it can be or not be without its subject, *viz.* the thing placed."[90] That is, Launay *begins* with a characterization of space according to which it is, if anything, a substance. Charleton, on the other hand, has a version very close to Gassendi's text that he uses "to authenticate this our Schism."[91] Whether it was from him, or more probably Gassendi himself, that Newton picked it up, is difficult to know. But it does emerge in his *De gravitatione et aequipondio fluidorum.*[92] Having proposed to overthrow the Cartesian philosophy with respect to extension, Newton rejects the trichotomy that extension be substance, accident, or nothing at all. It is not substance because it is not absolute in itself and is not active, and since it is conceivable without body and would not perish with a body that God might annihilate, it is not an accident; indeed it thus "approaches more nearly to the nature of substance." Using Gassendi's term (*affectio*) he calls it a disposition of all being.[93]

Locke has a celebrated passage in which he too rejects the substance ontology, and which, occurring where it does in his account of space, suggests that his source(s) would lead him to the absolutist conception. Despite the suggestion, . . . it is Bernier whose views here shed most light on Locke. By contrast to Bernier's line on space, the absolutist view is for a commonsense empiricist like Locke plainly a priori unsatisfactory. It is weird (the soul of dwarfs in the bodies of giants),[94] ill-defined (the question whether God is *in* space), and extravagant not just in being unparsimonious but in admitting the kind of entity it does. If substance and accident are unintelligible, a fortiori are space and time as a third category.

Finally, the Gassendist analysis of space raises a question with respect to the principle of sufficient reason. If space is infinite and homogeneous, and if this world occupies only a part of that space,[95] then why does it occupy the part of space that it does rather than some other; why does God create where He does rather than elsewhere? This is a very old problem with an enormous and difficult literature,[96] to which Leibniz's argument against the Newton-Clarke version of Gassendi's view is only the best known contribution. There are several philosophically plausible ways an upholder of the view might deal with the problem. One of them, however, is not through an appeal to a distorted authority. But I am afraid this is what the Gassendist position comes to, if there is a Gassendist position at all.

On behalf of ultramundane space Gassendi quotes, and Bernier translates, two brief texts from Augustine's *City of God* that deal with the topic. An argument is insinuated to the effect that unless space is infinite, the divine substance is limited by its ubiquity; that is, because God is everywhere, His place must be an infinite extension or He is not infinite. Limited space limits God. The upshot is that the divine substance must be conceived as though it were extended and diffused throughout infinite space.[97] The qualification *as though* is included "lest we imagine that the divine substance is extended in the manner of bodies." But the difference seems only to be that bodies are spatially (and temporally) limited. "As corporeal extension is said to be extended because it is not merely in a single point but is spread out through several parts of space, so the divine substance is held to be as it were extended [*quasi extensa*] because it exists not merely in a single place but in many, or rather in all places."[98] In these texts, at least, God is not said to be space, but only to be in space.

The context for the Augustinian texts on which the above dialectic is based is a discussion of God as creator. The immediate problem is the creation of the world in time: Why did God create at one time rather than another? This question was raised theoretically by the Epicureans[99] to show that God did not create at all. The problem is over mutability in God and sufficient reason. That God should act at one moment rather than at another indistinguishable from it means either He acts because of some change in Him or for no reason at all. To avoid what seems to be the only alternative to the Epicurean impiety, namely, that the world is created by God but without a beginning in time, Augustine argues that the question is no more legitimate than the question why He creates here rather than elsewhere. "For if they imagine that there were infinite stretches of time before the world existed, an infinity in which they cannot conceive of God's being inactive, *they will,* on the same showing, *imagine infinite stretches of space; and if anyone says that the omnipotent could not have been inoperative anywhere in that infinity, it will follow* that they are compelled to share the Epicurean fantasy of innumerable worlds."[100] Gassendi quotes and Bernier translates only the italicized material. The second text is also taken from its context: "Will they [who acknowledge that God is everywhere in His immaterial presence] say His substance is absent from those spaces beyond the world, that He is enclosed in the space of this world, which is so small in comparison with that infinity?" Augustine's point is that if God were in these infinite spaces, then the plurality of worlds would follow; hence He is not because as the very title of the chapter indicates, there is no space outside the world.[101]

Gassendi and Bernier do not attempt to legitimate infinite and homogeneous space by direct appeal to Augustine, because they themselves do not even raise his problem of sufficient reason. Their distorted texts are cited to show, independently of that problem, that Augustine found the notion of infinite ultramondane space intelligible, acceptable, or whatever. This is reflected in the various uses to which Bernier puts the texts. The proto-*Abrégé* follows Gassendi more or less closely as above. *Abrégé* 1 seems to use Augustine's texts less to argue that space is in fact infinite, or that beyond the occupied space of the world there is unoccupied space, than just to make the distinction between corporeal and incorporeal extension. It also ignores the problematic attempt to distinguish the senses in which bodies are in space and God is in space. *Abrégé* 2 merely reproduces the texts, introducing them with a remark about support for the view of the divine substance as spread out as it were in the imaginary spaces beyond the world, which is a view Bernier thought was held by Democritus, Epicurus, Lucretius, Nemesius, and the theologians.

What, then, to make of the distortion? Outright dissimulation is prima facie implausible, of course, and in any case unnecessary given the availability of acceptable ways of dealing with the problem. Just a mistaken reading is also improbable, but perhaps accounted for by the conceptual improbability, or difficulty at least, even in seeing a problem concerning sufficient reason. For the radical empiricist creation is a matter of sheer, unconstrained volition, or in nontheological terms, existence is fortuitous. Ultimately there is no reason why now and not earlier, why here and not there. That the sphere of what is not—of where God could have created but did not—should be infinite only serves to emphasize the ultimate lack of reason for the finite sphere of what is, of what He did create.[102] At this point the contrast with the Cartesian position is sharp. Here too extension is infinite, but here it is also real, whether material as for Descartes or intelligible as Malebranche would have liked it to be. If extension were merely finite, God would be less than God. In Platonic terms the world would be less than full and God would have been jealous and less than good. In Cartesian terms He would be a deceiver and the Euclidean picture of the world would be false. Given that He is not a deceiver, the existence of extension, whether created or uncreated, is far from fortuitous. Thus the significance of the Cartesian identification of matter and extension, which was sufficient but hardly necessary for the mathematization of nature. For with this identification the question, why here and not there, does not arise; for matter is everywhere it could possibly be.

Notes

1. See letters to Mersenne, December 18, 1629, AT [Descartes, *Oeuvres,* ed. C. Adam and P. Tannery. 1st ed. 1897–1913; 2d ed., CNRS, Paris: Vrin, 1964–75], 1:97; January 1630, ibid., pp. 112-13; March 4, 1630, ibid., p. 127; May 6, 1630, ibid., p. 148; or even as late as December 1638, AT, 2:464-65.

2. AT, 3:388-89.

3. July 22, 1641; AT, 3:416.

4. To Colvius, April 23, 1643; AT, 3:646.

5. To Mersenne, February 23, 1643; AT, 3:633.

6. To Noel, December 14, 1646; AT, 4:585-86.

7. The episode is recounted in Bougerel, *Pierre Gassendi,* pp. 306-8. See Jones, *Pierre Gassendi,* who gives more details on these personal relations (pp. 66-69) and also gives the substance of Gassendi's criticisms of the *Meditations* (pp. 135-88).

8. For the outline of my account, I have drawn heavily on the work of O. R. Bloch, to whom my debt will be apparent. Bloch first dealt with the topic in "Gassendi critique de Descartes"; he later elaborated many of these themes in *La philosophie de Gassendi: nominalisme, materialisme, et métaphysique.*

9. CSM [Descartes, *The Philosophical Writings,* trans. J. Cottingham, R. Stoothoff, and D. Murdoch. Cambridge: Cambridge University Press, 1985], 2:268; AT, 9:198.

10. Richard A. Watson takes Foucher's argument to be one of two major reasons for "the downfall of Cartesianism." See his book by that title.

11. CSM, 2:234; AT, 7:337-38.

12. *New Essays,* pp. 131-32.

13. *Des vrayes et des fausses idees; Oeuvres,* 38:199-200.

14. Bloch, "Gassendi critique," p. 232.

15. CSM, 2:179; AT, 7:257.

16. *Disquisitio Metaphysica; Opera,* 3:297a.

17. CSM, 2:100; AT, 7:140.

18. Bloch, "Gassendi critique," pp. 220-26.

19. *Opera,* 3:279a.

20. Ibid., 3:286a.

21. *Discourse on Method; CSM, 1:122-25; AT, 2:22-28.

22. *Opera,* 3:286a.

23. Cf. Gassendi's syllogistic reconstruction of Descartes's reasoning in *Meditations* 1 (3:279a).

24. *Opera,* 3:279b; *Selected Works,* p. 166.

25. *Opera,* 3:280a; *Selected Works,* p. 167.

26. Bloch, "Gassendi critique," p. 227.

27. *Opera,* 3:299b.

28. 2.1.16; 113.

29. *Opera,* 3:95-210.

30. 3:159a; *Selected Works,* p. 43. Cf. Locke: "All Things, that exist, being Particulars" (3.3.1; 409).

31. CSM, 2:35; AT, 7:51.

32. CSM, 2:212; AT, 7:304.

33. 2.23.33-35.

34. CSM, 2:255-56; AT, 7:371.

35. CSM, 2:189-90; AT, 7:271-72. See also CSM, 2:190-99; AT, 7:273: "When you go on to say that the perception of colour and hardness and so on is 'not vision or touch but is purely mental scrutiny', I accept this provided the mind is not taken to be really distinct from the imaginative faculty. You add that this scrutiny 'can be imperfect and confused or perfect and distinct depending on how carefully we concentrate on what the wax consists in.' But this does not show that the scrutiny made by the mind, when it examines the mysterious something that exists over and above all the forms, constitutes clear and distinct knowledge of the wax; it shows, rather, that such knowledge is constituted by the scrutiny made by the senses of all the possible accidents and changes which the wax is capable of taking on.

From these we shall certainly be able to arrive at a conception and explanation of what we mean by the term 'wax'; but the alleged naked, or rather hidden, substance is something that we can neither ourselves conceive nor explain to others."

36. CSM, 2:248-49; AT, 7:359-60.

37. *Opera,* 3:352b-353a.

38. Bracken, "Problems of Substance."

39. CSM, 2:256; AT, 7:371.

40. *Opera,* 3:352a; *Selected Works,* p. 222.

41. 3:353b; *Selected Works,* p. 223. Among those who have been sensitive to Locke's debt to Gassendi, François Duchesneau has produced perhaps the most extensive treatment of the question, but one that resulted in a conclusion precisely opposite to that drawn here. He emphasizes Gassendi's rejection of intellectual *pictures,* basing his case on texts from Bernier, Digby, and Gassendi's theory of vision. On this view, the perception of an idea is for Gassendi the mind's act of grasping the intelligible in the sensible given. I am rather persuaded by Bloch, who argues just the opposite from the model of Gassendi's theory of vision: "Vision is in no way the intuition of a cognitive content given in sensation, but a reconstruction by the mind of the reality of things from a content which is, not the [intelligible] translation of that reality [in the mind as per Duchesneau's interpretation according to the Aristotelian tradition], but the [causal] effect of it" (*La philosophie,* p. 20). Thus ideas are not intellectual, but they are yet pictures, which ceteris paribus are caused by what they picture. Of this difficult issue, much more below.

42. *Syntagma; Opera,* 1:179 ff; *Selected Works,* p. 383ff.

43. 1:180b.

44. 1:179b.

45. *locum constantem, & Tempus decurrens* (1:182a).

46. *Quantitatem, extensionemve quandam* (1:182a).

47. 1:182a-b; *Selected Works,* p. 385.

48. 1:179a.

49. Sambursky, "Place and space."

50. 1:182a; *Selected Works,* p. 384. See *Abrégé* 1, vol. 1: "it is inconceivable that a substance should be and that it should not be in some place" (p. 21). See also p. 19: Space must be uncreated since nothing is created unless in a place, and "it would be ridiculous to say that place is created in another place since this would go on to infinity."

51. *Essais physiques,* p. 103.

52. Sambursky, "Place and Space."

53. *Abrégé* 2, 2:399-400.

54. 1:183b-184a; *Selected Works,* p. 389. Also, 1:189b. Brundell points out that Gassendi here clearly drew upon the Jesuit *Conimbricenses* (*Pierre Gassendi,* p. 66).

55. Proto-*Abrégé,* p. 7.

56. *Abrégé* 1, 1:13.

57. *Principles* 2, 18; CSM, 1:231; AT, 8:50.

58. *Abrégé* 1, 1:13-14. The remark is dropped from *Abrégé* 2.

59. *Physiologia,* p. 68.

60. *Method,* p. 42.

61. *Physiologia,* p. 69.

62. See Heyd, "Philosophy"; Osler, "Providence" for the significance of voluntarist theology in this period.

63. *Essais physiques,* p. 76.

64. Ibid., p. 79.

65. Launay actually says "immense being" (p. 102). Gassendi, *Opera,* 1:190b.

66. *Essais physiques,* p. 101.

67. In fact, the incorporeal extension of the soul is somewhat greater than the corporeal extension of the body that imprisons it, since the soul of a dwarf can fill the body of a giant.

68. HR [Descartes, *The Philosophical Works,* trans. E. S. Haldane and G. R. T. Ross. Cambridge: Cambridge University Press, 1968. Ist ed., 1911], 1:242-43; AT, 8:24.

69. *Essais physiques,* p. 75.

70. In the heraldic sense: *la table d' attente.*

71. Proto-*Abrégé,* p. 4: "The first thing a physicist must do . . . is . . . to consider this space as the general place of all that has been produced . . . and that God may draw from His omnipotence." See *Abrégé* 1, 1:7-8; *Abrégé* 2, 2:1-2.

72. Bernier explains in *Abrégé* 1 that Gassendi thought that logic, the traditional first part of philosophy, was, if harmless, without great use: "if the eye sees, the ear hears . . . without any precepts, the understanding can reason well, seek the truth, find it and judge it without the aid of logic" (*au lecteur,* unpaginated). *Abrégé* 2 returns the logic to be outset of the work, although the treatment of space remains at the beginning of the physics.

73. Proto-*Abrégé,* p. 14.

74. *Abrégé* 1, 1:25.

75. *Abrégé* 2, 2:5, 10-11.

76. Proto-*Abrégé,* p. 13; *Abrégé* 1, 1:17-19; *Abrégé* 2, 2:12-13.

77. See *Syntagma; Opera,* 1:184b.

78. *Abrégé* 2, 2:10.

79. Archytas had argued that everything is in some place, hence because of the same regress, place must be nothing. See Sambursky, "Place and Space."

80. *Doubts* 1, p. 25.

81. Ibid., pp. 25-27.

82. *Doubts* 2, p. 387.

83. The Cartesian Antoine LeGrand later argued that "that which is Nothing can never constitute the Distance of *Bodies.*" Nor could distance be "founded in the *Bodies* themselves," for then relations of distance would never change (*Entire Body,* pt. 2, p. 2).

84. *Systême,* 1:286.

85. *Les principes,* p. 410.

86. *Doubts* 2, p. 398. With this conception of place Bernier can also answer the puzzle about Archytas's arrow: It would indeed go beyond the world but not *into* the void. With it he can also restore Archytas's argument to its original intent, which he does in effect arguing against Gassendi's view: How must everything be in a place when space, supposedly a real being, has no place?

87. *Opera,* 1:184a-185b. The text is taken verbatim from the *Animadversiones,* p. 614.

88. 1:21.

89. He also adds that (1) nothing can be its own place, because a body that moves does not carry its place with it, but leaves one and moves to another; (2) common sense tells us that place is different from the thing placed, and that since place is what receives bodies, it is both prior to and supposed by them.

90. *Essais physiques,* p. 79.

91. *Physiologia,* p. 66.

92. Which its editors date between 1664 and 1668 (p. 90).

93. *Unpublished papers,* pp. 99-100; trans. pp. 131-32. cf. *Syntagma, Opera,* 1:179a. The term does not appear in this connection in *Animadversiones* and therefore not in Charleton's account of space. I am thus inclined to agree with Westfall's contention that Newton here "drew his discussion of space and time directly from the *Syntagma*" ("Foundations," pp. 172-73, n. 5).

94. Locke of course is interested in metempsychosis (see his notes on Bernier) but only for purposes of thought experiments. He does not say that the soul of Castor in fact is ever in the body of Pollux, but only asks what we would say if it were.

95. *Opera,* 1:182a.

96. It has been systematically treated and made remarkably tractable by Sorabji.

97. praeter eandem concipimus infinitatem quasi extensionis, (*Opera,* 1:191b); comme diffuse & d'étendue (proto-*Abrégé,* p. 7).

98. Ibid.

99. Cicero, *De natura decorum* 1.9.21.

100. P. 434, corrected.

101. *De Civitate Dei,* p. 638. Augustine's points are faithfully conveyed by André Martin, however (*Philosophia,* 3:95).

102. As Launay put it, except for contemplating and loving Himself, God is inactive in those times and places in which He does not create, and if what He creates does not have the full temporal and spatial extension it might have, this is because He is "free and independent and consequently master of His actions" (*Essais physiques,* p. 104). Curiously, Launay initially gets the point of the Augustinian texts right when he argues that there *are not* innumerably many worlds. But later he falls in with the Gassendist interpretation when he argues that God *could* create innumerably many worlds or enlarge this one as it pleased Him, and since He cannot create a world without a place to put it in, ultramundane spaces must be admitted (*Essais physiques,* pp. 16, 101). The latter text raises the problem of sufficient reason at least obliquely. God must be where He acts, according to Launay, thus must be beyond the world in order (to be able) to create there.

Works Cited

Arnauld, A. *Des vrayes et des fausses idées, contre ce qu'enseigne l'auteur de la recherche de la vérité.* 1683. In *Oeuvres,* vol. 38.

_____. *Oeuvres.* Paris, 1775-83.

Bloch, Olivier René. "Gassendi critique de Descartes." *Revue philosophique de la France et de l'Etranger* 156 (1966): 217-36.

_____. *La philosophie de Gassendi: Nominalisme, matérialisme, et métaphysique.* The Hague: Martinus Nijhoff, 1971.

Bougerel, J. *Vie de Pierre Gassendi.* Paris, 1737.

Bracken, Harry M. "Some Problems of Substance among the Cartesians." *American Philosophical Quarterly* 1, no. 2 (April 1964): 129-37.

Descartes, R. *Oeuvres,* ed. C. Adam and P. Tannery. 1st ed. 1897-1913; 2d ed., CNRS, Paris: Vrin, 1964-75.

_____. *The Philosophical Writings,* trans. J. Cottingham, R. Stoothoff, and D. Murdoch. Cambridge: Cambridge University Press, 1985.

Duchesneau, François. *L'empirisme de Locke.* The Hague: Martinus Nijhoff, 1973.

Gassendi, P. *Opera.* Lyon, 1658.

_____. *The Selected Works,* trans. C. Brush. New York: Johnson Reprint, 1972.

Jones, H. *Pierre Gassendi, 1592-1655: An Intellectual Autobiography.* Nieuwkoop: B. DeGraaf, 1981.

Leibniz, G. W. *New Essays on Human Understanding,* trans. P. Remnant and J. Bennett. Cambridge: Cambridge University Press, 1981.

Locke, J. *An Essay Concerning Human Understanding,* ed. Peter H. Nidditch. Oxford: Clarendon Press, 1975; reprinted with corrections, 1979.

Watson, R. A. *The Downfall of Cartesianism.* The Hague: Martinus Nijhoff, 1968.

Margaret J. Osler (essay date 1994)

SOURCE: "Providence and Human Freedom in Christian Epicureanism: Gassendi on Fortune, Fate, and Divination," in *Divine Will and the Mechanical Philosophy: Gassendi and Descartes on Contingency and Necessity in the Created World,* Cambridge University Press, 1994, pp. 86-101.

[In the following excerpt, Osler explicates the voluntarism that permeates Gassendi's work, placing his development of a mechanical philosophy in the context of seventeenth-century theological controversies. The critic finds that Gassendi's insistence on human free will, in addition to divine free will, distinguishes him from other materialist thinkers, including Thomas Hobbes.]

> Fate is the decree of the divine will, without which nothing at all is done, . . . [and] Fortune is the concourse of events that, although unforeseen by men, nevertheless were foreseen by God.
>
> Pierre Gassendi, *Syntagma philosophicum*[1]

Having ensured that divine providence played a major role in his mechanical philosophy, Gassendi turned to the question of human freedom in Book III of the "Ethics," the last part of the *Syntagma philosophicum,* entitled "On Liberty, Fortune, Fate, and Divination."[2] In this concluding section of his magnum opus, Gassendi cast his discussion in the form of a debate among the major classical philosophies, particularly Stoicism and Epicureanism. The main issue was freedom—human and divine. While questions about fate, fortune, and divination may, at first glance, appear rather remote from the primary concerns of seventeenth-century natural philosophy, in fact they involve metaphysical issues central to the articulation of the mechanical philosophy: the extent of contingency and necessity in the world, the nature of causality, and the role of providence and the extent of human freedom in a mechanical universe.[3] Gassendi's treatment of these issues reflects his underlying voluntarism.

Since classical times, natural philosophers had dealt extensively with questions about fate, fortune, and divination. The concept of fate was central to Stoicism, which had explained the world as governed by a deterministic, rational ordering principle, the Logos. According to Stoic doctrine, fate is the expression of the Logos in the causal nexus of a deterministic universe.[4] This emphasis on causal necessity in the universe had provided foundations for the Stoic belief in astrology and other forms of divination, which were based on the assumption that every part of the universe is connected to every other by the Logos and that events in one realm (say, the heavens) can serve as signs for events taking place elsewhere (say, in human lives).[5] Stoic fate was directly opposed to chance, which the Epicureans had incorporated into the universe by means of the *clinamen* or random swerve of atoms that they introduced to account for the collision of atoms and for free will. While Stoicism was compatible with the idea of providence, it was often interpreted as ruling out human freedom. Epicureanism, which allowed for free will, explicitly denied any kind of providential account of the world.

The evident contradictions between both of these classical philosophies, on the one hand, and the Christian doctrines of divine freedom, providence, and human freedom, on the other, stimulated discussions among early Christian thinkers, among the most influential of whom—on these issues—were St. Augustine, who rejected both Epicureanism and Stoicism, and Boethius, who attempted to fuse them with orthodox theology.[6] These early Christian discussions seemed particularly relevant to the Renaissance humanists as they tried to come to grips with the recently recovered texts of the classical philosophers.[7] Although the themes of fate, fortune, and human freedom were ubiquitous in Renaissance writing, one context in which they were particularly relevant was the debate over astrology, which gained prominence following Marsilio Ficino's (1433-99) translation and publication of the Hermetic corpus and other magical-mystical literature.[8] Giovanni Pontano (1427/9-1503) and Giovanni Pico della Mirandola both argued against astrology on the grounds that it limits human freedom in unacceptable ways.[9]

Pomponazzi reasserted the legitimacy of astrology, in *De fato, de libero arbitrio et de praedestinatione,* completed in 1520.[10] Favoring Stoic metaphysics and ethics, he gave an account of contingency as it could be understood in a world ruled by deterministic laws. Contingency, according to Pomponazzi, is not an indication of indifference, "the possibility for an effect to be or not to be." Rather, it refers "only to things which sometimes happen and sometimes do not, such as whether or not it will rain next month. If it does rain, that happens necessarily." Likewise if it does not.[11] Since the human will falls within the "universal hierarchy of natural causes," our intuition of free will is an illusion based on ignorance of the true causes of our actions.[12] Pomponazzi took great pains to show how this kind of Stoic determinism was compatible with moral responsibility. "Everything is therefore subject to the providential order of fate."[13] Given what he construed as a choice between divine providence and human freedom, Pomponazzi opted for the divine.[14] However, in a self-contradiction that reveals the continuing pull of traditional Christian thought, he preserved human freedom by maintaining that "it is in the power of the will to will and to suspend an act—this freedom is preserved."[15] He noted that knowledge of freedom was the product of faith rather than of natural reason.[16]

Human freedom came under further assault at the hands of the Protestant reformers.[17] Luther concluded his debate with Erasmus with the resounding statement that human freedom is incompatible with divine foreknowledge:

> If we believe it to be true that God foreknows and predestines all things, that he can neither be mistaken in his foreknowledge nor hindered in his predestination, and that nothing takes place but as he wills it (as reason itself is forced to admit), then on the testimony of reason itself there cannot be any free choice in man or angel or any other creature.[18]

Calvin's doctrine of election similarly denied human freedom.[19] In his providential relationship to humanity, God determines how people choose and thereby obviates their free will. "God, whenever he wills to make way for his providence, bends and turns men's wills, even in external things; nor are they free to choose that God's will does not rule over their freedom."[20] In order to ensure God's freedom, Calvin was careful to distinguish his doctrine, "that particular events are generally testimonies of the character of God's singular providence," from the "Stoics' dogma of fate:"[21]

> We do not, with the Stoics, contrive a necessity out of the perpetual connection and intimately related series of causes, which is contained in nature; but we make God the ruler and governor of all things, who in accordance with his wisdom has from the farthest limit of eternity decreed what he was going to do, and now by his might carries out what he has decreed. From this we declare that not only heaven and earth and the inanimate creatures, but also the plans and intentions of men, are so governed by his providence that they are borne by it straight to their appointed end.[22]

In the Catholic world, these controversies came to the fore in the aftermath of the Council of Trent (1545-63), which had addressed the question of formulating doctrine in response to the reformers' challenge.[23] Gassendi's discussion of fate and free will falls clearly within this context. By insisting on human freedom as he did, Gassendi placed himself among the followers of the Jesuit Luis de Molina, whose treatise *Concordia liberi arbitrii cum gratiae donis, divina praescientia, providentia, praedestinatione et reprobatione* (1588) was adopted by his order in its renowned debate with the Dominicans on the relationship between divine grace and human free will.[24] The Spanish Jesuit Francisco Suárez adopted Molina's views, defending and expanding them into a small treatise written in 1594 in response to a request by Pope Clement VIII.[25] The Dominicans had emphasized divine omnipotence to such an extent that they considered God's decree as imposing itself on people, determining their future actions. Although the Dominicans argued that this determination does not destroy free will, the Jesuits rejected their argument, adopting instead the views of Molina that attempted to preserve divine omnipotence without sacrificing human freedom.[26] Whereas the Dominicans had claimed that God's foreknowledge of human actions makes it impossible for those actions to have any other outcome than what God foresees, Molina's account of God's foreknowledge of future contingents seemed to leave more play for human freedom. Molina described three kinds of knowledge that God has of future contingents: (1) his knowledge of naturally necessary states of affairs; (2) his *scientia media,* or knowledge of conditional future contingents (i.e., knowledge of what would follow from any given state of affairs); and (3) knowledge of his own causal contribution to any state of affairs.[27] It was Molina's concept of *scientia media* that enabled him to say that God's foreknowledge does not necessarily determine future human actions: God knows that, given certain circumstances, Peter will deny Christ; but that conditional knowledge does not necessitate Peter's denial.

Gassendi's approach to these questions in Book III of the "Ethics" rests on two important principles: that a proper understanding of the world must include divine freedom, creation, and providence and that the possibility of ethics—moral choice and judgment—requires human freedom. His humanist bent led him to consider these issues in the rhetorical context of a debate among the ancient philosophers, especially the Epicureans and the Stoics.

If divine freedom played a central role in Gassendi's philosophy of nature, human freedom was the cornerstone of his ethics.[28] Moral choice and judgment depend, he argued, on the possibility of those choices being taken freely and deliberately. Actions taken either by accident or by necessity do not merit praise or blame.[29] "Freedom (*libertas*) consists in indifference."[30] That is, the will and intellect are said to be free if they are equally able to choose one or another of possible options and are not in any way determined to one or the other.[31] Real freedom, understood as indifference, belongs only to rational beings and differs from what Gassendi called willingness (*libentia*). Willingness characterizes the actions of boys, brutes, and stones, agents lacking the capacity for rational choice.[32] Human freedom is also a concomitant of voluntarist theology; for if any human action were determined necessarily, the universe would contain some element of necessity that would restrict God's power and freedom.

Having articulated his underlying assumptions—namely, a voluntarist theology and a conception of human nature incorporating free will—Gassendi proceeded with his analysis of fortune, fate, and divination. Although he considered them in the context of ancient philosophy, this humanist device was a ploy for discussing some of the most controversial theological and natural philosophical issues of the early seventeenth century. These concepts challenged his

Christian, voluntarist, providential view of God, nature, and human nature, by calling for the elimination of either creation, providence, or free will.

Gassendi began his discussion of fortune and chance by adopting a standard, classical definition: Fortune is an unexpected consequence, a cause by accident. To illustrate his meaning, he cited Aristotle's example of a man who discovers treasure while digging in the ground to plant a tree.[33] Finding a treasure is a totally unexpected consequence of his act. While the digging preceded the discovery, it was not the cause of the discovery except accidentally, since the discovery of treasure is not the usual or natural outcome of digging in the ground. Such unexpected consequences are called fortuitous in connection with agents that act freely; they are called chance in connection with inanimate objects.[34] An example of chance would be the occurrence of a storm in the west at sunset. Both events—the storm and the sunset—are the outcome of natural causes, but their coincidence in space and time is both unpredictable and unanticipated. According to Gassendi, fortune and chance are both expressions of contingency in the world. Like fortune, chance is the name given to the kind of contingency that describes an event that may or may not happen in the future. An event that is said to be caused by chance or fortune is one that results from the unexpected concourse of several apparently unrelated causes. In the case of the unexpected discovery of the treasure, there is the concourse of the original burial of the treasure with the present digging in the ground.[35] Each event is the perfectly natural outcome of a series of causes. The two series are unrelated, however, and so their concourse is unexpected: Therein lies the element of chance or fortune, concepts that reflect our ignorance rather than the state of the world. "Fortune [or chance] is truly nothing in itself . . . only the negation of foreknowledge and of the intention of the events."[36]

Certain misunderstandings render the concept of fortune problematic. Those who reify fortune and call it divine—a position that even Epicurus had rejected—are ignorant of the real causes of the events in question.[37] Epicurus had, rather, equated fortune with chance and denied that "there is divine wisdom in the world."[38] He had thus compared life to a game of dice. Here he had erred, according to Gassendi, because he had failed to appreciate that divine providence touches every aspect of nature and of human life.[39]

Fortune and chance, understood as unanticipated outcomes of unexpected concourses of natural causes, can easily be incorporated into an orthodox philosophy of nature by including divine will and providence among the efficient causes operating in the world.[40] Opposing Epicurean materialism and emphasizing the limits of human knowledge, Gassendi thus believed he could reinterpret one of the important components of Epicureanism in a theologically suitable fashion. Accordingly, he defined fortune as "the concourse of events which, although unforeseen by man, were foreseen by God; and they are connected by a series of causes."[41] In other words, events that seem fortuitous to us are nevertheless providential, resulting from God's design, despite our ignorance of the causal sequences producing them.

Whereas fortune and chance raise questions about the nature of contingency, causality, and providence in the world, fate points to the complex problem of free will and determinism. Some interpretations of fate, as Gassendi understood or misunderstood them, seemed to incorporate a kind of natural necessity that would restrict both divine and human freedom. It is this necessitarian interpretation of the notion of fate—whether by ancient philosophers or contemporary theologians—to which Gassendi was primarily opposed.[42] The question of fate and its relation to free will had special relevance in the context of post-Reformation debates about free will. The reformers, especially the Calvinists, seemed to have denied human as well as divine freedom—at least regarding matters of salvation—with their doctrines of predestination and election. The Dominican approach to predestination and divine foreknowledge suffered from similar problems. In working out his own interpretation of the concept of fate in dialogue with the ancient philosophers, Gassendi participated in one of the most heated theological controversies of his own day.

He observed that there are two chief views about fate: that it is something divine and that it is merely natural. Among those who regarded fate as divine, he counted the Platonists and the Stoics. The former group defined fate as "the eternal God or that reason, which disposes all things from eternal time, and thus binds causes to causes."[43] In this sense, Plato (429-347 B.C.) had sometimes considered fate to be part of the soul of the world, sometimes "the eternal reason and law of the universe." The Stoics Zeno (366-c. 264 B.C.) and Chrysippus (280-206 B.C.) had defined fate as "the motive force of matter and the spiritual force and governing reason of the order of the universe." Seneca (c. 4 B.C.-65 A.D.) had gone so far as to identify fate with the god Jove.[44]

Despite the apparently theological and providential orientation of the Stoic interpretation of fate, Gassendi found its necessitarianism objectionable: "This necessity seems to be of such a kind that it completely removes the liberty of all human action and leaves nothing within our judgment."[45] Such negation of free will would deprive life of meaning. In a world ruled by fate, there would be no place for plans, prudence, or wisdom, since everything would happen according to fate. "All legislators would be either fools or tyrants, since they would command things [to happen] that were either always to be done or that we absolutely cannot do."[46] Since there would be no freedom of action, no action would be subject to moral judgment. All contingency in the universe would be eliminated. Consequently, all divination, prayer, and sacrifice would be rendered useless.[47]

Among those who considered fate to be something merely natural, Gassendi distinguished those who thought of fate as absolutely binding and those who did not. As Lisa Sarasohn has shown, Gassendi created a dialogue between Democritus (460-c. 356 B.C.) and Epicurus to represent the views of Hobbes in contrast to his own.[48] The hard determinism and materialism endorsed by Democritus in this section of the *Syntagma philosophicum* constitute the nightmare feared by Christian mechanical philosophers. Hobbes in fact held such views. His treatise *Of Liberty and Necessity,* in which he supported a deterministic position on the free-will controversy, was published without his permission in 1654 by the Anglican Bishop John Bramhall, who argued against Hobbes.[49] Hobbes then published *The Questions Concerning Liberty, Necessity, and Chance* (1656) which contained both Bramhall's treatise and his own replies.[50] Although this work was published after Gassendi's death, Gassendi was directly acquainted with Hobbes' views from their interactions in Paris around 1641 or possibly even earlier.[51]

In the dialogue between Democritus and Epicurus in Book III of the "Ethics," Gassendi put Hobbes' opinions in the words of Democritus, the ancient advocate of hard determinism. Democritus had held the view that "every event has a cause and that the same cause is always followed by the same effect" and that the truth of determinism rules out human freedom.[52] He conceived of fate as natural necessity. In Gassendi's presentation, Democritus' view was similar to that of the Stoics, shorn, however, of any remnant of theology: "Democritus taught . . . that Necessity is nothing other than . . . the motion, impact, and rebounding of matter, that is, of atoms, which are the matter of all things. Whence it can be understood that 'Material Necessity' is the cause of all things that happen."[53] Democritus claimed that since everything, including the human soul, is composed of atoms, there is no room for real freedom in the universe.[54] Not only freedom, but also error would be impossible in such a world.[55] And if everything were necessarily determined by the motions and collisions of atoms, there would be no room for divine providence.[56]

In contrast to Democritus, who maintained absolute necessity since nothing can impede a cause from producing its effect,[57] Epicurus believed that the necessity in nature is not absolute. Arguing on logical grounds, he claimed that it is impossible simultaneously to hold that all statements are either true or false and that there is absolute necessity in nature, for to do so would entail giving truth-value to statements about future contingents, something Epicurus regarded as impossible. Following Aristotle in his famous discussion of tomorrow's sea battle,[58] Epicurus "admitted this complex as truth, 'Either Hermachus will be alive tomorrow or he will not be alive.'" But Epicurus could not accept the possbility that either one of the disjuncts—"It is necessary that Hermachus be alive tomorrow" or "It is necessary that Hermachus not be alive tomorrow"—be true; for "There is no such necessity in nature."[59] Epicurus thought that necessity could apply only to statements about the past and present: The events described have already occurred or not occurred, and so statements describing them have a determined truth-value. However, statements about the future have an undetermined truth-value, so we cannot reason about them with necessity.[60] Since, according to Epicurus, we cannot have knowledge of future contingents, it follows that there is no such necessity in nature.[61]

As for events that occur by plan or by fortune, these involve human freedom, which Epicurus had tried to preserve by adding the *clinamen,* or random swerve, to the otherwise steady downward motion of the Democritean atoms. According to Gassendi, Epicurus had introduced the swerve with the explicit intention "that it shatter the necessity of fate and thus ensure the liberty of souls."[62] Despite Epicurus' good intentions, Gassendi did not find his solution to the free-will controversy convincing. Epicurus had thought that the unpredictability of the swerve preserves free will.[63] Gassendi did not agree. Events would still always happen by the same chain of necessary consequences. "What always happens by the same necessity would happen by a variety of motions, collisions, rebounds, swerves in a certain external series, like a chain of consequences."[64] Since Epicurus had argued that the soul consists of atoms, its choices would simply be determined by the long causal sequence of the material world. Gassendi concluded that the *clinamen* was therefore not a satisfactory explanation of human freedom.

Gassendi found all the traditional accounts of fate to be wanting, primarily for theological and ethical reasons. The deterministic, reductionist atomism of Democritus left room for neither divine providence nor free will:

> Therefore, the opinion of Democritus must be exploded inasmuch as it can by no means stand with the principles of the Sacred Faith (because of having removed from God the care and administration of things), and it is thus manifestly repugnant to the light of nature by which we experience ourselves to be free.[65]

The passion driving Gassendi's attack on Democritus can in part be explained by his identification of "Hobbes as Democritus reincarnated," for Gassendi found his contemporary's hard determinism entirely unacceptable.[66] Epicurus deserved criticism as well, despite his good intentions in attempting to preserve free will, for by denying the possibility of knowing future contingents, he had denied God such knowledge. He "thus supposes that there is no creation of things and no divine providence."[67]

In order to embrace the evident facts of both causal order and contingency within the bounds of his mechanical philosophy, Gassendi undertook a Christian reinterpretation of the concepts of fate, fortune, and chance, providing a providential understanding of these concepts, just as Augustine had done centuries earlier:[68]

> To the extent that Fate can be defended, so can Fortune. If we agree that Fate is the decree of the divine will, without which nothing at all is done, truly Fortune

is the concourse of events that, although unforeseen by men, nevertheless was foreseen by God; and they are the connected series of causes or Fate.[69]

Thus, fate is nothing more than God's decree, and fortune and chance are expressions of contingency in the world coupled with human ignorance of the causes of fortuitous events. Fortune, chance, and fate are not autonomous principles running the world. Even if all events have causes and even if God can foresee the unrolling of cause and effect—a foresight not available to humans—both the causes and their effects ultimately depend on divine will. The universe remains a contingent place.

Gassendi's reinterpretation of fortune, chance, and fate left plenty of room for the exercise of divine freedom and providence. The fact that certain events appear to be fortuitous in no way impairs divine omniscience. They appear fortuitous only because of the limitations of human knowledge:

> The word Fortune . . . indicates two things, the concourse of causes and the previous ignorance of events; Fortune can thus be admitted afterward with respect to man but not God; and on account of this . . . nothing stands in the way of our saying that Fortune is a part not only of Fate, but also of divine providence, which foresees for man what he cannot foresee [for himself].[70]

Far from imparting a randomness to life's events, fortune itself is an expression of divine foresight and providence. Fortune is an expression of human limitation, but it in no way impugns divine power and freedom.[71]

Reconciling fate with divine providence was not so difficult for Gassendi. A more challenging problem was to reconcile fate with free will. Here again he turned to theology for his solution, and here the connections between Gassendi's discussion and post-Reformation theology become explicit. His discussion was, in effect, a debate with the overly deterministic theologies of Calvin and the Dominicans: "We call Fate, with respect to men, nothing other than that part of Divine Providence that is called Predestination by theologians . . . in order that predestination and thus Fate can be reconciled with liberty."[72] Appealing to the vexatious doctrine of predestination seems an odd way to clarify anything. Indeed, Gassendi acknowledged that the problem of reconciling predestination and divine foreknowledge with human freedom had troubled both philosophers and theologians since antiquity.

God's foreknowledge of Peter's denial had challenged some philosophers and theologians because they had thought that such foreknowledge entailed a kind of fatalism that denies human freedom.[73] Peter's free will could be saved, but only at the expense of God's omniscience and veracity:

> Either God knew definitely and certainly that Peter would deny Christ, or he did not. It cannot be said that he did not know, because he predicted it and he is not a liar: and unless he knew, he would be neither omni-

scient nor God. Therefore, he knew it definitely and certainly. Thus, it could not be that Peter would not deny. If God knew and Peter did not deny . . . it would be argued of God that his foreknowledge was false and that he was a liar. If Peter cannot deny, then he is not free to deny or not deny. Therefore he is without freedom.[74]

In other words, either God's veracity and omniscience or Peter's free will must be denied. Gassendi found both alternatives unacceptable.

In order to resolve this difficulty, Gassendi invoked the Scholastic distinction between absolute necessity and necessity by supposition:

> For example, that double two is four or that yesterday comes before today is absolutely necessary, although that you lay the foundations of your house or leave the city is not necessary: nevertheless if you suppose that you will build your house or that you will be in the country, then for you to lay the foundation or leave the city is, I say, necessary from supposition. Truly it is manifest from this distinction, that absolute necessity hinders that by which a certain action is elicited, however that which is from supposition does not hinder (for he who will lay down a foundation absolutely can *not* lay it, and he who will leave the city can *not* leave).[75]

Molina's theory of *scientia media* provided Gassendi with a way of resolving these difficulties by interpreting the necessity of God's foreknowledge as necessity by supposition:[76]

> Peter's future denial was seen by God necessarily, but nevertheless by a necessity from supposition, because of which nothing of liberty is taken away. . . . [T]hus although it was determined from the beginning that [Peter] would deny him, he does it freely in whatever manner he did it; afterward, since he did it, it was necessary.[77]

Gassendi's concept of necessity contains a temporal component. The act of denial does not become necessary, despite being foreseen by God, until Peter commits it. Once the denial has occurred, it is part of the past that cannot be undone:

> If indeed when it is said that Peter denied necessarily this necessity is understood, not as something that was truly in Peter antecedently that forced him to act, but only now that it is in this time that is in the past and cannot not be past, thus the thing that is done by him is done . . . and cannot not be done by him.[78]

Necessity of this kind in no way impinges on divine freedom and omniscience, because God could foresee Peter's free choice. "Thus, it can be said that Peter denied not because God foresaw it, but God foresaw since Peter would deny."[79] God's knowledge of future events does not cause those events to happen; but, on account of his omniscience, he has foreknowledge because they will happen. Since some of those events are the acts of free agents, there is no contradiction between God's foreknowledge and human freedom.

Gassendi addressed at some length the question of how to interpret the doctrine of predestination. He rejected the Calvinist view that the members of the elect and the reprobate had been chosen from eternity. He also rejected the Dominican view that God's foreknowledge deprives human agents of their freedom. Instead, he opted for the more liberal, Molinist position. According to Gassendi, God created people with free will as well as the causal order of the world. He knows how an individual will respond in any particular situation, even though that individual will respond freely. In this way, God's foreknowledge in no way restricts the liberty of free agents.[80] Even if everything is included within the domain of divine decree, that inclusion does not eliminate human freedom, for God created free agents as well as determined ones.

If discussions about fate and fortune really concerned the roles of contingency and necessity in the universe, divination raised questions about the nature of causality. Divination had played a central role in Stoic thought, where it had been invoked to provide evidence for the causal interconnectedness of the universe.[81] For Gassendi, delineating the boundary between the natural and supernatural was an important part of the task of determining the limits of mechanical causality in the world. This problem was not unique to the mechanical philosophers. All natural philosophers in the period—Aristotelians and natural magicians, as well as mechanical philosophers—faced it in the questions raised by witchcraft, demonology, and other occult pursuits.[82]

The immediate context of Gassendi's concern with divination, as well as that of his contemporaries Mersenne, Naudé, and La Mothe le Vayer, was its notoriously naturalistic treatment by Pomponazzi in *De naturalium effectum admirandorum causis sive de incantationibus* (1556) and *De fato, de libero arbitrio et de praedestinatione* (1520). In order to account for many extraordinary effects without appealing to demons, Pomponazzi had sought to explain both natural and human history as determined by natural, astrological, and various occult causes. In so doing, he affirmed an Averroism far more radical than that condemned in 1277. The strong negative reaction to his books was exacerbated by his role in debates about the immortality of the soul.[83]

Whether or not Gassendi had actually read Pomponazzi's works himself, he doubtless knew about them from his friend Mersenne, who went to great lengths to refute Renaissance naturalism in *Quaestiones celeberrimae in Genesim* (1623) and *L'impiété des déistes* (1624).[84] Mersenne rejected the Renaissance naturalists as atheists because they "attribute everything to nature alone" and deny God a causal role in the world.[85] In particular, he attacked the naturalists' belief in astrology because it is contrary to the

teachings of the church fathers, because it is based on an unacceptable mysticism and a false theory of causation founded on the correspondence between macrocosm and microcosm, and because it is too restrictive of human freedom.[86] Moreover, "only true science, based on an idea of nature submissive to intelligible laws, would permit him to save religion, morality, and science."[87]

While Gassendi rejected Stoic fatalism and the more recent naturalism associated with it, he defended certain forms of divination on theological grounds. In the final chapter of Book III of the "Ethics," entitled "The Meaning of Divination, or the Foreknowledge of Future and Merely Fortuitous Things," Gassendi supported divination in opposition to Epicurus, whose blanket denial of the possibility that knowledge of future contingents might be compatible with human freedom had led him to reject the possibility of any kind of divination. That Epicurus was wrong, Gassendi argued, can be demonstrated straightaway by the fulfillment of the biblical prophecies.[88]

Gassendi began his discussion of divination with the consideration of demons, which some ancient thinkers had invoked as part of a naturalistic way of explaining how divination works. Demons concerned Gassendi, because the question of their existence bore on the deeper question of the causal order of the world and the boundaries between natural and supernatural causation. He rehearsed and rejected various ancient doctrines about demons—that they are particles of the *anima mundi*, that they have a corporeal nature, that they are halfway between humans and gods, that they move the heavenly spheres, that they are of some particular number or another.[89] The problem with all of these views is that they remove divine activity from the ordinary workings of the world. "They judged that it was alien to the divine majesty to care for all particulars himself,"[90] thereby impugning divine power by implying that God uses ministers to carry out his will because of some defect in his nature. Gassendi countered with a voluntarist argument: "God uses ministers, not because of disgrace, impotence, or need, but because he wished it for the state of things that is the world. He judged it congruous."[91] Reasserting nature's utter dependence on divine will, he noted that God, "if he had wished to institute another order, he would not have done a disgraceful thing nor would it testify to any impotence or need."[92] Unlike the highest prince in his realm, to whom the philosophers had compared him, God is actually present everywhere in the world, not just to his designated ministers. The philosophers had mistakenly substituted the activity of these demons for both God's general and special providence.[93] Since demons were generally understood to work by natural means, Gassendi sought to maintain a role for the supernatural by defending God's providential activity in the running of the world.

In fact, he believed that various orders of angels and demons do exist as purely spiritual beings, an opinion he based on "sacred scripture and . . . [which was] explained by theologians."[94] But there are also many false superstitions about the activity of these creatures, exploits that are exaggerated by the poets. There are

> many little stories which frequently fill your ears, from which you will often discover something difficult that is true, if you eliminate the fraud of impostors, the tricks of the crafty, the nonsense of old women, the easy credulity of the common people. Something must also be said about this kind of filthy magic, by which the unhappy person thinks himself carried away by he-goats. . . . [And] afterward, put to sleep by narcotic salves, they dream with a most vivid imagination [that they] were present in a most evil assemblage.[95]

Although these and other temptations and possessions actually exist—scripture, the lives of the saints, and the successful practice of exorcism attest to that fact—the point is to attend to our own spiritual and moral state, our relationship to God by virtue of his special providence, rather than to excuse our sins by blaming evil demons.[96] A proper understanding of demons had not been available to the ancient philosophers who did not possess either the true faith or sacred Scripture, which teach us both of their existence as spiritual beings and of the limits of their powers.

Gassendi had embarked on this long discussion of demons because some ancient advocates of divination had appealed to them in order to explain their practices.[97] Since it is sometimes possible to predict the future, as scripture attests, one must consider "whether the prediction was made by the intervention of demons or the craftiness of the soothsayers or the credulity of those who asked for it."[98] Although there *are* genuine cases of prophecy, many predictions are made of things that have natural causes and are "incapable of impediments, such as eclipses, risings of the stars, and other things of this kind, which depend on the determined disposition and constancy of the motions of the heavenly bodies."[99] In such cases, there is no need to appeal to anything beyond natural causes.

As for genuine divination, Gassendi repeated the traditional Stoic doctrine that there are two kinds. One, like astrology or the ancient interpretations of signs—such as the flight, songs, and feeding of birds or the casting of lots or the interpretation of dreams—depends on art. The other kind does not[100] In the closest approximation to a joke in the ponderous *Syntagma philosophicum,* Gassendi railed against "geomancers, hydromancers, aeromancers, pyromancers, and others . . . and last those astromancers or astrologers who . . . seek it from the stars," all of them practitioners of "artificial divination."[101] If astrology, which holds the principal place among the arts of divination is "inane and futile, the others ought to be no less inane and futile."[102] Gassendi thus denied that divination by art, the kind the Stoics valued most, is divination at all because it is nothing but the observation of regular sequences of natural events, whether or not we understand the causes of those sequences.

In fact, Gassendi argued, any genuine divination would presume the existence of events that do not have causes.[103]

Otherwise, nothing more would be involved in divination than the same kinds of conjectures used in any of the sciences that make predictions about future events. In all conjectural knowledge, we attend to the known causes of events and predict what will likely happen. Such predictions are conjectural, based on reasoning about our observed knowledge of the world. Divining is no different from this kind of conjectural science except that it frequently suffers from a deficit "of ratiocination and consultation."[104] The Stoics had agreed, but in advocating astrology, they had confounded inductive methods with divination by art, which is based on an empirical understanding of the deterministic nexus of the world.[105]

Gassendi's discussion of fortune, fate, and divination in Book III of the "Ethics" reveals his position on the major theological and ethical implications of the mechanical philosophy. His opposition to the hard determinism of Hobbes, the modern Democritus, was drawn from his voluntarist theology, which insisted on freedom, both human and divine. His emphasis on human freedom inclined him toward the more liberal, Molinist interpretation of predestination, probably the single most contentious issue in post-Reformation theology. His views on fortune, fate, and divination clearly situate him in the seventeenth-century debates about the philosophy of nature. He unambiguously advocated a baptized version of Epicurean atomism. By the same token, he clearly rejected the naturalistic Aristotelianism of Pomponazzi, the Stoic cosmological underpinnings of astrology, and the materialism of Hobbes. Gassendi's position on all these issues can be understood as reflecting his underlying theological assumptions, which informed his philosophy of nature at every level.

Notes

1. Pierre Gassendi, *Syntagma philosophicum,* in Gassendi, *Opera omnia,* 6 vols. (Lyon, 1658; facsimile reprint, Stuttgart-Bad Cannstatt: Friedrich Frommann Verlag, 1964), vol. 2, p. 840.

2. He had originally planned to include this section in the "Physics" as the conclusion of his discussion about God's role in the universe. For the dating of the "Ethics" and for the history of this section, see Louise Tunick Sarasohn, "The Influence of Epicurean Philosophy on Seventeenth Century Ethical and Political Thought: The Moral Philosophy of Pierre Gassendi," Ph.D. dissertation, University of California, Los Angeles, 1979, chap. 5. See also the seventeenth-century English translation of François Bernier's abridgement of Book III of the "Ethics," *Three Discourses of Happiness, Virtue, and, Liberty, collected from the works of the Learn'd Gassendus* (London: Awnsham & John Churchil, 1699).

3. See John Sutton, "Religion and the Failures of Determinism," in *The Uses of Antiquity: The Scientific Revolution and the Classical Tradition,* edited by Stephen Gaukroger (Dordrecht: Kluwer, 1991), pp. 25-51.

4. "Since the entire universe is governed by the divine *logos,* since, indeed, the universe is identical with the divine *logos,* then the universe, by definition, must be reasonable [*sic*]. The *logos* organizes all things according to the rational laws of nature, in which all events are bound by strict rules of cause and effect. Chance and accident have no place in the Stoic system. The causal nexus in the universe is identified with both fate and providence; fate, in turn, is rationalized and identified with the good will of the deity." Marcia L. Colish, *The Stoic Tradition from Antiquity to the Early Middle Ages,* 2 vols. (Leiden: E. J. Brill, 1985), vol. 1, pp. 31-2.

5. A. A. Long, *Hellenistic Philosophy: Stoics, Epicureans, Sceptics,* 2d edition (Berkeley: University of California Press, 1986), pp. 163-70; John M. Rist, *Stoic Philosophy* (Cambridge University Press, 1969), chap. 7; and S. Samburstky, *The Physics of the Stoics* (New York: Macmillan, 1959), pp. 65-71.

6. Antonio Poppi, "Fate, Fortune, Providence, and Human Freedom," in *The Cambridge History of Renaissance Philosophy,* edited by Charles B. Schmitt, Quentin Skinner, and Eckhard Kessler (Cambridge University Press, 1988), p. 642.

7. Ibid., pp. 644-50.

8. Ibid., pp. 650-1. See also Frances A. Yates, *Giordano Bruno and the Hermetic Tradition* (New York: Vintage, 1969; first published 1964), chaps. 2-4.

9. Poppi, "Fate, Fortune, Providence, and Human Freedom," pp. 651-2.

10. Ibid., p. 654.

11. Ibid., p. 655.

12. Ibid., p. 656.

13. Ibid.

14. Ibid., pp. 656-7.

15. Pietro Pomponazzi, *Libri quinque de fato, de libero arbitrio et de praedestinatione,* edited by R. Le May (Lugano, 1957), 3, 8, 10, as translated by Poppi, "Fate, Fortune, Providence, and Human Freedom," p. 659.

16. Ibid., p. 659. See also Sutton, "Religion and the Failures of Determinism," pp. 31-3.

17. For background on this controversy see Jan Miel, *Pascal and Theology* (Baltimore: Johns Hopkins University Press, 1969), pp. 1-58; Luis de Molina, *On Divine Foreknowledge (Part IV of the* Concordia*),* translated with an introduction and notes by Alfred J. Freddoso (Ithaca, N.Y.: Cornell University Press, 1988), Preface; and Dale van Kley, *The Jansenists and the Expulsion of the Jesuits from France, 1757-1765* (New Haven, Conn.: Yale University Press, 1975), chap. 1.

18. Martin Luther, *De servo arbitrio,* translated by Philip S. Watson and B. Drewery, in *Luther and Erasmus: Free Will and Salvation,* edited by E. Gordon Rupp and Philip S. Watson (Philadelphia: Westminster Press, 1969), p. 332.

19. John Calvin, *Institutes of the Christian Religion,* edited by John T. McNeill and translated by Ford Lewis Battles, 2 vols. (Philadelphia: Westminster Press, 1960), bk. III, chap. xxiv, sec. 5-6.

20. Ibid., bk. II, chap. iv, sec. 7.

21. Ibid., bk. I, chap. xvi, sec. 7.

22. Ibid., bk. I, chap. xvi, sec. 8.

23. See Hubert Jedin, *A History of the Council of Trent,* translated by Dom Ernest Graf, 2 vols. (London: Thomas Nelson, and St. Louis: Herder, 1957 and 1961; first published in German, Freiburg im Breisgau: Herder, 1957), vol. 2, chaps. 5-10. For summaries of the issues considered by the Council of Trent, see Steven Ozment, *The Age of Reform, 1250-1550: An Intellectual and Religious History of Late Medieval and Reformation Europe* (New Haven, Conn.: Yale University Press, 1980), pp. 407-9; and Hans J. Hillerbrand, *Men and Ideas in the Sixteenth Century* (Prospect Heights, Ill.: Waveland, 1969), pp. 91-6.

24. Poppi, "Fate, Fortune, Providence, and Human Freedom," p. 667. Sarasohn discusses Molina's influence on Gassendi at length. See Lisa T. Sarasohn, *Freedom in a Deterministic Universe: Gassendi's Ethical Philosophy* (Ithaca, N.Y.: Cornell University Press, forthcoming), chap. 5.

25. William Lane Craig, *The Problem of Divine Foreknowledge and Future Contingents from Aristotle to Suarez* (Leiden: E. J. Brill, 1988), p. 207; Calvin Normore, "Future Contingents," in *The Cambridge History of Later Medieval Philosophy,* edited by Norman Kretzmann, Anthony Kenny, and Jan Pinborg (Cambridge University Press, 1982), pp. 380-1.

26. See Molina, *On Divine Foreknowledge,* Preface. See also Rivka Feldhay, "Knowledge and Salvation in Jesuit Culture," *Science in Context, 1* (1987): 204-5.

27. Paraphrased from Molina, *On Divine Foreknowledge,* p. 23.

28. Lisa T. Sarasohn, "The Ethical and Political Philosophy of Pierre Gassendi," *Journal of the History of Philosophy, 20* (1982): 258-60.

29. Gassendi, *Syntagma philosophicum,* in *Opera omnia,* vol. 2, p. 821.

30. Ibid., p. 823.

31. A distinction of this kind between genuine freedom and necessitated choice has a long history, going back at least to Duns Scotus. See Miel, *Pascal and Theology,* p. 41. Gassendi's definition of *"libertas"* is very similar to that of Molina, who wrote: "Just

as, in order for an act to be a *sin* it is not sufficient that it be spontaneous, but is instead necessary that it be free in such a way that, when the faculty of choice consents to it, it has the power not to consent to it, given all the surrounding circumstances obtaining at that time, so too in order for there to be *merit* or for an act to be *morally* good—indeed, even in order for there to be a free act that is indifferent to moral good and evil—it is necessary that when the act is elicited by the faculty of choice, it be within the faculty's power not to elicit it, given all the circumstances obtaining at that time." Molina, *On Divine Foreknowledge,* disputation 53, pt. 2, sec. 17, pp. 224-5.

32. Gassendi, *Syntagma philosophicum,* in *Opera omnia,* vol. 2, p. 822. Lisa T. Sarasohn discusses Gassendi's concepts of *libertas* and *libentia* in "Motion and Morality: Pierre Gassendi, Thomas Hobbes, and the Mechanical World-View," *Journal of the History of Ideas, 46* (1985): 371-3; and in "The Ethical and Political Philosophy of Pierre Gassendi," p. 259. See also Sarasohn's extended discussion of these concepts in *Freedom in a Deterministic Universe,* chaps. 3 and 5.

33. Aristotle's example occurs in *Metaphysics,* V, 30 (1025a14-29), translated by W. D. Ross, in *The Complete Works of Aristotle,* edited by Jonathan Barnes, 2 vols. (Princeton, N.J.: Princeton University Press, 1984), vol. 2, p. 1619. For an extensive discussion of Aristotle's understanding of "coincidence" and "accident," see Richard Sorabji, *Necessity, Cause, and Blame: Perspectives on Aristotle's Theory* (Ithaca, N.Y.: Cornell University Press, 1980).

34. Gassendi, *Syntagma philosophicum,* in *Opera omnia,* vol. 2, p. 828.

35. Ibid.

36. Ibid., p. 829.

37. Ibid.

38. Ibid., p. 830.

39. Ibid., pp. 830-1.

40. Ibid.

41. Ibid., p. 840.

42. See Josiah B. Gould, "The Stoic Conception of Fate," *Journal of the History of Ideas, 35* (1974): 17-32.

43. Gassendi, *Syntagma philosophicum,* in *Opera omnia,* vol. 2, p. 830.

44. Ibid.

45. Ibid., p. 831.

46. Ibid., pp. 831-2.

47. Ibid., p. 832.

48. Sarasohn, *Freedom in a Deterministic Universe,* chap. 6.

49. Samuel I. Mintz, *The Hunting of Leviathan: Seventeenth-Century Reactions to the Materialism and Moral Philosophy of Thomas Hobbes* (Cambridge University Press, 1962), p. 110.

50. Thomas Hobbes, *The Questions Concerning Liberty, Necessity, and Chance, Clearly Stated and Debated between Dr. Bramhall, Bishop of Derry, and Thomas Hobbes of Malmesbury,* in *The English Works of Thomas Hobbes of Malmesbury,* edited by Sir William Molesworth, 11 vols. (London, 1839-45; reprinted Aalen: Scientia, 1962), vol. 5.

51. Sarasohn, *Freedom in a Deterministic Universe,* chap. 6.

52. Gassendi, *Syntagma Philosophicum,* in *Opera omnia,* vol. 2, pp. 830-2. I take this definition of "hard determinism" from Sutton, "Religion and the Failures of Determinism," p. 27.

53. Gassendi, *Syntagma philosophicum,* in *Opera omnia,* vol. 2, p. 834.

54. Ibid., p. 835.

55. Ibid., p. 834.

56. Ibid., p. 840.

57. Ibid., p. 837.

58. Aristotle, *De interpretatione,* translated by J. L. Ackrill, in *The Complete Works of Aristotle,* edited by Barnes, 18b7-25, vol. 1, p. 29.

59. Gassendi, *Syntagma philosophicum,* in *Opera omnia,* vol. 2, p. 837. Cicero discussed Epicurus' ideas about future contingents at some length. See Marcus Tullius Cicero, *De fato,* translated by H. Rackham (Cambridge, Mass: Loeb Classical Library, 1953) pp. 233-5.

60. The concept of necessity employed by Epicurus is not the same as that currently in vogue among twentieth-century philosophers. See Normore, "Future Contingents," pp. 358-81. See also the Introduction in William Ockham, *Predestination, God's Foreknowledge, and Future Contingents,* translated by Marilyn McCord Adams and Norman Kretzmann (New York: Appleton-Century-Crofts, 1969), pp. 1-33.

61. Similar ideas can be found among some of the Stoics. See Rist, *Stoic Philosophy,* p. 122.

62. Gassendi, *Syntagma philosophicum,* in *Opera omnia,* vol. 2, p. 837. Gassendi's analysis of the relationship between the swerve of atoms and free will is borne out by modern scholarship, although the main source for this doctrine appears to have been Lucretius, whom Gassendi cited extensively, rather than Epicurus. See Long, *Hellenistic Philosophy,* pp. 56-61; and Rist, *Epicurus,* pp. 90-9.

63. Gassendi, *Syntagma philosophicum,* in *Opera omnia,* vol. 2, p. 838.

64. Ibid.

65. Ibid., p. 840.

66. Sarasohn, "Motion and Morality," p. 369.

67. Gassendi, *Syntagma philosophicum,* in *Opera omnia,* vol. 2., p. 840.

68. Vincenzo Cioffari, "Fate, Fortune, and Chance," *Dictionary of the History of Ideas,* edited by Philip P. Wiener, 4 vols. (New York: Scribner, 1973), vol. 2, p. 230; Poppi, "Fate, Fortune, Providence, and Human Freedom," p. 642.

69. Gassendi, *Syntagma philosophicum,* in *Opera omnia,* vol. 2, p. 840.

70. Ibid.

71. This providential interpretation of chance was shared by Gassendi's English contemporary, the Puritan divine William Ames, who argued in his *Medulla theologica* (1623), that the appeal to lots is not an appeal to chance, but to providence: "There is no power of rendering judgment in contingent events themselves and no other fortune judging them than the sure providence of God; so it follows that judgment must be expected in a special way from God's providence. Pure contingency itself cannot be a principal cause in deciding any question, nor can the man for whom the event itself is purely contingent direct it to such an end. Therefore, such direction is rightly to be expected from a superior power." William Ames, *The Marrow of Theology,* translated by John D. Eudsden (Boston: United Church Press, 1968), II, xi, 10-11 (p. 272). See also Margo Todd, "Providence, Chance and the New Science in Early Stuart Cambridge," *Historical Journal,* 29 (1986): 697-711.

72. Gassendi, *Syntagma philosophicum,* in *Opera omnia,* vol. 2, p. 841.

73. Craig, *The Problem of Divine Foreknowledge,* p. 59.

74. Gassendi, *Syntagma philosophicum,* in *Opera omnia,* vol. 2, p. 841.

75. Ibid.; my emphasis. Gassendi's talk about the "absolute necessity" of mathematical truths here should not lead us to conclude that he abandoned his voluntarism. In his debate with Descartes, he defended an empiricist, probabilist account of the epistemological status of mathematics. See Chapter 6. See Pierre Gassendi, *Disquisitio metaphysica, seu dubitationes et instantiae adversus Renati Cartesii metaphysicam et responsa,* edited and translated into French by Bernard Rochot (Paris: J. Vrin, 1962), pp. 468-73; in *Opera omnia,* vol. 3, pp. 374-5.

76. Molina, *On Divine Foreknowledge,* p. 23. Sarasohn argues as well that Gassendi adopted the Molinist approach to the problem of predestination and divine foreknowledge. See Sarasohn, *Freedom in a Deterministic Universe,* chap. 5.

77. Gassendi, *Syntagma philosophicum,* in *Opera omnia,* vol. 2, p. 841.

78. Ibid.

79. Ibid., pp. 841-2.

80. Ibid., p. 844.

81. Sambursky, *Physics of the Stoics,* p. 66.

82. See Stuart Clark, "The Scientific Status of Demonology," in *Occult and Scientific Mentalities in the Renaissance,* edited by Brian Vickers (Cambridge University Press, 1984), pp. 351-74.

83. See Brian P. Copenhaver, "Astrology and Magic," p. 273; Poppi, "Fate, Fortune, Providence, and Human Freedom," pp. 653-60; and Eckhard Kessler, "The Intellective Soul," pp. 500-7, all in *The Cambridge History of Renaissance Philosophy,* edited by Schmitt, Skinner, and Kessler. On Pomponazzi's naturalism, see Étienne Gilson, "Autour de Pomponazzi: Problématique de l'immortalité de l'âme en Italie au début du XVIe siècle," *Archives d'histoire doctrinale et littéraire de Moyen Age, 28* (1961): 163-279. See also Paul Oskar Kristeller, *Eight Philosophers of the Renaissance* (Stanford, Calif.: Stanford University Press, 1964), chap. 5; Jean Céard, "Matérialisme et théorie de l'âme dans la pensée padouane: Le *Traité de l'immortalité de l'âme* de Pomponazzi," *Revue philosophique de France et l'étranger, 171* (1981): 25-48; and Olivier René Bloch, *La philosophie de Gassendi: nominalisme, matérialisme et métaphysique* (The Hague: Martinus Nijhoff, 1971), pp. 310-11.

84. Robert Lenoble, *Mersenne ou la naissance du mécanisme,* 2d edition (Paris: J. Vrin, 1971) chap. 3, esp. pp. 112-21.

85. Marin Mersenne, *Quaestiones celeberrimae in Genesim,* translated by William L. Hine, in "Marin Mersenne: Renaissance Naturalism and Renaissance Magic," in *Occult and Scientific Mentalities in the Renaissance,* edited by Brian Vickers (Cambridge University Press, 1984), p. 167.

86. Lenoble, *Mersenne ol la naissance du mécanisme,* pp. 128-33.

87. Ibid., p. 133; my translation. See also Sutton, "Religion and the Failure of Determinism," pp. 39-41.

88. Gassendi, *Syntagma philosophicum,* in *Opera omnia,* vol. 2, p. 847.

89. Ibid., pp. 849-51.

90. Ibid., p. 851.

91. Ibid.

92. Ibid.

93. Ibid., pp. 851-2.

94. Ibid., p. 851.

95. Ibid., pp. 852-3.

96. Ibid., p. 852.

97. It should be noted that the most important philosophical account of divination came from the Stoics, whose account was thoroughly materialistic, owing nothing to the personal agency of demons. See Sambursky, *Physics of the Stoics,* pp. 66-71.

98. Gassendi, *Syntagma philosophicum,* in *Opera omnia,* vol. 2, p. 853.

99. Ibid.

100. Sambursky, *Physics of the Stoics,* pp. 66-71. For the Ciceronian roots of this distinction, see *De Divinatione,* translated by William Armistead Falconer (Cambridge, Mass: Loeb Classical Library, 1953), I, 12, 24, 72-92; II, 26.

101. Gassendi, *Syntagma philosophicum,* in *Opera omnia,* vol. 2, p. 854. Apparently this list of various sorts of diviners had a long history. Isidore of Seville wrote as follows in his *Etymologies:* "Varro dicit divinationis quattor esse genera, terram, aquam, aerem et ignem. Hinc geomantiam, hydromantiam, aeromantiam, pyromantiam dictam." Isidore of Seville, *Etymologies,* edited by W. M. Lindsay (Oxford University Press, 1911), Lib. VIII, ix, line 13. I am grateful to Haijo Westra for bringing this point to my attention.

102. Gassendi, *Syntagma philosophicum,* in *Opera omnia,* vol. 2, p. 854. For a full account of Gassendi's rejection of astrology, see "Physics," sec. II, bk. VI, "De effectibus siderum," in ibid., vol. 1, pp. 713-52. This part of the *Syntagma* was translated into English in the seventeenth century. See Petrus Gassendus, *The Vanity of Judiciary Astrology. Or Divination by the Stars* (London: Humphrey Moseley, 1659). For the context of this polemic, see Jacques E. Halbronn, "The Revealing Process of Translation and Criticism," in *Astrology, Science, and Society: Historical Essays,* edited by Patrick Curry (Suffolk: Boydell Press, 1987), pp. 197-217. Sarasohn thoroughly discusses Gassendi's views on astrology and their relationship to his ethical theory in *Freedom in a Deterministic Universe,* chap. 4.

103. *Syntagma philosophicum,* in *Opera omnia,* vol. 2, p. 853.

104. Ibid., p. 855.

105. Sambursky, *Physics of the Stoics,* p. 67.

Lisa T. Sarasohn (essay date 1996)

SOURCE: "The Role of Freedom and Pleasure in the State and Society," in *Gassendi's Ethics: Freedom in a Mechanistic Universe,* Cornell University Press, 1996, pp. 142-67.

[In this excerpt, Sarasohn discusses the progress from Gassendi's idea of natural man to his construction of the social contracts that buttress a system of government. Fre-quently contrasting Gassendi's "Ethics" with the political philosophy of Thomas Hobbes, the critic emphasizes the importance to Gassendi of free will and the primary human drive for pleasure—tempered by prudence—in his notion of a just and moral society.]

GASSENDI'S POLITICAL PHILOSOPHY AND ITS CONTEXT

Human beings pursue what is pleasurable and conducive to life, and flee from what is painful and detrimental to life. Gassendi and Hobbes agreed on this fundamental human imperative—although Gassendi emphasized pleasure as the primary end, while Hobbes thought that the desire for self-preservation initiated human motion. Whatever the teleological substratum of choice and avoidance, Gassendi and Hobbes were in concord that the motivation for forming the state was a utilitarian calculation of the way life could best be lived.

For both, individual self-interest was the starting point for discussing not only how human beings act as individuals, but also how they act as members of society and the state. Both Gassendi and Hobbes, starting from the importance each saw in the passions, developed concepts of prudence, deliberation and social contract to explain how human beings emerged from a state of nature to become members of a polity that guarantees life and circumscribes choices.

Gassendi was one of the first thinkers to realize the implications of Hobbes's political ideas, just as he understood Hobbes's psychological maxims. But instead of simply rejecting Hobbes's ideas about nature, man, politics, and God, Gassendi subtly adapted them to his own Catholic and philosophic sensibilities.[1] Gassendi articulated his own political philosophy at the same time he confronted Hobbes's radical political ideas.

The French philosopher acknowledged that Hobbes's analysis of political behavior had some validity, as Gassendi's prefatory letter to the 1647 edition of *De Cive* makes clear:

> It is assuredly a work outside the common and worthy of being touched by all those who have a desire for elevated things. If I put aside what regards the Catholic religion, about which we disagree, I know no writer who scrutinizes more profoundly than he the subject that he treats in *De Cive.* . . . I know no one who has shown himself in philosophy more free from prejudice; no one who penetrates more into the matters upon which he theorizes.[2]

The differences between the Frenchman and his English friend lie most in how they defined reason and sociability. In Gassendi's analysis of human development, he emphasized human rationality and freedom of choice rather than Hobbes's stimulus to action, which was fear.

Gassendi believed that human beings possess the natural ability to reason and to create society. But with what criteria do they decide to do so? His answer shows that the basic coherence of his system lies in his explanation that human beings form societies "in which it would be permitted to live more comfortably, and thus to live more pleasurably; and they were led to this by nature, by reason of which they flee evil and strive after the good."[3] Pleasure, as the ultimate *telos,* is both the motivation for and the ultimate aim of human action, which in this case results in a social contract constituting civil society. The "good" itself is realized pleasure, and society is the medium for such pleasure. Thus, nature, by means of human nature, endowed man with the natural criterion, which initially motivated him to pursue the things necessary to life and consequently to devise things to make life more pleasurable.

While Gassendi rarely referred to God explicitly in his discussion of political philosophy, it seems clear that in his view nature is simply the immanent aspect of God's providential action: The instinctive search for pleasure, endowed by God, acts as the stimulus for societal development. Human beings form social pacts with one another as the natural result of the divinely ordained—but not determined—search for pleasure.

For Hobbes the social contract is artificial; law is imposed by the sovereign to curb man's natural passions. This cold-eyed evaluation of the origin of the state had vast ramifications for the rest of his political system. Hobbes intertwined the social contract, law, and the creation of a supreme and absolute authority so intricately that they can be separated only with the utmost difficulty. Human beings may have made the state, and created the sovereign authority, but the antithetical nature of the civil state to man's natural instincts means that this construction must be immutable—or crumble away completely.[4]

The naturalness of the pact that Gassendi envisioned is likewise crucial for his description of the civil state. In opposition to Hobbes, Gassendi adopted the view that the state, which reflects man's nature, is adaptable to changing circumstances—if the calculus of pleasure and pain dictates that change is necessary. Because the state exists to guarantee the pleasurable life, its citizens retain a power of consent.

It is important to understand that Gassendi was drawn to questions of political philosophy not only because of his relationship with Hobbes, but also for other reasons; most fundamentally, political philosophy was integral to the fabric of his moral philosophy. The three books of the "Ethics" consider, in order, happiness, virtue and fate, fortune and liberty. Gassendi's discussion of pleasure in the first book is intimately related to his theory of freedom in the third book. Not surprisingly, the second book, which contains Gassendi's political philosophy, is integrated into this structure.

In developing this schema in the "Ethics," particularly in the first two books, Gassendi followed the traditional division of the ethics course as it was taught in the French universities of the seventeenth century. According to L. W.

B. Brockliss, in his history of higher education in early modern France, "The seventeenth- and eighteenth-century ethics course was divided into two parts, *ethica generalis* and *ethica particularis.* The first dealt with man as an ethical individual; the second with the individual as a member of the family and the State; hence it was divided into economics and politics."[5]

Ethica generalis was devoted to the elucidation of the highest good, and although the professors followed an Aristotelian line, Gassendi's discussion of ethical theory essentially paralleled the university course. And just like his university contemporaries, Gassendi then turned from the general to the particular: man as a social and political being.

But politics was not just part of a pedagogical program in the seventeenth century, characterized by modern historians as "an age of crisis."[6] Major political upheavals—the Thirty Years War, the English Civil War, the Fronde in France—ripped through the rising nation-states. Many countries were struggling with the emergence of a strong centralized authority and its composition and relationship to the traditional orders of society. Gassendi's awareness of this turmoil is shown in a 1645 letter to his patron, Louis of Valois, commenting on everything from the English Civil War to the distribution of supplies in Lorraine.[7]

Although the crisis was reflected in every aspect of society and culture, it left its deepest mark in political theory. Some thinkers endorsed the new absolutism, while others developed systems of popular sovereignty and constitutionalism. Both defenders of the traditional rights of the aristocracy and apologists for religious rebellion adopted theories of social contract. The transformed Machiavellian concept of "reason of state" became increasingly popular at this time.[8] Hugo Grotius speculated on natural law and the law of nations. Gassendi was familiar with these schools of political thought and adapted elements of some, just as he absorbed various Hobbesian arguments.

Gassendi's philosophic work on Epicurus in the early 1630s also encouraged this interest in politics and its philosophic justification. Defending Epicurus against the charge of disparaging rhetoric—the most political of the liberal arts—in his 1633 *Vita* of the Greek philosopher, Gassendi challenged Cicero's claim that "the philosophy of Epicurus is useless for the political man."[9] Gassendi directly addressed the question of the relationship between religion and politics when discussing Epicurus's participation in public religious ceremonies, in which the Greek philosopher did not believe:

> He was present because the civil law and public tranquillity necessitated it: He condemned it because the soul gained no wisdom from it. . . . Inside, he was by his own law; outside, by the laws which oblige human society. Thus, at the same time he rendered what he owed to himself and to others. And I maintain that nothing could be more laudable, either in words or ac-

tions. . . . It is part of wisdom, that philosophers feel with a few, and as it is said, act with many.[10]

This stance certainly conflicted sharply with the ideals of Christian piety and Renaissance ideas of active citizenship and public responsibility. Both emphasized the ethical character of the state, a normative view which is absent here. Moreover, Gassendi's position reflects an almost Hobbesian double standard of private morality and public conformity—which somehow does not touch private integrity. But it demonstrates that questions of the nature of law, of obligation, and of the place of the individual within the state were important to Gassendi and integral to his study of Epicurus.

PRUDENCE AND PASSION

Gassendi's analysis of politics in Book 2 of the "Ethics" of the **Syntagma Philosophicum** is integrated within a general discussion of the virtues, beginning with a definition of prudence. Prudence is "a moral virtue, which moderates all the actions of our life correctly, both discerning good from evil, and useful from harmful, it prescribes what it is necessary to follow or avoid, and consequently it establishes men in a good and happy way of living." It is part of the intellectual faculty, although it is so closely related to moral action and the will "that it is intertwined and mingled with it and is customarily called 'the prince of Morality.'"[11]

This definition is by now familiar: Gassendi's account of prudence is another formula for the calculation of pleasure and pain. Prudence teaches the "art of life"—the very aim of ethics itself—in both the social and political spheres of human activity. Private prudence teaches an individual how to conduct his private and public life; political prudence teaches how the citizens of a state can live harmoniously and happily.[12]

At the very base of this doctrine of prudence is Gassendi's unshakable conviction of individual responsibility and freedom of choice, the ubiquitous characteristic of his entire ethical theory. Prudence dictates the moral virtues, "which reasonably are not moral unless it is understood that acts of this kind are done from voluntary choice." Prudence "is a habit of the mind, which is not certain, but conjectural; and in this it differs from science" (*scientia* as Aristotle defines it), because science has necessary things for its object, which cannot be otherwise. Prudence is directed toward contingent things, "which are or are not, thus they can be or be not." Prudence is a kind of art "in which the artificer cannot fail except by his own will" and it prescribes "the ends of virtue, when we pursue good things, and the opposite of these ends, when we pursue evil things." The general end of prudence is a happy and blessed life.[13]

Prudence is under our control since we construct our own moral lives. Moral action must be voluntary. Gassendi here used the term *ex electione voluntarieque,* "from voluntary choice," which is derived from *voluntas* or "will,"

but still conveys the meaning of a self-constituted or free choice. This contrasts with its near synonym *sponte,* which Gassendi usually used for a willing but not free choice. Prudential behavior is moral because it is free.

Gassendi's view of prudence contrasts sharply with Hobbes's definition. In *The Elements of Law,* Hobbes defined prudence simply as "nothing but to conjecture from experience."[14] The normative character of prudence is absent from Hobbes's account—although like Gassendi, Hobbes thought that prudential judgments are conjectural rather than certain. But in his discussion of prudence, Hobbes went further than Gassendi.

Since Hobbes dismissed the realist idea of extramental universals, he thought prudence—or reaching a conclusion based on past experiences—was extremely problematical. The meaning of justice, for example, may change with each particular circumstance. Thus, while past experiences are helpful in making choices, they do not result in a judgment with any supramental authority, except what is founded in individual opinion at the time of the judgment.[15]

Hobbes did not regard prudence as the God-endowed "prince of morality" because he downgraded the rationality of the deliberative process itself. Deliberation was for him a succession of appetites and fears that finally end in a non-voluntary act of will. Hobbes taught that human beings calculate during this deliberation, but such calculation is so connected to the passions and the act of will that it loses its character as a free rational decision.[16]

Hobbes, in *De Cive,* argued that man in the state of nature is motivated primarily by his passions, and most of all by fear—although in his calmer moments, man also possesses "right reason" in the sense of a practical reasoning ability. Thus, "the original of all great and lasting societies consisted not in the mutual good men had towards each other, but in the mutual fear they had of each other."[17]

All men, Hobbes argued, want to preserve their own lives, but since they are all equally capable of killing each other in the state of nature, and because there are some men who from vainglory want to dominate, men are forced by their own fear to constitute civil society. Hobbes defined mutual fear in a manner consistent with his psychological theories: "I comprehend in the word fear, a certain foresight of future evil; neither do I conceive flight the sole property of fear, but to distrust, suspect, take heed, provide so that they may not fear, is also incident to the fearful."[18]

Hobbes then argued that fear produces the decision to create the state:

> for every man, by natural necessity desires that which is good for him: nor is there any that esteems a war of all against all, which necessarily adheres to such a state, to be good for him. And so it happens, that through fear of each other we think it is fair to rid ourselves of this condition, and to get some fellows; and if

there needs must be war, it may yet not be against all men, nor without some helps.[19]

In psychological terms, Gassendi denied the Hobbesian arguments that humans are determined by their passions. He also denied the political consequences of the psychological necessitarianism: the necessary and immutable character of civil association. For Gassendi, passion does not proscribe the state, because prudence always allows human beings to calculate what is best for them—as individuals in the state of nature, and as members of the state.

THE STATE OF NATURE AND NATURAL RIGHT

Gassendi shared Hobbes's interest in the state of nature, but his approach to the question was initially historical. Gassendi began his discussion of political philosophy with a discussion of the state of nature as seen by the ancients, who portrayed it as either a golden or a bestial age. He did not believe that these views necessarily contradicted each other: There may have been a progressive degeneration from one to the other.

In fact, he found such a development posited in Book 5 of Lucretius's *De Rerum Natura,* the only extant description of Epicurean political theory. Book 5 clearly inspired Hobbes's description as well.[20] According to Gassendi's interpretation of the meaning of the text, Lucretius taught that man lived originally in a golden age, but because of the fear of violence and wild beasts, pity for the vulnerability of the weak, the inconveniences of the solitary life, and the lust of stronger men, he was impelled to enter society.[21]

Man then, according to Lucretius, created society and government out of the state of nature by means of a dual social contract, a first contract establishing society and then a second agreeing to obey legal codes. The aim of these contracts is to provide the peaceful environment vital to individual tranquillity and happiness. Gassendi commended the Lucretian analysis of why laws are obeyed: so that violence is contained and a peaceful life exists for the common good.[22]

But Gassendi was dissatisfied with the Epicurean discussion because it was sketchy on the nature of right and justice, both before and after the social contract, a problem Hobbes had also addressed.[23] Epicurus had described justice as a utilitarian contract in which men swore neither to harm nor be harmed by each other; it has no transcendent or absolute value or meaning.[24] After a long and erudite discussion, Gassendi rejected this concept and accepted the traditional legal definition of justice, *tribuendi cuique suum ius:* "to give to each one his own right."[25]

But, Gassendi admitted, "right" had been interpreted in different ways by different people. In particular, there had been much contention concerning whether someone has right by nature (the Stoic view) or by utility (the Epicurean view).[26] Gassendi believed that the only way to discover what human right is, and consequently, what justice

is, is to examine very closely man's beginnings in the state of nature and the subsequent development of the political state.[27] Just as Hobbes had, Gassendi returned to the constituent member of society—the individual in the state of nature—to determine the nature of natural right, political association, and justice.

Ethics professors in the French universities were also concerned with the state of nature. They equated it with the state of rational man before the Fall, that is, the state of a classical philosopher without the gift of grace. This idea was controversial. The Jansenists, notes Brockliss, thought "the idea was a Molinist subterfuge to mitigate the effects of the Fall; it was a theory used by 'laxist' theologians to suggest that God only deprived Adam of his supernatural not his natural powers, the latter, especially his reason, remaining unmarred."[28]

If the Jansenist accusation holds, it would suggest that Gassendi was inspired in his political philosophy as well as his moral psychology by the sixteenth-century Spanish Jesuit; Gassendi's political theory credits man with the full use of reason in the state of nature.

In his own description of the state of nature, Gassendi argued that an individual can be viewed in two ways:

> first absolutely, or according to himself, and as he is a man; then secondly, or comparatively, as he is related to others, and is a certain part or desires to be part of society. And certainly in the first way, he is viewed as solitary, and in a pure state of nature; that is, such as man is made by nature with all his parts, from which he is constructed, and with all his faculties, by which he is instructed.[29]

In this first, solitary state, man is not self-sufficient, in that he does not possess within himself all the things he needs to maintain life but must seek them externally. However, nature makes these necessities, food and shelter, easily obtainable, and endows man with the innate faculty of seeking for these things and transforming them into use. Gassendi concluded:

> Nature gave to man, so that he might exist, the faculty to maintain and to preserve himself. And Nature gave the ability to use all things which are necessary, conducive, and useful for his preservation. Furthermore, it is this faculty itself, which is the first right of nature; consequently, however often we use this faculty, we are judged to use a right of nature, and, in fact, the right of nature which is primary, or the most ancient gift of nature.[30]

Thus, man's first right is the ability to use anything that he considers necessary to preserve his own life. In the state of nature, moreover, "when one person desires and pursues something, there will be other who desire and pursue it equally; and hence will arise strife, rapine, and hatred."[31] The cause of contention in the state of nature is not that man is naturally violent or bestial, but rather that any man has a right to anything and that no one has a secure possession in what he uses. Although man appropriates goods and property in the state of nature, he does not hold them securely. Thus, while personal use of property exists in the state of nature, private ownership does not.

Up to this point, Gassendi's description of human beings in the state of nature is close to Hobbes's, if man is considered "absolutely, or according to himself, as he is a man."[32] That is, if man is considered apart from any social intercourse whatsoever. For both Hobbes and Gassendi, the first right human beings possess is self-preservation, and the result of everyone's effort to preserve himself is war.

Hobbes's definition of the character of the state of nature is well known: "it cannot be denied but that the natural state of men, before they entered into society, was a mere war, and that not simply, but a war of all men against all men." The root of this war of all against all is that "Nature hath given to every one a right to all" because everyone has the equal right to use anything or do anything to preserve himself."[33] These views have a clear tie to Gassendi's remarks about the state of nature in the "Ethics": "For in that bestial state, which is presumed free, it reasonably cost most dear, since as it was observed not long ago, there would be perpetual life and death combat, insofar as, everything belonging to everyone with equal right, no one could use anything for himself, but that another would seize it."[34]

Gassendi was invariably more wordy than Hobbes, but the message is the same. It is quite possible that this passage referred explicitly to Hobbes in the expression "since as it was observed not long ago."

But Gassendi believed that a state of war actually rarely existed in the state of nature, because a person not only exists as a solitary being, but also as a potential member of the social organism. In order to avoid constant war, people make pacts by which they exchange an uncertain right to everything for a certain right to something.[35] Thus, the fact that man can use his reason to avoid war, and consequently to make pacts to establish the state, is a second right of nature, and is as "natural" as the first right of nature.

"Therefore," Gassendi continued, so that man does not have to stay in this state, he "is made a sociable animal by nature." Nature "granted him the inclination to enter upon pacts, by means of which he might take council with one another and be turned into society rightly." Gassendi later made clear that natural right (*ius naturale*) can be taken in two ways: as man's faculty for maintaining life, common to all organic beings (*ius animale,* or animal right), and also as all his reasoning properties (*ius humanum,* or the right of man).[36] Both are equally natural and innate, but the latter enables man to realize that his interests would be served best by remitting to some extent his natural right in everything. It leads a man to make pacts with other men, who make similar remissions, leaving all with a defined

and secure right in those possessions remaining. It is at this point that private property in the traditional sense, or "mine and thine" as Gassendi called it, actually comes into being.

In his description of the *ius humanum,* Gassendi enumerated its abilities: "Of planning, or investigating, of teaching, or learning the various arts and especially the use of fire, of pacifying among themselves and joining together in society, and living in it by certain laws. And the laws of this kind are varied, as it is necessary, either by the occasion, or on account of some better utility urging."[37]

People also realize by the *ius humanum* that all needs will be more easily fulfilled by the mutual assistance of others. Gassendi called this initial period of social reciprocity "a state of modified nature," and it paralleled his secondary definition of man as part of society.[38] It seems, for Gassendi, that this stage of human development served as both a more advanced state of nature and the beginning of human society itself. It is a transitional state that contains both elements within itself.

Another contract during this state of modified nature protects the weak against the attacks of the stronger by establishing law and justice. These contracts are natural and the state of affairs and laws established by them are consequently also natural because they emanate from the faculty of human reason.[39] The *ius humanum* is transformed from a guide for individual action into a social dynamic propelling man into society.

Thus, Gassendi's social pact is natural, the outgrowth of natural reason:

> Because life was uncomfortable and dangerous in that ferocious state or state without pacts, people formed an assemblage, so that they could live more comfortably and delightfully. They did this because of their own natures which led them to flee evil and seek good. . . . Thus, from nature, the state can be no other than society, in which pacts are begun and preserved reciprocally. For this reason people determined in common to undertake these things among themselves, so that laws or narrowed rights are retained. Since laws are nothing else but pacts.[40]

This pact is vastly different from the pact Hobbes envisioned:

> Last of all, the consent of those brutal creatures is natural; that of man by contract only, that is to say, artificial. It is therefore no matter of wonder, if somewhat more is needful for man to the end that they live in peace. Wherefore consent or contracted society, without some common power whereby particular men may be ruled through fear or punishment, doth not suffice to make up that security which is requisite for the exercise of natural justice.[41]

Thus, for Hobbes the artificial construction of society by pact does not in itself provide a legitimate and obligatory set of laws—only the supreme authority can do that once the state is created.[42]

Gassendi's political philosophy, on the other hand, based legitimacy and obligation within the state on the voluntary actions of free agents creating a political society through social contracts, rather than the command of the supreme authority. Civil society, which is natural because it is the outcome of human nature, remains a construct of voluntary association emanating from the innate desire for pleasure. The purpose of such political bonds is to guarantee freedom and liberty to the individual. Gassendi wrote, "true and natural liberty is discovered rather in that society only, in which a man submits to the laws of society (this by his own approval or to his own advantage) and he does whatever is pleasing with what remains, and he possesses the right in his own goods, which no one can snatch away because of the public power which defends them."[43]

Gassendi has now determined what right is: Right is whatever remains in the power of the individual after he has established the pact. These original rights may be further limited because of utilitarian concerns, but although they have been limited, they remain "certain and free."[44]

CIVIL SOCIETY, THE STATE, AND THE RIGHT OF CONSENT

For Gassendi, the social contract sets up a limited arena of political liberties or laws, enforced by the supreme authority. But because Gassendi believed that man should always strive for happiness—inside the state as well as outside it—the establishment of the social contract was not the end of political development.

For Hobbes, human nature is static; the individual is always motivated by the same passions, and the laws of nature and human nature always reflect these psychological constants. The artificial construction of the social pact is the only dynamic moment in Hobbes's schema; afterwards, man is caught fast by his own nature and the state.

By contrast, Gassendi, while conceding a psychological constant in human behavior, believed that the prudential calculation of pleasure and pain led to constant revisions of human existence and therefore to human progress.

Gassendi elaborated these themes as he developed his political theory. He believed that although the original social contracts—to form society and to establish laws—removed many of the inconveniences of the state of nature, some remained. Accordingly, human beings—still guided by their reason to pursue what is best for themselves—make a third contract, to delegate authority to a government. Again borrowing from Lucretius, Gassendi explained, "Because it would be inconvenient for the whole multitude to come together to decide something, and individually (or even by tribe) to state an opinion, or to cast a vote; for this reason the multitude itself willingly (*sponte*) transfers the power either to a few people, or to some one person."[45] Government, then, is not divine—except incidentally, as a product of man's providentially inspired pursuit of pleasure. It is the result of volition, and it is natural because it is a product of natural reason.

J. W. Gough, in his history of political thought, calls this delegation of authority to government a "contract of government" or "contract of submission."[46] Bloch asserts that the dual or triple social contract—the contract of association and the contract of submission—found in Gassendi may be the earliest formulation of this complex kind of political theory articulated in the seventeenth century.[47] But while Gassendi's thinking does look forward to Locke and the liberal tradition of the eighteenth century, it also looks backward to the dual contract found in Lucretius.

Moreover, his work reflects social contract thinking from the middle ages, ideas further developed to justify rebellion and even tyrannicide by sixteenth-century Jesuit and Calvinist thinkers—who claimed that kings following the wrong religious formula were breaking social contracts with both God and the people. Humanist jurists of the late fifteenth century and sixteenth century employed similar contractual arguments, contending that ancient French history showed an aristocracy delegating its authority to a monarch by means of a social contract.[48]

Bloch's assertion that the state is not "properly founded" until the third contract is also open to interpretation. Gassendi never directly addressed the question, but he implied that some kind of state exists as soon as the multitude forms a society, and particularly after the society begins to make laws. "The laws, which are decreed in order to produce a civil society," he wrote at the end of his discussion of natural law, "are produced for the common utility or the common good." The words "civil society" seem to indicate that some kind of state is produced immediately by the establishment of law, an event which Gassendi clearly placed before any delegation of authority to leaders. Furthermore, when Gassendi spoke of "the highest power," he associated that power with the multitude who make laws, rather than with the government, which is created by the third contract.[49] If the making of law—in contrast to the creation of an institutional framework—is the mark of statehood, Gassendi clearly implied that the state predates government.

In a state structure, Gassendi maintained, sovereignty cannot be divided after it is transferred. It must reside in either the monarch, in the optimates, or in the people. Although a state may have a semblance of mixed government, in actuality only one unit possesses the supreme power, and this fact determines the nature of the state.

This analysis of the indivisibility of sovereignty is similar to Jean Bodin's, but Bodin and Gassendi differ fundamentally on the question of whether the people retain the right of consent to law.[50] Bodin, who was the foremost proponent of absolutism in the sixteenth century and still extremely influential in the seventeenth, did not envision any form of sovereignty residing in the people or arising from individuals in a state of nature. Bodin's state was formed when a sovereign power held a virtually unlimited ability to compose the law, which the citizens of the state were compelled to obey without question.[51]

Gassendi was responding to exigencies different from Bodin's. The sixteenth-century theorist was concerned with defending the inviolability of the state from the threatening dissolution of religious civil war. Absolute monarchy, a monarch *legibus solutus,* was the only response to the Calvinist and Jesuit justifications of tyrannicide and rebellion. Almost a hundred years later, new realities permitted Gassendi to utilize the "contract of submission" and to advocate a form of limited monarchy, drawing from but avoiding both the absolutism of Bodin and the radical resistance of the religious militants. The eclecticism of Gassendi's political thought is truly extraordinary.

Of the three traditional kinds of government, Gassendi favored monarchy because it provokes the fewest difficulties (one man can execute laws more efficiently than several), and those can be remedied by either succession or election. (Gassendi's casual reference to election shows his familiarity with Huguenot and constitutional arguments that monarchy was originally, and to some degree continuously, elective.)[52] Furthermore, he argued, empirical evidence shows that the rule of one is best: The home has one master, the army one general, the universe one ruler.[53] Gassendi consistently compared the state to the home.

But Gassendi designated boundaries of monarchical power. In his discussion of political prudence, he argued that the ruler's duties concerned particularly war and peace. In addition, "he should hold fixed in his soul the aim and end for the sake of which he rules, and to which he is subservient. This truly is the health, security, and utility of the people."[54] This claim duplicates the arguments of sixteenth-century Huguenot theorists, who proclaimed that magistrates were created for "the safety, the welfare and the conservation of the people" and who argued that kings should remember "it is due to the people, and for the sake of the people's welfare, that they exercise their power."[55]

Later, in his analysis **"Of Justice, Right, and Laws,"** Gassendi explicitly claimed that the people always retain some power of consent after the contract of government has been made: "next some laws were laid down by the princes; but it should be understood, nevertheless, that the consent of the people intervened, either expressly . . . or tacitly, because the power had been given and had been received mutually."[56]

Gassendi followed this passage with many of the arguments traditionally used by those arguing for some form of popular sovereignty. For example, he cited the *lex regia,* a principle taken from Roman law, which was interpreted to mean that when the *imperium* is granted to a ruler, it is delegated rather that irretrievably transferred,

and therefore sovereignty remains with the people. Gassendi also included a long discussion of the difference between a king—the shepherd of his people, who rules according to the law—and a tyrant—the wolf of his people, who cares only for himself.[57]

Gassendi believed that it is in the best interests of the king not to act like a tyrant. A king's chief aim, as for any man, should be tranquillity. For a king, as for any man, tranquillity is impossible without virtue, "because . . . the Prince is also a private man, for whom it is necessary always to possess a good character, and who will prove so much more suitable for ruling others, as much as he knows how to rule himself and order his own passions."[58]

Gassendi's good king will therefore conduct himself virtuously, for the good not only of his people, but of himself. The people will love and revere him, and he will live peacefully. But realizing that simple virtue will not always suffice in a world plagued by misguided subjects and external enemies, Gassendi provided detailed and intricate rules for running a country successfully. He advised the king to distribute justice "exquisitely," to tax justly and to inform the people why there are taxes, to maintain a strong army and to use spies, and to punish the leaders of sedition harshly, but to be lenient to the followers.[59] The government Gassendi described certainly is not constitutionalism, but neither is it absolutism. It has the flavor of Machiavelli and *raison d'etat,* yet another tradition Gassendi was happy to utilize in his own political philosophy.

In general, Gassendi was drawn to arguments against absolutism. Such arguments were traditionally associated with theories of social contract, and complemented his belief that government is the result of the voluntary desires of free individuals. The entire purpose of government is to secure the greatest happiness of the individual: The individual, therefore, will not give the government the irrevocable right to tyrannize him.[60]

Gassendi did not, however, draw any final implications from these arguments. He did not defend the right of the people to rebel; rather, he stated that it was in a person's best interest to obey the sovereign authority. During his discussion of public calamities—war, tyranny, the subversion of the state—he argued, "Since we may not change fate, or if you please, the decrees of eternal providence, it is better to soften the harshness by our own consent, rather than to exasperate them more by fruitless opposition."[61]

Gassendi insisted that one is obligated to obey the customs of any society while living in it, because "while either nature, or law, or custom may make a thing proper, it is nature itself which orders it to be maintained, insofar as it may serve the common good, on whose preservation depends the preservation of each individual, which is natural for everyone."[62]

This view seems to contradict the idea of the free creation of the state and continued voluntary consent after the state has been created. It reflects an ambiguity in the terminology Gassendi employed in this political discussion. He fairly often used the Latin *sponte,* meaning "voluntarily," when he discussed the social contract, rather than *libere,* meaning "freely." This choice implies that the formation of the state is natural and inevitable, leaving little room for the kind of free association that he usually advocated. To the extent that the state is the result of our natures, in their inevitable pursuit of pleasure, it comes into being willingly, but perhaps not freely.

This fact may explain why we are obligated to obey and not resist political authority. In the long run, happiness is better served by obeying than rebelling. The ambiguity in Gassendi's analysis originates in his dual concept of human nature: Man necessarily pursues pleasure, but through his reason, naturally makes free choices on how that pleasure is to be achieved.

Gassendi's ambiguous analysis of freedom and necessity in the creation of the state may reflect other semantic problems as well. Patrick Riley has argued that social contract theory from the time of Hobbes was "voluntarist," that the contract establishing the political state is legitimate because founded on the individual wills of the constituent members, freely willing whatever form the political state takes. This notion of the free will of individuals can be traced back to medieval theology, but it takes a particularly political turn in the seventeenth century: "consent or agreement based on will, understood as a moral 'faculty,' came to occupy a place in the seventeenth to the early nineteenth century political philosophy which it had never occupied before (not at least in the political, as distinguished from the moral and legal, realms)."[63]

Riley also argues that the primary ambiguities found in the theories of Hobbes and other political philosophers arise because "the will" is so variously and confusedly understood in early modern times. It can be viewed as a simple physiological movement in response to external stimuli, in which case human behavior is determined, or as a moral faculty which has the power, based on knowledge, freely to strive for and choose a certain moral action. The will, understood in the second sense, then obligates because someone "freely chooses something . . . which is not causally necessary." A free action is moral because it is based on the free choice of an individual, based on reason, to do or refrain from doing something. Unlike a stone, argues Riley, which must fall downward, human actions are not necessitated—because the will is free.[64]

It is in just this sense that Gassendi understood human beings as the free makers and participants in political society, although for him the ambiguous connotations of the human will suggested a psychological theory that associated freedom with the intellect rather than the will. For the French philosopher, the actions of the will were always caused and therefore, to some degree, necessitated.[65] Thus, when Gassendi used language drawn from the developing

voluntarist tradition, his political philosophy absorbed an element of ambiguity that made his theory less than consistent.

JUSTICE, UTILITY, AND THE LAWS OF NATURE

This seeming ambiguity—between the volitional and necessary origins of the state—is also reflected in Gassendi's concept of law. Law is a contract between people formed together in a particular society; Gassendi did not believe in a universal contract, a universal concept of justice. He noted that in different circumstances, such as when climate and terrain differ, societies develop differently—creating a great diversity of customs and laws. The particularity of the pact also means that there is no natural law among nations—particularly since one of the characteristics of law is its ability to compel, impossible among peoples of diverse customs.[66]

But this state of affairs does not mean that law is completely positive or conventional in nature. While Gassendi, like Hobbes, believed that there are no universal principles with a reified existence, he did find a kind of universalism in human nature itself. Although the particular laws themselves will differ depending on how and where they are made, the process by which they are established is natural (the *ius humanum*), and therefore the laws are natural even if not universal. That is, the same law is both natural and the product of positive choice, just as the social contract is the product of both instinct and deliberation.[67]

Gassendi experienced some of the same difficulties in deciding whether there is indeed some universal "law of nature" (*lex naturae*), existing before the creation of the state. On the one hand, he realized that natural law can be equated with natural instinct, which "is like a certain kind of spontaneous dictate" that leads us to eat, drink, procreate, and so forth. Presumably, obedience to such a law is voluntary (spontaneous), but not free. But there is another definition: "Natural law can be said to be found in man alone, insofar as reason is directed toward the nature of things . . . and thus the law of nature in these matters is nothing else than the law of reason or reason itself."[68]

In discussing the law of nature, Gassendi returned to the omnipresent binary composition of his ethical system. Clearly, natural instinct, when described as a "spontaneous dictate" (*spontaneum dictamen*) of human nature is the type of human freedom described elsewhere as *libentia* or willingness, while the secondary rational nature of humans is the same thing as *libertas* or the true human freedom.[69] When human beings act on instinct, their actions are voluntary; when they act on the basis of rational choice, they are free. Both states characterize men before and after the pact. Natural law spans the apparent contradiction between consent and obedience.

Once Gassendi had established the parameters of natural law, he felt he could establish some basic principles, which—if we disregard our "prejudices and preoccupations"—can be seen to characterize all humans. Essentially, in this discussion, he reiterated his view of the characteristics of human right and prudential action. First, "the most common and innate law in all men is that they pursue that which is good, advantageous, and gratifying, and they flee from what is evil, disadvantageous, and ungratifying." Not all men feel the same thing is a good, but all will seek what they perceive to be good. Second, "anyone loves himself more than the rest, or prefers good for himself, rather than another."[70] Here the egoism that found its original philosophic expression in ancient Epicureanism surfaced in the writings of the neo-Epicurean, where it underwrote an emerging individualistic moral code.

This conclusion has led Gianni Paganini to emphasize egoism and self-love in his analysis of Gassendi's political thought. He argues that this idea, adopted from Epicurus, was most difficult for Gassendi to reconcile with a Christianized Epicureanism. To Gassendi, argues Paganini, "self-love constitutes not only the motive of all ethical behavior, but also the cement of the political universe." Consequently, Gassendi's universe has lost any moral anchor and its members act only out of utilitarian expediency. In this argument, Gassendi duplicates Hobbes.[71]

This charge echoes a similar accusation directed against Epicurus himself, by both ancient and modern commentators. Epicurus had urged the wise man to withdraw from society in order to live in self-sufficient tranquillity, thinking only of himself. Cicero reacted to the implicit selfishness of this doctrine, by insisting that in Epicureanism, "Justice totters or rather I should say, lies already prostrate, so also with all those virtues which are discernible in social life and the fellowship of human society. For neither goodness nor generosity nor courtesy can exist" in such circumstances.[72] More modern critics have been equally scathing: Cyril Bailey accused Epicurus of "Egoistic Hedonism" and A. E. Taylor charged the philosopher with "moral invalidism."[73]

Other critics, however, from Seneca to more recent commentators such as Phillip Mitsis, David K. O'Connor, and P. A. Vander Waert, believe that Epicurean egoism can be accommodated to justice, fellowship, and even, in the case of Mitsis, altruism.[74] These critics, to varying degrees, emphasize the importance of happiness, community, and friendship in Epicurean philosophy, which links virtue, pleasure, and friendship so closely that the terms are virtually interchangeable. In Epicureanism, there can be no conflict between utilitarian and "pure" motives. People do things, including refraining from injustice and participating in social relationships, because they are useful and bring pleasure, a good both for the actors and others.[75]

Whether this interpretation is valid for the original philosophy remains open to question, but clearly Gassendi himself argued for an integration of utilitarian egoism and altruistic action. Immediately after proclaiming his second law of nature or reason, Gassendi argued that since it is natural to love those close to oneself like offspring, loving oneself is even more natural. Likewise, it is natural to love fellow citizens more than foreigners. It is even possible to love a friend so much that one could be willing to die for him if it brought one happiness and glory. Whatever service one person does for another will bring him some personal good, if nothing else "the consciousness of being a benefactor, which is of incomparable worth."[76]

Thus, for Gassendi, individual utility blends seamlessly into sociability and love for others. It does not concern him that the original spur for such action is a kind of selfishness, because the result is an ethics of caring. One of the most fundamental axioms of the neo-Epicurean's thought is that virtue and utility are indistinguishable from pleasure, the impetus to all actions, "the first accommodation of nature."[77]

So, when Paganini argues that Gassendi's endorsement of self-interest and utility links him closely to Hobbes, he emphasizes one element of Gassendi's thought at the expense of broader themes in the Frenchman's philosophy. Paganini rightly points out that Gassendi, in a discussion of Epicurus's *Principal Sayings* that was part of the ***Animadversiones in Decimum Diogenis Laertii*** (1649) sounded very Hobbesian in his discussion of Epicurean concepts of justice and injustice, which are founded completely on individual utility.[78] Gassendi goes so far as to equate man in the state of nature with a wolf, just as Hobbes did.

But Paganini acknowledges that Gassendi also accepted the idea that the rule of reason exists in the state of nature, allowing human beings to act for their common benefit. So, argues Paganini, Gassendi "oscillates between positive conventionalism and the traditional paradigm of rationality." However, Paganini argues that when Gassendi is true to his mechanistic psychology and utilitarian individualism, he falls squarely in the positivistic camp.[79]

But even in Gassendi's discussion of Epicurean concepts of justice, and immediately following the analogy he drew between some humans and wolfish animality, Gassendi clarified his interpretation by arguing that such animal behavior is aberrant—just as physical deformity is the exception rather than the norm of human appearance. Most people are guided by rationality, which leads human beings to practice the golden rule and to be good, kind, and gentle.[80] Thus, confronted with the teachings of both Epicurus and Hobbes, Gassendi maintained the basic rationality and sociability of human beings throughout his ethical writings.

Such rationality starts with care for oneself. So Gassendi's third law of nature in the "Ethics" states, "each one wishes to prolong life and the integrity and free use of the members and senses and all the faculties."[81] While self-preservation is the first right of animate beings, it counts only as the third law of nature. While right characterizes all creatures, law pertains only to human beings.

Lastly, Gassendi argued, "human beings are sociable and they live in society. . . . The reason why men are desirous of society, as we said before, is their mutual need which is devised by nature." Thus, society is constructed from human freedom and rationality, but at the same time is a product of a "nature" that manipulates human instinct to accomplish the creation of society. The Latin here is interesting too—Gassendi used *"machinata"* for devised, suggesting an almost mechanical origin of this naturally created social organism.[82] For this early proponent of the mechanical philosophy, there is not yet the rigid distinction between nature and artifact that will characterize the formation of the state for Hobbes.

After discussing the laws of nature, Gassendi turned for a second time to the nature of positive law within the state. The laws of civil society, or the state, are created by human beings after they have composed themselves into a society. Laws reflect the common utility of the people composing the state, each recognizing that the laws must be maintained for the common good, which includes each individual's good. Once again, expediency and utility are linked indissolubly with fellowship and altruism, with reason as the binding force. The ultimate validation of positive law is human prudence, which also obligates one to obey the law after it has been established.[83]

Even without positive law, rational men recognize the obligation to obey the golden rule, by imagining themselves in the place of other men. Such sympathetic projection is connected to the human conscience, "which is the best and most excellent councillor" a man can have. Thus, if all men were wise, "public justice would be unnecessary and useless."[84]

Both Gassendi and Hobbes realized that if all men followed the distates of prudence or right reason, the state itself would be superfluous. But Gassendi was more positive about man's eventual rise to wisdom than Hobbes was, and this optimism may underlie his vigorous espousal of a theory emphasizing the consent of the citizens as basic to the functioning of the state and the legitimacy of the positive law.[85] Nevertheless, given the nature of most men, Gassendi agreed with Hobbes that there must be some kind of coercive power behind the positive law. Human beings do not always act with prudence.

For Gassendi, the malleability of prudential behavior is grounded in the provisional nature of ethics itself. Hobbes believed he had founded a science of politics, a science more evident than physics itself, since it was based on a deductive knowledge of human behavior.[86] Gassendi's political philosophy rested on the probable and contingent, and therefore allowed more contingency in both political behavior and the study of politics.

As a political philosopher, Gassendi reflected a diverse spectrum of political theory, taking what he wanted from many prior formulations. In addition to Epicurean political philosophy, Gassendi used the ideas of proponents of both constitutionalism and absolutism. He also borrowed some notions from what Anthony Pagden calls the tradition of "political Aristotelianism"—a tradition of political thinking, reinvigorated by Thomas Aquinas, which sought the moral and universal origin of all forms of positive law, and grounded the state in natural morality and the law of nature. The adherents of this tradition, also called "ius-naturalism," felt they were constructing a "science" of politics, an *episteme*. Grotius and Samuel von Pufendorf are the most famous seventeenth-century adherents of this school of political philosophy. And like Gassendi, these natural rights philosophers connected right (*honestum*) and utility (*utile*) with natural law and the preservation of the state.[87] They saw no contradiction between utilitarian and social concerns.

Gassendi corresponded with Grotius, who was closely tied to Gassendi's patron, Peiresc.[88] According to Richard Tuck, Grotius was responding to the skeptical crisis of the seventeenth century, with its implicit moral relativism, by advancing a political philosophy that demonstrated that "there were at least two universal moral beliefs (the right of self-preservation and the ban on wanton injury), and that these minimalist ethics could be used as the basis for a universal moral science."[89] For Grotius, the principles of natural law are rooted in human reason and are consequently immutable and eternal.

Gassendi was close to this tradition when he posited a universal desire of self-preservation founded on the desire for pleasure, which is both instinctive and rational. For Gassendi, a psychological constant becomes a moral imperative, although the object of that constant is relative and transitory. But Gassendi did not reify natural law to the extent that Grotius had, because Gassendi's orientation was always to the individual who constituted society, rather than to any metaphysical principle detached from individuals.[90] The French philosopher also, of course, parted company with the natural law philosophers on the question of whether one could construct a "science" of politics, just as he rejected Hobbes's similar claim for his philosophy.

Gassendi's political philosophy is distinct in the way it combines elements from previous and contemporary political philosophies to support a new understanding of the role of the state and the individual within it. The pursuit of pleasure underlies the human constitution, and the emergence of societal custom and habit.

Thus, for Gassendi, the state itself is the product of both instinct and free choice. Civil society is both natural and a construct. It is the result of human passion—the desire for pleasure and avoidance of pain—but a passion circumscribed by reason or prudence and directed by a providential force, which finds the objects of its desires and aversions now in one thing and now in another.

In the next chapter, I demonstrate what some historians have claimed: that Gassendi is a precursor of political liberalism, and that his political and ethical thought strongly influenced John Locke. Gassendi did link ideas about liberty and the social contract formulated in earlier times to a sophisticated understanding and reformulation of Hobbesian ideas about the creation and nature of the state. Most fundamentally, Gassendi understood that an ethics based on freedom and pleasure had to accommodate a political philosophy that included both.

But in advocating these ideas, Gassendi avoided their most radical implications—the right of the individual to rebel against an authority who destroyed rights of life, liberty, and property. Temperamentally, Gassendi was one with Epicurus, who thought the wise man could best find tranquillity by withdrawing from participation in the state. Gassendi constructed a bold, influential political philosophy based on his view of human nature—but his own nature limited how far he would take it.

Notes

1. Bloch has noted that Gassendi's political ideas in Bk. 2 of the "Ethics" seem to be strongly affected by his knowledge of the philosophy of Thomas Hobbes, particularly when Gassendi deals with the state of nature, social contract theory, and the emergence of political man (Bloch, *Philosophie de Gassendi*, xxii-xxiii).

2. Quoted by Sortais, *Philosophie moderne*, 2:215.

3. Gassendi, "Ethics," in *SP*, *Opera*, 2:795. In all future citations, *Syntagma Philosophicum* will be referred to as SP. All translations made directly from the *Opera* are my own.

4. Hobbes's early political doctrines can be found in *Elements of Law* and *Philosophical Rudiments*, in *English Works of Thomas Hobbes*. *Philosophical Rudiments* is Hobbes's own translation of *De Cive* (1642), originally published in 1651.

5. Brockliss, *French Higher Education*, 216-27.

6. The best treatment of the "crisis of the seventeenth century" remains Rabb, *The Struggle for Stability in Early Modern Europe*.

7. Gassendi to Valois, January 5, 1645, in "Letters," *Opera*, 6:214-15. Many of Gassendi's letters to his friends comment on current affairs.

8. On reason of state, see William F. Church, *Richelieu and Reason of State* (Princeton, 1972), and Keohane, *Philosophy and the State*, 112-13, 241-42. Lionel Rothkrug, *Opposition to Louis XIV: The Political and Social Origins of the French Enlightenment* (Princeton, 1965), 82, states, "Words like expedience, necessity, self-interest, and the general welfare appear with increasing frequency in the early seventeenth century."

9. Pierre Gassendi, *De Vita et Moribus Epicuri*, in *Opera*, 5:233-34.

10. Ibid., 5:202.

11. Gassendi, "Ethics," in *SP*, *Opera*, 2:743, 737.

12. Ibid., 2:746-51.

13. Ibid., 2:734-44.

14. Hobbes, *Elements of Law*, 18.

15. Ibid., 18-19.

16. Ibid., 67-69.

17. Hobbes, *Philosophical Rudiments*, 5-6, 16. There is a good deal of debate in the recent literature on Hobbes about whether he was a "psychological egoist." I agree with those scholars who argue that he is. On this question, see Jean Hampton, *Hobbes and the Social Contract Tradition*, 9-24.

18. Hobbes, *Philosophical Rudiments*, 6n.

19. Ibid., 12.

20. Guyau, *Morale d'Épicure*, 198. Hobbes's contemporaries often accused him of being an Epicurean. See Richard S. Westfall, *Science and Religion in Seventeenth-Century England* (New Haven, 1958), 22, 108-9, and Richard Tuck, "The 'Modern' Theory of Natural Law," in *The Languages of Political Theory in Early-Modern Europe*, ed. Anthony Pagden (Cambridge, 1987), 107, who cites Pufendorf who believed that Hobbes was an Epicurean.

21. Lucretius, *On the Nature of the Universe*, 147-77.

22. Gassendi, "Ethics," in *SP*, *Opera*, 2:789. Lucretius's dual contract consists of a contract establishing society and a later agreement to obey legal codes (*On the Nature of the Universe*, 165-69).

23. Gassendi, "Ethics," in *SP*, *Opera*, 2:787-91.

24. Epicurus wrote: "Justice never is anything in itself, but in the dealings of men with one another in any place whatever and at any time it is a kind of compact not to harm or be harmed" (*Extant Remains*, 103). On Epicurus's political philosophy, see James H. Nichols, *Epicurean Political Philosophy: The De Rerum Natura of Lucretius* (Ithaca, 1972, 1976).

25. Gassendi, "Ethics," in *SP*, *Opera*, 2:786.

26. Ibid., 2:786-87. This was a common topic in the seventeenth century. See Tuck, "The 'Modern' Theory of Natural Law," 105.

27. Gassendi, "Ethics," in *SP*, *Opera*, 2:786-95.

28. Brockliss, *French Higher Education*, 219-20.

29. Gassendi, "Ethics," in *SP*, *Opera*, 2:794.

30. Ibid., 2:794-95.

31. Ibid.

32. Ibid.

33. Hobbes, *Philosophical Rudiments*, 9-11.

34. Gassendi, "Ethics," in *SP*, *Opera*, 2:755.

35. Ibid., 2:795.

36. Ibid., 2:795, 798. This distinction is part of the common parlance of the schools. See Brockliss, *French Higher Education*, 292-93.

37. Gassendi, "Ethics," in *SP, Opera*, 2:798.

38. Ibid., 2:795. This seems to duplicate Aristotle's "second nature," where custom arises from man's rational nature. See Brockliss, *French Higher Education*, 293, and Donald Kelley, "Civil Science in the Renaissance: The Problem of Interpretation," in *Languages of Political Theory*, 66.

39. Gassendi, "Ethics," in *SP, Opera*, 2:755, 795. The idea that man is naturally sociable but that it requires an act of will to establish society is not original with Gassendi. J. W. Gough, in *The Social Contract: A Critical Study of Its Development* (Oxford, 1936, 1957), traces this *topos* from its origin in Aristotle, through medieval social-contract theories, until it became fairly commonplace in the seventeenth century.

40. Gassendi, "Ethics," in *SP, Opera*, 2:795.

41. Hobbes, *Philosophical Rudiments*, 67-68.

42. Probably no part of Hobbes's political philosophy has received as much scholarly attention as the discussion of obligation and particularly what obligates in the state of nature. A good bibliography of the literature on obligation is given in Alan Ryan, "Hobbes and Individualism," 90-99.

43. Gassendi, "Ethics," in *SP, Opera*, 2:755.

44. Ibid., 2:799.

45. Ibid., 2:755.

46. Gough, *The Social Contract*, 1-7.

47. Olivier René Bloch, "Gassendi and the Transition from the Middle Ages to the Classical Era," *Yale French Studies* 49 (1973): 52.

48. Quentin Skinner, *The Foundations of Modern Political Thought, Vol. 2: The Age of Reformation* (Cambridge, 1978), 302-38; Keohane, *Philosophy and the State*, 316.

49. Gassendi, "Ethics," in *SP, Opera*, 2:801, 755, 795.

50. On Bodin's theory of the indivisibility of sovereignty, see Keohane, *Philosophy and the State*, 70-71, and Skinner, *Modern Political Theory*, 288-89.

51. Pierre Mesnard, "Jean Bodin," in *Encyclopedia of Philosophy*, 1:325-28.

52. Skinner, *Modern Political Theory*, 316-17.

53. Gassendi, "Ethics," in *SP, Opera*, 2:756-58.

54. Ibid., 2:758.

55. Quoted in Skinner, *Modern Political Theory*, 327.

56. Gassendi, "Ethics," in *SP, Opera*, 2:796.

57. Ibid., 2:757, 796. On the *lex regia*, see Skinner, *Modern Political Theory*, 130-40, 331. The *lex regia*

can also be used to justify absolutism, if consent is given irretrievably. In this discussion of consent, Gassendi's thought coheres closely to the traditional teaching of the universities. See Brockliss, *French Higher Education*, 255-56.

58. Gassendi, "Ethics," in *SP, Opera*, 2:659.

59. Ibid., 2:759-60.

60. Ibid., 2:755.

61. Ibid., 2:669-70.

62. Ibid., 2:778. A. Adam, "Gassendi: L'influence posthume," in *Pierre Gassendi: Sa vie et son oeuvre*, 170, believes that the idea of a natural right founded upon the laws, traditions, and manners of human beings, "lorsqu'il fonde ainsi un véritable empiricisme historique" is in its origins a Gassendist doctrine. It seems more likely that Gassendi was familiar with Aristotelian and early modern discussions of custom, where custom was viewed as a "second nature." Most early modern philosophers and jurists differentiated between nature and custom, and therefore would not view custom as natural in the way Gassendi did. On the history of the concept of custom, see Donald R. Kelley, "'Second Nature': The Idea of Custom in European Law, Society, and Culture," in *The Transmission of Culture in Early Modern Europe*, ed. Anthony Grafton and Ann Blair (Philadelphia, 1990), 131-61.

63. Patrick Riley, "How Coherent Is the Social Contract Tradition?" *Journal of the History of Ideas* 34 (1973): 548.

64. Ibid., 550-52.

65. On causal necessity, see Chap. 4 above.

66. Gassendi, "Ethics," in *SP, Opera*, 2:799.

67. Ibid., 2:797-801.

68. Ibid., 2:800.

69. In Gassendi's text, a willing or spontaneous action, *spontaneum*, is linked with "willingness," *libentia*. See "Ethics," in *SP, Opera*, 2:822-23.

70. Gassendi, "Ethics," in *SP, Opera*, 2:800.

71. Paganini, "Epicurisme et Philosophie," 33, 31.

72. Cicero, *On Ends*, 203.

73. Bailey, *Greek Atomists*, 515; A. E. Taylor, *Epicurus* (London, 1911), 22.

74. Mitsis, *Epicurus' Ethical Theory*, 98-128; P. A. Vander Waerdt, "The Justice of the Epicurean Wise Man," *Classical Quarterly* n.s. 37, no. 2 (1987): 402-22; and David K. O'Connor, "The Invulnerable Pleasures of Epicurean Friendship," *Greek, Roman, and Byzantine Studies* 30 (1989): 165-86.

75. This kind of interpretation can also be found in less recent critics. See Guyau, *Morale d'Épicure*, 139, and Festugière, *Epicurus and His Gods*, 62.

76. Gassendi, "Ethics," in *SP, Opera*, 2:801.

77. Ibid., 2:700.

78. Paganini, "Epicurisme et philosophie," 11-12.

79. Ibid., 17-18.

80. Pierre Gassendi, *Diogenis Laertii Liber X, cum nova Interpretione & Notis*, in *Opera*, 5:158-59.

81. Gassendi, "Ethics," in *SP, Opera*, 2:800.

82. Ibid., 2:800-801.

83. Ibid., 2:797-99.

84. Ibid., 2:802. On this, see Paganini, "Epicurisme et philosophie," 37-38.

85. Gassendi, "Ethics," in *SP, Opera*, 2:799.

86. On the notion of politics as science, see Tom Sorell, "The Science in Hobbes's Politics," in *Perspectives on Hobbes*, 7.

87. Anthony Pagden, "Introduction," in *The Languages of Political Theory in Early-Modern Europe*, 1-17.

88. Gassendi to Grotius, April 2, 1632, "Letters," *Opera*, 6:47. The tone of this letter is formal rather than intimate and it does not concern questions of political philosophy.

89. Tuck, "'Modern' Theory of Natural Law," 115. Gassendi's relationship with Grotius could use more study.

90. Paganini, "Epicurisme et philosophie," 33-34.

Works Cited

Bailey, Cyril B. *The Greek Atomists and Epicurus*. Oxford: Clarendon Press, 1928.

Bloch, Olivier René. "Gassendi and the Transition from the Middle Ages to the Classical Era." *Yale French Studies* 49 (1973): 43-55.

———. *La philosophie de Gassendi: Nominalisme, matérialisme, et métaphysique*. The Hague: Martinus Nijhoff, 1971.

Brockliss, L. W. B. *French Higher Education in the Seventeenth and Eighteenth Centuries: A Cultural History*. Oxford: Clarendon Press, 1987.

Church, William F. *Richelieu and Reason of State*. Princeton: Princeton University Press, 1972.

Cicero, Marcus Tullius. *On Ends [De Finibus]*. In A. A. Long and D. N. Sedley, eds. *Hellenistic Philosophy*. 2 vols. Cambridge: Cambridge University Press, 1987.

Epicurus. *Epicurus: The Extant Remains*. Trans. Cyril Bailey. Oxford: Clarendon Press, 1926.

Festugière, A. J. *Epicurus and His Gods*. Trans. C. W. Chilton. Oxford: Blackwell, 1955.

Gassendi, Pierre. *Opera Omnia*. 6 vols. Lyons, 1658; facsimile reprint, Stuttgart-Bad Cannstatt: Friedrich Frommann Verlag, 1964.

Gough, J. W. *The Social Contract: A Critical Study of its Development*. Oxford: Clarendon Press, 1957.

Guyau, J. M. *La Morale d'Épicure et ses rapport avec les doctrines contemporaines*. Paris: Félix Alcan, 1917.

Hampton, Jean. *Hobbes and the Social Contract Tradition*. Cambridge: Cambridge University Press, 1986.

Hobbes, Thomas. *Philosophical Rudiments Concerning Government*. In *The English Works of Thomas Hobbes of Malmesbury*. Ed. William Molesworth. London: J. Bohn, 1839-45; reprint, Aalen, Germany: Scientia, 1962.

Kelley, Donald R. "Civil Science in the Renaissance." In *The Languages of Political Theory in Early-Modern Europe*. Ed. Anthony Pagden. Cambridge: Cambridge University Press, 1987.

Keohane, Nannerl O. *Philosophy and the State in France: The Renaissance to the Enlightenment*. Princeton: Princeton University Press, 1980.

Mesnard, Jean. "La modernité de Bernier." In *Bernier et les Gassendistes*. Ed. Sylvia Murr. *Corpus: revue de philosophie* 20-21 (1992): 105-13.

Mitsis, Phillip. *Epicurus' Ethical Theory: The Pleasures of Invulnerability*. Ithaca: Cornell University Press, 1988.

Nichols, James H. *Epicurean Political Philosophy: The De Rerum Natura of Lucretius*. Ithaca: Cornell University Press, 1976.

O'Connor, David K. "The Invulnerable Pleasures of Epicurean Friendship." *Greek, Roman, and Byzantine Studies* 30 (1989): 165-86.

Paganini, Gianni. "Épicurisme et philosophie au XVIIème siècle. Convention, utilité et droit selon Gassendi." *Studi Filosofici* 12-13 (1989-1990): 4-45.

Rabb, Theodore K. *The Struggle for Stability in Early Modern Europe*. Oxford: Oxford University Press, 1975.

Riley, Patrick. "How Coherent Is the Social Contract Tradition?" *Journal of the History of Ideas* 34 (1973): 551-64.

Rothkrug, Lionel. *Opposition to Louis XIV: The Political and Social Origins of the French Enlightenment*. Princeton: Princeton University Press, 1965.

Ryan, Alan. "Hobbes and Individualism." In *Perspectives on Thomas Hobbes*. Ed. G. A. J. Rogers and Alan Ryan. Oxford: Clarendon Press, 1988.

Skinner, Quentin. *The Foundations of Modern Political Thought. Vol. 2: The Age of Reformation*. Cambridge: Cambridge University Press, 1978.

Sorell, Tom. *Hobbes*. London: Routledge & Kegan Paul, 1986.

Sortais, Gaston. *La philosophie moderne depuis Bacon jusqu'à Leibniz*. 2 vols. Paris: Paul Lethielleux, 1920-22.

Tuck, Richard. "The 'Modern' Theory of Natural Law." In *The Languages of Political Theory in Early-Modern Europe.* Ed. Anthony Pagden. Cambridge: Cambridge University Press, 1987.

Vander Waerdt, P. A. "The Justice of the Epicurean Wise Man." *Classical Quarterly* n.s. 37 no. 2 (1987): 402-22.

Westfall, Richard S. *Science and Religion in Seventeenth-Century England.* New Haven: Yale University Press, 1958.

FURTHER READING

Brett, G. S. *Gassendi.* London: Macmillan and Co., 1908, 307 p.

> Focuses mainly on Gassendi's *Physics*; discusses later views of Gassendi with an emphasis on Leibnitz.

Egan, Howard T. *Gassendi's View of Knowledge: A Study of the Epistemological Basis of His Logic.* Lanham, MD: University Press of America, 1984, 179 p.

> Examines both Gassendi's *Syntagma* and his earlier works to develop an account of his logic based on provisional knowledge.

Hervey, Helen. "Hobbes and Descartes in the Light of Some Unpublished Letters of the Correspondence between Sir Charles Cavendish and Dr. John Pell." *Osiris* 10 (1952): 67-90.

> Demonstrates the importance of Gassendi in the transmission of Epicureanism to England; reveals the animosity between Hobbes and Gassendi, on one side, and Descartes.

Jones, Howard. *Pierre Gassendi, An Intellectual Biography.* Nieuwkoop: B. deGraaf, 1981, 320 p.

> Offers an account of Gassendi's life and work; denies Gassendi any major importance in the history of philosophy.

Kargon, Robert Hugh. "Descartes, Gassend, and the Newcastle Circle." In his *Atomism in England from Hariot to Newton,* pp. 63-76. Oxford: Clarendon Press, 1966.

> Focuses on Gassendi's connection to the so-called Newcastle Circle, including Thomas Hobbes, William Petty, Kenelm Digby, and Margaret Cavendish (Duchess of Newcastle).

Kroll, Richard W. F. "The question of Locke's relation to Gassendi." *Journal of the History of Ideas* 45, No. 3 (1984): 339-359.

> Reviews arguments concerning Gassendi's influence on Locke's *Essay*; proposes that Locke's interest in Gassendi was just one part of the influence of Epicureanism.

Lennon, Thomas M. "Pandora; or, Essence and Reference: Gassendi's Nominalist Objection and Descartes' Realist Reply." In *Descartes and His Contemporaries: Meditations, Objections, and Replies,* edited by Roger Ariew and Marjorie Grene, pp. 159-181. Chicago: University of Chicago Press, 1995.

> Considers the debate between Descartes and Gassendi by focusing on the issue of the indivisibility of essences, especially the essence of one's idea of God.

Michael, Fred S., and Michael, Emily. "Corporeal Ideas in Seventeenth-Century Philosophy." *Journal of the History of Ideas* 50, No. 1 (1989): 31-48.

> Compares theories of ideas in the work of Descartes, Gassendi, Boyle, and Locke; argues the Gassendist account of human thought offers an important alternative to that of Descartes.

_____. "Early Modern Concepts of Mind: Reflecting Substance vs. Thinking Substance." *Journal of the History of Philosophy* 27, No.1 (1989): 29-48.

> Discusses the importance of the issues of immortality to seventeenth-century psychology; explicates Gassendi's concept of distinct rational and a corporeal souls.

_____. "A note on Gassendi in England." *Notes and Queries* [n.s. 37] 235, No. 3 (Sept. 1990): 297-299.

> Corrects earlier accounts of the transmission of Gassendi's work into England, detailing the history of their publication and translation into English, to assert Gassendi's status as the founder of modern empiricism.

Osler, Margaret J. "Baptizing Epicurean atomism: Pierre Gassendi on the immortality of the soul." In *Religion, Science, and Worldview: Essays in Honor of Richard S. Westfall,* edited by Margaret J. Osler and Paul Lawrence Farber, pp. 163-168. Cambridge: Cambridge University Press, 1985.

> Discusses Gassendi's views on man's immortality in the context of his project to reconcile Epicureanism with Christianity.

Pancheri, Lillian. "Pierre Gassendi, a forgotten but important man in the history of physics." *American Journal of Physics* 46, No. 5 (May 1978): 455-463.

> Argues for Gassendi's importance to physics as the first successful defender of the notion of time and space as real, independent entities; shows connections to Galileo and Newton.

Rogers, G. A. J. "Gassendi and the Birth of Modern Philosophy." Review Essay. *Studies in History and Philosophy of Science* 26, No. 4 (1995): 681-687.

> Reviews five French and English publications on Gassendi; considers the increased modern interest in Gassendi and the recognition of his importance.

Sarasohn, Lisa T. "The Ethical and Political Philosophy of Pierre Gassendi." *Journal of the History of Philosophy* 20, No. 3 (1982): 239-260.

Explicates Gassendi's *Ethics* as one of the first modern assertions of individual liberty and natural rights.

_____. "French Reaction to the Condemnation of Galileo, 1632-1642." *The Catholic Historical Review* 74, No. 1 (1988): 34-54.

Sheds light both on Gassendi's connection to Galileo and the European intellectual community and on the importance of his Catholicism.

_____. "Motion and Morality: Pierre Gassendi, Thomas Hobbes, and the Mechanical World-view." *Journal of the History of Ideas* 46, No. 3 (1985): 363-379.

Examines the connections between Hobbist and Gassendist theories of motion and their notions of man's nature and society; contrasts Hobbes' determinism with Gassendi's voluntarism.

Turner, A.J. "Pierre Gassendi: Astronomer and Natural Philosopher." *Interdisciplinary Science Reviews* 19, No. 2 (1994): 135-139.

Details some of Gassendi's scientific achievements to show how his work in astronomy, geology, and physics provided a foundation for his work in philosophy.

Pierre de Ronsard
1524-1585

French poet and critic.

The following entry presents recent critical discussion of Ronsard. For a survey of prior criticism, see *LC,* Volume 6.

INTRODUCTION

The central figure of the Pléiade poets—who sought to create a national literature in France to rival that of Renaissance Italy—Ronsard is considered the finest French lyric poet of the Renaissance. Patterning his verse upon the great works of classical antiquity, Ronsard is recognized for his contributions to the poetic forms of ode, sonnet, and elegy. In the two books of his *Sonnets pour Helene,* among his many works, he combined complex rhyme, picturesque imagery, and classical allusions and metaphors, thereby introducing what modern critics recognize as innovative poetic expressions to French literature. A renowned court poet in the later portion of his career, Ronsard was a champion of the established church and a defender of the monarchy. Ronsard is today regarded as the epitome of French Renaissance poetics.

BIOGRAPHICAL INFORMATION

Ronsard was born at the Château de la Possonière in the Vendômois region of France, the son of Louis de Ronsard, a minor nobleman, and Jeanne Chaudrier, a close relative of many of the aristocratic families of Touraine and Anjou. Except for a half year spent at the Collège de Navarre in Paris, Ronsard passed his early years in the Vendômois, where he was educated at home and acquired an abiding love for his native province that would later figure prominently in his poetry. At the age of twelve Ronsard was sent to court to serve as a page to members of the royal family. In 1538 he began a peripatetic career as a soldier and a diplomat. However, illness—the beginnings of a lifelong affliction with arthritis and deafness—forced him to abandon a diplomatic career. During his convalescence Ronsard determined to take up literature as a full-time occupation. Encouraged by the distinguished poet Jacques Peletier, Ronsard published his first work, "Ode de Pierre de Ronsard à Jacques Peletier," in 1547. Ronsard's first collection of poems, *Les quatre premier livres des odes,* met with considerable critical success. In subsequent works Ronsard diversified his style to include philosophical and scientific poetry. In 1558 or 1559, with his reputation firmly established, he was made official court poet, the re-

sponsibilities of which included writing occasional and honorary verse. Ronsard spent his last years mainly at Saint-Cosme Priory near Tours and at Croixval Priory, where he devoted himself to religious duties and to revising his works. Ronsard died at Saint-Cosme in 1585.

MAJOR WORKS

The poems of Ronsard's first major collection, *Les quatre premier livres des odes,* evince the themes, imagery, and style of his models from classical antiquity—principally Pindar and Horace—as they honor outstanding individuals, commemorate significant events, and celebrate the beauty of nature. The work contains Ronsard's best-known ode, "Ode à Michel de l'Hospital," composed in recognition of the man who defended Ronsard's views on poetic reform from one of its vocal detractors, Saint-Gelais. Ronsard's *Les amours, Continuation des amours,* and *Nouvelle continuation des amours,* which were inspired by the poet's love for a Florentine banker's daughter, Cassandre de Salviati, are a departure from the style and purpose of *Les quarter premiers livres.* Drawing from the poetry of Petrarch, the elaborate and sensual sonnets of *Les amours* treat conventional themes—unrequited love, solitude in a lover's absence, and erotic longing. In contrast, Ronsard's two books of Homeric poetry, *Les hymnes* and *Le second livre des hymnes,* published at about the same time as *Les amours,* are majestic, laudatory addresses and panegyrics to patrons and friends on philosophical, scientific, and aesthetic subjects. The publication of *Les oeuvres* in 1560 initiated Ronsard's second literary period, distinguished from the first by its public nature. In a number of alexandrine *discours,* or addresses, most notably *Discours des misères de ce temps* and *Remonstrance au peuple de France,* Ronsard used satire and invective for religious and political effect, discussing patriotism, Catholicism, and the French king's success in religious wars. Ronsard's most celebrated work, the extensive sonnet series *Sonnets pour Helene* is unlike any of the poet's other late verse in that it recalls Ronsard's earlier Petrarchan material, but with a more restrained and sincere tone. In the *Sonnets,* Ronsard explored the theme of love sacrificed for art while employing imagery drawn from classical myth. Ronsard's ambitious late work, *Les quatre premiers livres de la Franciade* was never completed. Ronsard offered an epic account of French history in the *Franciade,* linking in verse his nation's origins to the Trojan War as the Roman poet Vergil had done in his *Aeneid.* Ronsard's sole work of criticism, *Abrege de l'art poëtique françois,* was published anonymously. The work contains Ronsard's explication of his poetic theory, which suggests the importance of *mimesis,* or imitation of reality, combined with the creative imagination.

CRITICAL RECEPTION

In his day Ronsard claimed to have equaled the poetic achievement of the classical Greek poet Pindar, and certainly he enjoyed extraordinary critical and popular success. Soon after his death, his reputation declined significantly, and Ronsard's poetry suffered a period of neglect lasting nearly two centuries. By the early nineteenth-century, however, interest in his works had renewed, and in the twentieth century his poems have become the subject of rigorous academic inquiry and criticism. Critical regard has been focused on the nature of Ronsard's poetic theory, and the extent to which his works may be said to uphold the doctrines he outlined in his *Abrege de l'art poëtique françois.* Critics have also explored Ronsard's use of irony to transgress the poetic boundaries set by his classical models. Another primary area of contemporary critical interest has been Ronsard's participation in the ongoing Renaissance debate concerning the preeminence of one artistic form over all others, with scholars studying his claims that poetry should occupy the position of excellence above the visual arts. Additionally, critics have examined Ronsard's more marginal texts, including his early *Livret de folastries,* a work that can be described as almost pornographic, and which Ronsard suppressed during his later career. Overall, most modern scholars concur that

Ronsard gave to French literature something it had never before known, the concept of the creative imitation of the ancients. Thus, in regard to his poetic range and sustained innovation, Ronsard is widely viewed as the greatest French poet of his age.

PRINCIPAL WORKS

Avantentrée du Roy trescrestien à Paris (poetry) 1549

L'hyme de France (poetry) 1549

Ode de la paix (poetry) 1550

Les quatre premiers livres des odes de Pierre de Ronsard, ensemble son bocage (poetry) 1550

Les amours de P. de Ronsard vandomois, ensemble le cinqiesme de ses odes (poetry) 1552

Le cinquieme livre des odes, augmente; ensemble la harangue que fit Monseigneur le duc de Guise aus soudars de Mez le iour qu'il pensoit avoir l'assaut (poetry) 1553

Le livret de folastries à Janot Parisien (poetry) 1553

Les odes (poetry) 1553

Le bocage (poetry) 1554

Continuation des amours (poetry) 1555

Hymne de Bacus, avec la version latine de Iean Dorat (poetry) 1555

Les hymnes de P. de Ronsard a tresillustre et reverendissime Odet, cardinal de Chastillon [*Hercule Chrestien;* partial translation] (poetry) 1555

Les meslanges (poetry) 1555

Nouvelle continuation des amours (poetry) 1556

Le second livre des hymnes (poetry) 1556

Exhortation au camp du Roy pour bien combatre le iour de la bataille (poetry) 1558

Exhortation pour la paix (poetry) 1558

Chant de liesse, au Roy (poetry) 1559

Chant pastoral sur les nopces de Monseigneur Charles duc de Lorraine & Madame Claude fille II du Roy (poetry) 1559

Discours a treshault et trespuissant prince, Monseigneur le duc de Savoye; chant pastoral a Madame Marguerite, duchesse de Savoye, plus, XXIII inscriptions en faveur de quelques grands seigneurs (poetry) 1559

L'hymne de tresillustre prince Charles cardinal de Lorraine (poetry) 1559

Le paix, au Roy (poetry) 1559

Le second livre des meslanges (poetry) 1559

Suyte de l'hymne de tresillustre prince Charles cardinal de Lorraine (poetry) 1559

*Les oeuvres de P. de Ronsard, gentilhomme vandomois [*Songs and Sonnets of Pierre de Ronsard, Gentleman of Vendomois;* partial translation] (poetry) 1560

Elegie sur le despart de la Royne Marie retournant à son royaume d'Escosse (poetry) 1561

Continuation du discours des misères de ce temps, a la Royne (poetry) 1562

Discours des misères de ce temps, a la Royne mere du Roy [*A Discours of the Present Troobles in Fraunce, and*

Miseries of This Tyme, Compyled by Peter Ronsard Gentilman of Vandome, and Dedicated unto the Quene Mother] (poetry) 1562

Elegie sur les troubles d'Amboise, 1560 (poetry) 1562

Institution pour l'adolescence du Roy tres-chrestien Charles neufiesme de ce nom (poetry) 1562

Remonstrance au peuple de France (poetry) 1563

Responce de P. de Ronsard aux injures et calomnies (poetry) 1563

Les trois livres du recueil des nouvelles poesies (poetry) 1563

Abrege de l'art poëtique françois (criticism) 1565

Elegies, mascarades et bergerie (poetry) 1565

Les neus, ou nouvelles (poetry) 1565

Le septiesme livre des poemes (poetry) 1569

Le sixiesme livre des poemes (poetry) 1569

Les quatre premiers livres de la Franciade (poetry) 1572

Le tombeau du feu Roy tres-chrestien Charles IX, prince tres-debonnaire, tres-vertueux & tres-eloquent (poetry) 1574

Les estoilles a Monsieur de Pibrac, et deux responses a deux elegies envoyées par le feu Roy Charles à Ronsard (poetry) 1575

Le tombeau de tresillustre princesse Marguerite de France, duchesse de Savoye (poetry) 1575

Panegyrique de la renommee, a Henry Troisiesme, Roy de France & de Poloigne (poetry) 1579

Les derniers vers de Pierre de Ronsard (poetry) 1586

Oeuvres inédites de Pierre de Ronsard (poetry) 1855

Pierre de Ronsard: Oeuvres complètes. 20 vols. (poetry and criticism) 1914-75

*A later revision of this work (1578) contains *Le premier livre des sonnets pour Helene* and *Le second livre des sonnets pour Helene* [*Sonnets for Helen*].

CRITICISM

François Rigolot (essay date 1988)

SOURCE: "Ronsard's Pretext For Paratexts: The Case of the *Franciade*," in *SubStance: A Review of Theory and Literary Criticism,* No. 56, 1988, pp. 29-41.

[In the following essay, Rigolot examines Ronsard's theory of poetic mimesis as it is expressed in the prefaces to the Franciade.*]*

> "I could find no more excellent subject than this one"
>
> Ronsard, Preface to the *'Franciade'* (1572)

There has been much discussion in modern criticism (at least of late) of what is now commonly referred to as the *paratext,* that is, to paraphrase Gérard Genette's *Palimpsestes,* a number of signals (titles, prefaces, postfaces, footnotes, epigraphs, illustrations, etc.) which form the *entourage* of the text and, at the same time, constitute a major locus for the conditioning process of potential readers.[1]

In taking the prefaces of the *Franciade* as my object of study I intend neither to examine the theory of the heroic poem or epic—it has already been the object of much expert analysis[2]—nor to carry out a historical study that would position Ronsard in the evolving myth of the French people's Trojan origins.[3] Instead, choosing texts that are by nature explanatory, normative and prescriptive, I hope to surprise the poet in the act of intentionality. By "intentionality" I mean here not so much the explicitly declared intentions of the author—these should not always be taken at face value—as the implicit confessions capable of being gleaned from specific contradictions in the utterances of the discourse. Since all representation is a doubling of the self and the refashioning of a subject as an object, establishing the characteristic features of this object will allow us to understand better the subject's strategy in so composing it. Far from accepting at face value any advice to the "apprentice reader" (who is encoded as such in the prefatory discourse), I would like to attempt to unearth the semi- or largely unconscious projective symbolic system of the paratext, and to read, beyond the surface utterances that stage the fiction of the apprentice reader, the ambiguous projection of the Ronsardian theory of imitation.

The theoretical status of the imagination has of course been a subject of great interest to specialists of Ronsard and, more generally, to sixteenth-century scholars.[4] The concept of imagination, we are told, must be studied in the context of related notions of invention, imitation and fiction. Ronsard thus would be situated at the intersection of two main currents. One has a moral and didactic origin and would condemn "phantasie" as "mistress of falsehood"; the other proceeds from the rhetorical tradition and would welcome the ability of the mind to recreate ideas in different forms. Thus, beginning with the *Abbrégé de l'art poëtique françois* (1565), Ronsard dismisses "fantastic inventions" because they are the product of sick imagination, and can only conceive "a thousand monstrous forms lacking order and connection."[5] In the same work, however, our poet also sets forth a positive conception of the imagination, one growing out of a "natural good" and allowing the representation of "the ideas and the forms of everything that can be imagined."[6] This two-faced discourse on the imagination seems to express Ronsard's poorly articulated desire to restore the lost importance of rhetorical composition without abandoning the admonitions of the moralist tradition.

What exactly is there of this conceptual ambivalence in the corpus of successive prefaces of the *Franciade*? And is it not paradoxical to seek to discern an imaginary element in a place that it normally would tend to avoid? Discourse that "escorts" a text generally achieves its legitimacy by positing an equivalency of principle between its *saying* and the *doing* of the text it escorts. This conception supposes that the preface is deliberately located outside the realm of the imagination in order to ensure the rational apprehension of its critical object. However, the status of what is today called the *paratext* is not always so clearly delimited.[7] It is not certain, for example, that we can deny

to the peripheral sections certain characteristics traditionally attributed to what we conventionally call the "text" itself.

In addition, recent studies on the literature of Renaissance have taught us to distrust the distinctions, established with some haste although with the best of intentions, between prose and poetry, and between the theory and practice of writing. Terence Cave, in his excellent study, addressed the problem with respect to the notion of *copia*.[8] In Du Bellay, for example, it is no longer possible to assert that we can separate the theoretical discourse of the *Deffence et illustration de la langue françoise* from the *praxis* underlying that polemical manifesto. In fact, there is an oscillatory movement between "intention" and "performance," so that it would be useless to detach the *Deffence* from the rest of Du Bellay's work on the grounds that it supposedly follows different principles of composition.[9]

The preface of the first edition of the **Franciade** (1572) will receive the greatest share of our attention, both because it is certainly composed by Ronsard alone and because it is there that we are given, in the most immediate (most brutal? least considered?) way, the product of the prefacer's imagination. Repeating a favorite distinction of rhetoricians from Aristotle to Quintilian, Ronsard begins by warning his reader that, unlike the historian who seeks truth "without deception or pretence" (**Franciade,** 4), the poet must "stop at what is plausible."[10] This "plausible" is immediately defined by Ronsard as "what can be" or "what is already recognized by common opinion" (4). And he adds:

> I venture only to say (if my opinion should carry some weight) that the Poet who writes things as they are does not merit as much as he who feigns them and who draws as much as he can from the historian: not however in order to feign a fantastic Poetry like that of Ariosto the body of which is so deformed and monstruous that it resembles more the dreams of a man sick with a prolonged fever than the inventions of someone of sound health.
>
> (4)

There is a doubly negative attitude here that merits further attention. On the one hand, we witness the rejection of history in the name of the freedom of invention (history represents a subservience to reality because it "only admits the object as it is or was"). On the other hand, all "fantastic" imagination finds itself relegated to the domain of pathology because it neglects nature and lapses into teratology ("body . . . deformed and monstruous").[11] The use of the verb "to feign" (*feindre*) is interesting here because it denotes a keen awareness of the admissible limits of the imagination for the *feigneur,* that is to say, for the poet.[12] If history is that theoretical place characterized by the absence of the fictive (*feintise,* the non-imaginary), "fantastic poetry" on the contrary is marked by an excess of fiction (the delirium of the imaginary). The prefacer's discourse refuses to embrace both deficiency and excess, two extremes which cancel each other out before the natural and

learned blend of the perfect fiction where "frenzy" and "art" remain in perfect harmony.

Thus, from the beginning Ronsard marks out the boundaries of a permissible space in the poetic realm of the imaginary. He does not, however, wish to be alone in assuming such responsibilities; and this accounts for his citation of Homer and Virgil, whose works bear witness, he believes, to the same theoretical conception. Indeed, neither the *Iliad* nor the *Aeneid* is the work of an historian. Homer and Virgil did not seek to derive their subject from the verifiable reality of their culture for two reasons. First, they had definite political aims; Homer would have liked to "insinuate himself into the favor and good graces of the Eacides" (6-7) and Virgil sought to "merit the good grace of the Caesars" (7). This political aim was coupled with a very clear sense of their own poetic destinies. They wished to adopt or develop easily transposable myths, whether by exploiting well-known events acknowledged as such by their contemporaries (as Homer did with the Trojan War: "the report of such a war was acknowledged in the general opinion of men at that time" (7),) or by gathering such information from notable predecessors as they could legitimately put to good use (as did Virgil, reader of Homer and of the "old Annals of his time" from which he conceived the subject of his *Aeneid).*[13]

Ronsard has the same political and poetic aims; and he does not disguise that fact. On the one hand, he claims to have "an intense desire to honor the house of France" (8) and to sing the "heroic and divine virtues" of his prince, "King Charles IX" (8), whose "great victories" he does not hesitate to compare with those of "Charlemagne his grandfather" (9). On the other hand, he means to add his name to the long list of great epic poets by employing the same terms he had used to talk of Homer and Virgil. The subject that he treats is "founded on general knowledge" (9)—a phrase which echoes the description given, two pages earlier, of the intention attributed to the author of the *Iliad,* who exploited the "report" of the Trojan War and the "general opinion" that his contemporaries had of it (7). Moreover, if the *Aeneid* took its inspiration from the "old Annals of his time," the **Franciade** would be founded on a tradition "well established by the Annals" (7) and the "old beliefs of the Chronicles of France" (9).[14] The correspondence of vocabulary is striking; everything points to the French poet's self-conscious imitation of his ancient models. In rhetorical terms, he seeks to convince his reader that the *Idea* that moves him is no different in nature from that which rendered Homer and Virgil immortal. Hence the self-assurance with which he addresses us concerning his topic: "I could find no more *excellent subject* than this one"(9).

It matters little to Ronsard that subsequent readers might have doubts about his having chosen Trojan legends to give the French a sense of their national history.[15] For him the "excellence" of the subject is measured by its ability to emulate a pre-existing imaginary structure, one furthermore guaranteed by the endurance of ancient epics. The

success of the "heroic poem" is no mystery to him; three obvious conditions seem immediately to present themselves:

> 1) One should avoid both the *non-fiction* of History and the *sur-fiction* of "Fantasy."

> 2) One should rely on the authority of the Annals and the Chronicles, that is, on an acceptable and accepted tradition: what is called *plausible fiction.*

> 3) Ancient models should serve as inspiration for contemporary works because they offer proof of the validity of the two preceding conditions.

These conditions, reduced in practice to one alone, reveal clearly the degree of Ronsard's confidence in the theory of *imitation.* However, once the premises of his art have been laid out, the prefacer hastens to explain that practical considerations forced him to modify the historical particulars on which he based his fictions. Even in the first preface he writes, "I lengthened the canvas" (7). By this he means that he found necessary to invent certain episodes in order better to "imagine," that is to say, to represent the adventures of Francion. His choice of the word "canvas" or "cloth" (*toille*) is significant: it refers to the craft of the artisan, of the weaver (spelled variously as *tessier, tissier, texier, tixier*) fabricating textiles and texts. But the verb "lengthen" (*allonger*) is equally interesting, especially since it appears twice in the same context. Speaking of the genealogy of the French kings, Ronsard tells us that, unlike Virgil, he has had to take into account 63 sovereigns and that he was therefore obliged to "lengthen the paper" (5). The valorization of the poet's work is thus not a matter of *innovation* (an abrupt, qualitative leap of the imaginary) but of *amplification* ("lengthening" of the "cloth" and of the "paper," that is, of the already written texts, the ancient epics).[16]

In other terms, in this case Jakobsonian ones, one might say that the imagination (the imaginative, inventive, creative faculty) does not proceed by paradigmatic change along the axis of substitutions but by syntagmatic progression, along the axis of combination. And this is not merely a result of bending to the exigencies of the *translatio studii.* Refusing the "modern" challenge that pure metaphor represents, the *Franciade* seeks to assert itself naturally, by means of metonymic sliding—to the extent of supplying an eloquent suffix to the *Iliad.* In so doing, it follows the "natural good of the imagination" and not its unacceptable "fantastic inventions." There will be no break between the ancient text and the new poem: no cut in the "cloth," in the "paper" of universal Poetry; in short, it ensures that one will not encounter the "disjointed dreams of a madman."[17]

However, this conception of the "heroic poem" as a simple "lengthening" (*alongeail*) of the epic tradition of antiquity could be misleading. This metonymic process must not lead to a confusion of the historian's task: to set down the record of princes "thread by thread" (5) or "bit by bit" (336), with the poet's labor. In the middle of his first pref-

ace, Ronsard returns twice to consider the process of the poem's *conception*—attributing the most carnal sense to that word. He first establishes an equivalence between the intellectual faculty of the imagination and, in the physiological order, the act of childbirth: "Les espirts *conçoivent* aussi que les corps" ["Minds *conceive,* just as well as bodies."](8). This slightly awkward alexandrine, placed between an apology for the poem's title and an encomium of Charles IX, is illuminated by an explicit comparison found in the next paragraph: "Now just as women who are ready to *give birth* select a good atmosphere, a healthy house, a rich godfather before having their child, I have chosen the richest argument, the most beautiful verses and the most distinguished godfather in Europe to honor my book, and support my work." The idea of *parturition* replaces that of *amplification.* Ronsard does not lose sight of the fact that his *Franciade* must retrace poetically the *birth* of a great nation. His ambition, quite simply, is to *give birth* to France, but he cannot realize this ambition without "lengthening" the "cloth" of the ancient epic.

To give birth and to perpetuate the human race are notions intimately linked for the sixteenth-century mind. One need only to recall the famous letter of Gargantua to his son. The Poet, as progenitor, reproduces the will of the great Plasmatic Being. He knows that he can "acquire a sort of immortality and, in the waning of this transitory life, perpetuate his name and seed."[18] Ronsard is in fact so aware of this power that in the same phrase he associates his own glory with that of his king: "Possessed therefore of an intense desire to honor the house of France . . . and desiring *together* to perpetuate my renown everlastingly . . . I could find no more excellent subject than this one" (8-9). We have here a sort of verification of the *sententia* pronounced just before this: "minds conceive just as well as bodies." To conceive the *Franciade* is not to create something from nothing, but rather to accept the law of universal *reproduction,* celebrated by the *Roman de la Rose* and common to both minds and bodies. For Ronsard there is no difference between prolonging the Ancients' discourse (*l'allongement*) and perpetuating the Moderns' renown. It is not a question of choosing between the two; we must accept them *together* because—biologically, one might say—they are indivisible. What is more, the poet will not be induced to make his lyric heard (he will not be touched by "furor" and "enthusiasm") unless his "affections" are set in motion by the experience of the past.[19]

All this perhaps explains why the prefacer of the first edition devotes thirteen lines (in the Laumonier edition) to explain why he did not write the *Franciade* in alexandrines. In the second edition of the *Abbrégé de l'art poëtique françois* he had already given us a justification based on circumstances judged exterior to his will: "If I did not begin my Franciade in alexandrine verse, which I have brought (as you know) into vogue and honor, it is necessary to blame those who have the power to command me, and not my will, *because this is done against my wishes,* hoping one day to make it march in alexandrine step, but this time I must obey."[20] Thus in 1567 Ronsard tells us that it is by order of the king that he does not use a meter which nevertheless would be appropriate for a "solemn, lofty, and (if necessary to talk thus) altiloquent composition."[21] Five years later, the reason advanced is quite different. Alexandrines are now judged to be too "long" and too "subject," that is too alien to prosody, too similar to prose. Thus they are ill-suited to the task of "lengthening" the ancient epic and of "giving birth" to a new heroic form. It should be noted that the two explanations Ronsard proposes are not mutually exclusive. The possibility of the alexandrine's prosaic nature was raised as early as the first edition of the *Abbrégé,* even if expressed in the conditional tense: "[Alexandrines] *would fairly exude* prose, if they were not composed of distinguished, solemn, and resonant words, and of a rich rhyme, so that such richness might preclude a prose style."[22] That which remained menacing in 1565 became a concrete reality in 1572. The present tense is henceforth appropriate: "The shameful realization I have that it smacks too much of its prose [prevents me] from composing my work in alexandrine verse"(9). As for the royal interdiction, which figured prominently in the *extension* of the *Abbrégé* in 1567, it is not mentioned in any preface to the *Franciade.* The prefactory imagination simply cannot accommodate any tension between the poetic and the political projects. "Conception" can only occur with the harmonious and faithful cooperation of the two partners: the king and the poet are henceforth seen as co-participants, co-creators of the national hymn whose birth they celebrate.

This question so preoccupied Ronsard that he returned to the argument in the posthumous preface of 1587, this time placing it in the exordium of his text:

> PREFACE TO THE *FRANCIADE,*
> touching on the Heroic Poem.
> *To the apprentice reader:*
>
> You should not marvel, Reader, that I have not composed my *Franciade* in alexandrine verse . . .
>
> (331)

A single controlling idea runs through this entire paragraph on the alexandrine: it is summarized in a sentence placed between parentheses: "The prosaic style is the worst enemy of poetic elegance" (332), and the use of alexandrines is the easiest way of succumbing to this fault. The commentary of 1572 is amplified and made more radical to the extent that any meter of twelve syllables becomes completely unacceptable. The evolution of the alexandrines' prosaic character is clear: they "fearly exude prose" (in 1565); they "smack too much of their prose" (in 1572); they "smack too much of very facile prose, and are too enfeebled and limp" (in 1587).[23]

The birth of Ronsard's hero, Francion, of the *Franciade* and of France could not be evoked with such prose; what was needed was a voice that spoke the language of poetry and that was not liable to founder against the baser aspects of history. One thinks of the vigorous attack of 1587 launched against contemporary writers:

The majority of those writing in our time drag themselves, *enfeebled* [*the word was previously used to describe the alexandrine*], across the ground, like weak caterpillars [*what is more "limp" than a caterpillar!*], which no longer have the strength to climb to the treetops, and are satisfied with feeding on the base moisture of the earth, without seeking the nourishment of the high reaches [*where epic poetry resides!*], which they cannot attain because of their *feebleness.*

(337)

The alexandrine runs the risks of being the metrical medium of the "thing as it is" (4), of the "base moisture of the earth" (337), whereas what is needed is a medium suitable for *feigning,* which abandons pedestrian discourse in order to "climb to the treetops," there to dine on the "high reaches" (337).

It is this voice which the prefacer of 1572 treats at length when he invites the reader to speak his work, to "articulate it well" by reproducing faithfully the accents of the original song: "I will entreat only one thing of you, reader, which is to *articulate well* my verses and to adjust your voice to their sentiment; not as some read them, as missive, or as a few royal letters, but as a *well-articulated* Poem: and I beseech you once more, when you see this mark:!, to raise your voice slightly, so that you may render graceful that which you are reading" (12).

This emphasis on the *pronunciatio,* while following the traditional rhetorical prescriptions of the orators, here assumes particular importance in the context of Ronsard's rejection of the discourse of history. In the *Franciade* itself we learn, indeed, that Francus owes his name to an error of pronunciation. The passage is worth citing in the original French:

> Adonq Francus qui seul prince commande,
> Pront & gaillard au milieu de la bande,
> Voulant sa main d'une lance charger,
> D'Astyanax en Francus fit changer
> Son premier nom, en signe de vaillance
> Et des soldats fut nommé Porte-lance,
> Pheré-enchos, nom, des peuples vaincus
> Mal prononcé, & dit depuis Francus.
>
> (Book I, vv. 945-52, 76-77)

The onomastic remotivation from a learned etymology is not at all unusual here.[24] There are, however, two stages in this transformation of the name. First, in the conformity with the model of Homeric epithets, Astyanax becomes "Lance-bearer" (*Pheré-enchos*): this is the crucial moment when the identity of the hero finds itself translated into language and acknowledged by an act of speech. Next occurs the deformation of the name through ambiguity of Time: *Pheré-enchos* becomes *Francus.* Now, this second process is attributed to the "conquered people": it is they, the uncouth, who by their fault have obsured the Greek transparence of the heroic epithet. And it was not until Ronsard that the meaning of the original appellation could be recovered. In other words, without this poor historical pronunciation there would not have been any doubts about the Trojan origins of the *French:* they would have remained *Pheré-enchoi,* faithful descendants of the original *Lance-bearer. "Tantum pronunciatio potuit suadere malorum. . . ."*

Ronsard the prefacer thus possesses the wisdom to advance nothing that was not demonstrated previously by Ronsard the epic poet. His defense and illustration of the voice are all the more eloquent for it. It is probably with this goal in mind that the singer of France devoted the final lines of the initial preface to a seemingly minor topic, that of spelling: "Excuse, Reader, the printer's mistakes: for all the eyes of Argus would not pick them out well enough, especially in the first printing" (12). It does not seem likely that printing errors are Ronsard's only concern here, although in fact they were quite substantial.[25] In the dominant imaginary domain, that of praise of the voice, printing mistakes are mere trifles without interest, deserving of the reader's "excuse." The visual aspect of the text is only a necessary evil; what really matters is the oral participation in the poet's song. The ocular hypertrophy, symbolized by the hundredeyed giant, Argus, becomes ridiculous in the context of the all-powerful Poem: *carmen fictum, non figuratum:* song imagined and not represented on the page. For Ronsard is not Jean Lemaire de Belges (even if preoccupation with the Trojan origins of the French is common to both; he is not content to produce the "artifices," the optical illusions, of the "Great Rhetoric."[26]

In the same way, in order better to "adjust" and "elevate" his "voice" above the dissonant cacophonies, the reader/singer is invited to "close the mouths of those who are naturally envious of the property and honor of others" (12). When these mouths are closed, then will resound the triumphant *voice* of the *poeta vates,* free of parasitical interference. The mouth of the just, *Os ab Origine,* opens wide when the prefacer closes his discourse, as he emphasizes with a play on words: "J'ay *fermé* ce préface pour *fermer* leur bouche (des envieux)" ["I *shut* this preface in order to *shut* their mouths (those of the envious)"] (12). There could be no more convincing clausula for a reader completely prepared to welcome the plenitude of the Song.

This imaginary structure of the Voice will become noticeably richer in the Preface of 1587 where it takes on the form of a conflict between versifier and poet. The opposition, taken by Sebillet and Du Bellay from Quintilian (*Inst. orat.,* X, I, 89) is well known[27]: "There is as much difference between a Poet and a versifier, as between an old nag and a noble steed of Naples, or to choose an even better comparison, as between a venerable Prophet and a charlatan selling drugs" (335). In spite of what the common people might think, the versifier is merely a disguised writer of prose: he "composes rhymed prose" (336). He thus finds himself on the deaf side of writing, where Argus delights, unable to hear his *omnivoyance.* "On the contrary, the heroic Poet (. . . makes the Gods *converse* with men and men with Gods" (336). This dialogue, which

takes place between Heaven and Earth, concerns invention; it is coupled with another dialogue, this one on imitation, between the poet and the various authorities on whom he has drawn. Before Montaigne made it famous, Ronsard took from Virgil the image of the bee who, having "plundered flowers here and there" finally produces a honey "all its own"[28]: "In short, [the Poet] is a man who, as a bee *samples* and *sucks* all flowers, then disposes of his honey and profit depending on the timeliness of his arrival" (336). The verbs "sample" and "suck" refer to the buccal activity and not to manual work: once more the *logos* seeks to eliminate any monument either to graphic reproduction or to the craft of the writer.

Paradoxically, it is Amadis Jamyn, the devoted secretary of Ronsard, author of the *Argumens* of the **Franciade** and of several liminary pieces in verse, who comes to recall the Poet to his role as writer. The quatrain placed underneath the portrait of Charles IX, just before the "First Book," is a lesson in modesty for Ronsard as well as an encomium of the prince:

> Tu n'as, Ronsard, composé cet ouvrage,
> Il est forgé d'une royalle main,
> Charles scavant, victorieux & sage
> En est l'autheur, *tu n'es que l'escrivain.*

> A.I. (27)[29]

This denial of the Ronsardian "conception" of the work is quite a strange revelation in light of the great pains Ronsard took to impose the imaginary structure of his voice of the poet. Is this an indication that there is a counter-voice in the prefaces, camouflaged and repressed, which can only make itself heard indirectly, by means of the secretary's verses? Such a hypothesis is made all the more plausible if we consider that it would explain the addition of 1567 in the **Abbrégé de l'art poëtique,** discussed above, concerning the renunciation of the alexandrine.[30] The "tu n'es que l'escrivain" ("you are only the scribe") of Jamyn would be the imperative repetition of Ronsard's "il faut obeyr" ("I must obey"). And the verses would make quite clear what was only suggested in prose: "It is necessary to blame those who have the power to command me, and not my will."[31]

However, the myth of the voice is all the more powerful for its being bound up with the very reality of the language. Ronsard in fact comes out in favor of a "flourishing language (. . . lively and natural" (349), which is defined more and more by the use one makes of it than by the authority given to it. The vulgar tongue is superior to the learned one because it is shared by aristocrats ("Princes," "Magistrates") and bourgeois alike ("merchants and shop-keepers"). It circulates on all levels of society "in the same way as the commerce and traffic of coins" (350). In this sense, it serves as a link between the various elements of the nation, all of which the Poet aspires to join in discussion, just as the Gods and men are so joined (336). Such a vision of unity is, of course, a devoted illusion; but it is rooted in this "conception," unanimist before the fact, of an imaginary domain of the voice. The paradox affirms that the prefaces are addressed to "readers," specialists in the deciphering of letters. At a time when the reading public is limited, the *voice* of the Poet will, in fact, be the "common currency" of all those who *speak* the "maternal language"; and yet it will never be able to breach the dividing line traced by alphabetism and, imitating the great ancients ("as Homer did, with Hesiod, Plato, Aristotle, and Theophrastus, Virgil, Livy, Sallust, Lucretius and a thousand others"), speak "the same language as plowmen, valets and chambermaids" (351).

The desire for a unifying voice is probably the source, at least in part, of the preference accorded Homer in the Preface of 1572: "Moreover, I have modeled my work (of which these first four books will serve as an example) *rather on the natural facility of Homer than on the meticulous diligence of Virgil,* imitating as much as possible from both the craft and subject matter *built* more on plausibility than on truth" (5). In opting for the "natural facility" that he attributes to Homer, Ronsard only returns to a theme that is dear to him (the diatribe against *art* which he developed, beginning in 1552, in the **"Ode à Michel de l'Hospital"**); but he also inscribes his epic conception in a philosophy of language and proclaims the "right" to "living" languages (350), to "natural" language, "without difficulty," "without a schoolmaster" (350-51). In practice, however, as we shall see, he does not forget Virgil and his "meticulous diligence." For we must take into consideration the role that *art* plays in a discourse ostensibly against art, an art which counterbalances the desire for "natural birth." The quotation concerning the "natural facility of Homer" and the "meticulous diligence of Virgil" already bears witness to this. Did not Ronsard claim that he imitated the *craft* of the two poets "as much as possible" and that this craft is "built" on the plausible? The vocabulary of the plastic arts is here to remind us that procreation arising out of a state of frenzy cannot eschew careful composition, or the rules of art. In the first preface of the **Franciade,** Ronsard writes concerning the mythic voyage of his hero through Gaul, "On this foundation of plausibility I *built* my Franciade with his name" (8). And in the 1587 Preface he uses the same verb to denote an identical aim. "I *built* my Franciade, founded and based upon our old Annals, without concerning myself with its truth or falsity" (340). Yet because the "builder" is very sensitive to possible accusations that his composition is too "artful," he is careful to respond in advance to likely objections. For example, he anticipates the reader's censure of the length of Jupiter's speech at the beginning of Book I (vv. 33-156): "I do not doubt but that I will be accused of little artfulness by those saying that the harangue of Jupiter at the beginning of my first book is too long, and that I should not begin with it" (10). In fact, underlying the reproach of "little artfulness" is an accusation of an artfulness that is too visible, overdone, artificially long. But Ronsard defends himself by stating that such artfulness must be attributed to the model, to rules of the genre, to the necessities of action and, secondarily, to constraints inherent in the French language ("You must know that

thirty lines of Latin are worth more than sixty of our French" [10]). He justifies its length by showing that Virgil was guided by related principles in a similar passage of the *Aeneid* (I. 283ff.). That he should have recourse in this manner to the art of the model and the constraints of the language which increase the need for "artfulness" is indeed an important indication that the "meticulous diligence of Virgil" is, in many ways, more important to him than the "natural facility of Homer."

In the Foreword of 1573 Ronsard does not hesitate to compare himself to the most celebrated painter of Antiquity, Apelles, and to tell us that he has *corrected* his work "to render it more perfect": the **Franciade** will dare to "endure the filings and perfect polishings demanded by time" (3). The architectural and pictorial metaphors are considerably more developed in a passage from the Preface of 1587, in which the miserable hut of the historian undergoes a metamorphosis into a poet's sumptuous palace: "From a small hut [the Poets] create a magnificent Palace, which they enrich, gild and embellish with an exterior of marble, jasper and porphyry, with gillochis, ovolos, frontispieces and pedestals, friezes and capitals, and within, by paintings, raised tapestries, embossed with gold and silver" (340). Ronsard excels at constructing beforehand, in his prefaces, the grandiose dwelling which he will necessarily fail to create in his poem. For us, however, it is the intention that counts here: the resolution to "embellish," to "enlarge" his work (341), the "desire to enhance the language of [his] nation" (353). The fantasy of birth is not without an accompanying fantasy of construction.

Ronsard recognizes that the work is never halted in its development, in its march toward perfection. He even proclaims it forcefully as he notes the incompletion, the imperfection of his **Franciade.** In 1572 he both anticipates that "some other pedant in another's book will reprove me of not having followed the absolute rule of Poetry" (11), and tells the reader "that there is *no perfect book, mine even less so*" (11-12).

What we have here is not a simple expression of false modesty. In the Ronsardian imaginary space, the work is seen capable of being modified by changes in time, in the mood of the writer, or by suggestions from his friends. The "matter," certainly, will not change; but the manner of saying it, the form, is destined to undergo changes, whether by addition or subtraction[32]: "I shall be able, depending on the length of my life, the judgment and sincere opinion of my friends, to *increase or diminish* (my book), as one who does not swear by self-love, or by the persistency of his inventions" (12). This stance in favor of an open form, *opera aperta,* a text whose exact formulation remains subject to the fluctuation of time, will be taken up again in the very brief "Foreword" of 1573, as if the text's receptiveness were what Ronsard wished above all to affirm in his prefatory discourse. He writes that he is ready "to hear the judgment and the pronouncement of everyone" and "to receive any gracious *correction*" (3).

Returning to the question of "perfect polishings," the post-humous Preface of 1587 subordinates itself entirely to the authority of Horace. Three verses from *Ars poetica* serve as an epigraph to the long theoretical manifesto:

> Carmen reprehendite quod non
> Multa dies & multa litura coercuit, atque
> Praesectum decies non castigavit ad unguem.
>
> (vv. 292-94) (331)[33]

The apprentice poet must work for perfection while adhering to the principles of the prince of poeticians, that is, while avoiding "mediocrity": "You are not unaware, Reader, that a Poet must never be mediocre in his trade, nor learn his lessons half-way, but rather quite well, most excellently and *most perfectly:* mediocrity is an extreme vice in Poetry; it would be better never to get mixed up in it, and to learn another trade" (348). And yet languages are not perfect, poets make mistakes, and the art of perfecting can always be taken up again.[34]

Having discussed several examples of conceptual ambivalence in successive prefaces of the ***Franciade,*** we can say in conclusion that the prefatory discourse seems to embody, in both theory and practice, a number of complex and important oppositions: history *vs.* poetry, nature-inspiration *vs.* art-work, closure *vs.* openness. The succession of paratexts thus serves as a pretext for Ronsard to articulate the contradictory aspects of his poetics while, at the same time, staging the fiction of an "apprentice reader" whose credibility is meant to reinforce the imaginary structure of the poetic voice.

Notes

1. Gérard Genette, *Palimpsestes* (Paris: Seuil, 1982) 9-10.

2. I refer here to the bibliography established by Guy Demerson as an appendix in the new edition of Ronsard's *Oeuvres complètes,* ed. Paul Laumonier (Paris: Nizet, 1983) 378-380. Page numbers between parentheses in my text refer to vol. 16 of this edition.

3. For a look at the current state of this question see Bodo L. O. Richter, "Trojans or Merovingians? The Renaissance Debate Over the Historical Origins of France," *Mélanges à la mémoire de Franco Simone* (Geneva: Slatkine, 1982) 3:3-26.

4. Of special note is Grahame Castor's study, *Pléiade Poetics* (Cambridge UP, 1964) 119ff. and 172ff.

5. Ronsard, *Oeuvres complètes, supra* n2, 14: 25.

6. Michel Dassonville makes an association between the "natural good" of Ronsard and what Boileau will define as "a certain elevation of the spirit which makes us consider things in a favorable light" (*Traité du sublime,* ch. 6). Cf. "Ronsard à l'oeuvre," *Mélanges sur la littérature de la Renaissance à la mémoire de V.L. Saulnier* (Geneva: Droz, 1984) 364, n8.

7. On the notion of the *paratext,* see Gérard Genette's *Palimpsestes,* 9-10 and my *Texte de la Renaissance* (Geneva: Droz, 1982) 253ff.

8. Terence Cave, *The Cornucopian Text. Problems of Writing in the French Renaissance* (Oxford: Clarendon, 1979).

9. Ibid., xiv and xx.

10. In the Preface of 1587 one finds, "He holds as a very necessary maxim of his art, never to follow the truth step by step, but the verisimilar, and the possible" (336).

11. Horace himself did not speak with more eloquence (*Ars poetica,* vv. 408ff.). In the *Abbrégé de l'art poëtique françois,* Ronsard had already made the same criticism of "fantastic inventions." (Paris: Vendômois, 1565) 25.

12. Let us recall that *to feign* (Fr. *feindre*) retains the sense of the Latin *fingere,* itself a translation of the Greek *poiein* (to make, create). On this etymological justification, see *Pléiade Poetics, supra* n4, 120-22.

13. The posthumous Preface of 1587 adds that it is in reading the *Aeneid* that the poetic imagination of the future poet can develop: "such ecstatic descriptions, that you will read in such a divine author (. . . will make you a poet, though you had been a rock" (333).

14. The word "Chronicle" (*Chronique*) is used with reference to Virgil in 1587; it is perhaps an echo of the *Chroniques de France* of 1572. Instead of "well established by the Annals" one finds: "founded and based upon our old Annals."

15. P. Laumonier will echo these doubts: "Why did he not choose the eminently natural subject of Joan of Arc, delivering France from the English occupation?" (9, n1).

16. In 1587, after having lavished varying advice on his "apprentice reader," the prefacer adds: "Moreover, Reader, if I wished to instruct and inform you of all the precepts associated with Heroic Poetry, I would need a *ream of paper*" (348). This evinces a rather remarkable parallel between the lengthening of prose and that of poetry. It is as if in the imaginary domain of the preface the status of theory was somehow contaminated by that of practice.

17. Cf. *Abbrégé supra* n11, 14:13.

18. Rabelais, *Pantagruel,* ch. 8, ed. P. Jourda (Paris: Garnier, 1962) 1:256.

19. As Daniel Ménager writes, "the poetic project happens to be in deep complicity with heroic destiny." *Ronsard. Le roi, le poète et les hommes* (Geneva: Droz, 1979) 33.

20. *Abbrégé, supra* n11 14:25, addition of 1567-1573.

21. Ibid., text of 1565.

22. Ibid.

23. Cf. *Abbrégé, supra* n11, 14:25, addition of 1567-1573.

24. See my *Poétique et onomastique. L'Exemple de la Renaissance* (Geneva: Droz, 1977) concerning the theory of the remotivation of names.

25. Cf. Ronsard, *Oeuvres, supra* n2, 12, n3.

26. It should be noted that the Preface of 1587 also ends with brief observations on orthography; they are limited to vague proposals of reform and refer the reader to future remarks (353). The *Abbrégé*, for its part, was more eloquent on this subject, *supra* n11, 28-34.

27. Cf. T. Sebillet, *Art poëtique françois,* ed. F. Gaiffe (Paris: STFM, 1932) 19-20; J. Du Bellay *Deffense et illustration,* ed. H. Chamard (Paris: Didier, 1948) 173.

28. *Essais,* (Paris: Pléiade) 1:150-151a. Amadis Jamyn, in the first "Argument" of the *Franciade,* writes, "It resembles the bee, which in producing its honey makes use of every flower" (14).

29. As D. Ménager writes, the "invasive presence" of the King "reduces the poet to subordinate role." "The poet, simple 'scribe,' writes in his book that which the king, the only true 'author,' has inscribed in reality." *Ronsard, supra* n19, 289-90. The English translation of Jamyn's passage is as follows:

> You did not, Ronsard, compose this work,
> It is forged by a royal hand,
> Charles the learned, victorious and wise
> Is the author, you are but the scribe.

30. *Abbrégé, supra* n11, 14:25.

31. Ibid.

32. In connection with this see the thesis of Louis Terreaux, *Ronsard, Correcteur de ses oeuvres* (Geneva: Droz, 1968).

33. "Reject that poem which many days and many erasures have not subdued and ten times corrected to perfect accuracy."

34. Strangely enough, one might use Horace against Ronsard and recall that "sometimes the good Homer falls asleep" (*Ars poetica,* v. 359). Horace asked that poets be forgiven passing awkwardness if elsewhere they could point to brilliant successes.

Philippe Desan (essay date 1988)

SOURCE: "The Tribulations of a Young Poet: Ronsard from 1547 to 1552," in *Renaissance Rereadings: Intertext and Context,* pp. 184-202. Urbana: University of Illinois Press, 1988.

[In the following essay, Desan recounts Ronsard's early attempts to make a living as a poet.]

The poet has always been accorded a status well set off from that of other members of society. Poetic production and everyday necessities coexist only with difficulty, for the Muses' elect would seem to have other preoccupations than imagining themselves members of a civil and industrious society. The spirituality of poetry transcending material needs, the poet would subsist merely on rhymes and sparkling water, or even, as with Celadon in *L'Astrée,* on "cress and tears"; his always-gratuitous production would demand no real work. The image that we have of the poet is that of a demigod blackening pages of a book under the impulse of genius—no trace of monotonous labor. The poet simply grazes the surface of each page, pouring out illuminated visions; in the evening he falls asleep in peace and dreams of other poems, more beautiful still.

Clearly this is all a myth. Yet, as Claude Lévi-Strauss has effectively shown, we often organize our universe around myths which consequently become reality. One would then have to accept this nebulous idea of the poet. Nevertheless, the children of Calliope are also human beings, and must therefore pay their debts and feed themselves. Some among them even go so far as to consider their "art" a profession. It is this perception of poetry as *remunerable* work and the poet's self-recognition as a member of a market economy that interests me here.

Given the complete confusion of social stratification and the importance of poetry during the period, the sixteenth century would appear to be the privileged locus for the consideration of problems related to the mode of existence and the professional status of the poet in the midst of civil society. By poet, in this study, I mean male poet. There is some poetry written by women during the Renaissance, but it is a fact that the great majority of these women were already wealthy before they started writing. They belonged overwhelmingly to the aristocracy or the rising bourgeoisie, so for them poetry was never a way to make a living. Marguerite de Navarre is one very typical example. Likewise, Louise Labé, the daughter of a rich rope-maker from Lyon, obviously did not need to write poetry to earn a living. The opportunity to overcome social stratification and to become professionally successful as a poet was limited to men in the sixteenth century. Poetry was first perceived as a profession by men, and it is not a coincidence that the Pléiade poets were all men.

I will therefore take the poets of the Pléiade as the point of departure of my analysis, and will more particularly analyze the case of the young Ronsard who, in 1550, presents himself on the employment market with the hope of living off his pen. The period I consider in this study extends from 1547 to 1552; these dates, although somewhat arbitrary, correspond to the years when Ronsard started writing his first poems (1547) and when he received his first real financial reward for his poetry and became curé of Marolles (1552). Yet, in order to understand the professional path of Ronsard and the other poets of the Pléiade, it is necessary first to discuss the social structure of France during the sixteenth century.

The social organization of the French Renaissance is marked by the structural prevalence of three orders: the clergy, the nobility—further divided into *noblesse d'épée* and *noblesse de robe*—and finally the Third Estate, which embraces the rest of the people. This static organization, however, suffered a crisis as a result of the decline of the *noblesse d'épée* and the rise of the city bourgeoisie, which aspired to the rank of nobility through the purchase of offices and charges. The members of this new class arising out of the Third Estate were most often educated in the best universities and occupied the key posts in the state bureaucratic apparatus. These *robins* thus became jurisconsults, lawyers, procurators, intendants, and city councillors. The sale of offices allowed them to rise rapidly within the social hierarchy and to entitle themselves *sieurs* and even *gentilshommes*.[1] In order to cover rising state expenditures caused by costly wars, the king was forced to multiply the number of offices which could be purchased. Under Henri II the sale of these offices increased with a rapidity that inflamed further the antagonism between the "old" nobility and the younger rising class.[2]

The social inertia which had prevented mobility within French society for centuries, and which had thus preserved the stability and fixity of that society, was abruptly shattered, and "passage" from one order to another suddenly appeared possible for the first time. Money transformed lifestyles, offered a means to success, and became the object of much coveting. If one possessed sufficient savings, for example, one could buy an office; financial security would then often be guaranteed. But this means of social assertion had an important disadvantage, for the obligations connected with the office had to be conducted in person and the delegation of duties was not permitted. Thus, the officer was constrained to reside continuously and permanently where his office was located. One can easily understand why this "mode of subsistence" never became popular among the poets, who could not accept the restriction of residence imposed by François I in 1535 and reaffirmed in 1539. The poet of the sixteenth century had to follow his patron and move about constantly according to the dictates of the market. Further, if we consider the Pléiade poets, we see that most of them could not aspire to the most profitable offices because they did not possess the necessary capital to buy the best charges. The military profession, needless to say, also did not give the freedom of movement required by the poet. Strategies of social mobility were consequently quite restricted for those who decided to embark on a literary occupation.

Looking more closely at the lifestyle of the sixteenth-century poets, we find that the majority of these poets received their revenues in the form of ecclesiastical benefices, prebends, and sinecures in abbeys, rectories, and priories. They thus depended on the ecclesiastical order for survival and surrendered themselves almost completely to what Henri Weber has judiciously called "the chase for benefices."[3] How is this at-first-glance-baffling "vocation" to be explained? The answer lies in the manner in which ecclesiastical benefices were distributed during the six-teenth century. After the Concordat of Bologne (1516) between François I and Leo X, the so-called simple benefices could be granted directly by the king without referring to Rome. The concordat had in fact suppressed the election imposed by the Pragmatic Sanction for the regular benefices. These benefices were now at the disposal of the French sovereign, who had the power to recompense whomever he wanted under the condition that the recipient of the ecclesiastical benefice receive the tonsure. Even though residency was required for these simple benefices, there existed nonetheless the possibility of "legitimate" excuses, which opened the path to nonresidency. Charles Loyseau, a jurist at the end of the sixteenth century who has left us a treatise on the right to offices and benefices during this period, tells us that "the Casuists presently hold that the inveterate practices and customs excuse the necessity of residence on the location of the simple benefices."[4] It was permitted as well to transfer the task associated with the benefice onto someone else while continuing to receive the revenue associated with this benefice. Loyseau explains the attraction of such an indulgence: "Thus, the exercise rendered separable from the title, the labor from the payment, the office from the benefice, in short the spiritual from the temporal, the majority of the beneficiaries have had little trouble retaining the title and revenue of their benefice while discharging on others the labor of serving the poor."[5]

Only these simple benefices exempted the beneficiary from living in residence. They were in fact revenues with no obligation; this explains why these "simple benefices . . . consist more of revenue than of personal function."[6] It should not surprise us then if rectories, priories, presbyteries, and abbeys were much sought after by the poets and artists of the sixteenth century. Loyseau remarks on this subject that, during this time, "there is a large company of almoners, chaplains and clerks"[7] and that "one no longer chooses whom to award the offices of the Church, rather one gives the benefices to the men one wants to gratify."[8] Many poets thus chose to receive the tonsure and remained celibate so as to secure revenue from the ecclesiastical benefices they were awarded for having praised the prince. Such is the case with Ronsard, Du Bellay, Baïf, Pontus de Thyard, and a large number of their contemporaries. For example, from 1553 to 1557 the Vendômois poet was accorded the benefices of four provincial rectories.[9]

These benefices, however, were not so easily procured, and the poet who wanted to gain the favors of highly placed persons had to compose all sorts of occasional poems and commissioned pieces. Regarding the function of "official poet," Raymond Lebègue counts no fewer than six important tasks demanded the poet: (1) to eulogize the king, his family, and the highest civil servants, (2) to celebrate the events of the royal family, (3) to serve the royal politics in verse, (4) to contribute to court feasts, (5) to produce amorous poems on command, and (6) to provide occasional pieces.[10] It should also be noted that the pecuniary advantages of this post were far from being proportional to the prestige of such a function, and, despite the affirmations of Ronsard's first biographer, Claude Binet, our poet, though he received in 1554 the title of *poëte ordinaire du Roy,* was never fully paid for his services to Henri II.[11] It is only when Charles IX offered his patronage to the *Franciade* in 1560 that Ronsard was finally guaranteed shelter from material difficulties.

A substantial network of responsibilities and constraints, all bound to the profession of the poet, emerged in the sixteenth century and forces us to resituate poetic production within its larger socioeconomic context. The work of Ronsard attests to this constant awareness of and preoccupation with material security. In fact, Ronsard, who eventually became the greatest of the Pléiade poets, was compelled, at the beginning of his career, to establish himself among his fellow poets and to "make a living" laboriously before becoming the prince of poets. The competition was quite stiff at this time. If we take as a point of reference the number of poets who published their verses between 1545 and 1565 in the hope of attracting princely favors, we discover that the market for poetry was more than saturated. Of more than two thousand authors indexed by La Croix du Maine in his *Bibliothèque françoise,* approximately one-fourth are accorded the title of "poet." When Ronsard presented himself on the market as a poet in 1550 he not only had to attract the attention of the prince but also had to distinguish himself from the rest of his colleagues. While toying with the Muses, Ronsard had to seek the support of patrons who would allow him to devote himself entirely to his art without any pecuniary worries. The *Odes* demonstrate well this desire to overcome material problems. I now propose to read the *Odes* as a poetic paradigm in which the poet presents, in an academic fashion, all his knowledge of the art of rhymes according to the highest of models: Pindar and Horace. In this respect, the *Odes* also accompany the search for an occupation, and thus function as the young poet's request for employment.

In 1550, the poets attached to the king were François Habert—one of the last *rhétoriqueurs*—and Mellin de Saint-Gelais, a stubborn defender of Marotic poetry, who, as a result of the respect due his age and his white beard, controlled poetic production at the court. Ronsard was not even next at this time. Philibert Delorme—who, between 1547 and 1548, obtained three abbeys from the king in recompense for his poems, which were much appreciated at the Louvre, and who directly participated in the royal entry of Henri II into Paris in 1549—certainly preceded Ronsard. The Vendômois poet still seemed a novice and his poetic production remained somewhat meager.

In 1549, with the intention of attracting the favors of the princes, our poet published his **"Epithalame d'Antoine de Bourbon et Jeanne de Navarre,"** a celebration of their marriage the previous year. This enterprise sought to find a rich patron upon whom Ronsard could bestow his lyre. Apparently the effort achieved nothing, as Jeanne de Navarre remained deaf to Ronsard's eulogistic demand for employment. After this negative experience, the poet concentrated his effort directly on the royal person, as he probably began to realize that in the domain of the arts there can be no compromising: the first poet of France must be the poet of the king. All the same, the task was not so simple, and Ronsard suffered setback after setback. In 1549, for example, he saw himself refused the organization of the various festivities planned for the royal entry of Henri II into Paris. Jean Martin and Thomas Sebillet, the latter having published the previous year his *Art Poëtique François,*[12] were to be in charge of the ceremonies. Nonetheless, Ronsard published for the occasion an **"Avantentrée du Roi treschrestien à Paris,"** but, once more, the poem was not a success and did not receive the attention anticipated.

Ronsard always considered the production of occasional verses an indispensable activity, for as Daniel Ménager has noted, "even though the Court gives no official command, a poet of the Renaissance, since he depends on the Prince, cannot simply exempt himself from this task."[13] All the poets of that time had to devote a good part of their artistic production to this exercise, and the anecdotes of Ronsard and Du Bellay writing epitaphs for the dogs of Charles IX and the sparrow of Marguerite of Savoy are famous.

In 1549, Ronsard also had his **"Hymne de France"** printed by Michel Vascosan: He ends the poem with an appeal to the king, imitating Virgil's *Georgics:*

> As your poet, having first dared
> To have composed a rhyme to praise you,
> I beg that my lyre suits your pleasure.[14]

Once more the enterprise failed to attract the king's attention. The poet nevertheless did not despair; he would only be satisfied once he had gained the king's support:

> But my soul is only ravished
> By a burning desire
> To dare to attempt a work
> Which would content my great king
> So that the work's honey-sweetness
> Would so anoint his ear
> That I might find it facile
> To importune him for my well-being.[15]

Direct access to the monarch remaining for the moment impossible, Ronsard solicited protectors in the entourage of Henri II. Since it was not possible to flatter the king's ears directly, being still too accustomed to the "small Petrarchan sonnets or some delicacies of love"[16] from Mellin de Saint-Gelais and his disciples, the young poet therefore had to create a network of influential "friends" that would bring him closer to the royal person. It is a matter of strategy: because Henri II refused to hear the young poet, it had to be through the detour of his entourage that the latter would approach him. This might explain why Ronsard dedicated several poems to courtiers susceptible of appreciation in an attempt to make his poetry known to the royal family.

Ronsard was engaged in a search for friends, and by "friend" it is necessary to understand someone capable of speaking favorably of his poems at the court. Friendship is here defined in terms of belonging to a network of individuals who choose to aid each other, everyone being ready to intervene for the other if a reciprocal action could be expected. In a society where social mobility is still relatively slow, this system of mutual help was the only "rapid" way to success. It was therefore necessary to allure the patronage of men who had sufficient power at the court and to offer them the possibility of gain so that the relation might be mutually "profitable." It is important to note that what we now call the Pléiade poets originally grouped themselves under the name of *Brigade*—a word which evokes well the idea of military formation according to strict rules of membership. Organization into a group permitted the poets to "tighten ranks" and form a school in order to confront better the resistance of the poets "in place."

It is therefore not an accident if, among the great number of poets distributed all over France at this time, Ronsard, Du Bellay, Baïf, Belleau, Jodelle, and La Péruse all attended two small Parisian *collèges,* both located on the hill of Sainte-Geneviève. Baïf, Ronsard, and Du Bellay were students and friends of Dorat at the Collège de Coqueret, while Belleau, La Péruse, and Jodelle attended the courses of Muret at the Collège de Boncourt. These two institutions were not to be counted among the most prestigious *collèges* of the capital. We could ask ourselves at this point if the success of these poets did not come precisely from the fact that they knew how to organize themselves into a school and push to the extreme that esprit de corps necessary for their personal success, for the members of the Brigade were from 1547 to 1552 to follow the same road to poetic and social success and thus share the same interests.

Of course, schools and coteries disputed among themselves as to who occupied first place; such is the case, for example, with those who opposed the Marotic tradition, defended by Mellin, to the "new" poetry of the Pléiade poets. Yet, in all cases we have a comparable organization: the individual has power only insofar as he is recognized by the influential members of his profession and sustained by the rich members of the court. In the case of Ronsard, it suffices to count the odes dedicated to Baïf, Du Bellay, Belleau, Peletier, and other poets and friends from the Collège de Coqueret—Julien Peccate, Bertran Berger, and René d'Urvoy for example—in order to account for the cohesion that existed at that time among individuals of the same profession.[17]

On this point, the example of Pierre Paschal is illustrative. A Gascon poet and friend of the Pléiade authors until 1558, Paschal let it be known that he was preparing to draft a book inspired by Paul Emile's *Vies et eloges des hommes illustres* in order to laud the members of the Brigade. All the poets concerned regarded this plan with a favorable eye and rewarded Paschal *in advance* by inserting into their poems several flattering references to him. Ronsard even dedicated an entire ode to Paschal. However, this "payment" in advance revealed itself to be a bad investment, as Paschal quickly forgot his project when he gained the favor of Henri II and accepted the post of royal historiographer in 1558. The poets of the Pléiade who, through their praise of the Gascon poet, had directly participated in the establishment of his renown and thereby played an important part in his ascension to such a sought-after post demonstrated their fury when they discovered that they had been duped and that they would receive nothing in return for their investment. Ronsard, particularly infuriated by this lack of gratitude, composed a Latin invective against Paschal entitled **"Petri Paschali Elogium."**[18]

But the case of Paschal must ultimately be considered an exception. Other "friends" of Ronsard kept the bargain, "tit for tat" (*troque pour troq*) as the poet tells us. These "other friends" were particularly numerous at the court. In fact, the nobility and the ecclesiastical authorities represented the second important group that Ronsard had to seduce as they were, after all, the ones who held the purse strings and could assure a comfortable future to the poet. Ronsard had therefore "to sweeten the famous ones"[19] and transform himself into "a trumpeter / Of one and the other glory."[20] At this time his "shop [was] stocked with nothing but the drugs of praise and honor."[21] From 1547 to 1552 there were more important things for Ronsard to do than painting nature in rhyme. This would come later, after employment had been secured.

In order to succeed, Ronsard had to fight on two fronts: first he had to acquire a certain credit as a poet and, second, he needed to make himself sufficiently visible to the king to become the official poet. As Michel Dassonville points out, it is in the Pindaric ode, which had been introduced to Ronsard by his master, Dorat, that Ronsard saw the possibility of "reconciling the two ambitions which drove him for many years to please at the same time both the learned and the public at large."[22] Ronsard thus took for his model the greatest of Panhellenic poets who had been so skillful at capturing glory while at the same time accumulating an immense fortune for having lauded the rich citizens of Syracuse, Agrigente, Thebes, Argos, Athens, and Rhodes. As he rhymed his verses, Ronsard probably dreamed of the author of the *Olympics,* who had received 10,000 Athenian drachmas for having composed a dithyramb in honor of the Greek city.

Ronsard's project, however, did not unfold as expected—at least not at the beginning of the poet's career. Glory does not necessarily accompany material success. In attempting to gain both at once, the poet found himself confronted by a paradox, for it is difficult to please the learned and the princes in the same manner. By producing dithyrambs designed to gain the patronage of men of high rank, Ronsard brought upon himself the criticism of his fellow poets. His contemporary and friend, Etienne Pasquier, in a letter dating from 1555, reproaches Ronsard for his "half-courtly servitude" and closes his letter with the wish "that it will not come to pass that the good work of your pen should be used to the end of highly praising several we know not worthy of it."[23]

There also existed a problem of quantity for Ronsard in 1549; he lacked a poetic corpus sufficient for a first publication. Although he had already published a few poems, Ronsard did not have a book on the market. He therefore arduously put himself to the task and collected his compositions together with new unpublished work celebrating the monarch, for, as the poet would later declare, "the glory of kings is a fertile subject."[24] Ronsard even envisaged placing himself totally in the service of Henri II in order to recount in verse the deeds of the king and his family:

> Nevertheless the desire which goads my heart
> To demonstrate how I am your servant.[25]

At the beginning of 1550, Ronsard finally published a small octavo volume containing the first four books of the *Odes.* At the time he was just twenty-six years old; nevertheless, in the preface "Au lecteur," he immediately proclaimed himself the first poet of France: "But when you will call me the first French lyrical poet, and the one who has guided the others onto the path of this so honest labor, then you will bestow upon me that which is my due, and I will strive to make you understand that it is not unjustly that I have received it."[26] Mellin de Saint-Gelais felt the blow and rose to defend his own employment and status. It was after all his own place which he defended. The *rhétoriqueur* violently attacked Ronsard's poems in front of the king, Marguerite de Navarre, and her chancellor, Michel de l'Hospital. The favorite poet of the king ridiculed the hermetism, obscurity, and pedantry of certain odes, and for a time successfully diverted the king's favor.

Ronsard was fortunate enough, however, to find in the person of Michel de l'Hospital an influential protector at the court against the accusations of Saint-Gelais. To express his thanks for the intervention of the future chancellor of France, Ronsard dedicated to him one of the most beautiful odes describing the birth of the Muses. The same strategy was used on Jacques Bouju, Maître des requettes of the queen, who had also defended Ronsard, and Jean Martin, who wrote an "exposition" of the most difficult passages of the *Odes*—this exposition accompanying the first edition of the *Odes* in 1550.

Notwithstanding the moderate success of the *Odes,* Ronsard still awaited the recognition of his talent and the favors that usually follow such recognition:

> As one often sees the ship at port
> Attending the conduct of the wind
> Before departing, its swelling sail rising up
> To the side that the wind blows the stern,
> So, Prince, without stirring, I await
> Your royal favor, which I hope one day

> Will command me to make an honorable voyage
> Favorable to the winds of your fortune.[27]

The king kept him waiting and the Vendômois poet became more impatient "to taste the manna of royal grandeur."[28] Nevertheless Ronsard did not despair and he continued to refine the academism of his Pindaric odes. He had little choice, for he knew that before becoming the king's poet, he had first to impose himself as the French Pindar. With this goal in mind he imitated the Greek bard to the best of his ability in strophe, antistrophe, and epode. The mastery of the ancient poets became part of Ronsard's intellectual maturation; he could not and did not really wish to avoid this necessary stage of his poetic maturation. His authority as a poet needed to rest on something solid and directly linked to the humanist movement; the student found a master in Antiquity and applied himself to equaling his effort in the medium provided by the French language. Ronsard proceeded to offer the proof of his standing as an academic poet but also seemed aware of the fastidious nature of his odes. In fact, the result is not always brilliant, and Ronsard himself appears conscious of his lack of originality:

> Thus, following the gods, I beseech you to take
> Favorably this little gift as interest, while awaiting
> A present more perfect and worthy of a king,
> And that my Calliope will bear within me.[29]

Should we begrudge Ronsard his striving after the security of a decently remunerated occupation? We have a tendency to place the poet above society and do not think of him or her as an intriguer. This vision which we create of the poets is part of the false view we have of artistic production in general. Consider the situation of Ronsard. Before putting words into rhyme, Ronsard had first to operate in a world that was already socially and economically organized. It is precisely these existing preconditions that Jean-Paul Sartre has brilliantly analyzed in his study of Tintoretto. In Venice, at the same time as Ronsard wrote his odes, Tintoretto also had to confront painters of greater renown in order to gain part of the market for Venetian painting. As with Ronsard, Tintoretto had to "astonish, hit hard and impose himself"[30] to survive. Sartre has systematically deconstructed the vision we have of the "sublime" and lofty painters of the Italian Renaissance and he has transformed Jacopo into a laborer always on the lookout for a new contract.

What Sartre has shown for Tintoretto applies equally to Ronsard. The poet often speaks of the physical and technical aspect of his art; expressions like "laboring hand,"[31] "art of my thumb,"[32] "labor of my fingers,"[33] recur frequently in the *Odes,* and we have the sentiment that wooing the Muses requires much more than mere imagination: it is also necessary to do *physical* work in the elaboration of the poem. Isidore Silver has underlined the "craftsman" side of Ronsard's poetry by highlighting the laborious aspect of an apprenticeship which possesses none of the celestial grace one would often think to find with the poet.[34] It is perhaps because the poet must submit to material exigencies before devoting himself to the Muses that Ronsard considered his art as a "trade" (or a *traffic* in French): "I am the trader of the Muses"[35]—that is to say a merchant— Ronsard tells us. For it is in fact "merchandise" that the poet wished to exchange on the market.

Ronsard considered his writing as *labor,* and it is therefore not a coincidence if the word "labor" recurs as a leitmotif in the *Odes.*[36] In the preface of the 1550 edition, for example, the noun appears seven times in the space of five pages, most often in a context which leaves no ambiguity concerning its economic connotation. Ronsard also describes how he has written "industriously"[37] this volume and, in the first version of the ode "La Victoire de François de Bourbon" written in 1545, the Vendômois poet even considers himself as an "ingenious craftsman."[38] This idea of poetry as a professional occupation was again to be defended fifteen years later when, in his *Art poëtique,* Ronsard gave the following advice to his disciple Alphonse Delbene: "so far as human artifice, experience and labor permit, let me give you here several rules so that one day you can be the first in the knowledge of this so agreeable trade."[39]

At this point it is important to distinguish between *work* and *labor.* The first word is a generic term that implies a physical or intellectual process, while the second expression places work within a socioeconomic structure with all of its implications and therefore suggests a remuneration. It is for this reason that Ronsard perceived his poetic production in terms of its exchange value rather than its use value. The idea of poetry as a thing in itself which would be unrelated to the market is totally absent in the *Odes.* For Ronsard, poetry is part of the economic circuit and is consequently dependent on the laws of the market. Our poet was always conscious of the exchange value of his poetry; from the start, his odes had to be converted into money or gifts.[40] Endlessly he attempted to convince a potential patron that his verses had a price, and it is precisely the sum to be paid for fame and posterity that instigated the sighs and lamentations of the Vendômois poet. Ronsard frequently complained of the insufficient value that was accorded to his poetry and even drafted an ode "Contre les avaricieus" to this effect. The poet declared that he would content himself with what the king might offer if the present seemed appropriate for the investment of his labor. For many years Ronsard waited for a proper price:

> Prince, I send you this Ode
> Trading my verses in the same way
> A merchant trades his goods,
> Tit for tat: you who are rich,
> You, king of wealth, do not hesitate
> To exchange your gift for mine.
> Do not tire of offering,
> And you will see how I will accord
> The honor which I promise to sound
> When a present adorns my lyre.[41]

Ronsard defined the price of his verse as a long-term investment for the prince who wished to see himself glori-

fied for posterity. Poet of the powers in place, Ronsard enabled the monarch and princes to belong to a tradition that combined men and gods alongside one another. Mythical and real contemporary figures were united in the same discourse so that Apollo, Jupiter, Hercules, and Henri II became interchangeable. As critics have already noted, mythology was in fact the principal instrument of flattery at the court of Henri II.[42] Moreover, the written and thus "durable" form of his poems allowed Ronsard to offer the king eternal renown. As with Pindar, he praised his contemporaries as in the **"Usure a luimesme,"**[43] where he borrows the title given by Pindar to an ode to Agesidomas in the *Olympics:* Henri II here replaces the Greek hero. What Ronsard proposed to the king appears clearly in the following passage:

> Therefore your renown
> Will reach the heavens, animated
> By the labor of my hands:
> Such a durable treasure
> Describing the royal grandeur
> You should look upon favorably.[44]

Poetry possessed a functional aspect for Ronsard. The value of the poem is calculated in proportion to what it could yield to the person who becomes historically objectified in and by the verses. Much more than words artistically juxtaposed and beautifully arranged, poetry, in the sixteenth century, also served to establish differences between individuals and social classes. It contributed to the reinforcement of social order and instituted itself as a discipline designed to establish distinction. The beauty of the rhyme also served to define social classes and to distinguish between individuals:

> For Kings and Emperors
> Differ from laborors
> Only if someone sings their glory.[45]

As the seventh ode of the first book of the *Odes* would have us understand, no monument could better preserve the memory of kings than the poems promised by Ronsard. These "would render your renown alive," and the rhyme "could perpetuate your name,"[46] since "without the Muses the kings cannot live twice."[47] It is not enough for the prince to win battles, subjugate peoples, and accumulate a fortune; it is equally necessary for him to think of his glory for future generations. This offer of an existence for posterity was precisely the object of Ronsard's work: the *Odes* attempt to demonstrate the poet's mastery of this sort of exercise and accentuate his knowledge of the poetic tradition. Not only do the *Odes* emphasize the competence of the author to glorify the prince, but they also give credibility to his search for employment. On this point Ronsard is explicit:

> On the banks of Acheron: this glory is only
> Conceded by God to those daughters which Memory
> Conceived by Jupiter, to bestow upon those
> Who attract the poets with their gifts.[48]

In order to convince the sovereign of the importance of poetry, the poet was therefore forced to transform himself into a courtier. Nobody escaped the game of the adulators and the flatterers at the court of Henri II. Ronsard solicited and begged more than ever; in his demands he often showed some insolence and effrontery and even developed a theory of impudence:

> Impudence nourishes honor and the State.
> Impudence nourishes the screeching lawyers,
> Nourishes the courtiers, sustains the gendarmes.
> Impudence is today the best weapon
> One can enlist, even for the one
> Who wishes to succeed at court. . . . [49]

If impudence can provide the poet with the expected considerations, he will eventually become "the most impudent" and, like a "leech," he will never leave the prince's footsteps until he receives "the bait of a sweet favor."[50]

Helped by friends in high position, Ronsard had to frequent the immediate entourage of the king and praise the nobility. He spent a good part of his youth at the Louvre. However, although he was a regular attendant of the Parisian salons, Ronsard never became a good courtier and was in fact often maladroit. He revealed on several occasions his ignorance of the subtleties of the court[51] and complained later of the time he had lost because of these activities. In the second book of the *Melanges,* published in 1559, the poet admits his error to one of the most illustrious courtiers of his epoch—the cardinal of Chatillon, Odet de Coligny:

> Suddenly abandoning the Muses, I conceived
> Bishoprics, priories and abbeys, amazed
> To see myself transformed from a schoolboy
> Into a new courtier and restless court-bidder.
> Oh! That ambition unwillingly clothes itself!
> Thus I learned to take the path to the Louvre,
> Against my nature I learned to attend to
> Both your rising and your retiring.[52]

Ronsard had nevertheless to play the game and comply with the decorum of the court. Intrigues, alliances, and manipulations were the price to be paid in order to obtain the ecclesiastic positions and other compensations that could assure the poet's financial security. With this perspective in mind, Ronsard endeavoured to organize a "lobby," since before labor can be rewarded, it is first necessary that one's work be recognized:

> But it is necessary to bid the great gods of the court,
> To follow them, serve them, attend their table,
> To deliver before them a delectable story,
> To court them, watch them, and often bid their favor,
> Otherwise your labor will amount to no more than wind,
> Otherwise your science and your esteemed lyre,
> For lack of these, will dissipate like smoke.[53]

Ronsard clearly wrote his *Odes* in this prospect and from 1550 worked out what has justly been called a "theory of mendicancy."[54]

Impudence and mendicancy form the intrinsic polarities inherent in every ambitious young person. On one hand, it is in fact necessary to accept the authority of the potential patron who wields the hiring power, but on the other hand, it is equally important to show to the latter a certain detachment and aloofness that can eventually extend to the point of insolence and therefore indicate a certain autonomy and creative independence of the poet, showing his desire to place himself above the rest of job seekers. The *Odes* offer many examples of the interactions between these two poles that perhaps appear contradictory but are nonetheless strategically desirable. Impudence and mendicancy enabled Ronsard to sustain two discourses simultaneously: the poet new to the market of poetry addressed the prince with a sweet, soft-spoken tone—it is here the young man seeking his first employment who speaks to us—and, finally, in attempting to prove himself the equal of Pindar and master of the Muses, Ronsard could behave boldly and impudently before the king; his authority in poetry assured him this possibility. Thus, if Ronsard wished to secure employment and be accepted as the first poet of France, he had to maneuver between these two discourses with subtlety. What Ronsard sought to reconcile in the end are the two dreams of every beginner: glory and fortune.

In total we have observed five or six years of continual pursuit of a decently remunerated position. As we have seen, the long road of such an apprentice poet as Ronsard in search of first employment was not without hurdles. A sociological reading of the first writings of the Vendômois poet effectively permits us to ponder the function of the male poet during the sixteenth century, and highlights problems concerning the physical and material existence of these professionals of rhyme. We have seen how, by placing poetry and the poet within their social context, it is possible to raise questions of a conjectural nature concerning the ambiguous situation of the poet within a network of political and economic constraints. I have underlined several difficulties encountered by the poet at the beginning of his career, a period when it was not a question of describing what he desired but rather of imposing himself on the market and obtaining a first employment.

Notes

1. See the studies of Roger Doucet, *Les Institutions de la France au XVIe siècle,* 2 vols. (Paris: Editions A. et J. Picard, 1948); Roland Mousnier, *Les Hiérarchies sociales de 1450 à nos jours* (Paris: Presses Universitaires de France, 1969); and George Huppert, *Les Bourgeois Gentilshommes, An Essay on the Definition of Elites in Renaissance France* (Chicago: University of Chicago Press, 1977).

2. Roland Mousnier, *La Vénalité des offices sous Henri IV et Louis XIII* (Paris: Presses Universitaires de France, 1971); see the second chapter, "Les temps modernes: le XVIe siècle," pp. 35-92. See also Doucet, *Institutions de la France,* more particularly the chapter on "Le système bénéficial," pp. 693-718.

3. Henri Weber, *La Création poétique au XVIe siècle en France de Maurice Scève à Agrippa d'Aubigné* (Paris: Nizet, 1955); see the chapter on "La condition sociale des poètes et l'influence de la vie de cour," pp. 63-106.

4. Charles Loyseau, *Cinq Livres du Droict des Offices, suivis du Traitez des Seigneuries et de celui des Ordres* [1610]. I use here the edition of his *Œuvres complètes* published in Paris in 1666 by Alliot, p. 42 ("toutesfois les Casuistes tiennent qu'à present l'usage ou coustume inveterée excuse de resider aux Benefices simples" [my translation; all subsequent translations are mine]). On the legislation of ecclesiastical benefices during the sixteenth century, see Jean Gérardin, *Etude sur les bénéfices ecclésiastiques aux XVIe et XVIIe siècles* [1897] (Geneva: Slatkine Reprints, 1971).

5. Loyseau, *Cinq Livres du Droict des Offices,* p. 43 ("Ainsi donc l'exercise ayant esté fait separable du titre, le labeur du loyer, l'Office du Benefice: bref le spirituel du temporel, la pluspart des Beneficiers ont esté bien aises, en retenant le titre & revenu de leur Benefice, de se décharger de l'exercise & labeur des pauvres gens").

6. Loyseau, *Cinq Livres du Droict des Offices,* p. 460 ("les benefices simples . . . consist[ent] plus en revenu, qu'en fonction personelle").

7. Loyseau, *Cinq Livres du Droict des Offices,* p. 335 ("il y a une grande troupe d'Aumôniers, de Chappelains & de Clercs").

8. Loyseau, *Cinq Livres du Droict des Offices,* p. 460 ("on ne met plus par choix les hommes aux Offices de l'Eglise, mais on baille les Benefices aux hommes qu'on veut gratifier").

9. See Paul Bonnefon, "Ronsard ecclésiastique," *Revue d'Histoire Littéraire de la France* 2 (1895), 244-48. Though he had already been curé at the vicarage of Marolles associated with the diocese of Meaux since 1552, Ronsard ceded this charge in 1554 in order to become curé of Chally, as this vicarage, granted by the cardinal Jean Du Bellay, had revenues superior to those at Marolles. The curé of Chally replaced Ronsard at Marolles; yet the poet reserved for himself an annual rent of 50 livres on the occasion of this succession. In 1556 Ronsard obtained the vicarage of Evaillé, near Le Mans, and added the rent from this vicarage to that from Marolles. In 1557 he accepted a third benefice—the vicarage of Champfleur—granted by his friend Pisseleu, bishop of Condom. Ronsard renounced this latter charge in 1561, since he had in the meantime obtained the archdeaconry of Château-du-Loir. However, these three appointments yielded relatively little, and it was only under Charles IX that Ronsard replaced Amyot as abbot of Bellozane (1564) and was granted the priories of Saint-Cosme-lès-Tours (1565), Saint-Guingalois de Château-du-Loir (1569), and Saint-Cosme-lès-Montoire (1569). These last four priories and abbeys assured him good revenues. It is necessary to add that Ronsard received also the title of *aumonier ordinaire* (chaplain) of Charles IX and Henri III, a charge which guaranteed a pension of 1,200 livres per year. All those benefices acquired under the reign of Charles IX would not, however, increase after his death. Under Henri III the favors toward the poet became less frequent.

10. Raymond Lebègue, "Ronsard poète officiel," *Studi in onore di Vittorio Lugli e Diego Valeri* (Venise: Neri Pozza, 1961), pp. 373-87.

11. See the commentary of Paul Laumonier in *La Vie de P. de Ronsard* [1586], historical and critical introduction and commentary by Paul Laumonier (Geneva: Slatkine Reprints, 1969), p. 132.

12. On the royal entries during the sixteenth century, see Antoinette Huon, "Le thème du Prince dans les entrées parisiennes au XVIe siècle" and V. L. Saulnier, "L'entrée de Henri II à Paris et la révolution poétique de 1550," in Jean Jacquot, ed., *Les Fêtes de la Renaissance* (Paris: CNRS, 1956); and I. D. McFarlane, *The Entry of Henri II into Paris, 16 June 1549* (New York: Medieval & Renaissance Texts & Studies, 1982). See also the book of Josèphe Chartrou, *Les Entrées solennelles et triomphales à la Renaissance (1484-1551)* (Paris: Presses Universitaires de France, 1928).

13. Daniel Ménager, "Ronsard et le poème de circonstance," in Louis Terreaux, ed., *Culture et pouvoir au tempts de l'Humanisme et de la Renaissance* (Geneva, Paris: Slatkine & Champion, 1978), p. 319. On occasion poetry, see Predrag Matvejévitch, *La Poésie de circonstance, étude des formes de l'engagement poétique* (Paris: Nizet, 1971).

14. Ronsard, *Hymne de France* (ll. 217-19), in Paul Laumonier, ed. *Œuvres complètes,* 18 vols. (Paris: Société des Textes Français Modernes, 1914-67), I, 35 ("Moy ton Poëte, ayant premier osé / Avoir ton loz en ryme composé, / Je te supply, qu'à gré te soit ma lyre."). Unless otherwise indicated, all references to Ronsard are to this edition and appear in the text with the number of the book, ode, and lines in parentheses.

15. *Odes,* "A Bouju Angevin" (I, X, 17-24), I, 122-23 ("Mais mon ame n'est ravie / Que d'une brulante envie / D'oser un labeur tenter / Pour mon grand Roi contenter, / Afin que le miel de l'euvre / Son oreille oigne si bien, / Que facile je la treuve / L'importunan pour mon bien.")

16. *Odes,* "Au lecteur," I, 47 ("petit sonnet petrarquizé, ou quelque mignardise d'amour").

17. With respect to this subject, it should be noted that Ronsard often deleted from new editions odes which no longer served a particular function.

18. This text is reproduced in Pierre de Nolhac, *Ronsard et l'humanisme* (Paris: Champion, 1921), pp. 262-70.

19. *Odes,* "A Jouachim Du Bellai Angevin" (I, IX, 16), I, 109 ("emmieller les renoms").

20. *Ode de la Paix* (499-500), III, 35 ("sonneur / De l'une & de l'autre gloire").

21. *Odes,* "Au lecteur," I, 48 ("ma boutique n'est chargée d'autres drogues que de louanges, & d'honneurs").

22. Michel Dassonville, *Ronsard: étude historique et littéraire,* II, *A la conquête de la toison d'or (1545-1550)* (Geneva: Droz, 1970), 16.

23. Etienne Pasquier, *Choix de lettres sur la Littérature, la Langue et la Traduction,* published and annotated by D. Thickett (Geneva: Droz, 1956), pp. 5-6 ("servitude a demy courtisane," "que ne fissiez si bon marché de vostre plume à hault-louer quelques-uns que nous sçavons notoirement n'en estre dignes"). The Protestants Antoine de La Roche-Chandier and Bernard de Montméja also reproached Ronsard for his flattery and servility directed toward those of high rank. Our poet defended himself against these accusations in 1563 by writing a "Response de Pierre Ronsard, aux injures & calomnies de je ne sçay quels Predicantereaux & Ministreaux de Genéve," published in *Discours des Misères de ce temps.* On Ronsard's response, see Ullrich Langer, "A Courtier's Problematic Defense: Ronsard's 'Responce aux injures,'" *Bibliothèque d'Humanisme et Renaissance* 46, no. 2 (1984), 343-55.

24. *Second Livre des Meslanges,* "A Monsieur Du Thier" (7), X, 39 ("la gloire des Roys en suget est fertile").

25. *Odes,* "Au Roi Henri IIe de ce nom" (36-37), dedication of the third edition of the *Odes* appearing in 1555 and reproduced by Charles Guérin in his edition of the *Odes* (Paris: Editions du Cèdre, 1952), p. 4 ("Toutefois le desir qui le coeur m'aiguillonne / De te montrer combien je suis ton serviteur").

26. *Odes,* "Au lecteur," I, 43 ("Mais quand tu m'appelleras le premier auteur Lirique François, & celui qui a guidé les autres au chemin de si honneste labeur, lors tu me rendras ce que tu me dois, & je m'efforcerai te faire apprendre qu'en vain je ne l'aurai receu").

27. *Odes,* "Au Roi Henri II" (1-8); in Guérin, *Odes,* p. 145 ("Comme on voit le navire attendre bien souvent / Au premier front du port la conduite du vent / Afin de voyager, haussant la voile enflée / Du côté que le vent sa poupe aura soufflée, / Ainsi, Prince, je suis sans bouger, attendant / Que ta faveur royale aille un jour commandant / A ma nef d'entreprendre un chemin honorable / Du côté que ton vent lui sera favorable").

28. *Odes,* "Au lecteur," I, 50 ("gouter les mannes de la roialle grandeur").

29. *Odes,* "Au Roi Henri IIe de ce nom" (71-74); in Guérin, *Odes,* p. 5 ("Ainsi, suivant les dieux, je te suppli' de prendre / A gré ce petit don, pour l'usure d'attendre / Un présent plus parfait et plus digne d'un roi / Que jà ma Calliope enfante dedans moi.").

30. Jean-Paul Sartre, "Le séquestré de Venise: les fourberies de Jacopo," *Les Temps Modernes* no. 141 (Nov. 1957); text reproduced in *Situations IV* (Paris: Gallimard, 1964), pp. 291-346.

31. *Odes,* "A Michel de l'Hospital" (V, VIII, 6), III, 119 ("main laborieuse"); and "A Jan de la Hurteloire" (II, XIV, 15), I, 215 ("laborieuse main").

32. *Odes,* "A Jouachim Du Bellai Angevin" (I, IX, 14), I, 109 ("art de mon pouce").

33. *Odes,* "Au Seigneur de Carnavalet" (I, VI, 37), I, 92 ("labeur de mes dois").

34. Isidore Silver, "Ronsard poète rusé," *Cahiers de l'Association Internationale des Etudes Françaises* no. 22 (1970), 41-52.

35. *Odes,* "A Bertran Berger de Poitiers" (I, XV, 11), I, 139 ("Je suis le trafiqueur des Muses").

36. Ronsard uses the word "labeur" 152 times in his work. If one compares the frequency of this word with the rest of Ronsard's vocabulary—which extends to more than 12,000 words—one sees that this noun occupies the 430th position. The verbs "être," "faire," "avoir," "voir," etc., as well as a large number of adverbs and prepositions, evidently monopolize the top of the list. For more details on Ronsard's word usage, see A. E. Creore, *A Word-Index to the Poetic Works of Ronsard* (Leeds: W. S. Maney & Son, 1972).

37. *Odes,* "Au lecteur," I, 48 ("industrieusement").

38. *Odes,* "La Victoire de François de Bourbon" (I, V, 10), I, 83 ("ouvrier ingenieux").

39. *Abbrégé de l'Art Poëtique François,* XIV, 3 ("d'autant que l'artifice humain, experience & labeur le peuvent permettre, j'ay bien voulu t'en donner quelques reigles icy, afin qu'un jour tu puisses estre des premiers en la connaissance d'un si agreable métier").

40. Daniel Ménager has shown that the notion of "value" also occupies a central place in the *Hymnes;* in *Ronsard: le Roi, le Poète et les Hommes,* Travaux d'Humanisme et Renaissance, no. CLXIX (Geneva: Droz, 1979), p. 55. The "suyte de l'hymne au cardinal de Lorraine" illustrates well the preponderant importance of value in the *Hymnes.* Ménager believes, however, that in the end Ronsard refuses to "assign a price to his writing."

41. *Ode de la Paix* (469-78), III, 33-34 ("Prince, je t'envoie cette Ode, / Trafiquant mes vers à la mode /

Que le marchant baille son bien, / Troque pour troq': toi qui es riche, / Toi roi de biens, ne soi point chiche / De changer ton present au mien. / Ne te lasse point de donner, / Et tu verras comme j'acorde / L'honneur que je promai sonner / Quant un present dore ma corde").

42. Weber, *Création poétique,* p. 87.

43. *Odes,* "Usure a luimesme" (I, VII), I, 99-100.

44. *Odes,* "Au Seigneur de Carnavalet" (I, VI, 35-40), I, 92 ("Ores donq' ta renommée / Voira les cieus, animée / Par le labeur de mes dois: / Telle durable richesse / Sur la Roiale largesse / Heureuse estimer tu dois").

45. *Elegies, Mascarades et Bergerie,* "Ode à Monsieur de Verdun" (46-48), XIII, 258 ("Car les Rois & les Empereurs / Ne different aux laboureurs / Si quelcun ne chante leur gloire"). This ode was first published in 1565 in the *Elegies* before appearing in the later editions of the *Odes.*

46. *Odes,* "Usure a luimesme" (I, VII, 6, 8), I, 99 ("Ne feront vivre ton renom, / Pourra perpetuer ton nom").

47. *Odes,* "Au Roi Henri II" (117); in Guérin, *Odes,* p. 148 ("Sans les Muses deux fois les rois ne vivent pas").

48. *Odes,* "Au Roi Henri II" (119-22); in Guérin, *Odes,* p. 149 ("Aux rives d'Achéron: seulement cette gloire / Est de Dieu concédée aux filles que Mémoire / Conçut de Jupiter, pour la donner à ceux / Qui attirent par dons les poètes chez eux").

49. *Second Livre des Meslanges,* "Complainte contre Fortune" (423-28), X, 36-37 ("L'impudence nourrist l'honneur & les estas. / L'impudence nourrist les criards avocas, / Nourrist les courtizans, entretient les gendarmes: / L'impudence aujourd'hui sont les meilleures armes / Dont lon se puisse ayder, mesme à celuy qui veut / Parvenir à la court . . .").

50. *Second Livre des Meslanges* (431-41) ("le plus eshonté," "sangsue," "l'apast d'une douce faveur").

51. On the tactlessness of Ronsard before the court, see Michel Dassonville, *Ronsard: étude historique et littéraire,* and more particularly the third volume of his work, *Prince des poètes ou poète des Princes (1550-1556)* (Geneva: Droz, 1976), pp. 13-27.

52. *Second Livre des Meslanges,* "Complainte contre Fortune" (121-28), X, 22-23 ("Je conceu Eveschez, Prieurez, Abayes, / Soudain abandonnant les Muses, esbahyes / De me voir transformer d'un escolier contant / En nouveau courtizan, demandeur inconstant. / O que mal aisement l'ambition se couvre! / Lors j'apris le chemin d'aller souvent au Louvre, / Contre mon naturel j'apris de me trouver / Et a vostre coucher & à votre lever").

53. *Nouvelles Poésies,* "Compleinte a la Royne Mere du Roy" (296-302), XII, 186-87 ("Mais il te faut prier les grands dieux de la court, / Les suyvre, les servir, se trouver à leur table, / Discourir devant eux un conte delectable, / Les courtizer, les voir, & les presser souvent, / Autrement ton labeur ne seroit que du vent, / Autrement la science & ta lyre estimée / (Pour n'user de cet art) s'en iroit en fumée").

54. Isidore Silver, "Pierre de Ronsard: Panegyrist, Pensioner and Satirist of the French Court," *Romantic Review* 45 (1954), 92.

Lance K. Donaldson-Evans (essay date 1988)

SOURCE: "Demons, Portents, and Visions: Fantastic and Supernatural Elements in Ronsard's Poetry," in *Renaissance Rereadings: Intertext and Context,* pp. 225-35. Urbana: University of Illinois Press, 1988.

[In the following essay, Donaldson-Evans discusses the element of fantasy in Ronsard's poetry.]

For anyone who is familiar with much of the recent criticism devoted to *le fantastique,* the idea of viewing certain poetic texts of Ronsard as examples of this genre might well seem preposterous, anachronistic—indeed fantastic! First of all, Todorov, in his perceptive *Introduction à la littérature fantastique,* seems to preclude any such possibility when he states categorically: "We see now why the poetic reading constitutes a danger for the fantastic. If as we read a text we reject all representation, considering each sentence as a pure semantic combination, the fantastic could not appear . . . the fantastic can subsist only within fiction: poetry cannot be fantastic."[1]

A second problem confronting anyone rash enough to consider Ronsard from the perspective of the fantastic is the chronological dilemma. Many critics follow the lead of Castex in equating the rise of the fantastic with Romanticism. Now, while there is little doubt that the nineteenth century represents the Golden Age of fantastic literature, it is my contention—and fortunately I am not alone—that the fantastic is far from being a Romantic invention but is instead a phenomenon which resists such precise dating, one which occurs at least as early as the Renaissance.

However, for the moment, I want to return to the first problem and address Todorov's claim that poetry and the fantastic are incompatible. Obviously the first step in attempting to reconcile Todorov's view and my own is to arrive at a satisfactory working definition as to what constitutes the fantastic.

The etymological source of the word *fantastique* is a useful, indeed a necessary, place to begin: *fantaisie, fantastique, fantasque, fantasme* in all their meanings derive from the Greek verb *phantazein* (to make visible) and *phantazesthai* (to have visions) which produced the noun *phantasia* meaning "appearance" and later "phantom," as well as "faculty of imagination." So when Ronsard describes himself as being "fantastique d'esprit" as he does in **"L'Hymne de l'autonne,"** although the primary meaning of the adjective is something like "inventive" or perhaps even "visionary," it is neither illegitimate nor anachronistic to suggest important etymological and conceptual links between Ronsard's description of himself and the modern literary sense of *fantastique*. Of course, in sixteenth-century French, as Huguet's dictionary attests, the adjective *fantastique* also has a negative connotation, since it can mean "fou, insensé, extravagant" (mad or crazy). However, as madness was often considered to be related to the supernatural as well as to the process of literary creation, these meanings complement, without excluding, the etymological content of the word, a content which would be well known to a French Renaissance poet who had studied Greek at the Collège de Coqueret, as had Ronsard.

Perhaps one of the most practical definitions of the fantastic, however, is that given by Pierre-Georges Castex: "The fantastic is characterised by . . . the brutal intrusion of the mysterious into the context of everyday life."[2] Such a definition has the advantage of receiving the approval of Todorov himself and has been glossed by other critics such as Jacques Finné, who proposes the following version: "We can consider as fantastic any human being or in fact any entity encountered on the fringe of everyday human experience and whose sudden appearance violates the accepted rules of human existence."[3] It is this definition which I shall adopt as being the most fundamental account of the fantastic, a definition which aptly describes the many intrusions of the mysterious in Ronsard's verse as well as the many apparitions of beings which come from the periphery of everyday human experience.

Before proceeding, we need to return for a moment to Todorov for whom the *fantastique* is a peculiarly volatile, even fragile genre, being situated between *l'étrange* and *le merveilleux*. Indeed, for him, the *fantastique* lasts only as long as a certain hesitation either on the part of the reader or of one of the characters in a story as to whether apparently inexplicable events can be explained according to the laws of nature, or whether in fact they are the result of supernatural intervention. Once this hesitation passes, the *fantastique* will be incorporated either into the category of *l'étrange* (the supernatural explained) or *le merveilleux* (the supernatural accepted).[4] If we were to apply this criterion with total rigor, all the fantastic elements in Ronsard's verse would probably be assimilable to the *le merveilleux* and yet, as we shall see, there is often a feeling of the uncanny, which creates an atmosphere similar to that found in literature characterized "officially" as *fantastique*. In fact, Todorov's account of the fantastic is much less rigid than it first appears, and later in his text, when analyzing a story from the *Thousand and One Nights,* he recognizes the presence of supernatural beings as one of the pervasive features of the *fantastique:* "The other group of fantastic elements is based on the very existence of supernatural beings, such as the genie and the princess-sorceress, and on their power over human destiny. Both are capable of trans-

forming themselves and others, and both can fly or transport beings and objects in space, etc. This is one of the constants of the literature of the fantastic: the existence of supernatural beings more powerful than men."[5] In his hymn **"Les Daimons,"** Ronsard represents such supernatural beings and stresses their capacity for metamorphosis:

> Just as the Demons, whose body is so nimble,
> Pliable, supple, active, and transformable,
> Quickly change their shape, so that their agile body
> Is metamorphosed into whatever form it pleases:

(ll. 91-94)

. . . . .

> One ofttimes sees them changed into strange beasts,
> Their bodies cut into pieces: one of them has but a head,
> Another only eyes, another has but arms,
> While only the shaggy feet of yet another remain visible.

(ll. 99-102)[6]

If Todorov can include stories from the *Thousand and One Nights* in his discussion, it does not seem unreasonable to examine this particular Ronsard text, and in fact many others, from the perspective of the fantastic.

However, what of his objection that the *fantastique* and poetry are mutually exclusive? Once again we find ourselves confronted by a rigid definition which is less rigid than it appears. In the first place, Todorov himself admits that the differentiation he has already established between poetry and fiction (that fiction is representative while poetic images are nondescriptive) is a matter of degree rather than of binary opposition.[7] And if we move away from a structuralist/formalist approach, we can allow a certain referentiality, a certain fictionality to be inherent to some and perhaps all poetic genres. While "pure" lyric poetry might best be considered as a hermetic, self-referential verbal construct, other poetic genres, particularly in a period like the Renaissance, are replete with representational, fictional elements which cannot be reduced to a simple "verbal chain" or "semantic combination." Most of the Ronsard texts we are dealing with fall into such a referential category, which means that these examples of his poetry can in fact be considered to be perfectly legitimate vehicles for the *fantastique* (as, incidentally, Vax and Vircondelet among others, have already suggested).[8]

Most of the fantastic/supernatural elements in Ronsard's poetry are concentrated in the figure of the demon, that curiously ambiguous creature who makes his appearance in Ronsard's poetry quite early as a positive presence often associated directly with poetic inspiration. In the **"Ode à Joachim du Bellay"** from the first book of the *Odes,* Ronsard describes the ministrations of the demons to poets:

A Demon accompanies them,
The most learned Demon of all,
And he instructs them every night, as they dream
So that they learn from him without effort.
Although demigod, he is willing
Mere mortals to inform,
So that man, while yet asleep,
Can learn all knowledge.

(ll. 25-33)[9]

In texts such as this one, Ronsard's portrayal of the demons is positive: they are seen as benevolent manifestations of the supernatural world order which forms part of the poet's cosmos. They do not in any way constitute an incursion into the fantastic.

However, this is far from always being the case and when demons come to personify not only the good, but also the malevolent forces in the universe, it is then that they trigger the *frisson* and the hesitation which are signs of the fantastic. One of the texts where this is most clearly seen is the enigmatic **"Le Chat"** from *Le Premier Livre des Poemes.* This fascinating poem, which begins with a strongly affirmative declaration of religious faith ("God is omnipresent, and is everywhere active, / Beginning, end and middle / Of every living thing, and His soul is contained / In everything and gives life to all creatures, / Just as our soul gives life to our bodies" [ll. 1-5]),[10] quickly reveals a fundamental tension between faith and superstition, between the Christian and the pagan supernatural, a tension which is only superficially resolved in the final lines by the assertion of man's God-given preeminence over the animal kingdom. However, this closing affirmation stands in sharp contrast to the general movement of the poem. The initial paean of praise to an omnipresent divinity leads to a discussion of divination by means of animals, birds, and plants, and includes a number of examples which the poet claims come from his own personal experience.

Firstly, there is the story of the "Thessalienne," the daphne, a variety of laurel, upon which the poet had been lavishing his most careful attention ("I watered it, kept it free from weeds, dug up the soil around it / Morning and evening; my intention was / To use its branches to make a fine wreath for my head . . ." [ll. 77-79]). Mysteriously, one brief hour after having given the plant its morning watering, the poet found the formerly thriving plant dying. The only possible explanation was a supernatural one ("One hour later I found it uprooted / By a Demon; no mortal hand / Could have been responsible: it all happened too suddenly" [ll. 84-86]). This was not only an act of malevolence on the part of the Demon in question (and all this in a universe in which God is everywhere, infused in all beings), but a prophecy, since, subsequently, Ronsard fell ill and languished like the daphne, although, unlike the plant, he did not die. The "murder" (Ronsard calls it thus) of the daphne was coupled with another bad omen, as, two months later, one of his servants, mortally wounded by a horse's kick, called to him and fixed his eyes on him at the moment of his death. Both of these omens proved to be accurate and for eleven long months, Ronsard's broken body was wracked by persistent fever. While the attribution of Ronsard's illness to the intervention of a demon might seem to be simply a continuation of a long-standing tradition which goes back to biblical times, the omens themselves, particularly the mysterious death of the plant, represent precisely that transgression of natural laws, that brutal intrusion of the mysterious into everyday life, which constitute the very stuff of the fantastic.

The poet's dread reaches a paroxysm when, after more than a hundred lines, he finally turns his attention to the animal after which the poem is named. The "triste Chat" is the creature which has the most "esprit prophetique" (and which therefore should logically be one of the animals which is closest to God). However, the cat fills the poet with utter dread:

There was never a man living
Who hates cats more than I do;
I hate their staring eyes, their faces,
And when I see them, I flee from their presence,
Trembling all over from head to foot. . . .

(ll. 114-18)

Throughout this section of the poem a subtle link between demon, cat, and poet is established, a link which perhaps helps to explain the astonishing apprehension Ronsard feels for this particular animal. It is significant that the plant attacked and destroyed by the demon is a daphne, long associated with poetic creation, a plant which Ronsard specifically identifies with his own textual activity by stating that he intended to make a crown of laurel for himself from its leaves. As for the cat, Ronsard establishes a double correlation between it and poetic creation. Firstly, the adjective he uses to describe the dreaded animal is *triste,* an epithet which suggests melancholy, the temperament favourable to poetic production. Secondly the cat, like the demon, is endowed with prophetic powers, a gift also shared by the poet in Ronsard's literary universe. In this poem the demon (and the cat) represent the reverse face of the demon of poetic inspiration, and the dread Ronsard feels in the face of their intrusion into his everyday world is in fact a metonymy for the ultimate dread of any poet of any age: the fear of the Muses' flight, the phobia of poetic sterility. If all writing is about writing and all poetry about the poetic act, then the inscrutable and unpredictable intrusion of the fantastic into everyday life is the perfect figure for that most unpredictable of events: the outpouring of inspiration, variously seen by poets across the ages as the gift of the gods or as arising from some dark, demonic source.

Of course the poetic text where demons and demonology are most prevalent is the hymn **"Les Daimons."** This is a poem which has always particularly intrigued me and which has been the object of a great deal of commentary, thanks in part to Albert-Marie Schmidt's excellent critical edition. Nowhere is both the omnipresence and the ambiguity of the demon more abundantly clear. The demons are the inhabitants of the air and are thus intermediaries between the residents of the heavens (the angels and ultimately God) and those of the earth, mankind. Part air, part fire, their domain of predilection is the turbulent troposphere, "tousjours remply de vents, de foudres et d'orages." The demons are like their fellow inhabitants of this domain, the clouds, and, as we have already seen they have the same power of metamorphosis, the same ability to create monsters, except that the demons can bring these monsters to earth to frighten mortal men. Just as the air transmits to our eyes the images of objects in the material world, so the demons, creatures of air, transmit to the eyes of our mind, to our imagination, visions:

> Just as the Demons reveal their masquerades
> To our imagination which is capable of perceiving such things,
> Then our imagination transmits them to our minds,
> In the same fashion and way
> As it imagines them sleeping, or waking,
> Then our hearts are assailed by a sudden fear,
> Our hair stands up straight upon our heads,
> And from our brows, drop by drop,
> Sweat drips down to our feet.
> If we are abed, we dare not lift our arms,
> Nor even turn our body under the sheets;
> At such times we think we see our fathers
> Dead in their winding sheet, and we hear our poor, dead mothers,
> Speaking to us in the night, and we see in visions
> Our friends perishing in shipwrecks.

(ll. 125-38)[11]

And the list of *terreurs nocturnes* goes on as these supernatural creatures are presented as the source of such phenomena. As we can see from these verses, demons are held responsible for nightmares and portents. They are also associated with what many consider to be the fantastic subject par excellence: the ghost.

There are, however, good demons and it is through these creatures of the air that man receives the gift of prophecy:

> The good Demons come down to earth from the heavens
> To reveal the will of the Gods to us,
> And then transmit to God our prayers and actions.
> They free our fettered souls from our bodies
> To take them up there, so that they can imagine
> What we need to know for our instruction.
> They show us in the night, through marvelous dreams,
> The true presages of the good and ill that is to befall us.

(ll. 209-16)[12]

These good demons inspire no horror, just as the supernatural elements in fairy stories do not per se provoke fear, so perhaps we should modify Todorov's treatment of the relationship between the fantastic and the supernatural to state that benign supernatural beings and events do not produce the uncanny sensation associated with the fantas-

tic, while malevolent, capricious spirits do. In any case, Ronsard appears to be far more fascinated by the malevolent variety than by the good, and in subsequent verses of the poem he details the activities of the bad demons, which range from the transmission of "pestes, fiévres, langueurs" to the production of apocalyptic signs in the heavens:

> They make noises in the air to frighten us,
> They make our human eyes see two suns in the sky,
> They turn the moon black
> And cause a bloody rain to fall from the sky.

(ll. 225-28)

Ronsard then goes on to discuss "Incubes, Larves, Lares, Lemurs, Penates, et Succubes," all favorite subjects of later fantastic literature, and does not even neglect the somewhat playful, if frightening, activity of the poltergeists:

> They move seats, tables and tressles in the night,
> Keys, doors, sideboards, beds, chairs and stools,
> They count our treasure or hurl to the ground
> Now a sword, now a glass. . . .

(ll. 245-48)

However, the most striking example of *le fantastique* in this poem is the recital of an encounter with supernatural and diabolical beings which is found in lines 347-70. The poem's persona recounts how, one night, at the witching hour ("Un soir, vers la minuict . . .") he was on his way to visit his mistress when he found himself pursued by supernatural hellhounds ("I heard, or so it seemed to me, a barking pack / Of dogs following in my footsteps . . ." [ll. 351-52]). Leading the hunt is a disquieting skeletonlike figure mounted on a black horse, who stretches out his bony hand to Ronsard:

> I saw close to me on a large black horse
> A man who was nothing but bones,
> Holding out his hand to invite me to mount upon the horse behind him. . . .

(ll. 353-55)

The protagonist is seized with dread at the sight of these terrible apparitions and although he is wearing armor and is carrying a dagger, sword, and shield, he is nonetheless paralyzed with fear. It is only thanks to the remembrance that demons fear the naked blade of a sword, a remembrance which he sees as divinely inspired, that the poem's protagonist draws his weapon, with the result that the horrible specters flee. Ronsard's persona, when confronted by these demonic manifestations of the supernatural, gives voice to a feeling of dread which even his religious faith seems unable to overcome completely. The poem finishes with a prayer addressed to God which asks for protection from the evil variety of demonic forces and then, in an ironic twist which acts as a kind of poetic exorcism to dispel the fears which the poem has so eloquently expressed, Ronsard calls for the visitation of the demons upon the heads of those who are unappreciative of his poetry:

O Lord God, in whom I put my trust,
For the honor of your name, please grant,
Oh please, that never again will I find
Such apparitions in my path, but rather, Oh Lord,
Send them far from Christendom, send the Turks
These Goblins, Demons, Ghosts and Spirits,
Or else call them down upon the heads of those
Who dare say ill of the poems I sing on my new lyre.

(ll. 421-28)

The perfect revenge of the poet!

However, although demons (good and bad) are treated in many other texts of Ronsard in similar fashion to their portrayal in **"Le Chat"** and **"Les Daimons,"** they are not always associated with the uncanny and the fantastic. Even ghosts do not always give rise to a feeling of the numinous in Ronsard's verse. A case in point is the curious **"Prosopopée de Louys de Ronsard,"** a short work from the *Second Livre des Poemes* which recounts the appearing in a dream or a vision (it is not quite clear which) of Louis de Ronsard, the poet's deceased father. The poem purports to be a rebuttal of those philosophies which deny any immortality to the soul and is highly stylized with Vergilian overtones of Anchises appearing to Aeneas. It is just before dawn (the most propitious time for reliable dreams or visions) that the poet has this particular encounter with the supernatural:

I saw hovering over my bed an apparition,
Thin, without bones, which possessed the eyes, the face,
The body, the shape, and the voice
Of my dear father when he was of this world.

(ll. 9-12)[13]

The apparition becomes more frightening when it touches him three times, then leaves the bed three times, finally returning to take the poet's left hand and admonish him. What follows this evocation of the specter of his father is however quite unexceptional and we leave the threshold of the fantastic to fall into the sermon, since Louis's advice to his son is a standard paternal homily. At the end of his speech, Louis de Ronsard vanishes, leaving his son literally grasping at thin air:

but the shadowy Form,
Escaping from my clutch, flew away like the wind

and as night yields to day, the poet awakens, marveling ("tout esmerveillé"). Here the *merveilleux* is relatively benign, even if the image of the father is described as terrifying ("affreuse") in line 15, and the realm of the fantastic is approached from afar without being entered. What the supernatural frame of the poem does do, however, is to add interest to the rather banal advice the ghost gives to his son, advice he could have found in the Bible or in any number of pious treaties. Here the supernatural is an effective device to capture the reader's attention and to give weight to the father's words, although it does perhaps also

bear witness to Ronsard's abiding fascination with the fantastic in its most primal sense.

Are we then justified in considering Ronsard to be a *poète fantastique*? Perhaps not in the same way or to the same degree as some of the poets of the nineteenth century. I believe, however, we can legitimately describe certain elements in his work as fantastic and we can discover an uncanny, fantastic atmosphere in a small but significant number of his poems. If his brand of the *fantastique* belongs above all to Todorov's category of the *fantastique-merveilleux*, we are nonetheless in the presence of an embryonic *auteur fantastique* whose superstition is never fully conquered by his religious faith and who is able to portray effectively the feeling of the uncanny which results from the brutal intrusion of supernatural forces into everyday reality. The visceral fear of malevolent demons which Ronsard portrays so graphically in his poetry may well be the verbalization of that archetypal poetic fear: poetic impotence and sterility. Harold Bloom would perhaps see in this fear of the demon a metaphor for the anxiety of influence, since, as he says: "our daemon . . . came to us not from the fire but from our precursors."[14] However, no matter what psychological or literary explanations we might propose, the fact remains that Ronsard is a poet who is quite capable of provoking in his reader what Louis Vax has called "le frisson du fantastique."[15]

Notes

1. Tzvetan Todorov, *The Fantastic: A Structural Approach to a Literary Genre*, trans. Richard Howard (Cleveland: Case Western Reserve University Press, 1973), p. 60.

2. Pierre-Georges Castex, *Le conte fantastique en France de Nodier à Maupassant* (Paris: José Corti, 1951), p. 8 ("Le fantastique se caractérise . . . par une intrusion brutale du mystère dans le cadre de la vie réelle"). Unless otherwise indicated, all translations from the French are my own.

3. Jacques Finné, *La littérature fantastique* (Bruxelles: Editions de l'Université de Bruxelles, 1980), p. 13 ("Peut être considéré comme fantastique tout être humain ou toute entité dont la rencontre se situe en marge de l'expérience humaine courante; dont l'apparition viole les règles préétablies . . .").

4. Todorov, *Fantastic,* pp. 41ff.

5. Todorov, *Fantastic,* p. 109.

6. Pierre de Ronsard, *Oeuvres complètes,* ed. Paul Laumonier (Paris: Société des Textes Français Modernes, 1935), VIII ("Tout ainsi les Daimons qui ont le corps habile, / Aisé, souple, dispost, à se muer facile, / Changent bien tost de forme, et leur corps agile est / Transformé tout soudain en tout ce que leur plaist:" [ll. 91-94]; "Bien souvent on les voit, se transformer en beste, / Tronqués par la moytié: l'une n'a que la teste, / L'autre n'a que les

yeux, l'autre n'a que les bras, / Et l'autre que les piedz tous veluz par-à-bas" [ll. 99-102]).

7. Todorov, *Fantastic,* p. 59 ("Poetry too includes certain representative elements, and fiction properties which render the text, opaque, intransitive").

8. See Louis Vax, *La séduction de l'étrange* (Paris: Presses Universitaire de France, 1965) and Alain Vircondelet, *La poésie fantastique française* (Paris: Seghers, 1973).

9. Laumonier, I ("Un Démon les accompagne / Par-sur tous le mieux instruit, / Qui en songes toute nuit / Sans nul travail les enseigne, / Et demy-dieu ne desdeigne / De les aller informant, / Afin que l'homme en dormant / Toutes sciences appreigne" [ll. 25-33]).

10. Laumonier, XV, "Le Chat," ll. 1-5: ("Dieu est par tout, par tout se mesle Dieu, / Commencement, la fin et le milliue / De ce qui vit, et dont l'Ame est enclose / Par tout, et tient en vigueur toute chose, / Comme nostre ame infuse dans noz corps"). The French texts for the other sections of this poem are as follows: ll. 77-79 "Je l'arrosois, la cerclois et bechois / Matin et soir; la voyant je pensois / M'en faire au chef une belle couronne . . ."; ll. 84-86: "Une heure apres je la vis arrachée / Par un Démon; une mortelle main / Ne fist le coup: le fait fut trop soudain"; and ll. 114-18: "Homme ne vit qui tant haïsse au monde / Les Chats que moy d'une haine profonde; / Je hay leurs yeux, leur front et leur regard, / Et les voyant je m'enfuy d'autrepart, / Tremblant de nerfs, de veines et de membre' . . .".

11. "Les Daimons," ll. 125-38: "Tout ainsi les Daimons font leurs masqueures voir / A nostre fantaisie apte à les recevoir, / Puis nostre fantaisie à l'esprit les r'apporte / De la mesme façon et de la mesme sorte / Qu'elle les imagine ou dormant, ou veillant, / Et lors une grand'peur va noz coeurs assaillant, / Le poil nous dresse au chef, et du front, goutte-à-goutte, / Jusques à noz talons la sueur nous degoutte. / Si nous sommes au lict, n'osons lever les bras, / Ny tant soit peu tourner le corps entre les draps; / Adoncq' nous est advis que nous voyons noz peres / Morts dedans un linçueil, et noz defunctes meres / Parler à nous la nuict, et que voyons dans l'eau / Quelcun de noz amis perir dans un bateau." See also Albert-Marie Schmidt, *Les Daimons* (Paris: Albin Michel, 1939), for an excellent commentary on this poem.

12. "Les Daimons," ll. 209-16 ("Les bons viennent de l'air jusques en ces bas lieux / Pour nous faire sçavoir la volonté des Dieux, / Puis r'emportent à Dieu nos faictz et noz prieres, / Et detachent du corps noz ames prisonnieres / Pour les mener là-haut, à fin d'imaginer / Ce qui se doit sçavoir pour nous endoctriner. / Ils nous montrent de nuict par songes admirables / De noz biens et noz maux les signes veritables . . .").

The text of the other quotations from this hymn are as follows: ll. 225-28 ("Ilz font des sons en l'air pour nous espovanter, / Ilz font aux yeux humains deux Soleilz presenter, / Ilz font noircir la Lune horriblement hydeuse, / Et font pleurer le Ciel d'une pluye saigneuse"); ll. 245-48 ("Ilz remuent de nuict bancz, tables, et treteaux, / Clefz, huys, portes, buffetz, lictz, chaires, escabeaux, / Ou comptent noz tresors, ou gectent contre terre / Maintenant une espée, et maintenant un verre"); ll. 351-52 ("J'oüy, ce me sembloit, une aboyante chasse / De chiens qui me suyvoit pas-à-pas à la trace"); ll. 353-55 ("Je vy aupres de moy sur un grand cheval noir / Un homme qui n'avoit que les ôs, à le voir, / Me tendant une main pour me monter en crope"); and ll. 421-28 ("O Seigneur eternel, en qui seul gist ma foy, / Pour l'honneur de ton nom, de grace, donne moy, / Donne moy que jamais je ne trouve en ma voye / Ces paniques terreurs, mais, ô Seigneur, envoye / Loin de la Chrestienté, dans le païs des Turcz / Ces Larves, ces Daimons, ces Lares et Lemurs, / Ou sur le chef de ceux qui oseront mesdire / Des chansons que j'accorde à ma nouvelle lyre").

13. "Prosopopée," ll. 9-12: "j'apperceu sur mon lict une image / Gresle, sans oz, qui l'oeil et le visage, / Le corps, la taille, et la parole avoit / Du pere mien quand au monde il vivoit"; and ll. 61-62: "mais la nueuse Idole, / Fraudant mes doigts, ainsi que vent s'envole."

14. Harold Bloom, *The Anxiety of Influence* (London: Oxford University Press, 1973), p. 139.

15. Vax, *Séduction,* p. 60.

Jennifer Britnell (essay date 1989)

SOURCE: "Poetic Fury and Prophetic Fury," in *Renaissance Studies,* Vol. 3, No. 2, June, 1989, pp. 106-14.

[In the following essay, Britnell probes the connection between poetic and prophetic inspiration, using Ronsard as a principal example.]

In the Renaissance the poet's claim to divine inspiration was usually made in the context of Plato's four divine furies—poetry, the mysteries, prophecy, love. In this paper I shall look at certain aspects of the relationship between poetic fury and just one of the other forms of fury, prophecy. These two modes of inspiration are linked by the fact that in both cases the inspired person must express his inspiration in the form of verbal communication. Apollo, the god of prophecy, is also the patron of the Muses.

For both classical and later writers wishing to describe inspiration as divine fury, it was always rather easier to deal with prophecy than with poetry. Any discussion of the nature of poetry has to resolve a tension between technique and inspiration—between form and content, rhetoric and cognitive function. No such tension arises in the case of prophecy. The prophet proclaims the message he has been given by supernatural revelation; he is passing on otherwise unknowable knowledge.

For classical writers, prophecy suggested a range of activity reaching down from oracles to diviners. The example *par excellence* of prophetic fury was the Pythia at Delphi, who was so spectacularly overtaken by the god. Clearly highlighted in descriptions of the Pythia are the elements of alienation from normal mental processes, possession by a god and the imparting of otherwise inaccessible knowledge, but in an enigmatic guise.[1] Here is a recipe for prophetic fury. It should be noted, incidentally, that this knowledge is not necessarily a programme for the future: the prophet speaks out for the god, and may merely give advice and directions.[2]

The theory of the four furies is attractive to Renaissance Neoplatonic thought; it provides one of the connections between different levels of the spiritual hierarchy and one of the ways in which the human spirit is put in touch with the divine. When Ficino was commenting on Plato's description of the four furies in the *Ion,* he presented them as being in themselves a hierarchy of means by which the soul could be turned from diversity and disorder towards a unified state of adoration of God. In this hierarchy, poetic fury held the lowliest position; it was the first rung of the ladder, serving to induce harmony in the soul. The ladder ascends through mysteries and then prophecy to attain the pinnacle with love.[3] However, when commenting on the *Phaedrus,* Ficino admitted a wider scope for poetry by saying that it accompanied the other furies, because no man possessed by *furor* is content with ordinary speech.[4]

From the point of view of Renaissance poets, poetic fury was a dignifying notion, asserting their divine inspiration. But this dignity was lessened if its only function was to produce harmony. And so, as has been amply demonstrated by scholars, Pléiade poets did not on the whole exploit Ficino's hierarchy.[5] They preferred a higher view of poetic fury which sees it primarily as a means by which hidden universal truths are communicated to mankind through the intermediacy of the poet. Plato himself offers good authority for such a view, for in the *Ion* he illuminates the way in which God uses poets as ministers by comparing them to diviners and prophets: in all these cases, he says, God takes away their own minds in order that they shall utter words which are actually the words of God to men.[6] In this case it is of course quite difficult to make a distinction between prophetic and poetic fury, particularly when prophecy is not necessarily prediction. And indeed, poets are not concerned to make a clear distinction between prophecy and poetry; rather they exploit the similarity by using prophetic fury to serve as an illustrative figure, a means of understanding their high concept of poetic fury. This is particularly true of Ronsard, to whom I will return. Du Bellay is using the figure as a simile in *Regrets* VII

when his loss of poetic fury is compared to the Prophetess who ceases to feel the god and suddenly falls silent.[7]

The use of this figure presupposes that prophetic fury is more readily comprehensible to the reader and that it has a certain prestige. This brings us to the question of just how the Platonic theory of divine fury was syncretized with Christianity. The associations of the word *prophète* for a sixteenth-century reader would not instantly be oracles and diviners; rather they would be the prophets of the Old Testament, warning of God's wrath and foretelling the coming of Christ. Or they might be Christian prophets, above all St John on Patmos. Prophecy in Christian terms means announcing God's truth by the inspiration of the Holy Spirit. In Christian terms too it does not necessarily involve foretelling the future: thus a preacher who expounds God's word should be inspired by the spirit of prophecy.[8]

Through-going Neoplatonists and occultists simply merge the pagan and the Christian, seeking thereby to justify their thought system. Old Testament prophets march through Cornelius Agrippa's chapters on fury.[9] But what significance do such Christian associations of prophecy have for Pléiade poets laying claim to poetic fury? If prophetic fury is used to illustrate, explain and give prestige to poetic fury, then the Christian associations could be valuable. Richard Le Blanc in his translation of the *Ion* was happy enough to equate 'fureur poetique' with 'grace divine', without which no good works are possible.[10]

Ronsard is particularly interesting with regard to this question. His is the dominant voice in asserting the inspired nature of poetry and the descent of poetry from its origins with poet-theologians, like Orpheus. He is also the most consistent connector of prophecy and poetry. As Françoise Joukovsky has shown, very important in this connection is the figure of the sibyl.[11]

Sibyls appear in ancient literature as wise women foretelling the future. The priestess at Delphi was not a sibyl, but she may help to condition the most influential literary picture of a sibyl, which is that of the sixth book of the *Aeneid.* The Sibyl of Cumae leads Aeneas to her cave. 'Suddenly her countenance and her colour changed and her hair fell in disarray . . . Her bursting heart was wild and mad; she appeared taller and spoke in no mortal tones, for the God was nearer . . . ' Later 'the prophetess . . . ran furious riot in the cave, as if in hope of casting the God's power from her brain. Yet all the more did he torment her . . . crushed her and shaped her to his will.' Finally 'such were the words of mystery and dread which the Cumaean Sibyl spoke from her shrine; the cavern made her voice a roar as she uttered truth wrapped in obscurity . . . [At last] the frenzy passed and the mad mouth was still . . . '[12] Clearly we have here with Virgil's sibyl one of the most picturesque accounts available of possession by divine fury; Landino's commentary introduces at this point an explanation of all four furies,[13] and certainly this description of prophetic fury conditions Ronsard's account of his experience of poetic fury in his poem **"La Lyre"** addressed to Jean de Belot:[14]

> J'attends venir (certes je n'en ments point)
> Cette fureur qui la Sybile espoint:
> Mais aussi tost que par long intervalle
> Dedans mon coeur du Ciel elle devalle,
> Colere, ardent, furieux, agité,
> Je tramble tout soubz la divinité.
>
> (67-72)

And then, after the image of the torrential river rushing down from the mountains:

> Ainsi je cours de course desbridée,
> Quand la fureur en moy s'est desbordée
> Sans craindre rien, sans raison, ny conseil.
>
> (85-7)

Plainly here Ronsard is using the classical picture of prophetic inspiration to illuminate the concept of poetic inspiration. Here the sibyl is a very classical one. But Virgil himself was a major factor in the Christian prestige of the sibyl, because in the Fourth Eclogue, when he speaks of the return of the golden age with the birth of a baby, he calls it 'the last era in the Cumean song'.[15] For those who were to take the eclogue as referring to the birth of Christ, this confirmed the belief that the birth had been prophesied by the Cumean sibyl and by other sibyls.[16] In Virgil's time a considerable body of apocalyptic and messianic writing was circulating in the Empire under the name of the sibyl.[17] These and later texts were wrongly dated by early Christian writers; hence the conviction that a number of pagan prophetesses, some of great antiquity, had prophesied the coming of Christ. This belief was accepted throughout the middle ages. The prominence of sibyls increased in the early Renaissance; sibyls appear in religious art.[18] Often they balance the Old Testament prophets. In France the sibyls are found in carvings in churches, in woodcuts in Books of Hours and as characters in mystery plays. They get into lists of famous women.[19] They are in short by far the most accessible and popular manifestation of the *prisca theologia*.

I have recalled that background in order to underline just how familiar and meaningful the sibyl was to Ronsard's readers. As well as exploiting the sibyl as she appears in the *Aeneid*, Ronsard also sometimes expresses the analogy between sibyls and Old Testament prophets.[20] He links them, for example, in both the **"Hymne de la Justice"** and in **"Le Chat."** They have less prestige in **"Le Chat,"**[21] where they figure in a double descending hierarchy: men, women, animals—prophets of God, pagan sibyls, animals as means of augury. We start with prophets, evoked in a vocabulary at home in Christianity:

> Or come on voit qu'entre les homes naissent
> Miracles grands, des Prophetes qui laissent

> Un tesmoignage à la posterité
> Qu'ilz ont vescu pleins de divinité
>
> (43-6)

We then move on to sibyls—in a rather backhand version of the 'de claris feminis' motif:

> Et come on voit naistre ici des Sybilles
> Par les troupeaux des femmes inutiles:
>
> (47-8)

Finally we pass to animals, which, Ronsard says, are also able to indicate the future to us out of the Father's goodness. Thus the concept of augury by animals is acclimatized into a Christian world view:

> Ainsi voit-on, prophetes de nos maux,
> Et de noz biens, naistre des animaux,
> Qui le futur par signes nous predisent,
> Et les mortels enseignent et avisent.
> Ainsi le veult ce grand Pere de tous
> Qui de sa grace a tousjours soing de nous.
>
> (49-54)

In the **"Hymne de la Justice,"** however, the sibyls play a more dignified role.[22] Jupiter is told by 'Themis la devine' that, rather than destroy the human race, he must save it:

> Il faut pour la sauver que, de grace, illumines
> De ton esprit les coeurs des Sybilles devines,
> Des Prophetes aussi, qui seront tes prescheurs,
> Et, sans egard d'aucun, blasmeront les pecheurs,
> Pour reprendre en ton Nom de tous hommes le vice
> Attendant le retour de ta fille JUSTICE . . .
>
> (367-72)

The vocabulary is laden with Christian connotations—'prescheurs' rhyming with 'pecheurs', the prophet given the Judaeo-Christian role of preaching and reproving vice; the sense of 'grâce' is ambiguous in such a context.[23] Here the mention of the sibyls serves as a transition from the paganizing fable which has gone before to a suggestion of the Christian reading of this fable.

Now of course one of the prime texts concerning the four furies is the **"Ode à Michel de l'Hospital,"**[24] on the face of it a wholly pagan fiction. Although the full set of four furies is mentioned, the furies of poetry and prophecy are predominant and are very strongly linked. The little Muses ask to be given

> La tourbe des Chantres divins,
> Les Poëtes, et les Devins
> Et les Prophetes en partage.
>
> (350-2)

Their father Jupiter promises them that as well as 'science' they shall have his 'saincte fureur' (407-8); Jupiter will inspire Apollo, Apollo will inspire the Muses, and they, by Apollo's power, will enrapture 'les Poëtes saincts', who in their turn 'raviront la tourbe estonnée' (413-20)—thus suggesting a route by which knowledge of the divine is communicated to humanity.

So when the Muses begin to shoot their subtle flames, with whom do they begin?

> Du premier coup ont agité
> Le cuoeur prophette des Sybilles,
> Epoinct de leur divinité:

> (528-30)

The sibyls sing the future, but with great obscurity. Next mentioned are the ancient oracles, written in verse; then diviners, and next, their disciples, 'les Poëtes divins', the poet-theologians. After these 'Poëtes sainctz' come the 'vieux Poëtes humains' and then the 'prophetes Romains'—meaning here Latin poets. In other words, a descending, degenerating hierarchy. The reason for putting the sibyls at the top of a hierarchy of classical prophets would seem to be because of their Christian associations. So again, they can point the reader towards a Christian reading of the pagan fable. This is something which Ronsard did overtly in the *Abbregé de l'art poétique,* in which he describes the Muses as the daughters of Jupiter—'c'est à dire de Dieu'.[25] Having made this identification, he then proceeds to outline a similar history of poetry: the first divine poets wrote their 'Theologie allegorique' because of their contact with 'Oracles, Prophetes, Devins, Sybilles, Interpretes de songes'—all of whom come within the ambit of prophetic fury.

It will be noticed that in these accounts of the history of poetry, Ronsard, while ignoring the hierarchy of the four furies as described by Ficino, does draw upon another hierarchy in which poetry is not paramount. It is consistently shown as secondary to prophecy. However, as he uses it, this hierarchy does in fact function to the greater glory of poetry, because in the wake of prophecy poetry is revealing divine secrets, and the prophecy in whose steps she follows is imbued with weighty Christian connotations.

It seems that the parallel between prophetic and poetic fury is facilitated by a concept of prophecy which stresses the speaking forth of divine truth rather than foretelling the future. It is true that the parallel between the sibyls and the Old Testament prophets must rest on the prediction of the birth of Christ, but quite often the predictive side of prophecy is understated by poets who are using this comparative figure.[26] However, it is the predictive aspect of prophecy which everyone is really interested in, and for most people, then as now, this must have been the prime sense of the word. It is not surprising, then, that this more exciting aspect of prophecy should also have been claimed for the inspired poet, as it was for example by Amadis Jamyn who, when speaking of prophetic and poetic fury, claimed that Ronsard had made true predictions about the religious wars.[27]

I have been considering so far practising poets who illustrate and dignify their concept of poetic fury with reference to prophecy. I should like to conclude this paper with a brief reference to the reverse case. What about practising prophets? According to Christian belief the spirit of true prophecy comes from God, and it is a dangerous thing to claim that God has revealed the future to you, as the career of Postel and even more of Savonarola demonstrates. In France in the middle of the sixteenth century there was a foreteller of the future who cut himself off, both in the form and the content of his prophecy, from the medieval eschatological tradition which both Savonarola and Postel could be seen to be cultivating.[28] This prophet looked instead to a range of Renaissance occult sources of knowledge for his authority. I refer of course to Nostradamus, who abandoned narrative as a form for prophecy, espousing instead enigmatic verse.[29] What did he claim as the source of his knowledge? It would have been both dangerous and rather alien to his style to claim the inspiration of the Holy Spirit. And he was above all an astrologer. But clearly he wished to lay claim not only to astrological science but also to some sort of divine inspiration. To suggest the latter he intermingles in the preface to his first collection a Christian vocabulary with the terminology of Neoplatonism and of occult philosophy which provided the theoretical basis for the concept of divine fury. Even as he denies being inspired by a 'bacchante fureur' he suggests this context, as also with the Latin sentence: 'Soli numine divino afflati praesagiunt et spiritu prophetico particularia.'[30] And he goes on to say: 'Quant aux occultes vaticinations qu'on vient à recevoir par le subtil esprit de feu'—reminiscent of the Muse's subtle flames in Ronsard's ode—'. . . tout procedoit de la puissance divine du grand Dieu eternel, de qui toute bonté procede.'[31] To Henri II in 1558 he says, 'à un tresprudent, à un tressage Prince, j'ay consacré mes nocturnes & prophetiques supputations, composees plustost d'un naturel instinct: accompagné d'une fureur poëtique, que par reigle de poësie,—& la pluspart composé & accordé à la calculation Astronomique.'[32] So here, by a pleasing reversal, as prophetic fury has served to enhance the prestige of poetry, poetic fury is one of the factors suggested by the prophet as a source of his prophetic pronouncements. He makes the same suggestion in one of his letters.[33] Nostradamus is claiming to be more than just an astrologer; by exploiting what was as he wrote a very fashionable concept, he suggests a form of divine inspiration which has been integrated into contemporary patterns of thought and has a certain prestige, but which avoids the dangerous claim of direct revelation from the Holy Spirit.

Nostradamus received favourable comments from several Pléiade poets, particularly after the death of Henri II and the outbreak of religious war, both of which they considered he had truly prophesied. Of particular interest is Ronsard again in the **"Elegie à Guillaume des Autels"**—written in 1560, during the lifetime of Nostradamus.[34] Here Ronsard reviews the possible sources of Nostradamus's knowledge, once more a descending hierarchy of possibilities: God-given frenzy, a good daimon, a bad daimon, a natural gift of communication with the celestial, a natural melancholy temperament—whatever it was, his prophecy has proved true. Let us notice exactly how Ronsard formulates the first possibility which I paraphrased as 'God-given frenzy':

Ou soit que de grand Dieu l'immense eternité
Ait de Nostradamus l'entousiasme excité . . .

(175-6)

If we take 'eternité' as being one of the attributes of God himself, precisely that which makes past, present and future all one, and if we take 'entousiasme' as an inspiration or fury, this first suggestion is a perfect syncretization of Platonic prophetic fury in a contemporary Christian context. And 'entousiasme' was a word which was used for poetic frenzy as well. The fact that Nostradamus couched his prophecies in enigmatic verse, specifically stressing its difficulty and his wish to veil truth from the vulgar, is yet another feature of his work that could commend him to Pléiade poets, underlining as it did the parallelism which they were so pleased to exploit between prophetic and poetic inspiration and practice.

Notes

1. See H. W. Parke and D. E. W. Wormell, *The Delphic Oracle* (2 vols, Oxford, 1956). Most of the picturesque descriptions are late (e.g. Lucan, *Pharsalia*, v. 105-97. Plutarch, *De defectu oraculorum* 51), but stray remarks in earlier writers establish the factors noted here. After due preparation the Pythia sat on a tripod and fell into a trance, in which state she uttered mysterious words; these utterances were in the first person, but the 'I' was Apollo. Her sayings were then interpreted, in verse, by a male priest (the 'prophetes').

2. H. W. Parke, *Greek Oracles* (London, 1967); see also E. R. Dodds, *The Greeks and the Irrational* (California, 1951), 64-101. Very often the enquirer was seeking advice on ritual purification.

3. *Platonis . . . opera, additis Marsilii Ficini Argumentis at Commentariis* (Basle, 1561), 536-7.

4. *Commentaria in Platonem* (Florence, 1496), r4^v: Furens autem nullus est simplici sermone contentus. Sed in clamorem prorumpit et cantus et carmina.

5. See particularly the discussion in R. V. Merrill and R. J. Clements, *Platonism in French Renaissance Poetry* (New York, 1957), 118-44. F. Joukovsky-Micha, *Poésie et mythologie au XVIe siècle: quelques mythes de l'inspiration chez les poètes de la Renaissance* (Paris, 1969), provides a wealth of material: see especially pp. 123-85.

6. *Platonis . . . opera*, 539-40.

7. Other examples in Joukovsky-Micha, *Poésie et mythologie*, 132-40.

8. Prophecy as exposition of the word of God is one of the commonly accepted broad uses of the term, which can indeed be used for any supernatural illumination of the soul; see the introduction to A. Michael's article *prophétie* in the *Dictionnaire de théologie catholique*, ed. Vacant, etc., XIII, cols 708-11. See also M. A. Screech, *Ecstasy and the Praise of Folly* (London, 1980), 214-16, 223-40.

9. *De occulta philosophia* (Cologne, 1533), book 3, chs 45-9, pp. cccx-cccxvi.

10. *Le Dialogue de Plato, philosophie divin, intitulé Io*, trans. R. le Blanc (Paris, 1546), A2^v: Et veritablement, jouxte nostre philosophie evangelique nous croyons fidelement que nul bon oeuvre peult estre faict sans le sainct esprit, qui est la grace de Dieu . . . Et neantmoins qu'aulcuns poetes n'ayent eu la congnoissance de Jesus Christ, vray, et seul Dieu, si est-ce toutesfoys, qu'ilz n'ont faict aulcune bonne operation sans la grace predicte . . .

11. *Poésie et mythologie*, 141-72.

12. *Aeneid* VI, 42-101. English translation by W. F. Jackson Knight, Penguin Classics, 1956.

13. Landino's commentary on the word *furenti* in line 100, in for example *Virgilius cum commentariis quinque* (Venice, 1499), fol. ccxix^{r-v}.

14. Ronsard, *Oeuvres complètes*, ed. Laumonier (20 vols, Paris, 1914-75), XV, 19.

15. Line 4: Ultima Cumaei venit iam carminis aetas.

16. See Pierre Courcelle, 'Les exégèses chrétiennes de la quatrième églogue', *Rev Etud Anciennes*, 59 (1957), 294-319.

17. The texts were only known from fragments in early Christian writers until the discovery of a manuscript published in 1545 by Xystus Betuleius. The edition by C. Alexandre, *Oracula Sibyllina* (2 vols. Paris, 1841-56), contains prefaces from sixteenth-century editions. See also *The Old Testament Pseudepigrapha*, I, ed James H. Charlesworth (London, 1983), 317-472.

18. See Emile Mâle, *L'art religieux de la fin du moyen âge en France* (Paris, 1908), 267-96.

19. For example in Champier, *La Nef des dames vertueuses* (Paris, 1515); Bouchet, *Le Jugement poetic de l'honneur femenin* (Poitiers, 1538).

20. See particularly *L'Hercule chrestien*, lines 69-106, *Oeuvres*, ed. cit., VIII, 211-13, for a developed treatment of the sibyls as the vehicle of a secondary revelation to the gentiles.

21. *Oeuvres*, ed. cit., XV, 41.

22. *Oeuvres*, ed. cit., VIII, 65.

23. Laumonier here gives a note saying that the sense is 'de bonne grâce, de bon coeur', and in relation to *Le Chat*, line 54 quoted above, he suggests 'par sa faveur'. But a theological dimension seems undeniable in both cases.

24. *Oeuvres*, ed. cit., III, 118-63.

25. *Ibid.* XIV, 4.

26. A good example would be Olivier de Magny's treatment of the theme in his odes on behalf of Pierre de Paschal, *Odes,* ed. E. Courbet (2 vols, Paris, 1876), I, 73ff, e.g. p. 106: 'Les Poëtes, que Dieu fait naistre / Prophetes de sa deité, / Decouvrant par eux mille choses, / Et mille encor, et mille encloses / Au sein de la divinité.' But on the other side could be cited Ronsard's *Hymne de l'automne,* where the inspired poet 'predit toute chose avant qu'elle soit faite' as well as knowing 'la nature & les secrets des cieux' etc., (*Oeuvres,* ed. cit., XII, 47, ll. 13-24).

27. Amadis Jamyn, *Oeuvres poétiques, Premières poésies* . . . ed. S. M. Carrington (Geneva, 1973), *Avant-chant nuptial,* pp. 77-86, see lines 23-62.

28. On the medieval tradition see Marjorie Reeves, *The Influence of Prophecy in the Later Middle Ages* (Oxford, 1969).

29. There is no very satisfactory edition of the *Centuries;* for convenience I cite from that of A. Le Pelletier (2 vols, Paris, 1867). For bibliography see C. von Klinckowström, 'Die ältesten Ausgaben der "Propheties" des Nostradamus', *Z Bücherfreunde* (Leipzig, 1913), 361-72; also M. Chomarat, *Nostradamus entre Rhône et Saône* (Lyon, 1971) and *Bibliographie lyonnaise des Nostradamus* (Buenc, 1973). Literature on Nostradamus is notoriously unscholarly; there is useful material in E. Leoni, *Nostradamus, Life and Literature* (New York, 1961) and *Prophecies and Enigmas of Nostradamus,* trans. L. E. LeVert (New Jersey, 1979). Most welcome is Jean Dupèbe's scholarly edition of *Lettres inédites* (Geneva, 1983).

30. *Les Oracles de Michel de Nostredame,* ed. Le Pelletier. vol. II, preface dated 1555, p. 10. This is an elaboration of a sentence which concludes the first section of the pseudo-Ptolemaic *Centiloquium:* it is quoted as from Ptolemy by Cornelius Agrippa in his chapter *De vaticinio et furore,* p. cccxi: 'Soli numine afflati predicunt particularia'.

31. *Ibid.* 12.

32. *Ibid.* 146.

33. *Lettres,* ed. Dupèbe, letter XLI, dated 1562, p. 140: 'Itaque arrepto olorino calamo (anserinum enim ter recusavit), illo ipso dictante, veluti furore percitus poëtico, in tales versus proprupi . . .' See Dupèbe's note and his introduction, pp. 16-18.

34. *Oeuvres,* ed. cit., X, 358.

Ehsan Ahmed (essay date 1991)

SOURCE: "Pierre de Ronsard's *Odes* and the Law of Poetic Space," in *Renaissance Quarterly,* Vol. XLIV, No. 4, Winter, 1991, pp. 757-75.

[In the following essay, Ahmed argues that in the Odes *Ronsard transgresses the spatial boundaries that had hitherto defined poetry.]*

> Et faictes que toujours j'espie
> D'oeil veillant les secretz des cieulx,

> ("Ode à Michel de l'Hospital")

The **Odes** of 1550 and 1552 reveal Pierre de Ronsard's ambition to gain entry into the court of Henri II. In the 1550 preface to the **Odes,** Ronsard does not make the slightest effort to veil his literary and political objectives. He presents his **Odes** as a poetic challenge to Clément Marot's psalm translations of 1541 and 1543 with the discovery of an equally ancient lyric source, pagan rather than Hebraic, and he mounts an ad hominem attack on the court poet Mellin de Saint-Gelais in order to win Henri's favor. The poetry, however, places in evidence other preoccupations. The **Odes** describe and problematize the endless wanderings of a poetic subject who seeks to uncover the secrets not only of the ancient world but of the modern one as well.

The young Vendômois poet attempts to unify in his verse worlds fragmented by time and space. Tracing his patrons' history to ancient Greece and Rome becomes, in part, a way of creating an official place for himself in France. Within the metaphorical space of his poetry, however, he alters received spatial relationships so they will conform not to myth but to a new, higher form of reality. Ronsard's success comes from such a syncretic vision, but the legal ramifications weigh heavy upon his conscience—perhaps in light of the Sorbonne's condemnation of Marot's 1541 translation of sacred texts. Through his vernacular imitations, Ronsard relates his early modern world to an ancient poetic one that not only embraces an absolute and divine authority but also contradicts Church belief.[1]

Throughout the **Odes,** the poet makes continual reference to a certain law of propriety as he introduces ancient pagan elements in his verse. Although he recognizes the moral sanctions against classical paganism-revived, the poetic world of the **Odes** continually defies them and alludes to an unlimited possibility of creation. One can observe this conflict in the discursive, the historical, and the cosmological aspects of the **Odes.** Though these perspectives of meaning are analogous in structure and are often presented simultaneously, for the sake of exposition I shall separate them in order to demonstrate how the **Odes** are bound to a novel and problematic view of spatial relationships in sixteenth-century France. Ronsard's specific comments on the difficulty of combining ancient with modern elements are directly related to a vision he is trying to describe. Although Ronsard recognizes this need for propriety both formally and contextually, I argue that he nonetheless transgresses it. In fact, he plants the seeds of a poetic philosophy of infinite space which will resonate in the works of the Italian philosopher Giordano Bruno as he develops his own theory of the infinite which contributed directly to the scientific revolution at the end of the sixteenth century.[2]

THE LAW OF THE SONG

The **"Ode à Michel de l'Hospital,"** written in 1550 and published in 1552, appropriately marks the beginning of Ronsard's career as a court poet, while it recounts the origins of pagan poetry. The ode is given in recognition of l'Hospital's defense of Ronsard and his poetic reforms against the polemical attacks of Saint-Gelais. Through l'Hospital's efforts, Ronsard eventually was able to win the favor of Henri II.[3] The symbolic deference paid to the "loy de la Chanson" at the end of this poem could signal Ronsard's acceptance into the court, but the significance of this law in terms of discursive order is still greater:

> Mais la loy de la Chanson
> Ores ores me vient dire
> Que par trop en long je tire
> Les repliz de sa façon.
> Ore donque je ne puis
> Vanter la Fleur, tant je suis
> Pris d'un ardeur nompareille
> D'aller chez toy pour chanter
> Cest Ode, affin d'enchanter
> Ton soin charmé par l'oreille.
>
> (vv. 807-16)

(But the law of the Song / Now, now comes to tell me / That I draw out too long / The folds of its fashion. / Now I may no longer / Praise the Flower, so much am I / Seized by a passion without equal / To go to you and sing / This Ode, in order to captivate / You charmed through the ear.)

In spite of his much vaunted discovery of the ancient ode in his preface, Ronsard defines the relationship between the ode and the *chanson* as one between poetic innovation ("ode"), and poetic authority ("loy de la Chanson"). In search for authority, the chanson becomes the source of the ode, and the nature of poetic chronology becomes problematic, indeed reversed, in a poem that claims to uncover the pagan origin of poetry. Ronsard seems to submit his "ode" to the "loy de la Chanson" by syntactically placing it between the rhyme "chanter:enchanter" in the last verses, because the rhyme emphasizes the vernacular function of this ancient form; it "naturalizes" it. Particularly in light of Joachim Du Bellay's rejection of the term "chanson" in his *Deffence et Illustration de la langue françoyse* (1549), the use of it in this ode on lyric origins conveys a more ambivalent attitude towards the Ancients than Du Bellay would like to concede in the Pleiade's manifesto. The movement towards the Ancients is coupled with a movement back to France and an identification with its national lyric tradition. The expression, "the law of the song," derives from Pindar (Nemian, IV, v. 33) where the law, *tethmós,* refers to the just balance between a unified and yet diverse poetic discourse. Ronsard worries somewhat belatedly about transgressing this law in his most lengthy of Pindaric odes (composed of 816 verses). The poet real-izes at the closing of the poem that he has surpassed the limits of this lyric form and that he can no longer develop the encomium of Marguerite ("la Fleur"), the duchess of Berry and sister of Henri II, which he started in the preceding stanzas. He has drawn out the folds of the "chanson" too far in his eagerness to praise Michel de l'Hospital—so far that he begins to praise Marguerite as well. In view of this ancient law that prescribes an enclosed poetic field of diverse elements, the poet commits an act of impropriety by encompassing too many topics and overstepping formal boundaries. Though Pindar admits to the same infraction, his digressions are not so prolix as Ronsard's.[4]

Similar discursive improperieties recur earlier in the fifth epode of the **"Ode à Michel de l'Hospital,"** when Jupiter commands his daughters, the Muses, to perform "chansons" at a gathering of his divine court (V. 161 et passim). Once the Muses have gathered, they begin to tell the battle of the gods and the giants, known as the "Assaut des Geans et des Dieux." This account occupies the center of the poem and again emulates Pindar by embedding a digressive tale in an ode. While the Muses "accord" a discordant battle, Ronsard attempts to "accord" by means of imitation his chanson not with a Pindaric ode but with Hesiod's *Theogony* on the battle between the Titans and the Olympians.[5] Once the Muses have concluded their song, the poet, however, entones a discordant note:

> Juppiter qui tendoit l'oreille,
> La combloit d'un aize parfaict,
> Ravy de la voix nompareille
> Qui si bien l'avoit *contrefait:*
> Et retourné, rid en arriere
> De Mars, qui tenoit l'oiel fermé,
> Ronflant sur sa lance guerriere,
> Tant la Chanson l'avoit charmé.
>
> (vv. 319-26)

(Jupiter who was offering his ear, / Filled it (his ear) with complete joy, / Ravished by a voice beyond comparison / which had so well counterfeited it (the song): / And having turned, laughed behind him / At Mars, whose eyes were closed, / Snoring on his warrior staff, / So much the Song had pleased him.)

[The songs] have been reduced to one and impersonalized by the definite article. Moreover, this one voice did not sing the chanson but imitated it or more specifically parodied or counterfeited it ("contrefait").[6] Isidore Silver has remarked on the originality of this stanza but nonetheless queries: "How justify the tone of the passage?"[7] Could this be a reference to the imitator's own voice unwilling to efface itself behind the Muses, much less behind Hesiod? The battle song that causes Mars to snore ("ronflant") delights Jupiter. Ironically, Hesiod's poem on the origin of the world gives Ronsard the opportunity to render the identity of the original maker problematic; Jupiter's acknowledgement of Ronsard's pleasing distortion creates the impression of his actual presence at the god's court where he displays his ability to enchant even the greatest of divinities. The shifts that occur among the subjects and objects truly complicate the spatial order ("trop en long je tire / Les repliz") as Ronsard attempts to create a place for himself. From the perspective of Renaissance modes of intertextuality, one could say that Ronsard curries Henri's favor primarily through his heuristic imitations of the classical Greek poets Pindar and Hesiod.[8] But from a purely intrinsic point of view, one can analyze the shift as the displacement of the ancient and absolute center of poetic creation from the pagan divinities (i.e., the Muses) to the poet himself, so that their other worldliness assumes a relative value for the person speaking.

Du Bellay insists in the *Deffence* that young French poets compose French odes based on Latin and Greek examples and do so in a "consonant" manner. Ronsard ironizes that accord in his seminal ode on poetic origins. Margaret Ferguson writes that Du Bellay does not allow in his *Deffence* for "the possibility of an imitation that not only changes the ancient source but plays ironically on the change."[9] This feature distinguishes Ronsard's practice in his odes from Du Bellay's theoretical stance. While Du Bellay seeks a unified accord with Horace, Ronsard combines the voices of many. He even manages to distinguish his own voice among the divine ones by superimposing his voice on the Muses and wins the praise of Jupiter. His singularity becomes apparent when he draws attention to his own ability to write a counter-version of pagan history—again, "la voix qui le contrefait." He appropriates their authority in order to display his own creative power, and he identifies with the divine Ancients not as their epigone but as their equal. He rewrites their poetry, altering it, and indeed reversing the imagery in order to make a place for himself.

He transgresses the law of poetic space and propriety as he makes room for himself at the expense of his patrons, human and divine. In the opening verses of the **"Ode à Michel de l'Hospital,"** the theme of poetic space is foremost in Ronsard's thoughts as he wanders through fields of the Graces gathering flowers into crowns. In his travels, the first-person subject fashions a crown metaphorically by the joining verses:

> Errant par les champs de la Grace
> Qui peint mes vers de ses couleurs
> Sus les bords Dirceans j'amasse
> Le trésor des plus riches fleurs,
> Affin qu'en pillant je façonne
> D'une laborieuse main,
> La rondeur de ceste couronne.

> (vv. 1-7)

(Wandering in the fields of the Grace / Who paints my verse with her colors / By the side of the Dircean [fountain] I collect / Treasure from the richest flowers, / So that while culling I may fashion / With a skilled hand, / The roundness of this crown.)

The repeated deviations from the triadic pattern heightened by the initial placement of the word "errant" in the first verse can be taken as an assertion by the poet of his

role as the wandering discoverer. He inserts himself in the discourse at the risk of displacing his patron;[10] he fashions an oddly shaped crown around himself, symbolically marking a royal space protected from the "vulgaire." Ronsard leads the reader to believe the poet follows a pattern, but the **"Ode à Michel de l'Hospital"** represents a counter example to a unified discourse and provides counter histories to the ones he claims to imitate. Readers may be correct who view the poet's "errors" as ill-fashioned imitations of Pindar,[11] but Ronsard's deviations also articulate a novel and complex relationship—one which is not strictly an intertextual problem of imitation but more generally the quest for a poetic center in a world of unlimited diversity. The crown symbolized by the composition of the verses must be ample enough to give the poet freedom to wander *endlessly* and yet to *define* a place within the recognized bounds of the royal court. From a discursive point of view, herein lies the fundamental conflict of the *Odes*.

In his **"Ode de la Paix,"** Ronsard deprecates an abundant use of words and lauds brevity, but he will again disregard the law:

> Tousjous un propos deplaist
> Aus oreilles attendantes,
> Si plein outre reigle il est
> De parolles abondantes.
> Celui qui en peu de vers
> Etraint un sujet divers,
> Se mét au chef la couronne:
> De cette fleur que voici,
> Et de celle, et celle aussi,
> La mouche son miel façonne
> Diversement.

> (vv. 291-301)

(Always a subject is unpleasing / To the awaiting ears / If it surpasses the rule / With abundant words. / He who can contain in a few verses diverse subjects / May place the crown upon his head: /With this flower here / And there, and also there, / The bee fashions its honey / In a diverse manner.)

The plurality of voices and texts becomes central to the creation of an ode; Ronsard describes his craft ironically as that of a modest bee that "borrows" its honey from diverse sources—a theme developed in Horace's ode IV, ii, which Horace in turn borrows from Pindar's Pythia, X, vv. 53-54. The relationship between unity and diversity is central, because an overabundance of words is a transgression of the poetic law, "outre reigle," the same "loy de la Chanson" which Ronsard claims to observe in order to preserve the song's unity. He nonetheless abandons the encomiastic pattern in a blatantly immodest way to create a new history as he simultaneously admonishes one against such transgression. In the preface to the *Odes* he seeks the reader's praise for having traced an unknown path, having freely surmounted territorial boundaries:

> Si les hommes tant des siecles passés que du nostre, ont merité quelque louange pour avoir piqué diligemment aprés les traces de ceus qui courant par la carriere

de leurs inventions, ont de bien loin franchi la borne: combien davantage doit on vanter le coureur qui galopant librement par les campaignes Attiques, & Romaines osa tracer un sentier inconnu pour aller à l'immortalité?

(If men many centuries before ours merited some praise for having spurred [their horses] diligently after the traces of those who, racing on the career of discoveries, went well beyond the border: how much must one praise the racer who, galloping freely among the Attic and Roman countryside, dared to trace an unknown path to gain immortality?)[12]

It is the spirit of the unbound traveller which he tries to capture in his poetry but which unfailingly complicates the poetic discourse.

HISTORY AND PROPHECY

When Ronsard attempts to portray Henri II, Michel de l'Hospital, Marguerite de Valois, and others according to Pindar's example, he creates anachronistic settings for his sixteenth-century patrons. He tries to superimpose a national political patron onto a foreign poetic pattern, "un patron," and by doing so, he consciously crosses spatial boundaries. His identity becomes defined as the mediator between two worlds. To the extent that he attempts to reconcile pagan poetry with sixteenth-century court life, he resembles Marot's David who, as a divine prophet, mediates between the two spheres of heaven and earth. Moreover, as Christians uncover figures in the Old Testament to prophesy Christ's coming and to align the histories of the two peoples, Ronsard invents pagan prophesies of the founding of Paris in order to make the two worlds appear consecutive. In the preface to his translations, Marot explains David's experiences in terms of Christ. One can view Ronsard's prophetic history as an attempt to place an air of divine sanction over his verse. He regards it as venerable as the psalms. Marot establishes prophetic connections between the "Hebraïques" and the "Galliques" and between David and François I, whereas Ronsard creates an alternative history from Greece to Rome to France, from pagan gods to Henri II. To advance the parallel one more step, Ronsard wills into being concordant spiritual experiences between the pagan heros and the French through reviving ancient verse and mythologizing the birth of France as a modern and imperial state.

In the **"Ode de la Paix,"** Ronsard inserts a complex sequence of narratives in the middle of the ode; Vergil's *Aeneid* provides the main source of inspiration for this *translatio imperii*. The praise of Henri II which opens the poem leads quickly to the unfolding of a Franciade epyllion that traces a movement from the Creation to the Fall of Troy and to the founding of Paris (vv. 37-286). Issuing from this genealogical digression in an exaggerated Pindaric manner is the glorious descendant of Troy, Henri II. Ronsard justifies a place for himself at the French court, as if it were his natural right, by creating a similar place in history for his king; indeed, both were fated from the beginning of time. This victory ode marking the signing of the treaty between Henri II and Edward VI of England over France's reacquisition of Boulogne serves as a pretext for Ronsard to establish a place in France without limit for his poetic imagination.

Henri II is the prophesied heir from the Greek world. Through the voices of Cassandra and Andromache, Ronsard blends past, present, and future in an effort to surmount his historical limitations and yet to align his art with the prophetic arts of those two women.[13] Cassandra prophesies that Astyanax will found a new Troy on the Danube from which will emerge a group of settlers to found the city of Paris,[14] and Andromache foretells both of Paris becoming the eternal city, like Vergil's Rome, and of Henri's preeminence. Through these pagan prophets, Ronsard will chart a traditional "Catholic" succession of empires and letters from Greece to Rome and then to France. While the "timeless" evangelism of the psalms is preserved in Marot's reverential translation, Ronsard needs to amend mythological history to create an equally immortal image of Paris and Henri II.[15]

Once Ronsard has established the connection between Francus and Henri II and between Troy and Paris, he breaks the narrative line and banishes Francus from his ode:

> Fui donc Troien, toi et ta bande,
> Si ton Neveu me le commande
> J'irai bien tost pour te trouver.
>
> (vv. 284-86)

(Take flight Trojan, you and your troops, / If your Nephew commissions me [to write the epic] / I will come soon to find you.)

Again, as he did in the **"Ode à Michel de l'Hospital,"** the poet intervenes in the world which he is trying to represent. He exerts his influence over the descendants of Francus and in doing so advertises his ability to write a French epic for which he seeks Henri's commission: "Si ton Neveu me le commande."[16] Similar to the ode to l'Hospital, the center comes to represent the place of flight, an open space that can only be circumscribed by Henri's patronage. This divine history of Henri whose closure is alluded to remains nonetheless incomplete. This history is constructed in the ode through the infraction of the poetic law of unity which would be guaranteed, in this context, by the verisimilitude of events; yet the more diverse the events become, the less plausible they appear. The lyric subject unites the two peoples through a fictionalized account that he attempts to pass off as prophecy. Moreover, he hopes that his reader will accept this history as revealed truth. But later, in the "Epistre au lecteur" to his incomplete epic the *Franciade* (1572), Ronsard will criticize Ariosto for departing too far from the law of verisimilitude and for creating marvelous fables in the *Orlando Furioso*. Ronsard falls victim to his own judgment both in the **"Ode de la Paix"** and the *Franciade* as his efforts to posit unity between historically diverse cultures prove to be an impossibility.[17]

Adherence to this law of unity or verisimilitude has strong moral foundations. In the epyllion, Ronsard disregards the moral statement he makes at the opening of the ode as if it does not apply to him. There he observes, following Pindar's example, how aimlessness stems from royal pride (vv. 4-5, "De son heur outrecuidée / Court vague, sans estre guidée"; "From his proud happiness / He wanders, without being guided." Cf. Pindar Pythia V, str. 1). Morality is defined in spatial terms. Realizing toward the end of the ode that this poetic history has led himself astray, he invokes the Muse in a Pindaric manner to keep him from going farther adrift:

> Muse, repren l'aviron,
> Et racle la prochaine onde
> Qui nous baigne à l'environ
> Sans estre ainsi vagabonde.
>
> (vv. 287-90)

(Muse, resume the oar / And scrape the next wave / Which bathes our sides / Without thus being vagabond.)

Again, does the poet consider himself above moral reproach for his lack of proportion? In these verses the poet explains that his course is not self-determined but governed by a divine force, the Muse. Although he violates his own injunction against human pride—pride being an unsanctioned and indeed unlimited exploration of space—he looks to the Muse to authorize such a lofty undertaking. This problem of closure is recurrent; rather than seek this infinite space away from the court, he does so from the very center, as if again shaping a royal crown that gains him recognition as an epic poet and that sanctions his endless wandering among diverse topics. While the poetic and political crowns symbolically impose spatial order, the *tethmós,* they embody as well a prophecy of vast expansion for both Henri's empire and Ronsard's imagination. One can see at this point that the *Odes* both discursively and historically surpass the law of unity and tend to the realm of the marvelous as they attempt to encompass a myriad of seemingly disjointed concerns—be it the **"Ode à Michel de l'Hospital"** with topics ranging from the Battle of the Gods and the Giants to the genealogy of poets and the praise of too many patrons or the **"Ode de la Paix"** with the diverse and illustrious genealogy of Henri II. This same acceptance of the marvelous precedes a poetic belief in a world of infinite dimension.[18]

POETIC FLIGHT

Ronsard opens the *Quatre premiers livres des odes* in a work entitled **"Au Roi"** wherein he requests patronage from Henri in a twenty-verse prologue. If Henri gratifies Ronsard's mundane interests, the poet will place the king at the center of the ever-expanding poetic universe:

> L'aiant pour ma guide, SIRE,
> Autre bien je ne desire,
> Que d'apparoistre à tes yeux
> Le saint Harpeur de ta gloire,

> Et l'archer de ta memoire
> Pour la tirer dans les cieus.
>
> (vv. 15-20)

(Having you for my guide, Sir / I desire no other good / Than to appear before your eyes / As the holy Harpist of your glory / And the archer of your memory / In order to launch it into the heavens.)

Ronsard informs Henri II in this liminal ode that he, as poet, can perpetuate his king's memory as if he had the power to deify mortals, "Pour la tirer dans les cieus." Since the genealogy he creates for Henri is fictitious, glory is not equated with real acts but with the conservation of one's name for posterity, as suggested by the rhyme "gloire:memoire." If Henri II consents to be Ronsard's patron "ma guide" and secure for him a place as court poet, Ronsard will preserve the Valois king's name in the heavens. Memory becomes an explicit function of politics.

As Ronsard proceeds, he reveals a sense of poetic strength that appears to flourish quite independently of his king. The poet turns to his Muse and deliberates over whom he will glorify:

> Muse, bande ton arc dous,
> Muse ma douce esperance,
> Quel Prince fraperons nous,
> L'enfonçant parmi la France?
> Sera-ce pas nostre ROI,
> Duquel la divine oreille
> Humera cette merveille
> Qui n'obeist qu'à ma loi?
>
> (vv. 21-28)

(Muse, arm your sweet bow / Muse my sweet hope / Which Prince will we strike / Sending him throughout France? / Will it not be our KING, / Whose divine ear / Will drink up this marvel / Which only obeys my law?)

Ronsard describes his ability to glorify his king in an imperious manner because he views divine poetry as a sovereign would his kingdom: "Cette merveille / Qui n'obeist qu'à ma loi."[19] This "merveille" is the poetic space where familiarity is lost among objects of superhuman proportion. Here Ronsard explicitly abandons Pindar's law of poetic proportion. One can sense the poet's attempt to articulate this new law of poetry through his infractions of spatial and moral codes. Marsilio Ficino, in his commentary on Plato's *Phaedrus,* considers poetry to be ruled by one of the four divine madnesses in which the poet, as he composes, undergoes a state of rapture or alienation and holds a position outside the "customs of men"—a claim that Ronsard makes repeatedly for himself.[20] This alienated state is not only mirrored in the endlessly digressive form of the verses but can be understood only by one equally outside the law of mortals as the rhyme "divine oreille-:merveille" suggests.

It is noteworthy that a sixteenth-century definition of the "merveille" in terms of spatial law can be found in the writings of Michel de Montaigne. When writing about the divine nature of Vergil's poetry, Montaigne states that the "merveille" transcends the laws of human space:

> Au dernier [à Vergile], premier de quelque espace, mais laquelle espace il [un étudiant de poésie] jurera ne pouvoir estre remplie par nul espirit humain, il s'estonnera, il se transira. . . . Voicy merveille . . . la bonne, l'excessive, la divine [qui] est au dessus des regles et de la raison.

> (Regarding the latter [Vergil]—who is first by quite a distance, by a space that our student will swear no human mind can fill—he will be stunned and speechless. . . . Here is a wonder . . . the good, the supreme, the divine [which] is above rules and reason.)[21]

As Todorov observes in a recent work on the marvelous: "The function of the supernatural is to remove the text from the action of law and by the same token to transgress the very law."[22] Todorov uses the word "law" here also to mean the rule of verisimilitude. This rule is applicable to Ronsard's poetics in the **Odes** with the exception that this poet wants nonetheless to remain within the legal bounds of the royal court. Ronsard elevates his patron into the celestial orb through the transgression of the received laws of nature and of poetic history. The poet alone can transport Henri to the heavens with his winged words conveyed later in the rhyme "vers:univers" (vv. 53 and 56). He even justifies the extremity of his position in the preface (p. 48): "C'est le vrai but d'un poete Liriq de celebrer jusques à l'extremité celui qu'il entreprend de louer" ("It is the true goal of a lyric poet to celebrate *in extremis* the one he undertakes to praise"). In the second strophe, Ronsard thus passes from Henri II's glorification to his apotheosis:

> De Jupiter les antiques
> Leurs ecris embellissoient,
> Par lui leurs chants poetiques
> Commencoient, et finissoient,
> Prenant plaisir d'ouir dire
> Ses louanges à la lire:
> Mais Henri sera le Dieu
> Qui commencera mon mettre
> Et que j'ai voué de mettre
> A la fin et au meilieu.

> (vv. 29-38)

(With Jupiter, the ancients / Used to adorn their writings, / With him their poetic chants / They used to begin and finish, / Reaping pleasure from hearing / His praises sung on the lyre: / But Henri will be the God / Who will begin my meter / And who I vow to place / At the end and in the middle.)

Henri's deification is modeled on the invocation of Jupiter in ancient songs; Henri's presence in Ronsard's collection of songs offers a modern variation on this ancient formula. Ronsard needs to surpass the Ancients; whereas Jupiter occupies the beginning and the end, Henri will appear even in the middle. The poet controls the presence of his king in his verse and enables Henri to excel even Jupiter. The poet not only memorializes his patron but also deifies him.

The poetic image of deification recurs throughout the odes and reinforces the idea of a place beyond spatial and temporal measure.

The process of deification is Ronsard's innovation and an explicit deviation from Pindar.[23] In fact, Pindar emphasizes the difference between mortals and immortals and admonishes humans to respect their place. In Pythia III, v. 59f, he states: "With our mortal minds we should seek from the gods that which becomes us, knowing where we belong, and what lies before our feet. Dear soul of mine, never urge a life beyond mortality." Propriety is again based upon human measure. The pervasive attitude both in pagan and Christian morality prior to the scientific revolution was that the gods were the sole beings to partake in the infinite. Ronsard opposes the law of unity governed by verisimilitude only to uncover a higher law, like the one Montaigne conceived for Vergil. As Ronsard states in his address to Henri's deceased brother, Charles de Valois (II, iii, vv. 25-26): "Et nouvelles lois lui imposes / Nouveau citoien de là haut" ("And new laws you place upon him [Henri] / New citizen of the heavens"). Different rules apply in the marvelous space of the heavens—new rules that Ronsard tries to voice in his **Odes.** Though the gods may embody the infinite, the poet, according to Ronsard also can find himself in a world of infinite proportions—the experience of which he attempts to share.

When Henri made his entry into Paris in June, 1549, he was portrayed as Hercules by the humanist organizers, Jean Martin and Thomas Sebillet. Moreover, the organizing committee (which did not include any members from the Brigade or early Pléiade poets) focused on Hercules' divinization upon his death.[24] Shortly after the entry, Ronsard portrays the king as Jupiter, a living divinity, rather than as the apotheosized mortal; he creates a setting for the king more colossal than the streets of Paris.

Ronsard's desire to explore the unknown remains steadfast in the **Odes,** and it is voiced most defiantly in an ode to Joachim Du Bellay (I,ix) where he asserts that human nature has not limited his poetic flight. Although Horace claims in his celebrated ode IV,ii, "Pindarum quisquis studet aemulari," that anyone who attempts to imitate Pindar will share the fate of Icarus, Ronsard responds:

> Par une cheute subite
> Encor je n'ai fait nommer
> Du nom de Ronsard la mer
> Bien que Pindare j'imite.

> (vv. 165-168)

(With a sudden fall / Still I have not given the name / Ronsard to the sea / Although I imitate Pindar.)

The imitation of Pindar loses its literal, intertextual significance in the **Odes** and comes to mean for Ronsard to attempt the marvelous—hence, his defiance of Horace's caveat. Ronsard's vulgarization of Pindar demystifies the claims of this ancient lyricist without having to reduce himself to a humble creature; he writes a version of Icarus' success story, implying a new confidence in human powers which enables him to ascend to the heavens where truth is uncovered paradoxically through the "sins" of pagan hubris or Christian pride. In the later part of the century, Giordano Bruno (1548-1600) developed his revolutionary, metaphysical theory of infinite space which profoundly influenced the thinking of both philosophers and astronomers of the scientific revolution. At the century's midpoint, one can see such concepts trying to find an earlier poetic expression in Ronsard's odes. Ernst Cassirer notes that Bruno's belief in the infinite receives its strongest formulation in a sonnet inspired by Luigi Tansillo (1510-68) which Bruno rewrites in his third dialogue of his *Degl'eroici furori* (1585) in order to have Tansillo recite it as a personage of the dialogue. Like Ronsard, Bruno assumes a defiant Icarian stance:

> Poi che spiegat'ho l'ali al bel desio
> Quanto piu sott'il pie l'aria mi scorgo,
> Piu le veloci penne al vento porgo,
> E spreggio il mondo, e verso il ciel m'invio.
> Ne del figliuol di Dedalo il fin rio
> Fa che giu pieghi, anzi via piu risorgo.

(vv. 1-6)

(Now that I have given wings to that beautiful desire / the more I see the air under my feet / the more do I set my speedy feathers to the wind / and, disdaining the world, move toward the heavens. / Nor does the cruel end of the son of Daedalus / induce me to come down; in fact I climb higher.)[25]

Giordano Bruno posits in 1584 a theory of an unlimited corporeal universe in his metaphysical dialogue *La Cena de le ceneri*.[26] Resembling Ronsard's poetic world of unlimited space occupied by man himself, Bruno develops his notion of infinite space from a principle of plenitude. He uses the term "copia" not so much as a sixteenth-century generative principle of writing, as Terence Cave has demonstrated, but rather as a fundamental rule of cosmology.[27] Referring directly to Democritus and Epicurus, Bruno expresses his conviction in *De l'infinito, universo et mondi* (1584):

> Non sono fini, termini, margini, muraglia che ne defrodino e suttragano la infinita copia de la cose. Indi feconde è la terra ed il suo mare; indi perpetuo è il vampo del sole, summinstrandosi eternamente esca a gli voraci fuochi ed umori a gli attenuati mari; perche dall'infinito sempre nova copia di materia sottonasce.

(There are no ends, boundaries, limits or walls which can defraud or decrease the infinite copia of things. Therefore the earth and the ocean are fecund; therefore the sun's blaze is perpetual, so that eternally there is fuel for the voracious fires, and moisture for the attenuated sea. For from infinity an ever new copia of matter is born.)[28]

Both Koyré and Cassirer see the foundations of Bruno's infinite in poetics and not in mathematics or astronomy; yet his beliefs influenced modern science and philosophy as the works of Galileo and Descartes attest.[29] The notion

of the poet's unlimited flight conveyed by the defiant Icarus represents a fundamental shift in world view; humankind should test the limits of its condition. Bruno's belief that the marvels of the infinite were not exclusive to the Christian God led to his burning at the stake in Rome in 1600; the Church found the idea too dangerous, once the poetic veil was lifted.[30]

Unlike Bruno, Ronsard safely returns from celestial space to address mundane matters—namely, to reformulate the concept of human love. In a potent ode to Cassandre, he writes: "Amour n'a point de loi, / A sa grand' deité / Convient l'infinité" (II,v, vv. 10-12). ("Love has no longer any law / For her great divinity / Is suited the infinite.") The subsequent collections of **Amours** are suggestive of Bruno's copia, of a love without end and without a fixed perspective; they describe a universe where the poet no longer invests his beloved with an absolute value but rather a relative, transferrable one. Ronsard rejects the petrarchan mode to become the protean lyric subject who undergoes metamorphoses *ad infinitum* as he discovers new beloveds.[31] The relative and ever-changing status of Janne, Cassandre, Marie, and Hélène replaces the unequivocal position of Laura. Ronsard the poet inaugurates the modern age not only with novel forms of discourse, historical consciousness, world view, but also with a new poetics of amorous relations.

When Henri II finally accepted Ronsard into his court, Henri tacitly granted a privilege for the publication of a theory of infinite space which was not founded on astronomy but on poetry. Within the walls of the Louvre, Ronsard could become truly a marvelous poet and question the laws of nature *sine fine*.

Notes

1. Particularly in the *Ode à Michel de l'Hospital*, one reads of the ancient pagan poets being invested with the same divine authority as prophets. Inspired by Plato and Pindar, Ronsard portrays Jupiter as saying "Que les vers viennent de Dieu, / Non de l'humaine puissance" (vv. 475-76); Ronsard 3: 145. In the *Ode,* Ronsard then proceeds to invoke the Muses in a prayer to help him learn the secrets of the heavens (vv. 511-18). Also see his *Abbregé de l'art poëtique* (1565), where he defines this ancient period as a "theologie allegoricque": "La Poësie n'estoit au premier aage qu'un Theologie allegoricque, pour faire entrer au cervau des hommes grossiers par fables plaisantes et colorées les secretz qu'ilz ne pouvoyent comprendre, quand trop ouvertement on leur descouvroit la verité" (Ronsard 14: 4). The first editions (1550 and 1552) of Ronsard's odes will be cited; references to later editions will be used wherever it seems pertinent.

2. Koyré, 39, and passim.

3. For historical details of this event, see Nolhac, 178-87.

4. Ronsard, 1:44: "Des le méme tens que Clément Marot (seulle lumiere en ses ans de la vulgaire poësie) se travailloit à la poursuite de son Psautier, et osai le premier des nostres, enricher ma langue de ce nom Ode . . . affin que nul ne s'atribue ce que la verité commande estre à moi" ("At the same time that Clément Marot [the only light in these years of vernacular poetry] was working diligently on his psalter, I dared to be the first among our people to enrich my language with this word Ode . . . such that none may attribute to himself what truth shows to belong to me").

5. Du Bellay, 112-13, writes: "Chante moy ces odes incongnues encor' de la Muse Francoyse, d'un luc, bien accordé au son de la lyre Greque et Romaine."

6. Huguet defines "contrefaire" as to imitate; Huguet, 2: 497. Cotgrave, however, not only sees it as meaning to imitate but also to disfigure and to adulterate—that is, to alter.

7. Silver, 1937, 55.

8. Greene, 40, writes: "Heuristic imitations come to us advertising their derivation from the subtexts they carry with them, but having done that, they proceed to *distance themselves* from the subtexts and force us to recognize the poetic distance traversed. . . . The informed reader notes the allusion but he notes simultaneously the gulf in language, in sensibility, in cultural context, in world view, and in moral style." (The italics are mine.)

9. Ferguson, 285.

10. As Cave, 230-31, mentions, Ronsard paradoxically displaces Pindar and Michel de l'Hospital in order to portray himself as the wandering poet: "In a single syntactical movement, the initial metaphor of flower gathering (the figure of how the poem is made) is elaborated by successive layers of metonymy and periphrasis, introducing by allusion first the model-poet and then the patron. Neither is named. Pindar is displaced so that the poetic *je* can appropriate his *topoi*. . . . L'Hospital is the pretext, an empty place to be skirted by myths, narrations, and incrustations of *elocutio*."

11. Silver's thesis attempts to show Ronsard's emulation of Pindar to be an utter failure. Silver, 1937.

12. Ronsard borrows this topos of the poet-wanderer directly from Horace (*Epist*. I, xix, 21-22). See also I, iii, vv. 1-12, addressed to Marguerite de Valois, where Ronsard explains that he has to wander in order to find a new way to sing of her virtue which has been tainted by the Marotiques. For further study of this formulation, see Ahmed, 587-96.

13. See also ode I, xvi, where Ronsard explicitly considers himself and his poet friends: "Comme profettes des dieus" (v. 2).

14. In all subsequent editions of the ode and in the *Franciade*, Francus himself founds Paris, and not his descendants.

15. The *Franciade* epyllion functions as a means of founding a different literary tradition under Henri II. The epic that Ronsard was to write under Charles IX was intended to give a unified history to a France rent asunder by religious strife, while here the epyllion must be seen *a contrario* to widen those differences of spiritual and poetic identity between Marot and his school on the one hand and the young Ronsard on the other. The same story functions in opposing manners at two different historical moments. See Ménager, 277 and passim.

16. See Laumonier, 146-50, for background literary history of Ronsard's literary epic the *Franciade*.

17. Ronsard borrows Aristotle's distinction between the historian and the poet; the former tells things as they are, and the latter relates them as they could be. Ronsard cautions against poetic excess in the preface to the *Franciade,* 16: 4, though he is slow to heed his own advice: "J'ose seulement dire (si mon opinion a quelque poix) que le Poëte qui escrit les choses comme elles sont ne merite tant que celuy qui les feint et se recule le plus qu'il luy est possible de l'historien: non toutefois pour feindre une Poësie fantastique comme celle de l'Ariosto" ("I dare say only—if my opinion carries any weight—that the Poet who writes about things as they are does not merit so much as one who fictionalizes them and removes himself as far as possible from the historian: not so much, however, to create a Poetry so fantastic as Ariosto").

18. Cf. Hathaway, 160-61, who writes: "Many Renaissance writers were willing to say that the masterful solving of artistic problems was one of the chief sources of admiration or the marvelous. Hence they also stressed unity, or the reconciliation of unity and variety as a cause of the marvelous." For Ronsard, it is precisely the unsolved problem of unity and diversity which leads him to a poetic conception of infinite space.

19. It is perhaps noteworthy that the poet's law comes into direct conflict with the power of the king whom Ronsard describes in the opening stanza as "Le plus grand Roi qui se treuve, / Soit en armes ou en lois" (vv. 9-10). Under the pretense of serving his patron, Ronsard feels that his poetic strength is even greater than its former self.

20. Allen cites Ficino's *Commentarium in Phedrum* (Florence, 1496), chap. 4, iii: "Quicumque numine quomodolibet occupatur . . . et mores humanos excedit. Itaque occupatio hec sive raptus *furor* quidam et *alienatio* non iniuria nominatur" (italics mine).

21. Montaigne, "Du Jeune Caton," 1: 289-90; Frame, 1: 171.

22. Todorov, 167.

23. Joukovsky, 207, explains how Ronsard uses Pindaric imagery to deify mortals. However, Ronsard transforms Pindar's "foreign" images to create apotheotic scenes, and Pindar makes no explicit claims to possess deifying powers.

24. McFarlane, 58.

25. Cited in Cassirer, 189-90.

26. "Non è possibile giamai di trovar raggione semiprobabile per la quale sia margine di questo universo corporale; e per conseguenza ancora li astri che nel suo spacio si contengono, siino di numero finito" ("It is never possible to find a half-probable reason, why there may be a limit to this corporeal universe, and still by consequence, why the stars which are contained in its space, may be of finite number"); Bruno, 150.

27. Different from Bruno, who sees only the positive side of the infinite as a plenitude, Cave, 223-70, notes Ronsard's awareness of an emptiness undermining this everexpanding plenitude.

28. Cave, 361.

29. Koyré, 54; Cassirer, 188-91.

30. See Hathaway, 133-51, for debate with Church authorities on the usage of pagan marvels in Renaissance Italy.

31. For an explication of this continually altering subjectivity in Ronsard's *Amours,* see Rigolot, 187.

Bibliography

Ahmed, Ehsan. "Ronsard's 1550 *Odes:* Defining a Poetic Self." *Bibliothèque d'Humanisme et Renaissance* 3 (1987): 587-96.

Allen, J. B. *Marsilio Ficino and the Phaedran Charioteer.* Berkeley, 1981.

Blumenberg, Hans. *The Legitimacy of the Modern Age,* trans., Robert M. Wallace. Cambridge, MA, 1983.

Bruno, Giordano. *Dialoghi italiani,* ed. Giovanni Gentile. Florence, 1958.

Cassirer, Ernst. *The Individual and the Cosmos in Renaissance Philosophy,* trans. and ed. Mario Domandi. New York, 1963.

Cave, Terence. *The Cornucopian Text: Problems of Writing in the French Renaissance.* Oxford, Eng., 1979.

Cotgrave, R. *A Dictionarie of French and English Tongues (1611).* Columbia, SC, 1950.

Du Bellay, Joachim. *La Deffence et illustration de la langue françoyse,* ed. Henri Chamard. Paris, 1970.

Ferguson, Margaret W. "The Exile's Defense: Du Bellay's *Deffence et illustration de la langue françoyse.*" *PMLA* 93 (1978).

Funkenstein, Amos. *Theology and the Scientific Imagination from the Middle Ages to the Seventeenth Century.* Princeton, NJ, 1986.

Greene, Thomas. *The Light in Troy, Imitation and Discovery in Renaissance Poetry.* New Haven, 1982.

Hathaway, B. *Marvels and Commonplaces.* New York, 1968.

Horkheimer, Max, and Theodore W. Adorno. *The Dialectic of Enlightenment.* Trans. and ed. John Cumming. New York, 1972.

Huguet, E. *Dictionnaire de la langue française.* Paris, vols. 1925-67.

Hullot-Kentor, Robert. "Back to Adorno." *Telos* 81 (1989).

Joukovsky, Françoise. *La Gloire dans la poésie française et néolatine du XVIe siècle.* Geneva, 1969.

Koyré, Alexandre. *From the Closed World to the Infinite Universe.* New York, 1957.

Laumonier, Paul. *Ronsard, poète lyrique.* Paris, 1909.

McFarlane, I. D. *The Entry of Henri II into Paris, 16 June 1549.* Binghamton, 1982.

Ménager, Daniel. *Ronsard, le roi, le poète et les hommes.* Geneva, 1979.

Montaigne, Michel de. *Essais.* Ed. Pierre Villey. Paris, 1922.

———. *Essays.* Trans. and ed. Donald M. Frame. Stanford, 1976.

Nohlac, Paul. *Ronsard et l'Humanisme.* Paris, 1966.

Pindar. *The Odes.* Trans. and ed. Richmond Lattimore. Chicago, 1976.

Quint, David. *Origin and Originality in Renaissance Literature.* New Haven, 1983.

Rigolot, François. *Le Texte de la Renaissance.* Geneva, 1984.

Ronsard, Pierre de. *Oeuvres complètes,* 2nd ed. 20 vols. Ed. Paul Laumonier. Paris, 1914-74.

Silver, Isidor. *The Pindaric Odes of Ronsard.* Paris, 1937.

———. *Ronsard and the Hellenic Renaissance in France,* Part II, *Ronsard and the Grecian Lyre.* Geneva, 1981.

Todorov, Tzvetan. *Introduction à la littérature fantastique.* Paris, 1970.

Roberto E. Campo (essay date 1992)

SOURCE: "The Arts in Conflict in Ronsard's *Des peintures contenues dedans un tableau,*" in *Romance Quarterly,* Vol. 39, No. 4, November, 1992, pp. 411-24.

[In the following essay, Campo asserts that Ronsard's poem "Des peintures contenues dedans un tableau" can be interpreted "as an attack on the expressive weakness of painting" when compared to poetry.]

Jean Plattard once suggested that, like all the major French poets of the midsixteenth century, Pierre de Ronsard overwhelmingly preferred the narrative-type,[1] historical and mythological painting produced at the Château de Fontainebleau by artists such as Il Rosso and Primaticcio to the concurrent genre of courtly portraiture practiced by painters such as François Clouet and Corneille de Lyon: "Les poètes donnaient naturellement à ces peintures historiques et mythologiques la préférence sur les portraits."[2] The appeal, Plattard believed, was two-fold. On the one hand, there was "l'ampleur de la conception" (p. 492) of narrative painting—its conceptual magnitude, or ability to represent multiple (yet related) subject matters in a single frame. On the other hand, there was its "hardiesse et . . . liberté de l'imagination" (p. 492)—its imaginative boldness, as demonstrated by the ability of narrative painting to give form to the purely conceptual truths of ideal Nature (to borrow the Neoplatonic terminology of the period). For Plattard, Ronsard considered these qualities "comme caractéristiques du génie de la poésie et des arts en général" (p. 492).

There is no dispute that Ronsard greatly admired complexity and imaginative boldness in the arts and that he expressly sought to develop both qualities throughout his poetry.[3] However, it is far less certain that this admiration translated into a preference for narrative painting over portraiture. As I have shown in a study of the famous 1555 **"Elegie à Janet,"**[4] for example, Ronsard was well aware that these special qualities could also appear in portraits (especially in those by extraordinary talents like François Clouet, the official royal portraitist between 1541 and 1572). What is more, of the many poems on painting that Ronsard came to write during his career, only a few actually describe or allude to narrative pictures. Whereas Plattard's theory would imply a greater number of poems evoking historical or mythological pictures than works on portraits, an examination of Ronsard's poetry reveals just the opposite to be true.[5]

The doubts these observations raise about the tenability of Plattard's conclusions are the inspiration for the present essay. In brief, I shall analyze one of Ronsard's poems on a narrative picture in order to reassess, albeit in a preliminary way, how this art form is truly represented. Chosen for this purpose is a piece first published in the 1550 edition of the **Second livre des Odes**: **"Des peintures contenues dedans un tableau."**[6] This ode is especially relevant in two regards. On the one hand, it represents Ronsard's sole attempt to describe a narrative picture in the form of a painting. While many of his poems refer to scenes embroidered, engraved or etched upon cloaks, cups or lutes,[7] **"Des peintures"** stands apart in considering a design in paint on a two-dimensional, canvas-like surface. On the other hand, it is without dispute Ronsard's most

sustained effort at such a description. Of the 102 verses of the ode, 96 apply directly to the representation of the *tableau*—a five-part work consisting of three mythological episodes: the making of Jupiter's thunderbolt at Vulcan's forge (vv. 7-30), Jupiter's storm (vv. 31-48), and Juno's seduction of Jupiter (vv. 49-66); and two historical scenes: Charles V's 1535 armada assault against Tunis (vv. 67-90) and the imaginary capture of the Holy Roman Emperor by Henri II, who makes his triumphal entrance into Paris (vv. 91-102).

A direction for this investigation is suggested by the one point on which the in-depth, critical commentaries on **"Des peintures"** are most agreed: the thematic structure of the poem is unusually difficult to identify. Foremost among the problems noted are the very diversity of subjects presented—the apparent unrelatedness of the scenes that comprise the *tableau*—and the language and style of presentation—the exceptional concision and dryness with which the *peintures* are verbally rendered.[8]

These difficulties notwithstanding, in an essay entitled, "Ronsard the Painter: A Reading of 'Des peintures contenues dedans un tableau'," Philip Ford manages not only to shed considerable light on the troubling iconography of the individual scenes, but also to uncover a unifying thematic schema in the work as a whole.[9] Through a careful analysis of the ode's many subtle, intertextual allusions to classical antecedents—including Virgil's *Aeneid* (8) and *Georgics* (1, 3 and 4), Homer's *Iliad* (18 and 23) and Heraclitus's commentaries on Homeric allegories—this critic convincingly demonstrates that "the painting can be seen as an allegory representing the struggle over the years between French monarchs and the Holy Roman Emperor, with divine providence acting as the controlling force" (p. 42).

For all its great success, however, this study does little to explain why the ode should offer such resistance to interpretation, why the signifiers (the language and style) of the poem should be at such exceptional odds with its signified (the political-historical meaning of the work). The present investigation gives priority to this very matter—i.e., to the causes of and possible purposes behind the obscurity of the poem.

Until now four primary explanations have been offered. For Terence Cave, the thematic discontinuity and semantic opacity of the ode are the more-or-less inevitable products of the poet's fondness for Homer and, above all, Pindar. Especially pertinent is the quality of "copieuse diversité," or thematic and formal complexity, that characterizes the style of these authors, and which Ronsard expressly praises in his preface to the 1550 edition of the *Odes* (1:47: 11. 91-100) (pp. 164-66). For Brian Barron, on the other hand, these qualities relate to the nature of poetry itself. In particular, they reflect Ronsard's career-long struggle with his art's simultaneous, but conflicting tendencies toward description—the verbal representation of images and scenes, as in a picture—and narration—the *parole,* or discourse, that serves to link and explain the descriptions (pp. 268-72). Still another explanation is suggested, if only implicitly, by Philip Ford himself, in a more recent article on the nature of Ronsardian *ekphrasis* (the representation in words of a work of visual art).[10] There he argues that such qualities are in fact deeply rooted in Neoplatonic *ekphrasis,* the tradition whose paramount goal was the "révélation voilée d'idées métaphysiques et scientifiques, *que seuls les hommes sages et inspirés sauraient pénétrer*" (p. 82, my emphasis). Finally, in her study of ideal forms in the age of Ronsard, Margaret McGowan has concluded that the apparent incoherence of the poem is intended "to demonstrate the superior descriptive power of the poet." Despite its title, the ode is meant not to conjure up an actual painting, but rather to exemplify the poet's ability to create the *"idea"* (her emphasis) or a narrative picture (p. 81).

The particular merits of each theory aside, the diversity from one to the next plainly shows the lack of a consensus on the issue. With this in mind, I should like to offer yet another theory for consideration. In short, I would propose that the qualities of thematic discontinuity and conceptual obscurity in **"Des peintures"** might more properly relate to the nature of the narrative type of painting presented there. One might therefore suppose that these effects have been cultivated in order to demonstrate the expressive weaknesses of narrative pictures and, conversely, the corresponding strengths of poetry. One might even conclude that **"Des peintures"** articulates a position (perhaps Ronsard's own) within the *Paragone* debate of the Renaissance—the centuries-old dispute over the relative superiority of the arts revived in *quattrocento* Italy (hence the term "paragone": "comparison" in Italian) by theorist-painters like Leone Battista Alberti and, especially, Leonardo da Vinci.[11]

Evidence for this theory is present from the start, in the titles of the ode: both the original formulation, **"Des peintures contenues dedans un tableau,"** and the final version (first employed in 1555), **"Les peintures d'un Païsage."** From the form of the articles alone, for example, it is clear there will be some kind of opposition between the ideas of multiplicity (indicated by the plurals, "Des" and "Les") and unity (suggested by the singular, "un"). What is more, from the linking terms "contenues dedans" and "*d'*un," it is evident that a synthesis will develop, a dialectical relation whereby the first idea will subsume—and ultimately supplant—the second. In addition, since the plurals modify the word "peintures" in each version, it may be assumed that the notion of multiplicity should apply to painting and, in particular, to narrative painting (an expectation confirmed, we shall see, in the poem that follows). The idea of unity, on the other hand, may be linked to poetry. The key is the reference, in the final title, to the "Païsage." Although the term was already used to denote landscape painting by the middle of the sixteenth century,[12] its capitalization here[13] invites a meta-

phorical reading more in keeping with Ronsard's use of the word (uncapitalized) at the opening of his 1560 **"Elegie à Louis des Masures"**:

> Comme celui qui voit du haut d'une fenestre
> Alentour de ses yeux un *païsage* champestre,
>
> . . . . .
>
> Celuy qui list les vers que j'ay portraicts ici
> Regarde d'un trait d'œil meinte diverse chose
> Qui bonne & mauvaise entre en mon papier enclose.
>
> (10: 362-63, vv. 1-14, my emphasis)

Thus, to the extent the admirer of "un païsage champestre" is like the reader of the poem, it may be concluded that the "P/païsage" is a metaphor for the poem and, by extension, poetry. Finally, in so far as the *peintures* are "contenues dedans" the *Païsage,* it may be inferred that the art of poetry will effect the predicted synthesis, that the poem will bring oneness to the multipartite, narrative painting that follows.

What, though, is the precise nature of poetry's ability? The answer emerges with a clearer understanding of the concept of unity that develops within the poem itself. We therefore proceed to the opening stanza, the only more or less explicit, authorial reflection on the *tableau* as a whole:

> Tableau, que l'éternelle gloire
> D'un Apelle avouroit pour sien,
> Ou de quelque autre dont l'histoire
> Celebre le nom ancien,
> Tant la couleur heureusement parfaite
> A la Nature en son mort contrefaite.
>
> (vv. 1-6)

The implications underlying the paradoxical twist of verse 6 are especially important. Here, despite the hyperbolic salute to the perfection of the *tableau* in the first five lines—a perfection that even the legendary painters of Antiquity, including Apelle, would be tempted to envy—we learn that the Nature imitated is "en son mort." The negative connotation of this locution seems wholly at odds with the notions of joy, perfection and immortality that pervade the rest of the stanza. But what does this phrase, with its unusual use of the noun "mort" in the masculine, truly mean?

Following Edmond Huguet, for whom "le mort" denotes the "Etat" or "aspect d'une personne morte" (*Dictionnaire* 5, 340), Charles Guérin takes *en son mort* to mean "sur son image inanimée."[14] Paul Laumonier and Henri and Catherine Weber, on the other hand, arrive at a more figurative interpretation. They base it on Ronsard's use of the term in the first tercet of **Sonnet XXIII** of the 1578 *Second livre des sonets pour Helene*: "Vraye tu es farouche, & fiere en cruauté: / De toy fausse on jouyst en toute privauté. / Pres *ton mort* je m'endors, pres de luy je repose . . ." (17:265, my emphasis). Drawing on a reference to the lady's "forme douteuse" in an earlier verse (v. 5: "Je fusse mort d'ennuy dans ta forme douteuse"), these critics read "mort" in the masculine to mean "fantôme" or "apparition onirique."[15]

In the end, however, neither definition applies satisfactorily to the case at hand. Especially troublesome is how *le mort* should pertain to "Nature"—a term whose capitalization strongly suggests that it be taken in the broadest, Neoplatonic sense: i.e., as denoting both the physical world and the ideal realm of transcendent meanings and moral truths.

The solution, I believe, comes with Ronsard's reprise of the phrase in **"A mes Dames,"** a didactic poem published in the 1555 ***Troisieme livre des Odes***. Here, while reflecting on the education of Henri II's three young daughters, and, above all, on the importance of cultivating the powers of the mind at least as devotedly as the beauty of the body, the poet evokes the analogy of a painting as the first in a series of warnings against ignoring this wisdom.

> Peu de tans la beauté dure,
> Et le sang qui des Rois sort,
> Si de l'esprit on n'a cure:
> *Autant vaut quelque peinture*
> *Qui n'est vive qu'en son mort.*

> (7: 78, vv. 71-75, my emphasis)

Especially revealing is the opposition between "esprit"—which, in the context of the poem as a whole, can only be understood as the immortal, essential quality of mind (cf. vv. 76-85)—and "beauté"—one's perishable and, hence, inessential, physical attributes. Since the poet likens a woman whose only virtue is her beauty to a painting whose only life is "en son mort," it follows that this last phrase should designate the inessential qualities of a person or thing—that which belongs to the realm of superficial appearances, and which may therefore be said to stand in the same relation to one's true and immutable essence as Plato's shadows do to their respective Ideas. Thus considered, verse 6 of **"Des peintures"** may be read to say that, regardless of its perfection, the color of the *tableau* succeeds only in imitating the inessential realm of physical Nature, and, by extension, that narrative painting is unable to imitate the essential, abstract truths of ideal Nature.

Ronsard's conception of color as it relates to painting supports this theory. Not only does the poet firmly link color to the idea of physicality, but he regards it (and so physicality too) as an inextricable element of the painter's art. This point is driven home at the opening of his 1564 poetic lament to Marie Stuart, in the **"Elegie sur le depart de la Royne d'Escosse"**:

> Comme un beau pré despouillé de ses fleurs,
> *Comme un tableau privé de ses couleurs,*
> Comme le ciel, s'il perdoit ses estoilles,
> La mer ses eaux, la navire ses voiles,

> . . . . .

> Ainsi perdra la France soucieuse
> Ses ornemens, en perdant la beauté
> Qui fut sa fleur, *sa couleur,* sa clarté.

> (12: 193-94, vv. 1-10, my emphasis)

We remark, in particular, the connection between color—as much the *sine qua non* of painting as the other analogues for Queen Marie constitute the distinguishing features of their related places and objects—and the notion of physicality, metaphorically raised in the terms "ornemens" and "beauté."[16]

To return at last to the idea of unity and to the nature of poetry's special ability to unify, then, two primary conclusions may be drawn. First, we may infer that the attainment of unity depends, in an essential way, on the expression of ideal Nature. From the association, in the opening stanza, between physical Nature and painting, and the connection, in the titles, between painting and the idea of multiplicity, we find that physical Nature relates to both painting and multiplicity: physical Nature-painting-multiplicity. Accordingly, from the opposition, also in the titles, between multiplicity and unity, we may surmise that ideal Nature, as the antithesis of physical Nature (in Neoplatonic metaphysics), relates to unity: ideal Nature-unity. The second conclusion follows from the first. Given the affinity, likewise connoted in the titles, between unity and poetry, we may reason that poetry enjoys a privileged relationship with ideal Nature: ideal Nature-poetry-unity. Thus, in the same way painting is qualified to imitate physical Nature, poetry is uniquely able to imitate ideal Nature; and just as the relation of painting to multiplicity follows from its links with physicality, the power of poetry to effect unity derives directly from its special ability to express abstract, transcendent meanings and moral truths.

On a certain level, then, the titles and opening sestet of **"Des peintures"** may be said to advance the case for the superiority of poetry over painting in the imitation of ideal Nature and, thereby, to articulate (albeit implicitly) a position, on Neoplatonic grounds, in favor of the poet's art within the *Paragone* debate of the mid-sixteenth century. But what becomes of these ideas throughout the remainder of the poem? How are they reflected in the 96 verses devoted to the *tableau* itself? The answer, I propose, bears directly on the matter of the discontinuous style that characterizes the ode and obfuscates its political-historical, allegorical dimension. More precisely, I would suggest that the appearance of discontinuity throughout the *tableau* has been carefully cultivated in order to recreate the apparent disjointedness of a real narrative painting and, in so doing, to translate into words the expressive weaknesses of that visual art form.

The precise nature and specific effects of the two stylistic features most responsible for the discontinuity of the ode lend important support to this theory. First, there is Ronsard's obvious silence about the relatedness, the overall allegorical meaning, of the five *peintures* of the poem. Such reticence is highly unusual for Ronsard. Even in those poems where his debt to the stylistic diffuseness of Horace and Pindar is most apparent, the poet typically takes great care to insure detection of the unifying, thematic framework—whether through subtle allusion or overt commentary.[17]

Evidence of this exceptional silence appears from the beginning of the *tableau* description, in stanza 2:

> Où la grand bande renfrongnée
> Des Cyclopes laborieus,
> Est à la forge embesongnée,
> Qui d'un effort industrieus
> Haste un tonnerre, armure pour la destre
> De ce grand Dieu, à le ruer adestre.
>
> (vv. 7-12).

The opening relative pronoun, "Où," is deceiving. While its link to the first word of the ode, "Tableau," raises the expectation that stanza 2 will continue the authorial commentary begun in stanza 1, and, in the process, expand it by alluding to the unifying, political-historical message of the poem, in truth no such continuity arises. As the focus shifts instantly to the images themselves all allusions to the broader significance of the painting disappear. The poet offers nothing to contextualize the episodes that follow, and so, nothing to help the reader understand their overall meaning.

This silence continues throughout the poem, as may be seen in the striking abruptness of the concluding stanza of the work:

> Paris tient ses portes decloses
> Recevant son Roi belliqueur,
> Une grande nue de roses
> Pleut à l'entour du chef vainqueur.
> Les feus de joie ici & là s'alument,
> Et jusque au ciel les autels des Dieus fument.
>
> (vv. 97-102)

The ode simply ceases as the poet completes his account of the fifth painting. Once again Ronsard eschews all commentary, direct or indirect, that could help to establish the thematic unity underlying the five episodes of the *tableau*.

Contributing to the impression of authorial reticence are the phrases employed to conjoin the five *peintures*. Rather than use the customary signals of narrative emplotment, terms that might indicate something about the causal or temporal relationships between the various episodes, Ronsard opens each succeeding description with an allusion to some kind of spatial orientation. Moreover, the spatial cues selected are, in the end, nearly meaningless. However precise expressions like "Un peu plus haut" (v. 31) and "Au meilleu de" (v. 73) might first appear, they in fact never fulfill their referential promise. Missing is such essential information as the relative size of the various scenes and their orientation with respect to any of the standard, pictorial points of reference: top, bottom, left side, right side and center. The result is a sense of spatial randomness

and the fundamental paradox that the *tableau* in question is virtually impossible to visualize.[18]

But what could have inspired Ronsard's silence? His primary, textual model for the ode, Virgil's painted-shield episode in *Aeneid* 8 (11. 626-730), is significantly different in this regard. However elliptical its style or great its number of spatial connectives, this Latin antecedent never conceals its prophetic meaning from the reader. Clues about the underlying symbolism of the shield's iconography are provided on a variety of levels throughout the work.[19]

A likelier source of inspiration, I suggest, is the legendary analogy attributed to the classical Greek poet, Simonides of Keos: "Painting is mute poetry; poetry a speaking painting." Not only was this aphorism a favorite topic of artistic and poetic discussion throughout Renaissance Europe, but its echo clearly resonates in many of Ronsard's own poems (cf. the 1549 ode, **"A René d'Urvoi,"** vv. 1-4; his 1555 **"Elegie à Janet,"** vv. 95 and 192; and the 1567 "Elegie" to Marie Stuart, **"Bien que le trait de vostre belle face,"** vv. 71-76 and 137-46). On a certain level, then, the silence in **"Des peintures"** may be read as Ronsard's verbal equivalent of the muteness attributed to all the pictorial (and plastic) arts since distant Antiquity. More important, though, the sense of discontinuity and confusion to which this muteness gives rise may be regarded as manifestations of the inherently limited expressivity of narrative painting alluded to, in general terms, in the titles and opening stanza.

An examination of the second source of semantic incoherence in the poem upholds this reading. It is a matter of Ronsard's emphasis on the idea of present time throughout the ode. Like the silence, this feature—evident in the extraordinarily high number of present-tense verbs and present-progressive contructions (not to mention present participles used adjectivally)[20]—may be said to undermine any sense of emplotment, both within and between the various episodes. Much as the connecting terms considered previously substitute an illusion of spatiality for the idea of causality, the poet's emphasis on present time creates an impression of simultaneity that relentlessly subverts the possible chronology of the events recounted. There is more. With the apostrophes to the reader/spectator ("Vous") and the other more or less explicit references to the receptor sprinkled throughout the poem,[21] Ronsard injects a sense of *nowness* into this simultaneity. As a result, the events seem to take place both all at once and at the same moment in which the reader of the poem (the spectator of the painting) experiences them.

This sense of immediacy reaches a kind of climax midway through the present-tense description of the third *peinture* (vv. 49-66: Juno's amorous seduction of Jupiter). In verses 55-60, hence at the virtual (if not properly numerical) center of the poem, Ronsard introduces a parenthetic digression, likewise in the present tense, about a picture on the richly decorated "baudrier," or warrior's girdle, that the queen of the gods has borrowed from Venus (presumably in the hope that its aphrodisiac powers will help rekindle her husband's original amatory ardor):

> (Là, les amours sont portraits d'ordre,
> Celui qui donte les oiseaus,
> Et celui qui vient ardre & mordre
> Le cueur des Dauphins sous les eaus.
> Leandre, proie à l'amour inhumaine,
> Pendu aus flots noue où l'amour le meine.)

There can be little doubt that the three *amours* described in this passage—which Ford convincingly traces to Homer and the manifestations of Eros on Aphrodite's *cestos* in *Iliad* 14.214-17: spiritual love, impatient desire and maddening lust (37-38)—relate directly to the seduction theme of the *peinture* as a whole. Indeed, they may even symbolize the nuances of love at work in Juno's own heart and mind.

Still unclear, though, is why these images have been introduced as components of a miniature picture within this painting. Surely Ronsard owes nothing to Virgil. Never does the Roman author refer to a painting within the scenes on Aeneas' shield. Nor is it likely he drew inspiration from the Mannerist style of narrative painting practiced before or during the composition of **"Des peintures,"** in the late 1540s. However much painters of the day liked to juxtapose multiple scenes within a single frame,[22] contrary to what the *baudrier* stanza would imply, the number of contemporary narrative paintings found to include miniature versions of other pictures appears, in truth, rather small.[23]

Why too, we must wonder, has Ronsard marked off this passage in parentheses while simultaneously placing it at the center of the ode, one of the most privileged spots in the structure of any (pre-modernist) literary work? Insofar as the poet normally reserves this punctuation for purely subordinate, explicatory and personal digressions,[24] such a position would seem, on the surface, wholly inappropriate. It is true that, by evoking the "Dauphins sous les eaus" in verse 58, the *baudrier* stanza anticipates the more naturalistic breed of porpoises, the "Dauphins aus dos courbés," that "nouent / . . . follatrent & jouent" (vv. 71-72) in the first historical scene (vv. 67-90). Thus, on one level, these lines may be judged ideally located to prepare the transition from the mythological beginning of the ode (*peintures* 1-3) to its historical ending (*peintures* 4-5). Nevertheless, should not such an important structural function preclude the use of parentheses?

A solution to these queries may be found, I propose, in the contribution the *baudrier* sestet makes to the quality of simultaneity that develops in the ode. First, by including a description in the present tense of a miniature picture within the description, also in the present tense, of a painting that, we recall, is itself but a component of the present-tense description of the *tableau* as a whole, Ronsard succeeds in reinforcing the impression that all parts of the poem exist synchronously and, so again, in imitating in words a work of visual art (this time, the ability of a painting to present its multiple elements to the viewer at the same instant). Second, by enclosing this passage in parentheses while paradoxically placing it at the center of the ode, the poet manages not only to underscore his mimetic accomplishment, but also to draw attention to the subversive effects of such synchronousness on the ability of the narrative painter to express the transcendent meanings of ideal Nature. Indeed, by selecting this maneuver Ronsard may be said to assign a thematic role to this idea that rivals in importance the historical-allegorical message of the poem.[25]

This insistence on the disadvantages of pictorial simultaneity is, I believe, the most convincing evidence of Ronsard's involvement in the *Paragone* debate of the period. By addressing this feature, Ronsard confronts a central premise on which Renaissance art theorists—and, above all, Leonardo da Vinci[26]—based their claims for the painter's superiority over the poet. The 23rd treatise of Leonardo's *Trattato della pittura* (ca. 1498) raises this very issue in connection with another concern of the *Paragone* dispute, the relative worth of the senses of sight (the domain of the painter) and hearing (the province of the poet):

> La pittura ti rapresenta *in un'subito* la sua essentia nella uirtu uisius e per il proprio mezzo donde la impressiua riceue li obbietti naturali . . . ; e la poesia rifferisce il medesimo, ma con mezzo meno degno che l'occhio, il quale porta nella impressiua *più confusamente e con più tardità* le figurationi delle cose nominate, che non fa l'occhio. . . .

> ["Painting presents its subject to thee *in one instant* through the sense of sight, through the same organ that transmits the natural objects to the mind; . . . Poetry transmits the same subject through a sense which is less noble and which impresses on the mind the shapes of the objects it describes *more slowly and confusedly than the eye.* . . ."]

> (Richter, p. 61; my emphasis)

A similar argument appears in *Trattato* 22, only here Leonardo expands on the notion that a subject presented *all at once* by a painter is inherently more intelligible (and true to Nature[27]) than the same subject rendered by a poet through the time-bound medium of verbal language:

> Hor uedi, che differentia è dal udire raccontare una cosa, che dà piacere al occhio *con lunghezza di tempo,* o uederla *con quella prestezza,* che si uedono le cose naturali. et anchora che le cose de' poeti sieno con longho interuallo di tempo lette, spesse sono le uolte, che *le non sonno intese e bisogna farli sopra diuersi comenti,* de' quali rarissime uolte tali comentatori intendono, qual'fusse la mente del poeta . . . Ma l'opera del pittore *immediate è compresa* dalli suoi risguardatori.

> ["Now look what difference there is between listening *for a long time* to a tale about something which gives pleasure to the eye and actually seeing it *all at once* as works of nature are seen. Moreover, the works of poets are read at long intervals; *they are often not understood and require many explanations,* and commentators very

rarely know what was in the poet's mind . . . But the work of the painter is *immediately understood* by its beholders."]

(Richter, p. 60; my emphasis)

On a certain level, then, **"Des peintures"** may be read as a Ronsard's reply, on behalf of poetry, to Renaissance arguments like Leonardo's that ascribe the superiority of painting to its inherent synchronousness and immediate intelligibility.

To summarize, good grounds exist to assume that **"Des peintures"** does far more than allegorize the struggle between Henri II and Charles V and the role played by the gods in insuring a French victory. Based upon our examination of the title, the opening stanza and the principal features responsible for the obscure appearance of the work, we find that it may also be read as an attack on the expressive weaknesses of painting—specifically narrative painting—and that, perhaps, it represents a rebuttal to the theories exalting the painter over the poet advanced by Renaissance art theorists like Leonardo da Vinci.

Still uncertain, though, is how the ode has demonstrated the other thesis raised in the title and first sestet: the converse proposition which would place the superior ability to imitate ideal Nature in the pen of the poet. The answer, I submit, is surprisingly simple. For what clearer proof of this ability is there than the success of the poem in carrying at least two major ideas (its historical-allegorical message and, as the present study has attempted to show, a statement of Ronsard's position in the *Paragone* debate) and the fact that both ideas are—despite the discontinuous design of the work—comprehensible?

This last point raises one final question. Why are we able to understand the ode at all? If it is true that a narrative painting is "en son mort" with respect to ideal Nature, how is it **"Des peintures"** can coherently express any abstract concept after the effort Ronsard puts into imitating the two most essential properties of the pictorial arts, their muteness and visual synchronousness? The answer, I propose, relates to the nature of poetry itself. More precisely, it pertains to the intrinsic diachrony—or more properly, sequentiality—of poetry's medium of verbal language. For in the end, the ideas raised in this ode are too complex to be apprehended in an instant. They are the products of an evolution that depends upon the sequential disposition of words or, in the present case, upon the ode's movement from the first *peinture* to the fifth, from its mythological beginning to its historical end. Ronsard doubtless realizes this dependency. Indeed, it is the underlying reason for the simultaneous, opposing tendency of **"Des peintures"** toward confusion, as a *tableau,* and meaning, as a poem.

Notes

1. My understanding of "narrative painting" is based, in part, on the use of the term by Erwin and Dora Panofsky in "The Iconography of the Galerie François Ier at Fontainebleau," *Gazette des Beaux-Arts* (1958): 113-90. Equally influential, however, has been the definition advanced by Wendy Steiner in *Pictures of Romance* (University of Chicago Press, 1988), p. 2: "Of the many conditions contributing to [pictorial] narrativity, the most important are: that the painting present more than one temporal moment; that a subject be repeated from one moment to another; and that the subject be embedded in at least a minimally realistic setting."

2. Jean Plattard, "Les Arts et les artistes de la Renaissance française jugés par les écrivains du temps," *RHLF* 21 (1914): 481-502.

3. Cf. the preface to the 1550 edition of the *Odes* (1:47: 11. 91-100) and the *Abbregé de l'art poëtique françois* (especially on "invention": 14: 12ff).

4. "A Poem to a Painter: The *Elegie à Janet* and Ronsard's Dilemma of Ambivalence," *French Forum* 12 (1987): 273-87.

5. Cf. my unpublished doctoral dissertation, "Pierre and the *Paragone:* The Rivalry Between Poetry and Painting in the Works of Pierre de Ronsard" (diss. University of Pennsylvania 1989), pp. 69 and 187-221.

6. Pierre de Ronsard, *Œuvres complètes,* ed. Paul Laumonier, 1 (Paris: Hachette, 1931), 259-64. All citations of *Des peintures* are taken from this edition; all other citations of, or allusions to, Ronsard's works are likewise to Laumonier's edition and will be noted parenthetically, as appropriate, with references to volume, page and verse.

7. Cf., respectively, *Le ravissement de Cephale* (2: 133-47), *La Bergerie* (13: 75-131), *A sa guiterre* (1: 229-34) and *La Lyre* (15: 15-38).

8. Cf. Margaret McGowan, *Ideal Forms in the Age of Ronsard* (University of California Press, 1985), pp. 81, 83; Brian Barron, "'Ut Pictura poesis': un lieu commun de la Renaissance et son importance dans l'Œuvre de Ronsard" (diss. University of Edinburgh 1981), p. 269; Terence Cave, *Ronsard the Poet* (London: Methuen, 1973), p. 164.

9. *French Studies* 40 (1986): 32-44.

10. "La Fonction de l'ekphrasis chez Ronsard," *Ronsard en son IVe centenaire: L'Art de poésie,* ed. Yvonne Bellenger et al., *Etudes Ronsardiennes* II (Geneva: Droz, 1989).

11. For background on the *Paragone* between poetry and painting, see Jean Paul Richter, *The Literary Works of Leonardo da Vinci,* 3rd ed. (1883; rpt. New York: Phaidon, 1970) I, 13-22 and 41-68; Rensselaer Lee, *Ut Pictura Poesis: The Humanistic Theory of Painting* (New York: Norton, 1967), esp. pp. 56-61.; W. J. T. Mitchell, *Iconology: Image, Text, Ideology* (University of Chicago, 1986), esp. pp. 116-21., Leatrice Mendelsohn, *Paragoni: Benedetto Varchi's "Due Lezzioni" and Cinquecento Art Theory*

(University of Michigan Press, 1982). Regarding the *Paragone* in Ronsard's *Œuvre,* though between poetry and architecture, see Doranne Fenoaltea, *Du palais au jardain: l'architecture des "Odes" de Ronsard* (Etudes Ronsardiennes, 3), (Geneva: Droz, 1990), pp. 16-26.

12. Cf. the *Elegie à Louis des Masures* (10:362-70), esp. vv. 1-14. For more on the history of the word "païsage," see Huguet, *Dictonnaire de la langue française,* 5 (Paris: Didier, 1961). Cf., also, Lucile M. Golson, "Landscape Prints and Landscapists of the School of Fontainebleau," *Gazette des Beaux-Arts,* 73 (Feb. 1969): 95-110.

13. I base my comments on the rendering of the word as it consistently appeared in the body of the work beginning in 1555 and as Laumonier has transcribed it in his notes on editions (p. 259). It is nevertheless true that, in the *Table des Odes* for each edition in which the revised title was used (1555, 1560, 1567, 1571, 1573 and 1578), a lower-case "p" was supplied by the editor-publisher.

14. Guérin, *Les Odes de Ronsard* (Paris: Cèdre, 1952), p. 385.

15. Laumonier 17: 264-65; H. and C. Weber, *Les Amours de Pierre de Ronsard* (Paris: Garnier, 1963), p. 835.

16. Louis Le Caron notes the same essential link between painting and color in his fourth *Dialogue:* "Aucuns escrivent la fable estre en la poësie, ce que la couleur en la peinture, laquelle a plus de force que la ligne, pour faire regarder l'image bien tirée . . ." (*Dialogues,* eds. Joan A. Buhlmann and Donald Gilman [Geneva: Droz, 1986], p. 270).

17. Cf. the ode *A Michel de l'Hospital* (3:118-63). However complex this poem may be, Ronsard never lets us forget that the central story (relating the mythological origins of the muses and their divine powers) is above all an allegory intended to praise his friend and advocate, Michel de l'Hospital, and, by extension, to attack his detractors at court.

18. Cf. Cave (p. 164) and Ford (p. 32).

19. Cf. *Aeneid,* 11. 626-29: "Illic res Italas Romanorumque triumphos / haud vatum ignarus venturique inscius aevi / fecerat Ignipotens, illic genus omne futurae / stirpis ab Ascanio pugnataque in ordine bella." ["There the story of Italy and the triumphs of Rome had the lord of Fire fashioned, not unversed in prophecy, or unknowing of the age to come; there, every generation of the stock to spring from Ascanius, and the wars they fought one by one"] (*Virgil,* tran. H. Rushton Fairclough, 2 [Harvard University Press, 1954], 102-03).

20. Careful inspection uncovers 58 examples of the present tense (including passive forms) and 24 present-progressive constructions as compared to only three instances of the past tense.

21. Cf. the reference to "on" in verse 74. See also the analogies directed to the same receptor: "Comme un etang" (v. 30); "En forme de lances errans" (v. 46); "Egalle aus chans" (v. 48); and "Comme grandes forests" (v. 74). For more on the function of analogies as signals of the receptor-narratee, see Gerald Prince, "Introduction à l'étude du narrataire," *Poétique* 14 (1973): 178-96, esp. 185.

22. Cf. John Shearman, *Mannerism* (1967; rpt. New York: Penguin Books, 1979), pp. 21-22 and Jacques Bousquet, *Mannerism: The Painting and Style of the Late Renaissance,* tran. Simon Watson Taylor (New York: Braziller, 1964).

23. Admittedly, this observation is purely empirical and, so, remains open to amendment. For a complete list of the essays and art catalogues consulted on this matter, see my dissertation bibliography (pp. 243-46).

24. Cf., among many other poems, the ode *A Jouachim du Bellai Angevin* (1: 108-21, vv. 85, 106, 190) and the ode *A Bouju Angevin* (1: 121-25, vv. 5-6).

25. Françoise Joukovsky draws a similar conclusion in *Le Bel objet: les paradis artificiels de la Pléiade* (Paris: Champion, 1991), p. 61.

26. It is true that certain details of Leonardo's arguments would remain hidden until the first publication of the *Trattato,* in 1651 (in Paris). Nevertheless, thanks to France's frequent military, political and social exchanges with Italy (not the least relevant of which were Leonardo's associations with Louis XII in Milan, between 1506 and 1513, and his move to Amboise at the invitation of François I, in 1516), there can be little doubt that the essence of his thinking had reached French cultural leaders by the middle of the sixteenth century. For more on the history of the *Trattato* manuscripts, see Richter, pp. 5-11. For concrete evidence of Leonardo's legacy in early sixteenth-century France, see Geofroy Tory, *Champ Fleury,* ed. Gustave Cohen (Paris: Charles Bosse, 1931), pp. XIII (r), XXXIV (v), XXXV (r) and XLVI (v); and P. Durrieu, *Les Relations de Léonard de Vinci avec le peintre français Jean Perréal* (Paris: E. Leroux, 1919), pp. 7-8.

27. The relation between simultaneity and trueness to Nature receives its most striking development in Leonardo's battle-scene example. See *Trattato* 15 (Richter, p. 53) and *Trattato* 22 (Richter, p. 60).

Jerry C. Nash (essay date 1993)

SOURCE: "'Fantastiquant Mille Monstres Bossus': Poetic Incongruities, Poetic Epiphanies, and the Writerly Semiosis of Pierre de Ronsard," in *Romanic Review,* Vol. 84, No. 2, March, 1993, pp. 143-62.

In his latest study on an intriguing subject that was for him both "exhilarating" and "exasperating," Murray Krieger defines ekphrasis in these terms: "the literary representation of visual art, real or imaginary." The kind of ekphrasis that deals with the "real" is of course the art of mimesis, what Krieger calls "*enargeia* I," that is, the "sensible" or sense-oriented perception and portrayal of the mimetic real. Ekphrasis which strives to capture the "imaginary," a writer's art of semiosis, Krieger discusses as "*enargeia* II," that is, the "intelligible" or mind-oriented perception and portrayal of the semiotic imaginary.[1] My discussion of Pierre de Ronsard will consider only one side of his captivating poetic of ekphrasis, namely, his verbally semiotic presentations of the visual imaginary, his intelligible perceptions and creations of *enargeia* II. Other studies have already explored Ronsard's debt to the ekphrastic principle of imitation as it relates to and attempts to portray the mimetic real.[2] What remains is to examine this other discourse and level of meaning in Ronsard, his writerly semiosis of seeing and of showing which truly became a poetic obsession for him just as it did for Joachim Du Bellay and Maurice Scève, as I have written on elsewhere.[3]

Exhilarating and exasperating are indeed perfect ways to describe the writerly as well as readerly activity involved in the literary phenomenology of ekphrasis. This is especially the case when a poet is concerned with coming to terms with the imaginary real, with what another contemporary critic of Poetics, Michael Riffaterre, calls the "fictional truth" and triumph of semiosis over mimesis.[4] The exasperating side of Ronsard's poetic project can be seen in the many failure-poems one encounters in his ***Amours,*** such as the "eye-defeating" and thus art-defeating impasse which the poet acknowledges and describes early on in ***Cassandre*** XIX. [5] In addition to failure in love, the familiar thematics of unrequited love, this poem is also a statement about poetic sterility and poetic failure, and it is the beloved Cassandre herself in her Trojan role as prophetess who conveys this to the poet. His rewards and legacy, she tells him in the first two stanzas, can only be an early death and unaccomplished life, lackluster writings, and scorn and ridicule by his readers in the future. In sum, as Cassandre sees it: "Tu bastiras sur l'incertain du sable, / Et vainement tu peindras dans les cieulx." Worse still, Cassandre's dire and defeating predictions on the poet's failure and future seem to be confirmed by the ultimate sign of divine authority, as the poem's closural image "seals" the matter once and for all (i.e., the image of a lightning flash as an ill-fated omen which the poet "sees" on his "right" hand):

> Ainsi disoit la Nymphe qui m'afolle,
> Lors que le ciel pour *séeller* sa parolle
> D'un *dextre esclair* fut presage à mes yeulx.

Two other early poems are also about artistic failure: ***Cassandre*** XXVIII and **XXIX**. The reader does not have to wait until the ***Marie***-cycle of love poems to find confirmation of such a failure in poetic seeing and feeling and showing, contrary to what most critics, and especially Olivier Pot most recently, have argued.[6] *Cassandre* XXVIII is very revealing to show the poet showing the writing of mimesis as failure, or, to be more precise, to show the poet recognizing a failure in the sensible, sense-satisfying purpose of the mimetic vision and its writing. At first, the poet seems to be telling us that this ineffable beauty of Cassandre that has so enslaved him and caused his "senses" to "trouble" his reason *is* to be found in the many objects or entities of nature itself. This beauty the poet *does* see and feel through the perceiving senses of the body "*painted* in them":

> Je ne voy pré, fleur, antre, ny rivage,
> Champ, roc, ny boys, ny flotz dedans le Loyr,
> Que, *peinte en eulx,* il ne me semble *voyr*
> Ceste *beaulté* qui me tient en servage.

Up to this point, the mimetic vision and the writing of it are both working well for the poet. *But,* as the poet informs us in the poem's last tercet, when it comes to pursuing this beauty in them, he is left with the realization that Love has sent him forms that really have no substance, for they all seem to disappear ("s'enfuir"), leaving the poet with only an "empty real." Alongside deception in love, the poet is also pointing out to the reader another deception, that of mimetic perception and its portrayal. The *sensible* illusion and reality afforded by ekphrasis as mimesis are indeed deceptive and parallel the despair and deception and failure in love which the poet is also describing. As the poet poignantly puts it in the last line: "Et pour le vray je ne pren que le vuide."

This failure in the realist project, in mimetic art, that is, the inability of the poet to accept sensible perceptions or visions as real and meaningful and to turn them into adequate and self-satisfying words and images that succeed in bridging the gap between feeling and world, is also the subject of ***Cassandre*** XXIX. The first two quatrains of this sonnet also show the poet indulging an exceptionally sensible, highly sensual, even erotic fantasy, with the poet's arms imitating the intimate embrace of the vine-plant. Again, up to this point in the poem, things appear to be working well for the poet and for the reader. However, by the time we reach the end of this poem too, the poet's mimetic vision has been deconstructed and disintegrates completely, leaving him once again abandoned and dismayed:

> *Mais* ce *portraict* qui nage dans mes yeulx,
> *Fraude* tousjours ma joye entrerompuë.
> Et tu me fuis au meillieu de mon bien,
> Comme l'esclair qui se finist en *rien,*
> Ou comme au vent *s'esvanouit* la nuë.

In his "songe divin" of the mimetic real, which is the real subject and problem in this poem, the poet's vision of self as vine-plant enjoying physical intimacy with the beloved becomes ultimately a failed vision. The poet is literally left with "nothing" ("rien"), with the "self-consuming" ("s'évanouir") and unsatisfying vision and feeling and art of non-meaning and non-presence. This failure-poem, like the ones above, does not at all confirm the much discussed and much admired Pléiade realist project and its principle of ekphrasis as mimesis, an aesthetic and writerly principle which Henri Weber (in *La Création poétique . . .*) was one of the first to praise and to explore in Ronsard's poetic texts: Ronsard's "désir fondamental de cueillir *dans la réalité* les sensations les plus intenses pour en tirer une délectation exaltante"; or, as Weber continues to paint the picture of Ronsard as the successful poet in harmony verbally with depicting the mimetic real: " . . . aux mots mêmes qui *peignent le monde réel,* Ronsard sait en général associer par le seul effet du rythme *la joie de l'artiste* qui découvre ce monde, alors la *description* devient *poésie*" (125). As we have already seen, and there are other failure-poems in *Cassandre* one could turn to, such notions as "la joie de l'artiste" and indeed of poetry itself as ekphrasis are totally antithetical to the message being conveyed in **XIX, XXVII,** and **XXIX,** truly poems of despair and defeat in matters of love and of art.[7]

Fortunately however, *Cassandre* XIX does offer a clue as how to reverse artistic sterility and failure, and how to change despair and defeat into joy and poetry. Such a reversal begins, necessarily, with poems and statements such as those considered above which acknowledge failure, ones highlighting the very impossibility or at least the tenuousness and unacceptability of the mimetic project and process, with its sense-oriented aesthetic, in coming to terms with the ineffability of the love experience. Moreover, the best textual indication that mimetic failure is not Ronsard's final position on poetic seeing and showing lies in the ambiguity afforded in the closure of *Cassandre* XIX: the seemingly ill-fated omen of a lightning flash ("dextre esclair") on the poet's right hand. Can this image and sign, contrary to the view of Ronsard's various editors who have commented on it, not be interpreted differently, even in the exact opposite way as a *favorable* sign intended to lead the poet, and the reader, out of exasperation and failure to exhilaration and triumph? Elsewhere (**LVII**), the poet clearly signals that his torment and misfortune, like those of Sisyphus and Tantalus, are associated with a *left* hand. And in another place (**CLX**), perhaps even more revealing, we are told that his true potential as poet is to be found in "rightly" interpreting "intelligibly" ("dextrement") the prophecy of his fate. Only through a more intelligible perception and presentation, Ronsard reassures himself and his reader, can he as *poet* envision Cassandre/the Vendômois countryside (Gastine Forest, Loire River) raised to the poetic power of the Muse Thalia/ Mount Parnassus (Apollo's Laurel, Castalia Spring):

> Si dextrement l'augure j'ay receu,
> Et si mon oeil ne fut hyer déceu
> Des doulx regardz de ma doulce Thalie,
> Dorenavant *poëte me ferez,*

> Et par la France appellez vous serez,
> L'un mon laurier, l'aultre ma Castalie.

The "dextre esclair" in *Cassandre* XIX, as with the "dextrement" in the line above from **CLX,** may be a sign of melancholy, as Ronsard's various editors have presented it, but it also points to something the opposite. As pure metanoia, a change in direction of the mind and thus in poetic direction and definition, it stands as a sign of a *different* potential and way of writing and of showing, and of the potential success and miracle of the poet-pen-paper relationship in this different mode and aesthetic resisting and rejecting the realist aesthetic, opting instead to control its/ their own destiny. This image announces the poet's receptivity to an alternative semiotic kind of writing, an other mode of discourse which the poet acknowledges might be more apt and more satisfying epistemologically and literarily. To verbalize "intelligibly" visions of the ineffable, to capture in words through pen and paper the "flashing" significance and the realities not of this world but of mind and art, these are the poetic possibilities of a semiotic consciousness being suggested in *Cassandre* XIX and **CLX.** We have actually already begun to see this semiotic of the word at work in *Cassandre* CLX just quoted, in the magical visionary itinerary and transformation of Cassandre/ Vendôme becoming Thalia/Mount Parnassus. Thanks to the symbolic images of myth and allegory that increase the distance between signifier and signified, thanks to a reduced mimetic ambition whose increased unconcern with the things of the real world can better provide the poet and the reader with visionary access to the sacred and the ineffable, Ronsard's fabulous inventions or semiotic constructs will house not real people and real things and real spaces but will give life to and find *another* space and place for the verbal-visual ineffable in its infinite remove from such realities. Only then can the poet claim, as he does in **CLX,** that thanks to such marvelous non-mimetic creations: "Dorenavant *poëte me ferez.*"

There is no finer poem in all of Ronsard's works to help us see and understand and appreciate this poet's belief in and performance of a writerly semiosis and the brand of ekphrasis he was truly obsessed with than the *chanson,* **"Je veux chanter en ces vers ma tristesse,"** found in the *Amours de Marie.*[8] A song of melancholy and sadness turned into joyful vision and verbal presentation of this vision is precisely this poem's triumph. Ronsard's semiotic mode of presentation is what is being highlighted when the poet avows in lines 22-24 that his purpose in this poem is to "fantastiqu[er] mille monstres bossus, / Hommes, oiseaux, et Chimeres cornues." He is telling us that his art of semiosis, and his understanding now of ekphrasis, will necessarily be involved with poetic incongruities and aberrations ("mille monstres bossus"), from where poetic epiphanies will be derived, that is, will be created. However, before discussing these incongruous yet epiphanic creations, we do need to consider a great poem in the Italian Renaissance that served as an intertext, or rather a countertext, for Ronsard. The French poet's conscious rewriting of his Italian model will be of help in understanding the semiotic constructs of "Je veux chanter."

Ronsard's *chanson* is supposedly, and has been identified by all editors of Ronsard as being, an imitation of Petrarch's *Rime sparse* 127.[9] Petrarch's poem is about love's ecstasy and the clear mimetic analogies between the beauties of nature and Laura, the poet's beloved. In this poem, conventional ekphrasis as *enargeia* I is certainly at work where language functions on the level of imitation (*imitatio*) itself. Petrarch's poetic images, encapsulating the art of the mimetic real, vividly and credibly portray their natural-sign objects as if in a painting. The Italian poet is creating with his verbal "images" analogues to the visual images of the painter, thereby affirming the transferability of "things" between verbal and visual systems of representation. Like Ronsard, who tells us he must sing his song of grief if only in order to alleviate it or lessen it, Petrarch had similarly acknowledged in his own sorrowful song a therapeutic function of art:

> But still, however much of the story of my suffering I find written by his [Love's] very own hand, in the midst of my heart where I so often return, I shall speak out, because sighs take a truce and there is help for sorrow when one speaks. I say that although I gaze intent and fixed on *a thousand different things,* I see *only one lady* and her lovely face.

> (7-14)

But with the last idea just quoted from Petrarch, there is something new and very different from what Ronsard will write. Petrarch is already affirming for him the inseparability and the intense satisfaction of vision, focused on nature, on external reality, and the beloved object. His song will be concerned with the mimetic union and unity of "a thousand different *things*" on which the poet "gaze[s] intent and fixed" and where he "see[s] *only* one *lady* and her lovely face." The remainder of the poem is a description of these sensibly-felt "things" of the mimetic real that is Laura/Nature, that is, Laura as natural-sign objects. Her presence and absence parallel the luminous rising and dark setting of the sun:

> If I see the sun rise, I *sense* the approach of the light that enamors me; if setting at evening, I seem to *see* her when she departs, leaving all in darkness behind her.

> (66-70)

The sense-illuminating art of mimesis is, as Petrarch tells us, his principal poetic purpose in this poem, as it appears to be in the whole of the *Rime sparse:*

> . . . when the strange idea came to me to *tell* in so few pages in *how many places* the flower of all beauties, remaining in herself, has scattered her light.

> (87-90)

This is why the poet can believe that Laura as "light," as "the flower of all beauties," can bring him to see in and

through her the perfected excellence of nature itself. Whether he is "gazing at leaves on a branch or violets on the ground" (29-30), or viewing "from afar new snow on the hills" (43-44), or seeing "white with crimson roses in a vase of gold" (71-72), it is always the mimetic vision that permits him to see "the face of her who excels all other wonders with the three excellences gathered in her" (74-76), that is, the floral white, crimson, and gold above. This Italian poet has been conveying supernal beauty through the sensibly-signifying art of mimesis. He has been relying on a conventional sign system, one operating exclusively through the senses to connect signifier and signified, in order to portray the excellence and the pleasure derived from the mimetic picture.

As Ronsard's and indeed the Pléiade's acknowledged most eminent model poet, Petrarch was a master poet of mimesis, of ekphrasis as sense-oriented *enargeia* I. For him, the "veil" enclosing the ineffable beloved object and separating the poet from clear vision and representation of his vision of the ineffable is very thin indeed, so thin that the poet, through his sensible perceptions, is given access. In fact, for Petrarch this clear transparency between the human and the divine, between nature and the ineffable love object, is precisely what allows this sublimely mimetic poet the possibilities of aesthetic penetration. The writing of this mimetic potential is of course exquisite, full of sensory wonder and delight:

> I never saw after nocturnal rain the wandering stars going through the clear air and flaming between the dew and the frost, that I did not have before me *her lovely eyes* where leans my weary life, such as I *saw* them in the shadow of a lovely *veil.*

> (57-62)

Again, with Petrarch, the reader is witnessing what I have been referring to in Krieger as *enargeia* I, a "thinly-veiled mimesis" as opposed to the "opaque semiosis" of *enargeia* II. In his seminal and central Chapter 4, "The Verbal Emblem: The Renaissance," Krieger, turning to the Renaissance writer and critic Jacopo Mazzoni and from him to Longinus for aesthetic and writerly notions, gives us one of his best definitions of *enargeia* I, which we have been exploring above in Petrarch, and of *enargeia* II, which we shall turn to shortly in Ronsard:

> And if, as I have traced it, this distinction [between rhetoric and poetry in Mazzoni and Longinus] is projected into a distinction between . . . the mimetic dependence on an object outside the text and the text's independence of everything except the human mind that creates it, then it is a projection also of what I have claimed to be the distinction between *enargeia* I and *enargeia* II, between vivid (i.e., *transparently clear*) representation and vivid (i.e., intensely empathy-provoking) presentation.

> (126)

Following in the footsteps of Petrarch, Ronsard too is at times, as any reader of his poems must appreciate, a master poet of mimesis. This cannot be denied. In fact, his critical legacy hinges largely on his successes with *imitation*. He too is often able to "see" in external nature and in the "things" of this world (Petrarch) ineffable analogues in which to contain and through which to convey his "vision" of the beloved. This is the mimetically transcendent essence of *Hélène* III (Weber 420). Through transparent mimesis, the poet closes the gap between text and world, between signifier and signified. His universe depicted here is the same one painted earlier by Petrarch: the love vision, with the imperative "voy" being used five times to reinforce our understanding of this vision, finding a home, rest, and delight "en *ce monde si ample,*" in the same *worldly* divine illumination that Petrarch took refuge in: Hélène as the morning sun, her eyes as stars shining like a bright lantern in a temple, or the warm beam of her eyes bringing forth an eternal springtime, in a word, and controlling image, her "love radiance" ("ses flames amoureuses") embellishing the earth and enchanting the heavens. Hélène in this picture is, in the ultimate mimetic analysis, "des beautez le *portrait* & l'exemple" of the here-and-now "en *ce monde* si ample." She is mimesis personified.[10]

However, there is another, a totally different side to Ronsard, as I have been suggesting, one which can best be seen and appreciated by juxtaposing it with the poet's, and Petrarch's, mimetic side discussed above. This other side to Ronsard is, I believe, the artistic consequence of his doubts and questionings of mimetic portrayal, which we analyzed at some length at the beginning of this study. In his "different" creations, Ronsard will no longer be concerned with the mimetic art of representation, but with the semiotic art of presentation. Both poetic perspective and literary ontology are now radically different from what we have just observed in Ronsard and in Petrarch. This new verbal-visual writerly semiosis as ekphrasis is obsessed not with poetic similarities and unity but with poetic dissimilarities and incongruities, even with monsters and monstrosities and other aberrations of reality. This can all be seen in his poem-song, **"Je veux chanter en ces vers ma tristesse,"** one of his finest portrayals of poetic incongruities, and poetic epiphanies. As indicated earlier, this marvelous song is supposedly an imitation of Petrarch's Song 127. However, in Ronsard's version, the poet is deliberately subverting the mimetic value of Petrarch's pretext to highlight and emphasize another, perhaps more captivating process of signifying. As we shall see, he is clearly opting in for a semiotic mode of writing as both a resistance and a response to reality, and to mimetic representations of reality.[11]

The genesis of **"Je veux chanter"** is identical to that of *Rime sparse* 127. In the "absence" of Marie the beloved object (3: "Veu que je suis *absent* de ma maistresse"; 6: "Pour le départ de ma maistresse *absente*"), the only thing left for the poet to do is to sing his song of sorrow (5: "Pour ne mourir il faut donc que je chante"). Here there are obviously two meanings contained in the notion of absence. As with Petrarch, Ronsard's poet is separated from

the beloved, thus, a physical absence. Unlike in Petrarch, for Ronsard's poet the beloved is also absent *around him:* she is an object *"absented."* Thus, the poet can only construct, through mental and poetic images, the presentation of an absent reality. This reality is certainly not to be, and cannot be, found around him, for he cannot "see" it with the "body's eye" anywhere he looks. The sensible world, and the sensory instrument par excellence of perceiving this world—the poet's very eyes—will not lead the poet this time to transcendent seeing and showing, to ekphrasis and to epiphany. As the poet acknowledges once again his all-too-familiar impasse in sensible perception: "Tant par les *yeux* nos *esprits* sont *deceus*" (24).

Since the poet cannot see in anything real the beauty he looks for, he is forced to turn away from ordinary vision of the external world and to turn inward—to the inner eye, the "unreal" eye ("oeillade trompée") of the "mind-soul," as he calls it—for another source of vision. Mental imaging is clearly being made the prerequisite to poetic imaging, the mind's ability to conceive and produce pictures:

> Ainsi je vois d'une *oeillade trompée*
> Cette beauté dont je suis dépravé,
> Qui par les *yeux* dedans l'*âme* frappée,
> M'a *vivement* son *portrait* engravé.
>
> (29-32)

It is no longer the bodily, mimetic eye of "raison" connecting sight to actual presence, but the inner eye of "une fausse et vaine illusion" bestowing the creative insight of a presence-in-absence that the poet must now rely on for revelation and portrayal and meaning. Semiotic negation replaces logocentric affirmation as a poetic principle. Here is another of Ronsard's recognitions of this intriguing kind of semiotic seeing, which will lead the poet to showing in words the illusions of mind and art:

> Mais ma raison est si bien corrompue
> Par une *fausse et vaine illusion,*
> Que nuit et jour je la porte en la *vue,*
> *Et sans la voir j'en ai la vision.*
>
> (17-20)

His newly-acquired "deviant" kind of vision, as with its ineffable object, in frustrating and negating "reason" and normal or conventional sight is therefore called "une fausse et vaine illusion" ("une faulce imagination" as it is called in earlier editions), which permits the poet day and night to have "imaginings," that is, to visualize and verbalize both her and itself. Of course, the imaginings or creations of the poet's "fausse et vaine illusion" have nothing to do with the real world, hence the incongruous yet very apt wording Ronsard uses in designating his faculty of the imagination. They, and it, actually function to re-think and re-create this world. The contemplative and creative activity of the poet now is like the sailors who row with the "perception" of a broken oar (26-27: "En haute mer, à puissance de bras / Tirent la rame, ils l'imaginent torte") or, as the reader is also encouraged to see this impossible activity, like the sky-gazer "qui contemple les nues, / Fantastiquant mille monstres bossus, / Hommes, oiseaux et Chimeres cornues" (21-23). Needless to say, the reader is a very long way now from Petrarch's "flower of all beauties" in Song 127 and the "jardin" in *Hélène* III.

This highly incongruous, even monstrous, ineffable beauty to be perceived and portrayed so vividly by the "eye of the mind-soul" (29-32) is what the poet focuses on and pursues in the last two-thirds of this remarkable poem. Whether climbing in the mountains or walking in the woods alongside a stream, he avows how "tousjours à l'oeil ce *beau portrait* me suit" (36), that is, the "image" of this beauty of Marie as "beauté amère" which the poet's "unreal eye" has made in its moments of sublime derangement (29-32).[12] The verbal constructions "j'apperçoy" and "je pense voir," used eleven times to reinforce and give credibility to the workings of the poet's other, inner eye, introduce or dominate virtually every stanza that follows. "To perceive" is the same for Ronsard as "to think in order to see." Seeing as thinking precedes words as mental image precedes poetic image. Imagination is what turns mental image into poetic image. The creations of the poet's imagination are pure constructs of mind and art, of a writerly semiosis, which are now strangely yet credibly nonmimetic. This is why Ronsard refers to his faculty of imagination as "illusion," and as "fausse." This faculty is not at all real, but incredible, to the world, yet very real, credible, to the poet, for it satisfies and makes possible his own different and unique view of things. The poet's deviant imagination in the process of conceiving mental-verbal-visual monstrosities just may, in its unexpected and mimetically meaning-negating inventions, offer a better means of signifying the beauty of the ineffable. And it is not as much in Ronsard to visualize the verbal as it is to verbalize the visual (to turn thought and words into images). Which is to say that he is a poet intent on creating an other world more than he is a painter interested in depicting this world. To borrow the insightful words of John Berger which this writer-critic uses to indicate "another" (intelligible, mind-oriented) way of seeing, for Ronsard too "seeing [thought as imaging] comes before words." Ronsard now writes, not what he can see, but what he is capable of thinking and imagining.[13] This is really why Ronsard tells us so repeatedly in his *chanson:* "Je *pense* voir. . . ." Simply put, he turns to the mind, not to nature or external reality, for vision and creation.

Poetic incongruities of *enargeia* II are the products of this mental and linguistic operation and aberration, of Ronsard's other way of seeing and of writing. The reader's ability to participate in the poet's thoughts, even the most incongruous and outrageous and seemingly impossible, is crucial to Ronsard's writerly semiosis. This reader must share with the poet the challenge of the semiotic relationship between signs and referents, words, and things. One of Ronsard's favorite images and metaphors which the reader encounters in so many of his poems is of course the rose in its resplendent and ephemeral beauty, to which the poet mimetically equates the beauty of the beloved, usually with

an ulterior motive in mind. In "Je veux chanter" however, the natural-sign status of the rose is not one of similarity but of difference. The kind of rose that Ronsard sees this time in Marie does not conform to the real-life cycle of the rose in nature, with its fragile beauty and brief life span justifying the poet's plea of *carpe diem*. She/it *never* fades in the poet's mind, or imagination:

> Quand j'aperçois la rose sur l'épine,
> Je pense voir de ses lèvres le teint;
> La rose au soir de sa couleur décline,
> L'*autre* couleur *jamais* ne se déteint.
>
> (49-52)

Marie is indeed portrayed not through the transparently clear, sense-satisfying representation of mimesis but through the intensely empathy-provoking, intelligible presentation of the poet's semiotic consciousness. As an object existing in and being portrayed by mind, she is presented to the reader's mind not in an all resplendent and reassuring light but in the uneasy identification of her with intelligible, phantastic entities, such as the curved side of the Moon, that is, a bow and arrow ready to strike:

> Si le Croissant au premier mois j'avise,
> Je pense voir son sourcil ressemblant
> A l'arc d'un Turc qui la sagette a mise
> Dedans la coche et menace le blanc.
>
> (41-44)

In order to come to terms with and to depict the *chanson*'s overriding theme of presence-in-absence, the poet will also turn to the allegorical figure of "Cérès la blétière, / Ayant le front orné de son *présent*" to sustain him in the real absence around him of Marie (9-10). Or, he sees and portrays the beauty of Marie in the fantastic form and image of this ripening wheat whose frizzled blades as the result of plowing become the beloved's silk hair full of curls blowing in the wind:

> Si j'aperçois quelque champ qui blondoie
> D'épis frisés au travers des sillons,
> Je pense voir ses beaux cheveux de soie
> Epars au vent en mille crépillons.
>
> (37-40)

Ronsard too, like William Blake later, was able to see a "Heaven" in, of all things, a wild flower, in Marie as one of these "fleurs en quelque prée":

> Quand j'aperçois les fleurs en quelque prée
> Ouvrir leur robe au lever du Soleil,
> Je pense voir de sa face pourprée
> S'épanouir le beau lustre vermeil.
>
> (53-56)

And the wording "en *quelque* prée" is quite significant. It is just as meaningfully and intentionally indefinite as similar wording is later in another marvelous writer of semiosis, in Stéphane Mallarmé: "Je dis: *une* fleur!" For Mallarmé as for Ronsard, this imaginary or intelligible kind of flower as "l'*absente* de tous bouquets" is "la notion pure," that is, "*idée* même et suave."[14] In both poets, words are being used to call forth an intelligible reality of the imaginary as opposed to the sensible specific of the real: wild flowers in *some* meadow, those contained in a "meadow" within the mind of the poet, as opposed to actual flowers in one of the real world. Like Mallarmé's "absented" flower in *all* bouquets (i.e., in no real bouquet), which is this writer's mental-verbal image of "*idea* itself and sweet," Ronsard's own "images" of the verbally ineffable are also pure constructs of mind and art created to convey their own special world of a writerly semiosis. They do this by reducing mimetic fidelity and precision in order to capture the more indirect semiotic power of the aesthetic sign.

As such, Ronsard was also able to see, and to translate, his vision of the ineffable Marie in a wild oak tree:

> Si j'aperçois quelque chêne sauvage,
> Qui jusqu'au ciel élève ses rameaux
> Je pense voir sa taille et son corsage,
> Ses pieds, sa greve et ses jumeaux.
>
> (57-60)

Another semiotic re-creation of vision and of world can be seen in the "splashing noise" which the poet describes next as coming from a "clear" stream:

> Si j'entends *bruire* une fontaine *claire,*
> Je pense ouïr sa voix dessus le bord,
> Qui se plaignant de ma triste misère,
> M'appelle à soi pour me donner confort.
>
> (61-64)

In the very next stanza, the poet explains the real reason for all of these strange poetic and mental incongruities, his phantasms, his fantastic forms. They are the products of joyful melancholy:

> Voilà comment, *pour être fantastique,*
> En cent façons ses beautés j'aperçoi,
> Et *m'éjouis* d'être *mélancolique,*
> Pour recevoir tant de *formes* en moi.
>
> (65-68)

The recovery of semiotic vision from the melancholy associated with a perceived failure in mimetic perception and creation, of insight from sight, and the joyful portrayal of that new-found vision and order are Ronsard's ultimate triumph in "Je veux chanter." The poet is creating his own self-standing and self-satisfying universe in which he is *now* able to take utmost delight. Love for him is indeed the fury of a deranged and dissonant fantasy: "Nommant ce mal fureur de fantaisie" (71). There is no real cure for this melancholic disease of the poet's amorous pains, or at least no conventional cure for this "maladie" which "les médecins . . . savent bien juger" but "qui ne se peut par herbes soulager" (69-70, 72). His fate, like that of a few other committed love poets, is to suffer the happiness he can create from it, the happiness of his amorous pains in their state of unhappiness, these "amoureuses peines, / Dont le bonheur n'est sinon que malheur" (75-76).

But, as we have already seen, it is through this very sickness that health can be restored, through this unhappiness that happiness is possible, in the passage from an old (poetic) order and its failed expectations to creatively-renewed life, one in which the poet can loudly and defiantly proclaim: "Et m'éjouis d'être mélancolique"! The poet's melancholy is ultimately a positive, not negative, sign and a necessary and redeeming condition for semiotic production, for seeing and showing "dextrement" (**Cassandre** CLX: "intelligibly," "differently"). With this understanding, the poet's incongruities and aberrations, his *chanson,* are not really for him, as he hopes for his reader, so illusory or outlandish or unreal as they might appear at first. As the poet takes pains to reassure Marie on this crucial point, we read in the poem's last stanza: "ce n'est tromperie / Des visions que je raconte ici" (78-79). She and they—the poet's "amorous care"—are very real for him, and are even his epiphanies, for the poet carries them night and day in his mind (80). Giving new life and new meaning and new forms to the "black ink of melancholy" is truly Ronsard's triumph in this *chanson,* just as it was for Shakespeare in his own melancholic love lyrics, as Jean Starobinski has shown in his analysis of **Sonnet 114.** Ronsard too was able to transform the black ink of despair (Starobinski: "les désordres de l'esprit") into something of great human worth and value in the redemptive and liberating reality of art:

> Le fond ténébreux comporte la chance de l'éclat, si on lui superpose une matière lisse. Shakespeare le devine, en évoquant le miracle d'un amour qui resplendit, sauvé des ravages universels du Temps, dans l'encre noire du poème. . . . La mélancolie devenue encre devient enfin le tain grâce auquel l'image rayonne.[15]

And here is how Krieger describes the same triumph in Shakespeare, which, as I have been arguing, I also believe to have been Ronsard's. He too is concerned with, and quotes from, Shakespeare's Sonnet 114, a poem very close in semiotic perspective and mode to Ronsard's intriguing *chanson:* "To make of monsters and things indigest / Such cherubins as your sweet self resemble." He then will explain how, in Shakespeare as in other writers who share and develop the same deviant kind of perspective, such "strangely incongruous, dreamlike—if sometimes nightmarish—equivalences [can] abound in the redemption produced by monstrosity" and how "all readings [can] end in an identity—despite the great discrepancy—between sign and referent" (137). Sonnet 114's illusory metamorphosis of "monsters" and "things indigest" into "cherubins," in a word, its "magic semiotic," is achieved through the semiotic possibilities of the verbally intelligible image: "Through the alembic of his words the poet achieves his function as alchemist. . . . What the poet's eye sees has been transformed by the mind's power to superimpose its own seeing upon it, under the power of love that teaches the eye 'this alchemy'" (140).

What we have been discussing is of course the self-sufficiency and autonomy of the poetic text, the poem as ultimate intelligible image and universe, and its hermeneutic independence from everything but itself, and especially from the "real" world. This is exactly what Ronsard intends us to understand in his *chanson* when he acknowledges his own obsession with "fantastiquant mille monstres bossus, / Hommes, oiseaux, et Chimères cornues," that is, when he equates the beloved ineffable Marie with an ominous configuration of "le Croissant," with "Cérès la blétière," with "quelque champ qui blondoie / D'épis frisés au travers des sillons," with one of these "fleurs en quelque prée," with "quelque chêne sauvage," and so forth. These are the products of the mind's eye, of the poet's intelligible imagination (his "fausse et vaine illusion" or "faulce imagination" or "fureur de fantaisie"). Ronsard pushes poetic language and imagery and vision up to and at times beyond their usual referential intelligibility for meaning and value. This semiotic consciousness is what gives him vision of the absented Marie: "Et sans la voir [with 'sans l'avoir' also surely intended by Ronsard] j'en ai la vision." It is also what provides him with the *forms* in which to present his vision: "Pour recevoir tant de *formes* en moi."[16]

These forms of fantasy truly abound in Ronsard's *oeuvre*, his semiotic constructs which affirm their own charm of being and of not being. They are not limited to his love lyrics, though the latter are especially suited to his writerly semiosis. In **"La Lyre,"** for example, mind alone as creative intelligence is viewed as responsible for translating vision and constructing text:

> Quant à Pallas qui sort de la cervelle,
> C'est de l'esprit l'oeuvre toute nouvelle
> Que le penser luy [Jupiter] a fait concevoir.[17]

Ronsard is aligning himself here on the subject of poetic conception and creation with the most intelligible of all mythic figures and their accomplishments, with Jupiter and Minerva. Ronsard will also indicate what kind of lyric writing he is really intrigued by. The poet will affirm once again the necessity of his "fureur de fantaisie" so crucial, as we saw, to **"Je veux chanter,"** that is, his melancholic condition and inspiration for lyric writing:

> Quand la fureur me laisse, tout soudain
> Plume et papier me tombent de la main.
>
> (323)

He will specifically ask himself what kind of writing will best serve his purpose, will best translate the melancholic disposition of both Jean Belot, to whom **"La Lyre,"** is dedicated, and himself:

> Par quel escrit faut-il que je commence
> Pour envoyer des Muses la semence,
> J'enten mes vers, par toute Europe, à fin
> Que ton renom survive apres ta fin?
>
> (325)

Ronsard will give us the answer. Poetry aspiring to excellence and to permanence begins and ends in the mind of its author-reader, and above all else must speak to and captivate this mind with strange and novel creations. Invoking the inward-outward dichotomy and duality of Socrates as an apt image of Belot, and of himself, to convey this idea ("Lors de ta voix distile l'eloquence / Un vray Socrate," 326), Ronsard is obviously fascinated, as he hopes Belot and his reader will be, by this Socrates-image. For, as Ronsard sees it, its grotesque and highly incongruous exterior ("En front severe, en oeil melancolique," 325) does conceal an inner linguistic and creative charm capable of conceiving "dix mille odeurs *estranges et nouvelles* / . . . / Par la vertu de ta langue qui pousse / Un *hameçon* aux coeurs, tant elle est *douce*" (327). As is obvious by now, the poet is addressing himself as much as he is his friend and benefactor Belot in this poem, for the real subject of **"La Lyre,"** has to do with the aesthetics of a writerly semiosis, with Ronsard's own semiotically enticing "odeurs estranges et nouvelles."

Monstrously strange and novel images are also the subject of *Folastrie* VIII, which offers the reader another application or "writing" by Ronsard of *enargeia* II, of the intelligible operation of mind and art. This poem, like important sections of **"Je veux chanter,"** has to do with clouds, and a state of verbal-visual drunkenness and blindness:

> Je voy deçà, je voy delà,
> Je voy mille bestes cornues,
> Mille marmotz dedans les nues.
>
> (761)

> . . . . .

> Voyci deux nuages tous plains
> De Mores, qui n'ont point de mains,
> Ny de corps, et ont les visages
> Semblables à des chatz sauvages.
>
> (762)

Once again, the poet is on the semiotic path toward the epiphanic re-creation and redemption found in, created through, verbal-visual monstrosity. Through his intentionally "strange" images, the poet is also presenting a view of "drunkenness" as a textual reflection upon the creation of signs. Seen from a semiotic perspective, this view translates his awareness of the arbitrariness of signs and language, with one fictional, self-referential process of imaging (the seeing and showing here in clouds of "mille bestes cornues," of "mille mar*motz*") at work within another (the seeing and showing there in clouds of "Mores," of "chatz sauvages"). It is not too unreal to see here that Ronsard has constructed a semiotic *mise en abyme*. As self-referential fiction, this text is, I believe, calling into question the representational function of writing by emphasizing the ability of the poetic imagination to turn in upon itself and away from the real world. What the poet "sees" and shows in *Folastrie* VIII is, once again, the unique signifying creations of the poem, not conventional earthly objects.

Nowhere in Ronsard, finally, is his writerly semiosis, his intelligible art of mind over (mimetic) sense, so captivatingly shown and seen than in his painting-poem, **"L'Ombre du cheval"** (373), which I have saved for discussion last. This poem is a superb and magical embodiment of ekphrasis as *enargeia* II and the writing of the two principal features that define this kind of ekphrasis: "the literary depiction of a painting and also the figurative use of such a depiction" (Riffaterre 127), a definition we have been applying to Ronsard's texts throughout this study. It is written again to his friend Belot, ostensibly to thank him for a painting of a horse, but which Ronsard the *poet* prefers to read as a verbal emblem:

> Amy Belot, que l'honneur accompagne,
> Tu m'as donné non un cheval d'Espagne,
> Mais l'ombre vain d'un cheval par escrit,
> Que je comprens seulement en esprit.
> Je ne le puis ny par les yeux comprendre
> Ny par la main; il ne se laisse prendre,
> Chose invisible, et fantôme me suit,
> Ainsi qu'on voit en nos songes de nuit
> Se presenter je ne sçay quels images
> Sans corps, sans mains, sans bras et sans visages.

We have already seen this "horse," this mental monster, depicted above in the many verbal-visual constructs of Ronsard's ekphrasis as *enargeia* II. This time, the writerly ineffable is not a horse at all but "*l'ombre* vain d'un cheval *par escrit*," which can only be understood in the place where it was created, and where it must be read and interpreted—in the poet's and the reader's mind ("Que je comprens *seulement* en *esprit*"). As a "chose invisible, et fantôme," the horse in question cannot be comprehended by the eyes of the body ("Je ne le puis ny par les yeux comprendre"), nor through the sense of touch ("Ny par la main.") It is totally resistant to sensible perception. This horse must be visualized by the mind's eye just as one encounters "images" in a dream, that is, through intelligible perceptions totally lacking in sensible features (i.e., through images "*sans* corps, *sans* mains, *sans* bras et *sans* visages"). Of course, it is not a question in this poem of picturing a real horse at all, but of verbally conceiving "the imaging of the horse," the very title of the poem. This must take place at moments totally removed from reality, moments when mind and art are liberated from sensible reality, such as those of "drunkenness" or "blindness" (as we saw above in other poems), or those of sleep or the dream state, as the picture is being presented to us now:

> Ton cheval . . .
> Que seulement en dormant j'apperçoy;
> Car autrement ton cheval je ne voy.
> Plus en songeant ton cheval je me donne.

(373)

The horse in the poem, and to be correct one needs to say "*as* the poem," is distanced in every conceivable way from a real horse. This one does not gallop: "Mais ton cheval, fantôme, ne chemine" (374). But it does do other marvelous things, which a real horse cannot do:

> Il vole en l'air, boit en l'air, d'air se paist;
> C'est un corps d'air, l'air seulement luy plaist
> Et la fumée et le vent et le songe,
> Et dedans l'air seulement il s'allonge.

(374)

As with **"Je veux chanter," "L'Ombre du cheval"** is a captivating and convincing demonstration that the realist project is inherently incompatible with a view of the poetic text as a self-conscious and self-contained artifice. The ineffable existence or "world" of the "horse" portrayed so exquisitely in the above lines serves no other purpose than to affirm the ontological status of this "world" in the text, and the power of language to create the illusion that this "world" is "real." For in the final analysis, all that can really be said about this horse is that it is like these

> . . . jumens qui en tournant l'entrée
> De leur nature au vent Zephyrien,
> Sur le Printemps, *vont concevant de rien*.

(375)

"To go about conceiving nothing" as a principle and preoccupation of literary perception and discourse has been the real subject of this study of Ronsard's ekphrastic art. At the end of **"L'Ombre du cheval,"** Ronsard specifically calls this art of "nothing" his "vers raillards" (375). His is an art that is monstrously and incongruously "playful" or "witty" ("raillard"), an art which at its best is a playful statement on and performance of the autonomy of language itself. But this art of "nothing" should not be construed as trivial. Ronsard's writing of "rien" in "vers raillards" is always being related by the poet and owes its very existence to the poet's coming to terms with the Renaissance theoretical issue of literary re/presentation, with what today we view to be the tension between critical emphases on mimesis and metafictionality, on referentiality and self-referentiality. As we have seen in so many ways and forms, Ronsard's verbal-visual ineffable as "nothing," his writing of the "fantastic," requires a highly intelligible, incongruous, non-mimetic mode of presentation that replaces, as Todorov argues throughout his book on this subject, the mimetic credible as real with the semiotic fantastic as real.[18] This art of the fantastic is, to quote Krieger on this same point, one "that shifts the burden of the poem from its dependence on external objects of imitation and places it on the verbal inventions that respond to the visions produced by the poet's '*wit*'" (127). For a poet like Ronsard, as in the case of a poet like Mallarmé and his visions and constructs of "Rien" (Mondor/Jean-Aubry 27), this creative *wit* that is the ekphrastic mode of semiosis—the writerly brilliance of Ronsard's "vers *raillards*," or of his "*dextre* esclair" as we saw it presented at the beginning of this study—this wit is quite possibly the ultimate source of epiphany, of revelatory meaning.

In the end, however, it is up to the reader to assess the meaning and value of ekphrasis in Ronsard's texts. This reader will need to figure out in particular what Ronsard meant when he wrote, in qualifying his poetic creations and fictions: "ce n'est que Poësie" (Weber 318). The statement can best be understood, I believe, as poetry as pure invention of the mind and as reflector of its own self-contained system. Ronsard's fictitious mimesis thrives on the symbolic, visual malleability of the verbal image, on all these "ombre[s] vain[s] . . . par escrit" that are the writerly constructs of his opaque semiosis: Marie as the curved side of the Moon, the aesthetics of "La Lyre" ushering forth "dix mille odeurs estranges et nouvelles," the imaging of "mille monstres bossus" or of "mille bestes cornues," a pictured horse intelligibly depicted verbally, and so forth. Ronsard has only one word for all these strange but epiphanic creations. He calls them "Poësie."[19]

Notes

1. *Ekphrasis: The Illusion of the Natural Sign* (Baltimore: The Johns Hopkins University Press, 1992) 67ff., 93ff. Krieger's *Ekphrasis* is nothing less than seminal and has been very helpful in my own work on this subject in Renaissance poetry and poetics. We will be returning to him later in this essay. All italics in this study are mine, unless otherwise indicated, as are all translations into English.

2. See, among many others one could cite, the following representative studies: Henri Weber, *La Création poétique au XVIe siècle en France* (Paris: Nizet, 1955), especially 235-396 (wherein Ronsard figures prominently in the discussion of the love themes and imagery in the Pléiade production); Roberto E. Campo, "A Poem to A Painter: The *Elégie à Janet* and Ronsard's Dilemma of Ambivalence," *French Forum* 12 (1987): 273-87; Margaret M. McGowan, *Ideal Forms in the Age of Ronsard* (Berkeley: University of California Press, 1985); Donald Stone, Jr., *Ronsard's Sonnet Cycles: A Study in Tone and Vision* (New Haven: Yale University Press, 1966); Elaine Limbrick, "L'Oeil du poète: vision et perspective dans la poésie française de la Renaissance," *Etudes littéraires* 20 (1987): 13-26. The essay by Limbrick comes the closest to the aesthetic views on Ronsard which the present essay will develop. This critic is not, however, interested in the theoretical implications of ekphrasis, which I believe can be of great help in understanding a heretofore neglected side (critical and poetic: semiotic) of this Renaissance prince of poets.

3. The interest in and performance of a writerly semiosis, as opposed to a writerly mimesis, by Scève and Du Bellay are subjects explored in my book, *The Love Aesthetics of Maurice Scève: Poetry and Struggle* (Cambridge: Cambridge University Press, 1991), and my essay, "The Poetics of Seeing and Showing: Du Bellay's Love Lyrics," in Barbara C. Bowen and Jerry C. Nash, editors, *Lapidary*

Inscriptions: Renaissance Essays for Donald Stone, Jr. (Lexington: French Forum, 1991) 45-59.

4. This is the very title of Riffaterre's book, as well as the subject he treats therein: *Fictional Truth* (Baltimore: The Johns Hopkins University Press, 1990). More later from Riffaterre.

5. *Les Amours,* Henri and Catherine Weber, editors (Paris: Garnier, 1985).

6. This critical notion of Ronsard's constructive epistemology of inspiration (the idealism of Neo-Platonism) located in *Cassandre,* yielding to skeptical epistemology and artistic failure in *Marie* (mannerism), is a major structuring principle in Pot's discussion of Ronsard's love lyrics. See his *Inspiration et mélancolie: l'épistémologie poétique dans les Amours de Ronsard* (Geneva: Droz, 1990). I do not believe that evolution and sequentiality fully explain Ronsard's failure-poems. These surface throughout his love cycles and are connected to a perceived, and demonstrated, artistic failure in the realist project, to mimesis itself failing the poet, as much as they are to any notion of cyclical-epistemological evolution. This point will become more apparent as the present essay unfolds.

7. For other approaches to writerly impasses in other poems of Ronsard, see Terence Cave, "*Energeia:* Erasmus and the Rhetoric of Presence in the Sixteenth Century," *L'Esprit Créateur* 16 (1976): 5-19; and also Claude-Gilbert Dubois, "Itinéraire et impasses de la 'Vive Représentation' au XVIe siècle," in *La Littérature de la Renaissance: Mélanges d'histoire et de critique littéraires offerts à Henri Weber,* Marguerite Soulié and Robert Aulotte, editors (Geneva: Slatkine, 1984) 405-425.

8. I will be using here the edition by Albert-Marie Schmidt for quoting this *chanson* (80 lines, 20 quatrains) since it, unlike the Weber edition, gives the latest, and very important, emendations of this poem made by Ronsard himself in 1578-87. *Les Amours* (Paris: Gallimard, 1964). Since I quote from this poem so extensively, and since line numbers are not given by Schmidt, I am providing them to facilitate referencing.

9. Robert M. Durling, editor and translator, *Petrarch's Lyric Poems* (Cambridge, Massachusetts: Harvard University Press, 1976) 248-55.

10. This is the kind of interpretation presented so well by Stone 207-10.

11. Ronsard's writerly semiosis as *enargeia* II will also lend support to the view of more involvement by him in Renaissance Neo-Platonism than has been generally allowed by critics. As Krieger has argued and shown, *enargeia* II is the literary essence in the Renaissance of an ekphrastic, *verbally* art-defining Neo-Platonism. Through it, the "extravagant metaphysical demands of Christian Neo-Platonism" were met, precisely in observing the fundamental

distinction between the sensible reality of the profane, portrayed transparently as the mimetic real by the painter, or by a painterly-oriented poet, and the intelligible reality of the sacred and ineffable, presented opaquely as the verbal emblem by the writer: "For Renaissance Neo-Platonists, moved by a desire to save poetry and make it an instrument for our salvation, the potential object of imitation was, in the main, to vary with the art: a *sensible* object for the *visual* arts and an *intelligible* object for the *verbal* arts" (142).

12. Though he does not consider Ronsard, Jean-Michel Rabaté examines the aesthetics of "beauté amère" in his exciting book, *La Beauté amère: Fragments d'esthétiques* (Seyssel: Editions du Champ Vallon, 1986).

13. *Ways of Seeing* (London: British Broadcasting Corporation and Penguin Books, 1972) 7.

14. *Crise de vers,* Henri Mondor and G. Jean-Aubry, editors, Stéphane Mallarmé, *Oeuvres complètes* (Paris: Gallimard, 1945) 368.

15. "L'Encre de la mélancolie," *La Nouvelle Revue Française* 123 (1963): 423.

16. Ronsard's recognitions of his receptivity to the "forms" of the "mind's eye" clearly underscore his involvement in a writerly semiosis. As Riffaterre has shown (in *Fictional Truth*), this mode of seeing and of writing is always "opposed to referentiality, the assumed relationship between a sign and noverbal objects *taken to be reality*" (130). This is why "*form,* being obviously *contrived* [thus Ronsard's recognition of his '*faulce* imagination'], betrays the *hand* of its maker and signals fictionality [the 'dextre esclair' of Ronsard's 'fausse et vaine *illusion*']" (63). It should also be clear by now that I have altered the representational itinerary that Pot in his book argues to be Ronsard's. He interprets *Cassandre* in Neo-Platonic accents as all light and mimesis, and *Marie* as darkness and failure, whose "maniérisme . . . prend le parti inverse: *l'enjeu,* c'est simplement le *jeu*" (283, Pot's italics). He does however, at the end of his study, suggest that semiosis just may play a larger role in Ronsard's art than has been allowed (458). This notion is precisely what I have wished to explore in the present study, and to give to *Marie,* and to "Je veux chanter" in particular, a more positive assessment, as well as to other of Ronsard's less valued or less acclaimed texts, those that do not participate in the poet's project and triumph of mimesis.

17. Gustave Cohen, editor, Ronsard, *Oeuvres complètes* (Paris: Gallimard, 1950) II 324. The lines within poems in the Cohen edition are not numbered. My references are to page numbers. This edition and volume will be used for the remainder of Ronsard's poems, unless otherwise indicated.

18. Tzvetan Todorov, *Introduction à la littérature fantastique* (Paris: Seuil, 1970). Though more interested in the social role and implications of the fantastic, Todorov does offer many useful observations on the purely literary implications of the fantastic, such as we have been studying them in Ronsard. One is that "le fantastique permet de franchir certaines limites [of the mind, of mental and verbal perception] inaccessibles tant qu'on n'a pas recours à lui" (166). It does this through its compatibility with a writerly semiosis and its incompatibility with mimetic representation, through its "métaphysique du réel et de l'imaginaire" (176), through its "antithèse entre le verbal et le transverbal, entre le réel et l'irréel" (183).

19. Ronsard's writerly semiosis is also the kind of writing Hans Robert Jauss has in mind when he speaks of this "other, more essential world [which] opens up to us in and through the lyric experience." *Aesthetic Experience and Literary Hermeneutics,* Michael Shaw, translator (Minneapolis: University of Minnesota Press, 1982) 259. For Jauss too, as for Krieger, giving life and meaning to this "world" of mind and art is the objective and the challenge of both writing and reading.

Philip Ford (essay date 1993)

SOURCE: "Ronsard's Erotic Diptych: *Le ravissement de Cephale* and *Le defloration de Lede,*" in *French Studies,* Vol. XLVII, No. 4, October, 1993, pp. 385-403.

[In the following essay, Ford studies two odes by Ronsard that present erotic, mythological stories and draws allegorical and thematic parallels between both works.]

Throughout his poetic career, Ronsard seemed fascinated by the relationship between poetry and the visual arts. While art theorists at that time borrowed their vocabulary and approach to painting from the world of rhetoric, Ronsard often modelled his own literary technique on the mannerist works of art which proliferated under the Valois kings. Two early odes, **"Le Ravissement de Cephale"** (L. II. 133-47) and **"La Defloration de Lede"** (L. II. 67-79) offer an interesting example of a poetic diptych, worthy in its complexity of the frescoes at the palace of Fontainebleau.[1] First published in 1550 in the ***Quatre Premiers Livres des Odes,*** they share the same metre (heptasyllabic lines divided into *huitains*), the same basic structure, and the same theme (the love of a divinity for a mortal).

The *dispositio* of both these poems closely resembles the structure of Rosso's decorations in the Galerie François Ier, where a central narrative fresco is surrounded by an elaborate *inquadratura* which includes, amongst other elements, stucco or painted volets and cartouches. In the case of **"Le Ravissement de Cephale,"** the central narrative scene (lines 81-248, the *seconde pose*) presents the main events referred to in the title of the poem. The *inquadratura* (lines 1-80 and 249-88, the first and third *poses*) is concerned with preparations for the marriage of Peleus and Thetis, but within the first section, there is an ecphrasis, the equivalent, perhaps, of one of Rosso's cartouches, which depicts the storm scene on the cloak which is being prepared for Neptune by the nymphs. We shall see later that **"La Defloration de Lede"** follows a similar pattern.

Ronsard outlines the events of the Cephalus story in a series of little scenes which would not, in fact, be particularly explicit if we did not have Ovid's version of the story in mind (*Metamorphoses* VII. 694-VIII. 5).[2] According to the Roman poet, the story is as follows. Shortly after his marriage to Procris, Cephalus is abducted by Aurora who has fallen in love with him. He rejects the goddess's advances, but she persuades Cephalus to take on another form and test his wife's fidelity by trying to seduce her. He does so, offering Procris all kinds of gifts, and eventually, as she is wavering, he reveals his true identity. Procris, outraged, leaves and devotes herself to the pursuits of Diana, but Cephalus eventually apologizes and the couple are reconciled. A hound, and a javelin that always hits its target, gifts from Diana to Procris, are given by her to her husband. After years of happiness, Procris in turn becomes jealous of Cephalus when she is told that he may be having an affair with a nymph. She follows him early one morning, hiding in a bush as he lies on the ground after the exertions of the hunt and calling to the breeze, Aura, to come to him. A rustling betrays her presence, the javelin is hurled by Cephalus at what he suspects is a wild beast, and Procris dies in her husband's arms.

It is necessary to know these events for a complete understanding of Ronsard's reworking of the myth, even on a literal level. Procris is referred to only obliquely in an ambiguous latinate term of endearment ('Puis que j'ai tué ma vie . . . '; line 127),[3] the javelin is mentioned, but not explained, in an apostrophe (line 129-32), and none of the events leading up to Procris's death are elaborated. At the same time, Ronsard rearranges the traditional story in order to place the relationship between Aurora and Cephalus in the best possible light. In Ovid, it is Aurora who sows the seeds of jealousy in Cephalus's mind after his rejection of her; with Ronsard, the goddess does not become enamoured of him until after his wife's death. In Ovid, Aurora's abduction of the mortal is of short duration, whereas Ronsard emphasizes its permanent nature:

> Par force au ciel l'a monté,
> Où avecques lui encores
> Est maintenant à sejour,
> Et bien peu se soucie ores
> De nous allumer le jour.

(lines 244-48)

The subject of the myth is announced in the opening stanza of the *seconde pose,* and we are then presented with a picture of Amour, who overcomes Aurore as she prepares to light up the morning sky:

> Elle qui a de coutume
> D'allumer le jour, voulant
> L'allumer, elle s'allume
> D'un brandon plus violant:
> Passant les portes decloses
> Du ciel, elle alloit davant
> Çà & là versant ses roses
> Au sein du souleil levant.
>
> Son teint de nacre, & d'ivoire
> Le matin embellissoit,
> Et du comble de sa gloire
> L'Orient se remplissoit:
> Mais Amour en son courage
> N'endura de la voir là,
> Ains surmonté de sa rage
> Par ses roses se mella.

(lines 97-112)

The first of these two stanzas is a standard pictorial description of Aurora, but one which includes details which are more normally to be found together in paintings than in the classical poets. Ripa, in his *Iconologia,* describes Aurora as follows:[4]

> nel braccio sinistro un cestullo pieno di varii fiori, & nella stessa mano tiene una facella accesa, & con la destra sparge fiori.
>
> ([She has] a basket full of different flowers on her left arm, and in the same hand she is holding a burning torch, and is scattering flowers with her right hand.)

Ronsard reinforces the word-play based on *allumer* in lines 98-99 by playing on the ambiguous nature of the visual imagery of the torch (traditionally an attribute of both Dawn and Cupid) and of the roses (a symbol of Dawn and Venus). It is therefore all the more appropriate that Amour, in the next stanza, should mingle with the roses, which as a result of this juxtaposition are confirmed in their double significance (line 112).

Amour then makes Aurore see what will become the object of her desires:

> Elle vit dans un bocage
> Cephale parmi les fleurs,
> Faire un large marescage
> De la pluie de ses pleurs.

(lines 117-20)

He is cursing the javelin and the impermanent nature of the human condition:

> Ainsi disant il se pasme
> Sur le cors qui trépassoit,
> Et les reliques de l'ame
> De ses levres amassoit.

(lines 133-36)

The love that Aurore feels for Céphale makes her forsake the heavens ('Ja le ciel elle déprise', line 149). Ronsard describes the effects of Aurore's passion at length in lines

137-208, borrowing many details from Virgil's description of the effects of love on Dido (*Aeneid* IV. 54-89).

Aurore is guided by Love to Céphale, who is still lamenting, and she addresses him:

> Pourquoi pers tu de ton age
> Le printens à lamenter
> Une froide & morte image
> Qui ne peut te contenter?
> Elle à la mort fut sugette,
> Non pas moi le sang des Dieus,
> Non pas moi Nimphe qui jette
> Les premiers raions aus cieus:
> Reçoi moi donques, Cephale,
> Et ta basse qualité,
> D'un étroit lien égalle
> A mon immortalité.
> (lines 221-32)

He scorns her love, but Aurore pursues him, carries him heavenwards (in a later variant, 'comme un aigle qui serre / Un liévre en ses pieds donté') where, as we have already seen, they continue to live.

The way in which the myth is told raises a number of questions, as Ann Moss notes, referring to 'the extraordinarily oblique angles from which [Ronsard] tells the tales'.[5] Why is Procris never mentioned? Why are the Ovidian details passed over? In fact, the picture we are given of Cephalus is a highly ambiguous one. We see a young man, presumably beautiful, surrounded by flowers, and weeping into a pool. What do we have here other than a picture of Narcissus, weeping in frustration because he can never obtain the object of his love—himself?

> Je hai de vivre l'envie,
> Ce monde m'est odieus:
> Puis que j'ai tué ma vie
> A quoi me gardent les Dieus?
>
> (lines 125-28)

Or as Ovid's Narcissus exclaims:

> 'nec mihi mors gravis est posituro morte dolores,
> hic, qui diligitur, vellem diuturnior esset;
> nunc duo concordes anima monemur in una.'
> Dixit et ad faciem rediit male sanus eandem
> et lacrimis turbavit aquas . . . .
>
> (*Metamorphoses,* III. 471-75)

('Death is unimportant to me, as death will put an end to my grief; I wish that he who is loved would live longer; as it is, we two shall die together in one breath.' He concluded, and madly turned back to the same face, and disturbed the waters with his tears . . . .)

Even the picture of the fainting Céphale is ambiguous in the way that his actions are almost literally reflected by the beloved's corpse. Later we are told that Céphale, when approached by Aurore, 'Lui dedaignant sa priere / Fuit la supliante vois' (lines 233-34), or as Ovid writes of Narcissus and Echo:

> *ille fugit fugiensque* 'manus complexibus aufer!
> ante' ait 'emoriar, quam sit tibi copia nostri';
> rettulit illa nihil nisi 'sit tibi copia nostri!'
> *spreta* latet silvis . . .
>
> (*Metamorphoses* II. 390-93)

(He flees, and as he is fleeing says: 'Keep your hands from embracing me! I'd far sooner die, than I would give you power over me!' She replies simply: 'I would give you power over me!' Spurned, she lies hidden in the woods.)

Similarly, when Ronsard has Aurore exclaim:

> Pourquoi pers tu de ton age
> Le printens à lamenter
> Une froide & morte image
> Qui ne peut te contenter?
>
> (lines 221-24)

he surely has in mind the poet's exclamation to Narcissus in *Metamorphoses* III. 432-34:

> credule, quid frustra simulacra fugacia captas?
> quod petis, est nusquam; quod amas, avertere, perdes!
> ista repercussae, quam cernis, imaginis umbra est.

(Credulous boy, why do you try in vain to clasp a fleeting image? What you are seeking is nowhere. Turn aside, you will lose what you love! What you look upon is the shadow of a reflected picture.)

In other words, Ronsard's Céphale is twin brother to Narcissus, the traditional symbol of philautia, self-love: 'se cupit inprudens et, qui probat, ipse probatur' ('unwisely he desires himself and, in praising, he is himself what is praised').[6] However, in Ronsard's version of the story the young hero is saved, despite himself, through the intervention of heavenly love. Thus the poet is exploiting here a kind of visual and literary ambiguity which is present in some of the Fontainebleau frescoes, where, for example, the dying Adonis in the Galerie François Ier resembles a *pietà,* and the fresco depicting the twins of Catania contains a configuration similar to the traditional depiction of Aeneas carrying his father Anchises away from Troy after its sack by the Greeks.

However, perhaps the allegory can be pursued a little further. For the name Céphale is, of course, derived from the Greek word κεφαλη (= head). Thus, Cephalus, the rational mortal, deceived and disappointed by his earthly love of knowledge, is led to a blessed life of immortality in heaven by Love, through the agency of Dawn, a symbol of the onset of divine illumination. (In neo-Platonic terms, the beginnings of love are described by Ficino as rays of light emanating from the sun.[7] This, of course, also fits in with the ambiguity of the torch/roses image in lines 97-112, discussed above.)[8]

But what of the *inquadratura* of our poem? The first two stanzas and the five stanzas of the *tierce pose* are devoted to a description of the preparations for the marriage of Peleus and Thetis, and the prophecy of Themis concerning the birth of Achilles. Superficially, there is an obvious connection in that both the Peleus and Thetis myth and the central story of the poem deal with the union of a female divinity with a mortal man. This link may be suggested in line 261 where Themis says to Thetis: 'Bien qu'Inon soit ta compaigne.' Ino had leapt into the sea and drowned, but had been changed into the sea-goddess Leucothea by Neptune, at the request of Venus (Ovid, *Metamorphoses* IV. 531-42). Natalis Comes writes of Ino in his *Mythologiae:*

> Haec Ino vocata fuit postea Leucothea, & Dea maris existimata, ut ait Home. lib. 4. Odyss . . . . Leucothea, quae Matuta dicta est a Latinis, Aurora est.[9]

> (This Ino was subsequently called Leucothea, and considered a sea-goddess, as Homer says in book IV of the *Odyssey* [in fact, it is book V. 333-35]. Leucothea, who was called Matuta by the Romans, is Aurora.)

So, Ronsard appears to be emphasizing the links between Thetis and Ino/Aurora in his use of the periphrasis of line 261.

However, the opening of the poem contains details that are only distantly related to the Peleus and Thetis story. As Laumonier indicates, we seem to be dealing with a contamination of Catullus 64 and Virgil, *Georgics* IV. 333 et seq. But is the motive for this simply diversity? The scene described in the *Georgics* is Cyrene's river palace, where Aristaeus, her son, has come to discover why he has lost all his bees:

> At mater sonitum thalamo sub fluminis alti
> sensit. eam circum Milesia vellera Nymphae
> carpebant hyali saturo fucata colore, . . .
> inter quas curam Clymene narrabat inanem
> Volcani, Martisque dolos et dulcia furta,
> aque Chao densos divum numerabat amores.

> (*Georgics* IV. 333-35, 345-47)

(But his mother, in her chamber in the deep river, heard the sound. Around her, her nymphs were spinning Milesian fleeces, dyed in a rich sea-green hue . . . . Amongst them, Clymene was telling of the useless precautions of Vulcan, the tricks and stolen delights of Mars, and was numbering the many loves of the gods from Chaos onwards.)

The scene in Ronsard also recalls *Odyssey* XIII. 102 et seq., the cave of the Nymphs in Ithaca, to which the sleeping Odysseus is brought:

> Now at the harbour's head is an olive tree with spreading leaves, and hard by is a pleasant cave and a shady, sacred to the nymphs, that are called the Naiads. And therein are mixing bowls and jars of stone, and there moreover do bees hive. And there are great looms of stone, whereon the nymphs weave raiment of purple stain, a marvel to behold. And waters are therein welling evermore, and there are two gates to the cave, the one set toward the North Wind whereby men go down, but the portals toward the South pertain rather to the gods, whereby men may not enter; it is the way of the immortals.[10]

However, there are differences of detail in Ronsard's version:

> L'iver, lors que la nuit lente
> Fait au ciel si long sejour,
> Une vierge vigilente
> S'éveilla davant le jour:
> Et par les palais humides,
> Où les Dieus dormoient enclos,
> Hucha les seurs Neréides
> Qui ronfloient au bruit des flots.

> (lines 1-8)

(In a variant introduced in 1555, the 'palais' of line 5 becomes 'antres'.) Why does Ronsard insist on the fact that it is winter? In order to understand this section, we need to have in mind not only the Virgilian and Homeric texts, but also the allegorical explanations which concern them.

One of the most frequently published works of Homeric allegory in the sixteenth century was Porphyry's *Cave of the Nymphs,* and it seems more than likely that Ronsard has this work in mind in the ode under consideration.[11] Porphyry starts off by saying that since Homer's description is so full of obscurities, it must be allegorical, a notion that could equally be applied to Ronsard. The cave is both a symbol of the Cosmos and also a place of initiation into the mysteries of the Cosmos. The Naiads represent souls descending into corporeal generation, the stone looms stand for the bones on which they weave their own flesh and blood (the 'raiment of purple stain'). Porphyry also refers to the ancients speaking of the heavens as a robe, as if they were the garment of the heavenly gods. He writes of the two entrances to the Cave of the Nymphs:

> Taking the cave as an image and symbol of the Cosmos, Numenius and his pupil Cronius assert that there are two extremities in the heavens: the winter tropic than which nothing is more southern, and the summer tropic than which nothing is more northern. The summer tropic is in Cancer, the winter tropic is in Capricorn . . . . Of these Numenius and Cronius say that the gate through which souls descend is Cancer, but that they ascend through Capricorn.

Many of these details, then, could be applied to Ronsard's cave. His waking nymphs would symbolize waking souls, the robe they weave for Neptune quite explicitly represents the heavens and the seas, while the winter setting perhaps points towards the idea of the Tropic of Capricorn and the ascension of souls from corporeal existence to spiritual afterlife—the theme of the Cephalus story. It is also no coincidence that makes Ronsard choose the name Naïs (line 77) for the nymph who recounts this story, forming in this way a link with Homer's Naiads.

Turning now to the *Georgics,* we find one of the nymphs, Clymene, telling the story of the adultery of Ares and Aphrodite, 'aque Chao densos divum . . . amores'. The Ares and Aphrodite story was perhaps the most notorious of all the Homeric myths for those who, in the ancient world, considered Homer immoral. However, it was frequently allegorized, by Heraclitus the Rhetor amongst others, who sees Ares as representing discord and Aphrodite love, and their union as giving rise to Harmony.[12] A sixteenth-century reader would almost certainly have read the *Georgics* passage with some such explanation in mind. There would thus be a parallel here with the song of Virgil's nymph, Clymene, and Ronsard's Naïs, in that both nymphs are revealing a divine mystery.

In the same way, the ecphrasis devoted to Neptune's cloak takes up this theme of the equilibrium between the warring elements of the universe. These are symbolized by the silk and the gold thread used to weave the cloth ('D'une soie non commune, / Et d'un or en Cypre eleu . . .', lines 17-18). The gold here is clearly associated with Venus through the allusion to Cyprus, the island which is sacred to her, while, later on, the silk seems to represents the forces of discord:

> D'une soie & noire, & perse,
> Cent nuës entrelassoient,
> Qui d'une longue traverse
> Tout le serein effaçoient . . . .
>
> (lines 45-48)

The way in which these elements are inextricably woven together in the cloak symbolizes the eternal equilibrium between discord and love in the universe, with the god Neptune representing the forces of concord, both by his association with the gold—'Neptune i fut peint lui méme / Brodé d'or . . . '—and by his calming of the warring elements—'qui du danger / Tirant le marinier bléme / L'eau en l'eau faisoit ranger.' The rainbow which completes the cloak (lines 73-76) is both a biblical symbol of God's covenant with man after the Flood (Genesis 9. 12-17), and the goddess Iris who, according to Dorat, both announced and explained the secrets of the gods.[13]

Finally, there is the remaining part of our frame, the *tierce pose,* to consider. Themis, the goddess personifying Justice, predicts as she does in Pindar, *Isthmian Ode* 7, the birth of Achilles to Peleus and Thetis, 'Un qui donnera matiere / Aus Poëtes de chanter'. In celebrating the fact that 'Ses vertus reluiront comme / Les étoiles par les cieus', Ronsard mentions three particular deeds (all recalled by Pindar): the wounding of Telephus, the killing of Memnon, the son of Aurora and Tithonus, and the killing of Hector. Despite the apparently negative images of death introduced at the end of this poem, we are no doubt meant to have in mind the immortality won by all those, including Achilles, who, through their deeds of valour, achieve eternal fame by being celebrated in poetry.

"La Defloration de Lede" is addressed to Cassandre, and takes as its subject a fable which had already proved popular with painters, notably Leonardo da Vinci and Michelangelo.[14] The story may seem at first sight an odd one to dedicate to a mistress.[15] However, thanks to Proclus and other ancient thinkers, educated sixteenth-century readers would have been prepared to look for a mystical meaning behind the most shocking myths.[16]

As in the case of the Cephalus poem, the structure of this ode can be seen to resemble that of the Fontainebleau decoration. The central picture is made up of the rape of Leda (lines 137-200, the *tierce pose*). An important ecphrasis, describing the scenes of Leda's flower-basket, precedes this (lines 73-136, the *seconde pose*), and fulfils a function similar to that of Neptune's cloak in **"Le Ravissement de Cephale."** Lines 25-72 present us with the view of Jupiter, transformed into a swan through the effects of love, while in lines 201-32 the god prophesies the results of this love. The first 24 lines act as an introduction to the whole, and associate the poet with Jupiter. Our *in-quadratura* is thus a little more complex than was the case with the Cephalus ode, while the specific parallel drawn between the poet and Jupiter adds a further dimension to the poem.

The central scene which depicts the rape of Leda is, indeed, quite brutal. Having caught sight of the swan, she outstrips her companions in her eagerness to reach him (lines 137-44), and they frolic together beside the water (lines 145-52). Ronsard plays with the ambiguous nature of the bird in this section. Despite his animal appearance, he acts like a human ('Et l'oiseau qui tresaut d'aise, / S'en aproche tout humain', lines 146-47), and yet he is, of course, a god. It is the swan's beautiful singing that seduces Leda, and causes her to feel the stirrings of passion in her innermost being:

> Puis d'une gaie façon
> Courbe au dos l'une & l'autre aile,
> Et au bruit de sa chançon
> Il apprivoise la belle:
> La nicette en son giron
> Reçoit les flammes segrettes,
> Faisant tout à l'environ
> Du Cigne un lit de fleurettes.
>
> (lines 153-60)

The picture of the rape itself resembles very closely the Michelangelo painting, copied by Rosso Fiorentino for Fontainebleau. As in the painting, the swan's neck touches Leda's breasts (lines 165-66); his beak enters her mouth (lines 167-68), while he presses her body beneath his own (lines 171-72). Leda, both in the painting and the poem, is blushing (lines 177-78). After her deflowering, she immediately upbraids the bird, not so much, it seems, for committing the act itself as for being beneath her station:

> D'où viens tu, qui as l'audace
> D'aller ainsi violant
> Les filles de noble race?
>
> (lines 182-84)

The picture Ronsard presents is a highly graphic one: the white of the swan is contrasted with the green of the grass and the redness of Leda's lips and face, while the ground is strewn around with the plucked flowers, symbols of

Leda's own lost virginity (cf. lines 191-92). However, the fable may be construed as containing a mystery, as Edgar Wind argued in connection with the Michelangelo painting; Ronsard perhaps intended something similar in the framing sections of the poem.[17]

In lines 25-64, having likened himself to Jupiter, Ronsard goes on to describe the god's metamorphosis into a swan. The link between swans and the arts of music and poetry was well established long before the sixteenth century. Boccaccio in the *Genealogiae deorum gentilium* somewhat prosaically explains Jupiter's sexual conquest of Leda in terms of his beautifully seductive voice:

> The ancients may have invented the story of Jupiter's transformation into a swan because the swan sings sweetly. It is possible Jupiter too did this, and by the sweetness of his singing, as we have often seen occur, caused Leda to love and desire him.[18]

A rather more spiritual explanation may be found in Plato's *Phaedrus,* 251, where Socrates describes how, when someone sees an object of beauty, 'the stump of each feather under the whole surface of the soul swells and strives to grow from its root: for in its original state the soul was feathered all over'. In this image of Jupiter turning into a swan, we can see the union of poetry and music on the one hand with the effects of the erotic frenzy on the other, where the whiteness of the swan's feathers only emphasizes the purity of his soul.

Iconographically, the swan had been linked with music before the Leda ode, for example in a painting by Filippino Lippi dating from *c.* 1500, and entitled *Allegory of Music.* In this composition, Erato, the muse of music, is looking at an Apollonian swan with which two Cupids are playing. This painting is said to have links with Leonardo's own version of the Leda story.[19]

Lines 41-48 describe the *carcan* and gold and enamel chain which the swan wears around its neck:

> En son col meit un carcan,
> Avec une cheine, où l'Œuvre
> Du laborieus Vulcan
> Merveillable se déqueuvre.
> D'or en étoient les cerçeaus,
> Piolés d'aimail ensemble,
> A l'arc qui verse les eaus
> Ce bel ouvrage ressemble.

Laumonier suggests, not altogether convincingly, that this is 'soit pour faire croire à Léda qu'il est un cygne domestique et l'approcher plus aisément . . . , soit pour se parer par coquetterie et mieux séduire Léda' (L. II.70. n. 2). Although Ronsard uses the word 'carcan' a number of times in his poetry, it is generally in the sense of necklace, and there is never any chain attached. Lines 47-48 compare the chain to the rainbow. Now, there would be little point in the chain if it were not intended to be held by Leda, thus establishing a direct, physical connection between her and the swan. It seems likely, therefore, that the chain is an al-

lusion to the famous passage in Plato's *Io* concerning the magnet-like workings of inspiration:

> This [magnet] not only attracts iron rings, but induces in the rings the power to do the same themselves in turn—namely to attract other rings, so that sometimes a long chain of iron rings is formed, suspended from one another, all having the force derived from the stone. Thus the Muse herself makes people possessed, and from these possessed persons there hangs a chain of others, possessed with the same enthusiasm.[20]

> (*Io,* 533)

Thus, the swan, representing the Apollonian art of music, would inspire Leda through the chain. A similar image was used in the triumphal entry of Henri II into Paris in 1549, where the first arch was surmounted by a statue of the Gallic Hercules, bearing the features of François Ier:

> de sa bouche partoyent quatre chaisnettes, deux d'or, & deux d'argent, qui s'alloyent attacher aux oreilles des personnages dessus nommez: mais elles estoyent si treslaches, que chacun les pouuoit iuger ne seruir de contraincte: ains qu'ils estoyent voluntairement tirez par l'eloquence du nouuel Hercules, lequel a faict fleurir en ce Royaume les langues Hebraique, Grecque, Latine, & autres, beaucoup plus qu'elles n'ont iamais faict par le passé.[21]

An even closer iconographic parallel exists between this stanza and the Lippi *Allegory of Music,* already mentioned. In the painting, the swan is indeed wearing a 'carcan' attached to which is a curious ribbon with metal circles, held at one end by the Muse Erato, at the other by one of the *putti.* A sprig of laurel passes through the *carcan,* emphasizing the Apollonian connections. But what of the rainbow comparison in Ronsard? Iris, called periphrastically 'l'arc qui verse les eaus' (cf. Horace, *Ars poetica* 18, 'pluvius arcus'), was, as we have already noted, the female messenger of the gods, and acted as psychopomp. As such, she represents another link between heaven and earth, like the divine chain of the Muses itself.

The opening four lines of the next stanza (lines 49-52), describing the gold shining on the white feathers, might seem gratuitously decorative at first sight:

> L'or sus la plume reluit
> D'une semblable lumiere,
> Que le clair œil de la nuit
> Desus la nege premiere.

The gold here is compared to the moon ('le clair œil de la nuit'), the plumage to freshly-fallen snow ('la nege premiere'). The image is, visually, an extremely effective one, yet there is something wrong. Traditionally, it is the sun that is described in terms of gold, the moon in terms of silver; feathers, which are light and, as we have seen, signify the soul's ascent heavenwards, are here compared to snow, which is associated with coldness and downward movement towards the earth. What we have in this image, then, is a sacred marriage between sun and moon, gold and silver, heaven and earth, resulting in the portrayal of a perfect union between divine and mortal.

Jupiter's descent (lines 53-56) is then likened to that of an eagle falling upon a snake which is sloughing off its old skin (lines 57-60). Laumonier (L. II 71. n. I) points to the literary sources of eagles falling on snakes (Ovid, *Meta-morphoses* IV. 714-15) and snakes casting off their skins (Virgil, *Aeneid* II. 471-73 = *Georgics* III. 437-39); but he does not comment on the combination and consequent significance of these separate images. The eagle (called in the Ovid passage 'Iovis praepes') clearly represents Jupiter, the snake Leda.[22] Traditionally, the image of the eagle snatching up the serpent is a symbol of the spiritual victory of man's higher nature over his lower nature, of the union of spirit and matter. The snake sloughing off its skin, on the other hand, is a symbol of eternal youth, rejuvenation, resurrection of the soul, foreshadowing what Leda is to gain as a result of Jupiter's attentions. The stanza, and this section, ends with the swan arriving by Leda's side as she plays at the water's edge.

What is prefigured in this section, with its multiplicity of images, is borne out in the *quatrième pose* by Jupiter's words to Leda. Revealing his true identity, the god tells her that, because of his love, she is becoming part of an illustrious family: 'Tu seras incontinant / La belle seur de Neptune.'

The poem ends with two stanzas foretelling the outcome of the affair: Leda will produce two eggs, one containing Castor and Pollux, the other Helen, 'La beauté au ciel choisie'. Unlike other versions of the myth where Helen is joined by Clytemnestra, Ronsard chooses only to concentrate on the positive results of this story. The Dioscuri, tutelary gods who also act as psychopomps, were considered to be symbols of heavenly concord. Thus, harmony is one of the results of Jupiter's love for a mortal. The other result is heavenly beauty, in the shape of Helen.[23]

In his commentary on the *Symposium,* Ficino speaks of the workings of love. For him, beauty, harmony, and good are all synonymous. Earthly beauty is derived from a ray of light from the divine Sun, which creates an image of God in a beautiful mortal. There is a circular process when someone falls in love, a converting triad. Beauty leads to Love, which leads to a transcendent Pleasure, which in turn leads back to heavenly Beauty:

> [It is] a circle . . . inasmuch as it begins in God and attracts to Him, it is Beauty; inasmuch as, going across into the world, it captivates the world, we call it Love; and inasmuch as it returns to its source and with Him joins its labours, then we call it Pleasure. In this way, Love begins in Beauty and ends in Pleasure.[24]

This is precisely what happens in the Leda myth as recounted by Ronsard, where Leda's god-given beauty leads to the love of Jupiter, which in turn leads to divine pleasure, of which the result is beauty and harmony. Thus, the mystery of the central picture of the rape is to some extent explained by the narrative framework.

But what of the *seconde pose* devoted to the flower-basket and the list of flowers which Leda and her companions were collecting? Ronsard's immediate model is Moschus who, in his poem on the rape of Europa, includes a description of her flower-basket (Moschus 2. 37-62) and the scenes depicted on it. These themes concern Io, who had been changed into a heifer by Zeus, thus providing a neat bovine parallel to the events which form the main narrative of the poem, where Zeus changes himself into a bull.

Lines 65-72 in Ronsard's poem introduce Leda collecting flowers with her companions, and include a Horatian allusion to *Odes* III. 27. 29, as Laumonier indicates (L. II. 71. n. 3). Lines 73-96 describe a scene on the basket concerning the orbit of the sun. In a scene which resembles the description of Dawn in the Cephalus ode (L. II. 138. 97-108), Aurora is depicted, amidst golden clouds, strewing flowers across the sky, her unbound hair blown by the nostrils of the horses drawing the chariot of the Sun, which is hard on her heels.[25] As the sun orbits the earth, the muscles of the horses can be seen to stand out and 'leur puissance indontée / Se lasse sous les travaux / De la pénible montée' (lines 86-88). In the evening, the sun sinks into the sea, 'Jusqu'au fond de ce grand ventre'.

As Laumonier points out (L. II. 72. n. I), the description of the sun's orbit owes much to Ovid, *Metamorphoses* II. 63 et'seq.:

> ardua prima via est et qua vix mane recentes
> enituntur equi; medio est altissima caelo,
> unde mare et terras ipsi mihi saepe videre
> fit timor et pavida trepidat formidine pectus;
> ultima prona via est et eget moderamine certo:
> tunc etiam quae me subiectis excipit undis,
> ne ferar in praeceps, Tethys solet ipsa vereri.

> (The first part of the course is steep, and here the horses, fresh as they are in the early morning, can hardly make their way. In mid heaven it is extremely high, and to look down from there at the sea and land often causes even me to be afraid, and my heart quakes with trembling dread. The last part of the course is downhill and wants an assured control. Then even Tethys herself, who welcomes me in her waters below, fears that I may be carried down headlong.)

In this passage, we have the words of Apollo to his son Phaethon, describing the dangers of the course of the sun's chariot. As Panofsky points out, 'there is only one allegorical explanation of the myth of Phaethon: the fate of the daring mortal who had tried to defy human limitations was held to symbolize the fate of every *temerarius,* presumptuous enough to overstep the bounds of his allotted "state and situation"'.[26] However, the opposite is true of Apollo's description of his own journey, as well as of Ronsard's description, where the sun's course is, literally, a golden mean. However, Ronsard's use of the myth may well have a more specifically erotic significance.

In a famous passage, Socrates speaks, again in the *Phaedrus,* 247, of the soul's being like a charioteer drawn by two horses. When an individual falls in love with a beautiful person, the charioteer steers his course, being pulled towards vice by one horse, towards virtue by the other. The perfect course is that of the gods. Ronsard refers explicitly to the soul as charioteer, and to the ability of love to lead to knowledge, in *Les Amours* of 1552; thus, for example, L. IV. 24. 9-14:

> Le cheval noir qui ma Royne conduit
> Par le sentier où ma Chair la seduit,
> A tant erré d'une vaine traverse,
> Que j'ay grand peur, (si le blanc ne contraint
> Sa course vague, & ses pas ne refraint
> Dessoubz le joug) que ma raison ne verse.

and also:

> Par ce doulx mal j'adoray la beaulté,
> Qui me liant d'une humble cruaulté
> Me desnoua les liens d'ignorance.
> Par luy me vint ce vertueux penser,
> Qui jusqu'au ciel fit mon cuœur eslancer,
> Aillé de foy, d'amour & d'esperance.

>   (L. IV. 140-41. 9-14)

Thus, celestial love leads to knowledge. The mention of Aurora at the beginning of this description reinforces the idea. Ronsard emphasizes the arduous nature of the sun's course (lines 85-88) because the path of virtuous love is also hard. But the sun is rewarded when it returns to the sea, for it is commonly considered to be returning to its mistress Tethys (cf. Scève, *Délie* II).

By contrast, the descriptions in the remaining three stanzas present the other side of the coin, as we are shown here images of earthly love. The first one is the least obvious (lines 97-104). A shepherd sees a wolf approaching his sheep but is more intent on watching a snail climbing up a lily. Here, we have a symbol of purity and chastity, for lilies sprang up from the milk of Hera and are the attribute of Hera/Juno and Diana, as well as of the Virgin Mary. The snail, however, represents lust, both because of its association with mud (*limax/limus*) and because it was believed to be the only animal of its species to copulate.[27] Thus, the shepherd, intent on watching this scene of chastity outraged, is about to be punished by the loss of his sheep.

The picture of the satyrs in the next stanza (lines 105-12) is clearer. Satyrs are traditional symbols of lechery and of the lower instincts in general, for the lower halves of their bodies consist of the hind quarters of a goat. In 'folatrant', both satyrs lose what they were squabbling over, the milk, and hence, like the shepherd, are punished for their base instincts. Perhaps too there is an allusion to seminal fluid in the reference to the spilling of the milk, since satyrs are not generally associated with dairy products. The two fighting rams of the next stanza (lines 113-16) are yet an-

other symbol of virility and procreation in a stanza which ends with an allusion to Leda's loss of virginity.

Thus, the details of the description of the basket appear to have unity of theme, dealing with sacred and earthly love. They echo and reinforce the main theme of the painting, and indeed, help to throw light on it, while at the same time having a decorative function. The final two stanzas of the *seconde pose* present what had become in the classical world quite a common prelude to a scene of abduction: a picture of Leda with her companions picking flowers (cf. Ovid, *Fasti* VI. 425-44; Moschus, 2; and Claudian, *De raptu Proserpinae* II. 118-36). As we have seen, this too can be read allegorically: the plucking of flowers prefigures Leda's loss of virginity (unlike other accounts of the myth where Leda was already married to Tyndareus): compare, for example, Catullus, 62. 39-47 for a beautiful working of this theme, and lines 191-92 of this poem. Ronsard chooses a number of flowers with mythological connections. Those in lines 121-28, the narcissus, the hyacinth ('la lettre teinte au sang / Du Grec marri pour les armes'), and the heliotrope (or Clytie) all have amorous connotations, whether they be of self-love, homosexual love, or heterosexual love. The scarlet carnation also, of course, is a traditional symbol of passionate love.

Ronsard seems to have hesitated a great deal over the next stanza and to have been somewhat dissatisfied with his various versions. In 1587, 'bascinets' (line 131) becomes 'Coquerets'; but there is more doubt about the last three lines:

> 1550
> (Jettant sa charge odorante
> Et la rouge fueille aussi
> De l'immortel Amaranthe.)
> 1555-60
> (Jettant des fleurs l'odorante
> Moisson, & la fueille aussi
> De l'immortel Amaranthe.)
> 1567-84
> (Laissant la rose odorente
> Et la belle fueille aussy
> De l'immortel Amaranthe.)
> 1587
> De son Destin ignorante:
> De tant de fleurs que voicy
> Laisson la proye odorante.

Should we see anything allegorical in Leda's casting aside her flowers (or her rose) along with her amarant leaves (a symbol of immortality)? If our reading of the poem has been correct, she is far from losing a chance of immortality. Perhaps this is the reason why Ronsard attenuated the early 'Jettant' by replacing it with 'Laissant', and then finally abandoned any reference to leaving these plants behind.

Whatever the significance of individual details, Ronsard's general message is clear: inspired by the love of beauty, poetry and music themselves produce harmony and beauty. It is but a short step to relate this to the poet himself, and

Ronsard had done so in the opening lines of the ode (1-24). Through an allusion to Horace, Ronsard compares himself to Orpheus (lines 9-10):

> Mon luc qui des bois oiants
> Souloit alleger les peines

compare *Odes* I. 12. 9-12:

> arte materna rapidos morantem
> fluminum lapsus celerisque ventos,
> blandum et auritas fidibus canoris
> ducere quercus.

> (through his mother's skill delaying the swift flowing of rivers and the rapid winds, persuasive too to draw after him with his harmonious strings the listening oaks.)

There is also an allusion to Orpheus in lines 13-16:

> Et le souleil ne peut voir
> Soit quand le jour il apporte,
> Ou quand il se couche au soir
> Une autre douleur plus forte.

As Laumonier indicates (L. II. 68. n. 3), Ronsard has in mind here Virgil, *Georgics* IV. 465-66: 'te, dulcis coniunx, te solo in litore secum, / te veniente die, te decedente canebat' ('all alone on the lonely shore, he would sing of you, sweet wife, of you at the dawning of the day, of you at its setting'). We have already seen that Ronsard had this section of the *Georgics* in mind in the Cephalus ode.

Ronsard/Orpheus soon becomes Ronsard/Jupiter, however, in lines 25-32:

> Juppiter époinçonné
> De telle amoureuse rage,
> A le ciel abandonné,
> Son tonnerre, & son orage,
> Car l'Œil qui son cueur étraint
> Comme étraints ores nous sommes,
> Ce grand seigneur a contraint
> De tenter l'amour des hommes.

If, as we have already said seems likely, **"La Defloration de Lede"** and **"Le Ravissement de Cephale"** are companion pieces, what is the relationship between them? Clearly, like a diptych, they present different aspects of the same basic theme, the ravishment of a mortal by an immortal. On a more detailed level, there are further connections and parallels. Aurore, the protagonist of the Cephalus ode, figures in the flower-basket ecphrasis of the Leda poem; two descriptions of works of art, the swan's gold chain and Neptune's robe, conclude with an allusion to the rainbow; the sea, which on the flower-basket is presented with few details, takes up a good part of the description of Neptune's robe; Narcissus appears obliquely in both poems; and the Trojan war provides the background for the prophecies of both Jupiter and Themis. Similarly, both the ravished mortals fall into a deathlike swoon:

> Ses membres tombent peu forts,
> Et dedans la mort voisine
> Ses yeus ja nouoient . . . .

(L. II. 78. 197-99)

> Ainsi disant il se pasme
> Sur le cors qui trépassoit.

(L. II. 140. 133-34)

Both, however, are promised immortality.

It seems likely, therefore, that Ronsard is exploring various aspects of the experience of love and its inspirational properties in the two poems. In the Leda ode, the poet is represented as Jupiter, who through his plumage and swan's appearance is in turn associated with poetry. Inspired by the beauty of Leda/Cassandre, his love for her can ultimately produce the beauty and harmony of poetry, which will thus immortalize her. In the Cephalus ode, we see the same experience from a slightly different angle. This time, the mortal and rational Ronsard/Cephalus needs the divine inspiration of Cassandre/Aurore in order to achieve the rapture (*ravissement*) necessary to produce truly inspired poetry.

A number of conclusions can be drawn from this examination of the two odes. In the first place, we can see the importance of the individual details which go to make up the overall picture that Ronsard is creating. Apparently irrelevant items of decoration can have a symbolic value, acting as a parallel or a contrast to the main theme, or they can evoke in a concise form other mythological events. Secondly, we have seen that the structure of individual narrative poems, with a central theme surrounded by other, connected themes, builds up a picture which is complex but essentially unified. And finally, the connections between the two odes on both the thematic and the decorative level exemplify the way in which a consideration of the overall architecture of much of Ronsard's poetry can produce something more than simply the sum of the individual parts.[28]

To what extent would Ronsard's readers have appreciated the allegorical significance and thematic parallels of these two poems? Certainly, by placing them in different books of *Odes* even when they were first published, the poet is not going out of his way to draw attention to their similarities. And while some of the imagery would have been relatively accessible through its popularization in contemporary poetry and its use in the visual arts (Leda as the immortalized human soul, the swan as a symbol of music and poetry), other allusions would depend far more on the reader's ability to recognize specific allusions to classical texts, and to be aware of their allegorical meaning. The discovery of a unifying significance in a work of art may be an intellectually satisfying experience, but it is just one of a number of pleasures offered by Ronsard's poetry, It may well be, as Margaret McGowan has argued was the case with Renaissance poetry and music, that the harmony of the work itself was meant to create instinctively a corresponding sense of harmony in the reader.[29] And clearly, the poetry is there to be enjoyed on a purely aesthetic level. As with the frescoes of the Galerie François Ier, the sensuous beauty, wit, and harmony of Ronsard's work would have been appreciated by many more readers than those who would have grasped the intricacies of its thematic structure and allegorical significance.

Notes

1. References to Ronsard's works are to the (*Œuvres complètes,* edited by Paul Laumonier, and revised and completed by Isidore Silver and Raymond Lebègue, 20 vols (Paris, Hachette, Droz, Didier, 1914-75), abbreviated as L., and followed by volume number, page number, and line number. All references to Laumonier's commentary on the text are taken from his notes and will be indicated by bracketed page and note numbers.

2. Ovid also recounts or alludes to the story in the *Ars amatoria* III. 686-746, and *Amores* I. 13, 39-40.

3. The term *vita mea,* to refer to a poet's beloved, was used by Propertius (e.g. I. 2. I), but subsequently became very popular with neo-Latin poets.

4. Cesare Ripa, *Iconologia* (Padua, P. P. Tozzi, 1611), p. 36 (also available in a facsimile edition (New York and London, Garland Publishing, Inc., 1976)). The *editio princeps* was published in Rome in 1593.

5. Ann Moss, *Poetry and Fable: Studies in Mythological Narrative in Sixteenth-Century France* (Cambridge University Press, 1984), p. 126. The author considers the ode at length, pp. 125-32. See too her analysis of the Leda ode in 'New Myths for Old?', in *Ronsard in Cambridge: Proceedings of the Cambridge Ronsard Colloquium, 10-12 April 1985,* ed. by Philip Ford and Gillian Jondorf (Cambridge French Colloquia, 1986), pp. 55-66, (pp. 57-60).

6. *Metamorphoses* III. 425.

7. See especially Ficino's commentary on the *Symposium,* 2.3. For a modern edition of the work, see *Marsilio Ficino's Commentary on Plato's 'Symposium',* edited by Sears Reynolds Jayne, University of Missouri Studies, 19 (Columbia, University of Missouri, 1944).

8. Another, this time euhemeristic, explanation of the myth is offered by Heraclitus the Rhetor, commenting on the loves of Aurora and Orion (*Odyssey* v. 121). He explains the abduction as follows: 'When a young man of both noble birth and outstanding beauty died, they euphemistically called the early morning funeral cortège the abduction of Hemera [Day or Dawn], as if he had not died, but been snatched up through an amorous yearning.' See *Allégories d'Homère,* edited by Félix Buffière (Paris, Les Belles Lettres, 1962), 68, 5-6.

9. See *Mythologiae, sive explicationis fabularum libri decem,* first published in 1551. This explanation, which is probably based on Ovid, *Fasti* VI. 479, is cited from the 1584 edition of the *Mythologiae,* published in Frankfurt, f.241^r.

10. The translation is that of S. H. Butcher and A. Lang, *The Odyssey of Homer* (London, Macmillan, 1879), p. 210.

11. On the Cave of the Nymphs, see Félix Buffière, *Les Mythes d'Homère et la pensée grecque* (Paris, Les Belles Lettres, 1956), pp. 419-57 and appendix, and my articles 'Conrad Gesner et le fabuleux manteau', *Bibliothèque d'Humanisme et Renaissance,* 47 (1985), 305-20, and 'Ronsard and Homeric Allegory', in *Ronsard in Cambridge,* pp. 40-54. The text itself may be consulted in *The Cave of the Nymphs in the Odyssey: A Revised Text with Translation,* Arethusa Monographs, I (Buffalo, NY, Arethusa, 1969), whose translation is used here.

12. See Buffière edition of Heraclitus, ch. 69. The subject of the adultery of Mars and Venus was a very popular one with Renaissance artists; see, for example, Botticelli's treatment in the National Gallery, London.

13. On Iris, see my article 'Conrad Gesner et le fabuleux manteau', p. 316.

14. Leonardo's version, now surviving only in copies, hung in the palace of Fontainebleau (see Carlo Pedretti, *Leonardo: A Study in Chronology and Style* (Berkeley and Los Angeles, University of California Press, 1973), p. 97), as did a copy of Michelangelo's version, probably executed by Rosso Fiorentino, which is now in the National Gallery, London (see Cecil Gould, *National Gallery Catalogues: The Sixteenth-Century Italian Schools* (London, The National Gallery, 1975), pp. 150-52).

15. Compare the remarks of Michel Dassonville, *Ronsard: Étude historique et littéraire,* I. *Les Enfances Ronsard (1536-1545)* (Geneva, Droz, 1968), p. 244.

16. See my paper 'Ronsard and Homeric Allegory', p. 53.

17. See Edgar Wind, *Pagan Mysteries in the Renaissance,* revised edition (Oxford University Press, 1980), pp. 152-70.

18. *Genealogie deorum gentilium libri,* edited by Vincenzo Romano, 2 vols (Bari, Gius. Laterza & figli, 1951), p. 547.

19. See Wind, op. cit., and K. B. Neilson, *Filippino Lippi* (Cambridge, Mass., Harvard University Press, 1938), pp. 176 sq. This connection is disputed, however, by E. Panofsky, *Renaissance and Renascences in Western Art* (New York-San Francisco-London, Harper & Row, 1972), p. 203, n. 3. The painting is in the Kaiser-Friedrich-Museum, Berlin.

20. The translation is that of D. A. Russell, from *Ancient Literary Criticism: The Principal Texts, in*

New Translations, edited by D. A. Russell and M. Winterbottom (Oxford University Press, 1972), p. 43.

21. See *The Entry of Henri II into Paris 16 June 1549,* edited by I. D. McFarlane (Binghamton, NY, Center for Medieval & Early Renaissance Studies, 1982), ff. 3ʳ-4ʳ.

22. On snake symbolism, see Jane M. Drake-Brockman, 'Scève, the Snake and the Herb', *FS,* XXXIII (1979), 129-36, (p. 132). In the 'Ode sur les miseres des hommes' (L. v. 192-96), Ronsard alludes to the eternal youth of the snake in a section (lines 57-60) that recalls the *Jeunesse perdue* fresco in the Galerie François Iᵉʳ at Fontainebleau: 'Ah, que maudite soit l'Anesse / Qui, las! pour sa soif etancher / Au serpent donna la jeunesse / Que garder on devoit tant cher.'

23. For a discussion of the significance in Ronsard of Castor and Pollux, see my article 'Ronsard et l'emploi de l'allégorie dans *Le Second Livre des Hymnes', Bibliothèque d'Humanisme et Renaissance,* 48 (1981), 89-106, (pp. 99-104).

24. See Ficino, ed. cit., 2.2 (pp. 43 and 134).

25. Although Aurora is frequently spoken of by the ancients in terms of flowers to indicate her colour (*rosea, crocea*), she is never depicted as strewing flowers across the sky. However, both Ripa, as we have already seen, and Cartari portray her in this way, an obvious iconographic extension of the classical epithets, which in turn can be exploited in poetry.

26. *Studies in Iconology: Humanistic Themes in the Art of the Renaissance* (New York—San Francisco—London, Harper & Row, 1972), p. 219.

27. See Varro, *De lingua latina* 7. 64 ('limax ab limo, quod ibi vivit'), and Aristotle, *Generation of Animals* 762.a.31. Ronsard used similar images of negligence being punished elsewhere, for example in the *Bergerie* of 1564 (L. XIII. 89. 259-70).

28. Cf. Doranne Fenoaltea, *Du palais au jardin: L'Architecture des Odes de Ronsard,* Travaux d'Humanisme et Renaissance, 241 (Geneva, Droz, 1990).

29. See Margaret M. McGowan, *Ideal Forms in the Age of Ronsard* (Berkeley—Los Angeles—London, University of California Press, 1985), pp. 230-31.

Roberto E. Campo (essay date 1993)

SOURCE: "Pictorial Concerns in the Ronsardian *Exegi Monumentum,*" in *Sixteenth Century Journal,* Vol. XXIV, No. 3, Fall, 1993, pp. 671-83.

[In the following essay, Campo explores Ronsard's conception of the superiority of poetry over painting, as part of an on-going Renaissance debate concerning this matter.]

Critics have paid considerable attention to the Horatian commonplaces, *ut pictura poesis* and *exegi monumentum,* in French Renaissance literature over the past forty years. Before the 1980s, however, investigators of the first idea proceeded in very different directions from examiners of the second. As a rule, scholarship on *ut pictura poesis* focused primarily on the similarities—formal and thematic as well as expressive and functional—between the literary and plastic arts of early modern France. The rationale for this concern was provided by sixteenth- and seventeenth-century French and Italian theorists like Thomas Sebillet, Barthélemy Aneau, Jacques Peletier, Charles du Fresnoy, Lodovico Dolce, and Paolo Lomazzo.[1] These and other authors erroneously interpreted the *ut pictura poesis* passage in Horace's *Ars Poetica* (361-65), with its brief reflection on the parallel abilities of some poems and some paintings to provide pleasure however often or closely they are experienced, as either an affirmation of or a demand for the greater "sisterhood" of the verbal and visual arts.[2] The numerous essays of the 1950s-1970s exploring the mannerist and baroque elements common to all the arts of Renaissance France were consequences of such misreadings.[3]

The same three decades witnessed a substantially different approach to the sixteenth-century French *exegi monumentum* topos. This motif, adapted from the thirtieth and final ode of Horace's *Carminum liber* 3, maintained that monuments in verse are superior to monuments in bronze, stone, and paint for their greater ability to resist the ravages of time.[4] Critics attending to this topic commonly emphasized purely literary issues. One concern was etiology and influence: the ways in which sixteenth-century French monumental poetry appropriated the reflections on poetic immortality promulgated by antique authors like Horace, Pindar, and Propertius.[5] Another preoccupation involved thematics and stylistics: the status and articulation of the idea of perpetuation embedded in the recently revived theme of the poet as divine emissary.[6]

Thus, for many years *seizièmistes* gave little or no serious consideration to the possible theoretical links between the *exegi monumentum* topos and the concept of *ut pictura poesis* in French Renaissance literature. Two reasons may account for this neglect. First, there is the relative silence on this relation in the theoretical discourse of the period. Never do the *artes poeticae* of Thomas Sebillet, Joachim du Bellay, or Jacques Peletier, for instance, draw such a connection explicitly.[7] Then again, perhaps it derives from the ostensible incompatibility of the two ideas. Whereas the classical *exegi monumentum* presupposes the fundamental inequality of the verbal and plastic arts, traditional interpretations of *ut pictura poesis* stress the overall parity of words and pictures.[8]

Be that as it may, the *exegi monumentum* topos is first a comparison between texts and visual images and thereby shares essential conceptual ground with the *ut pictura poesis* idea. This truth has undoubtedly informed the more current trend in scholarship on these topics. Over the past decade or so critics such as Margaret McGowan and, most recently, Doranne Fenoaltea have set about charting the boundaries of this common terrain.[9] Heretofore, however, only one feature has been surveyed in any appreciable detail. Attuned to the emphasis on timeworn temples, tombs, and pyramids of the classical *exegi monumentum,* these critics have focused on the relations between the monumental poetry and the monumental architecture of Renaissance France—especially on the ways in which the sixteenth-century French *exegi monumentum* topos articulates what Fenoaltea calls the *"ut architectura poesis"* principle (a subsidiary concern of the *ut pictura poesis* concept).[10]

As fruitful as this new critical direction has proved to be, I would here like to open the examination of a different though equally important matter: the inscription of painting—the stated priority of *ut pictura poesis*—in the French Renaissance *exegi monumentum*. For this purpose, the monumental poetry of Pierre de Ronsard provides an ideal starting point. Nowhere is this inscription clearer and more problematic than in the many poems where the leader of the Pléiade school of poets explicitly addresses the relative ability of verses and pictures to guarantee immortality.[11]

Although inspired by the monumental poems of the Ancients, Ronsard's *exegi monumentum* pieces go well beyond their Latin and Greek antecedents. Some accomplish this by insisting on the eternalizing equivalence of the poetic and graphic arts—in line, as it were, with the popular (mis)understanding of *ut pictura poesis*. Other poems, however, engage the more problematic issue of artistic expressivity and, above all, the subject of the superiority of poetry over visual images in the expression of the celestial world, the highest order of truths in Neoplatonic metaphysics. Thus I would propose that, in addition to effecting significant variations in the traditional *exegi monumentum,* Ronsard takes advantage of this ancient topos to highlight fundamental, contemporary concerns about the expressive disparities between the verbal and pictorial arts. Further, I would suggest that, in so doing, the poet bespeaks his familiarity with—and engagement in—the ongoing *paragone* debate between poets and painters. This age-old polemic (revived in the Italian art treatises of the fifteenth century) underscored the inequalities of the various artistic media and thereby stood as the antithetical corollary to the parity-centered *ut pictura poesis* principle.

. . . . .

Evidence of Ronsard's disposition to explore variations in the traditional *exegi monumentum* first appears in an ode written in 1546,[12] his **"Epitaphe de François de Bourbon, Conte d'Anguian"** (*Odes* 2.20).[13] In the opening four quatrains of this encomium to the celebrated victor of Cérisoles, the poet makes two exceptional assertions. Initially, he insists that poetry and the visual arts enjoy an equal ability to grant immortality:[14]

> D'Homere grec la tant fameuse plume,
> Ou de Timante un tant fameus tableau,
> Durant leurs jours avoient une coutume
> D'arracher vifs les hommes du tumbeau.
> Je vous di ceus qui leur plaisoit encores
> Resusciter en depit de leur nuit
> Oblivieuse, *ores par l'encre, & ores*
> *Par la couleur,* eternisant leur bruit.

(The all-famous quill of Homer the Greek, or an all-famous picture of Timanthes, had a custom, in their days, of resting men alive from their tombs. I tell you of those whom it pleased to return to life, despite their oblivious night, *sometimes by ink and sometimes by color,* eternalizing their fame.)

(1:234, vv. 1-8: emphasis added)

As common as it was for authors since antiquity to match a timeless bard like Homer with a legendary artist like Timanthes (the famous Greek portraitist of the fourth century B.C. praised by Pliny in the *Natural History*[15]) when citing examples of the finest practitioners of poetry and painting, Ronsard breaks fundamental ties with tradition by characterizing the verbal and visual arts as equals in rescuing men from the "nuit Oblivieuse" (oblivious night) of death. At no time do Horace, Pindar, or their followers concede that the painter is a match for the poet in this domain.

The two quatrains that follow are equally extraordinary. However, now the emphasis shifts to the inherent immortality of virtue alone:

> Mais telles gens devoient leur second vivre,
> L'un au papier, l'autre à la toile, & non
> A *la vertu, qui sans l'aide du livre,*
> *Ou d'un tableau, consacre son renom.*
>
> *Ta vertu donc, seule te sert de tumbe,*
> *Sans mandier ne plume, ni oustils,*
> Car tout cela qui par la mort ne tumbe,
> Vit par desus cent vivans inutils.

(But such people owed their second life either to paper, or to canvas, and not to *virtue, which, without the aid of the book, or a picture, hallows one's renown. Therefore your virtue alone serves as your tomb, without beseeching quill or tools,* for all that does not fall by death lives more than a hundred that are alive but useless.)

(1:235, vv. 9-16: emphasis added)

Once again the poet takes a significant step away from the conventional *exegi monumentum*. In lines reminiscent of contemporary love lyrics and emblem epigrams,[16] Ronsard raises the possibility that, in certain rare instances, eternal fame may transcend both quill and brush: exceptional individuals like François de Bourbon may rely on virtue alone for a "second vivre" (second life).[17]

It has been suggested that the unorthodoxy of the **"Epi-taphe"** deserves little serious consideration. Relating this piece to the many Ronsardian *exegi monumentum* poems that present a more conventional view of preeminent power of poetry over death, Isidore Silver has dismissed one and the other deviation as "rhetorical flourishes" designed merely "to expedite the overture of an ode or to flatter its recipient."[18] Conclusions like these fall short, however, because they ignore the broader conceptual consequences of the poet's brazen literary iconoclasm. As real as the structural and encomiastic effects identified by Silver may be, their accomplishment alone would appear hardly able to justify a dissent that calls inevitably into question a mainstay among the age-old claims of poetry to supremacy over the plastic arts. Such trivial purposes would seem inherently inconsistent with such profound results.

One reading clearly obviates this objection. It is suggested by the priority accorded to the discussion about the relative durability of the arts in the linear deployment of the **"Epitaphe"**—by the sequential positioning of this discussion (vv. 1-16) before the review of François de Bourbon's military feats (vv. 17-36). That is, contrary to theories like Silver's, perhaps this poem is first an announcement of Ronsard's willingness to reappraise the traditional *exegi monumentum* and only secondarily an encomium to the hero of Cérisoles. Furthermore, given the syntactic primacy of the poetry-painting equation in particular, perhaps it is above all a reevaluation of the links between the *exegi monumentum* topos and the *ut pictura poesis* idea. Indeed, in this instance, it may even reflect an attempt to project the first idea through the homologizing lens of the second. This explanation would account not only for the larger implications of the innovations we have detected in the present work, but also for the problems that arise in Ronsard's most untraditional *exegi monumentum* poems.

A case in point is the ode **"A Bouju Angevin"** (*Odes* 4.2). This *exegi monumentum* piece from the fall of 1549[19] concerns and addresses Jacques Bouju, Ronsard's friend and advocate in the entourage of Henri II's sister, Marguerite de France. As before, the poet flouts convention in his reassessment of the relative perpetuating powers of poems and pictures. Despite the unmistakable echo of Horace's *CL* 3.30 throughout the second half of the poem (where we learn that Bouju needs no borrowed artistic favors to attain immortality since his own poetic achievements are already more lasting than the Colossus of Rhodes, Mausolos' tomb and the Pyramids of Egypt: 2:88-89, vv. 17-36),[20] Ronsard clearly accepts—indeed insists (witness the imperative)—that poetry and painting enjoy equal abilities to satisfy the seeker of everlasting life:

> Que celui qui s'estudie
> D'estre pour jamais vivant,
> La main d'un peintre mandie
> Ou l'encre d'un ecrivant!

(Let him who endeavors to live forever beseech the hand of a painter or the ink of a writer!)

(2:88, vv. 13-16)

Heretofore, this declaration has prompted the same reaction as the innovations in the **"Epitaphe"**: critics have dismissed it as a convenient and fundamentally meaningless rhetorical ploy.[21] This estimation must again be questioned, however, but not only because it ignores the implications outlined previously. It also overlooks, or at best underestimates, what the poem consistently says about the verbal and pictorial arts. Unlike the **"Epitaphe"**, in which virtue finally replaces ink and paint as the best source of immortality, this ode to Bouju resists all opportunities to challenge the preeminent perpetuating powers of the artist's brush and the poet's pen (even when the emphasis subsequently shifts to the Angevin's personal poetic prowess[22]). Thus this piece may be said to reflect not merely a willingness to reconsider the *exegi monumentum* topos in terms of the *ut pictura poesis* analogy, but a virtual commitment to do so.[23]

Such a commitment is similarly inscribed in the many *exegi monumentum* poems that would otherwise privilege poetic verses according to the traditional Horatian hierarchy of artistic permanence. In these cases, however, the novelty emerges in Ronsard's specific set of complaints against pictorial monuments.

The ode **"A René d'Urvoi"** (*Odes* 4.17), written between 1545 and 1549,[24] provides an illustration. In the middle of this sixty-four-verse tribute to Ronsard's former companion at the Collège de Coqueret, the flavor is unmistakably Horatian:

> Les vers sans plus t'ejouissent,
> Mes vers donq je t'ofrirai,
> Les vers seulement jouissent
> Du droit que je te dirai.
>
> Les Colonnes elevées,
> Ne les marbres imprimés
> De grosses lettres gravées,
> Ne les cuivres animés,
>
> Ne font que les hommes vivent
> En images contrefais,
> Comme les vers qui les suivent
> Pour témoins de leurs beaus fais.

(Verses alone give you joy; therefore I shall offer you my verses—only verses enjoy the power of which I shall tell you. Neither elevated columns, nor marble imprinted with great engraved letters, nor animated bronzes, make men live imitated in images as do verses that follow them as witnesses to their great deeds.)

(2:150, vv. 29-40)

Hence, like Horace, Ronsard insists that poetry is better able to immortalize its subjects than any plastic (including pictorial) "images."

On the reason why this should be so, however, Horace and Ronsard differ significantly. Whereas the Roman author follows Pindar in ascribing the perishability of plastic portraits to the mutability of physical materials,[25] Ronsard presents a more theoretical explanation, evoking Simonides of Ceos' famous *poesia pictura loquens*—"Painting is mute Poetry: Poetry a speaking Painting"[26]—and a subtle dose of Neoplatonic metaphysics to criticize the muteness of the visual arts in respect to the metaphysical and incorruptible, celestial world of pure forms and moral truths.[27] This direction is established in the first three quatrains:

> Je n'ai pas les mains apprises
> Au métier muet de ceus,
> Qui font une image assise
> Sus des piliers paresseus.
>
> Ma painture n'est pas mue
> Mais vive, & par l'univers
> Guindée en l'air se remue
> De sus l'engin de mes vers.
>
> Aujourdui faut que j'ataigne
> Au parfait de mon art beau,
> Urvoi m'a dit que je paigne
> Ses vertus en ce tableau.

(I lack the hands experienced in the mute profession of those who make an image seated upon loitering pedestals. My painting is not mute, but alive, and through the universe lifted into the air [it] moves upon the instrument of my verses. Today I must attain the perfection of my beautiful art; Urvoi told me to paint his virtues in this picture.)

(2:148-49, vv. 1-12)

For Ronsard, then, the painted portrait is perishable because it is "mue," or, as Laumonier explains, mute.[28] By mute, though, the author means more than merely nonverbal—i.e., more than just physical or, in the spirit of Pindar's ode for Pytheas of Aegina (*Nemea* 5), immobile.[29] He also means inexpressive or, more properly, unable to represent moral attributes like virtue and honor: qualities that belong, in the Neoplatonic universe, to the highest order of existence, the celestial realm of eternal forms and truths perceptible to the intellect. This notion is raised implicitly in the contrary characterization of the poem as a "peinture" that "n'est pas mue." Not only are verses *non*-physical, i.e., unfettered by materiality, but they are *meta*-physical, in the sense that their expressive ability reaches beyond the world of corporeal experience. This, we are led to infer, is why Urvoi has entrusted his "vertus" to a verbal portrait rather than to a visual one: he knows that Ronsard can achieve artistic perfection and, thus, an accurate representation of his metaphysical inner essence.

The link between the impermanence of pictures and their expressive limitations reappears, though with no further reference to muteness, in the ode **"Au Roy Henri II"** (1555 *Odes* 3.1), an *exegi monumentum* poem written in 1554[30] which solicits the king's moral and financial support for Ronsard's *Franciade* project.[31] The penultimate stanza is particularly revealing:

> Donques pour engarder que la Parque cruelle
> Sans nom t'ensevelisse en la nuit éternelle,

> Toujours ne faut avoir à gage des maçons
> Pour transformer par art une roche en maisons,
> Et toujours n'acheter avecques la main pleine
> Ou la medale morte, ou la peinture vaine.
> Mais il faut par bienfaits & par caresse d'yeus
> Tirer en ta maison les ministres des Dieus,
> Les Poëtes sacrés, qui par leur écriture
> Te rendront plus vivant que maison ni peinture.

(Thus to keep the cruel Fate from burying you, nameless, in the eternal night, you need not always hire masons to transform by art a rock into a house, nor always buy with [money-]filled hand either the dead medallion or the vain painting. But you must by favors and caressing eyes draw to your home the ministers of the Gods, the sacred Poets, who through their writing will render you more living than [can] house or painting.)

(7:32, vv. 137-46)

The implications of the adjective "vaine" (vain) at the rhyme of verse 142 are critical. More than connote empty, by its opposition to the adjective "pleine" (filled) at the rhyme of verse 141, or lifeless, by its parallel with the adjective "morte" (dead) at the caesura six syllables earlier, "vaine" must be understood in terms of both of these ideas. Accordingly, with respect to the meaning of the noun it modifies, "la peinture" (the painting), this adjective allows for two possible and significantly different readings. On the one hand, painting may be empty, or worthless, because it is subject to physical decay, or death. This interpretation would wholly concur with the *exegi monumentum* topos in the Horatian, Pindaric, and Propertian traditions, yet it would have no direct bearing on the matter of expressive potentials. On the other hand, a painting may be "morte," or lifeless, because it is empty, or unable to express metaphysical, essential qualities like personal virtue: properties which inherently pertain to the celestial world (in the Neoplatonic sense) and constitute the *sine qua non* of the portrait that is truly alive.

Although Ronsard avoids any explicit commentary privileging one of these readings above the other, his concluding remarks to Henri II on the inevitable merits of his proposed *Franciade* lend strong support to the second interpretation:

> Pour toi seul, je mettrai devant les yeus la poudre
> A tous mes devanciers, s'il plaist à ta grandeur . . .
> Qu'un jour me commander (d'un seul clin) que je face
> Ma Franciade tienne, où la Troïenne race
> De Francus ton ancestre, où les faits glorieus
> De tant de vaillans Roys qui furent tes aïeus,
> Où mesmes tes vertus y luiront évidantes,
> Comme luisent au ciel les étoilles ardantes
> Sortant de l'Ocean.

(For you alone, I will put dust in the eyes of all my predecessors, if it pleases your greatness . . . that one day you will command me (a wink will suffice) to make my Franciade yours, where the Trojan race of Francus, your ancestor, where the glorious deeds of so many valiant kings who were your forebears, where especially your virtues will shine conspicuous, as the burning stars shine in the sky when rising from the Ocean.)

(7:33, vv. 154-63)

Thus here, as in numerous other *exegi monumentum* poems,[32] Ronsard invests poetry with a special, if not unique, ability to represent personal inner virtues and, hence, to express concepts that, like the shining stars in heaven, belong to the highest order of existence in the Neoplatonic cosmos.

. . . . .

It is clear, then, that Ronsard's *exegi monumentum* poems reach well beyong their classical antecedents in their concern for the relations between monuments in words and monuments in paint (indeed, memorials in all of the plastic media). Some pieces emphasize the eternalizing equality of the poetic and pictorial arts; other works privilege poetry for its superior ability to express inner virtues, the metaphysical, essential qualities typically associated with the celestial realm in the Neoplatonic universe. In the former instances, we encounter a certain deference to the notion of artistic parity at the heart of the Renaissance *ut pictura poesis* principle; in the latter cases, we discover a virtual defiance of that principle. In fact, in the second group of poems, we detect signs of Ronsard's engagement, on the side of poetry, in the *paragone* debate between the poets and painters of his day.

The *paragone* was the polemical counterpart to the *ut pictura poesis* concept that focused on the unequal abilities of the various arts—most prominently, poetry and painting, but also sculpture, architecture, and music. Inspired by the Ancients' reflections on the hierarchy of human artistic endeavors, this dispute received its clearest expression in the art-theoretical treatises of *quattrocento* and *cinquecento* Italy (hence the term *paragone*: "comparison" in Italian).[33] However, on the specific issue of the relative durability of poetry and painting, the *Trattato della pittura* of Leonardo da Vinci unquestionably presents one of the most memorable statements. In *trattato* 19 not only does the great Florentine painter vehemently dispute peremptory poetic claims to superior permanence, but he also rejects the attempts to base such claims on the expressive preeminence of poetry. For as the picture of Calumny by the legendary ancient portraitist, Apelles, demonstrates,[34] painting is as able to represent abstract ideals as poetry.

> . . . potrà dire un poeta: io farò una fintione che significava cose grande; questo medesimo farà il pittore, come fece Apelle la calunnia. se uoi dicesti, la poesia è più eterna, per questo dirò essere piu eterne l'opere dun calderaio. chel tempo piu le conserva che le vostre o' nostre opere, niente dimeno è di poca fantasia; e la pittura si può, depingendo sopra rame con colori di vetro, farla molto piu etterna. noi per arte possiamo esser detti nipoti à dio. s'ella poesia s'estende in filosofia morale, e questa in filosofia naturale; se quella descrive l'operationi della mente, che considera quella, se la mente opera nei movimenti.

> (. . . if a poet should say: I will write a story which signifies great things, the painter can do likewise, for even so Apelles painted the Calumny. If you were to say that poetry is more lasting, I say the works of a coppersmith are more lasting still, for time preserves them longer than your works or ours; nevertheless they display little imagination. And a picture can be made more enduring by painting upon copper in enamel colours. We by our art may be called the grandchildren of God. If poetry treats of moral philosophy, painting has to do with natural philosophy. If poetry describes the working of the mind, painting considers the working of the mind as reflected in . . . movements. . . .)[35]

It has yet to be shown, of course, that Ronsard ever laid eyes on this or any other *paragone*-related passage in the *Trattato della pittura*. In fact, although Luca Pacioli attests to the existence of the *Trattato* (initially a mere collection of disparate notes) as early as 1498, a published version would not appear before the middle of the seventeenth century.[36] Nevertheless, the attacks against painting in the ode **"A René d'Urvoi"** and the 1555 ode **"Au Roy"** bear an unmistakable resemblance to the rebuttal against poetry in *trattato* 19. Their particular artistic biases aside, Ronsard and Leonardo are in striking agreement on the notion that the durability of an artform is intimately linked to its expressive strength. Presumably, then, ideas like Leonardo's were already on the minds of French literati by the mid-sixteenth century. What is more, they were already a central concern in the *exegi monumentum* poems of the foremost poet of Renaissance France.

But what would move Ronsard to address such ideas in the first place? Moreover, why would he propound a reductive characterization of painting that directly contradicts prevailing views on the representational and, especially, symbolic versatility of the pictorial arts?[37] Clearly Ronsard feels it necessary to adopt such a posture in defense of poetry. But why?

A lack of space prevents a full resolution of these queries here. Yet Fenoaltea is probably correct to insist that the "système du mécenat" (patronage system) of the period did much to incite Ronsard's commentaries on the relations between poetry and the other arts.[38] Competing for finite financial resources with visual artists whose plastic monuments could glorify a patron far more immediately and tangibly than any poet's verbal memorial, Ronsard was compelled to take the stand we have identified. However, whereas Fenoaltea has maintained that Renaissance poets sought primarily to produce images that were more "vivantes" (alive) than the painters' (i.e., to emulate above all the physicality of pictorial simulacra),[39] it is clear from the preceding analysis that Ronsard took this rivalry well into the domain of metaphysical expression.

Notes

An initial version of this essay was first presented in Chicago on December 27, 1990, at the annual convention of the Modern Language Association. I am indebted to the University of North Carolina at Greensboro and the

University Research Council, whose generous support during my first year and summer at UNCG greatly facilitated the completion of this project.

1. See T. Sebillet, *Art poétique françoys,* ed. Félix Gaiffe (Paris: Droz, 1932), 169; B. Aneau, *L'Imagination poétique,* (Lyons, 1552), 4; J. Peletier, *L'Art poétique,* ed. André Boulanger (Paris: Belles Lettres, 1930), 80; C. du Fresnoy *De arte graphica* (Paris, 1667), vv. 1-8; L. Dolce, *Dialogo della pittura intitolato l'Aretino* (Florence, 1735), 116; and P. Lomazzo, *Trattato dell'arte della pittura, scoltura, et architettura* (Milan, 1585), esp. 6.65.486. For more on these and other contemporary theorists of poetry and painting, see Rensselaer Lee, *Ut Pictura Poesis: The Humanistic Theory of Painting* (New York: Norton, 1967).

2. For an excellent analysis of the nuances of Horace's comments and an overview of the misunderstandings they have generated, see Wesley Trimpi, "The Meaning of Horace's 'Ut Pictura Poesis'," *Warburg and Courtauld Institutes* 36 (1973): 1-34. See also Jean H. Hagstrum, *The Sister Arts: The Tradition of Literary Pictorialism and English Poetry from Dryden to Gray* (Chicago: University of Chicago Press, 1958), 57-92, esp. 60-61.

3. Cf. Marcel Raymond, *Baroque et renaissance poétique* (Paris: Corti, 1955) and the introduction to his *La Poésie française et le maniérisme: 1546-1610* (Philadelphia: Temple University Press, 1972), Jean Rousset, *La Littérature de l'age baroque en France, Circé et le Paon* (Paris: Corti, 1953); Richard A. Sayce, "Ronsard and Mannerism: The *Elégie à Janet,*" *L'Esprit Créateur* 6 (1966): 234-47; Lance K. Donaldson-Evans, "Two Stages of Renaissance Style: Mannerism and Baroque in French Poetry," *French Forum* 7 (Sept. 1982): 210-23. It should be noted that, to date, such period-style criticism has been most copiously applied to Montaigne and his *Essais.* Pierre Bonnet presents a useful review of this material in his "Montaigne, le maniérisme et le baroque," *BSAM* 7-8 (July-Dec. 1973): 45-58.

4. The first eight verses are especially memorable:

Exegi monumentum aere perennius
regalique situ pyramidum altius,
quod non imber edax, non Aquilo impotens
possit diruere aut innumerabilis
annorum series et fuga temporum.
non omnis moriar multaque pars mei
vitabit Libitinam: usque ego postera
crescam laude recens.

(I have finished a monument more lasting than bronze and loftier than the Pyramids' royal pile, one that no wasting rain, no furious north wind can destroy, or the countless chain of years and the ages' flight. I shall not altogether die, but a mighty part of me shall escape the death-goddess. On and on shall I grow, ever fresh with the glory of after time.)

Horace: The Odes and Epodes, tr. Charles E. Bennett (Cambridge: Harvard University Press, 1968), 278-79

5. Cf. Horace, *Carminum Liber,* 3.30, 4.8-9; Pindar, *Pythia* 1 and 3; *Isthmia* 2 and 6; *Nemea* 4, 5, 7, 8, 9; and Propertius, *Carmina,* 3.2. For more on the history of this theme and its permutations during antiquity and the Middle Ages, see Ernst Curtius, *European Literature and the Latin Middle Ages,* tr. Willard R. Trask (Princeton: Princeton University Press, 1973), 476-77.

6. Both lines of inquiry are clearly represented in Paul Laumonier, *Ronsard poéte lyrique* (Paris: Hachette, 1923), 346-77; Henri Chamard, *Histoire de la Pléiade,* 4 vols. (Paris: Didier, 10939-40), esp. 1:291-93, 356-58, 2:274-75; Robert J. Clements, *Critical Theory and Practice of the Pléiade,* (Cambridge: Harvard University Press, 1942), 45-47, 79-83; Isidore Silver, *The Intellectual Evolution of Ronsard,* 2 vols. (St. Louis: Washington University, 1969-73), esp. 2:402-45.

7. In addition to the locations identified above (n. 1), see Sebillet, *Art poétique français,* 12-13; du Bellay, *La Deffence et illustration de la langue francoyse,* ed. Henri Chamard (Paris: Didier, 1970), 103-07, 181-82; and Peletier, *L'Art poétique,* 68. This is not to say, of course, that affinities are never assumed obliquely. Cf. du Bellay's comments on the contrasting durability of the linguistic (literary) and architectural (plastic) achievements of Ancient Rome: *Deffence,* 127-36, 183-84.

8. Cf. Lee, *Ut Pictura Poesis,* 3-9.

9. Margaret M. McGowan, *Ideal Forms in the Age of Ronsard* (Berkeley: University of California Press, 1985), esp. 51-88, 121-28; Doranne Fenoaltea, *Du palais au jardin: L'architecture des* Odes *de Ronsard,* Etudes Ronsardiennes, no. 3 (Geneva: Droz, 1990), 13-29.

10. Fenoaltea, *Du palais,* 16.

11. It is true, of course, that the majority of Ronsardian *exegi monumentum* poems focus only on the immortalizing power of poetry and make no explicit allusion to the plastic arts (cf. Silver, *Intellectual Evolution* 2:433-45). For obvious reasons, these pieces will be excluded from consideration in the present essay.

12. Laumonier, *Ronsard,* 40.

13. Unless otherwise stated, all references to the *Odes* are to the 1550 edition.

14. All citations of Ronsard's works are from the *Oeuvres complètes,* ed. Paul Laumonier, Isidore Silver, Raymond Lebègue, 20 vols. (Paris: Hachette, 1914-75). Henceforth they will be noted parenthetically, as appropriate, with references to

volume, page and verse in this edition. All English translations of Ronsard's poetry are my own.

15. Pliny, *Natural History,* 35.36.73-74.

16. Cf. *dizains* 23, 227: Maurice Scève, *Délie, object de plus haulte vertu,* ed. Eugène Parturier (Paris: Didier, 1961), 21, 158. See also, Alciati's emblem, "Ex litterarum studiis immortalitatem acquiri" (Immortality is achieved by literary studies), *Emblematum Libillus* (Paris: Christianus Wechelus, 1534), 45. Strictly speaking, however, none of these pieces evokes the *exegi monumentum* topos. In Scève's case, for example, the focus is the overall ineffability of the beloved's deific beauty and grace in the tradition of Ariosto, Britonio, and Tebaldeo. Similarly, Alciati's concern is the immortality of noble deeds and not the relative durability of the arts.

17. Cf. the judgment of virtue's immortality in verses 16-17 of the ode *Au Reverendissime Cardinal de Guise* (*Odes* 1.4; Laumonier, *Oeuvres* 1:80).

18. Silver, *Intellectual Evolution* 2:434.

19. Laumonier, *Ronsard,* 65.

20. For more on the fate of Bouju's poetry, see ibid., n. 7.

21. Cf. Silver, *Intellectual Evolution* 2:434.

22. It must again be emphasized that, for Ronsard, the important distinction lies between the durability of Bouju's poetry and that of all other artworks, whether pictures by a painter or verses by another poet (cf. 2:88, vv. 17-24). Hence, despite the subsequent Horatianesque attack upon plastic monuments alone (2:89, vv. 25-32), the poet never abandons his initial position on the immortalizing parity of the verbal and visual arts.

23. A similar conclusion may be drawn from the author's later comments on poetry and painting in the ode *Au Conte d'Alsinois* (*Odes* 5.11), written between 1551 and early 1552 (Laumonier, *Ronsard,* 85). Here Ronsard is particulary intrigued (perhaps even troubled) by the fortune of his good friend Nicolas Denisot du Mans, whose exceptional talents for both pen and brush are expected to render him doubly impervious to the oblivion of death (see Laumonier, *Oeuvres* 3:177-83, esp. 180-81, vv. 73-80).

24. Laumonier, *Ronsard,* 56; Silver, *Intellectual Evolution* 2:434.

25. Cf. Horace, *CL* 3.30, vv. 3-5, and Pindar, *Pythia* 6, vv. 6-14. The same notion is echoed by Propertius (3.2, vv. 17-27).

26. See Plutarch, *De Gloria Atheniensium,* 3.346f-347c.

27. In Neoplatonic thought, the celestial world typically contrasts with the realm of Nature, the inferior, terrestrial zone of corruptible form and matter. For a synopsis of this cosmology as articulated in the *Theologia Platonica* of the famous Renaissance Neoplatonist, Marsilio Ficino, see Erwin Panofsky, *Studies in Iconology: Humanistic Themes in the Art of the Renaissance* (Oxford: Oxford University Press, 1939; New York: Harper and Row, 1972), 131-33.

28. Laumonier, *Oeuvres* 2:148-49, n. 3.

29. See vv. 1-5: "No sculptor am I, that I should carve statues doomed to linger only on the pedestal where they stand. No! I would bid my sweet song speed from Aegina, in every argosy, and in every skiff, spreading abroad the tidings that the stalwart Pytheas, son of Lampon, hath won the crown for the pancratium at the Nemean games. . . . *The Odes of Pindar, Including the Principal Fragments,* tr. John Sandys (Cambridge: Harvard University Press), 359.

30. Laumonier, *Ronsard,* 149.

31. This is the epic poem featuring Francus, the son of the Trojan hero, Hector, and the legendary founder of the kingdom of France. The first and only four "chants" of this ill-fated, twenty-four-book project were published in 1572, seventeen years after the present ode.

32. Cf. *A René d'Urvoi* as well as the ode *Au Reverendissime Cardinal de Guise* (*Odes* 1.4; Laumonier, *Oeuvres* 1:79-82) and the ode *A Charles de Pisseleu* (*Odes* 2.18; Laumonier, *Oeuvres* 1:226-28, esp. vv. 21-44).

33. For more on the history of this debate, from antiquity through the Renaissance, see Jean Paul Richter, *The Literary Works of Leonardo da Vinci,* 3d ed., vol. 1 (New York: Phaidon, 1970), 13-22, 41-68.

34. The story of Apelles' Calumny was first recorded by Lucian in his *De Calumnia,* 5, though credit for its revival during the Renaissance goes to Leone Battista Alberti. See *Della pittura,* ed. Luigi Mallè (Florence: Sansoni, 1950), 103-05. On the significance of the Calumny anecdote for Renaissance Neoplatonists, see Panofsky, *Iconology,* 157-58.

35. Richter, *Literary Works* 1: 58.

36. Pacioli's testimony appears in a letter to Duke Lodovico Sforza dated 9 February 1498. For more on this letter and the complex history of Leonardo's document, see Richter, *Literary Works* 1:5-11.

37. It is well known that Renaissance Neoplatonists like Ficino and Pico della Mirandola attributed special symbolic and allegorical powers to visual images and the pictorial arts. Cf. E. H. Gombrich, "*Icones Symbolicae:* The Visual Image in Neo-Platonic Thought," *Warburg and Courtauld Institutes* 11 (1948): 163-92.

38. Fenoaltea, *Du palais,* 16. The same point is made by McGowan, *Ideal Forms,* 57. For more on the patronage system of sixteenth-century France, see

Henri Weber, *La Création poétique au XVIe siècle en France, de Maurice Scève à Agrippa d'Aubigné* (Paris: Librairie Nizet, 1955), 63-106.

39. Fenoaltea, *Du palais*, 25.

Jean M. Fallon (essay date 1993)

SOURCE: *Voice and Vision in Ronsard's 'Les Sonnets pour Helene.'* New York: Peter Lang, 1993, 142 p.

[*In the following excerpt, Fallon interprets Ronsard's* Sonnets pour Helene *cycle, seeing the work's final theme as one concerning love sacrificed for poetry.*]

Les Sonnets pour Helene recounts a story about growth— growth that involves action and stasis, expansion and reduction, choice and chance, progress and reversal.[1] The details of a lover's loss and a poet's progress emerge in the course of the two books of sonnets as the narrator struggles to record the quests of two personas in their search to realize their ultimate goals. The lover and the poet must each grapple with his complex role of imitator and creator of something unique. The lover's complaint bears traces of the traditional at times, for these pages repeat a familiar lament; yet the unique and inventive variations on an old theme impose a creative stamp on his words. The poet, too, calls up the familiar and weaves it with the new. He often sees himself as a creator, equating himself with Jupiter and other generative powers; yet he is also a product of the natural world, subject like the lover, to mortality. Much of the growth in these sonnets stems from the limits imposed by the threat of death, as well as from the nourishment provided by the hope of the eternal. What helps the poet may destroy the lover. Still, the voices of poet and lover are not necessarily always in conflict. In fact, they often merge and become indistinguishable, only to diverge again as they register the emotions and attitudes of two very different personalities.[2]

These voices are figured by the Dioscuri, the twins Castor and Pollux, mythological brothers of Helen of Troy, traditional guides to navigators and voyagers, and, as Gemini, zodiac sign of the month of May. Legend recounts that the brothers remained devoted and spiritually joined to one another, even when physically separated. They are associated with a partial immortality, as both brothers knew the underworld as well as the heavens.[3] Although explicit references to Castor and Pollux are rare in the text, their image is often invoked through allusions to twins of any kind, to stars, to events in Helene's life, to spring and to May, and to voyages at sea.[4] Notions of unity and opposition are inherent in the pair of Castor and Pollux as well as that of the poet and lover. Indeed, Castor and Pollux become symbols for the narrator's dual vocation. The figures of poet and lover are direct links to the tension between the immortal and the mortal. The poet allies himself with the immortals—the gods of Greek mythology, the Christian God, and above all to previous poets, who, though dead, enjoy an immortal existence through the posterity of their works. The figure of the poet is superior to that of the lover, for his work is the source of his immortality; this creation will not end with the dissolution of love but will spring forth from it. He is immortal because he fashions a creation that will outlast him. The love story, however, provides a sacrificial victim. The lover's growth is doomed from the outset by the choice of Helene as his subject. The lover chooses Helene because she is the most beautiful woman in history, a woman whose affections are worth a passionate, violent struggle. The poet selects Helene because he wishes to follow Homer, to glorify the poet's profession, to equate himself with the epic writer, even to create a form of epic within his sonnet cycle. A suggestion of epic appears in the first sonnet when the figures of the sea-guides Castor and Pollux are introduced:

> Ce premier iour de May, Helene ie vous iure
> Par Castor, par Pollux, vos deus freres iumeaux,
> Par la vigne enlassée à l'entour des ormeaux,
> Par les prez par les bois herissez de verdure,
> Par le nouueau Printemps, fils aisné de Nature,
> Par le cristal qui roule au giron des ruisseaux,
> Par tous les rossignols, miracle des oiseaux,
> Que seule vous serez ma derniere auenture.
>
> (I, I, ll. 1-8)[5]

The citing of the twins at the very opening of the work evokes the concept of a voyage, and the lines speak of an adventure about to begin. The notion of a voyage is a key element in many epics. In the *Sonnets pour Helene* in turn it metaphorically portrays the poet's growth as well as the lover's doomed courtship. This epic connotation is not gratuitous, for it points toward a preoccupation with a specific literary achievement, or rather, a literary failure. In the wake of the unfinished and unappreciated *Franciade* (1572-1578), Ronsard here manages to rechannel his frustrated urge to write the great French national epic into the composition of the *Sonnets pour Helene* (1584), the personal epic of his own poetic vocation. The poetic epic recounts the development of the poet, his belief in his creation, and the eternal glory which his poetry assures him.

Striking, too, in these opening lines is the system of coupling that we see in the images of Castor and Pollux, the vine entwined with the elms, the crystal rolling in the fold of the stream, the field stretching into the forest, and spring portrayed as Nature's offspring. Helene is *seule* both by placement of her name in the first line as a singular unit, not joined with another to form a pair, and in line eight where she is described as "seule vous." Helene's singular character already spells trouble for the unwitting lover who seeks to bind himself to her yet who throughout the pages of this book will succeed only in distancing himself from her. The first day of May suggests the promise of growth and fertility. The name "Helene" immediately casts doubt on the prognosis of the lover's growth because as such a fatal name, it connotes the destruction and death associated with the Trojan epic.[6] Thus, the failure of the one, essential pairing—the lover's union with Helene—

looms menacingly at the outset of the *Sonnets pour Helene.* The early model of the Dioscuri serves as a reminder that pairing in this work requires further consideration. Like the Castor and Pollux myth with its emphasis on union that is at times physical and at times spiritual, the issue of Helene's union with another may prove more complex. The narrator's initial failure to pair Helene with the lover permits a later union between Helene and the poet. Indeed, the remainder of this first sonnet affirms that the poet's adventure will dominate and eventually subjugate the lover's quest:

> Vous seule me plaisez, i'ay par election
> Et non à la volee aimé vostre ieunesse:
> Aussi ie prens en gré toute ma passion,
>
> Ie suis de ma fortune autheur, ie le confesse:
> La vertu m'a conduit en telle affection.
> Si la vertu me trompe adieu belle Maistresse.

(I, I, ll. 9-14)

The narrator confidently emphasizes his own power by the strong choice of verbs pertaining to control. Although he calls on Castor and Pollux, he is also relying heavily on himself and on his own guidance and control, conscious of his actions and motivations. His authorial voice speaks clearly in the last tercet, underlined by the word "autheur."[7] The repetition of "seule vous" and "vous seule" in lines eight and nine not only calls attention to Helene's singular nature but also underlines the speaker's assertion of his choice. We find here a juxtaposition of the narrator's two voices. One seeks direction for his voyage, while the other believes in his own power to steer his course. The more dominant, confident voice is that of the poet ready to embark on an adventure. The ensuing sonnets will sing of that epic and in so doing will tell the story of the sonnets' own creation. The lover's account will relate the sacrifice of love which permits the poet's voyage to begin.

In order to appreciate fully this idea of the sonnets' creation, we must examine closely the concept of voyage, for it shapes the overall textual framework of the *Sonnets pour Helene.* This framework consists of two, very different treatments of water as an image, one appearing in the sixth sonnet from the beginning of the work (I, VI) and the other beginning in the sixth sonnet from the end (II, LXII). Within the bounds created by this water framework, the lover's power weakens while the poet's gradually assumes full reign. The water image encourages the notion of voyage, the symbolic transformation from lover to poet via the textual adventure. We will analyze this demise of the lover's world and the evolution of the poet's and come to understand them first by defining the water framework and then by examining what transpires between the first and second frames.

The first water reference occurs in Book I, **Sonnet VI**:

> Dedans les flots d'Amour ie n'ay point de support,
> Ie ne voy point de Phare, & si ie ne desire

> (O desir trop hardy!) sinon que ma Nauire
> Apres tant de perils puisse gaigner le port.
>
> Las! deuant que payer mes voeux dessus le bort,
> Naufrage ie mourray: car ie ne voy reluire
> Qu'une flame sur moy, qu'une Helene qui tire
> Entre mille rochers ma Nauire à la mort.
>
> Ie suis seul me noyant de ma vie homicide,
> Choisissant un enfant, un aueugle pour guide,
> Dont il me faut de honte & pleurer & rougir.
>
> Ie ne sçay si mes sens, ou si ma raison tasche
> De conduire ma nef: mais ie sçay qu'il me fasche
> De voir un si beau port & n'y pouuoir surgir.

(I, VI)[8]

The narrator's attitude offers the image of a man limited in ability, the water being more powerful than he. By repeated use of negative expressions, he stresses his incapacity to help himself. His lack of control reduces him to passivity. The sonnet ends with the narrator neither safe on shore nor submerged in the seas. There is a strong downward movement in this sonnet, yet it is as if the downward pull—the drowning—is temporarily stalled. Castor and Pollux are notable for their absence because the narrator lacks navigational guides. A ploughing of the waters recalls the start of an epic adventure, but the narrator here has begun his trip without the benefit to the twins. Having called upon them in the opening sonnet, the narrator now either forgets or forsakes his sea-guides in this poem, only five sonnets further into the work, leaving open a greater possibility for a doomed adventure at sea.[9]

The verbs of verses six and nine—"ie mourray" and "ie suis seul"—have a pointedly negative content. The narrator's recognition of his isolation recalls the independent character attributed to Helene in the opening sonnet of the work: she appears so incapable of union with another. The narrator's negative knowledge influences his perception: in lines thirteen and fourteen the verb *savoir* is linked with the verb *voir.* In lines six and seven the narrator focuses his vision on Helene who pulls his ship toward the rocks. The mention of a vessel, "Nauire" in line seven and "nef" in line thirteen, reinforces the narrator's distance from the water. The downward motion, the movement to the interior of the medium is at work here. This removal from and control by the water contributes heavily to a perception that this first part of the water framework portrays and emphasizes the narrator as powerless. It is curious that a voyager in a sinking ship does not call upon Castor and Pollux to guide him, but chooses instead Love, personified by Cupid, "un enfant, un aueugle."[10] Both the issues of growth and development and of vision (or the lack of vision) are incorporated in the figure of Love. The narrator's dominant voice here is that of the lover whose growth has just begun in this sonnet when he realizes that he is *seul* and that Helene is distant and dangerous.[11] His choice of guide—a blind child who cannot in turn enhance the lover's sight—determines his vision.

Although we respond quickly to the lover's voice in this sonnet, both voices are present. The quatrains blame the Siren-like Helene for directing the boat to the rocks.[12] In the tercets, however, the thinking changes slightly. The narrator assumes more of the responsibility for his distress, using the first person, "me noyant, de ma vie homicide," and by accepting responsibility for having chosen his guide. In neglecting to call on the Dioscuri, he chooses to follow another guide and thereby substantially weakens the direction or control of his voyage. The narrator indicates that he feels not only sadness but also shame and embarrassment over his choice (l. 11). Embarrassment and shame imply an awareness of a mistake. The narrator recognizes his role in adding to the panic and anguish he feels, rather than viewing himself solely as a victim of Helene's actions. This cognizance of his own acts in tandem with the description of his emotions indicates that the narrator considers his feelings and reasoning powers as contributing factors to his problems, although he appears to be unsure of the precise cause. It is no accident that the sonnet ends on the verge of sight. To see, to know, and to be unable to act present the dilemma with which the narrator's two voices will struggle throughout the work. It angers him here to imagine the existence of "such a lovely port"—a safe haven and an end to a voyage, be it amorous or poetic. The final word, the verb "surgir" (to spring up) offsets the downward motion of the sonnet, in suggesting a springing upward. The very sound of the word "surgir" suggests "Surgères," the family name of Hélène (de Surgères), the woman to whom Ronsard addressed this cycle.[13] We will encounter in the latter half of the water framework another instance of a near-pun on a given name—that of Pierre—which we will contrast with this play on words.[14] Both instances imply the insertion of details from Ronsard's own life, a use of subjective matter which brings our attention to the poets's voice, to creation, as well as to self-glorification and self-preservation through these poems.

In spite of these positive signs, the sonnet ends on a note of hesitancy and irresolution. Indeed, the use of the present tense throughout, along with the final uncertainty about the narrator's safety or harm, leave the epic stalled. We have the beginning of a voyage but no further progress and no destination reached. The voyager is engulfed in waters which threaten to overwhelm him. While the narrator is far from reaching his port of call, he is beginning to see, although he does not yet incorporate the power of sight into his body of governing knowledge. He knows that he has wrongly chosen his guide and that there must be a new charting of direction. This recharting of the voyage will generate the changes encompassed within the water framework. It is important to understand and define this framework itself before analyzing what transpires to change the focus and tone so sharply from the opening use of water as an image to that in the final poems about water.

Rather than a single sonnet, the closing half of the water framework is a three-poem sequence. In the second part of the framework, water appears as a fountain which is purely the poet's creation, the product of his power.[15] The fountain is the subject of (1) **Sonnet II, LXXII,** (2) the **"Stances de la Fontaine d'Helene"** and finally (3) **Sonnet II, LXXIII.** This framing device—the water image—leaves five sonnets at the beginning of the *Sonnets pour Helene* which precede its appearance and five poems remaining after it. The change from *flots* in the first water sonnet to *fontaine* in the final sequence parallels the changes that the narrator experiences as he grows in his ability to control his environment.[16] The reduction in the body of water (from *flots* to *fontaine*) enables the narrator to increase his control over it. The transfer from the initial state of helplessness to the later one of power reflects the change in narrative voice from lover to poet. Moreover, the increase in the number of poems (from a single sonnet to a series of three poems) from the first frame to the second further underscores the emergence and development of the poet's dominance. While the lover need not perish in order for the poet to assume control, a process of transformation does occur, with the poet's voice incorporating the lover's into his own. The process is similar to the painting over of one canvas with another picture, where the first painting leaves traces which furnish some detail for the second, lasting image. In fact, the narrator in these sonnets records his own verbal self-portrait during the course of the work. Perfectly at ease in the art of creating and recreating images, the poet begins the culmination of his creative powers of representation—the fountain—which appears for the first time in **Sonnet II, LXXII,:**

> A fin que ton honneur coule parmy la plaine
> Autant qu'il monte au ciel engraué dans un Pin,
> Inuoquant tous les Dieux, & respandant du vin,
> Ie consacre à ton nom ceste belle Fontaine.
>
> Pasteurs, que vos tropeaux frisez de blanche laine
> Ne paissent à ces bords: y fleurisse le Thin,
> Et tant de belles fleurs qui s'ouurent au matin,
> Et soit dite à iamais la Fontaine d'Helene.
>
> Le passant en Esté s'y puisse reposer,
> Et assis dessus l'herbe à l'ombre composer
> Mille chansons d'Helene, & de moy luy souuienne.
>
> Quiconques en boira, qu'amoureux il deuienne:
> Et puisse en la humant, une flame puiser
> Aussi chaude qu'au coeur ie sens chaude la mienne.
>
> (II, LXXII)

The consecration of the fountain to Helene parallels the composition of *Les Sonnets pour Helene.* The completed poetic achievement—the cycle of sonnets—becomes the literal representation of the fountain, a *mise en abyme* (interior reduplication).[17] The artist erects both in the text and by the text his monument to Helene. The prohibiting of the shepherds and their flocks from drinking from the fountain preserves its purity and sets it apart from any other.[18] The poet will later add to his conception of this fountain in the **"Stances de la Fontaine d'Helene,"** continuing to exert his control over what the fountain is and what it represents, just as he does in the second quatrain and in the tercets of this sonnet. The verb "composer" (l. 10) is significant, too, for it emphasizes the increasing authorial control. In line eleven the narrator inserts a reference to himself ("and may he remember me"), thus associating himself directly with the fountain. This remembrance thus assures the narrator a lingering evocation with the fountain—the beginnings of his search for immortality. The last word of this sonnet, "mienne," like a signature further emphasizes the creator's role in achieving his creation. Helene is less important than either the fountain or the narrator, as the value shifts from the object or recipient of the narrator's words to the words themselves. The fountain is the source of the poet's vision, the flow of his mental images, and replaces the image of Helene.

The long **"Stances de la Fontaine d'Helene"** follows **Sonnet II, LXXII,** and is marked in the subtitle for singing or recitation by three persons. It is, as Laumonier's note informs us, full of allusions to Theocritus, Virgil, Horace, Ovid, Petrarch, Ariosto, the neo-Latins Navagero and Flamino and perhaps also to Propertius and Sannazar.[19] There are also allusions to Ronsard's own works—to sonnets in this cycle, and to two other works, *Les Amours* and **"L'Hylas."** The idea of so many references to so many other sources in a poem about a fountain evokes a reflection, a mirroring of one image into another. The evocation of reflection, in turn, recalls Narcissus. He appears, of course, frequently in other works by Ronsard, and although there is no single, dominant mythological personage in these **"Stances,"** the figure of Narcissus is central to the ideas of the fountain and of the representation of an image (or imitation): Narcissus fell in love with his reflection, an imitation. The concept of reflection and imitation reinforces this same notion in the **"Stances."** At one point one of the speakers entreats the moon to shine on the fountain: "Te mire dedans" (l. 76). Ronsard might well have addressed these same words to himself, for he uses portions of his own previously-published verses here in a poem about a fountain. In so doing, he parallels Narcissus's action at the edge of that legend's fountain, being both the "original" and the "imitation," creator and creation. The poet's double role recalls the issue of mortality and immortality, for he seeks to establish in the world something of lasting value, something that will outlive him. The monument to Helene, a fountain, becomes a metaphor of his poetic accomplishment and his claim to immortality. The closing words of the **"Stances,"** are spoken by the character "Le Poete," one of the three speakers indicated by Ronsard in the subtitle of this work. "Le Poete" closes the piece:

> Fontaine, ce-pendant de ceste tasse pleine
> Reçoy ce vin sacré que ie renuerse en toy:
> Sois ditte pour iamais la Fontaine d'Helene,
> Et conserue en tes eaux mes amours & ma foy.
>
> (ll. 85-88)

The phrase "pour iamais" appears three times in this series of fountain poems, and its repetition underlines the poet's

beseeching the fountain to preserve forever his love and his faith. *Les Sonnets pour Helene* records the lover's love and the poet's faith in his vision, with the sonnets remaining "pour iamais" the creation of the poet. After creating the fountain, the poet then pours into it the sacred wine which is swallowed up in the waters just as the lover's story is enveloped by the longer, more dominant "epic" of poetic glory. The lover's story is sacrificed to that of the poet's creation, with Love being forsaken so that a *text* about love might survive.

The poet further emphasizes his poetic creation in the **"Stances,"** most dramatically near the middle of the poem where the character "Le Premier" requests:

> Cesse tes pleurs, Hercule, et laisse ta Mysie,
> Tes pieds de trop courir sont jà foibles et las.
> Icy les Nymphes ont leur demeure choisie,
> Icy sont tes Amours, icy est ton Hylas.
>
> (ll. 33-36)

The words "Amours" and "L'Hylas" stand out since each is the title of a well-known work by Ronsard. **"L'Hylas"** (1569) in particular is noteworthy because the protagonist dies in a fountain. The poem, furthermore, concludes with one of Ronsard's most straightforward and often-quoted passages where he expounds upon his theory of poetry. In that passage, lines 417-430 of **"L'Hylas,"** Ronsard compares himself to a bee gathering his forces, stocking up for the winter:

> Mon Passerat, je resemble à l'Abeille
> Qui va cueillant tantost la fleur vermeille,
> Tantost la jaune: errant de pré en pré
> Volle en la part qui plus luy vient à gré,
> Contre l'Hyver amassant force vivres:
> Ainsy courant & fueilletant mes lires,
> J'amasse, trie & choisis le plus beau,
> Qu'en cent couleurs je peints en un tableau,
> Tantost en l'autre: & maistre en ma peinture,
> Sans me forcer j'imite la Nature,
> Comme j'ay fait en ce portrait d'Hylas
> Que je te donne, & si à gré tu l'as
> J'en aimeray mon present d'avantage
> D'avoir sceu plaire à si grand personnage.
>
> ("L'Hylas," ll. 417-430)[20]

Les Sonnets pour Helene portrays a movement of diurnal cycles, echoed often in the narrator's preoccupation with immortality, his fear of leaving no legacy as the winter of death approaches. The process of careful choice, advocated in the famous "bee passage" from **"L'Hylas"** is also central to the **"Stances,"** since the verses are modeled on so many other works. The concepts of imitation and creation converge in the figure of Narcissus who is, as is Ronsard, "Maistre en [sa] peinture (l. 425)," in that he creates his own image or self-portrait. However, Narcissus is initially unable to recognize his image as his own, thus he does not appreciate his ability to produce images. This flaw, moreover, proved fatal, leading directly to his death. This oversight or defect on the part of Narcissus may account for the lines in the **"Stances"** where the narrator refuses to identify with Narcissus: "Et non comme Narcisse . . ." (l. 24). In dividing the **"Stances"** into three parts spoken by "Le Premier," "Le Second," and "Le Poete," Ronsard seems intent on foregrounding the poetic identity and of merging the voices of all three to represent various aspects of the poet's character and his vision. Unlike Narcissus, Ronsard understands the nature of the image that he sees, recognizing its value for what it is—the product of his own artifice.

"L'Hylas" (1569, *Septieme Livre des Poèmes*) is a curious poem because the general narrative recounts the story of Hercules, to whom Ronsard addresses the beginning of the poem. The portion of the Hercules legend that Ronsard recounts is the loss of the young Hylas, Hercules's water-bearer. The young servant's death in a fountain so grieved the older hero that he did not return to Jason and the voyage of the *Argo*.[21] Once again we encounter, although rather indirectly, the notion of a disrupted voyage. Hylas's death, according to Ronsard's poem, is a sacrifice, so that the Argonauts' ship might be saved from evil: "Que la nauire est sauué de tout mal" (l. 308). The linking of a sacrifice in a fountain with a ship's preservation from harm recalls the water framework that opens and closes *Les Sonnets pour Helene* where the sacrifice of the lover's story permits the poetic voyage to reach its full sail.

If Hylas's death devastates Hercules, the encounter represents a passionate exchange for the young Hylas and his captor, the nymph Printine.[22] In **"L'Hylas"** we read:

> . . . en cependant Printine,
> Ardante au coeur d'une telle rapine,
> Sa gauche main finement approacha
> Et du garçon le col elle accrocha:
> Coup dessus coup le baise & le rebaise,. . . .

> (ll. 293-297)

It is significant that the text contains two versions of Hylas's death—the narrator's and Hylas's own. The two versions exemplify the concept of mirror images that a fountain might suggest, and the further reflection of the poem **"L'Hylas"** within the **"Stances"** presents yet another mirror—the vision of a mirror reflected. Here then is the beginning of a chain of reflected images, a chain that implies an infinite reflection of an image. The double versions of the same story also suggest an echo and thus certainly the figure of Echo in the Narcissus myth. Furthermore, the telling of one story within another parallels Ronard's use of Homer's Helen to tell his own story. In both the legends of Hylas and Narcissus, death in the fountain is a falling in, a giving way, a complete submergence of the self, culminating in the loss of contact with the rest of the world. Both, moreover, appear to lead to a happy afterlife for the victim—Hylas describes his life as happy: ". . . heureux ie vis ici" (**"L'Hylas,"** l. 396). In both stories, the loss is difficult for the survivors, Echo and Hercules.

Although the legends of Narcissus and Hylas present certain similarities, Ronsard establishes some fundamental differences between the two. First, Narcissus falls into and is enveloped by his own image whereas Hylas interacts with another, a separate and different individual who pulls him to his death. Hylas, furthermore, lives on through his voice, for he is able to speak to the grieving Hercules after his disappearance in the waters. He is then able to do what the poet in the *Sonnets pour Helene* hopes to do—to live eternally through the preservation of his voice. In the Narcissus myth, the lamenting voice and sighs belong to Echo, and the notion of immortality associated with Narcissus derives from the flower into which the latter is transformed. In the **"Stances,"** Ronsard makes reference to the Narcissus myth when "Le Second" expresses the wish: " . . . qu' Amour me transforme en un rocher sans ame / Et non comme Narcisse en une belle fleur" (**"Stances,"** ll. 23-24). The desire to be transformed, not into a flower as Narcissus was, but into a rock with no soul would enable the narrator to be a more enduring being. The word "rock" catches our attention, for Ronsard is making another of his quasi-onomastic games just as the verb "surgir" suggested "Surgères" in **Sonnet I, VI.** Another word for "rocher" is "pierre." It is probable that Ronsard has once again made reference to himself (to his first name, Pierre), inserting himself into his poem, mirroring his own identity in his verse. Each end of the water framework, then, contains hints of one character's name, and these two names counterbalance one another from opposite ends of the sonnet cycle, like the two halves of the water framework. The verb "surgir" suggests a leaping forward, appropriate for the beginning of a work, while the noun "rocher" adds a note of stasis, of grounding, as an anchor to the second half of this water framework. The narrator's early instability finds stability in the later allusion.

The lines which terminate **"L'Hylas"** constitute the aforementioned "bee passage" (ll. 417-430) wherein Ronsard explains his poetic theories concerning the role of the artist's conscious choice in his creations. Clearly the reference to Hylas in the **"Stances de la Fontaine d'Helene"** manifests the poet's belief in his role, in his art, in his actions, in his visions—something which the framework of the two water poem sequences has already implied. The fountain suggests a control that the poet achieves, and it presents a deliberate contrast to the overwhelming seas of the early sonnet.

Time and again in the **"Stances"** allusions to Ronsard's poems seize the reader's attention.[23] This long poem, then, functions repeatedly as a mirror, reflecting sonnets and poems from Ronsard's own repertoire, a function that places direct emphasis on the work of the poet, on the preservation and posterity of his works.[24] Among the more striking allusions in the **"Stances"** is the last speech offered by "Le Second":

> Aduienne apres mille ans qu'un Pastoureau desgoise
> Mes amours, & qu'il conte aux Nymphes d'icypres

Qu'un Vandomois mourut pour une Saintongeoise,
Et qu'encore son ame erre entre ces forests.

(ll. 77-80)

This passage resembles the ending of the **"Chanson,"** a poem which appears in the first book of the *Helene* sonnets, immediately following **Sonnet VI,** the first poem of the water framework. The tone of the **"Chanson"** is lighter, much less serious than **Sonnet VI,** but in the concluding lines the narrator foresees an inscription on his tombstone:

Dessus ma tombe engrauez mon soucy
En memorable escrit:
D'un Vandomois le corps respose icy,
Sous les Myrtes l'esprit.
Comme Pâris là bas faut que ie voise,
Non pour l'amour d'une Helene Gregeoise,
Mais d'une Saintongeoise.

("Chanson," ll. 43-49)

The tombstone initiates once again the issue of immortality, and the words engraved on a tombstone would, like a written text, remain "en memorable escrit" long after the death of the person in whose honor they were conceived. The choice of the words "memorable escrit" accentuates the eternal nature of the written creation. The identification of the narrator as "un Vandomois" in both the quotation from the **"Stances"** and the passage from the **"Chanson"** again positions Ronsard in his text. The notion of immortality is evoked in both passages, in the **"Chanson"** by the mentin of the "memorable escrit" and by the continued voicing of love for Helene. In the **"Stances"** we are told that one thousand years hence the story of the love of Ronsard the Vendomois for Helene the Saintongeoise will still be told, spouted forth ("degoisé"), as a fountain projects water, and that " . . . encore son ame erre entre ces forests" (l. 80). This idea of an eternally-wandering spirit precedes the mention by the narrator in the text of his wish to be transformed into "un rocher sans ame." The rock—the tomb—will be without "ame" because the narrator's soul will continue to wander in the forest. The spirit then is the eternal voice, the voice associated with Echo, and the immortal record of the poet's glory.

This separation of a grounded earthly body and a free-moving spirit occurs at various points in the *Sonnets pour Helene.* It relates to the earlier discussion of the separate but symbiotic twins, Castor and Pollux. Ronsard plays with Neo-Platonic concepts throughout this sonnet cycle, alternately promoting the superiority of the spiritual over the physical. Castor and Pollux furnish a convenient symbol for Ronsard since they represent separation, with one brother in the heavens and the other on earth, much like the linked but distinct soul and body of the narrator. Ronsard clearly prefers that the mind and body work in harmony, just as the corresponding voices of the poet and lover together produce the unity of this text.

The division of body and soul, however, parallels other dualities in the sonnet cycle. In the **"Stances"** we have noticed a tripartite composition, divided as it is into parts spoken by "Le Premier," "Le Second," and "Le Poete." Readers expecting a correspondence between "Le Premier" and "Le Second" with the personas of lover and poet will be unconvinced. It is "Le Poete" who clearly represents the voice and the perspective of the poet—perhaps even of the historical Ronsard—while "Le Premier" and "Le Second" reflect aspects of both lover and poet with no clear distinction to separate them. While "Le Second" speaks of a spirit still wandering in the forest, "Le Premier," too, allies himself to a creator of an eternally-lasting creation when he hypothesizes:

Si i'estois un grand Prince, un superbe edifice
Ie voudrois te bastir, où ie ferois fumer
Tous les ans à ta feste autels & sacrifice,
Te nommant pour iamais la Fontaine d'aimer.

("Stances," ll. 65-68)

We know that Ronsard was regarded for many years as the most important poet of his day, the Prince of Poets. "Le Premier" here speaks in the persona of the poet, for the "superbe edifice" is, in fact, the *Sonnets pour Helene.* Again we note the expression "pour iamais" (l. 68) in a fountain poem, suggesting the immortality attained by the poet throughout his creation. Although no clear dichotomy exists between "Le Premier" and "Le Second" with respect to the personas of lover and poet, the lover's voice does, however, grow ever fainter throughout the **"Stances,"** as references first to authorial functions, and then to Ronsard's and other poets' verses appear. The gradual merging of the two voices into one occurs much like the engulfing of the sacred wine by the waters of the fountain.

The whole construction of the **"Stances,"** functioning as a fountain, serves as real, tangible evidence of the poet's "source."[25] The poem emphasizes the poet's creative powers, his dominant control, leading ultimately to his supremacy: the final words of the **"Stances"** are spoken for the *first and only* time by the character "Le Poete." He gains total control at the end of the **"Stances"** just as the poet's voice assumes the command in the creation of the fountain poems. His closing words stress the role of the poet's voice and point toward some sort of fusion and resolution for the entire sonnet cycle. The **"Stances,"** in fact, make it clear that some kind of ending or closure to the *Sonnets pour Helene* is imminent, but it is a closure that includes the idea of an eternal resonance that contrasts directly with the dissolution of the love story. This blending of finality and eternity is a recurring motif in the body of Ronsard works, as the concluding sonnet of the earlier sonnet cycle *Les Amours* demonstrates. As we noticed, *Les Amours* is the second of Ronsard's prominent works ("L'Hylas" being the first) which is alluded to by name in the **"Stances."** The very last sonnet in the *Amours* collection salutes the dead Marie as follows: "Maintenant tu es viue & ie suis mort d'ennuy" (**"Epitaphe de Marie,"** l. 12, Sonnet XIII of "Sur la mort de Marie" in *Le Second*

Lieure des Amours). The work closes then with a death, with the finite limits of mortality imposed upon Marie the Angevine. The poet, however, reverses the order and views Marie as continuing to live while he pronounces himself emotionally dead.

In the **"Stances"** the eight lines of "Le Poete" which conclude the piece hint of both closure and eternity:

> Garçons ne chantez plus, jà Vesper nous commande
> De serrer nos troupeaux, les Loups sont ja dehors.
> Demain à la frescheur auec une autre bande
> Nous reuiendrons danser à l'entour de ces bords.
>
> (ll. 81-84)

The remaining lines constitute the previously-cited passage of the pouring of the wine into the waters of the fountain:

> Fontaine, ce-pendant de ceste tasse plaine
> Reçoy ce vin sacré que ie renuerse en toy:
> Sois ditte pour iamais la Fontaine d'Helene,
> Et conserue en tes eaux mes amours & ma foy.
>
> (ll. 85-88)

The termination of the lover's belief in his ability to love Helene parallels the notion of endings presented here. The poet's claim to lasting glory through the virtues of his creations underlines the notion of eternity. The fountain, the poet's source, will preserve and encourage the love and the faith or belief that the poet wants to recount. The "memorable escrit" which is the text itself, furnishes the tangible evidence of preservation. The lover's story, the *vin sacré,* is sacrificed in order to assure the continuance of the fountain. The insistence on the words "pour iamais" assure, in turn, the fountain's eternity. This structure makes it evident that the lover's story has ended, but that the poet's will necessarily continue into eternity *auec une autre bande.*

Sonnet II, LXXIII follows the **"Stances,"** concluding the group of fountain poems which comprise the second water framework:

> Il ne suffit de boire en l'eau que i'ay sacrée
> A ceste belle Helene, afin d'estre amoureux:
> Il faut aussi dormir dedans un antre ombreux,
> Qui a ioignant sa rive en un mont son entrée.
>
> Il faut d'un pied dispos danser dessus la prée.
> Et tourner par neuf fois autour d'un saule creux;
> Il faut passer la planche, il faut faire des voeux
> Au Pere Sainct Germain qui garde la contrée.
>
> Cela fait, quand un coeur seroit un froid glaçon,
> Il sentiroit le feu d'une estrange façon
> Enflamer sa froideur. Croyez ceste escriture.
>
> Amour du rouge sang des Geans tout souillé,
> Essuyant en ceste eau son beau corps despouillé.
> Y laissa pour iamais ses feux & sa teinture.
>
> (II, LXXIII)

The closing lines reaffirm the notion that love must be sacrificed in this work in order for the poetic adventure to succeed. Once again we read the words "pour iamais" which stress the poet's immortality. We now also encounter a curious series of actions that are supposed to point to becoming *amoureux,* according to the narrator. The actions—sleeping in a shadowy cave, dancing over the meadow, turning nine times around a hollow willow, passing the plank, making vows—all appear to belong to the realm of magic or nonsense. The narrator beseeches us, however, to believe these words: "Croyez ceste escriture" (l. 11). Readers may refuse to believe that these strange actions would leave one "amoureux" and thus not believe the "escriture." Or, they may believe in the written word and therefore accept the actions as leading to love. Since the lover's story began with the powerless tossing in the tumultuous waves of the first water poem, **Sonnet I, VI,** only to be overpowered by the overwhelming creative source represented here in these final water poems, we can assume that these words are spoken by an almost voiceless lover (and thus easily dismissed) or by a poet who cares about writing but knows little about love. The lover's voice simply does not reach his audience any longer, and it is therefore quite easy to dismiss this sonnet's four long, qualifying sentences which impart the curious and nonsensical actions leading to love. It takes little effort, finally, to sacrifice love and all that it entails to the shorter but more compelling sentence of the poem: "Croyez ceste escriture."

Sonnet II, LXXIII closes the water framework, leaving five poems to terminate *Les Sonnets pour Helene.* In similar fashion, we recall, five poems precede the first half of the water framework near the opening of the work. These two frames where water is featured present dramatically the transfer of control from lover to poet. The poems portray in theme and in tone the change in narrative voice from lover to poet. The sacrifice of the love story for the survival of the poet's story—his text—demonstrates vividly that Ronsard's main aim in writing this sonnet sequence was to narrate the growth of the writing process itself. The pretext of a lover's struggle disguises the more intriguing concern of the poetic adventure. This parallel and paradoxical pattern of growth that shapes the water framework serves as a blueprint for the overall development of the entire sonnet cycle. When the two books of sonnets which comprise the *Sonnets pour Helene* are read according to this initial framework, readers find that the development is manifest: love is sacrificed for poetry. We place our faith in the poetic narrative. The poet's voice is responsible for the growth of the poetic epic, for the symbolic voyage that he—and we—embark upon as we take up Ronsard's final sonnet sequence. He bids his followers believe now—and we do—in the power of the "memorable escrit."

Notes

1. Portions of this study were previously published in the *MIFLC Review,* 2 (October, 1992): 9-17. See Jean Fallon, "Following the Artist's Blueprint in *Les Sonnets pour Helene.*"

2. In her book, Kathleen Anne Perry has already written about Ronsard's use of a "flexible persona" in his poetry. She points to Ronsard's use of different narrators within a single poem, such as the "Voiage de Tours," and astutely remarks: "The mutability of the Petrarchan persona becomes, in Ronsard's work, a sort of shift in perspectives of a poet (or narrator) conscious of the context in which he is speaking." Kathleen Anne Perry, *Another Reality* (New York: Peter Lang Publishing, Inc., 1990) 134.

3. Pirrre Grimal, *The Dictionary of Classical Mythology,* trans. A. R. Maxwell-Hyslop (New York: Basil Blackwell Ltd., 1986) 140-141.

4. Ronsard recounts the legend of Castor and Pollux in his "L'Hynne III De Pollux et Castor, à Gaspar de Colligny." Verses 41-42 call our attention to the association with navigators: "Et qui sauuent encor les nauires forcées / Des homicides flots quand elles sont poussées. . . ."

5. All quotations from Ronsard's *Sonnets pour Helene* are taken from Pierre de Ronsard, as recorded in Paul Laumonier, ed. *Oeuvres Complètes de P. de Ronsard* (Paris: Librairie Alphonse Lemerre, 1914-1919). Laumonier uses word forms and spellings that Ronsard employed, keeping "Helene" unaccented, as Ronsard did, representing "u" for a modern "v" when it does not begin a word, "i" for "j," and preserving inconsistent spellings for the same word used within the body of the poems, as well as spellings of words which have changed since Ronsard used them. Laumonier also uses roman numerals to identify the sonnets, using a I or II to identify the book, followed by the sonnet number in roman numerals. For example, I, VI is the sixth sonnet in Book One. I have followed Laumonier's example in this study. Laumonier uses "IIII" instead of "IV." I have abbreviated the *Derniers Vers* by "D.V." in the one instance where I have quoted from that work. As a general practice, I quote the sonnets in full, but from the "Stances," the "Elegie," and the "Chanson," and from the long poem, "L'Hylas," I quote pertinent passages.

6. François Rigolot's exhaustive and riveting section of his 1977 book on onomastic notions in Renaissance poetry deals in great detail with the significance of the name "Hélène." He writes: "Le Nom est *fatal* en vérité (II, 9 & 3); et le sort tragique du *poète-amant* (emphasis mine) est marqué par cet emploi inconscient (mais sans doute conscient de la part de l'écrivain) du mot-clé de la thématique hélénique. . . . "Le jeu de la paronomase est donc justifié par le contexte; il est une *felix culpa* qui, critiquable sous la forme que lui donne le sonnet-définition, se rachète ensuite par les opérations métaphoriques qu'il permet pour le grand profit du texte poétique."

François Rigolot, *Poétique et Onomastique: L'Exemple de la Renaissance* (Geneva: Librairie Droz, 1977), 222.

7. Rigolot 226. He comments: "S'il y a élection de l'amour chez le personnage, il y a élection d'une technique scripturale chez l'auteur. Le déchiffrement d' "Hélène" est un long cheminement de la pensée qui correspond, en sens inverse, au lent encodage de l'âme par le sentiment amoureux."

8. The use of the words "nauire," "homicide," and "flots" in Sonnet I, VI recall Ronsard's "L'Hynne III De Pollux et Castor."

9. Philip Ford comments on the significance of the storm: "Set-piece storm descriptions are not uncommon in classical literature, with *Odyssey* 5. 291 sqq. serving as a model for such later scenes as Virgil's *Aeneid* I. 181 sqq. It is well known that Ronsard, like his teacher, Dorat, considered that the *Odyssey* represented an allegory of the human soul passing through the vicissitudes of life on to its homecoming in the afterlife. So, any depiction of a storm-tossed hero might be interpreted in this light." Philip Ford "Ronsard the Painter: A Reading of 'Des Peintures Contenues Dedans un Tableau,'" *French Studies: A Quarterly Review,* 40 (1) (January, 1986): 32-44. We can interpret this set-piece as illustrating in part the narrator's early situation before his progression to powerful poet.

10. For a discussion of the origins and development of Blind Cupid in Renaissance art and literature, see Erwin Panofsky, *Studies in Iconology: Humanistic Themes in the Art of the Renaissance* (New York: Harper & Row, Publishers, 1962) 95-128.

11. Malcolm Quainton, "The Love Poetry of Pierre de Ronsard: Convention and Beyond," *Durham University Journal,* 80 (2) (June, 1988): 193-199. He submits: "The star of Helen [is] by tradition harmful to mariners." Thus, whether the narrator refers to the star or to Helene's eyes as the light source that pulls him to the rocks, it is a negative light.

12. For another perspective on Ronsard's treatment of flames and shipwrecks, see Perry 195.

13. Quainton 197. He corroborates this view of Ronsard's use of this verb: "In particular, the verb *surgir* (line 14) [is] itself a play on the name of his lady, Hélène de Surgères."

14. Laurence Mall also reminds us of sixteenth century writers' fondness of incorporating their own names into their texts and of a fairly widespread use of onomastic games in Renaissance texts. Laurence Mall, "Nom et renom dans les *Sonets pour Helene* de Ronsard," *Australian Journal of French Studies:* 25 (2), (May-August, 1988): 115-131.

15. See Rigolot 221 where he notes the rhyming of "Helene" and "fontaine.

16. Perry 160. She sums up this image as follows: "Water contains within it the potential for destruction and creation, death and fertility. . . ."

17. John O'Brien mentions the *mise-en-abyme* as part of Ronsard's *Amours de Cassandre*. See John O'Brien, "Theatrum Catopticum: Ronsard's *Amours de Cassandre*," *The Modern Language Review,* 86 (2) (April, 1991): 298-309.

18. The fountain was, of course, an early inspiration for Ronsard in his Ode II, ix, "A la Fontaine Bellerie" which he had previously imitated from Horace's Ode III, xiii, "O Fons Bandusiae." As Ahmed notes in his article, Ronsard deifies the fountain by "depicting himself as the poetic source not of the Latin Bandusiae but the French Bellerie." E. Ahmed, "Ronsard's 1550 Odes: Defining a Poetic Self," *Bibliothèque d'Humanisme et Renaissance* 49 (3) (1987): 591-596.

19. Laumonier 207.

20. See Ronsard's poem "L'Hylas" with explanatory notes in Graham Castor and Terence Cave, eds. *Ronsard, Odes, Hymns and Other Poems* (Manchester: Manchester University Press, 1973) 229-238, and 285-286.

21. See Castor's and Cave's comments on Ronsard's interest in the *Argonautica* legends in his poetry in their *Ronsard, Odes, Hymns and Other Poems* 285-286.

22. In "L'Hylas" Ronsard uses two spellings: Printine and Printinne.

23. Barbara Welch has pointed out an element of Du Bellay's poetry which she calls his process of "s'entre-écrire". See Barbara L. Welch, "Subtextual Voice in Ronsard's 1552 *Amours* and Du Bellay's *Regrets*," *Romance Quarterly* 37 (4) (November, 1990): 397-407. It is easy to imagine Ronsard using his own words and images from his own previously written poems as a kind of subtext for his writing about writing. While Welch's article is instrumental in directing readers to a form of dialogue employed between Du Bellay and Ronsard in their works, we can understand Ronsard using something of the same sort in his reworkings of his own texts. Thus, the 1578 edition of the *Sonnets pour Helene* could have stimulated further comment in his 1584 version.

24. Terence Cave and Thomas Greene's numerous and cogent observations about Renaissance imitations of classical models have contributed to my understanding of Ronsard's self-referential material in his works. It is apparent that Ronsard uses some aspects of *imitatio* but it is to allude to his own previously-published poetry. See Terence Cave, *The Cornucopian Text: Problems of Writing in the French Renaissance* (Oxford: Oxford University Press, 1979), and Thomas Greene, *The Light in Troy: Imitation and Discovery in Renaissance Poetry* (New Haven: Yale University Press, 1982).

25. David Quint, *Origin and Originality in Renaissance Literature: Versions of the Source* (New Haven: Yale University Press, 1983). He explores the theme of the source as a locus of divinity and truth in Renaissance literature. See pages 21-30 in particular for a discussion of Ronsard's versions of the source in his "Ode a Michel de L'Hospital" and in his "Response aux injures et calomnies." Quint underlines these two poems as presenting "the divided aspirations of a poet who desires both to ground his verse in an authorized source and to establish his own identity as a literary creator: to be a source for other poets." Quint 30.

Catharine Randall (essay date 1996)

SOURCE: "Poetic License, Censorship and the Unrestrained Self: Ronsard's *Livret de folastries,*" in *Papers on French Seventeenth Century Literature,* Vol. XXIII, No. 45, 1996, pp. 449-62.

[In the following essay, Randall describes the trangressive and pornographic qualities of Ronsard's Livret de folastries.*]*

I. MAKING FREE WITH THE TEXT: RONSARD, LA FONTAINE AND A VOICE FROM VICE

One of the ways in which freedom of expression can be measured is through an examination of poetic license taken. "Poetic license" implies a censoring body, one overseeing the norms of expression. When censorship is ignored, or when limits are stretched, usually consciously (since poetry's very idiom—its formalism—renders an unconscious violation of norms fairly inconceivable), a politics develops and is demonstrated in that verse. This poetic politics mandates as privileged "licensing agency" the self, rather than the state.

In mid-sixteenth century France, while censorship was not explicitly codified, the standard of the *privilège du roi* certainly worked to maintain a policy regarding acceptable limits on speech. Such literary surveillance was particularly relevant to poetry, since at this time poetry was the privileged mode of communication for all noble and elevated matters, be they love affairs or affairs of state.

In the great majority of his publications, Pierre de Ronsard exercised his own system of self-correction and censorship both of himself as writer and of his readers. He generally did not encourage any unauthorized contact with his works; only those texts which he had personally corrected and perfected were permitted dissemination to the world at large.[1] In this way, he both internalized implicit public expectations for "censorship" at the time, and exalted himself as the preeminent "censoring" mechanism.

An unusual collection of poetry was published, at first anonymously, in Paris in 1553. This collection voiced no pretensions to grandeur or an elevated style; it seemed rather the aimless wanderings of a frivolous, erotic sensibility. What makes this volume so important, and what makes it so surprising that little critical attention has been directed its way, is that it was authored by Pierre de Ronsard, the official poetic voice for the court and arguably for his time. In the *Livret de folastries* a fascinating tension between public and private poetic personae can be read between the lines.

Ronsard, so involved in contemporary discussions of poetic theory, leader of the Pléïade, seems to have felt personally hamstrung by some of the effects of his theorizing. In the *Folastries,* he shapes a private, playful space in which to express interests, and to explore themes, at variance with official speech. However, he had some concerns about the book's reception, as his initial anonymous posture makes clear. In this he was not mistaken.

Although widely read by contemporaries, this little book was much decried, for a variety of reasons. First, otherwise sympathetic readers felt that the style of the book was too unravelled and too racy, not sufficiently stylistically *soigné,* not adequately "politically correct" for the day. Indeed, the *Livret* was, arguably, the first bona fide free verse construction of French literature,[2] composed primarily "en strophes et en vers libres."[3]

Ronsard chose never to integrate his *Folastries* into his collected works,[4] suggesting thereby a dissonance between public and private permission and vehicles for expression. This decision to set apart from the main body of his published material this self-consciously constructed work indicates a metaperspective on the former by the latter: in this regard, the *Folastries* convey personal truth, and are critical of the dissembling and polishing necessary to please in the public arena.[5] If the *Sonets pour Hélène, Marie* and *Cassandre* are examined by scholars as indicative of Ronsard's psychology of love, so much more so must the *Folastries* be considered as revealing an intimate, personal *prise de conscience* mediated through the body of the woman. The major difference between the three "officially received" collections and the *Folastries* is that the body of the woman is not necessarily—indeed, should not be—beloved. It is instead a commodity, an object appropriated to fulfil Ronsard's own purposes. In that sense, at least, the woman's body is employed pornographically. Lawrence Kritzman has noted that our reading patterns of the Ronsardian œuvre should aim at extracting from the text

> [une] stratégie du topos corporel . . . le texte ronsardien est investi des avatars du corps qui prennent la forme du langage . . . [ces corps] assur[ent] une représentation implicite de ce qui est apparemment inconnaissable.[6]

Thus, in writing the *Folastries,* Ronsard creates a decoding device for discerning an alternative, perhaps even counter-cultural, poetry: what his verses would say, were they only to find the tolerance for their audition. This device is defiant—sometimes erotic, sometimes obscene, certainly "unprincipled" in the light of formal expectations. It dares the reader to see beyond the public posture, to attend to an individual, self-indulgent stance. How free the verse? This verse is both very free, because so audacious, especially at the level of content, and very constrained, in that it arises dichotomously out of a condition of cultural constraint, and thereby cannot, in some measure, exist without those limitations. It both codifies and reacts against those norms.

Ronsard's publication of the admittedly occasionally obscene *Folastries* was further complicated by Protestant polemicists, against whom he had been waging a fierce verbal war with his *Discours sur les misères* and *Continuation des misères.* Delighted with his risk-taking self-revelations, Calvinist poets turned his text against him, upbraiding him for the immorality of the poems and using that to undermine his authority.[7]

Pornography, then, or at least what can be construed as pornographic in the *Folastries,* shows that the adjective "free" in "free verse" stands more for a personal pushing against constraint at the thematic level than an innovation at the formal level. Pornography, in this reading, is not a writing about sex solely, but also a text about the self situated within and reacting against constraint. Such a text ultimately becomes a critique of a political order perceived as oppressive or overly dominant. Lynn Hunt observes that:

> pornography [is] most often a vehicle for using the shock of sex to criticize . . . political authorities . . . Pornography . . . [is] a category of understanding . . . Its political and cultural meanings cannot be separated from its emergence as a category of thinking, representation and regulation.[8]

Thus, even though the *Folastries'* publisher did secure a *privilège,* publication of the bawdy book nevertheless caused Ronsard considerable awkwardness. Why, then, did this popular, much-respected court poet, versifier to kings, choose to compose such a volume? Why risk so much on so little? Was it, in fact, so little? What is the ultimate intent of the *Folastries,* and what is its effect?

II. DEMEANING DIMINUTIVES: DENYING BLAME IN THE *LIVRET*

The title of the *Livret* provides some clues as to its interpretation. "Livret" means "a little book," but also puns on the verb "livrer," both "to deliver" and "to free," as well as on the noun "livrée," or "domestic servant's uniform." The diminutive "livret" has the effect of purportedly diminishing the book's importance (and thus, perhaps, allowing its contents to go unscrutinized), while the tension inscribed between liberty and retainer may hint at a political perception on Ronsard's part that his unofficial utterances, his private self, may not be as publically acceptable as his courtier persona. "Folastries" contains "fol," or "crazy person", a conventional device for enabling a writer to make a bold statement yet remain uncriticized, as witnessed by Erasmus' *In Praise of Folly*. "Folastrie" is defined by Randle Cotgrave's 1610 *Dictionarie of the French and English Tongues* as "wanton or lascivious trickes." "Fol-as-" suggests a homophonic pun on the conventional way of announcing a proverbial utterance (such as "Fol est qui jette à ses pieds ce qu'il tient en ses mains"). Ronsard thereby lobbies for the facile popular acceptance, because of the "on dit" quality of the implicit aphoristic intertext, of the text. With this sort of title, including lechery, servitude, and proto-aphoristic pronouncement, Ronsard has already constructed a complex concatenation of text, sexual proclivity and political perspective. The ***Livret de folastries*** is, clearly, much more than a playful pastime or well-written bawdy book. Ronsard's attempt to dismiss its components as "vers raillars" (p. 4, v. 6) is obviously disingenuous, a mask for something more.

The contents of the ***Livret*** suggest interpretive paths. The first ***Folastrie*** takes pain to deculpabilize Ronsard; it is the fault of the woman that he writes such verse: "qu'éperdument j'ayme mieux / . . . éperdument asservie / De son grasset embonpoint . . ." (vv. 3-8). He creates the fiction of a man deprived of power, yearning after two women at once. He is sandwiched between them ("entre les dames" v. 191). This divided self accepts no responsibility; it is thus a very effective technique for concealing and protecting Ronsard. He is speechless ("Que dirai je davantage?" v. 136) except when she allows him voice through a pun: "elle me rend contant" (v. 28). The end of the ***Folastrie*** takes up the theme of censure; he protests (perhaps too much) that an entire litany of events and circumstances cannot keep him from his love:

> Ny le temps, ny son effort,
> Ny violence de mort,
> Ny les mutines injures,
> Ny les mesdisans parjures,
> Ny les trop sales broquards

> (p. 16, vv. 203-209 and passim)

yet the block of space devoted to this enumeration is so large as to dominate the text in importance, suggesting that his fear of censorship for incorrect speech is actually far greater than the passion he feels (and which he uses as a cipher to describe his fear of reprisals). In addition, Ronsard hides behind the figures of the women, in that he claims that they fear the villagers' criticism of their lewd behavior, while in actuality he is describing his own malaise resulting from others' characterizations of his writing. Power is the real issue here:

> . . . caquette de vostre honneur
> Et qu'il die: Ces deux belles,
> Qui font le jour les rebelles,
> Toute nuit d'un bras mignon
> Echaufent un compaignon,
> . . . Las, mignardes, je scay bien
> Qui vous empeche, & combien
> Le Tyran de ce vilage

> Vous souille de son langage,
> Mesdisant de vostre nom
> Qui plus que le sien est bon.

> (p. 15 vv. 170-182).

Not only the explicitly lubricious poems in the collection, but also the "monster poems" included there attest, maintains Françoise Jouvkovsky, to a fundamental perceived instability in Ronsard's world, what may be interpreted as an ontological insecurity regarding his ability to truly express his inner self through the medium of poetry as officially-crafted.[9] Treachery to one's master, similarly, is dismissively discussed in a poem again linked to sexuality, the ***Folastrie*** V, in which a dog betrays his master's illicit affair to the neighbors by barking outside the door of the room where the lovers are clandestinely entwined. The word "traistre" recurs with obsessional frequency: "desloyal et trasitre mastin . . . Ainsi, traistre, ton aboyer / Traistre . . . Mechant mastin . . . Si traistre à ton fidelle maistre" (pp. 36-38, vv. 13-59).

Finally, the *figura* upon which nearly all the poems in the collection are based - all the free verse poems, that is - offers some hermeneutic insights. The woman is always the *figura*, the medium for Ronsard's constrained expression. In this light, it is significant that the rhyme endings to many of the *Dithyrambes* included in the ***Folastries*** are feminine: "l'absence d'alternance régulière dans le genre de rimes [qui] se trouve d'un bout à l'autre dans la pièce . . . résulte de la liberté complète du rythme strophique . . ."[10] In addition, Ronsard employs the stylistic strategy of parenthetical utterance: the woman's remarks are often related within parentheses, as though to underscore that it is she, not Ronsard, who makes these bold statements, but also to remark upon the spatial constraint which was the lot of women in sixteenth-century France (and which Ronsard wants to adopt as his own, in order to represent the limits placed on his speech): "Et toutesfois ceste insensée . . . / A mille inventions. / Et quoy (dit elle) ma mignonne?" (p. 26, vv. 95-103). Ronsard's verse structure, further, closely imitates the actions of the women whose tales he recounts. For example, in ***Folastrie*** IV, Robin and Jaquet, goatherds, go to the fields to have a picnic, and eventually copulate. The outcome of the anecdote is represented early on in the poem by the embracing pattern of the verses describing their feeling for each other: "O amourettes doucelettes, / O doucelettes amourettes" (p. 31, vv. 7-8). When the couple eventually makes love, nature imitates art, showing the power Ronsard hopes to acquire through the construction of his verses, as the goats they have been guarding begin to copulate, too:

> A peine eut dit, qu'elle s'aproche,
> Et le bon Jaquet qui l'embroche,
> Fist trepigner tous les Sylvains
> Du dru maniment de ses reins.
> Les boucs barbus qui l'aguetèrent,
> Paillars, sur les chèvres montèrent

> (p. 34, vv. 91-96).

The frenzied movement of copulation is what Ronsard yearns for: *ébranlement, improvisation* and *liberation.* Similarly, the topos of the flea who alights on the mistress' breast sketches a bounding, aimless pattern, *á l'abandon,* subverting formalism:

> Que pleust à dieu que je peusse
> Pour un soir devenir puce . . .
> Qu'en glissant plat dessus elle,
> . . . Pour me suivre à l'abandon,
> . . . Suivoit par toute contrée

(pp. 40-41, vv. 35-63).

Elsewhere, Ronsard petitions "que j'erre sans fin" (p. 46, v. 80), and in his famous *Folastrie* on "L'Ivrogne", this random wandering produces text: "qui se transforme en cent nouvelles" (p. 51, v. 93).

The *Dithyrambes* that conclude the collection of **Folastries** dramatize the culmination of Ronsard's move toward liberated speech and free verse through the mouthpiece of the woman or of such ungovernable creatures as the flea; Bacchus is invoked, and language degenerates into a dionysian non-sense, utterly unfettered by formalistic constraints: "mes parolles sanglotent / Je ne scay quelz vers insensez . . . Evoé ïach ïach," (pp. 60-61, vv. 95-112), he shouts jubiliantly, at last untrammeled by formalistic expectations.

III. Speculations: Mirroring Constraint and Context

The **Folastries** line up in the development of a self-critical French discursive voice. That voice—developed through the recourse to free verse—expresses itself, in a different context but a similar genealogical derivation, a century later with La Fontaine, for example. Even though the context in which he writes exercises a more rigid and formalized surveillance of publications (Richelieu having founded the censoring institution of the Académie française in 1632), La Fontaine feels considerably less constricted. His verse is as free as Ronsard's, if not more so. Why is this the case?

These two literary figures form an instructive diptych, the two halves of which circumscribe a lacuna, an enigma that remains to be teased out. If Ronsard writes pornographics (about) politics—and I use (about) in parentheses to indicate that his text postures as other than it is, La Fontaine writes poetics about politics. La Fontaine's FABULA faces down Ronsard's FEMINA, as woman is the figure and voice through which Ronsard tries to speak. That is, Ronsard appears trapped in the Renaissance cycle of representationality in which verse seems to speak for itself, but in fact can only be heard through an intermediary or filter—in this case, that of the loose woman. The role of this woman is to deflect blame from the writer onto the whore.

For La Fontaine, on the other hand, nearly a century later, verse has itself become its own efficacy, verse possesses its own voice. Women are incidental and trifling figures for La Fontaine; he uses and abuses them poetically, and exculpates himself glibly:

> J'ai lieu d'apprehender des objections bien plus importantes. On m'en peut faire deux principales: l'une, que ce texte est licentieux; l'autre, qu'il n'epargne pas assez le beau sexe . . . Quant à la seconde objection, par laquelle on me reproche que ce livre fait tort aux femmes, on aurait raison si je parlais serieusement; mais qui ne voit que ceci est jeu, et par conséquent ne peut porter coup?

(La Fontaine, *Contes et nouvelles,* I, Préface, 556-7)

For La Fontaine, women are objects of play; Ronsard takes them with deadly seriousness. This shift from image to speech enacts one facet of the development of the discursive mode in French literature. A figure of speech thus becomes a mode of speech.

While Ronsard probes the boundary between social and political acceptability and salacious transgression,[11] La Fontaine's verse is able to go further. His poetry relaxes by pleasing itself with titillation, but aims at more: it develops its own politics of language that seeks to define itself against the backdrop of control by Richelieu, the throne and the new royal academies. Thus, what is important to him is less the morality, or immorality, of the woman's figure or the bawdy tale, but rather the potential power inherent in the language used to convey that form or story. His subject is liberating for his verse; unlike Ronsard, who seems to peek around the edges of his transgressive tales, La Fontaine uses their very subject matter as the legitimizing factor for his style: just as Renaissance theorists had deemed "un haut style" appropriate to a tragedy, or a "bas style" fitting for a comedy, La Fontaine says that pornography brings with it its own suitable style:

> On me dira que j'eusse mieux fait de supprimer quelques circonstances, ou tout au moins les déguiser. Il n'y aurait rien de plus facile; mais cela aurait affaibli le conte, et lui aurait ôté de sa grace. Tant de circonspection n'est nécessaire que dans les ouvrages qui promettent beaucoup de retenue dès l'abord, ou par leur sujet ou par la manière dont on les traite.

(*C et N,* I, p. 556)

In addition, he ascertains a legitimizing factor for his bawdy writing in the century itself, thereby exculpating his personal involvement:

> Apollon se plaignit aux neuf sœurs l'autre jour
> De ne voir presque plus de bons vers sur l'amour.
> Le siècle, disait-il, a gâté cette affaire:
> Lui nous parler d'amour! Il ne la sait pas faire.
> Ce qu'on n'a point au cœur, l'a-t-on dans ses écrits?
> J'ai beau communiquer de l'ardeur aux esprits . . .
> Les belles n'ayant pas disposé la matière,
> Amour, et vers, tout est fort à la cavalière.

(*C et N,* III, "Clymène: comédie," vv. 1-8, p. 777)

Pornography's style is its own excuse: you've been told up front, he tells his reader, to expect no more and no less than what you get, so don't complain:

> Voici les derniers ouvrages de cette nature qui partiront des mains de l'auteur: et par conséquent la dernière occasion de justifier ses hardiesses, et des licenses qu'il s'est données . . . [elles] sont inséparables . . . [de ce genre de pœsie].

(II, Préface, 603)

The power that such rhetoric masks is enormous. "Circonspection" disaggregates into components that reorient its meaning: "cir-CON-spection" licenses a global gaze at women's erogenous zones. Pornography, then gives La Fontaine the ability to express illicit matters. But it also allows him to make free with his textual models: as he would with a whore, he takes them and uses them for his own purposes and pleasure:

> Je me suis écarté de mon original.
> On en pourra gloser; on pourra me mécroire: . . .
> J'ai suivi mon auteur en deux points seulement:
> Points qui sont véritablement
> Le plus important de l'histoire.

("La Fiancée du roi de Garbe," II, vv. 9-16, p. 667)

Pornography as subject facilitates the liberty that he craves and requires. This liberty includes the freedom to rework precursors, to rewrite models, to form collages of several pre-texts, to insert his own perspective ("j'y mets du mien") wherever he so desires. For this process, he implies a mercantile transaction, just as a whore is procured for a fee:

> Boccace n'est le seul qui me fournit.
> Je vais parfois en une autre boutique . . .
> Je puise encore en un vieux magasin
> . . . quiconque en soit l'auteur.
> J'y mets du mien selon les occurrences:
> C'est ma coûtume; et, sans telles licenses,
> Je quitterais la charge du conteur.

("La servante justifiée," II, vv. 1-16, p. 637)

No explanation or justification is given; La Fontaine asserts boldly that "c'est ma coûtume;" censors and readers are required to accept this. At other times, La Fontaine coyly plays with the censor, offering just enough details to titillate, but not quite enough to warrant a censoring process:

> Et le chien? Le chien fit ce que l'amant voulût.
> Mais que voulût l'amant? censeur, tu m'importunes:
> Il voulût par ce chien tenter d'autres fortunes.
> D'une seule conquête est-on jamais content?

(*C et N*, III, "Le petit chien qui secoue l'argent et des pierreries," vv. 510-513, p. 776)

This otherwise fairly bold statement about bestiality cloaks itself in elliptical respectability and allusion at the very last moment. The prosaic tenor of the poetry facilitates such a ruse: prose can both spell things out and backpedal quickly; the suggestive quality of Ronsard's verse can get it into more trouble than La Fontaine's clarity or clear evasion.

The role of the *conte* or *nouvelle* as La Fontaine uses it is to convince, to winnow out disbelief through narrative strategies, as Ross Chambers has described in *The Oppositional Narrative*. Chambers asserts that La Fontaine

> has no other power to which to have recourse than 'the power of fable.' So, unlike the Orator, he does not interrupt his discourse in order to pounce; on the contrary he pursues his story to its end. He is not in the business of deceiving rhetorically so as to win on another terrain altogether; he wishes to gain his (own) oppositional ends, certainly, but he does it, not by arousing hopes and desires that are to be cruelly dashed, but through the satisfaction of narrative desires. So pleasure is his byword, for it is pleasure which, for him, equates with the power of fable.[12]

This is a new twist to Barthes' concept of *jouissance:* the text masturbates, arousing itself with pornography despite—or to spite—a situation in which pleasure is not physically realizable. The "fable develops the art of inhabiting a space possessed by the other," (Chambers, 65) in which "the 'narrative function' reproduces a discourse of power," (Chambers, 51) which it can then revise and undercut, predominantly through a strategy of irony.

For La Fontaine, then, the figure of the woman wanders through a theater of ironic situations. How does this take place? First, in his *Contes et nouvelles en vers* (1666; 1674), La Fontaine privileges a private place embedded within public space. This private area, what he calls his "cabinet" (I, 556), is doubly figured by the text which it shelters: the "petit receuil" (I, 556) of the text gathers itself (*recueillir*) to itself, rubbing against itself, pleasing itself for itself. It recognizes limits imposed on others ("je confesse qu'il faut en cela garder des bornes, et que les plus étroites sont les meilleures" I, 557), but it disregards those constraints for itself. The private space of the text, then, is characterized by freedom and self-fulfillment: "trop de scruple gâterait tout" (I, 557).

Another participant is invited into this private space; this is the reader. Now the text does not only rub itself, it rubs against the readers and, in so doing, is augmented: "jamais ce qu'on appelle un bon conte ne passe d'une main à l'autre sans recevoir quelque nouvel embellissement" II, 605). In this intercourse, the reader must also experience the seduction that the text exercises: "encore l'auteur n'aurait-il pas satisfait au principal point, qui est d'attacher le lecteur, de le réjouir, d'attirer malgré lui son attention, de lui plaire enfin (II, 603)." This "principal point" resonates with the great importance given to the final *pointe* of La Fontaine's fables, *contes* and *nouvelles*. The reader's *jouissance* "comes" at the last moment of the text, the culminating instance in which, with a phallic thrust, La Fontaine exposes his intentions and thrusts home with his wit.

Often, these textual ingressions are effected against the woman's figure, miming the act of intercourse verbally. In "La fiancée du roi de Garbe," for example, the tale concludes with a remonstrance to a woman bemoaning her lost virginity. "Ne m'allez point conter," (don't tell me any stories about it), this story asserts, thus denying to woman within the space of the text the right to voice her own story, "il est bon de garder sa fleur; / Mais, pour l'avoir perdu, il ne se faut pas pendre." (II, vv. 800-1, p. 686). She is thus doubly ravished; first, in the story; second, *by* the story. Randle Cotgrave's *Dictionarie of the French and English Tongues* corroborates this reading: he defines *pointe* as "a pricke . . . also, quicknesse, sharpnesse . . . the main point of an argument." The proliferation of *pointes* in La Fontaine's stylistic attests to the aggressive nature of his text. His verse is very free; Ronsard's is on the defensive, but La Fontaine goes on the offensive. Because of such assertiveness, La Fontaine can go beyond the private space in which his narration begins, and influence the public sphere: "Venons à la liberté que l'auteur se donne de tailler dans le bien d'autrui aussi bien que dans le sien propre" (II, 605).

Further, as narrative in the form of fable is employed by La Fontaine, encouraging a praxis (disclosure) rather than a stasis (image), it generates what Ronsard does not yet possess the resources—although he certainly demonstrates the inclination—to produce: "[censors/readers and author] are locked into a negotiation, an exchange with the works they seek to abridge."[13] In order that this "negotiation" occur, however, it is necessary that French poetry begin to slide toward a prose mode; the fable is one such possibility. "Censorship comes to loathe all that is uncertain. It loathes poetry"[14] precisely because it cannot negotiate or reason with it. La Fontaine, too, like Ronsard, experiences censorship; wanting to convert to Christianity on his deathbed, La Fontaine is blocked by his confessor who instructs him that unless he repents of his "contes infames"[15] he will be denied last rites. In light of this negative reception, it is interesting that La Fontaine, like Ronsard, speaks of his works as *folastries* and *bagatelles* (Préface, *Contes*, 555), apparently in this way seeking to discount their influence: "la gaiété de ces contes; elle passe légèrement" (I, 557). La Fontaine shows his concern to disguise their power by situating the production of his work in a situation of constraint:

> Voilà les principaux points sur quoi j'ai cru être obligé de me défendre. J'abandonne le reste aux censeurs: aussi bien serait-ce une entreprise infinie que de prétendre répondre à tout. Jamais la critique ne demeure court, ni ne manque de sujets de s'exercer: quand ceux que je puis prévoir lui seraient ôtés, elle en aurait bientôt trouvé d'autres.

> (I, 557)

Censorship and criticism seem omnipresent, but La Fontaine's verse will render them impotent. Criticism lurks everywhere; like the plainclothed vice squad cop luring whores on a crowded street at dusk, censorship writes its own plethora of possibilities: when one target removes itself, it determines more.

IV. CONCLUSION

Thus, if in a sense it is true that, as Paul Laumonnier avers, "c'est aux **Folastries** qui se rattachent notamment tous les recueils de poésies 'gaillardes' et 'satyriques' de la fin du XVIe siècle et du premier tiers du XVIIe,"[16] nevertheless La Fontaine breaks some of the strings of attachment to his model. Some of these ruptures are stylistic, some thematic, but all have the effect of circling around censorship rather than explicitly evading it, as Ronsard seems to feel the need to do. La Fontaine both lures and subsequently rejects the censor, wrapping him in coils of porn and poetry: the porn to seduce him, the poetry to ensnare him. While Du Bellay called Ronsard's verse "lawless verses," in fact his are not, because through their very avoidance of the implicit norm for speech and writing, they observe those conventions in a hyperactive way. La Fontaine's are the true lawless verses: writing within known constraints which he accepts, he underwrites them with his own new laws: laws of free speech jocularly uttered, concealing a barb, speech more powerful than the institution that tries to regulate it. He turns Richelieu's rhetoric of control against itself, riding rhetoric to a farther potential: if institutional control of speech is necessary, then poetry may posit itself as a metainstitution to, equally, patrol the purlieux of institutional speech. This is the real, and ultimate effect, of the *Contes et nouvelles en vers*. The strategies of domination and mastery exercised against the women therein serve, in the final analysis, to show the sway and dominion the figure of the woman wields within the rhetorical space: powerless, she knows power intimately, and adopts its masks and stratagems.

Notes

1. Richard Regosin, "Poétique et rhétorique de l'amour: le propre et l'impropre de la lecture de Ronsard," *Sur des vers de Ronsard,* Actes du colloque international Duke University, 11-13 Avril 1985, ed. Marcel Tetel (Paris: Aux amateurs de livres, 1990) 117. Regosin speaks of "Ronsard qui défend toute lecture inautorisée."

2. Pierre de Ronsard, *Œuvres complètes,* vol. 5, ed. P. Laumonnier (Paris: Didier, 1968) xiv.

3. *Ibid.* xiii.

4. *Ibid.* xvi.

5. *Ibid.*

6. Lawrence Kritzman, "Le corps de la fiction et la fiction du corps chez Ronsard," *Sur des vers de Ronsard: 1585-1985,* Actes du colloque international de Duke University, 11-13 Avril 1985, cd. Marcel Tetel (Paris: Aux Amateurs de Livres, 1990) 72.

7. *Ibid.* xix. "Une certaine opposition se manifeste parmi les membres du parlement, dont certains

manifestent des tendances au protestantisme. Même ses amis, tels Michel de l'Hôpital, le réprimandent et lui demandent d'écouter une inspiration plus chrétienne."

8. Lynn Hunt, *The Invention of Pornography* (New York: Zone, 1993) 10-11.

9. Françoise Jouvkovsky, *Le Bel Objet: les paradis artificiels de la Pléiade* (Geneva, 1991) 185. "On sait que le démon est instable par manque d'être, et par conséquent à la fois incomplet et soumis à des mutations." Was it perhaps to avoid censorship that Ronsard makes his texts "obscur" (187), that in them can be found "rien de préconçu" and "la seule loi est le hasard" (187)?

10. P. Laumonnier, ed. *Œuvres complètes*, 55.

11. The deliberate inclusion in the narrative fabric of Ronsard's poems in the *Folastries* of obscene, popular ribaldry and seamy vocabulary attests to a desire to shock and to break out of the confines enclosing normative correctness. In *Folastrie* III, for instance, Catin "exerce le mestier de l'un sur l'autre." In *Folastrie* IIII, the words "jauche moy," "chouser," "son petit cas" and "guignoit le tribart qui lui pendoit entre les jambes" occur. As Gregory de Rocher observes in "Ronsard's Dildo Sonnet: The Scandal of Poissy and Rasse des Noeux" in *Writing the Renaissance,* ed. Raymond La Charité (French Forum, 77, 1992): 149-167, Ronsard is "known to have exploited an extremely libertine vein during his early career in *Les Folastries.*"

12. Ross Chambers, *The Oppositional Narrative: Reading Oppositional Narrative* (University of Chicago, 1991) 65.

13. Michael Holquist, "Corrupt Originals: the Paradox of Censorship," *PMLA Special Issue on Censorship* (January 1994) 17.

14. *Ibid.,* footnote p. 56.

15. La Fontaine, *Œuvres completes,* (Paris: Gallimard, NRF, 1991) 1v.

16. Paul Laumonnier, ed. Ronsard, *Les folastries* (Paris: Didier, 1968).

Works Consulted

Anon., *Cabinet satyrique* (1618) (Paris: Fort, 1928).

Burt, Richard, ed. *The Administration of Aesthetics: Censorship, Political Criticism and the Public Sphere* (University of Minnesota Press).

Bourdieu, Pierre. "Censorship and the Imposition of Form," in *Language and Symbolic Power* (Harvard University Press, 1991).

Fleuret, F. *Les amoureux passe-temps* (Paris: Montaigne, 1925).

Holquist, Michael. "Corrupt Originals: the Paradox of Censorship," in *PMLA Special Issue on Censorship,* January 1994: 14-25.

Hunt, Lynn, ed. *The Invention of Pornography, 1500-1800* (New York: Zone, 1993).

Jansen, Sue Curry. *Censorship: The Knot that Binds Power and Knowledge* (Oxford University Press, 1988).

Lachèvre, Frédéric. *Recueils collectifs libres et satiriques* (Paris: Champion, 1914).

Macé, Jean. *Philippe contre les poetastres* (1555).

Patterson, Annabel. "Censorship," in *The Encyclopedia of Literature and Criticism* (London: Routledge, 1990).

Ronsard, Pierre de. *Œuvres complètes,* v. 5, ed. P. Laumonnier (Paris: Didier, 1968).

Cathy Yandell (essay date 1997)

SOURCE: "*Carpe Diem* Revisited: Ronsard's Temporal Ploys," in *Sixteenth Century Journal,* Vol. XXVIII, No. 4, 1997, pp. 1281-1302.

[In the following essay, Yandell investigates the carpe diem *theme in Ronsard's poetry and its relation to the poet's dread of aging.]*

> *For women are as Roses, whose faire flowre*
> *Being once displaid, doth fall that verie howre.*
>
> Orsino to Viola in Shakespeare's *Twelfth Night*
> (2:4:36-39)

The *carpe diem* ("pluck the day") motif, whose onomastic origins can be traced to Horace, permeates not only classical Greek and Latin poetry but also lyric poetry from fifteenth-century Italy to sixteenth-century Spain to seventeenth-century England.[1] Few students of English literature are unfamiliar with Robert Herrick's "Corinna's Going a Maying," John Donne's "The Anagram," William Shakespeare's Sonnets 3 and 4, or Andrew Marvell's "To His Coy Mistress." Similarly, in the Spanish tradition, Garcilaso de la Vega's "En tanto que de rosa y azucena," Luis de Góngora's "Micntras por compctir con tu cabcllo," Lupercio Leonardo de Argensola's "Ojalà suyo así llamar pudiera," and Francisco de Quevedo y Villegas's "A una mujer afeitada" form part of a large corpus of *carpe diem* poems. But it is perhaps in early modern France in general, and in the Pléiade in particular, that the *carpe diem* motif reaches its apogee. As Paul Laumonier humorously phrases it, "le vieux thème est dans l'air, et l'air en est saturé"[2] (the old theme is in the air, and the air is saturated with it). Pierre de Ronsard figures prominently in this tradition, which he both embraces and transforms.

Construed traditionally as "a compliment and an invitation" and more recently as "an instrument of seduction," *carpe diem* has received much critical mention but little sustained attention.[3] Perhaps this comparative dearth of scholarly scrutiny results from what appears to be a too obvious functioning of the literary motif. Even the most casual reader notes that the poet who invokes the *carpe diem* diem motif is attempting to convince the addressee, often through a comparison of the young girl to the ephemeral rose, that she should love him now while the time is ripe. But what is the nature of this tactic? How does it function, both rhetorically and psychologically? Is the poet's ultimate message an epicurean exhortation to "gather rosebuds while ye may," or do other rhetorical elements in the poems obfuscate that reading? Ronsard's *carpe diem* poems reveal not only multiple responses to these questions but also the poet's own assumptions about time, the topos that is explicitly problematized by the motif.

Ronsard's complex and original adaptation of the *carpe diem* motif can perhaps best be illustrated by juxtaposing his texts with the classical sources that he sets out to imitate. When Ronsard began to adopt the *carpe diem* motif in the mid-sixteenth century, a number of Latin, Greek, and more contemporary models were available to him. *The Greek Anthology* had been published in Florence in 1494 by Janus Lascaris and reprinted several times, including one printing in Paris by Josse Bade in 1531. Johannes Stobaeus's *Florilegium,* from which Ronsard borrowed many erotic-bacchic fragments, was published in Venice in 1535 by Bartholomeo Zanetti Casterzagense, in 1543 in Zurich by Froschoverus, and again in Basle in 1549 by Joannes Oporinus.[4] Horace's *Opera* and specifically the *Carmina* enjoyed a great popularity at the end of the fifteenth and the beginning of the sixteenth centuries, with numerous editions published in Venice, Florence, and then Paris (Simon de Colines, 1528). In addition to these classical sources, the *carpe diem* motif experienced a rebirth in the late-fifteenth-century Italian poetry of the *Petrarchisti,* Lorenzo de' Medici and Poliziano.[5] Ronsard also read Johannes Secundus, which led him to other neo-Latins, notably Marullus, whose *Epigrammata & Hymni* had been published in Florence in 1497 and in Paris in 1529.

Many subtle differences exist among the various sorts of *carpe diem* poems, but the most prototypical form of the genre features the older male poet, with distinctly erotic designs, exhorting the younger female addressee to take advantage of the present moment. Propertius urges Cynthia to taste of life's pleasures now, for her kisses will fall like petals from a festive garland (*Elegies,* II, 15). Ovid reminds a young Roman woman that years flow like water; she will regret having pushed away her lover as she lies in her solitary bed in later years. She should gather the rose before it wilts and falls of its own accord (*Ars Amatoria,* II, vv. 59-80). In this representative form, three constitutive elements interact within the space of the poem, all conflicting with a diametric opposite and creating a tension that the poem proposes to resolve: the rose in its withered avatar clashes with its vigorous, youthful representation; the poet in most cases expresses an explicit or implicit contention with the addressee; and the menacing future (illustrated by the projected declining, aging body of the addressee) opposes the epicurean present (incarnated in the currently glowing, youthful body of the addressee).

I will argue here that Ronsard's poet exploits these tensions in his *carpe diem* poems more explicitly than do his classical models and that his staging of the tensions betrays certain of the poet's attitudes toward temporality, gender, and the body. Consider as a first example the paradigmatic sonnet **"Je vous envoye un bouquet que ma main"** (1572) with respect to its most frequently cited model, Rufinus's "To Rhodoklea."[6]

> Here Rhodoklea
> is a garland
> a braid of delicate
> flowers laced
> by my own hands
> there are lilies
> roses
> moist anemones
> soft narcissus
> dark-gleaming violets
> wear it
> cease to be haughty
> both flowers and you
> will cease one day[7]
> Je vous envoye un bouquet que ma main
> Vint de trier de ces fleurs épanies:
> Qui ne les eust à ce vespre cuillies,
> Cheutes à terre elles fussent demain.
> Cela vous soit un exemple certain
> Que vos beautés, bien qu'elles soient fleuries,
> En peu de tems cherront toutes flétries,
> Et comme fleurs periront tout soudain.
> Le tems s'en va, le tems s'en va, ma Dame
> Las! le tems non, mais nous nous en allons,
> Et tost serons estendus sous la lame:
> Et des amours desquelles nous parlons
> Quand serons morts n'en sera plus nouvelle:
> Pour-ce aimés moi, ce pendant qu'estes belle.

(L., 7:152; P., 1:270)[8]

(I am sending you a bouquet that my hand / Just picked among these blossoming flowers / Tomorrow they would have fallen / Had no one picked them today. / Let this be an unmistakable lesson to you: / Your beauty, although it is flourishing / In little time will be gone / And like flowers, it will suddenly perish. / Time is fleeting, time is fleeting, my Lady / Alas! Not time, but we are fleeting, / and soon we will lie under stone. And of the loves we now speak, / there will be no more news when we are dead. / Thus love me now, while you are still beautiful.)

The tensions cited above generate the movement of both poems but much more obviously in the case of Ronsard. Both poems insist on the flight of time and both compare the young addressee to freshly picked flowers. Both poets highlight their own authority. Rufinus's narrator emphasizes his role of weaving together the garland, and Ronsard's speaker underscores that it is his own hand that picked the flowers in order to take advantage of their finest moment. In both cases, the poet fully intends to reap benefits from the addressee's beauty if she is so inclined. Rufinus's invitation, "wear it / cease to be haughty," is the suggestive equivalent of Ronsard's "Pour-ce aimés moy." In contrast to the concise idea of Rufinus's poem, however, the elaboration and development of the motif in the French sonnet create a quite different message.

The images of both poems lead to the conclusion that the lovers must act before death sets in: "both flowers and you / will cease one day," "cheutes à terre elles fussent demain," "comme fleurs periront tout soudain," "tost serons estendus sous la lame."[9] Ronsard's speaker, unlike Rufinus's, rhetorically identifies with the lady in that both poet and addressee will someday die: "le tems s'en va, ma Dame / Las! le tems non, mais nous nous en allons." Yet the identification of the first-person-plural pronoun extends only to death and not to the problem of aging. Given the paradigm of the older male poet/young girl, it is of course predictable that Ronsard would not conclude the sonnet with a reference to his own youth. The sonnet unfolds according to a principle of commonality, however, with one exception: both speaker and addressee will someday die, but within the rhetoric of the poem, only one of them will grow old. Five lines of the sestet proclaim the advent of death as the preeminent reason to love now, but the last line diverts the logical progression of the poem and substitutes the implication of the lady's eclipsed beauty ("while you are [still] beautiful") for their mutual death.

In Ronsard's sonnet the poet is thus rhetorically connected to the addressee through the use of the unifying first-person pronoun and then distanced from her through the pronounced shift back to the second person singular. The subjective dynamics within the poem mirror this tension. The poet establishes a connection with the addressee both by the implicit suggestion of sexual attraction and by his evocation of their mutual destiny. A severance between the poet and the addressee takes place, however, when Ronsard's speaker evokes her youthful beauty that will soon vanish. The shift from "nous" to "vous" and from "quand serons morts" to "ce pendant qu'estes belle" is reminiscent of Tonto's quintessential "what do you mean 'we,' Paleface?" By rhetorically joining the lady in their mutual expectation of death and then separating himself from her (from her loss of youth), Ronsard's poet manifests a more pronounced desire to gain mastery over both fleeting time and the lady's aging than does his classical model.[10] The 1567 elegy **"J'ay ce matin amassé de ma main"** provides another clear example of the poet's insistence on the flower's atrophy and loss of beauty rather than its death, but this time the poet magnifies the fusion of the flower and the addressee to illustrate the lady's vanishing desirability. Thomas Greene notes in Ronsard "the tendency of a woman's body to become a landscape and conversely, of a landscape to become her body, a tendency so subtle and pervasive as almost to merit the term *Joycean*."[11] This reciprocity develops particularly in the beginning of the elegy where the earth's bosom has produced a bouquet worthy of the lady's breast. It is doubtless not coincidental that in this elegy Ronsard's speaker

temporarily loses himself in a few uncharacteristically repetitive verses: "Elle est vermeille, et vous estes vermeille. / Sa blancheur est à la vostre pareille. / Elle est d'azur, vostre esprit et vos yeux / Ont pour couleur le bel azur des cieux. / Elle a le gris pour sa parure mise, / Et vous aimez la belle couleur grise" (L., 14:148; P., 2:353), insisting upon the collapse of modifiers and artfully coalescing the woman-flower so that the human and herbaceous qualities become interchangeable:

> Plus il ne reste à vous dire, maistresse,
> Que tout ainsi que ceste fleur se laisse
> Passer soudain, perdant grace et vigueur,
> Et tombe à terre atteinte de langueur,
> Sans estre plus des Amans desirée
> Comme une fleur toute desfigurée,
> Vostre âge ainsi verdoyant s'en-ira
> Et comme fleur sans grace perira.

> (L., 14:148; P., 2:354-55)

(It remains to be said, my lady, / That just as a flower fades suddenly, losing its grace and vigor, / And falls, languishing, to the ground / No longer desired by any lovers, / Like a disfigured flower, / [So] your flourishing age will flee / And like a flower will perish gracelessly.)

In this elegy it is the anthropomorphic flower, not the lady, replaced by the substantive "âge," who languishes, becomes disfigured, and fails to attract lovers. This referential indeterminacy that humanizes the flower also serves to dehumanize the addressee who "without grace will die." But once again, while death punctuates the poet's comparison, it is in no way the central problem posed by the elegy. There are six specific mentions of the loss of attractiveness to lovers and the deterioration of physical beauty in the elegy, whereas death (in the form of the verb "périr") figures only once.[12] Aging appears as a threat greater than death to the addressee in several of Ronsard's models as well,[13] but Ronsard's poet personalizes the temporal implications of the motif and accords them corporality, thus emphasizing the poet's authority in setting the clock forward. Ronsard's imitation of an epigram by Julianus from *The Greek Anthology* corroborates this claim:

> Maria is proud; but do thou, mighty Justice, take vengeance on the hauteur of that arrogant lass,—not by death, O Queen, but on the contrary may she reach the grey hairs of age, may her hard face come to wrinkles. May the grey hairs avenge my tears: may her beauty suffer for the error of her soul, as it was the cause of it.[14]

> Je ne veux point la mort de celle qui arreste
> Mon coeur en sa prison: mais, Amour, pour venger
> Mes larmes de six ans, fay ses cheveux changer,
> Et seme bien espais des neiges sur sa teste.
> Si tu veux, la vengeance est desja toute preste:
> Tu accourcis les ans, tu les peux allonger:
> Ne souffres en ton camp ton soudard outrager.
> Que vieille elle devienne, ottroyant ma requeste.
> Elle se glorifie en ses cheveux frisez,
> En sa verde jeunesse, en ses yeux aiguisez,

Qui tirent dans les coeurs mille pointes encloses.
Pourquoy te braves-tu de cela qui n'est rien?
La beauté n'est que vent, la beauté n'est pas bien,
Les beautez en un jour s'en-vont comme les roses.

(L., 17:245; P., 1:373)

(I do not wish the death of the one who holds / My heart in her prison. But Amor, to avenge / My tears of six years, change the color of her hair,/ And sow thick snow upon her head. / If you wish, vengeance is all ready./You shorten the years, you can lengthen them as well: Do not let your soldier be injured in your camp./ Make her old—grant my plea. / She glorifies in her curly locks, / In her green youth, in her sharp eyes / That pierce my heart with a thousand arrows. / Why do you play the gallant with something worthless? / Beauty is only wind, beauty is not a possession, / Beauties vanish in a day like roses.)

Ronsard's speaker, even while imploring Eros's aid, establishes his own voice from the outset ("je," "mon coeur," "mes larmes," "ton soudard"), which highlights his agency in the premature aging of the lady. The sixteenth-century poet insists more than does his Greek model upon the addressee's former beauty by furnishing concrete examples of the "before" as contrasted with the "after" ("cheveux frisez," "verde jeunesse," and "yeux aiguisez," which are all revealed to be ephemeral). Maintaining his authority in the physical realm, Ronsard omits the moral dimension introduced by Julianus ("May her beauty suffer for the error of her soul"). Ronsard's speaker (still the "je" introduced in the first quatrain) concludes his sonnet by evoking the transitory nature of beauty, as illustrated by two physical images: wind and roses. Thus once again Ronsard's poet rhetorically emphasizes his authority in the workings of time upon the lady and insists on her former beauty (and by extension the stakes involved in time's devastation of it) more than does the classical model.

Why, in these poems and elsewhere, is aging depicted as a fate worse than death? Why does the threat of the aging body prove to be such a prominent rhetorical strategy for Ronsard's poet, especially in comparison to his classical models? Female beauty in sixteenth-century France, as in fifteenth-century Italy, was a central preoccupation of artists and poets, to which the *Blasons poétiques du corps féminin* and many other works attest.[15] Judging from observations of male contemporaries, beauty and youth are not dissociable in the cultural sensibilities of early modern Europe. Vives's *Institution de la femme chrétienne,* first published in French translation in the 1540s, cites physical considerations as important factors in man's choosing a wife, and first mentioned among those is age.[16] Erasmus incites girls to marry while they are still "in the bloom of youth," which he specifies as about seventeen years old.[17] Similarly, Estienne Pasquier warns that girls should not delay marriage lest their perfect ripeness pass, and he estimates the ideal nubile age to be twenty years.[18] Aging women figure prominently as the subject of derision in a number of sixteenth-century proverbs collected by Le Roux de Lincy, including "Temps pommelé, pomme ridée et femme fardée ne sont pas de longue durée" (Hazy

weather, shriveled apple, and painted woman do not last long) and "Celuy qui prend la vieille femme, / Ayme l'argent plus que la dame" (He who takes an old wife loves money more than the lady).[19]

Thus it would appear that since youthful beauty is especially important to a woman in sixteenth-century France, at least from the perspectives cited, the threat of her losing that beauty by aging would be the most powerful of taunts. We could then agree with Henri Weber that in this poem Ronsard perhaps "a jugé que cet argument touchait plus directement l'orgueil féminin" (thought that this argument more directly touched feminine pride).[20] But that temptingly tidy conclusion fails to take into account the poet's terror about the future in general and about the effects of time on his own body in particular. As early as 1555 in "Quand je suis vingt ou trente mois / Sans retourner en Vandomois" (L., 7:98; P., 1:806), the poet at age thirty, to the bemusement of many twentieth-century readers, already laments that his youth is fleeting: "Mais tousjours ma jeunesse fuit, / Et la vieillesse qui me suit, / De jeune en vieillard me transforme" (my youth is continually fleeting, and old age follows me, transforming me from a young to an old man).

Ronsard's perennial consternation at the problem of aging is corroborated in Creore's *Word Index,* which cites over six hundred references to forms of "vieux" and over eight hundred to forms of "jeune." The poet's anxiety about growing old translates first into his privileging the moment of youth, which finds one of its earliest expressions in **"Dedans des Prés je vis une Dryade"** in the first book of the *Amours*:

> Dedans des Prez je vis une Dryade,
> Qui comme fleur s'assisoyt par les fleurs,
> Et mignotoyt un chappeau de couleurs,
> Eschevelée, en simple verdugade.
> De ce jour là ma raison fut malade,
> Mon cueur pensif, mes yeulx chargez de pleurs,
> Moy triste et lent: tel amas de douleurs
> En ma franchise imprima son oeillade.
> Là je senty dedans mes yeulx voller
> Un doulx venin, qui se vint escouler
> Au fond de l'ame: et depuis cest oultrage,
> Comme un beau lis, au moy de Juin blessé
> D'un ray trop chault, languist à chef baissée,
> Je me consume au plus verd de mon age.

(L., 4:53 [1552]; P., 1:55)

(In the meadow I saw a dryad / Sitting as a flower among flowers, / Sweetly donning a colorful hat, / Tousled, in a simple dress. / From this day forward my judgment grew weak, / My heart pensive, my eyes filled with tears, / I became sorrowful and slow. / Her gaze engraved such a heavy mark upon my liberty. / I felt a sweet venom fly into my eyes, flowing into the depths of my soul. And since this shattering event, / Just as a beautiful lily wounded by scorching rays in June / Languishes with its head bowed, / [So] I am wasting away in the prime of my youth.)

This sonnet enumerates love's melancholic effects on the poet, with a conclusion highlighting the speaker's youth. Reflections on the budding beauty of the dryad in the form of a flower immediately give way to the poet's Petrarchan introspection regarding his own state, translated by the predominance of first-person referents: "*ma* raison," "*mon* cueur pensif, *mes* yeulx," "moy triste et lent." The first tercet, troped in an *innamoramento,* elaborates the poet's condition brought about by the young dryad-flower.[21] The second tercet predictably exploits the image of the flower with its head down (recalling Virgil's description of the death of Euryalus in the *Aeneid,* IX, 435-37); but, quite unpredictably, the flower in the last tercet represents no longer the dryad but the poet himself, languishing as he is consumed by melancholy in his youth. This insistence on the poet's youth is certainly not a commonplace within the tradition of *innamoramento* poems.[22] What is even more striking in the sonnet and what distinguishes Ronsard from his classical models the most clearly is this substitution of the poet for the lady as the referent of the metaphorical flower.[23]

The woman-flower rhetorically metamorphosed into a man-flower within the space of the poem signals a blurring of genders as well as of identities. The substitution of one flower for the other once again stages a complex connection between poet and addresses; the Other both represents and does not represent himself, as evidenced in "Je vous envoie un bouquet" above. The Other is she who in amatory terms conquers him and whom he seeks to conquer, either by causing her aging within the poem (as in "Je ne veux point la mort") or by seeking her affection and her favors (as in the poem under consideration here), a connection often severed within the register of his *carpe diem* poems. The last line of the sonnet, completely focused on the poet's inner state (underscored by the reflexive verb form), insists on his separateness and summarizes his regrets about his own premature aging; in contrast to the "flower seated among flowers" who remains stable throughout the sonnet, the poet sees the "greenness" of his youth destroyed.

The attraction of youth for Ronsard lies not only in the promise of the future for the young poet, thwarted in the preceding poem, but also in an erotic proclivity for budding female sensuality in the aging poet:

> J'aime un bouton vermeil entre-esclos au matin,
> Non la rose du soir, qui au Soleil se lâche:
> J'aime un corps de jeunesse en son printemps fleury:
> J'aime une jeune bouche, un baiser enfantin
> Encore non souillé d'une rude moustache,
> Et qui n'a point senty le poil blanc d'un mary.

> (L., 17:326 [1569]; P., 1:453)

(I like a ruby bud half-opened in the morning / Not the rose of evening, which is weary in the sun, / I like a youthful body in its blossoming spring / I like a young mouth, a child-like kiss / Not yet sullied by a rough mustache, / And which has never felt a husband's grey beard.)

This implicit fusion of the pure, pristine young woman and the unspoiled morning rosebud recalls *Les triumphes de la noble et amoureuse dame et l'art de honnestement aymer* (1535) by Jean Bouchet, who espouses the theory that, like flowers, a young girl's beauty fades if she is kissed or touched too much, "car le lys representant virginité pert incontinent sa beauté par attouchemens" (because the lily representing virginity quickly loses its beauty by being handled).[24] While on the one hand, the poet in this context relishes the inexperienced lover, on the other, Ronsard's name has never figured among the advocates of preservation of female purity. Indeed, he chides the resisting Marie for despising nature (L., 7:254; P., 1:194) and for imagining honor "dedans son esprit sot" (L., 7:138; P., 1:273)(in her foolish mind).

The second book of the **"Sonnets pour Helene"** offers other examples of the poet's shunning societal strictures on sexual expression when such principles interfere with his erotic designs, as in the following 1578 sonnet:

> Cest honneur, ceste loy sont noms pleins d'imposture
> Que vous alleguez tant, sottement inventez
> De nos peres réveurs, par lesquels vous ostez
> Et forcez les presents les meilleurs de Nature,
> Vous trompez votre sexe et lui faites injure. . . .

> (L., 17:266; P., 1:460)

(This honor and this law that you ivoke so much are insidious, stupidly invented by our idle fathers. By [this honor], you abolish and constrain the best gifts of Nature, you deceive and abuse your sex. . . .)

Given Ronsard's unwavering adherence to orthodoxy in matters of state, as a fierce supporter of the kings he served, and religion, as a loyal Catholic, Ronsard's critique of contemporary sexual mores in this sonnet can be read as either exceptional or self-interested. I see evidence for both conclusions.

Challenging sexual mores in more comprehensive way, Ronsard launches a *boutade* in the **Continuation des Amours,** musing that if Petrarch didn't gain Laura's favors, the poet from Arezzo should never have continued his devotion to her for thirty years:

> . . . car à voir son escrit,
> Il estoit esveillé d'un trop gentil esprit
> Pour estre sot trente ans, abusant sa jeunesse,
> Et sa Muse, au giron d'une seule maitresse:
> Ou bien il jouissoit de sa Laurette, ou bien
> Il estoit un grand fat d'aymer sans avoir rien. . . .

> (L., 7:317;P., 1:168-69)

(Judging from his work, [Petrarch] had too fine a mind to be such a fool / for thirty years, wasting his youth and his Muse, attached to the same / lady. Either he was finding physical pleasure with his little Laura, / or else he was an idiot to love without getting anything. . . .)

In this passage Ronsard's speaker not only challenges Petrarch's inability to secure Laura's physical affection, but he also specifically deplores the loss of Petrarch's youth because of it.

In addition to Ronsard's unmitigated passion for youth, the poet's aversion to aging and the aged is revealed in countless poems, from the more general psychological reservations, "Pource je porte en l'ame une amere tristesse, / Dequoy mon pied s'avance aux faubourgs de vieillesse" (My soul carries a bitter sadness that I am headed for the realm of old age) (L., 18:42; P., 1:442),[25] to the specific fear of physical debility, "tant de malheurs / Que la vieillesse apporte, entre tant de douleurs . . ." (so many misfortunes that old age brings, amidst so much pain . . .) (L., 18:265—6; P., 2:612).

Several critics of Ronsard have concluded that the poet eventually rises above the questions of the flourishing or deteriorating physical body and accedes to a higher spiritual plane.[26] Indeed, Ronsard's speaker's sanguine tone when addressing the older "Sinope" in the first sonnet of a series devoted to her seems initially to mark the poet's acceptance of aging and its effects:[27]

> L'an se rajeunissoit en sa verde jouvence,
> Quand je m'épris de vous, ma Sinope cruelle;
> Seize ans estoyent la fleur de vostre âge nouvelle,
> Et vostre teint sentoit encore son enfance.
>
> Vous aviez d'une infante encor la contenance,
> La parolle, et les pas; vostre bouche estoit belle,
> Vostre front, et voz mains dignes d'une immortelle
> Et vostre oeil, qui me fait trespasser quand j'y pense.
>
> . . . . .
>
> Et si pour le jourd'huy voz beautez si parfaites
> Ne sont comme autrefois, je n'en suis moins ravy,
> Car je n'ay pas égard à cela que vous estes,
> Mais au dous souvenir des beautez que je vy.

> (L., 10:87; P., 1:277)

(The year was renewed in its fresh youth when I was taken with you, my cruel Sinope. Sixteen years were the flower of your new age, and your countenance seemed still in its childhood. You still had the look, the speech and the step of a royal daughter. Your forehead, your hands (worthy of an immortal) and your eyes make me die just thinking about them. . . . And if today your perfect beauties are no longer as they were before, I am none the less thrilled, for I do not heed what you are, but rather the sweet memory of the beauties I saw.)

The poet disconcerts the reader by the *pointe* of the last line, however, rejecting any stoic acceptance of the effects of age. Diverting the question of Sinope's diminishing beauty, the speaker retains instead the *image* of her more alluring youth. Sinope's current, faded incarnation is emphatically supplanted by the memory of her younger avatar. The poet thus in no way transcends the loss of the

young woman's beauty in favor of loftier considerations. On the contrary, he freezes in his mind the image of her former pulchritude by winding backward Mnemosyne's clock.

Here, as is so often the case in Ronsard's love lyrics, behind the problem of the Other looms the larger, more consuming question of the self. The fourth **"Sonnet à Sinope,"** which appears in the cycle shortly after **"L'an se rajeunissoit,"** sheds considerable light on the poet's regrets about his own aging and his jealousy of a younger suitor:

> Or de vostre inconstance accuser je me doy,
> Vous fournissant d'amy qui fut plus beau que moy,
> Plus jeune et plus dispos, mais non d'amour si forte.

> (L., 10:89; P., 1:278)

(Now I must blame myself for your inconstancy, / Furnishing you with a lover more handsome, / Younger and nimbler than I, but whose love is less strong.)

The poet consecrates the remaining sonnets to his loss of Sinope, culminating in the final poem where he renounces his quest: "C'est trop aymé, pauvre Ronsard, delaisse / D'estre plus sot, et le temps despendu / A prochasser l'amour d'une maistresse . . ." (L., 10:100; P., 1:278) (You have loved too much, poor Ronsard, cease / Being a fool and wasting time chasing after a mistress's love). Thus in light of the concluding sonnets of the cycle, the speaker's insistence on Sinope's declining beauty in the first sonnet can be glossed as a mask, a deflection, a substitute for the poet's discouragement about his own aging and his inveterate sense of loss.

What, then, is the relationship between Ronsard's apparent obsession with youth discernible throughout his work and the *carpe diem* poems? It seems clear from the preceding examples that the poet temporarily circumvents the question of his own aging (and of the alterity it represents) by projecting it onto the Other, incarnated textually in the female addressee.[28] The specific functioning of this projection is particularly apparent in Ronsard's 1550 **"A Janne impitoyable,"** which imitates Horace's ode "Ad Ligurinum" (IV, 10).[29] The odes of both Ronsard and his model are concerned with time's control over physical as well as psychological human destiny. They address, both rhetorically and psychologically, the dimension of aging that divides the self from itself, a phenomenon that Montaigne describes succinctly: "moy à cette heure et moy tantost sommes bien deux."[30] A commonplace in literary depictions of aging holds that the speaker does not recognize in the mirror his or her old face, which bears little resemblance to the "authentic" younger self. Horace's poet employs this image very convincingly when addressing the young Ligurinus:

> O crudelis adhuc et Veneris muneribus potens
> insperata tuae cum veniet pluma superbiae
> et, quae nunc umeris involitant, deciderint comae,
> nunc et qui color est puniceae flore prior rosae

mutatus, Ligurine, in faciem verterit hispidam,
dices "heu," *quotiens te speculo videris alterum,*
"quae mens est hodie, cur eadem non puero fuit,
vel cur his animis incolumes non redeunt genae?"

(Ah, how cruel you are while you are still master of
Venus' Gifts! / When your cheek of disdain comes to
be plumed with an unwelcome down, / When cascades
of your hair, falling in full waves to your shoulders
now, Start to thin and shed, when into rose-damask of
fleshly tint / Harshness comes and a changed roughness
of face, then, Ligurinus, then, / *As your mirror reflects
someone unknown,* you will protest: "Alas!, / What I
now understand, why did I not see as a lad? Or else, /
May I not have again cheeks unimpaired, suiting what
I know now?"[31]

Ronsard's ode threatens Janne with a similar fate:

Jeune beauté, mais trop outrecuidée
Des presens de Venus,
Quand tu voirras ta peau estre ridée
Et tes cheveux chenus,
Contre le temps et contre toy rebelle
Diras en te tançant:
"Que ne pensois-je alors que j'estois belle
Ce que je vais pensant?
Ou bien pourquoi à mon desir pareille
Ne suis-je maintenant?
La beauté semble à la rose vermeille
Qui meurt incontinent."
—Voilà les vers tragiques et la plainte
Qu'au ciel tu envoyras,
Incontinent que ta face dépainte
Par le temps tu voirras.
Tu sçais combien ardemment je t'adore,
Indocile à pitié,
Et tu me fuis, et tu ne veux encore
Te joindre à ta moitié.
O de Paphos et de Cypre regente,
Deesse aux noirs sourcis!
Plustost encor que le temps, sois vengente

. . . . .

Et du brandon dont les coeurs tu enflames
Des jumens tout autour,
Brusle-la moy, à fin que de ses flames
Je me rie à mon tour.

(L., 2:33-35; P., 1:761-62)

(Young beauty, too proud of Venus's gifts, when you
see your wrinkled skin and grey hair rebellious against
time and you, you'll chide yourself, saying "Why didn't
I think what I do now when I was beautiful? Or why
am I not as I wish now? Beauty, like the crimson rose,
dies suddenly."—You'll exclaim these tragic jeremiads
to the heavens, as you see your face quickly worn by
time. You know how ardently I love you, [but] obsti-
nate and unmerciful, you escape me, not wishing to
join your other half. O queen of Paphos and Cyprus,
goddess with black eyebrows! Even more than time,
take revenge and with the torch you use to ignite young
girls' hearts, fire her up for me, so that I can have my
turn to laugh.)

On a first reading, the poems appear to be identical in the
relationship between poet and addressee. Each poet desires
the young addressee, who has not reciprocated his love,
and both poets taunt the young object of desire, threatening old age and regret. But significant differences in the
poems arise in the poets' rhetorical strategies, and some of
these differences are attributable to the fact that Horace's
addressee is male whereas Ronsard's is female. Voltaire, in
his epistle to Horace, "n'a pas osé lui parler de son Ligurinus," and Laumonier, speaking of Horace in *Ronsard,
poète lyrique,* expresses the same reservation.[32] Though the
distinctions between the homoerotic lyric in Horace and
the heterosexual lyric in Ronsard would be compelling to
pursue, they extend beyond the scope of the present study.
What is of particular interest to us in this context are the
techniques by which Ronsard's poet once again establishes
a semblance of connection with the addressee, only to replace it with a more detached stance, thus highlighting the
sixteenth-century poet's mastery of the addressee and her
time.[33]

The structure of the odes initially appears similar, in that
both poems are predicated on an axis of when/then: *When*
all these physical changes befall you, both poets stipulate,
then you will see the light. Both addressees are made to
speak of their moment of alienation followed by cognition.
As the poems progress, however, a significant structural
difference between the two poems emerges. In the Horatian ode, the paternal speaker willingly relinquishes the
power of speech to his son/ lover so that youth articulates
his own belated discovery. Ligurinus thus has the last
word. In contrast, Ronsard's speaker frames the lady's
words (almost identical to Ligurinus's) within his own discourse, providing an exegesis and an elaboration such that
the concluding message remains the poet's own. The poet's
voice further enters the ode more explicitly in the form of
a monologue to the addressee in line 17, "Tu sçais bien
combien ardemment je t'adore," and the speaker's voice
continues to dominate the remainder of the poem. The
psychological underpinning of this form of *carpe diem,*
the rhetorical aging of a lover who spurns the poet, functions similarly in the two poems in that both poets seek
retribution for love refused. But Ronsard's ode far surpasses the Horatian ode in its depiction of difference and
conflict. In the Horatian ode, the speaker details Ligurinus's
present beauty in concrete terms, evoking his "cascades of
. . . hair, falling in full waves" and his "rosedamask of
fleshly tint," whereas Ronsard's speaker, apparently unwilling in this context to concede any semblance of com-
plimentary language, describes the lady's beauty simply as
"outrecuidée" (proud, haughty). In "Ad Ligurinum," the
relationship between the speaker and the addressee remains implicit, since the speaker is nowhere present in the
poem, and the only concrete indication of the speaker's
position emerges in the first words of the ode: "O crudelis.
. . ." The mirror image in line 6 of the Horatian ode
evinces a relationship in which both identity and alterity
are suggested and where, it could be argued, the *alter*
("different one") resembles the aged speaker more than he
resembles the youthful Ligurinus.

Ronsard's speaker, unlike Horace's, enters fully into the poem beginning in line 17, proclaiming his ardor, chastising Janne explicitly for fleeing his advances, and invoking Venus's vengeance upon her. Whereas in Horace, the conflict between narrator and narratee remains implicit, in Ronsard, the poem becomes a battlefield in which the speaker general triumphs, reserving for himself the last laugh. This last laugh adds a temporal dimension as well, since it transports the sonnet from the register of a future perspective of the present (the regrets of the young woman) back to the present ("Tu sçais combien ardemment je t'adore") and again the implied future of the imperative ("Brusle-la moy"), thus insisting even more on the tensions provoked by time's linear progression. Horace's ode, on the other hand, despite its insistence on fleeting time, remains rhetorically situated in the future. The Ronsardian ode thus stages the temporal tensions more dynamically both by its shift in time and by the intervention of the narrator. The sixteenth-century poet once again establishes his personal complicity with time and its powers more forcefully than does his classical model.

The tone Horace's poet adopts when directing a *carpe diem* poem to a male other than an elusive lover is, not surprisingly, even more complicitous than in his ode to Ligurinus. In the well-known "Aequam memento rebus in arduis," ("Remember, when life's path is steep," II, 3), addressed to Dellius, the tone of the ode suggests a vital connection between poet and addressee as the first counsels the second to partake of wines and perfumes "while Fortune and youth allow."

Several of Ronsard's poems on the subject of savoring the present moment, replete with wilting roses, are also addressed to men (as friends and colleagues, ostensibly, not as elusive lovers like Ligurinus), and in those odes and sonnets the poet establishes a tone of camaraderie, as in **"Verson ces roses en ce vin,"** dedicated to Aubert:

> La belle Rose du printemps,
> Aubert, admoneste les hommes
> Passer joyeusement le temps,
> Et pendant que jeunes nous sommes,
> Esbattre la fleur de nos ans. . . .
>
> (L.,7:190; P., 1:841)

(The beautiful spring rose, Aubert, incites men to pass the time joyously, and while we are young, to relish the flower of our years. . . .)

The explicit identification of the poet with the addressee predicates a kind of shared history that nullifies the conflict present in the motif when the addressee is a spurning female lover. Predictably, in this context Ronsard's menacing depictions of old age vanish and his epicurean urgings become egalitarian and untainted by spite.

Does Ronsard's speaker ever identify with a female addressee when he writes of the ravages of time? To a limited degree, yes. In **"Comme une belle fleur assise entre les fleurs,"** for example, the poet deplores "l'importune

vieillesse [qui] nous suit," and the tone reveals the poet's indisputable complicity with the female addressee. Yet it is "le coup d'Amour" and not the human body that withers and grows old in this poem: "Amour et les fleurs ne durent qu'un Printemps" (L., 17: 224; P., 1:364). In the 1550 ode **"Nimphe aus beaus yeus,"** also, Ronsard's poet allies himself with Cassandre by the first-person plural pronoun: "Incontinent nous mourrons . . . / Donc cependant que l'âge nous convie / De nous esbattre, esgayon nostre vie. / Ne vois-tu le temps qui s'enfuit, / Et la vieillesse qui nous suit" (L., 2:127-28; P., 1:807-8) (Suddenly we will die . . . / So while our age still bids us / To dally, let's make our lives more mirthful. / Don't you see that time is fleeing, / And old age follows us). In both of these examples, however, time's devastation remains abstract; the reader will note the absence of references to the aging poet's own body in the context of his exhortation to pluck the day.

In his extensive study of time in Ronsard, Malcolm D. Quainton concludes that for Ronsard, "human happiness and wisdom are seen to reside in a submission to the rhythmic variety of time and in a stoical acceptance of man's inevitable transience in the name of cosmic harmony."[34] But the poet writes in a multiplicity of registers.[35] I have argued that Ronsard's lyric poetry reveals an adamant attachment to youth and a pronounced terror of aging, neither of which is convincingly assuaged even in the **Derniers vers**. These attachments and fears, embodied in various corporal images throughout Ronsard's poetic corpus, find their most powerful expression in the *carpe diem* motif, which represents the poet's ultimate attempt to triumph over time and the aging body. Neither explicitly succumbing to Chronos's devastation of his own body nor stoically accepting it, as the above examples have illustrated, Ronsard's speaker in the *carpe diem* motif rhetorically masters the lady's time, ravishing her body by the ravaging of old age. Cassandre, Janne, and Hélène, all consigned at some point to a shriveled future within the poet's verses, function for Ronsard's speaker as his doubles whose bodies enact the aging the poet so forcefully dreads for himself elsewhere in his work.[36]

These physical projections into the future also reveal a paradoxical functioning of *carpe diem* in Ronsard's poetic corpus. While the motif's didactic message incites readers to relish the present moment, to round out, as it were, time's advancement, the repeated images contrasting youthful and aging bodies unfold in a mercilessly linear time frame. In *Physics*, Aristotle asserts that time is no more made up of instants than a line is made up of points. But as points can be established on a line, so Ronsard's employment of the *carpe diem* motif freezes in time fixed images of corporeal flowering and withering. Seizing textually not the moment but the human body, Ronsard's poet, rhetorically if not epistemologically, takes time into his hands and makes it his own.

Notes

1. From the ode to Leuconoë: "Carpe diem, quam minimum credula postero" (Reap the harvest of

today, putting as little trust as may be in the morrow!), *The Odes and Epodes,* trans. C. E. Bennett, Loeb Classical Library, 33 (Cambridge, Mass: Harvard UP, 1968), Ode I, 11, 32-33.

2. Paul Laumonier, *Ronsard, poète lyrique: Étude historique et littéraire* (Paris: Hachette, 1923; reprint, Geneva: Slatkine, 1972), 587.

3. Donald Stone, *Ronsard's Sonnet Cycles: A Study in Tone and Vision* (New Haven: Yale UP, 1966), 6; Elizabeth Berg, "Iconoclastic Moments: Reading the *Sonnets for Helene,* Writing the Portuguese Letters," in *The Poetics of Gender,* ed. Nancy K. Miller (New York: Columbia UP, 1986), 208. In their monumental studies of Ronsard and sixteenth-century poets, both Laumonier, *Ronsard, poète lyrique,* 560-634, esp. 581-91; and Henri Weber, *La création poétique au seizième siècle en France* (Paris: Nizet, 1955), 333-56, each devote a section to the *carpe diem* motif in the *Amours.* Stone, *Ronsard's Sonnet Cycles,* 6ff., treats the question briefly; and more recently Elizabeth Berg has given a feminist reading of the *Sonnets pour Helene* with some attention to the motif. Ricardo Quinones, *The Renaissance Discovery of Time* (Cambridge, Mass.: Harvard UP, 1972), is an excellent study that refers to *carpe diem* as an exhortation never to waste time, but there is no consideration of the motif as a rhetorical device. Richard Glasser, *Time in French Life and Thought,* trans. C. G. Pearson (Manchester: Manchester UP, 1972), 143, mentions *carpe diem* as an indication of the changing attitudes toward time and as the antidote to Ronsard's philosophy of the eternal: "Only that which resisted time was valuable and genuine," Glasser, *Time,* 168. See also Yvonne Bellenger, "Le vocabulaire de la journée et des moments dans la poésie du XVIe siècle," *Revue Belge de Philologie et d'Histoire* 5 (1977): 760-84; Tom Conley, *The Graphic Unconscious* (Cambridge: Cambridge UP, 1992), 106ff.; and Malcolm D. Quainton, *Ronsard's Ordered Chaos: Visions of Flux and Stability in the Poetry of Pierre de Ronsard* (Manchester: Manchester UP, 1980), 121-26.

4. For further development of these borrowings, see Laumonier, *Ronsard, poète lyrique,* 596-98; and Henri Chamard, *Histoire de la Pléiade* (Paris: Didier, 1939-1940), 70.

5. Lorenzo de Medici, *Poesie volgari* (Venice: Aldo Manuzio, 1554); Poliziano, Agnolo, and Lorenzo de Medici, *Canzone* (Florence: Giunti, 1568).

6. A number of other influences can be cited: Petrarch's "I'mi vivea" and more generally erotic epigrams from Asclepiades, Agathias, and Rufinus; see Laumonier, *Ronsard, poète lyrique,* 585-91; James Hutton, *The Greek Anthology in France and in the Latin Writers of the Netherlands to the Year 1800* (Ithaca: Cornell UP, 1946), 350-74; and Weber, *La création poétique,* 341-50. In most cases,

Ronsard does not imitate a single, indisputable work but rather conflates several sources. In this study I have chosen to work with the most obvious models, which lend themselves best to close readings when juxtaposed with the Ronsardian texts. But other classical sources that I have consulted also support the theses I advance here. For a very interesting study of the phenomenon of multiple sources in Ronsard, see Edwin Duval, "Ronsard's Conflation of Classical Texts," *Classical and Modern Literature: A Quarterly* 4 (1981): 255-66.

7. *Anthologia Palatina,* 5.74, in *The Greek Anthology,* trans. Alan Marshfield, ed. Peter Jay (Oxford: Oxford UP, 1973), 306.

8. The first of these (L.) refers to *Oeuvres complètes,* ed. Paul Laumonier (Paris: Société des Textes Français Modernes, 1914-1975); and the second (P.) to *Oeuvres complètes,* ed. Jean Céard, Daniel Ménager, and Michel Simonin, Bibliotheque de la Pléiade, 45-46, 2 vols. (Paris: Gallimard, 1993-1994).

9. Quainton, *Ronsard's Ordered Chaos,* 122, shows the progression of rhyming words of the octet and its depiction of the destruction wrought by time and the movement from life to death: "epanie, demain, fleuries, flétries, soudain."

10. Compare also the 1569 "Dame au gros coeur, pourquoy t'espargnes-tu?" (L., 15:121; P., 2:885) which Hutton, *Greek Anthology,* 361, calls a "mere translation" of an epigram by Asclepiades (5.85). Indeed, the idea of the two poems is identical except that Ronsard adds a dimension of physical aging absent from the original ("cependant que tu es jeune et belle"). Compare also "Douce beauté, meurdriere de ma vie" (L., 6: 219; P., 1:92).

11. Thomas M. Greene, *The Light in Troy: Imitation and Discovery in Renaissance Poetry* (New Haven: Yale UP, 1982), 205. See also François Rigolot, "Rhétorique de la métamorphose chez Ronsard," in *Textes et Intertextes: Études sur le seizième siècle pour Alfred Glauser,* ed. Floyd Grey and Marcel Tetel (Paris: Nizet, 1979), 152, who notes in the ode "Mignonne, allons voir" the alternation between the woman as rose and the rose as woman. See also *Oeuvres complètes de Ronsard,* ed. Gustave Cohen, Bibliotheque de la Pléiade, 2 vols. (Paris: Gallimard, 1950), 1:1081; and Husserl, cited by M. Merleau-Ponty, *Le visible et l'invisible* (Paris: Gallimard, 1964), 203.

12. However, as Leonard Johnson deftly points out, "with death once is enough" (note on the manuscript).

13. See Horace, *Carmina,* IV, x; Propertius, *Elegies,* III, xxv; Meleager's "Garland"; Hutton, *Greek Anthology,* 155.

14. *Anthologia Palatina,* 5.298, Hutton, *Greek Anthology,* 372.

15. See Elizabeth Cropper, "The Beauty of Women: Problems in the Rhetoric of Renaissance Portraiture," in *Rewriting the Renaissance: The Discourses of Sexual Difference in Early Modern Europe,* ed. Margaret W. Ferguson, Maureen Quilligan, and Nancy J. Vickers (Chicago: U Chicago P, 1986), 175-90; Ruth Kelso, *Doctrine for the Lady of the Renaissance* (Urbana: U Illinois P, 1956 and 1978), 136-209; Nancy J. Vickers, "Diana Described: Scattered Woman and Scattered Rhyme," *Critical Inquiry* 8 (1976): 265-79; Alison Saunders, *The Sixteenth-Century Blason Poétique* (Berne: Peter Lang, 1981); Cathy Yandell, *"A la recherche du corps perdu:* A Capstone of the Renaissance *blasons anatomiques," Romance Notes* 26(1986): 135-42.

16. Juan Luis Vives, *Institution de la femme chrétienne,* trans. Pierre de Changy (Lyon: S. Sabon, n.d.), 225. This passage is also reproduced in Guillerm, *Le miroir des femmes* (Lille: Presses Universitaires de Lille, 1983), 86.

17. *The Colloquies of Erasmus,* trans. Craig R. Thompson (Chicago: U Chicago P, 1975), 104.

18. Letter 10 of book 22, in *Lettres familières,* ed. Dorothy Thickett (Geneva: Droz, 1974), 408. Compare also Francesco Barbaro, *Deux livres de l'estat du mariage,* trans. Claude Joly (Paris: Guillaume de Luyne, 1567), 29, who recommends choosing a young wife because a younger woman will more willingly accept instructions. For further treatment of the question of age and marriageability in sixteenth-century Paris, see Barbara Diefendorf, *Paris City Councillors in the Sixteenth Century: The Politics of Patrimony* (Princeton: Princeton UP, 1983), 179ff.

19. Le Roux de Lincy, *Le Livre des proverbes français et leur emploi dans la littérature du Moyen Age et de la Renaissance* (Paris: A. Delahays, 1859), 1:133, 220. For other examples of this phenomenon, see Jacques Bailbé, "Le thème de la vieille femme dans la poésie satirique du 16e siècle et début du 17e siècle," *Bibliothèque d'Humanisme et Renaissance* 26 (1964): 98-119.

20. Laumonier, *La création poétique,* 347. Compare also his similar conclusion in Laumonier, *Ronsard poète lyrique,* 579.

21. Compare also Petrarch's *Rime Sparse,* CLIX, in *Petrarch's Lyric Poems,* ed. Robert Durling (Cambridge, Mass.: Harvard UP, 1976), 304.

22. Compare, for example, Petrarch, *Rime Sparse,* 1-3, pp. 36-39, 61, 138-39; Maurice Scève, *Delie,* I-XXX, in *Poètes du Seizième Siècle,* ed. Albert-Maric Schmidt (Paris: Gallimard, 1953), 75-85.

23. Weber, *La création poétique,* 248, notes simply that the lily referring to the poet joins and completes the evocation of spring flowers in the first quatrain. The sonnet "En vain pour vous ce bouquet je compose" (L., 15:212; P., 1:243-44) also includes a final image of the pining poet as wilting flower: "Comme je suis fany pour l'amour d'elle" (I am wilted out of love for her), whereas the epigram by Meleager on which it is based (5.143) limits the flower image to the addressee Heliodora. A comparison between the poet and the rose carries a different meaning in "Pren ceste rose aimable comme toy" (L., 15: 204; P., 1:72-73), where the poet's life of suffering, unlike that of the rose, is seen to have no end.

24. Jean Bouchet, *Les Triumphes de la noble et amoureuse dame, et l'art de honnestement aymer* (Paris: Galliot du Pré, 1535), 21.

25. Other passages are far too numerous to develop here. See, for example, "Epitaphe de Feu Monseigneur d'Annebault" (L., 13:182-83; P., 2:917); "Celuy qui est mort aujourdhuy" (L., 7:281; P., 1:785); and "Voicy le temps, Hurault, qui joyeux nous convie" (L., 17:380; P., 2:340). Gilbert Gadoffre, *Les Quatre saisons de Ronsard,* 13, 15, notes Ronsard's early obsession with death, but he also concludes that "Ronsard est un grand anxieux," which he attributes in large part to the tumultuous political and cultural environment of the second half of Ronsard's life. Compare also "Joyeuse suy ton nom qui joyeux te convie," verse 61, "Car l'age le meilleur s'enfuit dés la jeunesse" (For the best age already begins to escape us beginning in childhood) (L., 18:119; P., 2:298).

26. See, for example, Isidore Silver, *Ronsard and the Grecian Lyre,* vol. 3 (Geneva: Droz, 1987), 164; Quainton, *Ronsard's Ordered Chaos,* 110-15; Yvonne Bellenger, "Temps mythique et mythes du temps dans les Hymnes de Ronsard (*Hymnes* de 1555-56 et de 1563)," in *Le Temps et la durée dans la littérature au Moyen Age et à la Renaissance,* ed. Yvonne Bellenger (Paris: Nizet, 1986), 179-92.

27. Yvonne Bellenger, "Temps mythique," 178, in fact reads this poem as a confirmation of Ronsard's privileging love over beauty.

28. See Jean Laplanche and J.-B. Pontalis's definition of "projection," in *Dictionnaire de la psychanalyse,* ed. Roland Chemama (Paris: Presses Universitaires de France, 1981), 345: "the subject attributes to another the tendencies, desires, etc., that he repudiates in himself" (my translation).

29. Compare also Horace, *Carmina,* I, 25, vv. 9-19 and III, 26.

30. *Essais,* ed. Maurice Rat (Paris: Gallimard, 1962), 2:403 (III, 9). For a contemporary psychoanalytic reading of this question, see Kathleen Woodward, "The Mirror Stage of Old Age," in *Memory and Desire: Aging—Literature—Psychoanalysis,* ed. Kathleen Woodward and Murray M. Schwartz (Bloomington: Indiana UP, 1986).

31. Ode IV, 10, in *Odes and Epodes,* trans. Bennett, 324. The English translation is by Charles E. Passage, *The Complete Works of Horace* (New York: Frederick Ungar, 1983), my emphasis.

32. Laumonier, *Ronsard, poète lyrique,* 581.

33. Compare also Horace's "Ode to Lyce" (*Carmina,* IV, 13), a post-*carpe diem* apostrophe addressed to the now aged former lover. Here the poet is distanced from the female addressee throughout the ode, and the speaker's presence in the text is limited to two first-person references: "Audiuere, Lyce, di mea uota" (The gods, O Lyce, have heard my imprecations) and "Quid habes illius, illius, / quae spirabat amores, / quae me surpuerat mihi" (What remains now of that beauty that our love breathed, that overtook me . . . . On the poet's distance from himself and his own youth, see Michael C. Putnam, *Artifices of Eternity: Horace's Fourth Book of Odes* (Ithaca: Cornell UP, 1986), 227.

34. Quainton, *Ronsard's Ordered Chaos,* 127.

35. In the editors' introduction to the Pléiade reedition of Ronsard's works, they note Ronsard's ability to "se multiplier," in this case by his borrowing from other authors without engaging in servile imitation; *Oeuvres complètes,* ed. Céard, Ménager, and Simonin, 1:xxvi.

36. In a different context, Michel Simonin, "Hélène avant Surgères: pour une lecture humaniste des *Sonnets pour Hélène,*" in *Sur des vers de Ronsard, 1585-1985: Actes du colloque international,* ed. Marcel Tetel (Paris: Aux amateurs de livres, 1990), 127-43, has ably demonstrated the importance of the notions of *la gémellité* ("twinship") and of the double in the *Sonnets pour Hélène.*

Philip Ford (essay date 1997)

SOURCE: *Ronsard's 'Hymnes': A Literary and Iconographical Study.* Tempe, Ariz.: Medieval & Renaissance Texts & Studies, 1997, 337 p.

[In the following excerpt, Ford observes the sources, themes, and stylistic developments of Ronsard's early hymns.]

Les Hymnes sont des Grecs invention premiere.

(Ronsard, L. XVIII. 263. 1)

From our general discussion of iconographical aspects of Ronsard's poetry, it is clear that the prevailing philosophy of Neo-Platonism in humanist and artistic circles provided a strong unifying influence between the visual arts and poetry. It had a profound effect not only on the choice of subject, use of allegory, and interpretation of works of art, but also on their harmonious structure. Art aimed to please, move, and teach in line with the intentions of classical rhetoric, but perhaps more importantly, the harmony of art, albeit an imperfect copy of celestial harmony, could introduce peace and order into the frequently turbulent affairs of men.

Not all art, of course, was capable of achieving this end . . . In choosing to center this study on Ronsard's **Hymnes,** I was influenced by a number of considerations. Because these compositions are so varied in form and content, they offer a wide range of poetry, all written in the grand style, but spanning the whole of Ronsard's poetic career. By their very nature, they are likely to fall into the category of inspired poetry, and to embody some form of transcendent meaning. Their arrangement and rearrangement in successive editions of Ronsard's work offer evidence of the poet's ideas about *dispositio.* Finally, from the poetic point of view, they provide examples of his most successful poetry in the grand style. Dedicated usually to the influential and wealthy, they are in Ronsard's mind more abiding monuments than the decorated palaces to which many patrons devote their riches. This rivalry with the plastic arts leads Ronsard to attempt to produce his own poetic equivalents: temples, palaces, paintings and tapestries, gold and silver ware, etc.

With regard to *inventio* [in the **Hymnes**], we shall be concerned in general terms with the Neo-Platonic and mystic elements which were so important in grand poetry in the Renaissance. We shall consider the ways in which certain themes were treated by Ronsard, looking in particular at his exploitation of the pictorial imagery which helps to form his vision of the world. In investigating the structure of individual poems and their place in entire editions of Ronsard's works, we shall have regard to the organizational principles at work, and the ways in which structure, as in a decorated building or gallery, can be an aid to hermeneutics by establishing parallels and clarifying meaning. In the area of style, we shall be particularly interested in the extent to which Ronsard may have been influenced by Mannerism, and how far he diverged from some of its fundamental principles.

Before looking at Ronsard's early hymns, however, it will be useful to consider the literary antecedents on which he modelled his own poems, in order to determine what shaped his own approach to the genre. A number of classical models were at his disposal, of which the most important are the Homeric hymns, the hymns of Callimachus, and the Orphic hymns.[1] In his study and views of these collections, he would have been largely dependent on the erudition of humanist acquaintances, and particularly, no doubt, of his friend and mentor, Jean Dorat. For if by the middle of the sixteenth century there was no lack of annotated editions of Latin authors, this situation was very far from obtaining in the case of Greek literature. Generally, printers confined themselves to reproducing the text of a Greek writer, sometimes accompanied by the relevant scholia and, as the century progressed, by a Latin translation.[2] It is extremely rare to find introductory notes or a commentary even in the case of such an important poet as

Homer, although to make up for this deficiency, editors sometimes included the lives or comments of ancient writers (in the case of Homer, for example, the lives attributed to Plutarch, Herodotus, and Dio Chrysostom, all contained in the 1504 Aldine edition of Homer). However, even this is rare, and the reader is usually presented only with the bare Greek text.

On the whole, humanists were concerned with producing as accurate a text as possible, and Dorat must have devoted much of his teaching to philological questions. This emerges, for example, in the verses sent by Dorat requesting a manuscript of the Homeric hymns:[3]

> . . . fac Homeri
> Hymnorum mihi codicem vetustum
> Paulum commodites, sed ante primam
> Horam, namque hodie poema graecum
> Illud putre situque et ulcerosum
> Mendis aggrediar meo labore;

(Have the ancient manuscript of Homer's *Hymns* sent to me shortly, but before the first hour, for today I shall tackle that Greek poem which is decaying with mould and disfigured with errors.)

However, as is apparent in the manuscript notes of Dorat's lectures on Homer, he was also interested in the allegorical meaning of the hymns.[4]

> Praeterea aduertendum est quomodo quis se accingere debeat lectioni poetarum. Nam si fabulas meras legit nullam interpretationem uel moralem uel physicam ex his excerpens neque abstrusum sensum enucleet non minus profecto ineptus quam ille qui apud Aesopum murem cum Leone fabulantem solum legit interpretationem moralem negligit.

(Besides, we should point out how one ought to prepare to read the poets. For if one reads them as mere fables, without deriving any allegorical interpretation, be it moral or physical, or without laying open their hidden meaning, one is certainly no less foolish than someone who in Aesop only reads through the story of the mouse speaking to the lion, and neglects the moral interpretation.)

Ronsard was acquainted with all three of the Greek sources we have mentioned when he came to write his hymns, although he does not appear to have relied exclusively on any particular group in determining his own conception of the genre. Florent Chrestien, in a polemical poem concerning Ronsard, wrote:

> D'Aurat t'a expliqué quelques livres d'Homere,
> Quelques hymnes d'Orphee, ou bien de Callimach,
> Et pource incontinent tu fais de l'Antimach,
> Tu enfles ton gosier, pensant estre en la France
> Seul à qui Apollon a vendu sa science.[5]

(Dorat explained to you a few books of Homer, a few hymns of Orpheus or Callimachus, and as a result you immediately write bombastic poetry like Antimachus; you puff out your throat, thinking you are alone in France to whom Apollo has sold his knowledge.)

Since the three sources represent very different ways of approaching the genre, it will be useful to consider briefly their differences.

In the collection of the Homeric hymns known to the sixteenth century, the fragmentary first hymn to Dionysus and the important hymn to Demeter were both missing, while the collection ended with the epigram εἰς ξένους. The hymns are all devoted to divinities, are written in hexameters, and make use of the Homeric epic dialect, but apart from this, they extend in range from the three-line hymn 13 to December to the 580-line hymn to Hermes (hymn 4). The essential elements consist of an exordium (mentioning the particular qualities of the divinity) and a farewell formula, often encompassing a prayer. The longer hymns also contain a central narrative section of varying length, and it is possible that the shorter hymns which lack this are merely extracts, an opinion held by at least one editor of the hymns, F. Càssola.[6]

The Callimachean hymn is largely modelled on the Homeric, although it does present certain differences. While the poems are generally written in the epic language associated with Homer, two of the six hymns (5 and 6) are in the Doric dialect, and hymn 5 is in elegiac couplets and not hexameters. Moreover, gods are not invariably the dedicatees of the hymns (as is the case in hymn 4 to Delos and hymn 5 on the bath of Pallas). In structure, they broadly follow the Homeric model, although they tend to dispense with the formal and formulaic nature of the latter. While the Homeric hymn generally begins with a formal announcement of the subject of the poem ("I shall recall and not forget Apollo . . ." "Muse, sing of Hermes," etc.), Callimachus often chooses a more dramatic opening, especially, for example, in the second hymn, to Apollo:

> How Apollo's laurel is shaking! how the whole temple is shaking! Be off, be off, all you profane. Already Phoebus has touched with his divine foot the door's threshold.

The tone of Callimachus' hymns also differs considerably from that of his model, being more deliberately witty, and making a great display of recondite details concerning the gods, coupled with a tongue-in-cheek, deliberative treatment of popularly-held beliefs. Thus, in a section which Ronsard would imitate in his *Hinne de Bacus* (L. VI. 177. 7-16), he hesitates in the first hymn between Mount Ida and Arcadia as Zeus's birthplace:

> . . . which of the two, father, was lying? "The Cretans were alway liars." The Cretans even erected a tomb for you, lord; you who cannot die, who are eternal.

> (1. 7-9)

Moreover, Callimachus, in his Hellenistic erudition, piles up epithets and brief allusions to events connected with the divinity's life.

There is none of Callimachus' witty badinage in the third important group of hymns, traditionally attributed to Or-

pheus. Their time and place of composition have long intrigued scholars, but in his edition, Quandt agrees with Wilamowitz in attributing them to a single poet "not before the end of the second century AD, but before Nonnus [the fifth-century author of the *Dionysiaca*]."[7] As well as being addressed to divinities, these hymns are also dedicated to deified natural phenomena such as the Stars (7), the Sea (22), Death (87), Victory (33), Night (3), Fortune (72), and Nature (10). Generally speaking, they consist of an opening in which the subject is addressed in the first line. This is followed by a list, of varying length, of epithets, adjectival phrases, and relative clauses defining the divinity in all its various manifestations, and the hymn usually ends with a prayer. It is not infrequent for the same, at times apparently non-transferable epithets, to be attributed to different deities, and for a single deity to be given apparently contradictory properties. There is no narrative content in these hymns which, like most of the others we have considered, are written in hexameters in the Homeric dialect.

In his lectures on Homer, Dorat discusses the three collections as well as the *Odes* of Pindar. He is in no doubt that the Homeric hymns were written by Homer:

> Inscribuntur autem Homero. nonnulli tamen adhuc dubitant sitne germanum et legitimum opus illius: siquidem in isto opere quaedam uocabula singularia id est semel usurpata reperiuntur quae in alijs operibus minime usurpantur. Sed haec obiectio leuis est. sic Poetarum propria sunt quaedam uocabula ut apud Ouid. camella in fastis et apud Virgil. in culice et moreto et epigrammatis quae nusquam alijs in operibus inueniuntur.

(fol. 19^r)

> (Now, they are attributed to Homer. Nevertheless, some people are still in doubt as to whether this is a genuine, authentic work of his, since there are to be found in it a number of unique words, that is *hapax legomena,* which are not at all used in his other works. But this is an unimportant objection. Thus, some words are particular to poets, such as *camella* ["bowl"] in Ovid's *Fasti,* and in Virgil's *Culex, Moretum,* and *Epigrams,* which are not to be found elsewhere in their works.)

From the literary point of view, he is quite clear in his mind that the Homeric hymns are superior in quality, even to the works of Pindar, which both he and Ronsard admired:

> Quemadmodum uero inter tragicos tres palmam obtinere dicuntur Aeschylus augustus et magniloquens atque archaeus id est antiquus tum Euripides popularis forensis familiarior 3.us Sophocles intermedius unde duobus reliquis perfectior est habitus. Nam ut ait Gallus: "In medijs rebus gratia maior inest." Ita Homerus medium stylum tenuit inter Callimachum et Pindarum et proinde utrique praeponitur.

(fol. 19^v)

> (But just as amongst the tragic poets three are said to receive the victor's palm: Aeschylus, majestic, sublime,

and "archaios" or ancient; then Euripides, popular, persuasive, more familiar; and thirdly Sophocles, between the other two, so that he was considered more perfect; for as Gallus says: "There is greater enjoyment in the golden mean"; in the same way, Homer maintained an intermediate style between Callimachus and Pindar, and consequently he outdoes both of them.)

Thus, these three collections of hymns represent very different types of poem. The Romans handed down little to the Renaissance in the way of hymns, apart from the invocations of Lucretius to Venus and the Earth (1. 1-43); the Catullan hymn to Diana (34); the Horatian *Carmen saeculare* and odes such as 1. 10 to Mercury, 1. 21 to Diana and Apollo, and 1. 35 to Fortune; Virgil's eulogy to Italy (*Georgics* 2. 136-76); and a number of Claudian's compositions. However, it is the neo-Latin poet Marullus who seems to have exercised the most influence, after the Greeks, on Ronsard's concept of the hymn.

Marullus' *Hymni naturales* are much more varied in intention, tone, and meter than any of the previous collections of hymns.[8] Meters range from the hexameter (1. 1 and 5, 3. 1, and 4. 5), through the lyric meters, to the unusual galliambic meter (in 1. 6, the hymn to Bacchus), while the openings vary between direct invocations to the gods (e.g., "Te te, suprema maximi proles Iovis, / Innupta Pallas, invoco," 1. 2) and more meditative or dramatic beginnings, inspired by Callimachus ("Quis novus hic animis furor incidit? unde repente / Mens fremit horrentique sonant praecordia motu?," 3. 1).

Marullus is far more eclectic with regard to his sources than many previous critics have indicated. Ivo Bruns mentions the influence of Lucretius on the style, if not the philosophical content of the hymns, some of which he rightly claims are inspired by Neo-Platonism, and more specifically the works of Proclus.[9] Ciceri also sees Lucretian influences as well as Ovidian elements,[10] while Sainati, acknowledging the importance of Neo-Platonism on the philosophical content of the hymns, sees stylistic borrowings ranging from the Homeric hymns and Callimachus to Lucretius, Catullus, and Claudian.[11] These scholars also see the influence of Italian poets like Pontano, Sannazzaro, and thinkers such as Pico della Mirandola in Marullus' hymns, but none of them refers to the collection of the Orphic hymns and its influence on both the style and content of many of Marullus' poems. This is not the place to produce a detailed comparison of the hymns of Orpheus and Marullus, but a few indications of the areas where this influence is most important will be useful in characterizing Marullus' hymns, and hence the general concept of the hymn form which Ronsard ultimately took over.

In the first place, it is predominantly to the Orphic hymns that the Renaissance looked for models for the hymn of nature, the *hymnus naturalis*. The Homeric hymns had sung of deities or deified heroes, as had the hymns of Callimachus for the most part. The Orphic hymns constituted the only important collection handed down to the Renaissance of poems dedicated to natural phenomena: the Heav-

ens, the Stars, the Sun, the Aether, etc., and of Marullus' hymns, only 1. 5, the *Hymnus Aeternitati,* does not have a corresponding hymn in the Orphic collection. Of course, Marullus does not simply reproduce the Orphic hymn in Latin guise: his poems are generally longer and stylistically more varied. However, he does incorporate aspects of the Orphic hymns into his own compositions: the list of epithets and short descriptions attributed to the divinity being celebrated, the direct address at the start of the hymn, the prayer at the end, and the apparent inconsistency of attributing unique characteristics to more than one deity, or mutually exclusive properties to the same deity.

Such were the models available to Ronsard. In addition, he would have had at his disposal the theoretical writings of Menander the Rhetor in the Περι επιδεικτικγν. It was a section of this work (*On Hymns to the Gods*) which provided J. C. Scaliger with the material for his section on hymns in the *Poetices libri septem* of 1561.[12] Menander divides hymns into nine categories: invocatory hymns; valedictory hymns; hymns of nature; mythical hymns; genealogical hymns; fictitious hymns; votive hymns; deprecatory hymns; and, inevitably, mixed hymns, combining different aspects of the other categories. Menander had many more examples of hymns from a variety of authors than have survived to this day, including Sappho, Anacreon, Bacchylides, Parmenides, Empedocles, Simonides, but he does mention Orpheus as being one of the principal exponents of the hymns of nature or scientific hymn:

> Scientific hymns are such as were composed by Parmenides and Empedocles, expounding the nature of Apollo or of Zeus. Most of the hymns of Orpheus are of this kind.

> (1. 333)

Menander's editors, Russell and Wilson, doubt, however, that he is referring to the extant collection of Orphic hymns.

Menander devotes separate chapters to all these categories, providing a definition for each kind, discussing specific examples from verse and prose authors, and giving advice concerning their appropriateness for particular subjects and audiences, their length, and the poetic diction suitable for them. The categories most relevant to Ronsard's hymns are probably the natural hymns and the mythological hymns, though Ronsard does have examples of invocatory and fictitious hymns. Of the first kind, Menander says that it is most suitable for vivid, grandiose subjects ("The first point to be made is that this form does not suit the simpler writers, but does suit very well those with vigor and grandeur of conception," 1. 336), in which deities are considered as forces of nature:

> Such hymns are found, for example, when, in delivering a hymn to Apollo, we identify him with the sun, and discuss the nature of the sun, or when we identify Hera with air or Zeus with heat.

> (1. 337)

He writes in the same section that these hymns need not be explicitly about natural phenomena: "Some are written enigmatically, others in an overt manner." However, hymns of the first type, not being didactic, would generally be shorter than those of the second type. Menander also includes here a warning against the vulgarization of these hymns: "Such hymns should be carefully preserved and not published to the multitude or the people, because they look too unconvincing and ridiculous to the masses."

After discussing possible similarities between the mythical and genealogical hymns, Menander considers the former category more closely. These poems tend to be of greater length and complexity than some of the other kinds of hymn: "They are appropriate in a higher degree to the poet, since in his case the licence to speak at leisure and wrap up the subject in poetical ornament and elaboration produces no satiety or disgust" (1. 338). Menander particularly stresses the need for the skilful arrangement of the details of the myth, which should be spread out and not expounded straight away:

> Antidotes need to be applied, for the sake of brevity and charm; e.g., not introducing every detail in a direct form, but omitting some points, conceding some, introducing some by combination, sometimes claiming to give explanations, or not committing oneself to belief or disbelief.

> (1. 339)

Ronsard's concept of the hymn would have been influenced by the various sources and related theoretical writings discussed above, whether through the teachings of Dorat or as a result of his own reading. As is the case with so many literary notions in the Renaissance, this concept would almost certainly have been a somewhat complex one, an uneasy synthesis of the highly disparate elements which had survived from the ancient world. As Michel Dassonville remarks on the subject of Ronsard's early attempts at the genre:

> Attracted by numerous models, captivated by sources of inspiration which were Christian and pagan in turn, his mind clouded perhaps by the ode, which was still the only ancient genre which he had cultivated, influenced by, above all else, Pindar's sumptuous lyricism, Ronsard experienced some difficulty, it seems, in distinguishing the hymn from the ode.[13]

In the light of Dorat's discussion of the relative merits of Homer, Callimachus, and Pindar, this is not surprising. Dassonville rejects the attempts of Laumonier, Gustave Cohen, Chamard, and Schmidt to define and categorize the Ronsardian hymn, and prefers himself to provide a structural definition: the hymn is a tripartite poem consisting of a proem "souvent suivi d'un retour lyrique sur soi"; a central development; and a final wish, greeting, praise, or prayer for the poet or the dedicatee of the poem.[14] However, as it stands, this definition does not really differentiate between the Ronsardian hymn and the examples of the hymn form to be found amongst the ancients, and in par-

ticular the longer Homeric hymns. This can be done perhaps more effectively by considering the function of Ronsard's hymns, but in order to do this, it will be necessary to determine the poet's attitude towards the subjects with which he deals and the significance he attaches to the mythological content. It will also be useful to consider Ronsard's attitudes towards his models, in particular the three Greek collections of hymns, and Marullus.

It would, however, be dangerous to try to impose an uneasy unity on all those poems which Ronsard designates as *hymnes,* and still more so to criticize him for a lack of unity in them. As Francis Cairns remarks:

> "Hymn" therefore is not a genre in the sense in which propemptikon or komos is a genre. Nor is it a genre in the other common sense of the word, in which it is used to refer to kinds of literature like epic, elegy, or lyric; for these kinds of literature are each characterized by meter and length, and more important they are mutually exclusive. "Hymn" is not characterized by meter or by length, and hymns can be found in epic, elegy, lyric, etc.[15]

In fact, there is a gradual development in Ronsard's approach to the hymn, and his early examples tend to be based quite closely on one or more identifiable sources.

In dealing with Ronsard's hymns, we shall be looking at them not in isolation but in the context of their place in the various editions of the poet's works. We shall particularly concentrate on those poems which form part of the books of hymns. However, to start with, we shall consider briefly the five compositions which pre-date the first book of hymns, published in 1555.

Ronsard's interest in the hymn appears to begin in the autumn of 1549, when he published *L'Hymne de France* (L. I. 24-25), a poem which would remain in the collected books of hymns until the edition of 1572-73. The short **"Hinne à Saint Gervaise, et Protaise"** (L. II. 5-7), first published in the *Quatre premiers livres des Odes* of 1550, did not enjoy the same success, but the **"Hinne à la nuit,"** which first appeared in the same collection, disappeared from the 1560 collection of hymns, only to be included in the fourth book of hymns in the editions of 1567, 1571, and 1572-73. The **"Hymne triumphal sur le trépas de Marguerite de Valois, Royne de Navarre"** of 1551 (L. III. 54-78) was destined to take its place in the fifth book of *Odes,* but the *Hinne de Bacus* of 1555 appears in all the collective editions from 1560.

The fate of these early examples of the hymn underlines as much as anything else Ronsard's uncertainty about the nature of the genre at this time, particularly with regard to its form. Three of them were clearly considered by their author to be odes, while the *Hymne de France* and the *Hinne de Bacus,* written in decasyllables and alexandrines respectively, would provide the model for all subsequent examples of the genre. Before considering the 1555 col-

lection of *Les Hymnes,* it will be useful to consider the three early hymns which survived in later collections.

L'Hymne de France is in fact more of a panegyric than a hymn, being modelled, as Laumonier indicates, on Virgil's eulogy of Italy in *Georgics* 2. 136-76, though it incorporates a number of other sources as well. In the opening lines (1-16), the poet makes an address to his lyre, which is imbued with Orphic powers. For example, he writes:

> Tu peuz tirer les forez de leur place,
> Fleschir l'enfer, mouvoir les monts de Thrace,
> Voire appaiser le feu, qu'il ne saccaige
> Les verds cheveux d'un violé boucaige. . . .
>
> (lines 9-12)

(You can draw forests from their spot, move the Underworld, displace the mountains of Thrace, and even calm fire so that it does not destroy the green tresses of a profaned grove. . . .)

Line 17 then introduces the main theme, the praise of France, in comparison with other parts of the world. Ronsard ends the poem with a short valediction (lines 215-24), recommending to France his lyre, and thus providing a circular pattern to the hymn.

If the *Hymne de France* is something of a *contaminatio* of classical sources, the **"Hinne à la nuit,"** first published in the *Troisième Livre des Odes* of 1550, is, as Laumonier says, "d'un bout à l'autre la paraphrase d'une ode saphique du napolitain Pontano" (L. II. 21, n. 1). In many ways, it is curious that this poem was placed in the 1567 collection of hymns, having been treated more appropriately as an ode in 1560. It is certainly addressed to the Night, and contains a prayer at the end:

> Mai, si te plaist déesse une fin à ma peine,
> Et donte sous mes braz celle qui est tant pleine
> De menasses cruelles. . . .
>
> (L. II. 22. 25-27)

(Please, goddess, put an end to my pain, and tame beneath my arms the lady who is so full of cruel threats. . . .)

Yet the tone of the poem is sensual, and reminiscent of Latin and neo-Latin amatory verse, as well as certain aspects of the Pléiade's own "style mignard," as is evident from the following lines:

> Lors que l'amie main court par la cuisse, & ores
> Par les tetins, ausquels ne s'acompare encores
> Nul ivoire qu'on voie,
> Et la langue en errant sur la joüe, & la face,
> Plus d'odeurs, & de fleurs, là naissantes, amasse
> Que l'Orient n'envoie.
>
> (lines 13-18)

(When the lover's hand runs over the thigh, and now over the breasts, which remain unparalleled by any ivory one can see, and the tongue, in wandering over the cheek and the face, collects more fragrances and flowers, budding there, than the Orient sends forth.)

When it comes to the **Hinne de Bacus** of 1554, however, Ronsard seems to have a far clearer idea of what for him constitutes a hymn, and, not surprisingly, this poem appears in all the later collective editions of the hymns. By this time, it is clear from textual evidence that Ronsard has read and assimilated the full range of classical models: the Homeric hymns, Callimachus' hymns, the Orphic hymns, and Marullus' *Hymni naturales*. The **Hinne de Bacus** bears the marks of all of these collections: the wit of Callimachus, as evidenced in lines 7-16 on the birthplace of Bacchus, inspired by Callimachus 1. 7-9 on Zeus's birthplace, cited above; the lists of epithets and attributes which are typical of the Orphic hymns and of Marullus (see, for example, lines 165ff. and 231ff.); and the valediction which is normal in the Homeric hymns. For the first time, as we shall see, Ronsard brings together the elements that would contribute to the success of the later hymns.

Terence Cave has already considered this early hymn in some detail, and pointed to the popularity of the theme in the visual arts of the Renaissance, amongst which Titian's painting, is one of the finest examples.[16] Concentrating on the triumphal procession described in lines 109-32, he shows how the god's ambiguous nature is suggested visually by the juxtaposition of opposing forces—the regal qualities of the god suggested by the "manteau Tyrian" (line 113) contrasted with the violence of the lynxes who draw his chariot, for example. Other qualities are suggested by the composition of the crown he wears:

> Un chapelet de liz mellés de roses franches,
> Et de feuille de vigne, et de lhierre espars,
> Voltigeant, umbrageoit ton chef de toutes pars.
>
> (L. VI. 182. 114-16)

(A wreath of lilies mixed with red roses, scattered with vine leaves and ivy, tumbling about, shaded your head on all sides.)

Here, the various plants and flowers are traditional symbols of love (roses), immortality (the evergreen ivy and the lily), and fecundity (the vine). Bacchus and his train, then, represent a *discordia concors,* not only on a human but also on a cosmic level, as becomes clear in the final section of the poem where Bacchus is seen leading the cosmic dance (lines 274-76).

On the other hand, Cave does not discuss the first part of the poem in which Ronsard deals with the circumstances surrounding Bacchus' birth and nurture. A unique aspect of this concerns Juno's wish, in the course of her attempts to kill the young god, to feed him to her bitch:

> Junon n'attendit point, tant elle fut irée,
> Que sa charette à Paons par le ciel fust tirée,
> Ains faisant le plongeon se laisse toute aller
> A l'abandon du vent, qui la guidoit par l'ær
> Toujours fondant en bas sur la terre Indienne:

> Beante à ses talons la suivoit une chienne,
> Qu'expres elle amenoit, à fin de se venger
> Et faire ce bastard à sa chienne manger.
> Mais Inon qui previt par augures l'ambuche,
> Pour tromper la deesse, Athamante elle huche,
> Et lui conta comment Junon venoit charcher
> L'anfançon pour le faire en pieces detrancher:
> Athamante soudain le tapit contre terre,
> Et couvrit le berceau de fueilles de lhierre,
> De creinte que Junon en charchant ne le vist,
> Et qu'englotir tout vif à son chien ne le fist
> Ou de peur qu'autrement ne lui fist quelque offence.
>
> (L. VI. 179-80. 57-73)

(Juno was so enraged that she did not wait for her peacock chariot to be drawn through the sky, but, plunging down, she surrendered entirely to the wind, which guided her through the air as she sank down onto the land of India. Hard on her heels she was followed by a gaping she-dog which she brought on purpose to avenge herself and feed this bastard-child to her dog. But Ino, who through augury foresaw the ambush, in order to trick the goddess, called out to Athamas, and told him how Juno was coming to seek out the baby to have him hacked to pieces. Athamas at once conceals him on the ground and covers the cradle with ivy leaves, lest Juno see him in her search and have him swallowed alive by her dog, or harm him in some other way.)

Other elements in Ronsard's account of the birth of Bacchus are more traditional. Jupiter causes his mortal beloved, Semele, to become pregnant, whereupon Juno, in the shape of Semele's nurse, Beroë, persuades her rival to ask Jupiter to appear before her in all his splendor (lines 17-21), as a result of which Semele is killed by her lover's lightning bolts, and Bacchus is born prematurely. Jupiter hides his son in his thigh until it is time for him to be born (lines 27-30) and then transfers Bacchus to Nysa to be nurtured by Hippe (or Hipta), Ino and Athamas (lines 23-24, 31-48), or by nymphs (line 45).

There is some confusion in Ronsard's account, at times increased by later variants. For example, in lines 23-25:

> . . . ton pere marri
> A Nyse t'envoia pour y estre nourri
> Des mains d'Ippe, & d'Inon, d'Athame & Melicharse.

(. . . your distraught father sent you to Nysa to be nurtured by the hands of Hippe, Ino, Athamas, and Melicharses.)

Dorat's translation sheds both light and darkness on these lines:

> . . . iam tum genitor Nysam te misit alendum
> Hippaeque Inonique Athamantique & Meticharsae
> [*sic*].
>
> (Dorat, *Poematia* [1586], 376)

(. . . then your father sent you to Nysa to be nurtured by Hippe, Ino, Athamas, and Meticharses.)

"Ippe," then, is the Orphic goddess Hippa or Hipta, and "Athame," despite the 1584-1587 variant "la vieille Athame," is the husband of Ino, Athamas. "Melicharse" is presumably Melicertes, their son (see line 81 of this poem). The form "Melicharse" appears nowhere else in Ronsard's works, and is not found in ancient accounts of the myth, although according to Robert Graves, "Ino's younger son Melicertes is the Canaanite Heracles Melkarth ('protector of the city'), *alias* Moloch. . . ."[17] Dorat's "Mericharsae" is probably a typographical error.

The allegorical significance of the birth, as recounted by Ronsard, almost certainly represents the growth of the vine, an explanation frequent in the Renaissance mythographers. Natalis Comes would write, for example (fol. 155[v], *Mythologiae*):

> He is said to have been sewn into Jupiter's thigh, because the vine is extremely greedy for warmth. . . . Nymphs are said to have nurtured him after receiving him from his mother's ashes because the vine is of all trees the dampest, and its fruit, if properly watered, is much healthier and grows at the same time. He is said to have been transferred to Egypt because of the warmth of the region and the fertility of the soil, and the vine needs something similar to this region.

Finally, the details concerning Juno and her bitch must involve a physical interpretation like the other elements surrounding Bacchus' birth. Juno, as the lower air surrounding the earth, is accompanied late in summer by the dog-star which heralds excessive heat. Elsewhere, in **Les Bacchanales, ou le folatrissime voyage d'Hercueil pres Paris** (L. III. 184-217), Ronsard refers to "l'ardente Canicule" (line 148) as "la chienne" (line 155). In order to protect the vine from this heat, an ivy covering is used to shelter it, suggested by Athamas's covering of the cradle with ivy leaves.

Bacchus' growth (lines 83-92) and discovery of wine (lines 93-104) follow on logically from this, as does the spread of the use of wine, suggested by the triumphal procession of lines 105-32. Renaissance mythographers such as Conti emphasize the fact that in moderation, wine is a force for good ("quia cum moderatione sumptus utilis sit & bonus potus," fol. 150[v]), but drunk in excess, it leads to evil:

> For in conformity with the very nature of drunkards, lynxes, tigers, leopards, and panthers are said to follow him, and to pull his chariot. For wine marks those who drink immoderately with the characteristics and cruelty of these wild beasts, and renders them insane.
>
> (fol. 155[v])

As Cave indicates, this is suggested by the various forces present in Bacchus' retinue.

The ecstatic side of Bacchus is also, of course, emphasized by Ronsard, particularly since the Bacchic or mystic frenzy could inspire the poet. In the dithyrambic section of the hymn (lines 179ff.), this is applied by the poet to himself in terms reminiscent of poetic frenzy; [consider] lines 187-88:

> Je sen mon coeur trambler, tant il est agité
> Des poignans aiguillons de ta divinité
>
> (I can feel my heart tremble, so excited is it by the piercing goads of your godhead). . . .

The final main section of the poem sees Bacchus at work on a cosmic scale. As well as providing mankind with music, law, religion, etc., he also causes the rebirth of the world at springtime:

> Tu fais germer la terre, & d'estranges couleurs
> Tu revests les vers prés orguillis de leurs fleurs,
> Tu dedaignes l'enfer, tu restaures le monde
> De ta longue jeunesse, & la machine ronde
> Tu poises justement, & moderes le bal
> (Toy balant le premier) de ce grand animal.
>
> (lines 271-76)

(You cause the earth to sprout and you cloak with unwonted colors the green meadows, grown proud with their flowers; you disdain the Underworld, you restore the world with your long-lived youthfulness, and you balance exactly the round universe and control the dance of this great creature, with you being the first to dance.)

Although Bacchus is more normally associated with autumn, it is the Orphic god that Ronsard, following Marullus, has in mind here, as we can see from the *Hymnus Baccho* 50-54:

> Tibi ager viret almus, tu florea prata tepentibus
> Zephyris coloras, tu dissona semina ligas,
> In saecla mundo semper fugientia reparas
> Longa iuventa, tu libras pondera machinae
> Medioque terram suspendis in aere stabilem. . . .

(For *you* the bountiful field grows green, *you* give color to the flowery meadows through the warm west winds, *you* bind together different breeds, you restore the ever-fleeting generations in the universe with long-lasting youth, *you* balance the cosmic forces and hold the earth, unmoving, in mid air. . . .)

Marullus gives Bacchus, in other words, attributes similar to those of the Orphic god Amor who, as the creative principle in the universe, was variously referred to by the Orphics as Phanes, Protogonos, Dionysus, Eros, Metis, and Erikepaios; it is this form that Ronsard also appears to have in mind.[18]

Thus, there is a progress in the hymn from Bacchus as the earthly vine, through Bacchus as the god of wine and of mystic frenzy in the sublunar world, to Bacchus as the moving principle in the translunar world.

Although there is a certain coherence in this hymn, it is nevertheless slightly marred by confusing and confused ideas. In the first place, Ronsard has not worked out in his own mind the exact nature of his Bacchus. True, he wishes to emphasize the positive aspects of the god, as Cave points out, and to that end suppresses details concerning the ritual slaughter of animals (lines 93-104), the death of the god at the hands of the Giants (lines 151-64), and Bacchus' androgynous appearance (lines 85-92). Later on, however, he would restore some of these details in **"A Monsieur de Belot"** . . . and in the **"Hymne de l'Autonne"** . . . where the bisexual nature of Bacchus is an important element in the explanation of the various changes the earth undergoes throughout the year. Moreover, the confusion over the nymphs who raise Bacchus, and where they live (India or Arabia), along with an excessive reliance at times on Marullus lead to a less than clear idea of what Ronsard has in mind. This is typified by lines 282-83:

> Je te salüe à droit le Lychnite admirable
> Des homes & des Dieus . . .
>
> (I salute you in a fitting way, wondrous Lychnites of men and gods . . .)

which is Ronsard's version of: "Salve, benigne lychnita, deum et pater hominum" (Marullus, *Hymni Naturales* 1. 6. 58). Later, Marullus corrected "lychnita" to "licnita," but Ronsard, as Laumonier notes, has taken the word *lychnita* (in Greek λυχνιτης) in the sense of "lamp" and as such follows it with the two dependent objective genitives "des homes & des Dieus," whereas Marullus uses the word as an epithet of Bacchus ("bearing the sacred λικνον," or fan-shaped basket, carried on the head at the feast of Bacchus and containing mystical objects).

Despite these reservations, the hymn represents a turning point, for in it, Ronsard has developed the poetic voice which would form the basis of his style in the important 1555 collection of hymns. As Cave remarks:

> . . . the movement away from allegory in the strict [i.e., medieval] sense and towards metaphor has been brought about in part at least by this exploitation on a visual, decorative and rhythmic level of images which had earlier been treated schematically. . . . Ronsard clearly perceived the enduring value of myth as a means of embodying profound insights into man and the universe.

He is using here the principle of the "voile bien subtil" to conceal the various layers of meaning in the poem, as he would do in subsequent mythological hymns. On the stylistic level, the fertility associated with Bacchus is paralleled by a mannerist lexical profusion, notably in the epithets attributed to the god (e.g., lines 231-36), which add little to the meaning of the text but which contribute to the mystic, incantatory tone of the poem. The inspirational Dionysus had set him on the right path.

. . . . .

The later hymns would witness a refinement of the qualities which are apparent in the first of Ronsard's important mythological hymns. With the 1555 collection, he appears to develop a more unified vision, which is further modified in 1556 with the two largely narrative poems, **"L'Hymne de Calaïs, et de Zetes"** and **"L'Hymne de Pollux et de Castor."** With these changes comes an increasing appeal to the visual. As Albert Py remarks in his introduction to the *Hymnes*: [19]

> We shall allow ourselves to base on such indications the impression that, in Ronsard, the characterization of the subject of the hymn, through the aesthetic openings to which it invites us, tends to cause the language of the hymns to slip from the aural to the visual level. The voice sparks off images which present themselves to the sight more boldly than the voice makes itself heard. The song is matched with increasing insistence by a picture.

Notes

1. The first editions of these poems were all printed in Florence in 1488, 1494, and 1500 respectively. The Homeric hymns, generally appearing in editions of the complete works of Homer, were frequently reprinted in the first half of the sixteenth century, and the first Latin translation by Iodocus Velareus Verbrobanus appeared in Antwerp as early as 1528, while a later version is due to the work of Georgius Dartona (Venice, 1537). Most editions after 1542 include a Latin translation. French editions include those of Sebastianus Gryphius, Lyon, 1541 (reprinted 1542) and the Dartona translation, printed in Paris and Lyon in 1538. The Orphic hymns also appeared in several sixteenth-century editions, while the first Latin translation was prepared by Renatus Perdrierius (Bâle, 1555). Apart from a Latin version of the *Hymn to Artemis,* Callimachus does not seem to have been translated until relatively late, although a French edition of the original text appeared in Paris in 1549, at the Vascosan press. The information here is largely derived from the *Inni omerici,* edited by Filippo Cássola (Verona: Fondazione Lorenzo Valla, 1975); Ruth Bunker, *A Bibliographical Study of the Greek Works and Translations Published in France During the Renaissance: the Decade 1540-1550* (New York, 1939); *Orphei Hymni,* ed. Guilelmus Quandt (Berlin: Weidmann, 1955); and the Loeb edition of Callimachus.

2. See, for example, *Homeri omnia quae quidem extant opera, graece, adiecta versione latina ad uerbum* (Bâle: Brylingerus & Calybaeus, 1551).

3. Cited in Pierre de Nolhac, *Ronsard et l'humanisme* (Paris, 1921), 77, quoting from BN MS. lat. 8139, fols. 103-4.

4. MS. A 184, fols. 2-21 in the Biblioteca Ambrosiana, Milan. See my article, "Ronsard and Homeric Allegory" in *Ronsard in Cambridge,* and the two articles by Geneviève Demerson, "Qui peuvent être les Lestrygons?", *Vita Latina* 70 (1978), 36-42, and

"Dorat, commentateur d'Homère," in *Etudes seiziémistes offertes à M. le professeur V.-L. Saulnier,* THR 177 (Geneva: Droz, 1980), 223-34, as well as her book *Dorat en son temps: culture classique et présence au monde* (Clermont-Ferrand: Adosa, 1983), 181-86.

5. Taken from *Seconde Response de F. de la Baronie à Messire Pierre de Ronsard, Prestre-Gentihomme Vandomois, Evesque futur. Plus le Temple de Ronsard où la Legende de sa vie est briefvement descrite* (n.p., 1563), fol. Aiiii^r, cited in Isidore Silver, *Ronsard and the Hellenic Renaissance in France,* vol. 1, *Ronsard and the Greek Epic* (St. Louis: Washington University, 1961), 39.

6. Càssola, *Inni omerici,* p. xvii: "Gl'inni minori, che vengono considerati proemi allo stesso titolo degli altri, e più spesso si giudicano gli unici veri proemi, sono in generale estratti, e più precisamente esordi e congedi, di opere più estese."

7. Quandt, *Orphei hymni,* 44.

8. They may conveniently be consulted in Alessandro Perosa's edition of *Michaelis Marulli carmina* (Zürich: Thesaurus Mundi, 1951).

9. Ivo Bruns, "Michael Marullus: ein Dichterleben der Renaissance," *Preußische Jahrbücher* 74 (1893): 122ff. For other articles on Marullus' hymns, see Pier Luigi Ciceri, "Michele Marullo e i suoi 'Hymni naturales'," *Giornale storico della letteratura italiana* 64 (1914): 289 357; Dionysios Λ. Zakythenos, "Μιχαηλ Μαρουλλος Ταρχανιγτης Ελλην ποιητης τγν χρονγν της Αναγεννησεγς", Επετηρις Εταιρειας Βυζαντινγν Σπουδγν 5 (1928): 200-42; Benedetto Croce, "Michele Marullo Tarcaniota," in *Poeti e scrittori del pieno e del tardo Rinascimento,* 3 vols. (Bari: Laterza, 1945), 2: 267-380; and my article, "The *Hymni naturales* of Michael Marullus," in *Acta conventus neo-latini Bononiensis: Proceedings of the Fourth International Congress of Neo-Latin Studies,* ed. R. J. Schoeck, Medieval & Renaissance Texts & Studies, vol. 37 (Binghamton: MRTS, 1985), 475-82.

10. Ciceri, "Michele Marullo," pp. 323 and 329.

11. A. Sainati, "Michele Marullo," in *Studi di letteratura latina medievale e umanistica raccolti in occasione del suo ottantacinquesimo compleanno* (Padua: Antenore, 1972), 150.

12. Scaliger's remarks on the hymn are to be found in *Poetices libri septem* (Lyon: Antonius Vincentius, 1561), 1. 45 (p. 49), and 3. 92-95 (pp. 162-63). There is a modern edition of Menander by D. A. Russell and N. G. Wilson: *Menander Rhetor: Edited with Translation and Commentary* (Oxford: Clarendon Press, 1981). English quotations in this chapter are taken from this edition.

13. Michel Dassonville, "Éléments pour une définition de l'hymne ronsardien," *BHR* 24 (1962): 64. This article has subsequently been printed in *Autour des "Hymnes" de Ronsard,* ed. Madeleine Lazard (Geneva: Slatkine, 1984), 1-32.

14. "Éléments pour une définition," pp. 61-63 and 71.

15. Francis Cairns, *Generic Composition in Greek and Roman Poetry* (Edinburgh: Edinburgh University Press, 1972), 92.

16. See "The Triumph of Bacchus and its Interpretation in the French Renaissance: Ronsard's 'Hinne de Bacus.'"

17. Robert Graves, *The Greek Myths,* 2 vols. (Harmondsworth: Penguin Books, 1955, reprinted 1964), 1: 230.

18. Cf. my paper on Marullus' *Hymni naturales,* 478.

19. Published in Geneva, 1978, TLF 251. See p. 29.

FURTHER READING

Criticism

Ahmed, Ehsan. "'Quel Genre de Querelle?' Pierre de Ronsard and Janne." *Romance Notes* XXXVIII, No. 3 (Spring 1998): 255-61.

Interpretation of Ronsard's "A Janne Impitoiable" which explores the poem's "poetics of misogyny."

Bizer, Marc. "The Genealogy of Poetry According to Ronsard and Julius Caesar Scaliger." *Humanistica Lovaniensia: Journal of Neo-Latin Studies* XLIII (1994): 304-18.

Considers the Renaissance debate over the superiority of Homer or Vergil in regard to the critical views of Ronsard and his contemporary Scaliger.

Campo, Roberto E. *Ronsard's Contentious Sisters: The Paragone between Poetry and Painting in the Works of Pierre de Ronsard.* Chapel Hill: University of North Carolina Press, 1998, 277 p.

Extensive study of Ronsard's poems on painting and his place in the Renaissance controversy over the relative merits of the literary and visual arts.

Campion, Edmund J. "Classical Rhetoric and Ronsard's 'Elegie sur l'excellence de l'espirit des hommes.'" *Forum* XXIX, No. 1 (Winter 1988): 35-41.

Explores Ronsard's depiction of the classical theme of the dignity of man in "Elegie sur l'excellence de l'espirit des hommes."

Conley, Tom. "Ronsard's Sonnet-Pictures." In *The Graphic Unconscious in Early Modern French Writing,* pp. 70-90. Cambridge: Cambridge University Press, 1992.

Uncovers graphical and schematic representations in Ronsard's *Amours.*

Della Neva, Jo Ann. "Petrarch at the Portal: Opening Signals in *Les Amours* of Ronsard." *Revista di Letterature moderne e comparate* L, No. 3 (August-September 1997): 259-72.

Contends that Ronsard continued to use Petrarchan images in the later variants of his love poetry.

Duval, Edwin M. "The Place of the Present: Ronsard, Aubigné, and the 'Misères de ce Temps.'" *Yale French Studies,* No. 80 (1991): 13-29.

Investigates Agrippa d'Aubigné's poetic response to Ronsard's epic historical poem of 1562, Discours des misères de ce temps, which, Duval contends, corrects Ronsard's erroneous perception of contemporary events in France.

Fenoaltea, Doranne. "A Poetic Monument: Arrangement in Book I of Ronsard's 1550 *Odes.*" In *The Ladder of High Designs: Structure and Interpretation of the French Lyric Sequence,* edited by Doranne Fenoaltea and David Lee Rubin, pp. 54-72. Charlottesville: University Press of Virginia, 1991.

Focuses on formal, thematic patterns—in the shapes of rings and interlocking rings—in Ronsard's Odes.

Lewis, John. "Helen on Lesbos: A Sapphic Echo in Ronsard's *Sonnets pour Helene?*" *French Studies Bulletin,* No. 49 (Winter 1993): 4-8.

Mentions the significance of a Sapphic fragment to Ronsard's image of himself as an immortalized poet reposing in the mythic Elysian Fields.

Rocher, Gregory de. "Ronsard's Dildo Sonnet: The Scandal of Poissy and Rasse des Noeux." In *Writing the Renaissance: Essays on Sixteenth-Century French Literature in Honor of Floyd Gray,* edited by Raymond C. La Charité, pp. 149-64. Lexington, Ky.: French Forum, 1992.

Analyzes Ronsard's poem on the subject of female autoeroticism, and examines its use in a politico-religious dispute between Protestants and Catholics.

Smith, Malcolm C. *Ronsard & Du Bellay Versus Bèze: Allusiveness in Renaissance Literary Texts.* Geneva: Librairie Droz, 1995, 142 p.

Probes Ronsard's career-long feud with the French Reformer Théodore de Bèze concerning the poet's use of classical pagan authors rather than the Bible for literary inspiration.

Weinberg, Florence M. "Double Dido: Patterns of Passion in Ronsard's *Franciade.*" In *Lapidary Inscriptions: Renaissance Essays for Donald A. Stone, Jr.,* edited by Barbara C. Bowen and Jerry C. Nash, pp. 73-85. Lexington, Ky.: French Forum, 1991.

Responds to negative critical assessments of Ronsard's use of dual heroines in the Franciade. Weinberg maintains that this doubling serves the legitimate purpose of illustrating Ronsard's interpretation of classical ideas of love and morality.

Additional coverage of Ronsard's life and career is contained in the following source published by the Gale Group: *Poetry Criticism,* **Vol. 11.**

How to Use This Index

The main references

list all author entries in the following Gale Literary Criticism series:

BLC = *Black Literature Criticism*
CLC = *Contemporary Literary Criticism*
CLR = *Children's Literature Review*
CMLC = *Classical and Medieval Literature Criticism*
DA = *DISCovering Authors*
DAB = *DISCovering Authors: British*
DAC = *DISCovering Authors: Canadian*
DAM = *DISCovering Authors: Modules*
    DRAM: *Dramatists Module;* *MST:* *Most-Studied Authors Module;*
    MULT: *Multicultural Authors Module;* *NOV:* *Novelists Module;*
    POET: *Poets Module;* *POP:* *Popular Fiction and Genre Authors Module*
DC = *Drama Criticism*
HLC = *Hispanic Literature Criticism*
LC = *Literature Criticism from 1400 to 1800*
NCLC = *Nineteenth-Century Literature Criticism*
PC = *Poetry Criticism*
SSC = *Short Story Criticism*
TCLC = *Twentieth-Century Literary Criticism*
WLC = *World Literature Criticism, 1500 to the Present*

The cross-references

list all author entries in the following Gale biographical and literary sources:

AAYA = *Authors & Artists for Young Adults*
AITN = *Authors in the News*
BEST = *Bestsellers*
BW = *Black Writers*
CA = *Contemporary Authors*
CAAS = *Contemporary Authors Autobiography Series*
CABS = *Contemporary Authors Bibliographical Series*
CANR = *Contemporary Authors New Revision Series*
CAP = *Contemporary Authors Permanent Series*
CDALB = *Concise Dictionary of American Literary Biography*
CDBLB = *Concise Dictionary of British Literary Biography*
DLB = *Dictionary of Literary Biography*
DLBD = *Dictionary of Literary Biography Documentary Series*
DLBY = *Dictionary of Literary Biography Yearbook*
HW = *Hispanic Writers*
JRDA = *Junior DISCovering Authors*
MAICYA = *Major Authors and Illustrators for Children and Young Adults*
MTCW = *Major 20th-Century Writers*
NNAL = *Native North American Literature*
SAAS = *Something about the Author Autobiography Series*
SATA = *Something about the Author*
YABC = *Yesterday's Authors of Books for Children*

Literary Criticism Series
Cumulative Author Index

Anderson, Jon (Victor) 1940- . **CLC 9; DAM POET**
    See CA 25-28R; CANR 20
Anderson, Lindsay (Gordon)
    1923-1994 .... **CLC 20**
    See CA 125; 128; 146; CANR 77
Anderson, Maxwell 1888-1959 .... **TCLC 2; DAM DRAM**
    See CA 105; 152; DLB 7; MTCW 2
Anderson, Poul (William) 1926- .... **CLC 15**
    See AAYA 5; CA 1-4R, 181; CAAE 181; CAAS 2; CANR 2, 15, 34, 64; CLR 58; DLB 8; INT CANR-15; MTCW 1, 2; SATA 90; SATA-Brief 39; SATA-Essay 106
Anderson, Robert (Woodruff)
    1917- .... **CLC 23; DAM DRAM**
    See AITN 1; CA 21-24R; CANR 32; DLB 7
Anderson, Sherwood 1876-1941 ..... **TCLC 1, 10, 24; DA; DAB; DAC; DAM MST, NOV; SSC 1; WLC**
    See AAYA 30; CA 104; 121; CANR 61; CDALB 1917-1929; DA3; DLB 4, 9, 86; DLBD 1; MTCW 1, 2
Andier, Pierre
    See Desnos, Robert
Andouard
    See Giraudoux, (Hippolyte) Jean
Andrade, Carlos Drummond de CLC 18
    See Drummond de Andrade, Carlos
Andrade, Mario de 1893-1945 .... **TCLC 43**
Andreae, Johann V(alentin)
    1586-1654 .... **LC 32**
    See DLB 164
Andreas-Salome, Lou 1861-1937 ... **TCLC 56**
    See CA 178; DLB 66
Andress, Lesley
    See Sanders, Lawrence
Andrewes, Lancelot 1555-1626 .... **LC 5**
    See DLB 151, 172
Andrews, Cicily Fairfield
    See West, Rebecca
Andrews, Elton V.
    See Pohl, Frederik
Andreyev, Leonid (Nikolaevich)
    1871-1919 .... **TCLC 3**
    See CA 104
Andric, Ivo 1892-1975 .... **CLC 8;SSC 36**
    See CA 81-84; 57-60; CANR 43, 60; DLB 147; MTCW 1
Androvar
    See Prado (Calvo), Pedro
Angelique, Pierre
    See Bataille, Georges
Angell, Roger 1920- .... **CLC 26**
    See CA 57-60; CANR 13, 44, 70; DLB 171, 185
Angelou, Maya 1928- .... **CLC 12, 35, 64, 77; BLC 1; DA; DAB; DAC; DAM MST, MULT, POET, POP; WLCS**
    See AAYA 7, 20; BW 2, 3; CA 65-68; CANR 19, 42, 65; CDALBS; CLR 53; DA3; DLB 38; MTCW 1, 2; SATA 49
Anna Comnena 1083-1153 .... **CMLC 25**
Annensky, Innokenty (Fyodorovich)
    1856-1909 .... **TCLC 14**
    See CA 110; 155
Annunzio, Gabriele d'
    See D'Annunzio, Gabriele
Anodos
    See Coleridge, Mary E(lizabeth)
Anon, Charles Robert
    See Pessoa, Fernando (Antonio Nogueira)
Anouilh, Jean (Marie Lucien Pierre)
    1910-1987 .... **CLC 1, 3, 8, 13, 40, 50; DAM DRAM; DC 8**
    See CA 17-20R; 123; CANR 32; MTCW 1, 2

Anthony, Florence
    See Ai
Anthony, John
    See Ciardi, John (Anthony)
Anthony, Peter
    See Shaffer, Anthony (Joshua); Shaffer, Peter (Levin)
Anthony, Piers 1934- ..... **CLC 35;DAM POP**
    See AAYA 11; CA 21-24R; CANR 28, 56, 73; DLB 8; MTCW 1, 2; SAAS 22; SATA 84
Anthony, Susan B(rownell)
    1916-1991 .... **TCLC 84**
    See CA 89-92; 134
Antoine, Marc
    See Proust, (Valentin-Louis-George-Eugene-) Marcel
Antoninus, Brother
    See Everson, William (Oliver)
Antonioni, Michelangelo 1912- .... **CLC 20**
    See CA 73-76; CANR 45, 77
Antschel, Paul 1920-1970
    See Celan, Paul
    See CA 85-88; CANR 33, 61; MTCW 1
Anwar, Chairil 1922-1949 .... **TCLC 22**
    See CA 121
Anzaldua, Gloria 1942-
    See CA 175; DLB 122; HLCS 1
Apess, William 1798-1839(?) .... **NCLC 73; DAM MULT**
    See DLB 175; NNAL
Apollinaire, Guillaume 1880-1918 .. **TCLC 3, 8, 51; DAM POET; PC 7**
    See Kostrowitzki, Wilhelm Apollinaris de
    See CA 152; MTCW 1
Appelfeld, Aharon 1932- .... **CLC 23, 47**
    See CA 112; 133
Apple, Max (Isaac) 1941- .... **CLC 9, 33**
    See CA 81-84; CANR 19, 54; DLB 130
Appleman, Philip (Dean) 1926- .... **CLC 51**
    See CA 13-16R; CAAS 18; CANR 6, 29, 56
Appleton, Lawrence
    See Lovecraft, H(oward) P(hillips)
Apteryx
    See Eliot, T(homas) S(tearns)
Apuleius, (Lucius Madaurensis)
    125(?)-175(?) .... **CMLC 1**
    See DLB 211
Aquin, Hubert 1929-1977 .... **CLC 15**
    See CA 105; DLB 53
Aquinas,Thomas 1224(?)-1274 ...... **CMLC 33**
    See DLB 115
Aragon, Louis 1897-1982 .. **CLC 3, 22; DAM NOV, POET**
    See CA 69-72; 108; CANR 28, 71; DLB 72; MTCW 1, 2
Arany, Janos 1817-1882 .... **NCLC 34**
Aranyos, Kakay
    See Mikszath, Kalman
Arbuthnot, John 1667-1735 .... **LC 1**
    See DLB 101
Archer, Herbert Winslow
    See Mencken, H(enry) L(ouis)
Archer, Jeffrey (Howard) 1940- ...... **CLC 28; DAM POP**
    See AAYA 16; BEST 89:3; CA 77-80; CANR 22, 52; DA3; INT CANR-22
Archer, Jules 1915- .... **CLC 12**
    See CA 9-12R; CANR 6, 69; SAAS 5; SATA 4, 85
Archer, Lee
    See Ellison, Harlan (Jay)
Arden, John 1930- .... **CLC 6, 13, 15;DAM DRAM**
    See CA 13-16R; CAAS 4; CANR 31, 65, 67; DLB 13; MTCW 1

Arenas, Reinaldo 1943-1990 . **CLC 41; DAM MULT; HLC 1**
    See CA 124; 128; 133; CANR 73; DLB 145; HW 1; MTCW 1
Arendt, Hannah 1906-1975 .... **CLC 66,98**
    See CA 17-20R; 61-64; CANR 26, 60; MTCW 1, 2
Aretino, Pietro 1492-1556 .... **LC 12**
Arghezi, Tudor 1880-1967 .... **CLC 80**
    See Theodorescu, Ion N.
    See CA 167
Arguedas, Jose Maria 1911-1969 .... **CLC 10, 18; HLCS 1**
    See CA 89-92; CANR 73; DLB 113; HW 1
Argueta, Manlio 1936- .... **CLC 31**
    See CA 131; CANR 73; DLB 145; HW 1
Arias, Ron(ald Francis) 1941-
    See CA 131; CANR 81; DAM MULT; DLB 82; HLC 1; HW 1, 2; MTCW 2
Ariosto, Ludovico 1474-1533 .... **LC 6**
Aristides
    See Epstein, Joseph
Aristophanes 450B.C.-385B.C. .... **CMLC 4; DA; DAB; DAC; DAM DRAM, MST; DC 2; WLCS**
    See DA3; DLB 176
Aristotle 384B.C.-322B.C. .... **CMLC 31; DA; DAB; DAC; DAM MST; WLCS**
    See DA3; DLB 176
Arlt, Roberto (Godofredo Christophersen)
    1900-1942 .... **TCLC 29; DAM MULT; HLC 1**
    See CA 123; 131; CANR 67; HW 1, 2
Armah, Ayi Kwei 1939- . **CLC 5, 33; BLC 1; DAM MULT, POET**
    See BW 1; CA 61-64; CANR 21, 64; DLB 117; MTCW 1
Armatrading, Joan 1950- .... **CLC 17**
    See CA 114
Arnette, Robert
    See Silverberg, Robert
Arnim, Achim von (Ludwig Joachim von Arnim) 1781-1831 ..... **NCLC 5; SSC 29**
    See DLB 90
Arnim, Bettina von 1785-1859 .... **NCLC 38**
    See DLB 90
Arnold, Matthew 1822-1888 ..... **NCLC 6, 29; DA; DAB; DAC; DAM MST, POET; PC 5; WLC**
    See CDBLB 1832-1890; DLB 32, 57
Arnold, Thomas 1795-1842 .... **NCLC 18**
    See DLB 55
Arnow, Harriette (Louisa) Simpson
    1908-1986 .... **CLC 2, 7, 18**
    See CA 9-12R; 118; CANR 14; DLB 6; MTCW 1, 2; SATA 42; SATA-Obit 47
Arouet, Francois-Marie
    See Voltaire
Arp, Hans
    See Arp, Jean
Arp, Jean 1887-1966 .... **CLC 5**
    See CA 81-84; 25-28R; CANR 42, 77
Arrabal
    See Arrabal, Fernando
Arrabal, Fernando 1932- ... **CLC 2, 9, 18, 58**
    See CA 9-12R; CANR 15
Arreola, Juan Jose 1918-
    See CA 113; 131; CANR 81; DAM MULT; DLB 113; HLC 1; HW 1, 2
Arrick, Fran CLC 30
    See Gaberman, Judie Angell
Artaud, Antonin (Marie Joseph)
    1896-1948 .. **TCLC 3, 36; DAM DRAM**
    See CA 104; 149; DA3; MTCW 1
Arthur, Ruth M(abel) 1905-1979 ..... **CLC 12**
    See CA 9-12R; 85-88; CANR 4; SATA 7, 26

Ballard, J(ames) G(raham) 1930- . **CLC 3, 6, 14, 36; DAM NOV, POP; SSC 1**
See AAYA 3; CA 5-8R; CANR 15, 39, 65; DA3; DLB 14, 207; MTCW 1, 2; SATA 93

Balmont, Konstantin (Dmitriyevich) 1867-1943 .... **TCLC 11**
See CA 109; 155

Baltausis, Vincas
See Mikszath, Kalman

Balzac, Honore de 1799-1850 ... **NCLC 5, 35, 53; DA; DAB; DAC; DAM MST, NOV; SSC 5; WLC**
See DA3; DLB 119

Bambara, Toni Cade 1939-1995 ...... **CLC 19, 88; BLC 1; DA; DAC; DAM MST, MULT; SSC 35; WLCS**
See AAYA 5; BW 2, 3; CA 29-32R; 150; CANR 24, 49, 81; CDALBS; DA3; DLB 38; MTCW 1, 2

Bamdad, A.
See Shamlu, Ahmad

Banat, D. R.
See Bradbury, Ray (Douglas)

Bancroft, Laura
See Baum, L(yman) Frank

Banim, John 1798-1842 .... **NCLC 13**
See DLB 116, 158, 159

Banim, Michael 1796-1874 .... **NCLC 13**
See DLB 158, 159

Banjo, The
See Paterson, A(ndrew) B(arton)

Banks, Iain
See Banks, Iain M(enzies)

Banks, Iain M(enzies) 1954- .... **CLC 34**
See CA 123; 128; CANR 61; DLB 194; INT 128

Banks, Lynne Reid CLC 23
See Reid Banks, Lynne
See AAYA 6

Banks, Russell 1940- .... **CLC 37, 72**
See CA 65-68; CAAS 15; CANR 19, 52, 73; DLB 130

Banville, John 1945- .... **CLC 46, 118**
See CA 117; 128; DLB 14; INT 128

Banville, Theodore (Faullain) de 1832-1891 .... **NCLC 9**

Baraka, Amiri 1934- . **CLC 1, 2, 3, 5, 10, 14, 33, 115; BLC 1; DA; DAC; DAM MST, MULT, POET, POP; DC 6; PC 4; WLCS**
See Jones, LeRoi
See BW 2, 3; CA 21-24R; CABS 3; CANR 27, 38, 61; CDALB 1941-1968; DA3; DLB 5, 7, 16, 38; DLBD 8; MTCW 1, 2

Barbauld, Anna Laetitia 1743-1825 .... **NCLC 50**
See DLB 107, 109, 142, 158

Barbellion, W. N. P. TCLC 24
See Cummings, Bruce F(rederick)

Barbera, Jack (Vincent) 1945- .... **CLC 44**
See CA 110; CANR 45

Barbey d'Aurevilly, Jules Amedee 1808-1889 .... **NCLC 1; SSC 17**
See DLB 119

Barbour, John c. 1316-1395 .... **CMLC 33**
See DLB 146

Barbusse, Henri 1873-1935 .... **TCLC 5**
See CA 105; 154; DLB 65

Barclay, Bill
See Moorcock, Michael (John)

Barclay, William Ewert
See Moorcock, Michael (John)

Barea, Arturo 1897-1957 .... **TCLC 14**
See CA 111

Barfoot, Joan 1946- .... **CLC 18**
See CA 105

Barham, Richard Harris 1788-1845 .... **NCLC 77**
See DLB 159

Baring, Maurice 1874-1945 .... **TCLC 8**
See CA 105; 168; DLB 34

Baring-Gould, Sabine 1834-1924 ... **TCLC 88**
See DLB 156, 190

Barker, Clive 1952- .... **CLC 52;DAM POP**
See AAYA 10; BEST 90:3; CA 121; 129; CANR 71; DA3; INT 129; MTCW 1, 2

Barker, George Granville 1913-1991 .... **CLC 8, 48; DAM POET**
See CA 9-12R; 135; CANR 7, 38; DLB 20; MTCW 1

Barker, Harley Granville
See Granville-Barker, Harley
See DLB 10

Barker, Howard 1946- .... **CLC 37**
See CA 102; DLB 13

Barker, Jane 1652-1732 .... **LC 42**

Barker, Pat(ricia) 1943- .... **CLC 32, 94**
See CA 117; 122; CANR 50; INT 122

Barlach, Ernst (Heinrich) 1870-1938 .... **TCLC 84**
See CA 178; DLB 56, 118

Barlow, Joel 1754-1812 .... **NCLC 23**
See DLB 37

Barnard, Mary (Ethel) 1909- .... **CLC 48**
See CA 21-22; CAP 2

Barnes, Djuna 1892-1982 .... **CLC 3, 4, 8, 11, 29; SSC 3**
See CA 9-12R; 107; CANR 16, 55; DLB 4, 9, 45; MTCW 1, 2

Barnes, Julian (Patrick) 1946- .... **CLC 42; DAB**
See CA 102; CANR 19, 54; DLB 194; DLBY 93; MTCW 1

Barnes, Peter 1931- .... **CLC 5, 56**
See CA 65-68; CAAS 12; CANR 33, 34, 64; DLB 13; MTCW 1

Barnes, William 1801-1886 .... **NCLC 75**
See DLB 32

Baroja (y Nessi), Pio 1872-1956 ..... **TCLC 8; HLC 1**
See CA 104

Baron, David
See Pinter, Harold

Baron Corvo
See Rolfe, Frederick (William Serafino Austin Lewis Mary)

Barondess, Sue K(aufman) 1926-1977 .... **CLC 8**
See Kaufman, Sue
See CA 1-4R; 69-72; CANR 1

Baron de Teive
See Pessoa, Fernando (Antonio Nogueira)

Baroness Von S.
See Zangwill, Israel

Barres, (Auguste-)Maurice 1862-1923 .... **TCLC 47**
See CA 164; DLB 123

Barreto, Afonso Henrique de Lima
See Lima Barreto, Afonso Henrique de

Barrett, (Roger) Syd 1946- .... **CLC 35**

Barrett, William (Christopher) 1913-1992 .... **CLC 27**
See CA 13-16R; 139; CANR 11, 67; INT CANR-11

Barrie, J(ames) M(atthew) 1860-1937 .... **TCLC 2; DAB; DAM DRAM**
See CA 104; 136; CANR 77; CDBLB 1890-1914; CLR 16; DA3; DLB 10, 141, 156; MAICYA; MTCW 1; SATA 100; YABC 1

Barrington, Michael
See Moorcock, Michael (John)

Barrol, Grady
See Bograd, Larry

Barry, Mike
See Malzberg, Barry N(athaniel)

Barry, Philip 1896-1949 .... **TCLC 11**
See CA 109; DLB 7

Bart, Andre Schwarz
See Schwarz-Bart, Andre

Barth, John (Simmons) 1930- ... **CLC 1, 2, 3, 5, 7, 9, 10, 14, 27, 51, 89; DAM NOV; SSC 10**
See AITN 1, 2; CA 1-4R; CABS 1; CANR 5, 23, 49, 64; DLB 2; MTCW 1

Barthelme, Donald 1931-1989 ... **CLC 1, 2, 3, 5, 6, 8, 13, 23, 46, 59, 115; DAM NOV; SSC 2**
See CA 21-24R; 129; CANR 20, 58; DA3; DLB 2; DLBY 80, 89; MTCW 1, 2; SATA 7; SATA-Obit 62

Barthelme, Frederick 1943- ...... **CLC 36, 117**
See CA 114; 122; CANR 77; DLBY 85; INT 122

Barthes, Roland (Gerard) 1915-1980 .... **CLC 24, 83**
See CA 130; 97-100; CANR 66; MTCW 1, 2

Barzun, Jacques (Martin) 1907- ...... **CLC 51**
See CA 61-64; CANR 22

Bashevis, Isaac
See Singer, Isaac Bashevis

Bashkirtseff, Marie 1859-1884 .... **NCLC 27**

Basho
See Matsuo Basho

Basil of Caesaria c. 330-379 .... **CMLC 35**

Bass, Kingsley B., Jr.
See Bullins, Ed

Bass, Rick 1958- .... **CLC 79**
See CA 126; CANR 53; DLB 212

Bassani, Giorgio 1916- .... **CLC 9**
See CA 65-68; CANR 33; DLB 128, 177; MTCW 1

Bastos, Augusto (Antonio) Roa
See Roa Bastos, Augusto (Antonio)

Bataille, Georges 1897-1962 .... **CLC 29**
See CA 101; 89-92

Bates, H(erbert) E(rnest) 1905-1974 . **CLC 46; DAB; DAM POP; SSC 10**
See CA 93-96; 45-48; CANR 34; DA3; DLB 162, 191; MTCW 1, 2

Bauchart
See Camus, Albert

Baudelaire, Charles 1821-1867 . **NCLC 6, 29, 55; DA; DAB; DAC; DAM MST, POET; PC 1; SSC 18; WLC**
See DA3

Baudrillard, Jean 1929- .... **CLC 60**

Baum, L(yman) Frank 1856-1919 ... **TCLC 7**
See CA 108; 133; CLR 15; DLB 22; JRDA; MAICYA; MTCW 1, 2; SATA 18, 100

Baum, Louis F.
See Baum, L(yman) Frank

Baumbach, Jonathan 1933- .... **CLC 6,23**
See CA 13-16R; CAAS 5; CANR 12, 66; DLBY 80; INT CANR-12; MTCW 1

Bausch, Richard (Carl) 1945- .... **CLC 51**
See CA 101; CAAS 14; CANR 43, 61; DLB 130

Baxter, Charles (Morley) 1947- .... **CLC 45, 78; DAM POP**
See CA 57-60; CANR 40, 64; DLB 130; MTCW 2

Baxter, George Owen
See Faust, Frederick (Schiller)

Baxter, James K(eir) 1926-1972 .... **CLC 14**
See CA 77-80

Baxter, John
See Hunt, E(verette) Howard, (Jr.)

Bayer, Sylvia
See Glassco, John

Boyle, Mark
See Kienzle, William X(avier)
Boyle, Patrick 1905-1982 .... **CLC 19**
See CA 127
Boyle, T. C. 1948-
See Boyle, T(homas) Coraghessan
Boyle, T(homas) Coraghessan
1948- .... **CLC 36, 55, 90; DAM POP;**
SSC 16
See BEST 90:4; CA 120; CANR 44, 76;
DA3; DLBY 86; MTCW 2
Boz
See Dickens, Charles (John Huffam)
Brackenridge, Hugh Henry
1748-1816 .... **NCLC 7**
See DLB 11, 37
Bradbury, Edward P.
See Moorcock, Michael (John)
See MTCW 2
Bradbury, Malcolm (Stanley)
1932- .... **CLC 32, 61; DAM NOV**
See CA 1-4R; CANR 1, 33; DA3; DLB 14,
207; MTCW 1, 2
Bradbury, Ray (Douglas) 1920- .... **CLC 1, 3,**
10, 15, 42, 98; DA; DAB; DAC; DAM
MST, NOV, POP; SSC 29; WLC
See AAYA 15; AITN 1, 2; CA 1-4R; CANR
2, 30, 75; CDALB 1968-1988; DA3; DLB
2, 8; MTCW 1, 2; SATA 11, 64
Bradford, Gamaliel 1863-1932 .... **TCLC 36**
See CA 160; DLB 17
Bradley, David (Henry), Jr. 1950- ... **CLC 23,**
118; BLC 1; DAM MULT
See BW 1, 3; CA 104; CANR 26, 81; DLB
33
Bradley, John Ed(mund,Jr.) 1958- ... **CLC 55**
See CA 139
Bradley, Marion Zimmer 1930- ...... **CLC 30;**
DAM POP
See AAYA 9; CA 57-60; CAAS 10; CANR
7, 31, 51, 75; DA3; DLB 8; MTCW 1, 2;
SATA 90
Bradstreet, Anne 1612(?)-1672 ...... **LC 4, 30;**
DA; DAC; DAM MST, POET; PC 10
See CDALB 1640-1865; DA3; DLB 24
Brady, Joan 1939- .... **CLC 86**
See CA 141
Bragg, Melvyn 1939- .... **CLC 10**
See BEST 89:3; CA 57-60; CANR 10, 48;
DLB 14
Brahe, Tycho 1546-1601 .... **LC 45**
Braine, John (Gerard) 1922-1986 . **CLC 1, 3,**
41
See CA 1-4R; 120; CANR 1, 33; CDBLB
1945-1960; DLB 15; DLBY 86; MTCW 1
Bramah, Ernest 1868-1942 .... **TCLC 72**
See CA 156; DLB 70
Brammer, William 1930(?)-1978 ...... **CLC 31**
See CA 77-80
Brancati, Vitaliano 1907-1954 .... **TCLC 12**
See CA 109
Brancato, Robin F(idler) 1936- .... **CLC 35**
See AAYA 9; CA 69-72; CANR 11, 45;
CLR 32; JRDA; SAAS 9; SATA 97
Brand, Max
See Faust, Frederick (Schiller)
Brand, Millen 1906-1980 .... **CLC 7**
See CA 21-24R; 97-100; CANR 72
Branden, Barbara **CLC 44**
See CA 148
Brandes, Georg (Morris Cohen)
1842-1927 .... **TCLC 10**
See CA 105
Brandys, Kazimierz 1916- .... **CLC 62**
Branley, Franklyn M(ansfield)
1915- .... **CLC 21**
See CA 33-36R; CANR 14, 39; CLR 13;
MAICYA; SAAS 16; SATA 4, 68

Brathwaite, Edward (Kamau)
1930- ...... **CLC 11; BLCS; DAM POET**
See BW 2, 3; CA 25-28R; CANR 11, 26,
47; DLB 125
Brautigan, Richard (Gary)
1935-1984 .... **CLC 1, 3, 5, 9, 12, 34, 42;**
DAM NOV
See CA 53-56; 113; CANR 34; DA3; DLB
2, 5, 206; DLBY 80, 84; MTCW 1; SATA
56
Brave Bird, Mary 1953-
See Crow Dog, Mary (Ellen)
See NNAL
Braverman, Kate 1950- .... **CLC 67**
See CA 89-92
Brecht, (Eugen) Bertolt (Friedrich)
1898-1956 .... **TCLC 1, 6, 13, 35; DA;**
DAB; DAC; DAM DRAM, MST; DC
3; WLC
See CA 104; 133; CANR 62; DA3; DLB
56, 124; MTCW 1, 2
Brecht, Eugen Berthold Friedrich
See Brecht, (Eugen) Bertolt (Friedrich)
Bremer, Fredrika 1801-1865 .... **NCLC 11**
Brennan, ChristopherJohn
1870-1932 .... **TCLC 17**
See CA 117
Brennan, Maeve 1917-1993 .... **CLC 5**
See CA 81-84; CANR 72
Brent, Linda
See Jacobs, Harriet A(nn)
Brentano, Clemens (Maria)
1778-1842 .... **NCLC 1**
See DLB 90
Brent of Bin Bin
See Franklin, (Stella Maria Sarah) Miles
(Lampe)
Brenton, Howard 1942- .... **CLC 31**
See CA 69-72; CANR 33, 67; DLB 13;
MTCW 1
Breslin, James 1930-1996
See Breslin, Jimmy
See CA 73-76; CANR 31, 75; DAM NOV;
MTCW 1, 2
Breslin, Jimmy **CLC 4, 43**
See Breslin, James
See AITN 1; DLB 185; MTCW 2
Bresson, Robert 1901- .... **CLC 16**
See CA 110; CANR 49
Breton, Andre 1896-1966 .. **CLC 2, 9, 15, 54;**
PC 15
See CA 19-20; 25-28R; CANR 40, 60; CAP
2; DLB 65; MTCW 1, 2
Breytenbach, Breyten 1939(?)- . **CLC 23, 37;**
DAM POET
See CA 113; 129; CANR 61
Bridgers, Sue Ellen 1942- .... **CLC 26**
See AAYA 8; CA 65-68; CANR 11, 36;
CLR 18; DLB 52; JRDA; MAICYA;
SAAS 1; SATA 22, 90; SATA-Essay 109
Bridges, Robert (Seymour)
1844-1930 ... **TCLC 1; DAM POET; PC**
28
See CA 104; 152; CDBLB 1890-1914; DLB
19, 98
Bridie, James **TCLC 3**
See Mavor, Osborne Henry
See DLB 10
Brin, David 1950- .... **CLC 34**
See AAYA 21; CA 102; CANR 24, 70; INT
CANR-24; SATA 65
Brink, Andre (Philippus) 1935- . **CLC 18, 36,**
106
See CA 104; CANR 39, 62; INT 103;
MTCW 1, 2
Brinsmead, H(esba) F(ay) 1922- ...... **CLC 21**
See CA 21-24R; CANR 10; CLR 47; MAI-
CYA; SAAS 5; SATA 18, 78

Brittain, Vera (Mary) 1893(?)-1970 . **CLC 23**
See CA 13-16; 25-28R; CANR 58; CAP 1;
DLB 191; MTCW 1, 2
Broch, Hermann 1886-1951 .... **TCLC 20**
See CA 117; DLB 85, 124
Brock, Rose
See Hansen, Joseph
Brodkey, Harold (Roy) 1930-1996 ... **CLC 56**
See CA 111; 151; CANR 71; DLB 130
Brodskii, Iosif
See Brodsky, Joseph
Brodsky, Iosif Alexandrovich 1940-1996
See Brodsky, Joseph
See AITN 1; CA 41-44R; 151; CANR 37;
DAM POET; DA3; MTCW 1, 2
Brodsky, Joseph 1940-1996 ..... **CLC 4, 6, 13,**
36, 100; PC 9
See Brodskii, Iosif; Brodsky, Iosif Alexan-
drovich
See MTCW 1
Brodsky, Michael (Mark) 1948- .... **CLC 19**
See CA 102; CANR 18, 41, 58
Bromell, Henry 1947- .... **CLC 5**
See CA 53-56; CANR 9
Bromfield, Louis (Brucker)
1896-1956 .... **TCLC 11**
See CA 107; 155; DLB 4, 9, 86
Broner, E(sther) M(asserman)
1930- .... **CLC 19**
See CA 17-20R; CANR 8, 25, 72; DLB 28
Bronk, William(M.) 1918-1999 .... **CLC 10**
See CA 89-92; 177; CANR 23; DLB 165
Bronstein, Lev Davidovich
See Trotsky, Leon
Bronte, Anne 1820-1849 .... **NCLC 71**
See DA3; DLB 21, 199
Bronte, Charlotte 1816-1855 ...... **NCLC 3, 8,**
33, 58; DA; DAB; DAC; DAM MST,
NOV; WLC
See AAYA 17; CDBLB 1832-1890; DA3;
DLB 21, 159, 199
Bronte, Emily (Jane) 1818-1848 ... **NCLC 16,**
35; DA; DAB; DAC; DAM MST, NOV,
POET; PC 8; WLC
See AAYA 17;CDBLB 1832-1890; DA3;
DLB 21, 32, 199
Brooke, Frances 1724-1789 .... **LC 6, 48**
See DLB 39, 99
Brooke, Henry 1703(?)-1783 .... **LC 1**
See DLB 39
Brooke, Rupert (Chawner)
1887-1915 .... **TCLC 2, 7; DA; DAB;**
DAC; DAM MST, POET; PC 24; WLC
See CA 104; 132; CANR 61; CDBLB 1914-
1945; DLB 19; MTCW 1, 2
Brooke-Haven, P.
See Wodehouse, P(elham) G(renville)
Brooke-Rose, Christine 1926(?)- ...... **CLC 40**
See CA 13-16R; CANR 58; DLB 14
Brookner, Anita 1928- .... **CLC 32, 34, 51;**
DAB; DAM POP
See CA 114; 120; CANR 37, 56; DA3; DLB
194; DLBY 87; MTCW 1, 2
Brooks, Cleanth 1906-1994 . **CLC 24, 86, 110**
See CA 17-20R; 145; CANR 33, 35; DLB
63; DLBY 94; INT CANR-35; MTCW 1,
2
Brooks, George
See Baum, L(yman) Frank
Brooks, Gwendolyn 1917- ..... **CLC 1, 2, 4, 5,**
15, 49, 125; BLC 1; DA; DAC; DAM
MST, MULT, POET; PC 7;WLC
See AAYA 20; AITN 1; BW 2, 3; CA 1-4R;
CANR 1, 27, 52, 75; CDALB 1941-1968;
CLR 27; DA3; DLB 5, 76, 165; MTCW
1, 2; SATA 6
Brooks, Mel **CLC 12**
See Kaminsky, Melvin
See AAYA 13; DLB 26

Burroughs, William S(eward)
1914-1997 .. **CLC 1, 2, 5, 15, 22, 42, 75, 109; DA; DAB; DAC; DAM MST, NOV, POP; WLC**
See AITN 2; CA 9-12R; 160; CANR 20, 52; DA3; DLB 2, 8, 16, 152; DLBY 81, 97; MTCW 1, 2

Burton, Sir Richard F(rancis)
1821-1890 .... **NCLC 42**
See DLB 55, 166, 184

Busch, Frederick 1941- .... **CLC 7, 10, 18, 47**
See CA 33-36R; CAAS 1; CANR 45, 73; DLB 6

Bush, Ronald 1946- .... **CLC 34**
See CA 136

Bustos, F(rancisco)
See Borges, Jorge Luis

Bustos Domecq, H(onorio)
See Bioy Casares, Adolfo; Borges, Jorge Luis

Butler, Octavia E(stelle) 1947- .... **CLC 38, 121; BLCS; DAM MULT, POP**
See AAYA 18; BW 2, 3; CA 73-76; CANR 12, 24, 38, 73; DA3; DLB 33; MTCW 1, 2; SATA 84

Butler, Robert Olen (Jr.) 1945- .... **CLC 81; DAM POP**
See CA 112; CANR 66; DLB 173; INT 112; MTCW 1

Butler, Samuel 1612-1680 .... **LC 16, 43**
See DLB 101, 126

Butler, Samuel 1835-1902 . **TCLC 1, 33; DA; DAB; DAC; DAM MST, NOV; WLC**
See CA 143; CDBLB 1890-1914; DA3; DLB 18, 57, 174

Butler, Walter C.
See Faust, Frederick (Schiller)

Butor, Michel (Marie Francois)
1926- .... **CLC 1, 3, 8, 11, 15**
See CA 9-12R; CANR 33, 66; DLB 83; MTCW 1, 2

Butts, Mary 1892(?)-1937 .... **TCLC 77**
See CA 148

Buzo, Alexander(John) 1944- .... **CLC 61**
See CA 97-100; CANR 17, 39, 69

Buzzati, Dino 1906-1972 .... **CLC 36**
See CA 160; 33-36R; DLB 177

Byars, Betsy (Cromer) 1928- .... **CLC 35**
See AAYA 19; CA 33-36R; CANR 18, 36, 57; CLR 1, 16; DLB 52; INT CANR-18; JRDA; MAICYA; MTCW 1; SAAS 1; SATA 4, 46, 80; SATA-Essay 108

Byatt, A(ntonia) S(usan Drabble)
1936- ..... **CLC 19, 65; DAM NOV, POP**
See CA 13-16R; CANR 13, 33, 50, 75; DA3; DLB 14, 194; MTCW 1, 2

Byrne, David 1952- .... **CLC 26**
See CA 127

Byrne, John Keyes 1926-
See Leonard, Hugh
See CA 102; CANR 78; INT 102

Byron, George Gordon (Noel)
1788-1824 .... **NCLC 2, 12; DA; DAB; DAC; DAM MST, POET; PC 16; WLC**
See CDBLB 1789-1832; DA3; DLB 96, 110

Byron, Robert 1905-1941 .... **TCLC 67**
See CA 160; DLB 195

C. 3. 3.
See Wilde, Oscar

Caballero, Fernan 1796-1877 .... **NCLC 10**

Cabell, Branch
See Cabell, James Branch

Cabell, James Branch 1879-1958 .... **TCLC 6**
See CA 105; 152; DLB 9, 78; MTCW 1

Cable, George Washington
1844-1925 .... **TCLC 4; SSC 4**
See CA 104; 155; DLB 12, 74; DLBD 13

Cabral de Melo Neto, Joao 1920- ... **CLC 76; DAM MULT**
See CA 151

Cabrera Infante, G(uillermo) 1929- . **CLC 5, 25, 45, 120; DAM MULT; HLC 1**
See CA 85-88; CANR 29, 65; DA3; DLB 113; HW 1, 2; MTCW 1, 2

Cade, Toni
See Bambara, Toni Cade

Cadmus and Harmonia
See Buchan, John

Caedmon fl. 658-680 .... **CMLC 7**
See DLB 146

Caeiro, Alberto
See Pessoa, Fernando (Antonio Nogueira)

Cage, John (Milton,Jr.) 1912-1992 ... **CLC 41**
See CA 13-16R; 169; CANR 9, 78; DLB 193; INT CANR-9

Cahan, Abraham 1860-1951 .... **TCLC 71**
See CA 108; 154; DLB 9, 25, 28

Cain, G.
See Cabrera Infante, G(uillermo)

Cain, Guillermo
See Cabrera Infante, G(uillermo)

Cain, James M(allahan) 1892-1977 .. **CLC 3, 11, 28**
See AITN 1; CA 17-20R; 73-76; CANR 8, 34, 61; MTCW 1

Caine, Mark
See Raphael, Frederic (Michael)

Calasso, Roberto 1941- .... **CLC 81**
See CA 143

Calderon de la Barca, Pedro
1600-1681 .... **LC 23; DC 3; HLCS 1**

Caldwell, Erskine (Preston)
1903-1987 .. **CLC 1, 8, 14, 50, 60; DAM NOV; SSC 19**
See AITN 1; CA 1-4R; 121; CAAS 1; CANR 2, 33; DA3; DLB 9, 86; MTCW 1, 2

Caldwell, (Janet Miriam) Taylor (Holland)
1900-1985 .. **CLC 2, 28, 39; DAM NOV, POP**
See CA 5-8R; 116; CANR 5; DA3; DLBD 17

Calhoun, John Caldwell
1782-1850 .... **NCLC 15**
See DLB 3

Calisher, Hortense 1911- ..... **CLC 2, 4, 8, 38; DAM NOV; SSC 15**
See CA 1-4R; CANR 1, 22, 67; DA3; DLB 2; INT CANR-22; MTCW 1, 2

Callaghan, Morley Edward
1903-1990 ...... **CLC 3, 14, 41, 65; DAC; DAM MST**
See CA 9-12R; 132; CANR 33, 73; DLB 68; MTCW 1, 2

Callimachus c.
305B.C.-c.240B.C. .... **CMLC 18**
See DLB 176

Calvin, John 1509-1564 .... **LC 37**

Calvino, Italo 1923-1985 .... **CLC 5, 8, 11, 22, 33, 39, 73; DAM NOV; SSC 3**
See CA 85-88; 116; CANR 23, 61; DLB 196; MTCW 1, 2

Cameron, Carey 1952- .... **CLC 59**
See CA 135

Cameron, Peter 1959- .... **CLC 44**
See CA 125; CANR 50

Camoens, Luis Vaz de 1524(?)-1580
See HLCS 1

Camoes, Luis de 1524(?)-1580
See HLCS 1

Campana, Dino 1885-1932 .... **TCLC 20**
See CA 117; DLB 114

Campanella, Tommaso 1568-1639 .... **LC 32**

Campbell, John W(ood,Jr.)
1910-1971 .... **CLC 32**
See CA 21-22; 29-32R; CANR 34; CAP 2; DLB 8; MTCW 1

Campbell, Joseph 1904-1987 .... **CLC 69**
See AAYA 3; BEST 89:2; CA 1-4R; 124; CANR 3, 28, 61; DA3; MTCW 1, 2

Campbell, Maria 1940- .... **CLC 85; DAC**
See CA 102; CANR 54; NNAL

Campbell, (John) Ramsey 1946- ..... **CLC 42; SSC 19**
See CA 57-60; CANR 7; INT CANR-7

Campbell, (Ignatius) Roy (Dunnachie)
1901-1957 .... **TCLC 5**
See CA 104; 155; DLB 20; MTCW 2

Campbell, Thomas 1777-1844 .... **NCLC 19**
See DLB 93; 144

Campbell, Wilfred TCLC 9
See Campbell, William

Campbell, William 1858(?)-1918
See Campbell, Wilfred
See CA 106; DLB 92

Campion, Jane CLC 95
See CA 138

Campos, Alvaro de
See Pessoa, Fernando (Antonio Nogueira)

Camus, Albert 1913-1960 ...... **CLC 1, 2, 4, 9, 11, 14, 32, 63, 69, 124; DA; DAB; DAC; DAM DRAM, MST, NOV; DC 2; SSC 9;WLC**
See CA 89-92; DA3; DLB 72; MTCW 1, 2

Canby, Vincent 1924- .... **CLC 13**
See CA 81-84

Cancale
See Desnos, Robert

Canetti, Elias 1905-1994 .. **CLC 3, 14, 25, 75, 86**
See CA 21-24R; 146; CANR 23, 61, 79; DA3; DLB 85, 124; MTCW 1, 2

Canfield, Dorothea F.
See Fisher, Dorothy (Frances) Canfield

Canfield, Dorothea Frances
See Fisher, Dorothy (Frances) Canfield

Canfield, Dorothy
See Fisher, Dorothy (Frances) Canfield

Canin, Ethan 1960- .... **CLC 55**
See CA 131; 135

Cannon, Curt
See Hunter, Evan

Cao, Lan 1961- .... **CLC 109**
See CA 165

Cape, Judith
See Page, P(atricia) K(athleen)

Capek, Karel 1890-1938 ... **TCLC 6, 37; DA; DAB; DAC; DAM DRAM, MST, NOV; DC 1; SSC 36; WLC**
See CA 104; 140; DA3; MTCW 1

Capote, Truman 1924-1984 . **CLC 1, 3, 8, 13, 19, 34, 38, 58; DA; DAB; DAC; DAM MST, NOV, POP; SSC 2; WLC**
See CA 5-8R; 113; CANR 18, 62; CDALB 1941-1968; DA3; DLB 2, 185; DLBY 80, 84; MTCW 1, 2; SATA 91

Capra, Frank 1897-1991 .... **CLC 16**
See CA 61-64; 135

Caputo, Philip 1941- .... **CLC 32**
See CA 73-76; CANR 40

Caragiale, Ion Luca 1852-1912 ...... **TCLC 76**
See CA 157

Card, Orson Scott 1951- ..... **CLC 44, 47, 50; DAM POP**
See AAYA 11; CA 102; CANR 27, 47, 73; DA3; INT CANR-27; MTCW 1, 2; SATA 83

Cardenal, Ernesto 1925- .... **CLC 31; DAM MULT, POET; HLC 1; PC 22**
See CA 49-52; CANR 2, 32, 66; HW 1, 2; MTCW 1, 2

Chambers, Aidan 1934- .... **CLC 35**
See AAYA 27; CA 25-28R; CANR 12, 31, 58; JRDA; MAICYA; SAAS 12; SATA 1, 69, 108

Chambers, James 1948-
See Cliff, Jimmy
See CA 124

Chambers, Jessie
See Lawrence, D(avid) H(erbert Richards)

Chambers, RobertW(illiam)
1865-1933 .... **TCLC 41**
See CA 165; DLB 202; SATA 107

Chandler, Raymond (Thornton)
1888-1959 .... **TCLC 1, 7; SSC 23**
See AAYA 25; CA 104; 129; CANR 60;CDALB 1929-1941; DA3; DLBD 6; MTCW 1, 2

Chang, Eileen 1920-1995 .... **SSC 28**
See CA 166

Chang, Jung 1952- .... **CLC 71**
See CA 142

Chang Ai-Ling
See Chang, Eileen

Channing, William Ellery
1780-1842 .... **NCLC 17**
See DLB 1, 59

Chao, Patricia 1955- .... **CLC 119**
See CA 163

Chaplin, Charles Spencer
1889-1977 .... **CLC 16**
See Chaplin, Charlie
See CA 81-84; 73-76

Chaplin, Charlie
See Chaplin, Charles Spencer
See DLB 44

Chapman, George 1559(?)-1634 .... **LC 22; DAM DRAM**
See DLB 62, 121

Chapman, Graham 1941-1989 .... **CLC 21**
See Monty Python
See CA 116; 129; CANR 35

Chapman, John Jay 1862-1933 .... **TCLC 7**
See CA 104

Chapman, Lee
See Bradley, Marion Zimmer

Chapman, Walker
See Silverberg, Robert

Chappell, Fred (Davis) 1936- ..... **CLC 40, 78**
See CA 5-8R; CAAS 4; CANR 8, 33, 67; DLB 6, 105

Char, Rene(-Emile) 1907-1988 .... **CLC 9, 11, 14, 55; DAM POET**
See CA 13-16R; 124; CANR 32; MTCW 1, 2

Charby, Jay
See Ellison, Harlan (Jay)

Chardin, Pierre Teilhard de
See Teilhard de Chardin, (Marie Joseph) Pierre

Charles I 1600-1649 .... **LC 13**

Charriere, Isabelle de 1740-1805 .. **NCLC 66**

Charyn, Jerome 1937- .... **CLC 5, 8, 18**
See CA 5-8R; CAAS 1; CANR 7, 61; DLBY 83; MTCW 1

Chase, Mary (Coyle) 1907-1981 .... **DC 1**
See CA 77-80; 105; SATA 17; SATA-Obit 29

Chase, Mary Ellen 1887-1973 .... **CLC 2**
See CA 13-16; 41-44R; CAP 1; SATA 10

Chase, Nicholas
See Hyde, Anthony

Chateaubriand, Francois Renede
1768-1848 .... **NCLC 3**
See DLB 119

Chatterje, Sarat Chandra 1876-1936(?)
See Chatterji, Saratchandra
See CA 109

Chatterji, Bankim Chandra
1838-1894 .... **NCLC 19**

Chatterji, Saratchandra TCLC 13
See Chatterje, Sarat Chandra

Chatterton, Thomas 1752-1770 .... **LC 54; DAM POET**
See DLB 109

Chatwin, (Charles) Bruce
1940-1989 . **CLC 28, 57, 59; DAM POP**
See AAYA 4; BEST 90:1; CA 85-88; 127; DLB 194, 204

Chaucer, Daniel
See Ford, Ford Madox

Chaucer, Geoffrey 1340(?)-1400 .... **LC 17; DA; DAB; DAC; DAM MST, POET; PC 19; WLCS**
See CDBLB Before 1660; DA3; DLB 146

Chavez, Denise (Elia) 1948-
See CA 131; CANR 56, 81; DAM MULT; DLB 122; HLC 1; HW 1, 2; MTCW 2

Chaviaras, Strates 1935-
See Haviaras, Stratis
See CA 105

Chayefsky, Paddy CLC 23
See Chayefsky, Sidney
See DLB 7, 44; DLBY 81

Chayefsky, Sidney 1923-1981
See Chayefsky, Paddy
See CA 9-12R; 104; CANR 18; DAM DRAM

Chedid, Andree 1920- .... **CLC 47**
See CA 145

Cheever, John 1912-1982 ..... **CLC 3, 7, 8, 11, 15, 25, 64; DA; DAB; DAC; DAM MST, NOV, POP; SSC 1; WLC**
See CA 5-8R; 106; CABS 1; CANR 5, 27, 76; CDALB 1941-1968; DA3; DLB 2, 102; DLBY 80, 82; INT CANR-5; MTCW 1, 2

Cheever, Susan 1943- .... **CLC 18, 48**
See CA 103; CANR 27, 51; DLBY 82; INT CANR-27

Chekhonte, Antosha
See Chekhov, Anton (Pavlovich)

Chekhov, Anton (Pavlovich)
1860-1904 .... **TCLC 3, 10, 31, 55, 96; DA; DAB; DAC; DAM DRAM, MST; DC 9; SSC 2, 28;WLC**
See CA 104; 124; DA3; SATA 90

Chernyshevsky, Nikolay Gavrilovich
1828-1889 .... **NCLC 1**

Cherry, Carolyn Janice 1942-
See Cherryh, C. J.
See CA 65-68; CANR 10

Cherryh, C. J. CLC 35
See Cherry, Carolyn Janice
See AAYA 24; DLBY 80; SATA 93

Chesnutt, Charles W(addell)
1858-1932 .. **TCLC 5, 39; BLC 1; DAM MULT; SSC 7**
See BW 1, 3; CA 106; 125; CANR 76; DLB 12, 50, 78; MTCW 1, 2

Chester,Alfred 1929(?)-1971 .... **CLC 49**
See CA 33-36R; DLB 130

Chesterton, G(ilbert) K(eith)
1874-1936 . **TCLC 1, 6, 64; DAM NOV, POET; PC 28; SSC 1**
See CA 104; 132; CANR 73; CDBLB 1914-1945; DLB 10, 19, 34, 70, 98, 149, 178; MTCW 1, 2; SATA 27

Chiang, Pin-chin 1904-1986
See Ding Ling
See CA 118

Ch'ien Chung-shu 1910- .... **CLC 22**
See CA 130; CANR 73; MTCW 1, 2

Child, L. Maria
See Child, Lydia Maria

Child, Lydia Maria 1802-1880 .. **NCLC 6, 73**
See DLB 1, 74; SATA 67

Child, Mrs.
See Child, Lydia Maria

Child, Philip 1898-1978 .... **CLC 19, 68**
See CA 13-14; CAP 1; SATA 47

Childers, (Robert) Erskine
1870-1922 .... **TCLC 65**
See CA 113; 153; DLB 70

Childress, Alice 1920-1994 .. **CLC 12, 15, 86, 96; BLC 1; DAM DRAM, MULT, NOV; DC 4**
See AAYA 8; BW 2, 3; CA 45-48; 146; CANR 3, 27, 50, 74; CLR 14; DA3; DLB 7, 38; JRDA; MAICYA; MTCW 1, 2; SATA 7, 48, 81

Chin, Frank (Chew, Jr.) 1940- .... **DC 7**
See CA 33-36R; CANR 71; DAM MULT; DLB 206

Chislett, (Margaret) Anne 1943- ...... **CLC 34**
See CA 151

Chitty, Thomas Willes 1926- .... **CLC 11**
See Hinde, Thomas
See CA 5-8R

Chivers, Thomas Holley
1809-1858 .... **NCLC 49**
See DLB 3

Choi, Susan CLC 119

Chomette, Rene Lucien 1898-1981
See Clair, Rene
See CA 103

Chopin, Kate TCLC 5, 14; DA; DAB; SSC 8; WLCS
See Chopin, Katherine
See CDALB 1865-1917; DLB 12, 78

Chopin, Katherine 1851-1904
See Chopin, Kate
See CA 104; 122; DAC; DAM MST, NOV; DA3

Chretien de Troyes c. 12th cent.- .. **CMLC 10**
See DLB 208

Christie
See Ichikawa, Kon

Christie, Agatha (Mary Clarissa)
1890-1976 .... **CLC 1, 6, 8, 12, 39, 48, 110; DAB; DAC; DAM NOV**
See AAYA 9; AITN 1, 2; CA 17-20R; 61-64; CANR 10, 37; CDBLB 1914-1945; DA3; DLB 13, 77; MTCW 1, 2; SATA 36

Christie, (Ann) Philippa
See Pearce, Philippa
See CA 5-8R; CANR 4

Christine de Pizan 1365(?)-1431(?) .... **LC 9**
See DLB 208

Chubb, Elmer
See Masters, Edgar Lee

Chulkov, Mikhail Dmitrievich
1743-1792 .... **LC 2**
See DLB 150

Churchill, Caryl 1938- ...... **CLC 31, 55;DC 5**
See CA 102; CANR 22, 46; DLB 13; MTCW 1

Churchill, Charles 1731-1764 .... **LC 3**
See DLB 109

Chute, Carolyn 1947- .... **CLC 39**
See CA 123

Ciardi, John (Anthony) 1916-1986 . **CLC 10, 40, 44; DAM POET**
See CA 5-8R; 118; CAAS 2; CANR 5, 33; CLR 19; DLB 5; DLBY 86; INT CANR-5; MAICYA; MTCW 1, 2; SAAS 26; SATA 1, 65; SATA-Obit 46

Cicero, Marcus Tullius
106B.C.-43B.C. .... **CMLC 3**
See DLB 211

Cimino, Michael 1943- .... **CLC 16**
See CA 105

Cioran, E(mil)M. 1911-1995 .... **CLC 64**
See CA 25-28R; 149

Colman, George 1732-1794
See Glassco, John
Colt, Winchester Remington
See Hubbard, L(afayette) Ron(ald)
Colter, Cyrus 1910- .... **CLC 58**
See BW 1; CA 65-68; CANR 10, 66; DLB
33
Colton, James
See Hansen, Joseph
Colum, Padraic 1881-1972 .... **CLC 28**
See CA 73-76; 33-36R; CANR 35; CLR 36;
MAICYA; MTCW 1; SATA 15
Colvin, James
See Moorcock, Michael (John)
Colwin, Laurie (E.) 1944-1992 .... **CLC 5, 13,
23, 84**
See CA 89-92; 139; CANR 20, 46; DLBY
80; MTCW 1
Comfort, Alex(ander) 1920- ..... **CLC 7;DAM
POP**
See CA 1-4R; CANR 1, 45; MTCW 1
Comfort, Montgomery
See Campbell, (John) Ramsey
Compton-Burnett, I(vy)
1884(?)-1969 .... **CLC 1, 3, 10, 15, 34;
DAM NOV**
See CA 1-4R; 25-28R; CANR 4; DLB 36;
MTCW 1
Comstock, Anthony 1844-1915 ...... **TCLC 13**
See CA 110; 169
Comte, Auguste 1798-1857 .... **NCLC 54**
Conan Doyle, Arthur
See Doyle, Arthur Conan
Conde (Abellan), Carmen 1901-
See CA 177; DLB 108; HLCS 1; HW 2
Conde, Maryse 1937- .... **CLC 52, 92; BLCS;
DAM MULT**
See Boucolon, Maryse
See BW 2; MTCW 1
Condillac, Etienne Bonnot de
1714-1780 .... **LC 26**
Condon, Richard (Thomas)
1915-1996 ...... **CLC 4, 6, 8, 10, 45, 100;
DAM NOV**
See BEST 90:3; CA 1-4R; 151; CAAS 1;
CANR 2, 23; INT CANR-23; MTCW 1,
2
Confucius 551B.C.-479B.C. .. **CMLC 19; DA;
DAB; DAC; DAM MST; WLCS**
See DA3
Congreve, William 1670-1729 .... **LC 5, 21;
DA; DAB; DAC; DAM DRAM, MST,
POET; DC 2; WLC**
See CDBLB 1660-1789; DLB 39, 84
Connell, Evan S(helby), Jr. 1924- . **CLC 4, 6,
45; DAM NOV**
See AAYA 7; CA 1-4R; CAAS 2; CANR 2,
39, 76; DLB 2; DLBY 81; MTCW 1, 2
Connelly, Marc(us Cook) 1890-1980 . **CLC 7**
See CA 85-88; 102; CANR 30; DLB 7;
DLBY 80; SATA-Obit 25
Connor, Ralph TCLC 31
See Gordon, Charles William
See DLB 92
Conrad, Joseph 1857-1924 .... **TCLC 1, 6, 13,
25, 43, 57; DA; DAB; DAC; DAM
MST, NOV; SSC 9; WLC**
See AAYA 26; CA 104; 131; CANR 60;
CDBLB 1890-1914; DA3; DLB 10, 34,
98, 156; MTCW 1, 2; SATA 27
Conrad, Robert Arnold
See Hart, Moss
Conroy, Pat
See Conroy, (Donald) Pat(rick)
See MTCW 2
Conroy, (Donald) Pat(rick) 1945- ... **CLC 30,
74; DAM NOV, POP**
See Conroy, Pat

See AAYA 8; AITN 1; CA 85-88; CANR
24, 53; DA3; DLB 6; MTCW 1
Constant (de Rebecque), (Henri) Benjamin
1767-1830 .... **NCLC 6**
See DLB 119
Conybeare, Charles Augustus
See Eliot, T(homas) S(tearns)
Cook, Michael 1933- .... **CLC 58**
See CA 93-96; CANR 68; DLB 53
Cook, Robin 1940- .... **CLC 14;DAM POP**
See AAYA 32; BEST 90:2; CA 108; 111;
CANR 41; DA3; INT 111
Cook, Roy
See Silverberg, Robert
Cooke, Elizabeth 1948- .... **CLC 55**
See CA 129
Cooke, John Esten 1830-1886 .... **NCLC 5**
See DLB 3
Cooke, John Estes
See Baum, L(yman) Frank
Cooke, M. E.
See Creasey, John
Cooke, Margaret
See Creasey, John
Cook-Lynn, Elizabeth 1930- .. **CLC 93;DAM
MULT**
See CA 133; DLB 175; NNAL
Cooney, Ray CLC 62
Cooper, Douglas 1960- .... **CLC 86**
Cooper, Henry St. John
See Creasey, John
Cooper, J(oan) California (?)- .... **CLC 56;
DAM MULT**
See AAYA 12; BW 1; CA 125; CANR 55;
DLB 212
Cooper, James Fenimore
1789-1851 .... **NCLC 1, 27, 54**
See AAYA 22; CDALB 1640-1865; DA3;
DLB 3; SATA 19
Coover, Robert (Lowell) 1932- ...... **CLC 3, 7,
15, 32, 46, 87; DAM NOV; SSC 15**
See CA 45-48; CANR 3, 37, 58; DLB 2;
DLBY 81; MTCW 1, 2
Copeland, Stewart (Armstrong)
1952- .... **CLC 26**
Copernicus, Nicolaus 1473-1543 .... **LC 45**
Coppard, A(lfred) E(dgar)
1878-1957 .... **TCLC 5; SSC 21**
See CA 114; 167; DLB 162; YABC 1
Coppee, Francois 1842-1908 .... **TCLC 25**
See CA 170
Coppola, Francis Ford 1939- .... **CLC 16**
See CA 77-80; CANR 40, 78; DLB 44
Corbiere, Tristan 1845-1875 .... **NCLC 43**
Corcoran, Barbara 1911- .... **CLC 17**
See AAYA 14; CA 21-24R; CAAS 2; CANR
11, 28, 48; CLR 50; DLB 52; JRDA;
SAAS 20; SATA 3, 77
Cordelier, Maurice
See Giraudoux, (Hippolyte) Jean
Corelli, Marie 1855-1924 .... **TCLC 51**
See Mackay, Mary
See DLB 34, 156
Corman, Cid 1924- .... **CLC 9**
See Corman, Sidney
See CAAS 2; DLB 5, 193
Corman, Sidney 1924-
See Corman, Cid
See CA 85-88; CANR 44; DAM POET
Cormier, Robert (Edmund) 1925- ... **CLC 12,
30; DA; DAB; DAC; DAM MST, NOV**
See AAYA 3, 19; CA 1-4R; CANR 5, 23,
76; CDALB 1968-1988; CLR 12, 55;
DLB 52; INT CANR-23; JRDA; MAI-
CYA; MTCW 1, 2; SATA 10, 45, 83
Corn, Alfred (DeWitt III) 1943- .... **CLC 33**
See CA 179; CAAE 179; CAAS 25; CANR
44; DLB 120; DLBY 80

Corneille, Pierre 1606-1684 ..... **LC 28; DAB;
DAM MST**
Cornwell, David (John Moore)
1931- .... **CLC 9, 15; DAM POP**
See le Carre, John
See CA 5-8R; CANR 13, 33, 59; DA3;
MTCW 1, 2
Corso, (Nunzio) Gregory 1930- .... **CLC 1, 11**
See CA 5-8R; CANR 41, 76; DA3; DLB 5,
16; MTCW 1, 2
Cortazar, Julio 1914-1984 ... **CLC 2, 3, 5, 10,
13, 15, 33, 34, 92; DAM MULT, NOV;
HLC 1; SSC 7**
See CA 21-24R; CANR 12, 32, 81; DA3;
DLB 113; HW 1, 2; MTCW 1, 2
CORTES, HERNAN 1484-1547 .... **LC 31**
Corvinus, Jakob
See Raabe, Wilhelm (Karl)
Corwin, Cecil
See Kornbluth, C(yril) M.
Cosic, Dobrica 1921- .... **CLC 14**
See CA 122; 138; DLB 181
Costain, Thomas B(ertram)
1885-1965 .... **CLC 30**
See CA 5-8R; 25-28R; DLB 9
Costantini, Humberto 1924(?)-1987 . **CLC 49**
See CA 131; 122; HW 1
Costello, Elvis 1955- .... **CLC 21**
Costenoble, Philostene
See Ghelderode, Michel de
Cotes, Cecil V.
See Duncan, Sara Jeannette
Cotter, Joseph Seamon Sr.
1861-1949 ...... **TCLC 28; BLC 1; DAM
MULT**
See BW 1; CA 124; DLB 50
Couch, Arthur Thomas Quiller
See Quiller-Couch, SirArthur (Thomas)
Coulton, James
See Hansen, Joseph
Couperus, Louis (Marie Anne)
1863-1923 .... **TCLC 15**
See CA 115
Coupland, Douglas 1961- ..... **CLC 85; DAC;
DAM POP**
See CA 142; CANR 57
Court, Wesli
See Turco, Lewis (Putnam)
Courtenay, Bryce 1933- .... **CLC 59**
See CA 138
Courtney, Robert
See Ellison, Harlan (Jay)
Cousteau, Jacques-Yves 1910-1997 ... **CLC 30**
See CA 65-68; 159; CANR 15, 67; MTCW
1; SATA 38, 98
Coventry, Francis 1725-1754 .... **LC 46**
Cowan, Peter (Walkinshaw) 1914- .... **SSC 28**
See CA 21-24R; CANR 9, 25, 50, 83
Coward, Noel (Peirce) 1899-1973 . **CLC 1, 9,
29, 51; DAM DRAM**
See AITN 1; CA 17-18; 41-44R; CANR 35;
CAP 2; CDBLB 1914-1945; DA3; DLB
10; MTCW 1, 2
Cowley, Abraham 1618-1667 .... **LC 43**
See DLB 131, 151
Cowley, Malcolm 1898-1989 .... **CLC 39**
See CA 5-8R; 128; CANR 3, 55; DLB 4,
48; DLBY 81, 89; MTCW 1, 2
Cowper, William 1731-1800 .. **NCLC 8;DAM
POET**
See DA3; DLB 104, 109
Cox, William Trevor 1928- ... **CLC 9, 14, 71;
DAM NOV**
See Trevor, William
See CA 9-12R; CANR 4, 37, 55, 76; DLB
14; INT CANR-37; MTCW 1, 2
Coyne, P. J.
See Masters, Hilary

Cozzens, James Gould 1903-1978 . **CLC 1, 4, 11, 92**
See CA 9-12R; 81-84; CANR 19; CDALB 1941-1968; DLB 9; DLBD 2; DLBY 84, 97; MTCW 1, 2

Crabbe, George 1754-1832 .... **NCLC 26**
See DLB 93

Craddock, Charles Egbert
See Murfree, Mary Noailles

Craig, A. A.
See Anderson, Poul (William)

Craik, Dinah Maria (Mulock)
1826-1887 .... **NCLC 38**
See DLB 35, 163; MAICYA; SATA 34

Cram, Ralph Adams 1863-1942 ..... **TCLC 45**
See CA 160

Crane, (Harold) Hart 1899-1932 .... **TCLC 2, 5, 80; DA; DAB; DAC; DAM MST, POET; PC 3; WLC**
See CA 104; 127; CDALB 1917-1929; DA3; DLB 4, 48; MTCW 1, 2

Crane, R(onald) S(almon)
1886-1967 .... **CLC 27**
See CA 85-88; DLB 63

Crane, Stephen (Townley)
1871-1900 .... **TCLC 11, 17, 32; DA; DAB; DAC; DAM MST, NOV, POET; SSC 7; WLC**
See AAYA 21; CA 109; 140; CANR 84; CDALB 1865-1917; DA3; DLB 12, 54, 78; YABC 2

Cranshaw, Stanley
See Fisher, Dorothy (Frances) Canfield

Crase, Douglas 1944- .... **CLC 58**
See CA 106

Crashaw, Richard 1612(?)-1649 .... **LC 24**
See DLB 126

Craven, Margaret 1901-1980 .. **CLC 17;DAC**
See CA 103

Crawford, F(rancis) Marion
1854-1909 .... **TCLC 10**
See CA 107; 168; DLB 71

Crawford, Isabella Valancy
1850-1887 .... **NCLC 12**
See DLB 92

Crayon, Geoffrey
See Irving, Washington

Creasey, John 1908-1973 .... **CLC 11**
See CA 5-8R; 41-44R; CANR 8, 59; DLB 77; MTCW 1

Crebillon, Claude Prosper Jolyot de (fils)
1707-1777 .... **LC 1, 28**

Credo
See Creasey, John

Credo, Alvaro J. de
See Prado (Calvo), Pedro

Creeley, Robert (White) 1926- .. **CLC 1, 2, 4, 8, 11, 15, 36, 78; DAM POET**
See CA 1-4R; CAAS 10; CANR 23, 43; DA3; DLB 5, 16, 169; DLBD 17; MTCW 1, 2

Crews, Harry (Eugene) 1935- ..... **CLC 6, 23, 49**
See AITN 1; CA 25-28R; CANR 20, 57; DA3; DLB 6, 143, 185; MTCW 1, 2

Crichton, (John) Michael 1942- .... **CLC 2, 6, 54, 90; DAM NOV, POP**
See AAYA 10; AITN 2; CA 25-28R; CANR 13, 40, 54, 76; DA3; DLBY 81; INT CANR-13; JRDA; MTCW 1, 2; SATA 9, 88

Crispin, Edmund CLC 22
See Montgomery, (Robert) Bruce
See DLB 87

Cristofer, Michael 1945(?)- ... **CLC 28; DAM DRAM**
See CA 110; 152; DLB 7

Croce, Benedetto 1866-1952 .... **TCLC 37**
See CA 120; 155

Crockett, David 1786-1836 .... **NCLC 8**
See DLB 3, 11

Crockett, Davy
See Crockett, David

Crofts, Freeman Wills 1879-1957 .. **TCLC 55**
See CA 115; DLB 77

Croker, John Wilson 1780-1857 .... **NCLC 10**
See DLB 110

Crommelynck, Fernand 1885-1970 .. **CLC 75**
See CA 89-92

Cromwell, Oliver 1599-1658 .... **LC 43**

Cronin, A(rchibald) J(oseph)
1896-1981 .... **CLC 32**
See CA 1-4R; 102; CANR 5; DLB 191; SATA 47; SATA-Obit 25

Cross, Amanda
See Heilbrun, Carolyn G(old)

Crothers, Rachel 1878(?)-1958 .... **TCLC 19**
See CA 113; DLB 7

Croves, Hal
See Traven, B.

Crow Dog, Mary (Ellen) (?)- .... **CLC 93**
See Brave Bird, Mary
See CA 154

Crowfield, Christopher
See Stowe, Harriet (Elizabeth) Beecher

Crowley, Aleister TCLC 7
See Crowley, Edward Alexander

Crowley, Edward Alexander 1875-1947
See Crowley, Aleister
See CA 104

Crowley, John 1942- .... **CLC 57**
See CA 61-64; CANR 43; DLBY 82; SATA 65

Crud
See Crumb, R(obert)

Crumarums
See Crumb, R(obert)

Crumb, R(obert) 1943- .... **CLC 17**
See CA 106

Crumbum
See Crumb, R(obert)

Crumski
See Crumb, R(obert)

Crum the Bum
See Crumb, R(obert)

Crunk
See Crumb, R(obert)

Crustt
See Crumb, R(obert)

Cruz, Victor Hernandez 1949-
See BW 2; CA 65-68; CAAS 17; CANR 14, 32, 74; DAM MULT, POET; DLB 41; HLC 1; HW 1, 2; MTCW 1

Cryer, Gretchen (Kiger) 1935- .... **CLC 21**
See CA 114; 123

Csath, Geza 1887-1919 .... **TCLC 13**
See CA 111

Cudlip, David R(ockwell) 1933- .... **CLC 34**
See CA 177

Cullen, Countee 1903-1946 .... **TCLC 4, 37; BLC 1; DA; DAC; DAM MST, MULT, POET; PC 20; WLCS**
See BW 1; CA 108; 124; CDALB 1917-1929; DA3; DLB 4, 48, 51; MTCW 1, 2; SATA 18

Cum, R.
See Crumb, R(obert)

Cummings, Bruce F(rederick) 1889-1919
See Barbellion, W. N. P.
See CA 123

Cummings, E(dward) E(stlin)
1894-1962 .... **CLC 1, 3, 8, 12, 15, 68; DA; DAB; DAC; DAM MST, POET; PC 5; WLC**
See CA 73-76; CANR 31; CDALB 1929-1941; DA3; DLB 4, 48; MTCW 1, 2

Cunha, Euclides (Rodrigues Pimenta) da
1866-1909 .... **TCLC 24**
See CA 123

Cunningham, E. V.
See Fast, Howard (Melvin)

Cunningham, J(ames) V(incent)
1911-1985 .... **CLC 3, 31**
See CA 1-4R; 115; CANR 1, 72; DLB 5

Cunningham, Julia (Woolfolk)
1916- .... **CLC 12**
See CA 9-12R; CANR 4, 19, 36; JRDA; MAICYA; SAAS 2; SATA 1, 26

Cunningham, Michael 1952- .... **CLC 34**
See CA 136

Cunninghame Graham, R(obert)B(ontine)
1852-1936 .... **TCLC 19**
See Graham, R(obert) B(ontine) Cunninghame
See CA 119; DLB 98

Currie, Ellen 19(?)- .... **CLC 44**

Curtin, Philip
See Lowndes, Marie Adelaide (Belloc)

Curtis, Price
See Ellison, Harlan (Jay)

Cutrate, Joe
See Spiegelman, Art

Cynewulf c. 770-c. 840 .... **CMLC 23**

Czaczkes, Shmuel Yosef
See Agnon, S(hmuel) Y(osef Halevi)

Dabrowska, Maria(Szumska)
1889-1965 .... **CLC 15**
See CA 106

Dabydeen, David 1955- .... **CLC 34**
See BW 1; CA 125; CANR 56

Dacey, Philip 1939- .... **CLC 51**
See CA 37-40R; CAAS 17; CANR 14, 32, 64; DLB 105

Dagerman, Stig (Halvard)
1923-1954 .... **TCLC 17**
See CA 117; 155

Dahl, Roald 1916-1990 ...... **CLC 1, 6, 18, 79; DAB; DAC; DAM MST, NOV, POP**
See AAYA 15; CA 1-4R; 133; CANR 6, 32, 37, 62; CLR 1, 7, 41; DA3; DLB 139; JRDA; MAICYA; MTCW 1, 2; SATA 1, 26, 73; SATA-Obit 65

Dahlberg, Edward 1900-1977 .. **CLC 1, 7, 14**
See CA 9-12R; 69-72; CANR 31, 62; DLB 48; MTCW 1

Daitch, Susan 1954- .... **CLC 103**
See CA 161

Dale, Colin TCLC 18
See Lawrence, T(homas) E(dward)

Dale, George E.
See Asimov, Isaac

Dalton, Roque 1935-1975
See HLCS 1; HW 2

Daly, Elizabeth 1878-1967 .... **CLC 52**
See CA 23-24; 25-28R; CANR 60; CAP 2

Daly, Maureen 1921 .... **CLC 17**
See AAYA 5; CANR 37, 83; JRDA; MAICYA; SAAS 1; SATA 2

Damas, Leon-Gontran 1912-1978 .... **CLC 84**
See BW 1; CA 125; 73-76

Dana, Richard Henry Sr.
1787-1879 .... **NCLC 53**

Daniel, Samuel 1562(?)-1619 .... **LC 24**
See DLB 62

Daniels, Brett
See Adler, Renata

Dannay, Frederic 1905-1982 .. **CLC 11;DAM POP**
See Queen, Ellery
See CA 1-4R; 107; CANR 1, 39; DLB 137; MTCW 1

D'Annunzio, Gabriele 1863-1938 ... **TCLC 6, 40**
See CA 104; 155

de Man, Paul (Adolph Michel)
    1919-1983 .... CLC 55
    See CA 128; 111; CANR 61; DLB 67;
    MTCW 1, 2
De Marinis, Rick 1934- .... CLC 54
    See CA 57-60; CAAS 24; CANR 9, 25, 50
Dembry, R. Emmet
    See Murfree, Mary Noailles
Demby, William 1922- .... CLC 53; BLC 1;
    DAM MULT
    See BW 1, 3; CA 81-84; CANR 81; DLB
    33
de Menton, Francisco
    See Chin, Frank (Chew, Jr.)
Demetrius of Phalerum c.
    · 307B.C.- .... CMLC 34
Demijohn, Thom
    See Disch, Thomas M(ichael)
de Molina, Tirso 1580-1648
    See HLCS 2
de Montherlant, Henry (Milon)
    See Montherlant, Henry (Milon) de
Demosthenes 384B.C.-322B.C. ...... CMLC 13
    See DLB 176
de Natale, Francine
    See Malzberg, Barry N(athaniel)
Denby, Edwin (Orr) 1903-1983 .... CLC 48
    See CA 138; 110
Denis, Julio
    See Cortazar, Julio
Denmark, Harrison
    See Zelazny, Roger (Joseph)
Dennis, John 1658-1734 .... LC 11
    See DLB 101
Dennis, Nigel (Forbes) 1912-1989 ...... CLC 8
    See CA 25-28R; 129; DLB 13, 15; MTCW
    1
Dent, Lester 1904(?)-1959 .... TCLC 72
    See CA 112; 161
De Palma, Brian (Russell) 1940- ...... CLC 20
    See CA 109
De Quincey, Thomas 1785-1859 ...... NCLC 4
    See CDBLB 1789-1832; DLB 110; 144
Deren, Eleanora 1908(?)-1961
    See Deren, Maya
    See CA 111
Deren, Maya 1917-1961 .... CLC 16, 102
    See Deren, Eleanora
Derleth, August(William)
    1909-1971 .... CLC 31
    See CA 1-4R; 29-32R; CANR 4; DLB 9;
    DLBD 17; SATA 5
Der Nister 1884-1950 .... TCLC 56
de Routisie, Albert
    See Aragon, Louis
Derrida, Jacques 1930- .... CLC 24, 87
    See CA 124; 127; CANR 76; MTCW 1
Derry Down Derry
    See Lear, Edward
Dersonnes, Jacques
    See Simenon, Georges (Jacques Christian)
Desai, Anita 1937- ..... CLC 19, 37, 97; DAB;
    DAM NOV
    See CA 81-84; CANR 33, 53; DA3; MTCW
    1, 2; SATA 63
Desai, Kiran 1971- .... CLC 119
    See CA 171
de Saint-Luc, Jean
    See Glassco, John
de Saint Roman, Arnaud
    See Aragon, Louis
Descartes, Rene 1596-1650 .... LC 20, 35
De Sica, Vittorio 1901(?)-1974 .... CLC 20
    See CA 117
Desnos, Robert 1900-1945 .... TCLC 22
    See CA 121; 151

Destouches, Louis-Ferdinand
    1894-1961 .... CLC 9, 15
    See Celine, Louis-Ferdinand
    See CA 85-88; CANR 28; MTCW 1
de Tolignac, Gaston
    See Griffith, D(avid Lewelyn) W(ark)
Deutsch, Babette 1895-1982 .... CLC 18
    See CA 1-4R; 108; CANR 4, 79; DLB 45;
    SATA 1; SATA-Obit 33
Devenant, William 1606-1649 .... LC 13
Devkota, Laxmiprasad 1909-1959 . TCLC 23
    See CA 123
De Voto, Bernard (Augustine)
    1897-1955 .... TCLC 29
    See CA 113; 160; DLB 9
De Vries, Peter 1910-1993 ..... CLC 1, 2, 3, 7,
    10, 28, 46; DAM NOV
    See CA 17-20R; 142; CANR 41; DLB 6;
    DLBY 82; MTCW 1, 2
Dewey, John 1859-1952 .... TCLC 95
    See CA 114; 170
Dexter, John
    See Bradley, Marion Zimmer
Dexter, Martin
    See Faust, Frederick (Schiller)
Dexter, Pete 1943- .... CLC 34, 55;DAM POP
    See BEST 89:2; CA 127; 131; INT 131;
    MTCW 1
Diamano, Silmang
    See Senghor, Leopold Sedar
Diamond, Neil 1941- .... CLC 30
    See CA 108
Diaz del Castillo, Bernal 1496-1584 .. LC 31;
    HLCS 1
di Bassetto, Corno
    See Shaw, George Bernard
Dick, Philip K(indred) 1928-1982 ... CLC 10,
    30, 72; DAM NOV, POP
    See AAYA 24; CA 49-52; 106; CANR 2,
    16; DA3; DLB 8; MTCW 1, 2
Dickens, Charles (John Huffam)
    1812-1870 .... NCLC 3, 8, 18, 26, 37, 50;
    DA; DAB; DAC; DAM MST, NOV;
    SSC 17; WLC
    See AAYA 23; CDBLB 1832-1890; DA3;
    DLB 21, 55, 70, 159, 166; JRDA; MAI-
    CYA; SATA 15
Dickey, James (Lafayette)
    1923-1997 .... CLC 1, 2, 4, 7, 10, 15, 47,
    109; DAM NOV, POET, POP
    See AITN 1, 2; CA 9-12R; 156; CABS 2;
    CANR 10, 48, 61; CDALB 1968-1988;
    DA3; DLB 5, 193; DLBD 7; DLBY 82,
    93, 96, 97, 98; INT CANR-10; MTCW 1,
    2
Dickey, William 1928-1994 .... CLC 3, 28
    See CA 9-12R; 145; CANR 24, 79; DLB 5
Dickinson, Charles 1951- .... CLC 49
    See CA 128
Dickinson, Emily (Elizabeth)
    1830-1886 ..... NCLC 21, 77; DA; DAB;
    DAC; DAM MST, POET; PC 1; WLC
    See AAYA 22; CDALB 1865-1917; DA3;
    DLB 1; SATA 29
Dickinson, Peter (Malcolm) 1927- .. CLC 12,
    35
    See AAYA 9; CA 41-44R; CANR 31, 58;
    CLR 29; DLB 87, 161; JRDA; MAICYA;
    SATA 5, 62, 95
Dickson, Carr
    See Carr, John Dickson
Dickson, Carter
    See Carr, John Dickson
Diderot, Denis 1713-1784 .... LC 26
Didion, Joan 1934- .... CLC 1, 3, 8, 14, 32;
    DAM NOV
    See AITN 1; CA 5-8R; CANR 14, 52, 76;
    CDALB 1968-1988; DA3; DLB 2, 173,
    185; DLBY 81, 86; MTCW 1, 2

Dietrich, Robert
    See Hunt, E(verette) Howard, (Jr.)
Difusa, Pati
    See Almodovar, Pedro
Dillard, Annie 1945- .. CLC 9, 60, 115; DAM
    NOV
    See AAYA 6; CA 49-52; CANR 3, 43, 62;
    DA3; DLBY 80; MTCW 1, 2; SATA 10
Dillard, R(ichard) H(enry) W(ilde)
    1937- .... CLC 5
    See CA 21-24R; CAAS 7; CANR 10; DLB
    5
Dillon, Eilis 1920-1994 .... CLC 17
    See CA 9-12R; 147; CAAS 3; CANR 4, 38,
    78; CLR 26; MAICYA; SATA 2, 74;
    SATA-Essay 105; SATA-Obit 83
Dimont, Penelope
    See Mortimer, Penelope (Ruth)
Dinesen, Isak CLC 10, 29, 95; SSC 7
    See Blixen, Karen (Christentze Dinesen)
    See MTCW 1
Ding Ling CLC 68
    See Chiang, Pin-chin
Diphusa, Patty
    See Almodovar, Pedro
Disch, Thomas M(ichael) 1940- ... CLC 7, 36
    See AAYA 17; CA 21-24R; CAAS 4; CANR
    17, 36, 54; CLR 18; DA3; DLB 8; MAI-
    CYA; MTCW 1, 2; SAAS 15; SATA 92
Disch, Tom
    See Disch, Thomas M(ichael)
d'Isly, Georges
    See Simenon, Georges (Jacques Christian)
Disraeli, Benjamin 1804-1881 ... NCLC 2, 39,
    79
    See DLB 21, 55
Ditcum, Steve
    See Crumb, R(obert)
Dixon, Paige
    See Corcoran, Barbara
Dixon, Stephen 1936- .... CLC 52;SSC 16
    See CA 89-92; CANR 17, 40, 54; DLB 130
Doak, Annie
    See Dillard, Annie
Dobell, Sydney Thompson
    1824-1874 .... NCLC 43
    See DLB 32
Doblin, Alfred TCLC 13
    See Doeblin, Alfred
Dobrolyubov, Nikolai Alexandrovich
    1836-1861 .... NCLC 5
Dobson, Austin 1840-1921 .... TCLC 79
    See DLB 35; 144
Dobyns, Stephen 1941- .... CLC 37
    See CA 45-48; CANR 2, 18
Doctorow, E(dgar) L(aurence)
    1931- .... CLC 6, 11, 15, 18, 37, 44, 65,
    113; DAM NOV, POP
    See AAYA 22; AITN 2; BEST 89:3; CA 45-
    48; CANR 2, 33, 51, 76; CDALB 1968-
    1988; DA3; DLB 2, 28, 173; DLBY 80;
    MTCW 1, 2
Dodgson, Charles Lutwidge 1832-1898
    See Carroll, Lewis
    See CLR 2; DA; DAB; DAC; DAM MST,
    NOV, POET; DA3; MAICYA; SATA 100;
    YABC 2
Dodson, Owen (Vincent)
    1914-1983 .... CLC 79; BLC 1; DAM
    MULT
    See BW 1; CA 65-68; 110; CANR 24; DLB
    76
Doeblin, Alfred 1878-1957 .... TCLC 13
    See Doblin, Alfred
    See CA 110; 141; DLB 66
Doerr, Harriet 1910- .... CLC 34
    See CA 117; 122; CANR 47; INT 122
Domecq, H(onorio Bustos)
    See Bioy Casares, Adolfo

Domecq, H(onorio) Bustos
See Bioy Casares, Adolfo; Borges, Jorge Luis

Domini, Rey
See Lorde, Audre (Geraldine)

Dominique
See Proust, (Valentin-Louis-George-Eugene-) Marcel

Don, A
See Stephen, SirLeslie

Donaldson, Stephen R. 1947- .... **CLC 46; DAM POP**
See CA 89-92; CANR 13, 55; INT CANR-13

Donleavy, J(ames) P(atrick) 1926- .... **CLC 1, 4, 6, 10, 45**
See AITN 2; CA 9-12R; CANR 24, 49, 62, 80; DLB 6, 173; INT CANR-24; MTCW 1, 2

Donne, John 1572-1631 .... **LC 10, 24; DA; DAB; DAC; DAM MST, POET; PC 1; WLC**
See CDBLB Before 1660; DLB 121, 151

Donnell, David 1939(?)- .... **CLC 34**

Donoghue, P. S.
See Hunt, E(verette) Howard, (Jr.)

Donoso (Yanez), Jose 1924-1996 ... **CLC 4, 8, 11, 32, 99; DAM MULT; HLC 1; SSC 34**
See CA 81-84; 155; CANR 32, 73; DLB 113; HW 1, 2; MTCW 1, 2

Donovan, John 1928-1992 .... **CLC 35**
See AAYA 20; CA 97-100; 137; CLR 3; MAICYA; SATA 72; SATA-Brief 29

Don Roberto
See Cunninghame Graham, R(obert) B(ontine)

Doolittle, Hilda 1886-1961 . **CLC 3, 8, 14, 31, 34, 73; DA; DAC; DAM MST, POET; PC 5; WLC**
See H. D.
See CA 97-100; CANR 35; DLB 4, 45; MTCW 1, 2

Dorfman, Ariel 1942- ...... **CLC 48, 77; DAM MULT; HLC 1**
See CA 124; 130; CANR 67, 70; HW 1, 2; INT 130

Dorn, Edward (Merton) 1929- ... **CLC 10, 18**
See CA 93-96; CANR 42, 79; DLB 5; INT 93-96

Dorris, Michael (Anthony) 1945-1997 .... **CLC 109; DAM MULT, NOV**
See AAYA 20; BEST 90:1; CA 102; 157; CANR 19, 46, 75; CLR 58; DA3; DLB 175; MTCW 2; NNAL; SATA 75; SATA-Obit 94

Dorris, Michael A.
See Dorris, Michael (Anthony)

Dorsan, Luc
See Simenon, Georges (Jacques Christian)

Dorsange, Jean
See Simenon, Georges (Jacques Christian)

Dos Passos, John (Roderigo) 1896-1970 ... **CLC 1, 4, 8, 11, 15, 25, 34, 82; DA; DAB; DAC; DAM MST, NOV; WLC**
See CA 1-4R; 29-32R; CANR 3; CDALB 1929-1941; DA3; DLB 4, 9; DLBD 1, 15; DLBY 96; MTCW 1, 2

Dossage, Jean
See Simenon, Georges (Jacques Christian)

Dostoevsky, Fedor Mikhailovich 1821-1881 . **NCLC 2, 7, 21, 33, 43; DA; DAB; DAC; DAM MST, NOV; SSC 2, 33; WLC**
See DA3

Doughty, Charles M(ontagu) 1843-1926 .... **TCLC 27**
See CA 115; 178; DLB 19, 57, 174

Douglas, Ellen CLC 73
See Haxton, Josephine Ayres; Williamson, Ellen Douglas

Douglas, Gavin 1475(?)-1522 .... **LC 20**
See DLB 132

Douglas, George
See Brown, George Douglas

Douglas, Keith (Castellain) 1920-1944 .... **TCLC 40**
See CA 160; DLB 27

Douglas, Leonard
See Bradbury, Ray (Douglas)

Douglas, Michael
See Crichton, (John) Michael

Douglas, (George) Norman 1868-1952 .... **TCLC 68**
See CA 119; 157; DLB 34, 195

Douglas, William
See Brown, George Douglas

Douglass, Frederick 1817(?)-1895 .. **NCLC 7, 55; BLC 1; DA; DAC; DAM MST, MULT; WLC**
See CDALB 1640-1865; DA3; DLB 1, 43, 50, 79; SATA 29

Dourado, (Waldomiro Freitas) Autran 1926- .... **CLC 23, 60**
See CA 25-28R, 179; CANR 34, 81; DLB 145; HW 2

Dourado, Waldomiro Autran 1926-
See Dourado, (Waldomiro Freitas) Autran
See CA 179

Dove, Rita (Frances) 1952- .... **CLC 50, 81; BLCS; DAM MULT, POET; PC 6**
See BW 2; CA 109; CAAS 19; CANR 27, 42, 68, 76; CDALBS; DA3; DLB 120; MTCW 1

Doveglion
See Villa, Jose Garcia

Dowell, Coleman 1925-1985 .... **CLC 60**
See CA 25-28R; 117; CANR 10; DLB 130

Dowson, Ernest (Christopher) 1867-1900 .... **TCLC 4**
See CA 105; 150; DLB 19, 135

Doyle, A. Conan
See Doyle, Arthur Conan

Doyle, Arthur Conan 1859-1930 .... **TCLC 7; DA; DAB; DAC; DAM MST, NOV; SSC 12; WLC**
See AAYA 14; CA 104; 122; CDBLB 1890-1914; DA3; DLB 18, 70, 156, 178; MTCW 1, 2; SATA 24

Doyle, Conan
See Doyle, Arthur Conan

Doyle, John
See Graves, Robert (von Ranke)

Doyle, Roddy 1958(?)- .... **CLC 81**
See AAYA 14; CA 143; CANR 73; DA3; DLB 194

Doyle, Sir A. Conan
See Doyle, Arthur Conan

Doyle, Sir Arthur Conan
See Doyle, Arthur Conan

Dr. A
See Asimov, Isaac; Silverstein, Alvin

Drabble, Margaret 1939- ...... **CLC 2, 3, 5, 8, 10, 22, 53; DAB; DAC; DAM MST, NOV, POP**
See CA 13-16R; CANR 18, 35, 63; CD-BLB 1960 to Present; DA3; DLB 14, 155; MTCW 1, 2; SATA 48

Drapier, M. B.
See Swift, Jonathan

Drayham, James
See Mencken, H(enry) L(ouis)

Drayton, Michael 1563-1631 .... **LC 8; DAM POET**
See DLB 121

Dreadstone, Carl
See Campbell, (John) Ramsey

Dreiser, Theodore (Herman Albert) 1871-1945 .... **TCLC 10, 18, 35, 83; DA; DAC; DAM MST, NOV; SSC 30; WLC**
See CA 106; 132; CDALB 1865-1917; DA3; DLB 9, 12, 102, 137; DLBD 1; MTCW 1, 2

Drexler, Rosalyn 1926- .... **CLC 2, 6**
See CA 81-84; CANR 68

Dreyer, Carl Theodor 1889-1968 ...... **CLC 16**
See CA 116

Drieu la Rochelle, Pierre(-Eugene) 1893-1945 .... **TCLC 21**
See CA 117; DLB 72

Drinkwater, John 1882-1937 .... **TCLC 57**
See CA 109; 149; DLB 10, 19, 149

Drop Shot
See Cable, George Washington

Droste-Hulshoff, Annette Freiinvon 1797-1848 .... **NCLC 3**
See DLB 133

Drummond, Walter
See Silverberg, Robert

Drummond, William Henry 1854-1907 .... **TCLC 25**
See CA 160; DLB 92

Drummond de Andrade, Carlos 1902-1987 .... **CLC 18**
See Andrade, Carlos Drummond de
See CA 132; 123

Drury, Allen (Stuart) 1918-1998 .... **CLC 37**
See CA 57-60; 170; CANR 18, 52; INT CANR-18

Dryden, John 1631-1700 .... **LC 3, 21; DA; DAB; DAC; DAM DRAM, MST, POET; DC 3; PC 25; WLC**
See CDBLB 1660-1789; DLB 80, 101, 131

Duberman, Martin (Bauml) 1930- ...... **CLC 8**
See CA 1-4R; CANR 2, 63

Dubie, Norman (Evans) 1945- .... **CLC 36**
See CA 69-72; CANR 12; DLB 120

Du Bois, W(illiam) E(dward) B(urghardt) 1868-1963 ... **CLC 1, 2, 13, 64, 96; BLC 1; DA; DAC; DAM MST, MULT, NOV; WLC**
See BW 1, 3; CA 85-88; CANR 34, 82; CDALB 1865-1917; DA3; DLB 47, 50, 91; MTCW 1, 2; SATA 42

Dubus, Andre 1936-1999 ..... **CLC 13, 36, 97; SSC 15**
See CA 21-24R; 177; CANR 17; DLB 130; INT CANR-17

Duca Minimo
See D'Annunzio, Gabriele

Ducharme, Rejean 1941- ...., **CLC 74**
See CA 165; DLB 60

Duclos, Charles Pinot 1704-1772 .... **LC 1**

Dudek, Louis 1918- .... **CLC 11, 19**
See CA 45-48; CAAS 14; CANR 1; DLB 88

Duerrenmatt, Friedrich 1921-1990 ... **CLC 1, 4, 8, 11, 15, 43, 102; DAM DRAM**
See CA 17-20R; CANR 33; DLB 69, 124; MTCW 1, 2

Duffy, Bruce 1953(?)- .... **CLC 50**
See CA 172

Duffy, Maureen 1933- .... **CLC 37**
See CA 25-28R; CANR 33, 68; DLB 14; MTCW 1

Dugan, Alan 1923- .... **CLC 2, 6**
See CA 81-84; DLB 5

du Gard, Roger Martin
See Martin du Gard, Roger

See AAYA 19; CA 108; 113; CANR 35; INT
113

Gillian, Jerry
See Gilliam, Terry (Vance)

Gilliatt, Penelope (Ann Douglass)
1932-1993 .... **CLC 2, 10, 13, 53**
See AITN 2; CA 13-16R; 141; CANR 49;
DLB 14

Gilman, Charlotte (Anna) Perkins (Stetson)
1860-1935 .... **TCLC 9, 37; SSC 13**
See CA 106; 150; MTCW 1

Gilmour, David 1949- .... **CLC 35**
See CA 138; 147

Gilpin, William 1724-1804 .... **NCLC 30**

Gilray, J. D.
See Mencken, H(enry) L(ouis)

Gilroy, Frank D(aniel) 1925- .... **CLC 2**
See CA 81-84; CANR 32, 64; DLB 7

Gilstrap, John 1957(?)- .... **CLC 99**
See CA 160

Ginsberg, Allen 1926-1997 .... **CLC 1, 2, 3, 4,**
6, 13, 36, 69, 109; DA; DAB; DAC;
DAM MST, POET; PC 4; WLC
See AITN 1; CA 1-4R; 157; CANR 2, 41,
63; CDALB 1941-1968; DA3; DLB 5, 16,
169; MTCW 1, 2

Ginzburg, Natalia 1916-1991 .... **CLC 5, 11,**
54, 70
See CA 85-88; 135; CANR 33; DLB 177;
MTCW 1, 2

Giono, Jean 1895-1970 .... **CLC 4, 11**
See CA 45-48; 29-32R; CANR 2, 35; DLB
72; MTCW 1

Giovanni, Nikki 1943- .... **CLC 2, 4, 19, 64,**
117; BLC 2; DA; DAB; DAC; DAM
MST, MULT, POET; PC 19; WLCS
See AAYA 22; AITN 1; BW 2, 3; CA 29-
32R; CAAS 6; CANR 18, 41, 60;
CDALBS; CLR 6; DA3; DLB 5, 41; INT
CANR-18; MAICYA; MTCW 1, 2; SATA
24, 107

Giovene, Andrea 1904- .... **CLC 7**
See CA 85-88

Gippius, Zinaida (Nikolayevna) 1869-1945
See Hippius, Zinaida
See CA 106

Giraudoux, (Hippolyte) Jean
1882-1944 .... **TCLC 2, 7; DAM DRAM**
See CA 104; DLB 65

Gironella, Jose Maria 1917- .... **CLC 11**
See CA 101

Gissing, George (Robert)
1857-1903 .... **TCLC 3, 24, 47; SSC 37**
See CA 105; 167; DLB 18, 135, 184

Giurlani, Aldo
See Palazzeschi, Aldo

Gladkov, Fyodor (Vasilyevich)
1883-1958 .... **TCLC 27**
See CA 170

Glanville, Brian (Lester) 1931- .... **CLC 6**
See CA 5-8R; CAAS 9; CANR 3, 70; DLB
15, 139; SATA 42

Glasgow, Ellen (Anderson Gholson)
1873-1945 .... **TCLC 2, 7; SSC 34**
See CA 104; 164; DLB 9, 12; MTCW 2

Glaspell, Susan 1882(?)-1948 . **TCLC 55; DC**
10
See CA 110; 154; DLB 7, 9, 78; YABC 2

Glassco, John 1909-1981 .... **CLC 9**
See CA 13-16R; 102; CANR 15; DLB 68

Glasscock, Amnesia
See Steinbeck, John (Ernst)

Glasser, Ronald J. 1940(?)- .... **CLC 37**

Glassman, Joyce
See Johnson, Joyce

Glendinning, Victoria 1937- .... **CLC 50**
See CA 120; 127; CANR 59; DLB 155

Glissant, Edouard 1928- . **CLC 10, 68; DAM**
MULT
See CA 153

Gloag, Julian 1930- .... **CLC 40**
See AITN 1; CA 65-68; CANR 10, 70

Glowacki, Aleksander
See Prus, Boleslaw

Gluck, Louise (Elisabeth) 1943- .. **CLC 7, 22,**
44, 81; DAM POET; PC 16
See CA 33-36R; CANR 40, 69; DA3; DLB
5; MTCW 2

Glyn, Elinor 1864-1943 .... **TCLC 72**
See DLB 153

Gobineau, Joseph Arthur (Comte) de
1816-1882 .... **NCLC 17**
See DLB 123

Godard, Jean-Luc 1930- .... **CLC 20**
See CA 93-96

Godden, (Margaret) Rumer
1907-1998 .... **CLC 53**
See AAYA 6; CA 5-8R; 172; CANR 4, 27,
36, 55, 80; CLR 20; DLB 161; MAICYA;
SAAS 12; SATA 3, 36; SATA-Obit 109

Godoy Alcayaga, Lucila 1889-1957
See Mistral, Gabriela
See BW 2; CA 104; 131; CANR 81; DAM
MULT; HW 1, 2; MTCW 1, 2

Godwin, Gail (Kathleen) 1937- ..... **CLC 5, 8,**
22, 31, 69, 125; DAM POP
See CA 29-32R; CANR 15, 43, 69; DA3;
DLB 6; INT CANR-15; MTCW 1, 2

Godwin, William 1756-1836 .... **NCLC 14**
See CDBLB 1789-1832; DLB 39, 104, 142,
158, 163

Goebbels, Josef
See Goebbels, (Paul) Joseph

Goebbels, (Paul) Joseph
1897-1945 .... **TCLC 68**
See CA 115; 148

Goebbels, Joseph Paul
See Goebbels, (Paul) Joseph

Goethe, Johann Wolfgang von
1749-1832 . **NCLC 4, 22, 34; DA; DAB;**
DAC; DAM DRAM, MST, POET; PC
5; WLC
See DA3; DLB 94

Gogarty, Oliver St.John
1878-1957 .... **TCLC 15**
See CA 109; 150; DLB 15, 19

Gogol, Nikolai (Vasilyevich)
1809-1852 . **NCLC 5, 15, 31; DA; DAB;**
DAC; DAM DRAM, MST; DC 1; SSC
4, 29; WLC
See DLB 198

Goines, Donald 1937(?)-1974 . **CLC 80; BLC**
2; DAM MULT, POP
See AITN 1; BW 1, 3; CA 124; 114; CANR
82; DA3; DLB 33

Gold, Herbert 1924- .... **CLC 4, 7, 14, 42**
See CA 9-12R; CANR 17, 45; DLB 2;
DLBY 81

Goldbarth, Albert 1948- .... **CLC 5, 38**
See CA 53-56; CANR 6, 40; DLB 120

Goldberg, Anatol 1910-1982 .... **CLC 34**
See CA 131; 117

Goldemberg, Isaac 1945- .... **CLC 52**
See CA 69-72; CAAS 12; CANR 11, 32;
HW 1

Golding, William (Gerald)
1911-1993 ..... **CLC 1, 2, 3, 8, 10, 17, 27,**
58, 81; DA; DAB; DAC; DAM MST,
NOV; WLC
See AAYA 5; CA 5-8R; 141; CANR 13, 33,
54; CDBLB 1945-1960; DA3; DLB 15,
100; MTCW 1, 2

Goldman, Emma 1869-1940 .... **TCLC 13**
See CA 110; 150

Goldman, Francisco 1954- .... **CLC 76**
See CA 162

Goldman, William (W.) 1931- .... **CLC 1,48**
See CA 9-12R; CANR 29, 69; DLB 44

Goldmann, Lucien 1913-1970 .... **CLC 24**
See CA 25-28; CAP 2

Goldoni, Carlo 1707-1793 .... **LC 4; DAM**
DRAM

Goldsberry, Steven 1949- .... **CLC 34**
See CA 131

Goldsmith, Oliver 1728-1774 . **LC 2, 48; DA;**
DAB; DAC; DAM DRAM, MST, NOV,
POET; DC 8; WLC
See CDBLB 1660-1789; DLB 39, 89, 104,
109, 142; SATA 26

Goldsmith, Peter
See Priestley, J(ohn) B(oynton)

Gombrowicz, Witold 1904-1969 .... **CLC 4, 7,**
11, 49; DAM DRAM
See CA 19-20; 25-28R; CAP 2

Gomez de la Serna, Ramon
1888-1963 .... **CLC 9**
See CA 153; 116; CANR 79; HW 1, 2

Goncharov, Ivan Alexandrovich
1812-1891 .... **NCLC 1, 63**

Goncourt, Edmond (Louis Antoine Huot) de
1822-1896 .... **NCLC 7**
See DLB 123

Goncourt, Jules (Alfred Huot) de
1830-1870 .... **NCLC 7**
See DLB 123

Gontier, Fernande 19(?)- .... **CLC 50**

Gonzalez Martinez, Enrique
1871-1952 .... **TCLC 72**
See CA 166; CANR 81; HW 1, 2

Goodman, Paul 1911-1972 ..... **CLC 1, 2, 4, 7**
See CA 19-20; 37-40R; CANR 34; CAP 2;
DLB 130; MTCW 1

Gordimer, Nadine 1923- ...... **CLC 3, 5, 7, 10,**
18, 33, 51, 70; DA; DAB; DAC; DAM
MST, NOV; SSC 17; WLCS
See CA 5-8R; CANR 3, 28, 56; DA3; INT
CANR-28; MTCW 1, 2

Gordon, Adam Lindsay
1833-1870 .... **NCLC 21**

Gordon, Caroline 1895-1981 . **CLC 6, 13, 29,**
83; SSC 15
See CA 11-12; 103; CANR 36; CAP 1; DLB
4, 9, 102; DLBD 17; DLBY 81; MTCW
1, 2

Gordon, Charles William 1860-1937
See Connor, Ralph
See CA 109

Gordon, Mary (Catherine) 1949- .... **CLC 13,**
22
See CA 102; CANR 44; DLB 6; DLBY 81;
INT 102; MTCW 1

Gordon, N. J.
See Bosman, Herman Charles

Gordon, Sol 1923- .... **CLC 26**
See CA 53-56; CANR 4; SATA 11

Gordone, Charles 1925-1995 .... **CLC 1, 4;**
DAM DRAM; DC 8
See BW 1, 3; CA 93-96; 180; 150; CAAE
180; CANR 55; DLB 7; INT 93-96;
MTCW 1

Gore, Catherine 1800-1861 .... **NCLC 65**
See DLB 116

Gorenko, Anna Andreevna
See Akhmatova, Anna

Gorky, Maxim 1868-1936 ..... **TCLC 8; DAB;**
SSC 28; WLC
See Peshkov, Alexei Maximovich
See MTCW 2

Goryan, Sirak
See Saroyan, William

Gosse, Edmund (William)
1849-1928 .... **TCLC 28**
See CA 117; DLB 57, 144, 184

Gotlieb, Phyllis Fay (Bloom) 1926- .. **CLC 18**
See CA 13-16R; CANR 7; DLB 88

Gottesman, S. D.
See Kornbluth, C(yril) M.; Pohl, Frederik
Gottfried von Strassburg fl.
c.1210- .... **CMLC 10**
See DLB 138
Gould, Lois CLC 4, 10
See CA 77-80; CANR 29; MTCW 1
Gourmont, Remy (-Marie-Charles) de
1858-1915 .... **TCLC 17**
See CA 109; 150; MTCW 2
Govier, Katherine 1948- .... **CLC 51**
See CA 101; CANR 18, 40
Goyen, (Charles) William
1915-1983 .... **CLC 5, 8, 14, 40**
See AITN 2; CA 5-8R; 110; CANR 6, 71;
DLB 2; DLBY 83; INT CANR-6
Goytisolo, Juan 1931- . **CLC 5, 10, 23; DAM
MULT; HLC 1**
See CA 85-88; CANR 32, 61; HW 1, 2;
MTCW 1, 2
Gozzano, Guido 1883-1916 .... **PC 10**
See CA 154; DLB 114
Gozzi, (Conte) Carlo 1720-1806 .... **NCLC 23**
Grabbe, Christian Dietrich
1801-1836 .... **NCLC 2**
See DLB 133
Grace, Patricia Frances 1937- .... **CLC 56**
See CA 176
Gracian y Morales, Baltasar
1601-1658 .... **LC 15**
Gracq, Julien CLC 11, 48
See Poirier, Louis
See DLB 83
Grade, Chaim 1910-1982 .... **CLC 10**
See CA 93-96; 107
Graduate of Oxford, A
See Ruskin, John
Grafton, Garth
See Duncan, Sara Jeannette
Graham, John
See Phillips, David Graham
Graham, Jorie 1951- .... **CLC 48, 118**
See CA 111; CANR 63; DLB 120
Graham, R(obert) B(ontine) Cunninghame
See Cunninghame Graham, R(obert)
B(ontine)
See DLB 98, 135, 174
Graham, Robert
See Haldeman, Joe (William)
Graham, Tom
See Lewis, (Harry) Sinclair
Graham, W(illiam) S(ydney)
1918-1986 .... **CLC 29**
See CA 73-76; 118; DLB 20
Graham, Winston (Mawdsley)
1910- .... **CLC 23**
See CA 49-52; CANR 2, 22, 45, 66; DLB
77
Grahame, Kenneth 1859-1932 ...... **TCLC 64;
DAB**
See CA 108; 136; CANR 80; CLR 5; DA3;
DLB 34, 141, 178; MAICYA; MTCW 2;
SATA 100; YABC 1
Granovsky, Timofei Nikolaevich
1813-1855 .... **NCLC 75**
See DLB 198
Grant, Skeeter
See Spiegelman, Art
Granville-Barker, Harley
1877-1946 .... **TCLC 2; DAM DRAM**
See Barker, Harley Granville
See CA 104
Grass, Guenter (Wilhelm) 1927- ... **CLC 1, 2,
4, 6, 11, 15, 22, 32, 49, 88; DA; DAB;
DAC; DAM MST, NOV; WLC**
See CA 13-16R; CANR 20, 75; DA3; DLB
75, 124; MTCW 1, 2
Gratton, Thomas
See Hulme, T(homas) E(rnest)

Grau, Shirley Ann 1929- ... **CLC 4, 9;SSC 15**
See CA 89-92; CANR 22, 69; DLB 2; INT
CANR-22; MTCW 1
Gravel, Fern
See Hall, James Norman
Graver, Elizabeth 1964- .... **CLC 70**
See CA 135; CANR 71
Graves, Richard Perceval 1945- .... **CLC 44**
See CA 65-68; CANR 9, 26, 51
Graves, Robert (von Ranke)
1895-1985 .. **CLC 1, 2, 6, 11, 39, 44, 45;
DAB; DAC; DAM MST, POET; PC 6**
See CA 5-8R; 117; CANR 5, 36; CDBLB
1914-1945; DA3; DLB 20, 100, 191;
DLBD 18; DLBY 85; MTCW 1, 2; SATA
45
Graves, Valerie
See Bradley, Marion Zimmer
Gray, Alasdair (James) 1934- .... **CLC 41**
See CA 126; CANR 47, 69; DLB 194; INT
126; MTCW 1, 2
Gray, Amlin 1946- .... **CLC 29**
See CA 138
Gray, Francine du Plessix 1930- ..... **CLC 22;
DAM NOV**
See BEST 90:3; CA 61-64; CAAS 2; CANR
11, 33, 75, 81; INT CANR-11; MTCW 1,
2
Gray, John (Henry) 1866-1934 ...... **TCLC 19**
See CA 119; 162
Gray, Simon (James Holliday)
1936- .... **CLC 9, 14, 36**
See AITN 1; CA 21-24R; CAAS 3; CANR
32, 69; DLB 13; MTCW 1
Gray, Spalding 1941- ..... **CLC 49, 112; DAM
POP; DC 7**
See CA 128; CANR 74; MTCW 2
Gray, Thomas 1716-1771 .... **LC 4, 40; DA;
DAB; DAC; DAM MST; PC 2; WLC**
See CDBLB 1660-1789; DA3; DLB 109
Grayson, David
See Baker, Ray Stannard
Grayson, Richard (A.) 1951- .... **CLC 38**
See CA 85-88; CANR 14, 31, 57
Greeley, Andrew M(oran) 1928- ..... **CLC 28;
DAM POP**
See CA 5-8R; CAAS 7; CANR 7, 43, 69;
DA3; MTCW 1, 2
Green, AnnaKatharine 1846-1935 . **TCLC 63**
See CA 112; 159; DLB 202
Green, Brian
See Card, Orson Scott
Green, Hannah
See Greenberg, Joanne (Goldenberg)
Green, Hannah 1927(?)-1996 .... **CLC 3**
See CA 73-76; CANR 59
Green, Henry 1905-1973 .... **CLC 2, 13, 97**
See Yorke, Henry Vincent
See CA 175; DLB 15
Green, Julian (Hartridge) 1900-1998
See Green, Julien
See CA 21-24R; 169; CANR 33; DLB 4,
72; MTCW 1
Green, Julien CLC 3, 11, 77
See Green, Julian (Hartridge)
See MTCW 2
Green, Paul (Eliot) 1894-1981 .... **CLC 25;
DAM DRAM**
See AITN 1; CA 5-8R; 103; CANR 3; DLB
7, 9; DLBY 81
Greenberg, Ivan 1908-1973
See Rahv, Philip
See CA 85-88
Greenberg, Joanne (Goldenberg)
1932- .... **CLC 7, 30**
See AAYA 12; CA 5-8R; CANR 14, 32, 69;
SATA 25
Greenberg, Richard 1959(?)- .... **CLC 57**
See CA 138

Greene, Bette 1934- .... **CLC 30**
See AAYA 7; CA 53-56; CANR 4; CLR 2;
JRDA; MAICYA; SAAS 16; SATA 8, 102
Greene, Gael CLC 8
See CA 13-16R; CANR 10
Greene, Graham (Henry)
1904-1991 .... **CLC 1, 3, 6, 9, 14, 18, 27,
37, 70, 72, 125; DA; DAB; DAC; DAM
MST, NOV; SSC 29; WLC**
See AITN 2; CA 13-16R; 133; CANR 35,
61;CDBLB 1945-1960; DA3; DLB 13,
15, 77, 100, 162, 201, 204; DLBY 91;
MTCW 1, 2; SATA 20
Greene, Robert 1558-1592 .... **LC 41**
See DLB 62, 167
Greer, Richard
See Silverberg, Robert
Gregor, Arthur 1923- .... **CLC 9**
See CA 25-28R; CAAS 10; CANR 11;
SATA 36
Gregor, Lee
See Pohl, Frederik
Gregory, Isabella Augusta (Persse)
1852-1932 .... **TCLC 1**
See CA 104; DLB 10
Gregory, J. Dennis
See Williams, John A(lfred)
Grendon, Stephen
See Derleth, August (William)
Grenville, Kate 1950- .... **CLC 61**
See CA 118; CANR 53
Grenville, Pelham
See Wodehouse, P(elham) G(renville)
Greve, Felix Paul (Berthold Friedrich)
1879-1948
See Grove, Frederick Philip
See CA 104; 141, 175; CANR 79; DAC;
DAM MST
Grey, Zane 1872-1939 ... **TCLC 6;DAM POP**
See CA 104; 132; DA3; DLB 212; MTCW
1, 2
Grieg, (Johan) Nordahl(Brun)
1902-1943 .... **TCLC 10**
See CA 107
Grieve, C(hristopher) M(urray)
1892-1978 ..... **CLC 11, 19; DAM POET**
See MacDiarmid, Hugh; Pteleon
See CA 5-8R; 85-88; CANR 33; MTCW 1
Griffin, Gerald 1803-1840 .... **NCLC 7**
See DLB 159
Griffin, John Howard 1920-1980 ..... **CLC 68**
See AITN 1; CA 1-4R; 101; CANR 2
Griffin, Peter 1942- .... **CLC 39**
See CA 136
Griffith, D(avid Lewelyn) W(ark)
1875(?)-1948 .... **TCLC 68**
See CA 119; 150; CANR 80
Griffith, Lawrence
See Griffith, D(avid Lewelyn) W(ark)
Griffiths, Trevor 1935- .... **CLC 13, 52**
See CA 97-100; CANR 45; DLB 13
Griggs, Sutton Elbert
1872-1930(?) .... **TCLC 77**
See CA 123; DLB 50
Grigson, Geoffrey (Edward Harvey)
1905-1985 .... **CLC 7, 39**
See CA 25-28R; 118; CANR 20, 33; DLB
27; MTCW 1, 2
Grillparzer, Franz 1791-1872 .... **NCLC 1;
SSC 37**
See DLB 133
Grimble, Reverend Charles James
See Eliot, T(homas) S(tearns)
Grimke, Charlotte L(ottie) Forten
1837(?)-1914
See Forten, Charlotte L.
See BW 1; CA 117; 124; DAM MULT,
POET

Grimm, Jacob Ludwig Karl
1785-1863 .... NCLC 3, 77; SSC 36
See DLB 90; MAICYA; SATA 22

Grimm, Wilhelm Karl 1786-1859 .. NCLC 3,
77; SSC 36
See DLB 90; MAICYA; SATA 22

Grimmelshausen, Johann Jakob
Christoffelvon 1621-1676 .... LC 6
See DLB 168

Grindel, Eugene 1895-1952
See Eluard, Paul
See CA 104

Grisham, John 1955- ..... CLC 84;DAM POP
See AAYA 14; CA 138; CANR 47, 69;
DA3; MTCW 2

Grossman, David 1954- .... CLC 67
See CA 138

Grossman, Vasily (Semenovich)
1905-1964 .... CLC 41
See CA 124; 130; MTCW 1

Grove, Frederick Philip TCLC 4
See Greve, Felix Paul (Berthold Friedrich)
See DLB 92

Grubb
See Crumb, R(obert)

Grumbach, Doris (Isaac) 1918- . CLC 13, 22,
64
See CA 5-8R; CAAS 2; CANR 9, 42, 70;
INT CANR-9; MTCW 2

Grundtvig, Nicolai Frederik Severin
1783-1872 .... NCLC 1

Grunge
See Crumb, R(obert)

Grunwald, Lisa 1959- .... CLC 44
See CA 120

Guare, John 1938- .... CLC 8, 14, 29, 67;
DAM DRAM
See CA 73-76; CANR 21, 69; DLB 7;
MTCW 1, 2

Gudjonsson, Halldor Kiljan 1902-1998
See Laxness, Halldor
See CA 103; 164

Guenter, Erich
See Eich, Guenter

Guest, Barbara 1920- .... CLC 34
See CA 25-28R; CANR 11, 44, 84; DLB 5,
193

Guest, Edgar A(lbert) 1881-1959 .. TCLC 95
See CA 112; 168

Guest, Judith (Ann) 1936- .... CLC 8, 30;
DAM NOV, POP
See AAYA 7; CA 77-80; CANR 15, 75;
DA3; INT CANR-15; MTCW 1, 2

Guevara, Che CLC 87; HLC 1
See Guevara (Serna), Ernesto

Guevara (Serna), Ernesto
1928-1967 .... CLC 87; DAM MULT;
HLC 1
See Guevara, Che
See CA 127; 111; CANR 56; HW 1

Guicciardini, Francesco 1483-1540 ..... LC 49

Guild, Nicholas M. 1944- .... CLC 33
See CA 93-96

Guillemin, Jacques
See Sartre, Jean-Paul

Guillen, Jorge 1893-1984 .... CLC 11; DAM
MULT, POET; HLCS 1
See CA 89-92; 112; DLB 108; HW 1

Guillen, Nicolas (Cristobal)
1902-1989 ... CLC 48, 79; BLC 2; DAM
MST, MULT, POET; HLC 1; PC 23
See BW 2; CA 116; 125; 129; CANR 84;
HW 1

Guillevic, (Eugene) 1907- .... CLC 33
See CA 93-96

Guillois
See Desnos, Robert

Guillois, Valentin
See Desnos, Robert

Guimaraes Rosa, Joao 1908-1967
See CA 175; HLCS 2

Guiney, LouiseImogen 1861-1920 .. TCLC 41
See CA 160; DLB 54

Guiraldes, Ricardo (Guillermo)
1886-1927 .... TCLC 39
See CA 131; HW 1; MTCW 1

Gumilev, Nikolai (Stepanovich)
1886-1921 .... TCLC 60
See CA 165

Gunesekera, Romesh 1954- .... CLC 91
See CA 159

Gunn, Bill CLC 5
See Gunn, William Harrison
See DLB 38

Gunn, Thom(son William) 1929- .. CLC 3, 6,
18, 32, 81; DAM POET; PC 26
See CA 17-20R; CANR 9, 33; CDBLB
1960 to Present; DLB 27; INT CANR-33;
MTCW 1

Gunn, William Harrison 1934(?)-1989
See Gunn, Bill
See AITN 1; BW 1, 3; CA 13-16R; 128;
CANR 12, 25, 76

Gunnars, Kristjana 1948- .... CLC 69
See CA 113; DLB 60

Gurdjieff, G(eorgei) I(vanovich)
1877(?)-1949 .... TCLC 71
See CA 157

Gurganus, Allan 1947- .. CLC 70;DAM POP
See BEST 90:1; CA 135

Gurney, A(lbert) R(amsdell), Jr.
1930- ..... CLC 32, 50, 54; DAM DRAM
See CA 77-80; CANR 32, 64

Gurney, Ivor (Bertie) 1890-1937 ... TCLC 33
See CA 167

Gurney, Peter
See Gurney, A(lbert) R(amsdell), Jr.

Guro, Elena 1877-1913 .... TCLC 56

Gustafson, James M(oody) 1925- ... CLC 100
See CA 25-28R; CANR 37

Gustafson, Ralph (Barker) 1909- ..... CLC 36
See CA 21-24R; CANR 8, 45, 84; DLB 88

Gut, Gom
See Simenon, Georges (Jacques Christian)

Guterson, David 1956- .... CLC 91
See CA 132; CANR 73; MTCW 2

Guthrie, A(lfred) B(ertram),Jr.
1901-1991 .... CLC 23
See CA 57-60; 134; CANR 24; DLB 212;
SATA 62; SATA-Obit 67

Guthrie, Isobel
See Grieve, C(hristopher) M(urray)

Guthrie, Woodrow Wilson 1912-1967
See Guthrie, Woody
See CA 113; 93-96

Guthrie, Woody CLC 35
See Guthrie, Woodrow Wilson

Gutierrez Najera, Manuel 1859-1895
See HLCS 2

Guy, Rosa (Cuthbert) 1928- .... CLC 26
See AAYA 4; BW 2; CA 17-20R; CANR
14, 34, 83; CLR 13; DLB 33; JRDA;
MAICYA; SATA 14, 62

Gwendolyn
See Bennett, (Enoch) Arnold

H. D. CLC 3, 8, 14, 31, 34, 73; PC 5
See Doolittle, Hilda

H. de V.
See Buchan, John

Haavikko, Paavo Juhani 1931- .. CLC 18, 34
See CA 106

Habbema, Koos
See Heijermans, Herman

Habermas, Juergen 1929- .... CLC 104
See CA 109; CANR 85

Habermas, Jurgen
See Habermas, Juergen

Hacker, Marilyn 1942- ...... CLC 5, 9, 23, 72,
91; DAM POET
See CA 77-80; CANR 68; DLB 120

Haeckel, Ernst Heinrich (Philipp August)
1834-1919 .... TCLC 83
See CA 157

Hafiz c. 1326-1389 .... CMLC 34

Hafiz c. 1326-1389(?) .... CMLC 34

Haggard, H(enry) Rider
1856-1925 .... TCLC 11
See CA 108; 148; DLB 70, 156, 174, 178;
MTCW 2; SATA 16

Hagiosy, L.
See Larbaud, Valery (Nicolas)

Hagiwara Sakutaro 1886-1942 ..... TCLC 60;
PC 18

Haig, Fenil
See Ford, Ford Madox

Haig-Brown, Roderick (Langmere)
1908-1976 .... CLC 21
See CA 5-8R; 69-72; CANR 4, 38, 83; CLR
31; DLB 88; MAICYA; SATA 12

Hailey, Arthur 1920- ..... CLC 5; DAM NOV,
POP
See AITN 2; BEST 90:3; CA 1-4R; CANR
2, 36, 75; DLB 88; DLBY 82; MTCW 1,
2

Hailey, Elizabeth Forsythe 1938- ..... CLC 40
See CA 93-96; CAAS 1; CANR 15, 48; INT
CANR-15

Haines, John (Meade) 1924- .... CLC 58
See CA 17-20R; CANR 13, 34; DLB 212

Hakluyt, Richard 1552-1616 .... LC 31

Haldeman, Joe (William) 1943- .... CLC 61
See Graham, Robert
See CA 53-56, 179; CAAE 179; CAAS 25;
CANR 6, 70, 72; DLB 8; INT CANR-6

Hale, Sarah Josepha (Buell)
1788-1879 .... NCLC 75
See DLB 1, 42, 73

Haley, Alex(ander Murray Palmer)
1921-1992 . CLC 8, 12, 76; BLC 2; DA;
DAB; DAC; DAM MST, MULT, POP
See AAYA 26; BW 2, 3; CA 77-80; 136;
CANR 61; CDALBS; DA3; DLB 38;
MTCW 1, 2

Haliburton, Thomas Chandler
1796-1865 .... NCLC 15
See DLB 11, 99

Hall, Donald (Andrew, Jr.) 1928- ...... CLC 1,
13, 37, 59; DAM POET
See CA 5-8R; CAAS 7; CANR 2, 44, 64;
DLB 5; MTCW 1; SATA 23, 97

Hall, Frederic Sauser
See Sauser-Hall, Frederic

Hall, James
See Kuttner, Henry

Hall, James Norman 1887-1951 ..... TCLC 23
See CA 123; 173; SATA 21

Hall, Radclyffe
See Hall, (Marguerite) Radclyffe
See MTCW 2

Hall, (Marguerite) Radclyffe
1886-1943 .... TCLC 12
See CA 110; 150; CANR 83; DLB 191

Hall, Rodney 1935- .... CLC 51
See CA 109; CANR 69

Halleck, Fitz-Greene 1790-1867 .... NCLC 47
See DLB 3

Halliday, Michael
See Creasey, John

Halpern, Daniel 1945- .... CLC 14
See CA 33-36R

Hamburger, Michael (Peter Leopold)
1924- .... CLC 5, 14
See CA 5-8R; CAAS 4; CANR 2, 47; DLB
27

Hamill, Pete 1935- .... CLC 10
See CA 25-28R; CANR 18, 71

Hamilton, Alexander
1755(?)-1804 .... NCLC **49**
See DLB 37
Hamilton, Clive
See Lewis, C(live) S(taples)
Hamilton, Edmond 1904-1977 .... CLC **1**
See CA 1-4R; CANR 3, 84; DLB 8
Hamilton, Eugene (Jacob) Lee
See Lee-Hamilton, Eugene (Jacob)
Hamilton, Franklin
See Silverberg, Robert
Hamilton, Gail
See Corcoran, Barbara
Hamilton, Mollie
See Kaye, M(ary) M(argaret)
Hamilton, (Anthony Walter) Patrick
1904-1962 .... CLC **51**
See CA 176; 113; DLB 191
Hamilton, Virginia 1936- .... CLC **26;DAM**
MULT
See AAYA 2, 21; BW 2, 3; CA 25-28R;
CANR 20, 37, 73; CLR 1, 11, 40; DLB
33, 52; INT CANR-20; JRDA; MAICYA;
MTCW 1, 2; SATA 4, 56, 79
Hammett, (Samuel) Dashiell
1894-1961 .... CLC **3, 5, 10, 19, 47; SSC**
17
See AITN 1; CA 81-84; CANR 42; CDALB
1929-1941; DA3; DLBD 6; DLBY 96;
MTCW 1, 2
Hammon, Jupiter 1711(?)-1800(?) . NCLC **5;**
BLC 2; DAM MULT, POET; PC 16
See DLB 31, 50
Hammond, Keith
See Kuttner, Henry
Hamner, Earl (Henry), Jr. 1923- ...... CLC **12**
See AITN 2; CA 73-76; DLB 6
Hampton, Christopher (James)
1946- .... CLC **4**
See CA 25-28R; DLB 13; MTCW 1
Hamsun, Knut TCLC **2, 14, 49**
See Pedersen, Knut
Handke, Peter 1942- ... CLC **5, 8, 10, 15, 38;**
DAM DRAM, NOV
See CA 77-80; CANR 33, 75; DLB 85, 124;
MTCW 1, 2
Handy, W(illiam) C(hristopher)
1873-1958 .... TCLC **97**
See BW 3; CA 121; 167
Hanley, James 1901-1985 ..... CLC **3, 5, 8, 13**
See CA 73-76; 117; CANR 36; DLB 191;
MTCW 1
Hannah, Barry 1942- .... CLC **23, 38, 90**
See CA 108; 110; CANR 43, 68; DLB 6;
INT 110; MTCW 1
Hannon, Ezra
See Hunter, Evan
Hansberry, Lorraine (Vivian)
1930-1965 ..... CLC **17, 62; BLC 2; DA;**
DAB; DAC; DAM DRAM, MST,
MULT;DC 2
See AAYA 25; BW 1, 3; CA 109; 25-28R;
CABS 3; CANR 58; CDALB 1941-1968;
DA3; DLB 7, 38; MTCW 1, 2
Hansen, Joseph 1923- .... CLC **38**
See CA 29-32R; CAAS 17; CANR 16, 44,
66; INT CANR-16
Hansen, Martin A(lfred)
1909-1955 .... TCLC **32**
See CA 167
Hanson, Kenneth O(stlin) 1922- .... CLC **13**
See CA 53-56; CANR 7
Hardwick, Elizabeth (Bruce)
1916- .... CLC **13; DAM NOV**
See CA 5-8R; CANR 3, 32, 70; DA3; DLB
6; MTCW 1, 2

Hardy, Thomas 1840-1928 .. TCLC **4, 10, 18,**
32, 48, 53, 72; DA; DAB; DAC; DAM
MST, NOV, POET; PC 8; SSC 2;WLC
See CA 104; 123; CDBLB 1890-1914;
DA3; DLB 18, 19, 135; MTCW 1, 2
Hare, David 1947- .... CLC **29, 58**
See CA 97-100; CANR 39; DLB 13;
MTCW 1
Harewood, John
See Van Druten, John (William)
Harford, Henry
See Hudson, W(illiam) H(enry)
Hargrave, Leonie
See Disch, Thomas M(ichael)
Harjo, Joy 1951- ...... CLC **83; DAM MULT;**
PC 27
See CA 114; CANR 35, 67; DLB 120, 175;
MTCW 2; NNAL
Harlan, Louis R(udolph) 1922- .... CLC **34**
See CA 21-24R; CANR 25, 55, 80
Harling, Robert 1951(?)- .... CLC **53**
See CA 147
Harmon, William (Ruth) 1938- .... CLC **38**
See CA 33-36R; CANR 14, 32, 35; SATA
65
Harper, F. E. W.
See Harper, Frances Ellen Watkins
Harper, Frances E. W.
See Harper, Frances Ellen Watkins
Harper, Frances E. Watkins
See Harper, Frances Ellen Watkins
Harper, Frances Ellen
See Harper, Frances Ellen Watkins
Harper, Frances Ellen Watkins
1825-1911 ...... TCLC **14; BLC 2; DAM**
MULT, POET; PC 21
See BW 1, 3; CA 111; 125; CANR 79; DLB
50
Harper, Michael S(teven) 1938- ... CLC **7, 22**
See BW 1; CA 33-36R; CANR 24; DLB 41
Harper, Mrs. F. E. W.
See Harper, Frances Ellen Watkins
Harris, Christie (Lucy) Irwin
1907- .... CLC **12**
See CA 5-8R; CANR 6, 83; CLR 47; DLB
88; JRDA; MAICYA; SAAS 10; SATA 6,
74
Harris, Frank 1856-1931 .... TCLC **24**
See CA 109; 150; CANR 80; DLB 156, 197
Harris, George Washington
1814-1869 .... NCLC **23**
See DLB 3, 11
Harris, Joel Chandler 1848-1908 ... TCLC **2;**
SSC 19
See CA 104; 137; CANR 80; CLR 49; DLB
11, 23, 42, 78, 91; MAICYA; SATA 100;
YABC 1
Harris, John (Wyndham Parkes Lucas)
Beynon 1903-1969
See Wyndham, John
See CA 102; 89-92; CANR 84
Harris, MacDonald CLC **9**
See Heiney, Donald (William)
Harris, Mark 1922- .... CLC **19**
See CA 5-8R; CAAS 3; CANR 2, 55, 83;
DLB 2; DLBY 80
Harris, (Theodore) Wilson 1921- ..... CLC **25**
See BW 2, 3; CA 65-68; CAAS 16; CANR
11, 27, 69; DLB 117; MTCW 1
Harrison, Elizabeth Cavanna 1909-
See Cavanna, Betty
See CA 9-12R; CANR 6, 27, 85
Harrison, Harry (Max) 1925- .... CLC **42**
See CA 1-4R; CANR 5, 21, 84; DLB 8;
SATA 4
Harrison, James (Thomas) 1937- ...... CLC **6,**
14, 33, 66; SSC 19
See CA 13-16R; CANR 8, 51, 79; DLBY
82; INT CANR-8

Harrison, Jim
See Harrison, James (Thomas)
Harrison, Kathryn 1961- .... CLC **70**
See CA 144; CANR 68
Harrison, Tony 1937- .... CLC **43**
See CA 65-68; CANR 44; DLB 40; MTCW
1
Harriss, Will(ard Irvin) 1922- .... CLC **34**
See CA 111
Harson, Sley
See Ellison, Harlan (Jay)
Hart, Ellis
See Ellison, Harlan (Jay)
Hart, Josephine 1942(?)- .... CLC **70;DAM**
POP
See CA 138; CANR 70
Hart, Moss 1904-1961 .... CLC **66;DAM**
DRAM
See CA 109; 89-92; CANR 84; DLB 7
Harte, (Francis) Bret(t)
1836(?)-1902 ... TCLC **1, 25; DA; DAC;**
DAM MST; SSC 8; WLC
See CA 104; 140; CANR 80; CDALB 1865-
1917; DA3; DLB 12, 64, 74, 79, 186;
SATA 26
Hartley, L(eslie) P(oles) 1895-1972 ... CLC **2,**
22
See CA 45-48; 37-40R; CANR 33; DLB
15, 139; MTCW 1, 2
Hartman, Geoffrey H. 1929- .... CLC **27**
See CA 117; 125; CANR 79; DLB 67
Hartmann, Eduard von
1842-1906 .... TCLC **97**
Hartmann, Sadakichi 1867-1944 ... TCLC **73**
See CA 157; DLB 54
Hartmann von Aue c.
1160-c.1205 .... CMLC **15**
See DLB 138
Hartmann von Aue 1170-1210 ...... CMLC **15**
Haruf, Kent 1943- .... CLC **34**
See CA 149
Harwood, Ronald 1934- .... CLC **32; DAM**
DRAM, MST
See CA 1-4R; CANR 4, 55; DLB 13
Hasegawa Tatsunosuke
See Futabatei, Shimei
Hasek, Jaroslav (Matej Frantisek)
1883-1923 .... TCLC **4**
See CA 104; 129; MTCW 1, 2
Hass, Robert 1941- .... CLC **18, 39, 99;PC 16**
See CA 111; CANR 30, 50, 71; DLB 105,
206; SATA 94
Hastings, Hudson
See Kuttner, Henry
Hastings, Selina CLC **44**
Hathorne, John 1641-1717 .... LC **38**
Hatteras, Amelia
See Mencken, H(enry) L(ouis)
Hatteras, Owen TCLC **18**
See Mencken, H(enry) L(ouis); Nathan,
George Jean
Hauptmann, Gerhart (Johann Robert)
1862-1946 .... TCLC **4; DAM DRAM**
See CA 104; 153; DLB 66, 118
Havel, Vaclav 1936- ... CLC **25, 58, 65; DAM**
DRAM; DC 6
See CA 104; CANR 36, 63; DA3; MTCW
1, 2
Haviaras, Stratis CLC **33**
See Chaviaras, Strates
Hawes, Stephen 1475(?)-1523(?) .... LC **17**
See DLB 132
Hawkes, John (Clendennin Burne, Jr.)
1925-1998 .. CLC **1, 2, 3, 4, 7, 9, 14, 15,**
27, 49
See CA 1-4R; 167; CANR 2, 47, 64; DLB
2, 7; DLBY 80, 98; MTCW 1, 2

Hawking, S. W.
See Hawking, Stephen W(illiam)
Hawking, Stephen W(illiam) 1942- . **CLC 63, 105**
See AAYA 13; BEST 89:1; CA 126; 129; CANR 48; DA3; MTCW 2
Hawkins, Anthony Hope
See Hope, Anthony
Hawthorne, Julian 1846-1934 .... **TCLC 25**
See CA 165
Hawthorne, Nathaniel 1804-1864 . **NCLC 39; DA; DAB; DAC; DAM MST, NOV; SSC 3, 29; WLC**
See AAYA 18;CDALB 1640-1865; DA3; DLB 1, 74; YABC 2
Haxton, Josephine Ayres 1921-
See Douglas, Ellen
See CA 115; CANR 41, 83
Hayaseca y Eizaguirre, Jorge
See Echegaray (y Eizaguirre), Jose (Maria Waldo)
Hayashi, Fumiko 1904-1951 .... **TCLC 27**
See CA 161; DLB 180
Haycraft, Anna 1932-
See Ellis, Alice Thomas
See CA 122; CANR 85; MTCW 2
Hayden, Robert E(arl) 1913-1980 . **CLC 5, 9, 14, 37; BLC 2; DA; DAC; DAM MST, MULT, POET; PC 6**
See BW 1, 3; CA 69-72; 97-100; CABS 2; CANR 24, 75, 82; CDALB 1941-1968; DLB 5, 76; MTCW 1, 2; SATA 19; SATA-Obit 26
Hayford, J(oseph) E(phraim) Casely
See Casely-Hayford, J(oseph) E(phraim)
Hayman, Ronald 1932- .... **CLC 44**
See CA 25-28R; CANR 18, 50; DLB 155
Haywood, Eliza (Fowler)
1693(?)-1756 .... **LC 1, 44**
See DLB 39
Hazlitt, William 1778-1830 .... **NCLC 29**
See DLB 110, 158
Hazzard, Shirley 1931- .... **CLC 18**
See CA 9-12R; CANR 4, 70; DLBY 82; MTCW 1
Head, Bessie 1937-1986 .... **CLC 25, 67; BLC 2; DAM MULT**
See BW 2, 3; CA 29-32R; 119; CANR 25, 82; DA3; DLB 117; MTCW 1, 2
Headon, (Nicky) Topper 1956(?)- ..... **CLC 30**
Heaney, Seamus (Justin) 1939- ..... **CLC 5, 7, 14, 25, 37, 74, 91; DAB; DAM POET; PC 18; WLCS**
See CA 85-88; CANR 25, 48, 75; CDBLB 1960 to Present; DA3; DLB 40; DLBY 95; MTCW 1, 2
Hearn, (Patricio) Lafcadio (Tessima Carlos)
1850-1904 .... **TCLC 9**
See CA 105; 166; DLB 12, 78, 189
Hearne, Vicki 1946- .... **CLC 56**
See CA 139
Hearon, Shelby 1931- .... **CLC 63**
See AITN 2; CA 25-28R; CANR 18, 48
Heat-Moon, William Least CLC 29
See Trogdon, William (Lewis)
See AAYA 9
Hebbel, Friedrich 1813-1863 .... **NCLC 43; DAM DRAM**
See DLB 129
Hebert, Anne 1916- ..... **CLC 4, 13, 29; DAC; DAM MST, POET**
See CA 85-88; CANR 69; DA3; DLB 68; MTCW 1, 2
Hecht, Anthony (Evan) 1923- ...... **CLC 8, 13, 19; DAM POET**
See CA 9-12R; CANR 6; DLB 5, 169
Hecht, Ben 1894-1964 .... **CLC 8**
See CA 85-88; DLB 7, 9, 25, 26, 28, 86

Hedayat, Sadeq 1903-1951 .... **TCLC 21**
See CA 120
Hegel, Georg Wilhelm Friedrich
1770-1831 .... **NCLC 46**
See DLB 90
Heidegger, Martin 1889-1976 .... **CLC 24**
See CA 81-84; 65-68; CANR 34; MTCW 1, 2
Heidenstam, (Carl Gustaf) Verner von
1859-1940 .... **TCLC 5**
See CA 104
Heifner, Jack 1946- .... **CLC 11**
See CA 105; CANR 47
Heijermans, Herman 1864-1924 .... **TCLC 24**
See CA 123
Heilbrun, Carolyn G(old) 1926- .... **CLC 25**
See CA 45-48; CANR 1, 28, 58
Heine, Heinrich 1797-1856 .... **NCLC 4, 54; PC 25**
See DLB 90
Heinemann, Larry (Curtiss) 1944- .. **CLC 50**
See CA 110; CAAS 21; CANR 31, 81; DLBD 9; INT CANR-31
Heiney, Donald (William) 1921-1993
See Harris, MacDonald
See CA 1-4R; 142; CANR 3, 58
Heinlein, Robert A(nson) 1907-1988 . **CLC 1, 3, 8, 14, 26, 55; DAM POP**
See AAYA 17; CA 1-4R; 125; CANR 1, 20, 53; DA3; DLB 8; JRDA; MAICYA; MTCW 1, 2; SATA 9, 69; SATA-Obit 56
Helforth, John
See Doolittle, Hilda
Hellenhofferu, Vojtech Kapristian z
See Hasek, Jaroslav (Matej Frantisek)
Heller, Joseph 1923- .. **CLC 1, 3, 5, 8, 11, 36, 63; DA; DAB; DAC; DAM MST, NOV, POP; WLC**
See AAYA 24; AITN 1; CA 5-8R; CABS 1; CANR 8, 42, 66; DA3; DLB 2, 28; DLBY 80; INT CANR-8; MTCW 1, 2
Hellman, Lillian (Florence)
1906-1984 .. **CLC 2, 4, 8, 14, 18, 34, 44, 52; DAM DRAM; DC 1**
See AITN 1, 2; CA 13-16R; 112; CANR 33; DA3; DLB 7; DLBY 84; MTCW 1, 2
Helprin, Mark 1947- .... **CLC 7, 10, 22, 32; DAM NOV, POP**
See CA 81-84; CANR 47, 64; CDALBS; DA3; DLBY 85; MTCW 1, 2
Helvetius, Claude-Adrien 1715-1771 .. **LC 26**
Helyar, Jane Penelope Josephine 1933-
See Poole, Josephine
See CA 21-24R; CANR 10, 26; SATA 82
Hemans, Felicia 1793-1835 .... **NCLC 71**
See DLB 96
Hemingway, Ernest (Miller)
1899-1961 .... **CLC 1, 3, 6, 8, 10, 13, 19, 30, 34, 39, 41, 44, 50, 61, 80; DA; DAB; DAC; DAM MST, NOV; SSC 1, 25, 36; WLC**
See AAYA 19; CA 77-80; CANR 34; CDALB 1917-1929; DA3; DLB 4, 9, 102, 210; DLBD 1, 15, 16; DLBY 81, 87, 96, 98; MTCW 1, 2
Hempel, Amy 1951- .... **CLC 39**
See CA 118; 137; CANR 70; DA3; MTCW 2
Henderson, F. C.
See Mencken, H(enry) L(ouis)
Henderson, Sylvia
See Ashton-Warner, Sylvia (Constance)
Henderson, Zenna (Chlarson)
1917-1983 .... **SSC 29**
See CA 1-4R; 133; CANR 1, 84; DLB 8; SATA 5
Henkin, Joshua CLC 119
See CA 161
Henley, Beth CLC 23; DC 6

See Henley, Elizabeth Becker
See CABS 3; DLBY 86
Henley, Elizabeth Becker 1952-
See Henley, Beth
See CA 107; CANR 32, 73; DAM DRAM, MST; DA3; MTCW 1, 2
Henley, William Ernest 1849-1903 .. **TCLC 8**
See CA 105; DLB 19
Hennissart, Martha
See Lathen, Emma
See CA 85-88; CANR 64
Henry, O. TCLC 1, 19; SSC 5; WLC
See Porter, William Sydney
Henry, Patrick 1736-1799 .... **LC 25**
Henryson, Robert 1430(?)-1506(?) ...... **LC 20**
See DLB 146
Henry VIII 1491-1547 .... **LC 10**
See DLB 132
Henschke, Alfred
See Klabund
Hentoff, Nat(han Irving) 1925- .... **CLC 26**
See AAYA 4; CA 1-4R; CAAS 6; CANR 5, 25, 77; CLR 1, 52; INT CANR-25; JRDA; MAICYA; SATA 42, 69; SATA-Brief 27
Heppenstall, (John) Rayner
1911-1981 .... **CLC 10**
See CA 1-4R; 103; CANR 29
Heraclitus c. 540B.C.-c.450B.C. .... **CMLC 22**
See DLB 176
Herbert, Frank (Patrick)
1920-1986 .... **CLC 12, 23, 35, 44, 85; DAM POP**
See AAYA 21; CA 53-56; 118; CANR 5, 43; CDALBS; DLB 8; INT CANR-5; MTCW 1, 2; SATA 9, 37; SATA-Obit 47
Herbert, George 1593-1633 ..... **LC 24; DAB; DAM POET; PC 4**
See CDBLB Before 1660; DLB 126
Herbert, Zbigniew 1924-1998 ..... **CLC 9, 43; DAM POET**
See CA 89-92; 169; CANR 36, 74; MTCW 1
Herbst, Josephine (Frey)
1897-1969 .... **CLC 34**
See CA 5-8R; 25-28R; DLB 9
Heredia, Jose Maria 1803-1839
See HLCS 2
Hergesheimer,Joseph 1880-1954 .... **TCLC 11**
See CA 109; DLB 102, 9
Herlihy, James Leo 1927-1993 .... **CLC 6**
See CA 1-4R; 143; CANR 2
Hermogenes fl. c. 175- .... **CMLC 6**
Hernandez, Jose 1834-1886 .... **NCLC 17**
Herodotus c.484B.C.-429B.C. .... **CMLC 17**
See DLB 176
Herrick, Robert 1591-1674 .... **LC 13; DA; DAB; DAC; DAM MST, POP; PC 9**
See DLB 126
Herring, Guilles
See Somerville, Edith
Herriot, James 1916-1995 ...... **CLC 12;DAM POP**
See Wight, James Alfred
See AAYA 1; CA 148; CANR 40; MTCW 2; SATA 86
Herrmann, Dorothy 1941- .... **CLC 44**
See CA 107
Herrmann, Taffy
See Herrmann, Dorothy
Hersey, John (Richard) 1914-1993 .... **CLC 1, 2, 7, 9, 40, 81, 97; DAM POP**
See AAYA 29; CA 17-20R; 140; CANR 33; CDALBS; DLB 6, 185; MTCW 1, 2; SATA 25; SATA-Obit 76
Herzen, Aleksandr Ivanovich
1812-1870 .... **NCLC 10, 61**
Herzl, Theodor 1860-1904 .... **TCLC 36**
See CA 168

Herzog, Werner 1942- .... **CLC 16**
  See CA 89-92
Hesiod c. 8th cent. B.C.- .... **CMLC 5**
  See DLB 176
Hesse, Hermann 1877-1962 ... **CLC 1, 2, 3, 6,
  11, 17, 25, 69; DA; DAB; DAC; DAM
  MST, NOV; SSC 9; WLC**
  See CA 17-18; CAP 2; DA3; DLB 66;
  MTCW 1, 2; SATA 50
Hewes, Cady
  See De Voto, Bernard (Augustine)
Heyen, William 1940- .... **CLC 13, 18**
  See CA 33-36R; CAAS 9; DLB 5
Heyerdahl, Thor 1914- .... **CLC 26**
  See CA 5-8R; CANR 5, 22, 66, 73; MTCW
  1, 2; SATA 2, 52
Heym, Georg (Theodor Franz Arthur)
  1887-1912 .... **TCLC 9**
  See CA 106; 181
Heym, Stefan 1913- .... **CLC 41**
  See CA 9-12R; CANR 4; DLB 69
Heyse, Paul (Johann Ludwigvon)
  1830-1914 .... **TCLC 8**
  See CA 104; DLB 129
Heyward, (Edwin) DuBose
  1885-1940 .... **TCLC 59**
  See CA 108; 157; DLB 7, 9, 45; SATA 21
Hibbert, Eleanor Alice Burford
  1906-1993 .... **CLC 7; DAM POP**
  See BEST 90:4; CA 17-20R; 140; CANR 9,
  28, 59; MTCW 2; SATA 2; SATA-Obit 74
Hichens, Robert (Smythe)
  1864-1950 .... **TCLC 64**
  See CA 162; DLB 153
Higgins, George V(incent) 1939- ... **CLC 4, 7,
  10, 18**
  See CA 77-80; CAAS 5; CANR 17, 51;
  DLB 2; DLBY 81, 98; INT CANR-17;
  MTCW 1
Higginson, Thomas Wentworth
  1823-1911 .... **TCLC 36**
  See CA 162; DLB 1, 64
Highet, Helen
  See MacInnes, Helen (Clark)
Highsmith, (Mary) Patricia
  1921-1995 ... **CLC 2, 4, 14, 42, 102;
  DAM NOV, POP**
  See CA 1-4R; 147; CANR 1, 20, 48, 62;
  DA3; MTCW 1, 2
Highwater, Jamake (Mamake)
  1942(?)- .... **CLC 12**
  See AAYA 7; CA 65-68; CAAS 7; CANR
  10, 34, 84; CLR 17; DLB 52; DLBY 85;
  JRDA; MAICYA; SATA 32, 69; SATA-
  Brief 30
Highway, Tomson 1951- .... **CLC 92;
  DAC;DAM MULT**
  See CA 151; CANR 75; MTCW 2; NNAL
Higuchi, Ichiyo 1872-1896 .... **NCLC 49**
Hijuelos, Oscar 1951- .... **CLC 65; DAM
  MULT, POP; HLC 1**
  See AAYA 25; BEST 90:1; CA 123; CANR
  50, 75; DA3; DLB 145; HW 1, 2; MTCW
  2
Hikmet, Nazim 1902(?)-1963 .... **CLC 40**
  See CA 141; 93-96
Hildegard von Bingen 1098-1179 . **CMLC 20**
  See DLB 148
Hildesheimer, Wolfgang 1916-1991 .. **CLC 49**
  See CA 101; 135; DLB 69, 124
Hill, Geoffrey (William) 1932- ...... **CLC 5, 8,
  18, 45; DAM POET**
  See CA 81-84; CANR 21; CDBLB 1960 to
  Present; DLB 40; MTCW 1
Hill, George Roy 1921- .... **CLC 26**
  See CA 110; 122
Hill, John
  See Koontz, Dean R(ay)

Hill, Susan (Elizabeth) 1942- .... **CLC 4, 113;
  DAB; DAM MST, NOV**
  See CA 33-36R; CANR 29, 69; DLB 14,
  139; MTCW 1
Hillerman, Tony 1925- ... **CLC 62;DAM POP**
  See AAYA 6; BEST 89:1; CA 29-32R;
  CANR 21, 42, 65; DA3; DLB 206; SATA
  6
Hillesum, Etty 1914-1943 .... **TCLC 49**
  See CA 137
Hilliard, Noel (Harvey) 1929- .... **CLC 15**
  See CA 9-12R; CANR 7, 69
Hillis, Rick 1956- .... **CLC 66**
  See CA 134
Hilton, James 1900-1954 .... **TCLC 21**
  See CA 108; 169; DLB 34, 77; SATA 34
Himes, Chester (Bomar) 1909-1984 ... **CLC 2,
  4, 7, 18, 58, 108; BLC 2; DAM MULT**
  See BW 2; CA 25-28R; 114; CANR 22;
  DLB 2, 76, 143; MTCW 1, 2
Hinde, Thomas **CLC 6, 11**
  See Chitty, Thomas Willes
Hine, (William) Daryl 1936- .... **CLC 15**
  See CA 1-4R; CAAS 15; CANR 1, 20; DLB
  60
Hinkson, Katharine Tynan
  See Tynan, Katharine
Hinojosa(-Smith), Rolando (R.) 1929-
  See Hinojosa-Smith, Rolando
  See CA 131; CAAS 16; CANR 62; DAM
  MULT; DLB 82; HLC 1; HW 1, 2;
  MTCW 2
Hinojosa-Smith, Rolando 1929-
  See Hinojosa(-Smith), Rolando (R.)
  See CAAS 16; HLC 1; MTCW 2
Hinton, S(usan) E(loise) 1950- .... **CLC 30,
  111; DA; DAB; DAC; DAM MST,
  NOV**
  See AAYA 2; CA 81-84; CANR 32, 62;
  CDALBS; CLR 3, 23; DA3; JRDA; MAI-
  CYA; MTCW 1, 2; SATA 19, 58
Hippius, Zinaida **TCLC 9**
  See Gippius, Zinaida (Nikolayevna)
Hiraoka, Kimitake 1925-1970
  See Mishima, Yukio
  See CA 97-100; 29-32R; DAM DRAM;
  DA3; MTCW 1, 2
Hirsch, E(ric) D(onald),Jr. 1928- ..... **CLC 79**
  See CA 25-28R; CANR 27, 51; DLB 67;
  INT CANR-27; MTCW 1
Hirsch, Edward 1950- .... **CLC 31, 50**
  See CA 104; CANR 20, 42; DLB 120
Hitchcock, Alfred (Joseph)
  1899-1980 .... **CLC 16**
  See AAYA 22; CA 159; 97-100; SATA 27;
  SATA-Obit 24
Hitler, Adolf 1889-1945 .... **TCLC 53**
  See CA 117; 147
Hoagland, Edward 1932- .... **CLC 28**
  See CA 1-4R; CANR 2, 31, 57; DLB 6;
  SATA 51
Hoban, Russell (Conwell) 1925- . **CLC 7, 25;
  DAM NOV**
  See CA 5-8R; CANR 23, 37, 66; CLR 3;
  DLB 52; MAICYA; MTCW 1, 2; SATA
  1, 40, 78
Hobbes, Thomas 1588-1679 .... **LC 36**
  See DLB 151
Hobbs, Perry
  See Blackmur, R(ichard) P(almer)
Hobson, Laura Z(ametkin)
  1900-1986 .... **CLC 7, 25**
  See CA 17-20R; 118; CANR 55; DLB 28;
  SATA 52
Hochhuth, Rolf 1931- .. **CLC 4, 11, 18; DAM
  DRAM**
  See CA 5-8R; CANR 33, 75; DLB 124;
  MTCW 1, 2

Hochman, Sandra 1936- .... **CLC 3, 8**
  See CA 5-8R; DLB 5
Hochwaelder, Fritz 1911-1986 .... **CLC 36;
  DAM DRAM**
  See CA 29-32R; 120; CANR 42; MTCW 1
Hochwalder, Fritz
  See Hochwaelder, Fritz
Hocking, Mary (Eunice) 1921- .... **CLC 13**
  See CA 101; CANR 18, 40
Hodgins, Jack 1938- .... **CLC 23**
  See CA 93-96; DLB 60
Hodgson, William Hope
  1877(?)-1918 .... **TCLC 13**
  See CA 111; 164; DLB 70, 153, 156, 178;
  MTCW 2
Hoeg, Peter 1957- .... **CLC 95**
  See CA 151; CANR 75; DA3; MTCW 2
Hoffman, Alice 1952- .... **CLC 51;DAM NOV**
  See CA 77-80; CANR 34, 66; MTCW 1, 2
Hoffman, Daniel (Gerard) 1923- . **CLC 6, 13,
  23**
  See CA 1-4R; CANR 4; DLB 5
Hoffman, Stanley 1944- .... **CLC 5**
  See CA 77-80
Hoffman, William M(oses) 1939- ..... **CLC 40**
  See CA 57-60; CANR 11, 71
Hoffmann, E(rnst) T(heodor) A(madeus)
  1776-1822 .... **NCLC 2; SSC 13**
  See DLB 90; SATA 27
Hofmann, Gert 1931- .... **CLC 54**
  See CA 128
Hofmannsthal, Hugo von
  1874-1929 ...... **TCLC 11; DAM DRAM;
  DC 4**
  See CA 106; 153; DLB 81, 118
Hogan, Linda 1947- ... **CLC 73;DAM MULT**
  See CA 120; CANR 45, 73; DLB 175;
  NNAL
Hogarth, Charles
  See Creasey, John
Hogarth, Emmett
  See Polonsky, Abraham (Lincoln)
Hogg, James 1770-1835 .... **NCLC 4**
  See DLB 93, 116, 159
Holbach, Paul Henri Thiry Baron
  1723-1789 .... **LC 14**
Holberg, Ludvig 1684-1754 .... **LC 6**
Holden, Ursula 1921- .... **CLC 18**
  See CA 101; CAAS 8; CANR 22
Holderlin, (Johann Christian) Friedrich
  1770-1843 .... **NCLC 16; PC 4**
Holdstock, Robert
  See Holdstock, Robert P.
Holdstock, Robert P. 1948- .... **CLC 39**
  See CA 131; CANR 81
Holland, Isabelle 1920- .... **CLC 21**
  See AAYA 11; CA 21-24R, 181; CAAE 181;
  CANR 10, 25, 47; CLR 57; JRDA; MAI-
  CYA; SATA 8, 70; SATA-Essay 103
Holland, Marcus
  See Caldwell, (Janet Miriam) Taylor
  (Holland)
Hollander, John 1929- .... **CLC 2, 5, 8, 14**
  See CA 1-4R; CANR 1, 52; DLB 5; SATA
  13
Hollander, Paul
  See Silverberg, Robert
Holleran, Andrew 1943(?)- .... **CLC 38**
  See CA 144
Hollinghurst, Alan 1954- .... **CLC 55, 91**
  See CA 114; DLB 207
Hollis, Jim
  See Summers, Hollis (Spurgeon, Jr.)
Holly, Buddy 1936-1959 .... **TCLC 65**
Holmes, Gordon
  See Shiel, M(atthew) P(hipps)
Holmes, John
  See Souster, (Holmes) Raymond

Klein, A(braham) M(oses)
1909-1972 . **CLC 19; DAB; DAC; DAM MST**
See CA 101; 37-40R; DLB 68

Klein, Norma 1938-1989 .... **CLC 30**
See AAYA 2; CA 41-44R; 128; CANR 15, 37; CLR 2, 19; INT CANR-15; JRDA; MAICYA; SAAS 1; SATA 7, 57

Klein, T(heodore) E(ibon) D(onald)
1947- .... **CLC 34**
See CA 119; CANR 44, 75

Kleist, Heinrich von 1777-1811 ...... **NCLC 2, 37; DAM DRAM; SSC 22**
See DLB 90

Klima, Ivan 1931- .... **CLC 56;DAM NOV**
See CA 25-28R; CANR 17, 50

Klimentov, Andrei Platonovich 1899-1951
See Platonov, Andrei
See CA 108

Klinger, Friedrich Maximilianvon
1752-1831 .... **NCLC 1**
See DLB 94

Klingsor the Magician
See Hartmann, Sadakichi

Klopstock, Friedrich Gottlieb
1724-1803 .... **NCLC 11**
See DLB 97

Knapp, Caroline 1959- .... **CLC 99**
See CA 154

Knebel, Fletcher 1911-1993 .... **CLC 14**
See AITN 1; CA 1-4R; 140; CAAS 3; CANR 1, 36; SATA 36; SATA-Obit 75

Knickerbocker, Diedrich
See Irving, Washington

Knight, Etheridge 1931-1991 . **CLC 40; BLC 2; DAM POET; PC 14**
See BW 1, 3; CA 21-24R; 133; CANR 23, 82; DLB 41; MTCW 2

Knight, Sarah Kemble 1666-1727 .... **LC 7**
See DLB 24, 200

Knister, Raymond 1899-1932 .... **TCLC 56**
See DLB 68

Knowles, John 1926- . **CLC 1, 4, 10, 26; DA; DAC; DAM MST, NOV**
See AAYA 10; CA 17-20R; CANR 40, 74, 76; CDALB 1968-1988; DLB 6; MTCW 1, 2; SATA 8, 89

Knox, Calvin M.
See Silverberg, Robert

Knox, John c. 1505-1572 .... **LC 37**
See DLB 132

Knye, Cassandra
See Disch, Thomas M(ichael)

Koch, C(hristopher) J(ohn) 1932- .... **CLC 42**
See CA 127; CANR 84

Koch, Christopher
See Koch, C(hristopher) J(ohn)

Koch, Kenneth 1925- ..... **CLC 5, 8, 44;DAM POET**
See CA 1-4R; CANR 6, 36, 57; DLB 5; INT CANR-36; MTCW 2; SATA 65

Kochanowski, Jan 1530-1584 .... **LC 10**

Kock, Charles Paul de 1794-1871 . **NCLC 16**

Koda Shigeyuki 1867-1947
See Rohan, Koda
See CA 121

Koestler, Arthur 1905-1983 ... **CLC 1, 3, 6, 8, 15, 33**
See CA 1-4R; 109; CANR 1, 33; CDBLB 1945-1960; DLBY 83; MTCW 1, 2

Kogawa, Joy Nozomi 1935- .. **CLC 78; DAC; DAM MST, MULT**
See CA 101; CANR 19, 62; MTCW 2; SATA 99

Kohout, Pavel 1928- .... **CLC 13**
See CA 45-48; CANR 3

Koizumi, Yakumo
See Hearn, (Patricio) Lafcadio (Tessima Carlos)

Kolmar, Gertrud 1894-1943 .... **TCLC 40**
See CA 167

Komunyakaa, Yusef 1947- .... **CLC 86, 94; BLCS**
See CA 147; CANR 83; DLB 120

Konrad, George
See Konrad, Gyoergy

Konrad, Gyoergy 1933- .... **CLC 4, 10, 73**
See CA 85-88

Konwicki, Tadeusz 1926- .... **CLC 8, 28, 54, 117**
See CA 101; CAAS 9; CANR 39, 59; MTCW 1

Koontz, Dean R(ay) 1945- .... **CLC 78; DAM NOV, POP**
See AAYA 9, 31; BEST 89:3, 90:2; CA 108; CANR 19, 36, 52; DA3; MTCW 1; SATA 92

Kopernik, Mikolaj
See Copernicus, Nicolaus

Kopit, Arthur (Lee) 1937- ..... **CLC 1, 18, 33; DAM DRAM**
See AITN 1; CA 81-84; CABS 3; DLB 7; MTCW 1

Kops, Bernard 1926- .... **CLC 4**
See CA 5-8R; CANR 84; DLB 13

Kornbluth, C(yril) M. 1923-1958 .... **TCLC 8**
See CA 105; 160; DLB 8

Korolenko, V. G.
See Korolenko, Vladimir Galaktionovich

Korolenko, Vladimir
See Korolenko, Vladimir Galaktionovich

Korolenko, Vladimir G.
See Korolenko, Vladimir Galaktionovich

Korolenko, Vladimir Galaktionovich
1853-1921 .... **TCLC 22**
See CA 121

Korzybski, Alfred (Habdank Skarbek)
1879-1950 .... **TCLC 61**
See CA 123; 160

Kosinski, Jerzy (Nikodem)
1933-1991 .... **CLC 1, 2, 3, 6, 10, 15, 53, 70; DAM NOV**
See CA 17-20R; 134; CANR 9, 46; DA3; DLB 2; DLBY 82; MTCW 1, 2

Kostelanetz, Richard(Cory) 1940- ... **CLC 28**
See CA 13-16R; CAAS 8; CANR 38, 77

Kostrowitzki, Wilhelm Apollinaris de
1880-1918
See Apollinaire, Guillaume
See CA 104

Kotlowitz, Robert 1924- .... **CLC 4**
See CA 33-36R; CANR 36

Kotzebue, August (Friedrich Ferdinand) von
1761-1819 .... **NCLC 25**
See DLB 94

Kotzwinkle, William 1938- ..... **CLC 5, 14, 35**
See CA 45-48; CANR 3, 44, 84; CLR 6; DLB 173; MAICYA; SATA 24, 70

Kowna, Stancy
See Szymborska, Wislawa

Kozol, Jonathan 1936- .... **CLC 17**
See CA 61-64; CANR 16, 45

Kozoll, Michael 1940(?)- .... **CLC 35**

Kramer, Kathryn 19(?)- .... **CLC 34**

Kramer, Larry 1935- .. **CLC 42; DAM POP; DC 8**
See CA 124; 126; CANR 60

Krasicki, Ignacy 1735-1801 .... **NCLC 8**

Krasinski, Zygmunt 1812-1859 .... **NCLC 4**

Kraus, Karl 1874-1936 .... **TCLC 5**
See CA 104; DLB 118

Kreve (Mickevicius),Vincas
1882-1954 .... **TCLC 27**
See CA 170

Kristeva, Julia 1941- .... **CLC 77**
See CA 154

Kristofferson, Kris 1936- .... **CLC 26**
See CA 104

Krizanc, John 1956- .... **CLC 57**

Krleza, Miroslav 1893-1981 .... **CLC 8,114**
See CA 97-100; 105; CANR 50; DLB 147

Kroetsch, Robert 1927- .... **CLC 5, 23, 57; DAC; DAM POET**
See CA 17-20R; CANR 8, 38; DLB 53; MTCW 1

Kroetz, Franz
See Kroetz, Franz Xaver

Kroetz, Franz Xaver 1946- .... **CLC 41**
See CA 130

Kroker, Arthur (W.) 1945- .... **CLC 77**
See CA 161

Kropotkin, Peter (Aleksieevich)
1842-1921 .... **TCLC 36**
See CA 119

Krotkov, Yuri 1917- .... **CLC 19**
See CA 102

Krumb
See Crumb, R(obert)

Krumgold, Joseph (Quincy)
1908-1980 .... **CLC 12**
See CA 9-12R; 101; CANR 7; MAICYA; SATA 1, 48; SATA-Obit 23

Krumwitz
See Crumb, R(obert)

Krutch, JosephWood 1893-1970 .... **CLC 24**
See CA 1-4R; 25-28R; CANR 4; DLB 63, 206

Krutzch, Gus
See Eliot, T(homas) S(tearns)

Krylov, Ivan Andreevich
1768(?)-1844 .... **NCLC 1**
See DLB 150

Kubin, Alfred (Leopold Isidor)
1877-1959 .... **TCLC 23**
See CA 112; 149; DLB 81

Kubrick, Stanley 1928-1999 .... **CLC 16**
See AAYA 30; CA 81-84; 177; CANR 33; DLB 26

Kumin, Maxine (Winokur) 1925- ..... **CLC 5, 13, 28; DAM POET; PC 15**
See AITN 2; CA 1-4R; CAAS 8; CANR 1, 21, 69; DA3; DLB 5; MTCW 1, 2; SATA 12

Kundera, Milan 1929- . **CLC 4, 9, 19, 32, 68, 115; DAM NOV; SSC 24**
See AAYA 2; CA 85-88; CANR 19, 52, 74; DA3; MTCW 1, 2

Kunene, Mazisi (Raymond) 1930- ... **CLC 85**
See BW 1, 3; CA 125; CANR 81; DLB 117

Kunitz, Stanley (Jasspon) 1905- .. **CLC 6, 11, 14; PC 19**
See CA 41-44R; CANR 26, 57; DA3; DLB 48; INT CANR-26; MTCW 1, 2

Kunze, Reiner 1933- .... **CLC 10**
See CA 93-96; DLB 75

Kuprin, Aleksandr Ivanovich
1870-1938 .... **TCLC 5**
See CA 104

Kureishi, Hanif 1954(?)- .... **CLC 64**
See CA 139; DLB 194

Kurosawa, Akira 1910-1998 .... **CLC 16, 119; DAM MULT**
See AAYA 11; CA 101; 170; CANR 46

Kushner, Tony 1957(?)- .... **CLC 81; DAM DRAM; DC 10**
See CA 144; CANR 74; DA3; MTCW 2

Kuttner, Henry 1915-1958 .... **TCLC 10**
See Vance, Jack
See CA 107; 157; DLB 8

Kuzma, Greg 1944- .... **CLC 7**
See CA 33-36R; CANR 70

Kuzmin, Mikhail 1872(?)-1936 ...... **TCLC 40**
See CA 170

Lazarus, Emma 1849-1887 .... NCLC 8
Lazarus, Felix
    See Cable, George Washington
Lazarus, Henry
    See Slavitt, David R(ytman)
Lea, Joan
    See Neufeld, John (Arthur)
Leacock, Stephen (Butler)
    1869-1944 . TCLC 2; DAC; DAM MST
    See CA 104; 141; CANR 80; DLB 92;
    MTCW 2
Lear, Edward 1812-1888 .... NCLC 3
    See CLR 1; DLB 32, 163, 166; MAICYA;
    SATA 18, 100
Lear, Norman (Milton) 1922- .... CLC 12
    See CA 73-76
Leautaud, Paul 1872-1956 .... TCLC 83
    See DLB 65
Leavis, F(rank) R(aymond)
    1895-1978 .... CLC 24
    See CA 21-24R; 77-80; CANR 44; MTCW
    1, 2
Leavitt, David 1961- ...... CLC 34;DAM POP
    See CA 116; 122; CANR 50, 62; DA3; DLB
    130; INT 122; MTCW 2
Leblanc, Maurice (Marie Emile)
    1864-1941 .... TCLC 49
    See CA 110
Lebowitz, Fran(ces Ann) 1951(?)- ... CLC 11,
    36
    See CA 81-84; CANR 14, 60, 70; INT
    CANR-14; MTCW 1
Lebrecht, Peter
    See Tieck, (Johann) Ludwig
le Carre, John CLC 3, 5, 9, 15, 28
    See Cornwell, David (John Moore)
    See BEST 89:4; CDBLB 1960 to Present;
    DLB 87; MTCW 2
Le Clezio, J(ean) M(arie) G(ustave)
    1940- .... CLC 31
    See CA 116; 128; DLB 83
Leconte de Lisle, Charles-Marie-Rene
    1818-1894 .... NCLC 29
Le Coq, Monsieur
    See Simenon, Georges (Jacques Christian)
Leduc, Violette 1907-1972 .... CLC 22
    See CA 13-14; 33-36R; CANR 69; CAP 1
Ledwidge, Francis 1887(?)-1917 .... TCLC 23
    See CA 123; DLB 20
Lee, Andrea 1953- ... CLC 36; BLC 2; DAM
    MULT
    See BW 1, 3; CA 125; CANR 82
Lee, Andrew
    See Auchincloss, Louis (Stanton)
Lee, Chang-rae 1965- .... CLC 91
    See CA 148
Lee, Don L. CLC 2
    See Madhubuti, Haki R.
Lee, George W(ashington)
    1894-1976 .... CLC 52; BLC 2; DAM
    MULT
    See BW 1; CA 125; CANR 83; DLB 51
Lee, (Nelle) Harper 1926- . CLC 12, 60; DA;
    DAB; DAC; DAM MST, NOV; WLC
    See AAYA 13; CA 13-16R; CANR 51;
    CDALB 1941-1968; DA3; DLB 6;
    MTCW 1, 2; SATA 11
Lee, Helen Elaine 1959(?)- .... CLC 86
    See CA 148
Lee, Julian
    See Latham, Jean Lee
Lee, Larry
    See Lee, Lawrence
Lee, Laurie 1914-1997 . CLC 90; DAB;DAM
    POP
    See CA 77-80; 158; CANR 33, 73; DLB
    27; MTCW 1

Lee, Lawrence 1941-1990 .... CLC 34
    See CA 131; CANR 43
Lee, Li-Young 1957- .... PC 24
    See CA 153; DLB 165
Lee, Manfred B(ennington)
    1905-1971 .... CLC 11
    See Queen, Ellery
    See CA 1-4R; 29-32R; CANR 2; DLB 137
Lee, Shelton Jackson 1957(?)- .... CLC 105;
    BLCS; DAM MULT
    See Lee, Spike
    See BW 2, 3; CA 125; CANR 42
Lee, Spike
    See Lee, Shelton Jackson
    See AAYA 4, 29
Lee, Stan 1922- .... CLC 17
    See AAYA 5; CA 108; 111; INT 111
Lee, Tanith 1947- .... CLC 46
    See AAYA 15; CA 37-40R; CANR 53;
    SATA 8, 88
Lee, Vernon TCLC 5; SSC 33
    See Paget, Violet
    See DLB 57, 153, 156, 174, 178
Lee, William
    See Burroughs, William S(eward)
Lee, Willy
    See Burroughs, William S(eward)
Lee-Hamilton, Eugene (Jacob)
    1845-1907 .... TCLC 22
    See CA 117
Leet, Judith 1935- .... CLC 11
Le Fanu, Joseph Sheridan
    1814-1873 ..... NCLC 9, 58; DAM POP;
    SSC 14
    See DA3; DLB 21, 70, 159, 178
Leffland, Ella 1931- .... CLC 19
    See CA 29-32R; CANR 35, 78, 82; DLBY
    84; INT CANR-35; SATA 65
Leger, Alexis
    See Leger, (Marie-Rene Auguste) Alexis
    Saint-Leger
Leger, (Marie-Rene Auguste)
    AlexisSaint-Leger 1887-1975 .... CLC 4,
    11, 46; DAM POET; PC 23
    See CA 13-16R; 61-64; CANR 43; MTCW
    1
Leger, Saintleger
    See Leger, (Marie-Rene Auguste) Alexis
    Saint-Leger
Le Guin, Ursula K(roeber) 1929- ..... CLC 8,
    13, 22, 45, 71; DAB; DAC; DAM MST,
    POP; SSC 12
    See AAYA 9, 27; AITN 1; CA 21-24R;
    CANR 9, 32, 52, 74; CDALB 1968-1988;
    CLR 3, 28; DA3; DLB 8, 52; INT CANR-
    32; JRDA; MAICYA; MTCW 1, 2; SATA
    4, 52, 99
Lehmann, Rosamond (Nina)
    1901-1990 .... CLC 5
    See CA 77-80; 131; CANR 8, 73; DLB 15;
    MTCW 2
Leiber, Fritz (Reuter,Jr.) 1910-1992 . CLC 25
    See CA 45-48; 139; CANR 2, 40; DLB 8;
    MTCW 1, 2; SATA 45; SATA-Obit 73
Leibniz, Gottfried Wilhelmvon
    1646-1716 .... LC 35
    See DLB 168
Leimbach, Martha 1963-
    See Leimbach, Marti
    See CA 130
Leimbach, Marti CLC 65
    See Leimbach, Martha
Leino, Eino TCLC 24
    See Loennbohm, Armas Eino Leopold
Leiris, Michel (Julien) 1901-1990 ..... CLC 61
    See CA 119; 128; 132
Leithauser, Brad 1953- .... CLC 27
    See CA 107; CANR 27, 81; DLB 120

Lelchuk, Alan 1938- .... CLC 5
    See CA 45-48; CAAS 20; CANR 1, 70
Lem, Stanislaw 1921- .... CLC 8, 15, 40
    See CA 105; CAAS 1; CANR 32; MTCW
    1
Lemann, Nancy 1956- .... CLC 39
    See CA 118; 136
Lemonnier, (Antoine Louis) Camille
    1844-1913 .... TCLC 22
    See CA 121
Lenau, Nikolaus 1802-1850 .... NCLC 16
L'Engle, Madeleine (Camp Franklin)
    1918- .... CLC 12; DAM POP
    See AAYA 28; AITN 2; CA 1-4R; CANR 3,
    21, 39, 66; CLR 1, 14, 57; DA3; DLB 52;
    JRDA; MAICYA; MTCW 1, 2; SAAS 15;
    SATA 1, 27, 75
Lengyel, Jozsef 1896-1975 .... CLC 7
    See CA 85-88; 57-60; CANR 71
Lenin 1870-1924
    See Lenin, V. I.
    See CA 121; 168
Lenin, V. I. TCLC 67
    See Lenin
Lennon, John (Ono) 1940-1980 .. CLC 12, 35
    See CA 102
Lennox, Charlotte Ramsay
    1729(?)-1804 .... NCLC 23
    See DLB 39
Lentricchia, Frank(Jr.) 1940- .... CLC 34
    See CA 25-28R; CANR 19
Lenz, Siegfried 1926- .... CLC 27;SSC 33
    See CA 89-92; CANR 80; DLB 75
Leonard, Elmore (John, Jr.) 1925- . CLC 28,
    34, 71, 120; DAM POP
    See AAYA 22; AITN 1; BEST 89:1, 90:4;
    CA 81-84; CANR 12, 28, 53, 76; DA3;
    DLB 173; INT CANR-28; MTCW 1, 2
Leonard, Hugh CLC 19
    See Byrne, John Keyes
    See DLB 13
Leonov, Leonid (Maximovich)
    1899-1994 .... CLC 92; DAM NOV
    See CA 129; CANR 74, 76; MTCW 1, 2
Leopardi, (Conte) Giacomo
    1798-1837 .... NCLC 22
Le Reveler
    See Artaud, Antonin (Marie Joseph)
Lerman, Eleanor 1952- .... CLC 9
    See CA 85-88; CANR 69
Lerman, Rhoda 1936- .... CLC 56
    See CA 49-52; CANR 70
Lermontov, Mikhail Yuryevich
    1814-1841 .... NCLC 47; PC 18
    See DLB 205
Leroux, Gaston 1868-1927 .... TCLC 25
    See CA 108; 136; CANR 69; SATA 65
Lesage, Alain-Rene 1668-1747 .... LC 2, 28
Leskov, Nikolai (Semyonovich)
    1831-1895 .... NCLC 25; SSC 34
Lessing, Doris (May) 1919- ... CLC 1, 2, 3, 6,
    10, 15, 22, 40, 94; DA; DAB; DAC;
    DAM MST, NOV; SSC 6; WLCS
    See CA 9-12R; CAAS 14; CANR 33, 54,
    76; CDBLB 1960 to Present; DA3; DLB
    15, 139; DLBY 85; MTCW 1, 2
Lessing, Gotthold Ephraim 1729-1781 . LC 8
    See DLB 97
Lester, Richard 1932- .... CLC 20
Lever, Charles (James)
    1806-1872 .... NCLC 23
    See DLB 21
Leverson, Ada 1865(?)-1936(?) .... TCLC 18
    See Elaine
    See CA 117; DLB 153

See AAYA 13; AITN 2; CDALB 1865-
1917; DLB 8, 12, 78, 212; SATA 18

London, John Griffith 1876-1916
See London, Jack
See CA 110; 119; CANR 73; DA; DAB;
DAC; DAM MST, NOV; DA3; JRDA;
MAICYA; MTCW 1, 2

Long, Emmett
See Leonard, Elmore (John, Jr.)

Longbaugh, Harry
See Goldman, William (W.)

Longfellow, Henry Wadsworth
1807-1882 .... **NCLC 2, 45; DA; DAB;
DAC; DAM MST, POET; WLCS**
See CDALB 1640-1865; DA3; DLB 1, 59;
SATA 19

Longinus c. 1st cent. - .... **CMLC 27**
See DLB 176

Longley, Michael 1939- .... **CLC 29**
See CA 102; DLB 40

Longus fl. c. 2nd cent. - .... **CMLC 7**

Longway, A. Hugh
See Lang, Andrew

Lonnrot, Elias 1802-1884 .... **NCLC 53**

Lopate, Phillip 1943- .... **CLC 29**
See CA 97-100; DLBY 80; INT 97-100

Lopez Portillo (y Pacheco),Jose
1920- .... **CLC 46**
See CA 129; HW 1

Lopez y Fuentes,Gregorio
1897(?)-1966 .... **CLC 32**
See CA 131; HW 1

Lorca, Federico Garcia
See Garcia Lorca, Federico

Lord, Bette Bao 1938- .... **CLC 23**
See BEST 90:3; CA 107; CANR 41, 79;
INT 107; SATA 58

Lord Auch
See Bataille, Georges

Lord Byron
See Byron, George Gordon (Noel)

Lorde, Audre (Geraldine)
1934-1992 ... **CLC 18, 71; BLC 2; DAM
MULT, POET; PC 12**
See BW 1, 3; CA 25-28R; 142; CANR 16,
26, 46, 82; DA3; DLB 41; MTCW 1, 2

Lord Houghton
See Milnes, Richard Monckton

Lord Jeffrey
See Jeffrey, Francis

Lorenzini, Carlo 1826-1890
See Collodi, Carlo
See MAICYA; SATA 29, 100

Lorenzo, Heberto Padilla
See Padilla (Lorenzo), Heberto

Loris
See Hofmannsthal, Hugo von

Loti, Pierre **TCLC 11**
See Viaud, (Louis Marie) Julien
See DLB 123

Lou, Henri
See Andreas-Salome, Lou

Louie, David Wong 1954- .... **CLC 70**
See CA 139

Louis, Father M.
See Merton, Thomas

Lovecraft, H(oward) P(hillips)
1890-1937 ...... **TCLC 4, 22; DAM POP;
SSC 3**
See AAYA 14; CA 104; 133; DA3; MTCW
1, 2

Lovelace, Earl 1935- .... **CLC 51**
See BW 2; CA 77-80; CANR 41, 72; DLB
125; MTCW 1

Lovelace, Richard 1618-1657 .... **LC 24**
See DLB 131

Lowell, Amy 1874-1925 .... **TCLC 1, 8; DAM
POET; PC 13**
See CA 104; 151; DLB 54, 140; MTCW 2

Lowell, James Russell 1819-1891 .... **NCLC 2**
See CDALB 1640-1865; DLB 1, 11, 64, 79,
189

Lowell, Robert (Traill Spence, Jr.)
1917-1977 .... **CLC 1, 2, 3, 4, 5, 8, 9, 11,
15, 37, 124; DA; DAB; DAC; DAM
MST, NOV; PC 3; WLC**
See CA 9-12R; 73-76; CABS 2; CANR 26,
60; CDALBS; DA3; DLB 5, 169; MTCW
1, 2

Lowenthal, Michael (Francis)
1969- .... **CLC 119**
See CA 150

Lowndes, Marie Adelaide (Belloc)
1868-1947 .... **TCLC 12**
See CA 107; DLB 70

Lowry, (Clarence) Malcolm
1909-1957 .... **TCLC 6, 40; SSC 31**
See CA 105; 131; CANR 62; CDBLB 1945-
1960; DLB 15; MTCW 1, 2

Lowry, Mina Gertrude 1882-1966
See Loy, Mina
See CA 113

Loxsmith, John
See Brunner, John (Kilian Houston)

Loy, Mina **CLC 28; DAM POET; PC 16**
See Lowry, Mina Gertrude
See DLB 4, 54

Loyson-Bridet
See Schwob, Marcel (Mayer Andre)

Lucan 39-65 .... **CMLC 33**
See DLB 211

Lucas, Craig 1951- .... **CLC 64**
See CA 137; CANR 71

Lucas, E(dward) V(errall)
1868-1938 .... **TCLC 73**
See CA 176; DLB 98, 149, 153; SATA 20

Lucas, George 1944- .... **CLC 16**
See AAYA 1, 23; CA 77-80; CANR 30;
SATA 56

Lucas, Hans
See Godard, Jean-Luc

Lucas, Victoria
See Plath, Sylvia

Lucian c. 120-c. 180 .... **CMLC 32**
See DLB 176

Ludlam, Charles 1943-1987 .... **CLC 46,50**
See CA 85-88; 122; CANR 72

Ludlum, Robert 1927- .... **CLC 22, 43; DAM
NOV, POP**
See AAYA 10; BEST 89:1, 90:3; CA 33-
36R; CANR 25, 41, 68; DA3; DLBY 82;
MTCW 1, 2

Ludwig, Ken **CLC 60**

Ludwig, Otto 1813-1865 .... **NCLC 4**
See DLB 129

Lugones, Leopoldo 1874-1938 ...... **TCLC 15;
HLCS 2**
See CA 116; 131; HW 1

Lu Hsun 1881-1936 .... **TCLC 3; SSC 20**
See Shu-Jen, Chou

Lukacs, George **CLC 24**
See Lukacs, Gyorgy (Szegeny von)

Lukacs, Gyorgy (Szegeny von) 1885-1971
See Lukacs, George
See CA 101; 29-32R; CANR 62; MTCW 2

Luke, Peter (Ambrose Cyprian)
1919-1995 .... **CLC 38**
See CA 81-84; 147; CANR 72; DLB 13

Lunar, Dennis
See Mungo, Raymond

Lurie, Alison 1926- .... **CLC 4, 5, 18, 39**
See CA 1-4R; CANR 2, 17, 50; DLB 2;
MTCW 1; SATA 46

Lustig, Arnost 1926- .... **CLC 56**
See AAYA 3; CA 69-72; CANR 47; SATA
56

Luther, Martin 1483-1546 .... **LC 9, 37**
See DLB 179

Luxemburg, Rosa 1870(?)-1919 ..... **TCLC 63**
See CA 118

Luzi, Mario 1914- .... **CLC 13**
See CA 61-64; CANR 9, 70; DLB 128

Lyly, John 1554(?)-1606 .... **LC 41; DAM
DRAM; DC 7**
See DLB 62, 167

L'Ymagier
See Gourmont, Remy (-Marie-Charles) de

Lynch, B. Suarez
See Bioy Casares, Adolfo; Borges, Jorge
Luis

Lynch, B. Suarez
See Bioy Casares, Adolfo

Lynch, David (K.) 1946- .... **CLC 66**
See CA 124; 129

Lynch, James
See Andreyev, Leonid (Nikolaevich)

Lynch Davis, B.
See Bioy Casares, Adolfo; Borges, Jorge
Luis

Lyndsay, Sir David 1490-1555 .... **LC 20**

Lynn, Kenneth S(chuyler) 1923- ...... **CLC 50**
See CA 1-4R; CANR 3, 27, 65

Lynx
See West, Rebecca

Lyons, Marcus
See Blish, James (Benjamin)

Lyre, Pinchbeck
See Sassoon, Siegfried (Lorraine)

Lytle, Andrew (Nelson) 1902-1995 ... **CLC 22**
See CA 9-12R; 150; CANR 70; DLB 6;
DLBY 95

Lyttelton, George 1709-1773 .... **LC 10**

Maas, Peter 1929- .... **CLC 29**
See CA 93-96; INT 93-96; MTCW 2

Macaulay, Rose 1881-1958 .... **TCLC 7, 44**
See CA 104; DLB 36

Macaulay, Thomas Babington
1800-1859 .... **NCLC 42**
See CDBLB 1832-1890; DLB 32, 55

MacBeth, George (Mann)
1932-1992 .... **CLC 2, 5, 9**
See CA 25-28R; 136; CANR 61, 66; DLB
40; MTCW 1; SATA 4; SATA-Obit 70

MacCaig, Norman (Alexander)
1910- .... **CLC 36; DAB; DAM POET**
See CA 9-12R; CANR 3, 34; DLB 27

MacCarthy, Sir (Charles Otto) Desmond
1877-1952 .... **TCLC 36**
See CA 167

MacDiarmid, Hugh **CLC 2, 4, 11, 19, 63; PC
9**
See Grieve, C(hristopher) M(urray)
See CDBLB 1945-1960; DLB 20

MacDonald, Anson
See Heinlein, Robert A(nson)

Macdonald, Cynthia 1928- .... **CLC 13, 19**
See CA 49-52; CANR 4, 44; DLB 105

MacDonald, George 1824-1905 .... **TCLC 9**
See CA 106; 137; CANR 80; DLB 18, 163,
178; MAICYA; SATA 33, 100

Macdonald, John
See Millar, Kenneth

MacDonald, John D(ann)
1916-1986 .. **CLC 3, 27, 44; DAM NOV,
POP**
See CA 1-4R; 121; CANR 1, 19, 60; DLB
8; DLBY 86; MTCW 1, 2

Macdonald, John Ross
See Millar, Kenneth

Macdonald, Ross **CLC 1, 2, 3, 14, 34, 41**
See Millar, Kenneth

Mannheim, Karl 1893-1947 .... **TCLC 65**
Manning, David
   See Faust, Frederick (Schiller)
Manning, Frederic 1887(?)-1935 ... **TCLC 25**
   See CA 124
Manning, Olivia 1915-1980 .... **CLC 5, 19**
   See CA 5-8R; 101; CANR 29; MTCW 1
Mano, D. Keith 1942- .... **CLC 2, 10**
   See CA 25-28R; CAAS 6; CANR 26, 57;
   DLB 6
Mansfield, Katherine TCLC 2, 8, 39; DAB;
   SSC 9, 23; WLC
   See Beauchamp, Kathleen Mansfield
   See DLB 162
Manso, Peter 1940- .... **CLC 39**
   See CA 29-32R; CANR 44
Mantecon, Juan Jimenez
   See Jimenez (Mantecon), Juan Ramon
Manton, Peter
   See Creasey, John
Man Without a Spleen, A
   See Chekhov, Anton (Pavlovich)
Manzoni, Alessandro 1785-1873 .... **NCLC 29**
Map, Walter 1140-1209 .... **CMLC 32**
Mapu, Abraham (ben Jekutiel)
   1808-1867 .... **NCLC 18**
Mara, Sally
   See Queneau, Raymond
Marat, Jean Paul 1743-1793 .... **LC 10**
Marcel, Gabriel Honore 1889-1973 . **CLC 15**
   See CA 102; 45-48; MTCW 1, 2
March, William 1893-1954 .... **TCLC 96**
Marchbanks, Samuel
   See Davies, (William) Robertson
Marchi, Giacomo
   See Bassani, Giorgio
Margulies, Donald CLC 76
Marie de France c. 12th cent. - ..... **CMLC 8;**
   PC 22
   See DLB 208
Marie de l'Incarnation 1599-1672 ...... **LC 10**
Marier, Captain Victor
   See Griffith, D(avid Lewelyn) W(ark)
Mariner, Scott
   See Pohl, Frederik
Marinetti, Filippo Tommaso
   1876-1944 .... **TCLC 10**
   See CA 107; DLB 114
Marivaux, Pierre Carlet de Chamblain de
   1688-1763 .... **LC 4; DC 7**
Markandaya, Kamala CLC 8, 38
   See Taylor, Kamala (Purnaiya)
Markfield, Wallace 1926- .... **CLC 8**
   See CA 69-72; CAAS 3; DLB 2, 28
Markham, Edwin 1852-1940 .... **TCLC 47**
   See CA 160; DLB 54, 186
Markham, Robert
   See Amis, Kingsley (William)
Marks, J
   See Highwater, Jamake (Mamake)
Marks-Highwater, J
   See Highwater, Jamake (Mamake)
Markson, David M(errill) 1927- .... **CLC 67**
   See CA 49-52; CANR 1
Marley, Bob CLC 17
   See Marley, Robert Nesta
Marley, Robert Nesta 1945-1981
   See Marley, Bob
   See CA 107; 103
Marlowe, Christopher 1564-1593 ...... **LC 22,**
   47; DA; DAB; DAC; DAM DRAM,
   MST; DC 1; WLC
   See CDBLB Before 1660; DA3; DLB 62
Marlowe, Stephen 1928-
   See Queen, Ellery
   See CA 13-16R; CANR 6, 55

Marmontel, Jean-Francois 1723-1799 .. **LC 2**
Marquand, John P(hillips)
   1893-1960 .... **CLC 2, 10**
   See CA 85-88; CANR 73; DLB 9, 102;
   MTCW 2
Marques, Rene 1919-1979 ..... **CLC 96; DAM**
   MULT; HLC 2
   See CA 97-100; 85-88; CANR 78; DLB
   113; HW 1, 2
Marquez, Gabriel (Jose) Garcia
   See Garcia Marquez, Gabriel (Jose)
Marquis, Don(ald Robert Perry)
   1878-1937 .... **TCLC 7**
   See CA 104; 166; DLB 11, 25
Marric, J. J.
   See Creasey, John
Marryat, Frederick 1792-1848 .... **NCLC 3**
   See DLB 21, 163
Marsden, James
   See Creasey, John
Marsh, (Edith) Ngaio 1899-1982 .... **CLC 7,**
   53; DAM POP
   See CA 9-12R; CANR 6, 58; DLB 77;
   MTCW 1, 2
Marshall, Garry 1934- .... **CLC 17**
   See AAYA 3; CA 111; SATA 60
Marshall, Paule 1929- .. **CLC 27, 72; BLC 3;**
   DAM MULT; SSC 3
   See BW 2, 3; CA 77-80; CANR 25, 73;
   DA3; DLB 157; MTCW 1, 2
Marshallik
   See Zangwill, Israel
Marsten, Richard
   See Hunter, Evan
Marston, John 1576-1634 .... **LC 33; DAM**
   DRAM
   See DLB 58, 172
Martha, Henry
   See Harris, Mark
Marti (y Perez), Jose (Julian)
   1853-1895 ...... **NCLC 63; DAM MULT;**
   HLC 2
   See HW 2
Martial c. 40-c. 104 .... **CMLC 35; PC 10**
   See DLB 211
Martin, Ken
   See Hubbard, L(afayette) Ron(ald)
Martin, Richard
   See Creasey, John
Martin, Steve 1945- .... **CLC 30**
   See CA 97-100; CANR 30; MTCW 1
Martin, Valerie 1948- .... **CLC 89**
   See BEST 90:2; CA 85-88; CANR 49
Martin, Violet Florence
   1862-1915 .... **TCLC 51**
Martin, Webber
   See Silverberg, Robert
Martindale, Patrick Victor
   See White, Patrick (Victor Martindale)
Martin du Gard, Roger 1881-1958 . **TCLC 24**
   See CA 118; DLB 65
Martineau, Harriet 1802-1876 .... **NCLC 26**
   See DLB 21, 55, 159, 163, 166, 190; YABC
   2
Martines, Julia
   See O'Faolain, Julia
Martinez, Enrique Gonzalez
   See Gonzalez Martinez, Enrique
Martinez, Jacinto Benavente y
   See Benavente (y Martinez), Jacinto
Martinez Ruiz, Jose 1873-1967
   See Azorin; Ruiz, Jose Martinez
   See CA 93-96; HW 1
Martinez Sierra, Gregorio
   1881-1947 .... **TCLC 6**
   See CA 115

Martinez Sierra, Maria (de laO'LeJarraga)
   1874-1974 .... **TCLC 6**
   See CA 115
Martinsen, Martin
   See Follett, Ken(neth Martin)
Martinson, Harry (Edmund)
   1904-1978 .... **CLC 14**
   See CA 77-80; CANR 34
Marut, Ret
   See Traven, B.
Marut, Robert
   See Traven, B.
Marvell, Andrew 1621-1678 .. **LC 4, 43; DA;**
   DAB; DAC; DAM MST, POET; PC
   10; WLC
   See CDBLB 1660-1789; DLB 131
Marx, Karl (Heinrich) 1818-1883 . **NCLC 17**
   See DLB 129
Masaoka Shiki TCLC 18
   See Masaoka Tsunenori
Masaoka Tsunenori 1867-1902
   See Masaoka Shiki
   See CA 117
Masefield, John (Edward)
   1878-1967 ..... **CLC 11, 47; DAM POET**
   See CA 19-20; 25-28R; CANR 33; CAP 2;
   CDBLB 1890-1914; DLB 10, 19, 153,
   160; MTCW 1, 2; SATA 19
Maso, Carole 19(?)- .... **CLC 44**
   See CA 170
Mason, Bobbie Ann 1940- ... **CLC 28, 43, 82;**
   SSC 4
   See AAYA 5; CA 53-56; CANR 11, 31, 58,
   83; CDALBS; DA3; DLB 173; DLBY 87;
   INT CANR-31; MTCW 1, 2
Mason, Ernst
   See Pohl, Frederik
Mason, Lee W.
   See Malzberg, Barry N(athaniel)
Mason, Nick 1945- .... **CLC 35**
Mason, Tally
   See Derleth, August (William)
Mass, William
   See Gibson, William
Master Lao
   See Lao Tzu
Masters, Edgar Lee 1868-1950 .... **TCLC 2,**
   25; DA; DAC; DAM MST, POET; PC
   1; WLCS
   See CA 104; 133; CDALB 1865-1917; DLB
   54; MTCW 1, 2
Masters, Hilary 1928- .... **CLC 48**
   See CA 25-28R; CANR 13, 47
Mastrosimone, William 19(?)- .... **CLC 36**
Mathe, Albert
   See Camus, Albert
Mather, Cotton 1663-1728 .... **LC 38**
   See CDALB 1640-1865; DLB 24, 30, 140
Mather, Increase 1639-1723 .... **LC 38**
   See DLB 24
Matheson, Richard Burton 1926- ...... **CLC 37**
   See AAYA 31; CA 97-100; DLB 8, 44; INT
   97-100
Mathews, Harry 1930- .... **CLC 6, 52**
   See CA 21-24R; CAAS 6; CANR 18, 40
Mathews, John Joseph 1894-1979 .. **CLC 84;**
   DAM MULT
   See CA 19-20; 142; CANR 45; CAP 2;
   DLB 175; NNAL
Mathias, Roland (Glyn) 1915- .... **CLC 45**
   See CA 97-100; CANR 19, 41; DLB 27
Matsuo Basho 1644-1694 .... **PC 3**
   See DAM POET
Mattheson, Rodney
   See Creasey, John
Matthews, Brander 1852-1929 .... **TCLC 95**
   See DLB 71, 78; DLBD 13

Matthews, Greg 1949- .... **CLC 45**
See CA 135

Matthews, William (Procter,III)
1942-1997 .... **CLC 40**
See CA 29-32R; 162; CAAS 18; CANR 12,
57; DLB 5

Matthias, John (Edward) 1941- .... **CLC 9**
See CA 33-36R; CANR 56

Matthiessen, Peter 1927- ... **CLC 5, 7, 11, 32,
64; DAM NOV**
See AAYA 6; BEST 90:4; CA 9-12R; CANR
21, 50, 73; DA3; DLB 6, 173; MTCW 1,
2; SATA 27

Maturin, Charles Robert
1780(?)-1824 .... **NCLC 6**
See DLB 178

Matute (Ausejo), Ana Maria 1925- .. **CLC 11**
See CA 89-92; MTCW 1

Maugham, W. S.
See Maugham, W(illiam) Somerset

Maugham, W(illiam) Somerset
1874-1965 ... **CLC 1, 11, 15, 67, 93; DA;
DAB; DAC; DAM DRAM, MST, NOV;
SSC 8; WLC**
See CA 5-8R; 25-28R; CANR 40; CDBLB
1914-1945; DA3; DLB 10, 36, 77, 100,
162, 195; MTCW 1, 2; SATA 54

Maugham, William Somerset
See Maugham, W(illiam) Somerset

Maupassant, (Henri Rene Albert) Guy de
1850-1893 .... **NCLC 1, 42; DA; DAB;
DAC; DAM MST; SSC 1; WLC**
See DA3; DLB 123

Maupin, Armistead 1944- .... **CLC 95;DAM
POP**
See CA 125; 130; CANR 58; DA3; INT
130; MTCW 2

Maurhut, Richard
See Traven, B.

Mauriac, Claude 1914-1996 .... **CLC 9**
See CA 89-92; 152; DLB 83

Mauriac, Francois (Charles)
1885-1970 .... **CLC 4, 9, 56; SSC 24**
See CA 25-28; CAP 2; DLB 65; MTCW 1,
2

Mavor, Osborne Henry 1888-1951
See Bridie, James
See CA 104

Maxwell, William (Keepers,,Jr.)
1908- .... **CLC 19**
See CA 93-96; CANR 54; DLBY 80; INT
93-96

May, Elaine 1932- .... **CLC 16**
See CA 124; 142; DLB 44

Mayakovski, Vladimir (Vladimirovich)
1893-1930 .... **TCLC 4, 18**
See CA 104; 158; MTCW 2

Mayhew, Henry 1812-1887 .... **NCLC 31**
See DLB 18, 55, 190

Mayle, Peter 1939(?)- .... **CLC 89**
See CA 139; CANR 64

Maynard, Joyce 1953- .... **CLC 23**
See CA 111; 129; CANR 64

Mayne, William (James Carter)
1928- .... **CLC 12**
See AAYA 20; CA 9-12R; CANR 37, 80;
CLR 25; JRDA; MAICYA; SAAS 11;
SATA 6, 68

Mayo, Jim
See L'Amour, Louis (Dearborn)

Maysles, Albert 1926- .... **CLC 16**
See CA 29-32R

Maysles, David 1932- .... **CLC 16**

Mazer, Norma Fox 1931- .... **CLC 26**
See AAYA 5; CA 69-72; CANR 12, 32, 66;
CLR 23; JRDA; MAICYA; SAAS 1;
SATA 24, 67, 105

Mazzini, Guiseppe 1805-1872 .... **NCLC 34**

McAlmon, Robert (Menzies)
1895-1956 .... **TCLC 97**
See CA 107; 168; DLB 4, 45; DLBD 15

McAuley, James Phillip 1917-1976 .. **CLC 45**
See CA 97-100

McBain, Ed
See Hunter, Evan

McBrien, William Augustine 1930- .. **CLC 44**
See CA 107

McCaffrey, Anne (Inez) 1926- .... **CLC 17;
DAM NOV, POP**
See AAYA 6; AITN 2; BEST 89:2; CA 25-
28R; CANR 15, 35, 55; CLR 49; DA3;
DLB 8; JRDA; MAICYA; MTCW 1, 2;
SAAS 11; SATA 8, 70

McCall, Nathan 1955(?)- .... **CLC 86**
See BW 3; CA 146

McCann, Arthur
See Campbell, John W(ood, Jr.)

McCann, Edson
See Pohl, Frederik

McCarthy, Charles, Jr. 1933-
See McCarthy, Cormac
See CANR 42, 69; DAM POP; DA3;
MTCW 2

McCarthy, Cormac 1933- ...... **CLC 4, 57, 59,
101**
See McCarthy, Charles, Jr.
See DLB 6, 143; MTCW 2

McCarthy, Mary (Therese)
1912-1989 .. **CLC 1, 3, 5, 14, 24, 39, 59;
SSC 24**
See CA 5-8R; 129; CANR 16, 50, 64; DA3;
DLB 2; DLBY 81; INT CANR-16;
MTCW 1, 2

McCartney, (James) Paul 1942- . **CLC 12, 35**
See CA 146

McCauley, Stephen (D.) 1955- .... **CLC 50**
See CA 141

McClure, Michael (Thomas) 1932- ... **CLC 6,
10**
See CA 21-24R; CANR 17, 46, 77; DLB
16

McCorkle, Jill (Collins) 1958- .... **CLC 51**
See CA 121; DLBY 87

McCourt, Frank 1930- .... **CLC 109**
See CA 157

McCourt, James 1941- .... **CLC 5**
See CA 57-60

McCourt, Malachy 1932- .... **CLC 119**

McCoy, Horace (Stanley)
1897-1955 .... **TCLC 28**
See CA 108; 155; DLB 9

McCrae, John 1872-1918 .... **TCLC 12**
See CA 109; DLB 92

McCreigh, James
See Pohl, Frederik

McCullers, (Lula) Carson (Smith)
1917-1967 .... **CLC 1, 4, 10, 12, 48, 100;
DA; DAB; DAC; DAM MST, NOV;
SSC 9, 24;WLC**
See AAYA 21; CA 5-8R; 25-28R; CABS 1,
3; CANR 18; CDALB 1941-1968; DA3;
DLB 2, 7, 173; MTCW 1, 2; SATA 27

McCulloch, John Tyler
See Burroughs, Edgar Rice

McCullough, Colleen 1938(?)- .... **CLC 27,
107; DAM NOV, POP**
See CA 81-84; CANR 17, 46, 67; DA3;
MTCW 1, 2

McDermott, Alice 1953- .... **CLC 90**
See CA 109; CANR 40

McElroy, Joseph 1930- .... **CLC 5, 47**
See CA 17-20R

McEwan, Ian (Russell) 1948- .... **CLC 13, 66;
DAM NOV**
See BEST 90:4; CA 61-64; CANR 14, 41,
69; DLB 14, 194; MTCW 1, 2

McFadden, David 1940- .... **CLC 48**
See CA 104; DLB 60; INT 104

McFarland, Dennis 1950- .... **CLC 65**
See CA 165

McGahern, John 1934- .... **CLC 5, 9, 48;SSC
17**
See CA 17-20R; CANR 29, 68; DLB 14;
MTCW 1

McGinley, Patrick (Anthony) 1937- . **CLC 41**
See CA 120; 127; CANR 56; INT 127

McGinley, Phyllis 1905-1978 .... **CLC 14**
See CA 9-12R; 77-80; CANR 19; DLB 11,
48; SATA 2, 44; SATA-Obit 24

McGinniss, Joe 1942- .... **CLC 32**
See AITN 2; BEST 89:2; CA 25-28R;
CANR 26, 70; DLB 185; INT CANR-26

McGivern, Maureen Daly
See Daly, Maureen

McGrath, Patrick 1950- .... **CLC 55**
See CA 136; CANR 65

McGrath, Thomas (Matthew)
1916-1990 ..... **CLC 28, 59; DAM POET**
See CA 9-12R; 132; CANR 6, 33; MTCW
1; SATA 41; SATA-Obit 66

McGuane, Thomas (Francis III)
1939- .... **CLC 3, 7, 18, 45**
See AITN 2; CA 49-52; CANR 5, 24, 49;
DLB 2, 212; DLBY 80; INT CANR-24;
MTCW 1

McGuckian, Medbh 1950- .... **CLC 48; DAM
POET; PC 27**
See CA 143; DLB 40

McHale, Tom 1942(?)-1982 .... **CLC 3, 5**
See AITN 1; CA 77-80; 106

McIlvanney, William 1936- .... **CLC 42**
See CA 25-28R; CANR 61; DLB 14, 207

McIlwraith, Maureen Mollie Hunter
See Hunter, Mollie
See SATA 2

McInerney, Jay 1955- ..... **CLC 34, 112;DAM
POP**
See AAYA 18; CA 116; 123; CANR 45, 68;
DA3; INT 123; MTCW 2

McIntyre, Vonda N(eel) 1948- .... **CLC 18**
See CA 81-84; CANR 17, 34, 69; MTCW 1

**McKay, Claude TCLC 7, 41; BLC 3;
DAB;PC 2**
See McKay, Festus Claudius
See DLB 4, 45, 51, 117

McKay, Festus Claudius 1889-1948
See McKay, Claude
See BW 1, 3; CA 104; 124; CANR 73; DA;
DAC; DAM MST, MULT, NOV, POET;
MTCW 1, 2; WLC

McKuen, Rod 1933- .... **CLC 1, 3**
See AITN 1; CA 41-44R; CANR 40

McLoughlin, R. B.
See Mencken, H(enry) L(ouis)

McLuhan, (Herbert) Marshall
1911-1980 .... **CLC 37, 83**
See CA 9-12R; 102; CANR 12, 34, 61;
DLB 88; INT CANR-12; MTCW 1, 2

McMillan, Terry (L.) 1951- .... **CLC 50, 61,
112; BLCS; DAM MULT, NOV, POP**
See AAYA 21; BW 2, 3; CA 140; CANR
60; DA3; MTCW 2

McMurtry, Larry (Jeff) 1936- .. **CLC 2, 3, 7,
11, 27, 44; DAM NOV, POP**
See AAYA 15; AITN 2; BEST 89:2; CA
5-8R; CANR 19, 43, 64; CDALB 1968-
1988; DA3; DLB 2, 143; DLBY 80, 87;
MTCW 1, 2

McNally, T. M. 1961- .... **CLC 82**

McNally, Terrence 1939- ... **CLC 4, 7, 41, 91;
DAM DRAM**
See CA 45-48; CANR 2, 56; DA3; DLB 7;
MTCW 2

McNamer, Deirdre 1950- .... **CLC 70**

McNeal, Tom CLC 119

McNeile, Herman Cyril 1888-1937
See Sapper
See DLB 77
McNickle, (William) D'Arcy
1904-1977 .... **CLC 89; DAM MULT**
See CA 9-12R; 85-88; CANR 5, 45; DLB
175, 212; NNAL; SATA-Obit 22
McPhee, John (Angus) 1931- .... **CLC 36**
See BEST 90:1; CA 65-68; CANR 20, 46,
64, 69; DLB 185; MTCW 1, 2
McPherson, James Alan 1943- .. **CLC 19, 77;**
BLCS
See BW 1, 3; CA 25-28R; CAAS 17;
CANR 24, 74; DLB 38; MTCW 1, 2
McPherson, William (Alexander)
1933- .... **CLC 34**
See CA 69-72; CANR 28; INT CANR-28
Mead, George Herbert 1873-1958 . **TCLC 89**
Mead, Margaret 1901-1978 .... **CLC 37**
See AITN 1; CA 1-4R; 81-84; CANR 4;
DA3; MTCW 1, 2; SATA-Obit 20
Meaker, Marijane (Agnes) 1927-
See Kerr, M. E.
See CA 107; CANR 37, 63; INT 107;
JRDA; MAICYA; MTCW 1; SATA 20,
61, 99; SATA-Essay 111
Medoff, Mark (Howard) 1940- ... **CLC 6, 23;**
DAM DRAM
See AITN 1; CA 53-56; CANR 5; DLB 7;
INT CANR-5
Medvedev, P. N.
See Bakhtin, Mikhail Mikhailovich
Meged, Aharon
See Megged, Aharon
Meged, Aron
See Megged, Aharon
Megged, Aharon 1920- .... **CLC 9**
See CA 49-52; CAAS 13; CANR 1
Mehta, Ved (Parkash) 1934- .... **CLC 37**
See CA 1-4R; CANR 2, 23, 69; MTCW 1
Melanter
See Blackmore, R(ichard) D(oddridge)
Melies, Georges 1861-1938 .... **TCLC 81**
Melikow, Loris
See Hofmannsthal, Hugo von
Melmoth, Sebastian
See Wilde, Oscar
Meltzer, Milton 1915- .... **CLC 26**
See AAYA 8; CA 13-16R; CANR 38; CLR
13; DLB 61; JRDA; MAICYA; SAAS 1;
SATA 1, 50, 80
Melville, Herman 1819-1891 ..... **NCLC 3, 12,**
29, 45, 49; DA; DAB; DAC; DAM
MST, NOV; SSC 1, 17; WLC
See AAYA 25; CDALB 1640-1865; DA3;
DLB 3, 74; SATA 59
Menander c. 342B.C.-c. 292B.C. ... **CMLC 9;**
DAM DRAM; DC 3
See DLB 176
Menchu, Rigoberta 1959-
See HLCS 2
Menchu, Rigoberta 1959-
See CA 175; HLCS 2
Mencken, H(enry) L(ouis)
1880-1956 .... **TCLC 13**
See CA 105; 125; CDALB 1917-1929; DLB
11, 29, 63, 137; MTCW 1, 2
Mendelsohn, Jane 1965(?)- .... **CLC 99**
See CA 154
Mercer, David 1928-1980 .... **CLC 5;DAM**
DRAM
See CA 9-12R; 102; CANR 23; DLB 13;
MTCW 1
Merchant, Paul
See Ellison, Harlan (Jay)
Meredith, George 1828-1909 .. **TCLC 17, 43;**
DAM POET
See CA 117; 153; CANR 80; CDBLB 1832-
1890; DLB 18, 35, 57, 159

Meredith, William (Morris) 1919- .... **CLC 4,**
13, 22, 55; DAM POET; PC 28
See CA 9-12R; CAAS 14; CANR 6, 40;
DLB 5
Merezhkovsky, Dmitry Sergeyevich
1865-1941 .... **TCLC 29**
See CA 169
Merimee, Prosper 1803-1870 ... **NCLC 6, 65;**
SSC 7
See DLB 119, 192
Merkin, Daphne 1954- .... **CLC 44**
See CA 123
Merlin, Arthur
See Blish, James (Benjamin)
Merrill, James (Ingram) 1926-1995 .. **CLC 2,**
3, 6, 8, 13, 18, 34, 91; DAM POET; PC
28
See CA 13-16R; 147; CANR 10, 49, 63;
DA3; DLB 5, 165; DLBY 85; INT CANR-
10; MTCW 1, 2
Merriman, Alex
See Silverberg, Robert
Merriman, Brian 1747-1805 .... **NCLC 70**
Merritt, E. B.
See Waddington, Miriam
Merton, Thomas 1915-1968 ..... **CLC 1, 3, 11,**
34, 83; PC 10
See CA 5-8R; 25-28R; CANR 22, 53; DA3;
DLB 48; DLBY 81; MTCW 1, 2
Merwin, W(illiam) S(tanley) 1927- ... **CLC 1,**
2, 3, 5, 8, 13, 18, 45, 88; DAM POET
See CA 13-16R; CANR 15, 51; DA3; DLB
5, 169; INT CANR-15; MTCW 1, 2
Metcalf, John 1938- .... **CLC 37**
See CA 113; DLB 60
Metcalf, Suzanne
See Baum, L(yman) Frank
Mew, Charlotte (Mary) 1870-1928 .. **TCLC 8**
See CA 105; DLB 19, 135
Mewshaw, Michael 1943- .... **CLC 9**
See CA 53-56; CANR 7, 47; DLBY 80
Meyer, Conrad Ferdinand
1825-1905 .... **NCLC 81**
See DLB 129
Meyer, June
See Jordan, June
Meyer, Lynn
See Slavitt, David R(ytman)
Meyer-Meyrink, Gustav 1868-1932
See Meyrink, Gustav
See CA 117
Meyers, Jeffrey 1939- .... **CLC 39**
See CA 73-76, 181; CAAE 181; CANR 54;
DLB 111
Meynell, Alice (Christina Gertrude
Thompson) 1847-1922 .... **TCLC 6**
See CA 104; 177; DLB 19, 98
Meyrink, Gustav TCLC 21
See Meyer-Meyrink, Gustav
See DLB 81
Michaels, Leonard 1933- ...... **CLC 6, 25;SSC**
16
See CA 61-64; CANR 21, 62; DLB 130;
MTCW 1
Michaux, Henri 1899-1984 .... **CLC 8, 19**
See CA 85-88; 114
Micheaux, Oscar (Devereaux)
1884-1951 .... **TCLC 76**
See BW 3; CA 174; DLB 50
Michelangelo 1475-1564 .... **LC 12**
Michelet, Jules 1798-1874 .... **NCLC 31**
Michels, Robert 1876-1936 .... **TCLC 88**
Michener, James A(lbert)
1907(?)-1997 .... **CLC 1, 5, 11, 29, 60,**
109; DAM NOV, POP
See AAYA 27; AITN 1; BEST 90:1; CA
5-8R; 161; CANR 21, 45, 68; DA3; DLB
6; MTCW 1, 2

Mickiewicz, Adam 1798-1855 .... **NCLC 3**
Middleton, Christopher 1926- .... **CLC 13**
See CA 13-16R; CANR 29, 54; DLB 40
Middleton, Richard (Barham)
1882-1911 .... **TCLC 56**
See DLB 156
Middleton, Stanley 1919- .... **CLC 7, 38**
See CA 25-28R; CAAS 23; CANR 21, 46,
81; DLB 14
Middleton, Thomas 1580-1627 .... **LC 33;**
DAM DRAM, MST; DC 5
See DLB 58
Migueis, Jose Rodrigues 1901- .... **CLC 10**
Mikszath, Kalman 1847-1910 .... **TCLC 31**
See CA 170
Miles, Jack CLC 100
Miles, Josephine (Louise)
1911-1985 .. **CLC 1, 2, 14, 34, 39; DAM**
POET
See CA 1-4R; 116; CANR 2, 55; DLB 48
Militant
See Sandburg, Carl (August)
Mill, John Stuart 1806-1873 .... **NCLC 11, 58**
See CDBLB 1832-1890; DLB 55, 190
Millar, Kenneth 1915-1983 ..... **CLC 14;DAM**
POP
See Macdonald, Ross
See CA 9-12R; 110; CANR 16, 63; DA3;
DLB 2; DLBD 6; DLBY 83; MTCW 1, 2
Millay, E. Vincent
See Millay, Edna St. Vincent
Millay, Edna St. Vincent
1892-1950 .... **TCLC 4, 49; DA; DAB;**
DAC; DAM MST, POET; PC 6;
WLCS
See CA 104; 130; CDALB 1917-1929;
DA3; DLB 45; MTCW 1, 2
Miller, Arthur 1915- ...... **CLC 1, 2, 6, 10, 15,**
26, 47, 78; DA; DAB; DAC; DAM
DRAM, MST; DC 1; WLC
See AAYA 15; AITN 1; CA 1-4R; CABS 3;
CANR 2, 30, 54, 76; CDALB 1941-1968;
DA3; DLB 7; MTCW 1, 2
Miller, Henry (Valentine)
1891-1980 .... **CLC 1, 2, 4, 9, 14, 43, 84;**
DA; DAB; DAC; DAM MST, NOV;
WLC
See CA 9-12R; 97-100; CANR 33, 64;
CDALB 1929-1941; DA3; DLB 4, 9;
DLBY 80; MTCW 1, 2
Miller, Jason 1939(?)- .... **CLC 2**
See AITN 1; CA 73-76; DLB 7
Miller, Sue 1943- .... **CLC 44;DAM POP**
See BEST 90:3; CA 139; CANR 59; DA3;
DLB 143
Miller, Walter M(ichael, Jr.) 1923- ... **CLC 4,**
30
See CA 85-88; DLB 8
Millett, Kate 1934- .... **CLC 67**
See AITN 1; CA 73-76; CANR 32, 53, 76;
DA3; MTCW 1, 2
Millhauser, Steven (Lewis) 1943- .... **CLC 21,**
54, 109
See CA 110; 111; CANR 63; DA3; DLB 2;
INT 111; MTCW 2
Millin, Sarah Gertrude 1889-1968 ... **CLC 49**
See CA 102; 93-96
Milne, A(lan) A(lexander)
1882-1956 ..... **TCLC 6, 88; DAB; DAC;**
DAM MST
See CA 104; 133; CLR 1, 26; DA3; DLB
10, 77, 100, 160; MAICYA; MTCW 1, 2;
SATA 100; YABC 1
Milner, Ron(ald) 1938- .... **CLC 56; BLC 3;**
DAM MULT
See AITN 1; BW 1; CA 73-76; CANR 24,
81; DLB 38; MTCW 1

Morgan, Janet 1945- .... CLC 39
See CA 65-68

Morgan, Lady 1776(?)-1859 .... NCLC 29
See DLB 116, 158

Morgan, Robin (Evonne) 1941- .... CLC 2
See CA 69-72; CANR 29, 68; MTCW 1;
SATA 80

Morgan, Scott
See Kuttner, Henry

Morgan, Seth 1949(?)-1990 .... CLC 65
See CA 132

Morgenstern, Christian 1871-1914 .. TCLC 8
See CA 105

Morgenstern, S.
See Goldman, William (W.)

Moricz, Zsigmond 1879-1942 .... TCLC 33
See CA 165

Morike, Eduard (Friedrich)
1804-1875 .... NCLC 10
See DLB 133

Moritz, Karl Philipp 1756-1793 .... LC 2
See DLB 94

Morland, Peter Henry
See Faust, Frederick (Schiller)

Morley, Christopher (Darlington)
1890-1957 .... TCLC 87
See CA 112; DLB 9

Morren, Theophil
See Hofmannsthal, Hugo von

Morris, Bill 1952- .... CLC 76

Morris, Julian
See West, Morris L(anglo)

Morris, Steveland Judkins 1950(?)-
See Wonder, Stevie
See CA 111

Morris, William 1834-1896 .... NCLC 4
See CDBLB 1832-1890; DLB 18, 35, 57,
156, 178, 184

Morris, Wright 1910-1998 .. CLC 1, 3, 7, 18,
37
See CA 9-12R; 167; CANR 21, 81; DLB 2,
206; DLBY 81; MTCW 1, 2

Morrison, Arthur 1863-1945 .... TCLC 72
See CA 120; 157; DLB 70, 135, 197

Morrison, Chloe Anthony Wofford
See Morrison, Toni

Morrison, James Douglas 1943-1971
See Morrison, Jim
See CA 73-76; CANR 40

Morrison, Jim CLC 17
See Morrison, James Douglas

Morrison, Toni 1931- . CLC 4, 10, 22, 55, 81,
87; BLC 3; DA; DAB; DAC; DAM
MST, MULT, NOV, POP
See AAYA 1, 22; BW 2, 3; CA 29-32R;
CANR 27, 42, 67; CDALB 1968-1988;
DA3; DLB 6, 33, 143; DLBY 81; MTCW
1, 2; SATA 57

Morrison, Van 1945- .... CLC 21
See CA 116; 168

Morrissy, Mary 1958- .... CLC 99

Mortimer, John (Clifford) 1923- ..... CLC 28,
43; DAM DRAM, POP
See CA 13-16R; CANR 21, 69; CDBLB
1960 to Present; DA3; DLB 13; INT
CANR-21; MTCW 1, 2

Mortimer, Penelope(Ruth) 1918- .... CLC 5
See CA 57-60; CANR 45

Morton, Anthony
See Creasey, John

Mosca, Gaetano 1858-1941 .... TCLC 75

Mosher, Howard Frank 1943- .... CLC 62
See CA 139; CANR 65

Mosley, Nicholas 1923- .... CLC 43, 70
See CA 69-72; CANR 41, 60; DLB 14, 207

Mosley, Walter 1952- .... CLC 97; BLCS;
DAM MULT, POP
See AAYA 17; BW 2; CA 142; CANR 57;
DA3; MTCW 2

Moss, Howard 1922-1987 ...... CLC 7, 14, 45,
50; DAM POET
See CA 1-4R; 123; CANR 1, 44; DLB 5

Mossgiel, Rab
See Burns, Robert

Motion, Andrew (Peter) 1952- .... CLC 47
See CA 146; DLB 40

Motley, Willard (Francis)
1909-1965 .... CLC 18
See BW 1; CA 117; 106; DLB 76, 143

Motoori, Norinaga 1730-1801 .... NCLC 45

Mott, Michael (Charles Alston)
1930- .... CLC 15, 34
See CA 5-8R; CAAS 7; CANR 7, 29

Mountain Wolf Woman 1884-1960 .. CLC 92
See CA 144; NNAL

Moure, Erin 1955- .... CLC 88
See CA 113; DLB 60

Mowat, Farley (McGill) 1921- .... CLC 26;
DAC; DAM MST
See AAYA 1; CA 1-4R; CANR 4, 24, 42,
68; CLR 20; DLB 68; INT CANR-24;
JRDA; MAICYA; MTCW 1, 2; SATA 3,
55

Mowatt, Anna Cora 1819-1870 ..... NCLC 74

Moyers, Bill 1934- .... CLC 74
See AITN 2; CA 61-64; CANR 31, 52

Mphahlele, Es'kia
See Mphahlele, Ezekiel
See DLB 125

Mphahlele, Ezekiel 1919- ... CLC 25; BLC 3;
DAM MULT
See Mphahlele, Es'kia
See BW 2, 3; CA 81-84; CANR 26, 76;
DA3; MTCW 2

Mqhayi, S(amuel) E(dward) K(runeLoliwe)
1875-1945 .... TCLC 25; BLC 3;DAM
MULT
See CA 153

Mrozek, Slawomir 1930- .... CLC 3, 13
See CA 13-16R; CAAS 10; CANR 29;
MTCW 1

Mrs. Belloc-Lowndes
See Lowndes, Marie Adelaide (Belloc)

Mtwa, Percy (?)- .... CLC 47

Mueller, Lisel 1924- .... CLC 13, 51
See CA 93-96; DLB 105

Muir, Edwin 1887-1959 .... TCLC 2, 87
See CA 104; DLB 20, 100, 191

Muir, John 1838-1914 .... TCLC 28
See CA 165; DLB 186

Mujica Lainez, Manuel 1910-1984 ... CLC 31
See Lainez, Manuel Mujica
See CA 81-84; 112; CANR 32; HW 1

Mukherjee, Bharati 1940- .... CLC 53, 115;
DAM NOV
See BEST 89:2; CA 107; CANR 45, 72;
DLB 60; MTCW 1, 2

Muldoon, Paul 1951- .... CLC 32, 72;DAM
POET
See CA 113; 129; CANR 52; DLB 40; INT
129

Mulisch, Harry 1927- .... CLC 42
See CA 9-12R; CANR 6, 26, 56

Mull, Martin 1943- .... CLC 17
See CA 105

Muller, Wilhelm NCLC 73

Mulock, Dinah Maria
See Craik, Dinah Maria (Mulock)

Munford, Robert 1737(?)-1783 .... LC 5
See DLB 31

Mungo, Raymond 1946- .... CLC 72
See CA 49-52; CANR 2

Munro, Alice 1931- .... CLC 6, 10, 19, 50, 95;
DAC; DAM MST, NOV; SSC 3;
WLCS
See AITN 2; CA 33-36R; CANR 33, 53,
75; DA3; DLB 53; MTCW 1, 2; SATA 29

Munro, H(ector) H(ugh) 1870-1916
See Saki
See CA 104; 130; CDBLB 1890-1914; DA;
DAB; DAC; DAM MST, NOV; DA3;
DLB 34, 162; MTCW 1, 2; WLC

Murdoch, (Jean) Iris 1919-1999 ... CLC 1, 2,
3, 4, 6, 8, 11, 15, 22, 31, 51; DAB;
DAC; DAM MST, NOV
See CA 13-16R; 179; CANR 8, 43, 68; CD-
BLB 1960 to Present; DA3; DLB 14, 194;
INT CANR-8; MTCW 1, 2

Murfree, Mary Noailles 1850-1922 ... SSC 22
See CA 122; 176; DLB 12, 74

Murnau, Friedrich Wilhelm
See Plumpe, Friedrich Wilhelm

Murphy, Richard 1927- .... CLC 41
See CA 29-32R; DLB 40

Murphy, Sylvia 1937- .... CLC 34
See CA 121

Murphy, Thomas (Bernard) 1935- ... CLC 51
See CA 101

Murray, Albert L. 1916- .... CLC 73
See BW 2; CA 49-52; CANR 26, 52, 78;
DLB 38

Murray, Judith Sargent
1751-1820 .... NCLC 63
See DLB 37, 200

Murray, Les(lie) A(llan) 1938- .... CLC 40;
DAM POET
See CA 21-24R; CANR 11, 27, 56

Murry, J. Middleton
See Murry, John Middleton

Murry, John Middleton
1889-1957 .... TCLC 16
See CA 118; DLB 149

Musgrave, Susan 1951- .... CLC 13, 54
See CA 69-72; CANR 45, 84

Musil, Robert (Edler von)
1880-1942 .... TCLC 12, 68; SSC 18
See CA 109; CANR 55, 84; DLB 81, 124;
MTCW 2

Muske, Carol 1945- .... CLC 90
See Muske-Dukes, Carol (Anne)

Muske-Dukes, Carol (Anne) 1945-
See Muske, Carol
See CA 65-68; CANR 32, 70

Musset, (Louis Charles) Alfredde
1810-1857 .... NCLC 7
See DLB 192

Mussolini, Benito (Amilcare Andrea)
1883-1945 .... TCLC 96
See CA 116

My Brother's Brother
See Chekhov, Anton (Pavlovich)

Myers, L(eopold)H(amilton)
1881-1944 .... TCLC 59
See CA 157; DLB 15

Myers, Walter Dean 1937- ..... CLC 35; BLC
3; DAM MULT, NOV
See AAYA 4, 23; BW 2; CA 33-36R; CANR
20, 42, 67; CLR 4, 16, 35; DLB 33; INT
CANR-20; JRDA; MAICYA; MTCW 2;
SAAS 2; SATA 41, 71, 109; SATA-Brief
27

Myers, Walter M.
See Myers, Walter Dean

Myles, Symon
See Follett, Ken(neth Martin)

Nabokov, Vladimir (Vladimirovich)
1899-1977 .... CLC 1, 2, 3, 6, 8, 11, 15,
23, 44, 46, 64; DA; DAB; DAC; DAM
MST, NOV; SSC 11; WLC
See CA 5-8R; 69-72; CANR 20; CDALB
1941-1968; DA3; DLB 2; DLBD 3;
DLBY 80, 91; MTCW 1, 2

Nagai Kafu 1879-1959 .... TCLC 51
  See Nagai Sokichi
  See DLB 180
Nagai Sokichi 1879-1959
  See Nagai Kafu
  See CA 117
Nagy, Laszlo 1925-1978 .... CLC 7
  See CA 129; 112
Naidu, Sarojini 1879-1943 .... TCLC 80
Naipaul, Shiva(dhar Srinivasa)
  1945-1985 .... CLC 32, 39; DAM NOV
  See CA 110; 112; 116; CANR 33; DA3;
  DLB 157; DLBY 85; MTCW 1, 2
Naipaul, V(idiadhar) S(urajprasad)
  1932- .... CLC 4, 7, 9, 13, 18, 37, 105;
  DAB; DAC; DAM MST, NOV
  See CA 1-4R; CANR 1, 33, 51; CDBLB
  1960 to Present; DA3; DLB 125, 204,
  206; DLBY 85; MTCW 1, 2
Nakos, Lilika 1899(?)- .... CLC 29
Narayan, R(asipuram) K(rishnaswami)
  1906- . CLC 7, 28, 47, 121; DAM NOV;
  SSC 25
  See CA 81-84; CANR 33, 61; DA3; MTCW
  1, 2; SATA 62
Nash, (Fredric) Ogden 1902-1971 . CLC 23;
  DAM POET; PC 21
  See CA 13-14; 29-32R; CANR 34, 61; CAP
  1; DLB 11; MAICYA; MTCW 1, 2; SATA
  2, 46
Nashe, Thomas 1567-1601(?) .... LC 41
  See DLB 167
Nashe, Thomas 1567-1601 .... LC 41
Nathan, Daniel
  See Dannay, Frederic
Nathan, George Jean 1882-1958 .... TCLC 18
  See Hatteras, Owen
  See CA 114; 169; DLB 137
Natsume, Kinnosuke 1867-1916
  See Natsume, Soseki
  See CA 104
Natsume, Soseki 1867-1916 .... TCLC 2, 10
  See Natsume, Kinnosuke
  See DLB 180
Natti, (Mary) Lee 1919-
  See Kingman, Lee
  See CA 5-8R; CANR 2
Naylor, Gloria 1950- .... CLC 28, 52; BLC 3;
  DA; DAC; DAM MST, MULT, NOV,
  POP; WLCS
  See AAYA 6; BW 2, 3; CA 107; CANR 27,
  51, 74; DA3; DLB 173; MTCW 1, 2
Neihardt, John Gneisenau
  1881-1973 .... CLC 32
  See CA 13-14; CANR 65; CAP 1; DLB 9,
  54
Nekrasov, Nikolai Alekseevich
  1821-1878 .... NCLC 11
Nelligan, Emile 1879-1941 .... TCLC 14
  See CA 114; DLB 92
Nelson, Willie 1933- .... CLC 17
  See CA 107
Nemerov, Howard (Stanley)
  1920-1991 .... CLC 2, 6, 9, 36; DAM
  POET; PC 24
  See CA 1-4R; 134; CABS 2; CANR 1, 27,
  53; DLB 5, 6; DLBY 83; INT CANR-27;
  MTCW 1, 2
Neruda, Pablo 1904-1973 .. CLC 1, 2, 5, 7, 9,
  28, 62; DA; DAB; DAC; DAM MST,
  MULT, POET; HLC 2; PC 4; WLC
  See CA 19-20; 45-48; CAP 2; DA3; HW 1;
  MTCW 1, 2
Nerval, Gerard de 1808-1855 ... NCLC 1, 67;
  PC 13; SSC 18
Nervo, (Jose) Amado (Ruiz de)
  1870-1919 .... TCLC 11; HLCS 2
  See CA 109; 131; HW 1

Nessi, Pio Baroja y
  See Baroja (y Nessi), Pio
Nestroy, Johann 1801-1862 .... NCLC 42
  See DLB 133
Netterville, Luke
  See O'Grady, Standish (James)
Neufeld, John (Arthur) 1938- .... CLC 17
  See AAYA 11; CA 25-28R; CANR 11, 37,
  56; CLR 52; MAICYA; SAAS 3; SATA
  6, 81
Neville, Emily Cheney 1919- .... CLC 12
  See CA 5-8R; CANR 3, 37, 85; JRDA;
  MAICYA; SAAS 2; SATA 1
Newbound, Bernard Slade 1930-
  See Slade, Bernard
  See CA 81-84; CANR 49; DAM DRAM
Newby, P(ercy) H(oward)
  1918-1997 .... CLC 2, 13; DAM NOV
  See CA 5-8R; 161; CANR 32, 67; DLB 15;
  MTCW 1
Newlove, Donald 1928- .... CLC 6
  See CA 29-32R; CANR 25
Newlove, John(Herbert) 1938- .... CLC 14
  See CA 21-24R; CANR 9, 25
Newman, Charles 1938- .... CLC 2, 8
  See CA 21-24R; CANR 84
Newman, Edwin (Harold) 1919- ...... CLC 14
  See AITN 1; CA 69-72; CANR 5
Newman, John Henry 1801-1890 .. NCLC 38
  See DLB 18, 32, 55
Newton, (Sir)Isaac 1642-1727 .... LC 35, 52
Newton, Suzanne 1936- .... CLC 35
  See CA 41-44R; CANR 14; JRDA; SATA
  5, 77
Nexo, Martin Andersen
  1869-1954 .... TCLC 43
Nezval, Vitezslav 1900-1958 .... TCLC 44
  See CA 123
Ng, Fae Myenne 1957(?)- .... CLC 81
  See CA 146
Ngema, Mbongeni 1955- .... CLC 57
  See BW 2; CA 143; CANR 84
Ngugi, James T(hiong'o) CLC 3, 7, 13
  See Ngugi wa Thiong'o
Ngugi wa Thiong'o 1938- .. CLC 36; BLC 3;
  DAM MULT, NOV
  See Ngugi, James T(hiong'o)
  See BW 2; CA 81-84; CANR 27, 58; DLB
  125; MTCW 1, 2
Nichol, B(arrie) P(hillip) 1944-1988 . CLC 18
  See CA 53-56; DLB 53; SATA 66
Nichols, John(Treadwell) 1940- .... CLC 38
  See CA 9-12R; CAAS 2; CANR 6, 70;
  DLBY 82
Nichols, Leigh
  See Koontz, Dean R(ay)
Nichols, Peter (Richard) 1927- .... CLC 5, 36,
  65
  See CA 104; CANR 33; DLB 13; MTCW 1
Nicolas, F. R. E.
  See Freeling, Nicolas
Niedecker, Lorine 1903-1970 ..... CLC 10, 42;
  DAM POET
  See CA 25-28; CAP 2; DLB 48
Nietzsche, Friedrich (Wilhelm)
  1844-1900 .... TCLC 10, 18, 55
  See CA 107; 121; DLB 129
Nievo, Ippolito 1831-1861 .... NCLC 22
Nightingale, Anne Redmon 1943-
  See Redmon, Anne
  See CA 103
Nightingale, Florence 1820-1910 ... TCLC 85
  See DLB 166
Nik. T. O.
  See Annensky, Innokenty (Fyodorovich)

Nin, Anais 1903-1977 ..... CLC 1, 4, 8, 11, 14,
  60; DAM NOV, POP; SSC 10
  See AITN 2; CA 13-16R; 69-72; CANR 22,
  53; DLB 2, 4, 152; MTCW 1, 2
Nishida, Kitaro 1870-1945 .... TCLC 83
Nishiwaki, Junzaburo 1894-1982 .... PC 15
  See CA 107
Nissenson, Hugh 1933- .... CLC 4, 9
  See CA 17-20R; CANR 27; DLB 28
Niven, Larry CLC 8
  See Niven, Laurence Van Cott
  See AAYA 27; DLB 8
Niven, Laurence Van Cott 1938-
  See Niven, Larry
  See CA 21-24R; CAAS 12; CANR 14, 44,
  66; DAM POP; MTCW 1, 2; SATA 95
Nixon, Agnes Eckhardt 1927- .... CLC 21
  See CA 110
Nizan, Paul 1905-1940 .... TCLC 40
  See CA 161; DLB 72
Nkosi, Lewis 1936- ... CLC 45; BLC 3; DAM
  MULT
  See BW 1, 3; CA 65-68; CANR 27, 81;
  DLB 157
Nodier, (Jean) Charles (Emmanuel)
  1780-1844 .... NCLC 19
  See DLB 119
Noguchi, Yone 1875-1947 .... TCLC 80
Nolan, Christopher 1965- .... CLC 58
  See CA 111
Noon, Jeff 1957- .... CLC 91
  See CA 148; CANR 83
Norden, Charles
  See Durrell, Lawrence (George)
Nordhoff, Charles(Bernard)
  1887-1947 .... TCLC 23
  See CA 108; DLB 9; SATA 23
Norfolk, Lawrence 1963- .... CLC 76
  See CA 144; CANR 85
Norman, Marsha 1947- .... CLC 28; DAM
  DRAM; DC 8
  See CA 105; CABS 3; CANR 41; DLBY
  84
Normyx
  See Douglas, (George) Norman
Norris, Frank 1870-1902 .... SSC 28
  See Norris, (Benjamin) Frank(lin, Jr.)
  See CDALB 1865-1917; DLB 12, 71, 186
Norris, (Benjamin) Frank(lin,Jr.)
  1870-1902 .... TCLC 24
  See Norris, Frank
  See CA 110; 160
Norris, Leslie 1921- .... CLC 14
  See CA 11-12; CANR 14; CAP 1; DLB 27
North, Andrew
  See Norton, Andre
North, Anthony
  See Koontz, Dean R(ay)
North, Captain George
  See Stevenson, Robert Louis (Balfour)
North, Milou
  See Erdrich, Louise
Northrup, B. A.
  See Hubbard, L(afayette) Ron(ald)
North Staffs
  See Hulme, T(homas) E(rnest)
Norton, Alice Mary
  See Norton, Andre
  See MAICYA; SATA 1, 43
Norton, Andre 1912- .... CLC 12
  See Norton, Alice Mary
  See AAYA 14; CA 1-4R; CANR 68; CLR
  50; DLB 8, 52; JRDA; MTCW 1; SATA
  91
Norton, Caroline 1808-1877 .... NCLC 47
  See DLB 21, 159, 199

Norway, Nevil Shute 1899-1960
See Shute, Nevil
See CA 102; 93-96; CANR 85; MTCW 2

Norwid, Cyprian Kamil
1821-1883 .... **NCLC 17**

Nosille, Nabrah
See Ellison, Harlan (Jay)

Nossack, Hans Erich 1901-1978 .... **CLC 6**
See CA 93-96; 85-88; DLB 69

Nostradamus 1503-1566 .... **LC 27**

Nosu, Chuji
See Ozu, Yasujiro

Notenburg, Eleanora (Genrikhovna) von
See Guro, Elena

Nova, Craig 1945- .... **CLC 7, 31**
See CA 45-48; CANR 2, 53

Novak, Joseph
See Kosinski, Jerzy (Nikodem)

Novalis 1772-1801 .... **NCLC 13**
See DLB 90

Novis, Emile
See Weil, Simone (Adolphine)

Nowlan, Alden (Albert) 1933-1983 . **CLC 15;**
DAC; DAM MST
See CA 9-12R; CANR 5; DLB 53

Noyes, Alfred 1880-1958 .... **TCLC 7;PC 27**
See CA 104; DLB 20

Nunn, Kem CLC 34
See CA 159

Nye, Robert 1939- ... **CLC 13, 42;DAM NOV**
See CA 33-36R; CANR 29, 67; DLB 14;
MTCW 1; SATA 6

Nyro, Laura 1947- .... **CLC 17**

Oates, Joyce Carol 1938- .. **CLC 1, 2, 3, 6, 9,**
11, 15, 19, 33, 52, 108; DA; DAB;
DAC; DAM MST, NOV, POP; SSC
6;WLC
See AAYA 15; AITN 1; BEST 89:2; CA
5-8R; CANR 25, 45, 74; CDALB 1968-
1988; DA3; DLB 2, 5, 130; DLBY 81;
INT CANR-25; MTCW 1, 2

O'Brien, Darcy 1939-1998 .... **CLC 11**
See CA 21-24R; 167; CANR 8, 59

O'Brien, E. G.
See Clarke, Arthur C(harles)

O'Brien, Edna 1936- ..... **CLC 3, 5, 8, 13, 36,**
65, 116; DAM NOV; SSC 10
See CA 1-4R; CANR 6, 41, 65; CDBLB
1960 to Present; DA3; DLB 14; MTCW
1, 2

O'Brien, Fitz-James 1828-1862 ..... **NCLC 21**
See DLB 74

O'Brien, Flann CLC 1, 4, 5, 7, 10, 47
See O Nuallain, Brian

O'Brien, Richard 1942- .... **CLC 17**
See CA 124

O'Brien, (William) Tim(othy) 1946- . **CLC 7,**
19, 40, 103; DAM POP
See AAYA 16; CA 85-88; CANR 40, 58;
CDALBS; DA3; DLB 152; DLBD 9;
DLBY 80; MTCW 2

Obstfelder,Sigbjoern 1866-1900 ..... **TCLC 23**
See CA 123

O'Casey, Sean 1880-1964 .... **CLC 1, 5, 9, 11,**
15, 88; DAB; DAC; DAM DRAM,
MST; WLCS
See CA 89-92; CANR 62;CDBLB 1914-
1945; DA3; DLB 10; MTCW 1, 2

O'Cathasaigh, Sean
See O'Casey, Sean

Ochs, Phil 1940-1976 .... **CLC 17**
See CA 65-68

O'Connor, Edwin(Greene)
1918-1968 .... **CLC 14**
See CA 93-96; 25-28R

O'Connor, (Mary) Flannery
1925-1964 .... **CLC 1, 2, 3, 6, 10, 13, 15,**
21, 66, 104; DA; DAB; DAC; DAM
MST, NOV; SSC 1, 23;WLC
See AAYA 7; CA 1-4R; CANR 3, 41;
CDALB 1941-1968; DA3; DLB 2, 152;
DLBD 12; DLBY 80; MTCW 1, 2

O'Connor, Frank CLC 23; SSC 5
See O'Donovan, Michael John
See DLB 162

O'Dell, Scott 1898-1989 .... **CLC 30**
See AAYA 3; CA 61-64; 129; CANR 12,
30; CLR 1, 16; DLB 52; JRDA; MAI-
CYA; SATA 12, 60

Odets, Clifford 1906-1963 ..... **CLC 2, 28, 98;**
DAM DRAM; DC 6
See CA 85-88; CANR 62; DLB 7, 26;
MTCW 1, 2

O'Doherty, Brian 1934- .... **CLC 76**
See CA 105

O'Donnell, K. M.
See Malzberg, Barry N(athaniel)

O'Donnell, Lawrence
See Kuttner, Henry

O'Donovan, Michael John
1903-1966 .... **CLC 14**
See O'Connor, Frank
See CA 93-96; CANR 84

Oe, Kenzaburo 1935- .... **CLC 10, 36, 86;**
DAM NOV; SSC 20
See CA 97-100; CANR 36, 50, 74; DA3;
DLB 182; DLBY 94; MTCW 1, 2

O'Faolain, Julia 1932- .... **CLC 6, 19, 47, 108**
See CA 81-84; CAAS 2; CANR 12, 61;
DLB 14; MTCW 1

O'Faolain, Sean 1900-1991 ...... **CLC 1, 7, 14,**
32, 70; SSC 13
See CA 61-64; 134; CANR 12, 66; DLB
15, 162; MTCW 1, 2

O'Flaherty, Liam 1896-1984 .... **CLC 5, 34;**
SSC 6
See CA 101; 113; CANR 35; DLB 36, 162;
DLBY 84; MTCW 1, 2

Ogilvy, Gavin
See Barrie, J(ames) M(atthew)

O'Grady, Standish (James)
1846-1928 .... **TCLC 5**
See CA 104; 157

O'Grady, Timothy 1951- .... **CLC 59**
See CA 138

O'Hara, Frank 1926-1966 .... **CLC 2, 5, 13,**
78; DAM POET
See CA 9-12R; 25-28R; CANR 33; DA3;
DLB 5, 16, 193; MTCW 1, 2

O'Hara, John (Henry) 1905-1970 . **CLC 1, 2,**
3, 6, 11, 42; DAM NOV; SSC 15
See CA 5-8R; 25-28R; CANR 31, 60;
CDALB 1929-1941; DLB 9, 86; DLBD
2; MTCW 1, 2

O Hehir, Diana 1922- .... **CLC 41**
See CA 93-96

Ohiyesa
See Eastman, Charles A(lexander)

Okigbo, Christopher (Ifenayichukwu)
1932-1967 ... **CLC 25, 84; BLC 3; DAM**
MULT, POET; PC 7
See BW 1, 3; CA 77-80; CANR 74; DLB
125; MTCW 1, 2

Okri, Ben 1959- .... **CLC 87**
See BW 2, 3; CA 130; 138; CANR 65; DLB
157; INT 138; MTCW 2

Olds, Sharon 1942- ... **CLC 32, 39, 85; DAM**
POET; PC 22
See CA 101; CANR 18, 41, 66; DLB 120;
MTCW 2

Oldstyle, Jonathan
See Irving, Washington

Olesha, Yuri(Karlovich) 1899-1960 .... **CLC 8**
See CA 85-88

Oliphant,Laurence 1829(?)-1888 ... **NCLC 47**
See DLB 18, 166

Oliphant, Margaret (Oliphant Wilson)
1828-1897 .... **NCLC 11, 61; SSC 25**
See DLB 18, 159, 190

Oliver, Mary 1935- .... **CLC 19, 34, 98**
See CA 21-24R; CANR 9, 43, 84; DLB 5,
193

Olivier, Laurence(Kerr) 1907-1989 .. **CLC 20**
See CA 111; 150; 129

Olsen, Tillie 1912- .... **CLC 4, 13, 114; DA;**
DAB; DAC; DAM MST; SSC 11
See CA 1-4R; CANR 1, 43, 74; CDALBS;
DA3; DLB 28, 206; DLBY 80; MTCW 1,
2

Olson, Charles (John) 1910-1970 .. **CLC 1, 2,**
5, 6, 9, 11, 29; DAM POET; PC 19
See CA 13-16; 25-28R; CABS 2; CANR
35, 61; CAP 1; DLB 5, 16, 193; MTCW
1, 2

Olson, Toby 1937- .... **CLC 28**
See CA 65-68; CANR 9, 31, 84

Olyesha, Yuri
See Olesha, Yuri (Karlovich)

Ondaatje, (Philip) Michael 1943- .... **CLC 14,**
29, 51, 76; DAB; DAC; DAM MST; PC
28
See CA 77-80; CANR 42, 74; DA3; DLB
60; MTCW 2

Oneal, Elizabeth 1934-
See Oneal, Zibby
See CA 106; CANR 28, 84; MAICYA;
SATA 30, 82

Oneal, Zibby CLC 30
See Oneal, Elizabeth
See AAYA 5; CLR 13; JRDA

O'Neill, Eugene (Gladstone)
1888-1953 .... **TCLC 1, 6, 27, 49; DA;**
DAB; DAC; DAM DRAM, MST; WLC
See AITN 1; CA 110; 132; CDALB 1929-
1941; DA3; DLB 7; MTCW 1, 2

Onetti, Juan Carlos 1909-1994 ... **CLC 7, 10;**
DAM MULT, NOV; HLCS 2; SSC 23
See CA 85-88; 145; CANR 32, 63; DLB
113; HW 1, 2; MTCW 1, 2

O Nuallain, Brian 1911-1966
See O'Brien, Flann
See CA 21-22; 25-28R; CAP 2

Ophuls, Max 1902-1957 .... **TCLC 79**
See CA 113

Opie, Amelia 1769-1853 .... **NCLC 65**
See DLB 116, 159

Oppen, George 1908-1984 .... **CLC 7, 13,34**
See CA 13-16R; 113; CANR 8, 82; DLB 5,
165

Oppenheim, E(dward) Phillips
1866-1946 .... **TCLC 45**
See CA 111; DLB 70

Opuls, Max
See Ophuls, Max

Origen c. 185-c. 254 .... **CMLC 19**

Orlovitz, Gil 1918-1973 .... **CLC 22**
See CA 77-80; 45-48; DLB 2, 5

Orris
See Ingelow, Jean

Ortega y Gasset, Jose 1883-1955 ... **TCLC 9;**
DAM MULT; HLC 2
See CA 106; 130; HW 1, 2; MTCW 1, 2

Ortese, Anna Maria 1914- .... **CLC 89**
See DLB 177

Ortiz, Simon J(oseph) 1941- . **CLC 45; DAM**
MULT, POET; PC 17
See CA 134; CANR 69; DLB 120, 175;
NNAL

Orton, Joe CLC 4, 13, 43; DC 3
See Orton, John Kingsley
See CDBLB 1960 to Present; DLB 13;
MTCW 2

See CANR 38, 83; JRDA; MAICYA; SAAS
3; SATA 4, 72, 109

Patton, George S. 1885-1945 .... **TCLC 79**

Paulding, James Kirke 1778-1860 ... **NCLC 2**
See DLB 3, 59, 74

Paulin, Thomas Neilson 1949-
See Paulin, Tom
See CA 123; 128

Paulin, Tom CLC 37
See Paulin, Thomas Neilson
See DLB 40

Pausanias c. 1st cent. - .... **CMLC 36**

Paustovsky, Konstantin (Georgievich)
1892-1968 .... **CLC 40**
See CA 93-96; 25-28R

Pavese, Cesare 1908-1950 .. **TCLC 3; PC 13;**
SSC 19
See CA 104; 169; DLB 128, 177

Pavic, Milorad 1929- .... **CLC 60**
See CA 136; DLB 181

Pavlov, Ivan Petrovich 1849-1936 . **TCLC 91**
See CA 118; 180

Payne, Alan
See Jakes, John (William)

Paz, Gil
See Lugones, Leopoldo

Paz, Octavio 1914-1998 . **CLC 3, 4, 6, 10, 19,**
51, 65, 119; DA; DAB; DAC; DAM
MST, MULT, POET; HLC 2; PC
1;WLC
See CA 73-76; 165; CANR 32, 65; DA3;
DLBY 90, 98; HW 1, 2; MTCW 1, 2

p'Bitek, Okot 1931-1982 .... **CLC 96; BLC 3;**
DAM MULT
See BW 2, 3; CA 124; 107; CANR 82; DLB
125; MTCW 1, 2

Peacock, Molly 1947- .... **CLC 60**
See CA 103; CAAS 21; CANR 52, 84; DLB
120

Peacock, ThomasLove 1785-1866 .. **NCLC 22**
See DLB 96, 116

Peake, Mervyn 1911-1968 .... **CLC 7, 54**
See CA 5-8R; 25-28R; CANR 3; DLB 15,
160; MTCW 1; SATA 23

Pearce, Philippa CLC 21
See Christie, (Ann) Philippa
See CLR 9; DLB 161; MAICYA; SATA 1,
67

Pearl, Eric
See Elman, Richard (Martin)

Pearson, T(homas) R(eid) 1956- .... **CLC 39**
See CA 120; 130; INT 130

Peck, Dale 1967- .... **CLC 81**
See CA 146; CANR 72

Peck, John 1941- .... **CLC 3**
See CA 49-52; CANR 3

Peck, Richard (Wayne) 1934- .... **CLC 21**
See AAYA 1, 24; CA 85-88; CANR 19, 38;
CLR 15; INT CANR-19; JRDA; MAI-
CYA; SAAS 2; SATA 18, 55, 97; SATA-
Essay 110

Peck, Robert Newton 1928- .... **CLC 17; DA;**
DAC; DAM MST
See AAYA 3; CA 81-84; CANR 31, 63;
CLR 45; JRDA; MAICYA; SAAS 1;
SATA 21, 62, 111; SATA-Essay 108

Peckinpah, (David) Sam(uel)
1925-1984 .... **CLC 20**
See CA 109; 114; CANR 82

Pedersen, Knut 1859-1952
See Hamsun, Knut
See CA 104; 119; CANR 63; MTCW 1, 2

Peeslake, Gaffer
See Durrell, Lawrence (George)

Peguy, Charles Pierre 1873-1914 ... **TCLC 10**
See CA 107

Peirce, Charles Sanders
1839-1914 .... **TCLC 81**

Pellicer, Carlos 1900(?)-1977
See CA 153; 69-72; HLCS 2; HW 1

Pena, Ramon del Valle y
See Valle-Inclan, Ramon (Maria) del

Pendennis, Arthur Esquir
See Thackeray, William Makepeace

Penn, William 1644-1718 .... **LC 25**
See DLB 24

PEPECE
See Prado (Calvo), Pedro

Pepys, Samuel 1633-1703 .... **LC 11; DA;**
DAB; DAC; DAM MST; WLC
See CDBLB 1660-1789; DA3; DLB 101

Percy, Walker 1916-1990 .... **CLC 2, 3, 6, 8,**
14, 18, 47, 65; DAM NOV, POP
Sec CA 1-4R; 131; CANR 1, 23, 64; DA3;
DLB 2; DLBY 80, 90; MTCW 1, 2

Percy, William Alexander
1885-1942 .... **TCLC 84**
See CA 163; MTCW 2

Perec, Georges 1936-1982 .... **CLC 56, 116**
See CA 141; DLB 83

Pereda (y Sanchez de Porrua), Jose Mariade
1833-1906 .... **TCLC 16**
See CA 117

Pereda y Porrua, Jose Maria de
See Pereda (y Sanchez de Porrua), Jose
Maria de

Peregoy, George Weems
See Mencken, H(enry) L(ouis)

Perelman, S(idney) J(oseph)
1904-1979 .. **CLC 3, 5, 9, 15, 23, 44, 49;**
DAM DRAM; SSC 32
See AITN 1, 2; CA 73-76; 89-92; CANR
18; DLB 11, 44; MTCW 1, 2

Peret, Benjamin 1899-1959 .... **TCLC 20**
See CA 117

Peretz, Isaac Loeb 1851(?)-1915 ... **TCLC 16;**
SSC 26
See CA 109

Peretz, Yitzhok Leibush
See Peretz, Isaac Loeb

Perez Galdos, Benito 1843-1920 ... **TCLC 27;**
HLCS 2
See CA 125; 153; HW 1

Peri Rossi, Cristina 1941-
See CA 131; CANR 59, 81; DLB 145;
HLCS 2; HW 1, 2

Perrault, Charles 1628-1703 .... **LC 3, 52**
See MAICYA; SATA 25

Perry, Brighton
See Sherwood, Robert E(mmet)

Perse, St.-John
See Leger, (Marie-Rene Auguste) Alexis
Saint-Leger

Perutz, Leo(pold) 1882-1957 .... **TCLC 60**
See CA 147; DLB 81

Peseenz, Tulio F.
See Lopez y Fuentes, Gregorio

Pesetsky, Bette 1932- .... **CLC 28**
See CA 133; DLB 130

Peshkov, Alexei Maximovich 1868-1936
See Gorky, Maxim
See CA 105; 141; CANR 83; DA; DAC;
DAM DRAM, MST, NOV; MTCW 2

Pessoa, Fernando (Antonio Nogueira)
1888-1935 .... **TCLC 27; DAM MULT;**
HLC 2; PC 20
See CA 125

Peterkin, Julia Mood 1880-1961 ...... **CLC 31**
See CA 102; DLB 9

Peters, Joan K(aren) 1945- .... **CLC 39**
See CA 158

Peters, Robert L(ouis) 1924- .... **CLC 7**
See CA 13-16R; CAAS 8; DLB 105

Petofi, Sandor 1823-1849 .... **NCLC 21**

Petrakis, Harry Mark 1923- .... **CLC 3**
See CA 9-12R; CANR 4, 30, 85

Petrarch 1304-1374 .... **CMLC 20; DAM**
POET; PC 8
See DA3

Petronius c. 20-66 .... **CMLC 34**
See DLB 211

Petrov, Evgeny TCLC 21
See Kataev, Evgeny Petrovich

Petry, Ann (Lane) 1908-1997 ... **CLC 1, 7, 18**
See BW 1, 3; CA 5-8R; 157; CAAS 6;
CANR 4, 46; CLR 12; DLB 76; JRDA;
MAICYA; MTCW 1; SATA 5; SATA-Obit
94

Petursson, Halligrimur 1614-1674 .... **LC 8**

Peychinovich
See Vazov, Ivan (Minchov)

Phaedrus c. 18B.C.-c. 50 .... **CMLC 25**
See DLB 211

Philips, Katherine 1632-1664 .... **LC 30**
See DLB 131

Philipson, Morris H. 1926- .... **CLC 53**
See CA 1-4R; CANR 4

Phillips, Caryl 1958- . **CLC 96; BLCS; DAM**
MULT
See BW 2; CA 141; CANR 63; DA3; DLB
157; MTCW 2

Phillips, David Graham
1867-1911 .... **TCLC 44**
See CA 108; 176; DLB 9, 12

Phillips, Jack
See Sandburg, Carl (August)

Phillips, Jayne Anne 1952- .... **CLC 15, 33;**
SSC 16
See CA 101; CANR 24, 50; DLBY 80; INT
CANR-24; MTCW 1, 2

Phillips, Richard
See Dick, Philip K(indred)

Phillips, Robert(Schaeffer) 1938- ..... **CLC 28**
See CA 17-20R; CAAS 13; CANR 8; DLB
105

Phillips, Ward
See Lovecraft, H(oward) P(hillips)

Piccolo, Lucio 1901-1969 .... **CLC 13**
See CA 97-100; DLB 114

Pickthall, Marjorie L(owry) C(hristie)
1883-1922 .... **TCLC 21**
See CA 107; DLB 92

Pico della Mirandola, Giovanni
1463-1494 .... **LC 15**

Piercy, Marge 1936- .... **CLC 3, 6, 14, 18, 27,**
62
See CA 21-24R; CAAS 1; CANR 13, 43,
66; DLB 120; MTCW 1, 2

Piers, Robert
See Anthony, Piers

Pieyre de Mandiargues, Andre 1909-1991
See Mandiargues, Andre Pieyre de
See CA 103; 136; CANR 22, 82

Pilnyak, Boris TCLC 23
See Vogau, Boris Andreyevich

Pincherle, Alberto 1907-1990 .... **CLC 11, 18;**
DAM NOV
See Moravia, Alberto
See CA 25-28R; 132; CANR 33, 63; MTCW
1

Pinckney, Darryl 1953- .... **CLC 76**
See BW 2, 3; CA 143; CANR 79

Pindar 518B.C.-446B.C. ..... **CMLC 12;PC 19**
See DLB 176

Pineda, Cecile 1942- .... **CLC 39**
See CA 118

Pinero, Arthur Wing 1855-1934 ... **TCLC 32;**
DAM DRAM
See CA 110; 153; DLB 10

Powys, T(heodore) F(rancis)
1875-1953 .... **TCLC 9**
See CA 106; DLB 36, 162

Prado (Calvo),Pedro 1886-1952 ..... **TCLC 75**
See CA 131; HW 1

Prager, Emily 1952- .... **CLC 56**

Pratt, E(dwin) J(ohn)
1883(?)-1964 .... **CLC 19; DAC; DAM POET**
See CA 141; 93-96; CANR 77; DLB 92

Premchand TCLC 21
See Srivastava, Dhanpat Rai

Preussler, Otfried 1923- .... **CLC 17**
See CA 77-80; SATA 24

Prevert, Jacques (Henri Marie)
1900-1977 .... **CLC 15**
See CA 77-80; 69-72; CANR 29, 61;
MTCW 1; SATA-Obit 30

Prevost, Abbe (Antoine Francois)
1697-1763 .... **LC 1**

Price, (Edward) Reynolds 1933- ... **CLC 3, 6, 13, 43, 50, 63; DAM NOV; SSC 22**
See CA 1-4R; CANR 1, 37, 57; DLB 2; INT CANR-37

Price, Richard 1949- .... **CLC 6, 12**
See CA 49-52; CANR 3; DLBY 81

Prichard, Katharine Susannah
1883-1969 .... **CLC 46**
See CA 11-12; CANR 33; CAP 1; MTCW 1; SATA 66

Priestley, J(ohn) B(oynton)
1894-1984 .... **CLC 2, 5, 9, 34; DAM DRAM, NOV**
See CA 9-12R; 113; CANR 33;CDBLB 1914-1945; DA3; DLB 10, 34, 77, 100, 139; DLBY 84; MTCW 1, 2

Prince 1958(?)- .... **CLC 35**

Prince, F(rank) T(empleton) 1912- .. **CLC 22**
See CA 101; CANR 43, 79; DLB 20

Prince Kropotkin
See Kropotkin, Peter (Aleksieevich)

Prior, Matthew 1664-1721 .... **LC 4**
See DLB 95

Prishvin, Mikhail 1873-1954 .... **TCLC 75**

Pritchard, William H(arrison)
1932- .... **CLC 34**
See CA 65-68; CANR 23; DLB 111

Pritchett, V(ictor) S(awdon)
1900-1997 ...... **CLC 5, 13, 15, 41; DAM NOV; SSC 14**
See CA 61-64; 157; CANR 31, 63; DA3; DLB 15, 139; MTCW 1, 2

Private 19022
See Manning, Frederic

Probst, Mark 1925- .... **CLC 59**
See CA 130

Prokosch, Frederic 1908-1989 ...... **CLC 4, 48**
See CA 73-76; 128; CANR 82; DLB 48; MTCW 2

Propertius, Sextus c.
50B.C.-c.16B.C. .... **CMLC 32**
See DLB 211

Prophet, The
See Dreiser, Theodore (Herman Albert)

Prose, Francine 1947- .... **CLC 45**
See CA 109; 112; CANR 46; SATA 101

Proudhon
See Cunha, Euclides (Rodrigues Pimenta) da

Proulx, Annie
See Proulx, E(dna) Annie

Proulx, E(dna) Annie 1935- ... **CLC 81;DAM POP**
See CA 145; CANR 65; DA3; MTCW 2

Proust,
(Valentin-Louis-George-Eugene-)Marcel
1871-1922 . **TCLC 7, 13, 33; DA; DAB; DAC; DAM MST, NOV; WLC**
See CA 104; 120; DA3; DLB 65; MTCW 1, 2

Prowler, Harley
See Masters, Edgar Lee

Prus, Boleslaw 1845-1912 .... **TCLC 48**

Pryor, Richard (Franklin Lenox Thomas)
1940- .... **CLC 26**
See CA 122; 152

Przybyszewski, Stanislaw
1868-1927 .... **TCLC 36**
See CA 160; DLB 66

Pteleon
See Grieve, C(hristopher) M(urray)
See DAM POET

Puckett, Lute
See Masters, Edgar Lee

Puig, Manuel 1932-1990 .... **CLC 3, 5, 10, 28, 65; DAM MULT; HLC 2**
See CA 45-48; CANR 2, 32, 63; DA3; DLB 113; HW 1, 2; MTCW 1, 2

Pulitzer, Joseph 1847-1911 .... **TCLC 76**
See CA 114; DLB 23

Purdy, A(lfred) W(ellington) 1918- ... **CLC 3, 6, 14, 50; DAC; DAM MST, POET**
See CA 81-84; CAAS 17; CANR 42, 66; DLB 88

Purdy, James (Amos) 1923- .... **CLC 2, 4, 10, 28, 52**
See CA 33-36R; CAAS 1; CANR 19, 51; DLB 2; INT CANR-19; MTCW 1

Pure, Simon
See Swinnerton, Frank Arthur

Pushkin, Alexander (Sergeyevich)
1799-1837 .... **NCLC 3, 27; DA; DAB; DAC; DAM DRAM, MST, POET; PC 10; SSC 27; WLC**
See DA3; DLB 205; SATA 61

P'u Sung-ling 1640-1715 .... **LC 49; SSC 31**

Putnam, Arthur Lee
See Alger, Horatio, Jr.

Puzo, Mario 1920-1999 .... **CLC 1, 2, 6, 36, 107; DAM NOV, POP**
See CA 65-68; CANR 4, 42, 65; DA3; DLB 6; MTCW 1, 2

Pygge, Edward
See Barnes, Julian (Patrick)

Pyle, Ernest Taylor 1900-1945
See Pyle, Ernie
See CA 115; 160

Pyle, Ernie 1900-1945 .... **TCLC 75**
See Pyle, Ernest Taylor
See DLB 29; MTCW 2

Pyle, Howard 1853-1911 .... **TCLC 81**
See CA 109; 137; CLR 22; DLB 42, 188; DLBD 13; MAICYA; SATA 16, 100

Pym, Barbara (Mary Crampton)
1913-1980 .... **CLC 13, 19, 37, 111**
See CA 13-14; 97-100; CANR 13, 34; CAP 1; DLB 14, 207; DLBY 87; MTCW 1, 2

Pynchon, Thomas (Ruggles, Jr.)
1937- ..... **CLC 2, 3, 6, 9, 11, 18, 33, 62, 72; DA; DAB; DAC; DAM MST, NOV, POP; SSC 14;WLC**
See BEST 90:2; CA 17-20R; CANR 22, 46, 73; DA3; DLB 2, 173; MTCW 1, 2

Pythagoras c. 570B.C.-c.500B.C. .. **CMLC 22**
See DLB 176

Q
See Quiller-Couch, SirArthur (Thomas)

Qian Zhongshu
See Ch'ien Chung-shu

Qroll
See Dagerman, Stig (Halvard)

Quarrington, Paul (Lewis) 1953- ..... **CLC 65**
See CA 129; CANR 62

Quasimodo, Salvatore 1901-1968 ..... **CLC 10**
See CA 13-16; 25-28R; CAP 1; DLB 114; MTCW 1

Quay, Stephen 1947- .... **CLC 95**

Quay, Timothy 1947- .... **CLC 95**

Queen, Ellery CLC 3, 11
See Dannay, Frederic; Davidson, Avram (James); Lee, Manfred B(ennington); Marlowe, Stephen; Sturgeon, Theodore (Hamilton); Vance, John Holbrook

Queen, Ellery, Jr.
See Dannay, Frederic; Lee, Manfred B(ennington)

Queneau, Raymond 1903-1976 ..... **CLC 2, 5, 10, 42**
See CA 77-80; 69-72; CANR 32; DLB 72; MTCW 1, 2

Quevedo, Francisco de 1580-1645 .... **LC 23**

Quiller-Couch, Sir Arthur(Thomas)
1863-1944 .... **TCLC 53**
See CA 118; 166; DLB 135, 153, 190

Quin, Ann (Marie) 1936-1973 .... **CLC 6**
See CA 9-12R; 45-48; DLB 14

Quinn, Martin
See Smith, Martin Cruz

Quinn, Peter 1947- .... **CLC 91**

Quinn, Simon
See Smith, Martin Cruz

Quintana, Leroy V. 1944-
See CA 131; CANR 65; DAM MULT; DLB 82; HLC 2; HW 1, 2

Quiroga, Horacio (Sylvestre)
1878-1937 .... **TCLC 20; DAM MULT; HLC 2**
See CA 117; 131; HW 1; MTCW 1

Quoirez, Francoise 1935- .... **CLC 9**
See Sagan, Francoise
See CA 49-52; CANR 6, 39, 73; MTCW 1, 2

Raabe, Wilhelm (Karl) 1831-1910 . **TCLC 45**
See CA 167; DLB 129

Rabe, David (William) 1940- .. **CLC 4, 8, 33; DAM DRAM**
See CA 85-88; CABS 3; CANR 59; DLB 7

Rabelais, Francois 1483-1553 ...... **LC 5; DA; DAB; DAC; DAM MST; WLC**

Rabinovitch, Sholem 1859-1916
See Aleichem, Sholom
See CA 104

Rabinyan, Dorit 1972- .... **CLC 119**
See CA 170

Rachilde 1860-1953 .... **TCLC 67**
See DLB 123, 192

Racine, Jean 1639-1699 .. **LC 28; DAB;DAM MST**
See DA3

Radcliffe, Ann (Ward) 1764-1823 ... **NCLC 6, 55**
See DLB 39, 178

Radiguet, Raymond 1903-1923 ...... **TCLC 29**
See CA 162; DLB 65

Radnoti, Miklos 1909-1944 .... **TCLC 16**
See CA 118

Rado, James 1939- .... **CLC 17**
See CA 105

Radvanyi, Netty 1900-1983
See Seghers, Anna
See CA 85-88; 110; CANR 82

Rae, Ben
See Griffiths, Trevor

Raeburn, John (Hay) 1941- .... **CLC 34**
See CA 57-60

Ragni, Gerome 1942-1991 .... **CLC 17**
See CA 105; 134

Rahv, Philip 1908-1973 .... **CLC 24**
See Greenberg, Ivan
See DLB 137

Raimund, Ferdinand Jakob
1790-1836 .... **NCLC 69**
See DLB 90

Raine, Craig 1944- .... **CLC 32, 103**
See CA 108; CANR 29, 51; DLB 40

Raine, Kathleen (Jessie) 1908- ..... **CLC 7, 45**
See CA 85-88; CANR 46; DLB 20; MTCW 1

Rainis, Janis 1865-1929 .... **TCLC 29**
See CA 170

Rakosi, Carl 1903- .... **CLC 47**
See Rawley, Callman
See CAAS 5; DLB 193

Raleigh, Richard
See Lovecraft, H(oward) P(hillips)

Raleigh, Sir Walter 1554(?)-1618 .. **LC 31, 39**
See CDBLB Before 1660; DLB 172

Rallentando, H. P.
See Sayers, Dorothy L(eigh)

Ramal, Walter
See de la Mare, Walter (John)

Ramana Maharshi 1879-1950 .... **TCLC 84**

Ramoacn y Cajal, Santiago
1852-1934 .... **TCLC 93**

Ramon, Juan
See Jimenez (Mantecon), Juan Ramon

Ramos, Graciliano 1892-1953 .... **TCLC 32**
See CA 167; HW 2

Rampersad, Arnold 1941- .... **CLC 44**
See BW 2, 3; CA 127; 133; CANR 81; DLB 111; INT 133

Rampling, Anne
See Rice, Anne

Ramsay, Allan 1684(?)-1758 .... **LC 29**
See DLB 95

Ramuz, Charles-Ferdinand
1878-1947 .... **TCLC 33**
See CA 165

Rand, Ayn 1905-1982 ...... **CLC 3, 30, 44, 79; DA; DAC; DAM MST, NOV, POP; WLC**
See AAYA 10; CA 13-16R; 105; CANR 27, 73; CDALBS; DA3; MTCW 1, 2

Randall, Dudley (Felker) 1914- .... **CLC 1; BLC 3; DAM MULT**
See BW 1, 3; CA 25-28R; CANR 23, 82; DLB 41

Randall, Robert
See Silverberg, Robert

Ranger, Ken
See Creasey, John

Ransom, John Crowe 1888-1974 .. **CLC 2, 4, 5, 11, 24; DAM POET**
See CA 5-8R; 49-52; CANR 6, 34; CDALBS; DA3; DLB 45, 63; MTCW 1, 2

Rao, Raja 1909- ...... **CLC 25, 56; DAM NOV**
See CA 73-76; CANR 51; MTCW 1, 2

Raphael, Frederic (Michael) 1931- ... **CLC 2, 14**
See CA 1-4R; CANR 1; DLB 14

Ratcliffe, James P.
See Mencken, H(enry) L(ouis)

Rathbone, Julian 1935- .... **CLC 41**
See CA 101; CANR 34, 73

Rattigan, Terence (Mervyn)
1911-1977 .... **CLC 7; DAM DRAM**
See CA 85-88; 73-76; CDBLB 1945-1960; DLB 13; MTCW 1, 2

Ratushinskaya, Irina 1954- .... **CLC 54**
See CA 129; CANR 68

Raven, Simon (Arthur Noel) 1927- .. **CLC 14**
See CA 81-84

Ravenna, Michael
See Welty, Eudora

Rawley, Callman 1903-
See Rakosi, Carl
See CA 21-24R; CANR 12, 32

Rawlings, Marjorie Kinnan
1896-1953 .... **TCLC 4**
See AAYA 20; CA 104; 137; CANR 74; DLB 9, 22, 102; DLBD 17; JRDA; MAI-CYA; MTCW 2; SATA 100; YABC 1

Ray, Satyajit 1921-1992 .. **CLC 16, 76; DAM MULT**
See CA 114; 137

Read, Herbert Edward 1893-1968 ..... **CLC 4**
See CA 85-88; 25-28R; DLB 20, 149

Read, Piers Paul 1941- .... **CLC 4, 10, 25**
See CA 21-24R; CANR 38; DLB 14; SATA 21

Reade, Charles 1814-1884 .... **NCLC 2, 74**
See DLB 21

Reade, Hamish
See Gray, Simon (James Holliday)

Reading, Peter 1946- .... **CLC 47**
See CA 103; CANR 46; DLB 40

Reaney, James 1926- ... **CLC 13; DAC; DAM MST**
See CA 41-44R; CAAS 15; CANR 42; DLB 68; SATA 43

Rebreanu, Liviu 1885-1944 .... **TCLC 28**
See CA 165

Rechy, John (Francisco) 1934- ...... **CLC 1, 7, 14, 18, 107; DAM MULT; HLC 2**
See CA 5-8R; CAAS 4; CANR 6, 32, 64; DLB 122; DLBY 82; HW 1, 2; INT CANR-6

Redcam, Tom 1870-1933 .... **TCLC 25**

Reddin, Keith .... **CLC 67**

Redgrove, Peter (William) 1932- . **CLC 6, 41**
See CA 1-4R; CANR 3, 39, 77; DLB 40

Redmon, Anne .... **CLC 22**
See Nightingale, Anne Redmon
See DLBY 86

Reed, Eliot
See Ambler, Eric

Reed, Ishmael 1938- .. **CLC 2, 3, 5, 6, 13, 32, 60; BLC 3; DAM MULT**
See BW 2, 3; CA 21-24R; CANR 25, 48, 74; DA3; DLB 2, 5, 33, 169; DLBD 8; MTCW 1, 2

Reed, John (Silas) 1887-1920 .... **TCLC 9**
See CA 106

Reed, Lou .... **CLC 21**
See Firbank, Louis

Reeve, Clara 1729-1807 .... **NCLC 19**
See DLB 39

Reich, Wilhelm 1897-1957 .... **TCLC 57**

Reid, Christopher (John) 1949- .... **CLC 33**
See CA 140; DLB 40

Reid, Desmond
See Moorcock, Michael (John)

Reid Banks, Lynne 1929-
See Banks, Lynne Reid
See CA 1-4R; CANR 6, 22, 38; CLR 24; JRDA; MAICYA; SATA 22, 75, 111

Reilly, William K.
See Creasey, John

Reiner, Max
See Caldwell, (Janet Miriam) Taylor (Holland)

Reis, Ricardo
See Pessoa, Fernando (Antonio Nogueira)

Remarque, Erich Maria
1898-1970 ... **CLC 21; DA; DAB; DAC; DAM MST, NOV**
See AAYA 27; CA 77-80; 29-32R; DA3; DLB 56; MTCW 1, 2

Remington, Frederic 1861-1909 ...... **TCLC 89**
See CA 108; 169; DLB 12, 186, 188; SATA 41

Remizov, A.
See Remizov, Aleksei (Mikhailovich)

Remizov, A. M.
See Remizov, Aleksei (Mikhailovich)

Remizov, Aleksei (Mikhailovich)
1877-1957 .... **TCLC 27**
See CA 125; 133

Renan, Joseph Ernest 1823-1892 .. **NCLC 26**

Renard, Jules 1864-1910 .... **TCLC 17**
See CA 117

Renault, Mary .... **CLC 3, 11, 17**
See Challans, Mary
See DLBY 83; MTCW 2

Rendell, Ruth (Barbara) 1930- . **CLC 28, 48; DAM POP**
See Vine, Barbara
See CA 109; CANR 32, 52, 74; DLB 87; INT CANR-32; MTCW 1, 2

Renoir, Jean 1894-1979 .... **CLC 20**
See CA 129; 85-88

Resnais, Alain 1922- .... **CLC 16**

Reverdy, Pierre 1889-1960 .... **CLC 53**
See CA 97-100; 89-92

Rexroth, Kenneth 1905-1982 .... **CLC 1, 2, 6, 11, 22, 49, 112; DAM POET; PC 20**
See CA 5-8R; 107; CANR 14, 34, 63; CDALB 1941-1968; DLB 16, 48, 165, 212; DLBY 82; INT CANR-14; MTCW 1, 2

Reyes, Alfonso 1889-1959 ... **TCLC 33; HLCS 2**
See CA 131; HW 1

Reyes y Basoalto, Ricardo Eliecer Neftali
See Neruda, Pablo

Reymont, Wladyslaw (Stanislaw)
1868(?)-1925 .... **TCLC 5**
See CA 104

Reynolds, Jonathan 1942- .... **CLC 6, 38**
See CA 65-68; CANR 28

Reynolds, Joshua 1723-1792 .... **LC 15**
See DLB 104

Reynolds, Michael Shane 1937- .... **CLC 44**
See CA 65-68; CANR 9

Reznikoff, Charles 1894-1976 .... **CLC 9**
See CA 33-36; 61-64; CAP 2; DLB 28, 45

Rezzori (d'Arezzo), Gregorvon
1914-1998 .... **CLC 25**
See CA 122; 136; 167

Rhine, Richard
See Silverstein, Alvin

Rhodes, Eugene Manlove
1869-1934 .... **TCLC 53**

Rhodius, Apollonius c. 3rd
cent.B.C.- .... **CMLC 28**
See DLB 176

R'hoone
See Balzac, Honore de

Rhys, Jean 1890(?)-1979 ...... **CLC 2, 4, 6, 14, 19, 51, 124; DAM NOV; SSC 21**
See CA 25-28R; 85-88; CANR 35, 62; CD-BLB 1945-1960; DA3; DLB 36, 117, 162; MTCW 1, 2

Ribeiro, Darcy 1922-1997 .... **CLC 34**
See CA 33-36R; 156

Ribeiro, Joao Ubaldo (Osorio Pimentel)
1941- .... **CLC 10, 67**
See CA 81-84

Ribman, Ronald (Burt) 1932- .... **CLC 7**
See CA 21-24R; CANR 46, 80

Ricci, Nino 1959- .... **CLC 70**
See CA 137

Rice, Anne 1941- .... **CLC 41; DAM POP**
See AAYA 9; BEST 89:2; CA 65-68; CANR 12, 36, 53, 74; DA3; MTCW 2

Rice, Elmer (Leopold) 1892-1967 ...... **CLC 7, 49; DAM DRAM**
See CA 21-22; 25-28R; CAP 2; DLB 4, 7; MTCW 1, 2

Rice, Tim(othy Miles Bindon)
1944- .... **CLC 21**
See CA 103; CANR 46

Rich, Adrienne (Cecile) 1929- ... **CLC 3, 6, 7, 11, 18, 36, 73, 76, 125; DAM POET; PC 5**
See CA 9-12R; CANR 20, 53, 74; CDALBS; DA3; DLB 5, 67; MTCW 1, 2

Rich, Barbara
See Graves, Robert (von Ranke)

Rich, Robert
See Trumbo, Dalton

Richard, Keith CLC 17
See Richards, Keith

Richards, David Adams 1950- .... **CLC 59; DAC**
See CA 93-96; CANR 60; DLB 53

Richards, I(vor) A(rmstrong) 1893-1979 .... **CLC 14, 24**
See CA 41-44R; 89-92; CANR 34, 74; DLB 27; MTCW 2

Richards, Keith 1943-
See Richard, Keith
See CA 107; CANR 77

Richardson, Anne
See Roiphe, Anne (Richardson)

Richardson, Dorothy Miller 1873-1957 .... **TCLC 3**
See CA 104; DLB 36

Richardson, Ethel Florence (Lindesay) 1870-1946
See Richardson, Henry Handel
See CA 105

Richardson, Henry Handel TCLC 4
See Richardson, Ethel Florence (Lindesay)
See DLB 197

Richardson, John 1796-1852 .... **NCLC 55; DAC**
See DLB 99

Richardson, Samuel 1689-1761 ...... **LC 1, 44; DA; DAB; DAC; DAM MST, NOV; WLC**
See CDBLB 1660-1789; DLB 39

Richler, Mordecai 1931- ...... **CLC 3, 5, 9, 13, 18, 46, 70; DAC; DAM MST, NOV**
See AITN 1; CA 65-68; CANR 31, 62; CLR 17; DLB 53; MAICYA; MTCW 1, 2; SATA 44, 98; SATA-Brief 27

Richter, Conrad (Michael) 1890-1968 .... **CLC 30**
See AAYA 21; CA 5-8R; 25-28R; CANR 23; DLB 9, 212; MTCW 1, 2; SATA 3

Ricostranza, Tom
See Ellis, Trey

Riddell, Charlotte 1832-1906 .... **TCLC 40**
See CA 165; DLB 156

Ridgway, Keith 1965- .... **CLC 119**
See CA 172

Riding, Laura CLC 3, 7
See Jackson, Laura (Riding)

Riefenstahl, Berta Helene Amalia 1902-
See Riefenstahl, Leni
See CA 108

Riefenstahl, Leni CLC 16
See Riefenstahl, Berta Helene Amalia

Riffe, Ernest
See Bergman, (Ernst) Ingmar

Riggs, (Rolla) Lynn 1899-1954 ..... **TCLC 56; DAM MULT**
See CA 144; DLB 175; NNAL

Riis, Jacob A(ugust) 1849-1914 ..... **TCLC 80**
See CA 113; 168; DLB 23

Riley, James Whitcomb 1849-1916 .... **TCLC 51; DAM POET**
See CA 118; 137; MAICYA; SATA 17

Riley, Tex
See Creasey, John

Rilke, Rainer Maria 1875-1926 .. **TCLC 1, 6, 19; DAM POET; PC 2**
See CA 104; 132; CANR 62; DA3; DLB 81; MTCW 1, 2

Rimbaud, (Jean Nicolas) Arthur 1854-1891 .... **NCLC 4, 35; DA; DAB; DAC; DAM MST, POET; PC 3; WLC**
See DA3

Rinehart, Mary Roberts 1876-1958 .... **TCLC 52**
See CA 108; 166

Ringmaster, The
See Mencken, H(enry) L(ouis)

Ringwood, Gwen(dolyn Margaret) Pharis 1910-1984 .... **CLC 48**
See CA 148; 112; DLB 88

Rio, Michel 19(?)- .... **CLC 43**

Ritsos, Giannes
See Ritsos, Yannis

Ritsos, Yannis 1909-1990 .... **CLC 6, 13, 31**
See CA 77-80; 133; CANR 39, 61; MTCW 1

Ritter, Erika 1948(?)- .... **CLC 52**

Rivera, Jose Eustasio 1889-1928 ... **TCLC 35**
See CA 162; HW 1, 2

Rivera, Tomas 1935-1984
See CA 49-52; CANR 32; DLB 82; HLCS 2; HW 1

Rivers, Conrad Kent 1933-1968 .... **CLC 1**
See BW 1; CA 85-88; DLB 41

Rivers, Elfrida
See Bradley, Marion Zimmer

Riverside, John
See Heinlein, Robert A(nson)

Rizal, Jose 1861-1896 .... **NCLC 27**

Roa Bastos, Augusto (Antonio) 1917- .... **CLC 45; DAM MULT; HLC 2**
See CA 131; DLB 113; HW 1

Robbe-Grillet, Alain 1922- .... **CLC 1, 2, 4, 6, 8, 10, 14, 43**
See CA 9-12R; CANR 33, 65; DLB 83; MTCW 1, 2

Robbins, Harold 1916-1997 ..... **CLC 5; DAM NOV**
See CA 73-76; 162; CANR 26, 54; DA3; MTCW 1, 2

Robbins, Thomas Eugene 1936-
See Robbins, Tom
See CA 81-84; CANR 29, 59; DAM NOV, POP; DA3; MTCW 1, 2

Robbins, Tom CLC 9, 32, 64
See Robbins, Thomas Eugene
See AAYA 32; BEST 90:3; DLBY 80; MTCW 2

Robbins, Trina 1938- .... **CLC 21**
See CA 128

Roberts, Charles G(eorge) D(ouglas) 1860-1943 .... **TCLC 8**
See CA 105; CLR 33; DLB 92; SATA 88; SATA-Brief 29

Roberts, Elizabeth Madox 1886-1941 .... **TCLC 68**
See CA 111; 166; DLB 9, 54, 102; SATA 33; SATA-Brief 27

Roberts, Kate 1891-1985 .... **CLC 15**
See CA 107; 116

Roberts, Keith (John Kingston) 1935- .... **CLC 14**
See CA 25-28R; CANR 46

Roberts, Kenneth (Lewis) 1885-1957 .... **TCLC 23**
See CA 109; DLB 9

Roberts, Michele (B.) 1949- .... **CLC 48**
See CA 115; CANR 58

Robertson, Ellis
See Ellison, Harlan (Jay); Silverberg, Robert

Robertson, Thomas William 1829-1871 .... **NCLC 35; DAM DRAM**

Robeson, Kenneth
See Dent, Lester

Robinson, Edwin Arlington 1869-1935 ... **TCLC 5; DA; DAC; DAM MST, POET; PC 1**
See CA 104; 133; CDALB 1865-1917; DLB 54; MTCW 1, 2

Robinson, Henry Crabb 1775-1867 .... **NCLC 15**
See DLB 107

Robinson, Jill 1936- .... **CLC 10**
See CA 102; INT 102

Robinson, Kim Stanley 1952- .... **CLC 34**
See AAYA 26; CA 126; SATA 109

Robinson, Lloyd
See Silverberg, Robert

Robinson, Marilynne 1944- .... **CLC 25**
See CA 116; CANR 80; DLB 206

Robinson, Smokey CLC 21
See Robinson, William, Jr.

Robinson, William, Jr. 1940-
See Robinson, Smokey
See CA 116

Robison, Mary 1949- .... **CLC 42, 98**
See CA 113; 116; DLB 130; INT 116

Rod, Edouard 1857-1910 .... **TCLC 52**

Roddenberry, Eugene Wesley 1921-1991
See Roddenberry, Gene
See CA 110; 135; CANR 37; SATA 45; SATA-Obit 69

Roddenberry, Gene CLC 17
See Roddenberry, Eugene Wesley
See AAYA 5; SATA-Obit 69

Rodgers, Mary 1931- .... **CLC 12**
See CA 49-52; CANR 8, 55; CLR 20; INT CANR-8; JRDA; MAICYA; SATA 8

Rodgers, W(illiam) R(obert) 1909-1969 .... **CLC 7**
See CA 85-88; DLB 20

Rodman, Eric
See Silverberg, Robert

Rodman, Howard 1920(?)-1985 .... **CLC 65**
See CA 118

Rodman, Maia
See Wojciechowska, Maia (Teresa)

Rodo, Jose Enrique 1872(?)-1917
See CA 178; HLCS 2; HW 2

Rodriguez, Claudio 1934- .... **CLC 10**
See DLB 134

Rodriguez, Richard 1944-
See CA 110; CANR 66; DAM MULT; DLB 82; HLC 2; HW 1, 2

Roelvaag, O(le) E(dvart) 1876-1931 .... **TCLC 17**
See CA 117; 171; DLB 9

Roethke, Theodore (Huebner) 1908-1963 .... **CLC 1, 3, 8, 11, 19, 46, 101; DAM POET; PC 15**
See CA 81-84; CABS 2; CDALB 1941-1968; DA3; DLB 5, 206; MTCW 1, 2

Rogers, Samuel 1763-1855 .... **NCLC 69**
See DLB 93

Rogers, Thomas Hunton 1927- .... **CLC 57**
See CA 89-92; INT 89-92

Rogers, Will(iam Penn Adair) 1879-1935 ... **TCLC 8, 71; DAM MULT**
See CA 105; 144; DA3; DLB 11; MTCW 2; NNAL

Rogin, Gilbert 1929- .... **CLC 18**
See CA 65-68; CANR 15

Rohan, Koda TCLC 22
See Koda Shigeyuki

Rohlfs, Anna Katharine Green
See Green, Anna Katharine

Rohmer, Eric CLC 16
See Scherer, Jean-Marie Maurice

Rohmer, Sax TCLC 28
See Ward, Arthur Henry Sarsfield
See DLB 70

Roiphe, Anne (Richardson) 1935- .. **CLC 3, 9**
   See CA 89-92; CANR 45, 73; DLBY 80;
      INT 89-92
Rojas, Fernando de 1465-1541 .... **LC 23;**
      HLCS 1
Rojas, Gonzalo 1917-
   See HLCS 2; HW 2
Rojas, Gonzalo 1917-
   See CA 178; HLCS 2
Rolfe, Frederick (William Serafino Austin
      Lewis Mary) 1860-1913 .... **TCLC 12**
   See CA 107; DLB 34, 156
Rolland, Romain 1866-1944 .... **TCLC 23**
   See CA 118; DLB 65
Rolle, Richard c. 1300-c.1349 .... **CMLC 21**
   See DLB 146
Rolvaag, O(le) E(dvart)
   See Roelvaag, O(le) E(dvart)
Romain Arnaud, Saint
   See Aragon, Louis
Romains, Jules 1885-1972 .... **CLC 7**
   See CA 85-88; CANR 34; DLB 65; MTCW
      1
Romero, Jose Ruben 1890-1952 .... **TCLC 14**
   See CA 114; 131; HW 1
Ronsard, Pierre de 1524-1585 ..... **LC 54; PC**
      11
Rooke, Leon 1934- ... **CLC 25, 34;DAM POP**
   See CA 25-28R; CANR 23, 53
Roosevelt, Franklin Delano
      1882-1945 .... **TCLC 93**
   See CA 116; 173
Roosevelt, Theodore 1858-1919 ..... **TCLC 69**
   See CA 115; 170; DLB 47, 186
Roper, William 1498-1578 .... **LC 10**
Roquelaure, A. N.
   See Rice, Anne
Rosa, Joao Guimaraes 1908-1967 ... **CLC 23;**
      HLCS 1
   See CA 89-92; DLB 113
Rose, Wendy 1948- .. **CLC 85; DAM MULT;**
      PC 13
   See CA 53-56; CANR 5, 51; DLB 175;
      NNAL; SATA 12
Rosen, R. D.
   See Rosen, Richard (Dean)
Rosen, Richard (Dean) 1949- .... **CLC 39**
   See CA 77-80; CANR 62; INT CANR-30
Rosenberg, Isaac 1890-1918 .... **TCLC 12**
   See CA 107; DLB 20
Rosenblatt, Joe CLC 15
   See Rosenblatt, Joseph
Rosenblatt, Joseph 1933-
   See Rosenblatt, Joe
   See CA 89-92; INT 89-92
Rosenfeld, Samuel
   See Tzara, Tristan
Rosenstock, Sami
   See Tzara, Tristan
Rosenstock, Samuel
   See Tzara, Tristan
Rosenthal, M(acha) L(ouis)
      1917-1996 .... **CLC 28**
   See CA 1-4R; 152; CAAS 6; CANR 4, 51;
      DLB 5; SATA 59
Ross, Barnaby
   See Dannay, Frederic
Ross, Bernard L.
   See Follett, Ken(neth Martin)
Ross, J. H.
   See Lawrence, T(homas) E(dward)
Ross, John Hume
   See Lawrence, T(homas) E(dward)
Ross, Martin
   See Martin, Violet Florence
   See DLB 135

Ross, (James) Sinclair 1908-1996 ... **CLC 13;**
      DAC; DAM MST; SSC 24
   See CA 73-76; CANR 81; DLB 88
Rossetti, Christina (Georgina)
      1830-1894 . **NCLC 2, 50, 66; DA; DAB;**
      DAC; DAM MST, POET; PC 7; WLC
   See DA3; DLB 35, 163; MAICYA; SATA
      20
Rossetti, Dante Gabriel 1828-1882 . **NCLC 4,**
      77; DA; DAB; DAC; DAM MST,
      POET; WLC
   See CDBLB 1832-1890; DLB 35
Rossner, Judith (Perelman) 1935- . **CLC 6, 9,**
      29
   See AITN 2; BEST 90:3; CA 17-20R;
      CANR 18, 51, 73; DLB 6; INT CANR-
      18; MTCW 1, 2
Rostand, Edmond (Eugene Alexis)
      1868-1918 .... **TCLC 6, 37; DA; DAB;**
      DAC; DAM DRAM, MST; DC 10
   See CA 104; 126; DA3; DLB 192; MTCW
      1
Roth, Henry 1906-1995 ..... **CLC 2, 6, 11, 104**
   See CA 11-12; 149; CANR 38, 63; CAP 1;
      DA3; DLB 28; MTCW 1, 2
Roth, Philip (Milton) 1933- ... **CLC 1, 2, 3, 4,**
      6, 9, 15, 22, 31, 47, 66, 86, 119; DA;
      DAB; DAC; DAM MST, NOV, POP;
      SSC 26; WLC
   See BEST 90:3; CA 1-4R; CANR 1, 22, 36,
      55; CDALB 1968-1988; DA3; DLB 2, 28,
      173; DLBY 82; MTCW 1, 2
Rothenberg, Jerome 1931- .... **CLC 6, 57**
   See CA 45-48; CANR 1; DLB 5, 193
Roumain, Jacques (Jean Baptiste)
      1907-1944 ...... **TCLC 19; BLC 3; DAM**
      MULT
   See BW 1; CA 117; 125
Rourke, Constance (Mayfield)
      1885-1941 .... **TCLC 12**
   See CA 107; YABC 1
Rousseau, Jean-Baptiste 1671-1741 ...... **LC 9**
Rousseau, Jean-Jacques 1712-1778 .... **LC 14,**
      36; DA; DAB; DAC; DAM MST; WLC
   See DA3
Roussel, Raymond 1877-1933 .... **TCLC 20**
   See CA 117
Rovit, Earl (Herbert) 1927- .... **CLC 7**
   See CA 5-8R; CANR 12
Rowe, Elizabeth Singer 1674-1737 ..... **LC 44**
   See DLB 39, 95
Rowe, Nicholas 1674-1718 .... **LC 8**
   See DLB 84
Rowley, Ames Dorrance
   See Lovecraft, H(oward) P(hillips)
Rowson, Susanna Haswell
      1762(?)-1824 .... **NCLC 5, 69**
   See DLB 37, 200
Roy, Arundhati 1960(?)- .... **CLC 109**
   See CA 163; DLBY 97
Roy, Gabrielle 1909-1983 .... **CLC 10, 14;**
      DAB; DAC; DAM MST
   See CA 53-56; 110; CANR 5, 61; DLB 68;
      MTCW 1; SATA 104
Royko, Mike 1932-1997 .... **CLC 109**
   See CA 89-92; 157; CANR 26
Rozewicz, Tadeusz 1921- .... **CLC 9, 23;DAM**
      POET
   See CA 108; CANR 36, 66; DA3; MTCW
      1, 2
Ruark, Gibbons 1941- .... **CLC 3**
   See CA 33-36R; CAAS 23; CANR 14, 31,
      57; DLB 120
Rubens, Bernice (Ruth) 1923- .... **CLC 19, 31**
   See CA 25-28R; CANR 33, 65; DLB 14,
      207; MTCW 1
Rubin, Harold
   See Robbins, Harold

Rudkin, (James) David 1936- .... **CLC 14**
   See CA 89-92; DLB 13
Rudnik, Raphael 1933- .... **CLC 7**
   See CA 29-32R
Ruffian, M.
   See Hasek, Jaroslav (Matej Frantisek)
Ruiz, Jose Martinez CLC 11
   See Martinez Ruiz, Jose
Rukeyser, Muriel 1913-1980 . **CLC 6, 10, 15,**
      27; DAM POET; PC 12
   See CA 5-8R; 93-96; CANR 26, 60; DA3;
      DLB 48; MTCW 1, 2; SATA-Obit 22
Rule, Jane (Vance) 1931- .... **CLC 27**
   See CA 25-28R; CAAS 18; CANR 12; DLB
      60
Rulfo, Juan 1918-1986 ...... **CLC 8, 80; DAM**
      MULT; HLC 2; SSC 25
   See CA 85-88; 118; CANR 26; DLB 113;
      HW 1, 2; MTCW 1, 2
Rumi, Jalal al-Din 1297-1373 .... **CMLC 20**
Runeberg, Johan 1804-1877 .... **NCLC 41**
Runyon, (Alfred) Damon
      1884(?)-1946 .... **TCLC 10**
   See CA 107; 165; DLB 11, 86, 171; MTCW
      2
Rush, Norman 1933- .... **CLC 44**
   See CA 121; 126; INT 126
Rushdie, (Ahmed) Salman 1947- .... **CLC 23,**
      31, 55, 100; DAB; DAC; DAM MST,
      NOV, POP; WLCS
   See BEST 89:3; CA 108; 111; CANR 33,
      56; DA3; DLB 194; INT 111; MTCW 1,
      2
Rushforth, Peter (Scott) 1945- .... **CLC 19**
   See CA 101
Ruskin, John 1819-1900 .... **TCLC 63**
   See CA 114; 129; CDBLB 1832-1890; DLB
      55, 163, 190; SATA 24
Russ, Joanna 1937- .... **CLC 15**
   See CANR 11, 31, 65; DLB 8; MTCW 1
Russell, George William 1867-1935
   See Baker, Jean H.
   See CA 104; 153; CDBLB 1890-1914;
      DAM POET
Russell, (Henry) Ken(neth Alfred)
      1927- .... **CLC 16**
   See CA 105
Russell, William Martin 1947- .... **CLC 60**
   See CA 164
Rutherford, Mark TCLC 25
   See White, William Hale
   See DLB 18
Ruyslinck, Ward 1929- .... **CLC 14**
   See Belser, Reimond Karel Maria de
Ryan, Cornelius(John) 1920-1974 ...... **CLC 7**
   See CA 69-72; 53-56; CANR 38
Ryan, Michael 1946- .... **CLC 65**
   See CA 49-52; DLBY 82
Ryan, Tim
   See Dent, Lester
Rybakov, Anatoli (Naumovich)
      1911-1998 .... **CLC 23, 53**
   See CA 126; 135; 172; SATA 79; SATA-
      Obit 108
Ryder, Jonathan
   See Ludlum, Robert
Ryga, George 1932-1987 .... **CLC 14; DAC;**
      DAM MST
   See CA 101; 124; CANR 43; DLB 60
S. H.
   See Hartmann, Sadakichi
S. S.
   See Sassoon, Siegfried (Lorraine)
Saba, Umberto 1883-1957 .... **TCLC 33**
   See CA 144; CANR 79; DLB 114
Sabatini, Rafael 1875-1950 .... **TCLC 47**
   See CA 162

Sabato, Ernesto (R.) 1911- .... CLC 10, 23;
DAM MULT; HLC 2
See CA 97-100; CANR 32, 65; DLB 145;
HW 1, 2; MTCW 1, 2

Sa-Carniero, Mario de 1890-1916 . TCLC 83

Sacastru, Martin
See Bioy Casares, Adolfo

Sacastru, Martin
See Bioy Casares, Adolfo

Sacher-Masoch, Leopold von
1836(?)-1895 .... NCLC 31

Sachs, Marilyn (Stickle) 1927- .... CLC 35
See AAYA 2; CA 17-20R; CANR 13, 47;
CLR 2; JRDA; MAICYA; SAAS 2; SATA
3, 68; SATA-Essay 110

Sachs, Nelly 1891-1970 .... CLC 14, 98
See CA 17-18; 25-28R; CAP 2; MTCW 2

Sackler, Howard (Oliver)
1929-1982 .... CLC 14
See CA 61-64; 108; CANR 30; DLB 7

Sacks, Oliver (Wolf) 1933- .... CLC 67
See CA 53-56; CANR 28, 50, 76; DA3; INT
CANR-28; MTCW 1, 2

Sadakichi
See Hartmann, Sadakichi

Sade, Donatien Alphonse Francois, Comtede
1740-1814 .... NCLC 47

Sadoff, Ira 1945- .... CLC 9
See CA 53-56; CANR 5, 21; DLB 120

Saetone
See Camus, Albert

Safire, William 1929- .... CLC 10
See CA 17-20R; CANR 31, 54

Sagan, Carl (Edward) 1934-1996 .... CLC 30,
112
See AAYA 2; CA 25-28R; 155; CANR 11,
36, 74; DA3; MTCW 1, 2; SATA 58;
SATA-Obit 94

Sagan, Francoise CLC 3, 6, 9, 17, 36
See Quoirez, Francoise
See DLB 83; MTCW 2

Sahgal, Nayantara (Pandit) 1927- .... CLC 41
See CA 9-12R; CANR 11

Saint, H(arry) F. 1941- .... CLC 50
See CA 127

St. Aubin de Teran, Lisa 1953-
See Teran, Lisa St. Aubin de
See CA 118; 126; INT 126

Saint Birgitta of Sweden c.
1303-1373 .... CMLC 24

Sainte-Beuve, Charles Augustin
1804-1869 .... NCLC 5

Saint-Exupery, Antoine (Jean Baptiste
Marie Roger) de 1900-1944 .... TCLC 2,
56; DAM NOV;WLC
See CA 108; 132; CLR 10; DA3; DLB 72;
MAICYA; MTCW 1, 2; SATA 20

St. John, David
See Hunt, E(verette) Howard, (Jr.)

Saint-John Perse
See Leger, (Marie-Rene Auguste) Alexis
Saint-Leger

Saintsbury, George (Edward Bateman)
1845-1933 .... TCLC 31
See CA 160; DLB 57, 149

Sait Faik TCLC 23
See Abasiyanik, Sait Faik

Saki TCLC 3; SSC 12
See Munro, H(ector) H(ugh)
See MTCW 2

Sala, George Augustus NCLC 46

Salama, Hannu 1936- .... CLC 18

Salamanca, J(ack) R(ichard) 1922- .. CLC 4,
15
See CA 25-28R

Salas, Floyd Francis 1931-
See CA 119; CAAS 27; CANR 44, 75;
DAM MULT; DLB 82; HLC 2; HW 1, 2;
MTCW 2

Sale, J. Kirkpatrick
See Sale, Kirkpatrick

Sale, Kirkpatrick 1937- .... CLC 68
See CA 13-16R; CANR 10

Salinas, Luis Omar 1937- ..... CLC 90; DAM
MULT; HLC 2
See CA 131; CANR 81; DLB 82; HW 1, 2

Salinas (y Serrano), Pedro
1891(?)-1951 .... TCLC 17
See CA 117; DLB 134

Salinger, J(erome) D(avid) 1919- .. CLC 1, 3,
8, 12, 55, 56; DA; DAB; DAC; DAM
MST, NOV, POP; SSC 2, 28; WLC
See AAYA 2; CA 5-8R; CANR 39; CDALB
1941-1968; CLR 18; DA3; DLB 2, 102,
173; MAICYA; MTCW 1, 2; SATA 67

Salisbury, John
See Caute, (John) David

Salter, James 1925- .... CLC 7, 52, 59
See CA 73-76; DLB 130

Saltus, Edgar (Everton) 1855-1921 . TCLC 8
See CA 105; DLB 202

Saltykov, Mikhail Evgrafovich
1826-1889 .... NCLC 16

Samarakis, Antonis 1919- .... CLC 5
See CA 25-28R; CAAS 16; CANR 36

Sanchez, Florencio 1875-1910 .... TCLC 37
See CA 153; HW 1

Sanchez, Luis Rafael 1936- .... CLC 23
See CA 128; DLB 145; HW 1

Sanchez, Sonia 1934- .... CLC 5, 116; BLC 3;
DAM MULT; PC 9
See BW 2, 3; CA 33-36R; CANR 24, 49,
74; CLR 18; DA3; DLB 41; DLBD 8;
MAICYA; MTCW 1, 2; SATA 22

Sand, George 1804-1876 ..... NCLC 2, 42, 57;
DA; DAB; DAC; DAM MST, NOV;
WLC
See DA3; DLB 119, 192

Sandburg, Carl (August) 1878-1967 . CLC 1,
4, 10, 15, 35; DA; DAB; DAC; DAM
MST, POET; PC 2; WLC
See AAYA 24; CA 5-8R; 25-28R; CANR
35; CDALB 1865-1917; DA3; DLB 17,
54; MAICYA; MTCW 1, 2; SATA 8

Sandburg, Charles
See Sandburg, Carl (August)

Sandburg, Charles A.
See Sandburg, Carl (August)

Sanders, (James) Ed(ward) 1939- ... CLC 53;
DAM POET
See CA 13-16R; CAAS 21; CANR 13, 44,
78; DLB 16

Sanders, Lawrence 1920-1998 .... CLC 41;
DAM POP
See BEST 89:4; CA 81-84; 165; CANR 33,
62; DA3; MTCW 1

Sanders, Noah
See Blount, Roy (Alton), Jr.

Sanders, Winston P.
See Anderson, Poul (William)

Sandoz, Mari(e Susette) 1896-1966 .. CLC 28
See CA 1-4R; 25-28R; CANR 17, 64; DLB
9, 212; MTCW 1, 2; SATA 5

Saner, Reg(inald Anthony) 1931- .... CLC 9
See CA 65-68

Sankara 788-820 .... CMLC 32

Sannazaro, Jacopo 1456(?)-1530 .... LC 8

Sansom, William 1912-1976 .... CLC 2, 6;
DAM NOV; SSC 21
See CA 5-8R; 65-68; CANR 42; DLB 139;
MTCW 1

Santayana, George 1863-1952 .... TCLC 40
See CA 115; DLB 54, 71; DLBD 13

Santiago, Danny CLC 33

See James, Daniel (Lewis)
See DLB 122

Santmyer, Helen Hoover 1895-1986 . CLC 33
See CA 1-4R; 118; CANR 15, 33; DLBY
84; MTCW 1

Santoka, Taneda 1882-1940 .... TCLC 72

Santos, Bienvenido N(uqui)
1911-1996 .... CLC 22; DAM MULT
See CA 101; 151; CANR 19, 46

Sapper TCLC 44
See McNeile, Herman Cyril

Sapphire
See Sapphire, Brenda

Sapphire, Brenda 1950- .... CLC 99

Sappho fl. 6th cent. B.C.- ..... CMLC 3; DAM
POET; PC 5
See DA3; DLB 176

Saramago, Jose 1922- .... CLC 119;HLCS 1
See CA 153

Sarduy, Severo 1937-1993 .... CLC 6, 97;
HLCS 1
See CA 89-92; 142; CANR 58, 81; DLB
113; HW 1, 2

Sargeson, Frank 1903-1982 .... CLC 31
See CA 25-28R; 106; CANR 38, 79

Sarmiento, Domingo Faustino 1811-1888
See HLCS 2

Sarmiento, Felix Ruben Garcia
See Dario, Ruben

Saro-Wiwa, Ken(ule Beeson)
1941-1995 .... CLC 114
See BW 2; CA 142; 150; CANR 60; DLB
157

Saroyan, William 1908-1981 ... CLC 1, 8, 10,
29, 34, 56; DA; DAB; DAC; DAM
DRAM, MST, NOV; SSC 21; WLC
See CA 5-8R; 103; CANR 30; CDALBS;
DA3; DLB 7, 9, 86; DLBY 81; MTCW 1,
2; SATA 23; SATA-Obit 24

Sarraute, Nathalie 1900- . CLC 1, 2, 4, 8, 10,
31, 80
See CA 9-12R; CANR 23, 66; DLB 83;
MTCW 1, 2

Sarton, (Eleanor) May 1912-1995 ..... CLC 4,
14, 49, 91; DAM POET
See CA 1-4R; 149; CANR 1, 34, 55; DLB
48; DLBY 81; INT CANR-34; MTCW 1,
2; SATA 36; SATA-Obit 86

Sartre, Jean-Paul 1905-1980 . CLC 1, 4, 7, 9,
13, 18, 24, 44, 50, 52; DA; DAB; DAC;
DAM DRAM, MST, NOV; DC 3; SSC
32; WLC
See CA 9-12R; 97-100; CANR 21; DA3;
DLB 72; MTCW 1, 2

Sassoon, Siegfried (Lorraine)
1886-1967 . CLC 36; DAB; DAM MST,
NOV, POET; PC 12
See CA 104; 25-28R; CANR 36; DLB 20,
191; DLBD 18; MTCW 1, 2

Satterfield, Charles
See Pohl, Frederik

Saul, John (W. III) 1942- ...... CLC 46; DAM
NOV, POP
See AAYA 10; BEST 90:4; CA 81-84;
CANR 16, 40, 81; SATA 98

Saunders, Caleb
See Heinlein, Robert A(nson)

Saura (Atares), Carlos 1932- .... CLC 20
See CA 114; 131; CANR 79; HW 1

Sauser-Hall, Frederic 1887-1961 ...... CLC 18
See Cendrars, Blaise
See CA 102; 93-96; CANR 36, 62; MTCW
1

Saussure, Ferdinand de
1857-1913 .... TCLC 49

Savage, Catharine
See Brosman, Catharine Savage

Savage, Thomas 1915- .... CLC 40
See CA 126; 132; CAAS 15; INT 132

Savan, Glenn 19(?)- .... **CLC 50**
Sayers, Dorothy L(eigh)
1893-1957 .... **TCLC 2, 15; DAM POP**
See CA 104; 119; CANR 60; CDBLB 1914-
1945; DLB 10, 36, 77, 100; MTCW 1, 2
Sayers, Valerie 1952- .... **CLC 50, 122**
See CA 134; CANR 61
Sayles, John (Thomas) 1950- . **CLC 7, 10, 14**
See CA 57-60; CANR 41, 84; DLB 44
Scammell, Michael 1935- .... **CLC 34**
See CA 156
Scannell, Vernon 1922- .... **CLC 49**
See CA 5-8R; CANR 8, 24, 57; DLB 27;
SATA 59
Scarlett, Susan
See Streatfeild, (Mary) Noel
Scarron
See Mikszath, Kalman
Schaeffer, Susan Fromberg 1941- ..... **CLC 6,
11, 22**
See CA 49-52; CANR 18, 65; DLB 28;
MTCW 1, 2; SATA 22
Schary, Jill
See Robinson, Jill
Schell, Jonathan 1943- .... **CLC 35**
See CA 73-76; CANR 12
Schelling, Friedrich Wilhelm Josephvon
1775-1854 .... **NCLC 30**
See DLB 90
Schendel, Arthur van 1874-1946 ... **TCLC 56**
Scherer, Jean-Marie Maurice 1920-
See Rohmer, Eric
See CA 110
Schevill, James (Erwin) 1920- .... **CLC 7**
See CA 5-8R; CAAS 12
Schiller, Friedrich 1759-1805 . **NCLC 39, 69;
DAM DRAM**
See DLB 94
Schisgal, Murray (Joseph) 1926- .... **CLC 6**
See CA 21-24R; CANR 48
Schlee, Ann 1934- .... **CLC 35**
See CA 101; CANR 29; SATA 44; SATA-
Brief 36
Schlegel, August Wilhelmvon
1767-1845 .... **NCLC 15**
See DLB 94
Schlegel, Friedrich 1772-1829 .... **NCLC 45**
See DLB 90
Schlegel, Johann Elias (von)
1719(?)-1749 .... **LC 5**
Schlesinger, Arthur M(eier),Jr.
1917- .... **CLC 84**
See AITN 1; CA 1-4R; CANR 1, 28, 58;
DLB 17; INT CANR-28; MTCW 1, 2;
SATA 61
Schmidt, Arno (Otto) 1914-1979 ...... **CLC 56**
See CA 128; 109; DLB 69
Schmitz, Aron Hector 1861-1928
See Svevo, Italo
See CA 104; 122; MTCW 1
Schnackenberg, Gjertrud 1953- .... **CLC 40**
See CA 116; DLB 120
Schneider, Leonard Alfred 1925-1966
See Bruce, Lenny
See CA 89-92
Schnitzler, Arthur 1862-1931 . **TCLC 4; SSC
15**
See CA 104; DLB 81, 118
Schoenberg, Arnold 1874-1951 ...... **TCLC 75**
See CA 109
Schonberg, Arnold
See Schoenberg, Arnold
Schopenhauer, Arthur 1788-1860 .. **NCLC 51**
See DLB 90
Schor, Sandra (M.) 1932(?)-1990 ..... **CLC 65**
See CA 132
Schorer, Mark 1908-1977 .... **CLC 9**
See CA 5-8R; 73-76; CANR 7; DLB 103

Schrader, Paul (Joseph) 1946- .... **CLC 26**
See CA 37-40R; CANR 41; DLB 44
Schreiner, Olive (Emilie Albertina)
1855-1920 .... **TCLC 9**
See CA 105; 154; DLB 18, 156, 190
Schulberg, Budd (Wilson) 1914- .. **CLC 7, 48**
See CA 25-28R; CANR 19; DLB 6, 26, 28;
DLBY 81
Schulz, Bruno 1892-1942 .. **TCLC 5, 51; SSC
13**
See CA 115; 123; MTCW 2
Schulz, Charles M(onroe) 1922- .... **CLC 12**
See CA 9-12R; CANR 6; INT CANR-6;
SATA 10
Schumacher, E(rnst) F(riedrich)
1911-1977 .... **CLC 80**
See CA 81-84; 73-76; CANR 34, 85
Schuyler, James Marcus 1923-1991 .. **CLC 5,
23; DAM POET**
See CA 101; 134; DLB 5, 169; INT 101
Schwartz, Delmore (David)
1913-1966 ... **CLC 2, 4, 10, 45, 87; PC 8**
See CA 17-18; 25-28R; CANR 35; CAP 2;
DLB 28, 48; MTCW 1, 2
Schwartz, Ernst
See Ozu, Yasujiro
Schwartz, John Burnham 1965- .... **CLC 59**
See CA 132
Schwartz, Lynne Sharon 1939- .... **CLC 31**
See CA 103; CANR 44; MTCW 2
Schwartz, Muriel A.
See Eliot, T(homas) S(tearns)
Schwarz-Bart, Andre 1928- .... **CLC 2, 4**
See CA 89-92
Schwarz-Bart, Simone 1938- ... **CLC 7;BLCS**
See BW 2; CA 97-100
**Schwitters, Kurt (Hermann Edward Karl
Julius)** 1887-1948 .... **TCLC 95**
See CA 158
Schwob, Marcel (Mayer Andre)
1867-1905 .... **TCLC 20**
See CA 117; 168; DLB 123
Sciascia, Leonardo 1921-1989 .. **CLC 8, 9, 41**
See CA 85-88; 130; CANR 35; DLB 177;
MTCW 1
Scoppettone, Sandra 1936- .... **CLC 26**
See AAYA 11; CA 5-8R; CANR 41, 73;
SATA 9, 92
Scorsese, Martin 1942- .... **CLC 20, 89**
See CA 110; 114; CANR 46, 85
Scotland, Jay
See Jakes, John (William)
Scott, Duncan Campbell
1862-1947 .... **TCLC 6; DAC**
See CA 104; 153; DLB 92
Scott, Evelyn 1893-1963 .... **CLC 43**
See CA 104; 112; CANR 64; DLB 9, 48
Scott, F(rancis) R(eginald)
1899-1985 .... **CLC 22**
See CA 101; 114; DLB 88; INT 101
Scott, Frank
See Scott, F(rancis) R(eginald)
Scott, Joanna 1960- .... **CLC 50**
See CA 126; CANR 53
Scott, Paul (Mark) 1920-1978 ...... **CLC 9, 60**
See CA 81-84; 77-80; CANR 33; DLB 14,
207; MTCW 1
Scott, Sarah 1723-1795 .... **LC 44**
See DLB 39
Scott, Walter 1771-1832 . **NCLC 15, 69; DA;
DAB; DAC; DAM MST, NOV, POET;
PC 13; SSC 32; WLC**
See AAYA 22; CDBLB 1789-1832; DLB
93, 107, 116, 144, 159; YABC 2
Scribe, (Augustin) Eugene
1791-1861 ..... **NCLC 16; DAM DRAM;
DC 5**
See DLB 192

Scrum, R.
See Crumb, R(obert)
Scudery, Madeleine de 1607-1701 .... **LC 2**
Scum
See Crumb, R(obert)
Scumbag, Little Bobby
See Crumb, R(obert)
Seabrook, John
See Hubbard, L(afayette) Ron(ald)
Sealy, I. Allan 1951- .... **CLC 55**
Search, Alexander
See Pessoa, Fernando (Antonio Nogueira)
Sebastian, Lee
See Silverberg, Robert
Sebastian Owl
See Thompson, Hunter S(tockton)
Sebestyen, Ouida 1924- .... **CLC 30**
See AAYA 8; CA 107; CANR 40; CLR 17;
JRDA; MAICYA; SAAS 10; SATA 39
Secundus, H. Scriblerus
See Fielding, Henry
Sedges, John
See Buck, Pearl S(ydenstricker)
Sedgwick, Catharine Maria
1789-1867 .... **NCLC 19**
See DLB 1, 74
Seelye, John (Douglas) 1931- .... **CLC 7**
See CA 97-100; CANR 70; INT 97-100
Seferiades, Giorgos Stylianou 1900-1971
See Seferis, George
See CA 5-8R; 33-36R; CANR 5, 36; MTCW
1
Seferis, George CLC 5, 11
See Seferiades, Giorgos Stylianou
Segal, Erich (Wolf) 1937- . **CLC 3, 10; DAM
POP**
See BEST 89:1; CA 25-28R; CANR 20, 36,
65; DLBY 86; INT CANR-20; MTCW 1
Seger, Bob 1945- .... **CLC 35**
Seghers, Anna CLC 7
See Radvanyi, Netty
See DLB 69
Seidel, Frederick (Lewis) 1936- .... **CLC 18**
See CA 13-16R; CANR 8; DLBY 84
Seifert, Jaroslav 1901-1986 .. **CLC 34, 44, 93**
See CA 127; MTCW 1, 2
Sei Shonagon c. 966-1017(?) .... **CMLC 6**
Séjour, Victor 1817-1874 .... **DC 10**
See DLB 50
Sejour Marcou et Ferrand, Juan Victor
See Séjour, Victor
Selby, Hubert, Jr. 1928- .... **CLC 1, 2, 4, 8;
SSC 20**
See CA 13-16R; CANR 33, 85; DLB 2
Selzer, Richard 1928- .... **CLC 74**
See CA 65-68; CANR 14
Sembene, Ousmane
See Ousmane, Sembene
Senancour, Etienne Pivert de
1770-1846 .... **NCLC 16**
See DLB 119
Sender, Ramon (Jose) 1902-1982 ...... **CLC 8;
DAM MULT; HLC 2**
See CA 5-8R; 105; CANR 8; HW 1; MTCW
1
Seneca, Lucius Annaeus c. 1-c.
65 .... **CMLC 6; DAM DRAM; DC 5**
See DLB 211
Senghor, Leopold Sedar 1906- .... **CLC 54;
BLC 3; DAM MULT, POET; PC 25**
See BW 2; CA 116; 125; CANR 47, 74;
MTCW 1, 2
Senna, Danzy 1970- .... **CLC 119**
See CA 169
Serling, (Edward) Rod(man)
1924-1975 .... **CLC 30**
See AAYA 14; AITN 1; CA 162; 57-60;
DLB 26

Serna, Ramon Gomez de la
See Gomez de la Serna, Ramon
Serpieres
See Guillevic, (Eugene)
Service, Robert
See Service, Robert W(illiam)
See DAB; DLB 92
Service, Robert W(illiam)
1874(?)-1958 .... TCLC 15; DA; DAC;
DAM MST, POET; WLC
See Service, Robert
See CA 115; 140; CANR 84; SATA 20
Seth, Vikram 1952- .... CLC 43, 90;DAM
MULT
See CA 121; 127; CANR 50, 74; DA3; DLB
120; INT 127; MTCW 2
Seton, CynthiaPropper 1926-1982 ... CLC 27
See CA 5-8R; 108; CANR 7
Seton, Ernest (Evan) Thompson
1860-1946 .... TCLC 31
See CA 109; CLR 59; DLB 92; DLBD 13;
JRDA; SATA 18
Seton-Thompson, Ernest
See Seton, Ernest (Evan) Thompson
Settle, Mary Lee 1918- .... CLC 19, 61
See CA 89-92; CAAS 1; CANR 44; DLB
6; INT 89-92
Seuphor, Michel
See Arp, Jean
Sevigne, Marie (de Rabutin-Chantal)
Marquise de 1626-1696 .... LC 11
Sewall, Samuel 1652-1730 .... LC 38
See DLB 24
Sexton, Anne (Harvey) 1928-1974 ..... CLC 2,
4, 6, 8, 10, 15, 53; DA; DAB; DAC;
DAM MST, POET; PC 2; WLC
See CA 1-4R; 53-56; CABS 2; CANR 3,
36; CDALB 1941-1968; DA3; DLB 5,
169; MTCW 1, 2; SATA 10
Shaara, Jeff 1952- .... CLC 119
See CA 163
Shaara, Michael (Joseph, Jr.)
1929-1988 .... CLC 15; DAM POP
See AITN 1; CA 102; 125; CANR 52, 85;
DLBY 83
Shackleton, C. C.
See Aldiss, Brian W(ilson)
Shacochis, Bob CLC 39
See Shacochis, Robert G.
Shacochis, Robert G. 1951-
See Shacochis, Bob
See CA 119; 124; INT 124
Shaffer, Anthony (Joshua) 1926- ..... CLC 19;
DAM DRAM
See CA 110; 116; DLB 13
Shaffer, Peter (Levin) 1926- .. CLC 5, 14, 18,
37, 60; DAB; DAM DRAM, MST; DC
7
See CA 25-28R; CANR 25, 47, 74; CD-
BLB 1960 to Present; DA3; DLB 13;
MTCW 1, 2
Shakey, Bernard
See Young, Neil
Shalamov, Varlam (Tikhonovich)
1907(?)-1982 .... CLC 18
See CA 129; 105
Shamlu, Ahmad 1925- .... CLC 10
Shammas, Anton 1951- .... CLC 55
Shange, Ntozake 1948- .... CLC 8, 25, 38, 74;
BLC 3; DAM DRAM, MULT; DC 3
See AAYA 9; BW 2; CA 85-88; CABS 3;
CANR 27, 48, 74; DA3; DLB 38; MTCW
1, 2
Shanley, John Patrick 1950- .... CLC 75
See CA 128; 133; CANR 83
Shapcott, Thomas W(illiam) 1935- .. CLC 38
See CA 69-72; CANR 49, 83
Shapiro, Jane CLC 76

Shapiro, Karl (Jay) 1913- . CLC 4, 8, 15, 53;
PC 25
See CA 1-4R; CAAS 6; CANR 1, 36, 66;
DLB 48; MTCW 1, 2
Sharp, William 1855-1905 .... TCLC 39
See CA 160; DLB 156
Sharpe, Thomas Ridley 1928-
See Sharpe, Tom
See CA 114; 122; CANR 85; INT 122
Sharpe, Tom CLC 36
See Sharpe, Thomas Ridley
See DLB 14
Shaw, Bernard TCLC 45
See Shaw, George Bernard
See BW 1; MTCW 2
Shaw, G. Bernard
See Shaw, George Bernard
Shaw, George Bernard 1856-1950 .. TCLC 3,
9, 21; DA; DAB; DAC; DAM DRAM,
MST; WLC
See Shaw, Bernard
See CA 104; 128; CDBLB 1914-1945;
DA3; DLB 10, 57, 190; MTCW 1, 2
Shaw, Henry Wheeler 1818-1885 .. NCLC 15
See DLB 11
Shaw, Irwin 1913-1984 .... CLC 7, 23, 34;
DAM DRAM, POP
See AITN 1; CA 13-16R; 112; CANR 21;
CDALB 1941-1968; DLB 6, 102; DLBY
84; MTCW 1, 21
Shaw, Robert 1927-1978 .... CLC 5
See AITN 1; CA 1-4R; 81-84; CANR 4;
DLB 13, 14
Shaw, T. E.
See Lawrence, T(homas) E(dward)
Shawn, Wallace 1943- .... CLC 41
See CA 112
Shea, Lisa 1953- .... CLC 86
See CA 147
Sheed, Wilfrid (John Joseph) 1930- . CLC 2,
4, 10, 53
See CA 65-68; CANR 30, 66; DLB 6;
MTCW 1, 2
Sheldon, Alice Hastings Bradley
1915(?)-1987
See Tiptree, James, Jr.
See CA 108; 122; CANR 34; INT 108;
MTCW 1
Sheldon, John
See Bloch, Robert (Albert)
Shelley, Mary Wollstonecraft (Godwin)
1797-1851 ..... NCLC 14, 59; DA; DAB;
DAC; DAM MST, NOV; WLC
See AAYA 20; CDBLB 1789-1832; DA3;
DLB 110, 116, 159, 178; SATA 29
Shelley, Percy Bysshe 1792-1822 .. NCLC 18;
DA; DAB; DAC; DAM MST, POET;
PC 14; WLC
See CDBLB 1789-1832; DA3; DLB 96,
110, 158
Shepard, Jim 1956- .... CLC 36
See CA 137; CANR 59; SATA 90
Shepard, Lucius 1947- .... CLC 34
See CA 128; 141; CANR 81
Shepard, Sam 1943- .... CLC 4, 6, 17, 34, 41,
44; DAM DRAM; DC 5
See AAYA 1; CA 69-72; CABS 3; CANR
22; DA3; DLB 7, 212; MTCW 1, 2
Shepherd, Michael
See Ludlum, Robert
Sherburne, Zoa (Lillian Morin)
1912-1995 .... CLC 30
See AAYA 13; CA 1-4R; 176; CANR 3, 37;
MAICYA; SAAS 18; SATA 3
Sheridan, Frances 1724-1766 .... LC 7
See DLB 39, 84

Sheridan, Richard Brinsley
1751-1816 .. NCLC 5; DA; DAB; DAC;
DAM DRAM, MST; DC 1; WLC
See CDBLB 1660-1789; DLB 89
Sherman, Jonathan Marc CLC 55
Sherman, Martin 1941(?)- .... CLC 19
See CA 116; 123
Sherwin, Judith Johnson 1936-
See Johnson, Judith (Emlyn)
See CANR 85
Sherwood, Frances 1940- .... CLC 81
See CA 146
Sherwood, Robert E(mmet)
1896-1955 .... TCLC 3; DAM DRAM
See CA 104; 153; DLB 7, 26
Shestov, Lev 1866-1938 .... TCLC 56
Shevchenko, Taras 1814-1861 .... NCLC 54
Shiel, M(atthew) P(hipps)
1865-1947 .... TCLC 8
See Holmes, Gordon
See CA 106; 160; DLB 153; MTCW 2
Shields, Carol 1935- .... CLC 91, 113;DAC
See CA 81-84; CANR 51, 74; DA3; MTCW
2
Shields, David 1956- .... CLC 97
See CA 124; CANR 48
Shiga, Naoya 1883-1971 ...... CLC 33;SSC 23
See CA 101; 33-36R; DLB 180
Shikibu, Murasaki c. 978-c. 1014 ... CMLC 1
Shilts, Randy 1951-1994 .... CLC 85
See AAYA 19; CA 115; 127; 144; CANR
45; DA3; INT 127; MTCW 2
Shimazaki, Haruki 1872-1943
See Shimazaki Toson
See CA 105; 134; CANR 84
Shimazaki Toson 1872-1943 .... TCLC 5
See Shimazaki, Haruki
See DLB 180
Sholokhov, Mikhail (Aleksandrovich)
1905-1984 .... CLC 7, 15
See CA 101; 112; MTCW 1, 2; SATA-Obit
36
Shone, Patric
See Hanley, James
Shreve, Susan Richards 1939- .... CLC 23
See CA 49-52; CAAS 5; CANR 5, 38, 69;
MAICYA; SATA 46, 95; SATA-Brief 41
Shue, Larry 1946-1985 .... CLC 52;DAM
DRAM
See CA 145; 117
Shu-Jen, Chou 1881-1936
See Lu Hsun
See CA 104
Shulman, Alix Kates 1932- .... CLC 2,10
See CA 29-32R; CANR 43; SATA 7
Shuster, Joe 1914- .... CLC 21
Shute, Nevil CLC 30
See Norway, Nevil Shute
See MTCW 2
Shuttle, Penelope (Diane) 1947- .... CLC 7
See CA 93-96; CANR 39, 84; DLB 14, 40
Sidney, Mary 1561-1621 .... LC 19, 39
Sidney, Sir Philip 1554-1586 .... LC 19, 39;
DA; DAB; DAC; DAM MST, POET
See CDBLB Before 1660; DA3; DLB 167
Siegel, Jerome 1914-1996 .... CLC 21
See CA 116; 169; 151
Siegel, Jerry
See Siegel, Jerome
Sienkiewicz, Henryk (Adam Alexander Pius)
1846-1916 .... TCLC 3
See CA 104; 134; CANR 84
Sierra, Gregorio Martinez
See Martinez Sierra, Gregorio
Sierra, Maria (de la O'LeJarraga) Martinez
See Martinez Sierra, Maria (de la
O'LeJarraga)

Smith, Martin Cruz 1942- .... **CLC 25; DAM MULT, POP**
See BEST 89:4; CA 85-88; CANR 6, 23, 43, 65; INT CANR-23; MTCW 2; NNAL

Smith, Mary-Ann Tirone 1944- .... **CLC 39**
See CA 118; 136

Smith, Patti 1946- .... **CLC 12**
See CA 93-96; CANR 63

Smith, Pauline (Urmson)
1882-1959 .... **TCLC 25**

Smith, Rosamond
See Oates, Joyce Carol

Smith, Sheila Kaye
See Kaye-Smith, Sheila

Smith, Stevie CLC 3, 8, 25, 44; PC 12
See Smith, Florence Margaret
See DLB 20; MTCW 2

Smith, Wilbur (Addison) 1933- .... **CLC 33**
See CA 13-16R; CANR 7, 46, 66; MTCW 1, 2

Smith, William Jay 1918- .... **CLC 6**
See CA 5-8R; CANR 44; DLB 5; MAICYA; SAAS 22; SATA 2, 68

Smith, Woodrow Wilson
See Kuttner, Henry

Smolenskin, Peretz 1842-1885 .... **NCLC 30**

Smollett, Tobias (George) 1721-1771 ... **LC 2, 46**
See CDBLB 1660-1789; DLB 39, 104

Snodgrass, W(illiam) D(e Witt)
1926- .... **CLC 2, 6, 10, 18, 68; DAM POET**
See CA 1-4R; CANR 6, 36, 65, 85; DLB 5; MTCW 1, 2

Snow, C(harles) P(ercy) 1905-1980 ... **CLC 1, 4, 6, 9, 13, 19; DAM NOV**
See CA 5-8R; 101; CANR 28; CDBLB 1945-1960; DLB 15, 77; DLBD 17; MTCW 1, 2

Snow, Frances Compton
See Adams, Henry (Brooks)

Snyder, Gary (Sherman) 1930- . **CLC 1, 2, 5, 9, 32, 120; DAM POET; PC 21**
See CA 17-20R; CANR 30, 60; DA3; DLB 5, 16, 165, 212; MTCW 2

Snyder, Zilpha Keatley 1927- .... **CLC 17**
See AAYA 15; CA 9-12R; CANR 38; CLR 31; JRDA; MAICYA; SAAS 2; SATA 1, 28, 75, 110

Soares, Bernardo
See Pessoa, Fernando (Antonio Nogueira)

Sobh, A.
See Shamlu, Ahmad

Sobol, Joshua CLC 60

Socrates 469B.C.-399B.C. .... **CMLC 27**

Soderberg, Hjalmar 1869-1941 ...... **TCLC 39**

Sodergran, Edith (Irene)
See Soedergran, Edith (Irene)

Soedergran, Edith (Irene)
1892-1923 .... **TCLC 31**

Softly, Edgar
See Lovecraft, H(oward) P(hillips)

Softly, Edward
See Lovecraft, H(oward) P(hillips)

Sokolov, Raymond 1941- .... **CLC 7**
See CA 85-88

Solo, Jay
See Ellison, Harlan (Jay)

Sologub, Fyodor TCLC 9
See Teternikov, Fyodor Kuzmich

Solomons, Ikey Esquir
See Thackeray, William Makepeace

Solomos, Dionysios 1798-1857 .... **NCLC 15**

Solwoska, Mara
See French, Marilyn

Solzhenitsyn, Aleksandr I(sayevich)
1918- .. **CLC 1, 2, 4, 7, 9, 10, 18, 26, 34, 78; DA; DAB; DAC; DAM MST, NOV; SSC 32; WLC**
See AITN 1; CA 69-72; CANR 40, 65; DA3; MTCW 1, 2

Somers, Jane
See Lessing, Doris (May)

Somerville, Edith 1858-1949 .... **TCLC 51**
See DLB 135

Somerville & Ross
See Martin, Violet Florence; Somerville, Edith

Sommer, Scott 1951- .... **CLC 25**
See CA 106

Sondheim, Stephen (Joshua) 1930- . **CLC 30, 39; DAM DRAM**
See AAYA 11; CA 103; CANR 47, 68

Song, Cathy 1955- .... **PC 21**
See CA 154; DLB 169

Sontag, Susan 1933- .... **CLC 1, 2, 10, 13, 31, 105; DAM POP**
See CA 17-20R; CANR 25, 51, 74; DA3; DLB 2, 67; MTCW 1, 2

Sophocles 496(?)B.C.-406(?)B.C. .... **CMLC 2; DA; DAB; DAC; DAM DRAM, MST; DC 1; WLCS**
See DA3; DLB 176

Sordello 1189-1269 .... **CMLC 15**

Sorel, Georges 1847-1922 .... **TCLC 91**
See CA 118

Sorel, Julia
See Drexler, Rosalyn

Sorrentino, Gilbert 1929- .. **CLC 3, 7, 14, 22, 40**
See CA 77-80; CANR 14, 33; DLB 5, 173; DLBY 80; INT CANR-14

Soto, Gary 1952- .... **CLC 32, 80; DAM MULT; HLC 2; PC 28**
See AAYA 10; CA 119; 125; CANR 50, 74; CLR 38; DLB 82; HW 1, 2; INT 125; JRDA; MTCW 2; SATA 80

Soupault, Philippe 1897-1990 .... **CLC 68**
See CA 116; 147; 131

Souster, (Holmes) Raymond 1921- .... **CLC 5, 14; DAC; DAM POET**
See CA 13-16R; CAAS 14; CANR 13, 29, 53; DA3; DLB 88; SATA 63

Southern, Terry 1924(?)-1995 .... **CLC 7**
See CA 1-4R; 150; CANR 1, 55; DLB 2

Southey, Robert 1774-1843 .... **NCLC 8**
See DLB 93, 107, 142; SATA 54

Southworth, Emma Dorothy Eliza Nevitte
1819-1899 .... **NCLC 26**

Souza, Ernest
See Scott, Evelyn

Soyinka, Wole 1934- .... **CLC 3, 5, 14, 36, 44; BLC 3; DA; DAB; DAC; DAM DRAM, MST, MULT; DC 2; WLC**
See BW 2, 3; CA 13-16R; CANR 27, 39, 82; DA3; DLB 125; MTCW 1, 2

Spackman, W(illiam) M(ode)
1905-1990 .... **CLC 46**
See CA 81-84; 132

Spacks, Barry (Bernard) 1931- .... **CLC 14**
See CA 154; CANR 33; DLB 105

Spanidou, Irini 1946- .... **CLC 44**

Spark, Muriel (Sarah) 1918- ..... **CLC 2, 3, 5, 8, 13, 18, 40, 94; DAB; DAC; DAM MST, NOV; SSC 10**
See CA 5-8R; CANR 12, 36, 76; CDBLB 1945-1960; DA3; DLB 15, 139; INT CANR-12; MTCW 1, 2

Spaulding, Douglas
See Bradbury, Ray (Douglas)

Spaulding, Leonard
See Bradbury, Ray (Douglas)

Spence, J. A. D.
See Eliot, T(homas) S(tearns)

Spencer, Elizabeth 1921- .... **CLC 22**
See CA 13-16R; CANR 32, 65; DLB 6; MTCW 1; SATA 14

Spencer, Leonard G.
See Silverberg, Robert

Spencer, Scott 1945- .... **CLC 30**
See CA 113; CANR 51; DLBY 86

Spender, Stephen (Harold)
1909-1995 .... **CLC 1, 2, 5, 10, 41, 91; DAM POET**
See CA 9-12R; 149; CANR 31, 54; CD-BLB 1945-1960; DA3; DLB 20; MTCW 1, 2

Spengler, Oswald (Arnold Gottfried)
1880-1936 .... **TCLC 25**
See CA 118

Spenser, Edmund 1552(?)-1599 ..... **LC 5, 39; DA; DAB; DAC; DAM MST, POET; PC 8; WLC**
See CDBLB Before 1660; DA3; DLB 167

Spicer, Jack 1925-1965 .... **CLC 8, 18, 72; DAM POET**
See CA 85-88; DLB 5, 16, 193

Spiegelman, Art 1948- .... **CLC 76**
See AAYA 10; CA 125; CANR 41, 55, 74; MTCW 2; SATA 109

Spielberg, Peter 1929- .... **CLC 6**
See CA 5-8R; CANR 4, 48; DLBY 81

Spielberg, Steven 1947- .... **CLC 20**
See AAYA 8, 24; CA 77-80; CANR 32; SATA 32

Spillane, Frank Morrison 1918-
See Spillane, Mickey
See CA 25-28R; CANR 28, 63; DA3; MTCW 1, 2; SATA 66

Spillane, Mickey CLC 3, 13
See Spillane, Frank Morrison
See MTCW 2

Spinoza, Benedictus de 1632-1677 .... **LC 9**

Spinrad, Norman (Richard) 1940- ... **CLC 46**
See CA 37-40R; CAAS 19; CANR 20; DLB 8; INT CANR-20

Spitteler, Carl (Friedrich Georg)
1845-1924 .... **TCLC 12**
See CA 109; DLB 129

Spivack, Kathleen (Romola Drucker)
1938- .... **CLC 6**
See CA 49-52

Spoto, Donald 1941- .... **CLC 39**
See CA 65-68; CANR 11, 57

Springsteen, Bruce (F.) 1949- .... **CLC 17**
See CA 111

Spurling, Hilary 1940- .... **CLC 34**
See CA 104; CANR 25, 52

Spyker, John Howland
See Elman, Richard (Martin)

Squires, (James) Radcliffe
1917-1993 .... **CLC 51**
See CA 1-4R; 140; CANR 6, 21

Srivastava, Dhanpat Rai 1880(?)-1936
See Premchand
See CA 118

Stacy, Donald
See Pohl, Frederik

Stael, Germaine de 1766-1817
See Stael-Holstein, Anne Louise Germaine Necker Baronn
See DLB 119

Stael-Holstein, Anne Louise Germaine Necker Baronn 1766-1817 .... **NCLC 3**
See Stael, Germaine de
See DLB 192

Stafford, Jean 1915-1979 .. **CLC 4, 7, 19, 68; SSC 26**
See CA 1-4R; 85-88; CANR 3, 65; DLB 2, 173; MTCW 1, 2; SATA-Obit 22

Stafford, William (Edgar)
1914-1993 .. CLC 4, 7, 29; DAM POET
See CA 5-8R; 142; CAAS 3; CANR 5, 22;
DLB 5, 206; INT CANR-22

Stagnelius, Eric Johan 1793-1823 . NCLC 61

Staines, Trevor
See Brunner, John (Kilian Houston)

Stairs, Gordon
See Austin, Mary (Hunter)

Stairs, Gordon
See Austin, Mary (Hunter)

Stalin, Joseph 1879-1953 .... TCLC 92

Stannard, Martin 1947- .... CLC 44
See CA 142; DLB 155

Stanton, Elizabeth Cady
1815-1902 .... TCLC 73
See CA 171; DLB 79

Stanton, Maura 1946- .... CLC 9
See CA 89-92; CANR 15; DLB 120

Stanton, Schuyler
See Baum, L(yman) Frank

Stapledon, (William) Olaf
1886-1950 .... TCLC 22
See CA 111; 162; DLB 15

Starbuck, George (Edwin)
1931-1996 .... CLC 53; DAM POET
See CA 21-24R; 153; CANR 23

Stark, Richard
See Westlake, Donald E(dwin)

Staunton, Schuyler
See Baum, L(yman) Frank

Stead, Christina (Ellen) 1902-1983 ... CLC 2,
5, 8, 32, 80
See CA 13-16R; 109; CANR 33, 40; MTCW
1, 2

Stead, William Thomas
1849-1912 .... TCLC 48
See CA 167

Steele, Richard 1672-1729 .... LC 18
See CDBLB 1660-1789; DLB 84, 101

Steele, Timothy (Reid) 1948- .... CLC 45
See CA 93-96; CANR 16, 50; DLB 120

Steffens, (Joseph) Lincoln
1866-1936 .... TCLC 20
See CA 117

Stegner, Wallace (Earle) 1909-1993 .. CLC 9,
49, 81; DAM NOV; SSC 27
See AITN 1; BEST 90:3; CA 1-4R; 141;
CAAS 9; CANR 1, 21, 46; DLB 9, 206;
DLBY 93; MTCW 1, 2

Stein, Gertrude 1874-1946 .... TCLC 1, 6, 28,
48; DA; DAB; DAC; DAM MST, NOV,
POET; PC 18; WLC
See CA 104; 132; CDALB 1917-1929;
DA3; DLB 4, 54, 86; DLBD 15; MTCW
1, 2

Steinbeck, John (Ernst) 1902-1968 ... CLC 1,
5, 9, 13, 21, 34, 45, 75, 124; DA; DAB;
DAC; DAM DRAM, MST, NOV; SSC
37;WLC
See AAYA 12; CA 1-4R; 25-28R; CANR 1,
35; CDALB 1929-1941; DA3; DLB 7, 9,
212; DLBD 2; MTCW 1, 2; SATA 9

Steinem, Gloria 1934- .... CLC 63
See CA 53-56; CANR 28, 51; MTCW 1, 2

Steiner, George 1929- ... CLC 24;DAM NOV
See CA 73-76; CANR 31, 67; DLB 67;
MTCW 1, 2; SATA 62

Steiner, K. Leslie
See Delany, Samuel R(ay, Jr.)

Steiner, Rudolf 1861-1925 .... TCLC 13
See CA 107

Stendhal 1783-1842 .... NCLC 23, 46; DA;
DAB; DAC; DAM MST, NOV; SSC
27; WLC
See DA3; DLB 119

Stephen, Adeline Virginia
See Woolf, (Adeline) Virginia

Stephen, SirLeslie 1832-1904 .... TCLC 23
See CA 123; DLB 57, 144, 190

Stephen, Sir Leslie
See Stephen, SirLeslie

Stephen, Virginia
See Woolf, (Adeline) Virginia

Stephens, James 1882(?)-1950 .... TCLC 4
See CA 104; DLB 19, 153, 162

Stephens, Reed
See Donaldson, Stephen R.

Steptoe, Lydia
See Barnes, Djuna

Sterchi, Beat 1949- .... CLC 65

Sterling, Brett
See Bradbury, Ray (Douglas); Hamilton,
Edmond

Sterling, Bruce 1954- .... CLC 72
See CA 119; CANR 44

Sterling, George 1869-1926 .... TCLC 20
See CA 117; 165; DLB 54

Stern, Gerald 1925- .... CLC 40, 100
See CA 81-84; CANR 28; DLB 105

Stern, Richard (Gustave) 1928- ... CLC 4, 39
See CA 1-4R; CANR 1, 25, 52; DLBY 87;
INT CANR-25

Sternberg, Josefvon 1894-1969 .... CLC 20
See CA 81-84

Sterne, Laurence 1713-1768 .. LC 2, 48; DA;
DAB; DAC; DAM MST, NOV; WLC
See CDBLB 1660-1789; DLB 39

Sternheim, (William Adolf) Carl
1878-1942 .... TCLC 8
See CA 105; DLB 56, 118

Stevens, Mark 1951- .... CLC 34
See CA 122

Stevens, Wallace 1879-1955 ...... TCLC 3, 12,
45; DA; DAB; DAC; DAM MST,
POET; PC 6; WLC
See CA 104; 124; CDALB 1929-1941;
DA3; DLB 54; MTCW 1, 2

Stevenson, Anne (Katharine) 1933- ... CLC 7,
33
See CA 17-20R; CAAS 9; CANR 9, 33;
DLB 40; MTCW 1

Stevenson, Robert Louis (Balfour)
1850-1894 . NCLC 5, 14, 63; DA; DAB;
DAC; DAM MST, NOV; SSC 11; WLC
See AAYA 24; CDBLB 1890-1914; CLR
10, 11; DA3; DLB 18, 57, 141, 156, 174;
DLBD 13; JRDA; MAICYA; SATA 100;
YABC 2

Stewart, J(ohn) I(nnes) M(ackintosh)
1906-1994 .... CLC 7, 14, 32
See CA 85-88; 147; CAAS 3; CANR 47;
MTCW 1, 2

Stewart, Mary (Florence Elinor)
1916- .... CLC 7, 35, 117; DAB
See AAYA 29; CA 1-4R; CANR 1, 59;
SATA 12

Stewart, Mary Rainbow
See Stewart, Mary (Florence Elinor)

Stifle, June
See Campbell, Maria

Stifter, Adalbert 1805-1868 .. NCLC 41; SSC
28
See DLB 133

Still, James 1906- .... CLC 49
See CA 65-68; CAAS 17; CANR 10, 26;
DLB 9; SATA 29

Sting 1951-
See Sumner, Gordon Matthew
See CA 167

Stirling, Arthur
See Sinclair, Upton (Beall)

Stitt, Milan 1941- .... CLC 29
See CA 69-72

Stockton, Francis Richard 1834-1902
See Stockton, Frank R.
See CA 108; 137; MAICYA; SATA 44

Stockton, Frank R. TCLC 47
See Stockton, Francis Richard
See DLB 42, 74; DLBD 13; SATA-Brief 32

Stoddard, Charles
See Kuttner, Henry

Stoker, Abraham 1847-1912
See Stoker, Bram
See CA 105; 150; DA; DAC; DAM MST,
NOV; DA3; SATA 29

Stoker, Bram 1847-1912 .... TCLC 8; DAB;
WLC
See Stoker, Abraham
See AAYA 23; CDBLB 1890-1914; DLB
36, 70, 178

Stolz, Mary (Slattery) 1920- .... CLC 12
See AAYA 8; AITN 1; CA 5-8R; CANR 13,
41; JRDA; MAICYA; SAAS 3; SATA 10,
71

Stone, Irving 1903-1989 .. CLC 7;DAM POP
See AITN 1; CA 1-4R; 129; CAAS 3;
CANR 1, 23; DA3; INT CANR-23;
MTCW 1, 2; SATA 3; SATA-Obit 64

Stone, Oliver (William) 1946- .... CLC 73
See AAYA 15; CA 110; CANR 55

Stone, Robert (Anthony) 1937- ... CLC 5, 23,
42
See CA 85-88; CANR 23, 66; DLB 152;
INT CANR-23; MTCW 1

Stone, Zachary
See Follett, Ken(neth Martin)

Stoppard, Tom 1937- ... CLC 1, 3, 4, 5, 8, 15,
29, 34, 63, 91; DA; DAB; DAC; DAM
DRAM, MST; DC 6; WLC
See CA 81-84; CANR 39, 67; CDBLB 1960
to Present; DA3; DLB 13; DLBY 85;
MTCW 1, 2

Storey, David (Malcolm) 1933- . CLC 2, 4, 5,
8; DAM DRAM
See CA 81-84; CANR 36; DLB 13, 14, 207;
MTCW 1

Storm, Hyemeyohsts 1935- .... CLC 3;DAM
MULT
See CA 81-84; CANR 45; NNAL

Storm, Theodor 1817-1888 .... SSC 27

Storm, (Hans) Theodor (Woldsen)
1817-1888 .... NCLC 1; SSC 27
See DLB 129

Storni, Alfonsina 1892-1938 . TCLC 5; DAM
MULT; HLC 2
See CA 104; 131; HW 1

Stoughton, William 1631-1701 .... LC 38
See DLB 24

Stout, Rex(Todhunter) 1886-1975 ...... CLC 3
See AITN 2; CA 61-64; CANR 71

Stow, (Julian) Randolph 1935- ... CLC 23, 48
See CA 13-16R; CANR 33; MTCW 1

Stowe, Harriet (Elizabeth) Beecher
1811-1896 .... NCLC 3, 50; DA; DAB;
DAC; DAM MST, NOV; WLC
See CDALB 1865-1917; DA3; DLB 1, 12,
42, 74, 189; JRDA; MAICYA; YABC 1

Strachey, (Giles)Lytton 1880-1932 . TCLC 12
See CA 110; 178; DLB 149; DLBD 10;
MTCW 2

Strand, Mark 1934- .... CLC 6, 18, 41, 71;
DAM POET
See CA 21-24R; CANR 40, 65; DLB 5;
SATA 41

Straub, Peter (Francis) 1943- . CLC 28, 107;
DAM POP
See BEST 89:1; CA 85-88; CANR 28, 65;
DLBY 84; MTCW 1, 2

Strauss, Botho 1944- .... CLC 22
See CA 157; DLB 124

Streatfeild, (Mary) Noel
1895(?)-1986 .... CLC 21
See CA 81-84; 120; CANR 31; CLR 17;
DLB 160; MAICYA; SATA 20; SATA-
Obit 48

Stribling, T(homas) S(igismund)
1881-1965 .... **CLC 23**
See CA 107; DLB 9

Strindberg, (Johan) August
1849-1912 .... **TCLC 1, 8, 21, 47; DA;**
DAB; DAC; DAM DRAM, MST; WLC
See CA 104; 135; DA3; MTCW 2

Stringer, Arthur 1874-1950 .... **TCLC 37**
See CA 161; DLB 92

Stringer, David
See Roberts, Keith (John Kingston)

Stroheim, Erich von 1885-1957 ..... **TCLC 71**

Strugatskii, Arkadii (Natanovich)
1925-1991 .... **CLC 27**
See CA 106; 135

Strugatskii, Boris (Natanovich)
1933- .... **CLC 27**
See CA 106

Strummer, Joe 1953(?)- .... **CLC 30**

Strunk, William, Jr. 1869-1946 ...... **TCLC 92**
See CA 118; 164

Stryk, Lucien 1924- .... **PC 27**
See CA 13-16R; CANR 10, 28, 55

Stuart, Don A.
See Campbell, John W(ood, Jr.)

Stuart, Ian
See MacLean, Alistair (Stuart)

Stuart, Jesse (Hilton) 1906-1984 ... **CLC 1, 8,**
11, 14, 34; SSC 31
See CA 5-8R; 112; CANR 31; DLB 9, 48,
102; DLBY 84; SATA 2; SATA-Obit 36

Sturgeon, Theodore (Hamilton)
1918-1985 .... **CLC 22, 39**
See Queen, Ellery
See CA 81-84; 116; CANR 32; DLB 8;
DLBY 85; MTCW 1, 2

Sturges, Preston 1898-1959 .... **TCLC 48**
See CA 114; 149; DLB 26

Styron, William 1925- .... **CLC 1, 3, 5, 11, 15,**
60; DAM NOV, POP; SSC 25
See BEST 90:4; CA 5-8R; CANR 6, 33, 74;
CDALB 1968-1988; DA3; DLB 2, 143;
DLBY 80; INT CANR-6; MTCW 1, 2

Su, Chien 1884-1918
See Su Man-shu
See CA 123

Suarez Lynch, B.
See Bioy Casares, Adolfo; Borges, Jorge
Luis

Suassuna, Ariano Vilar 1927-
See CA 178; HLCS 1; HW 2

Suckow, Ruth 1892-1960 .... **SSC 18**
See CA 113; DLB 9, 102

Sudermann, Hermann 1857-1928 .. **TCLC 15**
See CA 107; DLB 118

Sue, Eugene 1804-1857 .... **NCLC 1**
See DLB 119

Sueskind, Patrick 1949- .... **CLC 44**
See Suskind, Patrick

Sukenick, Ronald 1932- .... **CLC 3, 4, 6, 48**
See CA 25-28R; CAAS 8; CANR 32; DLB
173; DLBY 81

Suknaski, Andrew 1942- .... **CLC 19**
See CA 101; DLB 53

Sullivan, Vernon
See Vian, Boris

Sully Prudhomme 1839-1907 .... **TCLC 31**

Su Man-shu TCLC 24
See Su, Chien

Summerforest, Ivy B.
See Kirkup, James

Summers, Andrew James 1942- .... **CLC 26**

Summers, Andy
See Summers, Andrew James

Summers, Hollis (Spurgeon, Jr.)
1916- .... **CLC 10**
See CA 5-8R; CANR 3; DLB 6

Summers, (Alphonsus Joseph-Mary
Augustus) Montague
1880-1948 .... **TCLC 16**
See CA 118; 163

Sumner, Gordon Matthew CLC 26
See Sting

Surtees, Robert Smith 1803-1864 .. **NCLC 14**
See DLB 21

Susann, Jacqueline 1921-1974 .... **CLC 3**
See AITN 1; CA 65-68; 53-56; MTCW 1, 2

Su Shih 1036-1101 .... **CMLC 15**

Suskind, Patrick
See Sueskind, Patrick
See CA 145

Sutcliff, Rosemary 1920-1992 .... **CLC 26;**
DAB; DAC; DAM MST, POP
See AAYA 10; CA 5-8R; 139; CANR 37;
CLR 1, 37; JRDA; MAICYA; SATA 6,
44, 78; SATA-Obit 73

Sutro, Alfred 1863-1933 .... **TCLC 6**
See CA 105; DLB 10

Sutton, Henry
See Slavitt, David R(ytman)

Svevo, Italo 1861-1928 .. **TCLC 2, 35; SSC 25**
See Schmitz, Aron Hector

Swados, Elizabeth (A.) 1951- .... **CLC 12**
See CA 97-100; CANR 49; INT 97-100

Swados, Harvey 1920-1972 .... **CLC 5**
See CA 5-8R; 37-40R; CANR 6; DLB 2

Swan, Gladys 1934- .... **CLC 69**
See CA 101; CANR 17, 39

Swarthout, Glendon (Fred)
1918-1992 .... **CLC 35**
See CA 1-4R; 139; CANR 1, 47; SATA 26

Sweet, Sarah C.
See Jewett, (Theodora) Sarah Orne

Swenson, May 1919-1989 ...... **CLC 4, 14, 61,**
106; DA; DAB; DAC; DAM MST,
POET; PC 14
See CA 5-8R; 130; CANR 36, 61; DLB 5;
MTCW 1, 2; SATA 15

Swift, Augustus
See Lovecraft, H(oward) P(hillips)

Swift, Graham (Colin) 1949- ...... **CLC 41, 88**
See CA 117; 122; CANR 46, 71; DLB 194;
MTCW 2

Swift, Jonathan 1667-1745 ..... **LC 1, 42; DA;**
DAB; DAC; DAM MST, NOV, POET;
PC 9; WLC
See CDBLB 1660-1789; CLR 53; DA3;
DLB 39, 95, 101; SATA 19

Swinburne, Algernon Charles
1837-1909 .... **TCLC 8, 36; DA; DAB;**
DAC; DAM MST, POET; PC 24; WLC
See CA 105; 140; CDBLB 1832-1890;
DA3; DLB 35, 57

Swinfen, Ann CLC 34

Swinnerton, Frank Arthur
1884-1982 .... **CLC 31**
See CA 108; DLB 34

Swithen, John
See King, Stephen (Edwin)

Sylvia
See Ashton-Warner, Sylvia (Constance)

Symmes, Robert Edward
See Duncan, Robert (Edward)

Symonds, John Addington
1840-1893 .... **NCLC 34**
See DLB 57, 144

Symons, Arthur 1865-1945 .... **TCLC 11**
See CA 107; DLB 19, 57, 149

Symons, Julian (Gustave)
1912-1994 .... **CLC 2, 14, 32**
See CA 49-52; 147; CAAS 3; CANR 3, 33,
59; DLB 87, 155; DLBY 92; MTCW 1

Synge, (Edmund) J(ohn) M(illington)
1871-1909 . **TCLC 6, 37; DAM DRAM;**
DC 2
See CA 104; 141; CDBLB 1890-1914; DLB
10, 19

Syruc, J.
See Milosz, Czeslaw

Szirtes, George 1948- .... **CLC 46**
See CA 109; CANR 27, 61

Szymborska, Wislawa 1923- .... **CLC 99**
See CA 154; DA3; DLBY 96; MTCW 2

T. O., Nik
See Annensky, Innokenty (Fyodorovich)

Tabori, George 1914- .... **CLC 19**
See CA 49-52; CANR 4, 69

Tagore, Rabindranath 1861-1941 ... **TCLC 3,**
53; DAM DRAM, POET; PC 8
See CA 104; 120; DA3; MTCW 1, 2

Taine, Hippolyte Adolphe
1828-1893 .... **NCLC 15**

Talese, Gay 1932- .... **CLC 37**
See AITN 1; CA 1-4R; CANR 9, 58; DLB
185; INT CANR-9; MTCW 1, 2

Tallent, Elizabeth (Ann) 1954- .... **CLC 45**
See CA 117; CANR 72; DLB 130

Tally, Ted 1952- .... **CLC 42**
See CA 120; 124; INT 124

Talvik, Heiti 1904-1947 .... **TCLC 87**

Tamayo y Baus, Manuel
1829-1898 .... **NCLC 1**

Tammsaare, A(nton) H(ansen)
1878-1940 .... **TCLC 27**
See CA 164

Tam'si, Tchicaya U
See Tchicaya, Gerald Felix

Tan, Amy (Ruth) 1952- . **CLC 59, 120; DAM**
MULT, NOV, POP
See AAYA 9; BEST 89:3; CA 136; CANR
54; CDALBS; DA3; DLB 173; MTCW 2;
SATA 75

Tandem, Felix
See Spitteler, Carl (Friedrich Georg)

Tanizaki, Jun'ichiro 1886-1965 ... **CLC 8, 14,**
28; SSC 21
See CA 93-96; 25-28R; DLB 180; MTCW
2

Tanner, William
See Amis, Kingsley (William)

Tao Lao
See Storni, Alfonsina

Tarantino, Quentin(Jerome) 1963- . **CLC 125**
See CA 171

Tarassoff, Lev
See Troyat, Henri

Tarbell, Ida M(inerva) 1857-1944 . **TCLC 40**
See CA 122; 181; DLB 47

Tarkington, (Newton) Booth
1869-1946 .... **TCLC 9**
See CA 110; 143; DLB 9, 102; MTCW 2;
SATA 17

Tarkovsky, Andrei (Arsenyevich)
1932-1986 .... **CLC 75**
See CA 127

Tartt, Donna 1964(?)- .... **CLC 76**
See CA 142

Tasso, Torquato 1544-1595 .... **LC 5**

Tate, (John Orley) Allen 1899-1979 .. **CLC 2,**
4, 6, 9, 11, 14, 24
See CA 5-8R; 85-88; CANR 32; DLB 4,
45, 63; DLBD 17; MTCW 1, 2

Tate, Ellalice
See Hibbert, Eleanor Alice Burford

Tate, James (Vincent) 1943- ..... **CLC 2, 6, 25**
See CA 21-24R; CANR 29, 57; DLB 5, 169

Tavel, Ronald 1940- .... **CLC 6**
See CA 21-24R; CANR 33

Taylor, C(ecil) P(hilip) 1929-1981 .... **CLC 27**
See CA 25-28R; 105; CANR 47

Taylor, Edward 1642(?)-1729 ..... **LC 11; DA; DAB; DAC; DAM MST, POET**
See DLB 24

Taylor, Eleanor Ross 1920- .... **CLC 5**
See CA 81-84; CANR 70

Taylor, Elizabeth 1912-1975 ..... **CLC 2, 4, 29**
See CA 13-16R; CANR 9, 70; DLB 139; MTCW 1; SATA 13

Taylor, Frederick Winslow
1856-1915 .... **TCLC 76**

Taylor, Henry (Splawn) 1942- .... **CLC 44**
See CA 33-36R; CAAS 7; CANR 31; DLB 5

Taylor, Kamala (Purnaiya) 1924-
See Markandaya, Kamala
See CA 77-80

Taylor, Mildred D. **CLC 21**
See AAYA 10; BW 1; CA 85-88; CANR 25; CLR 9, 59; DLB 52; JRDA; MAICYA; SAAS 5; SATA 15, 70

Taylor, Peter (Hillsman) 1917-1994 .. **CLC 1, 4, 18, 37, 44, 50, 71; SSC 10**
See CA 13-16R; 147; CANR 9, 50; DLBY 81, 94; INT CANR-9; MTCW 1, 2

Taylor, Robert Lewis 1912-1998 .... **CLC 14**
See CA 1-4R; 170; CANR 3, 64; SATA 10

Tchekhov, Anton
See Chekhov, Anton (Pavlovich)

Tchicaya, GeraldFelix 1931-1988 ... **CLC 101**
See CA 129; 125; CANR 81

Tchicaya U Tam'si
See Tchicaya, Gerald Felix

Teasdale, Sara 1884-1933 .... **TCLC 4**
See CA 104; 163; DLB 45; SATA 32

Tegner, Esaias 1782-1846 .... **NCLC 2**

Teilhard de Chardin, (Marie Joseph) Pierre
1881-1955 .... **TCLC 9**
See CA 105

Temple, Ann
See Mortimer, Penelope (Ruth)

Tennant, Emma (Christina) 1937- .. **CLC 13, 52**
See CA 65-68; CAAS 9; CANR 10, 38, 59; DLB 14

Tenneshaw, S. M.
See Silverberg, Robert

Tennyson, Alfred 1809-1892 ... **NCLC 30, 65; DA; DAB; DAC; DAM MST, POET; PC 6; WLC**
See CDBLB 1832-1890; DA3; DLB 32

Teran, Lisa St. Aubin de **CLC 36**
See St. Aubin de Teran, Lisa

Terence c. 184B.C.-c. 159B.C. ...... **CMLC 14; DC 7**
See DLB 211

Teresa de Jesus, St. 1515-1582 .... **LC 18**

Terkel, Louis 1912-
See Terkel, Studs
See CA 57-60; CANR 18, 45, 67; DA3; MTCW 1, 2

Terkel, Studs **CLC 38**
See Terkel, Louis
See AAYA 32; AITN 1; MTCW 2

Terry, C. V.
See Slaughter, Frank G(ill)

Terry, Megan 1932- .... **CLC 19**
See CA 77-80; CABS 3; CANR 43; DLB 7

Tertullian c. 155-c. 245 .... **CMLC 29**

Tertz, Abram
See Sinyavsky, Andrei (Donatevich)

Tesich, Steve 1943(?)-1996 .... **CLC 40, 69**
See CA 105; 152; DLBY 83

Tesla, Nikola 1856-1943 .... **TCLC 88**

Teternikov, Fyodor Kuzmich 1863-1927
See Sologub, Fyodor
See CA 104

Tevis, Walter 1928-1984 .... **CLC 42**
See CA 113

Tey, Josephine **TCLC 14**
See Mackintosh,Elizabeth
See DLB 77

Thackeray, William Makepeace
1811-1863 ...... **NCLC 5, 14, 22, 43; DA; DAB; DAC; DAM MST, NOV; WLC**
See CDBLB 1832-1890; DA3; DLB 21, 55, 159, 163; SATA 23

Thakura, Ravindranatha
See Tagore, Rabindranath

Tharoor, Shashi 1956- .... **CLC 70**
See CA 141

Thelwell, Michael Miles 1939- .... **CLC 22**
See BW 2; CA 101

Theobald, Lewis, Jr.
See Lovecraft, H(oward) P(hillips)

Theodorescu, Ion N. 1880-1967
See Arghezi, Tudor
See CA 116

Theriault, Yves 1915-1983 .... **CLC 79; DAC; DAM MST**
See CA 102; DLB 88

Theroux, Alexander (Louis) 1939- .... **CLC 2, 25**
See CA 85-88; CANR 20, 63

Theroux, Paul (Edward) 1941- ..... **CLC 5, 8, 11, 15, 28, 46; DAM POP**
See AAYA 28; BEST 89:4; CA 33-36R; CANR 20, 45, 74; CDALBS; DA3; DLB 2; MTCW 1, 2; SATA 44, 109

Thesen, Sharon 1946- .... **CLC 56**
See CA 163

Thevenin, Denis
See Duhamel, Georges

Thibault, Jacques Anatole Francois
1844-1924
See France, Anatole
See CA 106; 127; DAM NOV; DA3; MTCW 1, 2

Thiele, Colin (Milton) 1920- .... **CLC 17**
See CA 29-32R; CANR 12, 28, 53; CLR 27; MAICYA; SAAS 2; SATA 14, 72

Thomas, Audrey (Callahan) 1935- .... **CLC 7, 13, 37, 107; SSC 20**
See AITN 2; CA 21-24R; CAAS 19; CANR 36, 58; DLB 60; MTCW 1

Thomas, Augustus 1857-1934 .... **TCLC 97**

Thomas, D(onald) M(ichael) 1935- . **CLC 13, 22, 31**
See CA 61-64; CAAS 11; CANR 17, 45, 75; CDBLB 1960 to Present; DA3; DLB 40, 207; INT CANR-17; MTCW 1, 2

Thomas, Dylan (Marlais)
1914-1953 ... **TCLC 1, 8, 45; DA; DAB; DAC; DAM DRAM, MST, POET; PC 2; SSC 3; WLC**
See CA 104; 120; CANR 65; CDBLB 1945-1960; DA3; DLB 13, 20, 139; MTCW 1, 2; SATA 60

Thomas, (Philip) Edward
1878-1917 .... **TCLC 10; DAM POET**
See CA 106; 153; DLB 98

Thomas, Joyce Carol 1938- .... **CLC 35**
See AAYA 12; BW 2, 3; CA 113; 116; CANR 48; CLR 19; DLB 33; INT 116; JRDA; MAICYA; MTCW 1, 2; SAAS 7; SATA 40, 78

Thomas, Lewis 1913-1993 .... **CLC 35**
See CA 85-88; 143; CANR 38, 60; MTCW 1, 2

Thomas, M. Carey 1857-1935 .... **TCLC 89**

Thomas, Paul
See Mann, (Paul) Thomas

Thomas, Piri 1928- .... **CLC 17;HLCS 2**
See CA 73-76; HW 1

Thomas, R(onald) S(tuart) 1913- ...... **CLC 6, 13, 48; DAB; DAM POET**
See CA 89-92; CAAS 4; CANR 30; CDBLB 1960 to Present; DLB 27; MTCW 1

Thomas, Ross(Elmore) 1926-1995 .... **CLC 39**
See CA 33-36R; 150; CANR 22, 63

Thompson, Francis Clegg
See Mencken, H(enry) L(ouis)

Thompson, Francis Joseph
1859-1907 .... **TCLC 4**
See CA 104; CDBLB 1890-1914; DLB 19

Thompson, Hunter S(tockton)
1939- ... **CLC 9, 17, 40, 104; DAM POP**
See BEST 89:1; CA 17-20R; CANR 23, 46, 74, 77; DA3; DLB 185; MTCW 1, 2

Thompson, James Myers
See Thompson, Jim (Myers)

Thompson, Jim (Myers)
1906-1977(?) .... **CLC 69**
See CA 140

Thompson, Judith **CLC 39**

Thomson, James 1700-1748 ... **LC 16, 29, 40; DAM POET**
See DLB 95

Thomson, James
1834-1882 .... **NCLC 18;DAM POET**
See DLB 35

Thoreau, Henry David 1817-1862 .. **NCLC 7, 21, 61; DA; DAB; DAC; DAM MST; WLC**
See CDALB 1640-1865; DA3; DLB 1

Thornton, Hall
See Silverberg, Robert

Thucydides c.455B.C.-399B.C. ...... **CMLC 17**
See DLB 176

Thurber, James (Grover)
1894-1961 .... **CLC 5, 11, 25, 125; DA; DAB; DAC; DAM DRAM, MST, NOV; SSC 1**
See CA 73-76; CANR 17, 39; CDALB 1929-1941; DA3; DLB 4, 11, 22, 102; MAICYA; MTCW 1, 2; SATA 13

Thurman, Wallace (Henry)
1902-1934 .... **TCLC 6; BLC 3; DAM MULT**
See BW 1, 3; CA 104; 124; CANR 81; DLB 51

Tibullus, Albius c. 54B.C.-c.
19B.C. .... **CMLC 36**
See DLB 211

Ticheburn, Cheviot
See Ainsworth, William Harrison

Tieck, (Johann) Ludwig
1773-1853 .... **NCLC 5, 46; SSC 31**
See DLB 90

Tiger, Derry
See Ellison, Harlan (Jay)

Tilghman, Christopher 1948(?)- .... **CLC 65**
See CA 159

Tillinghast, Richard (Williford)
1940- .... **CLC 29**
See CA 29-32R; CAAS 23; CANR 26, 51

Timrod, Henry 1828-1867 .... **NCLC 25**
See DLB 3

Tindall, Gillian (Elizabeth) 1938- ...... **CLC 7**
See CA 21-24R; CANR 11, 65

Tiptree, James, Jr. **CLC 48, 50**
See Sheldon, Alice Hastings Bradley
See DLB 8

Titmarsh, Michael Angelo
See Thackeray, William Makepeace

Tocqueville, Alexis (Charles Henri Maurice Clerel, Comte) de 1805-1859 . **NCLC 7, 63**

Tolkien, J(ohn) R(onald) R(euel)
1892-1973 .. **CLC 1, 2, 3, 8, 12, 38; DA; DAB; DAC; DAM MST, NOV, POP; WLC**
See AAYA 10; AITN 1; CA 17-18; 45-48; CANR 36; CAP 2; CDBLB 1914-1945;

CLR 56; DA3; DLB 15, 160; JRDA;
MAICYA; MTCW 1, 2; SATA 2, 32, 100;
SATA-Obit 24

Toller, Ernst 1893-1939 .... **TCLC 10**
See CA 107; DLB 124

Tolson, M. B.
See Tolson, Melvin B(eaunorus)

Tolson, Melvin B(eaunorus)
1898(?)-1966 .... **CLC 36, 105; BLC 3;**
DAM MULT, POET
See BW 1, 3; CA 124; 89-92; CANR 80;
DLB 48, 76

Tolstoi, Aleksei Nikolaevich
See Tolstoy, Alexey Nikolaevich

Tolstoy, Alexey Nikolaevich
1882-1945 .... **TCLC 18**
See CA 107; 158

Tolstoy, Count Leo
See Tolstoy, Leo (Nikolaevich)

Tolstoy, Leo (Nikolaevich)
1828-1910 .. **TCLC 4, 11, 17, 28, 44, 79;**
DA; DAB; DAC; DAM MST, NOV;
SSC 9, 30; WLC
See CA 104; 123; DA3; SATA 26

Tomasi di Lampedusa, Giuseppe 1896-1957
See Lampedusa, Giuseppe (Tomasi) di
See CA 111

Tomlin, Lily CLC 17
See Tomlin, Mary Jean

Tomlin, Mary Jean 1939(?)-
See Tomlin, Lily
See CA 117

Tomlinson, (Alfred) Charles 1927- .... **CLC 2,**
4, 6, 13, 45; DAM POET; PC 17
See CA 5-8R; CANR 33; DLB 40

Tomlinson, H(enry) M(ajor)
1873-1958 .... **TCLC 71**
See CA 118; 161; DLB 36, 100, 195

Tonson, Jacob
See Bennett, (Enoch) Arnold

Toole, John Kennedy 1937-1969 ..... **CLC 19,**
64
See CA 104; DLBY 81; MTCW 2

Toomer, Jean 1894-1967 .... **CLC 1, 4, 13, 22;**
BLC 3; DAM MULT; PC 7; SSC 1;
WLCS
See BW 1; CA 85-88; CDALB 1917-1929;
DA3; DLB 45, 51; MTCW 1, 2

Torley, Luke
See Blish, James (Benjamin)

Tornimparte, Alessandra
See Ginzburg, Natalia

Torre, Raoul della
See Mencken, H(enry) L(ouis)

Torrence, Ridgely 1874-1950 .... **TCLC 97**
See DLB 54

Torrey, E(dwin) Fuller 1937- .... **CLC 34**
See CA 119; CANR 71

Torsvan, Ben Traven
See Traven, B.

Torsvan, Benno Traven
See Traven, B.

Torsvan, Berick Traven
See Traven, B.

Torsvan, Berwick Traven
See Traven, B.

Torsvan, Bruno Traven
See Traven, B.

Torsvan, Traven
See Traven, B.

Tournier, Michel (Edouard) 1924- .... **CLC 6,**
23, 36, 95
See CA 49-52; CANR 3, 36, 74; DLB 83;
MTCW 1, 2; SATA 23

Tournimparte, Alessandra
See Ginzburg, Natalia

Towers, Ivar
See Kornbluth, C(yril) M.

Towne, Robert(Burton) 1936(?)- ...... **CLC 87**
See CA 108; DLB 44

Townsend, Sue CLC 61
See Townsend, Susan Elaine
See AAYA 28; SATA 55, 93; SATA-Brief
48

Townsend, Susan Elaine 1946-
See Townsend, Sue
See CA 119; 127; CANR 65; DAB; DAC;
DAM MST

Townshend, Peter (Dennis Blandford)
1945- .... **CLC 17, 42**
See CA 107

Tozzi, Federigo 1883-1920 .... **TCLC 31**
See CA 160

Traill, Catharine Parr 1802-1899 .. **NCLC 31**
See DLB 99

Trakl, Georg 1887-1914 .... **TCLC 5;PC 20**
See CA 104; 165; MTCW 2

Transtroemer, Tomas (Goesta)
1931- .... **CLC 52, 65; DAM POET**
See CA 117; 129; CAAS 17

Transtromer, Tomas Gosta
See Transtroemer, Tomas (Goesta)

Traven, B. (?)-1969 .... **CLC 8, 11**
See CA 19-20; 25-28R; CAP 2; DLB 9, 56;
MTCW 1

Treitel, Jonathan 1959- .... **CLC 70**

Tremain, Rose 1943- .... **CLC 42**
See CA 97-100; CANR 44; DLB 14

Tremblay, Michel 1942- .... **CLC 29, 102;**
DAC; DAM MST
See CA 116; 128; DLB 60; MTCW 1, 2

Trevanian CLC 29
See Whitaker, Rod(ney)

Trevor, Glen
See Hilton, James

Trevor, William 1928- .. **CLC 7, 9, 14, 25, 71,**
116; SSC 21
See Cox, William Trevor
See DLB 14, 139; MTCW 2

Trifonov, Yuri (Valentinovich)
1925-1981 .... **CLC 45**
See CA 126; 103; MTCW 1

Trilling, Lionel 1905-1975 .... **CLC 9, 11, 24**
See CA 9-12R; 61-64; CANR 10; DLB 28,
63; INT CANR-10; MTCW 1, 2

Trimball, W. H.
See Mencken, H(enry) L(ouis)

Tristan
See Gomez de la Serna, Ramon

Tristram
See Housman, A(lfred) E(dward)

Trogdon, William (Lewis) 1939-
See Heat-Moon, William Least
See CA 115; 119; CANR 47; INT 119

Trollope, Anthony 1815-1882 ... **NCLC 6, 33;**
DA; DAB; DAC; DAM MST, NOV;
SSC 28; WLC
See CDBLB 1832-1890; DA3; DLB 21, 57,
159; SATA 22

Trollope, Frances 1779-1863 .... **NCLC 30**
See DLB 21, 166

Trotsky, Leon 1879-1940 .... **TCLC 22**
See CA 118; 167

Trotter (Cockburn), Catharine
1679-1749 .... **LC 8**
See DLB 84

Trout, Kilgore
See Farmer, Philip Jose

Trow, George W. S. 1943- .... **CLC 52**
See CA 126

Troyat, Henri 1911- .... **CLC 23**
See CA 45-48; CANR 2, 33, 67; MTCW 1

Trudeau, G(arretson) B(eekman) 1948-
See Trudeau, Garry B.
See CA 81-84; CANR 31; SATA 35

Trudeau, Garry B. CLC 12

See Trudeau, G(arretson) B(eekman)
See AAYA 10; AITN 2

Truffaut, Francois 1932-1984 ... **CLC 20, 101**
See CA 81-84; 113; CANR 34

Trumbo, Dalton 1905-1976 .... **CLC 19**
See CA 21-24R; 69-72; CANR 10; DLB 26

Trumbull, John 1750-1831 .... **NCLC 30**
See DLB 31

Trundlett, Helen B.
See Eliot, T(homas) S(tearns)

Tryon, Thomas 1926-1991 .. **CLC 3, 11;DAM**
POP
See AITN 1; CA 29-32R; 135; CANR 32,
77; DA3; MTCW 1

Tryon, Tom
See Tryon, Thomas

Ts'ao Hsueh-ch'in 1715(?)-1763 .... **LC 1**

Tsushima, Shuji 1909-1948
See Dazai Osamu
See CA 107

Tsvetaeva (Efron), Marina (Ivanovna)
1892-1941 .... **TCLC 7, 35; PC 14**
See CA 104; 128; CANR 73; MTCW 1, 2

Tuck, Lily 1938- .... **CLC 70**
See CA 139

Tu Fu 712-770 .... **PC 9**
See DAM MULT

Tunis, JohnR(oberts) 1889-1975 .... **CLC 12**
See CA 61-64; CANR 62; DLB 22, 171;
JRDA; MAICYA; SATA 37; SATA-Brief
30

Tuohy, Frank CLC 37
See Tuohy, John Francis
See DLB 14, 139

Tuohy, John Francis 1925-1999
See Tuohy, Frank
See CA 5-8R; 178; CANR 3, 47

Turco, Lewis (Putnam) 1934- ..... **CLC 11, 63**
See CA 13-16R; CAAS 22; CANR 24, 51;
DLBY 84

Turgenev, Ivan 1818-1883 .... **NCLC 21; DA;**
DAB; DAC; DAM MST, NOV; DC 7;
SSC 7; WLC

Turgot, Anne-Robert-Jacques
1727-1781 .... **LC 26**

Turner, Frederick 1943- .... **CLC 48**
See CA 73-76; CAAS 10; CANR 12, 30,
56; DLB 40

Tutu, Desmond M(pilo) 1931- .... **CLC 80;**
BLC 3; DAM MULT
See BW 1, 3; CA 125; CANR 67, 81

Tutuola, Amos 1920-1997 ...... **CLC 5, 14, 29;**
BLC 3; DAM MULT
See BW 2, 3; CA 9-12R; 159; CANR 27,
66; DA3; DLB 125; MTCW 1, 2

Twain, Mark TCLC 6, 12, 19, 36, 48, 59; SSC
34; WLC
See Clemens, Samuel Langhorne
See AAYA 20; CLR 58, 60; DLB 11, 12,
23, 64, 74

Tyler, Anne 1941- . **CLC 7, 11, 18, 28, 44, 59,**
103; DAM NOV, POP
See AAYA 18; BEST 89:1; CA 9-12R;
CANR 11, 33, 53; CDALBS; DLB 6, 143;
DLBY 82; MTCW 1, 2; SATA 7, 90

Tyler, Royall 1757-1826 .... **NCLC 3**
See DLB 37

Tynan, Katharine 1861-1931 .... **TCLC 3**
See CA 104; 167; DLB 153

Tyutchev, Fyodor 1803-1873 .... **NCLC 34**

Tzara, Tristan 1896-1963 ...... **CLC 47; DAM**
POET; PC 27
See CA 153; 89-92; MTCW 2

Uhry, Alfred 1936- .. **CLC 55; DAM DRAM,**
POP
See CA 127; 133; DA3; INT 133

Ulf, Haerved
See Strindberg, (Johan) August

Vigny, Alfred (Victor) de
1797-1863 .. **NCLC 7; DAM POET; PC 26**
See DLB 119, 192
Vilakazi, Benedict Wallet
1906-1947 .... **TCLC 37**
See CA 168
Villa, Jose Garcia 1904-1997 .... **PC 22**
See CA 25-28R; CANR 12
Villarreal, Jose Antonio 1924-
See CA 133; DAM MULT; DLB 82; HLC 2; HW 1
Villaurrutia, Xavier 1903-1950 ...... **TCLC 80**
See HW 1
Villiers de l'Isle Adam, Jean Marie Mathias Philippe Auguste, Comte de
1838-1889 .... **NCLC 3; SSC 14**
See DLB 123
Villon, Francois 1431-1463(?) .... **PC 13**
See DLB 208
Vinci, Leonardo da 1452-1519 .... **LC 12**
Vine, Barbara CLC 50
See Rendell, Ruth(Barbara)
See BEST 90:4
Vinge, Joan (Carol) D(ennison)
1948- .... **CLC 30; SSC 24**
See AAYA 32; CA 93-96; CANR 72; SATA 36
Violis, G.
See Simenon, Georges (Jacques Christian)
Viramontes, Helena Maria 1954-
See CA 159; DLB 122; HLCS 2; HW 2
Virgil 70B.C.-19B.C.
See Vergil
See DLB 211
Visconti, Luchino 1906-1976 .... **CLC 16**
See CA 81-84; 65-68; CANR 39
Vittorini, Elio 1908-1966 .... **CLC 6, 9, 14**
See CA 133; 25-28R
Vivekananda, Swami 1863-1902 .... **TCLC 88**
Vizenor, Gerald Robert 1934- .... **CLC 103; DAM MULT**
See CA 13-16R; CAAS 22; CANR 5, 21, 44, 67; DLB 175; MTCW 2; NNAL
Vizinczey, Stephen 1933- .... **CLC 40**
See CA 128; INT 128
Vliet, R(ussell) G(ordon)
1929-1984 .... **CLC 22**
See CA 37-40R; 112; CANR 18
Vogau, Boris Andreyevich 1894-1937(?)
See Pilnyak, Boris
See CA 123
Vogel, Paula A(nne) 1951- .... **CLC 76**
See CA 108
Voigt, Cynthia 1942- .... **CLC 30**
See AAYA 3, 30; CA 106; CANR 18, 37, 40; CLR 13, 48; INT CANR-18; JRDA; MAICYA; SATA 48, 79; SATA-Brief 33
Voigt, Ellen Bryant 1943- .... **CLC 54**
See CA 69-72; CANR 11, 29, 55; DLB 120
Voinovich, Vladimir (Nikolaevich)
1932- .... **CLC 10, 49**
See CA 81-84; CAAS 12; CANR 33, 67; MTCW 1
Vollmann, William T. 1959- .. **CLC 89; DAM NOV, POP**
See CA 134; CANR 67; DA3; MTCW 2
Voloshinov, V. N.
See Bakhtin, Mikhail Mikhailovich
Voltaire 1694-1778 .... **LC 14; DA; DAB; DAC; DAM DRAM, MST; SSC 12; WLC**
See DA3
von Aschendrof, BaronIgnatz
See Ford, Ford Madox
von Daeniken, Erich 1935- .... **CLC 30**
See AITN 1; CA 37-40R; CANR 17, 44

von Daniken, Erich
See von Daeniken, Erich
von Heidenstam, (Carl Gustaf) Verner
See Heidenstam, (Carl Gustaf) Verner von
von Heyse, Paul (Johann Ludwig)
See Heyse, Paul (Johann Ludwig von)
von Hofmannsthal, Hugo
See Hofmannsthal, Hugo von
von Horvath, Odon
See Horvath, Oedoen von
von Horvath, Oedoen
See Horvath, Oedoen von
von Liliencron, (Friedrich Adolf Axel) Detlev
See Liliencron, (Friedrich Adolf Axel) Detlev von
Vonnegut, Kurt, Jr. 1922- . **CLC 1, 2, 3, 4, 5, 8, 12, 22, 40, 60, 111; DA; DAB; DAC; DAM MST, NOV, POP; SSC 8; WLC**
See AAYA 6; AITN 1; BEST 90:4; CA 1-4R; CANR 1, 25, 49, 75; CDALB 1968-1988; DA3; DLB 2, 8, 152; DLBD 3; DLBY 80; MTCW 1, 2
Von Rachen, Kurt
See Hubbard, L(afayette) Ron(ald)
von Rezzori (d'Arezzo), Gregor
See Rezzori (d'Arezzo), Gregor von
von Sternberg, Josef
See Sternberg, Josef von
Vorster, Gordon 1924- .... **CLC 34**
See CA 133
Vosce, Trudie
See Ozick, Cynthia
Voznesensky, Andrei (Andreievich)
1933- .... **CLC 1, 15, 57; DAM POET**
See CA 89-92; CANR 37; MTCW 1
Waddington, Miriam 1917- .... **CLC 28**
See CA 21-24R; CANR 12, 30; DLB 68
Wagman, Fredrica 1937- .... **CLC 7**
See CA 97-100; INT 97-100
Wagner, Linda W.
See Wagner-Martin, Linda (C.)
Wagner, Linda Welshimer
See Wagner-Martin, Linda (C.)
Wagner, Richard 1813-1883 .... **NCLC 9**
See DLB 129
Wagner-Martin, Linda (C.) 1936- .... **CLC 50**
See CA 159
Wagoner, David (Russell) 1926- .... **CLC 3, 5, 15**
See CA 1-4R; CAAS 3; CANR 2, 71; DLB 5; SATA 14
Wah, Fred(erick James) 1939- .... **CLC 44**
See CA 107; 141; DLB 60
Wahloo, Per 1926-1975 .... **CLC 7**
See CA 61-64; CANR 73
Wahloo, Peter
See Wahloo, Per
Wain, John (Barrington) 1925-1994 . **CLC 2, 11, 15, 46**
See CA 5-8R; 145; CAAS 4; CANR 23, 54; CDBLB 1960 to Present; DLB 15, 27, 139, 155; MTCW 1, 2
Wajda, Andrzej 1926- .... **CLC 16**
See CA 102
Wakefield, Dan 1932- .... **CLC 7**
See CA 21-24R; CAAS 7
Wakoski, Diane 1937- ...... **CLC 2, 4, 7, 9, 11, 40; DAM POET; PC 15**
See CA 13-16R; CAAS 1; CANR 9, 60; DLB 5; INT CANR-9; MTCW 2
Wakoski-Sherbell, Diane
See Wakoski, Diane

Walcott, Derek (Alton) 1930- .... **CLC 2, 4, 9, 14, 25, 42, 67, 76; BLC 3; DAB; DAC; DAM MST, MULT, POET; DC 7**
See BW 2; CA 89-92; CANR 26, 47, 75, 80; DA3; DLB 117; DLBY 81; MTCW 1, 2
Waldman, Anne(Lesley) 1945- .... **CLC 7**
See CA 37-40R; CAAS 17; CANR 34, 69; DLB 16
Waldo, E. Hunter
See Sturgeon, Theodore (Hamilton)
Waldo, Edward Hamilton
See Sturgeon, Theodore (Hamilton)
Walker, Alice (Malsenior) 1944- ... **CLC 5, 6, 9, 19, 27, 46, 58, 103; BLC 3; DA; DAB; DAC; DAM MST, MULT, NOV, POET, POP; SSC 5; WLCS**
See AAYA 3; BEST 89:4; BW 2, 3; CA 37-40R; CANR 9, 27, 49, 66, 82; CDALB 1968-1988; DA3; DLB 6, 33, 143; INT CANR-27; MTCW 1, 2; SATA 31
Walker, David Harry 1911-1992 ...... **CLC 14**
See CA 1-4R; 137; CANR 1; SATA 8; SATA-Obit 71
Walker, Edward Joseph 1934-
See Walker, Ted
See CA 21-24R; CANR 12, 28, 53
Walker, George F. 1947- . **CLC 44, 61; DAB; DAC; DAM MST**
See CA 103; CANR 21, 43, 59; DLB 60
Walker, Joseph A. 1935- .... **CLC 19; DAM DRAM, MST**
See BW 1, 3; CA 89-92; CANR 26; DLB 38
Walker, Margaret (Abigail)
1915-1998 .... **CLC 1, 6; BLC; DAM MULT; PC 20**
See BW 2, 3; CA 73-76; 172; CANR 26, 54, 76; DLB 76, 152; MTCW 1, 2
Walker, Ted CLC 13
See Walker, Edward Joseph
See DLB 40
Wallace, David Foster 1962- ..... **CLC 50, 114**
See CA 132; CANR 59; DA3; MTCW 2
Wallace, Dexter
See Masters, Edgar Lee
Wallace, (Richard Horatio)Edgar
1875-1932 .... **TCLC 57**
See CA 115; DLB 70
Wallace, Irving 1916-1990 .... **CLC 7, 13; DAM NOV, POP**
See AITN 1; CA 1-4R; 132; CAAS 1; CANR 1, 27; INT CANR-27; MTCW 1, 2
Wallant, Edward Lewis 1926-1962 ... **CLC 5, 10**
See CA 1-4R; CANR 22; DLB 2, 28, 143; MTCW 1, 2
Wallas, Graham 1858-1932 .... **TCLC 91**
Walley, Byron
See Card, Orson Scott
Walpole, Horace 1717-1797 .... **LC 49**
See DLB 39, 104
Walpole, Hugh (Seymour)
1884-1941 .... **TCLC 5**
See CA 104; 165; DLB 34; MTCW 2
Walser, Martin 1927- .... **CLC 27**
See CA 57-60; CANR 8, 46; DLB 75, 124
Walser, Robert 1878-1956 ...... **TCLC 18;SSC 20**
See CA 118; 165; DLB 66
Walsh, Jill Paton CLC 35
See Paton Walsh, Gillian
See AAYA 11; CLR 2; DLB 161; SAAS 3
Walter, Villiam Christian
See Andersen, Hans Christian

Wambaugh, Joseph (Aloysius, Jr.)
1937- .... **CLC 3, 18; DAM NOV, POP**
See AITN 1; BEST 89:3; CA 33-36R;
CANR 42, 65; DA3; DLB 6; DLBY 83;
MTCW 1, 2

Wang Wei 699(?)-761(?) .... **PC 18**

Ward, Arthur Henry Sarsfield 1883-1959
See Rohmer, Sax
See CA 108; 173

Ward, Douglas Turner 1930- .... **CLC 19**
See BW 1; CA 81-84; CANR 27; DLB 7,
38

Ward, E. D.
See Lucas, E(dward) V(errall)

Ward, Mary Augusta
See Ward, Mrs. Humphry

Ward, Mrs.Humphry 1851-1920 ... **TCLC 55**
See DLB 18

Ward, Peter
See Faust, Frederick (Schiller)

Warhol, Andy 1928(?)-1987 .... **CLC 20**
See AAYA 12; BEST 89:4; CA 89-92; 121;
CANR 34

Warner, Francis (Robert lePlastrier)
1937- .... **CLC 14**
See CA 53-56; CANR 11

Warner, Marina 1946- .... **CLC 59**
See CA 65-68; CANR 21, 55; DLB 194

Warner, Rex(Ernest) 1905-1986 .... **CLC 45**
See CA 89-92; 119; DLB 15

Warner, Susan (Bogert)
1819-1885 .... **NCLC 31**
See DLB 3, 42

Warner, Sylvia (Constance) Ashton
See Ashton-Warner, Sylvia (Constance)

Warner, Sylvia Townsend
1893-1978 .... **CLC 7, 19; SSC 23**
See CA 61-64; 77-80; CANR 16, 60; DLB
34, 139; MTCW 1, 2

Warren, Mercy Otis 1728-1814 ..... **NCLC 13**
See DLB 31, 200

Warren, Robert Penn 1905-1989 .. **CLC 1, 4,
6, 8, 10, 13, 18, 39, 53, 59; DA; DAB;
DAC; DAM MST, NOV, POET; SSC
4;WLC**
See AITN 1; CA 13-16R; 129; CANR 10,
47;CDALB 1968-1988; DA3; DLB 2, 48,
152; DLBY 80, 89; INT CANR-10;
MTCW 1, 2; SATA 46; SATA-Obit 63

Warshofsky, Isaac
See Singer, Isaac Bashevis

Warton, Thomas 1728-1790 ...... **LC 15;DAM
POET**
See DLB 104, 109

Waruk, Kona
See Harris, (Theodore) Wilson

Warung, Price 1855-1911 .... **TCLC 45**

Warwick, Jarvis
See Garner, Hugh

Washington, Alex
See Harris, Mark

Washington, Booker T(aliaferro)
1856-1915 ...... **TCLC 10; BLC 3; DAM
MULT**
See BW 1; CA 114; 125; DA3; SATA 28

Washington, George 1732-1799 .... **LC 25**
See DLB 31

Wassermann, (Karl)Jakob
1873-1934 .... **TCLC 6**
See CA 104; 163; DLB 66

Wasserstein, Wendy 1950- .. **CLC 32, 59, 90;
DAM DRAM; DC 4**
See CA 121; 129; CABS 3; CANR 53, 75;
DA3; INT 129; MTCW 2; SATA 94

Waterhouse, Keith(Spencer) 1929- .. **CLC 47**
See CA 5-8R; CANR 38, 67; DLB 13, 15;
MTCW 1, 2

Waters, Frank(Joseph) 1902-1995 ... **CLC 88**
See CA 5-8R; 149; CAAS 13; CANR 3, 18,
63; DLB 212; DLBY 86

Waters, Roger 1944- .... **CLC 35**

Watkins, Frances Ellen
See Harper, Frances Ellen Watkins

Watkins, Gerrold
See Malzberg, Barry N(athaniel)

Watkins, Gloria 1955(?)-
See hooks, bell
See BW 2; CA 143; MTCW 2

Watkins, Paul 1964- .... **CLC 55**
See CA 132; CANR 62

Watkins, Vernon Phillips
1906-1967 .... **CLC 43**
See CA 9-10; 25-28R; CAP 1; DLB 20

Watson, Irving S.
See Mencken, H(enry) L(ouis)

Watson, John H.
See Farmer, Philip Jose

Watson, Richard F.
See Silverberg, Robert

Waugh, Auberon (Alexander) 1939- .. **CLC 7**
See CA 45-48; CANR 6, 22; DLB 14, 194

Waugh, Evelyn (Arthur St. John)
1903-1966 .. **CLC 1, 3, 8, 13, 19, 27, 44,
107; DA; DAB; DAC; DAM MST,
NOV, POP; WLC**
See CA 85-88; 25-28R; CANR 22; CDBLB
1914-1945; DA3; DLB 15, 162, 195;
MTCW 1, 2

Waugh, Harriet 1944- .... **CLC 6**
See CA 85-88; CANR 22

Ways, C. R.
See Blount, Roy (Alton), Jr.

Waystaff, Simon
See Swift, Jonathan

Webb, (Martha) Beatrice (Potter)
1858-1943 .... **TCLC 22**
See Potter, (Helen) Beatrix
See CA 117; DLB 190

Webb, Charles (Richard) 1939- .... **CLC 7**
See CA 25-28R

Webb, James H(enry), Jr. 1946- ...... **CLC 22**
See CA 81-84

Webb, Mary (Gladys Meredith)
1881-1927 .... **TCLC 24**
See CA 123; DLB 34

Webb, Mrs. Sidney
See Webb, (Martha) Beatrice (Potter)

Webb, Phyllis 1927- .... **CLC 18**
See CA 104; CANR 23; DLB 53

Webb, Sidney (James) 1859-1947 .. **TCLC 22**
See CA 117; 163; DLB 190

Webber, Andrew Lloyd .... **CLC 21**
See Lloyd Webber, Andrew

Weber, Lenora Mattingly
1895-1971 .... **CLC 12**
See CA 19-20; 29-32R; CAP 1; SATA 2;
SATA-Obit 26

Weber, Max 1864-1920 .... **TCLC 69**
See CA 109

Webster, John 1579(?)-1634(?) ... **LC 33; DA;
DAB; DAC; DAM DRAM, MST; DC
2; WLC**
See CDBLB Before 1660; DLB 58

Webster, Noah 1758-1843 .... **NCLC 30**
See DLB 1, 37, 42, 43, 73

Wedekind, (Benjamin) Frank(lin)
1864-1918 .... **TCLC 7; DAM DRAM**
See CA 104; 153; DLB 118

Weidman, Jerome 1913-1998 .... **CLC 7**
See AITN 2; CA 1-4R; 171; CANR 1; DLB
28

Weil, Simone (Adolphine)
1909-1943 .... **TCLC 23**
See CA 117; 159; MTCW 2

Weininger, Otto 1880-1903 .... **TCLC 84**

Weinstein, Nathan
See West, Nathanael

Weinstein, Nathan von Wallenstein
See West, Nathanael

Weir, Peter (Lindsay) 1944- .... **CLC 20**
See CA 113; 123

Weiss, Peter (Ulrich) 1916-1982 .. **CLC 3, 15,
51; DAM DRAM**
See CA 45-48; 106; CANR 3; DLB 69, 124

Weiss, Theodore (Russell) 1916- ... **CLC 3, 8,
14**
See CA 9-12R; CAAS 2; CANR 46; DLB 5

Welch, (Maurice) Denton
1915-1948 .... **TCLC 22**
See CA 121; 148

Welch, James 1940- ..... **CLC 6, 14, 52; DAM
MULT, POP**
See CA 85-88; CANR 42, 66; DLB 175;
NNAL

Weldon, Fay 1931- . **CLC 6, 9, 11, 19, 36, 59,
122; DAM POP**
See CA 21-24R; CANR 16, 46, 63; CD-
BLB 1960 to Present; DLB 14, 194; INT
CANR-16; MTCW 1, 2

Wellek, Rene 1903-1995 .... **CLC 28**
See CA 5-8R; 150; CAAS 7; CANR 8; DLB
63; INT CANR-8

Weller, Michael 1942- .... **CLC 10, 53**
See CA 85-88

Weller, Paul 1958- .... **CLC 26**

Wellershoff, Dieter 1925- .... **CLC 46**
See CA 89-92; CANR 16, 37

Welles, (George) Orson 1915-1985 .. **CLC 20,
80**
See CA 93-96; 117

Wellman, John McDowell 1945-
See Wellman, Mac
See CA 166

Wellman, Mac 1945- .... **CLC 65**
See Wellman, John McDowell; Wellman,
John McDowell

Wellman, ManlyWade 1903-1986 ..... **CLC 49**
See CA 1-4R; 118; CANR 6, 16, 44; SATA
6; SATA-Obit 47

Wells, Carolyn 1869(?)-1942 .... **TCLC 35**
See CA 113; DLB 11

Wells, H(erbert) G(eorge)
1866-1946 . **TCLC 6, 12, 19; DA; DAB;
DAC; DAM MST, NOV; SSC 6; WLC**
See AAYA 18; CA 110; 121; CDBLB 1914-
1945; DA3; DLB 34, 70, 156, 178;
MTCW 1, 2; SATA 20

Wells, Rosemary 1943- .... **CLC 12**
See AAYA 13; CA 85-88; CANR 48; CLR
16; MAICYA; SAAS 1; SATA 18, 69

Welty, Eudora 1909- ..... **CLC 1, 2, 5, 14, 22,
33, 105; DA; DAB; DAC; DAM MST,
NOV; SSC 1, 27; WLC**
See CA 9-12R; CABS 1; CANR 32, 65;
CDALB 1941-1968; DA3; DLB 2, 102,
143; DLBD 12; DLBY 87; MTCW 1, 2

Wen I-to 1899-1946 .... **TCLC 28**

Wentworth, Robert
See Hamilton, Edmond

Werfel, Franz (Viktor) 1890-1945 ... **TCLC 8**
See CA 104; 161; DLB 81, 124

Wergeland, Henrik Arnold
1808-1845 .... **NCLC 5**

Wersba, Barbara 1932- .... **CLC 30**
See AAYA 2, 30; CA 29-32R; CANR 16,
38; CLR 3; DLB 52; JRDA; MAICYA;
SAAS 2; SATA 1, 58; SATA-Essay 103

Wertmueller, Lina 1928- .... **CLC 16**
See CA 97-100; CANR 39, 78

Wescott, Glenway 1901-1987 ... **CLC 13;SSC
35**
See CA 13-16R; 121; CANR 23, 70; DLB
4, 9, 102

Wesker, Arnold 1932- ... **CLC 3, 5, 42; DAB; DAM DRAM**
See CA 1-4R; CAAS 7; CANR 1, 33; CD-BLB 1960 to Present; DLB 13; MTCW 1

Wesley, Richard (Errol) 1945- .... **CLC 7**
See BW 1; CA 57-60; CANR 27; DLB 38

Wessel, Johan Herman 1742-1785 .... **LC 7**

West, Anthony (Panther)
1914-1987 .... **CLC 50**
See CA 45-48; 124; CANR 3, 19; DLB 15

West, C. P.
See Wodehouse, P(elham) G(renville)

West, (Mary) Jessamyn 1902-1984 ... **CLC 7, 17**
See CA 9-12R; 112; CANR 27; DLB 6; DLBY 84; MTCW 1, 2; SATA-Obit 37

West, Morris L(anglo) 1916- .... **CLC 6, 33**
See CA 5-8R; CANR 24, 49, 64; MTCW 1, 2

West, Nathanael 1903-1940 .... **TCLC 1, 14, 44; SSC 16**
See CA 104; 125; CDALB 1929-1941; DA3; DLB 4, 9, 28; MTCW 1, 2

West, Owen
See Koontz, Dean R(ay)

West, Paul 1930- .... **CLC 7, 14, 96**
See CA 13-16R; CAAS 7; CANR 22, 53, 76; DLB 14; INT CANR-22; MTCW 2

West, Rebecca 1892-1983 ... **CLC 7, 9, 31, 50**
See CA 5-8R; 109; CANR 19; DLB 36; DLBY 83; MTCW 1, 2

Westall, Robert (Atkinson)
1929-1993 .... **CLC 17**
See AAYA 12; CA 69-72; 141; CANR 18, 68; CLR 13; JRDA; MAICYA; SAAS 2; SATA 23, 69; SATA-Obit 75

Westermarck, Edward 1862-1939 . **TCLC 87**

Westlake, Donald E(dwin) 1933- .... **CLC 7, 33; DAM POP**
See CA 17-20R; CAAS 13; CANR 16, 44, 65; INT CANR-16; MTCW 2

Westmacott, Mary
See Christie, Agatha (Mary Clarissa)

Weston, Allen
See Norton, Andre

Wetcheek, J. L.
See Feuchtwanger, Lion

Wetering, Janwillem van de
See van de Wetering, Janwillem

Wetherald, Agnes Ethelwyn
1857-1940 .... **TCLC 81**
See DLB 99

Wetherell, Elizabeth
See Warner, Susan (Bogert)

Whale, James 1889-1957 .... **TCLC 63**

Whalen, Philip 1923- .... **CLC 6, 29**
See CA 9-12R; CANR 5, 39; DLB 16

Wharton, Edith (Newbold Jones)
1862-1937 .... **TCLC 3, 9, 27, 53; DA; DAB; DAC; DAM MST, NOV; SSC 6; WLC**
See AAYA 25; CA 104; 132; CDALB 1865-1917; DA3; DLB 4, 9, 12, 78, 189; DLBD 13; MTCW 1, 2

Wharton, James
See Mencken, H(enry) L(ouis)

Wharton, William (a pseudonym) CLC 18, 37
See CA 93-96; DLBY 80; INT 93-96

Wheatley (Peters), Phillis
1754(?)-1784 ...... **LC 3, 50; BLC 3; DA; DAC; DAM MST, MULT, POET; PC 3; WLC**
See CDALB 1640-1865; DA3; DLB 31, 50

Wheelock, John Hall 1886-1978 .... **CLC 14**
See CA 13-16R; 77-80; CANR 14; DLB 45

White, E(lwyn) B(rooks)
1899-1985 . **CLC 10, 34, 39; DAM POP**
See AITN 2; CA 13-16R; 116; CANR 16, 37; CDALBS; CLR 1, 21; DA3; DLB 11, 22; MAICYA; MTCW 1, 2; SATA 2, 29, 100; SATA-Obit 44

White, Edmund (Valentine III)
1940- .... **CLC 27, 110; DAM POP**
See AAYA 7; CA 45-48; CANR 3, 19, 36, 62; DA3; MTCW 1, 2

White, Patrick (Victor Martindale)
1912-1990 . **CLC 3, 4, 5, 7, 9, 18, 65, 69**
See CA 81-84; 132; CANR 43; MTCW 1

White, Phyllis Dorothy James 1920-
See James, P. D.
See CA 21-24R; CANR 17, 43, 65; DAM POP; DA3; MTCW 1, 2

White, T(erence) H(anbury)
1906-1964 .... **CLC 30**
See AAYA 22; CA 73-76; CANR 37; DLB 160; JRDA; MAICYA; SATA 12

White, Terence deVere 1912-1994 .... **CLC 49**
See CA 49-52; 145; CANR 3

White, Walter
See White, Walter F(rancis)
See BLC; DAM MULT

White, Walter F(rancis)
1893-1955 .... **TCLC 15**
See White, Walter
See BW 1; CA 115; 124; DLB 51

White, William Hale 1831-1913
See Rutherford, Mark
See CA 121

Whitehead, Alfred North
1861-1947 .... **TCLC 97**
See CA 117; 165; DLB 100

Whitehead, E(dward) A(nthony)
1933- .... **CLC 5**
See CA 65-68; CANR 58

Whitemore, Hugh (John) 1936- .... **CLC 37**
See CA 132; CANR 77; INT 132

Whitman, Sarah Helen (Power)
1803-1878 .... **NCLC 19**
See DLB 1

Whitman, Walt(er) 1819-1892 .. **NCLC 4, 31, 81; DA; DAB; DAC; DAM MST, POET; PC 3; WLC**
See CDALB 1640-1865; DA3; DLB 3, 64; SATA 20

Whitney, Phyllis A(yame) 1903- ...... **CLC 42; DAM POP**
See AITN 2; BEST 90:3; CA 1-4R; CANR 3, 25, 38, 60; CLR 59; DA3; JRDA; MAICYA; MTCW 2; SATA 1, 30

Whittemore, (Edward) Reed (Jr.)
1919- .... **CLC 4**
See CA 9-12R; CAAS 8; CANR 4; DLB 5

Whittier, John Greenleaf
1807-1892 .... **NCLC 8, 59**
See DLB 1

Whittlebot, Hernia
See Coward, Noel (Peirce)

Wicker, Thomas Grey 1926-
See Wicker, Tom
See CA 65-68; CANR 21, 46

Wicker, Tom CLC 7
See Wicker, Thomas Grey

Wideman, John Edgar 1941- ...... **CLC 5, 34, 36, 67, 122; BLC 3; DAM MULT**
See BW 2, 3; CA 85-88; CANR 14, 42, 67; DLB 33, 143; MTCW 2

Wiebe, Rudy (Henry) 1934- .. **CLC 6, 11, 14; DAC; DAM MST**
See CA 37-40R; CANR 42, 67; DLB 60

Wieland, Christoph Martin
1733-1813 .... **NCLC 17**
See DLB 97

Wiene, Robert 1881-1938 .... **TCLC 56**

Wieners, John 1934- .... **CLC 7**
See CA 13-16R; DLB 16

Wiesel, Elie(zer) 1928- .... **CLC 3, 5, 11, 37; DA; DAB; DAC; DAM MST, NOV; WLCS**
See AAYA 7; AITN 1; CA 5-8R; CAAS 4; CANR 8, 40, 65; CDALBS; DA3; DLB 83; DLBY 87; INT CANR-8; MTCW 1, 2; SATA 56

Wiggins, Marianne 1947- .... **CLC 57**
See BEST 89:3; CA 130; CANR 60

Wight, James Alfred 1916-1995
See Herriot, James
See CA 77-80; SATA 55; SATA-Brief 44

Wilbur, Richard (Purdy) 1921- ..... **CLC 3, 6, 9, 14, 53, 110; DA; DAB; DAC; DAM MST, POET**
See CA 1-4R; CABS 2; CANR 2, 29, 76; CDALBS; DLB 5, 169; INT CANR-29; MTCW 1, 2; SATA 9, 108

Wild, Peter 1940- .... **CLC 14**
See CA 37-40R; DLB 5

Wilde, Oscar 1854(?)-1900 .... **TCLC 1, 8, 23, 41; DA; DAB; DAC; DAM DRAM, MST, NOV; SSC 11; WLC**
See CA 104; 119; CDBLB 1890-1914; DA3; DLB 10, 19, 34, 57, 141, 156, 190; SATA 24

Wilder, Billy CLC 20
See Wilder, Samuel
See DLB 26

Wilder, Samuel 1906-
See Wilder, Billy
See CA 89-92

Wilder, Thornton (Niven)
1897-1975 .. **CLC 1, 5, 6, 10, 15, 35, 82; DA; DAB; DAC; DAM DRAM, MST, NOV; DC 1; WLC**
See AAYA 29; AITN 2; CA 13-16R; 61-64; CANR 40; CDALBS; DA3; DLB 4, 7, 9; DLBY 97; MTCW 1, 2

Wilding, Michael 1942- .... **CLC 73**
See CA 104; CANR 24, 49

Wiley, Richard 1944- .... **CLC 44**
See CA 121; 129; CANR 71

Wilhelm, Kate CLC 7
See Wilhelm, Katie Gertrude
See AAYA 20; CAAS 5; DLB 8; INT CANR-17

Wilhelm, Katie Gertrude 1928-
See Wilhelm, Kate
See CA 37-40R; CANR 17, 36, 60; MTCW 1

Wilkins, Mary
See Freeman, Mary E(leanor) Wilkins

Willard, Nancy 1936- .... **CLC 7, 37**
See CA 89-92; CANR 10, 39, 68; CLR 5; DLB 5, 52; MAICYA; MTCW 1; SATA 37, 71; SATA-Brief 30

William of Ockham 1285-1347 ..... **CMLC 32**

Williams, Ben Ames 1889-1953 .... **TCLC 89**
See DLB 102

Williams, C(harles) K(enneth)
1936- .... **CLC 33, 56; DAM POET**
See CA 37-40R; CAAS 26; CANR 57; DLB 5

Williams, Charles
See Collier, James L(incoln)

Williams, Charles (Walter Stansby)
1886-1945 .... **TCLC 1, 11**
See CA 104; 163; DLB 100, 153

Williams, (George) Emlyn
1905-1987 .... **CLC 15; DAM DRAM**
See CA 104; 123; CANR 36; DLB 10, 77; MTCW 1

Williams, Hank 1923-1953 .... **TCLC 81**

Williams, Hugo 1942- .... **CLC 42**
See CA 17-20R; CANR 45; DLB 40

Woolf, Virginia Adeline
See Woolf, (Adeline) Virginia
See MTCW 2
Woollcott, Alexander (Humphreys)
1887-1943 .... **TCLC 5**
See CA 105; 161; DLB 29
Woolrich,Cornell 1903-1968 .... **CLC 77**
See Hopley-Woolrich, Cornell George
Wordsworth, Dorothy 1771-1855 .. **NCLC 25**
See DLB 107
Wordsworth, William 1770-1850 .. **NCLC 12, 38; DA; DAB; DAC; DAM MST, POET; PC 4; WLC**
See CDBLB 1789-1832; DA3; DLB 93, 107
Wouk, Herman 1915- ... **CLC 1, 9, 38; DAM NOV, POP**
See CA 5-8R; CANR 6, 33, 67; CDALBS; DA3; DLBY 82; INT CANR-6; MTCW 1, 2
Wright, Charles (Penzel, Jr.) 1935- .. **CLC 6, 13, 28, 119**
See CA 29-32R; CAAS 7; CANR 23, 36, 62; DLB 165; DLBY 82; MTCW 1, 2
Wright, Charles Stevenson 1932- ... **CLC 49; BLC 3; DAM MULT, POET**
See BW 1; CA 9-12R; CANR 26; DLB 33
Wright, Frances 1795-1852 .... **NCLC 74**
See DLB 73
Wright, Frank Lloyd 1867-1959 .... **TCLC 95**
See CA 174
Wright, Jack R.
See Harris, Mark
Wright, James (Arlington)
1927-1980 .... **CLC 3, 5, 10, 28; DAM POET**
See AITN 2; CA 49-52; 97-100; CANR 4, 34, 64; CDALBS; DLB 5, 169; MTCW 1, 2
Wright, Judith (Arandell) 1915- ..... **CLC 11, 53; PC 14**
See CA 13-16R; CANR 31, 76; MTCW 1, 2; SATA 14
Wright, L(aurali) R. 1939- .... **CLC 44**
See CA 138
Wright, Richard (Nathaniel)
1908-1960 .... **CLC 1, 3, 4, 9, 14, 21, 48, 74; BLC 3; DA; DAB; DAC; DAM MST, MULT, NOV; SSC 2; WLC**
See AAYA 5; BW 1; CA 108; CANR 64;CDALB 1929-1941; DA3; DLB 76, 102; DLBD 2; MTCW 1, 2
Wright, Richard B(ruce) 1937- .... **CLC 6**
See CA 85-88; DLB 53
Wright, Rick 1945- .... **CLC 35**
Wright, Rowland
See Wells, Carolyn
Wright, Stephen 1946- .... **CLC 33**
Wright, Willard Huntington 1888-1939
See Van Dine, S. S.
See CA 115; DLBD 16
Wright, William 1930- .... **CLC 44**
See CA 53-56; CANR 7, 23
Wroth, LadyMary 1587-1653(?) .... **LC 30**
See DLB 121
Wu Ch'eng-en 1500(?)-1582(?) .... **LC 7**
Wu Ching-tzu 1701-1754 .... **LC 2**
Wurlitzer, Rudolph 1938(?)- .... **CLC 2, 4, 15**
See CA 85-88; DLB 173
Wyatt, Thomas c. 1503-1542 .... **PC 27**
See DLB 132
Wycherley, William 1641-1715 ...... **LC 8, 21; DAM DRAM**
See CDBLB 1660-1789; DLB 80
Wylie, Elinor (Morton Hoyt)
1885-1928 .... **TCLC 8; PC 23**
See CA 105; 162; DLB 9, 45

Wylie, Philip(Gordon) 1902-1971 ..... **CLC 43**
See CA 21-22; 33-36R; CAP 2; DLB 9
Wyndham, John CLC 19
See Harris, John (Wyndham Parkes Lucas) Beynon
Wyss, Johann David Von
1743-1818 .... **NCLC 10**
See JRDA; MAICYA; SATA 29; SATA-Brief 27
Xenophon c. 430B.C.-c.354B.C. .... **CMLC 17**
See DLB 176
Yakumo Koizumi
See Hearn, (Patricio) Lafcadio (Tessima Carlos)
Yamamoto, Hisaye 1921- .... **SSC 34; DAM MULT**
Yanez, Jose Donoso
See Donoso (Yanez), Jose
Yanovsky, Basile S.
See Yanovsky, V(assily) S(emenovich)
Yanovsky, V(assily) S(emenovich)
1906-1989 .... **CLC 2, 18**
See CA 97-100; 129
Yates, Richard 1926-1992 .... **CLC 7, 8, 23**
See CA 5-8R; 139; CANR 10, 43; DLB 2; DLBY 81, 92; INT CANR-10
Yeats, W. B.
See Yeats, William Butler
Yeats, William Butler 1865-1939 .... **TCLC 1, 11, 18, 31, 93; DA; DAB; DAC; DAM DRAM, MST, POET; PC 20; WLC**
See CA 104; 127; CANR 45; CDBLB 1890-1914; DA3; DLB 10, 19, 98, 156; MTCW 1, 2
Yehoshua, A(braham) B. 1936- .. **CLC 13, 31**
See CA 33-36R; CANR 43
Yep, Laurence Michael 1948- .... **CLC 35**
See AAYA 5, 31; CA 49-52; CANR 1, 46; CLR 3, 17, 54; DLB 52; JRDA; MAICYA; SATA 7, 69
Yerby, Frank G(arvin) 1916-1991 . **CLC 1, 7, 22; BLC 3; DAM MULT**
See BW 1, 3; CA 9-12R; 136; CANR 16, 52; DLB 76; INT CANR-16; MTCW 1
Yesenin, Sergei Alexandrovich
See Esenin, Sergei (Alexandrovich)
Yevtushenko, Yevgeny (Alexandrovich)
1933- .... **CLC 1, 3, 13, 26, 51; DAM POET**
See CA 81-84; CANR 33, 54; MTCW 1
Yezierska, Anzia 1885(?)-1970 .... **CLC 46**
See CA 126; 89-92; DLB 28; MTCW 1
Yglesias, Helen 1915- .... **CLC 7, 22**
See CA 37-40R; CAAS 20; CANR 15, 65; INT CANR-15; MTCW 1
Yokomitsu Riichi 1898-1947 .... **TCLC 47**
See CA 170
Yonge, Charlotte(Mary)
1823-1901 .... **TCLC 48**
See CA 109; 163; DLB 18, 163; SATA 17
York, Jeremy
See Creasey, John
York, Simon
See Heinlein, Robert A(nson)
Yorke, Henry Vincent 1905-1974 ..... **CLC 13**
See Green, Henry
See CA 85-88; 49-52
Yosano Akiko 1878-1942 ..... **TCLC 59;PC 11**
See CA 161
Yoshimoto, Banana CLC 84
See Yoshimoto, Mahoko
Yoshimoto, Mahoko 1964-
See Yoshimoto, Banana
See CA 144
Young, Al(bert James) 1939- . **CLC 19; BLC 3; DAM MULT**
See BW 2, 3; CA 29-32R; CANR 26, 65; DLB 33

Young, Andrew (John) 1885-1971 ...... **CLC 5**
See CA 5-8R; CANR 7, 29
Young, Collier
See Bloch, Robert (Albert)
Young, Edward 1683-1765 .... **LC 3, 40**
See DLB 95
Young, Marguerite (Vivian)
1909-1995 .... **CLC 82**
See CA 13-16; 150; CAP 1
Young, Neil 1945- .... **CLC 17**
See CA 110
Young Bear, Ray A. 1950- ...... **CLC 94;DAM MULT**
See CA 146; DLB 175; NNAL
Yourcenar, Marguerite 1903-1987 ... **CLC 19, 38, 50, 87; DAM NOV**
See CA 69-72; CANR 23, 60; DLB 72; DLBY 88; MTCW 1, 2
Yuan, Chu 340(?)B.C.-278(?)B.C. . **CMLC 36**
Yurick, Sol 1925- .... **CLC 6**
See CA 13-16R; CANR 25
Zabolotsky, Nikolai Alekseevich
1903-1958 .... **TCLC 52**
See CA 116; 164
Zagajewski, Adam PC 27
Zamiatin, Yevgenii
See Zamyatin, Evgeny Ivanovich
Zamora, Bernice (B. Ortiz) 1938- .. **CLC 89; DAM MULT; HLC 2**
See CA 151; CANR 80; DLB 82; HW 1, 2
Zamyatin, Evgeny Ivanovich
1884-1937 .... **TCLC 8, 37**
See CA 105; 166
Zangwill, Israel 1864-1926 .... **TCLC 16**
See CA 109; 167; DLB 10, 135, 197
Zappa, Francis Vincent, Jr. 1940-1993
See Zappa, Frank
See CA 108; 143; CANR 57
Zappa, Frank CLC 17
See Zappa, Francis Vincent, Jr.
Zaturenska, Marya 1902-1982 .... **CLC 6,11**
See CA 13-16R; 105; CANR 22
Zeami 1363-1443 .... **DC 7**
Zelazny, Roger(Joseph) 1937-1995 ... **CLC 21**
See AAYA 7; CA 21-24R; 148; CANR 26, 60; DLB 8; MTCW 1, 2; SATA 57; SATA-Brief 39
Zhdanov, Andrei Alexandrovich
1896-1948 .... **TCLC 18**
See CA 117; 167
Zhukovsky, Vasily (Andreevich)
1783-1852 .... **NCLC 35**
See DLB 205
Ziegenhagen, Eric CLC 55
Zimmer, Jill Schary
See Robinson, Jill
Zimmerman, Robert
See Dylan, Bob
Zindel, Paul 1936- ..... **CLC 6, 26; DA; DAB; DAC; DAM DRAM, MST, NOV; DC 5**
See AAYA 2; CA 73-76; CANR 31, 65; CDALBS; CLR 3, 45; DA3; DLB 7, 52; JRDA; MAICYA; MTCW 1, 2; SATA 16, 58, 102
Zinov'Ev, A. A.
See Zinoviev, Alexander (Aleksandrovich)
Zinoviev, Alexander (Aleksandrovich)
1922- .... **CLC 19**
See CA 116; 133; CAAS 10
Zoilus
See Lovecraft, H(oward) P(hillips)
Zola, Emile (Edouard Charles Antoine)
1840-1902 .... **TCLC 1, 6, 21, 41; DA; DAB; DAC; DAM MST, NOV; WLC**
See CA 104; 138; DA3; DLB 123
Zoline, Pamela 1941- .... **CLC 62**
See CA 161

Literary Criticism Series
Cumulative Topic Index

This index lists all topic entries in Gale's *Classical and Medieval Literature Criticism, Contemporary Literary Criticism, Literature Criticism from 1400 to 1800, Nineteenth-Century Literature Criticism,* and *Twentieth-Century Literary Criticism.*

Young Playwrights Festival
  1988-CLC 55: 376-81
  1989-CLC 59: 398-403
  1990-CLC 65: 444-8

LC Cumulative Nationality Index

LC Cumulative Title Index

Title Index

Title Index

Title Index

Title Index